The
Garland
CLASSICS OF
FILM LITERATURE

REPRINTED IN PHOTO-FACSIMILE
IN 32 VOLUMES

BEST FILM PLAYS
1943-44

John Gassner
and
Dudley Nichols

GARLAND PUBLISHING, INC. • NEW YORK & LONDON • 1977

This edition reprinted by arrangement
with Crown Publishers, Inc.

Library of Congress Cataloging in Publication Data

Main entry under title:

Best film plays, 1943-44.

(The Garland classics of film literature ; 11)
Reprint of the 1945 ed. published by Crown,
New York.
CONTENTS: Gassner, J. The film play annual.--
Nichols, D. Writer, director, and film.--Wanger, W.
The motion picture industry and the war effort.
[etc.]
1. Moving-picture plays. I. Gassner, John,
1903-1967. II. Nichols, Dudley, 1895-   II. Se-
ries.
PN1997.A1B372   1977   822'.03   76-52102
ISBN 0-8240-2875-9

Printed in the United States of America

BEST FILM PLAYS
OF 1943-1944

BEST FILM PLAYS OF 1943-1944

Edited by
JOHN GASSNER
and
DUDLEY NICHOLS

CROWN PUBLISHERS
NEW YORK

Copyright 1945
by
CROWN PUBLISHERS

CASABLANCA: Screenplay of the Warner Brothers photoplay "Casablanca," copyright 1943 by Warner Brothers Pictures, Inc.

DRAGON SEED: Screenplay of the Metro-Goldwyn-Mayer Studios photoplay "Dragon Seed," copyright 1944 by Loews' Incorporated.

GOING MY WAY: Screenplay of the Paramount photoplay, "Going My Way," copyright 1944 by Paramount Pictures Inc. Lyrics of the Johnny Burke and James Van Heusen songs *The Day After Forever, Going My Way*, and *Swinging On A Star*, copyright 1944 by Burke & Van Heusen Inc.

HAIL THE CONQUERING HERO: Screenplay of the Paramount photoplay, "Hail the Conquering Hero," copyright 1943 by Paramount Pictures Inc.

THE MIRACLE OF MORGAN'S CREEK: Screenplay of the Paramount photoplay "The Miracle of Morgan's Creek," copyright 1943 by Paramount Pictures, Inc.

THE MORE THE MERRIER: Screenplay of the Columbia Pictures photoplay "The More the Merrier," copyright 1943 by Columbia Pictures Corporation.

THE OX-BOW INCIDENT: Screenplay of the Twentieth Century-Fox photoplay "The Ox-Bow Incident," copyright 1942 by Twentieth Century-Fox Film Corporation.

THE PURPLE HEART: Screenplay of the Twentieth Century-Fox photoplay "The Purple Heart," copyright 1944 by Twentieth Century-Fox Film Corporation.

WATCH ON THE RHINE: Screenplay of the Warner Brothers photoplay "Watch on the Rhine," copyright 1943 by Warner Brothers Pictures, Inc.

WILSON: Screenplay of the Twentieth Century-Fox photoplay "Wilson," copyright 1944 by Twentieth Century-Fox Film Corporation.

WARNING: These motion pictures in their printed forms are designed for the reading public only. All motion picture and dramatic rights in them are fully protected by copyrights, in both the United States and Canada, and no public or private performance—professional or amateur—may be given without the written permission of the copyright owner. As the courts have also ruled that the public reading of a play or scenario for pay or where tickets have been sold constitutes a public performance, no such reading may be given except under the conditions above stated. Anyone wilfully disregarding the copyright owner's right renders himself liable to prosecution.

Published simultaneously in Canada by Ambassador Books Ltd.

Second Printing, June 1945

PRINTED IN THE UNITED STATES OF AMERICA
AMERICAN BOOK—STRATFORD PRESS, INC., NEW YORK

ACKNOWLEDGMENTS

As in the previous "20 Best Film Plays," I am under great obligation to Dudley Nichols for his collaboration, to the first patron of the project Sidney Buchman, to my friendly mentor Benjamin Sonnenberg, and to Walter Wanger for encouragement. This time, Mr. Wanger went to the trouble of contributing to the present book, so that my debt to him has been doubled. Many friends of the previous project are also responsible for this initial volume of an annual "Best Film Plays" because of their generous cooperation on "20 Best Film Plays": Messrs. J. Robert Rubin, Charles Koerner, Jacob Wilk, William Dozier, James J. Geller, John Byram, Frank Capra, Louis K. Sidney, Samuel Goldwyn, and Harry Cohn.

I am also grateful to the critics Bosley Crowther, Howard Barnes, Frederick Babcock, George Freedley, Charles Lee, Charles Wagner, Archer Winsten and John T. McManus. A wealth of encouragement and in some cases advice came from them. If other motion picture and book critics were to be mentioned their names would be legion. I must, however, single out Jesse Zunser, the editor of Cue Magazine, for the time and thought he devoted to discussing the new volume with me. The presence of photographs in it is directly attributable to him.

I am deeply indebted to William Morris for supporting the project with his facilities, and to Margerie Lyon (whose help in clearances was again invaluable) and Albert Taylor of the Morris office. To Crown Publishers' editors, Edmund Fuller and Bertha Krantz. To my counselling friends, Robert Gessner, Leopold Atlas and Morris Ebenstein. And to my wife, Mollie Gassner, for tireless editorial assistance in preparing copy and reading proofs.

For permissions, my thanks go to the executive heads of Metro-Goldwyn-Mayer, Twentieth Century-Fox, Warner Brothers, Paramount and Columbia Pictures Corporation, as well as to the owners, publishers and agents of original published material mentioned on the title pages—especially to Lillian Hellman, Bennett Cerf, Saxe Commins, and Miss Pearl Buck's literary representative David Lloyd. As usual, the legal staffs of the motion picture companies bore the brunt of the burden of clearances, so that I must be especially grateful to Sidney Justin and Miss Harriet Nystuen of Paramount, George Wasson and E. C. de Lavigne of Twentieth Century-Fox, F. L. Hendrickson of MGM, Morris Ebenstein of Warner Brothers, and Duncan G. Cassell of Columbia Pictures Corp. And I have many creditors in the studios for kindnesses in clearing titles and providing stills.

In conclusion, I acknowledge a very great debt to Jacob Wilk, Leo McCarey, Preston Sturges, and Darryl F. Zanuck for facilitating the inclusion of the screenplays in the present volume. Mr. Zanuck should, indeed, head the list of patrons for enabling me to present two of his notable productions, for his Introduction to *Wilson,* and for the trouble he took to clarify problems attendant upon including it.

J. G.

CONTENTS

A FILM PLAY ANNUAL, by John Gassner ix

WRITER, DIRECTOR AND FILM, by Dudley Nichols xxi

THE MOTION PICTURE INDUSTRY AND THE WAR EFFORT,
by Walter Wanger xxxi

PREFACE TO *Wilson*, by Darryl F. Zanuck 1

WILSON, by Lamar Trotti 7

THE PURPLE HEART, by Jerome Cady 89

GOING MY WAY, by Frank Butler and Frank Cavett
Based on a story by Leo McCarey 149

THE MIRACLE OF MORGAN'S CREEK, by Preston Sturges . . 223

WATCH ON THE RHINE, by Dashiell Hammett
Based on the stage play by Lillian Hellman 299

DRAGON SEED, by Marguerite Roberts and Jane Murfin
Based on the novel by Pearl S. Buck 357

THE MORE THE MERRIER, by Robert Russel, Frank Ross, Richard Flournoy and Lewis Foster
Based on a story by Robert Russel and Frank Ross 451

THE OX-BOW INCIDENT, by Lamar Trotti
Based on the novel by Walter Van Tilburg Clark 511

HAIL THE CONQUERING HERO, by Preston Sturges 561

CASABLANCA, by Julius J. & Philip G. Epstein and Howard Koch
Based on a play by Murray Burnett and Joan Alison 631

NOTE: Credits to screenwriters, authors of original material, producers and directors are in accordance with instructions from the motion picture studios. In no case have the editors departed from this rule, as the granting of credits does not lie within their discretion.

A FILM PLAY ANNUAL

By John Gassner

When Dudley Nichols and I projected *20 Best Film Plays* we got hold of a Tartar. We had entertained an innocent notion of presenting a number of screenplays as reading for the public, and expected to call it a day. But by the time we went to press, it became apparent that one oversized volume could not contain all the noteworthy screenplays of the past. I still receive letters offering suggestions for a supplementary omnibus. And no sooner was our book published than it seemed obligatory for us to start an annual "best film plays" series.

If, as we maintained, the screenplay had become a new literary medium which reached untold millions *via* the screen, reflected our age for better or worse, and affected the thought and behavior patterns of the multitude, the annual accumulation of new film dramas could not be entirely ignored. If, as we also believed, it was of some importance to screenwriters to be published like other writers, we could not overlook the obligation to print some of the best work they continued to write. Since enough people proved their interest in reading the scripts, and because aspiring writers seemed eager for them, the pressure could not be entirely disregarded. And, finally, we had to heed the most seductive of all temptations, that of a sense of duty, possibly mistaken, to the potentially superb artistic and social medium of film-making. I say "potentially," of course, because so long as the eagle's feet are shackled by an ignominious censorship it cannot get off the ground often enough, or fly very far. It was conceivable that the enterprise would strengthen the hearts of the minority that endeavors to justify the existence of Hollywood for other purposes than mere profit.

We were loath to prepare an "annual" not only because we can ill afford the time, but because such a volume can easily suggest an egregious pretension—that of setting ourselves up as arbiters of the motion picture world. There is an Academy of Motion Picture Arts and Sciences for this purpose, the New York critics make annual selections of best films, as do individual motion picture critics no doubt everywhere, and *Film Daily* holds a nation-wide poll which provides a sufficient test of the popularity of the year's output. Such a book would also be expected to be more inclusive than one publishable volume could possibly be; not all of the worthier film plays could be published, some would be unavailable, and the clearance of others would take too long to meet any annual deadline. Inclusion, moreover, of the vast amount of data entailed in any survey of the gigantic entertainment industry, even the mere lists of films and casts, would be out of the question. We were, after all, not confronted with Mr. Burns Mantle's professional theatre which unfolds a mere hundred plays annually! Nor could we consider the possibility of saving space by synopsizing the screenplays without negating our very first principle—that summary destroys the integrity of this form of composition, which is distinctive only insofar as it reflects the mobile medium that it serves.

Nevertheless, having established the practice of publishing noteworthy film plays and found an acceptable form of presenting them, we could not disengage ourselves gracefully. The same reasons that motivated the publication of the previous volume apply to the present one. The screenplay remains a vital dramatic form, no matter how deficient in ultimate stylistic refinement, at least for the present; no matter how substance is often perverted by business acting in collusion with priggish censoriousness. And the recent period covered by this book (we had to limit ourselves to the twelve months between August 1943 and August 1944, except in the case of two films that were released earlier) brought forth a number of screenplays that are likely to prove gratifying for one reason or another. Most of the material, besides (*Going My Way, Wilson, Casablanca, The Miracle of Morgan's Creek, Hail the Conquering Hero, The More the Merrier,* and *The Purple Heart*), had not reached the reader in any other form—that is, as a published novel or as a produced play. The authors of the screenplays functioned as expert writers for a lively contemporary medium, and deserved to be published, at least for their creative part in the film. And finally, we were agreed that although a motion picture is obviously never complete, never really a "motion picture," except on the screen, there are gratifications in reading the scripts that went into production.

We decided to assemble this initial volume on the simplest possible principle—that of presenting ten available screenplays which impressed us as being well above average, and as possessing qualities of interest in one or more respects. If it happened, since we are not conscious of any personal singularity, that our inclusions were also popular, so much the better; and fortunately, such films as *Wilson, Going My Way, Casablanca, Watch on the Rhine, The Miracle of Morgan's Creek,* and *Hail the Conquering Hero* have already won public and critical acclaim. If it happened that our partiality to certain other films was not supported by widespread popularity, we could stand by personal conviction. In the present volume, for example, *The Ox-Bow Incident* was a box-office failure and scored only twelve votes in the *Film Daily's* 1943 poll, yet I would willingly forego a dozen films that have received ten times as many credits. Since the collection is happily unofficial, and makes no Olympian claims for the editors, personal taste, and opinion could have their day. Anyone is free to draw up another list equally good, if not better, or abide by *Film Daily's* ten "best."

Even so, I should explain that our editorial choice could not be exercised with complete liberty. Some films were omitted because of legal tangles or difficulty in clearances—two specific instances are *A Guy Named Joe* and *The Song of Bernadette;* and *Madame Curie* had to be dropped at the last moment for lack of space. Also there were notable war documentaries to which publication in this volume might do scant, if any, justice. Our consolation lay in the possibility that the included screenplays would reveal virtues rewarding to the general reader and the student, and that they would serve as examples of the best that Hollywood had had to offer in twelve bustling months and as some indication of observable trends on the higher levels of motion picture production.

Wilson and *The Ox-Bow Incident* may remind us that Hollywood can put on its thinking cap now and then, although it prefers to stand bareheaded on most occasions. They are dramas of political and social thought, and may be acclaimed both for their importance and rarity in the field. It may be sheer ignorance on my part, but I can recall only a few other films of the period that tried even half successfully to grapple with a point of view at all: the worthy "B" picture *Power of the Press; None Shall Escape,* which dealt with the trial of war criminals; *Address Unknown,* which dramatized the deterioration of personal morale in the Nazi inferno; *Happy Land,* which sought an affirmation in our ability to weather other crises in our history, and the controversial *Lifeboat.*

The Purple Heart and *Dragon Seed,* along with *Casablanca* and *Watch on the Rhine,* represent the considerably larger segment of films that treated various aspects of the war, among which degrees of distinction were attained during our twelve months by *So Proudly We Hail, The Sullivans, The Cross of Lorraine, Sahara, Cry Havoc, Gung Ho, The Story of Dr. Wassell, Corvette K-225, Thirty Seconds Over Tokyo, The North Star,* and a number of documentaries like *Memphis Belle, Report from the Aleutians,* and the *Why We Fight* series. Only the field of melodrama is completely unrepresented by any of our serious films, although I am not aware of any severe loss here, *Shadow of a Doubt* having come too early and *Double Indemnity* too late for our period. Only *Gaslight* may be missed here, and some may clamor for *The Curse of the Cat People.* Character drama was likewise at an ebb, though *Random Harvest* scored great popularity.

Our selections, *Hail the Conquering Hero, The Miracle of Morgan's Creek*, and *The More the Merrier*, are representative of another sizable group of pictures that dealt with the war-time scene in America, and applied the salve of humor to irritations on the home front. They are to be distinguished from the less successfully realized serious treatments of the home front in terms of pathos and sentiment which reached the ultimate proportions in David O. Selznick's popular *Since You Went Away*. And our three riotous screenplays do very well by the species of farce-comedy and extravaganza at which Hollywood has been excelling. The superior *Holy Matrimony, The Human Comedy, Princess O'Rourke, Arsenic and Old Lace, See Here Private Hargrove,* and sundry other comedies falling into our arbitrary period might have claims to recognition. But the three published here will be generally recognized as possessing more than average merit.

Finally, *Going My Way*, while standing in a class by itself, may well represent two trends in film production simultaneously: the small trend toward motion pictures that satisfied a craving for spiritual values, among which *The Song of Bernadette* won special acclaim, and, if only indirectly, the continued popularity of musical films, among which *Cover Girl* will be recalled for its simple freshness as musical comedy, and *Lady in the Dark* for its ambitious pageant-like divagation into the curiosa of Freudian psychology. Neither screen fantasy, which might have been best represented by *A Guy Named Joe,* nor film biography, sufficiently exhibited by *Wilson*, can be said to have constituted a trend. The dearth of fantasy, whose philosophic possibilities were lightly outlined in *It Happened Tomorrow*, and whose solace in times of stress was touchingly demonstrated by *Happy Land*, is surprising. And the sparseness of biography after notable achievements in the field ever since *Pasteur* is explicable, though it is to be regretted. Recovering the past and drawing inspiration from great lives like Wilson's and Madame Curie's comprise a very imperative obligation to Hollywood's vast and not too informed public. It is possible, however, that the immediacy of the present overshadowed the past.

The volume, in addition, can make some claim to representativeness, in the sense that it exhibits the continued progress of some of Hollywood's more creative spirits. The already amply recognized achievements of Darryl F. Zanuck were notably augmented by his productions of *Wilson* and *The Purple Heart*. Hal Wallis delivered two more impressive productions with *Casablanca* and *Watch on the Rhine*. Lamar Trotti climbed higher with the screenplays of *Wilson* and *The Ox-Bow Incident*. Preston Sturges attained the zenith of his preëminence as both writer and director with *The Miracle*

A FILM PLAY ANNUAL xiii

of Morgan's Creek and *Hail the Conquering Hero*. Pandro S. Berman came off with more honors as producer of *Dragon Seed*. Henry King, who made his director's mark as early as 1921 with *Tol'able David*, lifted his record to new altitudes with *Wilson* as well as *The Song of Bernadette*. Leo McCarey, responsible for both the story and the direction of *Going My Way*, reached the peak of his distinguished career. George Stevens scored again as director with *The More the Merrier*, Lewis Milestone with *The Purple Heart*, and William A. Wellman with *The Ox-Bow Incident*. And among Hollywood's actors an ascent is traceable in numerous instances: in Bing Crosby's transmutation of his popular talent in *Going My Way*, the long delayed emergence into screen prominence of the old Abbey Theatre's Barry Fitzgerald, the further exhibition of Aline MacMahon's unusual capacities in *Dragon Seed*, Eddie Bracken's double triumph in Preston Sturges' extravaganzas, Humphrey Bogart's performance in *Casablanca*, Paul Lukas' superb portrait in *Watch on the Rhine*, and the discovery of Alexander Knox as a redoubtable screen actor in *None Shall Escape* and in the difficult role of Wilson.

In short, it may be noted that this volume, though consisting of only ten films, cannot fail to reflect the Hollywood scene to some degree—virtually with no conscious effort on our part, except my request of some report on Hollywood's war activities from the President of the Academy.

Whether the overall record is encouraging or discouraging depends upon one's point of view, upon the patience of thoughtful observers with the various limitations of the industry, upon how gracefully they can accept the disappointment of fond expectations for an art form whose potentialities loom larger the more one thinks of them. It is not surprising that executives, who are concerned with the practical business of making a dollar, tend to be optimistic, while the artists, who know what wonders they would like to perform on the screen, are most given to desperation.

On behalf of the semi-detached observer who writes this introduction, I can only report that although very much inclined to be grateful for small favors and to give Hollywood the benefit of every doubt, he fears that *in toto* film achievements fall too far short of their promise. What, with notable exceptions, is omitted by author or studio often comprises the most solid substance of plot and meaning. The logic of the resolution of a screenplay seems too often meager or hurried. The upshot of too many films is disproportionately small by comparison with the labor of preparation or the expository matter. The tendency is to follow the line of least resistance, or the line of least difficulty in comprehension, character analysis, and social import. For reasons that are generally ascribed to the Hays office but may also be attributed to the contagion of a lazy-minded attitude, to a flabby pursuit of the matter and idea, too much gets irretrievably lost in filmmaking. The obituary notice on many a fine intention may well read *"spurlos versenkt."*

I cannot also avoid the suspicion that those excellent cinematic devices, the dissolve and the fade-out, serve as a seduction. Every craftsman will probably rise up in indignant protest against this amateur deduction, for without these devices films would never have made any progress; without them cinematic art would be static, ponderous, and dull. Yet the temptation of evasion is always present in the technique. While writers for the stage are frequently guilty of relegating crucial events or decisions to the wings or to intermissions, those responsible for the final screenplay (the writer-producer-director-cutter combinations) seem too inclined to discharge an obligation by dissolving or "fading out" a scene and skipping to something else. This has never been the way of major art, which has invariably squeezed the last drop out of some matter. Take the example of *The Iliad, The Divine Comedy, Hamlet, War and Peace, The Brothers Karamazov,* the Parthenon frieze, the *St. Matthew's Passion,* Beethoven's Opus No. 131, or what you will! Or even something as short as *Riders to the Sea* or the Toccata and Fugue in D Minor, or something compact but completely realized as a Cézanne still life. Work of this order creates the impression that the inherent possibilities of the matter have been exhausted by the creator.

It is an impression too rarely given by films, into which have gone such an expenditure of money and endeavor and the mechanical resources of the wonder-making machine age. No doubt Hollywood's more intelligent craftsmen could write a book-length explanation, citing all the intrinsic and extrinsic evils of a collaborative, constantly interrupted, star-harassed, censorship-ridden, business-dominated mass production enterprise. My reference to dissolves and fade-outs is intended to be more metaphorical than literal. It is perhaps most apropos when considered as a symbol of evasion, and slickness, and sloth—of want or fear of concentration on the thing in hand, on the experience, whether serious or comic, to be evoked. That is the respect in which the facile and too-ready use of dissolve and fade-out appears to me literally an evil—a temptation too subverting and demoralizing. All the more so, since it is of the essence of film art. All the more so because it is so easy to justify oneself, wrap the robes of righteousness about oneself, and proclaim that it was all done *pour l'art.* How often do we resort to the dissolve, for instance, *not* to make full use of the film medium, but to cheat on content and force?

That the filmic devices can be employed to master the material, to unfold its true substance, has already been too forcefully demonstrated to take excuses at their face value. We need only recall films like *Potemkin* or *Carnival in Flanders,* or, on home grounds, *The Informer* and *The Grapes of Wrath.* Whenever a current film approximates fullness of realization, it communicates magnitude, it is possessed of a splendor bright or sultry, it communicates something more than the mediocrity that passes for success. In this resides the as yet infrequently realizable dream of Hollywood's finest artists.

That this isn't always wanted by the public, especially in the case of serious film drama, is a claim that Hollywood's executives, who must take into account the risks of heavy investment, can substantiate more often than not. The cynic bird in us may, indeed, occasionally croak that the best way to destroy the lassitude of film-making is to kill its mass audience. . . . But there are less quixotic courses open to us: Some are seemingly "impractical," like making films for special distribution to avoid the Dracula of Hays office licensing; of making them outside of Hollywood and cooperatively, in order to escape the burden of high costs and, with that, avoid the expense of spirit in a waste of shame. Some courses are more plainly practical, such as making more "B" budget pictures that rely on an exploitable idea rather than on stars and scenic glitter; or in the case of "A" pictures, simply taking the not too great risk of bludgeoning the public with story development, characterization, and other matters, on the chance that one may *overwhelm* the spectator. It has been known to "work" and pay dividends. It was such a chance that the Theatre Guild took when it produced the exceptionally profitable nine-act *Strange Interlude.* It is the procedure of that shrewd showman David Selznick in the currently successful film *Since You Went Away,* which, though criticized for its clichés and sentimentality, left the bulk of its audience limp enough to get at least the illusion of magnitude. The next step, the achievement of the truly great instead of the merely gargantuan, may come from aspiration but never from lethargy and casualness. Someone once called Victor Hugo a "Michelangelo in terra cotta," but even that is artistically preferable to an Edgar A. Guest. And be it added that subject and point of view are also encompassed in this question. A *"B"* idea picture must at least start with an idea, and the comparative inexpensiveness of production permits the risk of forthright treatment, while an "all out" elaborated *"A"* picture may lend importance to an even cautiously introduced idea through the largeness of the frame and of the personal story containing it. That this largeness is not necessarily a matter of length but of intensity, of packing a film with relevant matter, goes without saying. Pictures are not to be appreciated by the yard measure. Last year unreeled twenty-three pictures that ran two hours or over, but this was not in itself an assurance of superiority; it did not make most of them better than, or equal to, *Going My Way*. (As a matter of fact, large chunks of the so-called final screenplay were omitted on the screen—and to great advantage, if I may say so.) But too often cutting lops off the most essential substance, or the general pattern is skimpy from the very start.

In varying degrees, the screenplays of the present collection possess the merits of "fullness." When one sits down with them even in print, it is as though one sat down to some semblance of a dinner rather than to a quick lunch—a sandwich and a milk-shake. We get the savor of a full course in the meat of *Wilson, The Purple Heart, Dragon Seed, The Ox-Bow Incident, Casablanca* and *Watch on the Rhine*, in the spiritual fare of *Going My Way*, and on the haphazardly heaped-up cafeteria tray of *Hail the Conquering Hero, The Miracle of Morgan's Creek,* and *The More the Merrier!*

Wilson belongs in the book by reason of its tradition-breaking concern with a tragic political career whose failure had momentous consequences to be told only in terms of the blood, sweat and tears of a world in travail; whose defeat, and the manner in which it came about, may sound warnings as we get ready to reconstitute the world; whose aspiration should, nonetheless, serve as an inspiration in the days to come. That *Wilson* reaches the widespread millions of America instead of a small circle of preconvinced Broadway intellectuals is an added measure of its timely importance. The film may not characterize Wilson in all his human complexity, and may not tell the entire story of the failure of Versailles, since the plane of treatment is broad and simple. It may fail to take into sufficient account the complex antagonisms of Europe, the power-politics of the powder-keg continent, as well as the post-war progressive promptings so tragically aborted by the men in the saddle; and too little is made of the economic quicksands in which good will and the men of good will were doomed to flounder. Yet, it is no small accomplishment to show as much as *Wilson* succeeds in recapitulating on the screen without becoming ineffectually sprawling, and without courting the confusion that would have resulted from too complicated an analysis. The film is purposeful and poignant, and, as Bosley Crowther pointed out, there is "an impulse of action" in its "special pleading for an international idea envisioning permanent peace."

The accomplishment must strike us as all the greater when we consider the risks run by its producers (to the tune of $5,200,000, it is reported), and the opposition they knew it would engender in an industry which is fair prey for every pressure group. There is irony in the fact that Hollywood is apt to be damned as zealously when it opens its mouth as when it keeps it shut, when it faces the realities as when it shuns them. A box-office, as well as a prestige, victory for *Wilson,* moreover, held promise of victories for the film colony's most forward-looking leaders. If *Wilson* succeeded, there would be no telling how often Hollywood might venture to grapple with themes on which opinion was divided. Indubitably there is great danger in the power of the film once it acquires the habit of pleading causes, since it can be employed for evil as well as good, depending upon who uses it. Yet nothing risked, nothing gained. And a colorless and impotent neutrality is a negative virtue which may also become a great vice. The world has suffered too horribly from sins of omission, from failure to take up arms promptly enough against a sea of troubles. For these reasons, quite apart from detailed merits of treatment, *Wilson* stands first in this collection, as one mark of progress in the social efficacy of screen drama.

On a different, and yet not entirely unrelated, level of prominence stands *Going My Way.* It is another screenplay revolving around men of good will, a tribute to those who move in small ways its wonders to perform; who taking fire from the empyrean of a faith, bring it down in individual portions to the common earth of common men. Of all recent spiritual screen dramas, *Going My Way* proved to be closest to everyday light without losing but actually gaining radiance, revealed itself as most engagingly related to ordinary humanity, and managed to dispense its meaning with the greatest freedom from debatable hypothesis and with the greatest gayety. If a little sentimentality crept into it, it was not the kind for which apologies are urgently in order. If the benevolent course of action, if the limited social service and the good will in the film cannot be regarded, at least by some of us, as a panacea (it has been tried so often by individuals and groups without saving the world from its disasters!), that need hardly trouble the sceptic. *Going My Way* makes no immoderate claims for creed or policy that we can feel called upon to refute. Its contagion is of the spirit, and its validity is unimpeachable on this score, and also on the score of its recognizably human portraiture. The excellent blending in *Going My Way,* of drama and music, is, moreover, as singular an accomplishment as Hollywood has delivered in many years.

Naturally—or shall we say, unnaturally—we are more often compelled to take a stand in which the morality, though just as valid, is less innocent, and covered with the dust and blood of conflict. This was, and still remains, the most pressing fact of our day. *Casablanca* and *Watch on the Rhine* were the two recent films that approached that challenge most dramatically. In both instances, citizens of America were involved in the struggle while the nation stood officially aloof. In both instances, the problem was treated with more than average perception and intensity. Each film proved effective in its own way. If *Casablanca* traded in exotic atmosphere, in romance and melodrama, and in sentiment masquerading as toughness in the Hemingway manner, it did so with an exemplary expertness of suspense and tension. It is at least a lesson in film contrivance, and to some purpose—which is fairly unusual. If *Watch on the Rhine* remained a worthy stage play somewhat literally transferred to another medium, its earnestness and general solidity of characterization gave the screen a telling, concentrated human drama.

Among the non-documentary war films that exhibited the struggle on foreign soil, *The Purple Heart* and *Dragon Seed* were noteworthy because both were rooted in human character. *The Purple Heart,* with a plot tensely wound around the execution of the first American flyers to bomb Tokyo, derived stature from the mold of American heroism. The hypothetically created trial may be subject to scepticism as all hypothesis is, but in common with many movie-goers the editors found the story engrossing and the characters uplifting—all the more so because these were so assembled as to provide a cross-section of an American generation compounded of many racial strains. *Dragon Seed,* whatever shortcomings appeared on the screen from a miscegenation of accents, commended itself in drawing strength from the common people of China, from a democratic will that all responsible American observers have united to extol, and that none would like to see frustrated. Deriving human authenticity from the pen of Pearl Buck, *Dragon Seed* possessed respect for the common man's share in the war and brought a geographically remote people closer to us.

The Ox-Bow Incident made exceptional claims to distinction with a realistic treatment of American frontier life and a relentless examination of the genesis and momentum of mob violence. Few films of any year possessed such concentrated story-telling and such an insistent pulse-beat. Its grimness was too unpalatable for an audience so consistently treated to lemon drops and candy bars by the purveyors of entertainment, but it would be difficult to find many instances of grimness put to better use, without gratuitous sensationalism, and without synthetic horrors.

As for the comedies, *The More the Merrier* was an excellent example of racy humor, framed by the American scene and enlivened with the dry idiom and boisterous manners which are recognizably our own. It was the best of the comedies treating the overcrowded, war-time Washington of the innumerable government agencies, civil service employees, and priority-bent visiting businessmen whose conglomerate efforts, despite avalanches of complaint, somehow launched the most stupendous war effort in history. An odd romance in this atmosphere, and one involving the bread-and-butter people instead of Hollywood's ordinarily glamorous couples, added a welcome common touch. If zany comedies have a justification (who shall say that they don't?), *The More the Merrier* was, in spite of some exhaustion of its contrivance, an example of how they are to be made.

In *The Miracle of Morgan's Creek* and *Hail the Conquering Hero,* Preston Sturges once more exemplified his facility for employing the hoary tricks of farcical contrivance in a manner that seems fresh and somehow overwhelming. In both instances, as usual, Sturges performs as an agile Puck who plucks at the threadbare sleeves of average sentiment, pulls the most respectably knotted tie or ribbon awry, and douses us with cold water without somehow getting our dander up. There is even a trace of acid in the liquid; it spots publicly cherished notions and practices, and yet keeps us rolling in the aisles. If he is jester-laureate to the American people, he has earned the title because his mimicry is faultless, and because, like all expert wearers of motley, he knows how to whirl us about while he slapsticks us. Bosley Crowther has aptly described this as Sturges' "irrepressible impudence." But set in his clown's make-up are eyes that are alternately sharp and moistly warm, and they leave us wondering whether we can make him out. It is this small challenge to curiosity, this uncertainty as to his intention that make the difference between his tomfoolery on the screen and most men's. Perhaps that is also why he gets by the Hays office where others fail. This feat was indeed the greatest miracle in his *Miracle of Morgan's Creek!* Does not *The Miracle* play hob with conventional views on marriage and legitimacy, and yet leave the public content? Does not *Hail the Conquering Hero* constitute perhaps the brashest travesty on hero-worship since *The Playboy of the Western World,* and yet salve audiences with compassion for the 4F Eddie Bracken hero? The cynic or the social critic can find aid and comfort in Sturges' work, if not perhaps without suspicion that the nimble fellow may not be actually so tough-minded, while the sentimentalist is sure to be gratified—though not without the disquieting feeling that his leg is being pulled.

In closing, it may be noted that without intentional timing, the present volume started going to press on a special occasion. In the year 1944, the American motion picture industry, concerning which Marc Connelly aptly said that "Mother Science gave it a premature birth and Father Opportunism sent it out to work before it could walk," reached its fiftieth anniversary—which still makes it an infant by comparison with the three-thousand-year-old theatre. Fifty years ago, any stout Cortez with a nickel to spend could go to a "Kinetoscope Parlor" in New York and watch Annie Oakley firing a gun for fifteen seconds. Birthday congratulations are in order, although with these might go a reminder, adopted from Hollywood's Nunnally Johnson, concerning many products of maturing technique: "It isn't worth all the extra trouble you have to go through to get a worse picture."

New York, February, 1945.

Note: The texts used in this book are the final shooting scripts. Necessarily, however, in the nature of film making many changes and deletions occur in the shooting and film editing. Whenever a brief sequence occurs which did not appear in the released film, it has been enclosed in heavy brackets. When it seemed absolutely necessary, shooting scripts were collated with dialogue and continuity transcripts of the film.

WRITER, DIRECTOR AND FILM

By DUDLEY NICHOLS

A film is essentially the product of the writer, the director, and the actor. And since the actor generally submits his personality, feeling and imagination to the will of the director, it is fairly true to say that the film is the active product of writer and director. This is by no means to derogate the actor. The creative director will modify his material frequently to give the actor's individuality a fuller scope, to inspire his particular imagination, to implant that conviction from which emotion flows. But no one actor makes a play and it is the director's task to integrate the creative gifts of all who participate in the making of the film. For this reason alone the gifted director must always remain the dominant force in the making of a film. This is by no means to derogate the writer.

There are so few film directors of this first rank that they can make only a small proportion of the films demanded by the public. At a lower level of directorial accomplishment the gifted film-writer may become the dominant personality, impressing his own style upon the film to be made, giving it integrity, while the director follows his lead. Any work of art must have an individual style, therefore one individual must dominate its production.

This is simple enough in painting or literature where one person completes the task. But in a medium such as film, requiring manifold talents and skills, it becomes at times extremely difficult. Talents and skills are embodied in individuals who have wills and personalities of their own. To dominate and weld this collection of skills and talents into one instrument the person who undertakes the task must be a man of action as well as an artist; and only rarely are these two conflicting temperaments unified in one person. The man of action is almost never an artist and the artist is almost never a man of action.

This accounts perhaps for the scarcity of first-rank film directors. It accounts for the difficulty of a gifted writer turned producer and steering a motion picture through to completion. One must virtually be two people and one of these is always trying to get the upper hand. But whoever succeeds will achieve a recognizable style in the finished work. That is the final test in film which decides whether the worker is an artist or an artisan—*style*. The signature of the great film director is in every frame of his film; and how few they are in the aggregate of film directors throughout the world. This statement cannot be made about film-writers because their work is not the end-product but is the first step in a collective creation unless they follow through with the director to the final stage of the cutting-room, in which case they achieve a true collaboration with the director.

The truth is that there is no point in debating the relative importance of writer and director. The able director attracts the able writer and vice versa, and they hold each other in the highest respect, each acknowledging the other's contribution. Each knows a good deal about the other's work. They are akin. They must both be story-tellers in the ancient sense, trying to fascinate their fellows by setting forth the struggles, fears and hungers of imagined characters in the most flexible medium of expression man has yet invented.

There is a tendency to say that the writer has only become important since films began to talk. Nothing is more untrue. Twenty-five years ago, when D. W. Griffith was making his masterpieces, he instinctively sought, as a dramatist in film, the collaboration of writers. Of course they were not then called film-writers or screen-writers. A writer is a writer no matter what his technique—a teller of tales and perhaps a critic of life if in addition to imagination he also possesses a mind that perceives values. Griffith did not need his writers at his side. Like Shakespeare he took his stories where he found them—*Broken Blossoms* from Thomas Burke, *The Birth of a Nation* from a second-rate historical novelist; even the threadbare old melodrama *Way Down East* served his purpose. Collaborating in a sense with such writers, he was able by his own genius to create masterpieces, just as Shakespeare found the seed of *Hamlet* in Saxo Grammaticus or in Belleforest's *Histoires Tragiques*. The point is that the relationship between writer and film director is a natural and inevitable one.

When it came to making an original film such as *Intolerance,* Griffith again drew upon the writers of the past, from the Bible to medieval history, threading into that complicated structure a modern story of his own which was inspired by published reports of a social investigation of the period. Griffith was always a moralist, a fierce critic of social injustice, a poet tender with love. He was perhaps more of a writer than any of the film directors who have followed him. While his films could tell themselves without "titles," he was always experimenting with words, trying to find new ways of using words in conjunction with his imagery, and he longed for sound and music to such an extent that for his later films he created elaborate sound effects and had special scores composed.

These references to David Griffith are not so much a digression as they seem, for anyone who decides to work creatively in film, whether as writer or director, must in a sense follow in the footsteps of Griffith. He must always fight for freedom of the screen. Griffith wanted film to be as large and free as literature. Always a fighting man himself, he gave to the world a free and exciting medium of expression. It is a provocative thing to observe what has happened to that freedom in less than a generation, while technical proficiency in film-making has developed by leaps and bounds. Today, when the cinema has become so technically perfect that it is possible to express with poetic force almost anything within the scope of the imagination, it is next to impossible to say anything which questions fixed power and established authority.

I am not speaking of the United States alone. Wherever films are made, power and prejudice and politics have built their barricades around the camera. One does not mean to say that this is something to bewail, it is very likely the inevitable consequence of discovering that the cinema has the power to shape the mind of the peoples of the world. The power of the image over the mind has always been immediate. You can almost trace the great epochs of painting by the response of the mass mind in those periods. In medieval times when the Church was the paramount authority, there was no place for the heretical painter or for any master however great who would question any fixed idea on which that authority was based. The endless energies that nowadays are directed towards limiting the expressiveness of film, towards fencing the camera into one arid pasture where life is lovely and nothing is wrong with the world, is a testimonial to the power and greatness of the cinema. It is a challenge to the artist to fight for truth and honesty as he has always had to fight if he were worth his salt. There is nothing to deplore so long as there are film-makers who will strive to make better and bolder films.

All this is by way of saying that not only is it idle to argue the relative importance of writer and director in films but it is essential that they work in the closest harmony and collaboration. Show me a superior film and I will show you where this harmony existed. There is no room for egoistic clash in the relationship between writer and director. One must work with mutual respect and humility, serving only the end-product—the film. In a way it is like song-writing: both words and music are requisite. To a film-maker, the words you will find printed in these screenplays are dead without their music. It is like reading the score of a song without hearing the music. And by music one means, of course, not audible music, but the flow of imagery—that visible metric flow of human sharps and flats and grace notes which have been the counterpart of music for all great filmmakers from Griffith on. It is the painter's music in kinetic transformation. Without this music there is no song. The words are dead, cinematically speaking. Words and music are required—the writer and the director.

Just as in song-writing, the occasionally gifted man may combine both functions. But the mechanism of film production has become so difficult and complicated that very few first-rank men in the field have the required energies. The first-rate director must be a good deal of a writer and the competent film-writer something of a director, which is only to say that they must thoroughly know their medium. The nearer truth is that the writer and director are viewing the imagined film from different perspectives. The writer, without writing down the exact music, must finally visualize the film in its entirety, for only in this way can he give it flow and form. The director is writing within each sequence, each scene, making the words and images evoke the mood or feeling he is after.

One is speaking now of pure creation in film, of the ideal film, which is almost never possible in the field of commercial film production. But one must study the ideal film to come to grips with the problems. Regardless of what one may think of the bulk of films as they are, one must respect the medium, whose potentialities have hardly been touched. And one must continuously endeavor to discriminate between it and other media of expression. For a true film is not a photographed play or novel or short story, although it may very likely find its seed in such sources. It is something that exists by laws of its own, drawing life from many sources but having its own world of being. As well say that Michelangelo's Madonna is simply a sculptured imitation of its model. Of course it is not; it is the spirit and passion of the sculptor poured into a massive container, it is a portion of space rendered visible in the image of maternity, it is an infinitude of things but it is not a copy of life; it is a work of art, which cannot be defined except by word-images which are themselves sparks of poetry. It cannot be defined because its root-stalk, life, cannot be defined. No more is *Hamlet* a "dramatized version" of the source-stories Shakespeare found; he made it a poetic tragedy that was entirely new, a work of art that lived afresh in its own world, that had cut its birth-cords by pure creative power.

To mention such comparisons is perhaps to risk the risibility of those who smile upon the current cinema because it is employed almost entirely for mass entertainment. Yet these same people do not devalue literature because of the pulp magazines or the character of fiction in the large circulation weeklies. The history of literature is long and they can point to the masterpieces. The history of the cinema is short and by comparison there are few master-works. Yet given time they will arrive.

One of the great lacks of the cinema so far has been its deficiency in perceptive criticism. There are some critics of course who evaluate successive films as they appear, according to their personal lights, but few men have written critically about the medium itself. Those most equipped to do so are too busy making films or trying to make films. Sometimes even these men have no critical judgment, but work by instinct and often brilliantly by the "intelligence of the heart" and in consequence of long apprenticeship. It is true one must work instinctively when one is actually making a film— or making anything in the realm of art—but behind the intuitive passion should lie a critical attitude, a conscious understanding of what one is doing, to be called upon during the rest periods. An artist without a theory, said Da Vinci, is like a ship-captain without a compass. The cinema is no longer the kinetoscope of Edison. Imagination and feelings have been poured into its mechanism and the little machine, now technically but not artistically perfected, has become at least potentially an instrument of man's spirit. So far we have had much practice and little theory in this new realm of cinema. Until a sound critical work shall be produced we must individually bend our energies to a fuller understanding of what cinema is. The first requirement is that we discriminate between film-writing and all other forms of writing, between film-making and all other dramatic and narrative art forms. I do not propose to discuss these matters in detail here; in fact I profess no capacity for that task, but one can point out the immense confusion that exists in the minds of even talented writers between stage and screen. The fact that films are shown in theaters inclines the casual thinker to identify the two things. So great is the confusion that one frequently finds a stage play being unrolled on the screen, and a motion picture being presented on the stage, even if the producers are unaware of the fact.

It is an over-simplification to say that the stage is the realm of the word and the screen the dominion of the image, yet that is where critical thinking must commence. A word is a symbolic image at one or more removes, sometimes a clot of images. As the intellect refines and complicates these word-images they recede toward abstraction, they lose impact and poetic power; though what they lose in visual force they frequently gain in music. The poet is always trying to restore the force of image to the word. The classic theater—and only in the classic does one find purity of form—is the theater of the word, of great rhetoric, of impassioned speech where the act is secondary—the act being only a poker, so to speak, to stir the fire of passion into blazes of poetry. The great theater *is not intimate,* it is neither written nor staged for only the first three rows. We see the actors move, but posture and gesture count for more than facial expression and we are impassioned by their words, by the grief or laughter of their hearts giving peculiar timbre and inflection to the voice. Nothing but the extreme act competes with the effectiveness of the word. The theater is the secure stronghold of verbal drama and uttered poetry, though it is a place for the eye as well as the ear.

In the cinema the values are reversed. Paradoxical as it may sound when one considers the vast auditoriums in which films are presented nowadays, it *is the only intimate theater.* It is a hundred times more intimate than the stage ever dreamt of being, even in Strindberg's tiny theater when that genius was unconsciously striving for a cinematic form in which everything should become symbolic, seeking a realism of the spirit—a super-realism. The audience, no matter how large, is one person—*the camera*—peering closely into eyes and faces, invisibly sitting in the very laps of the actors so to speak, a secret spy that like an invisible sprite can roam the world at will. Nothing is secret from these key-hole spectators of the cinema. They feel so close to the actors that they identify themselves with, or put themselves into imaginary relationships with, the popular players to a degree that is fantastic. Fanatical is a better word, for they are called "fans." It is the very intimacy of the screen that induces this devotion to a pitch that sometimes seems to be a kind of horrifying mass-hysteria. True, this fanaticism for star performers is promoted by the merchants of motion pictures but that alone does not account for the phenomenon. It could not be promoted if the dream-basis of intimacy were not present. The film-going multitudes see their favorite actors more clearly and intimately than they see those around them in real life, more clearly than they see their own faces in the mirror. How, after all, can they see their own faces in a "close-up" ten feet tall? It is the heroic magnification which the Greeks sought in representing their gods on the stage, sought by primitive mechanism such as stilts and masks, lacking the perfected machine.

It is idle to speak, as partisans of the stage sometimes do, of "live actors" and "shadow actors," of *round* actors and *flat* actors. Such people have never viewed an effective film without prejudice, for as any spectator knows the imagination quickly surrenders to the screen and its world of illusion. The phenomenon of the film fan proves the point. It may be that an uncritical intelligence surrenders more easily, but certainly the mass of people finds on the screen the illusion of reality. It is a **very dense** materialism of mind that would hold the stage to be a more powerful illusion than the screen. Both are illusory of course. Seen from the right perspective all life is illusion. The poet deals in illusion—and poetry is the animating spirit of all the arts.

In pointing out this intimacy of the screen one imputes no deficiency to the stage. Far from it. But it does indicate one great divergence of the two arts which must summon forth a divergent method: and it is method we are searching for. When a theatrical art has become this intimate, *the word* at once begins to lose its power. *Nor does this tarnish the glory of the word.* It only means that there is a more economical eloquence at hand, the eloquence of the eyes and the human face and a number of other revealing things when closely observed. The human face can only speak emotions, perhaps; it is limited in the expression of ideas; and in abstract thought it is utterly dumb. But in emotions, which are the main business of the dramatist, it is the most eloquent thing in the world. Oscar Wilde said something to the effect that if you want to know what a woman is saying look at her, don't listen. It was not all jest. Words can lie, the eyes and face can seldom do so. It would be truer to say that if you want to know what a person under stress of humor or tragedy is feeling, look at that person, don't listen. If you can magnify the face to the size of a film "close-up," words tend to become superfluous; and in art, which demands the most exacting economy, the one intolerable thing is superfluity.

This is only the primer stage of our inquiry. The camera is not confined to the human face. The film can make the spectator look at anything under the sun in a split second. A hand, a broken fingernail, a letter, an empty glass, a cigarette stub, an empty chair, a range of mountains or a drop of dew can be made to fill the screen. Everything visible in the world can be instantaneously made a symbol at the poet's will. And by the device of montage these symbols can flow together or follow one another in a stream, arriving at new relationships and provoking new meanings as easily as the poet builds his lines into a poem, the whole attaining a significance far greater than the meaning of any single line or image, a significance that embodies all parts of the poem and yet rises above them and is something else again.

This aspect of the cinema gives a symbolic range that even Strindberg never dreamt of. It opens the door wide for the great poets of the future who will work in film. It shows us that film is not limited to the dramatic and narrative forms but can also find its counterpart in all the poetic forms. It was a poet, David Griffith, who first discovered this range in film. He found the suggestive power of arranging "close-ups" of objects. There has been other experimentation along this line but no film-maker has bent his full energies towards the goal. It is quite possible when the poet arrives who will be also a master of film, to write lyric and epic "verse" in a montage of pure imagery. A Whitman could compose in film. Pare Lorentz, for instance, has experimented along this line. One feels new ground broken in his film "The River."

Intimacy, montage, magnification and ability to concentrate the spectator's attention on one minute detail at any given instant are not the only qualities wherein cinema differs from the classic theater; but they can serve as a starting point in pursuit of a sound theory. Montage—or "cutting" as we call it in Hollywood—is of course not entirely absent from the stage. I recall a conversation, some years ago at Yalta, with Eisenstein on this matter. When you are with Eisenstein you talk montage. He observed that even in the theater a good director is using some of the principles of film montage—that is, he keeps directing attention to this or that detail of the action taking place on the stage. Sometimes this attention is directed by a curious movement of the actor, sometimes by his remaining motionless, though generally movement and grouping are used. But the effect is not absolute and compulsive as in the cinema, which shuts everything from view except the detail which the director wishes to force upon the eye of the audience. Concentration is forced upon the spectator with an impact unknown to the stage.

One more misconception needs to be cleared up in this attempt to discriminate between stage and screen, and that is to point out the error of the common belief that the screen is the medium of pantomime. In the days of the silent film, of course, pantomime was employed a great deal. The unthinking jumped to the conclusion that since the actor could not speak in words he had to convey his thoughts and feelings by means of pantomime. This was obviously wrong because the expressiveness of pantomime is extremely limited, its range of ideas small, its scale of emotions primitive. Anyone could observe in a Griffith film, for instance, that emotions were produced among the spectators which went far beyond the alphabet of pantomime. I recall Mr. Griffith's reply one night a year or two ago when after we had run one of his old films, *Broken Blossoms,* with a group of friends, someone present remarked to him about the power of the film's pantomime: "What pantomime? There's no pantomime in the picture at all—only attitudes." It was perfectly true. He knew very well that he had discarded pantomime as being too limited to express what he wanted to say and had employed something very old in the theater—attitude. But he had employed it in a new way and with a closeness of vision and a compulsion of attention which were beyond the reach of the stage. Attitude in cinema is for the "medium shot" what the human face is for the "close-up"; they are closely related and must be wielded in the same way.

But space limits further analysis of the nature of cinema and its infinite possibilities of development. I realize we have only opened the door a crack and taken a generalized glimpse—perhaps only a glimpse at the obvious. Experimentation is necessary and the means of production have become so costly, alas, that there is small disposition to experiment.

But lacking the costly materials and machinery for actual experimentation, those who love film must continue to experiment with their minds and attempt to arrive at a sound theory, which can be formulated as a stepping-stone to the development of the medium. The first step is certainly to discriminate more clearly between stage and screen so that we shall cease to flounder about in both fields. This calls for work from both drama critics and film critics. Nor should either condescend toward the craft of the other, for what we do not cherish we cannot understand. They, of course, like the film-writers and directors who have contributed too little to theory, have the excuse that they live in a furious world where there is not enough time for thought.

In conclusion I really should set down my Last Will and Testament because I have recklessly used the words "art" and "artist" a good deal. Of course I have been talking about *ideal* film, about the medium itself apart from the problems of production in what has become a great industry. In the world we live in every art, especially if it tends to be popular, becomes an industry. We have the publishing industry no less than the film industry. The point to remember is that these industries are kept alive by fresh creative minds, individuals who seek out the compass of theory just as the electrical and other industries are kept vital by inventors and scientifically creative minds enriched by knowledge and theory. Yet the film industry has been taken in so often by spurious "artists" that it is gun-shy and there is no more damning word to apply to a director, writer or other film-worker in Hollywood. I am fortunate to know a number of directors in Hollywood who are artists but I will keep their secret. The cat is out of the bag of course with regard to D. W. Griffith; and may I point out that, though he wears his years lightly and is a vital man full of young enthusiasm, he is not making any films? No doubt he is trying to live down the fact that he is an artist. I apologize to him for having revived the calumny, though I have no doubt that he will be around to shoot me if this book should fall into his hands.

In conclusion let me make one further apology, for having omitted the producer and other people who are important to the making of a film. In general I have preferred not to speak of producers; but one must admit that there are great exceptions—men who love the motion picture and combine audacity and imagination to bring off achievements that the writer and director, being not too bright in the world of money, could never manage.

HOLLYWOOD, February, 1945.

THE MOTION PICTURE INDUSTRY AND THE WAR EFFORT

By WALTER WANGER

When future historians write the story of World War II a bright chapter will be assigned to the contributions of America's motion picture industry in winning the war.

Although there is no yardstick to measure the proportion of the film industry's share in prosecuting this war, these contributions have been positive and real. We have no gross tonnage, no total mileage, no fabulous figures of productivity to gauge how much we did and how effective we were. Nevertheless, America's foremost spokesmen in all fields of the war endeavour—the President of the United States, outstanding members of the Federal Government, chiefs of the Army, Navy and Air Force, members of the State Department and other vital Governmental offices, and by no means least of all the G. I.s in foxholes and sailors below deck—all of these have expressed eloquent testimony to Hollywood's varied and important share in bringing this conflict to a victorious conclusion.

Whereas aircraft companies can count by planes, and whereas munitions plants can count by shell casings, Hollywood has no easy standard of measurement. Yet, the thousands of personal appearances of Hollywood entertainers in every theatre of war, on the home front, in hospitals here in the United States have done much to boost morale and sell the War Bonds which are financing this war. The thousands of training films made by Hollywood's finest technicians and craftsmen, furnished free to all branches of the Armed Forces, have received the highest commendations from our Army and Navy leaders. As for the G. I.s themselves, the following statement by a soldier in some distant foxhole on one of America's battlefields, is certainly the most touching tribute of all, and in some respects the most important. "Movies for us out here," wrote the G. I., "are like a couple of hours at home." There is little that I can add to a tribute like that.

A few hours after the terrible news of Pearl Harbor the motion picture industry had already begun the herculean task of organizing its productive capacities for the war effort. Before the tragedy of Hawaii the motion picture industry had been cooperating with various governmental agencies in fulfilling the needs of America's training and defense program. But the

Report from Walter Wanger, President of the Academy of Motion Picture Arts and Sciences, on the contribution of the motion picture industry to the war effort of the United States.

actuality of war called upon Hollywood, as it called upon every other industry and community in America, to strain its resources and capacities to the limit.

In the three years since Pearl Harbor, the United States has put over 12,000,000 trained and equipped men into the field. Their equipment—the best of any nation in the world, and recognized as the most powerful—is the product of America's great producing industries. But its training fell largely to one—the motion picture industry. Washington authorities knew long before Pearl Harbor that the motion picture film was the one most effective instrument of instruction for everything from how to fire a sixteen-inch gun to the problems of how to store field kitchen equipment. The High Command of the Armed Forces turned to the film companies for their help in this sudden emergency; and the studios responded by turning over all their facilities and manpower to the monumental job ahead.

Hollywood personnel—from producer to technician—had been watching with more than passing interest the type of training and "educational" films which our enemies and our allies had been turning out. The Academy of Motion Picture Arts and Sciences itself sponsored several showings of British documentaries dealing with Britain's war effort, and also showed several German propaganda films which were exhibited before German people and conquered people as well as its Army and Navy personnel; pictures like "Victory over Poland" and "The March Through the East of Europe" are two examples.

Hollywood saw these pictures, observed them carefully, and then improved on them. The motion picture industry has long known its responsibility as the producer of the world's most effective medium of communication. This knowledge was put to immediate work, and with tremendous effectiveness when the word came to America to roll up its sleeves for war.

Civilian and Service morale can never be measured. Men who have studied both home front and battle front attitudes, however, express it this way: "There is no *degree* of morale; either it's there, or it isn't." Entertainment from Hollywood served both our men at the fighting front, and civilians at home producing for the war effort. But more important to the fighting front are the three or four films weekly, reduced from the established 35mm size to 16mm, which are sent to every theatre of war activity in the world to entertain our fighting men. This is the touch of home which has come to mean so much to Americans everywhere.

Statistics are always dry; yet the number of persons involved and the mileage covered by camp entertainers must run into celestial figures. No theatre of the war has been neglected, and entertainers like Bing Crosby and Bob Hope, for example, have literally lost their front line audiences in the middle of a show because the men were called to a sudden attack.

Earlier in the War the Research Council of the Academy of Motion Picture Arts and Sciences had established a program of turning out all-important training films. Once the tempo of war speeded this program up, the Council moved forward with clock-like precision to undertake the tremendous training film program. At the request of the Army Signal Corps, the Council pooled the experience and knowledge of its technicians and, working through a stream-lined committee of twenty, solved problems connected with the production of training films, and their exhibition in mobile as well as stationary theatres.

Studios working together established photographic schools at no cost to the United States Government. Trained technicians stood side by side with raw recruits to learn combat photography under the direction of Hollywood's best craftsmen. The result is that the United States has the best combat photographers of any in the world.

The motion picture industry established at no cost to the Government the largest Navy Radar Training School in the country in Chicago. In three years some 35,000 Radar operators have been graduated from this one school alone, an eloquent example of the determination of the film industry to give the country its best.

According to figures published by the Army Overseas Motion Picture Service, an audience of 32,000,000 are seeing Hollywood's films without charge each month. A further breakdown reveals that there are at least 3,000 showings daily for men in service in every part of the globe, from the Aleutians to Burma, from Ascension Island to Aachen.

But again these are figures, and they are meaningless in the largest sense of what this war is about. The fact that Hollywood and the motion picture industry have offered the Government its product, its talent, its goods free, without cost of any kind—incidentally, the only American industry to do so—is another fact of which the industry is proud. But here again this gesture is but a symbol of what the motion picture industry can mean to America and the rest of the world.

The motion picture industry is looking ahead to the needs of a postwar world, intent upon binding up its wounds and pressing forward into the future. Films can and must play an important part in the establishing of the world of tomorrow. The effectiveness of motion pictures as an educator has been dramatically established again and again in training companies throughout the nation. The value of films as a medium of entertainment, a moment's welcome release from the bitterness of war, has also been well established. And the value of films as an instrument of peace, an instrument in establishing good will is reflected in its value as an instrument of propaganda for war. We are fighting to maintain supremacy of a way of life respected and imitated throughout the world; and our Union now extends to our Allies and makes us, in the largest sense, citizens of a world composed of a community of nations. In the world of the future, all nations—former foes as well as friends—will be vitally concerned with mutual examination, interpretation and the complete understanding of common aims. Films are the one interpretative medium which can make this world one harmonious whole, with all of its component parts working for the common good. The motion picture industry will be called upon to undertake the greatest sales campaign of its fifty years of history; the motion picture industry must be prepared to "sell" the world to the world.

And we of the film industry realize that we can serve our own and America's interests best when we also serve the causes of freedom, justice, tolerance and international understanding.

PREFACE TO "WILSON"

By Darryl F. Zanuck

An idea for a motion picture production seldom arrives full-blown at its proper destination.

The birth of such an idea may be the result of chance or of some sudden flash of insight. It usually is. But the process of developing and bringing it to acceptable maturity is one filled with pain and frustration, clamor and insomnia.

The motion picture *Wilson* had such a birth. The pattern held true except for one rather dramatic detail. The war and my own experiences on the fighting fronts played their full part in fashioning this film.

Originally, the idea for a motion picture based on the life of Woodrow Wilson came simply as a by-product. For some time, I had been mulling over another idea altogether—a picture dealing with the life of the late Samuel Gompers, the great labor leader. It seemed to me at the time that a constructive, carefully documented film about Gompers would not only be a worthwhile undertaking from a dramatic standpoint but that it might also contribute something to lessening the tensions developing in our economic system.

But as I continued to delve into the subject, with the aid of Lamar Trotti, one of the screen's most capable writers, I found myself more and more often confronted with the name of Woodrow Wilson, the record of his accomplishments and the part he played in Gompers' career. Naturally, I was familiar, rather hazily, to be true, with Wilson's achievements, but this close perusal of the man's record, his great vision and his courage convinced me that here indeed was a subject worthy of cinematic consideration.

Consequently, we dropped the Gompers project for the time being and shifted to the story of Wilson. However, our research activities into President Wilson's life had been in progress for only a short time when the nation was plunged into war. I became a colonel in the Army Signal Corps and naturally, in the press of new activities dealing with the making of training and documentary films, the civilian projects on which I had been engaged were pretty well forgotten.

As the war progressed and I was shifted from one fighting front to another, I found the idea which had so intrigued me at the studio being revived by a continuing series of grim experiences.

I saw how destructive of humanity war was, and how innocent of its causes were those who had to do the fighting. Again and again as I saw our boys dying and suffering the thought occurred: why had not something been done to prevent this futile sacrifice?

Subsequently, the same thoughts were echoed in various forms by fighting men wherever the fortune of war took me—in the foxholes of Africa and Tunisia, in Commando boats off the coast of France, in Canada, England and Ireland and remote, far-off spots like Bathurst, in British Gambia. They were expressed at times lamely and gropingly, in the language of men unaccustomed to thinking of international issues. But they were also expressed at other times with a force and fervor which were almost frightening. These men seemed to feel, whether dimly or clearly, that they had been let down somewhere along the line. They may not have known exactly who was to blame, or why or how, but they felt and they knew that a better, saner world was possible. They had come to realize, many of them, that Wilson had foreseen this and tried to prevent it, but that he had somehow been balked and beaten.

Such experiences, of course, could not but revive my dormant interest in President Wilson as a motion picture subject. In fact, my interest rose to such a pitch I proposed that the government undertake to make it as a documentary to show the mistakes of the past so they could be avoided in the future. The proposal was rejected. I realize now that it wasn't a project for the government. But the matter continued to grip my interest as a production to mark my return to the studio. I therefore wired Lamar Trotti to take up where we had left off and prepare a tentative script.

After being placed on the inactive list a year later, I plunged at once into the task of preparing the picture for production. Immediately, I discovered myself face to face with a number of highly perplexing problems, not the least of which was the mere physical task of bringing a subject of such vast scope to the screen under the various material limitations imposed by the government. The want of a nail, I discovered, could not only lose battles. It could also raise hob with production plans.

The foremost of these problems, however, and the one requiring immediate solution, was one of approach. The history of Hollywood's ventures into the field of contemporary affairs had not been a particularly happy one. There were two reasons for this. We had learned, through bitter experience, that any attempt to deal realistically with the problems of the day was bound to bring down on us a flood of vituperation and criticism from special groups. It did not seem to matter how worthy or well intentioned such attempts might be. We were vulnerable in the sense that the screen did not seem to enjoy the same privileges of expression accorded the press or the radio. Reprisals were often threatened and in some cases carried out. They were carried out, for example, when a Senate committee, dominated by isolationists, called the entire motion picture industry on the carpet to accuse us of war-mongering a short time before the attack on Pearl Harbor. I had been a witness at that farcical hearing and was well aware of the lengths to which some groups would go to shackle this vital medium.

The result had been to make the industry wary of any subject dealing with the concrete problems affecting the nation and the world. Occasionally such a picture has come through. I had produced several myself, among them *The Grapes of Wrath* and *The Ox-bow Incident*. But the risk each time was so great and the complications so vexing that such pictures seemed hardly worth the effort and pain.

Yet, after my experiences on the fighting fronts, I was determined to make *Wilson* regardless of the headaches. Here I must add that many members of the Twentieth Century-Fox organization opposed the idea as entailing too great a risk. They argued from motives which were utterly sincere. However, many others supported me. In looking back, it seems to me that the future of the motion picture industry is in safe hands when men are willing to gamble their professional reputations and their money simply to do a job which they feel is worth doing.

I knew from experience that criticism from outside quarters would not be long in coming. I knew I would be accused of partisanship, of playing politics, of advancing the Rooseveltian cause for a fourth term or pleading for the election of my good friend, the late Wendell Willkie, a truly great man. I was not disappointed. The drumfire began almost simultaneously with the announcement of the plans for the picture. It has abated somewhat now but I still hear from the self-appointed critics.

Yet, none of this was in my mind. I could not see then and certainly cannot see now how anyone can quarrel with the projection of a man who almost literally had given up his life to the cause of peace. I could not possibly see any partisanship in such an undertaking, no matter what the special pleaders might say. Therefore, we dismissed these objections and went ahead.

The other problem was much more pressing and local. It concerned the box office fate of pictures which had attempted to break into new and controversial ground. With a few rare exceptions, they had not done well. *The Grapes of Wrath* was a financial success but it had been backed up by a great novel which had had a phenomenal sale. On the other hand, *The Ox-bow Incident,* a story of mob violence and its dreadful consequences, had been a flop. In spite of its significance and its dramatic value, our records showed that it had failed to pay its way. In fact, its pulling power was less than that of a Laurel and Hardy comedy we made about the same time.

It became obvious to myself and my associates, therefore, that we would have to underscore the dramatic and entertainment values inherent in the subject. This was not a cynical decision made in the hope of profit, as some have charged. It goes far deeper than that. For no motion picture, no matter how fine or constructive, is greater than its audience. By that I mean that a picture must have an audience.

To be truly successful, to make its point, a picture must be a financial success at the box office. It must be seen by the maximum number of people. If it fails at the box office it merely means, particularly in a serious film, that the point has failed to get across. Artistically and technically, it may be perfect. But unless people wish to see it and do, it is still a failure. It has failed because it was made to be seen.

You could, of course, blame the public, but that would be self-deception. It had always seemed to me that subjects of great social significance could be made acceptable to the great masses of our public by the proper employment of the techniques we had used so often and so well in films made simply for entertainment. The fault, in other words, too often lies not with the public but with ourselves. We have simply failed to utilize our resources and our talents for providing entertainment. We had turned out pictures of meaning and of value but we had not presented the subject properly. They had been grim and perhaps dull, and the public, very properly, had ignored their existence.

Consequently, as we progressed with the planning of *Wilson*, many of the details were changed in the interest of wider popular appeal. Originally we had intended to make *Wilson* in black and white, but later, in spite of the enormous added costs entailed, we decided to film it in Technicolor. I believe everyone will agree that the chromatic values thus given the picture add immensely to its dramatic force.

The change meant much more than simply a shift from black and white to color. It meant the automatic elimination of hundreds of feet of newsreel film of the Wilson era which we had managed to obtain at great cost and labor. It meant extensive changes in the sets and wardrobes and the complete revision of the plans for the make-up of the hundreds of characters in the picture.

The point is important not so much because of the great added expense involved but because it so well illustrates the imponderables which must be quickly dealt with in productions of this serious type. For once such films are launched, it is impossible to hold back. *Wilson* was in the nature of an experiment. In all modesty, I can say that it was the greatest experiment of its kind ever attempted in Hollywood. The presentation of a controversial subject on such a scale had never before been undertaken, particularly in the face of such physical obstacles and the attacks to which we were being subjected. We felt that if the experiment were to succeed it would have to have all we could give it. Otherwise, we would be blameworthy. We would blame ourselves for hedging or stinting. At stake, we all felt, was more than the fate of this one picture, no matter how costly. The future of the motion picture industry as an incalculable force for good also was in the balance. For we well knew that no other company would dare to take the risks involved in bringing vital, contemporary problems to the screen if *Wilson,* in movie parlance, laid an egg.

Therefore, the decisions were made. They brought the cost of the picture from an original estimate of less than $2,000,000 to more than $4,000,000.

The physical details of transferring Mr. Trotti's splendid scenario to the screen were not the least of the problems which we had to face. A picture of this type needs a degree of close and intelligent cooperation, seldom required in any other field. A single prop man can quite easily and unintentionally undo the work of a hundred artists and a fractious performer can make even the sunniest of California days bleak and depressing. Creative artists are temperamental folk. They would not be creative otherwise. Their talents must be blended, supervised and channelized in any undertaking of this kind. It is a task requiring great patience, great understanding and great tact. In this particular instance, we were fortunate.

The choice of Alexander Knox to portray the title role was one of those blessed accidents which make movie making both a great gamble and a stimulating profession. For weeks we had frantically cast about for an individual able, by training and personal force, to depict the President. It was not our intention to find someone closely resembling Wilson. That, we felt, would be caricature. What we desperately needed and wanted was a trained actor, not well known, to delineate the character of the President, to project the fervor and the idealism which animated him and the cold stubbornness which he could display whenever he felt a principle at stake. No established, big-name actor would do for the reason that his gestures and expressions, his smallest movements, would be familiar to millions of movie goers. The essential portrait of Wilson which we desired would necessarily be distorted.

In this emergency, we decided to make a recording of the dialogue in the screenplay to give us a chance to judge by ear the dramatic effectiveness of what we had. To portray Wilson in this recording, we called in Knox, who was all but unknown to film audiences. Some years before he had played a supporting role in one of our films, *This Above All.* That recording by Knox proved so moving and dramatic we knew we had our man. There is no great natural similarity between Knox and Wilson. Yet, I am certain that the picture did not suffer thereby. Certainly, the critics have hailed his performance in this difficult role as one of the finest the screen has afforded.

But if physical similarity to the subject was not important in the case of Knox, it was quite otherwise as regards the host of historical figures to be portrayed. They would be delineated but briefly. There was no chance of developing a rounded portrait through speech and action. And finally, these figures were familiar to millions of Americans still living.

The task of assembling a proper supporting cast, therefore, proved extremely difficult. We needed not only competent players but also men who could qualify in their physical make-up. We combed the Hollywood lists thoroughly and time after time until we obtained approximately what we desired. Our make-up department filled in the rest.

Here and there, I have heard a few complaints regarding the selection of Geraldine Fitzgerald for the part of the second Mrs. Wilson. I must confess to a feeling of impatience at such criticism. It is based mostly on the grounds that Miss Fitzgerald does not bear a close physical resemblance to the subject. To my mind, it was no more important that she look exactly like Mrs. Wilson than that Knox measure up in outward form to the President. She appears in the picture long enough to define the essential character of the woman who had such a decisive influence on the President's life. Very few have taken exception to her performance, which is what counts.

The choice of Henry King as director was all but automatic. Time after time, he had demonstrated his ability to handle sensitively and with fine intelligence screen subjects of great sweep and power. We felt highly fortunate in having him for *Wilson*.

Lamar Trotti rates far more than mere honorable mention for his contribution to the whole. A motion picture is never better than the screen play which is its essence and foundation. For him, *Wilson* became a labor of love.

It was truly a monumental job of research and writing which he accomplished single-handed. I know very few others who could have done it.

Wilson, in a literal sense, therefore represents the ideas of many men which I have humbly appropriated. In another sense, it is a tribute to these men—a tribute paid in the hope that it will contribute its measure toward bringing a better world into being.

December 1, 1944.

DARRYL F. ZANUCK'S
Production of

WILSON

(*A Twentieth Century–Fox Picture*)

Screenplay by LAMAR TROTTI

Produced by DARRYL F. ZANUCK

Directed by HENRY KING

The Cast

WOODROW WILSON	Alexander Knox
PROFESSOR HENRY HOLMES	Charles Coburn
EDITH WILSON	Geraldine Fitzgerald
JOSEPH TUMULTY	Thomas Mitchell
ELLEN WILSON	Ruth Nelson
SENATOR HENRY CABOT LODGE	Sir Cedric Hardwicke
WILLIAM G. McADOO	Vincent Price
GEORGE FELTON	William Eythe
ELEANOR WILSON	Mary Anderson
MARGARET WILSON	Ruth Ford
JOSEPHUS DANIELS	Sidney Blackmer
JESSIE WILSON	Madeleine Forbes
ADMIRAL GRAYSON	Stanley Ridges
EDDIE FOY	Eddie Foy, Jr.
COLONEL HOUSE	Charles Halton
SENATOR E. H. JONES	Thurston Hall
EDWARD SULLIVAN	J. M. Kerrigan
JIM BEEKER	James Rennie
HELEN BONES	Katherine Locke
SECRETARY LANSING	Stanley Logan
CLEMENCEAU	Marcel Dalio
WILLIAM JENNINGS BRYAN	Edwin Maxwell
LLOYD GEORGE	Clifford Brooke
VON BERNSTORFF	Tonio Selwart
SENATOR WATSON	John Ince
SENATOR BROMFIELD	Charles Miller

Film Editor—BARBARA McLEAN

Screenplay of the Twentieth Century–Fox photoplay "Wilson," copyright 1944 by Twentieth Century–Fox Film Corporation. By permission of Darryl F. Zanuck and Twentieth Century–Fox Film Corp.

WILSON
PART ONE

The opening title fades in, reading:

>SOMETIMES THE LIFE
>OF A MAN MIRRORS THE LIFE OF
>A NATION. THE DESTINY OF
>OUR COUNTRY WAS CRYSTALLIZED
>IN THE LIFE AND TIMES OF
>WASHINGTON AND LINCOLN . . .
>AND PERHAPS, TOO, IN THE LIFE
>OF ANOTHER PRESIDENT . . .

VOICES SINGING (*over narrative titles*).

>Of thee I sing—
>Land where my fathers died,
>Land of the pilgrims' pride—

This dissolves to another title:

>. . . THIS IS A STORY OF
>AMERICA—AND THE STORY OF
>A MAN . . . WOODROW WILSON
>28TH PRESIDENT
>OF THE UNITED STATES

VOICES SINGING (*continued*).

>From every mountain side
>Let freedom ring.

This fades out and another title fades in, reading:

>PRINCETON UNIVERSITY
>1909

And this dissolves to a long view of the PRINCETON CAMPUS. We see the Princeton chimes and then the campus —with young men walking about and lounging on the lawn. This scene cuts to a BUILDING on the campus, with a boy riding on a bicycle up the walk toward it. Then we see PROSPECT AVENUE —the street of the undergraduate clubs, as carriages drive along the street and people walk along the sidewalk.

This dissolves to the PRINCETON FOOTBALL FIELD. The Princeton band, in

Copyright 1944, by *20th Century-Fox Film Corporation*.

black and gold uniforms, is marching out on the field, playing "Crash Through that Line of Blue." The band leader marches out in front, twirling his baton, stepping high. This cuts to the ROOTING SECTION: The Princeton students are cheering wildly. Many of them wear sweaters and the funny little hats then common to college students.

The YALE TUNNEL, as seen from above: The Yale team comes through the tunnel and runs out on the field. Off-scene we hear the strains of a band playing "Boola-Boola," and wild cheering. Then opposite the ENTRANCE TUNNEL, the Princeton team runs out on the field. Off-scene the cheering becomes even louder and "Crash Through that Line of Blue" dominates the music.

We see the PRINCETON STANDS, with a group of Princeton students on their feet, waving Princeton pennants and cheering wildly. The view moves over to a smaller group including WOODROW WILSON, President of Princeton, his wife, ELLEN, and his three daughters, MARGARET, JESSIE and NELL, and PROFESSOR HOLMES. Wilson and Holmes carry canes with Princeton pennants on them. Wilson and the girls are on their feet, and he is alive with interest in what is going on below.

> WILSON (*excitedly*). Now if coach only has sense enough to put Felton in at left half!
>
> NELL (*seriously*). Is Felton good, Father?
>
> WILSON (*giving her an incredulous look*). Good? My dear Nell, Felton is the greatest broken field runner since Willie Heston of Michigan!
>
> NELL (*squashed*). Oh.

The SCORE BOARD: It is the beginning of the second half. The score is Princeton—0, Yale—0. Over this continue cheering and band music. This cuts to the PLAYING FIELD as the two teams line up for the second half kick-off. Then FELTON is seen at close view in football togs, playing half-back. He wets his lips, and looks off intently. He is very tense and eager.

We get a full view of the FIELD as the referee blows his whistle and Yale kicks off to Princeton, followed by a telescopic view as Felton receives the ball near his own goal line and comes up the field—his teammates forming an effective flying wedge which enables him to get through and to start on his way toward a touchdown.

The PRINCETON STANDS: Wilson and the girls are on their feet, yelling wildly, Wilson making short, staccato shouts and pounding with his cane.

> WILSON (*excitedly*). It's Felton! It's Felton! Go it, Felton!

The PLAYING FIELD: Felton has almost reached the Yale goal line when suddenly he is overtaken by a Yale man and brought down by a vicious tackle. The ball flies out of his arms. A Yale man scoops it up and gallops off toward the Princeton goal, pursued by the almost stunned Princeton team. We get a close view of FELTON on the ground, looking off, horrified, and then see the play continuing.

The PRINCETON STANDS: Wilson is still going crazy, yelling at the top of his voice.

> WILSON. Stop him! Stop him!

The PLAYING FIELD: The Yale man dodges the last Princeton player and goes over for a touchdown.

The PRINCETON STANDS, catching the edge of the ROOTING SECTION: A groan goes up from the Princeton rooters, while from across the field comes the sound of triumphant Yale, cheering to the strains of "Boola-Boola." Almost everybody sinks down dejectedly. Wilson is stunned—his hat is crushed down over his ears and he slumps into his seat. Ellen and the girls look at him in some amusement. Nell leans toward him and then her eyes twinkle.

NELL (*with mock accusation*). Felton!

As Wilson groans inwardly, the music of "Boola-Boola" and the cheering of the triumphant Yale fans continue.

HOLMES (*with mock disgust*). Felton!

This dissolves to a closeup of the SCOREBOARD:

Team	1st Half	2nd Half	Game
PRINCETON	0	0	0
YALE	0	6	6

VOICES (*singing over this scene*).
Fight—fight for Yale
The sons of Eli are—

This cuts to a fairly long view of the PRINCETON TUNNEL as the voices continue to sing over the scene.

VOICES (*singing*).
—out for glory
On to the fray—
We'll tell to Princeton the same old story
The cry is on—on they come
We'll raise the slogan of Yale triumphant
Smash—bang—we'll rip poor Princeton!
Whoop it up for Yale today.
Fight—fight for Yale—
The sons of Eli are out for glory
On to the fray—
We'll tell to Princeton the same old story
The cry is on—on they come

We'll raise the slogan of Yale triumphant
Smash—bang—we'll rip poor Princeton!
Whoop it up for Yale today.

This dissolves to the STADIUM. It is late afternoon. The game is just over; the crowd is leaving, while the music of "Boola-Boola" and the cheering come over. We see the Wilsons and Professor Holmes coming out of the grandstand with the crowd. A newsboy is hawking afternoon papers. Wilson is very dejected. Professor Holmes seems to be slyly amused by Wilson's woebegone look.

ELLEN (*to Wilson, her eyes twinkling mischievously*). Don't fret, dear. I think it is very sweet of our boys to let Yale win. After all, they're our guests.

Wilson stops, looks at her, starts to say something, then gives up. When he looks off ahead again, he sees someone and calls out.

WILSON. Oh, Felton!

NEAR THE PRINCETON TUNNEL: The Princeton team is limping off the field, the men dirty and tired, very depressed and unhappy. One man is being helped along by a couple of others. Defeat hangs heavy over them. Toward the end of the line of boys is Felton. He is covered with mud and looks "all in." More than any of the others he is sunk in gloom. He draws the back of his hand across his nose and looks up as he hears his name called.

FELTON (*as he hears Wilson calling out his name*). Yes, sir. (*Wilson leans over and pats Felton on the back.*)

WILSON (*a reassuring smile on his face*). Never mind, Felton. You played a great game. Everybody's entitled to a fumble now and then.

For a moment their eyes meet.

FELTON (*in a low voice, as he moves on*). Thank you, sir.

Meanwhile, in the background, Holmes is to be seen whispering something into the newsboy's ear. He also appears to hand the newsboy a coin. The newsboy turns quickly to Wilson as Holmes, an innocent look on his face, catches up with the Wilsons.

NEWSBOY (*very serious*). Are you Mr. Wilson?

WILSON (*surprised*). Yes.

NEWSBOY. You President of Princeton?

WILSON. I am.

NEWSBOY. Then why the heck don't you get a football team?

At first Wilson is startled, then he cannot help grinning. The others hold back their laughter. Wilson looks up sharply at Holmes. Holmes puts on his most innocent look, as if butter would not melt in his mouth.

WILSON (*to the newsboy*). I've been thinking about that myself, young man. If you know anybody who wants to swap a good half-back for a rather moth-eaten Professor of Economy, here's your man.

He points to Holmes, grins, and walks on. The girls laugh and go with him, leaving Holmes and the newsboy staring after them. Then a close view shows HOLMES and the NEWSBOY looking after the Wilsons.

NEWSBOY. We didn't do so good—did we, Prof?

Holmes grins and does the business of pushing back his hat, then goes on.

[This dissolves to PROSPECT AVENUE, in Princeton, in the late afternoon, the view moving across "FRATERNITY ROW" —the street of the luxurious undergraduate clubs. As Wilson and his family come along, FELTON is just emerging from one of the houses, carrying a couple of suitcases. As the boy cuts around a tree on the front lawn he bumps smack into Wilson.

FELTON. Oh—excuse me!

He is startled and a little nonplussed, not only because of the accident but because he hadn't expected to see Wilson.

WILSON (*touching his hat*). Good afternoon, Felton.

FELTON. Goodbye, sir. . . . (*Then quickly catching himself*) I mean, good afternoon, sir.

As he moves off hurriedly, Wilson shoots a sharp glance after the boy, then he stops.

WILSON (*to Ellen and the girls*). Excuse me. (*As they go on, he turns and calls to the boy.*) Just a moment, Felton. (*Felton stops, and Wilson comes up to him.*) You're leaving Princeton?

FELTON (*after a slight hesitation*). Yes, sir.

WILSON. Why?

FELTON. It just didn't work out, that's all.

WILSON. What didn't work out?

FELTON (*evasively*). Oh—a lot of things.

WILSON. Such as—?

FELTON. Well, these upperclass clubs for one thing.

WILSON. What about the clubs?

FELTON. Everything! The way they're run! What they're doing to Princeton!

WILSON (*with quiet insistence*). I wish you'd say exactly what you mean, Felton.

The boy looks at Wilson and his jaw sets. Then he sets his suitcases down.

FELTON (*angrily*). I came down here to get an education, not to join a country club!

WILSON (*quietly*). Go on.

FELTON (*with a sweeping gesture*). Just look at these houses! Every one of them out to see how much money they can spend—trying to outshine the other! Half the men in school afraid even to walk past them because somebody might think they're bootlicking!

WILSON. But aren't you a member of a club yourself?

FELTON. Yes, sir—or at least I was—until I realized what a bunch of snobs we are.

WILSON. Are you suggesting that members of a social organization haven't the right to choose their own friends?

FELTON. Of course not! But that doesn't mean they've got to act as if they were better than everybody else just because their fathers happen to have a million dollars or something.

WILSON. Well, I must say you seem to feel very strongly about it.

FELTON (*earnestly*). Yes, sir, I do. You see, I'd always thought Princeton was a great University. I'd heard my father talk about it—and *you*, too. I thought it was a place where you could learn something—not only out of books, but how to live in a country like ours. But what chance have you got with a bunch of fellows who act as if they never even heard the word democracy?

WILSON (*calmly*). I agree with you, Felton. I think you're absolutely right to leave.

FELTON (*surprised*). You do, sir?

WILSON. In fact, I've felt as you do for a long time. It's very gratifying and encouraging to find some of our most promising young men with backbone enough to do something about it—even if it is only running away. (*Again touching his hat*) Good afternoon.

And he moves off, leaving Felton staring after him in bewilderment. Felton picks up his bags and starts off. Then he stops again and looks back, still puzzled.

This dissolves to a view of the PRINCETON CHIMES sending their mellowed tones out over the campus; the view then moves across the PRINCETON CAMPUS, and dissolves to the CORRIDOR of the ADMINISTRATION BUILDING, a dignified, Gothic structure. Ten or twelve men—members of the Board of Trustees—are just coming out of Wilson's office. They appear closer. The expressions on their faces indicate that something important is afoot. Several of the men are frowning grimly; others are merely thoughtful and perplexed; one or two even seem pleased. Felton is seated here, just outside of Wilson's office, as if waiting for an appointment. He looks off at the trustees. As the more angry ones pass the camera they give vent to their feelings.

FIRST TRUSTEE. The man's out of his mind!

SECOND TRUSTEE. I've been a trustee of this university for twenty years and I've never heard such nonsense!

THIRD TRUSTEE. Why can't he ever leave things alone?

Felton sits there, a glimmer of a smile on his face, looking after the departing trustees.

WILSON'S OFFICE: Wilson is seated at his typewriter. Throughout the scene he continues to peck away. Professor Holmes, his closest friend—and incidentally, his severest critic—is watching him reflectively out of the corner of his eye, while he fiddles with his pipe. Professor Holmes carries his tobacco loose in his coat pocket and is forever spilling it over himself and the floor. Holmes looks at Wilson with a twinkle in his eye, and a chuckle.

HOLMES. It's a pity you don't play poker, Woodrow—I've never seen a man who could bluff with such a straight face.

The view cuts to WILSON. He looks up with a questioning, rather amused glance.

WILSON. Bluff? We've been friends for twenty years. Have you ever known me to bluff?

This cuts back to HOLMES.

HOLMES. Good heavens! You don't mean you're actually going through with this thing!

This cuts to WILSON, with a very wide grin in which there is a bit of a challenge.

WILSON. And why not?

This cuts back to HOLMES (and the film cuts back and forth as the two men continue their conversation).

HOLMES. But my dear man, you can't just up and abolish these clubs overnight.

WILSON. I'm not talking about an *overnight* idea—it's something I have given a great deal of thought to—for a long time.

HOLMES. If we haven't any clubs where do you think our well-heeled alumni are going to sleep when they come down here for football games?

WILSON (*with a dry smile*). I must admit that's one phase of the problem I have utterly failed to consider.

HOLMES. When you started lecturing them about "luxury" and "snobbishness" and "special privilege" they thought you were attacking them as *individuals*.

WILSON (*surprised*). But there was nothing personal in what I said! I merely asked that these clubs be taken over and turned into living quarters for the University as a whole—not restricted to a relatively unimportant minority.

HOLMES. No wonder people say you're cold and standoffish—that you're just an egotistical, ambitious schoolteacher with a one-track mind.

WILSON (*with a sly smile*). And what do *you* say, Henry?

HOLMES. I say you're a Scotch Presbyterian and Scotch Presbyterians are the most obstinate people in the world!

WILSON. Don't worry, Henry. Remember there's Irish in me, too. I like a good fight.

HOLMES (*shaking his head*). Good night, Mr. Wilson. You're impossible.

WILSON (*with a grin*). Good night, Mr. Holmes. I agree with you.

This dissolves to the PRINCETON CLUB in New York at night, and then to a close view of a NEWSPAPER HEADLINE— a small head—probably in the second section of the paper. It reads:

> PRINCETON PROFESSOR CALLS
> FOR DEMOCRACY IN EDUCATION

Over this we hear the clicking of billiard balls. The view draws back to reveal the billiard room in a New York club. It is richly furnished: A group of men, most of them in evening clothes, playing pool. One of them— whom we will call BROWN—is shooting.

BROWN (*as he makes several shots*). I advise you gentlemen not to make the mistake of thinking this Wilson scheme is just a fight against your boys' club. I *know* the man. I was in his class at school. If he can put this over in the holy name of Democracy, there's no telling what he'll try next. Then where'll you be?

We get a close view of a MAN WHO IS READING A NEWSPAPER. As he lowers the paper we see that it is Professor Holmes.

HOLMES (*pointing*). Right where you are, Charlie—behind the eight-ball.

The others laugh. THE EIGHT-BALL appears at close range, and this dissolves to a brief montage of the FACES OF CROWDS—STUDENTS—ALUMNI—WILSON, over which comes applause, hand-clapping, booing. We see headlines, too, indicating the progress of the fight. (Not banner lines. One and two-column headlines—probably in the second section of newspapers.) A New Jersey paper headline reads:

> ALUMNI ATTACK WILSON'S CLUB PLAN
> College President Called
> Traitor to His Own Class

A New York paper headline reads:
> WILSON CARRIES FIGHT TO COUNTRY
> "Princeton not for sale,"
> says President in Fighting Speech
> to Alumni

This dissolves to the FRONT PAGE OF A NEW JERSEY PAPER, the headline reading:

> STUDENTS CHEER WILSON BUT
> VOTE TO RETAIN CLUBS
> Wilson Denies He Will Resign

The view pulls back to disclose SENATOR EDWARD (BIG ED) JONES, his nephew, JIM BEEKER, and an associate, ED SULLIVAN, the three overlords of New Jersey politics, all seated in a bootblack stand having their shoes shined by three colored boys. This is a narrow shoe-shine stand, beyond which we see street traffic. (As the men talk we hear the snap of the bootblacks' shining rags.) We do not know who these men are at the time. Jones is puffing a big black cigar.

BEEKER (*thoughtfully*). This schoolteacher's sure getting himself plenty of publicity. Look, he's pushed our clam bake right off the front page!

He shows a photo of a political rally on the inside page to Jones.

SULLIVAN (*shaking his head*). Yeh, but he got licked. That kind of publicity don't do nobody any good.

Jones considers this for a moment, then he looks at the paper again.

JONES. I wouldn't be too sure about that. He's put up a good fight—all that talk about equality. And besides, the people are for him.

He takes a long pull on his cigar, and cocks one eye.

JONES (*thoughtfully*). I wonder if he's a Democrat.

As the other two men look at him, the view dissolves to] the LIVING ROOM of PROSPECT HOUSE, the president's home at PRINCETON. It is night, and Wilson, Ellen, and the girls are gathered around the piano singing a gay, lilting, yet nostalgic song: "Put on Your Old Grey Bonnet," Margaret playing the accompaniment. Wilson has a sweet, clear tenor, Margaret a trained voice. Ellen and the other two girls have pleasant but untrained voices. . . . During the song the front doorbell rings and a moment later JENNY, an Irish maid, passes the open door on her way to answer it.

At the FRONT DOOR Jenny opens it to reveal JONES, BEEKER and SULLIVAN. Jones is an extraordinary character. He has the suave distinction of a man of power and place, together with the face of an innocent child. He is the political overlord of New Jersey, and according to his lights, not a bad man. . . . Beeker, whose political creed may be summed up in the words: "You do something for me and I'll do something for you," is a lesser Ed Jones. . . . Sullivan is the more typical district leader—the man who gets out the votes, keeps the boys in line, and safeguards the Organization. . . . (The song coming over.)

WILSON AND FAMILY (*singing*).
"Put on your old gray bonnet
With the blue ribbon on it
While I hitch old
Dobbin to the shay—
Through the fields of clover
We'll drive on to Dover
On our golden wedding day, etc."

JONES. Is Mr. Wilson in?

JENNY. Yes, sir.

JONES (*impressively*). Tell him that Senator Edward Jones would like to see him, please.

JENNY (*standing aside*). Will you come into the study?

The HALL of PROSPECT HOUSE: The three men come in, put their hats on a marble-top table, and follow the maid toward the study. . . . As they pass the open door of the living room, they see Wilson and Nell, their backs to the door, doing a soft-shoe dance while Margaret continues to play and the others to hum. The three politicians look at him in some amazement.

SULLIVAN (*in a low voice*). Is *that* him? (*As Jones nods solemnly*) Say, what kind of a Professor *is* he? (*Jones gives him a warning look as Jenny opens the door to the study.*)

JENNY. I'll tell Mr. Wilson you're here.

WILSON'S STUDY: Books spill all over the place—shelves of them. The three politicians come in and look around curiously.

SULLIVAN. Not a bad layout for a schoolteacher.

JONES. The college owns it. They just let him live here.

SULLIVAN. Free?

Big Ed nods, and Sullivan moves over to inspect the books.

SULLIVAN (*grinning and winking*). You know, Ed, I think it'd be kinda nice if the State did something like this for us boys.

As Big Ed chuckles, Sullivan scans the titles on a set of books, and we get a close view of THREE BOOKS as Sullivan reads their titles aloud.

SULLIVAN'S VOICE. "History of the American People"—"Constitutional Government"—"Mere Literature"—

SULLIVAN (*astonished*). Say! Did you know he wrote these *himself!*

As he starts to pull out one of the books a sound at the door causes him to put it back hastily. He turns as Wilson comes in, a rather puzzled smile on his face but courteous as always.

WILSON. Good evening, gentlemen.

JONES. Good evening, Professor. I'm Senator Jones.

WILSON (*smiling*). Big Ed? (*The Senator laughs good-naturedly, and they shake hands.*)

JONES. That's right. (*Presenting the other two*) This is my nephew, Jim Beeker—and my old friend, Ed Sullivan. Professor Wilson. (*Wilson shakes hands with the two men.*)

WILSON. How do you do, gentlemen? Won't you sit down?

JONES. Thank you.

The men sit down. There is a slight pause.

WILSON. Well, Senator, what can I do for you?

JONES (*holding his reply for a moment so as to give it proper importance*). Mr. Wilson, how would you like to be Governor of New Jersey?

WILSON (*surprised*). Governor?

JONES (*smiling and nodding*). There's a strong progressive movement running in this country. People are looking for a change.

WILSON (*amazed*). Yes, but why me? I'm not a politician.

BEEKER (*smiling*). No, but this fight you've put up at Princeton has got a lot of people talking.

WILSON (*with a wry smile*). I was defeated at Princeton.

JONES (*waving this aside*). Oh, people don't take these schoolboy matters as seriously as you do, Professor. All they see is that you're against special privilege, and that's enough for them.

SULLIVAN (*smiling*). Besides, your books on how to run a government are known all over the world.

Wilson, as is his habit at such moments, has taken off his glasses and is holding them in one hand while he gently rubs his eyes with the other.

WILSON. You've read my books, Mr. Sullivan?

Sullivan looks at Jones, who chuckles.

JONES. Let's say we've *heard* them spoken of very highly.

Wilson laughs as he takes out his handkerchief and polishes his glasses.

WILSON (*with a smile*). Of course, gentlemen, this is all very flattering, but to be perfectly frank with you, Senator, you're barking up the wrong tree. I'm a schoolteacher, which must make me something of an idiot in the eyes of a lot of good people. (*As Sullivan nods in agreement, Wilson looks around with mock furtiveness; in a whisper*) What's even worse, I'm a Southern Democrat in a Yankee stronghold.

The politicians laugh indulgently.

JONES. We just won't tell **anybody** about that, Professor.

WILSON. Besides, you must realize this isn't the sort of decision I can make overnight.

JONES. Take your time, Professor, there is no hurry. The convention is still a long way off. (*As they get up*) Well, we'd better not take any more of your time, Professor. I know how busy you are. Come along, boys.

Wilson opens the door for them and they start out. We see them in the HALLWAY as he conducts them toward the door, then the DOORWAY of the LIVING ROOM opens, and the heads of Jessie, Margaret, and Nell are seen as they peek out into the hallway at their father and his guests, taking care not to be seen.

THE HALLWAY:

JONES (*as they go to the door*). Mr. Wilson, I have a feeling that this— shall we say casual meeting—is going to be the beginning of a very delightful association for all of us. Indeed, I regard it as the beginning of a new era in the State of New Jersey, one upon which we will all look back with everlasting pride.

Wilson glances at him out of the corner of his eye but says nothing. Instead he crosses to the front door and opens it.

At the FRONT DOOR Wilson shakes hands with Jones and there are ad libs of "Good night—Good night."

JONES (*pausing*). You will think it over now, Professor?

WILSON (*grinning*). I'll do better than that, Senator. I'll have *my wife* think it over.

They laugh and exit. Wilson closes the door and stands for a moment in deep thought, unmistakably interested, but wary and uncertain. Then he turns and starts back to the living room.

In the HALLWAY, the three girls hurry to meet him, full of excited curiosity.

NELL (*in a low voice*). Was that really "Big Ed" himself?

WILSON. In person.

ELLEN. What did he want?

WILSON (*lightly—to cover his real feelings*). Nothing of any importance. He merely wants me to run for Governor. (*And he goes into the living room.*)

THE LIVING ROOM, as his wife and daughters follow him into the room:

JESSIE. Governor?

NELL. Jerusalem!

MARGARET. You? Governor?

Wilson pretends to be indignant that they should think so little of his chance.

WILSON (*with haughty finality*). And why not?

They pursue him in an excited cluster as he walks on, playing the game of dismissing them.

ELLEN. What did you tell them?

WILSON (*barging right into a table, tossing off their curiosity*). Oh— that I'd think it over—and ask *your* permisison.

ELLEN (*dismayed*). Woodrow! You didn't!

WILSON (*with mock gravity as he picks up a volume from the table, not paying the slightest attention to them apparently*). Have I ever done anything foolish without asking your permission? (*He opens the book and pretends to fasten his mind to an important page.*)

ELLEN. Woodrow, look at me! (*He lets go of the book and does so.*) I know you haven't any personal ambition just to hold office. But you must admit the opportunity *is* rather unusual.

WILSON. So it is—so it is.

ELLEN. You must get awfully tired sometimes of a mere talking profession.

WILSON (*dropping his teasing for a moment and looking at her quietly*). You're quite right, my dear. I will admit there are moments when the academic life has its drawbacks. (*Then energetically throwing off the temptation*) But the idea of a man of my age suddenly giving up a nice comfortable way of life and launching out on a sea of "ifs" and "buts"! It sounds like the account of a fool. (*He turns away, refusing it in his mind.*)

ELLEN (*pursuing him, her tone insistent*). But Woodrow, you've *always* been interested in politics.

WILSON (*stopping and looking at her; hesitating for a moment before he finds the answer in his mind*). Only as an observer on the sidelines, my dear.

The girls have swept around behind him and cut off his further retreat. Nell points the book (which she took from him) accusingly in his face.

NELL. What about the time when you were a student at the University of Virginia and wrote your father you'd made up your mind to be a Senator?

JESSIE (*with excited triumph*). Yes— and had cards printed—"Senator Thomas Woodrow Wilson."

WILSON (*forced to smile*). A youthful indiscretion! (*Sternly to Nell*) I was young then, young lady—*very young.* About *your* mental age. (*Then to Ellen, seriously*) Besides, you know perfectly well, I have certain responsibilities to Princeton.

ELLEN. Your work at Princeton is done, and you know it. You believe in the principles of democratic equality and the abolition of any special privilege class. If these things are worth while at all, don't they apply to all the people, not just to Princeton?

He looks at his wife and the girls silently and thoughtfully for a moment, obviously disturbed.

WILSON. You mean you really think I should seriously consider it?

ELLEN (*sincerely*). I do, Woodrow. I most assuredly do.

He looks at her for a moment, then at the girls.

THE GIRLS (*shouting in chorus*).
Of course we do!
Certainly!
You'd make a beautiful Governor!

He looks at them for another moment and forces a smile.

WILSON (*teasingly*). I declare, I never met such a collection of ambitious women in my life! (*As Ellen and the girls smile*) But I warn you, if I do go into this thing—and mind you, I'm not saying I will!—you're going to have to kiss all the babies—*You*— and *you*—and *you*—and *you!* That's one thing I draw the line on.

As the girls burst into laughter and Nell throws her arms about him, the scene dissolves to a view of WILSON surrounded by a cheering crowd of people.

WILSON

A mother is holding a baby upright into his face to be kissed. He looks at it, gulps, sees the determined look in the woman's eyes, closes his eyes and kisses it.

This dissolves to a STREET IN JERSEY CITY at night. Through a tough, boss-controlled neighborhood, moves a torchlight procession, led by a uniformed band playing the stirring old tune "Tammany." In the line of march are the loyal and vociferous Democrats of New Jersey, many of them carrying signs reading:

> FOR GOVERNOR
> WOODROW WILSON—
> THE MAN OF THE HOUR
>
> A VOTE FOR WILSON
> IS A VOTE FOR CLEAN GOVERNMENT
>
> WIN WITH WILSON—
> THE PRINCETON SCHOOLMASTER

Other signs indicate that the marchers are members of various Democratic clubs, Loyal Sons of Erin, etc. . . . In a flag-draped automobile of the period ride Big Ed Jones, Beeker and Mr. Sullivan. They are bowing right and left. . . . On the sidewalk are many members of the opposition, greeting the parade with boos, catcalls, and derisive laughter. . . . Running alongside the band are about a dozen Dead End kids singing at the top of their lungs.

KIDS.
Tammany, Tammany!
Stick together at the polls,
You'll get long green wampum rolls,
Tammany, Tammany,
Politicians get positions,
Tammany!

This dissolves to A THEATRE AUDITORIUM at night, with the STAGE at the end. Wilson stands on the stage beneath a huge "Wilson for Governor" banner, facing his first political rally—a lone figure in a dark suit against a light drop. Outwardly at least, he is calm and in perfect command of himself. Off-scene there is a veritable bedlam of band music and cheering. The AUDITORIUM is filled with noisy voters and their families, many of whom have come to heckle and boo, as well as to cheer. A band occupies two upper boxes. Then we see the PRINCETON DELEGATION. In the front of the gallery is a group of students, led by Felton, who are lending vocal support to their champion. At the moment they are giving an organized "Wilson Rah!"

BOYS (*cheering*).
Ray	Ray	Ray
Tiger	Tiger	Tiger
Sis	Sis	Sis
Boom	Boom	Boom
Ah — — — — — — — — —
Wilson!	Wilson!	Wilson!

A full view shows WILSON on the STAGE facing the din. He raises his hand for quiet, but the shouting gets even worse. Then we see ELLEN and the THREE GIRLS, seated in about the third or fourth row, watching Wilson nervously. Professor Holmes is seated just in front of them. He is shaking his head, as if bewildered by it all.

ELLEN (*nervously—shouting above the din*). Do you really think they'll like him?

NELL. Now, Mother, stop worrying. They'll love him.

ELLEN. But he's never had any experience with people like these before.

NELL (*grimly*). Neither have *they* had any experience with a man like *him* before.

In a BOX, Big Ed, Beeker and Sullivan are seated in full view of the audience, applauding. Several of their followers are in the box with them. Then we see the STAGE again as Wilson holds up his hand for quiet, and the shouting and band music die down.

> WILSON. Now, ladies and gentlemen, I am going to let you in on a little secret. Many of my friends are very much worried about this campaign. They tell me I'm conducting it in the worst possible way because—it appears—I'm asking you people to *think*.

There is a fresh outburst of laughter and yelling and raucous catcalling. Then Wilson holds up his hand for quiet, and grins.

> WILSON. On the other hand, my opponents are even more worried, because they expected my speeches to be mere academic lectures on government—filled with glittering generalities that have nothing to do with the situation in New Jersey. Apparently they've deluded themselves into thinking that I've had no political experience! Good heavens, no political experience! I wonder if these gentlemen have ever attended a Faculty meeting—or seen the wives of the Trustees in action? (*Once more he pauses and grins at the audience. And again there is a general roar of laughter and applause.*)

The FRONT ROW of the BALCONY: JOSEPH TUMULTY, a round-faced Irishman, and a distinguished-looking old jurist, look at each other. Then Tumulty gets to his feet, cups his hands to his lips and calls out.

> TUMULTY. That's all very amusing, Mr. Wilson, but why don't you tell us what kind of a deal you've made with the bosses?

At this, in the AUDITORIUM, there is an angry outburst from the Party supporters, coupled with applause from those who are skeptical. There are cries of "Throw him out!" and people rise—look up at Tumulty. This is followed by a close view of a COUPLE of IRATE PARTY WORKERS in BIG ED's BOX.

> FIRST MAN. Who's that bird?

> SULLIVAN. Joe Tumulty—one of them Irish lawyers in the Legislature—claims he's a Democrat. But he ain't voted right once! *Not once!*

On the STAGE, however, Wilson is unruffled, as he motions the crowd to be quiet.

> WILSON. I've made no deal with anyone.

In the BALCONY:

> TUMULTY. I suppose you're going to deny there's even such a thing as a boss system in New Jersey?

In the AUDITORIUM, TUMULTY in the foreground: We see WILSON on the stage in the background. Again there is an angry outburst, hissing and booing.

> WILSON. No—the existence of the boss system is notorious.

> TUMULTY. Then what are you going to do about it?

> WILSON. Bend all my energies to breaking it up.

There is a moment of stunned silence at this, and people turn and look up at the box where Big Ed, Beeker and Sullivan are seated. Big Ed continues to smile amiably, not the least ruffled; Sullivan, however, has a worried look on his face. In the BALCONY, Tumulty continues his questioning.

TUMULTY. When you say bosses, do you mean Big Ed Jones, Jim Beeker and Ed Sullivan?

This provokes another angry outburst, and several people seated behind Tumulty lean forward and try to push him into his seat. For a moment a riot is threatened. The jurist turns and brings his walking-stick down on the head of one of Tumulty's assailants.

On the STAGE:

WILSON (*looking up at Big Ed*). Of course I mean Big Ed. I feel about him exactly as I feel about every other boss—whether he's a Democrat or a Republican.

The audacity again silences the crowd in the AUDITORIUM, with WILSON in the foreground.

WILSON. Senator Jones understands exactly how I feel. In fact, just so there would be no misunderstanding about it, he's given me his word that in *no circumstances* will he permit his name to be presented to the Legislature as a candidate for re-election to the United States Senate —an office for which I consider him utterly unfitted.

People in the auditorium are now looking up at Big Ed, stunned, waiting for a cue from him.

TUMULTY rises and looks toward Big Ed's box.

TUMULTY. What do *you* say, Big Ed?

In the BOX: Big Ed, still smiling amiably, rises and waves to the crowd in endorsement of the statement.

BIG ED. I say the candidate speaks for the Party.

In the AUDITORIUM, at this sign, vigorous applause once more breaks out, and hats are thrown into the air. We see the BAND as it strikes up "Hot Time in the Old Town Tonight." In the BALCONY, Tumulty and the other skeptics begin to cheer and applaud vigorously, following which we see ELLEN and the GIRLS, Ellen applauding as wildly as anyone else in the audience. Her hat is down over one eye. Nell straightens her mother's hat.

NELL (*warningly*). Mother! . . . Suppose somebody sees you?

ELLEN. Let them!

Holmes is gloomily shaking his head as he looks at the cheering crowd—still unable to grasp it.

In the BOX, Big Ed continues to smile. Sullivan, however, is still worried.

JONES. Great! Great! He'll win in a walk!

SULLIVAN. Yeah, but suppose he means it?

JONES. Nonsense! They had him in a corner. What else *could* he say?

SULLIVAN (*still dubious*). Just the same, I don't like the cut of that fellow's jaw.

JONES. I tell you, he's something new in politics—a scholar and a gentleman with ideals and principles. (*To the group of plug-uglies*) You can't beat that when it comes to electioneering.

SULLIVAN (*unconvinced*). I got as many ideals and principles as anybody, Ed, but I still don't know what the boys in the downtown wards of Jersey City are going to say with nothing better than that to go on.

ELLEN and the GIRLS:

ELLEN (*excitedly—to Holmes*). Wasn't he wonderful?

HOLMES (*turning to her*). The most idiotic campaign speech in the whole history of politics! (*Ellen and the girls look at him in amazement.*)

ELLEN (*shocked*). I don't understand.

HOLMES. He *means* what he says!

And he gets up, puts on his hat, and starts out. As the cheering and band music continue, we see Felton leading the cheering.

This dissolves to a LARGE BANNER reading: JERSEY CITY DEMOCRATIC HEADQUARTERS, and then to THE DEMOCRATIC HEADQUARTERS on election night. A noisy celebration is in progress. Big Ed, Beeker and Sullivan are here with the ward heelers and Party small-fry. (All the Tammany gore possible. Shirt-sleeves, big black cigars, spittoons, posters, cartoons.) A bar has been set up and beer is flowing freely. A man in shirt-sleeves and big mustache is crossing to the blackboard to record the latest returns. One worker—with a black eye, a bloody nose, and a big grin—is just breezing in, followed by half a dozen of his helpers.

WORKER (*triumphantly*). We didn't lose a single vote in the Eighth Ward.

There is a cheer at this and Sullivan slaps the worker on the shoulder.

SULLIVAN. That's the spirit, my boy. You do right by the Party and the Party'll do right by you.

Off-scene we hear a man's voice.

VOICE. At 9:18 P.M. twenty-two counties reporting.

They all turn as a man in shirt-sleeves starts to chalk up the score:

LEWIS 312,809
WILSON 587,632

This provokes a fresh cheer. Men crowd around Big Ed and the other bosses, congratulating them.

VOICES. Great work, Boss!
Looks like we've got the Legislature, too! Biggest landslide in history!

Several begin to sing: "For He's a Jolly Good Fellow." The victory—*obviously*—belongs to the Bosses!

This dissolves to the HALL OF PROSPECT HOUSE at night. Wilson, Ellen and the girls face a battery of photographers and newspapermen. They are being pushed and pulled, ordered to look this way and that, while a flood of questions is hurled at each of them.

PHOTOGRAPHERS. This way, Governor!
Hey, you girls! Get in closer!
Look up at him, Mrs. Wilson!
How about a big smile—everybody?

A close view of PROFESSOR HOLMES shows him looking on with quiet but unconcealed amusement. One of the reporters turns to him.

REPORTER. Quite an upset, Professor.

HOLMES (*dryly*). Any election is an upset, young man, if you happen to be unfortunate enough to be elected. (*The reporter laughs.*)

Then we see the WILSONS:

NEWSPAPERMEN (*trying to interview them at the same time*). Where you going to live, Mrs. Wilson?
You girls engaged?
How's it feel to be a Governor's daughter?
What's the first move, Governor?

WILSON (*as he is tugged at this way and that*). If you'll wait a minute, gentlemen, I'll be glad to write out a statement.

NEWSPAPERMAN. Oh, that's all right, Governor. Just give us some personal stuff—something the people'll be interested in.

HOLMES. Go ahead, Woodrow. Tell 'em what you like for breakfast— a few *important* things like that.

He shoots an amused glance at Wilson, who looks at him and scowls. Meanwhile, the scene is becoming more and more turbulent and disordered, the helpless victims overcome by the situation. Wilson's face becomes more and more grim.

WILSON (*in a low voice, out of the corner of his mouth*). Do I have to put up with this sort of thing—in my own home?

ELLEN (*sotto voce*). Yes, my dear —every day from now until the end of your life. (*As he looks at her, horrified*) So you might as well get used to it and—smile.

As he steels himself for the ordeal and forces a broad, *toothy* smile, and the flashlight pans explode, the scene fades out.

PART TWO

PROSPECT HOUSE fades in. Horse-drawn moving vans are standing in front of the house. Packers are bringing out furniture. Several small children are playing hop-scotch on the sidewalk, taking it all in. Then we see the LIVING ROOM: First a close view of an OIL PAINTING as hands reach in and take it from the wall, then, as the view draws back, a scene of confusion. Much of the furniture is gone. Two men are carrying out the piano, Margaret moving alongside urging them to be careful. Wilson, himself, is seated on a chair glancing through his mail. Ellen and Nell are packing bric-à-brac and wrapping china figures in wads of old newspapers. Jessie is coming in with a tray holding a tea set, and is having difficulty balancing it. There are cries of "Look out!" "Look out!" until she guides it safely across and sets it down on a table, the others breathing a sigh of relief.

ELLEN. I never before realized what possessions mean. I'll never own another thing as long as I live.

As she carefully packs a small china figure, one of the movers approaches Wilson's chair.

MOVER. Excuse me, Governor.

Wilson gets up—his hands full of mail.

WILSON. Oh, yes, of course.

He backs off into the path of other movers who are carrying out a sofa. They brush him aside. Suddenly Nell cries out in dismay.

NELL. Here's that horrible picture again! I thought I'd destroyed them!

She unfolds a newspaper, and Jessie and Ellen lean over to look at it, following which we see a NEWSPAPER PICTURE of the WILSONS, taken on the night of the election. It is far from flattering. Wilson has a big, toothy smile on his face. Margaret is looking terribly stern. Only Jessie has come off with honor. Then the group around the newspaper reappears.

NELL (*indignantly*). We ought to sue them!

JESSIE. And look at Margaret! You'd think she was a militant suffragette or something—ready to throw a brick at a policeman.

ELLEN. And your poor father! How can they print such things?

NELL (*handing the picture to her father*). If *I* were Governor, there'd be a law against it!

Wilson glances at the paper. Then he grins and recites with gestures the limerick which he often quoted.

WILSON.
"For beauty I am not a star
There are hundreds more handsome by far,
But my face I don't mind it,
For I am behind it,
It's the people in front that I jar."

As he starts toward another chair, a mover shakes his head and takes it almost literally from under him. Wilson shrugs and steps aside and into the table which threatens to overturn. As he hastily grabs for it, the tea set falls with a crash.

The scene dissolves to the GOLD DOME of the STATE CAPITOL in New Jersey, and then to GOVERNOR WILSON'S OFFICE, where Wilson is seated at his desk facing three members of the Legislature. His desk as always is clean and orderly. On one corner, however, lies a folded newspaper.

WILSON. The Legislature has had sufficient time to digest the contents of this bill, gentlemen. I must insist, therefore, that it be brought to a vote immediately—regardless of the opposition. (*The Legislators nod.*)

FIRST LEGISLATOR. You're right, Governor. We've got the votes. (*Smiling*) I say let's go ahead and let 'em howl.

As Wilson smiles broadly a door in the background opens and Joseph Tumulty comes in.

WILSON. Yes, Tumulty?

TUMULTY. Excuse me, Governor, but Senator Jones and Mr. Beeker have arrived.

The smile fades from Wilson's face and his expression hardens a bit.

WILSON (*quietly*). Thank you, Tumulty. Send them in, please. (*As Tumulty exits, Wilson turns to the Legislators.*) Will you gentlemen excuse me? This is a matter of considerable importance.

LEGISLATORS (*getting to their feet*). Of course, Governor. Good morning, Governor. Don't worry about a thing.

WILSON. Good day, gentlemen.

As the men file out of the second door, Tumulty opens the other door and permits Senator Jones and Beeker to come in. The Senator is his usual beaming, hearty self and his voice booms out in greeting as the Legislators are going out the other door.

JONES. Good morning, Ed—Joe—Bill—

LEGISLATORS (*ad libbing*). Good morning, Senator—Ed. Mr. Beeker.

As the door closes behind the Legislators, Senator Jones and Beeker, still beaming, cross toward Wilson's desk. Tumulty goes out, closing the door behind him.

JONES (*his hand out*). Good morning, Mr. Governor. Beautiful day.

BEEKER (*bowing*). Governor.

Wilson remains at his desk, still quiet and reserved. He makes no movement to rise and shake hands with the Senator.

WILSON (*quietly*). Good morning, gentlemen. Sit down, please.

JONES (*with a laugh*). Thank you, sir.

He seats himself in one of the chairs and Beeker takes one next to him.

JONES (*smiling*). You sent for me?

Wilson turns and picks up the newspaper from the desk.

WILSON (*quietly*). Did you authorize this statement to the effect that you have decided to be a candidate for the United States Senate?

JONES (*with hearty good humor*). Well, at the insistence of many of my friends, Governor—

WILSON (*cutting in*). But you publicly stated that in no circumstances would you be a candidate!

JONES (*with an indulgent chuckle*). A man says a lot of things in the heat of a campaign, Governor.

WILSON (*sharply*). But to go back on your word less than a year after the election would be outrageous and indecent!

JONES. Oh come, come, Governor. People don't take these matters as seriously as you do. They've probably forgotten all about it.

WILSON (*coldly*). I beg to differ with you, Senator. I have not forgotten, nor have the people.

BEEKER. But surely if the Party feels Uncle Ed's the man for the job—

WILSON. The people who elected me have already decided that he's not.

JONES (*indulgently*). Now hold on, Governor. Let's get one thing clear. *I* nominated you. *I* elected you.

WILSON (*quietly*). Then you should have exercised better judgment in your choice.

There is a brief pause. Jones and Beeker look at each other.

JONES (*placatingly*). Would you be satisfied to announce your opposition publicly and let it go at that?

WILSON (*cold as ice*). If you insist in going through with such bald-faced deceit, I shall have no recourse but to fight you with every means in my power.

Again there is a brief pause.

BEEKER (*with a sneer—to Big Ed*). Well, it looks to me as if the Professor here expects to give us the bum's rush and run this whole show to suit himself.

WILSON. I consider your language coarse, Mr. Beeker, and your manners offensive. However, you seem to have grasped the idea perfectly.

JONES. I don't want to quarrel with you, Governor. I know how seriously you take all these reform issues and how hard you've worked. But what you need is a *nice long rest*.

Wilson goes over to the door, opens it, and stands aside to let the men out.

WILSON (*quietly*). Good day, Senator.

The babylike expression is gone from Jones' face now. He glares at Wilson, then stalks out of the room. Beeker follows, pausing at the door.

BEEKER. Be sensible, Governor. We know you've got your eye on the

White House. But what chance do you think you'd have for the nomination if your own State organization is against you?

WILSON (*quietly*). Get out.

BEEKER (*in a sudden burst of anger*). You're no gentleman!

WILSON. You're no judge!

As he closes the door on the two men, the scene dissolves to the HALL OUTSIDE WILSON'S ROOM, and Beeker comes out, his face flaming with anger.

BEEKER (*as they start off*). Are you going to let him get away with that?

JONES (*his voice hard—determined*). Get on the telephone. Get Ed Sullivan!

The DOOR to the PARLOR of the WILSON SUITE is opened and Margaret, Jessie, and Nell are again peeking out but being careful not to be seen. Over this comes Jones' voice.

JONES' VOICE. This Wilson fellow might as well find out right at the beginning that I can be just as tough as he is! And a whole lot tougher!

This dissolves to the DEMOCRATIC HEADQUARTERS at night as one of the plug-uglies yanks a Wilson poster off the wall. The view draws back to reveal Jones, Beeker, and Sullivan surrounded by about twenty men. Jones is in a fighting temper.

JONES. You men get busy! Look up his bank account! Dig into his past! There's no such thing as a perfect specimen! He's stubbed his toe somewhere along the line, and when you find out what it is, trip him—and trip him hard!

To emphasize this command he slams his fist on the desk and looks around belligerently, as if to see if anybody is opposing him. There is a moment's silence and one of the men in the room —small, about five foot two, wearing a derby—shakes his head.

SMITH. Count me out, Ed. I'm climbing on the other side of the fence while the climbing's good.

JONES. You're doing what?

SMITH. It's no use, Ed. This gink's got the people with him. Look at all these reforms he's got them howling for. (*Very earnestly*) I always say, Ed, you can't lick reform for at least *two years* after it gets started. I got a hunch if anybody gets tripped it's gonna be you. (*They look at him in astonishment.*) Goodbye, boys.

Then he turns and starts out, leaving them looking after him in amazement.

SMITH (*tipping his derby*). It was a nice organization while it lasted.

This dissolves to the FRONT PAGE of a NEWSPAPER. The headline reads: WILSON SMASHES JONES' TRY FOR SENATE. On the front page is a large cartoon showing a political boss labeled "Jones" being booted out of an office by a foot labeled "Wilson." The cartoon reads: CLOISTERED PROFESSOR VANQUISHES THE BIG BOSS. . . . The view then draws back to disclose a wooden bowl as a spoon dips in and takes out some spaghetti, and continues to draw back to reveal Big Ed Jones, Beeker, and Ed Sullivan, seated in the booth of an Italian restaurant—having lunch. Jones is studying the cartoon, a look of complete bewilderment on his baby-like face. Beeker glares angrily as he eats. Sullivan is attacking a plate of spaghetti and washing it down with gulps of red wine.

JONES (*shaking his head*). I still don't understand it. He seemed like such a nice fellow, too.

SULLIVAN. I told you I didn't like the cut of that fellow's jaw.

JONES. What gets me is the way newspapers all over the country are picking this up—making him out a hero.

SULLIVAN. It'd be just like that darnfool convention to go on and nominate him for President now, whether we like it or not.

BEEKER (*gloomily*). And with the Republicans split wide open between Teddy Roosevelt and Taft they can elect him, too.

JONES (*philosophically*). Well, if you ask me, that'd be a whole lot better than having him hanging around New Jersey.

And on these words the scene fades out.

PART THREE

A distant view of the GOLD DOME of the STATE CAPITOL fades in, and then dissolves to GOVERNOR WILSON'S OFFICE, where Joe Tumulty is talking on the telephone.

TUMULTY. I'll tell Governor Wilson you called, the minute he returns. . . . Thank you, sir. (*As he hangs up there is a rap at the door.*) Come in.

The door opens and Felton comes in, accompanied by two Princeton students. They wear those college boys' hats of the period. One student wears a sweater with the letter "P" on it. Felton has several papers in his hands which he puts down on the desk in front of Tumulty.

FELTON. Hello, Mr. Tumulty.

TUMULTY. Hello, boys. (*Indicating the papers*) What's that?

FELTON. More applications for Wilson-for-President clubs. (*Reading*) "Rochester — Atlanta — (*then grinning*) Oyster Bay"—

TUMULTY. What? That's Teddy Roosevelt's *home town!*

SECOND STUDENT (*grinning*). I came from there, too, Mr. Tumulty.

They look at one another and laugh. The telephone rings and Tumulty turns to pick it up.

TUMULTY. Governor Wilson's office. . . . This is his secretary. . . . Oh, yes, Congressman. How do you do? . . . I'm sorry. The Governor's out of town on a *very important mission*. . . . I wish I could tell you where he is, but it's something very much on his heart, something I'm sure *you'd* approve of. . . . Yes, indeed—I'll tell him the moment he gets back. . . . Goodbye, Congressman. Goodbye. . . . (*He hangs up, and grins.*)

This dissolves to the STAGE of the PALACE THEATRE in NEW YORK. A man and six or eight girls are doing a number—"Moonlight Bay." It concludes and the singers move off. Then we see the FRONT ROW of the theatre, from which Governor Wilson and Ellen are following the show with evident delight. They are applauding vigorously. Suddenly Professor Holmes leans over from the second row and touches Wilson on the shoulder.

HOLMES (*as Wilson turns*). Official business, no doubt.

WILSON (*with a laugh*). It's odd, but it seems something *important* like this comes up at least once a week.

ELLEN. Yes, every time the Palace changes its program. (*They laugh at this.*)

HOLMES. Well, they tell me you've been taking to politics like a billy goat to tin cans—raising Cain all over the place. (*As Wilson chuckles*) No wonder they want to kick you upstairs into the White House.

WILSON. Oh, you don't want to take these "Wilson-for-President" clubs too seriously. Remember a lot of people still regard me as a pretty dangerous fellow.

HOLMES. And so you are! But it's too late now. I've already planked out five dollars to help bamboozle the public.

WILSON (*shaking his head*). Just throwing it away.

HOLMES (*nodding*). Maybe. But then Teddy Roosevelt's a Harvard man, isn't he? Bill Taft's from Yale. I'd give five dollars of my money any day to get a Princeton boy a crack at both those outfits in one game.

As Wilson and Ellen laugh, there is a burst of applause, and they turn back to the stage. We then see that a card has been set on the easel near the wings of the STAGE. It reads: LEW DOCKSTADER * AND HIS FAMOUS IMPERSONATIONS. Then LEW DOCKSTADER comes on dressed as Teddy Roosevelt—in blackface—grinning broadly—showing teeth—saying "Bully! Dee-lighted!" etc. He carries an elephant gun and is dressed in Rough Rider costume.

This dissolves to the CIVIC AUDITORIUM in BALTIMORE. Over the entrance is a huge sign reading: DEMOCRATIC NATIONAL CONVENTION OF 1912. . . . A uniform band is just going into the building, playing "Dixie." Following it is a milling, jostling, good-natured crowd of vociferous, wild-eyed Democrats. It is a hot day and the men have their coats over their arms and handkerchiefs under their collars. Some of the delegates carry signs with pictures of their favorites: WOODROW WILSON, OSCAR W. UNDERWOOD, JUDSON HARMON, CHAMP CLARK, WILLIAM JENNINGS BRYAN. And the scene dissolves to the CONVENTION HALL. All we see is a mass of posters and banners reading ALABAMA—NEW YORK—GEORGIA—PENNSYLVANIA — CALIFORNIA — NEW JERSEY — NORTH CAROLINA, etc. Over this is a bedlam of sound—rebel yells and band music. Then we see the CONVENTION PLATFORM, where the Chairman pounds with his gavel for attention.

CHAIRMAN (*in a great booming voice*). The Chair has the honor to present to you that *great* Democrat—that peerless leader who never sold the truth to serve the hour—the *great Commoner* himself—Nebraska's favorite son—William Jennings Bryan!

A tumultuous shout goes up—a mingling of cheering and booing—as BRYAN steps forward in his shirt sleeves, waving a palm-leaf fan.

BRYAN. Mr. Chairman! I move that in this crisis in our Party's career, this convention declare itself unalterably opposed to the nomination of *any candidate* who is representative of or under obligation to Wall Street, to Tammany Hall, or to any other privilege-hunting and favor-seeking class—

---

* In the final film, as released, this scene was replaced by a scene featuring Eddie Foy.

Even Bryan's mighty voice is drowned out in the cheering and booing that greets this. For passions here are inflamed, and it is to be a knock-down-drag-out fight all the way. Then on the BANDSTAND the band suddenly bursts into "Onward, Christian Soldiers," played in a martial tempo.

The SPEAKERS' STAND comes to view and the scene follows JOSEPHUS DANIELS as he comes running up the steps calling out above the din:

DANIELS. Mac! *McAdoo!*

On the SPEAKERS' STAND, then, WILLIAM GIBBS MCADOO rises and hurries forward in answer to the summons.

MCADOO. Here—*Daniels!*

Another man—WILLIAM MCCOMBS—Wilson's campaign manager hurries in from behind McAdoo. All are excited. Then we focus on the GROUP as Daniels and McAdoo meet. Daniels is very excited.

DANIELS (*panting from his run*). McAdoo—we'd better get Wilson on the telephone at the Governor's Mansion at Sea Girt. I don't like the way this Bryan thing's going.

MCADOO (*as McCombs joins them*). Neither do I. But McCombs is his manager. Let's see what he says.

MCCOMBS. It's too early. Besides, the Associated Press—every newspaper in New York has a direct wire to the Governor's place. He probably already knows what's going on.

This dissolves to the GOVERNOR'S HOUSE at SEA GIRT. Tents have been set up on the lawn for the use of newspapermen. Over the tents are signs reading: NEW YORK TIMES—NEW YORK WORLD—ASSOCIATED PRESS, etc. A telegrapher is typing out the news as it comes in. Wilson, Tumulty, and several others stand around. Suddenly Tumulty, who is looking over the telegrapher's shoulder, groans.

TUMULTY. That William Jennings Bryan! He's trying to steal the nomination for himself!

WILSON (*smiling*). What's he done now, Tumulty?

TUMULTY. Got his band playing hymns.

As Wilson and the others laugh, the scene dissolves to the CONVENTION PLATFORM. It is night now, and a delegate with a rich, fruity Southern voice is speaking.

DELEGATE. It is my great honor and distinguished privilege to place in nomination for the exalted office of President of the United States, that great statesman from Alabama—Oscar W. Underwood!

A great cheer goes up at this, and on the BANDSTAND, the band bursts into "Oh, Susannah" and voices pick up the words. The scene then wipes off and we see the PLATFORM again as another delegate is speaking.

DELEGATE. I give you that great statesman from Missouri—that great servant of the Common Man—the Honorable Champ Clark!

Another mighty cheer goes up, and on the BANDSTAND, the band strikes up the "Houn' Dawg Song," following which a Clark parade starts in the AISLE of the CONVENTION HALL, placards with pictures of Clark leading the way—men singing "Houn' Dawg Song." A girl dressed as Miss Columbia, waving a flag, is borne on the shoulders of several men. This scene wipes off, and we see Judge Westcott speaking from the PLATFORM.

JUDGE WESTCOTT. New Jersey appreciates the honor of placing before this convention as a candidate for the Presidency of the United States, the seer and philosopher of Princeton—the Princeton schoolmaster—Woodrow Wilson!

An even mightier cheer greets this, and on the BANDSTAND the band strikes up "School Days," following which delegates favorable to Wilson—McAdoo, McCombs, Daniels, et al.—start a parade on the CONVENTION FLOOR behind huge portraits of their candidate, singing as they go. Over this come opposition boos, catcalls and the flaunting of the pictures of Clark and Underwood.

This scene dissolves to a GOLF COURSE near SEA GIRT, where Wilson, dressed in long white trousers, is addressing his ball, preparatory to digging it out. Professor Holmes, his partner, wears knickers. Just as Wilson draws back for his swing, a breathless Tumulty rushes in, a sheaf of telegrams in his hand. A couple of Negro caddies, with golf clubs, stand near by.

TUMULTY. Governor! Governor! (*As Wilson pauses*) Here're the results of the first ballot! (*Reading*) Clark, 440; Wilson, 324; Underwood, 117. . . .

HOLMES. Humph! Sounds kind of like our golf score!

WILSON. Thank you, Tumulty. (*And he starts to address his ball again.*)

TUMULTY (*pleading*). Those reporters have been after me all morning, Governor. Won't you say something?

WILSON (*after a moment's thought*). Yes. You may tell them that Governor Wilson received the news of the first ballot in a *riot of silence*. . . . Fore!

And he swings, lifts the ball out neatly, and looks after it. The others react with astonishment at his coolness in the face of all the excitement. Wilson turns and looks at Holmes and grins broadly.

This dissolves to the CONVENTION HALL at night. A delegate in the New York section is on his feet.

DELEGATE. Mr. Chairman!

We see the PLATFORM as the Chairman's gavel falls.

CHAIRMAN. The chair recognizes the leader of the New York Delegation—the Honorable Charles Murphy of Tammany Hall. (*A burst of booing greets this.*)

MURPHY (*seen close*). New York wishes at this time to change its ballot and to cast its *ninety votes* for the next President of the United States—Champ Clark of Missouri!

We see the MISSOURI DELEGATION as the Clark supporters leap up on chairs, yelling and shrieking, trying to start a stampede to their candidate. The "Houn' Dawg Song" blares out again, and the men shout it lustily.

This dissolves to the FRONT HALL at SEA GIRT the next day. Tumulty is on the telephone. Wilson and his family are gathered around.

TUMULTY (*turning from the phone*). It's William McCombs, Governor. He wants to talk to you personally.

WILSON (*taking the phone*). Yes?

The WILSON HEADQUARTERS in Convention Hall: Here McCombs, a thin, nervous, high-strung man, is on the phone. We hear faintly the Convention shouting and the band.

MCCOMBS (*excitedly*). The jig's up, Governor! It looks like a stampede for Clark. This last parade's been going on for over an hour already. You've got to send me a wire withdrawing your name. I can't hold your delegates any longer.

We see WILSON at the PHONE.

WILSON. What's the score now?

Back in the WILSON HEADQUARTERS, MC-COMBS on the phone:

MCCOMBS. Clark 556—Wilson 350½. But I tell you it's hopeless. No candidate yet has ever received a majority without being nominated. I told you all along we should have made some kind of deal with that New York delegation!

We again see WILSON at the phone.

WILSON. What's Bryan going to do?

MCCOMBS at the phone in the WILSON HEADQUARTERS:

MCCOMBS. He's been hoping he could play you and Clark off against each other—then get the nomination for himself. But it's too late. We're licked. It'll be Clark on the next ballot.

We again see WILSON at the phone, now surrounded by members of his family.

WILSON. Just a moment. (*Turning from the phone*) McCombs sounds pretty excited. He thinks I should send a wire releasing my delegates.

TUMULTY (*groaning*). I knew it—I knew it all along! That Tammany Hall!

HOLMES. I always wondered why the Democrats picked a jackass for their mascot—now I know.

Wilson looks up at Ellen. We know he is thinking of her disappointment more than his own. Ellen smiles at him, chin up.

ELLEN. It's all right, Woodrow. At least we will be able to get away for a holiday.

WILSON. Thank you, my dear.

He smiles, pleased by her acceptance of the news, then turns back to the telephone.

WILSON (*into the phone*). Well Mc-Combs, I—Hello? . . . Hello? . . .

The WILSON HEADQUARTERS: McCombs is being pushed aside from the phone by a tall beak-nosed man—WILLIAM G. MCADOO. The latter's face is dark with anger. At his side is JOSEPHUS DANIELS.

MCADOO. Here—let me have that phone. Hello, Governor! Governor! William G. McAdoo speaking! I just heard what McCombs told you. But he's dead wrong! You can't withdraw now! Clark'll never be able to get a two-thirds vote! Wait! Here's Josephus Daniels! He'll tell you the same thing! (*And he pushes Daniels to the phone.*)

DANIELS. He's right, Governor! You're stronger than ever! Your delegates'll stick if it takes all summer!

WILSON at the phone, surrounded by his eager, excited family: He turns from the phone to Ellen.

WILSON. That's odd. My convention manager tells me we're defeated, but McAdoo and Daniels say I can't lose. What do you think, Ellen?

ELLEN (*promptly*). That you have nothing to lose by staying in.

WILSON (*with a smile*). That is what I think—so I will stay in. (*He turns to the phone.*) Hello, McAdoo? . . . Thank my friends and tell them we'll see it through.

He turns from the phone and his wife, linking her arm in his, looks at him with a tender smile as the scene dissolves to the CONVENTION HALL at night. A band is playing the "Houn' Dawg Song" and a Clark parade is still in full blast—men yelling, screaming, sweating—the delegates dog-tired but determined to force the issue. Then we see DANIELS and MCADOO in the NEW JERSEY DELEGATION standing beneath the Wilson banner watching the parade and listening to the music.

DANIELS (*grimly*). If they don't stop that fool song soon, I'm going to take a real hound out there and kick him around.

MCADOO (*grabbing his arm*). You can't! They'd lynch you and we need every Wilson vote we can get!

The CLARK PARADE: The music and cheering continue. Pandemonium is reigning. But this is followed by a view of the NEBRASKA DELEGATION on the floor. William Jennings Bryan gets to his feet. He holds a palm-leaf fan in his hand—he is coatless.

BRYAN (*shouting above the tumult*). Mr. Chairman!

On the PLATFORM, the chairman pounds his gavel.

CHAIRMAN. For what purpose does the gentleman from Nebraska arise?

The NEBRASKA DELEGATION:

BRYAN. To explain my vote.

We get a view of the CONVENTION with BRYAN in the foreground. Instantly there is a fresh outburst. Cries of "Sit down!" "Throw him out!" "Regular order!" "Go on!" "Let him speak!" etc., rise above the hooting and yelling.

BRYAN. Speaking for myself, and for any of the delegation who may decide to join me, I shall withhold my vote from Champ Clark—or from any other candidate as long as New York's vote is recorded for him—

Pandemonium really breaks out now. Desperately men struggle to reach Bryan to prevent his speaking—jumping across chairs, wild with anger as they scent what is coming. Several of those near him seize Bryan and try to force him down.

BRYAN (*as he struggles to brush his assailants aside*).—and cast it for Nebraska's second choice—*Woodrow Wilson!*

The NEW JERSEY DELEGATION: McAdoo, Daniels and other supporters of Wilson are now going mad with excitement. Off-scene the cheering and booing and band music is "terrific." "School Days" now dominates the music, although several of the men have their heads together and are baying like hound dogs!

This dissolves to the FRONT LAWN of SEA GIRT as Tumulty dashes out of a tent and sprints across the lawn, shouting as he goes.

TUMULTY. Governor! Governor!

Behind him race the reporters—about twenty-five of them. As Tumulty's cries continue, Wilson, Ellen, the girls, and others hurry out of the house.

TUMULTY. It's all over! You've been nominated on the forty-sixth ballot!

He turns and begins to wave his arms frantically. Wilson looks quickly at Ellen, and she takes his hand. The girls are excited and thrilled.

WILSON (*quietly*). Well, my dear, I'm afraid we won't have that holiday after all.

As she smiles at him through sudden tears, band music is heard off-scene.

They all look off in astonishment. And what they see is A BRASS BAND in uniform coming from behind the row of pup tents. It is playing "Hail to the Chief."

At the FRONT PORCH, Wilson and his family are still looking off in amazement as Tumulty hurries up to them. He grabs the Governor's hand and shakes it, almost overcome with emotion and excitement. The reporters follow.

NELL (*awed*). They're playing "Hail to the Chief."

WILSON (*smiling—to Tumulty—indicating the band*). Is that some of your work?

TUMULTY. I've had them hiding out there for two days.

WILSON (*amused*). Suppose I hadn't been nominated?

TUMULTY (*grinning*). Oh, I'd made arrangements for them to fold their tents, and like the Arabs, silently steal away.

Wilson and the girls laugh, and Tumulty grins sheepishly. We then see the FRONT YARD with the band marching up to the front porch playing the stirring "Hail to the Chief," and the scene fades out.

PART FOUR

A TWENTY-FOUR SHEET POSTER fades in. It shows Wilson as a knight-in-armor mounted on a Democratic Donkey, charging head-on at a bespectacled Bull Moose with the face and teeth of Teddy Roosevelt, while a G.O.P. Elephant, looking suspiciously like William Howard Taft, gingerly walks away from the scene. Above the poster are the words: VOTE DEMOCRATIC. And we hear lively exciting music—"Dixie."—Suddenly through the poster crashes a speeding train, and this dissolves to the view of a TRAIN rushing through the night, the music rising to a crescendo. Over it is superimposed a newspaper headline reading: WILSON TAKES THE NEW FREEDOM TO COUNTRY. Then this dissolves to the REAR PLATFORM of the TRAIN, on which Wilson—backed by Ellen, his daughters, Tumulty, McAdoo, Daniels and McCombs—is speaking.

WILSON. When I speak to you of business and government—of capital and labor—of privilege and equal opportunities—my only purpose is to rehabilitate Democracy. . . .

We see the FACES of the LISTENERS—cotton farmers in blue jeans. We hear light applause as Wilson's voice continues.

WILSON'S VOICE. . . . And to prove to the world that the Democratic system can successfully meet the economic, industrial and social problems that confront us . . .

This wipes to the SPEAKERS' TABLE, at night, with a GROUP OF BUSINESS MEN listening to Wilson (the camera moving across their faces).

WILSON'S VOICE. . . . Because I believe as Lincoln did, that Democracy—with all its faults and failures—if properly guided and interpreted, holds the future of the world. . . .

This is followed by a very long view of MADISON SQUARE GARDEN at night, and we see Wilson—alone—standing in the ring under a great light addressing the audience. All lights are out in the Garden except the ones on the platform, so that all we see around the figure of Wilson is blackness. It is as though we were seeing and hearing him from the top gallery.

WILSON. My great dream is that, as the years go on, the world will turn to America more and more for those moral inspirations which lie at the basis of all freedom. And that America will come into the full light of the day when all the world shall know she puts human rights above all other rights, and that her flag is not only the flag of America, but the flag of humanity.

As he pauses and the applause and cheering become a roar, the scene dissolves to a view of TIMES SQUARE on election night. A wildly cheering crowd jam-packs the streets, noisy in the typical American fashion, while we again hear "School Days" . . . Then we see the side of the TIMES BUILDING, on which the words "WILSON SWEEPING THE NATION" are flashed on a screen from a stereopticon machine, followed by a picture of Wilson, and the cheering becomes one mighty roar.

This dissolves to a view of WILSON'S HOUSE in CLEVELAND LANE, in Princeton, at night, and this to WILSON'S STUDY. Wilson stands alone at the window, his back turned. After a moment the door opens softly and Ellen comes in, a couple of telegrams in her hand. Wilson turns and looks at her. Their eyes meet for a moment, then without a word she reaches up and kisses him.

ELLEN (*indicating the telegrams*). I thought you'd like to see these.

(*Reading*) "I cordially congratulate you on your election and extend to you my best wishes for a successful administration. William Howard Taft." . . . "The American people by a great plurality have conferred upon you the highest honor in their gift. I congratulate you thereon. Theodore Roosevelt."

There is a long pause. He is visibly moved, sobered by this great new responsibility.

WILSON (*from the depths of his soul*). President—of—the—United States!

She nods, and for a long moment they stand together in silence. Then, off-scene, the faint strains of voices lifted in song are heard. Both turn toward the window and listen as the singing comes nearer.

ELLEN (*softly—moved*). It's the students, Woodrow. They're coming to serenade you.

The exterior of the HOUSE: The Princeton students, many of them carrying torches, are slowly drifting toward the house in Cleveland Lane, singing "Old Nassau." As they come up to the house, the door opens and Ellen and Wilson step out, followed by the girls, Tumulty, Professor Holmes and several other friends and relatives. As the song ends, one of the students—Felton—calls out:

FELTON. Congratulations, Mr. President!

Professor Holmes drags a rocking chair forward and Wilson gets up on it, Felton and another student stepping up and holding it. There is a long pause as Wilson struggles to regain control of his emotions.

WILSON. I have no feeling of triumph tonight; only a sense of solemn responsibility. I know only too well the very great task ahead of me, and I look pleadingly to you—the young men of America—to stand behind me, to support me. That's all I can say except—good night and God bless you.

There are tears in his eyes as he finishes, and in Felton's, too. For a moment the boys are silent. Then one of the students leads them in the Wilson cheer.

STUDENTS (*cheering*).
Ray	Ray	Ray
Tiger	Tiger	Tiger
Sis	Sis	Sis
Boom	Boom	Boom
Ah —	— —	— —
Wilson	Wilson	Wilson

Softly the strains of "Old Nassau" are again taken up and, as the song swells, the scene fades out.

PART FIVE

The WHITE HOUSE, seen in daylight, fades in to the faint strains of "My Country, 'Tis of Thee," and dissolves to a view of the GREAT SEAL OF THE UNITED STATES, in the floor just inside the White House. Then the view moves from the Seal to a group of people standing in the entrance hall of the White House. Wilson, Ellen and their daughters are coming in from the inauguration, followed by members of the inauguration party and their families. They include members of the Cabinet, the Chief Justice, and Professor Holmes. Assembled here are members of the White House staff—IKE HOOVER, the chief usher, the President's military aides, Negro attendants, and farther back the White House domestic staff. The faces are smiling at them in friendly welcome. Hoover steps forward and bows.

HOOVER. Mr. President, I'm Hoover, the chief usher.

WILSON (*holding out his hand*). How do you do, Hoover. This is Mrs. Wilson and my daughters, Miss Margaret, Miss Jessie and Miss Eleanor.

HOOVER (*bowing and smiling*). It occurred to me, Mr. President, that you and Mrs. Wilson would like to inspect your living quarters before luncheon.

WILSON. Thank you.

HOOVER. This way, sir. We'll take the elevator. (*And he conducts the family toward the rear corridor.*)

WILSON (*smiling as he passes the White House staff*). Thank you.

As they move off, the scene dissolves to the Wilsons, who like any other American family moving into a new home, are eagerly inspecting their rooms, testing the beds, examining the furniture, the fixtures, the pictures, the view.

MARGARET. Why, Mother, it's lovely!

NELL. I thought it was going to be grand and overpowering, and it's not at all! It's just a home!

WILSON (*teasingly*). Does it amaze you so much that our predecessors also had good taste?

Jessie suddenly appears at the door leading into the next room.

JESSIE. Come, look at my room! (*As they flow toward her room*) I'm sure it must be the one in which Abigail Adams used to hang out her laundry.

MARGARET. No. *That* was the East Room. I looked it up.

JESSIE'S ROOM: It, too, is a very charming room—large and airy. Over the fireplace is a large portrait of Dolly Madison. Jenny, the maid, is in the room unpacking a bag.

NELL (*as they come in*). Oh hello, Jenny. I see you got here all right.

JENNY. Oh, yes'm.

JESSIE (*indicating the portrait*). Mistress Dolly Madison! And don't anyone dare tell me *she* didn't sleep here!

NELL (*looking around*). Can't you almost *feel* them!

JESSIE (*shuddering*). Heavens! You don't think the house is haunted, do you?

WILSON. Well, a lot of them were extremely reluctant to leave here in their lifetimes!

The girls laugh, while Ellen, who has crossed to the mantelpiece, indicates a brass plaque.

ELLEN (*reading*). "In this room Abraham Lincoln signed the Emancipation Proclamation of January 1, 1863, whereby four million slaves were given their freedom and slavery forever prohibited in the United States!"

JESSIE (*awed*). Imagine! And in *my* room!

JENNY. I met the cook and she didn't look down her nose at me at all! You'd think she would—cooking in the White House!

Wilson and Ellen exchange amused glances, but Jenny is unaware of this.

JENNY. And Miss Nell, guess what! They've got *three* automobiles here! And an electric!

NELL (*overjoyed*). No!

JENNY. Yes'm, they have. I saw the chauffeur and he said we could use them whenever we wanted to.

WILSON. That's not bad for a family that's never even owned a horse and buggy.

Wilson says this with a little smile, but we know that he realizes just how far they have come to have three automobiles at their command. As he and Ellen start out, Nell drops an arm around Jessie's waist.

NELL (*whispering*). I still wish we were having an inaugural ball. It'd be such fun!

JESSIE. Father hates a lot of fuss.

NELL (*sighing*). I know. Just like Thomas Jefferson. Only—just for tonight! I wish he was a—a Republican!

JESSIE (*warningly*). Shh!—

WILSON'S SUITE: A grate fire is burning. In one corner of the bedroom is an oversized bed. Wilson stands beside it, as the girls come in.

WILSON (*quietly*). President Lincoln's bed.

NELL (*marveling at its size*). He must have been an awfully big man!

WILSON (*without turning*). He was.

Ellen has opened her handbag. Now she brings out three small packages of jewelry, a brooch, a ring and a string of pearls.

ELLEN (*smiling*). My dears, your father and I have a little gift for each of you—in commemoration of this day.

GIRLS (*excitedly*). Oh, Mother, how wonderful!

As the girls admire the small inexpensive pieces of jewelry, Wilson—unobserved by the others—steps up behind Ellen and, before she knows it, fastens a pendant around her neck.

ELLEN (*as she sees what he is doing*). Woodrow!

There is a broad smile on his face. The girls, forgetting their own gifts, crowd happily around their mother to admire hers.

ELLEN (*deeply moved*). Woodrow—it's beautiful! But why did you? I mean how did you—?

WILSON (*smiling*). Well, as you know, I borrowed a little money from the bank to pay my campaign expenses and—this was left over.

ELLEN. But Woodrow, it's *too* nice!

WILSON (*his eyes twinkling*). Perhaps, but then you mustn't forget I've got a better job now—shorter hours and more pay.

As they laugh, there is a knock at the door.

WILSON (*calling out*). Come in.

The door opens and the Negro butler —COATS—a big handsome fellow with shiny teeth—appears.

COATS. Excuse me, Mr. President, but luncheon is served.

WILSON. Thank you—?

COATS. Coats, sir.

WILSON. Thank you, Coats.

All start at once for the door, Ellen and the girls still admiring their gifts.

COATS (*grinning broadly*). Howdy, Miss Ellen. You don't remember me, do you?

ELLEN (*stopping, looking at him quizzically*). No, I—

COATS. My family lived right behind yours in Rome, Georgia. My mother did your mother's washing for close on to thirty years, I reckon.

ELLEN (*delighted*). Why how nice to have somebody from *down home* in the house!

COATS (*delighted*). Yes, ma'am, Miss Ellen, it's going to be mighty nice for me, too—having some ladies and gentlemen around here that speak my language.

As they all laugh and go out, the scene fades out.

PART SIX

A title fades in. It reads:

"DURING HIS FIRST YEAR IN OFFICE PRESIDENT WILSON INITIATED ONE PIECE OF SOCIAL LEGISLATION AFTER ANOTHER . . ."

This is followed by a series of glimpses of various BILLS. We see Wilson signing his name to one, affixing his seal to another, stamping another. (These brief scenes are almost in montage.) They are such bills as the FEDERAL RE-

SERVE BANK ACT, the ADAMSON EIGHT-HOUR LAW, the CLAYTON ANTI-TRUST ACT, the UNDERWOOD-TARIFF, and the FEDERAL TRADE COMMISSION. We see on each bill its title.

This dissolves to the CORRIDOR leading from TUMULTY'S OFFICE to the EXECUTIVE OFFICE ANTEROOM. Joseph Tumulty is just coming out, bearing several documents. He is whistling "Moonlight Bay." Then we see the ANTEROOM of the PRESIDENT'S OFFICE as Tumulty comes in. The room is crowded with visitors waiting to see the President. Some are seated on narrow, straight-back chairs which line the room. Others stand in little groups talking in low tones. The door to Wilson's office opens, and a group of Senators file out and cross to get their light spring overcoats. They look none too well pleased. They talk while putting on their coats.

FIRST SENATOR (*grumbling*). I don't know what I came here for anyhow. He didn't want *my* advice.

SECOND SENATOR. Nor anybody else's, Senator.

THIRD SENATOR. Once he's made up his mind, nothing in Heaven or earth's going to change him.

FOURTH SENATOR. I thought he was very patient and considerate. At least he *listened* to *our* side of it.

FIRST SENATOR. Oh, he was polite enough. But somehow he always makes me feel like an unruly schoolboy. I catch myself being afraid he's going to reach out and rap me over the knuckles.

SECOND SENATOR (*as he struggles into his coat*). Strange that a man who wants to save humanity should find it so difficult to loosen up and deal with a few human beings.

FIRST SENATOR. Oh, all these starry-eyed idealists are just the same! Think anybody who opposes them is in league with the devil.

As they start out, SENATOR HENRY CABOT LODGE of Massachusetts comes into the room. Senator Lodge is thin, white-haired, aristocratic, with a white beard. He smiles enigmatically.

LODGE. Good morning, gentlemen.

FIRST SENATOR (*as they go by*). Senator Lodge. (*A colored attendant takes his hat and coat.*)

SECOND SENATOR (*jovially*). Well, Senator! I didn't expect to find *you here!*

LODGE (*with a trace of humor*). Oh yes, we Republicans still do business with the Government *occasionally*.

The Senators look at him wonderingly, then go out. As they leave, Tumulty greets Lodge.

TUMULTY. Good morning, Senator Lodge.

LODGE. Mr. Tumulty, will you announce me to the President?

TUMULTY. Yes, of course, Senator.

As he turns and starts toward the President's office, he sees Colonel House just coming in. He stops.

TUMULTY. Colonel House! Welcome home!

HOUSE. Hello, Tumulty. (*They shake hands briefly.*)

HOUSE (*to Senator Lodge*). Senator.

LODGE (*coolly*). Colonel House.

TUMULTY. Go right in, Colonel. The Governor's waiting for you.

HOUSE. Thank you.

As he goes toward the President's door, Tumulty turns to Lodge.

TUMULTY. I'm sorry, Senator, but Colonel House has just got back from Europe and the President is anxious to see him on a very important matter. You don't mind waiting just a minute, do you?

Lodge continues to smile, but his eyes harden.

LODGE. Not at all.

As he sits down we hear from the President's office, Wilson greeting his friend House.

WILSON'S VOICE. House!

HOUSE'S VOICE. Governor!

As the door closes we hear Wilson's voice again.

WILSON'S VOICE. I've missed you.

A close view of TUMULTY shows him looking at Lodge, worried, seeing trouble brewing. He wipes his forehead, then picks up a newspaper from the table beside him and goes to Lodge.

TUMULTY. Have you seen the morning paper, Senator?

LODGE (*coldly*). Yes.

Tumulty looks at him anxiously, then off at Wilson's office. The scene moves with Tumulty as he goes across to the window and stops. The camera then swings past him and through the window we view Ellen at work in a rose garden beyond. Then we see the ROSE GARDEN, where Ellen is clipping rose bushes. As the view moves closer, we hear her humming faintly "Put On Your Old Grey Bonnet." And this dissolves to the UPPER HALLWAY—at the door leading to the family living room. Nell and Jessie, in evening clothes, are just coming out followed by two men also in evening clothes, McAdoo and Francis Sayre.

MCADOO (*to Nell*). For the daughter of a college professor, you know less about the problems of finance than anyone I have ever met. (*They all laugh.*)

JESSIE. How would a college professor know about finance—he hasn't any!

NELL. Why is it everyone expects us to be intellectual giants who talk about nothing but opera and literature?

JESSIE. People don't realize that we've spent all our lives in a college town.

MCADOO. If you ask me, I'd say you're really the most frivolous young ladies in Washington!

By this time they have reached the head of the stairs, and stopped.

JESSIE. If you will wait downstairs while we say good night to Mother and Father—we'll only be a minute.

MCADOO AND SAYRE. Certainly . . . Of course . . .

They move down the stairs as the girls go into the FAMILY SITTING ROOM. Nell opens the door, and she and Jessie go in. Wilson and Ellen are alone here; Ellen in front of an easel at work on one of her still-life paintings; Wilson is in a deep chair, immersed in a book.

NELL (*kissing Ellen*). Good night, Mother.

ELLEN. Good night, dear. Have a good time. (*As Nell goes to Wilson, Jessie kisses Ellen.*)

JESSIE (*admiring the painting*). It's beautiful, Mother! How do you do it?

ELLEN (*disparagingly*). Oh, it's far from finished.

WILSON is seen close as Nell bends over to kiss him, and we see that he is reading a detective story: "Murder on the Waterfront."

NELL. Have you guessed the murderer yet?

WILSON (*smiling*). It has to be the sweet old grandmother. She's the only one without a motive.

As Nell laughs and hurries off, Jessie kisses him.

JESSIE. Good night, Father.

WILSON. Good night, dear.

As the girls hurry out, closing the door behind them, Wilson again opens his book.

WILSON (*already reading again*). Where are they off to?

ELLEN. Oh, somewhere to dance. (*Smiling*) I believe Mr. McAdoo is quite adept at the "Turkey Trot."

Wilson grimaces at the word—returns to his book—Ellen to her painting.

WILSON. Haven't I seen that young man with Jessie before?

ELLEN. Any number of times, my dear.

WILSON. I talked with him at dinner. He struck me as being exceptionally intelligent. (*Looking up with a grin*) Schoolteacher, isn't he?

ELLEN. Yes.

WILSON (*trying to remember*). What's his name again?

ELLEN (*casually—busy with her work*). Francis Sayre. And the next time you see him, Woodrow, I suggest that you really get acquainted with him, because I have an idea you're going to be his father-in-law.

WILSON (*looking up at her in amazement*). What? ! ! !

ELLEN (*quietly*). It seems young people will get those foolish ideas, even if they do live in the White House.

WILSON (*jealous*). But—but—!

ELLEN. As I expect Nell and Mr. McAdoo also are discovering.

WILSON (*flabbergasted*). Nell!—McAdoo—my Secretary of Treasury?

ELLEN (*with a smile*). Well, the child's been taking an amazing interest in finance lately.

As the full force of this news strikes him, he looks at her blankly. With a smile she gets up and goes to him. Then we see ELLEN and WILSON close together. Ellen sits down on the sofa beside Wilson. Wilson is still bewildered by the amazing news he had heard about his daughters. Ellen is amused at his "Life With Father" attitude. In a rather quiet, awed voice, Wilson speaks, half to himself.

WILSON. Nell and McAdoo . . . Jessie and—what did you say his name is?

ELLEN (*her eyes twinkling*). Francis Sayre, my dear. . . . Francis Sayre—schoolteacher.

He gives her a quick look. She puts her hands over his and smiles up at him. The humor of the whole situation finally reaches him and he relaxes and smiles, too.

The scene dissolves to WILSON'S OFFICE at night. First there is a closeup of a TYPEWRITER, a typewritten page in the machine, revealing the last paragraph, which reads: . . . "Therefore, my policy of watchful waiting insofar as the Mexican situation is concerned, must remain unchanged. However, I wish to thank you for your kind suggestions. Sincerely, Woodrow Wilson." The view then draws back to reveal Wilson at the typewriter. He is wearing an old bathrobe. He has been writing the letter. Tumulty is with him. As Wilson pulls the sheet out of the typewriter and signs it we see a weary Tumulty trying to stifle a yawn. Wilson hands him the letter.

WILSON. Have this delivered to Senator Lodge, first thing in the morning by special messenger.

TUMULTY. Yes, sir.

WILSON. Thank you, Tumulty. Good night.

TUMULTY. Good night, Governor.

Suppressing another yawn, he turns and leaves. Wilson starts to gather up his papers, preparing to leave the office. Suddenly he hears Nell's laughter off-scene. All else in the house is quiet—everyone apparently fast asleep. Wilson looks up puzzled and glances at his watch. It is 12:45, and he shrugs. Now we hear Jessie's laughter off-scene. Again he looks up. A jealous look on his face, he rises, snaps off the light and moves quickly to the door which opens on the portico.

As Wilson steps out on the PORTICO in the moonlight and looks around again he hears Nell's laughter. He sees: Off the portico William McAdoo, his Secretary of Treasury, teaching Nell Wilson how to do the Bunny Hug as they are both laughing. A close view of WILSON then shows him looking off in their direction rather sternly: He is tempted to stop them. Then with a helpless gesture, he turns back toward the room. At this moment, Jessie's laughter is heard from the other direction and he looks off at her. He sees: At the other end of the portico, Jessie and Francis Sayre, and Sayre's arm is about Jessie's shoulder. Then WILSON, again seen close, looks paternally indignant as he wonders what is going on around here. Again he is tempted to put a stop to this nonsense. But he loses his courage, turns and tiptoes softly back into the room. We then see a CHAIR turned over in WILSON'S OFFICE —books scattered on the floor, and the view moving up, discloses the figure of WILSON hastily retreating through the door in the background.

This dissolves to the family LIVING ROOM at night: Margaret is at the piano, surrounded by Wilson, Jessie and Nell, playing and singing: "By the Light of the Silv'ry Moon." Ellen and Wilson's young cousin, HELEN BONES, are seated in a corner of the room at work on an invitation list. Wilson looks off at his wife. COL. HOUSE is seated in a corner, looking on with smiling eyes.

WILSON. Wait a minute, Margaret. (*As Margaret breaks off playing*) Ellen, come help us out.

ELLEN (*looking up*). I can't! I promised Helen we'd finish this invitation list tonight. (*At this Wilson, Nell and Jessie go to Ellen and Helen.*)

WILSON (*with a smile at Helen*). Poor Helen Bones! I told you what you were letting yourself in for when you took this job as Ellen's secretary.

HELEN (*laughing*). Yes, Cousin Woodrow, but you didn't tell me what a White House wedding is like.

NELL (*her arm encircling Jessie's waist*). It's all Jessie's fault. If only she hadn't decided to get married.

JESSIE. Well, I like that! What about your own wedding?

NELL. That's different. I'm marrying Mac, and he lives here in Washington, but you have to go and marry somebody who lives at the other end of nowhere.

WILSON (*teasingly*). Perhaps I ought to fire Bryan and make Frank Sayre Secretary of State, just so we can keep Jessie at home.

NELL. You can all joke about it all you want! Just the same this is the first break in the family. We've never been separated before—any of us.

There is a long pause after this. It is obvious that this thought is weighing on the minds of all of them.

ELLEN (*getting up*). Well, Helen, if these people are going to be so blue, perhaps I had better join them after all. (*As she starts for the piano*) Though goodness knows why they need *my* voice. They know I never could sing a note.

This breaks the mood, and they all laugh and again gather around Margaret at the piano. Margaret starts to play and they sing. Suddenly Nell looks at her mother, whose face is distorted with sudden pain. Ellen reaches out and steadies herself against the piano.

NELL (*alarmed*). Mother! What's the matter? Are you ill?

The music and singing end abruptly, and they all look at Ellen who is obviously unwell.

ELLEN (*weakly—leaning against the piano*). I don't know . . . I'm all right. Just a little faint.

Instantly Wilson and the girls, very much alarmed, help her into a chair and gather around her solicitously. Colonel House comes over, too.

JESSIE (*frightened*). Mother, you aren't going to be sick?

ELLEN (*forcing a smile*). I'm just a little dizzy, that's all.

WILSON (*to Margaret*). Ring for some water!

As Margaret turns to obey, he takes Ellen's hand and begins to chafe it. Colonel House comes over and joins the family group.

NELL (*kneeling beside her mother's chair*). You've been doing too much.

WILSON. It's all this entertaining. You can't keep it up.

ELLEN. But that's my job. The President has to entertain.

WILSON (*firmly*). Not if it's going to affect your health! (*After a slight pause*) Come and lie down.

ELLEN. Nonsense! I feel perfectly all right again. I'll just sit here for a moment while you go on with your song.

NELL. Not tonight!

ELLEN. Please! I insist.

There is a pause. They are all obviously upset. Wilson and the girls look at her, and then at one another. Wilson nods, and without a word, Margaret turns back to the piano and they follow.

ELLEN (*smiling*). It'll sound much better without me.

Margaret begins to play again and their voices join in. But something of the zest has gone. As he sings Wilson keeps watching Ellen, who continues to smile as if nothing were the matter. Colonel House, too, is watching her.

This dissolves to the ROSE GARDEN, seen in daylight. Ellen's rose bush is now in full bloom covered with red roses. Then the rose garden dissolves into a view of ELLEN'S BEDROOM at night: Margaret sits beside her mother, fanning her, while Nell and Jessie hover close by. Ellen looks very ill and wasted since we last saw her.

ELLEN. Washington's so hot in the summer, I wish you girls didn't feel you had to sit here with me.

MARGARET. We like it here.

ELLEN. Your poor father. He's hardly been out of that chair for a week. Why don't you take him for a drive —or down the Potomac on the yacht?

NELL. There'll be time enough for that when you're on your feet again (*There is a slight pause.*)

JESSIE. Where is Father now?

ELLEN. I made him lie down. He looked so tired.... Besides, I wanted to speak to you girls—alone. (*She motions to Nell and Jessie.*) Sit here —beside me.

Nell and Jessie sit on the edge of the bed, and she gives them each a hand. Margaret continues to fan her.

ELLEN (*smiling*). Of course I'm sure I'm going to be all right, but if anything *should* happen to me, I want you girls to promise me one thing.

NELL. Mother! Don't even say such things!

ELLEN. Your father is a great man. Promise me you won't let him be a *lonely* great man.

MARGARET. Mother! Please!

ELLEN. More than anyone I've ever known he needs sympathy and loyalty and companionship. Remember he's very shy—and sensitive. Not many people understand him. They think he's cold—and unbending. They can't see how tenderhearted and eager he is to give himself to his friends.

JESSIE (*in a whisper*). Mother!

ELLEN. He needs a woman's love and attention and understanding—someone he can turn to and trust. A wife is as much a part of him as his very mind—or heart. (*Proudly*) I know— because I have been his wife. (*She looks searchingly, pleadingly at the girls. Then she whispers.*) Promise? (*The girls nod.*)

NELL. Of course we promise. But mother, it's ridiculous of you to talk like this. You'll be up and about in no time, and you know it.

As Ellen smiles, the scene dissolves to the LIVING ROOM—upstairs. It is day. A uniformed trained nurse, carrying a tray with surgical supplies, is coming along the hall. As she approaches the door, we see Wilson and his three daughters seated on a sofa. Wilson gets quickly to his feet and follows the nurse, so that when she opens Ellen's door he can catch a glimpse of Ellen in bed, a doctor and another nurse bending over her. The nurse with the tray looks at him sympathetically, then goes on into the room, closing the door behind her. Wilson turns back toward the girls. His face is gaunt, his eyes haggard, as if he had not slept for days. Nell takes his hand and draws him down beside her. They sit there for a moment in silence, then look up again as Tumulty comes in.

TUMULTY (*hesitantly*). Senator Carter Glass telephoned, Governor. He wants to know if he can see you this afternoon about that Federal Reserve Bank matter?

Wilson stares at Tumulty for a moment, gathering his thoughts. Then he shakes his head.

WILSON. Tell him he'll have to excuse me. I can think of nothing while Ellen is like this.

TUMULTY. All right, Governor. He'll understand. (*He looks at Wilson, then turns away.*)

MARGARET (*worried about him*). Father, you promised Mother you'd play golf this afternoon.

WILSON. I know—but I can't.

Again he gets to his feet and nervously tiptoes to Ellen's door to listen. The girls look at him, helplessly. Then Jessie gets up, goes over to him, and once more leads him back to the sofa.

WILSON (*after a pause*). I can't bear the thought of her suffering.

JESSIE. Father! Please! She wouldn't want you to feel like this.

WILSON. She's always been the most radiant person I've ever known. For thirty years I've never had a thought in which she didn't enter. (*Brokenly*) I can't—I couldn't go on without her. (*There is a long pause.*) I'll never forget the first time I ever saw her. I was practicing law—in Atlanta. I had to go to Rome, Georgia, on business. Her father was the Presbyterian minister. I went to his church.—I'm afraid I couldn't have told you what the sermon was about.

NELL. She saw you, too. She always said she was glad she had on her prettiest hat.

WILSON. I don't think any two people were ever so happy—when I was teaching at Bryn Mawr and at Princeton—when you girls were babies . . . (*Then with a flash of anger*) It's *this place* that's killing her!

MARGARET (*comfortingly*). She's been happy here, Father—and so proud of you!

WILSON. She's done too much! I didn't realize it!

NELL. She wouldn't have been happy doing any less.

There is another long pause. Then suddenly the door to Ellen's room opens. All jump to their feet as DR. CARY GRAYSON comes out.

WILSON. Well, Grayson?

GRAYSON. She's sleeping now. So far as I can tell, there's no great change since yesterday—just a gradual weakening.

WILSON. There's no hope?

His eyes seek Grayson's. The latter cannot lie to him.

GRAYSON. Medical science is not the last word, Mr. President. We can only wait and see.

As Wilson nods, the scene moves to a close view of his face, and we see that his eyes are filled with tears.

This dissolves to the FRONT DOOR of the WHITE HOUSE in daylight. A great bow of heavy black crepe hangs from the knob. One of the colored attendants stands on duty there; a couple of subdued visitors are entering. Over this come softly the strains of "Nearer, My God, to Thee." But there is a discordant undernote, too, for—from far off—we hear, faintly, the cries of newsboys:

NEWSBOYS. Extra! All about the war! Extra! All about the war!

We then see the WHITE HOUSE FLAG flying at half mast. The music continues, but now the cries of the newsboys are closer—and clearer.

NEWSBOYS. Extra! Germany Declares War! England and France Mobilizing. Russia to March, says Czar! Austria Attacks Serbia! Extra! All about the war! Extra!

This dissolves to a view of the ENTRANCE to the LIVING ROOM at night. Margaret, Helen Bones and Col. House open the door and start into the room. They stop and look off. Then we see Wilson standing alone in the dimly lit room looking out of the window. Slowly he turns—unaware of the presence of the two girls and House—and goes slowly to the piano. The view draws closer to him and we see in his face what the loss of Ellen means to him. At the piano he hesitates, then idly, almost unconscious of his action, he picks out several notes of "Put On Your Old Grey Bonnet." His eyes are filled with tears. At the DOORWAY, Margaret, Helen and Col. House quietly close the door, not wishing to intrude.

MARGARET (*in a whisper*). If there were only something we could do— some way we could help.

This dissolves to a view of ELLEN'S ROSE GARDEN. All the petals are off the roses now. They lie scattered on the ground about the bush. The scene fades out.

PART SEVEN

The WHITE HOUSE GROUNDS fade in. There is snow on the ground. This dissolves to a STREET CORNER, where several newsboys are calling extras and selling papers like hot cakes, people frantically grabbing for them.

NEWSBOYS. Extra! Lusitania torpedoed off coast of Ireland! Over one hundred American lives lost! Extra! German sub sinks Lusitania! Fifteen hundred die! Extra!

CITIZENS. Cold-blooded murder! Piracy! Wholesale slaughter!

We get a close view of a MAN AT A BAR.

MAN. We'll be at war with Germany in a week!

This wipes off, disclosing a MAN IN A BARBER'S CHAIR, a towel over his face.

MAN. It's not our war! Why should we get mixed up in it?

This wipes off, disclosing a MAN ON A BOOTBLACK STAND reading a paper.

MAN. If Americans don't want to get hurt, let them stay home!

This wipes off, showing TWO MEN WALKING, one with a paper.

FIRST MAN. I bet Teddy Roosevelt would know what to do if he was in the White House.

This cuts to the OFFICE of two Senators, one standing in the center of the room, the second seated in the foreground with his head bowed.

SENATOR. More than one hundred murdered on the high seas and that man in the White House too proud to fight!

This dissolves to the CABINET ROOM in the White House. First, a close view shows Wilson seated at the head of the table, listening to a stormy debate on the very issue which is dividing the country: War or peace. He looks older, and his hair is beginning to whiten noticeably.

VOICES (*coming over*). But we have no choice! These Huns must be taught a lesson! We can't stand by and watch the rest of the world slipping into anarchy! We've got to declare war!

By now the view has pulled back to reveal Wilson's Cabinet. At his right sits Bryan, the great Pacifist—at his left McAdoo, now his son-in-law. The Cabinet is about evenly divided between those demanding war and those crying for peace. In general, Bryan, McAdoo, Daniels and Burleson favor peace. Lane, Garrison, and Houston lean toward a declaration of war.

BRYAN (*heatedly*). No! No! Our people were warned to stay off that ship! How do we know it wasn't carrying munitions?

GARRISON (*furiously*). Nonsense! That's nothing but German propaganda!

HOUSTON. Congress is all set to act! It'll back us up in a minute!

MCADOO. But what about the people?

GARRISON. Don't worry about the people! They're good and mad!

LANE. Read your newspapers!

GARRISON (*pointing*). If you don't believe it, just look out that window!

HOUSTON (*appealing directly to Wilson*). Mr. President, do you know people are saying openly that this administration lacks courage?

WILSON (*his jaw set*). They may call me a coward or anything else they wish! I won't be rushed into this war!

The forcefulness of this statement produces a shocked silence. All look at Wilson.

LANE (*shocked*). Does that mean you're going to overlook the most dastardly crime of which any civilized nation has ever been guilty?

WILSON (*struggling to remain calm*). No, I shall warn the German Government—in the strongest terms of which I am capable—that in the future it will be held to *strict accountability*.

GARRISON (*with just a trace of sarcasm*). Another note?

WILSON (*with a flash of anger*). Yes, another note!

GARRISON. But these Germans pay no attention to notes! The only thing they understand is force!

WILSON. I agree. The Germans are bullies of the worst sort. I doubt if they'll keep faith with anyone. But I'm not so much concerned with what the Germans do as I am with our own responsibility which is *to keep out of this war if possible*, so that at the right time we can offer ourselves as the only nation in the world with sufficient strength and influence to bring about a decent and lasting peace.

There is a slight pause. Lane and Garrison look at each other.

WILSON (*continuing*). The vast majority of Americans expect me to keep my head and save them from this awful mess. I don't want them to say when the casualty lists start coming in: "Why did Wilson have to move so fast? Why didn't he make at least one more effort?"

Again he pauses. Several of his Cabinet Members are obviously displeased. Only Bryan, Daniels, and McAdoo nod with evident approval.

LANE. But have you considered what this policy of uncertainty is doing to our economy?

HOUSTON. Cotton down to six cents! Our goods rotting on the wharves, afraid to go to sea! Our farmers and railroads facing ruin!

WILSON (*cold as ice*). I haven't thought to consider this war in terms of dollars and cents!

MCADOO (*nodding*). Nor have the fathers and mothers of this country, Mr. President!

Wilson gets to his feet, obviously deeply moved by this debate.

WILSON. No, gentlemen, it would be the easiest thing in the world for me, as President, to ask for a declaration of war. The man on horseback is always a hero. But I wouldn't have to do the fighting. Some poor farmer's boy or the son of some great family would have to do the fighting and the dying. When I ask them to do that, I want to be very sure that what they're dying for is worthwhile. . . . Good morning.

And under the stress of his great emotions, he turns and quickly leaves the room. Members of the Cabinet rise, and look after him in silence.

This dissolves to the OVAL ROOM at night. Wilson stands at a window looking out, a troubled and lonely man. After a moment he turns and goes to his desk, drops into his chair and inserts a sheet of paper in his typewriter. The door in the background opens, and Margaret comes in with a glass of milk and a small plate of sandwiches, which she sets down in front of him. He looks up at her and smiles faintly.

WILSON. Thank you, my dear.

MARGARET. You really should be in bed, Father. It's very late.

WILSON. I'll go along directly.

She looks down at him, deeply concerned, wanting to comfort him, but helpless to do so. He leans his head against her.

WILSON. Wouldn't it be nice if we could run away from it all?

A far-away look comes into his eyes. He speaks slowly, reminiscently, with a faint trace of a smile.

WILSON. Once upon a time your mother and I did just *that*—I'd been working very hard on the first draft of "Mere Literature"—without saying a word to anyone at the University, we slipped out for a holiday in the country. . . . I think it was just about the most perfect two weeks I have ever known—we tramped in the hills, slept in the sun, and walked alone at night under the stars.

There is a long, quiet pause. Then he continues, not looking at Margaret, but almost out into the past.

WILSON. Your mother was a very wonderful woman, Margaret—she had that rare quality of always being close to you, when you wanted her . . . when you needed her . . .

Then, with a sigh, he straightens up. Margaret looks down at him for a moment, then she turns and goes out. The view moves with her as she moves to the door, fighting back the tears. Suddenly the sound of his typewriter keys is heard as he begins to pound out his latest note to the German Government.

The scene dissolves into the FRONT PAGE of a NEWSPAPER, the headline reading:

"GERMANY YIELDS TO WILSON'S DEMANDS: AGREES TO CURB SUBMARINE WARFARE
President Outlines Sweeping New Preparedness Program—"

The view draws back to reveal Senator Lodge and several other Senators having lunch in a corner of the Senate Restaurant. One of them is reading the newspaper.

FIRST SENATOR. How long will Germany live up to it?

LODGE. As long as it suits her convenience.

SECOND SENATOR. I suppose we'll have to go along with Wilson's Preparedness Program.

LODGE (*sharply*). Not *his* Preparedness Program! Ours! (*With cold anger*) We started it! *We* pushed it when he would have nothing to do with it! Now he's trying to take it over—claim it for himself—because he thinks it's good politics! But never mind that! It has to be done! Not only will we have to go along, we'll have to lead the way—put aside any thought of Party—do what we can to save this country!

As the others nod assent, the scene fades out.

PART EIGHT

The WHITE HOUSE LAWN fades in. It is spring. The fountain is playing and the trees are budding. This dissolves to the REAR BASEMENT ENTRANCE of the White House. Wilson and Dr. Grayson are just coming in from a game of golf. They wear plus-fours. Both are wet to the skin, their shoes muddy, water dripping from their caps. Through the door we see an automobile. A secret service man opens the door for them. The scene moves with them to the elevator. Grayson pushes the button and the elevator door opens.

GRAYSON. Well, Mr. President, Teddy Roosevelt can't say you haven't adopted at least *one* of his policies.

WILSON (*as he gets in*). What's that?

GRAYSON. The strenuous life. (*As Wilson laughs lightly, the elevator starts up.*)

The interior of the ELEVATOR as it goes up: Suddenly it stops and the door jerks open. Two thoroughly drenched women start to get in. Their shoes are covered with mud, rain is dripping from their hats. They are HELEN BONES and EDITH BOLLING GALT. They stop quickly as they see who is in the car.

EDITH (*quickly*). Oh, the President.

WILSON (*a quick laugh*). Looking the worse for wear, I'm afraid.

Mrs. Galt has drawn back quickly.

HELEN. Hello, Cousin Woodrow.

WILSON. Come in.

The women hesitate a minute, then laugh, a bit embarrassed. They get into the elevator.

HELEN. Cousin Woodrow, I want you to know my friend, Mrs. Galt.

WILSON (*smiling*). I'm delighted, Mrs. Galt.

EDITH (*bowing*). Mr. President!

HELEN. Of course you know Doctor Grayson.

EDITH. Oh, very well! For a long time.

GRAYSON. Have you forgotten I introduced her to you?

HELEN (*as the elevator starts up again*). We've been for a walk in the rain and I persuaded Edith to come back here for tea with Margaret and me.

WILSON. Tea? Sounds delicious. May we come too?

HELEN (*appealing to Edith*). Shall we let them?

EDITH (*smiling*). As patriotic citizens, I don't see how we could very well say "no."

She has a soft, pleasant voice, great beauty, and unmistakable Southern charm.

WILSON. You're from the South, Mrs. Galt?

EDITH (*with a bright smile*). I had the honor to be born in the same State as you, Mr. President—Virginia.

HELEN. She's a descendant of Pocahontas.

WILSON (*smiling*). Well—*that is* Virginia! (*Again they laugh and the elevator stops.*)

The UPPER CORRIDOR, as the women get out followed by the President and Dr. Grayson: For the briefest moment, Wilson's eyes meet Edith's. Then the group breaks up.

WILSON. We shan't keep you waiting long.

Helen leads Edith off in one direction—Wilson and Grayson going off in the other.

HELEN. Don't hurry. Give us time to freshen up a bit.

We watch WILSON and GRAYSON as they walk away. Grayson glances back over his shoulder.

GRAYSON. Charming woman.

WILSON (*nodding*). Very.

This dissolves to the OVAL ROOM in the late afternoon. Edith, Helen, Margaret and Grayson are seated in front of an open fire having tea, while Wilson stands in front of them, leaning against the mantel. The men have changed their clothes—the women have cleaned their shoes and powdered their noses.

WILSON. Do you play golf, Mrs. Galt?

EDITH (*her eyes twinkling*). I've played a few times, Mr. President, and perhaps this will give you a faint idea of *how well!* The last time I played I was about two hundred yards from the green on the ninth hole—and I asked my caddy if he thought I could make it with my mashie. (*With a Negro accent*) "Yes ma'am, you can make it—allowin' you hit it often enough!"

They all laugh, Wilson with quick enjoyment. Margaret looks at her father —then at Helen. Both smile, happy to see him laugh for the first time in months.

As this dissolves we see the WHITE HOUSE TOURING CAR, Helen Bones and Edith Galt riding in the back seat of the touring car, with a secret service man in a jump-seat on each side of them. Wilson is riding up front with a uniformed chauffeur. The girls talk quietly.

HELEN. We're going down the Potomac next week-end on the yacht—would you like to join us, Edith?

EDITH. I'd love to—but I promised to visit the Hastings in Virginia.

HELEN. That's a shame. I'd hoped you could come—Cousin Woodrow will be *terribly* disappointed.

EDITH (*pleasantly surprised*).—The President asked for me?

As Helen nods her head in the affirmative and starts to reply, one of the secret service men coughs or does some piece of business which indicates his intimate presence. His hat blows off.

EDITH (*whispering, with an amused glance*). I can't for the life of me understand why they call it *Secret* Service.

As both girls laugh, the scene dissolves to EDITH'S HOUSE in Washington. A messenger has got out of a car and is going toward the door. We see him ring the bell, and the door is opened by a colored maid, to whom he hands a package. Then we see EDITH'S LIVING ROOM, Edith seated reading as the maid comes in and hands her the package.

EDITH. Thank you.

Edith unwraps the package to reveal a book. Puzzled, she glances at the title, then opens it. Inside is a note. Slowly she reads it—half aloud—just enough of the words to convey the full meaning.

EDITH. "My dear Mrs. Galt: I have ordered a copy of 'Round My House' through the bookseller, but while we are waiting for it, I take the liberty of sending you a copy from the Congressional Library. I hope it will give you a little pleasure. I covet nothing more than to give you pleasure—you have given me so much."

A closeup of EDITH shows her reading the signature: "Woodrow Wilson." She looks up from the sheet of paper, a puzzled look on her face, wondering. Then this dissolves to EDITH'S DRESSING ROOM at night. There is a rap at the door and Edith's voice calls: "Come in." The door opens and the same maid comes in with a box of flowers, which she brings in and puts on a table. (The camera moves in on the box of flowers. A pair of hands come in —open the box—and take out a card. Camera then pulls back to reveal Edith, dressed for dinner.) The room has several large but simple mirrors. Edith glances at the card, and reads it silently —then aloud.

EDITH (*amused*). "You are the only woman I know who can wear an orchid. Generally it's the orchid that wears the woman. W.W."

She smiles, then turns to the mirror—tries the orchid first at her waist, then on her shoulder, as the scene dissolves to the SOUTH PORTICO of the WHITE HOUSE. It is a lovely summer's evening. Wilson and Edith are standing looking out across the moon-drenched lawn (Camera shooting up at them from below. Slowly camera moves in.) Edith wears a white satin dress with creamy lace, an orchid, as usual, on her shoulder. He is in blue coat and white trousers. There is a long moment of silence.

WILSON. I think this is my favorite spot at the White House.

EDITH. It *is* lovely.

A long pause follows. Then he suddenly leans forward tense and grave.

WILSON. I asked Margaret and the others to leave us alone for a while, that I might have an opportunity to say something to you.

EDITH (*unsuspecting*). Yes?

WILSON. I need you, Edith. Will you be my wife?

She looks at him in astonishment, obviously unprepared for this.

EDITH. Mr. President!

WILSON (*quickly — impulsively*). I know this comes as a shock to you. Perhaps I've been too impulsive—but if I'm to continue to make opportunities to see you, I must speak.

Edith looks at his intense, eager face, aware of a great enveloping emotion.

EDITH. But, Mr. President, how can you be sure? You've known me only a few months.

WILSON. Time is not always measured in weeks, or months. In the last year I've lived a lifetime of loneliness and heartache. You've changed all that—given me hope that happiness is still possible.

There is a slight pause as she considers this.

EDITH (*gently*). Have you spoken to your daughters?

WILSON. Yes. They tell me they already love and admire you—that nothing could make them happier.

EDITH (*seeking words to express her feelings*). But I've never thought of you except as the President. . . . I've had no training for the responsibilities of such a life.

WILSON. Would you rather I'd not spoken?

EDITH (*frankly*). No. Any woman would be touched to be told that she could be of help to one in your position—in times like these. . . . But I'd have to have time to know you—to see you—to be with you.

WILSON (*tensely*). Do you want to see me?

EDITH (*frankly*). Yes. I do.

WILSON. Then I'll wait. (*He looks at her, and there is a long pause.*) But in all fairness to you, there's something you must understand.

EDITH. Yes?

WILSON. There's a spotlight on this house. Whoever comes here is observed and discussed. Everything I say is quoted—sometimes even correctly. (*As she smiles*) No matter how I try, I can't protect you from gossip.

EDITH (*smiling*). I'm not afraid of gossip.

WILSON. It would be even worse if I came to *your* house.

EDITH. But surely you have the right to choose your own friends!

WILSON (*with a wry little smile*). In this job I'm not sure I have any rights at all.

EDITH (*after some slight pause*). And this gossip you speak of—will it hurt you—what you're doing?

WILSON. It's you I'm thinking about —not myself!

EDITH (*smiling*). In that case, I suggest we go on exactly as we have in the past. As to being your wife— if it has to be "yes" or "no" at once, then I'm afraid it will have to be— "no."

He looks at her—like a hurt little boy.

WILSON (*earnestly*). Won't you at least give me the hope that you might change your mind—that maybe when you do know me better—?

EDITH (*smiling*). I'd be less than a woman, Mr. President—if I didn't reserve that right.

And she leans back and looks out over the lawn, a quiet and tender smile on her lips.

This dissolves to a BASEBALL PARK. Wilson and Edith are seated in a box with Tumulty, Nell, McAdoo, and a couple of Secret Service men. Edith again wears orchids. Wilson has a ball in his hand. With a smile on his face he rises and tosses it out on the field. A great cheer goes up. A newsreel cameraman leaps up and quickly shoots a picture of Wilson and Edith. The cameraman is a jaunty fellow clad in knickers, with his cap on backwards. We then see in the BASEBALL STANDS, a couple of women and a man at close view: The women nudge each other and look off at the Wilson box.

FIRST WOMAN. That's *her!*

SECOND WOMAN (*in a low voice*). I hear she was out on his yacht last week, too.

MAN. I know she was up to his summer home at Cornish.

ANOTHER SECTION OF STANDS: There is a close view of a man's ear; a man behind him leans forward and whispers something. We do not hear what he is saying, but we do hear the voice of the man whose ear is visible.

MAN. With an election coming up, too!

This dissolves to EDITH'S LIVING ROOM at night, with DR. GRAYSON seen close, standing with his back to the fire. There is a long pause. Obviously he is worried and upset.

GRAYSON. There's no use beating about the bush, Edith. You know about the whispers—the gossip— that's going on.

A close view of EDITH shows her seated in a chair across from him. She nods.

GRAYSON (*seen with her in a wider scene*). He heard about it today. Naturally he would be the last to hear. But I've never seen him so angry in my life. His lips went white —his hands shook. I think if he could get his hands on those scandalmongers he'd forget he's President.

EDITH (*quickly*). No, he mustn't do that!

GRAYSON. What's worse, some of his own friends are mixed up in it. They're afraid a second marriage will prevent his re-election.

EDITH (*quietly*). And what do you think?

GRAYSON. That his own political fortunes don't make any difference to him. It's you.

There is a slight pause. Then Edith gets up and walks across the room to him.

EDITH. Nothing must stand in the way of his re-election. I'd never forgive myself if I were the cause of his defeat.

GRAYSON (*quietly*). He's the President of the United States, but first of all he's a man. And he loves you. (*As she half turns toward him*) To do what he has to do he needs you, Edith. (*There is a long pause as she considers this.*)

EDITH (*quietly*). Thank you, Doctor Grayson. It was very kind of you to tell me all this. I shall write him my decision.

As she holds out her hand, the scene dissolves to WILSON'S OFFICE at night. He is pacing up and down the floor like a caged tiger. Once he goes to the telephone and picks it up.

VOICE (*through the telephone*). Yes, Mr. President.

WILSON. Get me Mrs.—(*He pauses.*)

VOICE. Yes, Mr. President?

WILSON. No, never mind.

He replaces the receiver on the hook. Again he paces the floor. Obviously he is a man deeply in love. And this dissolves to EDITH'S LIVING ROOM at night. Edith is seated at her writing desk—a sheet of notepaper before her. The camera moves in, and across her shoulder we see her write the word: "Dearest."

This dissolves to the CORRESPONDENTS' ROOM in the WHITE HOUSE. A couple of White House reporters are playing chess. One or two are working at typewriters. Tumulty strolls in and looks on for a moment, his nonchalant manner carefully concealing the fact that he bears important news. The reporters greet him affably.

REPORTER (*without looking up from the game*). What's the news, Joe?

TUMULTY. Not a thing, boys. How's it with you?

SECOND REPORTER. No notes to Germany? (*As Tumulty shakes his head*) No sinkings? (*As he again shakes his head*) No messages to Congress about us being too proud to fight?

TUMULTY. Sorry—just the usual routine.

Casually he sets several news releases on the table in front of the players. As he turns away, one of the reporters leans forward and glances at the news release. Suddenly he grabs the sheet, and bolts out of his chair like a madman, knocking over the chessmen. The others, realizing something big is going on, leap for the papers. Then we hear a reporter reading excitedly into a telephone.

REPORTER. "The announcement was made today of the engagement of Mrs. Norman Galt of this city and President Woodrow Wilson."

As the others rush for telephones, and Tumulty grins, the scene dissolves into a WHITE HOUSE INVITATION reading:

"THE PRESIDENT AND MRS. WILSON
request the pleasure of the company of
THE VICE-PRESIDENT AND MRS. MARSHALL
at a reception to be held at
THE WHITE HOUSE
*Thursday evening, January the tenth
nineteen hundred and sixteen
at nine-thirty o'clock.*"

This dissolves to the LOWER FLOOR of the WHITE HOUSE at night. A brilliant and spectacular assemblage is gathered for a White House diplomatic reception: women in evening dresses—diplomats in uniforms, many countries represented. Music is being played. Next we see the MARINE BAND, the players in scarlet coats. Suddenly they begin to play "Hail to the Chief." This is followed by a full view of the CROWD, as the people turn toward the arch and look up.

The UPPER CORRIDOR: Wilson and Edith, escorted by their military and naval aides, members of the Cabinet and their wives, and members of the family, begin to form a procession, the President and Edith in the lead. Edith wears a white gown brocaded in silver. There is a pomp and beauty to the show, and yet a gracious simplicity, too. Wilson and Edith are smiling. Then we see the STAIRWAY as the President and Edith lead the way down the stairs. As they come forward, an aisle opens up for them.—In the procession we spot Holmes, Felton and Colonel House.

In the EAST ROOM, too, guests are assembled as the President and his party come in to form a receiving line. People bow to them, and smile.

And now we see a GROUP of SENATORS standing in line to greet the President. They are the same men who were in Senator Lodge's office, but Lodge is *not* among them.

FIRST SENATOR (*in a low, sarcastic voice*). His Imperious Majesty appears to be in good spirits tonight.

SECOND SENATOR (*smiling*). Time will remedy that.

THIRD SENATOR (*hopefully*). Then you really think we have a chance to defeat him in November?

SECOND SENATOR. Not defeat, Senator. *Obliterate!*

They continue to smile and bow as the Wilsons pass by. Finally, we see the BLUE ROOM in the White House, with Wilson and Edith and their party in the receiving line. The guests file by greeting them, and the scene fades out.

PART NINE

A HOT DOG STAND, with a canopy over the top, fades in. Several men in shirt sleeves are gathered around. Hot dogs are being sold and the man selling them is like a spieler at a circus:

MAN. Hot dogs! Get your hot dogs! You can't enjoy the Convention, folks, without a hot dog!

On the canopy is a sign:
NATIONAL DEMOCRATIC CONVENTION 1916
RE-ELECT WOODROW WILSON

The people buying hot dogs have small bamboo canes with pennants reading: "WILSON 1916."

Next we see the DEMOCRATIC NATIONAL CONVENTION, a quartette on a platform singing: "We Take Off Our Hats to You, Mr. Wilson"—a corny campaign song of the day.

QUARTETTE (*singing*).
"We take off our hats to you,
Mr. Wilson.
Our hats are off to you.
You're the man of the hour,
You've stood like a tower,
And know what to do for the
Red, White and Blue, etc."

They turn and lift their hats to a big portrait of Woodrow Wilson as they sing one full chorus.

This dissolves to a RESTAURANT where a woman is standing on a stairway, singing:
"I didn't raise my boy to be a soldier,
I brought him up to be my pride and joy, etc."

And this cuts to a CABARET where a woman stands on the stage, singing the lines,
"He's got those big blue eyes like you, Daddy,
Reminds me of you all the time, etc."

This scene wipes off to reveal a LARGE BANNER reading "REPUBLICAN NATIONAL CONVENTION 1916." Over this comes wild cheering. Then we see a BAND of about thirty pieces playing "National Emblem," and then another PLATFORM behind which is a big picture of Charles Evans Hughes.

This wipes off disclosing a huge "WILSON FOR PRESIDENT" LITHOGRAPH in CONVENTION HALL, and standing beside it, pointing at Wilson, is a Democratic orator with a deep bull-like voice.

ORATOR. He kept us out of war!

There comes the sound of cheering, and this scene wipes off, revealing a Republican orator standing in the back of an old-fashioned car, in the midst of a group of about thirty overall-clad working-men.

ORATOR. Woodrow Wilson is the most incompetent, vacillating, insincere and cowardly leader this nation has ever endured!

There are cheers, and boos. After this, scene after scene wipes off in quick succession:

We see a second DEMOCRATIC ORATOR in front of a RAILROAD STATION, with Democratic posters in the background reading: "WHO BROKE THE MONEY TRUSTS?"—"WHO KEPT US OUT OF WAR?"—"WHO EXTENDED THE PARCEL POST?" "WILSON."

ORATOR. He kept us out of war! (*His words are greeted with cheers and applause.*)

A second REPUBLICAN ORATOR is holding forth in the back of a TRUCK, Republican posters showing Belgium raped.

ORATOR. We must rid ourselves of this college sissy and once again substitute *action* for elocution. (*Cheers. Boos.*)

A third DEMOCRATIC ORATOR on a THEATRE STAGE, posters in the background reading: "VOTE FOR WILSON!"—"PEACE WITH HONOR!"

ORATOR. He kept us out of war!

A third REPUBLICAN ORATOR, at a BANQUET SPEAKERS' TABLE, a poster reading: "WATCHFUL WAITING FOR WHAT?"

ORATOR. Wilson and his dynasty—his heirs and assigns—anybody who with bended knee has served his purposes must be driven from all control, from all influence upon the Government of the United States.

A fourth DEMOCRATIC ORATOR—a BANDSTAND in the PARK with a poster reading: "PROSPERITY! PREPAREDNESS!" in the background.

ORATOR. He kept us out of war!

A fourth REPUBLICAN ORATOR—a PARK BANDSTAND with a poster in the background reading: "AS MAINE GOES, SO GOES THE NATION. MAINE HAS GONE FOR HUGHES!"

ORATOR (*into a microphone*). While we watch the world in flames, we must not forget what is happening here at home under our very noses.

The view moves up from the speaker to a VOICE MAGNIFIER, the orator's voice continuing.

ORATOR'S VOICE. Private initiative is being stifled. Business is being put into a strait-jacket. Industry is being hamstrung!—All under this false claim that this is democracy, when as a matter of fact it is nothing but the blundering of a starry-eyed idealist trying to make a dream world.

A fifth DEMOCRATIC ORATOR—A man in shirt sleeves and galluses—on a FREIGHT LOADING PLATFORM of a railroad station.

ORATOR. He kept us out of war!

He leans forward until he is bent double and points off, whereupon the scene cuts to a close view of a BAND, with horses and buggies in the background, as it breaks into "Dixie."

This dissolves to the FRONT PAGE of the NEW YORK TIMES, on which a double headline reads:

20,000,000 AMERICANS GO TO POLLS TODAY. FORECAST SWEEPING REPUBLICAN VICTORY

Over this come the strains of "Sidewalks of New York." Side by side are two-column photographs of the rival candidates—WILSON AND HUGHES. And this dissolves to the BLUE ROOM in the White House on election night. First there is a view of Wilson standing and reading from a sheet of paper.

WILSON (*reading*). "A weak and imbecile man—the weakest I ever knew in a high place . . ."

Then the view draws back gradually as he continues, and we see with the Wilsons, Nell, Jessie, Margaret, Frank Sayre, Professor Holmes, and other friends and supporters. Edith is pouring after-dinner coffee.

WILSON (*reading*). "If I wanted to paint a despot, a man perfectly regardless of every constitutional right of the people, I would paint his hideous form."

He pauses and looks around. Edith has stopped pouring. She and the girls are highly indignant.

NELL. That's outrageous!

WILSON (*reading on*). "When he goes out of office next March, the whole country, except thieves, cowards, public plunderers, office holders and traitors, will rejoice."

EDITH (*angrily*). Woodrow, this is the last straw! You've got to do something about it! They have no right to say such things about you—even to win an election!

WILSON (*pretending to be surprised*). Oh, they weren't talking about *me*. That's what they said about Abraham Lincoln when he was running for re-election in 1864.

He laughs and puts the paper back into his pocket and takes a cup of coffee from his wife. The others are still seething with indignation. Edith, however, smiles.

HOLMES. I understand Teddy Roosevelt says you're the most incompetent man ever to occupy the office, Woodrow—worse even than Thomas Jefferson.

This provokes a smile all around. Wilson laughs for a moment, then his face grows sober.

WILSON (*seriously*). Frankly, I've been more concerned with what our own side has been saying. All this prating about "He kept us out of war!" As if I, or anyone else, can look into the future and see what is, or is not, to be. Any little German lieutenant can put us into the war tomorrow by some new outrage on the sea tonight.

HOLMES. Would you mind very much if you should be defeated?

WILSON (*frankly*). Well, I don't suppose any man wants to see his policies repudiated.

NELL. They tell me the betting in Wall Street closed at ten to eight against you, Father.

WILSON (*smiling and leaning toward her*). Well, I hope you didn't take any of it.

As he bends over, he sees Tumulty standing in the doorway, a tragic look on his face.

WILSON. Yes, Tumulty? (*Tumulty comes in toward him.*)

TUMULTY (*almost too moved to speak*). Governor, the *New York Times* has just conceded the election of Mr. Hughes.

There is a moment of shocked silence. Then there is an outburst of indignant outcries of "No!" "It's impossible!" "I don't believe it!" All turn and look at Wilson, who takes the news without a change of expression.

HOLMES (*looking at his watch*). But how can they be sure? It's only nine o'clock. They're still at the polls in the West.

Edith reaches out and takes Wilson's hand—smiles at him as if to say "It's all right."

WILSON (*thoughtfully*). Yes, it does seem rather early. However, the *Times* is generally right. (*Then lightly*) In the meanwhile, I see no reason for despair. The Government's not going to collapse just because I've been left at home. Hughes is an honest man and a very capable one.

HOLMES (*with broad grin*). As a matter of fact, I understand his own people are inclined to refer to him simply as "Wilson with whiskers."

WILSON (*smiles, and turns to Edith*). Of course my wife may feel that the country's judgment is a bit warped.

EDITH (*with an answering smile*). I can think of nothing except that you will be free of all this—that at least we can be alone.

WILSON (*gratefully*). Thank you, my dear. (*Turning to Margaret*) And now, Margaret, let's see if we can't do something to cheer these other people up. A song, perhaps, to which —with your permission, sir—(*bowing to Holmes*)—I shall add my golden tenor.

He looks around at the doleful group and smiles. Suddenly Margaret's fighting spirit comes back, too. Her chin goes up and, as if nothing had happened, she starts to play "Crash Through That Line of Blue." First Wilson, then the others, join in valiantly, even Professor Holmes adding his wavering voice to the chorus.

The scene dissolves to the REPUBLICAN HEADQUARTERS at night, with a sign on the window reading: "REPUBLICAN NATIONAL HEADQUARTERS."

Then we see the ROOM. It is filled with pictures of Hughes and Republican campaign slogans. The Party members —including some of the Senators we know—are staging a triumphant Indian

War Dance, whooping and hollering as they prance around the room in celebration of the great victory. Senator Lodge, while too dignified to join in the festivities, looks on with a smile.

This dissolves to WILSON'S BEDROOM, next day, as Edith hurries in.

EDITH (*excitedly*). Woodrow! Mr. Tumulty's just had word that late returns from the West show a definite swing to you—that you still have a chance!

From out of the bathroom, Wilson sticks his lathered face, his shirt open, towel around his neck.

WILSON. Really? . . . Well, I wouldn't put too much stock in that, my dear. Tumulty's inclined to be a bit optimistic at times, you know.

This dissolves to the FRONT DOOR of HUGHES' HOME at night. Here a group of reporters are facing a formal English butler.

REPORTER. May we see Mr. Hughes?

SERVANT. The President has gone to bed. He left word he was not to be disturbed.

REPORTER. Well, when the *President* wakes up, give him this and tell him you're not so sure he's President after all.

Whereupon he hands the servant a newspaper. As the latter looks down at it, we see a HEADLINE which reads:

"WILSON RE-ELECTED
CALIFORNIA'S VOTE SWINGS NATION"

And on the servant's startled look, the scene dissolves to the BLUE ROOM. It is evening, and a gay and triumphant scene is in progress. Wilson and Edith are here with members of his family, Cabinet, Holmes, Colonel House and all his friends. They are congratulating him and there is a note of rejoicing in the scene. Daniels steps up and takes the President's hand. Servants are passing punch and sandwiches. Among the guests is Felton.

FELTON. I never gave up, Mr. President. Not for one minute.

WILSON (*smiling*). Well, I did. I'd have sold out pretty cheaply election night.

MC ADOO. You just got through by the skin of your teeth in the electoral college, but you polled three million more popular votes than in 1912. That's not to be laughed at.

WILSON (*to Edith, lightly*). Why on earth any man should want a job like this for another four years is beyond me. (*He pauses—then with engaging frankness*) But I confess I *did* want it.

As he smiles and others press forward to shake his hand, the scene fades out.

PART TEN

[A close view of a DEATH-HEAD HUSSAR HAT, resting on a desk, fades in. Then the view draws back and we see sitting behind the desk the German Kaiser. Standing at one side is the Crown Prince. Four or five Junker officers of the High Command, including the Admiral of the Fleet, are with the Kaiser. The room has only a desk. Behind it on the wall is a large map, draped at one side with purple velvet. The Kaiser has evidently come to a decision of some kind, for he reaches for his pen and with a flourish puts his signature to an official paper which lies on his desk. Then he rises, and hands the paper to one of his aides.

KAISER. *Senden Sie das sofort zum Grafen Bernstorff!*]

This dissolves to the EXTERIOR of the WHITE HOUSE on a rainy January night. A limousine is just pulling up in front of the house. Two men get out and hurry up the steps. A uniformed usher opens the door and they go in. Then we see the HALLWAY as the men come in. They are ROBERT LANSING, Secretary of State, and COUNT VON BERNSTORFF, the German Ambassador.

LANSING. Has the President retired?

USHER. Yes, sir.

LANSING. Wake him, please. Tell him that Mr. Lansing, Secretary of State, and His Excellency, Count von Bernstorff, the German Ambassador, are here, and that we must see him at once.

The usher hesitates for a moment, but the grave, tense manner of the Secretary sweeps away his scruples.

USHER. Will you wait in the East Room, sir?

As the two men start off, the scene dissolves to the EAST ROOM at night. Here Lansing and the Count are seated in stiff-backed chairs. . . . Lansing is obviously upset. As a sound is heard at the door, both get quickly to their feet. Wilson comes in.

LANSING. Mr. President.

VON BERNSTORFF. Mr. President.

WILSON. Mr. Lansing. Your Excellency. (*Puzzled*) What is it, gentlemen?

LANSING (*greatly agitated*). Mr. President, I'm sorry to disturb you at such an hour, but Count von Bernstorff has just handed me another note from his government.

WILSON. Yes?

LANSING. Beginning *tomorrow,* Germany will resume its policy of unrestricted submarine warfare—

VON BERNSTORFF (*hastily*). We have no other choice, Mr. President.

LANSING.—and will sink on sight—and without warning—any neutral vessel entering European waters.

Wilson stares at Von Bernstorff, hardly able to believe his ears.

VON BERNSTORFF. With certain exceptions, of course.

LANSING (*irony in his voice*). Yes, I believe one American ship will be permitted to sail from a designated port each week—provided it is properly lighted and marked.

Wilson continues to stare at Von Bernstorff incredulously. The latter is obviously ill at ease.

VON BERNSTORFF. We deeply regret the necessity of this decision, Mr. President, and we sincerely hope you will not permit it to interfere with your noble efforts to bring about peace with our enemies.

WILSON (*coldly*). Sit down, sir! (*Von Bernstorff drops into a chair.*)

LANSING. We also have received indisputable proof within the last hour that the German Government has been using our own State Department cables in an effort to foment trouble between this country and Mexico.

WILSON (*white with anger*). What?

LANSING. With California, New Mexico, and parts of Texas as bait.

VON BERNSTORFF (*with a flash of Prussian anger*). I deny any such thing, Mr. President!

LANSING. The proof is overwhelming, Mr. President. There can be no doubt.

Von Bernstorff has visibly paled. He clutches the knob of his walking stick to keep his hands from shaking. Wilson looks at him and for a moment one thinks he might even attack the German agent. . . . Then he begins to speak—quietly at first, but with mounting passion as he goes on.

WILSON. Count von Bernstorff, for more than two years this Government has exercised every restraint in its efforts to remain neutral in this conflict. But you and your military masters apparently are determined to deny us that right.

VON BERNSTORFF. But I assure you, sir—

WILSON (*ignoring the interruption*). Every way we turn we run into a blank wall of German cruelty and stupidity. Every time we think we've escaped, you blindly—and *deliberately*—block us with some new outrage!

VON BERNSTORFF (*rising—full of German indignation*). Mr. President! . . .

WILSON. Sit down. Won't you Germans ever be civilized? Won't you ever learn to keep your word? Or to regard other peoples as men, women and children of flesh and blood and not as inferiors to be treated as you see fit—all in the name of your discredited German Kultur and race superiority?

VON BERNSTORFF (*again rising*). I wish to withdraw, Mr. President. . . .

WILSON. We are not exactly fools. We know about the spies and conspirators you've sent amongst us in an effort to corrupt our opinions through lies and rumors, and of your ceaseless attempts to sabotage our industries and commerce. (*Waving aside an interruption*) Unfortunately, some of our own people have fallen in with your plans, and day after day I see them going up and down this country doing your work, crying out in their innocence that this is "just another European war" which can't touch America—building up false illusions of safety and security—appealing to our ancient traditions of isolation—while you smile behind their backs and go right ahead with your evil plans of world conquest and exploitation.

VON BERNSTORFF (*again rising*). I bid you good night, Mr. President.

WILSON. You will wait until I have concluded, Count von Bernstorff. (*A*

Tumulty: That William Jennings Bryan! He's trying to steal the nomination for himself.

Wilson: We have no selfish ends to serve. We desire no conquest, no dominion, no material compensation for the sacrifices we shall freely make . . .

Wilson signs the Treaty of Versailles.

Wilson: I'm afraid I'm more concerned with what this young lady and her generation think of me than I am with what the present lords of the earth have to say.

Von Bernstorff sinks down again) Is your Kaiser so contemptuous of American military prowess? Does he think we're so weak and disunited—just because we prefer peace to war—that we will not fight in any circumstances? Or is he so drunk with power that he can't understand that such action will unite this nation as never before in its history—and that he has made it clear at *last* that this is, in truth, a fight for freedom and decency against the most evil and autocratic power the world has ever seen? (*Turning to Lansing*) Mr. Lansing, you will hand His Excellency, Count von Bernstorff, his passports immediately. (*To Von Bernstorff*) Good night, sir!

Count von Bernstorff gets to his feet and clicks his heels, speechless before the wrath of the President. Then he turns and marches out of the room, followed by Lansing, who bows to the President before he exits. Wilson stands looking after them for a moment in deep thought, and the scene draws in to afford a close view revealing the struggle and sense of outrage which Von Bernstorff's announcement has produced. Slowly he turns and crosses and stands in front of the great, dimly-lit portrait of Washington, the scene moving with him, as we hear faintly the strains of "Yankee Doodle." Then a whispering voice states the age-old theory of isolation.

VOICE. "Why, by interweaving our destiny with that of any part of Europe, entangle our peace and prosperity in the toils of European ambition, rivalry, interest, humor, or caprice?"

In deep and troubled thought, he slowly goes to stand in front of the portrait of Lincoln. As he stares up into the homely face of the Civil War President, the music changes softly to "Battle Hymn of the Republic," and again a whispering voice speaks the plea of humanity.

VOICE. "That government of the people, by the people, and for the people, shall not perish from the earth."

As he stands there silent, summoning strength out of the past, the scene dissolves to WILSON'S OFFICE, where WILSON is seated at his tyepwriter, his face grim and taut as he types—every nerve tense, concentrated. The view moves close and tilts (leans) forward to read what he has written. Over his shoulder we see the words:

. . . "To be in fact nothing less than war against the government and people of the United States; that it formally accept that state of belligerency which has thus been thrust upon it."

Suddenly his hand reaches in, grasps the piece of paper, and is about to tear it out of the machine, but he hesitates, controls himself, and as the view draws back quickly, he gets to his feet, turns from the typewriter, and crosses the room in an agony of indecision. As he goes, he beats one closed fist against the open palm of his other hand.

This is followed by a full view of WILSON'S OFFICE, dimly lit, the only light being the one over his typewriter. Wilson paces the entire length of the room, then stops for a moment at the window, draws aside the curtains and peers out into the darkness. We get the feeling of a small figure, a figure of loneliness and despair in this huge room, fighting a shattering problem alone. In the background a door opens and Edith comes in. He turns quickly at the sound. As Edith speaks, she is full of sympathy—her voice tender, pleading.

EDITH (*from the door*). Is there anything I can get you, Woodrow? It's after four o'clock.

Wilson takes a step toward her. His voice is a cry of agony, of despair.

WILSON. Isn't there something else I could do?

EDITH (*as she starts toward him*). They've given you no choice, Woodrow!

WILSON (*coming toward her tense, pleadingly*). But am I doing right? Isn't there some way—some—

EDITH (*still going toward him—breaking in*). How else can you deal with these mad men? How can there possibly be any peace or sanity in the world as long as they are in power?

They meet near his desk. His face is tense, drawn. He has been through hell and his voice, his speech, his manner reveal how near the breaking point he is as he sees his dreams of peace shattered—and by a word from himself, too.

WILSON. Yes, I know. But if only there were some organization capable of meeting this problem—of settling it without fighting—killing—destroying—

EDITH (*impassionedly*). Maybe this war's the only way men can be brought to their senses, Woodrow, and taught to live at peace with one another like civilized human beings!

He picks up a paperweight from his desk which he pounds against his hand to emphasize and to accentuate his answer.

WILSON (*with equal passion*). If I didn't think that!—If I didn't believe that this time the world would really unite and cooperate!—If I thought for one moment this was going to be just another chapter in the long and bloody history of war, I'd never—*never*— (*He struggles to control himself as he turns and looks at the manuscript in the typewriter.*)

EDITH (*putting her hands on his shoulders*). No one who knows the fight you've put up can ever doubt that!

He turns and looks at her. Their eyes hold for a moment. Hers are strong, steady and unwavering, and he seems to gain strength from her. Then he turns and drops into a chair in front of his typewriter, and stares at the words he has written.

WILSON (*quietly*). You realize it will mean the end of the world we've known. Everything we've fought for —every social gain we've made—will be lost. (*Edith moves over close to him, and looks down at him.*)

EDITH. Only for a little while, my dear.

WILSON (*staring past her*). Our whole energy will be devoted to one thing — *destruction*. Liberalism — humanitarianism—everything we hold dear will have to go by the board. To beat Germany we'll have to be just as *brutal*—and *ruthless*—and *cynical* as she is.

EDITH (*quietly, leaning toward him*). Is that too high a price to pay if this should really be "the war to end all wars"?

WILSON (*looking up at her questioningly*). But *will* it be? Can we be sure? *Are* the people ready to understand and to work together?

EDITH (*with conviction*). The *people* —yes!

As the full significance of this hits him, the whole meaning and purpose of the war become clear to him at last. There is another pause fraught with meaning, all his faith in the people revived. His jaw sets with sudden determination. He is now ready to go through with it.

WILSON (*as he turns again to the typewriter*). The *people*—yes!

And he starts with renewed hope and vigor and faith to finish what he started to write, Edith watching him sympathetically.

WILSON (*briskly, as he types*). Will you ask Tumulty to come in—he'll want to send this to the printers.

This dissolves to the CAPITOL at night, the view directed at the DOME. It is raining. This dissolves to the HOUSE OF REPRESENTATIVES at night, as viewed from the GALLERY. A very grave Wilson is addressing a joint session of the Congress.

WILSON. With profound sense of the solemn and even tragic character of the step I am taking and of the grave responsibilities which it involves, I advise that the Congress declare the recent course of the Imperial German Government. . . .

Now we see WILSON, with the court reporters and Secret Service men in the foreground.

WILSON (*continuing*). . . . to be in fact nothing less than war against the Government and people of the United States; that it formally accept that status of belligerency which has thus been thrust upon it.

The FLOOR OF CONGRESS comes into view. Chief Justice White, wearing the robes of his office, suddenly raises his hands above his head and brings them together approvingly, at the same time letting out a mighty Rebel yell. Then the scene begins to move through the Congress as Wilson's speech continues, and we see the various reactions of the nation's law-makers, Supreme Court members, and the Cabinet. Here men applaud, others cheer. A few sit in silence, heads bowed. One woman Congressman is weeping. LaFollette throws up his hands in despair.

WILSON'S VOICE. In so doing, let us make clear to all the world what our motives and objectives are. We have no selfish ends to serve. We desire no conquest, no dominion, no material compensation for the sacrifices we shall freely make. We are but one of the champions of the rights of mankind. We shall be satisfied when those rights have been made as secure as the faith and freedom of nations can make them. . . .

The scene moves to the GALLERY, where Edith, Holmes, and Wilson's daughters sit, listening to the speech—and past their faces. They lean forward, intent on every word, knowing what it costs him to say them.

WILSON'S VOICE. It is a fearful thing to lead this great peaceful people into war. But the right is more precious than peace, and we shall fight for the things which we have always carried nearest our hearts. . . .

A close view of WILSON (shooting up at him, past the men who are taking notes):

WILSON.—For Democracy, for the right of those who submit to authority to have a voice in their own governments, for the rights and liberties of small nations, for a universal dominion of right by such a concert of free peoples as shall bring peace and safety to all nations and make the world itself at last free.

A close view of SENATOR LODGE applauding is followed by a close view of WILSON as he concludes.

> WILSON. To such a task we can dedicate our lives and our fortunes, everything we are and everything that we have, with the pride of those who know that the day has come when America is privileged to spend her blood and her might for the principles that gave her birth and happiness and the peace which she has treasured. . . .

There are tears in his eyes.

> WILSON. God helping her, she can do no other!

He pauses. There is a brief pause, then a mighty roar and applause. We see the FLOOR OF CONGRESS, men standing, applauding, cheering (not quite all, however); WILSON listening to the applause, then lifting his eyes toward the gallery; and finally EDITH, leaning forward toward Wilson, her face full of sympathy and understanding. There are tears in her eyes as the scene fades out.

PART ELEVEN

THE WAR: A crashing, stirring rendition of "Over There." The progress of the war itself is to be shown in terms of newsreel shots in the theatre with the proscenium arch visible, and through the songs of the period. . . . In the beginning we see a BLINDFOLDED MAN, Vice-President Marshall, drawing the first draft number; AMERICAN BOYS in civilian clothes marching off to war, suitcases in hand; ROOKIES drilling. "Over There" played and sung. . . . Shots of AMERICAN INDUSTRY being mobilized—steel pouring—ships being launched—weapons of war forged. Over this come the words and music of "Tipperary." . . . Shots of a LIBERTY LOAN DRIVE participated in by Mary Pickford and Charlie Chaplin; A STREET on a gasless Sunday—horses—pedestrians; SIGNS IN WINDOWS (emphasizing rationing program)—"Meatless Tuesday"—"Give Till It Hurts"; HOUSEWIVES lined up in front of butcher shops. Over this comes "Keep the Home Fires Burning." . . . Shots of AMERICAN SOLDIERS marching through the streets; TANK AND OTHER MOBILE EQUIPMENT on parade; SOLDIERS in maneuvers; a RED CROSS PARADE. Over this the music of "K-K-K-Katy." . . . Shots of AMERICAN TROOPS IN FRANCE: Men on the way to the front—plowing through the mud—living in trenches. Over this the music of "Goodbye Broadway, Hello France."

This dissolves to the BLUE ROOM. Wilson is facing Colonel House, who is seated near him.

> WILSON (*leaning forward*). Go to Europe. Say to our associates in this war that we not only assent to a unified command—we insist upon it.

This dissolves to the PRESIDENT'S LIVING ROOM at night. Wilson is facing Josephus Daniels, Secretary of the Navy. Both are standing. Models of a Liberty ship and destroyer are on the desk.

> DANIELS. I am pleased to report, Mr. President, that your suggestion to employ convoys has resulted in the delivery of one million American

soldiers to France without the loss of a single life.

This dissolves to WILSON'S OFFICE. Wilson is facing Barney Baruch.

WILSON. Baruch, as head of the War Industries Board, you are my right arm and my right eye in all forms of supply.

BARUCH. Thank you, Mr. President. (*Wilson links his arm in Baruch's, and they start to go out.*)

WILSON (*as they walk*). I understand that in your college days you were an outstanding amateur boxer.

BARUCH (*smiling*). Well, at least I was a boxer, Mr. President.

WILSON (*grinning*). Good. It'll come in handy.

This dissolves to the OVAL ROOM, where Wilson is sitting at his desk signing commissions which Edith is placing before him.

WILSON (*with a smile*). Commissions—commissions! Good Heavens! How many second lieutenants are there?

Edith smiles and removes them as fast as he scribbles his name on them.

The door to the anteroom opens and Margaret appears. Wilson looks up.

MARGARET. Excuse me, Father, but there's somebody here who wants to say goodbye to you.

And she smiles and steps aside as Felton appears in the doorway, a big smile on his face. Felton is wearing a uniform with one silver bar on his shoulder—a first lieutenant.

WILSON (*quickly dropping his pen and his face lighting up with pleasure, he gets to his feet*). Well, Lieutenant! Come in—come in!

FELTON (*with a grin as he comes forward*). Hello, Mr. President . . . Hello, Mrs. Wilson.

EDITH (*smiling*). I must say this is a well-dressed army!

Wilson goes forward to greet Felton. They shake hands warmly. Margaret has closed the door in the background and is coming forward to join them.

FELTON. I don't want to take your time, Mr. President—I just wanted to say "so long" before I shove off.

WILSON. You're leaving soon?

FELTON (*grinning*). I'm afraid that's a military secret, sir. (*Wilson and the two women join heartily in the laughter.*)

WILSON. And quite right, too.

Then quickly the laughter dies. Wilson looks at the boy and realizes what Felton is going off to face—at his own command, too.

WILSON (*his voice choked*). Well, take care of yourself, Felton—

FELTON (*equally stirred*). Yes, sir, I will.

WILSON.—and—don't be too impatient with us.

FELTON. No, sir—I'll try not to be.

There is a long pause. Wilson puts an arm around the boy's shoulders.

WILSON. Well, son—

For the first time he seems to be at a loss for words—to be groping—as if saying goodbye to his own son.

WILSON.—goodbye.

FELTON. Goodbye, sir.

WILSON. And thank you for coming to see me. Thank you very much—very much.

Their eyes hold for a moment. Then the boy abruptly turns and hurries off. Wilson stands watching him go. Edith moves to his side.

This dissolves to a canteen in a Railway Station. There is a crowd of soldiers to whom coffee is being dispensed over a long counter by several women and young girls. We then see a GROUP OF YOUNG SOLDIERS as one of them points.

FIRST BOY. Sure, it's her!

SECOND BOY. Aw, don't kid me!

FIRST BOY. Well, go on and ask her then. See for yourself.

SECOND BOY. Okay, I will.

He starts off, the view moving with him through the crowd and over to a coffee urn. A woman is just drawing a cup of coffee. As she turns we see that it is Edith. She smiles at the soldier— a tall, raw-boned country boy.

SECOND BOY. Say, lady! They been trying to tell me you're the President's wife.

EDITH (*amused*). Really?

SECOND BOY. They can't string me!

EDITH. You don't think I look the part?

SECOND BOY. I say you don't!

EDITH (*smiling*). I agree with you. But when you come back from France, if you'll come to the White House, I'll do my best to look as I should. (*And she hands him the cup of coffee.*) Or, better still, why don't you speak to the President himself about it.

And she indicates someone out of sight. As the boy turns, his face drops in astonishment and the cup slips from his hands and falls to the floor with a crash, for Wilson is coming toward him.

WILSON (*smiling*). Slippery, aren't they?

SECOND BOY (*bewildered*). But you're the—the—!

WILSON (*helping to pick up the pieces*). In this war, even the President has to do K.P. occasionally.

The other boys crowd around, eager to shake hands with the President and his wife. There are boys of all nationalities. Wilson, happy and at ease with them, grasps their hands and the barriers that ordinarily exist between a President and the people are forgotten.

BOYS (*pushing to get to him*).
Hi, Mr. President!
Hello there, Mr. President!
I never thought I'd get to shake hands with you!
Boy! I can't wait to write home!
Shucks, they'll say we're lying!

Wilson pauses in front of one of the boys.

WILSON. Where are you from, young man?

FIRST BOY (*with a trace of a German accent*). Milwaukee, Sir.

WILSON. German?

FIRST BOY (*proudly*). My father was German. I'm just an American.

WILSON (*to the next boy*). And you?

SECOND BOY. My name's Vespucci, Mr. President. But I'm just an American, too.

THIRD BOY (*a youngster with a big grin*). I guess there's something funny about all of us, Mr. President. Mike yonder's a Bohunk. Me, I'm just Irish. Tex here claims he's just from plain Texas.

TEX (*grinning*). At least there ain't nobody told me any different yet.

They all laugh at this. Then Wilson's face grows sober.

WILSON. This is all very interesting, boys, and I want you to remember it. (*As they grow quiet to listen*) Here we are—men of all races—with different backgrounds and ancestries—working together for a common purpose. That's what's made America what it is—and that's what the whole world must learn to do some day.

He pauses and looks around. The music has stopped, and more and more men are crowding into the room to listen to him.

WILSON. I know there are some people who say that this is just another war to protect the great fortunes, or for some other economic reason. But don't believe them! If anybody tries to tell you that universal peace is just an idle dream, tell him he's a liar! Say your President said that you're fighting this war so there won't have to be any more wars. And that when we get through with it, we're going to sit down with the people of other countries who feel as we do and work out some plan which will make it unnecessary for boys like you—and your sons—to have to go out and shoot one another. Maybe we'll call it a League—or maybe we'll call it something else. But whatever it is, that's what you boys are going to France for. And with the help of God, that's what you're going to get! Now goodbye boys, and—God bless you all.

There is a moment of silence, then the raucous voice of a Sergeant is heard.

SERGEANT'S VOICE. Company, fall in! All right, you guys! Get back on that train! What are you tryin' to do—hold up the war?

The Sergeant pushes his way through the DOOR. He is big and tough, and he doesn't stand for foolishness. One of the soldiers tries to stop him.

SOLDIER (*in a low voice*). Take it easy, Sarge! We been talking to the President!

SERGEANT (*a regular Sergeant Quirt*). Sez you?

And he pushes on. Suddenly, however, he sees the President. A horrified look comes into his face. In a wider scene, we then see Wilson and Edith laughing. The Sergeant turns and beats a pell-mell retreat, to the raucous laughter of his outfit.

This dissolves into a NEWSPAPER HEADLINE reading:

"WILSON GIVES CONGRESS PROGRAM
FOR WORLD PEACE"

and the headline dissolves to the HOUSE OF REPRESENTATIVES where Wilson is addressing Congress with the court reporters in the foreground. Then the scene draws in slowly.

WILSON. For our part we see very clearly that unless justice is done to others it will not be done to us. The program of the world's peace, therefore, is *our* program; and that program, the only possible program, is based, as we see it, on these *Fourteen Points*.

This scene wipes off to disclose the PRESS ROOM of the CAPITOL where reporters are relaying the message to their papers. From each we catch an outstanding phrase of the famous Fourteen Points.

FIRST REPORTER. . . . Open covenants —openly arrived at. . . .

SECOND REPORTER. . . . Freedom of the seas. . . .

THIRD REPORTER. . . . Free trade. . . .

FOURTH REPORTER. . . . Self-determination. . . .

FIFTH REPORTER. . . . An impartial adjustment of all colonial claims. . . .

SIXTH REPORTER. . . . The League of Nations. . . .

The scene dissolves into a DESK CALENDAR, giving the date October 6, 1918. A hand comes in and turns the page, and this dissolves to the FAMILY SITTING ROOM at night. There is a grate fire burning, and in front of it sit EDITH, WILSON, and NEWTON BAKER, Secretary of War. They sit in silence for a moment, Wilson in deep and sober thought.

WILSON (*after a pause*). Did you bring this month's casualty figures, Baker?

Baker reaches in his pocket and brings out a slip of paper.

BAKER. This is not one of my most pleasant tasks, Mr. President.

WILSON (*reaching for it*). I know. (*He takes the slip from Baker, and stares at it for a moment.*) A hundred and twelve thousand of our boys dead so far.

BAKER. That's only an approximation, Mr. President. All the figures are not in, of course.

WILSON. A hundred and eighty-three thousand six hundred and twelve wounded.

BAKER. The fighting's been heavy—almost ceaseless—in the last weeks.

EDITH (*sympathetically*). Woodrow, you mustn't let your mind dwell on these things. You must try to think instead of what these boys are dying for.

WILSON (*nodding*). I know. . . . But a hundred and twelve thousand *dead*.

He sits for a moment staring at the piece of paper. Then there is a knock at the door.

WILSON. Come in.

As Wilson looks up Tumulty opens the door and comes in. He is excited.

TUMULTY. Governor!

WILSON. Yes?

TUMULTY (*handing Wilson a cable*). Governor! Here's a message that has just come from the Swiss Minister.

Wilson takes the cable, opens it and reads to himself. Edith watches him closely.

WILSON (*reading aloud*). "The German Government requests the President of the United States to take steps for the restoration of peace. . . ."

EDITH (*joyously*). Woodrow!

BAKER. Mr. President!

WILSON (*reading*). "The basis to be the program laid down by the President in his Fourteen Points."

He looks up and across at Edith, and there are tears in both their eyes.

WILSON (*in a whisper*). Thank God.

This dissolves into a picture of CHURCH BELLS ringing, accompanied by sirens screaming and a bedlam of sound, in turn dissolving to A STREET IN WASH-

INGTON at night. The President's car is trying in vain to get through a solid mass of hysterically happy people. Secret Service men are helpless to prevent their leaping on the car to cheer the smiling President and his wife as the scene fades out.

The EAST ROOM of the White House then fades in. It is night, and we first see PADEREWSKI playing his Minuet. The view then draws back to disclose Wilson, Edith, and a group, in evening clothes, seated on gold chairs listening. Professor Holmes, Nell, McAdoo, Margaret, a few Senators, and Secretary Lansing are among those present. As the group is fully revealed, the music ends. There is a quick burst of polite applause. Then the President rises, and of course so does everyone else. A buzz of conversation flows through the room. Servants come in with trays of sandwiches and punch.

Next we see the GROUP around the PRESIDENT, consisting of Holmes, Lansing, and Edith; and during the scene Daniels and McAdoo come up.

HOLMES. So you're going to Paris to write the Peace, are you?

WILSON (*smiling*). And to buy my wife a new bonnet.

HOLMES. You think that's a smart thing to do?

EDITH (*laughing*). To buy me a bonnet?

HOLMES. To get mixed up in that bunch of wildcats over there.

WILSON. I don't know how smart it is, but I consider it most essential.

A servant offers sandwiches and punch. As they help themselves the conversation continues.

LANSING (*a little frightened*). Mr. President, I was wondering—it's only a thought, mind you—if your influence would not be even greater if you stayed here—served as a sounding board? If mistakes were made, you could repudiate them.

WILSON (*coldly*). I hope no mistakes will be made. (*And this response is followed by a brief pause.*)

HOLMES (*biting into a sandwich*). Humph! Lettuce sandwich! (*As they laugh*) Whom will you take with you?

WILSON. Lansing, of course. House. (*After draining a glass of punch*) A military adviser—General Bliss, probably—

HOLMES. I mean somebody from the Senate. Remember they have to approve any Treaty you agree to.

WILSON. Whom have you in mind?

HOLMES. Well, Senator Lodge is Chairman of the Foreign Relations Committee—and a very practical man. (*To a servant*) Here, give me another one of those sandwiches—but one with some meat in it!

WILSON. That's the trouble. Too many treaties have already been written by practical men. (*Shaking his head, firmly*) No, if I take anyone from the other Party it will be a man like Henry White.

HOLMES. You mean the one with the whiskers?

WILSON. He's served in our embassy in Paris. He knows Europe.

MCADOO. May I point out, Mr. President, that this is the heyday of nationalism among nations. In Paris you will meet the ablest politicians in the world—practical men, many of whom will be concerned not so much with peace as with national boundaries, indemnities, new balances of power. Many of our own people here at home will share their views. It might be wise to have some practical man along to cope with such people.

WILSON (*firmly*). I agree as to the situation, Mac. But I disagree as to the solution. In a world full of practical men, more practical men would hinder rather than help. Our great hope lies not in me, nor in any other individual, but in the power of right. People all over the world—the common people—have set their hearts and minds against selfish nationalism. They have paid with their blood and treasure. I *must go*—not alone as President of the United States, but as the spokesman for these peoples, of whatever nationality. Our own people expect me to go. To do anything less is unthinkable.

HOLMES (*as Lansing and McAdoo exchange discouraged glances*). Well, I suppose if your mind's made up, there's nothing we can do about it. Still, if it were up to me, I'd take Lodge. I'd put him right out in front—let him help carry the load. (*As Wilson shakes his head determinedly*) Of course, I'd keep my eye on the little—excuse me, Edith—on his little goatee.

And as he takes another sandwich, the scene fades out.

PART TWELVE

A TITLE fades in. It reads:

"AND SO THE PRESIDENT WENT TO EUROPE TO WRITE THE PEACE, TO BE GREETED EVERYWHERE AS A SAVIOUR—AS THE MAN WHO HAD STOPPED A WORLD WAR."

This dissolves to a NEWSREEL THEATRE, in which a newsreel is showing the Wilsons arriving in Paris, being driven through the streets, and being acclaimed by thousands. Then we get a close view of WILSON and EDITH in a carriage, smiling and waving. Then the NEWSREEL shows the Wilsons in London, riding in the Royal Coach, followed by a close view of WILSON and EDITH responding to the cheers of the London populace. Next the NEWSREEL shows the Wilsons in Italy, the crowds greater, followed by a close view of WILSON and EDITH on a balcony, waving to the throng. The NEWSREEL finally presents the Wilsons in Paris, crowds surging through the streets, across which are banners—"VIVE WILSON!" followed by a close view of THE BIG FOUR—Wilson, Lloyd George, Clemenceau and Orlando on a terrace of a French chateau. They are being photographed and are conscious of it, and each one teasingly tries to make the other take the central position.*

A close view shows a SENATOR reading a Washington newspaper on which is a headline reading:

ALLIED POWERS ACCEPT LEAGUE OF NATIONS AS PART OF PEACE TREATY
President Wilson Hailed as World Saviour

---
* All the above newsreel shots are in black and white.

FIRST SENATOR (*with a scornful snort*). They tell me in Italy they're even burning candles in front of his picture!

The scene draws back to reveal a group of seven or eight Senators in Senator Lodge's office. The Senators, one after another, sign a paper on Lodge's desk. Lodge himself has nothing to say. His face is cold and forbidding. He contents himself with blotting the signatures with a roller blotter as the Senators sign.

SECOND SENATOR. "Kaiser" Woodrow! Or is it "Saint" Woodrow now?

THIRD SENATOR. He's having a field day, all right! But wait till that old Tiger, Clemenceau, gets through with him. He'll be lucky to come back with his shirt.

FIRST SENATOR (*tersely*). It's America's shirt I'm worrying about!

FOURTH SENATOR (*chuckling as he gets through signing*). This'll put a fire cracker under him! Maybe now he'll realize there is such a thing as the Senate and the Constitution! All this business about remaking the map of Europe—giving away this—giving away that—talking about America not having any *material interests* in this war! What about the money we lent them?

FIRST SENATOR. I don't think we need worry, gentlemen.

He takes up the document which they have been signing, and waves it at them, a smile on his face.

FIRST SENATOR. We now have the names of thirty-seven members of the United States Senate affixed to this document.

There is a light laugh at this. Then the Second Senator turns to Lodge, who as yet has said nothing.

SECOND SENATOR. Senator Lodge, you haven't expressed yourself. Are you still with us?

LODGE (*as cold as ice*). My views on the subject are well known, gentlemen. Nothing that has occurred here or in Europe has caused me to change them.

FIRST SENATOR. And you will introduce the resolution yourself?

LODGE (*as he takes the paper from the Senator*). I should consider it an honor to do so, sir.

This dissolves to a ROOM in WILSON'S PARIS HEADQUARTERS at night. Wilson, Lansing, Clemenceau, Lloyd George, Orlando, House and several Aides and Secretaries are assembled for the session. Wilson, Clemenceau, Lloyd George, Orlando and House are bending over a table on which is spread out a map of Europe. (Clemenceau as usual wears grey gloves.)

CLEMENCEAU (*pointing to a map*). Mr. President, France can accept no treaty that does not include the Saar Basin and all territory west of the Rhine.

WILSON (*in quick anger*). But France has no right to that land! It belongs to the people who live on it!

CLEMENCEAU (*with a shrug*). They can go where they please. My government demands the land and its resources, and so do our people.

WILSON (*sternly*). But that's impossible! When the Germans surrendered it was on condition that we protect their rights. That is written in the Armistice. You yourself signed it.

CLEMENCEAU (*stubbornly*). The Germans forfeited their rights in this war. They are murderers.

WILSON (*very much agitated*). Monsieur Clemenceau, I will never be a party to such an agreement. It violates everything we said we were fighting for. To take part of Germany—that has always been part of Germany—and cede it to France is nothing short of theft!

CLEMENCEAU (*dryly*). You live in America, Mr. Wilson, with an ocean on either side. You can afford to be lenient with your enemies.

WILSON. If you are not prepared to abide by the solemnly accepted terms of the Armistice, I might as well go home.

CLEMENCEAU (*hitting the desk suddenly*). And if such opposition to our just claims is continued, I might as well resign.

WILSON (*angrily*). You are breaking your word!

CLEMENCEAU (*just as heatedly*). And you are pro-German!

For a moment the two leaders glare at each other threateningly.

LLOYD GEORGE (*quickly—soothingly*). Gentlemen—gentlemen. Let us consider these matters calmly. I am sure that we *all* believe in the self-determination clause of the Fourteen Points.

WILSON (*holding tight rein on his emotions*). It is not right to do wrong even to make peace. Besides, the Covenant of the League of Nations is sufficient guarantee of France's safety. Under its provisions should Germany ever become hostile again Great Britain and America will instantly rise to the defense of France. (*To Lloyd George*) Is that not so, Mr. Prime Minister?

LLOYD GEORGE (*nodding*). It is so stated in the Covenant.

CLEMENCEAU. That's all very well, Mr. President, when you speak of what America will or will not do. But are you prepared to *guarantee* what America will do?

WILSON. *I am.*

CLEMENCEAU. Are you aware that a bloc of thirty-seven Senators has signed a resolution stating that the League, as you propose it, is not acceptable to the American people?

WILSON. I am perfectly aware of that document, Monsieur. However, I should like to remind you that these men do not compose the entire Senate, nor do they reflect the opinion of the American people, regardless of party. (*Wilson seen close*) As a matter of fact, some of the leading members of the Republican Party, including former President William Howard Taft, and Charles Evans Hughes, have expressed approval of the League, and I will also give you my word for this, too, Monsieur—if these thirty-seven men, who represent no opinion but their own, dare to try to block, to thwart, to betray the first honest attempt of the world to achieve a permanent peace (*Wilson now seen standing by Lloyd George, who is seated, with Lansing also seated and others seen in the background through the door*) the American people will rise in their anger and (*bringing his fist down on the table*) thrash them as they would an alien enemy landing on their shores!

This cuts to a fairly close view of Clemenceau as he bows to Wilson.

CLEMENCEAU. Mr. President, I bow (*bowing again*) to you. (*As both are standing at the table at which Lloyd George, Orlando and others are seated*) Shall we resume our discussions?

This dissolves to the HALL OF MIRRORS, and then into a view of WILSON and the AMERICAN DELEGATES as they approach the table to sign the Treaty of Peace—a path opening for them. Then we see the GERMAN DELEGATION, a dozen stolid Prussians looking on with angry sullen faces.

EDITH and MARGARET are standing on tiptoes looking across the heads of intervening people toward Wilson, who is then seen close as he accepts a gold pen and prepares to sign his name. As he writes, the view comes closer and focuses on HIS HAND, and we see him scribble his name across the document. The music over this scene is loud and prophetically discordant.

This dissolves to SENATOR LODGE'S OFFICE, with Lodge seated at his desk writing. His secretary comes in and approaches him.

SECRETARY. Excuse me, Senator Lodge, but there are several newspapermen outside who'd like to speak to you for a moment. They want to know how you feel about the Treaty —especially about the League of Nations.

LODGE (*turning slowly in his chair and looking up*). You may tell the gentlemen of the press that whatever I have to say about this matter will be said on the floor of the United States Senate.

SECRETARY. Yes, sir.

As the secretary turns away, Lodge looks after her, a faint smile on his face, and the scene fades out.

PART THIRTEEN

A view of the GEORGE WASHINGTON at sea fades in, and dissolves to the DECK at night. Wilson and Edith are strolling arm-in-arm in the moonlight looking out at the water. He looks tired and ill. In fact, the change in him is shocking. Wilson wears a light overcoat and cap, Edith has a scarf around her throat. They walk for a moment in silence.

EDITH. It'll be nice to be home again.

He nods. But his thoughts seem far away. There is a slight pause.

EDITH (*casually*). Woodrow—this Treaty—are you satisfied with it?

WILSON (*after a slight pause*). It might have been worse.

A slight shiver passes through him. Edith leans forward and draws his coat closer about his throat to protect him from the night air.

EDITH. Sometimes, Woodrow, I think you were the only one who really meant what we said we were fighting for.

WILSON (*with a sigh*). I got so tired of telling them that a Treaty of revenge will one of these days put into power men who will use revenge as an excuse for their own ambitions! (*His voice suddenly hard*) But they couldn't forget that fifty years ago the Germans marched into Paris and dictated the terms of peace. Now all they could say was—"It's our turn."

EDITH. Clemenceau?

WILSON. He wasn't the worst. At least he was frank about it. But think of Italy—Japan—openly admitting they went to war for strips of land! Boasting they paid a million lives for them!

EDITH. I know, Woodrow. But at least you got what you really went for—the League. (*He looks at her and nods.*)

WILSON. Yes, the League is the vital and compelling part of the Treaty. Whatever mistakes we made about boundaries, reparations, disarmament, or colonies, the League will be in a position to arbitrate and rectify . . . as soon as the passions and resentments of war have had time to die.

There is a long pause. They cross to the rail, stop and look off.

EDITH. I wonder if the people realize that if you hadn't gone to Paris there'd have been no League?

WILSON. The people—perhaps. (*With a kind of bitterness*) My friends in the Senate—? (*He leaves the thought unfinished.*)

EDITH (*bitterly*). You mean Lodge!

WILSON (*his eyes growing cold*). He's not the only one. Some of our own Party. Jim Reed of Missouri, for instance. Apparently he's gone even further. He's just as much opposed as Borah or Hiram Johnson, or any other of the "Irreconcilable Battalion of Death."

EDITH. But William Howard Taft—Hughes—they're Republicans and they're for the League—almost as much as you.

WILSON. Yes, they've been splendid. But unfortunately they're not in a position to vote in the Senate.

EDITH (*consolingly*). You mustn't worry, Woodrow. They may talk a lot, but they won't dare stand in the way of something the whole world needs. (*His eyes meet hers. His jaw comes up and he nods.*)

WILSON. You're right! They won't dare!

While he says this with firmness, we see in his eyes a little bit of doubt and apprehension, however. At this moment Admiral Grayson comes up to them, carrying a cablegram.

GRAYSON. Excuse me, Mr. President—I thought you might like to have this at once.

WILSON. Thank you (*He takes the cablegram and opens it.*)

WILSON (*to Edith*). Excuse me.

He reads the cable, a grave look on his face, then hands it to Edith, who reads it, likewise grave-faced. As their eyes meet, and without telling us what is in the cable, the scene dissolves into a NEWSPAPER HEADLINE:
"SENATE OPENS FIGHT ON LEAGUE OF NATIONS
Demands 46 Qualifying Amendments"

Then the view draws back to reveal Holmes reading the paper. He and Edith are in the Oval Room of the White House. It is day. Dr. Grayson is just coming from the adjacent bedroom, stuffing his stethoscope into his pocket. Edith's face is grave, drawn with anxiety.

GRAYSON. The only trouble with him is that he's tired, Edith. That influenza he had in Paris took a lot out of him.

EDITH (*her distress evident in her eyes as she clasps and unclasps her hands*). If he could only relax—sleep—

HOLMES (*gruffly*). I know what's the matter with him—*Senatitis!*

GRAYSON (*with a smile at Holmes*). Yes—but unfortunately that's one kind of *headache* I don't know how to prescribe for.

There is a sound at the door and they all turn and look off as the door of Wilson's room opens and the President comes in. Edith and Holmes get to their feet.

WILSON (*smiling as he crosses to Edith*). I told you there was nothing wrong, Edith—just a summer cold.

EDITH (*forcing an answering smile*). I know. I only wanted to be sure. (*As she straightens the handkerchief in his coat pocket*) But you must promise me, Woodrow, that the *moment* this matter is settled we'll get away from here.

GRAYSON. What you need, Mr. President, is a vacation—exercise—

HOLMES (*gruffly*). Even your kind of golf is better than being cooped up in this place this kind of weather.

WILSON (*with a dry grin at Holmes*). Thank you, Mr. Holmes. Perhaps I can use that argument on Senator Lodge.

There is a knock at the door. Wilson turns and calls off.

WILSON. Yes? (*The door opens and Tumulty comes in.*)

TUMULTY. It's ten o'clock, Governor. Senator Lodge and members of the Foreign Relations Committee are waiting in your office.

WILSON. Thank you, Tumulty. I'm coming. (*To Edith*) Goodbye, my dear. (*Bending over and kissing her*) Have a nice day.

EDITH (*earnestly, restraining him for a moment*). Woodrow, promise me that you'll be careful—that you won't allow yourself to be upset.

WILSON (*suddenly sober*). Don't worry, my dear. If necessary I'll get down on my hands and knees.

As the three look at him, his voice breaks for just a moment, and we realize how important this coming meeting is to him.

WILSON. When it comes to the League I—I have no pride.

And he turns and hurries out. Edith, Holmes and Grayson look after him as he closes the door behind him, their faces filled with concern.

This dissolves to WILSON'S OFFICE. Wilson is seated, facing the Foreign Relations Committee composed of sixteen Senators. Senator Lodge is placed a slight distance in front of the Committee, in order to emphasize the personal nature of the fight between Wilson and Lodge. Throughout Lodge's manner is frigidly polite. Wilson is trying desperately to keep a tight rein on his tongue and his feelings.

(The entire attitude of Lodge is changed. We must feel that he is ice-cold. He knows that he has the President where he wants him and he makes the most of it. He is never rude, but he is sharp, bitter, and at times *almost* rude. He does not pause between speeches or speak slowly. He cracks back at Wilson; and the Senators who sit behind him should be far more keenly interested than they now appear to be. While this is not a fight, it should have the semblance of a fight—a bitter clash.)

WILSON. Gentlemen, I asked you here in the hope that we might come to some understanding about the League of Nations.

LODGE (*smiling*). I don't mean to be facetious, Mr. President, but whose understanding? Yours? Or ours?

WILSON. One we can mutually uphold.

LODGE. In view of our stated positions, I wonder if that isn't expecting a great deal.

WILSON. Senator, I'm sure we all have only one purpose in common—to serve the best interests of the American people.

LODGE. But apparently we have very different ideas as to what constitutes their best interests.

WILSON. In that case, shouldn't we at least try to reconcile our differences?

LODGE. The Treaty would have been approved by the Senate weeks ago if it weren't attached to your League.

WILSON (*quietly*). Not *my* League, Senator. I didn't originate it. I wish I had. It's been the dream of men in every generation since the Sermon on the Mount. I'm merely one of its proponents.

Lodge moves as if to say something, but before he can begin Wilson goes right on.

WILSON. As a matter of fact, I would be more inclined to call it *your* League. For I seem to recall that in 1916 you yourself advanced the thought that the nations would have to unite for peace, and that there would have to be an international police force to enforce it.

Again Lodge moves as if to interrupt or to protest.

LODGE. Just a moment—

Wilson does not stop talking. He continues:

WILSON. Indeed, I have here, Senator, an excerpt from an address which you delivered May 27, 1916, at the new Willard Hotel in Washington before the League to Enforce Peace, in which you said: (*He reads.*) "I know the difficulties which arise when we speak of anything which seems to involve an alliance. But I do not believe that when Washington warned us against entangling alliances he meant for one moment that we should not join with the other civilized nations of the world if a method could be found to diminish war and encourage peace."

Lodge is angry that Wilson has bested him in front of the other Senators, and he speaks in cold terms.

LODGE. The fact that a man happens to have changed his mind does not bear on the merits of any question! And even if a man happens to be a convert, some good work has been done by converts since the days of St. Paul to the present time. Besides, in my wildest dreams I never contemplated pledging American arms and economic sanctions every time some ambitious ruler in Europe or Asia covets the lands and resources of another. We'd be constantly involved in broils and quarrels that are none of our business!

WILSON. Yet, let me remind you that in every discussion of the peace during the war we promised the world—

LODGE. I beg your pardon. *You* promised.

WILSON. *This government* promised that some way would be found to avoid such catastrophes as we have just been through. Other powers have accepted the principles of the League. It's inconceivable to me that we, who advanced it, should go back on our word.

LODGE (*snapping out his reply*). Accept the Senate reservations and the Senate will accept the League.

The men behind Lodge nod in the affirmative.

WILSON. I have no objections, gentlemen, to a resolution containing any clarifying reservations the Senate sees fit to make. But to change the Treaty itself is impossible, and I will never agree to it. This nation's honor is at stake.

LODGE. If that is your unalterable view, Mr. President, I'm afraid we won't get very far. (*He starts to rise.*)

WILSON. Just a moment, Senator. (*Earnestly—pleadingly*) Perhaps we've made mistakes—all of us. But regardless of the Treaty and what you individually may think of it, or of *those* who wrote it, let me remind you that the League is irrevocably attached to it. And the League is the only hope the world has to avoid wars in the future. Unless you can advance a better idea, I beg of you to consider that and to help save that hope.

LODGE. I, too, have my ideals, Mr. President, and one of them is *peace!* But a realistic peace that we can surely maintain—one which will not siphon off the power, the prestige and the resources of the United States! If you had wanted my views on this matter you could have very easily obtained them *before* you went to Paris—*before* you made concessions to the Statesmen of Europe—*before* you burned your bridges behind you!

At this the scene cuts to show the silent reaction of Wilson. He is desperately endeavoring to restrain himself. Lodge finishes in a cold, almost sarcastic tone.

LODGE. This is *not* the age of miracles, Mr. President, nor of miracle-workers.

He sits down, and Wilson rises for a last speech.

WILSON. America has but two choices, gentlemen. It must accept a League of Nations or it must live with a gun in its hand. It's for the people to decide. Thank you for coming here, (*With a bow*) Goodbye.

The members of the Committee rise, say good-day, and file out. Wilson stands at his desk, his face grim, set with determination. As the door closes on the last Senator, he presses a couple of buzzers on his desk. A moment later Tumulty comes in through one door, Edith through another.

WILSON (*quietly*). Tumulty, you may start making arrangements at once for our trip.

EDITH (*hurrying in*). Woodrow!

WILSON. I'll have no more haggling with that man! I'll stump the country—let the people know exactly what's at stake!

TUMULTY (*concerned*). But, Governor, you know what Doctor Grayson said. You can't afford to take the risk.

WILSON (*sharply*). I promised the young men of this country that we were fighting this war to end wars! Now it's up to me to see that we meant what we said!

EDITH (*pleading*). But, Woodrow, for my sake, why don't you do what they ask—accept the Senate's reservations—get this awful quarrel settled!

WILSON. Don't you desert me, too ... (*His voice breaks—almost a sob.*) I couldn't—stand—that!

EDITH (*anxiously*). But, my dear, I'm only thinking of you—of your health.

WILSON. I have no *right* to accept any changes. And even if I did, don't you see they'd come back tomorrow with forty-six more? It's nothing but a scheme to kill the League entirely.

EDITH. Forgive me, Woodrow. I should have known. (*Then she looks around.*) But, oh my dear, if they had only developed the radio, wireless, so that you could sit here and talk to them, without having to go out in all this heat.

This scene dissolves to SENATOR LODGE'S OFFICE at night. Several Senators are gathered here—the Irreconcilables. Several of the men are in evening clothes —white ties.

LODGE. Somebody must trail him across the country—speak everywhere he speaks. The people must understand exactly what this League would let them in for. (*Addressing a Senator*) Would you care to undertake the job, Senator?

A large gray-haired, elderly Senator nods.

SENATOR (*emphatically*). Gladly!

The scene dissolves to a re-enactment of THE FIGHT FOR THE LEAGUE: Here we see a fighting President battling against illness and mounting nervous strain, taking his case to the highest court in the land—the People—while a powerful opposition contends with him for mastery over the minds of the electorate. (The effect should be almost that of a fist fight, one side hitting hard, the other returning blow for blow.) ... Each speech is in a different background. Throughout, there is yelling, applause, booing, punctuated by cries of "Impeach him," etc. ... Fading in and out as we need it, is a MAP of the United States on which we follow the line of travel, beginning in Washington and going to Columbus, Ohio; Richmond; Indiana; St. Louis, Missouri; Billings, Montana; Portland; Oregon; Tacoma, Washington; Seattle; Oakland, California; San Francisco; Palo Alto; Berkeley; Los Angeles; San Diego; Sacramento; Salt Lake City; Denver; and Pueblo. The background of the map is black, the line marking the progress of the tour is white. ... Over this is superimposed a HEADLINE reading: PRESIDENT TAKES LEAGUE FIGHT TO THE PEOPLE. ... As the line comes from Washington to Columbus, the Map fades out. There is a closeup of WILSON on a train, visible behind him the shoulders of secret service men, as he speaks:

WILSON. A war in which civilization has been bled white must not end in a mere victory of arms and a new balance of power. We must not—we *cannot*—stop short of our goal!

This wipes off to a long view of a THEATRE. The Senator we saw with Lodge is speaking.

OPPONENT. The fundamental question is: Do you want American boys to police the world? Do you want American blood to uphold, maintain, and preserve Old World governments?

His words are greeted by cries of "No! No!" and "Stay out!" as the scene wipes off to a STADIUM PRIZEFIGHT RING at night, affording a close view of WILSON.

WILSON. The passions of the world are not dead. The revelries are not cooled. The need for united action is more urgent than ever. But there can be no united action—no League of Nations—in the true sense without America's participation!

This wipes off similarly to a picture of the opposing Senator speaking at a BANQUET TABLE.

OPPONENT. Let's think of America for a change. God gave us two oceans. Who's going to be foolish enough to attack us?

There are cries of "Stay out!" "Impeach him!" as the scene wipes off to AN AUDITORIUM PLATFORM on which WILSON is speaking. The change in him is even greater now.

WILSON. The isolation of the United States is at an end—not because we choose to go into the politics of the world, but because by the sheer genius of our people and the growth of our power we have become a determining factor in the world. And make no mistake about this. Germany wants us to remain isolated. She wants to see at least one great nation left out of this combination which she would never again dare face.

A closer view of EDITH and GRAYSON shows Edith watching her husband with mounting concern. Felton is in the background.

EDITH (*in a whisper*). He can't—he can't go on like this!

This wipes off to a close view of a ONE-ARMED SOLDIER IN UNIFORM, and a PLATFORM AGAINST A WALL WITH BUNTING.

OPPONENT. I ask you one question. What is this League of Nations but a political organization which will take away the authority of the Congress of the United States, and put it into the hands of foreign governments. We boys who fought this war have brought a militant, arrogant Germany to her knees. What we want now is to get back to our American way of life!

This dissolves to a PULLMAN CAR as the train is slowing up for a stop, passing through railroad yards. Wilson is sunk in a chair, his eyes closed, a look of pain and utter weariness in his face. Edith, Grayson and Tumulty are looking at him, deeply perturbed. Felton in the background is watching, too.

GRAYSON (*gravely*). Mr. President, you'll have to give up this trip and return to Washington at once.

WILSON (*wearily, without opening his eyes*). That's impossible!

GRAYSON. It's not only possible, it's imperative.

WILSON. But I can't stop now. The people are beginning to understand. If I desert them now, they will be confused and misled.

EDITH (*as Grayson looks appealingly at Edith*). Forty speeches in twenty-two days—in seventeen States! Nobody could stand that.

WILSON. But I'm scheduled to speak here in Pueblo. The people are waiting for me. There're several points that still need to be explained—

EDITH. Perhaps you can come to Pueblo later.

The train is already coming to a halt. Through the windows we see the figures of people waiting and we hear their cheers.

EDITH (*sitting down beside him, taking his hand*). Believe me, my dear, I wouldn't ask you to stop if there were the slightest chance that you could go on. But you'll only kill yourself. And you must live—if only to carry on the fight.

Their eyes meet, and he shakes his head, and slowly gets to his feet.

WILSON. I must go on. I'm all right.

Edith and Grayson have risen and stand beside him, holding his arms. They look at one another anxiously, but helplessly. With a great effort he pulls himself together, summons his strength, and starts out. The cheering of the crowd continues. As he goes, Edith, Grayson, Felton and Tumulty stand where they are, looking after him. The view rests on them as the cheering of the crowd becomes a roar and we know that Wilson is facing them. Then we see the REAR PLATFORM of the TRAIN, with WILSON, seen close, making his final plea. He is near the breaking point now.

WILSON. I feel like asking the Secretary of War to get the boys, who went across the water to fight, together on some field where I could go and see them, and I would stand up before them and say: Boys, I told you before you went across the seas that this was a war against wars, and I did my best to fulfill that promise, but I am obliged to come to you in mortification and shame and say I have not been able to fulfill the promise. You are betrayed. You fought for something that you did not get. And the glory of the armies and the navies of the United States is gone like a dream in the night, and there ensues upon it, in the suitable darkness of the night, the nightmare of dread which lay upon the nations before this war came, and there will come some time, in the vengeful Providence of God, another struggle in which, not a few hundred thousand fine men from America will have to die, but as many millions as are necessary to accomplish the final freedom of the peoples of the world.

There are tears in his eyes. He has gradually become more and more strained and weaker as he has come nearer the end of the speech. Now he pauses, but we have the feeling that there is to be more of the speech. He pauses for a long moment, tries desperately to go on. He whips up the last bit of his energy, but it is impossible.

WILSON. I will—

He looks down at the crowd, realizes that he cannot continue, that he is finished. Then, almost in a whisper, he adds:

WILSON. I—thank you for coming—

We definitely feel that the man has reached the breaking point, that this is the beginning of the stroke. He waits for a moment. The crowd is moved, touched, somehow aware of his condition. Wilson turns and slowly gropes his way back into the Pullman. The view then draws back with him as he walks like one in a daze back into the car where Edith, Grayson and Tumulty are waiting. For a moment he pauses, sways a bit. Edith, Felton and Grayson quickly step up beside him and help him into a chair. He slumps down, all his strength gone. Edith draws the shade nearest to him, sits down beside him and his head falls against her shoulder. Her arms go around him.

WILSON (*with a sigh*). I'm so—tired.

EDITH (*holding him close for a moment; quietly*). Mr. Tumulty, will you please tell the newspapermen that we're returning to Washington at once.

WILSON (*crying out*). No—no.

Tumulty looks at her, is about to say something; then, afraid to speak, he simply nods and goes out. Grayson bends down and helps Wilson to his feet and starts leading him off toward his bedroom. Edith waits behind, to get hold of herself. Then, like one in a dream, she starts to lower the other shades of the car, following which the scene dissolves to a picture of the TRAIN rushing through the night. The windows of the Presidential car are dark and foreboding as the scene fades out.

PART FOURTEEN

THE WHITE HOUSE fades in at night, a few lights gleaming from the windows, following which we see the WHITE HOUSE GATE, with a group of anxious men and women standing before it and looking at the house. Over this comes a newsboy's voice, calling extras.

NEWSBOY'S VOICE. President Suffers Nervous Breakdown! Extra! Read all about it! Extra!

This dissolves to WILSON'S BEDROOM. Wilson lies in bed, a very sick man. Admiral Grayson and two other doctors are huddled together in consultation. A nurse is bending over Wilson. Grayson goes out, leaving the doctors behind. Then we see the LIVING ROOM, UPSTAIRS, as Grayson comes out and carefully closes the door to the sickroom. Edith, Tumulty, Professor Holmes, and Daniels are waiting—pale, silent. This is a family council-of-war, as it were.

GRAYSON. His whole left side is paralyzed, but his mind is perfectly clear and untouched.

EDITH (*simply*). Will he recover?

GRAYSON. He'll improve with time. But for the present, he needs rest and quiet—release from every disturbing problem.

TUMULTY. But how is that possible when everything that comes to the President is a problem?

EDITH. Wouldn't it be better for him to resign—let Mr. Marshall succeed him?

GRAYSON (*shaking his head*). He's staked his life on getting the League ratified. If he resigns now this great incentive to recovery will be gone.

DANIELS. Besides, his resignation would have a very bad effect on the country—for that matter, on the whole world.

GRAYSON. Our thought is that you have everything of an official nature come to you. You can weigh the importance of each matter—and in consultation with the heads of the various departments, decide what he must see and what can safely be left to others—In this way you can be of great service to your husband, Edith.

Edith looks from one to the other uncertainly. Holmes nods.

EDITH. I can't do it! It's too great a responsibility!

HOLMES. Even if his life may depend upon it?

Edith looks from one to the other. Each nods gravely.

EDITH. In that case, there can be but one answer. I'll try.

The scene fades out.

PART FIFTEEN

A BANNER fades in. It reads: FOR PRESIDENT—WILLIAM G. MCADOO. . . . This is followed by a BANNER reading: FOR PRESIDENT—JAMES COX OF OHIO. . . . This in turn is succeeded by a BANNER reading: DEMOCRATIC NATIONAL CONVENTION—SAN FRANCISCO 1920. . . . Over this comes band music of "Dixie," and through it we catch the voices of men speaking. (It is a confused, noisy scene suggesting another National Convention.)

VOICES (*swallowed by the band*). Mr. Chairman, I give you that great Democrat. . . .
Mr. Chairman, in this moment of peril. . . .
Mr. Chairman, our great leader in Washington. . . .

This dissolves to the SOUTH PORTICO of the White House. Wilson is seated in a wheelchair in the sun. Edith, Nell, Margaret and Jessie are with him. His five-year-old granddaughter is playing on the floor beside him. They are having tea, all waiting on him.

WILSON (*with a teasing smile at Edith*). Well, *Mrs.* President, what's on tap for today?

EDITH (*firmly*). Woodrow, don't you dare call me that! You know very well I've never made *one* decision without your knowledge and consent.

WILSON (*smiling*). I know it—and *you* know it—but do our enemies know it?

EDITH. I'm not concerned with what our enemies know!

WILSON. Oh, but you should listen to them, my dear. You'll learn a great deal.

NELL. Such as what, Father?

WILSON (*smiling at his wife*). Well, during the war, for instance, I never would have dreamed that Edith was a German spy if I hadn't kept my ears open.

EDITH. Nor, I suppose, that you'd bargained with Wall Street to bring on the war in the first place!

WILSON (*nodding*). For that matter, I never would have even suspected I was insane if the Senate hadn't sent the Honorable Albert Fall to look me over.

EDITH. That man!

WILSON (*his eyes twinkling*). I'd always been told that Teddy Roosevelt put those bars on our windows to keep his children from falling out—when all of the time it seems you girls put them there to keep me in.

He laughs; it isn't exactly a laughing matter to the others, but Wilson seems to take it all very good-naturedly.

NELL. I don't see how you can take it so calmly, Father. I'd scratch their eyes out.

EDITH. No, Woodrow handled Senator Fall beautifully. As he was leaving, that gentleman said: "Mr. President, the Senate is praying for you." Whereupon your father, without batting an eye, asked: "Which way, Senator?"

Even the girls laugh now, and Wilson chuckles at the memory. The little girl comes over and stands beside his chair. He puts a hand on her head, feeds her a cookie.

WILSON. I'm afraid I'm more concerned with what this young lady and her generation think of me than I am with what the present lords of the earth have to say.

He looks at the child fondly for a moment, then turns to Edith.

WILSON. No memoranda today?

EDITH. They've passed the Volstead Act over your veto.

WILSON (*showing no surprise or resentment*). Well, now we'll have Prohibition . . . I trust. (*He looks up to see Joseph Tumulty hurrying toward him.*)

WILSON. Well, Tumulty?

TUMULTY. Governor, the Democrats have just nominated James Cox of Ohio!

There is a buzz of excitement from the women, and Wilson looks at Tumulty thoughtfully.

WILSON (*quietly*). Cox on one side—and Harding on the other. . . . (*He looks off.*) Cox for the League—Harding against it. . . . Well, now the lines are drawn. It's clearly up to the people to decide.

This dissolves to the WHITE HOUSE CORRESPONDENTS' ROOM at night. A special wire service has been set up, and a telegrapher is typing the news as it comes in. Tumulty, grave-faced, stands beside him. The operator tears a sheet out of his machine and hands it to Tumulty. The latter reads it and then turns and goes out.

This dissolves to the BLUE ROOM, where Wilson, Edith, the girls, Professor Holmes and Dr. Grayson are seated, awaiting the news. Most of them are depressed, but Wilson is as calm as ever. Nobody says anything. They look up as Tumulty comes in.

TUMULTY (*with difficulty*). Mr. President, it appears that Senator Harding has won an overwhelming victory. (*He pauses.*) Senator Harding has just issued a statement to the American people declaring that the League of Nations is now a closed incident.

Everyone looks at Wilson, who sits for a moment, as if stunned, unable to believe it.

WILSON (*quietly*). Thank you, Tumulty.

There is another long pause. It is like a house of death. Then he gets to his feet.

WILSON (*to Edith*). Well, Edith, if these good people will excuse us—

EDITH (*rising and taking his arm*). Yes, Woodrow.

WILSON (*as they go toward the door*). Good night.

The others murmur good night, then are silent. The door closes behind the Wilsons.

NELL. Professor Holmes, if Father *had* taken Senator Lodge to Paris with him, do you think the results might have been different?

HOLMES. It's possible. I'm not sure.

MARGARET. I hear so many people say that Father lacks the human touch —that he doesn't know how to get along with people. Do you suppose if he'd been able to compromise—to play politics—?

HOLMES. He wouldn't be Woodrow Wilson if he could do that. (*Puffing on his pipe*) Back at Princeton it was just the same. He put up a great fight against the club system, and he was beaten. I urged him then to compromise, but he said it was not in his nature to compromise with what he knew to be wrong. I told him he was making a mistake—that he was too idealistic. But I'm no longer sure I was right. In the end, I expect, the world'll discover that only the ideals count.

As they look at him, deeply impressed, the scene dissolves to a full view of the CAPITOL in daylight, and then to the PRESIDENT'S ROOM in the CAPITOL. Wilson and Edith are here with members of the Cabinet—Wilson seated at a small table signing last-minute bills. As he concludes, he looks up and smiles.

WILSON. I'm sorry I won't be able to stay for the inauguration ceremonies, but Mr. Harding and Mr. Coolidge have been kind enough to excuse me. I told them it was bad enough for the Senate to throw me down, without my stumbling and falling up the steps on my own account.

The others try to smile at this, but it is too tragically true for any real smiling. Wilson gets to his feet, grasping his cane. Then he and Edith start to shake hands with the members of his official family. As the men move by him many are near tears. Some look at him, just nod and try to smile. He and Edith go through the ordeal quietly with simply "Thank you, Daniels," "Good luck, Baker. We've taken a house on 'S' Street. We expect to see you there often." Baker holds his hand for a long time. Both want to say something— find it very difficult.

BAKER. Goodbye, Mr. President.

WILSON (*smiling*). Just Woodrow Wilson now. (*At this Baker turns and looks off at the clock.*)

BAKER. You still have one minute to go, Mr. President.

Wilson looks at the clock, too, and we get a close view of the CLOCK which shows that it is exactly 11:59, and then again see the PRESIDENT'S ROOM as the members of the Cabinet continue to file by saying "Goodbye, Mr. President." He calls each by name, smiles, nods. As the last man is passing, a Committee of Senators and Representatives appears in the doorway, led by Senator Lodge. Wilson looks up.

WILSON (*quietly*). Senator Lodge.

LODGE. Mr. President, a joint committee of the House and Senate are here to notify you that the Congress has completed the business before it, and now stands ready to adjourn, unless you have some further message.

There is a slight pause. Wilson looks past Lodge toward the clock on the wall; we get a close view of the CLOCK and see that it is now only a few seconds before twelve o'clock; then we again see the PRESIDENT'S ROOM.

WILSON (*coldly*). The President has nothing further to communicate. Good-day, sir.

There is a moment of silence. Then the clock begins to strike twelve. Edith takes his arm, and together they start out of the room, the Senators and Cabinet members opening an aisle for them. The music has started, and, as they go out, begins to swell.*

The scene dissolves to the "s" STREET HOUSE at night—a few people passing, looking off at the house; then to the DINING ROOM in "s" STREET HOUSE where Edith and Wilson are seated at the table. The Negro butler—Scott—is removing the dessert plates. There is a brief pause. One gets a feeling of loneliness—of strangeness in the new surroundings.

* NOTE: On the screen, the film ends at this point as Wilson's cabinet bids him goodbye, voices singing
"Long may our land be bright
With freedom's holy light,
Protect us by Thy Might,
Great God, our King."

EDITH (*smiling across the table at him*). Well, Woodrow—our first dinner in our own home. (*As he nods*) I'm afraid it hasn't been very exciting.

WILSON. I wonder if you know how exciting it has been?

EDITH (*touched*). Thank you, Woodrow.

WILSON. Of course, it *is* rather difficult to realize that I no longer have the responsibilities that go with the presidency. (*With a wry little smile*) Now I'm simply an *Ex*-President.

There is another brief pause, then Edith gets up and goes around and sits beside him.

EDITH. In a few days you'll be just as busy as you ever were.

WILSON. Yes, I expect there'll be plenty to do. Perhaps I'll even find time to get at that book I've dedicated to you.

She looks at him, realizes he is trying to put a good face on it, and—understanding this—she does not comment. Instead she turns to Scott who is clearing the last dishes from the table.

EDITH. We'll have our coffee in the living room, Scott.

She rises and Wilson gets to his feet. Together they start out of the room, Wilson using his cane, the scene moving with them to the door of the living room where they stop—surprised looks on their faces. They see: Gathered in the living room Jessie, Nell, Margaret, Frank Sayre, McAdoo, Holmes, all smiling toward him and Edith. There are cheerful greetings: "Hello, Father." "Hello, Edith." Then EDITH and WILSON, as they smile, come into the room. The three girls come forward, fussing over him, helping him to his chair in front of the fire, "Sit here, Father." "Would you like a stool for your feet?"

WILSON (*smiling broadly*). I've never had so much service in my life. I'm glad there's at least one Party with which I'm still in favor.

As they laugh, the door opens and Scott comes in with a large tray of coffee. He sets it in front of Edith. On the tray is a cablegram.

SCOTT (*handing the cable to Wilson*). This just came, Mr. President.

WILSON (*taking the cable*). Thank you.

He opens it and reads. Edith has begun to pour the coffee. Holmes has found an easy chair and is fiddling with his pipe. Margaret is seated at the piano, facing the room. The other two girls hover about their father. As Wilson reads, a pleased smile crosses his face, and without a word he hands the cable to Edith. She reads it—looks up at him—smiles—then as everyone looks to her, she reads it aloud.

EDITH. "Stockholm, Sweden . . . Woodrow Wilson was today awarded the Nobel Peace Prize for his efforts in behalf of the League of Nations."

Instantly there are cries of congratulations and rejoicing, Jessie leaning over to hug Wilson. Edith looks across at him, smiles—then carefully folds the cablegram and puts it in her gown over her heart.

WILSON (*smiling*). Well, you see, there's life in the old boy yet.

McAdoo steps up to Wilson.

MCADOO. What do you think will happen now, Mr. President? (*As Wilson looks up at him*) Can we ever hope for peace—a real understanding between nations—now that we have turned our back on the League?

WILSON (*quietly*). Yes. I'm not one of those who have the slightest anxiety about the eventual triumph of the things I've stood for. The fight's just begun. You and I may never live to see it finished. But that doesn't matter. The ideals of the League aren't dead just because a few obstructive men now in the saddle say they are. The dream of a world united against the awful wastes of war is too deeply imbedded in the hearts of men everywhere.

Suddenly his face wrinkles in a smile and he turns and looks at his old friend Holmes, who is puffing away in the corner.

WILSON. And I'll even make this concession to Providence—it may come about in a *better* way than we proposed.

There is a long moment of silence after this. Suddenly the sound of voices singing "Old Nassau" breaks in. All turn startled toward the window, from beyond which the chorus of men's voices is coming. Wilson and Edith look at each other, puzzled. Only old Holmes smiles knowingly.—Margaret stops playing. All rise, and Holmes moves toward the window.

NELL (*going to Wilson*). Father—they haven't forgotten. They've come to serenade you.

Wilson nods and looks across at Holmes, who smiles at him. He is deeply—deeply touched.

EDITH. Woodrow—will you go out to them?

Again he nods. She puts his cane in his hand and helps him to his feet. Margaret hurries out of the room ahead of them, and the others follow. As he comes into the hall, Margaret drapes a cape about her father's shoulders. Nell gets his hat to protect him from the night air. He smiles his silent thanks.

We see the STREET IN FRONT OF WILSON'S HOME at night. Several hundred people are gathered here in front of Wilson's door. A few students from Princeton —many of them alumni of the University. Scattered in the crowd are soldiers—a few West Point cadets (in Washington for the Inauguration Parade)—a few women and others (attracted out of curiosity perhaps). They are singing "Old Nassau," just as the boys sang it so long ago at Princeton.

Then Wilson and Edith step out, followed by the girls, McAdoo, Sayre, and Holmes. They stand listening as the song rises. As before, Holmes joins in the singing. In a closeup we see Wilson's face, his eyes filled with tears, moved by this demonstration of affection and confidence. Edith looks at him, proud and happy and takes his hand. Finally we look past WILSON (reverse shot) into the faces of the singers, as the song swells and swells, rising in volume until it seems a great multitude must be singing. As it reaches its final note and fades away, the scene fades out.

DARRYL F. ZANUCK'S
Production of

THE PURPLE HEART

(A Twentieth Century-Fox Picture)

Screenplay by JEROME CADY

Produced by DARRYL F. ZANUCK

Directed by LEWIS MILESTONE

The Cast

CAPTAIN HARVEY ROSS	Dana Andrews
LIEUTENANT ANGELO CANELLI	Richard Conte
SERGEANT HOWARD CLINTON	Farley Granger
SERGEANT JAN SKVOZNIK	Kevin O'Shea
LIEUTENANT PETER VINCENT	Donald Barry
MRS. ROSS	Trudy Marshall
LIEUTENANT WAYNE GREENBAUM	Sam Levene
LIEUTENANT KENNETH BAYFORTH	Charles Russell
SERGEANT MARTIN STONER	John Craven
JOHANA HARTWIG	Tala Birell
GENERAL ITO MITSUBI	Richard Loo
MITSURU TOYAMA	Peter Chong
PETER VOROSHEVSKI	Gregory Gaye
KARL KEPPEL	Torben Meyer
LUDWIG KRUGER	Kurt Katch
MANUEL SIVA	Martin Garralaga
KARL SCHLESWIG	Erwin Kalser
BORIS EVENIK	Igor Dolgaruki
FRANCISCO DE LOS SANTOS	Nestor Paiva
PAUL LUDOVESCU	Alex Papana
YUEN CHIU LING	H. T. Tsiang
MOY LING	Benson Fong
ADMIRAL KENTARA YAMAGICHI	Key Chang
ITSUBI SAKAI	Allen Jung
POLICE CAPTAIN	Wing Foo
COURT CLERK	Paul Fung
PROCURATOR	Joseph Kim
COURT STENOGRAPHER	Luke Chan
TOMA NAGOTA	Beal Wong
HANK MORRISON	Marshall Thompson

Film Editor—DOUGLASS BIGGS

Screenplay of the Twentieth Century-Fox photoplay "The Purple Heart," copyright 1944 by Twentieth Century-Fox Film Corporation. By permission of Twentieth Century-Fox Film Corporation.

THE PURPLE HEART

"Out of the dark mists of the Orient have come no details of the actual fate of the heroic American aviators forced to earth in the bombing of Tokio. Perhaps those details will never be known. The Japanese Government, in mingled hate and fear, announced only that some were executed. This picture, therefore, is the author's conception of what may well have happened, based upon unofficial reports."

PART ONE

A FOREWORD fades in, with impressive, dignified music:

"The most highly prized of all decorations with which the United States recognizes the valor of its warriors is the Order of the Purple Heart. Established during the War of the Revolution by General George Washington, the Purple Heart is awarded only to soldiers whose blood has been spilled in the defense of our country. It is to those gallant Americans who have given, and are giving, their life's blood for the United States, that this motion picture is humbly dedicated."

This dissolves into a close view of a TOKIO COURTROOM—disclosing a huge Japanese flag, inlaid in the wall. The view draws back slowly and we see that a door beneath, and to one side of the flag, is opening and the CLERK is entering. He is an aged, excitable, wizened little Japanese, wearing the formal black gown and cap, edged in purple. As he enters, the scene draws back further and we see that the courtroom is large, and situated in a modern type of building. Its furnishings are Occidental and but for the flag inlaid in the wall, the room might easily be mistaken for a courtroom anywhere in America or England. Immediately below the flag is the judges' platform. On it is a semi-circular desk, behind which are three chairs. On the platform, to the right and left of the semi-circular desk, are chairs and smaller desks used by the clerk and the police procurator. On the floor immediately below the platform are the witness box to the left, and the prisoners' box to the right; the witness box contains no chair. At the rear of the room is a projection machine, not immediately identifiable as such because it is covered with a canvas cover. The rest of the room is given over to the chairs for spectators, and, at one side, a table for press correspondents. There are double doors at the center of the rear of the room, a single door behind the judges' platform, and another single door giving off to the right behind the prisoners' box. Japanese soldiers, armed with rifles, stand stiffly at attention four feet apart, in a row extending around all walls save the one with the flag. As the view draws back to show us all this, the clerk has reached his desk. He does not sit down, but remains standing, looking toward the rear doors, and nods to a Jap major, off scene. Thereupon we get a reverse view and see this Japanese major opening the double rear doors.

A line of civilians appears in the doorway single file, each person armed with credentials. The first man in line is LUDWIG KRUGER, a German, who wears

---

Copyright, 1944, *by Twentieth Century-Fox Film Corporation.*

a swastika pin in his lapel. He hands his credentials to an officer, who has taken his position beside the door.

KRUGER (*announcing himself*). Ludwig Kruger, *Muencher Abend Zeitung*.

The officer checks a list of names and returns Kruger's credentials, and he enters the courtroom. Next in line is BORIS EVENIK, a Bulgarian. He announces himself and presents his credentials which read:

> Boris Evenik,
> *Slovo,* Sofia

Evenik's credentials are checked and returned and he is permitted to enter. So far not a word has been spoken. The third man in line is PETER VOROSHEVSKI, a huge gorilla-like amiable Russian. He announces himself and presents his credentials which read:

> Peter Voroshevski,
> *The Red Star,* Moscow

The Jap officer checks the credentials with the list and returns them to Voroshevski. Both he and Voroshevski speak together:

Credentials not in order. So sorry.

The Jap officer looks a little annoyed, but makes no comment as Voroshevski, not concerned in the slightest, slouches to one side and stands grinning almost contemptuously as other correspondents are admitted. The next man is FRANCISCO DE LOS SANTOS, an Argentinean, who hands the officer his credentials. Santos is a pompous, exceedingly polite man, impeccably dressed, who gives the impression that on occasion he might have a hot temper.

VOROSHEVSKI (*stepping aside as Santos presents his credentials*). Good morning, Comrade Santos.

SANTOS. Francisco de los Santos, *El Mundo,* Buenos Aires.

The officer studies the credentials thoughtfully while Santos taps his toe impatiently. The officer finally approves with a salute and allows Santos to enter.

SANTOS (*inclining his head courteously*). Thank you.

Santos enters the courtroom, Voroshevski looking after him thoughtfully. Next in line is a couple—JOHANA HARTWIG and TOMA NOGATO. Johana is a blonde, phlegmatic but almost pretty woman of thirty. Despite her prettiness her face is hard, her mouth grim though sensuous, her eyes brilliant, darting, sadistic. She wears a Nazi swastika pin.

TOMA NOGATO is a dapper little Japanese, five or six years younger than Johana, good-looking in a Japanese way. Voroshevski grins at them and addresses Johana.

VOROSHEVSKI. Good morning, comrades.

Johana's eyes flash furiously and her lips tighten, but she says nothing. Voroshevski grins to himself. Johana hands her credentials to Toma who hands both his and hers to the officer.

JOHANA. Johana Hartwig, D.N.B. News Agency, Berlin.

TOMA. Toma Nogato, Domei, Tokio.

The officer bows—the first time he has bowed—and passes them inside, as KARL SCHLESWIG, an Austrian, steps up.

SCHLESWIG (*presenting credentials*). Karl Schleswig, Vienna *Tageblatt*.

He is passed inside giving way to PAUL LUDOVESCU, a highly perfumed and dainty Roumanian. As Ludovescu presents his cards, he notices Voroshevski lolling in the corridor.

LUDOVESCU (*to the officer, but looking at Voroshevski, puzzled*). Paul Ludovescu, Nationalist Syndicate, Bucharest.

The officer returns the credentials and Ludovescu sorts them carefully before putting them into his pocket. As he does this, MANUEL SIVA, a fussy, irritable little man appears, spies Voroshevski, stops and tips his hat to the Russian.

SIVA (*to Voroshevski*). Good morning, Senhor Voroshevski. Aren't you going to attend the trial?

VOROSHEVSKI. No, Comrade Siva. My credentials are not in order.

Siva makes a sympathetic clucking noise and is about to turn away when Voroshevski stops him.

VOROSHEVSKI. And I wouldn't be surprised if yours are not.

SIVA (*indignant*). Absurd.

VOROSHEVSKI (*grinning*). Yes, isn't it?

Siva scowls at him, nods courteously to Ludovescu who is watching in some surprise, and pompously presents his credentials to the Japanese officer.

SIVA. Manuel Siva, *Diario de Noticias*, Lisbon.

The officer looks at the credentials and hands them back.

OFFICER. Credentials not in order— so sorry.

Siva throws Voroshevski a look of surprise then turns indignantly to the officer.

SIVA. Just a minute! I am an accredited correspondent the same as the others——

OFFICER. If you wish to file complaint please consult honorable Bureau of Enlightenment.

SIVA (*truculently*). Is there something you don't want me to see? What sort of trial is this?

He starts to peek in through the doorway. The Jap calls out "Soldiers" in Japanese; these come up and block his path. Siva quickly steps back.

At this the scene cuts to the CORRESPONDENTS' TABLE where Kruger, Evenik, Johana, Toma and the others have taken their places. Ludovescu enters the box.

LUDOVESCU. They wouldn't admit Voroshevski or Siva. Why won't they admit them?

SANTOS. I wonder. All these precautions—these soldiers—(*Turning to Johana and Toma*) Is this to be a *military* trial?

Johana looks at him, her face telling us nothing, then shrugs.

KRUGER. How can it be? This is a *civil* court.

TOMA. I can tell better after I see who the judges are.

EVENIK (*examining his credentials*). "You are invited to represent your newspaper at a most important hearing in the Imperial Criminal Court—" (*Looking at the others*) "Invited"—I was picked up yesterday by the police—examined for two hours, and last night my rooms were searched.

SANTOS. So were mine. I knew it the minute I discovered the plumbing was out of order. You'd think by now they'd know I wouldn't plug my own drain pipe with secret documents.

Vincent: That's one crate we won't deliver to the Chinese.

Ling: . . . my guests found no method of carrying out their promise. I am still in excellent health.

Ross: When my time comes to walk, I hope I can do as well.

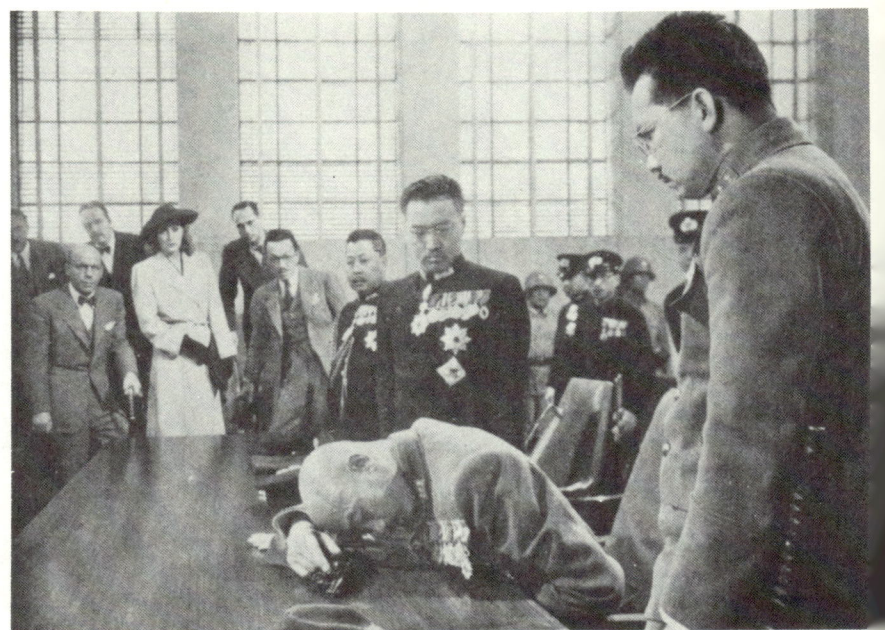

General Mitsubi acknowledges defeat with suicide.

TOMA. It happened to all of us. You should not be offended.

JOHANA. Toma is right. After all, we must remember that Japan is at war.

This cuts to the DOUBLE DOORS at the rear of the COURTROOM, and into the court files a group of high-ranking officers in the Japanese army. GENERAL ITO MITSUBI of the Ministry of Intelligence leads them. Mitsubi is a rather tall, trim, precise, deadly Japanese militarist. The other officers are members of his staff.

TOMA (*calling out to the others*). General Mitsubi!

We then see him and his aides cross the room to a table.

The CORRESPONDENTS' BACKS are now visible as they turn, look over their shoulders, and react to the sight of those impressive officers.

KRUGER (*awed*). General Mitsubi!

SANTOS. Who?

TOMA. Mitsubi—Chief of the Military Intelligence.

LUDOVESCU (*looking back toward the rear door*). Look, Santos!

All the correspondents crane their heads further, looking back toward the rear doors as we next see ADMIRAL KENTARA YAMAGICHI. He enters accompanied by his staff of naval officers, actually the same number of men as have accompanied Mitsubi. Yamagichi is a stout, sea-going Jap, his round head bald as an egg.

The correspondents' wonder and curiosity reach new heights.

TOMA (*reverently*). Admiral Yamagichi! Commander of the Imperial Fleet.

The correspondents begin producing notebooks and pencils in their eagerness to take notes, but continue looking back toward Yamagichi and his staff. Then we see the Admiral and his staff come forward to the two front rows to the left of the courtroom. General Mitsubi and his staff are standing in the two front rows to the right. The Admiral, the General and their staffs bow ceremoniously to one another. Then all sit down, and then the correspondents, seen again, begin writing notes hurriedly—all except Toma and Johana.

[The OLD CLERK now appears seated at his desk. He looks up from some writing and glares off toward the correspondents, then pounds his desk with his fist and screeches loudly.

CLERK. No notebooks! No pencils!

The CORRESPONDENTS' TABLE is seen again as the clerk's voice comes over, this time in a higher pitch.

CLERK'S VOICE. No notebooks! No pencils!

TOMA (*smiling at the others*). Please excuse the Honorable clerk. Your notebooks and pencils have disturbed him.

SANTOS (*indignant*). How can we make an accurate report without notes?

TOMA. We are not here as correspondents. We are here as guests. If you will read your invitation, I am sure you will find I am correct.

Santos looks at him dubiously then turns and begins conferring with Evenik in whispers as the clerk's voice again is heard.]

CLERK'S VOICE. The judges of this court will now exercise their powers—

The entire COURTROOM now is shown, with attention on the clerk who is standing and addressing the courtroom, which despite the presence of correspondents, witnesses and soldiers is nearly empty; its emptiness providing a sombre, foreboding note: The clerk continues.

CLERK. —according to law in the name of the Emperor!

He peers around the room and notices that although everyone else has risen, Santos and Evenik are still conferring in whispers.

CLERK (*angrily*). Up! Stand! Everybody up! Stand!

Santos and Evenik come to their feet. The clerk nods to a soldier who opens the door immediately behind the judges' platform.

This cuts to the JUDGES' PLATFORM, the view focussed on the door beneath the flag, as a soldier opens it, and a procession of dignitaries enters. First is the PROCURATOR, an unemotional Japanese of middle age. He wears the black court robes and is escorted by two uniformed policemen who will remain standing behind his chair during the trial. Next come two associate judges, JUDGE KINOTO and JUDGE YAKAMISHI, each slightly beyond middle age, highly cultured and intelligent looking, each wearing the traditional court robes. The procurator comes to his desk, and remains standing, his two policemen standing behind him. The associate judges come to the semi-circular desk and remain standing, beside chairs at either end of it. The center chair is empty.

The door beneath the flag is then seen closer as MITSURU TOYAMA enters. Toyama is the most powerful man in Japan. He is the head of the Black Dragon Society. His word frightens even the Emperor. He is majestic, austere. His face is the perfection of the Japanese mask of imperturbability. His features are fine, cleanly chiseled—and cruel. Slowly, he walks forward to his place in the center of the semi-circular desk, the view moving with him. And at this the scene cuts to the CORRESPONDENTS' TABLE as the correspondents lean forward, stunned, scarcely believing their eyes.

JOHANA (*breathless*). It is old Toyama!

TOMA (*thunderstricken*). Toyama!

LUDOVESCU (*awed*). Mitsuru Toyama!

TOMA (*breathless*). —the greatest political power in the Empire.

SANTOS. Isn't he also the head of the Black Dragon Society?

Toma looks at Santos as if almost afraid to answer.

TOMA (*in a whisper*). When Toyama speaks, even the Emperor listens.

LUDOVESCU (*to Evenik*). "Trembles" is more the word.

The entire COURTROOM is next seen as Toyama reaches his desk. The judges, the clerk, the procurator and his two policemen turn and face the flag. As if manipulated by puppet strings, they all bow ceremoniously to the flag, then turn and exchange solemn bows with one another.—This cuts to the JUDGES' PLATFORM as the judges, clerk and procurator sit down. Toyama turns formally to the procurator.

TOYAMA. You have prepared the evidence?

The procurator gets up and crosses to the judges' table, bringing with him a voluminous dossier of papers, which he hands to Toyama with another bow. He turns and marches back to his chair and seats himself. Toyama lays the dossier aside and speaks to the clerk.

TOYAMA. All witnesses are present?

The clerk stands up, and instantly the scene cuts to a view of the guards and soldiers at the door. YUEN CHIU LING, a thin oldish man, and his studious-looking son MOY LING enter, come forward into the room, and sit down, Ling removing the felt hat he has been wearing.

CLERK (*bowing*). All witnesses are present.

[Toyama nods and looks out over the courtroom toward the press table.

TOYAMA. Before this trial begins, I wish to repeat to the honorable representatives of the international press that they have been honored by an invitation to attend the most important criminal matter which has ever been presented before this court.

At the CORRESPONDENTS' TABLE the correspondents listen attentively as Toyama's voice comes over.

TOYAMA'S VOICE. It is a matter which is intended to receive the fullest publicity, at the proper time. However, the nature of this crime is of such monstrous proportions that until you are given official permission to release the story to your newspapers, this court imposes upon you, and each of you, an oath of secrecy, bound by your own consciences.

TOYAMA appears in a close view as he continues to address the correspondents.

TOYAMA. If, as an individual, any of you has any reluctance to assume this sacred responsibility, you will withdraw now.

The correspondents are seen as Santos half rises from his chair, as if to leave, following which TOYAMA is seen looking at Santos sharply.

TOYAMA. And you?

The correspondents appear resigned as Santos sinks back in his chair. Johana smiles at Toma.

JOHANA (*in a whisper*). Our Argentine friend is learning slowly—but he is learning.

The Judges' stand is now seen as Toyama nods to the correspondents.

TOYAMA. Your decision has been noted.] (*To the clerk*) Have the defendants brought into the courtroom.

The clerk appears in close view as he turns and gestures to the soldiers, who guard the prisoners' door. Following this gesture, the view moves slowly to the prisoners' DOOR as the soldiers open it; the harsh rasp of the turning doorknob resounding through the courtroom like the crack of doom. The door then is seen closer as it is opened, and through it we can see a long, narrow corridor, which gives off into an L. The corridor is brightly lighted by bulbs in the ceiling. One of the soldiers calls into the corridor, his voice echoing and resounding hollowly.

SOLDIER (*in Japanese*). Bring in the prisoners.

Far back in the corridor we hear this order repeated sharply in Japanese and its echoes, too, ring and reverberate through the corridor. We hear next the shuffling of feet of a small group of men, walking slowly, out of sight around the corner of the L, the footsteps sounding harsh and high pitched on the cement floor. Presently shadows appear on the wall as the group approaches the turn of the L.

The view moves around the courtroom, fixing on the faces of General

Mitsubi and his staff, Admiral Yamagichi and his staff, the judges, clerk and procurator, the ring of silent, motionless soldiers, rigid at attention around the wall. Over all of this, the footsteps, clashing on the cement floor, come closer, closer. The moving view ends on the correspondents, and is followed by a closer view of the CORRESPONDENTS staring in the direction of the prisoners' door, fascinated. Johana's emotions are stirring, sensuously, and her eyes are bright, her lips parted moistly as she knots and unknots a corner of her handkerchief. The footsteps offscene pass from cement onto a wooden floor, and come closer, then finally stop.

And now TOYAMA and the CLERK are seen looking toward and down at the prisoners, who are out of sight. Toyama's face is cold, implacable, his eyes motionless in their sockets.

CLERK. The prisoners will respond as their names are called.

A close view shows the CLERK picking up a list of names, while softly, as if from a great distance, we hear "The Army Air Corps Song" (instrumental only) which continues until the last flier has been identified.

CLERK. Captain Harvey Ross.

The scene moves slowly from the clerk to the first man in the prisoners' box. This man is CAPTAIN HARVEY ROSS, one of the American fliers who bombed Tokio. He is wearing his leather flying jacket over a G. I. shirt. His trousers are regulation dungarees. His name is stenciled above the breast pocket of his jacket, and his flying wings are still pinned to his shirt. Ross is a tall, lean, muscular man in his late twenties, who speaks with a Texas twang. He has a droll, dry, western humor. He is a steady man, nothing heroic about him, but he gives the impression of tremendous strength of spirit.

ROSS (*raising his hand*). Captain Ross.

CLERK'S VOICE. Lieutenant Kenneth Bayforth.

The moving view discloses the next man in line. This is LIEUTENANT BAYFORTH. He is a blonde, curly-headed young man, some few years younger than Ross. Like Ross, he wears his leather jacket, G. I. uniform and silver wings. He is of an inherently good nature, but we get no trace of his sense of humor now as he raises his hand.

BAYFORTH. Lieutenant Bayforth.

CLERK'S VOICE. Lieutenant Angelo Canelli.

The view moves to the next prisoner: He is LIEUTENANT ANGELO CANELLI. A fine, sensitive Italian boy, no more than nineteen now—he lied about his age to enlist in the air force. He is an artist, a devout Catholic, and has the sensitive, spiritual face which these give to him.

CANELLI. Lieutenant Canelli.

CLERK'S VOICE. Sergeant Martin Stoner.

The view moves to another prisoner: SERGEANT STONER, about twenty-eight, might have been a scholar in civilian life. He has a slender, ascetic face and figure, and his voice is soft, well modulated and cultured, as from years of study. We shall discover that he is an omnivorous reader and a devotee of poetry.

STONER. Sergeant Stoner.

CLERK'S VOICE. Lieutenant Peter Vincent.

The moving view then reveals LIEUTENANT VINCENT, who is a rough, tough, brawling New York Irishman, a former commercial test pilot. His jaw juts out pugnaciously as if he would like to spit in the eye of every Japanese present, and his eyes flash with hatred as he raises his hand.

VINCENT. Lieutenant Vincent.

CLERK'S VOICE. Sergeant Jan Skvoznik.

The view moves to SERGEANT JAN SKVOZNIK. He is a hulking big fellow, about twenty-four, with an enormous head and the shoulders and torso of a stevedore. He is a "professional amateur" football player, and summer-time toiler in a steel mill.

SKVOZNIK. Sergeant Skvoznik.

CLERK'S VOICE. Lieutenant Wayne Greenbaum.

As the scene moves, we next see LIEUTENANT GREENBAUM: He is as rough and tough in his own way as Vincent, but possessed of a philosophical sense of humor which at times is not above being ribald. He raises his hand.

GREENBAUM. Lieutenant Greenbaum.

CLERK'S VOICE. Sergeant Howard Clinton.

Last of all we see SERGEANT CLINTON, the baby of the outfit. Clinton is heartbreakingly young, almost incongruous in a soldier's uniform. We recognize in him the one member of the group who may break if anyone does. His eyes are wide and terrified as he raises his right hand.

CLINTON (*almost in a whisper*). Sergeant Clinton.

All the FLIERS are now visible with the judges' platform in the background.

CLERK. You may be seated.

The fliers sit down, and the music of "The Army Air Corps Song" ceases. Ross, obviously the spokesman for the group, remains on his feet, looking at the court, apparently trying to choose words with which to address them.

ROSS. If it isn't asking too much, sir, I'd like to know what this is all about.

TOYAMA (*coldly*). You wish to make inquiries?

ROSS. Yes, I do.

TOYAMA. Speak.

ROSS. Are we being put on trial?

TOYAMA. That is correct.

ROSS. On what charge?

TOYAMA. You will be informed in due time.

ROSS. Excuse my ignorance, your honor, but back home we'd be entitled to a lawyer or something.

TOYAMA. You will have adequate counsel to defend you.

ROSS. Thank you, sir.

Greenbaum tugs at Ross' sleeve and Ross leans over. Greenbaum half rises and whispers in his ear. Ross nods and again addresses the court.

ROSS. Oh, yeah. We would appreciate someone from the Swiss Legation or the Red Cross.

Toyama makes a slight negative gesture with his hand.

TOYAMA. Your counsel has already been appointed by the court.

Toyama nods to the clerk who calls out.

CLERK. Itsubi Sakai.

An enigmatic Japanese, wearing the robe and cap which counsels wear in Japanese courtrooms, bustles forward and takes his place at a small desk adjoining the prisoners' box.

TOYAMA. You may have a brief conference with the defendants.

A group view of the FLIERS shows them looking at Sakai dubiously as he bows to the court, turns and smiles at them.

SAKAI. My name is Sakai. Princeton —class of '31.

GREENBAUM (*scowling at him*). My name is Greenbaum. City College of New York. Class of '39. (*He turns to Ross.*) Sir, may I say something to the court?

ROSS. Go ahead, Greenie—we're all in this together.

GREENBAUM (*turning to Sakai*). Do you mind?

SAKAI (*turning toward the court*). I object.

This cuts to the THREE JUDGES.

TOYAMA. Speak.

GREENBAUM (*standing up*). Your honor, I have had some experience with law, and I know that as prisoners of war, no civil court in the world has any jurisdiction over us. I refer you to the Geneva treaty, and I quote: "Combatants who are captured are entitled to that protection which their own state is unable to afford them. Their lives, ceasing to be *jura publica* under the dominion of belligerency, have become *jura universalia*, when seen from one point of view and *jura privata* when seen from another; thus by a double portal they re-enter the sphere of normal relations. Though separated for the time being from any political community, they once more belong to humanity and to themselves. And as of their lives, *so of their liberties*. It is of their combatant liberty *alone* that belligerency can dispose."

The entire courtroom has been staring at Greenbaum, astounded at his presentation of his argument. Toyama is probably the most taken aback of anyone, but as Greenbaum concludes, his eyes narrow coldly.

GREENBAUM (*concluding*). So you see you can't try us in a civil court, and I therefore move that the charges be dismissed—whatever they are.

This cuts to the CORRESPONDENTS' TABLE while Santos, the Argentinean correspondent, leans over excitedly, and whispers to Evenik, the Bulgarian.

SANTOS. He is absolutely right. This court has no jurisdiction over them.

Johana silences him with a warning, impatient glance and they return their attention to the court, Johana continuing to tie and untie the knot in his handkerchief. This cuts to the JUDGES' PLATFORM.

TOYAMA. The crime of which you are guilty is a violation of international law. The Emperor's government finds no basis on which you may seek immunity under the articles of war.

The FLIERS are seen as Greenbaum slowly sits down, realizing he has lost the point.

GREENBAUM (*to Sakai*). What does he mean—the crime of which we are guilty? Before the trial even starts? What gives out here?

SAKAI (*apologetically*). So sorry, but under Japanese law, every prisoner is assumed to be guilty until he proves his innocence.

Ross and Greenbaum exchange worried glances. It is obvious they are going to get no cooperation out of Mr. Sakai. Ross looks at Sakai sharply.

> ROSS. All right, Princeton. As long as we're stuck with you, at least find out what we're charged with. (*Drily*) If that isn't asking too much.

> SAKAI (*agreeably*). Not at all.

He rises and bows to the judges.

> SAKAI. The prisoners wish to be informed of the nature of the charges against them.

The JUDGES' PLATFORM appears.

> TOYAMA. The procurator will read the indictment.

We get a close view of the PROCURATOR as he reads the indictment.

> PROCURATOR. Whereas the defendants have been identified as members of the armed forces of the United States of America, an enemy with which the Japanese Empire is at war—

A moving view picks out the faces of the fliers who show no further emotion as the procurator continues to read. They realize that this whole trial is a mockery and can have but one finish. The procurator's voice comes over.

> PROCURATOR'S VOICE. And whereas on the eighteenth day of April in the year 1942, the cities of Tokio, Yokohama, Nagoya, Kobe and Osaka were bombed by enemy aircraft. And whereas the above mentioned members of the armed forces of the United States while bombing the above mentioned cities, diverted their attack from military objectives—

The PROCURATOR is seen close as he continues to read.

> PROCURATOR. —and dropped their bombs upon non-military installations such as schools, hospitals and temples of worship—

This cuts to the CORRESPONDENTS' TABLE as Santos leans over and whispers to Kruger.

> SANTOS (*indignant whisper*). This is completely false! I was in Tokio—

Kruger glares at him, and they both look toward the procurator whose voice continues. Then we see him reading at the JUDGES' PLATFORM.

> PROCURATOR. And whereas the defendants flew at low altitudes and directed their machine gun fire into crowds, killing many women and children—

The clerk pounds his desk with his fist and screeches shrilly.

> CLERK (*in his terrible English*). Brutality! Brutality!

The procurator, not much surprised at the outburst, continues reading.

> PROCURATOR. Therefore the Emperor's government demands the conviction of the defendants for the crime of *murder*.

He closes the dossier and sits down at his desk.

The FLIERS are seen leaping to their feet in furious incredulity. They shout out their feelings in savage protest.

> FLIERS. What do you mean, murder! You're nuts! That's a lie, and you know it! You can't do that to us! You don't know what you're talking about!

The procurator is pounding for silence, and roaring "Silence!" The clerk is jumping up and down, screaming "Brutality! Brutality!" The entire courtroom is in an uproar. Vincent points his finger at Toyama.

> VINCENT. We never machine-gunned anybody! We hit our targets and nothing else!
>
> ROSS (*seizing Vincent to quiet him*). Level off! (*To all of them*) We'll speak our piece when the time comes.

More impressed by this than by the soldiers who have surrounded them, the fliers subside, and order is restored.

This cuts to the JUDGES' PLATFORM. Toyama has made a notation in his notebook on the desk before him and nods to the clerk.

> TOYAMA. Summon the first witness.
>
> CLERK. Yuen Chiu Ling.

LING and his son, MOY, appear in a close view, and as Ling starts to rise, his son places a hand on his arm and whispers to him in Chinese.

> MOY (*in Chinese*). Please, honorable father! Don't do it.
>
> LING (*angrily, in Chinese*). Silence, unrespectful one!

Ling rises, smiles apologetically at the court, and goes forward. Moy slumps back in his seat, unhappily. Next, Ling reaches the witness box and steps into it. He is bowing and smiling, obviously badly frightened and wishing to make a good appearance.

> LING (*reading from the paper handed to him*). I affirm that according to my conscience I will speak the truth, adding nothing and concealing nothing.

Ling produces a seal and stamps the paper. Toyama begins questioning Ling.

> TOYAMA. Your name?
>
> LING. Yuen Chiu Ling.
>
> TOYAMA. Your nationality?
>
> LING. Chinese.
>
> TOYAMA. Where is your home?
>
> LING. Kunwong.
>
> TOYAMA. You hold an official position there?
>
> LING. I am Governor of Kunwong province.
>
> TOYAMA. Where were you on the day the bombing took place.
>
> LING. At my home.
>
> TOYAMA. Did you see any of the defendants on that date?
>
> LING. Yes, excellency.
>
> TOYAMA. Describe the circumstances.

Ling nods and as he starts to speak, the scene draws in to a close view of the obsequiously bowing witness, with the American fliers appearing in the background.

> LING. I learned of the bombing over my radio. The first reports were confusing and contradictory as to the number of planes involved, and the amount of damage caused. As night approached, Radio Tokio warned that the American planes were believed headed across China. Still later, other reports claimed the storm was forcing many of the planes down.

And now as he speaks the scene cuts to a full view of SKY AND MOUNTAINS at night. An American B-25 bomber is winging through the storm.

> LING'S VOICE. One of them was reported to have crashed in the mountains—

As we watch, the plane crash-lands. Then another bomber, storm-tossed, is seen coming in to a landing in the water.

LING'S VOICE. —Another was believed to have fallen into the sea—

The plane lands on the choppy water, nosing down into the waves, tail up.

LING'S VOICE. —Then it was reported that one of the planes was in the vicinity of Kunwong—

We now get a full view of the countryside. It is night, and a storm is raging. The countryside is in total, obliterating darkness. Thunder rolls overhead, and an occasional blinding flash of lightning reveals that a downpour of rain is falling. This also reveals that we are on a rutty, winding country road, its mud churned to gumbo by the storm. Coming into view is a spotlight, on an automobile. This spotlight darts its beam through the darkness—from one side of the road to the other, then up at the rocky hillside at one side of the road—a finger of light, questing, searching, never still.

A closer view shows the spotlight, darting its beam about, searchingly. We now hear the muffled, slow rhythm of the car's engine, as the car moves slowly along. Then comes another sound—the sound of the marching feet of a body of men, slogging through the mud. The spotlight stops, almost as if physically listening, then abruptly, it is switched off.

A night scene of a ROAD appears, on which a patrol of Japanese infantry, possibly ten or fifteen men, on foot, splashes through the mud, crossing the intersection of a crossroad. We hear a command, barked in Japanese—

VOICE. Close up those ranks.

As the patrol passes by, there is an interval of complete darkness, then, beyond the crossroad, the spotlight flashes on again, and resumes its eerie poking into the darkness.

The spotlight again appears as it moves forward. Again the muffled rhythm of the car's motor is heard. But now, over the sound of the storm and the chug of the motor, comes a new sound—the distant, but approaching sound of an airplane. Closer and closer it comes, louder and louder. The spotlight hesitates, then points straight up—a pigmy attempt at spotlighting the airplane. The camera follows the beam of light up into the sky, reaches the end of it, and proceeds on up into the darkness. A brief interval of nothing but complete blackness of sky and storm, then a flash of lightning reveals another American B-25, lunging through the storm, tossed about as a leaf in a hurricane.—This is followed by a close view of the bomber, bucking and tossing as the storm throws it about. On the fuselage, we can see lettered the words: "MRS. MURPHY."

The interior of the PILOT'S COMPARTMENT then comes into view with Captain Ross at the controls and Lieutenant Vincent beside him. Their faces are tense and worried. Sergeant Clinton, his youthful face equally taut, stands in the doorway behind them, peering first at the rainswept windshield, then at the instruments on the dash. Vincent is leafing through a small book.

VINCENT (*spelling*). W-o-n—w-o-o. Oh, oh. Here it is.

ROSS. Here what is?

VINCENT. The place where the old man told us to land. (*He reads.*) "Woosang—population 8000—principal city of Sangpo Province." (*He looks at Ross.*) Can you imagine the reception we're going to get? We step out of the ship—shake hands with the Governor and say, "Here you are, brother, a nice new B-25 with the compliments of Uncle Sam —and you're getting fifteen more just like it." (*He resumes reading.*) "The principal industries of Woosang are agriculture, weaving and pottery. It is noted for the beauty of its scenery. . ." (*He peers out of the window as lightning flashes.*) . . . and, brother, this ain't it!

Ross flips the key of the plane's interphone system. Clinton instantly leaves and goes back into the fuselage.

ROSS. Pilot to navigator.

This cuts to the FUSELAGE where Greenbaum is at his chart desk. Hank Morrison, a big, easy-going, farmer type of boy, is braced against one wall, consuming a sandwich and a cup of coffee. Clinton enters from the cockpit as Greenbaum answers on the interphone. Clinton and Morrison lean over to listen on Greenbaum's earphones, which he holds loose from his head so that all can hear.

GREENBAUM. Navigator to pilot. Go ahead, sir.

ROSS' VOICE. How are we doing, Greenie?

GREENBAUM. Wind velocity has altered. Better compensate to 64. (*He looks at the others.*) Will we make it?

In the interior of the COCKPIT, Ross glances at the gas gauge.

ROSS. Not a chance.

Greenbaum and the others in the interior of the FUSELAGE look increasingly worried.

GREENBAUM. Not even if we pick up a tailwind?

ROSS' VOICE. Not even if we could all get out and push.

In the interior of the COCKPIT, Vincent shakes his head gravely as Ross speaks into the interphone.

ROSS. Prepare to abandon ship. I'll try to get above this weather to give us a better break. That's an *order*.

In the interior of the FUSELAGE, Greenbaum and the others react to the order. For a moment they are tense and silent, then try to snap out of it and make an effort to appear casual.

GREENBAUM. Right, sir.

[He flips off the key and removes the headphones, then turns and fiddles with a short wave radio set.

MORRISON. What's the use of monkeying with that. It's a cinch Radio Tokio won't tell us where we are.

GREENBAUM. Quiet! I got something!

Out of the radio comes music and a Japanese song, marred by static.

CLINTON (*trying to be lighthearted*). If we've got to crash-land by radio, I'd rather come in on a prayer.

MORRISON. And a high note from Dinah Shore.

GREENBAUM (*turning off the radio*). You heard the Skipper. We're not gonna crash, we're gonna hit the silk. Get rolling.

Morrison and Clinton snap out of it and instantly begin getting into their 'chutes and chin-strap jumping helmets. Greenbaum picks up a roll of charts from his navigator's table and looks at them gloomily.

GREENBAUM (*wailing*). Why was I ever born! Sometimes I hate my old man. Fought a war to make the world safe for his children—that's me. And lookit. Three months honest work and I got to tear it all up.

MORRISON. So what? You're always doing that. Writing and tearing—writing and tearing. What are you always writing anyway?

He takes the charts from Greenbaum and looks at them. The backs are covered with bars of music and snatches of lyrics.

MORRISON. Songs? I thought you were a lawyer.

GREENBAUM. So did I.

MORRISON (*returning the charts to Greenbaum*). No kidding—what made you give it up?

GREENBAUM. That's another thing my old man couldn't get for me—a practice.

As he starts tearing up his charts, he is suddenly attracted by something he sees.

Then we see that CLINTON is struggling to get into a parachute, but not having much luck because of the pitching of the plane. He looks tense and worried. He wipes his forehead. Looking up, he sees Greenbaum watching him, and reacts in annoyance at being detected in what seems to be a weak moment.

CLINTON. What are you looking at?

GREENBAUM. Don't let it get you, Clint. We're all shaking in our pants.

MORRISON. Not me—I know I won't die until my time comes and then nothing can stop it.

GREENBAUM. That's the way to feel. Just remember your basic—when you gotta go—go.

CLINTON (*wrestling with the parachute*). Remember *your* basic. This is no time for jokes.

But a lunge of the plane half throws Clinton to the floor, and partially entangles him in the parachute straps. Greenbaum helps him to his feet and starts buckling him into his 'chute.

GREENBAUM (*pretending disgust*). Here, let me do it! (*To Morrison*) See this, Morrison? This is the kind of service you get when you're in the Blue Book. Three nurses to change your didies when you're born. Private schools so you don't have to associate with the proletariat. A doctor if you sneeze and a specialist to wipe your nose. (*He finishes buckling the 'chute and smacks Clinton on the seat-pack.*) There you are, m'lord.

CLINTON (*grinning*). Thank you, my good man. Remind me to mention you in my will.

GREENBAUM (*all seriousness*). Remember to keep your legs out of the shrouds, or you might be falling head down. It's a wonderful view, but things fall out of your pockets.

A wider angle shows Morrison coming forward, dragging a vast amount of canned food. One large package and two small ones, tied together with rope.

MORRISON. Break it up, you two. I can't jump with all this. You gotta give me a hand.

GREENBAUM. What are you going to do—set up a delicatessen store in China?

MORRISON. I'm willing to die when my time comes, but I don't want it to be from hunger. (*He holds up various cans gloatingly.*) Chicken soup, double strength—pork and beans, from Boston—chile con carne, the pride of Texas. Corned beef hash —did I ever tell you how my mother used to make it? She used to—

GREENBAUM (*resignedly, to Clinton*). His mother is in again. (*He turns to Morrison, pleadingly.*) Look, Hank. You heard the Skipper's orders. Soon we may be facing our Maker. Do us a favor—let us live the last few minutes of our lives without hearing for the nine millionth time about your old lady's cooking! (*He flips the key and speaks into the interphone.*) Navigator to pilot. All clear back here. We can break up housekeeping any time. (*Looking at Morrison*) The sooner the better!

In the interior of the COCKPIT, Ross and Vincent are now eying the instrument panel grimly. Then we see the instrument panel; the gas gauge shows almost completely empty. Thereupon we again see the men in the cockpit. Vincent is looking at Ross meaningly as Ross speaks into the interphone.

ROSS. Roger, stand by. (*To Vincent*) Have you cleaned out your pockets yet?

VINCENT. I never had anything in them.

ROSS (*slipping off his earphones*). Take over. I want to get rid of some stuff.

Vincent takes over the controls. Ross reaches inside his jacket and takes out a worn, frayed letter and opens it. Then a close shot shows ROSS looking at the letter tenderly.—On the LETTER (inserted into the scene) we see the heading, in a childish scrawl:

"Dear Daddy"

Pasted to a corner is a snapshot of a belligerent-looking youngster of about five or six, holding two or three scrambling puppies.—Ross looks at Vincent sheepishly.

ROSS. Did I read you the last one?

Ross and Vincent are seen together, as Vincent, without taking his eyes from the controls, recites from memory.

VINCENT. "Dear Daddy. Mama loves you, Grandpa loves you. Calamity Jane has eight new puppies and they love you. At night I say my prayers for my daddy.

x x x x x x x x x x x x x x x x x x x x x

These are kisses for my daddy. Please come home soon so we can go hunting.

> Your loving son,
> Tim"

ROSS. You left out a line. (*Reciting*) I love my daddy. Mostest and—(*softly*) mostest.—Kids are funny. They make up words.

VINCENT. That Tim of yours is quite a proposition.

ROSS (*warmly*). You can say that again.

VINCENT. I never could figure how he came by that red hair.

ROSS. My grandfather on my mother's side. He was a policeman.

VINCENT. Oh.

Ross looks at the letter for the last time and partially turns away from Vincent. Then ROSS appears in a close view as he touches the letter and snapshot shyly to his lips—then tears them up and throws them through an aperture in the window; following which VINCENT and ROSS again are seen together. Vincent looks surprised.

VINCENT. What'd you do that for?

ROSS (*bitterly*). Don't let them find anything on you that isn't G. I.

VINCENT (*after a thoughtful pause*). Sometimes I'm glad I never got married. This is one of the times. . . .

Suddenly one of the motors starts to spit. Ross instantly snaps on his earphones and takes the controls.

ROSS (*into the interphone*). Pilot to navigator ... All men come forward with your 'chutes. We're going to chance it from the forward escape hatch. (*To Vincent*) Go ahead—I'll set the automatic.

Vincent gets up and starts out of the cockpit, as Ross sets the automatic pilot.]

The interior of the FUSELAGE appears as Vincent enters from the cockpit, and starts getting into the 'chute.

VINCENT. Any idea at all where we are, Greenie?

GREENBAUM. We're over China.

VINCENT. Splendid—that narrows things down considerably.

Ross enters, lurches into the center of the group, and starts putting on a parachute.

ROSS. Well, men, if anything happens to me, Lt. Vincent is in command. This is your first trip with him, but he's a fine officer and a great flier. It cost the government $40,000 apiece to make fliers out of you and me, but Lt. Vincent laid the same aeronautical education right in Uncle Sam's lap for free. He was a commercial pilot before the rest of us knew the difference between a propeller and a windsock. Stick to him, trust his judgment. He'll get you through if anybody can. (*He looks around at them.*) Lt. Vincent will jump first, then Sgt. Clinton, then Sgt. Morrison, then Lt. Greenbaum. I will go last.—I've set the ship on a circular course, so she won't be far away when she hits. If she burns when she crashes we'll all see the flames and meet there. If she doesn't burn, each man look for her. Whoever finds her, burn her. She must not fall into Japanese hands and the rest of us can use the fire as a beacon. (*He turns and slaps Vincent on the back.*) Okay, boys. This is the end of the line.

Vincent nods, and without expression, makes his way aft and opens the door. Without a look back, he dives out into the night. The others, already lined up to jump, follow quickly—Clinton, then Morrison, then Greenbaum. As Greenbaum gets to the door, he pauses, looks around affectionately at the plane, then says:

GREENBAUM. So long, Mrs. Murphy. I'll bet you never thought you'd have a Greenbaum in love with you.

He jumps. Ross, last in line, takes a quick look around the ship before following, his unhappiness at losing his beloved ship apparent in his eyes.

A RICE PADDIE comes into full view. A flash of lightning reveals Vincent as his parachute drifts down and he lands. He sinks to his knees in the swampy mud and his parachute drags him fifteen or twenty feet through the ooze before he can collapse it and free himself from it. The 'chute is now so watersoaked and caked with mud that Vincent abandons it without another thought. He looks around, undecidedly, producing a flashlight and casting its beam about cautiously, partially shielding the light with his fingers. Rain continues to drench the rice paddie, the wind is blowing a gale, and occasional lightning flashes shatter the darkness as thunder claps roll and reverberate. Vincent finally starts off to the right, floundering and stumbling through the mud.

VINCENT is then seen moving about. He slogs his way through the rice paddie, sometimes going almost to his knees, sometimes halted altogether by a particularly furious gust of wind. To avoid this, he half turns, and begins making his way backward against the wind, but suddenly, he trips over something, falls backward and sits down in the mud. Exasperated, he gets to one knee, but suddenly stops, in this position, and throws the beam of his flashlight on the object over which he has stumbled.

A close view shows a man's foot, wearing a G. I. shoe of the U. S. Army. A few inches of muddy, water-soaked dungaree pants are visible above the shoe top.—Vincent's face is seen at close view as he reacts to the foot, still held by the beam of the flashlight. Slowly the beam travels up the body— the ankle, the knee, thigh and torso until it reaches the face and identifies the man as Captain Ross, who is knocked cold. His collapsed parachute is still attached.

Ross and Vincent are seen together as Vincent, still on one knee, flounders to Ross, cuts his 'chute free and lifts his head and shoulders from the mire. He opens one of Ross' eyes and looks into it, then goes to work on Ross, massaging his cheeks violently, flexing Ross' arms to assist respiration, etc., much as a second works on a punch-drunk fighter between rounds. Finally Ross opens his eyes, shakes his head, and looks around groggily. Vincent watches him anxiously.

> VINCENT. Time to get up, Skipper. We've arrived. (*Ross wakes up and shakes his head to clear it.*) You all right?
>
> ROSS. I think so.

He tries his arms and legs, finds them in order, and gets to his feet.

> ROSS. Nothing broken, as far as I can tell.

> VINCENT (*glowering*). You scared the pants off of me. I was commencing to think you really meant that little speech you made upstairs.
>
> ROSS (*looking around*). See any of the others?
>
> VINCENT. I've seen nothing but mud.

The sound of the airplane is heard, circling near, its engines missing and popping. They look aloft, following the direction of the sound with their eyes.

> ROSS. Mrs. Murphy sounds like she's getting ready.

The plane's motors miss and backfire violently, then stop altogether. We can hear the whine of wind through its controls as it goes into a dive. This sound continues for a brief moment, then we hear a tremendous crash somewhere far offscene.

> VINCENT (*gloomily*). That's one crate we won't deliver to the Chinese.

[The two men start toward the direction of the sound, stumbling and floundering through the mire. Ross, leading the way, uses his flashlight cautiously, switching it on and off. Suddenly he stops, the beam of his flashlight focused on something on the ground. He leans over and picks it up, holding it for Vincent to see.—ROSS (seen close) is holding up a can of corned beef.

> ROSS (*calling*). Morrison! Hank! Hank Morrison!

Ross and Vincent are seen together, waiting. There is no answer.

> VINCENT. Maybe he got a mouthful of mud, the same as you.
>
> ROSS (*nodding*). Use your flashlight.

He throws the beam of his flashlight in one direction, and Vincent throws his in the opposite direction so that they are standing back to back, revolving slowly in a circle. Suddenly, Ross stops, holding the beam of his flashlight rigid. Vincent whirls and throws his light at the same spot on the ground, and an expression of horror begins to grow on their faces.—Then a close view discloses three cans of food, part of Morrison's main bundle, the bundle itself, half burst open and partially buried in the mud. A man's broken arm protrudes into view—the rest of him back, out of sight.—The two men are seen standing frozen in horror.

VINCENT. His chute didn't open.

ROSS (*after a long, silent pause*). He was one swell guy— It doesn't seem possible, we were all up there together just a few minutes ago—and now he's gone.

VINCENT. I never knew him as well as the rest of you—but I liked him. All he ever talked about was his mother—and her cooking. He was sure proud of her.

ROSS. Yes. I know. He worshipped her. . . . Get his dog-tag and his bracelet— We'll want to send them on.

Vincent walks toward the body as ROSS, seen close, watches Vincent, offscene. We can hear Vincent floundering around in the darkness. Ross has been deeply touched by the death.

Vincent rejoins Ross. He is holding Morrison's dog-tag and crash bracelet, and is examining them in the beam of his flashlight.

VINCENT (*after a long pause*). It's funny how you know a guy so long, but never *really* know him.

ROSS (*surprised*). What do you mean?

VINCENT. How long has Sergeant Morrison been with you?

ROSS. Why—about two years.

VINCENT. Listen to this. (*He reads from the tag.*) Morrison—Henry Joseph. Blood type A—Religion, Lutheran. In case of death notify— guardian—Superintendent, City Orphanage, St. Paul, Minnesota.

ROSS (*stunned*). No father—and even his mother was just—something he made up . . .

VINCENT (*after a pause*). I've got an idea Hank's seeing his mother for the first time, right about now. (*He glances heavenward, just for a moment, then with forced casualness*) Well—that's how it is.

Vincent and Ross move on as another part of the RICE PADDIE comes into view: A parachute, disengaged from one of the fliers, and blown along by the wind, tumbles and balloons as it blows out of the scene. Then for a moment we see nothing but the stormswept rice paddie, and hear nothing but the wind. — Finally, as the view continues to move, we pick up Greenbaum, who is fighting his way through the storm. He is soaking wet, caked with mud; his teeth are chattering with cold and fear. He looks apprehensively around as he flounders along. Suddenly, he stops, whips out his .45, drops to one knee and challenges sharply.

GREENBAUM. Who goes there? (*Receiving no answer*) Speak up, or I'll shoot!

A lightning flash reveals that he is quite alone—no one near. Disgusted, he continues slogging along. As he does—although his lips do not move, we can hear his voice—his mental voice—talking to him.

GREENBAUM'S MENTAL VOICE. Come on, Greenbaum! Snap out of it! You want to die of fright? Get your mind off of this—whip up a number. (*Thus adjured by himself, Greenbaum starts singing.*)

GREENBAUM (*singing*). China, is there any place finer—

GREENBAUM'S MENTAL VOICE. Naw, that's been done.

GREENBAUM (*singing*). I've got a hole in my umbrella, on a rainy, rainy, day—

GREENBAUM'S MENTAL VOICE. It's no use, Greenbaum. Sing something you know.

GREENBAUM (*singing*). Nothing can stop the Army Air Corps—except the weather—nothing can stop the Army Air Corps.

As he sings this, another parachute billows past, blown by the wind. Greenbaum reacts in excited delight to the hope that there may be other members of the party about. He looks around, calling loudly.

GREENBAUM. Hey! Skipper! Captain Ross—sir! It's me—Greenie! (*Receiving no answer*) Lieutenant Vincent? (*Receiving no answer*) Hey, Hank! Hank Morrison!

This time, Clinton's voice is heard, calling from far off in the darkness.]

CLINTON'S VOICE. Hey-y-y!

Clinton's light goes on far down the rice paddie on the same level with Greenbaum's as his voice comes over.

CLINTON'S VOICE (*far off*). Hey! Hey! Gre-ee-nie!—It's me—Clint.

Clinton waves his light vigorously, and the lights starts bobbing, to indicate Clinton's floundering as he runs.

Greenbaum reacts in relief and delight and starts toward Clinton's light, throwing his flashlight around in a circular motion.

GREENBAUM. Clinton! Hey, it's me.

A long moving scene shows the two lights as they begin moving toward one another. Clinton's light indicates a fall. He gets up and resumes running, then Greenbaum's light indicates a fall, but he, too, gets up and his light moves toward Clinton. The view moves in until Greenbaum and Clinton meet. —They then appear in a close view as they embrace and start dancing around in delight; their flashlights bobbing and revolving in a crazy dance of joy. The two boys are laughing and pummeling one another in an ecstasy of happiness over their meeting, for the moment oblivious of their mud-soaked condition. Then as they step back, Greenbaum looks at Clinton critically, then down at himself.

GREENBAUM. What did we fall into? We're covered with some kind of mud.

CLINTON. Call it mud if you care to, but you needn't be so polite. We're in a rice field.

GREENBAUM (*holding his nose*). Rice! Fooey! I'll never touch the stuff again —even with raisins.

Suddenly the sound of an explosion is heard. They whirl quickly and look into the distance—where a shot of flame can be seen billowing up in the rain-filled darkness.

GREENBAUM. It's Mrs. Murphy! (*They start out toward the flames.*)

[A moving view of the road now appears as the Japanese patrol previously seen is slogging along through the mud. It stops suddenly as the Japanese officer calls out in Japanese. Far offscene, much farther than when previously seen is the flare of the burning plane.

OFFICER (*in Japanese*). Halt!

He looks off, reacts, and barks out another command.

OFFICER (*in Japanese*). Double time!

The patrol starts forward at a trot.]

Another section of the road appears in complete darkness over which comes the sound of the storm. After a moment, we can also hear the chugging sound of an automobile motor, and the spotlight previously seen turns a corner of the road and begins to come into view. As it fills the screen, it stops, and the spotlight is turned off. A moving view through the darkness picks up two flashlights moving toward the flames of the burning airplane at the extreme right. As we watch, the two flashlights reach the flames. Then we see the spotlight as it is turned on and the car starts again.

The BURNING AIRPLANE now appears as Ross, Vincent, Greenbaum and Clinton are pumping one another's hands and clapping each other's shoulders in delight.

GREENBAUM (*shaking hands with Vincent*). Hey, no reflection on you, Vincent, but I'm sure glad we still got the same skipper.

CLINTON (*shaking hands with Ross*). So am I.

VINCENT. So am I, sir.

ROSS (*drily*). Thanks, fellows—so am I. That's too bad—Mrs. Murphy kept a good house.

VINCENT (*grinning*). As long as you *are* here, Captain, how about moving us away from this fire? This place may be crawling with Japs.

[CLINTON (*looking around*). What about Hank?

GREENBAUM. I hope he sees this bonfire before the Japs do.

ROSS. Hank is dead.

Greenbaum and Clinton look from one to the other of the officers, shocked and dumbfounded.

GREENBAUM (*after a pause*). It's funny. It ought to break me up, but I don't feel a thing. He talked so often about getting it.

He squats down on the ground as though he, too, has suddenly become a fatalist. Clinton squats down beside him, he, too, looking thoroughly dejected.

CLINTON. He was a complete fatalist. "Why worry?" he used to say. "When your number's up, it's up." There is a great deal to be said for his viewpoint.

Ross looks at them sharply, realizing that he is on the verge of inheriting two new fatalists. He clutches Greenbaum and Clinton affectionately by their collars and lifts them to their feet.

ROSS. There's also a great deal to be said for mine—"God helps those who help themselves." (*He gives them an affectionate shove.*) Pack 'em up, laddies—we gotta think about ourselves.

The fliers disappear from sight.]

The interior of a car is seen through the windshield. We look directly over the steering wheel. We cannot see the occupants of the car, but we do see the beam of the spotlight piercing the gloom ahead of the car, and lighting the rainswept road. A hand suddenly turns the spotlight on the right hand side of the road. Through the windshield we see the four fliers just climbing onto the road from the rice paddie.

They instantly dive out of sight behind the embankment.

Behind the EMBANKMENT the fliers appear, flattened on the ground, with their guns drawn. Then as we get a close view of the CAR from the fliers' angle the door is thrown open.—The FLIERS are crouching behind the rocks. Ross has his .45 leveled toward the spotlight.

ROSS (*calling out*). If you're coming out—come out with your hands up.

A silhouette steps out with hands up, followed by a second figure.

VINCENT. (*delighted*). They understand you! We're among friends.

ROSS. Not so fast, Vinnie. There are Quislings even among the Chinese. (*Calling out*) Who are you?

The SPOTLIGHT now discloses a hand which reaches into the gleam of the light, and turns it. It reflects on the grinning, impish face of Lieutenant Bayforth!—Ross, Greenbaum, Clinton and Vincent gaze thunderstricken at Bayforth. But their astonishment instantly gives way to delight, as Ross lets out a whoop of joy.

ROSS. It's Georgia Tech!

VINCENT (*shouting*). Bayforth!

The four men instantly leap from behind the embankment.—A wider angle shows the four men reaching Bayforth. They literally toss him into the air, yelling and singing. Skvoznik, Canelli and Stoner climb from the car and stand watching, grinning broadly.

THE FLIERS (*singing lustily*).
He's a rambling wreck from Georgia Tech,
And a heckuva engineer,
A heckuva, heckuva, heckuva, heckuva, heckuva engineer.
And just like all good fellows
He drinks his whiskey clear.
He's a rambling wreck from Georgia Tech,
And a heckuva engineer.

The song ends in a wild yell as Clinton, Greenbaum, Ross and Vincent spy Bayforth's crew standing by laughing. Greenbaum and Clinton rush toward them, and they dance and caper about, yelling and pounding one another.

Ross, Bayforth and Vincent watch the men and grin happily.

ROSS. What happened to your ship?

BAYFORTH. I crashed her landing in this goo.

ROSS. Did you burn her?

BAYFORTH. I didn't have to. She sunk out of sight. Burke was killed.

We now see the Chinese governor and informer LING, with MOY, his son, at his elbow.

LING (*respectfully*). Please! Forgive the intrusion, gentlemen. It is not safe to stay here.

Ross, seeing Ling for the first time, eyes him suspiciously.

ROSS (*to Bayforth*). You haven't introduced me to your friend, Lieutenant.

LING (*bowing to Ross*). I am Yuen Chiu Ling, governor of Kunwong province. This is my son, Moy.

ROSS (*shaking hands with the two Chinese*). Well, howdy, gentlemen. Glad to know you.

VINCENT and BAYFORTH are seen together as Vincent speaks *sotto voce* to Bayforth.

VINCENT. Where did you pick him up?

BAYFORTH (*sotto voce*). A couple of miles down the road. Said he was out looking for us.

ROSS, BAYFORTH, VINCENT, LING and MOY form a group in which Ling is smiling at Ross.

LING. All China is grateful to you for the blow at Tokio, Captain.

ROSS (*quickly*). How do you know about that?

LING. Radio Tokio has talked of nothing else all day.

GREENBAUM (*joining them; eagerly*). How did we do? Was there much damage?

LING. One moment they announce no damage, the next they say fires are raging out of control. First they say there were no casualties, then they estimate the casualties may exceed four thousand.

VINCENT (*happily*). Sounds like we put the fear of God into them.

LING (*seriously*). No. The Japanese do not fear God. They fear only bombs.

We see LING and MOY, Moy watching his father anxiously as Ling looks at the fliers meaningly.

LING. No doubt, Captain, you have a secret base you are trying to reach. Perhaps I can guide you?

The FLIERS are seen closely, as Ross looks at them, then at Ling.

ROSS. That's very kind of you, Governor, but we can't tell you where we're going any more than we can tell you where we came from. Those are our orders.

LING (*bowing his head, apologetically*). A million pardons. I should not have asked. It was stupid of me.

GREENBAUM (*sidling up to Ross*). May I make a suggestion, Captain?

Ross looks at him. Greenbaum fingers his .45 and offers it to Ross behind Bayforth's back.

GREENBAUM (*sotto voce*). Maybe he'll *lend* us his station wagon.

Ling apparently has overheard this, for he smiles at Ross and speaks earnestly.

LING (*seen close*). My humble car is at your disposal. You have done much for China. But Japanese patrols are all around us. You must not travel in these clothes—you expose yourselves to much danger. And you must eat and rest—my house is not far.

Moy unexpectedly speaks to his father in Chinese.

MOY (*in Chinese*). Please! Father! You must not!

LING (*sharply, in Chinese*). I have told you—do not interfere! (*In English to the fliers*) My son joins me in urging you—to accept our invitation.

ROSS, seen close, thinks this over for a long moment, studying the faces of the other boys, but they obviously are looking to him for a decision so he finally turns and smiles at Ling.

ROSS. Okay, governor. We'll take a chance. If you're on the level, we'll never know how to thank you enough. But if you cross us, we'll certainly know how to kill you.

Ling seems to regard this as some sort of joke for he starts laughing.

The scene dissolves to the COURTROOM, affording a close view of LING standing in the witness box, as he continues testifying.

LING. As your excellencies can see, my guests found no method of carrying out their promise. (*He bows sardonically to the fliers.*) I am still in excellent health.

A close view of the judges, shows TOYAMA making a note in his book, writing as he asks his next question.

> TOYAMA. The court is particularly interested in any conversations in which the defendants mentioned the targets struck by their bombs.

This cuts to LING in the witness box as he bows, servilely. (The fliers are seen listening as he proceeds with his testimony.)

> LING. Yes, excellency. Mistaking me for a possible accomplice, these men (*pointing at the fliers*) were in a boisterous and boastful mood. They laughed as they told me how they machine-gunned children at play in a school yard—how they destroyed hospital after hospital, temple after temple. The court can well imagine how contemptible I felt having these monsters share my table—even if it was only for the purpose of detaining them until Japanese troops arrived.
>
> CLERK (*jumping up, and pounding the table*). Brutality! Brutality!

At this the scene cuts to the FLIERS, and Ross comes to his feet quickly.

> ROSS (*furiously, to Toyama*). This man is a liar! Sure, we told him we hit our targets,—but they weren't hospitals, temples or schools. They were oil storage centers, airports, and shipyards. That's what we hit, and that's what we told him!

Ling looks at Ross contemptuously, then turns to the court.

> LING. Excellencies—my son was present at all times. He will gladly corroborate my statements—if your excellencies think it is necessary.
>
> TOYAMA (*seen close*). The court has no cause to suspect the witness of perjury. (*To Ling*) You may step down.

The scene cuts to the FLIERS as Greenbaum jumps to his feet furiously.

> GREENBAUM. Hey! Just a minute here! We got a right to cross-examine! (*To Sakai*) Work on that guy. Break him down.
>
> SAKAI (*with apologetic surprise*). Our law does not permit cross-examination unless the court suspects the witness did not tell all of the truth.

Greenbaum glares at him, about to explode, but Bayforth stops him, grabbing him by the shoulder.

> BAYFORTH. Look—look—what's the use, fellows? This is a lynching.

The entire COURTROOM is seen now as Ling starts back to his seat, and the clerk calls the next witness.

> CLERK. General Ito Mitsubi.

General Mitsubi rises and starts forward, passing Ling who is returning to his seat. Ling bows, humbly, and continues.

Ling sits down in his seat beside Moy who remains impassive as Ling smiles at him as much as to say: "I did well didn't I?" Moy sits motionless, refusing to look at Ling but we can see there are tears in his eyes.—The COURT seen in full view as Mitsubi reaches the witness box and faces the court.

> MITSUBI (*reading, as the clerk hands him the oath on a paper*). "I affirm that according to my conscience will speak the truth, adding nothing and concealing nothing."

The clerk sits down, and Toyama addresses Mitsubi.

TOYAMA. Your name and rank.

MITSUBI. Ito Mitsubi, General in command of military intelligence.

TOYAMA. Following the bombings, did your department photograph the result of the attacks on Tokio, Yokohama, Nagoya, Kobe and Osaka?

MITSUBI. It did.

TOYAMA. Specifically, did you prepare motion pictures showing civilian casualties?

MITSUBI, seen closer, glances unemotionally toward the fliers, then nods.

MITSUBI. Yes, excellency.

TOYAMA'S VOICE. Are you ready to display them to the court?

MITSUBI. Yes, excellency.

And Mitsubi turns and signals to two non-commissioned officers seated among the witnesses.—These step instantly to the projection machine which has been set up in the rear of the courtroom. Other soldiers quickly draw the Venetian blinds at the windows, plunging the court into dim, half-light. Still another soldier quickly pulls down a rolled-up screen which hangs on the wall on one side. These movements are all simultaneous, and lightning-like, as if from careful rehearsal.—We see the PROJECTION MACHINE as the non-coms return from the windows and flick a switch on the projector, throwing a square of dazzling white light onto the screen. The other inserts a small glass stereopticon slide into the machine. Then the COURTROOM is seen in full view as the first picture is flashed onto the screen. It shows an Oriental street with the wreckage of a temple of some sort in the foreground. Blasted vehicles, including automobiles and horse-drawn carts, litter the pavement, along with the corpses of horses and the sprawled bodies of a dozen or more civilian casualties.

MITSUBI (*seen at full view; without emotion*). This is where American bombs fell in Mizumachi Street in Yokohama.

The correspondents JOHANA and SANTOS are seen together, looking at the screen in fascination. Johana's lips are parted —it is not a smile, but a symptom of enormous emotion. Santos looks badly puzzled as Mitsubi's voice comes over.

MITSUBI'S VOICE. The court will notice the wreckage of the Diajingu shrine and the many civilian casualties.

Mitsubi and the soldier at the projection machine appear again.

MITSUBI. Here you see the result of bombing and machine gunning in Nagoya. Eight hundred civilian casualties, and the Buddhist temple of Eihoji destroyed.

The CORRESPONDENTS' TABLE is seen in a fairly close view, as Santos half rises to his feet, staring at the screen.

SANTOS (*in a hoarse whisper*). That is not an actual air raid!

JOHANA (*sharply*). Santos! Be still!

SANTOS. Those pictures were taken during an air raid drill! Before Japan was even at war! (*To the others*) You know! We were all there!

TOMA (*significantly*). [You could be mistaken, Santos.] I wasn't there.

Santos slowly relaxes, and stares in the direction of the FLIERS, who are next seen staring horrified at the screen. Their earlier tension has almost reached the breaking point, and even Ross, the best controlled of them all, is twitching nervously.

> MITSUBI'S VOICE. This is what happened when the Americans brutally bombed Shimbashi station in Tokio—

A fairly close view discloses the SCREEN on which is seen the tangled wreckage of a bombed railroad station—possibly the famous one with the crying baby seated in the foreground.

> MITSUBI'S VOICE. —which, although it was a railroad terminal, was not a military objective, but was, on the other hand, crowded with civilians attempting to flee to a place of safety.

Suddenly a wild, piercing scream of mortal agony is heard, and we see the courtroom being plunged into pandemonium by the scream.

TOYAMA in a close view is seen rising to his feet, a thundercloud of anger.

> TOYAMA (*in Japanese*). Order! Raise the blinds!

A fairly close view shows the soldiers scrambling to raise the Venetian blinds, restoring light in the courtroom, as Toyama is staring down into the courtroom, astounded.—And now the CORRESPONDENTS have turned in their seats and are looking back, their eyes wide and staring. Following which, we see the FLIERS, looking into the crowd, incredulously: LING is slumped forward in his chair, dead. MOY stands over him, erect, proud, smiling. He is wiping the blade of a long knife on a silk handkerchief, looking straight at Toyama. MOY is then seen at close view, his eyes flashing proudly.

> MOY. This, at least, excellency, is the truth . . . (*Turning to the fliers*) I am a soldier of China. My father has answered to his Honorable ancestors for your betrayal.

Attention is now focused on the judges' stand, as Toyama points a steady, unemotional finger at Moy.

> TOYAMA (*in Japanese*). Arrest that man!—Take him out!

Soldiers seize Moy. He hands one of them the knife with a slight bow, and they start leading him out. Other soldiers start carrying out Ling's body, and as the soldiers lead Moy past the fliers, en route to the door leading into the prison, Ross speaks to the others.

> ROSS. Come on, fellows, stand up for a man.

The fliers get to their feet, smiling at Moy. Moy bows, humbly, smiling, and is led away. The boys sit down, their eyes following Moy until he disappears through the door.

The scene cuts to the JUDGES' STAND as Toyama sits down, and the door closes behind Moy.

> TOYAMA. The court regrets this interruption and especially deplores its nature. The Chinese are a treacherous people. Try as we will to enlighten and guide them—they remain barbarians who will strike down even their own flesh and blood, if the price is high enough . . . It is the opinion of this court that the honorable Yuen Chiu Ling was killed by a paid assassin—fortunately not before he could testify. (*To Mitsubi*) General Mitsubi, I believe we can spare ourselves further visual testimony. Can you tell the court the base from which these prisoners came?

> MITSUBI (*seen at close view as he glances at the fliers*). Yes, excellency. As a result of our preliminary investigation, we have every reason to believe that they came from an aircraft carrier—

The FLIERS react in consternation to this—their secret betrayed. Their consternation grows as Mitsubi speaks.

MITSUBI'S VOICE. —of the Hornet type.

But at this the scene cuts to ADMIRAL YAMAGICHI as he rises to his feet apologetically.

YAMAGICHI. I trust your excellencies will pardon my inexcusable interruption.

This cuts to TOYAMA and MITSUBI. They are looking toward Yamagichi in surprise.

TOYAMA (*inclining his head*). Admiral Yamagichi.

YAMAGICHI (*seen close as he turns to Mitsubi, apologetically*). General Mitsubi, your brilliance in matters of military investigation is famous throughout the empire.

He bows to Mitsubi, and we see Mitsubi bowing politely to Yamagichi.

YAMAGICHI. I therefore rebuke myself for calling to your attention certain matters which you must already have investigated most exhaustively. (*Turning to Toyama*) Certain—ah—findings of a naval board of inquiry. (*To Mitsubi*) In a spirit of the most respectful cooperation, I should like to place these findings at your excellency's disposal—(*to Toyama*)—in private.

MITSUBI, at close range is seen looking at Yamagichi inscrutably. Finally, he bows, courteously.

MITSUBI. I am grateful for your excellency's assistance.

The manner in which he says "assistance" is the only indication that he resents Yamagichi's intrusion at all.

TOYAMA (seen close) looks quickly at Mitsubi, getting the implication in the word "assistance." He looks down at the court.

TOYAMA (*sharply*). The prisoners will be removed. General Mitsubi and Admiral Yamagichi will wait upon me in my chambers in five minutes. Court is adjourned—until tomorrow at the same hour.

The judges rise, and the clerk pops to his feet, smiting his desk.

CLERK. Up! Stand! Everybody! Up! Stand!

The COURTROOM is seen in full view as everyone rises. The judges and court attachés bow to the flag and file out. Soldiers start leading the fliers toward their door, and the doors close behind them.

The scene dissolves to TOYAMA'S CHAMBERS. Here TOYAMA (seen close) is seated behind his desk, his face stern and implacable.

TOYAMA. The purposes of this trial are threefold:
First: To appease public clamor and reassure the populace.
Second: To serve notice on our enemies as to what their fliers may expect in the event of future raids.
Third: To defeat the master plan behind this attack—a plan designed to divide our strength and force us on the defensive.

The view moves back, revealing MITSUBI and YAMAGICHI, who, flanked by their staffs, are ranged about the room, listening respectfully as Toyama continues.

TOYAMA. If the American murderers came from Russia, Japan must keep thousands of planes in the air over the Russian border, twenty-four hours a day, week in and week out, on constant alert. On the possibility that they came from a base in China, we must employ more thousands of planes, patrolling every mile of the Chinese frontier. And if they came from an aircraft carrier, we must immobilize important units of our navy, on defensive patrol of our home waters. (*He looks at them, meaningly.*) *The Emperor has charged this court with the responsibility of learning the exact base from which this attack was launched.* I will countenance no political bickering between the army and the navy. (*To Mitsubi*) You are convinced the American planes came from a carrier? (*Mitsubi nods.*) And you, Admiral Yamagichi —you disagree?

YAMAGICHI. I would not so far humiliate either the general or myself. I merely wish your excellency to consider certain facts.

MITSUBI. If it is proved that I am in error, I shall feel that I have falsely accused the imperial navy of negligence, and I shall apologize with my life.

Yamagichi inclines his head in acknowledgment. As he does, a soldier enters and hands Mitsubi a note. He opens it, reads it, then turns to Toyama.

MITSUBI (*to Toyama*). With your excellency's permission, I believe I can produce immediate proof of my contention.

TOYAMA. Proceed.

Mitsubi nods to an aide who goes to the door, opens it, and brings in SABURO GOTO, a frightened man, in the uniform of a sailor in the Japanese navy, who stares around at the impressive assemblage in awe. Mitsubi barks a sharp question at him.

MITSUBI. What is your name?

GOTO. Saburo Goto, excellency.

MITSUBI. You are a sailor in the Japanese navy?

GOTO. Yes, excellency.

MITSUBI. Where were you on the morning of April 18th?

GOTO. On my ship, the Ni-ju-ni-nichi Maru, a converted trawler. We were on patrol eight hundred miles at sea.

MITSUBI. Tell us what happened.

GOTO. We were sunk by an enemy vessel.

MITSUBI. At what time of day was this?

GOTO. Shortly after eight o'clock in the morning.

MITSUBI (*turning triumphantly to Toyama*). I submit, excellency, that the sinking of this man's ship by a carrier at eight o'clock in the morning, would time perfectly with the arrival of the bombers over Tokio at midday.

YAMAGICHI (*interrupting*). One moment, please. (*To Goto*) You have been taught to identify enemy vessels of various types?

GOTO. Yes, excellency.

YAMAGICHI. Describe the type of enemy vessel which sank you.

GOTO. I cannot tell you, excellency.

MITSUBI (*sharply*). Why not?

GOTO. I was below deck in the boiler room when we were hit—and yet was the only survivor.

He says this as if somewhat mystified by the workings of fate, but Yamagichi gestures impatiently.

YAMAGICHI. You did not yourself see the enemy ship?

GOTO. When I came to the surface and recovered consciousness, I saw only the wreckage of our own ship. It was raining and the visibility was poor.

YAMAGICHI (*turning to Toyama*). Your excellency, this man's ship was patrolling an area which the navy has heavily mined. It is not uncommon for a mine to break loose, and sink or damage one of our own vessels. *I* submit that such an accident is far more probable than the presence of an enemy carrier—in a zone which the imperial navy regards as impregnable.

TOYAMA (*after some thought*). I cannot accept this man's testimony as conclusive proof of anything.

MITSUBI (*to Goto*). That is all. You may go.

Mitsubi sits down reflectively as Goto leaves. Admiral Yamagichi turns to one of his aides who hands him a roll of charts.

YAMAGICHI. I have some technical information, excellency, which I consider conclusive proof that the American planes could not have come from a carrier.

He unrolls the charts and pins the first to a chart board which occupies one wall.

As YAMAGICHI pins the chart to the wall, we see it at close range. It is the blueprint of an American B-25 bomber. The next chart he pins up is the blueprint of an American aircraft carrier.

YAMAGICHI. The American planes which bombed Japan have been officially identified as the type known as the B-25 bomber. It has a wingspread of 67 feet, and an overall length of 54 point 1875 feet.

The GROUP, seen at fairly close range, is watching Yamagichi as he makes his various points, indicating the charts with a finger as he does so.

YAMAGICHI. This is the largest type of American aircraft carrier—the Hornet type.

YAMAGICHI, at close view continues his explanation, pointing alternately to the prints of the plane and the carrier.

YAMAGICHI. It has a flight deck which is 809 point 6 feet in length. The presence on this flight deck of sixteen B-25's would reduce the deck space by more than two-thirds—

He draws a line which cuts the deck of the carrier by two-thirds—a heavy crayon line made with a dramatic sweep of the arm.

YAMAGICHI. —making a take-off at sea *mathematically impossible.*

TOYAMA, in a close view, is seen looking sharply at Mitsubi.

TOYAMA. Can you refute these facts?

MITSUBI (*stiffly*). I should like time to examine them.

TOYAMA (*pointedly*). I expect this examination to be completed without delay. (*To both*) *Again, I wish to remind you of the Emperor's personal interest in this matter.* (*Both Mitsubi and Yamagichi bow.*) You are excused, gentlemen.

And the two officers and their staffs start filing out.

[This scene dissolves to the exterior of the PRISON and the COURTYARD viewed from the outside of the yard, toward the huge double gates which are just being opened. On either side of the gates, is a crowd of Japanese civilians. Men, women and children, are gesticulating and shouting and are being held back by armed soldiers. Marching into the yard is a troop of imperial cadets—boys from five to eight years old, under command of a young Japanese infantry lieutenant. As the gates swing open wide, they continue on, marching into the yard until they are completely inside.

JAP LIEUTENANT (*in Japanese*). Halt. (*The cadets halt, and he barks more orders.*) Columns of one. (*This is executed.*) First column—right face. (*This is executed.*) Second column—left face.

This also is executed, and now the cadets stand in two single lines facing one another, forming a lane. The view focused on the cadets shows them awaiting and obeying further orders.

JAP LIEUTENANT (*in Japanese*). First column, eyes right. Second column, eyes left.

All the boys turn their eyes toward the gate. We see now that they are dressed in uniforms which mimic those of adult Japanese soldiers, and that each boy wears at his belt the knife which is given to every Jap boy when he becomes five years old. Following their gaze we see the prison gate, as a huge limousine pulls in, heavily escorted by motorcycle troops. Outside, the crowd breaks through the cordon of soldiers and rushes toward the gates, which soldiers from the inside close in their faces. An officer steps forward and opens the door of the huge car from which emerge the fliers. As they get out of the car, they see the double line of Japanese boys, in front of them; and, against a wall at one side, the dead bodies of two Chinese, which guards are preparing to take away. The firing squad which has executed them, is shouldering arms and marching away.

As the fliers are horror-stricken at the sight of this atrocity, Ross decides to try to lift the spirits of his men, and grins at them, a bit wryly, as he indicates the Japanese cadets.

ROSS. Well, fellows, looks like we're going to be Exhibit A for the rising sons of—the rising sun.

OFFICER (*sharply, to Ross*). You walk. Slow.

Ross, alone, starts for the double row of boys, the view moving with him.

As he walks between these rows of Japanese boys, he looks down at them and smiles, following which we see a row of cadets' faces, some of them wearing heavy glasses, as Ross marches between the rows. They eye him malevolently.—Then Ross is about to pass from view, and behind him comes Greenbaum, the second of the fliers to walk the gauntlet. Greenbaum is looking at the kids with amusement.—All of them are seen looking at big Greenie with hate and blood lust in their eyes.—Then Greenbaum, seen at close range, stops suddenly in his tracks, whirls on one row of cadets, and shouts at them, unexpectedly.

GREENBAUM. Boo!

The cadets leap backward in alarm, several of them almost falling, as Greenbaum, chuckling, continues on his way. The Jap officer screams at him in Japanese. In the background, then, we see Vincent starting through the gauntlet.

The JAIL CORRIDOR comes into view disclosing the cell block which is in three tiers. The fliers are brought in and marched up a spiral stairway to the second tier.—This cuts to the CATWALK of the second tier of CELLS as the fliers march to a tank cell at one end. As they reach it, Ross, Greenbaum, Clinton and Vincent halt at the left side of the door. Bayforth, Canelli, Stoner and Skvoznik step to the right side of the door. One of the soldiers barks an order, in bad English.

JAP SOLDIER (*pointing to their feet*). Shoe. Take off shoe.

The fliers begin removing their shoes and placing them in a row in front of the cell. One of Vincent's shoes sticks a little. He gives it an unusually hard pull and it flies off and out of his hand, rolling almost to the edge of the catwalk. He breaks ranks to retrieve it. As he bends over to pick it up, one of the soldiers reverses his rifle and clips Vincent on the chin with the gun butt, knocking him down. Vincent staggers to his feet, and the soldier back-slaps him across the face. Other soldiers promptly close in with their bayonets, holding the fliers motionless, as they attempt to leap to Vincent's assistance. —A close view shows VINCENT getting to his feet, his face contorted with pain, and then we see the JAP SOLDIER grinning triumphantly at Vincent. He tosses a remark to his comrades over his shoulder in Japanese.

JAP SOLDIER (*laughing, in Japanese*). That will teach him a lesson!

The FLIERS taut with suppressed fury, start filing into the cell and this cuts to a JAPANESE LISTENING ROOM where a technician is listening at a small loud-speaker, which is connected with the boys' cell. Through this speaker can be heard the boys entering the cell below, throwing themselves upon mattresses. We also hear Vincent's gasping as he tries to regain his breath, and his infuriated voice.

VINCENT'S VOICE. I'm going to kill one of those—

His next word is lost in a loud clang as the cell door is slammed shut and locked. We pick up the tail end of Vincent's speech.

VINCENT'S VOICE. —if it's the last thing I ever do!]

This cuts to the FLIERS' CELL, littered with thin mattresses and thinner quilts which are the only bedding. In one corner a large bucket filled with water provides the only toilet facilities. The fliers disperse themselves around the cell, some flopping onto mattresses, others sitting with their backs against the wall, still others pacing restlessly.

SKVOZNIK. You know, I've been thinking and thinking, and I can't figure out what made that monkey say we came from an aircraft carrier.

Greenbaum, whose attention has been attracted to something apparently high on the wall, whirls suddenly on Skvoznik.

GREENBAUM. He was just trying to get the navy's goat, you dope.

Greenbaum pantomimes that there is a microphone concealed in the cell, and then we see the JAPANESE LISTENING ROOM: a Japanese military technician sits at a table on which is a small loud-speaker, obviously connected with the cell. Coming from the speaker is the unintelligible sound of whispers. The Jap places his ear close to the speaker and turns it up to full volume to decipher the whisper. Instead, out of the radio comes a loud blast.

SKVOZNIK'S VOICE (*surprised*). YEAH?

GREENBAUM'S VOICE. YEAH!

The blast almost shatters the Jap's ear drums, and he recoils from the radio set with an alacrity which almost upsets his chair.

This cuts to the FLIERS' CELL, where Skvoznik has crossed to the cell door and calls to the guard, who paces by outside.

SKVOZNIK. Hey! Mr. Moto, when do we eat?

The guard continues on without responding. Skvoznik turns to the others, woebegone.

SKVOZNIK. I'm as hungry as the guy who wanted to eat Charley Chaplin in *The Gold Rush.*

ROSS (*grinning*). That's why they made us take off our shoes—afraid we'd eat them.

SKVOZNIK (*taking a notch in his belt*). I'm not kidding. You guys are starting to look like chickens to me. (*He eyes Greenbaum speculatively.*) Click, click.

GREENBAUM (*pretending alarm*). Captain Ross!

The fliers roar with laughter as Skvoznik chases Greenbaum around and Greenbaum pretends to be a chicken.

In the CELL, the fliers whisper to each other and pass the word down the line to Ross.

FLIERS. There's a microphone up there—they can hear what you say . . .

Suddenly the rattling of an iron door is heard, and a view of the ADJOINING CELL discloses MOY LING pressing close to the cell wall on which he has been knocking with his fist. He calls to Ross in the next cell.

MOY LING. It is I, Moy Ling.

In the FLIERS' CELL the boys react to Moy Ling's presence.

ROSS. It's our Chinese friend! Gentlemen, I propose that we elect him an honorary member of our squadron. All in favor, say aye.

FLIERS (*roaring it out like a resounding cheer*). AYE!

ROSS (*smiling*). Did you hear that, Moy Ling?

A closeup shows Ling's eyes lighting up, and he straightens proudly.

MOY LING. Yes, my captain. (*He pauses wistfully.*) I wish to explain why I did not act sooner than I did. It required much time to decide to kill my own father.

The fliers stand silently, awed by Moy's simple speech, then look in the direction of the corridor from which comes the sound of a cell door opening.—It is Moy's cell which is being opened by a guard, accompanied by two soldiers. They lead him out and march him down the corridor past the door to the fliers' cell. As they pass on out of sight, attention is focussed on the FLIERS' CELL: Ross looks through the bars.

ROSS (*in deep appreciation*). I'd have him on my team, any time. . . .

[A Japanese attendant pushes a perambulator into view. On it is a bucket of rice and a stack of small wooden bowls. He begins dishing out rice into the bowls.—The fliers react in pleased surprise at the thought of food.

SKVOZNIK. Chow!

GREENBAUM. Mess call!

The men line up—Ross, Vincent, Bayforth and Greenbaum in one line Skvoznik, Canelli, Stoner and Clinton in the other.—And then we get a close view of them at the door as the attendant hands a bowl of rice to Ross, who passes it back. The attendant hands another bowl to Skvoznik, who hands it back. The view moves back as the two rice bowls are handed back until they reach Greenbaum and Clinton. Greenbaum looks at his bowl, disgusted.

GREENBAUM. Rice!

Dubiously he tastes a small morsel of it, then notices Clinton looking at him meaningly.

GREENBAUM (*defensively*). Okay! So I'm a liar!

They eat, although obviously without much relish. Stoner is eating his rice suspiciously.

STONER. According to Jonathan Swift, it was a courageous man who first ate an oyster. What would Swift call me if I ate this?

ROSS. A scavenger.

SKVOZNIK. Not only is it terrible, but there's not enough of it.

CANELLI (*philosophically*). It will probably keep body and soul together.

BAYFORTH. Which explains why the Japanese have no souls.

SKVOZNIK (*woefully as he finishes his rice and holds up his empty bowl*). Look! Two mouthfuls and it's all gone.

Ross, under the guise of kidding, but actually sympathetic for the big fellow, crosses to where Skvoznik sits on the floor, and places before Skvoznik his own bowl in which a little rice remains.

ROSS (*to the others*). Bring your leavings to our starving comrade, gents. (*Like a barker*) Give until it hurts. Every little bit helps. Small contributions thankfully received. Step right up and leave your contributions. The Japs are not going to starve Jan Skvoznik.

The other fliers are placing their bowls in a row before Skvoznik. Various quantities of rice remain in each bowl.

ROSS. If they do, it'll be over our dead bodies.

GREENBAUM. Mind you, captain, it's not that I begrudge him the food out of my own mouth, but if this happens every meal, it *will* be over our dead bodies.

Skvoznik is happily stuffing himself from the remaining bowls, stacking them as he empties them.

SKVOZNIK (*mouth full*). Gee, thanks, fellows. Sure you don't want it?]

The guard now appears, unlocks and opens the door of the FLIERS' CELL.

GUARD. Captain Ross?

ROSS. Yes?

GUARD. You come.—(*In Japanese*) Shoes!

Ross goes back, slips on his shoes and gets his coat.

ROSS. Well, boys, I'll see you again. Soon—I hope.

The others nod in acknowledgment, and Ross is led out, the guard locking the door behind him. The fliers cluster at the door, peering anxiously down the corridor as Ross is led away, each busy with his own thoughts.

The scene cuts to MITSUBI'S OFFICE, large, high-ceilinged, severely furnished. There are chairs around the walls, and in the center of the room is a long conference table. A door opens at one side and Ross is ushered in by a soldier.

SOLDIER. You wait.

Before Ross can answer, he closes the door and Ross is left quite alone. He stands undecided for a moment, then sits down on the edge of one of the chairs. This does not look so terrifying, he decides, yet he is alert, every sense straining for some indication of danger. But as he sits undisturbed and nothing happens, he relaxes a little, purses his lips and begins whistling a soft, tuneless cowboy whistle, such as a cowboy might make when riding along alone. Presently his attention is attracted by the sound of a door opening. Ross turns, and into the room comes KARL KEPPEL, of the Swiss Red Cross. Keppel is an earnest, sincere man of about fifty, his appearance typically that of a career diplomat. Ross looks at him in surprise, glad to see a white man, but still on guard. Keppel hurries to him excitedly.

KEPPEL (*breathless*). Captain Ross?

ROSS. Yes, sir.

KEPPEL. At last! My name is Keppel —Karl Keppel of the Swiss Red Cross.

ROSS (*beaming—shaking hands*). Well, now, I'm *mighty* glad to see you, sir.

KEPPEL. And *I* to see you. Ever since I learned you Americans were captured I have been trying desperately to reach you, but nobody would admit knowing anything about you— where you were, or what had happened to you. I would still be cooling my heels in somebody's office if it had not been for General Mitsubi.

At the mention of Mitsubi's name, Ross' face falls and he eyes Keppel suspiciously.

ROSS. Mr. Keppel, may I see your credentials?

KEPPEL (*surprised*). Captain Ross!

ROSS. We're charged with murder, Mr. Keppel. General Mitsubi is a star witness for the prosecution.

KEPPEL (*fishing for his papers*). Murder? You are on trial?

ROSS (*sarcastically*). In a civilian criminal court, *Mr. Keppel*. They say we bombed and machine-gunned civilians and are not entitled to be considered prisoners of war.

Keppel produces his credentials and hands them to Ross.

KEPPEL (*indignantly*). I will get word to Washington immediately! They will take steps to stop this outrage!

Ross examines Keppel's credentials, and his suspicions are removed. He returns the credentials, smiling.

ROSS. Forgive me for being suspicious, Mr. Keppel—but you see the spot we're in.

KEPPEL (*pocketing his credentials*). I do indeed, and I shall do everything in my power to help you. I will come again and report my progress. Meanwhile, captain, goodbye and good luck to you and your men.

ROSS (*emotionally*). Thank you, sir.

Keppel smiles and starts for the door, but as he reaches it, it opens and Mitsubi enters. He bows and smiles to Keppel.

MITSUBI. Um—could you spare *me* a moment, Mr. Keppel?

KEPPEL. I am at your service, General.

MITSUBI (*taking his arm and strolling him to the table*). Captain Ross no doubt told you of the charges against him and his men?

KEPPEL. Yes, sir, he did.

MITSUBI. Tell me—Mr. Keppel—in your opinion can Washington force us to drop these charges?

KEPPEL. It most certainly can—and will. Remember, there are over a hundred thousand Japanese nationals in internment camps in the United States.

MITSUBI. Thank you very much, Mr. Keppel. Your observations are most interesting. If there is anything further I can do for you, don't hesitate to call upon me.

He bows. Keppel nods and leaves. Mitsubi turns to Ross.

MITSUBI. Sit down, please.

Mitsubi turns and leans against the table, studying Ross, who sits down and watches him narrowly.

MITSUBI. Ever been in California, Captain?

ROSS. Lots of times.

MITSUBI. Recently?

ROSS (*with a shy smile*). Now look here, General, I aim to be as obliging as I can under the circumstances, but you're a soldier and an officer, and you know as well as I do that I can't answer any questions. So to save time and wear and tear on both of us, I suggest we skip it.

MITSUBI (*after a moment*). I admire your frankness, Captain. I was only *curious* about Santa Barbara. I lived there for some time. Worked on a fishing boat.

ROSS (*smiling*). And charted every inch of water from San Diego to Seattle.

MITSUBI (*smiling*). Those charts will be useful some day.

ROSS (*still trying to be pleasant and make the best of it*). Don't bet on it, General.

MITSUBI (*after a moment*). Perhaps you do not believe Japan will win the war?

ROSS. Me and 140,000,000 others.

MITSUBI. You still doubt it? After Singapore? Hong Kong? The Indies? Thailand? May I remind you, Captain—in five months we have changed from a "have not" nation to the world's largest "have" nation. We control sixty-five percent of the world's tin, eighty-five percent of the world's copper, ninety percent of the world's rubber. And in the conquered areas alone, we have four hundred million workers developing these resources.

ROSS. We have a few resources, too. The bombing of Japan was rather resourceful, don't you think?

Mitsubi sits on the edge of the desk, staring at Ross complacently.

MITSUBI. A mere token raid, Captain. (*He looks at Ross sharply.*) Our important buildings have been constructed to withstand any catastrophe.

ROSS. Makes it tough on the little guys who live in the paper houses, doesn't it, General?

MITSUBI. Don't depend upon a panic among our people. They are conditioned to shock. Our earthquakes have been valuable in *that* respect. (*He rises and looks at Ross earnestly.*) No, Captain. Japan is united in this war, through Emperor worship and—(*his eyes narrowing*)—hate for all foreigners, white or otherwise. The Japanese will win. He wears wood fiber clothes, cardboard shoes; he cheerfully eats one-third of his usual diet; he works fourteen hours a day, seven days a week. (*His eyes gleam.*) And our soldiers—ask your troops at Bataan. We do not leave any place that we want. You must kill us. We will win this war because *we are willing to sacrifice ten million lives!* (*He smiles.*) How many lives is the white man willing to sacrifice? (*Ross returns Mitsubi's stare unemotionally.*)

ROSS (*after a long pause*). Your figures sound mighty impressive. From all I've heard, your soldiers fight like cornered rats—no offense, General! But I still can't answer your questions.

MITSUBI (*with a change of attack*). Tell me, Captain Ross—do you share Mr. Keppel's opinion? Do you believe your government can help you?

ROSS. I don't know. I don't know what to think. All I know, is that if you do anything to us, the people back home aren't going to forget it.

MITSUBI. Would it surprise you to learn that I thoroughly agree with Mr. Keppel? Washington *will* act as soon as they receive the news. But—

ROSS (*looking at him grimly*). But—will Washington receive the news? Is that what you mean?

MITSUBI. That depends upon you—and me. If you will tell the *truth* and admit that you came from a carrier, I will permit Mr. Keppel's message to go through to Washington. (*Ross looks at Mitsubi for some time before replying.*)

ROSS (*finally*). Even if I trusted you, General, my orders forbid me to tell anything but my name, rank and serial number. And I don't trust you.

MITSUBI (*inclining his head slightly*). Very well. That's your decision.

He presses a button on the desk. A door opens and a soldier enters. Mitsubi signals for the soldier to take Ross away. Ross starts out, but as he reaches the door, the door on the opposite side of the room opens and a soldier leads Skvoznik into the room. Skvoznik reacts to the sight of Ross.

SKVOZNIK. Captain Ross, sir!

Ross whirls, sees him, and his face tightens. Then his eyes go to Mitsubi.

MITSUBI. You see, Captain Ross, you are not my only prisoner. Must I remind you that a chain is no stronger than its weakest link?

Ross does not answer, merely stands there looking at him.

MITSUBI. Is there anything you wish to say to your comrade before you go?

Ross looks from Mitsubi to Skvoznik, then back again. The implications in Mitsubi's threat are quite clear. This is to be the beginning of torture! He can save Skvoznik by talking—but he can save the HORNET by not talking. He looks back to Mitsubi as Skvoznik watches anxiously.

ROSS. I have *nothing* to say.

Skvoznik's face relaxes into a defiant grin. Mitsubi turns to the soldier guarding Ross.

MITSUBI. Return him to his cell.

The soldier leads Ross out, closing the door.

MITSUBI (*to Skvoznik*). Sit down, please. (*The guard closes the door.*)

The scene cuts to the FLIERS' CELL. The boys are pacing up and down like caged animals, waiting for the return of either Skvoznik or Ross as we hear the sound of approaching footsteps. The boys instantly lie down, or sit down, or crouch on their hams. The guard opens the door to admit Ross who removes his shoes before entering. The boys wait until the door is closed and locked and the guard has resumed his pacing before anyone speaks. Clinton finally breaks the silence.

CLINTON. They took Skvoznik.

ROSS. I know. He was brought into Mitsubi's office.

GREENBAUM. What's going on up there?

ROSS. Mitsubi wants to know where our bombers came from. If Skvoznik doesn't tell, he'll keep after us one by one.

VINCENT. Skvoznik wouldn't tell. I know the guy. He'd die first!

STONER. He's strong as an ox. He worked every summer as an iron puddler—right alongside his old man.

GREENBAUM. Boy, was he tough on a football field—

CLINTON. Sure, he made All-American.

CANELLI. Best game he ever played, he played with three broken ribs. They won't get anything out of him —he'll take all they've got.

As he says this, we suddenly hear the sound of a squad of men marching up outside the prison. A voice calls in Japanese.

VOICE (*in Japanese*). Squad halt. (*The marchers halt.*) Ready. (*The click of rifles*) Aim. (*A pause*) Fire!

There is a staccato burst of rifle fire. During all this, the fliers stand tense, frozen to silence, horrified at the thought that the victim of that firing squad has been Skvoznik. Outside, we hear the firing squad marching away. Shaken, trembling, the fliers sink to the floor, some lying, some sitting, others crouching.

CLINTON (*biting his lips*). Do you suppose that was—Skvoznik?

ROSS. I don't know—I don't know what to think—we'll just have to wait—and see. . . .

The boys speak in whispers, as if almost talking to themselves. They all rush to the bars of the cell to look out, —all but Clinton. Ross stops and comes back to stand beside him.

ROSS. Scared, kid?

CLINTON. I wonder if we can take it —all the way, I mean?

ROSS (*remembering Mitsubi*). I wonder.

CLINTON. It's the fear of being afraid that frightens me more than anything else.

ROSS. Just remember what the old man told you—fear has nothing to do with cowardice—a fellow is only yellow when he lets his fear make him quit. I had it so bad when we took off—my hands were shaking, my heart was pounding so loud I thought everybody could hear it. If I was alone and nobody around, I don't know whether or not I could have made it. And now we'd better change the subject.

Ross goes to the background and sits down. Clinton walks past the others and stands by Greenbaum, who places his arm around his shoulder. The scene fades out.

PART TWO

The ANTEROOM to the PRISON CELLS fades in as footsteps and a bell are heard. Feet start coming down the circular staircase that leads down to the anteroom, and the view moves with MITSUBI as he walks down the steps.—He goes to the Guard at the gate in the background: The Guard opens the door and Mitsubi walks on as the door is closed. This cuts to the CORRIDOR between the prison cells and we see him walking past them and looking down at the men asleep. In succession, we see Vincent asleep on the floor; Clinton turning on his mattress; Greenbaum and Stoner; Bayforth, with others in the background; Ross, seen close.

ROSS' VOICE (*as he turns in his sleep*). Pilot to navigator—pilot to navigator—Roger—Roger—Roger.

We hear the hissing and pounding of waves, then the subdued rumble of airplane motors being warmed up and the occasional screech of a bosun's whistle. To this is added the ad lib of excited, ethereal voices.

VOICES. Army pilots, man your planes . . . Army pilots, man your planes . . . Take off now? Why! We're not due to take off for thirty-six hours . . . Got to do it now, that Jap trawler saw us. She may have radioed Tokio before we hit her . . . So long, kid, see you in Chungking . . . Thanks for the ride, sailor, we'll do as much for you sometime.

Now another voice breaks in, sharp, peremptory, commanding.

SECOND VOICE. Attention, men!

The other voices become quiet, although in the background the airplane motors continue to warm up.

SECOND VOICE. If any of you are forced down, destroy your ship at once. We don't want to take any chance on the Japs tracing you back to this carrier. Whatever the cost, *protect the Hornet!*

Other voices instantly pick up the last line, repeating it over and over in an exciting crescendo.

VOICES. Protect the Hornet! Protect the Hornet! Protect the Hornet!

Over this now comes the crashing thunder of a bomber taking off, then another, and another, as the voices continue to chant "Protect the Hornet." Slowly the montage of sound dies away, leaving Ross staring around the cell at his men. After another moment, and Mitsubi's disembodied voice (in Ross' thoughts) intrudes, softly, almost gently.

MITSUBI'S VOICE. Must I remind you, Captain, a chain is no stronger than its weakest link? Weakest link—weakest link.

Mitsubi's shadow moves across Ross' face as Mitsubi takes a few steps along the cell unseen. Ross opens his eyes and looks around. He raises himself up on his elbow.—This cuts to a close view of MITSUBI standing outside the cell, looking down at Ross. He drops the cigarette he is smoking.—This cuts to ROSS, seen close, as he looks toward Mitsubi.—Then we see MITSUBI turning and starting to leave; and after this, ROSS, whose eyes follow Mitsubi. He starts to rise.—He moves across the cell over the sleeping men, stops at the bars, and looks after the retreating Mitsubi as the scene fades out.

Then the CENSOR'S OFFICE fades in. It is night. Keppel enters and goes to a Japanese attaché who is at work behind a counter. Several other attachés are seen at work in the background, although the office is not large.

KEPPEL. My name is Keppel—of the Swiss Red Cross. I would like to see Mr. Oraki.

ATTACHÉ (*courteously*). Concerning what, please?

KEPPEL (*producing a sheet of paper*). He would not approve this message. I have revised it according to his suggestions.

ATTACHÉ (*taking the paper*). Thank you. I will call it to his attention. Please return tomorrow.

KEPPEL. But this message must be sent *now!* At once!

ATTACHÉ (*apologetically*). So sorry. It will take time.

KEPPEL (*indignantly*). Time! Time! That is one thing I cannot spare!

ATTACHÉ (*regretfully*). If you wish to file a complaint, may I suggest that you contact the honorable *Minister* of Intelligence?

Keppel stares at him furiously, and realizes he is up against a stone wall.

KEPPEL. Thank you. I shall!

He turns and leaves as the view draws in to hold the ATTACHÉ in a close view. As the door is heard opening, the attaché tears up the message and throws the pieces into a waste basket.

This cuts to the COURTROOM at the rear doors. Admiral Yamagichi and his staff are entering, and Santos has joined the other correspondents at their table. As Yamagichi and his staff reach their places, they bow to General Mitsubi and his staff, who have entered and are just taking their places. The army punctiliously returns the navy's bows. The CLERK'S VOICE is heard booming.

CLERK'S VOICE. The judges of this court will now exercise their powers in accordance with the law, and by authority of the emperor. Up! Stand! Everybody! Up! Stand!

The entire courtroom comes to its feet as the three judges, the procurator and his police escort enter, bow to the flag, then to each other, and sit down. Everyone else sits down.—Now a fairly close view shows the JUDGES' PLATFORM as Toyama nods to the clerk, who turns and calls out to someone not in sight.

CLERK. Bring in the defendants.

We then see the PRISONERS' DOOR as the soldiers open it and one of them calls into the corridor.

SOLDIER (*in Japanese*). Bring in the defendants.

His voice echoes back through the corridor, and we hear the shuffling of feet far back out of sight. The view moves back and forth until it is holding the door in a close view as the first American enters. This is Ross. Behind him come Vincent, Bayforth, Greenbaum, Clinton, Stoner and Canelli. We see the face of each man as he comes out, and notice that Skvoznik is missing! Also, we see in the faces of the others a drawn, anxious look while at the CORRESPONDENTS' TABLE Santos is looking in the direction of the prisoners in surprise.

SANTOS. Today there are only seven!

Johana, her eyes gleaming with emotional tension, looks up at him with an innocent smile.

JOHANA. Perhaps one is indisposed.

The clerk's voice is again heard at this point.

CLERK'S VOICE. You may be seated.

Attention is focused on the PRISONERS' BOX as the boys sit down. They are looking around for some sign of Skvoznik, their apprehension growing by the second as they realize he is not in the room.

TOYAMA is now seen closely as he looks toward General Mitsubi.

TOYAMA. General Mitsubi.

A close view shows MITSUBI rising to his feet with Yamagichi and his staff in the background watching with interest.

MITSUBI. With your excellency's permission, I should like to question one of the prisoners.

TOYAMA. Proceed.

MITSUBI (*calling out*). Sergeant Jan Skvoznik.

Sakai instantly and unexpectedly gets to his feet.

SAKAI (*to Toyama*). I wish to apologize to the court for the absence of this defendant. He became ill during the night. I must request that he be excused from further testimony.

MITSUBI (*sarcastically*). I am deeply touched by Mr. Sakai's concern for his client.

A fairly close view of the FLIERS shows their faces ashen with concern for Skvoznik's safety as Mitsubi's voice is again heard.

MITSUBI'S VOICE. However, I have only a few questions which I am sure will not inconvenience this poor, sick American.

MITSUBI (*seen, as he continues*). I have taken the liberty of having him brought here.

TOYAMA (*rebukingly to Sakai*). This court has no patience with malingering. (*To Mitsubi*) You may question the witness.

MITSUBI (*bowing*). Thank you, excellency.

CLERK (*in Japanese*). Bring him in.

The PRISONERS come into view with attention focused on the prisoners' door. They look anxiously at the door as a guard opens it and calls inside.

GUARD (*in Japanese*). Bring him in.

A moving view shows the FLIERS looking off toward the door through which Skvoznik must enter. On their faces we see fear for their comrade and an agonizing suspense. They would show hope, but they know there is none. From the corridor comes the sound of slow halting footsteps coming closer and closer, while our attention is directed to the PRISONERS' DOOR as two soldiers lead Skvoznik into the room, each grasping him by an elbow. There are no marks of violence on the big fellow, no scars or bruises, but his face is ashen white with a sickly, sickening pallor of one already dead. In his eyes we see the lack of consciousness-of-being which is customary in idiots. His lips are parted in a pathetic half smile, the last smile of hurt and bewilderment, as if in his last lucid moment he was wondering, wistfully, "Why would they do this?"—This cuts to the FLIERS, their eyes widening in horror. One or two of them half rise but are pushed back into their seats by soldiers.

The CORRESPONDENTS show their reaction to this spectacle: In the eyes of Johana and Toma is the lustful brilli ance of a bull-fight spectator watching the dying throes of a gallant bull whose mighty strength has been shattered by torture.—This cuts to the WITNESS BOX as the soldiers lead Skvoznik to the box and assist him into it. Mitsubi strides into view purposefully and faces him.

MITSUBI. State your name.

A close view shows Skvoznik staring at Mitsubi as if he had not heard or, as if hearing, he had not understood.

SKVOZNIK (*trying to answer, his voice an almost indistinguishable mumble*). Name—name—?

Next MITSUBI and SKVOZNIK are seen together as Mitsubi prompts him, the fliers appearing in the background.

MITSUBI. Your name is Jan Skvoznik?

SKVOZNIK. Skvoznik? Skvoznik—

The FLIERS are wrenched by an almost physical torture at the sight of the tragic figure of their comrade. Canelli, his face working with emotion, is unable to endure any more. He leaps to his feet, crying out wildly.

CANELLI. Stop it! You fiends! *Stop it!*

The entire courtroom looks at Canelli, who cries out again, in the agony of his emotion.

CANELLI. Look at him! Sick! He was never sick a day in his life! That's what *they've* done to him—the dirty, crawling—

A close view shows TOYAMA slapping the desk with the flat of his hand angrily.

TOYAMA. Silence!

CANELLI, now seen close, whirls and faces the correspondents.

CANELLI. If you are newspapermen, why do you sit there?—Why don't you rush out of here—scream the shame of this from every headline— (*A soldier rushes toward him.*) —from every radio—

The soldier hits Canelli on the head with his gun, knocking him to the floor. Other soldiers seize Canelli and start dragging him out.—At this, Vincent vaults out of the box and with two mighty blows knocks the two soldiers unconscious. But other soldiers rush from their places at the wall and at bayonet point force the other fliers to remain where they are. The entire courtroom is in an uproar.

A close view shows the CLERK doing a veritable devil's dance of fury, brandishing his skinny fists and screeching unintelligibly in Japanese, while TOYAMA appears standing erect, terrible in his wrath, shouting for order.

TOYAMA. Order! Order!

The COURTROOM is seen in full view as Vincent and Canelli are dragged out and the other fliers, persuaded by bayonets, sit down, their eyes blazing their fury.—Then TOYAMA, seen close, stares out over the courtroom as quiet is restored. He looks toward the correspondents.

TOYAMA. I will instruct the correspondents to ignore this fanatical outburst which was staged with the obvious purpose of enlisting your sympathies.

The CORRESPONDENTS are seen looking toward Toyama, whose voice comes over.

TOYAMA'S VOICE. This court is endeavoring to present the facts fairly and impartially despite the ghastly nature of the crime of which the prisoners are guilty.

We then see TOYAMA looking from the correspondents toward the fliers.

TOYAMA. However, the temper of the court is being severely tried by the persistent misconduct of the defendants.

At this Greenbaum half rises to his feet, but Ross pulls him back.

TOYAMA (*speaking more sternly, as a result of Greenbaum's move*). I will warn them now that any future demonstrations will be dealt with more firmly. (*He turns to Mitsubi.*) Proceed with the testimony, General Mitsubi.

The JUDGES are now seen as Mitsubi faces them: They are reacting to a sudden off-stage noise and exchanging curious glances.—We get a full view of the COURTROOM as Mitsubi starts to address the court. But as he does, the crowd noises off-stage are suddenly joined by a clamor of whistles and bells. The judges and Mitsubi look irritably toward the windows, and as they do the judges' door opens and an attaché hurries and crosses quickly to the clerk and hands him a note.

The clerk opens the note, and reacts in tremendous astonishment, and leaps to his feet. The view moves with him to the judges' bench where he hands the note to Toyama with an obsequious bow. Toyama looks at him in annoyance, accepts the note, reads it, and instantly comes to his feet, his eyes glistening. He hands the note to his associate judges who read it, and also get to their feet.—The entire courtroom is puzzled by the strange actions of the judges. Their amazement grows as the judges, without a word, leave their benches and file out of the courtroom, and the CLERK, seen closely, snatches off his cap, waves it excitedly, and screeches loudly.

CLERK. Banzai! Banzai! Corregidor has fallen! Corregidor has fallen!

A fairly close view of the FLIERS shows their reaction to this calamitous news.

CLERK'S VOICE. The Philippines are ours! Banzai! Banzai!

The COURTROOM goes wild with the joy of victory.—JOHANA and TOMA embrace in delight; and the soldiers around the walls toss their caps and shout "Banzai! Banzai!"—Mitsubi, Yamagichi and their staffs draw their swords and start doing a wild samurai sword dance. Mitsubi goes to the prisoners' box. He stands looking at them, smiling, while behind them, on the wall, we see the shadows of the officers doing the wild, fanatical, samurai dance with hysterical yells and screeches coming over the shot. Mitsubi turns and looks back at the celebrating officers. The fliers follow the direction of his gaze.

MITSUBI (*turning to them, grinning*). What do you think of your illustrious General MacArthur *now*? He escaped capture by *running away!*

ROSS. Don't be too disappointed, General. You'll meet him again.

MITSUBI. You approve of his action?

ROSS. Whole-heartedly. It was realistic.

MITSUBI. I think so, too. It is a wise man who knows where courage ends and stupidity begins.

ROSS. I get it.

MITSUBI. General MacArthur abandoned Corregidor when he saw defense was useless. Yet you stupidly insist on protecting the carrier from which you came—when it no longer needs your protection.

ROSS. General MacArthur undoubtedly received orders to leave. Our orders remain unchanged. I imagine he found his orders as difficult to obey as we find ours.

Mitsubi looks at the men for a long minute and sees no hope of persuading them to talk. Finally he nods.

MITSUBI. As you wish. (*To the guards*) Remove the prisoners.

A wider view shows the fliers being led out of the courtroom, and around them the samurai sword dance rises to a new fury.

The scene dissolves to the interior of a JAP DRINKING PLACE. In the street outside we can hear the celebrating Japanese. The door opens and Santos enters with Keppel. Through the open door we can see Jap crowds on the street outside, hysterical in their celebration. Some of them are brandishing fists toward Santos and Keppel and yelling wildly.

Santos and Keppel, badly frightened, close the door, glad to be out of the dangerous crowd. Santos looks off, sees what he wants, and nods to Keppel, who follows him to a SMALL TABLE where Siva, the Portuguese correspondent, and Voroshevski, the Russian, are seated over a bottle of sherry. Siva is unhappy.

SIVA. Twice, within an hour, I narrowly escaped with my life. The Japanese treat me as if I am an enemy.

VOROSHEVSKI (*surprised*). Of course, Siva! To them, Portugal and Russia are neutral enemies, Germany and Italy are friendly enemies, and England and America are belligerent enemies. The Japanese draw a very fine distinction.

Now Santos and Keppel reach the two men.

SANTOS. Good afternoon—comrades.

Voroshevski and Siva do a double-take and look up. Voroshevski glowers at Santos.

VOROSHEVSKI. Why aren't you celebrating the Axis victory?

SANTOS (*uncomfortably*). You both know Mr. Keppel of the Swiss Red Cross.

SIVA. Of course.

VOROSHEVSKI. How are you, Mr. Keppel? (*Insistently, to Santos*) Why aren't you celebrating the victory?

SANTOS. I have turned in my credentials. I have resigned my position. I am thoroughly ashamed.

Voroshevski instantly becomes the soul of hospitality.

VOROSHEVSKI. Won't you gentlemen join us? (*Keppel and Santos sit down.*)

KEPPEL. Thank you, thank you.

SANTOS. Mr. Keppel has a favor to ask. I will let him tell his own story. He needs help desperately.

KEPPEL. The thing is, I'm trying to get a message to Washington, but every—

And at this the scene dissolves to the interior of the JAP LISTENING ROOM. It is early evening, and Mitsubi and the Japanese operator are listening at the loud speaker which connects with the boys' cell. Faintly we hear Skvoznik groaning almost imperceptibly. Then we hear the regular, rhythmic footsteps of the guard pacing the iron catwalk outside the cell. Through this sound the scene dissolves to the CATWALK outside the cells where the guard, pacing his station, passes the fliers' cell. As he passes the door to their cell, we get a glimpse of the interior. Low key lighting in the corridor casts skeletal shadows over the fliers. Skvoznik lies on a mattress in a corner. Ross squats beside him, and Greenbaum leans over Ross' shoulder anxiously. The others, Stoner, Clinton and Bayforth are sprawled around on their mattresses.

GREENBAUM. How is he?

ROSS. The same. He'll always be the same, I guess.

STONER (*tensely, indicating Canelli's empty mattress*). What about Canelli? (*He indicates Vincent's mattress.*) And Vincent? That's what I want to know.

ROSS (*quietly*). Take it easy, Stoner.

STONER. It's night—and they're not back yet—

ROSS (*comfortingly*). Well, whatever is happening to them, at least we know they haven't talked. That's one thing.

Back in the LISTENING ROOM—Mitsubi and the operator are still listening. Mitsubi gestures in disgust and presses a button. A soldier enters.

MITSUBI (*in Japanese*). Return the two *Americans* to their cells.

This cuts to a full view of the FLIERS' CELL: Ross is still squatting beside Skvoznik, watching for some sign of improvement which of course does not come. Skvoznik continues to stare blankly into space. The other boys are crouched around counting the seconds, waiting for the return of Vincent and Canelli. Somewhere, far offscene, a door rasps as it is unlocked. After what seems an eternity, it clangs shut. Approaching footsteps sound on the iron catwalk. Slowly, the boys half rise to their feet, not knowing what to expect or fear. Shadows appear on the wall outside, then the figures of some soldiers, half supporting Canelli, whose right arm is in a sling and carrying Vincent, who is unconscious, on a stretcher. The fliers stare silently as the soldiers unlock the door and shove Canelli into the cell. Two other soldiers carry Vincent's unconscious body in and dump him unceremoniously on a mattress. Too horror-stricken to move, the fliers stare at Canelli and Vincent. Greenbaum regains his senses long enough to rush at the soldiers, intending to strangle one or both of them, crying "What did you do to him—just let me out." But the guard slaps him, slams the door in his face and locks it. Greenbaum stands quivering with frustrated fury, then turns and crosses to where the others are clustered around Vincent.—We then see Ross examining Vincent, the others watching. Ross looks up.

ROSS. He's alive. That's about all.

The others straighten, shaking their heads in futile sympathy. They turn to where Canelli is seated on the floor, his face drawn with pain. His right arm is broken, and hangs in a sling.

GREENBAUM. What'd they do to you, kid?

CANELLI (*attempting a smile*). What you see.

This cuts to a semi-close view of CANELLI and BAYFORTH seated on the floor, the other fliers behind them.

CANELLI (*looking around at them wistfully*). I intended to continue studying art if I came through this war. The way things look, I guess I'll have to change my plans. Don't mind so much but it's sure gonna be tough on my folks. From the first moment I drew a three-legged cow with a crayon, my father dreamed of a second Michelangelo. Together with my mother, he saved every penny for years to send me to Italy to study.

When the day came for me to go, Italy was in the war, and on the wrong side. I could not go—and I could not stay, either. I had said goodbye to too many people. You know how it is. So I went to New York. "There are fine schools there," I told my parents. Instead, I enlisted. I wanted to fight the thing that had spoiled my father's dream. As far as he knows, I'm still in New York, painting beautiful pictures. I'm glad.—How's Vincent?

The GROUP OF FLIERS are seen at close view: they are deeply touched by Canelli's piteous story. Vincent, unconscious, groans a little. Ross looks down at him, then at the others.

ROSS (*who had knelt down beside Vincent, rising*). He's still out.

CANELLI (*looking at Vincent*). You know what he said just before he passed out?

ROSS. Hold it, Angelo. (*Grimly, to the group*) We don't know who will be next, or how soon.

He turns, and goes to a corner near Skvoznik and sits down. The others scatter, Stoner sitting down on a mattress, facing the door, Clinton and Greenbaum sitting down side by side, Bayforth sitting down between Canelli and Clinton.—Next we see STONER, at close view, sitting against a wall. He looks down at his left wrist and runs his fingers over it—the sun tan is marred by a band of white where a wristwatch once was worn. This apparently starts a train of thought, and after a moment Stoner looks up, his eyes then staring toward the cell door, as he wanders off.

[We see what Stoner sees:* the barred door and beyond it, the stone wall of the prison, with a small window set in it. Over this comes an arpeggio of distant, almost celestial music as the view moves toward the cell door—through it—to the stone wall and through that, too, to the night outside, and the screen is filled with a beautiful, white, moonlit cloud, drifting through the night.

STONER'S VOICE.
Ah! Love! Could thou and I with Fate conspire
To grasp this sorry scheme of things entire—

Softly, a girl's voice picks up the next lines—the voice of Anne, his sweetheart.

ANNE'S VOICE.
Would not we shatter it to bits—and then
Re-mould it nearer to the heart's desire!

STONER'S VOICE (*in hushed surprise*). Anne!

ANNE'S VOICE. Hello, Martin. I heard you.

STONER'S VOICE. Yes I—I hoped you would, but I didn't think—I didn't dare hope— (*A slight pause*) "Re-mould it nearer to our heart's desire." Do you still remember it?

ANNE'S VOICE.
Yes, Martin. Every word!
(*A slight pause*)
Ah, Moon of my delight, who know'st no wane,
The Moon of Heaven is rising once again—
How oft hereafter rising shall she look
Through this same Garden, after me, —in vain.

---

* The following sequence appeared in the shooting script instead of the one that appeared on the screen.

And when Thyself, with shining
   Foot shall pass
Among the Guests, star scattered on
   the grass,
And in thy joyous errand reach the
   spot
Where I made one—turn down an
   empty glass!

As her voice ceases and the celestial music again is heard, the view begins pulling back, past the window and the stone wall and into the cell and we are again on Stoner. He is sitting where he was, looking down at the wrist where the watch once was, and he is smiling.]

We see STONER as Ross is working over Vincent. Stoner looks up strangely.

STONER. "How do I love thee? Let me count the ways."

ROSS (*looking up toward him*). What?

STONER. Oh, that's what Anne had inscribed in the wrist watch she gave me.

ROSS. Oh. (*And he proceeds to dip a cloth in a pail of water.*)

STONER. "How do I love thee? Let me count the ways."

At this we get a close view of the barred window. The sky is seen through the bars, and an arpeggio of distant, almost celestial music is heard.

STONER'S VOICE.
"I love thee to the depth and breadth
   and height
My soul can reach, when feeling out
   of sight—(*The camera moves closer, past the clouds, to the clouds in the sky—*)
For the ends of Being and ideal
   Grace." (*A white cloud drifts by.*)

ANNE'S VOICE. "I love thee to the level of every day's most quiet need, by sun and candle-light."

STONER'S VOICE. Anne!

ANNE'S VOICE. Hello, Martin.

STONER'S VOICE. Hello.

ANNE'S VOICE.
"I love thee freely, as men strive for
   right;
I love thee purely, as they turn from
   praise;
I love thee with the passion put to
   use
In my old griefs, and with my childhood's faith.
I love thee with a love I seemed to
   lose
With my lost saints—I love thee with
   the breath,
Smiles, tears, of all my life!—and if
   God choose,
I shall but love thee better after
   death."

We see STONER again, with ROSS in the background looking at him.

STONER (*repeating*).
"And if God choose,
I shall but love thee better after
   death."

He smiles, looks down at his wrist, while ROSS dips the cloth in the pail of water. The view moves to afford a closeup of ROSS wrapped in thought, then moves down to ROSS' HANDS as he wrings the water from the cloth, then to drops of water falling into the bucket of water.

This has apparently started a train of thought for Ross, and the scene dissolves to a closeup of a BUCKET. A boy's hands are seen wringing out a cloth, and the moving view discloses Tim, a small boy of five or six.—This cuts to a scene in which ROSS and his wife appear. We see his wife, a Texas girl, wearing Levi's boots and Stetson, standing on the bottom rail of the corral, her elbows resting on the top rail. She is looking down into the corral. Ross rushes to the corral gate, and is about to open it, but his wife stops him with a gesture. He climbs onto the lower rail of the corral, still holding the bucket, which he partially lowers into the corral as he, too, rests his elbows on the top rail. He and his wife start smiling proudly as their son, Tim, dressed as near like his father as possible, walks over to a newborn foal, which has not yet got to its feet, and proudly sponges it off, a cowhand in the background leaning against a rail, watching.

We see ROSS and his WIFE looking down at the boy and the colt, and beaming proudly; then TIM and the COLT as the latter staggers to its feet and unsteadily trots across the corral. Tim folds his hands behind his back and teeters on his boot heels, very grown up.

ROSS and his WIFE are again seen, laughing merrily at Tim.—A dog runs up to TIM, brushing around his feet, his tail wagging.—Then we see Ross and his wife at the bucket. She dips her hands in and flicks some water in his face. He retaliates, and they laugh gaily. He grabs her hands and holds them.

This dissolves to a closeup of the BUCKET with Ross kneeling over it— Vincent lying on a mattress on the floor. We are once more in the cell, with Ross looking down at the bucket of water, a far-away smile in his eyes. He takes the cloth and places it on Vincent's forehead.

This cuts to CLINTON and GREENBAUM. Clinton, his head buried in his hands, is lost in thought. Greenbaum looks at him. Clinton does not notice. Greenbaum looks at him more closely. Clinton still does not notice. Greenbaum jogs his leg.

GREENBAUM. You, too, Clint?

Clinton recalls himself to reality with a start. Greenie grins at him.

CLINTON. I guess I was pretty far away.

GREENBAUM (*laughing*). Personally, I'd settle for a nice juicy steak.

CLINTON. Boy! Was *I* far away from here!

GREENBAUM (*morosely*). You're lucky. *I* got the kind of thoughts that don't cooperate. The kind that insist on sticking to the trouble at hand. The kind that keep saying: "Who do you think you're kidding, Greenbaum?"

CLINTON. My thoughts played a trick on me, too. One time when I was a little boy, I got lost. I stopped a policeman and asked him how to find my home. When I told him who I was, he offered to take me there. "Please don't," I said. "Just tell me where I live. I want to find it myself." (*He looks back at Greenbaum.*) He laughed and said he understood, and told me how to find my home. (*Turning away from Greenbaum*) I asked him his name. "The boys at the station house call me Joe," he said. Until I joined the army he was the only person I ever knew who let me do anything for myself. It was Joe my thoughts took me to just now. (*He laughs a little and looks back at Greenbaum.*) I don't know why.

Greenbaum looks at him, shaking his head resignedly.

GREENBAUM. Not your girl. Not your old man. Not your mama. A cop named Joe! Huh— (*He leans his head on the bars of the cell.*) Rich people!

The scene cuts to ROSS, BAYFORTH and VINCENT. Bayforth is leaning with his head tilted back against the wall, wrapped in thought. Ross is squatting beside Vincent, watching him. He decides to move him into a more comfortable position. He calls over his shoulder.

ROSS. Bayforth. (*Bayforth doesn't answer, and Ross looks around.*) Bayforth. Give me a hand.

Bayforth recalls himself to reality with a start, and assists Ross to readjust Vincent's position, during the following dialogue.

BAYFORTH. Sorry, Captain. You just brought me back from the greatest little state in the union.

ROSS. What's Georgia got that Texas doesn't have?

BAYFORTH (*simply*). My home.

ROSS (*gently*). How right you are.

They finish making Vincent more comfortable, and as they do, we hear the cell door being unlocked. Ross and Bayforth instantly leap to their feet and turn and face the door.—The CELL DOOR is then seen from the corridor as the guard unlocks it. Two soldiers, armed with rifles, are behind him. The guard opens the door and stands in the doorway, looking around at the fliers, whom we see in the background inside the cell, as the view moves around the faces of the fliers. Each man is tense, grim, expecting to hear his name called. The view is focused on ROSS, but the voice of the guard is heard.

GUARD'S VOICE. Sergeant Clinton. You come.

At the mention of Clinton's name, Greenbaum takes an involuntary step toward Clinton, calling out "Howard!" but Clinton stops him with a gesture.

CLINTON. Don't worry, Greenie. This is the second time in my life that I've been allowed to find my own way home. I think I can make it.

Slowly he starts walking toward the door.—Clinton walks his "last mile" with closeups of the remaining uninjured fliers—Greenbaum, Bayforth, Stoner and Ross.—Clinton walks through the door, with the guard following and the soldiers bringing up the rear. The guard slams the door shut and we again see the JAP LISTENING ROOM: Mitsubi and the operator are listening on the dictaphone. Through it we hear the sound of the key being turned in the lock downstairs and the sound of the soldiers leading Clinton away. Mitsubi smiles in anticipation, rises and leaves.

This cuts to the PRISON CORRIDOR. [Greenbaum rushes to the door, grabs the bars and bangs his forehead against the bars once, twice. Blood trickles from his forehead. Ross rushes in and seizes his shoulder, steadying him.

GREENBAUM. A kid! He's just a kid!

ROSS. You're wrong, Greenie. He's a man. When my time comes to walk, I hope I can do as well.]

Greenbaum and Bayforth look through the bars; they then go back in the cell and sit down on the floor, where the other fliers are now seated. Then the scene fades out.

PART THREE

The INTERIOR CORRIDOR outside the FLIERS' CELL fades in. It is dawn. There is a change of lighting in the set, and from what we can see of the fliers, they have spent a restless, sleepless night. The door at the end of the corridor opens and Clinton is escorted toward his cell by two Jap sentries.—We get a close view of the FLIERS as they react to the return of Clinton. He is not bruised or beaten in any way. He seems terribly tired and his features are strained. The boys stare at him.

THE FLIERS. Not a scratch— Never even touched you, Howard.

They pull him into the cell.

THE FLIERS. Nice going— Look at him—he's good as new— Oh, don't worry, but I'm going to slug you for scaring me to death.—What's the idea of being AWOL all night— Just in time for breakfast— What did you do—scare Mitsubi— What did they have to say to you?—

But Greenbaum, in the foreground, stops and stares at him, for Clinton has not said a word.—This cuts to a close view of CLINTON: He tries to answer. His lips move and we see his tongue, but his voice is gone.—The other fliers just stare at him suspiciously now.— Thereupon GREENBAUM turns to them.

GREENBAUM. Wait a minute. I know what you're thinking, but it's not true— (*Looking at Clinton*) Go on, Howard, tell them you didn't talk up there—go on, tell them— (*Grabbing his coat, shaking him*)— Say something, Howard—talk—talk. (*He stops.*) You can talk—can't you?

We then get a closer view of CLINTON, as Stoner steps forward to him. CLINTON shakes his head to Greenbaum's question.

STONER. They did torture him.

BAYFORTH (*approaching*). They must have tortured him or something—he can't speak.

ROSS (*also approaching him*). Is that it—is that what they did?

Clinton shakes his head—"Yes," turns, and walks back deeper into the cell, Stoner and Bayforth looking after him. —Stoner starts after him, but is pulled back by Ross. The fliers disperse around the cell. Greenbaum, starting to follow, puts his hands to his throat.

The scene cuts to the CORRIDOR as the door opens and the attendant enters with the perambulator containing the food and eating bowls. The view moves with him as he pushes the perambulator to the cell containing the fliers.— This cuts to a full view of the CELL where Skvoznik and Vincent lie quietly on their mattresses, alive, but bereft of reason. Clinton and Canelli sit against a wall, their heads drooping on their chests. Ross, Greenbaum and Stoner are slouched around, utterly despondent under the pressure of the endless waiting, the deadly suspense. They lift their eyes dully as the attendant outside strikes the bars with his ladle and shoves a bowl of food between the bars. Ross gets to his feet, takes the bowl and hands it to Stoner. The attendant hands through another which Ross gives to Greenbaum. Greenbaum instantly turns toward Clinton.—We then see CANELLI, CLINTON and GREENBAUM as Greenbaum offers Clinton the bowl of rice. Clinton shakes his head silently, and Greenbaum gives the bowl to Canelli.—Then the attendant sets some tin cups containing a weak, warm tea inside the bars and continues on his way. Ross picks up a cup of tea. Greenbaum does likewise, then again turns toward Clinton.—We see STONER taking his food as the attendants wheel the perambulator out. He goes back and sits down on the floor, next to Vincent lying on his mattress. Stoner lifts a mouthful of food in his fingers, but as he does he shudders in revulsion.

A close view discloses CLINTON as Greenbaum leans down and tries to offer him a cup of tea. Clinton shakes his head, smiling apologetically.

GREENBAUM. Please try.

Clinton puts his hand up to his throat.

GREENBAUM. It's tea, Clint—it'll be good for you.

Greenbaum pats his shoulder and places the tea on the floor beside him, then turns away.

Greenbaum picks up the last remaining cup of tea which the guard placed inside the cell. As he does, Stoner suddenly puts his bowl of food on the floor. His eyes fill with tears. He raises the cup of tea to his lips and tries to drink.

STONER. I can't stand any more! I can't stand it!

He throws himself on his stomach, buries his face in his arms and begins sobbing.

This cuts to the JAP LISTENING ROOM. Mitsubi and the operator are listening to the loudspeaker.—This cuts to the FLIERS' CELL, with Stoner in the foreground, sobbing. ROSS starts toward him, and kneels next to him.

ROSS (*very gently*). Stoner.

STONER (*controlled by an effort*). Yeah—yes, sir.

ROSS (*gently*). I was just figuring up. Today's my birthday.

BAYFORTH. Happy birthday, Captain—

CANELLI (*raising his cup*). Happy birthday, Captain.

ROSS (*to Stoner*). Aren't you going to drink with me, Stoner?

At this, Stoner looks at Ross, then raises his cup in a toast.

STONER. In a cup of General Somebody's stinkingly bitter tea, I drink to your very good health, sir.

ROSS. Thank you, gentlemen.

This cuts to the JAPANESE LISTENING ROOM. Mitsubi pounds his hand on the loud speaker furiously, realizing that Stoner's breakdown has been halted, and goes out angrily.—Then we see the FLIERS again

CANELLI. How old are you today, sir?

ROSS (*smiling at the group*). Thirty. Getting to be an old man. (*He drinks.*)

STONER. Thirty! (*Quoting*)
"Has there any old fellow got mixed with the boys?
If there has, throw him out without making a noise." (*He drinks some tea.*)

ROSS. Carry on, Stoner. You're making me feel younger.

STONER. I don't know whether I remember:—
"Hang the catalogue's cheat and the almanac's spite.
Old Time is a liar, we're twenty tonight.
We're twenty, we're twenty, who says we are more?
He's tipsy, young jackanapes, show him the door.

We've a trick, we young fellows, you
    may have been told,
Of talking in public as if we were
    old."

GREENBAUM slumps down beside Clinton and Canelli, to listen.

STONER'S VOICE.
"That boy we call 'doctor' and this
    we call 'judge'
It's a neat little fiction, of course, it's
    all fudge."

Then we again see STONER and Ross, with Canelli and Bayforth behind them.

STONER.
"Yes, we're boys, always playing
    with sword or with pen.
And I sometimes have asked, shall
    we ever be men?
Shall we always be youthful and
    laughing and gay,
'Till the last dear companion drops
    smiling away?" (*He raises his cup in a toast.*)
"Then here's to our boyhood, its gold
    and its gray,
The stars of its winters, the dews of
    its May."

But now the door is heard opening, and the fliers look up.—A soldier is standing at the DOOR. A guard opens the door. The soldier steps up.

SOLDIER. Lieutenant Bayforth.

Without a word, Bayforth gets up and leaves the cell. The Jap sentries escort him down the corridor. The other boys look after him.—They turn forward as Stoner speaks:

STONER (*softly, at close view*).
"And when we have done with our
    lifelasting toys,
Dear Father, take care of Thy children, the boys. . . ."

A series of semi-closeups follows: CLINTON's own physical suffering is now augmented by the terror of what he knows will happen to Bayforth. His eyes seek the face of Captain Ross.— We see in Ross' face what Clinton sees —a consuming, agonizing sympathy for his "boys" which is almost more than mortal man can bear.—The sight of Ross' suffering is more than Clinton can bear. He dips a finger into the cup of tea beside him and starts writing on the floor beside him. As he does, he reaches out of frame and touches Greenbaum on the arm to attract his attention.

GREENBAUM, CLINTON and CANELLI are seen together. Greenbaum turns and watches Clinton who continues writing on the floor, dipping his finger in the tea. But what he is writing horrifies Greenbaum, who leaps to his feet and goes over to Ross.

GREENBAUM (*thunderstricken*). Harvey!—Harvey!

ROSS (*to Greenbaum*). What is it?

GREENBAUM. It's Clinton. He says— if they do to Bayforth what they did to him and the others, he's going to talk.

This cuts to the JAPANESE LISTENING ROOM, with the radio operator glued to the loudspeaker.—Then we see ROSS and GREENBAUM, looking back.

ROSS. If he feels he must talk, then only God and his conscience should stop him.

In the LISTENING ROOM the operator smiles triumphantly, turns the loudspeaker off, picks up the microphone and speaks into it.

OPERATOR (*in Japanese*). General Mitsubi, please—Mitsubi.

The scene cuts to the CORNER of an ORIENTAL ROOM where General Mitsubi and two other army officers, whom we have seen at the trial, are seated on mats on the floor, drinking tea and being served by three Geisha girls in the traditional fashion with much kneeling. On the floor in front of them, we see several blueprints of an aircraft carrier. Obviously they have been studying the blueprints and trying to break down the Admiral's theory.—Then as one of the Geisha girls refills his cup of tea, MITSUBI points to the blueprint.

MITSUBI (*in Japanese*). —we must disprove this theory.

At this point Mitsubi looks up, upon hearing someone, and we next see a Japanese officer entering rather hurriedly, saluting Mitsubi, and handing him a message.—A close view then shows MITSUBI reading the message. His eyes light up, and he gets to his feet, excitedly.

MITSUBI (*in Japanese*). One of our prisoners has decided to talk. *Sergeant Clinton* has told his companions that if any harm befalls *Lieutenant Bayforth,* he will no longer keep silent!

(Although the above speech is in Japanese, we definitely hear the names *Clinton* and *Bayforth* in English, and the audience will be able to surmise that Mitsubi knows of Clinton's threat to talk if Bayforth is tortured.)*

[The scene dissolves to the RUSSIAN EMBASSY, where Voroshevski stands before a desk behind which is the Russian ambassador. On the wall behind him is a Russian flag.

AMBASSADOR. Your message has been given to the Japanese minister of intelligence. I am still waiting to hear from him.

The scene wiping off, we see the PORTUGUESE EMBASSY, where Siva is standing before his ambassador's desk. A Portuguese flag is prominently displayed on the wall.

AMBASSADOR. I am still waiting to hear from the Japanese minister of intelligence.

This scene wipes off to the ARGENTINE EMBASSY, where Santos is standing before the ambassador's desk. The Argentine flag is on the wall.

AMBASSADOR. I have no answer. Perhaps I shall not get one. After all, this is really none of our affair.

And the scene wipes off to the JAPANESE MINISTRY OF INTELLIGENCE, where Keppel is standing before the desk behind which sits the Japanese minister of intelligence.

MINISTER (*apologetically*). So sorry. I still have no answer.]

The scene dissolves to the COURTROOM with attention focused on the JUDGES' DOOR as Toyama and his associate judges enter and proceed to their various places. The VOICE of the clerk comes over.

CLERK. Up! Stand! Everybody! Up! Stand!

Everyone rises in the courtroom. The prisoners have not yet been brought in. The judges, as usual, bow to the flag, then to one another, and the entire courtroom sits down.—YAMAGICHI and his STAFF are next seen as Yamagichi sits down, turns and bows.—After this we see MITSUBI, with his STAFF, and as he sits down Mitsubi catches Yamagichi's bow, and returns it in kind.—Then the PRISONERS' DOOR is opened by guards and the fliers are brought in—

---

* On the screen, it is a Geisha girl who brings Mitsubi the message, and upon reading it he smiles and tears it up.

seven of them. Bayforth is missing.— The prisoners are led to their box, and as they sit down, Toyama speaks from the bench.

TOYAMA (*looking down at Mitsubi*). General Mitsubi.

MITSUBI (*stepping forward confidently, almost gaily*). I have only two more witnesses to call. I think your excellencies will find further testimony is not necessary.

TOYAMA (*looking down at Mitsubi*). Proceed.

MITSUBI (*bowing and smiling confidently*). Thank you, excellencies. (*He turns toward the prisoners' door.*) Lieutenant Kenneth Bayforth.

We see the FLIERS turn and look toward the prisoners' door, apprehensive of what they will see; then the CORRESPONDENTS, the view favoring Toma and Johana, who are looking toward the prisoners' door, eager for some new sight of torture.

The PRISONERS' DOOR is opened and a guard leads Bayforth into the room. At first glance, he seems to have been unharmed, then we are aware that his hands are encased in leather gloves.— A close view shows CLINTON staring off toward Bayforth, and we know he has seen those gloves. Clinton looks as if he were about to rise in protest but Greenbaum's fist closes sharply on Clinton's arm, commanding him to self-control and Clinton subsides into his seat.—Then the COURTROOM is seen in full view as Bayforth is led to the witness stand, and enters the box. The clerk raises his hand.

CLERK. Do you affirm that according to your conscience you will speak the truth, adding nothing and concealing nothing?

The FLIERS are seen waiting, watching for Bayforth to take the oath. BAYFORTH, at close range, looks at his brother fliers, then at the clerk.

BAYFORTH. I give my word as a soldier and an officer that anything I say will be the truth.

MITSUBI (*turning to Bayforth*). You are aware, Lieutenant Bayforth, of the nature of the information that is desired from you?

ADMIRAL YAMAGICHI looks at his staff meaningly, and smothers a yawn. Mitsubi is off on the same old tangent!— We then see the JUDGES' STAND, the view favoring Bayforth and Mitsubi as Bayforth finally looks Mitsubi in the eye and nods.

BAYFORTH. Yes, sir. I am.

MITSUBI. And are you now willing to provide this information to the court?

BAYFORTH, seen close, looks at Mitsubi without emotion, then down at his hands, then back at Mitsubi.

BAYFORTH. No, I'm not.

MITSUBI looks at Bayforth with an inscrutable expression.—We see the FLIERS relax in relief, and then we get a glimpse of the JUDGES as Toyama looks down at Mitsubi, perplexed.

MITSUBI (*enjoying Toyama's suspense*). Thank you, Lieutenant Bayforth.

We see YAMAGICHI and his STAFF look toward Mitsubi, a little puzzled, but not yet worried.—Then MITSUBI and BAYFORTH appear together as Mitsubi nods to Bayforth.

MITSUBI. You may step down.

As Bayforth steps down, Mitsubi turns toward the fliers' box.

MITSUBI. Sergeant Howard Clinton! Take the stand.

The FLIERS instantly turn and look toward Clinton as he rises slowly to his feet. This is the last moment of defense—if Clinton talks, their entire gallant stand against an empire has gone for nothing.—Now attention is focused on GREENBAUM and CLINTON as Greenbaum looks up at Clinton inscrutably, but whether his glance conveys pleading, hope, or resignation, we cannot divine. He merely pats Clinton's arm as Clinton moves to leave the box.

Bayforth enters the box as Clinton moves past the other fliers to leave the box. As Clinton passes the others, each man—except Vincent and Skvoznik—give him some sign of encouragement, or forgiveness. A handclasp, a slap on the back, a courageous smile—these are the weapons given Clinton as he steps out to face his persecutors.

In the correspondents' corner Johana's and Toma's eyes are alight with fervid expectation, and gloating over Clinton's apparent defeat. Then we get a full view of the COURTROOM as Clinton takes his place in the box, Mitsubi facing him, Sakai (the Japanese lawyer) at the table in the background, the fliers in the prisoners' box far in the background.

MITSUBI. Sergeant Clinton, you have a statement which you wish to make to the court at this time?

SAKAI (*rising*). I wish to apologize to the court for this defendant's inability to answer. He became ill during the night and suffered the loss of his voice.

MITSUBI (*imperturbably*). In that case —we will provide the prisoner with other means of communication. (*Calling to an officer in Japanese*) Paper!

At this an officer hands him paper and pencil, and Mitsubi turns to Clinton.

MITSUBI (*in English*). Write your statement.

Clinton takes the paper and pencil and starts writing.—This cuts to the FLIERS as they lean forward tensely; to Yamagichi and his staff waiting, their lips parted breathlessly; to a view of the CORRESPONDENTS, with Kruger turning to Johana and Toma, nodding. Then we see CLINTON handing the paper to Mitsubi, but putting one paper in his pocket.

MITSUBI looks down at the paper, and his face falls. He crushes the note in his hand and turns toward Toyama.

TOYAMA. Well, General Mitsubi?

MITSUBI (*a bit crestfallen but still hopeful*). The defendant points out that since he is physically unable to talk, he has appointed a brother officer to speak for him. (*Ross stands up, expecting to be called.*) (*Mitsubi turns toward the fliers.*) Lieutenant Greenbaum. (*To Clinton*) You may step down.

We get a fairly close view of the FLIERS as Greenbaum rises to his feet. The others look at him tensely. Then Clinton comes up to Greenbaum, looks at him smiling, and hands him the note which he put into his pocket. Ross stands aside letting Greenbaum out of the box, and Clinton steps into it. He and Ross sit down and Greenbaum goes to the witness box, where he reads the note.

MITSUBI faces Greenbaum, smiling in sardonic ingratiation.

MITSUBI. Read the court the information Sergeant Clinton wishes to reveal.

GREENBAUM, seen close, with Mitsubi in the foreground and correspondents and guards in the background, looks at him for a long time, and finally nods.

GREENBAUM (*striking his hand against the box, forcefully*). Gladly. General Mitsubi, thanks to your dictaphone, you heard me say last night that if Lieutenant Bayforth was tortured, Sergeant Clinton would speak. (*He looks toward the prisoners' box.*) Well—there sits Lieutenant Bayforth —and Sergeant Clinton keeps his word.

GREENBAUM (*turning to Mitsubi*). He speaks gratefully of the pain you inflicted upon him—pain which cleared the mists from his eyes and showed him with the sharpness of torture exactly why you must know where our bombers came from. He speaks of the military strength with which you must patrol the Russian frontier (*leaning forward to Mitsubi tantalizingly*)—if that is where we came from. (*He straightens up.*) He speaks of the forces with which you must guard against attack from China, in case we came from there. He speaks of your naval power, forced onto the defensive, because we might have come from a carrier. He speaks of eight soldiers—unknown, imprisoned, without hope. Eight insignificant guys —who have your whole army, your whole navy, and your whole air force, tied up in a knot. (*Pointing at the paper in his hand*) These are the things of which he speaks in this moment of pain and agony and— pride. (*He crushes the paper in his hand.*) And now *I'll* speak, for myself. On the day when you give Skvoznik back his mind, and Vincent his senses—on the day when you restore the use of Canelli's arms and Bayforth's hands—on the day when you give Clinton back his voice—on that day I'll tell you what you want to know—(*glaring at Mitsubi*) *and not one second sooner.*

Then the COURTROOM is seen in full view. All save the fliers sit stunned and silent at Greenbaum's outburst, but the fliers are on their feet, cheering while Toyama rises and shrieks "Order, Order!"

At this YAMAGICHI relaxes, and smiles at his staff officer. Then we see TOYAMA looking down at Mitsubi for a long minute.

TOYAMA. General Mitsubi, have you any further evidence?

MITSUBI turns and faces the judges, saying "Yes, excellency." He is near the end of his rope, but he has one card left to play. He gestures to an aide, who steps forward and hands Mitsubi an official-looking envelope. Mitsubi calls to Greenbaum "Step down," and Greenbaum walks back to the prisoners' box. Then Mitsubi breaks the seal, removes a document and brings it to Toyama, who takes it, without emotion, and looks at it.—YAMAGICHI exhibits renewed interest. Mitsubi is pulling a fast one, and Yamagichi doesn't like it. —The FLIERS, looking from Mitsubi to Toyama, are puzzled.

TOYAMA finishes reading the paper and, without showing it to the other judges, returns it to Mitsubi.

TOYAMA (*without emotion*). Very well. Proceed.

Mitsubi takes the paper, returns it to his pocket, and bows to the court.

MITSUBI. Thank you, excellency.

He turns and crosses to the fliers' box, the view moving with him.—He reaches the fliers' box and stands before it, looking at the fliers with a new expression on his face—one of defeat, one of pleading, one almost of desperation.

MITSUBI. I have been authorized by a power so high I dare not mention his honorable name, to request the court to dismiss the charges against you.

We see the FACES of the FLIERS mirroring their reaction of this unexpected attack—for attack is what they instantly recognize.—YAMAGICHI is increasingly perplexed and concerned over Mitsubi's craftiness.—In the correspondents' corner Toma and Johana exchange startled glances.—Then the FLIERS and MITSUBI are seen together as Mitsubi faces them heavily. He is firing his last broadside, and he knows it.

MITSUBI. After all, you are only soldiers fighting for your country, a situation every Japanese can understand.

The FLIERS react as his words come over.

MITSUBI'S VOICE. When you bombed schools and hospitals, you were only acting under orders. It is your commanding officers who are guilty, it is they who should be on trial.

The fliers are almost unable to believe their ears as Mitsubi continues.—Then we see MITSUBI turning toward the court.

MITSUBI. I, therefore, request the court that this trial be ended, and the charges against these prisoners be dismissed.

Ross and the other fliers stare at Mitsubi, thunderstricken, unable to believe their ears.—The CORRESPONDENTS are reacting excitedly. Johana and Toma exchange incredulous and horror-stricken looks. Are the fliers to escape after all? —Then TOYAMA, seen close with the two other judges, looks down at the fliers paternally.

TOYAMA. The court is disposed to show every leniency toward these soldiers.

At a fairly close view we see the FLIERS as overwhelming joy comes over their faces, only to be shattered by Toyama's next words.

TOYAMA'S VOICE. *Provided*——

The view widens to include TOYAMA as he continues.

TOYAMA. —that they inform this court of the identities of their commanding officers, so that they may be punished when Japan has won the war, and that they further inform this court as to the exact location of the base from which they came, so that immediate steps may be taken to prevent a recurrence of the monstrous murder of civilians.

Ross gets to his feet, and addresses Toyama.

ROSS. And what happens to us if the charges against us are dismissed?

TOYAMA. If you accept, you will be removed to a military prison camp and shown the consideration to which all legitimate prisoners of war are entitled.

ROSS. And if we refuse to accept—your honor?

TOYAMA. You will be found guilty as charged—and you will be executed

Ross sits down and looks questioningly at the others. Mitsubi steps forward and speaks eagerly.

MITSUBI. I beg you, do not answer hastily. Realize what this means to you. We already have thousands of British and American prisoners of war. Although Japan never signed the Geneva Convention, we nevertheless respect its provisions. Yo will live in a camp with your fellow soldiers—you will be well fed and well clothed—you will be contacted by the Red Cross, and you will be able to send letters to your loved ones at home! Think, Captain Ross! Lieutenant Bayforth—you other men—we are offering you your lives. You have only to accept.

ROSS. How do we actually *know* you'll do as you say? You can promise us anything—

MITSUBI (*pointing to the Press*). The members of the international press are present. They are your witnesses. And furthermore, the Imperial Court's decision will be handed down in writing and certified copies deposited with the Swiss Legation.

Ross and the other fliers exchange looks. Ross turns to Mitsubi.

ROSS. After what my men have been through this is a tempting offer, and we know the Swiss can be trusted—but—

MITSUBI (*to Toyama*). I request that the defendants be granted a few minutes to discuss their decision in private.

TOYAMA. The request is granted. (*To the guards*) Remove the prisoners to my chambers.

The scene dissolves to the CONFERENCE ROOM. The fliers enter and disperse themselves around the room as the door closes. Ross turns to them.

ROSS (*generally*). Well, men, for one moment, this undemocratic hole has given us the democratic privilege of majority rule. It seems we're the jury which must decide whether its own members shall live or die.

GREENBAUM. I suggest we discuss it thoroughly before taking a vote.

CANELLI (*interrupting quietly*). A man who is half dead is half decided. I am not qualified to vote. (*He looks at his broken arm.*)

BAYFORTH (*looking at his gloved hands*). Canelli is right. The choice belongs to those of you who have something to live for.

Clinton crosses to Canelli and Bayforth who are sitting side by side, nods to them affirmatively, and sits down beside them. Ross looks at them for a long moment, barely controlling his tears, then shakes his head.

ROSS. No. You've been tortured and have given your blood. You faced death and remained silent. As long as I, too, faced only death, I believed that my courage could equal yours. Now I am not facing death, but life. And I feel that only those who have known torture can weigh its value, and are entitled to vote.

STONER. The captain speaks for me.

GREENBAUM. And for me.

Thus they are aligned—Bayforth, Canelli and Clinton and Ross, Greenbaum and Stoner. For a moment there is indecision, an impasse. The men look at one another, each man silently offering his life to his comrades. Then, suddenly, without any change of expression whatever, Vincent begins speaking for the first time since he was tortured. (*He is not singing.*)

VINCENT (*slowly*). Mine eyes have seen the glory of the coming of the Lord—

All instantly turn and look at him thunderstricken. They wait for him to continue.

ROSS (*prompting him*). He is trampling out the vineyard where the—

VINCENT. —where the grapes of wrath are stored. He has loosed the fateful—

ROSS. Lightning—

VINCENT. —of his terrible, swift sword— His truth—

ROSS. —is marching—

VINCENT. His truth is marching on. Glo—glory.

As the men stare at Vincent spellbound, ROSS begins singing softly, and they all, except Vincent, join him.

THE FLIERS (*singing*).
Glory, glory, hallelujah!
Glory, glory, hallelujah!
Glory, glory, hallelujah!
His truth is marching on!

ROSS (*quietly*). I guess it needed a wisdom more profound than ours. I see it clearly now. It is not a majority rule, it is one for all and all for one. And each of us must bear on his conscience the responsibility for Vincent and Skvoznik.

Ross picks up a pad and some pencils from the conference table. He begins tearing sheets from the pad, then looks across the room at Canelli's broken arm and Bayforth's crippled hands and realizes those two will not be able to write. He lays the pad and pencils aside and thinks for a moment. His eyes go to a Japanese vase, sitting on a side table. He gets an idea, starts to unpin his wings, and picks up the vase.

ROSS. This will be a secret ballot. The man who thinks we ought to talk will drop his wings in here—broken. The man who wants us to remain silent will drop his wings into the vase—unbroken. If there is one pair of broken wings in this vase, we'll tell the Japs what they want to know. (*He looks around at the group.*) Is it agreed?

The boys nod in the affirmative, and call out "Agreed." Ross removes his wings as he says the next line.

ROSS. In this way, none of us will ever know *which one* decided to talk.

He holds the vase under the edge of the table so that no one can see whether his wings go in whole or broken. He drops his wings.

We get a close view of GREENBAUM as he removes his wings. He looks across at Clinton. His pity for the boy is evident in his eyes. Greenbaum looks down at the wings in his hands, and makes a movement with his hands which can easily be mistaken for the gesture of breaking them—although we are not certain. Then we see the others step forward, one after another, and drop their wings into the vase, beneath the edge of the table. Canelli removes his wings with his left hand. Stoner removes Bayforth's wings for him and places them in Bayforth's cupped, gloved hands. We see it would be possible for him to break the wings if he wished, but we do not see if he does.—This cuts to the DOOR as, without ceremony, a soldier opens it.

SOLDIER. Time is up.

A full view shows the group of fliers around the table, Ross in the foreground. He has collected the last pair of wings. He looks into the vase, then toward the soldier.

ROSS. We're ready.

The scene then cuts to the COURTROOM as the fliers are led in from the judge's chambers. There is dead, absolute silence. Ross is carrying the Japanese vase.—MITSUBI has rejoined his staff. He and his men stare in the direction of the fliers, whose footfalls echo.—YAMAGICHI and his STAFF are seen as their eyes follow the fliers.—The JUDGES watch as the fliers cross the courtroom.—The CORRESPONDENTS follow the fliers as they reach the prisoners' box. Then we see the entire COURTROOM as Toyama looks toward the fliers who are now seated in their box.

TOYAMA. Have you reached a decision?

Ross rises and holds up the vase.

ROSS. It is in here.

TOYAMA, seen close, appears puzzled.—ROSS hands the vase to the soldier nearest the box. The soldier hands it to one nearer the judges' stand. It is handed from one soldier to another, then to the clerk, who rises and brings it to Toyama. Toyama looks at it, bewildered, shakes it, and is surprised that it rattles. Then we again see the FLIERS as Ross looks at Toyama.

ROSS. If you find one pair of broken wings in that vase, we will speak. That is our decision.

TOYAMA, seen close, takes one unbroken wing from the vase and lays it on the desk before him. He takes out another.—YAMAGICHI and his STAFF watch breathlessly.—One by one, the FLIERS are seen in closeups watching as Toyama takes out an unbroken wing from the vase.

Finally TOYAMA, seen close, removes the rest of the wings. He shakes the vase, but nothing more comes out. And this cuts to the FLIERS, with the correspondents in the background.

ROSS (smiling). Thanks, fellows.

This cuts to a view of MITSUBI and YAMAGICHI, with guards behind them, and we see Mitsubi unbotton one button on his coat and place his right hand inside. Then we again see TOYAMA.

TOYAMA. Captain Ross—is this your final word?

This cuts to a close view of ROSS, a guard standing in the background against the wall.

ROSS. No, excellency. It's true we Americans don't know very much about you Japanese, and never did—and now I realize you know even less about us. You can kill us—all of us, or part of us. But, if you think that's going to put the fear of God into the United States of America and stop them from sending other fliers to bomb you, you're wrong—dead wrong. They'll blacken your skies and burn your cities to the ground and make you get down on your knees and beg for mercy. This is your war—you wanted it—you asked for it. And now you're going to get it—and it won't be finished until your dirty little empire is wiped off the face of the earth!

There is a closeup of Clinton as he smiles, followed by a view of all the fliers as they rise and cheer.

VOICES. Hurray.

At this point, however, a pistol shot rings out. We see a curl of smoke rising, and MITSUBI is seen seated on his chair, crouching low behind the table, only his torso showing. Then we see his body slumped over the table, while YAMAGICHI and other officers stand looking at him.

TOYAMA (at the Judge's stand). The defendants, and each of them, are found guilty of the crime of murder as set forth in the indictment.

We get a moving view of the FACES of the FLIERS as Toyama's voice comes over.

TOYAMA'S VOICE. They will be removed from the courtroom and given into the custody of the military prison until such time as the sentence of death is executed upon their bodies.

The FLIERS come into view as they listen to the sentence stolidly, then the scene moves to the prisoners' door with an officer and guards. We hear voices in Japanese calling *"Take out the prisoners,"* the officer turning to deliver the command which is echoed in the corridor behind the door.—In the CORRIDOR, then, we see the fliers being led from the courtroom. And as they walk forward we hear the strains of "The Army Air Corps Song," following which each of the fliers, with others in the background, is seen in a closeup walking forward.

The faces of the boys are alight with exaltation, touched with glory. Theirs is the triumph, and theirs the victory. Each grinning face, every glistening eye, emphasizes their pride. Ross, Greenbaum, Stoner, Clinton, Canelli, Bayforth—even Vincent and Skvoznik march out of that courtroom hand in hand with destiny and imperishable glory, as the strains of "The Army Air Corps Song" rise to a crashing crescendo and the boys, in FULL CLOSEUP pass before us and into history.

VOICES (*rising in song as the* FLIERS *walk forward*).
Up we go
(*Closeup of* BAYFORTH)
Into the wild blue yonder
Climbing high into the sun.
(*Closeup of* GREENBAUM)
Here they come, zooming to meet our thunder
At 'em boys, give
(*Close up of* STONER, *guards in the background*)
her the gun.
Down we dive, spouting our flames from under
(*Closeup of* VINCENT)
Off with one terrible roar—
We live in fame or go
(*Closeup of* SKVOZNIK)
down in flame—boy—
Nothing can stop the Army Air Corps—
We live
(*A close view of all the fliers marching forward, faces alight with exaltation, touched with glory*) in fame or go down in flame—boy—Nothing can stop
(*The scene dissolving to a picture of the Purple Heart before the picture fades out*)
the Army Air Corps.

GOING MY WAY

(A Paramount Picture)

Screenplay by Frank Butler *and* Frank Cavett

Story by Leo McCarey

Produced and Directed by Leo McCarey

The Cast

FATHER O'MALLEY	Bing Crosby
GENEVIEVE LINDEN	Risë Stevens
FATHER FITZGIBBON	Barry Fitzgerald
FATHER TIMOTHY O'DOWD	Frank McHugh
TED HAINES	James Brown
HAINES, SR.	Gene Lockhart
CAROL JAMES	Jean Heather
MR. BELKNAP	Porter Hall
TOMASO BOZANNI	Fortunio Bonanova
MRS. CARMODY	Eily Malyon
OFFICER PATRICK McCARTHY	Tom P. Dillon
TONY SCAPONI	Stanley "Stash" Clements
HERMAN LANGERHANKE	Carl "Alfalfa" Switzer
MRS. QUIMP	Anita Bolster

ROBERT MITCHELL BOY CHOIR

Film Editor—Leroy Stone

Screenplay of the Paramount photoplay "Going My Way," copyright 1944 by Paramount Pictures Inc. By permission of Paramount Pictures Inc. Lyrics of the Johnny Burke and James Van Heusen songs *The Day After Forever*, *Going My Way*, and *Swinging On A Star*, copyright 1944 by Burke and Van Heusen, Inc. By permission of Burke and Van Heusen, Inc.

GOING MY WAY

PART ONE

AN UPPER WINDOW fades in. This window is on the corner of a four-story, brownstone mansion. Once an exclusive residence, it has long since been converted into ill-conditioned flats, and is now moldering into slow decay. The sun is dropping down behind the Palisades, and street noises, typical of such a locality, drift up into the scene. The location is somewhere on the north side of West 49th Street, New York City. Leaning backward out of the window, cleaning it, is a woman. This is MRS. QUIMP. Mrs. Q. is fortyish, flat-breasted, ominous. She owns a moist, peaked nose, a malicious tongue, and a talent for purveying gossip. Her voice is adenoidal, metallic, startling, and it gives one the impression of being filtered through a Jew's-harp. She is referred to locally, and without affection, as "The Quimp." She spits on an obstinate dust speck, scrapes it off with her thumbnail, gives it a final swipe with a cloth, and starts to squirm back into the room. As she turns, facing the street, a MAN'S VOICE, pleasant and friendly, floats up from the street below:

MAN'S VOICE. Excuse me, Ma'am . . .

The Quimp "deflates" onto the window-sill, cups her chin in the palm of her hand, and stares down toward the voice.

A bird's-eye view of the STREET below: Standing on the sidewalk, a young Roman Catholic Priest is beaming up at Mrs. Quimp. He carries an ancient suitcase, and is in the act of raising a stiff straw hat. He is an extremely friendly young man with an engaging smile. This is FATHER "CHUCK" O'MALLEY.

O'MALLEY. Could you please tell me the way to St. Dominic's?

MRS. QUIMP, seen in a large head-closeup: Her little gimlet eyes bore voraciously into the priest below. The pressure of her chin on the palm of her hand has "scrunched" her lipless mouth upwards so that it almost touches her nose. She makes no immediate answer.

MRS. QUIMP (*through her nose*). Huh?

Copyright 1944, by Paramount Pictures Inc.

FATHER O'MALLEY'S face is tilted up. His smile broadens.

O'MALLEY. I say—I'm looking for St. Dominic's.

MRS. QUIMP is leaning her face on the palm of her hand; her mouth opens and shuts like a snapping-turtle.

MRS. QUIMP. Why?

We see the BROWNSTONE MANSION, with Father O'Malley on the sidewalk, Mrs. Quimp above, and the windows beside and above The Quimp. The scene also shows a brief flight of steps leading up to the entrance.

O'MALLEY. Well—I guess I'm sort of going to work there.

MRS. QUIMP. The new assistant, eh? And you can't even find the church (*His eyes twinkling, O'Malley shakes his head.*) Then all I can say is young man, you're off to a might bad start. (*Then like a bullet out of a gun*) What's your name?

O'MALLEY. Father O'Malley. Charles Patrick Francis O'Malley. (*With a friendly smile*) What's yours?

During the above a woman's head has popped out of the window alongside Mrs. Quimp; another one, directly above her. They are the good-natured faces of poor, hard-working women. Before The Quimp can reply, the woman in the window alongside, a ponderous 250-pounder, supplies the information.

FIRST WOMAN (*shouting down*). Her name's Quimp. Hattie *Quimp!*

She laughs heartily, her whole body shaking like jelly. The second woman above takes it up from there.

SECOND WOMAN (*shouting down to O'Malley*). Oh, you'll see a lotta *her*, you will! At St. Dominic's she's a reg'lar two-a-day-er.

The Quimp's head pivots on its scrawny neck from one woman to the other. Her gimlet eyes gleam malevolently.

FIRST WOMAN (*nodding*). Very religious. Burns *candles!*

SECOND WOMAN (*"thumbs" at The Quimp*). Candles and scandals!

We see MRS. QUIMP sticking her head out of the window.

MRS. QUIMP. I could tell you plenty about them, too! And if I did, they'd have to leave the neighborhood. (*She starts to withdraw, hits her head on the window, cries out, "Oh!" and disappears.*)

SECOND WOMAN. If you're looking for St. Dominic's, Father, it's a block up and to the left.

With a little gesture of his hand, and "Thank you!" O'Malley turns and starts up the street.

This dissolves to a section of a STREET in the vicinity of St. Dominic's. In the street a baseball game is in progress; the players, tough little mugs all, ranging in age from twelve to fifteen. A grocery delivery truck, making its last round, draws up to the curb.

Carrying his suitcase, Father O'Malley walks briskly across the foreground. He notes the spectators of the baseball game lounging on the steps of their houses, in the open windows above. It is a tough neighborhood, all right. Slowing down, but not stopping, he watches the game. The scene then moves with FATHER O'MALLEY, with the baseball game in the background, and brings O'Malley toward an extremely small boy playing right-field. O'Malley stops.

O'MALLEY (*to the youngster*). How's it going?

YOUNGSTER. Aw, slow. Ain't nuttin' come my way all afternoon. (*Then suddenly*) Watch right-field fer me a minute, will yuh, Father? I gotta run over to de house. (*Then screaming off to his friends*) Hey, fellas—de Father's standin' in fer me, see? Be right back!

And before O'Malley can do anything about it, the youngster is racing across the street. There is a chorus of "Okay! Okay!" and the game continues. O'Malley sets down his suitcase and gravely accepts the responsibility of right-field. And at that precise moment the batter cracks a high one directly toward him, and the cheering is terrific.

The ball is a high one, and O'Malley, with professional ease, sets himself, judges the distance and (*followed by the camera*) starts to back up. Faster and faster, and passing the delivery truck, he backs across the road. As he reaches the opposite sidewalk, the ball, far too high, comes into view and with a terrific crash sails through the second-story window of a brownstone house. Glass tinkles onto the sidewalk.

At the crash of broken glass the game breaks up. In four seconds there is not a player on the field.

Outside the BROWNSTONE MANSION: Expectantly, O'Malley is looking up at the broken window as the head and shoulders of a man emerge violently: a middle-aged man, his anger repressed and embittered. This is MR. BELKNAP.

> O'MALLEY (*with a friendly smile*). Would you mind throwing the ball back? (*And at this Mr. Belknap sizzles gently.*)
>
> BELKNAP (*with fearful restraint*). What do you think you're doing?
>
> O'MALLEY. I'm a substitute right-fielder.

Abruptly, Belknap disappears: then reappears almost immediately.

> BELKNAP (*slamming the ball down*). I'll be right down and talk to you.

The ball rolls across the street and under the delivery truck. O'Malley trots after it and with careful regard for his clothes gets gingerly onto his hands and knees and crawls under the truck to retrieve the ball.

A STREET-SPRINKLER appears. This juggernaut, spouting a heavy geyser of water (seen at a low angle), rolls fatefully toward the delivery truck, momentarily obscures O'Malley beneath it, and passes on in a backwash of water, scraps of paper and orange-peel. Momentarily paralyzed by the catastrophe, O'Malley, his back turned, is kneeling beneath the truck. Two pairs of feet—a man's and a woman's—come into the scene and stop.

Soaked, wretchedly bedraggled, O'Malley withdraws himself and rises. And the view rising with him brings him face to face with Mr. Belknap and The Quimp. They are watching him, academically, bitterly, as O'Malley favors them with a sheepish grin.

> MRS. QUIMP (*through her nose*). Still lookin' fer St. Dominic's?
>
> MR. BELKNAP. Playing with a lot of kids—smashing people's windows. . . . You ought to be ashamed of yourself.

O'Malley shakes the water out of his pants.

> O'MALLEY (*apologetically*). I don't feel too good about it.
>
> BELKNAP. A big, grown-up man. (*Pointing, bitterly*) And look at you.
>
> MRS. QUIMP. And a priest besides. (*Belknap scowls at her.*) You just wait 'til I tell Father Fitzgibbon.
>
> BELKNAP (*turning on her*). You keep outa this, will you? (*Waving her away*) Go on. Go on. (*Indicating O'Malley*) This is between him and me.

The Quimp bridles, tosses her head and "sniffs" herself away in the direction of a grocery store.

> O'MALLEY (*to Belknap*). Honestly I'm sorry about the window.
>
> BELKNAP. Yeah—but being sorry don't fix it.

O'Malley thrusts his hand into his sodden pants pocket.

> O'MALLEY. Of course I expect to pay for it . . .

Withdrawing his hand, he is embarrassed to discover only a couple of dimes and a nickel.

BELKNAP (*indicating the money, nastily*). Not with *that* you won't.

O'MALLEY. All right, I'll send it.

BELKNAP. When? . . . Priests never have money. (*O'Malley nods, and Belknap starts to speak.*)

O'MALLEY (*checking him*). Now, wait a minute, my good man. I said I'd pay for it. I said I'm sorry. What else can I say after I say I'm sorry?

BELKNAP. Aw, that ain't the idea. It's the principle of the thing. Priests didn't ought to go around breaking windows. (*Pause, then*) Sets a bad example for the children.

O'MALLEY (*helplessly*). You got me stymied. I'm contrite, I'm penitent. I've told you I'm sorry.

BELKNAP. Yeah, you told me that twice, but that—

O'MALLEY (*heading him off*). Yes, I know—that doesn't fix your window. Look—I think you're just playing hard to get along with. (*From the pocket of his coat he produces a rosary.*) Maybe some security would help?

He displays the rosary, a beautiful thing of ebony, silver, and mother-of-pearl.

O'MALLEY. It was given to me . . . (*Handing it to Belknap*) Why don't you keep it 'til I make good? Maybe you'd feel better.

Handling it as though it were red-hot, Belknap examines the rosary with minute attention.

O'MALLEY (*pointing to the crucifix*). Mother-of-pearl . . . (*Pause, then*) Now, if that'll hold you— (*He pulls his sodden coat away from his chest.*) I'll run along and get out of these wet clothes.

Leaving Belknap staring doubtfully at the rosary in his hand, O'Malley starts briskly across the street toward where his grip is parked on the curb. Belknap fingers the rosary, frowns, comes to a decision. He calls out after O'Malley.

BELKNAP. Hey—*you!*

The view moves with him as he overtakes O'Malley on the curb across the street.

BELKNAP (*dangling the rosary*). Here—I got no use for this. In the first place, I don't believe in it—matter of fact, I don't believe in anything.

O'MALLEY. I believe that.

BELKNAP. I'm an atheist. (*Handing the rosary to O'Malley*) And besides, I'm superstitious.

O'MALLEY (*pocketing the rosary*). All right. And don't worry—I'll see that your window's mended. So forget it.

BELKNAP. How can I forget it? (*Pointing up*) That's *my* room—and until it's fixed I'll have to sleep in my wife's room.

O'Malley gives him a funny, searching look: tries to figure out an answer to *this* one. Failing, he shakes his head, and with a little shrug starts away in the direction of St. Dominic's, as, drifting into the scene, come the strains of "Santa Lucia" played on a hurdy-gurdy.*

Wet to the skin, his collar a wilted rag, O'MALLEY strides briskly toward the entrance to the St. Dominic's Parish House. In so doing he passes the owner of the hurdy-gurdy, an amiable, pic-

* On the screen, Father O'Malley's encounter with the street-sprinkler follows this scene instead of preceding it.

turesque old Italian. O'Malley picks up "Santa Lucia," and sings a happy little eight-bar obbligato. This brings him to the door of the Parish House. He concludes the obbligato with a gesture of his hand toward the Italian. As he rings the bell . . .

The scene dissolves to FATHER FITZGIBBON'S STUDY: It is a spacious room, mellowed with age and wear. There are many books, some religious prints on the wall, and a large fireplace. There is a window-recess through which we see the secluded loveliness of the church gardens. In the recess there is a large desk, and here sits FATHER FITZGIBBON. He is an old man, disintegrating under the weight of his years. He is absent-minded, irritable and stubborn. He speaks with an Irish brogue, and his humor is barbed, sometimes painfully so. On the desk there is a small tea-tray.

Pacing up and down in front of his desk is a tall, thin, extremely well-dressed, middle-aged man. This is MR. TED HAINES, SR. His manner is a little feverish, a little jumpy, a little off the beam. Sitting in a chair, nursing his hat, is MR. TED HAINES, JR., a delightful young man and a breezy, cheery talker.

HAINES, SR. (*across the desk, to Fitzgibbon*). But, Father Fitzgibbon, why do you want a new furnace?

FITZGIBBON (*mildly plaintive*). Because, last winter, Mr. Haines, in the month of November alone, four of my parishioners took to their beds with pneumonia. 'Twas only by a miracle that I, meself, pulled through. (*A pause, then pathetically*) It would only cost six hundred and thirty-two dollars . . . complete with automatic damper.

HAINES. But, Father Fitzgibbon, I didn't come here to put in a new furnace.

TED. I think you ought to give him his furnace, Dad. It would warm people's hearts, and maybe his collections would be bigger.

With a dirty look, Haines, Sr. tries to squelch his son. He turns to Fitzgibbon.

HAINES. No, no, son, improvements are out now. Now, Father—

FITZGIBBON. That was good, what he said. That—was good.

HAINES. Oh, well, he's new to our business. Now, Father—

FITZGIBBON. No furnace, huh?

HAINES. No furnace. Now, Father, here is my business. You owe the Knickerbocker Savings and Loan Company (*spreading the fingers of his right hand*) five payments on the mortgage, and if these aren't taken care of I'm afraid the Knickerbocker Savings and Loan will have to take necessary action. Huh? (*He bites the end off a cigar, puts it in his mouth.*) Why don't you make that the subject of your sermon next Sunday. Tell it to your people. "The Lord loveth a cheerful giver."

The old priest picks up a legal document in a blue binding. On the cover we catch the word "MORTGAGE."

FITZGIBBON (*dryly*). Oh, I can imagine meself sayin' that in Mass next Sunday. What a sermon that would be, Mr. Haines! (*He adjusts his glasses, turns over the cover of the document, and enunciates solemnly.*) The text of me sermon this mornin' is taken from the—from the mortgage according to Mr. Haines—from the first to the twenty-third clause (*Looking up from the document, at Haines*) Very dull, you know.

HAINES. Oh, but that's your business —keep it bright, huh? No, but seriously, Father, we've made a bad loan, and we want our money back.

FITZGIBBON. Well, you'll get it somehow.

HAINES. Oh! Well, now, that's all I wanted to know. Well, good day, Father. (*To Ted*) Come on, son.

[As Ted gets up, Haines, Sr., explodes into a terrific sneeze.

FITZGIBBON (*mildly*). The furnace . . .]

Father and son start toward the door, and we see them then coming out of FATHER FITZGIBBON'S STUDY together.

TED (*as the door closes behind them*). You can't foreclose, Dad. I've read up about it. There's never been a Catholic Church foreclosure in the history of New York.

HAINES. There's always a first time, isn't there?

TED. Don't you think you're a little harsh with him, Dad?

HAINES (*stiffening his forearm with a jerk*). You've got to be. Never loan money to a church. (*Closing his hand*) When you try to close in on 'em, everybody thinks you're a heel.

TED (*brightly, as they walk away*). Well, aren't you?

HAINES (*brusquely*). Yes.

As they walk out of the scene, MRS. CARMODY appears, knocks at the door, and goes into Father Fitzgibbon's study. Mrs. Carmody, Father Fitzgibbon's housekeeper, is well on in years, and from long association with her employer has acquired many of his characteristics. She is tall, gray, dignified, and very erect. A grim face and a sharp tongue, however, hide the inherent warmness of her heart.

FATHER FITZGIBBON'S STUDY: Mrs. Carmody enters, crosses to the desk, and picks up the tea-tray.

FITZGIBBON (*as she does so*). Ah, Mrs. Carmody, has young O'Malley come yet?

MRS. CARMODY. He's here (*with peculiar significance*)—but he insisted on changing his clothes before seeing you.

FITZGIBBON (*nodding, pleased*). That's nice . . . tidying himself up a bit.

At that moment, the exuberant voice of O'Malley is heard from the direction of the landing above, singing "Santa Lucia."

O'MALLEY'S VOICE (*getting nearer*). "Hark, how the sailors' cry
Joyously echoes nigh,
Santa Lucia! Santa Lucia!"

Father Fitzgibbon catches Mrs. Carmody's eye, and the old priest's eyebrows flip up like window-shades. Then the voice subsides, and there is a knock on the door. The view in the study expands as Mrs. Carmody opens the door wide, and O'Malley enters. He is wearing sneakers, white flannel trousers that have seen better days, and a sweatshirt, across the front of which is stenciled: *Property of The St. Louis Browns.*

O'Malley favors Fitzgibbon with an engaging smile, and makes a friendly little gesture.

O'MALLEY. Hello, Father.

A closeup of FATHER FITZGIBBON shows him staring incredulously from behind his desk at this apparition. A closeup of MRS. CARMODY shows her also staring at O'Malley in amazement. Then we see a considerable portion of the STUDY as with a grim shake of her head, Mrs. Carmody goes out past O'Malley and closes the door, while, without taking his eyes off O'Malley, Father Fitzgibbon rises slowly, and slowly comes around his desk. His hands clasped behind his back, he walks up and down in front of O'Malley, examining him as though he were Exhibit "A" in a freak museum.

o'MALLEY (*cheerfully*). I'm your new Curate, Father. You'll excuse my appearance.

FITZGIBBON (*sighing, shaking his head*). No. No. It isn't possible. The Bishop may hold a grudge against me. He may think I've got a mouthful of clover and can't preach— (*shaking his head again*) but even the Bishop wouldn't do *a thing like this* to me.

O'Malley looks himself over and chuckles as he sees Father Fitzgibbon's point.

o'MALLEY. Yes—I see what you mean.

Fitzgibbon, seen close at the desk, points a tremulous finger at O'Malley.

FITZGIBBON. Young man, may I ask if that is the—ah—official garb of our Order in St. Louis?

o'MALLEY. Had a little trouble on the way over, Father. (*Shaking his head ruefully*) I guess this just isn't my day.

Fitzgibbon says nothing. Hands clasped behind his back, he studies O'Malley clinically. O'Malley starts to fill his pipe.

o'MALLEY (*indicating the pipe*). Do you mind?

O'Malley spills some tobacco on the floor. Father Fitzgibbon points it up with a cold stare. Embarrassed now, O'Malley picks up the tobacco, two or three grains at a time, and puts it back into his pipe. He pulls out a match, raises one leg to strike it on the seat of his pants when, catching Fitzgibbon's eye, he checks himself and strikes it on a combination ash try and matchbox on the corner of the desk. In so doing, he upsets and spills the whole works on the floor. Getting down on his hands and knees, and under Fitzgibbon's reproving stare, he starts to pick up the matches.

o'MALLEY. You see, Father, this just isn't my day.

He replaces the matches and lights his pipe. Fitzgibbon sits down, leans across the desk, and studies him closely.

FITZGIBBON. Young man, as a matter of curiosity, how did you ever come to be a priest?

O'Malley gives him a startled look, but before he can reply a telephone bell rings, and Father Fitzgibbon picks up the receiver.

We see a PHONE BOOTH, and through the glass, Mrs. Quimp at the phone. We cannot hear what she is saying, but by her expression and the rapid movement of her nutcracker-jaws, we know she is pouring out a load of dirt. And this cuts to the STUDY: O'Malley is obviously the subject of the conversation, because Father Fitzgibbon, with the receiver to his ear, at the desk, is looking him over from head to foot.

FITZGIBBON (*into the phone*). Well well, you don't say . . . Ummmph . . . you don't say . . . (*Nodding* Ummmph . . . (*Eying O'Malley* Yes—I can quite believe it.

O'Malley, sure that he is being talked about, leans forward and indicates the phone.

O'MALLEY (*sotto voce*). Mrs. Quimp?

The old man stiffens, is about to shake his head "no," when O'Malley wags a forefinger at him warningly. Thinking better of it, Father Fitzgibbon nods his head "yes."

FITZGIBBON (*into the phone*). No, no, Mrs. Quimp—no, indeed. (*Pause— He winces.*) Not at all, Mrs. Quimp —sure I'd be the last to accuse *you* of gossip. (*Wincing again*) Indeed I appreciate your good intentions— they're of the very best, I'm sure. . . . Thank you, Mrs. Quimp. . . . Goodbye, Mrs. Quimp! (*He hangs up.*)

O'MALLEY (*sheepishly*). I guess she told you, eh?

FITZGIBBON. Yes. The garrulous old biddy. (*Severely*) Young man, I'm afraid you're off to a very bad start.

O'MALLEY (*unable to resist it*). That's what *she* told me. (*Very contritely*) I'm sorry, Father.

FITZGIBBON. Smashing people's windows. Tsk, tsk, tsk! Most regrettable. And that reminds me, I was going to ask you something . . . (*Drawing his hand absently-mindedly across his face, then*) Oh yes, I know. . . . Young man, how did you ever become a priest?

But again the telephone rings, and Father Fitzgibbon picks up the receiver. He listens a moment, then frowns.

FITZGIBBON (*into the phone*). Chuck who? (*Voice high*) Father Chuck . . .

O'MALLEY (*sotto voce*). That's *me*.

Fitzgibbon hands him the receiver, and leaning across the desk, O'Malley settles himself to talk.

O'MALLEY (*into the phone*). Hello? (*Exuberantly*) Timmy? How are you, Timmy? Just got in, Timmy! . . . Well, what d'you know! (*To Father Fitzgibbon*) That's Father Timothy—old friend of mine—went to school together. (*Singing into the phone*) "Hail, Alma Mater, thy time-honored halls, etc."

Through the receiver we hear the fine voice of Father Timothy singing tenor at the other end: "Shall echo with our praise, etc." And as Father Fitzgibbon glares, the scene cuts to ST. JOSEPH'S PARISH HOUSE where FATHER TIMOTHY, at the telephone, is just concluding his "Hail, Hail!" into the telephone. He is a joyful little tubby personality; full of life, full of bounce, bubbling with energy.

TIMOTHY. Hey, Chuck—can you talk? (*Pause, then*) Oh . . . well, then I'll do the talking. How does the old man impress you?

O'Malley, seen in FATHER FITZGIBBON'S STUDY at the desk, with the receiver at his ear, eyes Fitzgibbon appraisingly.

O'MALLEY (*ruefully, into the phone*). You're a big help . . . it's hard to say. Time will tell. (*Pausing, chuckling*) Uh-uh! . . . Can't I tell you when I see you? (*Chuckling again*) Yes—it'd be much better. (*Pause, then*) All right, Timmy— make it soon. (*He hangs up, then turns to Fitzgibbon, indicating the phone.*) Great little man.

Fitzgibbon grunts non-committally, sits down at his desk and again draws his hand absent-mindedly across his face.

FITZGIBBON. Let me see—where were we? I know, I know—I was going to ask you something.

O'MALLEY (*hurriedly*). That's right, you were going to ask me if I wanted to see the church.

FITZGIBBON. So I was. So I was.

The old man rises and starts toward the door. Then a close view shows Father Fitzgibbon opening the door for O'Malley, and as O'Malley goes through ahead of him, we see for the first time that on the back of O'Malley's sweater is a rather wild-looking Mickey Mouse cartoon. Father Fitzgibbon's reaction is ludicrous. Mumbling to himself, he steps back into the room, takes a coat off a hook, and starts out after O'Malley.

The scene dissolves to the CHURCH GARDEN. The place is surprisingly reminiscent of an Old World monastery garden, with neat gravel paths skirting well-kept flower beds. A small fountain bathes a diminutive rock garden and bird bath. There is a little shrine in the brick wall to the rear. Beneath an old pear tree, in one corner, there are a few hickory chairs clustered about a table. Beyond the garden wall we see the back ends of tenement houses: a maze of fire-escapes, clothes-lines, bedclothes put out for airing, and flowerpots on window-sills. The scene follows Father Fitzgibbon and Father O'Malley as they walk leisurely across the gardens toward the church. Now wearing the coat Father Fitzgibbon brought out for him, O'Malley is looking the place over, appraising its beauty.

O'MALLEY (*with sincerity*). I like this. It's beautiful.

FITZGIBBON. Thank you.

O'MALLEY (*after a pause*). Father—how long have you been here?

FITZGIBBON. Forty-five years ... forty-six in July.

O'MALLEY. How old is the church?

FITZGIBBON. The same. (*With pride*) I built it.

O'MALLEY (*with great feeling*). I only hope that some day I can say I built as much.

Fitzgibbon gives him a funny little look, and grunts non-committally. The moving view has brought them to the fountain. It is quite beautiful, water cascading into the bird bath, into the basin filled with water-lilies.

O'MALLEY (*staring at it*). That's nice.

FITZGIBBON (*simply*). The birds like it. They're good company. (*He pauses a moment, then*) Listen.

From the pear tree comes the twittering of birds. O'Malley whistles a musical bird-call. The birds answer him. This pleases the old man.

O'MALLEY and FITZGIBBON, the old man slightly in the lead, move forward a few paces, and O'Malley, dropping behind, steps over onto a strip of lawn and, kneeling down, examines something in the grass.

FITZGIBBON (*thinking O'Malley is still alongside*). Yes—I have taken a great deal of pleasure in my garden. Many years of hard work have gone into its making, but it's been worth it. Yes, you'll find this a very pleasant place in which to meditate—you do meditate, don't you?

O'MALLEY (*laughing*). Oh yes, sure.

FITZGIBBON'S VOICE (*as he goes ahead and out of sight*). Now, I'll show you the church.

O'Malley is still behind him. Fitzgibbon continues moving toward the steps. He turns, watching, as O'Malley picks up a clover leaf and straightens up.

O'MALLEY (*rising*). Hmm, for a minute I thought I'd found a four-leaf clover ... (*He laughs.*) But I guess this just isn't my day.

FITZGIBBON (*blandly*). Would you like to see the church?

O'MALLEY (*hastily*). Oh, yes.

A SIDE ENTRANCE to the SANCTUARY: We see a gravel path and a four-foot privet hedge, both paralleling the entrance. In the background Father Fitzgibbon is coming toward the privet hedge and O'Malley running across the lawn to catch up with him. Father Fitzgibbon passes through the narrow cut in the privet hedge and starts up the steps to the Sanctuary. Running in at an angle, and taking the privet hedge in a vaulting jump, O'Malley runs up the steps, slows down and enters the Sanctuary. Father Fitzgibbon stops, looks back as though gauging the height of the privet hedge, shakes his head helplessly, and follows his assistant into the Sanctuary.

The SANCTUARY, with the ALTAR: The church proper is in the same key as the rest of St. Dominic's: dark, gloomy, barren, and in need of repair. Scattered about in the nave are three or four old ladies and old men, saying their rosaries. The side door opens and the two priests enter. We then see FATHER FITZGIBBON and O'MALLEY closer as they go on up into the chancel and pause before the altar for a deep devotion. O'Malley now leads the way to a side altar. As they reach it, he kneels, blesses himself, prays, rises, takes out two candles from a receptacle, lights and places them in candle holders—pantomiming to Fitzgibbon "That's for you and me." Fitzgibbon digs into his pocket and fumbles for money. At this O'Malley restrains him and drops a coin in the candle repository. Pleased, Fitzgibbon smiles at him.

O'MALLEY (*as he does so*). I love the symbolism of the candles—the light of faith shining in a pagan world—sort of keeping vigil for you while we're busy . . . (*aside*) and boy, how I need it.

He turns and extends his hand to Father Fitzgibbon. The old man hesitates, then takes it reluctantly, as the scene fades out.

PART TWO

The CHURCH GARDENS fade in. It is morning, and reading his office, Father Fitzgibbon is walking slowly up and down the garden path. The old man's gait is feeble but measured; his lips frame the words he is reading. At the end of a lap, and without removing his eyes from the book, he pulls off one of his old carpet slippers, shakes out a pebble, replaces the slipper and resumes his tramp. Then the other end of the lap brings him face-to-face with an assortment of luggage. Mildly surprised, the old man sees an ancient trunk, a couple of suitcases, a golf-bag and clubs, and a tennis racket in a press and water-proof cover. His interest sharpens.

FITZGIBBON (*calling out*). Mrs. Carmody . . . Mrs. Carmody!

He is about to call again when Mrs. Carmody enters hastily from the Parish House. She is carrying the old man's clerical collar.

FITZGIBBON (*indicating the luggage, testily*). Mrs. Carmody—whose is all this—ah—impedimenta?

MRS. CARMODY. Father O'Malley's. The men just brought it.

The old priest eyes it sardonically, prods

the golf-bag with his toe, and makes a great show of looking for something.

FITZGIBBON (*sarcastically*). And where, may I ask, is his fishpole?

MRS. CARMODY (*getting it from behind the trunk*). Here.

FITZGIBBON. Ummmmmph! . . . Where is he?

MRS. CARMODY. Oh, he left early this morning. The young man doesn't sleep as late as you do, you know. (*As the old man starts away*) Come here—you've forgotten your collar.

FITZGIBBON (*feeling his neck*). Ummmmph . . . So I did. So I did.

Turning the old man around, Mrs. Carmody starts to put on his collar: has a little difficulty with the collar-stud in the back of his shirt. Father Fitzgibbon squirms and fidgets like a small boy having his ears washed.

MRS. CARMODY (*jerking the collar*). Stand still. (*Fixing it*) There.

She leaves him, and starts toward the door of the Parish House. Then Fitzgibbon, looking off, sees: The AREAWAY as O'Malley enters, coming toward the garden. He is carrying an old-fashioned bushel-basket. The basket has a lid.

O'Malley goes toward the table under the pear tree. He is wearing the suit he wore the previous day, now sponged and pressed. Father Fitzgibbon starts toward him. AT THE TABLE, then, O'Malley tosses his hat onto a chair, sets the basket on the table, and wipes the perspiration from his forehead. Fitzgibbon ambles into the scene, and eyes the basket.

O'MALLEY (*cheerfully*). Good morning, Father.

FITZGIBBON (*nodding*). Been to market, eh? Better leave such trifles to Mrs. Carmody. You should have been making parish calls.

O'MALLEY. I have. (*He indicates the basket.*) Old Mrs. McDowd—the one with the big house and the rheumatism—she sent you a present.

FITZGIBBON (*brightening*). She did, eh? *Very* generous of her, I must say. A fine, Christian woman, Mrs. McDowd—has the proper spirit. (*Comes eagerly to the table, watching O'Malley fumble with the hasps on the lid of the basket*) Something to eat, I dare say? (*Rubbing his hands expectantly*) Preserves, no doubt? Maybe jam or pickled pigs' feet. Mrs. McDowd is famous for her pigs' feet. Possibly some brandied peaches? (*Licking his lips*) If there's one thing I'm partial to, it's a nice, big jar of brandied peaches. Aren't you?

O'MALLEY (*sheepishly*). Uh-huh . . .

O'Malley lifts the lid and commences to ladle out, one by one, five tiny puppies, setting them on the table. Father Fitzgibbon's disappointment is ludicrous. He eyes the pups bitterly.

FITZGIBBON (*shaking his head*). They're too young, O'Malley—much too young to be separated from their mother.

O'MALLEY (*setting down the last pup*). That's what she said.

And on this, O'Malley brings forth the embarrassed mother and sets her on the table with her hungry offspring.

FITZGIBBON (*stiffly*). The joy of giving is indeed a pleasure—especially when you get rid of something you don't want. Mrs. McDowd is full of those tricks. When her husband died she sent me his umbrella, his long flannel underwear, and his truss.

Two or three of the pups have "plunked" off the table onto the lawn and are exploring Father Fitzgibbon's flower beds. With a startled exclamation, the old priest starts to round them up. At this O'Malley looks up and we see what he sees: Father Timothy O'Dowd is coming toward O'Malley. O'Malley goes to meet him, and they greet each other enthusiastically. O'Dowd starts singing "Hail, Alma Mater" and O'Malley joins him, till they both sing lustily.

O'MALLEY AND TIMOTHY (*shaking hands*). Chuck!
Timmy!
How long's it been, Chuck?
Four, five years. Five, anyway. (*O'Malley takes his arm.*) Come on over and meet Father Fitzgibbon!

They go to where Father Fitzgibbon is dumping the pups into the basket. As fast as he puts them in, others scramble out. O'Malley and Timothy O'Dowd come up to him.

O'MALLEY. Father Fitzgibbon, this is my old friend, Father O'Dowd. We've been friends since we were knee-high to a niblick. He was our local Huckleberry Finn. . . . He believes in laugh and the world laughs with you, and if you cry—you cry all by yourself. (*Timothy beams appropriately.*)

Father Fitzgibbon has got the pups into the basket and put the lid on. He eyes O'Dowd without enthusiasm.

TIMOTHY (*to Fitzgibbon*). I dropped by to see if Father O'Malley could play a little golf this afternoon.

FITZGIBBON. Oh, you did. . . . Where's your parish?

TIMOTHY (*with a gesture*). Over here —St. Joseph's.

FITZGIBBON. What time do you say your Morning Mass?

TIMOTHY. Six o'clock.

FITZGIBBON (*nodding*). Uh—ummh! Now, about your golf. . . . I can't answer for you, but at St. Dominic's we have very little time for games of golf—and such like. And if you were working for me, all I can say is *you* wouldn't have time for it ayther.

TIMOTHY (*to O'Malley*). It's lucky for me, then, I'm at St. Joseph's! (*He beams.*)

FITZGIBBON (*sourly*). It's my hope St. Joseph's is able to say the same.

O'MALLEY (*chuckling*). He's got you there, Timmy. Father, you ought to come 'round with us sometime. It's a great game.

TIMOTHY. Sure, Father—we'd teach you. A man's never too old to learn.

O'MALLEY. Lots of fresh air on a golf-course.

FITZGIBBON. And profanity, too. (*Emphatically*) No—a golf-course is nothing but a pool room moved outdoors.

TIMOTHY (*laughing with O'Malley*). You mind if I use that one sometime, Father?

O'MALLEY (*as he and Timothy smile*). Seriously, Father—why don't you take it up?

TIMOTHY. I've got half my parish playing.

FITZGIBBON. Perhaps if they didn't play so much golf you would hear more confessions.

TIMOTHY. I find the more golf they play the less they have to confess! (*He beams at O'Malley.*)

For over a moment Father Fitzgibbon eyes Timothy academically, then speaks inquiringly.

FITZGIBBON. Young man, would you mind telling me just how you ever became a priest?

O'MALLEY. We blindfolded him and he thought he was joining the Elks.

But at that moment Mrs. Carmody's head pops out of Father Fitzgibbon's study window.

MRS. CARMODY. Father Fitzgibbon, you're wanted on the telephone.

And so with a mumbled "Excuse me," Father Fitzgibbon exits toward the study.

TIMOTHY (*nodding off in the direction of Fitzgibbon*). Does he know?

O'MALLEY (*sharply*). Does he know what?

TIMOTHY. That you're in charge?

O'MALLEY (*concerned*). How did you know?

TIMOTHY. I didn't . . . but I gathered as much when I heard you were here. He's getting old. Everybody knows St. Dominic's is in a bad way. It'll take a young man with a lot of fight to pull it out.

O'MALLEY. Look, Timmy — don't mention it to anybody, will you? (*Timothy shakes his head.*) You see, when I saw the Bishop it was our understanding that if I came here Father Fitzgibbon was to remain as Pastor, and I was to straighten out St. Dominic's . . . without hurting his feelings.

TIMOTHY. You're in charge, but you're not? (*O'Malley nods.*) I don't think I'd like an assignment like that . . . (*As an afterthought*) But the Bishop couldn't very well put him out to pasture, could he?

At that moment Fitzgibbon enters. He looks from one to the other.

FITZGIBBON (*to Timothy*). What is this I hear about a pasture?

TIMOTHY (*fumbling*). Well—uh—Father, I—I was saying to him—(*pointing to O'Malley*) the next time I come *past yure* church I'll drop in and see you.

He looks at O'Malley over Fitzgibbon's shoulder, and the look says, "God forgive me!" He tips his hat nervously to Fitzgibbon, backs away, turns and leaves.

FITZGIBBON (*briskly, to O'Malley*). Mrs. Quimp just phoned. Her landlord's throwing her out again. She wants somebody to come right down. You'd better go. See what you can do.

O'MALLEY (*picking up his hat and starting away*). Glad to, Father.

FITZGIBBON (*calling after him*). Mrs. Quimp lives at—

O'MALLEY (*interrupting him*). I know—"candles and scandals!"

As Father Fitzgibbon stares after him, shaking his head helplessly, the scene dissolves to the CHURCH ENTRANCE and the STREET. As Father O'Malley breezes out onto the street, he passes Haines, Sr. He checks O'Malley.

HAINES (*faintly sarcastic*). Bet you're the new assistant—the one who's going to get St. Dominic's out of all its trouble. (*O'Malley nods, and laughs.*)

O'MALLEY. And I'll bet *you're* all the trouble. (*Pause, then*) I'll wager you're the man with the mortgage

HAINES (*a bit taken aback*). Oh, so you've heard about the mortgage.

O'MALLEY. All churches have mortgages. It isn't respectable for a church not to have one. (*Extending his hand*) My name's O'Malley.

HAINES (*taking it, a little reluctantly*). Mine's Haines—Ted Haines, Sr.

O'MALLEY. Nice meeting you—maybe we'll want to touch you for a little more. We could do with a new paint job. (*Turning to leave*) You look like a man it'd be a pleasure to do business with.

With a "S'long" gesture, he walks briskly away. Not quite knowing how to take it, Haines stares after him, takes a few steps forward, and follows him with his eyes.

This dissolves to the BROWNSTONE FRONT. O'Malley appears, looks the building over, and starts up the steps. He stops abruptly as from within come the sounds of violence, the hurried clumping of feet down a flight of wooden stairs. The door flies open and two hefty house-movers back out hastily. They are followed immediately by Ted Haines, Jr. As young Haines backs hurriedly down the steps, a broom, wielded by Mrs. Quimp, descends square on top of his head, crushing his natty felt hat down over his ears. We get a fleeting glimpse of the infuriated Quimp, and then she disappears, slamming the door behind her. Extricating himself from his felt hat, young Haines finds himself face-to-face with Father O'Malley. He grins cheerfully.

TED. Hello, Father. The Quimp and I were just discussing you.

Restoring his hat to shape, he moves down the steps with O'Malley.

TED (*as they reach the bottom of the steps*). I represent the Knickerbocker Savings and Loan Company, and inasmuch as Mrs. Quimp declines to pay her rent, the Knickerbocker Savings and Loan Company refuses to offer her any further hospitality.

He pulls out his pipe, pats his pockets for his tobacco pouch, but apparently hasn't got it.

O'MALLEY (*offering him his pouch*). Is she very far in arrears?

TED (*taking the pouch*). In the opinion of the Knickerbocker Savings and Loan, any arrears are too far. (*Sniffing the tobacco, starting to fill his pipe*) Mrs. Quimp has paid us nothing for six months. (*Indicating the pouch*) Thanks, Father.

O'MALLEY (*pulling out his pipe*). I think it's mighty fine of you to show Mrs. Quimp so much leniency.

TED (*holding up a cautioning hand*). Just a minute—the Knickerbocker Savings and Loan would be very much embarrassed if the rumor got around that they had shown leniency to anybody. (*Solemnly*) The corporation has no soul, Father.

The two men light their pipes, sharing Ted's match-box.

TED (*indicating the step*). Sit down, Father.

There is a close view of O'MALLEY and TED as O'Malley sits down on the lower step and Ted leans against the railing. Their pipes are both going well.

O'MALLEY. Suppose the poor old woman doesn't have any place to go?

TED (*breezily*). The Knickerbocker Savings and Loan is not a charitable institution like St. Dominic's. We have our investors to think of—

O'MALLEY (*nodding gravely*). I know . . . three and a half percent and security.

TED (*nodding*). With us it's just a matter of cold-blooded business, Father. (*He sits down on the step beside O'Malley.*) While with *you*—it's different. (*Prodding O'Malley with his pipe*) You haven't got anything and you don't want anything. That's your business—and people respect you for it. But I'm not in your business, see? And if *I* haven't got anything and don't want anything—*I'm a bum.*

O'MALLEY (*shaking his head thoughtfully*). Surely there ought to be something we can do about it.

TED (*emphatically*). I don't know what you're going to do about it— (*He jumps up.*) But we're going to throw that old fuddleduck out on her ear!

He makes a move as though to summon the house-movers. Jumping up, O'Malley restrains him.

O'MALLEY (*confidentially*). Look—why don't you give her a break—why don't you give her another month to make good in?

Ted shakes his head, and starts again to move her out. Again O'Malley restrains him.

O'MALLEY. At St. Dominic's we'll guarantee that much of her indebtedness.

TED. St. Dominic's! (*He guffaws.*) I see you haven't been around long, Father. Why, St. Dominic's is in worse shape than The Quimp. My old man happens to own the mortgage, and he says—

O'MALLEY (*interrupting*). Oh—so your father holds the mortgage, eh?

TED. You're darned right he holds it, and confidentially, I think he'd like to find a way to foreclose . . . wants to tear down the church and make a parking lot out of it. (*Laughing breezily*) Oh, he's a *very* disliked man—and I'm sort of following in his footsteps.

O'MALLEY. Junior, huh? (*He pauses, then*) Well, getting back to Mrs. Quimp—

TED (*cutting in briskly*). Don't worry about her—she's as good as on the sidewalk right now. (*Calling off*) Hey, Mike—put a shoulder to that door!

We see Mike and his companion lumbering toward the steps.

O'MALLEY (*to Mike and his companions*). Wait a minute, fellows . . . (*He turns earnestly to young Haines.*) Ever thought that here's a chance to do something really fine?

TED (*flatly*). No.

O'MALLEY. Well, think about it. Try opening up your heart. Forget the Knickerbocker Savings and Loan for a while and be yourself. Try a little charity. (*He smiles engagingly.*) "Bread upon the waters—Do unto others"—and all that sort of thing. Believe me—it pays off.

Ted makes a great show of being touched. Basically, he's a fine kid, and we think he likes O'Malley. Now, however, we feel he's just putting on an act.

TED (*with a little too much emotion*). Father, you've affected me deeply. I'll do it for you. (*Then, with his old briskness*) But, mark my words, if she doesn't pay up in thirty days I'll throw the old bat right out on her— (*O'Malley raises a restraining hand.*) So help me! (*He grins a wide friendly grin.*) You know, if I don't watch my step, Father—I'm sure going to grow up to be an awful heel. (*They both laugh, then with a gesture to the movers*) Okay, fellas— see you here in thirty days.

o'malley. I appreciate this, Mr. Haines. After all, it isn't what you take from others that matters—it's what you *give*. And would you give me back my tobacco?

Haines laughs, fumbles in his pocket and hands the pouch back.

ted. Okay, Father. . . . You've got to watch me every minute! (*He laughs gustily, and they both start down the street in opposite directions.*)

The scene dissolves to a STREET along which moves a LARGE TRUCK loaded with crates of live poultry. On the back of the truck a gang of young hoodlums, including most of the participants in the preceding baseball game, are expertly breaking open the crates and releasing the birds. The truck passes O'Malley coming from the opposite direction. He stops dead in sheer amazement, as the air is suddenly filled with turkeys, chickens and ducks, gobbling, squawking, flying in all directions. He turns and starts after the truck. Next we see the CAB OF THE TRUCK where, upon hearing the squawking of poultry, the driver looks in the rear-view mirror. The MIRROR shows the air and the street filled with poultry, and the young hoodlums dropping off the truck. Then, brakes screaming, the truck slams to a stop. The young hoodlums are grabbing up whatever birds are handiest. Shouting bloody-murder, the outraged driver leaps out of the truck.

o'malley, momentarily, stands dumbfounded. (Over the scene we hear the shouts of the driver and the terrified squawking of the poultry. Then, abruptly, the shrill blast of a police whistle, and O'Malley dashes out of sight.) The STREET is then seen in turmoil: It is a melee of young hoodlums, squawking poultry, flying feathers, and a surge of pedestrians who join with the driver in a mad scramble to retrieve the birds. As two cops, one of them McCarthy, come pounding into the scene, the young hoodlums scatter with whatever booty they have managed to scoop up. Finally, we see o'malley, with the best intentions in the world, racing in hot pursuit of a fine white duck.

The scene dissolves to the WALL of the CHURCH GARDENS as the uproar from the street drifts into the scene. From the other side of the wall, the head of one of the young hoodlums pops up like a periscope. He is a Teutonic-looking kid, with a closely-cropped blond head. This is HERMAN LANGERHANKE. He scans the garden, which is apparently deserted, then disappears. Almost immediately another youngster's head pops into view. He is a handsome, curly-headed young Italian boy of about thirteen. This is TONY SCAPONI, leader of the gang. Tony heaves himself up onto the wall, sits astride of it, and reaching down, reappears with a fine, big turkey-gobbler. Then, extending his hand, he yanks young Herman up onto the wall beside him. They look around furtively, then drop down into the garden. Stealthily, cautiously, they proceed across the garden.

Then they appear in the CORNER of the CHURCH, on one side. The turkey-gobbler is under Tony's arm, while Tony's right hand is muffling its outcries. And now, coming forward, on the other side, deep in meditation, is Father Fitzgibbon. A few moments, and simultaneously the two factions meet, the two youngsters running smack into the startled old man. The boys jump a foot, and back up.

FITZGIBBON (*mildly*). Ah . . . good afternoon, boys! (*And momentarily, the two boys are paralyzed.*)

TONY (*feebly*). 'Lo, Fadder . . .

At that moment, wriggling its head out of Tony's grip, the turkey uncorks a prolonged gobble; and spotting the bird, Father Fitzgibbon's eyes light up.

FITZGIBBON. A fine fat bird you got there, boys.

TONY (*gulping*). Yes, Fadder . . . (*Shooting a scared glance at Herman*) Me an' Hoiman—we wuz— uh—we wuz sorta bringin' it over to yuh. (*Thrusting the turkey toward Father Fitzgibbon*) It's—uh—sort of a present. Ain't it, Hoiman? (*And Herman nods convulsively, muttering, "Uh-yeah."*)

FITZGIBBON (*delighted*). Well, now —that's very generous of you—such a fine bird and all. (*To Herman*) And where, may I ask, did you get it?

HERMAN (*paralyzed*). We—uh—we sorta—

TONY (*interrupting, hurriedly*). We won it in a raffle—uh—over to— (*a wide gesture*) de pitcher thee-ayter.

FITZGIBBON. Well, well, now—just think of that. (*Pause, then*) But surely your mother—

TONY (*quickly*). Aw, 'cept at Christmas—Ma don't like toikey.

FITZGIBBON (*beaming*). She doesn't, eh? Then that's most fortunate for me. (*Tucking the turkey securely under his arm*) There's nothing I'm more partial to than a fine Tom-turkey . . . (*licking his lips*) roasted —with dressing. (*Nodding*) I do indeed appreciate your kindness, boys.

TONY. Aw—it ain't nuttin'.

FITZGIBBON. On the contrary, boys . . . I appreciate the thought behind it. Small luxuries, as well as small sacrifices, are ofttimes the most Godly. (*He pats them both on their heads pontifically.*) Well, bless you both—and convey my kind regards to your good mothers and fathers.

A closeup of FITZGIBBON shows the turkey flapping its wings furiously and we see him struggling with it helplessly, trying to hold it.

TONY (*running to him and taking the bird from him*). Okay, Fadder. We'll see you later.

FITZGIBBON. Take it—take it inside— inside the kitchen to the housekeeper.

The two boys eye each other and exit hurriedly. Father Fitzgibbon brushes himself off.

At this the scene dissolves quickly to a close view of an OVEN. The door is open, and the turkey, now brown, sizzling and luscious, is being basted by Mrs. Carmody's loving hands. Then we see the PARISH DINING ROOM at night. The table is set for dinner.

O'MALLEY (*entering with Father Fitzgibbon*). I'm sorry, Father, but I disagree with you. Young Haines acted very reasonably.

O'Malley pulls out a chair for the old man and eases it under him as he sits

MCCARTHY. Evenin', Ma'am. I'm wantin' to see Father O'Malley

MRS. CARMODY. Father O'Malley's at his dinner now. Maybe you'll take a seat.

McCarthy and the boys enter, the two kids awed, scared stiff. As Mrs. Carmody closes the door, O'Malley enters from the dining room, napkin in hand. Mrs. Carmody goes toward the kitchen.

O'MALLEY. Hello, McCarthy.

MCCARTHY (beaming). Good evenin', Father. (Indicating Herman and Tony) Well—I brung 'em. (Pointing) Tony Scaponi—Herman Langerhanke.

O'MALLEY. That's fine.

His manner is not patronizing. On the contrary, he treats them as adults, his equals.

O'MALLEY (extending his hand to the youngsters). Hyah, Tony—hyah, Herman.

The two boys shake hands in limp silence, and stare at O'Malley uncomfortably.

O'MALLEY (to McCarthy). You needn't wait, McCarthy.

MCCARTHY (dubiously). Well—okay, Father.

He favors the two youngsters with a warning scowl and leaves ponderously, closing the door. The two youngsters exchange a quick glance of relief.

O'MALLEY. Well, fellows—I hear you and the mob are great baseball fans. (The two only give him a bewildered nod.) Saturday, the Yanks are playing the St. Louis Browns. How about me taking you and the gang?

Tony and Herman cannot believe their ears. They eye each other, and the look says, "Is he nuts?"

O'MALLEY. You see, St. Louis is my home town. I can get all the passes I want.

Again Tony and Herman exchange a look. They just can't believe it.

O'MALLEY. Well, how about it?

HERMAN (gulping). Sure . . . I guess so. (He looks at Tony for confirmation.)

TONY. Yeah. . . . I guess de fellas'd be glad to.

O'MALLEY (briskly). Okay. It's a date, then. Meet me here Saturday around noon.

Still incredulous, the kids nod as O'Malley opens the door.

O'MALLEY. Now, run along home to your dinner . . . and I'll finish mine. (He winks significantly at the two kids.) Turkey!

For a moment it doesn't register, and then they both react with a terrific "double-take." O'Malley starts to close the door.—Then the scene cuts back to the dining room (a close view at the table). Mrs. Carmody has just served the vegetables and is leaving toward the kitchen. Father Fitzgibbon has completed the carving of the turkey. He has served both himself and O'Malley. O'Malley enters briskly, sits down and helps himself to vegetables.

FITZGIBBON (as O'Malley sits down). Let's see—uh—where was I? I know, I know—

O'MALLEY (grinning). What made me become a priest?

down at the table. O'Malley then sits opposite him.

FITZGIBBON (*as he unfolds his napkin*). And why not? You guaranteed Mrs. Quimp's rent, didn't you?

O'MALLEY. Of course I did.

FITZGIBBON (*acidly*). St. Dominic's can't afford such obligations—and besides, I expected you to counsel Mrs. Quimp—not to adopt her.

Before O'Malley can answer, Mrs. Carmody sails into the room from the kitchen, holding aloft a fine brown, luscious turkey on a large platter. With a flourish, she sets it before Father Fitzgibbon. O'Malley sees the turkey, gives it a ludicrous "double take," and catches Mrs. Carmody's eye.

O'MALLEY. Ah—*hot* turkey!

MRS. CARMODY. Hot—of course it's hot. (*And she goes out.*)

Father Fitzgibbon, keeping his eyes fixed squarely on the turkey, says grace.

FITZGIBBON. Bless us, O Lord! And these Thy gifts, which we are about to . . . (*His voice fades into a mumble—he concludes with a jerk.*) Amen.

O'MALLEY. Amen.

And then with one swoop, Father Fitzgibbon falls on the turkey with the carving tools, O'Malley eying him thoughtfully for a moment.

O'MALLEY (*tentatively*). Father—do you know a youngster by the name of Tony Scaponi?

His carving tools poised in mid-air, Father Fitzgibbon looks up, immediately on the defensive.

FITZGIBBON. And what about him?

O'MALLEY. Well, this afternoon—

FITZGIBBON (*flatly*). Tony comes from a fine, upstanding Catholic family . . . (*As an afterthought*) Eleven children. Sure, I know Tony —as fine a lad as there is in the parish.

O'MALLEY. The police don't think so.

FITZGIBBON. Oh—they *don't*, eh?

O'MALLEY. No. And if something isn't done about it young Tony and his pals'll wind up in a reform school.

FITZGIBBON. Who told ye that?

O'MALLEY. The police.

FITZGIBBON (*snorting*). You've been listening to Patrick McCarthy, no doubt. Well, he hasn't been to Mass in the last ten years.

O'MALLEY. Maybe. But McCarthy's right about those kids—they're terrorizing the whole neighborhood.

FITZGIBBON (*pounding the table*). Not another word, d'ye hear?! The way the police talk, you'd think every lad in the parish was a criminal. (*Eying the turkey*) I'll have you know the very food before us was put here by two of the very lads the police are so maliciously slandering . . . and Tony Scaponi was one of 'em. (*He recommences to carve the turkey*) I gave 'em my blessings—

O'MALLEY. And they gave you the bird.

At that moment, we hear the doorbell ring, and the scene cuts to the HALL. Mrs. Carmody appears and opens the front door to admit police officer PATRICK MCCARTHY with Tony Scaponi and Herman in tow. Officer McCarthy, 250 pounds of New York's finest, is middle-aged, enormous.

GOING MY WAY 167

FITZGIBBON. No, no. It was about young Tony. What was it the police were accusing him of? (*The old man has now picked up a luscious turkey-drumstick.*)

O'MALLEY. Stealing, Father.

FITZGIBBON (*bristling*). Stealing? Stealing *what*?

O'MALLEY (*quietly*). Turkeys.

The old man stiffens, the turkey-drumstick halfway to his mouth. In a portentous silence, Fitzgibbon looks at the remains of the turkey on the table, then at the drumstick in his hand. He knows what O'Malley is thinking, and O'Malley knows he knows.

FITZGIBBON (*feebly*). Did the poor man get his—uh—turkeys back?

O'MALLEY (*nodding solemnly*). All but *one*.

FATHER FITZGIBBON, seen close as the view moves up to him, eyes the drumstick in his hand hungrily. He fights against the temptation to eat it, and slowly, catching O'Malley's eye, lowers the drumstick to the plate. O'Malley smilingly passes him the bread, and Fitzgibbon takes a slice, saying, "Thank you," as the scene fades out.

PART THREE

THE PARISH HOUSE LIVING ROOM fades in. O'Malley is seated at the piano, playing. [The scene dissolves to the PARISH HOUSE RECEPTION ROOM in the morning. Father O'Malley is at an ancient piano. Thoughtfully, abstractedly, he is playing sacred music. The door opens. TWO OLD LADIES move timidly, almost apologetically, into the room. O'Malley, playing softly, nods, and smiles to them. After a moment's hesitation:

FIRST OLD LADY (*shyly*). Good morning, Father—we would like to make a confession.

O'Malley turns and looks at them; a closeup shows their faces are calm, serene—the faces of two ancient Madonnas; then we see the GROUP as a slow, kindly smile transfigures O'Malley's face.

O'MALLEY (*gently*). Have you done anything wrong?

OLD LADIES (*in unison*). No, Father. Oh, no!

O'MALLEY. Then, run along . . .

Murmuring, "Yes, Father," the two old ladies back out of the room. O'Malley resumes playing.]

The door opens, this time to admit Officer McCarthy. With him is a slim, lovely girl in her late 'teens. She is definitely not "Big City" but has a world of self-assurance. This is CAROL JAMES. At the moment she is sullenly defiant, and carries a chip on her most attractive shoulder. O'Malley turns on the bench.

O'MALLEY. Ah, McCarthy. How are you?

MCCARTHY (*beaming*). Mornin', Father—you open fer bizness?

O'MALLEY. Always open for business, McCarthy. What is it?

McCarthy comes forward with the girl. She gives a little defiant toss of her head.

MCCARTHY. I gotta problem, Father . . . seems like it's more yours than mine. (*"Thumbing" the girl*) It's her.

O'Malley looks at the girl and smiles. She frowns, twitches her shoulders, and the movement says: "Yes—and what are you going to do about it?" Smiling, O'Malley indicates a chair. The girl shakes her head. O'Malley nods for McCarthy to go ahead.

MCCARTHY (*ponderously*). Well, Father—it's like this. Last night I'm walkin' me beat, see—and who d'ya think I runs into?

O'MALLEY (*indicating the girl*). Her.

MCCARTHY. Uh-uh! Mrs. Quimp. "Officer McCarthy," she sez (*imitating The Quimp's nasal drone*), "if you'll take the trouble to go 'round the corner you'll find a girl . . . I been watchin' her, and she ain't up to no good." (*Resuming his normal voice*) You know how the old stool-pigeon talks.

O'Malley turns and looks at the girl, and a closeup of Carol shows her meeting O'Malley's gaze with the calm, bored intolerance of youth.

MCCARTHY'S VOICE. Well, Father, I goes around the corner and there, like The Quimp sez, I finds *her*— She's lookin' in Wineberger's Delicatessen Store window.

A close view of the three:

MCCARTHY. Well, I looks at her and I sizes her up. One of those things, I think, so I'm about to say to her— (*a little "Move-along-there" flip of his hand*) "Look, sister—not on my beat," when she turns, and right away I see I'm outa line. (*Nodding toward the girl*) You follow me, Father?

O'Malley studies the girl, and nods.

MCCARTHY. Well, to get down to it, I find she's run away from home an' broke . . . don't know a soul in town. (*Carol closes her eyes, with a gesture of absolute boredom.*) So, instead of bookin' her, I take her home. It was all right with the Missus—for *one* night, but if she stays any longer, well—(*He looks at Carol.*) I guess Mrs. McCarthy, good woman that she is, is no different from any other wife. (*Significantly*) You follow me, Father?

O'MALLEY (*solemnly*). Yes, I follow you.

MCCARTHY. So, anyways, she tells us she left home on account of her folks not understanding her. (*Closing his eyes painfully and beating his breast*) Says she can't *breathe*—says they don't understand her—tryin' to run her life for her!

Carol's boredom is abysmal. She draws in her breath, and rolls her eyes heavenward.

MCCARTHY. She claims whenever they say anything to her, she just goes—(*pantomiming broadly*) *all to pieces!* We tried arguin' with her, Father—but she's a tough one. (*Sincerely outraged*) She thinks "honor thy father and thy mother" is a bellylaugh! (*Mopping his brow, moving toward the door*) Well, Father— guess I'll let you pick it up from there. She'll give you all the lowdown. (*As an afterthought*) Says her name's *Carol James.*

O'MALLEY. All right, McCarthy. (*Whereupon, with a "S'long" gesture, McCarthy leaves, closing the door.*)

O'MALLEY (*to Carol*). Better sit down.

She does, and O'Malley sits opposite her. Then we see them close as, leaning forward, he gives her a friendly smile.

O'MALLEY. Well, Carol—suppose you give me *your* side of it?

CAROL (*shrugging*). It's just about like he said.

O'MALLEY. Don't get along with your folks, eh?

CAROL. No.

O'MALLEY. And you're going to leave home?

CAROL (*emphatically*). Oh, I've left.

O'MALLEY. Unnn . . . (*Pause, then*) How are you fixed for funds?

CAROL. I haven't any. That's how I met Officer McCarthy . . . (*Then, with the arrogant confidence of youth*) Oh, but I'll get by.

There is a pause. Carol calmly adjusts her hat. O'Malley eyes her thoughtfully.

O'MALLEY. Why don't you go home?

CAROL (*stiffening with exasperation*). You, too? (*Teeth and hands clenched*) I tell you at home I can't breathe!

O'MALLEY. Parents, eh?

CAROL (*jumping up at this, the words tumbling out*). They're intolerable! We don't agree on anything! (*Indicating her hair*) Don't like the way I do my hair! (*With gestures*) My eyebrows—too much lipstick—(*indicating the top of her dress*) too something or other! (*Extending her long, red nails*) Too long! (*Touching the hem of her dress*) Too short! Do *you* think it's too short?

O'MALLEY (*after a pause*). No-o-o . . .

CAROL (*hotly*). They even object to my boy-friends! And if they *do* let me go out, they say—(*Imitating her parents*) "Where are you going? Come home early! Come right home after the show!" (*She flops helplessly into her chair*) And no matter how early I get in—it's always too late. If I say we ran out of gas, they say I'm lying.

O'MALLEY (*with a little smile*). Are you?

And for the first time, Carol smiles too. It's a "swell" smile. She nods.

CAROL. Sometimes.

O'MALLEY. Have you ever thought of having your boy-friends over to the house?

A closeup of CAROL shows her exasperation; she rolls her eyes heavenward and blows her hair up off her forehead.

CAROL. Now you talk like *they* do! I tell you, I can't have them over to the house because Grandma sleeps in the living room! By nine o'clock we have to be off the couch—she needs it for her bed. (*With a helpless gesture*) Can you imagine?

O'MALLEY and CAROL: O'Malley nods portentously. He can imagine it very well.

O'MALLEY. Did you ever think that maybe there's two sides to it—that maybe you're a little unreasonable?

CAROL (*bridling*). I'm *eighteen*!

O'MALLEY (*nodding his head solemnly*). O-o-oh . . . eighteen. Tsk-tsk-tsk. As old as that. (*After a pause*) You know, when I was eighteen, I thought my father was pretty dumb . . . but when I was twenty-one, I was surprised to find out how much he'd learned in three years. (*O'Malley laughs, but Carol doesn't think this is funny at all.*) Well, now you're in New York—what do you propose to do?

CAROL (*with great assurance*). I'm going to get a job—I'm a singer.

O'MALLEY. Well, so you're a singer, eh? Any good?

CAROL. Of *course* I'm good.

O'MALLEY. What makes you think so?

CAROL (*exasperated*). Well—I—I'm just good, that's all.

O'MALLEY (*rising*). Would you like to sing something for me? Maybe I can help you. (*Modestly*) I'm supposed to be a pretty good judge.

CAROL. Oh, you wouldn't know the kind of stuff *I* know.

O'MALLEY (*moving toward the piano*). How do you know?

We see the RECEPTION ROOM as O'Malley sits down at the PIANO and plays a few chords in a popular vein.

CAROL (*surprised*). Oh . . . (*She gets up and comes toward the piano.*) Do you happen to know "Day After Forever"?

O'MALLEY (*nodding*). What key? (*He makes a guess at her range and starts to play the introduction.*)

CAROL. Would you mind dropping it a little?

O'Malley does so, and she begins to sing "Day After Forever." Her voice is definitely good, but her gestures are corny, stilted, God-awful. A closeup of O'MALLEY shows him making a half-turn, sneaking a look at her. Her voice impresses him.—CAROL is seen singing, but in an emotional high-spot, she makes a particularly appalling gesture.—At this a closeup of O'MALLEY shows him wincing, and turning his head away.—Finally, Carol concludes her number at the piano, and O'Malley turns on the piano-bench.

THE LYRIC (*sung by Carol*).
All day tomorrow
I'll be whispering your name,
And the day after forever
I know I'll do the same.

Maytime or winter,
I won't let you out of sight.
And the day after forever
We'll talk about tonight.

Your laughter is a melody
That I'll remember long.
It plays upon my heart strings,
It's my favorite song.

All through a lifetime
I'll be loving you, and then
On the day after forever—
I'll just begin again. (*She turns and looks up toward O'Malley smiling.*)

CAROL. Well, what do you think?

O'MALLEY. You've got a pretty good voice . . . (*Carol beams.*) But instead of so much of this— (*He rises and "pantomimes" some of her more ludicrous gestures.*) You'd do better if you put more feeling into the lyrics. Y'know, the fellow went to a lot of trouble writing those lyrics. (*He smiles.*) Don't you think you owe him a break?

CAROL. Well, for instance, Father?

She sits down at the piano, and plays the opening bars of the song. O'Malley hesitates a moment, then goes into it, singing it with great feeling.

O'MALLEY (*singing*).
All day tomorrow
I'll be whispering your name,

And the day after forever,
I know I'll do the same.

Maytime or winter,
I won't let you out of sight,
And the day after forever
We'll talk about tonight.

CAROL (*seen in a closeup as she smiles understandingly*). I see what you mean, Father. (*She is startled by the quality of his voice.*)

O'MALLEY (*seen close*). Supposing you try it then, huh? Just speak the words.

CAROL (*speaking the lines*). Your laughter is a melody That I'll remember long.

O'MALLEY. That's it.

CAROL. It plays upon my heart strings.

O'MALLEY. Now sing it.

CAROL (*singing*). It's my favorite song. All through a lifetime—

But now, while we hear her singing, "I'll be loving you," and then both of them singing, "And then on the day after tomorrow, I'll just begin again," we see Father Fitzgibbon coming down the landing, leaning on the bannister, looking down and listening.

O'MALLEY (*stopping his accompaniment*). What's that— (*singing*) A-gain?

CAROL. Well, I was imitating you, Father.

O'MALLEY. Did I do that?

CAROL. Oh, definitely.

O'MALLEY. Well, maybe, but I didn't do that— (*Singing*) And the day after forever,
We'll talk about tonight.
(*Speaking*) There's no thought behind that at all. (*Snapping his fingers*) (*Singing*) We'll talk about to— (*Speaking*) What has that got to do with the song?

But at this point O'Malley looks up, and sees Fitzgibbon, and Carol follows his gaze. We see Fitzgibbon staring at them, thunderstruck.

O'MALLEY (*a little sheepishly*). Hello, Father. (*Under Fitzgibbon's cold, disapproving stare*) The young lady has come to us for help.

At this, Father Fitzgibbon advances on Carol, who rises. He eyes her a moment.

FITZGIBBON. So it's work you're wantin'?

CAROL (*eagerly*). Yes, Father.

FITZGIBBON (*rubbing his chin thoughtfully*). Well, I think maybe I can place you. (*Carol's face lights up.*) What would ye think of a little general house-work? (*To O'Malley*) Mrs. Scaponi, with all those children— (*To the deflated Carol*) Eleven! (*To O'Malley*) Twelve—in October. (*To Carol*) I think maybe she could use you.

CAROL (*through her teeth*). I'm not looking for that kind of work. I'm a singer.

FITZGIBBON (*sardonically*). Well, now —and where, may I ask, do you expect to find employment? In some cool, airy night club? (*She nods.*) Any prospects?

CAROL. Well—no—not exactly.

FITZGIBBON. And you're willing to starve rather than to push a broom. . . . You have a home, I presume?

O'MALLEY. She just left it.

FITZGIBBON (*with finality*). Then you go right back to your parents. (*Snorting*) A fine little girl like you —singin' in a place like the—uh— Blue Goose or something.

CAROL. Well, you've got to start some place, Father.

FITZGIBBON. Nonsense! Being a good wife and a mother is a good enough start for you! Like your *own* mother.

CAROL (*bitterly*). You haven't seen my mother. (*She's had enough. She turns to O'Malley.*) Goodbye, Father —and thanks. (*And she starts toward the door.*)

FITZGIBBON (*pointing an admonishing finger*). And you go home and *stay* home till the right man comes along.

CAROL (*turning at the door*). The right man'll never come near *our* house! (*She adjusts her hat with a vicious jerk.*) And don't worry, *I'll get by.*

She turns and walks out of the room, shutting the door. At this O'Malley hesitates, and then, with a quick look at Father Fitzgibbon, he starts after her.

Outside the CLOISTER: Carol comes out of the Parish House and starts toward the gate to the street. There is defiance and determination in every move of her body. A moment, and O'Malley, coming out of the Parish House, starts after her. We then see O'MALLEY and FITZGIBBON.

O'MALLEY. Father! (*Fitzgibbon turns and steps forward to him.*) Do you think you could let me have ten, Father?

FITZGIBBON. Huh?

O'MALLEY. Ten dollars. She's all alone. She hasn't a thing.

FITZGIBBON (*reluctantly*). Oh—

O'MALLEY. Open up our hearts, huh? Ten dollars.

FITZGIBBON (*opening his purse, and turning away from O'Malley, who gestures "Just a minute" to Carol out of sight*). How about five, huh?

O'MALLEY. Five? No, no, ten—ten!

Fitzgibbon hands a bill to him, and the view moves with O'MALLEY as he goes to Carol standing outside the doorway.

O'MALLEY. Carol, I didn't like the way you said that "I'll get by!" Here's a little (*holding out the bill*) something to tide you over.

CAROL (*moved but hesitant*). Oh, but —but, Father, I—

O'MALLEY (*insistent*). It's all right. It's not charity. It's a loan.

CAROL (*as she accepts it, and puts it into her bag*). Well, thanks. I can use it. I appreciate it.

Together, they start toward the gate. O'Malley opens it.

CAROL (*extending her hand*). Goodbye, Father.

O'MALLEY (*shaking hands*). Good luck, Carol. (*A pause, then*) I guess there's a lot I could have said—advice and so forth—but I'm afraid you wouldn't have paid any attention. (*He pantomimes "In one ear and out the other."*) After all, you know, you *are* eighteen.

Their eyes meet. She gives him a warm smile.

CAROL. Don't worry, Father—I'll be all right.

O'MALLEY. I know you will, Carol.

CAROL (*with the familiar toss of her head*). I'll get by.

O'MALLEY (*wincing*). Don't say that! (*She starts out into the street—and he calls after her.*) And don't forget, let's hear from you.

CAROL (*calling back*). All right, Father. Goodbye.

She turns and starts down the street. For a moment O'Malley stares after her thoughtfully, and thoughtfully closes the gate. At that moment the church bells above him begin to ring sonorously, and as he starts slowly back toward the Parish House, the scene fades out.

PART FOUR

The STREET outside St. Dominic's, with people passing, fades in. Then we see the CHURCH BASEMENT. It is large, and with its concrete floor, huge furnace and scattered junk, typical. A flight of wooden steps leads up out of the cellar. Tony and his gang are here—Tony and Herman a little apart. Like young cattle in a corral, the youngsters are restless, suspicious, constantly on the verge of a stampede.

HERMAN (*to the others*). Hey, fellas! Whatta we doin' hangin' aroun' here for? (*The boys gather around him.*)

BOYS. Yeah—wassa idea, Tony? Aw—les' scram! Wadda we come here for, anyways?

TONY (*pushing through the boys and stepping up to Herman; tough*). 'Cause I promised O'Malley—dat's what for!

HERMAN. Why?

TONY (*laughing*). 'Cause I said so, see!

There are scattered, windy noises of derision. Herman has gone up the steps of the cellar. He leans over the rail, points to surplices on a clothes line, and lets out a yell.

HERMAN. Hey, fellas! (*Indicating the surplices*) Look! Waist panty-coats.

There is a rush of youngsters into the scene.

BOYS. Yeah!— Lace petticoats!

HERMAN (*a tough little mug; whirling on Tony, snarling*). Reg'lar woisenberg, ain'tcha! Foist t'ing yuh know he'll charm us into dem t'ings!

The smallest of them all, a youngster who will later be identified as "Pitch-Pipe", pipes up.

PITCH-PIPE. Yeah—make altar boys outa us!

Another outburst of "Le's scram! Le's get outa here! Yeah—'fore it's too late!" There is a movement toward the steps. But Tony jumps up ahead of them, and faces them.

TONY. Now, hold it! Foist guy up— I kick his teeth out, see? (*As they hesitate*) Now, look, youse—O'Malley's a right guy! Diden rat on us about da toikeys, did he? Took us to da baseball game, diden he? Bought us hot-dogs, diden he? Gonna take us to a pitcher, ain't he? (*There are a few murmurs of assent.*) Okay, den —give da guy a break!

HERMAN (*contemptuously*). Daaaaah!

He starts up the steps. But Tony shoves him backward, jumps down, grabs him by the front of his shirt, and spins him around. As he cocks his right for a vicious drive at Herman's mouth, he spots O'Malley coming down the steps. In a continuation of his movement, Tony swings Herman around to face O'Malley.

TONY (*pointing*). Say hello to da Fadder!

HERMAN (*feebly*). 'Lo, Fadder . . .

O'MALLEY (*genially*). Hiya, fellas!

As he comes down the steps into the basement they draw back. O'Malley is wearing a pair of dark-gray flannel slacks, his old "St. Louis Browns" sweat-shirt, a "St. Louis Browns" windbreaker, and a baseball cap. The youngsters are staring, pop-eyed at what he is wearing. They come forward, examining him with awe.

TONY. Hey, Fadder—where'd yuh get dat outfit?

O'MALLEY. Oh, it's the St. Louis Browns. I told you . . . I used to work out with them. They—they thought I brought 'em luck. And when I left town they made me a present of it.

HERMAN (*as there is an awed murmur*). Oh, that's just the outfit to wear in a cellar.

He laughs at his own joke. O'Malley and the other kids laugh, too.

O'MALLEY. Oh you! Knocking my team! (*Eying them*) Well, fellas, I guess you fellas wonder why I asked you down here, huh?

TONY (*out of the corner of his mouth*). Hey, Fadder—I want to talk to you a minute, can I?

He nods a "Come-on-over-here," and he and O'Malley, saying, "Pardon me, boys," start out of the scene together, the others watching them suspiciously.

A CORNER of the CELLAR: O'Malley and Tony stop at a pillar.

O'MALLEY. Something on your mind, Tony?

TONY. Well, Fadder—uh—so's yuh won't have no beef comin', I'm layin' it on da line. Okay?

O'MALLEY (*smiling*). Okay!

TONY. Okay! Well, Fadder— (*A nod of his head toward the gang*) Dey's here—like I promised. But you shoulda hoid 'em squawk! Worse dan dat toikey.

O'MALLEY (*laughing with Tony*). Oh, the turkey.—They did, eh?

TONY. Yeah. Dey figgered bein' a priest yuh wuz gonna slip 'em da ole routine. Poisonally, I'm fa givin' yuh a break. An' what I sez wid da gang *goes*.

O'MALLEY. Swell of you, Tony.

TONY (*dismissing it with a gesture*) Aw—pig dust! (*Then, very seriously*) But da way it is now, Fadder —I'm on da hook fa yuh, see? I'm responsible fa yuh, see?

O'MALLEY (*nodding*). I won't let you down, Tony.

TONY. Well, mebbe yuh won't, but I'm tellin' yuh—yuh step outa line just once, and me an' da gang'll drop yuh like yuh wuz a hot patayta. Okay?

O'MALLEY. Okay. (*They shake hands.*) Now, can I talk to 'em?

TONY. Oh, sure. Go ahead.

O'Malley, followed by Tony, steps toward the gang. He looks them over. They are sullen, restless, suspicious.

O'MALLEY. Well, fellas, I'm not going to do much talking. Like Tony here, I'm going to lay it right on the line. I asked you down here to do me a favor. (*Pause, then*) St. Dominic's needs a choir—and I want to start one.

This is met with little enthusiasm: murmurs, a restless scuffling of feet.

O'MALLEY. I know what you're thinking—but it isn't going to be that way at all. It's going to be fun—and believe me, I like fun as much as you do. And if it doesn't work out that way—if you think I'm trying to slip something over on you—then, like Tony says, you can drop me like a hot patayta.

The boys make no comment; they let O'Malley hang there.

O'MALLEY (*after a moment*). You fellas figure I'm pretty much of a long-shot, don't you? Well, I think you're all pretty good sports—not scared to take a chance. (*He smiles.*) Even on a long-shot. Whatta you say? You going to give me a break?

There is still no answer.

TONY. Well, Fadder, dat depends. What is it?

O'MALLEY. Well, how many of you fellas know "Three Blind Mice"?

The gang exchange startled looks. A moment, and one of them raises a cautious hand, calling out, "I know it," and then glances at the boy next to him sheepishly. O'Malley tries to be encouraging: "One—two. Any more?" Three or four more follow.

TONY (*impatiently*). Aw, come on, yuh all know it. (*Whereupon all the boys raise their hands.*)

O'MALLEY. Everybody knows it?

TONY. Sure.

O'MALLEY. Fine. (*But he looks in Herman's direction, and exclaims.*) What's the matter with him over there?

TONY. Oh, Hoiman? He's—he's poutin'. Hey, Hoiman!

We see Herman going up the stairs. On hearing Tony, he stops, looks at the hanging surplices disgustedly, shakes his head, and continues up the steps. Then we see Tony and the other boys with O'Malley.

TONY (*to O'Malley*). He's got a good bass voice. D'yuh want him?

O'MALLEY (*nodding*). Well, certainly, Tony.

TONY (*confidently, starting after Herman*). You got 'im, Fadder! (*He starts up the steps.*)

O'MALLEY (*returning to his problem*). Now, let's see. We've got to divide this up some way.

THE GARDEN as Herman comes out: As he passes a fine stained-glass window Tony overtakes him, grabs him and spins him around.

TONY. Hey, Hoiman! Wait a minute! The Fadder wants to see ya.

HERMAN (*yelling*). Well, I don't want to see the Fadder.

At this, Tony, gangster-fashion, backhands him viciously in the mouth.

TONY (*as Herman starts to protest*). Sssssssh! ("*Shushing*" *him with both hands*)

HERMAN (*bewildered*). Why—

TONY (*slapping his head back and forth again*). Will you keep quiet? Will you, please?

HERMAN (*goggle-eyed*). Don't hit me on the head! (*As Tony merely "shushes" him*) You make me dopey!

TONY. You are dopey. Now keep quiet.

Again, as Herman starts to speak, Tony back-hands him, and again "shushes" him in a whisper. Then he grabs him and swings him around.

TONY. Come here! Now, look. He wants a bass singer.

HERMAN (*yelling*). I ain't a bass singer.

TONY (*slapping again*). You are a bass singer.

HERMAN (*raging*). Why am I a bass singer?!

TONY (*slapping again*). That burns me up!

HERMAN (*now wobbly*). My head! My head!

TONY (*slapping*). Will you go down, please? Will you go down? (*As Herman opens his mouth, he gets another slap.*) Now keep quiet. Okay?— Let's go.

HERMAN (*giving up*). Okay. (*And Tony leads him back.*)

Then we see Father Fitzgibbon coming up the garden path. He stops at a hedge. He looks at it and makes a few feeble attempts to jump the hedge as O'Malley did, and gives up. Instead he walks around it, looks back at it longingly, and starts up the steps. This dissolves into the CHURCH as the old priest comes to a side altar and kneels. He bows his head, closes his eyes, in prayer. Suddenly, however, from the basement below comes a blast of sound: it is the boys and O'Malley singing "Three Blind Mice."

BOYS.
"Three blind mice,
Three blind mice,
See how they run,
See how they run."

The old priest stiffens where he kneels. His lips purse ominously. He rubs the back of his neck, tries to concentrate, as the voices continue.

BOYS.
"They all ran after the farmer's wife,
She cut off their tails with the carving knife.
Did you ever see such a sight in your life, etc."

He finally gives up, crosses himself, rises, and goes out.

This dissolves to the HALLWAY as Fitzgibbon comes down the steps and goes over to Mrs. Carmody, who is standing at the foot of the stairs.

MRS. CARMODY. It's none of my business, Father . . . but sometimes the things we do in haste are the things we most regret. Think it over awhile. If you *really* feel you must see the Bishop—

FITZGIBBON (*emphatically*). That, I do.

MRS. CARMODY. The boys are better off here than running the streets. I'm sure that was Father O'Malley's idea.

FITZGIBBON. I'm a tolerant man, Mrs. Carmody, but there are some things that get under my skin, and "Three Blind Mice" is one of them.

MRS. CARMODY. But he's young, Father. (*The old man snorts.*) Sure, and I'll admit it . . . maybe a wee bit impulsive . . . but I know he means well. (*Then, significantly, almost a warning*) And after all, the Bishop *did* put him here.

FITZGIBBON. Yes, and the Bishop'll put him some place else. I'm going to ask to have Father O'Malley transferred. (*He puts on his glasses and starts to leave.*)

For the first time Fitzgibbon is aware of Mrs. Carmody's distress. He interprets it as sympathy for O'Malley.

FITZGIBBON (*patting her arm*). Don't worry. It'll not be a bad report I'm making. I'll just be telling the Bishop that on matters of policy this young man and I differ—that we don't see eye-to-eye—and I'd be happier if he were sent some other place.

The moving scene has brought them to an ancient hat and coat rack. Fitzgibbon reaches for his coat, but Mrs. Carmody checks him.

MRS. CARMODY (*pleading, very distressed*). It's a long, hard way you've come, Father. Forty-five years, and most of the time carrying other people's burdens. Time's come now when you should rest on your oars —take things a mite easier. Look around a bit—(*smiling wistfully*) enjoy the scenery. Let somebody else carry the load for you . . . (*smiling again*) and sure, Father O'Malley's got a strong pair of shoulders.

For a moment Father Fitzgibbon hesitates, and then starts convulsively as from the basement of the church the sound of "Three Blind Mice" bursts out again.

FITZGIBBON. See what I mean. (*Reaching for his hat and coat*) No. No. I've got to see the Bishop!

The old man commences to struggle into his coat, and with a sigh of resignation Mrs. Carmody helps him. As the song continues, the old man adjusts his muffler and puts on his hat. He opens the door and starts out. Mrs. Carmody, snatching his umbrella from the rack, overtakes him and thrusts it into his hand. As the old priest shuffles away, Mrs. Carmody, staring after him, shakes her head, and the gesture says: "No good will come of this."

This dissolves into a closeup of the clock showing 4:28, and then into the BASEMENT as the clock keeps ticking. We get a full view with O'Malley standing, facing the seated boys.

O'MALLEY. Well, we've got our sections now, and I'm going to give each section a note, and we'll put them all together and we'll have a chord. Take this section first. Here's your note. (*Singing*) Bah. Got that? Let me hear it.

ONE BOY (*singing*). Ahhhh.

O'MALLEY. Oh, I thought we had some singers here! I want to hear everybody in this section. Big now! Let me hear it.

We get a full view of O'Malley and the boys as the first section sings a note.

O'MALLEY. That's good! Second section, here's your note.

We see O'Malley closer as he sings Ba, ba. Ba.

O'MALLEY. You got that? Let me hear it. (*And now the second section sings a note. But one boy, called Elmer, sings a sour note.*)

O'MALLEY (*seen close*). Oh, we got a cruller in there somewhere! Who's that? You? (*Turning to the boy*) What's your name?

ELMER. My name's Elmer.

O'MALLEY. Elmer. Your voice is changing or something, isn't it?

ELMER. Yeah, I guess so, Father.

O'MALLEY. I think we'll have to drop you down a bracket. You get over here in the third section. Elmer is a switch-hitter, it seems. (*As the boys laugh*) Let me hear that second section again. (*Singing*) Ba, ba. (*As the second section sings a note*) Oh, that's great. Now, the third section. Here's your note. (*Singing*) Ba, ba, ba. Got that? (*As the third section sings a note*) Elmer, you sing like you were made for this section. (*Now seen close*) Now we're gonna drop way down in the basement. Watch this now. This is—this is tricky. Everybody take a toe hold. (*Singing*) Ba, ba, ba, ba. That's your note. (*Singing*) Ba. Let me hear it. (*As the fourth section sings a note*) Oh, there's a pink one in there somewhere!

TONY. That wasn't me!

O'MALLEY. What did you sing?

TONY. Uh—(*He sings a note and his voice breaks.*)

Tony rises, and glares at the boys as they laugh.

O'MALLEY (*clearing his throat*). Sit down, Tony. Okay, everybody together now. (*Tony sits down.*) You've got your notes— (*Singing*) Ba, ba, ba, ba. Now we'll hit them all together and we've got a nice chord. (*Seen close*) You ready? Everybody take a deep breath now.

We see the first section. They inhale deeply.

O'MALLEY. Let's hear it.

We see the first section again. They sing a chord. The view moves past other boys singing, to Tony and Herman. They react, pleased with themselves. Then the scene dissolves to a full view of O'Malley and the boys.

O'MALLEY. Now you've got chord number one, chord number two, chord number three. Put those three chords together and we can sing a song. (*Seen close*) Now I'll hold up the fingers and those will be your signals. Watch the signals now. Make out I'm the catcher and I'm giving you the signals—one, two, three. Ready? (*He wiggles his fingers.*)

We see the BASEMENT full of boys.

O'MALLEY'S VOICE. Here's your note now. (*We see him singing.*) Bah. (*He sings, holding up his fingers, signalling the chords. The boys hum throughout the scene.*)

O'MALLEY (*singing*).
Silent night,
Holy night,
All is calm, all is bright.
'Round yon virgin, mother and child
Holy infant, so tender and mild,
Sleep in heavenly peace,
Sleep in heavenly peace.

O'MALLEY. Oh, that's fine, boys. Thanks very much. Want to call a day? There's still enough light outside for some baseball.

BOY. Let's sing some more, Father.

SECOND. Yeah, let's go ahead.

BOYS. Yeah, come on. Let's sing some more.

The scene fades out.

PART FIVE

The HALL of the PARISH HOUSE fades in. It is evening. Bustling down the hall, Mrs. Carmody switches on the lights. She is about to turn into the dining room when the sound of a key fumbling into the lock of the front door attracts her attention. As she stares at the door it opens slowly to reveal Father Fitzgibbon. He looks older, more feeble. Something has happened to him; something has crushed him. He turns, fumbles the door shut. Mrs. Carmody's face floods with pity and tenderness. She goes to him quickly, starts to help the old man off with his hat and coat.

MRS. CARMODY (*with forced cheerfulness*). Well, Father—did you see the Bishop?

The old man, his thoughts elsewhere, nods his head bleakly. Mrs. Carmody gives him a searching look, and says no more.

FITZGIBBON (*starting down the passage*). Would ye give Father O'Malley me compliments . . . Ask him if he'd mind stepping into me study.

This cuts to FATHER FITZGIBBON'S STUDY: The curtains are drawn; the fire burns brightly. A desk lamp throws a cheerful glow. The old man comes in and closes the door. He pauses, looks around the room, sees its warmth and cheer. He crosses to the fireplace, stares at the old clock ticking over the mantelpiece. He's thinking: "Forty-five years of it—and it's been good." The door opens and O'Malley comes in. The old man turns and, with his back to the fire, faces O'Malley.

O'MALLEY (*cheerfully*). You wanted me, Father?

Father Fitzgibbon draws his hand across his face—the old familiar, absent-minded gesture.

FITZGIBBON. Yes . . . So I did. So I did.

With a visible effort, Fitzgibbon drags himself back to the realities of the moment. With great deliberation, he points to his own chair behind the desk.

FITZGIBBON. Sit down . . . sit down.

O'Malley looks at the chair, then quizzically at the old man. Without pointing it up, he sits down in another chair, pulls out his tobacco-pouch and starts to fill his pipe. Fitzgibbon moves away from the fire toward O'Malley.

There is a close view of O'MALLEY and FITZGIBBON as Fitzgibbon eyes O'Malley for a moment thoughtfully. The old priest's attitude toward O'Malley has undergone a complete metamorphosis. He is very polite, almost humble.

FITZGIBBON. Father O'Malley . . . (*He clears his throat.*) I've been to see the Bishop.

O'MALLEY (*beaming*). Is that so? Fine.

FITZGIBBON. And I want to be frank with you . . . (*He clears his throat again.*) I must admit my purpose in going to see the Bishop was to have you transferred.

A closeup of O'MALLEY follows: He is in the act of lighting his pipe. He freezes, the match poised in mid-air. For a moment he stares at Fitzgibbon uneasily, then blows out the match, drops it into an ash tray.

O'MALLEY. Oh . . . (*A pause, then*) I'm sorry you don't like me, Father.

FITZGIBBON. I don't dislike *anyone*. It's just that I disagree with you.

O'Malley gets up. He eyes the old man searchingly. His attitude is of a man wondering just how much the other fellow has been told.

O'MALLEY. What did the Bishop say when you told him?

FITZGIBBON. He didn't say anything . . . (*A wry little smile*) Y'see, I didn't get around to telling him.

O'MALLEY (*surprised and puzzled*). Well . . . what happened?

FITZGIBBON. D'ye mind if I tell it in my own way? (*He walks back to the fire, then faces O'Malley.*) Well, the Bishop received me most cordially. He said I was looking very well . . . for my age. After a bit of talk, he congratulated me on my forty-five years at St. Dominic's—(*with a little nod*)—a remarkable memory. He said it was monument to—(*with a vague gesture*)—to the fact that I built it.

O'MALLEY (*noncommittally*). Coming from the Bishop, that's certainly a fine compliment.

FITZGIBBON (*seen close*). Then I told him I had come to talk about *you*. That seemed to disturb him. He asked me to sit down, and gave me a cigar . . . and a very good cigar it was. Then he began to tell me what a fine young man you were—capable —progressive . . . how much confidence he had in you. (*He walks toward O'Malley, and cocks his head knowingly.*) He even told me that he had a nice talk with you before you reported to me.

O'Malley is wretchedly ill at ease. He knows that what he feared has been said.

FITZGIBBON. Of course, he didn't tell me what you two talked about. (*With a little gesture*) He didn't have to. I could read it in the good man's eyes . . . When you get to my age, y'can do that, y'know . . . Well, after a little more of telling me how progressive you were, he asked me why I'd come. And knowing what was on his mind, and to spare him the embarrassment of having to tell me—y'know the Bishop wouldn't hurt anybody—I put him at his ease. (*He pauses and clears his throat.*) "Bishop," I said, "the very thing that's in *your* mind is in mine. It's the very thing I've come to see ye about . . . I want ye to put young Father O'Malley in charge of St. Dominic's."

O'MALLEY (*aghast*). You did?

FITZGIBBON (*nodding*). And under the circumstances, a forgivable falsehood. The Bishop seemed much relieved. He complimented me on my ability to think so clearly . . . at my age—at my ability to face the inevitable.

The poignancy of the old man's defeat has moved O'Malley deeply.

O'MALLEY (*low-voiced*). Then, what happened?

FITZGIBBON. That was all . . . (*Pointing to the desk and chair*) So now you're in charge. And if me cooperation means anything, I want ye to know that ye'll have it.

O'MALLEY. Oh, Father! Why can't we go along just as we have been?

FITZGIBBON. No, no, no, you're—

you're in charge now. (*He swings his chair around for him.*) Sit down.

O'MALLEY (*protesting*). No, Father.

There is a long pause. In the silence the clock on the mantelpiece ticks loudly.

FITZGIBBON (*insistent*). Yes, sit down. I'll familiarize you with the—

O'MALLEY (*embarrassed*). There's no hurry about it. We can do that at any time, Father.

FITZGIBBON (*stubbornly*). Well, is there anything you would like me to do—I mean, now?

O'Malley's emotion chokes him. He manages to shake his head.

O'MALLEY. Nothing.

FITZGIBBON. Then, if ye—if ye don't mind, I'll—I'll lie down a while before dinner.

O'MALLEY (*quietly*). All right, Father.

In another dreadful silence, the old man walks feebly to the desk and lays down a large bunch of keys.

FITZGIBBON. Here are the keys to everything.

Looking very old and feeble, he goes to the door, and there he turns.

FITZGIBBON. When you and the Bishop had your little talk—it was more or less along those lines, wasn't it?

Deeply moved, O'Malley nods his head in admission. The old man goes out, closing the door noiselessly behind him.

At the DESK, overcome with emotion, O'Malley stares at the closed door. After a moment his eyes wander to the desk, its chair, its ancient seat—worn and smooth. He fingers the keys, abstractedly, unhappily. A moment, and Mrs. Carmody enters. She carries a small tea-tray, and her eyes show signs of tears hastily dried. She sets the tea-tray on the desk. There is no resentment in her, only sorrow.

MRS. CARMODY (*quietly*). If you want anything, Father, there's a bell-push on the corner of the desk ... he always used it.

O'Malley glances at her. A closeup of MRS. CARMODY shows that tears shine in her eyes and overflow. Then we see her turning without a word, and leaving. And a closeup of O'MALLEY shows him staring bleakly at the door for a moment.

This dissolves to the PARISH DINING ROOM at night. The view is drawing back from Father Fitzgibbon's empty chair. Dinner is set for two. O'Malley is pacing restlessly back and forth. He looks at his watch, and at that moment Mrs. Carmody appears at the door leading into the kitchen.

MRS. CARMODY. I think you'd better start without him. Looks like he's not coming down for dinner.

O'Malley nods, pulls out his chair, sits down and unfolds his napkin. Mrs. Carmody re-enters with the first course, sets it on the table.

O'MALLEY. Well, he said he wanted to take a little nap.

MRS. CARMODY. He didn't look well, did he, when he came in this evening?

O'MALLEY (*shaking his head*). Go see if he's awake. If he's coming down, I'll wait for him.

She leaves hurriedly through the door leading into the hall.

We then see O'MALLEY at the TABLE as he helps himself to a portion of meat and vegetables. Again, he looks at his watch, then stares without any interest at all at the food before him. He picks up his knife and fork, sets them down again and rises abruptly. Then the view moves with him as he crosses the room, pulls back the drapes and stares out. A heavy rain is drumming against the window. Two pedestrians with umbrellas hurry past, leaning against the wind and the storm. He settles the drapes back into place, and comes back to the table and starts pacing aimlessly. He stops dead in his tracks as he hears MRS. CARMODY's feet thumping hurriedly down the hall stairs. She bursts in, frightened, breathless, calling, "Father O'Malley!"

O'MALLEY. What is it?

MRS. CARMODY (*anguished*). Father, he's gone! Took his bag—his nightgown's gone—so's his toothbrush—his hat and coat! He's gone.

O'MALLEY (*alarmed*). Where would he go?

MRS. CARMODY. That's what I can't imagine! An old man like him—out in all this rain . . . and he didn't even take his rubbers.

For a moment they eye each other helplessly. Then O'Malley goes out without saying a word. We see him, next, going to the hat rack in the foyer, getting his coat, and starting to put it on. Mrs. Carmody follows him in and opens the door. We hear a heavy downpour.

This scene dissolves to a close view of McCarthy. With the rain running in rivulets down his black rubber coat, McCarthy is at a police telephone callbox. With the receiver to his ear, he is listening. Just back of him, his hands in the pockets of his raincoat, his shoulders hunched against the storm, the rain dripping off the brim of his hat, stands O'Malley.

MCCARTHY (*into the phone*). Okay . . . sure—but keep at it, will you? (*A pause, then*) Naw—you can't miss 'im—a little guy—old. Got a grip and an umbrella . . . Okay! (*He hangs up, and turns a worried face to O'Malley.*) Nothing yet, Father. They're gonna check the hospitals—the subways. (*As he sees O'Malley's distress*) Look—take it easy, will you, Father? (*A comforting pat on his shoulder*) And ye'd better go home—no use the two of us getting drowned. (*He takes O'Malley by the elbow and propels him out of sight.*)

O'MALLEY. All right, but you call me the minute you hear anything.

MCCARTHY. I will, Father.

O'MALLEY. I don't care what time it is.

MCCARTHY. I will, Father.

And as O'MALLEY leaves, the scene fades out.

The HALLWAY of St. Dominic's fades in, and we get a close view of the wall clock, the handles showing it is 11:25. This dissolves to the HALL later on, the clock ticking on. Mrs. Carmody is seated on a bench with her head on her hand and her eyes closed. She opens her eyes, raises her head, and looks toward O'Malley. O'Malley's head is between his hands. And now he raises his head and opens his eyes.

MRS. CARMODY. Shall I make some coffee?

O'MALLEY. Huh? Hmm? Oh, no thank you.

Mrs. Carmody's eyes close and her head drops onto her hand again.

Then we see the exterior of the CHURCH as McCarthy is coming forward, followed by the reluctant Fitzgibbon, while the rain is coming down in buckets. McCarthy crosses and opens the gate. But Fitzgibbon lingers behind. McCarthy gestures for him to come on.

MCCARTHY. Come on! (*As Fitzgibbon continues to hesitate*) Now what's the matter?

FITZGIBBON (*moving close to him*). If you don't mind, I'd—I'd rather go in by myself.

MCCARTHY. If you don't mind, I found you and I'm goin' to deliver you personally.

FITZGIBBON. But that's not necessary. There's no reward, you know. It's goin' to be a little difficult and I'd rather explain to Father O'Malley in me own way, and I can do that better when you're not around.

Fitzgibbon starts to enter through the gate, then stops.

MCCARTHY. Okay. But if you want my advice, you'll just tell him you've been a bad boy and you ran away from home and you're sorry.

FITZGIBBON (*belligerently*). Huh! And if you want my advice, you'll go to church on Sunday and say you haven't been to Mass in ten years and that you're sorry. Huh!

Fitzgibbon goes inside. McCarthy grins and closes the gate.

In the HALL: Slowly, the door opens. A gust of wind and rain drives in. The door opens six inches, a foot—revealing Father Fitzgibbon—a frustrated, soaked, unhappy little man. Like a small runaway boy, thwarted by the terrors of the night, he has come home. He sees Mrs. Carmody and O'Malley.

FITZGIBBON (*with a sheepish little gesture*). Hello . . .

O'MALLEY rises. His emotions are mixed: relief, a desire to put the old man across his knee and spank him. MRS. CARMODY rises. Her feelings are much the same as O'Malley's. Then we see the old man coming in, fumbling the door shut behind him. Fitzgibbon makes a brave show of covering up his utter weariness.

FITZGIBBON (*as they approach him*). If ye don't mind—I've come back . . . (*nodding portentously*) but only temporarily.

They humor him as though he were a child, nodding and murmuring agreement to anything he says. The old man is fortifying himself against the humiliation of his return.

FITZGIBBON. Until me plans are more formulated, maybe you wouldn't mind letting me stay. Oh, I'll be no bother to ye . . . (*He sneezes violently.*)

O'Malley and Mrs. Carmody support him and try to ease him out of his dripping coat and hat.

O'MALLEY (*as though to a child*). Here, Father . . . let's get you out of these wet clothes and get you to bed, huh?

FITZGIBBON (*nodding*). But I don't expect me old room . . . that's *yours*, now.

O'MALLEY (*humoring him*). Oh, I haven't moved in yet.

Mrs. Carmody and O'Malley are leading him forward and up the STAIRS, supporting Father Fitzgibbon between them.

FITZGIBBON. No, no—I insist. That's *your* room ... I'll sleep on a cot—anywhere. (*As Mrs. Carmody and O'Malley make soothing noises*) I'll not even be bothering ye for me food ... I'll eat out.

O'MALLEY. We'll talk about that later. Mrs. Carmody will bring you something on a tray.

FITZGIBBON. Pray, don't bother ye'-selves. I'm not a bit hungry. I—I—I—

MRS. CARMODY (*nodding*). Come now, Father—just a wee snack. I've been keeping it for you on the stove. (*The old man shakes his head stubbornly.*)

O'MALLEY (*rolling the words on his tongue*). A nice, juicy cut of roast beef — Yorkshire pudding — (*To Mrs. Carmody*) And there were some boiled onions, too—weren't there?

MRS. CARMODY (*catching on*). Oh, yes, and some asparagus ... with buttered breadcrumbs.

O'MALLEY (*smacking his lips*). And golden-brown potatoes. And—(*as an afterthought*)—a nice hot cup of coffee?

By this time Father Fitzgibbon is fairly drooling. He looks from one to the other, and as though conferring upon them a great favor:

FITZGIBBON. We-e-ll ... well ... if ye insist—just a small portion of—of everything.

O'MALLEY (*smiling at Mrs. Carmody*). Good.

As Mrs. Carmody hurries down the stairs, O'Malley urges the old man down the upper hall ...

This dissolves to FATHER FITZGIBBON'S BEDROOM. Nightgowned, stuffed, Father Fitzgibbon is propped up amongst his pillows. On the coverlet before him is a large tray, every plate on it clean as a whistle. As we come in, O'Malley is sitting on the foot of the bed, Mrs. Carmody nearby. Father Fitzgibbon has an air of deep humility, a little overdone.

FITZGIBBON (*pushing aside the tray, to Mrs. Carmody*). I hope it wasn't too much trouble for ye, Mrs. Carmody.

MRS. CARMODY (*picking up the tray*). No trouble at all, Father.

FITZGIBBON. I feel I should help ye with the dishes, Mrs. Carmody—but ... (*He fingers his nightgown.*)

MRS. CARMODY. Don't worry about the dishes ... (*Indicating them to O'Malley*) It's not much washing they'll be needing.

She picks up the tray and exits. With a sigh of satisfaction Father Fitzgibbon leans back on the pillows.

O'MALLEY (*feeling the old man's hand*). You're still cold, Father. You know, you were drenched to the skin. You need something to warm you up. (*Confidentially*) You wouldn't have a wee drop of the crature around would you? (*As the old man hesitates*) It'll stop you from catching cold. (*As the old man still hesitates*) I'll have one with you. I was out too—to get an evening paper.

FITZGIBBON (*capitulating*). Well, in that case ...

O'MALLEY (*rising*). I'll ask Mrs. Carmody where she keeps it.

FITZGIBBON (*pointing off*). If ye'll look in the bookcase yonder ...

O'Malley starts toward the bookcase, and we see that it is a Mid-Victorian affair with glass doors and a cupboard at the bottom.

FITZGIBBON'S VOICE. Ye'll find it behind "The Life of General Grant" . . . it's a present from me mother.

Delving behind the books, O'Malley extracts a small, oblong box. He opens it, and a little music-box arrangement in the lid tinkles an Irish lullaby. And picking up two glasses en route, he comes to Father Fitzgibbon, the music-box tinkling softly.

O'MALLEY (*indicating the box; with a rich Irish brogue*). A bit of auld Ireland, eh?

FITZGIBBON (*nodding*). Yes. Every Christmas since I left, me old mother sends me one of these. (*He takes the box from O'Malley.*) With a degree of abstinence, it becomes my calendar . . . I get a little behind during Lent, but it comes out even at Christmas.

The old man takes out the bottle, closes the lid of the box and pours out two small drinks, and hands one of them to O'Malley. Then we see on the wall behind O'Malley a photographic portrait in a large oval frame.

FITZGIBBON (*pointing with the bottle to the photograph on the wall*). That's—that's me mother.

O'Malley turns and looks at the picture closely. It depicts a lovely young woman of about thirty. Her clothes are early nineteenth century.

O'MALLEY (*after a pause, with great sincerity*). She's very beautiful.

This delights Fitzgibbon. He turns, looking off at the picture.

FITZGIBBON. Of course, that was taken some time ago . . . she's ninety now.

(*After a pause, wistfully*) You know, Father O'Malley, I always planned that as soon as I got a few dollars ahead, I would go back to the old country and see my mother. (*The old man smiles up at the picture, and then at O'Malley.*) Would ye believe it—that was forty-five years ago, and every time I got a few dollars ahead there always seemed to be some other need for it.

O'Malley looks at the old man, and with a warm smile nods his complete understanding.

O'MALLEY (*nodding*). Yes . . . there was always somebody who seemed to need it more than you did . . . (*He turns and looks at the picture again.*) Well, let's drink to your mother. (*He raises his glass toward the picture.*) Here's hoping that you'll see her soon.

The old man is about to drink when he checks himself.

FITZGIBBON. What about *your* mother, eh?

O'MALLEY. I'm afraid I don't remember much about her. She died when I was quite young.

FITZGIBBON. Oh . . . Well, let's drink to both of them, anyway.

O'MALLEY (*touched*). Thank you, Father.

They touch their glasses, drink, set them down. With a sigh of contentment, the old man lies back on his pillows, turns his head sideways, and contemplates the picture of his mother on the wall. O'Malley sits down on the bed, beside him. Fitzgibbon nods toward the picture.

FITZGIBBON (*with a wistful, reminiscent smile*). Oh, you'd like her . . .

(*with a quick look at O'Malley*) and she'd like you, too. She has a song in *her* heart. She was always singing through the house . . .

He seems to be reflecting, almost listening. It is as though he were trying to draw to him old memories.

FITZGIBBON. I can almost hear her now.

A moment, and he rises up on his pillows, looking earnestly at O'Malley.

FITZGIBBON. M'boy—d'ye by any chance know— (*He purses up his lips.*) "Too-ra-loo-laroo?"

The old man glances at the picture on the wall, and leaning forward, O'Malley starts to sing softly. The lovely old Irish lullaby is poignant and nostalgic. The old man nods eagerly, and then with a sigh of sheer ecstasy, sinks back amongst his pillows. He takes one more glance at the picture of his mother, and then as O'Malley's voice seems to fill the small bedroom with the haunting memories of old Ireland, the old man's eyes close wearily.

O'MALLEY, humming, tiptoes to the switch, turns off the light, and starts toward the door, believing him to be asleep. At this we see Fitzgibbon opening his eyes; and saying, "Good night," he closes his eyes again.—O'Malley, about to go out, turns, looks back, laughs, and shakes his head, tickled at the old man's deception. Then he goes out and closes the door behind him as the scene fades out.

PART SIX

The exterior of a THEATRE fades in at night. A large poster announces the latest exploits of "Hopalong Cassidy." There is the usual ebb and flow of pedestrian activity. There is a trickle of people out of the theatre and through the lobby as the early-evening show terminates. Amongst them, and headed by O'Malley, come Tony and his gang. They are tired, but happy. The view follows them to the sidewalk, where there is a bus stop sign. There is horseplay en route, simulated popping of six-shooters, the galloping of Cassidy's pinto riding to the rescue cowboy "Yip-Heee's!" and Indian war-cries. There is a shrill yelp from Pitch-Pipe as Herman Langerhanke, burying his hands in the youngster's hair, makes a too realistic effort to scalp him. O'Malley intervenes hastily.

O'MALLEY. All right, fellas—break it up, break it up. (*As he restores order*) Here, Tony—here's the bus fare. You fellas go right home and get to bed. Remember—I'm responsible for you. (*As a final admonition*) Rehearsal in the morning.

TONY (*disappointed*). Aw gee, Fadder—ain'tcha comin' wid us?

O'MALLEY. No. I'm going to walk. Got a sermon on Sunday— (*Making a show of pressing his fingers against his forehead*) I've got to think up something to say. (*Confidentially*) It's an extra-special one for you parents—(*winking at them*) on how to bring up children.

The youngsters chuckle, and there is chorus of: "Good night, Fadder!" "Good night!" "Good night!" "Gee—and tanks fa da show!" "It was swell!" "See yuh termorrow!" With a little "S'long" gesture, O'Malley walks away down the street. As he does so, a bus rumbles in to the stop and the kids swarm aboard.

We see O'Malley as, with his hands in the pockets of his coat, he walks briskly along. The bus overtakes him, and from the top, where the kids are, comes the strains of "The Calliope" number. O'Malley grins, and as the bus rolls onward the scene dissolves to another view of O'MALLEY moving along. O'Malley flips up the collar of his coat, snaps down his hat-brim, hunches his shoulders and increases his pace. A little way, and he comes past the intersection of an alley. A girl, wearing a beautiful mink coat, comes hurrying toward him. She passes him almost on the run, and makes a right turn into the alley. O'Malley stops dead and stares after her. One feels that he has recognized her. A moment, and the girl pops back around the corner. Their eyes meet through the drizzle of rain.

GIRL (*uncertainly*). Chuck? (*Then recognizing him, ecstatically*) *Chuck!*

She comes running toward him.

O'MALLEY (*as they meet*). Jenny!

They shake hands warmly, eye each other appraisingly, like old friends long separated. The girl is in her middle twenties, utterly charming, poised, and bubbling with humor. This is GENEVIEVE LINDEN.

JENNY (*with great feeling*). It's good to see you!

O'MALLEY. It's good to see you, too, Jenny. Where were you going?

JENNY. To work—and I'm late. Come along!

She grabs his hand and literally drags him around the corner. Then we see the girl hurrying down the alley, the astonished O'Malley in tow. As they turn into a door, the scene cuts to the STAGE DOOR of the METROPOLITAN OPERA HOUSE. She is dragging O'Malley by the hand. Jenny hurries in and up a brief flight of steps. At the head of the steps, they whisk past a doorman reading an evening paper at his desk. Then they are BACKSTAGE, amid a scattering of technicians, prop-men, and costumed extras. There is all the excitement and activity before an evening performance. As they pass a "flat," O'Malley jerks Jenny to a stop. Stencilled on the "flat," he reads:

PROPERTY OF THE METROPOLITAN
OPERA CO.

O'MALLEY (*pointing to it in amazement*). Say—what are you doing here?

JENNY. This is where I work.

A jerk of her hand and she and O'Malley are on the move again.

O'MALLEY. Wait a minute! (*Again he stops her, and looks around.*) But it's Carmen!

Jenny giggles happily, and nods her head. She opens the door of a dressing room suite and starts in.

O'MALLEY (*on the threshold*). What do you play—one of the spectators at the bull-fight?

Jenny whips a rose out of a vase, puts it between her teeth and, hand on hip, strikes a pose.

JENNY. *I'm Carmen!*

She laughs as though this were a terrific joke. O'Malley laughs, too.

O'MALLEY (*incredulously*). *Jenny Tuffle—Carmen?*

JENNY. Oh, I've changed that—it's Genevieve Linden.

O'MALLEY (*nodding*). O-oh . . . How long have you been in town?

JENNY (*ecstatically excited*). This is it . . . this is the opening night! . . . I was singing *Carmen* in Rio—they heard me, and—and said would you do it here—(*with a wide gesture*) *here!* Can you imagine?

O'MALLEY. Jenny Tuffle in the Metropolitan . . .

A maid comes from the interior of the dressing room, toward the door and starts to remove Jenny's coat.

JENNY. Come on, Effie, I'm terribly late. (*To O'Malley*) Well, make yourself comfortable, Chuck— (*With a gesture*) Y'know, I have to get on with it. (*Accompanied by the maid, she starts across the sitting room.*)

O'Malley hesitates, then steps in, leaving the door open. It is comfortably furnished, typical. There are easy-chairs, many flowers. A door leads into the dressing-room proper. Looking around, O'Malley sits down on the edge of a chair. It is so situated that it is impossible for him to see into the dressing room.

JENNY'S VOICE (*with mock accusation*). I don't know why I'm even talking to you.

O'MALLEY. No?

JENNY'S VOICE. Why didn't you write?

O'MALLEY (*starting to remove his overcoat*). I *did* write.

Jenny, at the make-up table in her dressing room, now wearing a simple dressing-robe of fine, heavy white material, is fastening it up at the throat. Her maid, laying out some cosmetics before the mirror, goes out.

JENNY (*sitting down before the mirror*). I know you did, but why did you stop?

O'MALLEY'S VOICE (*from the sitting room*). Well, didn't I tell you?

Jenny picks up a brush and starts to brush her hair vigorously.

JENNY. No, you didn't— (*Then grimly*) But you're going to.

A man in full evening dress comes in through the open door into the SITTING ROOM. He is an Italian, has dignity and sartorial genius. This is TOMASO BOZZANNI, Jenny's conductor. He is politely and mildly surprised to see O'Malley. He raps on the door of the dressing room.

BOZZANNI. Jenny—please, I want to ask just a small favor.

JENNY'S VOICE. Hello, Tommy . . . what is it?

BOZZANNI (*sardonically*). Tonight, would you be so good as to glance occasionally at my baton? (*He pantomimes with an imaginary baton.*) Tonight, let us not race—let us try just for one time to finish together.

Jenny's delightful laugh tinkles from the dressing room. Bozzanni gestures to O'Malley, and the gesture says, "She is hopeless!"

JENNY'S VOICE (*laughing*). All right, Tommy, I promise—cross my heart. And, Tommy—do *me* a favor. Meet Chuck O'Malley—he's a very old friend of mine. Chuck—Signor Tomaso Bozzanni.

In the SITTING ROOM, Chuck rises. The two men shake hands.

BOZZANNI (*eying O'Malley as they do so, mildly surprised*). Chock?

O'MALLEY (*with a grin*). That's what she always calls me.

JENNY'S VOICE. You haven't told me yet, Chuck . . . Why did you stop writing?

O'MALLEY. I did tell you—in my last letter.

JENNY (*seen in her dressing room*). Which letter was that?

O'MALLEY (*in the sitting room as Bozzanni walks to the door, flipping open a cigarette case and lighting a cigarette indifferently*). I guess that must have been the letter you didn't get.

JENNY (*laying down her brush, staring into the mirror thoughtfully*). You wrote me in Rome . . . in Florence . . . Naples . . . Vienna . . . Budapest . . . (*She enumerates the letters with the thumb and fingers of her right hand.*)

As she enumerates his letters, she smiles wistfully. One feels that her thoughts are drifting back through time, that she remembers vividly not only the place, but almost the very hour that his letters reached her.

JENNY. Then I went to Switzerland . . . and I found one of your letters waiting for me in Lucerne. (*Her voice and her eyes are almost ecstatic.*) You should have been there, Chuck. It was the week before Christmas . . . There was a quaint little post office—I walked down to it in the snow. The moon was so bright that I read your letter on the way home. And I answered it . . . that night. (*She pauses, then wistfully*) And that letter in Lucerne was the last one I got. From there I went to South America—but there were no more letters. (*Turning her head toward the door*) What happened, Chuck?

As there is no answer from the sitting room, she rises quickly, and goes to the door of the sitting room.

JENNY. Chuck—what happened?

Slowly the expression on her face changes as she sees O'MALLEY. His unbuttoned coat, revealing his priestly clothes, explains everything. There is a great serenity about him; a great dignity. JENNY, seen close at the door, says nothing for a moment, then she speaks in a hushed voice.

JENNY. Father Chuck . . . (*With a catch in her voice, a little gesture of bewilderment, a little smile*) It'll take me a little while to get used to that. (*Another pause, and now she is in complete control of herself, and she speaks very brightly.*) Where's your parish, Father?

In the SITTING ROOM, leaning against the wall, looking from one to the other, Bozzanni has been watching the drama unfold. O'Malley has risen.

O'MALLEY. St. Dominic's. (*With a gesture*) Over there—about ten blocks. You remember Timmy?

JENNY. Tim O'Dowd . . . Yes, of course I do.

O'MALLEY (*nodding*). He's at St. Francis now. He's a priest, too.

JENNY (*smiling*). Oh, dear old Timmy . . . can you imagine that?

There is a brief pause. Then O'Malley looks at his watch.

O'MALLEY. Well . . . I'll have to be getting along.

JENNY (*as he makes a motion as though to leave; hastily*). Oh, please don't go ... (*To Bozzanni*) Tommy, he can stand in the wings, can't he?

BOZZANNI. It would be a privilege.

JENNY (*to O'Malley, as he hesitates*). Please. (*To Bozzanni*) He and I started together—in a school play—"The Flamingo and the Rose."

O'MALLEY (*giving Bozzanni a sheepish little look*). I'd love to, if you're sure it won't—

JENNY (*cutting in*). It won't do anything but bring me luck.

O'MALLEY. I can't stay long—I have a choir rehearsal in the morning.

JENNY. Just a little while, then ... (*To Bozzanni*) You know, Tommy, Father O'Malley was the first one to tell me that I could sing.

BOZZANNI (*to O'Malley, with a sly look at Jenny; laughing*). Maybe one day I will tell her the same thing.

He takes Father O'Malley's arm and they start out. Walking away, Bozzanni glances back at Jenny.

BOZZANNI (*to O'Malley, sotto voce*). If she listens to you, Father, it is possible that you could persuade her to listen just once to me. (*With a gesture of his hand*) Watch the baton!

As they walk out, we get a closeup of JENNY. For a moment she watches them without any expression at all, and then turns back into her dressing room.

This dissolves to the STAGE of the METROPOLITAN OPERA HOUSE—in the wings where O'Malley stands in the foreground, looking toward the stage. Here, as Carmen, Jenny is singing an aria; we see a closeup of her singing, then of O'MALLEY listening, completely enraptured with the quality and loveliness of her voice; we get close views of BOZZANNI as he conducts the orchestra and he looks appealingly toward Jenny; of JENNY as she sings on serenely, paying no attention whatever to him or his baton, and of BOZZANNI looking toward the wings and shrugging toward O'Malley with a gesture that says, "You see what I mean?" and of O'MALLEY looking at Bozzanni, and also gesturing as though to concede, "She's hopeless!"

Finally we get a larger view of the WINGS of the STAGE, O'Malley in the foreground, technicians and some costumed extras listening entranced to the conclusion of Jenny's aria. As she concludes, the house rocks with applause. She takes a bow, moves toward the wings and O'Malley, taking more bows en route. Breathless, her eyes like stars, she comes in to O'Malley as the applause swells and swells.

JENNY. How was it?

O'MALLEY (*laughing*). Why ask me? (*Indicating the frantically applauding audience*) Go on—go on—get back!

Jenny returns onstage. She takes more bows, acknowledging the applause which is tumultuous; and still bowing, she comes back to O'Malley in the wings.

O'MALLEY (*starting to leave*). Goodbye, Jenny ...

JENNY. Good-bye, Chuck ... I'll be down to see you.

The applause swells crescendo, and once more Jenny goes onstage, O'Malley walking away. He stops and glance back. Jenny is blowing kisses to the audience. She looks in his direction, and blows him a kiss, too. With a little "S'long" gesture, O'Malley walks out of sight. Then, as the Opera House resounds to "Bravos!" whistles, and thunderous applause, the scene fades out.

PART SEVEN

[The interior of the CHURCH fades in and we see Father Fitzgibbon. In the deserted church, he is a small and pathetically lonely figure. With a dust cloth, he is making a great show of dusting one of the pews. O'Malley enters from the sacristy, and hurries toward him. O'Malley comes in. The old man is very preoccupied with the business of dusting. O'Malley restrains his exasperation.

O'MALLEY (*sotto voce*). What are you doing?

FITZGIBBON (*looking up, too innocently*). Dusting.

O'MALLEY. You know you don't have to do that.

FITZGIBBON. Just trying to be useful ... I'm sure I don't want to be a burden to ye.

Fitzgibbon picks up a prayer book, dusts it meticulously. Gently, O'Malley takes the dust rag and the prayer book from the old man and sets them down. He takes him by the arm and leads him toward the exit.

O'MALLEY. Mrs. Quimp wants to see you, Father.

FITZGIBBON (*mildly*). Me? Why don't you tell her ... you're the one to talk to.

O'Malley winces, knowing full well that the old man is putting on a little act to make him feel badly, and the scene dissolves to the CHURCH GARDENS —under the pear tree—where, stiff as a ramrod, Mrs. Quimp is sitting on the edge of a chair. Droning metallically through her adenoids, she is talking to Father Fitzgibbon.

MRS. QUIMP. So—you can draw your own conclusions.

O'Malley passes in the background, and Father Fitzgibbon beckons him.]

We see O'Malley crossing the CHURCH GARDENS and approaching Father Fitzgibbon.

O'MALLEY. You wanted to see me, Father?

O'Malley comes toward them. Fitzgibbon's attitude is humble, but inwardly we feel that he is gloating a little over what he has to say.

FITZGIBBON. Yes, yes. Mrs Quimp here, good woman that she is—(*sly emphasis on the latter*) has come here with a bit of disturbing information ... and I think it more properly should be brought to your attention.

O'MALLEY. Nice work, Mrs. Quimp. What is it?

FITZGIBBON (*as The Quimp bridles and sniffs disdainfully*). Mrs. Quimp, suppose you tell Father O'Malley in your own words.

MRS. QUIMP (*the snapping turtle*). You'd better tell him, Father.

FITZGIBBON (*only too happy to oblige*). Huh? Ah, well—your little songbird, who, I might add, although without funds was too proud to push a broom, is feathering her nest in her own manner. And I can only say, if Mrs. Quimp's observations are correct, a very fine manner it is. (*He pauses, clasps his hands behind his back, and rocks on his heels.*) It seems, Father O'Malley, that the young lady in question has an apartment directly across from Mrs. Quimp's—uh—bedroom. And according to Mrs. Quimp, young Ted Haines comes early and stays so late that—

O'MALLEY (*with a nod at The Quimp*).—that she can't get any sleep.

MRS. QUIMP (*bridling and sniffing*). Queer, I must say. Young Haines is willing to throw me out without so much as a how-d'you-do! (*A moist sniff*) But with this young *lady*—and, mark you, there are other words I could find to call her—his attitude is different. He's much more lenient. (*Right in O'Malley's face*) Don't you think that's strange?

O'MALLEY (*eying her*). Ummh ... that's a question. (*A little throwaway gesture*) People do funny things, you know.

FITZGIBBON. Fine goings-on, Father O'Malley. 'Tis plain as the nose on your face.

O'MALLEY. The nose on whose face, Father?

FITZGIBBON. Umh? ... Well, never mind whose face it's on; we must face it. (*To Mrs. Quimp*) Excuse us a moment.

He takes O'Malley's arm and leads him out of scene, then we see them together alone.

FITZGIBBON (*sotto voce*). This is a serious matter, Father O'Malley. (*Then slyly*) Since you're so familiar with the case, I think you should handle it ... I'll handle the *little sins*.

As O'Malley folds his arms and gives him a strange look ... the scene fades out.

The scene dissolves to the STAIRWAY of an APARTMENT HOUSE: The stair-carpet is worn, the walls are in need of paint. The view follows O'Malley as he ascends the stairs. Into the scene, from above, muffled through a door, comes the sound of Carol's voice singing, "I'll be loving you . . ." from "The Day After Forever." It is sung with more sincerity than we last heard it. O'Malley pauses, looks up and nods his appreciation. Then he hurries up the last two steps, crosses the hall and knocks at one of the doors. The song breaks off.

CAROL'S VOICE. Come in!

Then we see CAROL'S APARTMENT, which has the high ceiling and spaciousness inherited from the old brownstone mansion. It has been freshly painted and decorated, inexpensively, but clean, neat and chintzy. There is a new baby-grand piano in one corner. Carol has turned on the bench to face the door. Young Ted Haines is near her. As O'Malley comes in, Carol jumps up quickly. Ted comes forward, not the least bit abashed.

TED. (*delighted*). Hello, Father! Come in!

O'MALLEY (*coming in and closing the door*). Hello, Carol.

CAROL. Hello, Father.

O'MALLEY (*smiling*). I heard you ... that's more like it.

CAROL. Thank you, Father. Maybe it's because I'm putting more meaning into the words.

We get a close view of the three as O'Malley walks into the center of the room. He deliberately looks the apartment over, appraises it. Ted and Carol exchange a swift glance. They know only too well how the situation must appear to him.

O'MALLEY. Hmm! Very nice here, isn't it? Very nice.

TED (*quickly*). Now, before you go any further, Father—

O'MALLEY (*cutting in*). You mean it's all in my mind?

TED. That's right.

CAROL. Yes, I'm sure you're just dying to know the details, Father—so sit down and I'll tell you. (*She eases him into a chair, then throws herself into the part.*) Well, I was going down the street, minding my own business, too, when who do you think just happened by—purely by accident, of course—and pulled up alongside of the curb?

O'MALLEY (*snapping his fingers and pointing at Ted*). Mr. Ted Haines, Jr.!

CAROL (*snapping her fingers*). Right! And what do you think his approach was? (*Nodding at Ted*) *You* tell him.

TED (*with mock dignity*). I prefer not to remember.

CAROL. Well, being a woman, *I* do. His exact words were: "Hey, good-lookin'—what's cookin'?"

O'MALLEY (*shaking his head*). Tsk, tsk, tsk!

TED (*to Carol*). Aw, now, wait a minute! (*To O'Malley*) What I said was: "Who do you know that I know?"

O'MALLEY. You know, that's worse.

CAROL. Well, that was that—and with practically no more of a buildup than that, he asked me to lunch.

TED. Well—who knows? It might've worked. It's been known to.

CAROL. So after I'd cooled him off, I came back here — Y'know — no money, no job—expecting to be thrown out any minute . . . There was a knock on the door—when I said to myself, "Here it comes!" . . . And who do you think was there?

O'MALLEY (*snapping his fingers and pointing at Ted*). Junior!

CAROL (*snapping her fingers*). Right! I was so surprised!

TED. So was I!

O'MALLEY. All right, up to here—we're all surprised.

CAROL. Naturally, before throwing me out he had to know a little about me, so in a few well-chosen sentences I gave him the details—sort of like I told you.

O'MALLEY. And you hit the jack-pot!

TED. Well, I wouldn't call it a jack-pot, exactly, Father. We had the apartment vacant—and it seemed a shame to throw her out. (*A pause, then defiantly*) Well, anyway, what's wrong with that?

O'MALLEY (*gravely*). Nothing that I know of—up to here.

TED. Well, as I was saying—it seemed a shame to throw her out—

O'MALLEY (*in an undertone*). Like Mrs. Quimp . . .

TED. Well, that's different.

O'Malley glances at Carol, then back at Ted.

O'MALLEY. I can see that, obviously . . .

TED. Look, Father—she told me about going to see you, that you wanted to help her . . . (*O'Malley nods.*) Well, you haven't got a corner on helping people, have you? . . . And besides, I've practically got her lined up in a job.

CAROL. Yes, and as soon as I get it, I'm going to pay him back—(*looking at Ted*) every nickel of it.

TED. And oh, by the way, Father . . . (*He pulls out his wallet.*) I understand she owes you ten.

He takes out a ten-dollar bill and hands it to O'Malley. O'Malley takes it and says nothing. We get a closeup of CAROL and TED. They are so refreshing, so eager, so delightful. Then we see the three, as both Ted and Carol are looking at O'Malley, waiting for him to speak. His eyes shift from them to the brand-new piano.

O'MALLEY. That's a nice-looking piano.

TED (*defiantly*). Well, she needs it, doesn't she? She's a singer—she's got to practice!

O'MALLEY (*nodding*). Very thoughtful . . . But aren't pianos kind of expensive these days?

TED. I asked her first if she could play a ukulele.

O'MALLEY (*with a shrug*). Oh, well—then, naturally—

TED. Yeah, naturally. (*As both laugh*) Carol tells me you can play, Father. Why don't you try it out and see if I got a good buy?

CAROL (*eagerly*). Yes, play something for us, Father.

O'Malley gets up and goes toward the piano, and we then see him close as he casually fingers the keys with one hand, and sits down and plays a few chords: the sort one would use for the "tuning" of a piano. The chords assume form, become a melody. With his elbows on the piano, and cupping his chin on his hands, Ted listens appreciatively. O'Malley hits a few sonorous bass chords.

TED (*to O'Malley*). Would you mind us asking *you* a few questions? (*O'Malley smiles and nods "go ahead."*) Look, where'd you get that wicked left hand?

Carol, leaning on the opposite side of the piano from Ted, cups her chin in her hands and stares at O'Malley, who is then seen very close as he is playing softly now, the two youngsters leaning on the piano watching him.

O'MALLEY (*laughing*). Well—I was always interested in music. Used to write a bit of it at school, had a little band—used to play for dances. —O'Malley's Orioles! (*Playing a little more*) You know, at one time I had to make quite a decision—write the nation's songs— (*He is kidding on this last.*) or go my way.

TED. Any regrets, Father?

O'MALLEY. Regrets? No . . . I get a great happiness out of helping people realize that religion isn't this . . . (*He grimaces mournfully and gestures both hands down to the floor.*) taking all the fun out of everything —but this— (*He smiles and gestures, bringing both hands upward.*) It can be bright—bring you closer to happiness . . . Do you go to church,

Ted? (*As Ted reacts*) Or should I change the subject? (*As Ted nods*) Here's something you might try . . . When your conscience—you know, that little fellow on your shoulder— starts whispering to you—don't stick your fingers in your ears—give him a break.

TED. But if you want to do things badly enough, Father, that little fellow can't stop you from doing them.

O'MALLEY (*smiling*). No, but he can stop you from having a good time while you're doing them. (*He plays a few more chords on the piano.*) Now, if I could set what I mean to music I could be much more eloquent. (*Still playing softly*) It would sound simpler—you'd remember it. (*He stops playing and looks at the two youngsters.*) The spoken word can sometimes be pretty dull.

Chins cupped in their hands, the two youngsters are now leaning eagerly across the piano.

CAROL. You mean *sing* your sermons, Father?

O'MALLEY. Yes, kind of.

CAROL (*after a pause*). Have you ever had anything published?

O'MALLEY. Well, no.

TED. Well, play us one of your unpublished ones.

O'Malley appears to think a moment. He glances at her, and we get a large closeup of CAROL, who looks so young, so bright and eager, then of TED, who looks so wholesome, so typically Young America.

O'Malley plays the opening bars of "Going My Way?" then sings it with great feeling.

THE LYRIC (*sung by O'Malley*).
This road leads to Rainbowville,
Going My Way?
Up ahead is Bluebird Hill,
Going My Way?
Just pack a basket full of wishes,
And off you start with Sunday morning in your heart.
Round the bend you'll see a sign,
Dreamers' Highway.
Happiness is down the line,
Going My Way?
The smiles you gather will look well on you.
Oh, I hope you're Going My Way, too.

The two youngsters watch him, and slowly the inherent significance of what he is telling them in music hits them both. They eye each other, and each knows that the other knows. Finally, O'Malley concludes the number. There is a silence. The two youngsters neither move nor speak. O'Malley rises.

O'MALLEY (*softly*). Well, I think I'll leave you on that . . . (*He turns to them.*)

We then see the youngsters, who are deeply stirred.

O'MALLEY (*warmly*). Good-bye, Carol. Good-bye, Ted.

The youngsters never move from where they are leaning across the piano. They watch O'Malley in silence as he picks up his hat, crosses to the door and goes out. The door closes quietly behind him. Ted and Carol make no movement, as they stare at the door . . .

CAROL (*pensively*). Nice thought— "Going My Way"—isn't it?

TED (*respectfully*). He's quite a fellow.

The scene fades out.

[We see the BROWNSTONE MANSION as O'Malley comes quickly down the steps, looks off and sees ACROSS THE STREET (from O'Malley's angle) Father Fitzgibbon and Mrs. Quimp standing near the entrance to The Quimp's residence. The old man beckons to O'Malley.

O'MALLEY, dodging the traffic, starts on the run across the street. Narrowly averting being hit by a truck, he comes in to Father Fitzgibbon and The Quimp. The old man is doing his best to hide his curiosity; Mrs. Quimp isn't.

MRS. QUIMP (*drooling, hopefully*). Well, Father—was it just like I thought?

O'MALLEY. I don't know, Mrs. Quimp —what *did* you think?

Mrs. Quimp bridles, tosses her head and "boops" up the steps in a huff. Father Fitzgibbon turns confidentially to O'Malley.

FITZGIBBON (*eyebrows up, sotto voce*). Well, what *did* happen?

O'Malley gives the old man a reproachful stare, shakes his head, and the gesture says, "Tsk, tsk, tsk!" At that moment, the scream of an ambulance siren from around the corner blasts into the scene. O'Malley, leaving Father Fitzgibbon, turns and hurries in the direction of the sound.

We see FATHER FITZGIBBON'S STUDY as Father Fitzgibbon is entering. He just sits down when Mrs. Carmody knocks and sails in—mad.

MRS. CARMODY. *That woman's* here again!

FITZGIBBON (*throwing up his hands in desperation*). Can't you get rid of her—can't I be out on a sick call or something?

MRS. CARMODY. Sorry—I tried that one. It didn't work . . . she saw you come in, and she says— (*Mimicking The Quimp*) "It's very important!"

FITZGIBBON. Well—show her in.

In the HALLWAY Mrs. Carmody comes to Mrs. Quimp, who is waiting.

MRS. CARMODY. Father is very busy. He'll see you for just *two* minutes. (*The two women exchange glares.*)

MRS. CARMODY (*to herself, as The Quimp goes into the study*). The divil fly away with the likes of yez!

Mrs. Quimp enters the STUDY, and stands fidgeting.

MRS. QUIMP. Oh . . . er . . . hem. . . .

Father Fitzgibbon keeps her standing while he pretends to be busy at his desk.

FITZGIBBON (*without looking up*). Well, Mrs. Quimp, who's going to the dogs in the parish today?

MRS. QUIMP (*severely*). It's not them that's *in* the parish, today . . . it's somebody that's trying to *run* the *parish!* (*Tossing her head, she looks at him severely.*)

FITZGIBBON (*looking up, sharply*). Indeed! Indeed! Now, my good woman, suppose you leave off the usual beatin' around the bush and come to the point. What is it?

MRS. QUIMP. Well, if you *must* know, it's about *one* of the priests. (*Defiantly—she sits back for the reaction. She gets it.*)

FITZGIBBON (*sarcastically*). As there are only two of us, and you are coming to *me* . . . (*pointing to himself*) it wouldn't require the F.B.I. to know that you are talking about

Father O'Malley. What's he done now?

MRS. QUIMP. Well, far be it from me to say a word against the man of God, but I do think you should know what *they* are sayin' about him.

FITZGIBBON (*dryly*). Meaning by *they*—mostly YOU—*Mrs. Quimp and yourself*, perhaps. Well, what are *they* saying?

MRS. QUIMP (*warming up*). First of all, he's been associatin' with all the riff-raff of the parish—talkin' with all the tramps and hoboes—an' makin' friends of the worst young hoodlums in the neighborhood—dressin' them up like choir boys.

FITZGIBBON (*wiping off a smile*). Terrible, terrible! Almost as bad as the Lord with his publicans and sinners . . . What else?

MRS. QUIMP. Why—the scandalous way he's actin'—goin' 'round in golf clothes . . . playin' the pianner . . . and singin' all over the place—and it's not all church music either, Your Reverence. (*This she says with a nod and knowing wink.*)

FITZGIBBON (*shaking his head*). Tsk, tsk. It's *orffull* . . . orfull—against all the rubrics—trying to put a little joy into religion, eh? . . . To make it more attractive for the youngsters. . . . It's turrible. We'll have to take David and his harp out of the Bible. What else?

MRS. QUIMP (*excited—quite mad by this time*). And I haven't mentioned the worst thing of all. *They* are *all* tawkin' about it . . . his encouragin' that young woman to sing—the one what ran away from home . . . (*Lowering her voice to a shocked whisper*) They was at the pianner together—singin' *love songs!!* (*Pausing to let it sink in*) And . . . him a priest!

FITZGIBBON (*in mock shock, repeating*). Tsk, tsk . . . and him a priest . . . trying to keep a young girl off the streets . . . tsk, tsk . . . shades of Mary Magdalen!! What are we coming to? . . . What else?

MRS. QUIMP (*shouting*). What else? Glory be to God, Father . . .

FITZGIBBON (*interrupting, eagerly*). Why, didn't you hear what happened at Brogans'?

MRS. QUIMP (*eagerly, leaning forward*). No . . . no!

FITZGIBBON. Why, he spent the last three nights there. (*Pausing to let it sink into the shocked Quimp, then adding*) He was sitting up with poor Pat Brogan, who was dying . . .

The Quimp wilts and sits back. Father Fitzgibbon is enjoying it immensely. He continues.

FITZGIBBON. And the Widow O'Reilly affair was worse . . . (*The Quimp sits up again and leans forward eagerly.*) Every Friday last month he was seen coming out of her house early in the morning (*He lets it sink in, then adds, softly.*) Her son, little Michael, is a cripple, you know—and he looks forward to Father O'Malley's Communion call every Friday morning.

The Quimp again wilts at this.

FITZGIBBON (*shaking his head and laughing*). I'm afraid you're getting behind on your news. "They" (*nodding significantly*) haven't told you half of the *orffull* things Father O'Malley's been mixed up in since he came—all the comfort and joy he's bringing every day to those in trouble and sorrow . . . True, his methods are a bit unconventional at times, I admit— (*The sounds of "Calliope" and voices of altar boys come up to them. Father Fitzgibbon hears it and waves toward the window with his hand.*) *His* ways are not always my ways, but—I have to admit—(*chuckling to himself*) that with his smile and song, he often reaches those I've failed to reach. (*Then rising and leading Mrs. Quimp toward the door*) I wouldn't worry too much about *his*—(*significantly*) soul, Mrs. Quimp.

Mrs. Carmody appears at the door, a suppressed smile on her face. She's evidently been listening. Just as they are leaving Father Fitzgibbon calls them back.

FITZGIBBON. Oh, Mrs. Quimp . . . here's a riddle for you to think over while you are saying your prayers. Do *you* know why the sidewalks of Holland—are the cleanest in the world? (*He asks it with a smile and a high-pitched voice and waits—catching Mrs. Carmody's eye.*)

The Quimp, now completely wilted, shakes her head in bewilderment. Father Fitzgibbon answers with mock seriousness.

FITZGIBBON. Because . . . everybody sweeps before his own door! . . . Good-bye, Mrs. Quimp—God bless you.

Mrs. Carmody turns Mrs. Quimp around, giving Father Fitzgibbon a sly wink, and shows The Quimp out, as the scene fades out.]

PART EIGHT

The exterior of ST. DOMINIC's fades in, with Father Fitzgibbon standing on the church steps. Father O'Dowd and Jenny appear.

O'DOWD. Good morning, Father.

FITZGIBBON. Good morning.

O'DOWD. I'd like to present Miss Genevieve Linden. Jenny, this is Father Fitzgibbon.

JENNY. Good morning, Father.

FITZGIBBON. Howdy do.

O'DOWD. She's a singer.

FITZGIBBON (*on his guard*). Huh? Oh. Lookin' for work?

O'DOWD. Oh, no, no, Father! She sings at the Metropolitan Opera House.

FITZGIBBON (*cordially now*). Well, now, it's a great privilege to meet you, Miss Linden. You've come quite a ways in the world.

JENNY. Well, I—I—

FITZGIBBON. Travel extensively?

JENNY. Yes, quite a bit.

FITZGIBBON. Ah, and where's your home?

JENNY. Well, I just bought a home on Long Island.

FITZGIBBON (*with careful strategy*). Well! A nice home?

JENNY. Very lovely.

FITZGIBBON (*genially*). Well, now in that case, undoubtedly you'd be interested in a crazy quilt. We're rafflin' it off.

O'DOWD (*as Jenny and O'Dowd exchange amused glances and she opens her purse*). Again? Tch, tch, tch!

FITZGIBBON (*severely*). We're tryin' to raise a little money, Father O'Dowd.

O'DOWD. I see.

FITZGIBBON (*to Jenny*). How many?

JENNY. I'll take them all. How much are they?

FITZGIBBON. Be ten dollars. (*Fitzgibbon flips tickets, hands them to her, and takes the money.*) Thank you. And I hope you win it.

JENNY. Thank you.

O'DOWD (*playfully*). And I hope you win it, too, Jenny, then perhaps you'll donate it to our church and we can raffle it off over there all over again.

FITZGIBBON (*troubled*). Oh, I'd hate to see that crazy quilt leavin' the parish.

O'DOWD (*as Jenny and he laugh*). Where's the Pied Piper and his merry little men?

FITZGIBBON. Down in the basement.

O'DOWD (*starting toward the basement*). Thank you, Father. Come, Jenny.

JENNY. Good-bye, Father.

FITZGIBBON. Good-bye. Thank you.

O'DOWD. Congratulations on selling all your tickets.

O'Dowd follows Jenny, and as Father Fitzgibbon takes another book of tickets out of his pocket, the scene dissolves to the BASEMENT where Father O'Malley and his boys are singing, "Do-do, da-da, do-do, da-da, do-o-o-o-o, da-da-ta-da." Jenny and Father Timothy come quietly down the steps and move quietly up behind the youngsters as they sing. O'Malley sees them, but Jenny signals "Go ahead!" and the singing continues.

JENNY and TIMOTHY are seen close: The girl is deeply moved by the beauty of the youngsters' voices. She catches Father O'Dowd's eye. In pantomime he conveys his impression, "Terrific!" Then we see the whole group of boys again as the number concludes and Jenny and Timothy move around the group toward O'Malley. The youngsters eye her with awe.

O'MALLEY (*to Jenny*). Like some more?

JENNY. Uh-huh.

O'MALLEY. You're our first audience, you know. (*Turning to the boys*) Ready, boys? (*The boys sing a chord, but O'Malley doesn't like it, cries out, "Oh!" while Jenny and O'Dowd laugh; he twists his ear, as if to shut out the sound, and the boys stop singing.*)

O'MALLEY. Of course, we have our serious side. Would you like to hear the boys sing something nice?

JENNY (*smiling*). Uh-hmm.

O'MALLEY. Something with a little more beauty?

JENNY. Yes, very much.

O'Malley sits down at the piano and plays the introduction.

O'MALLEY AND BOYS (*singing*). Ave Maria, gratia plena. (*As we see the boys, then O'Malley close*) Maria, gratia plena. (*As we get a closeup of*

Jenny listening with pleasure) Maria, gratia plena. (*As O'Malley looks toward her*) Ave, Ave dominus. (*As we see both O'Malley and Jenny*) Dominus—(*Jenny joining O'Malley and the boys*)—tecum. (*Jenny and the boys without O'Malley*) Benedicta tu in mulieribus—(*A closeup of Jenny*).

JENNY (*singing*). Et benedictus, et benedictus fructus ventris. (*As the boys sing the obbligato*) Ventris, Tui, Jesus. (*The boys singing the obbligato*) Ave Maria.

JENNY AND BOYS. Ave Maria. Amen.

The anthem concludes. The youngsters applaud Jenny with wild enthusiam.

O'MALLEY. Very well done, boys. (*Dismissing them*) That's all.

JENNY (*glowing with pleasure; to the boys*). Thank you so much. (*The boys utter confused exclamations in reply.*)

O'MALLEY (*as we see the boys filing out*). See you all tomorrow, huh?

We see O'Malley, O'Dowd and Jenny watching the boys, who are going out.

JENNY (*moved*). Oh, they're angels! They've got something you lose when you get older.

O'Dowd looks unhappy, and O'Malley turns and looks up at him.

O'MALLEY. What's the matter, Timmy?

O'DOWD (*flustered*). Nothing—nothing. That was beautiful, Chuck—beautiful.

O'MALLEY. Oh, of course, we don't get Miss Genevieve Linden of the Metropolitan down here every day—nor Deems O'Dowd, either.

O'DOWD. Oh, now wait a minute, wait a minute.

JENNY (*seen in a closeup*). I'm glad to see you've kept up your interest in music, Father. Are you writing anything any more?

O'MALLEY. Oh, yes. I have a little song here now that Timmy's going to take to a publisher. Very good friend of his, and—and if he likes it, that might be the answer to all our troubles.

We see O'Malley and O'Dowd, as the latter reaches into an inside pocket and pulls out a folded sheet of music then looks toward Jenny and sadly shakes his head. O'Malley turns, and sees the music in O'Dowd's hand. O'Dowd hands it to him.

O'DOWD. I have bad news for you. I've been to the publisher, Chuck. He wasn't interested—wouldn't even look at it. Said they were loaded up.

JENNY (*seen in a closeup*). May I see it? (*The music is handed to her.*)

Jenny lays the manuscript on top of the piano and studies it.

O'DOWD (*to O'Malley*). So you're still in trouble.

O'MALLEY. Wouldn't even look at it, eh?

O'DOWD. Oh, he just glanced at it. Said it was too— (*Fluttering his fingers, pantomiming ethereal quality*) Said it wanted more— (*Pantomiming "low-down"*) Boy, I looked at some of their hits: (*He shakes his head.*) "It was hut-sut time on the rilla-rye . . . " (*O'Malley has sunk dejectedly onto the piano-bench.*) And there was another one—I couldn't even understand the words . . . A fellow lost his girl in Salt Lake City, then he goes on to say that the altitude is 5400 feet, average temperature 73, that the place is noted for gold, silver, copper, grain. But it doesn't make any difference to this fellow—(*with a lift of his eyebrows*) 'cause he lost his Sugar.

O'Malley has been setting the last part of Timothy's speech to appropriate music.

O'MALLEY (*playing appropriately*). Yes, I know that type of song, Timmy . . . (*A few chords*) But I don't think it would very properly come from me. Can you imagine "Beat Me Eight to the Bar"—by Daddy O'Malley? (*He hangs his head in shame over the piano keys.*)

JENNY (*looking up from the sheet of music*). I like this . . . (*Thoughtfully*) "Going My Way." Have you got another copy of this? (*As O'Malley nods*) Then may I have this one?

O'MALLEY. Of course.

JENNY. Will you autograph it for me?

O'Malley takes a fountain pen from Father O'Dowd, puts the sheet of music on top of the piano, leans over it a moment and then writes.

JENNY. Thank you . . . Well, I'm afraid I must hurry along. (*To O'Dowd*) Father Tim, can I drop you off?

O'DOWD. You can, thank you.

O'MALLEY (*handing the music to her*). There you are.

JENNY (*taking it*). Thank you. (*Starting out*) Good-bye.

O'MALLEY (*sadly*). Good-bye.

Jenny goes out, but O'Dowd stands waiting and O'Malley turns to him blankly.

O'DOWD (*explaining*). My pen, Father.

O'MALLEY (*handing him the pen*). Oh! Oh, yes.

O'Dowd goes after Jenny, and the scene fades out.

PART NINE

THE QUIMP'S HOUSE fades in as The Quimp is droning nasally to Haines, Sr.

MRS. QUIMP. So—you can draw your own conclusions. It was me that turned the girl over to the police in the first place. Then, when I found out it was your son who was keeping company— (*She coughs dryly.*) If you get what I mean . . . I just wouldn't have felt right if I hadn't told you.

HAINES. I'm very much obliged to you, Mrs. Quimp, for your information.

MRS. QUIMP. You're welcome, I'm sure. After all, Mr. Haines, it's what we do for others that counts. (*Hopefully*) Would you like me to go with you?

HAINES (*dryly*). No. I think I can handle it.

As he leaves her, the scene dissolves to the HALLWAY of CAROL'S APARTMENT. Haines strides in and knocks belligerently on the door. A moment and Carol, in negligee, opens it. Brushing her aside, Haines barges in. This cuts to the APARTMENT as, startled, Carol closes the door and follows Haines. Haines glowers around the room. Over near the window we find the remains of a breakfast set for two. A man's lounging robe is tossed carelessly over the back of a chair.

CAROL (*coming up to Haines*). Who are you?

HAINES (*barking*). I want a word with you—that's who I am!

CAROL (*trying to suppress a little giggle*). You must be his father.

HAINES (*appraising her*). How old are you?

CAROL (*with the old toss of her head*). I'm eighteen.

HAINES. Hmm . . . well, that's good.

At that moment, booming lustily from the bathroom, comes the voice of young Ted Haines singing, "In my arms—in my arms—ain't I never gonna get a girl in my arms, etc." Haines, Sr., stiffens, glares at the girl with narrowed eyes, and then glares off in the direction of the sound. A moment, and the bathroom door bangs open, and out comes Ted. He is barefooted, wears a pair of beige slacks and a white under-vest. He is slicked up and freshly shaved. He is singing lustily and executing a mad sort of little dance to the rhythm of the song. He fails to see his father, who is standing near the wall, dances up to Carol, and, still singing, takes her up in his arms and starts to pirouette. She tries to pantomime to him that his father is there. Ted, puzzled, says "What?" But she gestures again, and he swings around. Ted is not the least abashed.

TED (*setting Carol on her feet*). Hello, Dad. (*Picking up the lounging robe, he struggles into it.*)

HAINES (*apoplectically, indicating the robe*). That's mine!

TED. Yeah . . . I had it altered. (*At this Haines chokes, then recovers.*)

HAINES. Where've you been the last two weeks?

TED (*with wide, ecstatic gestures*). In a blue heaven, dancing on pink clouds . . . (*indicating Carol*) and she came in on a moonbeam.

HAINES (*explosively*). That's a lie . . . I had you followed!

TED. Tsk-tsk-tsk! That wasn't cricket, Dad. When you were my age, did I follow you around? (*As Carol giggles*) Everything I say kills her.

HAINES. It kills me. Do you realize this is one of my apartments.

TED. Oh yes, I had it redecorated.

Carol's mirth gets away with her. This infuriates Haines. Ted has dropped into a chair and is putting on his socks and shoes.

HAINES (*turning on Carol furiously*). You better take it easy! Do you know, I can have you thrown out of town. (*To Ted—busy with his shoes*) Maybe I know something about her you don't know—she was picked up on the street by the police.

TED (*easily*). Oh, I know that. Maybe we know something that you don't know—we're *married*.

HAINES (*staggered*). Married!

Getting up, Ted takes Carol's left hand and draws Haines' attention to a wedding ring.

HAINES (*snarling*). Oh, I'll have that annulled.

TED (*shaking his head*). Uh-uh. You can only get 'em annulled when they're not right in the first place—and this one was right. We both said something about "till death do us part." *(To Carol)* Remember? *(Carol nods wistfully.)*

HAINES *(ominously)*. Where were you married?

TED *(with a jerk of his thumb)*. St. Dominic's ... Father O'Malley.

HAINES. O'Malley! A secret marriage, eh? Well, he's put his foot in it this time.

TED. No, it wasn't a secret. It was in all the papers.

HAINES. I didn't see it!

With his foot up on the arm of a chair, Ted is tying his shoe-lace.

TED. Well, you never get past the financial column.

HAINES. Don't be impertinent. *(To Carol)* Young woman, do you know how he's planned to support you? You know, he's quit his job.

CAROL. Oh, that's all right—I'll take care of him.

TED. Sure. She's working.

HAINES. Oh, so you'd live off your wife!

TED *(revelling in it)*. Well, Mother was a big help to you, wasn't she—until you got on your feet? *(He looks at Carol and she giggles.)*

HAINES. That was entirely different. I've made something of myself. *(His face contorts in a spasm of self-analysis. He looks at Ted, hoping to be reassured.)*

Ted, seated on the arm of the couch, looks at him curiously.

TED. Yes, Dad, you certainly have.

HAINES. Look, son—haven't you any shame? *(Ted shakes his head and beams "No.")* No pride? *(Again Ted shakes his head "No.")* You've really slipped—you've lost everything.

A wonderful ecstatic smile floods Ted's face. He shakes his head.

TED. I haven't lost anything, Dad. *(He looks at Carol.)* I've found something. Well, darling, I guess I'd better get dressed.

The two youngsters exchange a smile, and it's a smile "out of this world." Ted goes toward the bedroom, and as the girl stares after him, we know she has found something, too.

HAINES. I—I think I am a failure as a father.

CAROL *(smiling strangely)*. I don't think so.

TED'S VOICE *(calling from the bedroom)*. Honey, will you get me my hat?

CAROL. Oh, I'll get it.

The girl goes in another direction, leaving Haines standing there fuming, baffled, defeated.

CAROL *(returning)*. You'll have to forgive the way we've been acting today, Dad. We were a little hysterical. I guess we were both a little—well, mad.

HAINES. Well, I'm mad, too! Quitting his job like that and running off and getting married.... I don't know, this—this younger generation doesn't seem to have any sense—

But just then the door behind Carol opens and Ted comes in. Haines freezes dead in his tracks, his jaw dropping as Ted enters from the bedroom. He has put on a shirt, and is just finishing tying his tie, and the thing that chills Haines, Sr., is the fact that on the collar of the boy's shirt is the single gold-bar of an Army Lieutenant. Carol gives Ted his Army hat. He takes it and puts it on squarely. Carol shakes her head, and standing in front of him, adjusts it rakishly over one eye. Then, taking his two hands in hers, she leans back and appraises him. Suddenly, they are in each other's arms. He holds her close, kisses her; her arms go around his neck. This is something more than an embrace—one feels that this is something they want to remember. A close-up shows HAINES, SR., stunned, bewildered.

The two youngsters separate. Ted tilts up her chin and looks into her eyes.

TED. So long, Sweet.

CAROL (*in a whisper*). God bless you . . .

Ted, starting out, passes his father.

TED (*with a little gesture of his hand*). Good-bye, Dad. That plane you gave me did the trick. (*He indicates the Air Corps insignia.*) When they found out about my six hundred hours in the air—they said, "Okay, Bud, we want you," and— Be nice to her, Dad. She'll grow on you.

From a table near the door, he picks up a small leather kit. Bereft of words, Haines watches Ted pause at the door. The youngster looks back at Carol. Momentarily their eyes meet. Then, with a pathetic little gesture, Carol pantomimes "Get going!" and Ted leaves, closing the door.

HAINES (*whispering*). Good-bye, boy.

Wrenching his eyes from the door, Haines turns to Carol. The girl's eyes are tremulous, misty. She's sobbing.

CAROL (*looking up at Haines, trying to smile through her tears*). Well, he's gone, Dad.

The scene fades out.

PART TEN

The HALLWAY of the METROPOLITAN OPERA HOUSE fades in. Father O'Dowd is at a wall phone. There is lettering stencilled on a flat against the wall: PROPERTY OF METROPOLITAN OPERA CO.

TIMOTHY (*into the phone*). Look, Max, you've got to do this for me and I don't want any arguments! (*After a pause*) Now, wait a minute —I've been to a lot of trouble to arrange this so grab your hat and a taxi and get over here! (*Pause; then*) Yes, *now*—right this minute! (*Grinning*) And if you don't, I'll put the Irish curse on you. (*He hangs up.*)

The MUSIC PUBLISHERS' OFFICE: The office is small, prosperous, typical. Three men with three cigars are lolling untidily around a conference table littered with sheet-music. A fourth, MAX DOLAN, is just hanging up the phone. The four men are fattish, fortyish, sartorial sunbursts. This is the firm of Dolan, Lilley, Burke, and Van Heusen, Music Publishers.

MAX (*in a husky voice, indicating the phone*). That's Father O'Dowd, a friend of mine.

LILLEY (*smiling*). What did he want, a donation?

MAX. No. A pal of his has got a song. He's plugging it—and *what* a plug. Get this—Father O'Dowd's grabbed off the Metropolitan Opera House, their full orchestra conducted by Tomaso Bozzanni, the star, Genevieve Linden, and a choir of thirty voices. All this fuss to put over a song written by a pal of his. Now they're all waiting over at the Met for *us*. Can you imagine such a thing?

Then as the three partners shake their heads, the scene dissolves to the STAGE of the METROPOLITAN. The house is completely dark. Work-lights illuminate the stage. On-stage we see Jenny, Bozzanni and various kinds of technicians. O'Malley and his youngsters are filing across the stage. Jenny and Bozzanni walk over to meet them. We see them shake hands.

JENNY (*in great spirits, to Bozzanni*). Tommy—here's Father O'Malley and his Merry Little Men. He doesn't know it, but they're going to sing for us. (*To O'Malley*) Aren't you?

O'MALLEY. Now, wait a minute, Jenny. We came over to hear *you*.

JENNY. Yes, I know, but please— Tommy has simply *got* to hear these youngsters.

BOZZANNI (*beaming to O'Malley*). Please—just a little something.

And now we see JENNY with the boys in the background.

JENNY (*singing as the boys hum*).
This road leads to Rainbowville,
Going My Way?

We see O'Dowd, Max and the publishers. O'Dowd turns and looks inquiringly at Max.

JENNY (*heard singing as the boys continue humming throughout the scenes*).
Up ahead is Bluebird Hill,
Going My Way?
(*As we see the whole group*)
Just pack a basket full of wishes
And off you start—

We see O'Malley directing, the boys in the background.

JENNY (*heard singing*).
With Sunday morning in your heart.

We see Jenny, with the boys in the background.

JENNY.
Round the bend you'll see a sign,
Dreamers' Highway.
Happiness is down the line,
Going My Way?

We see O'Dowd, Max and the publishers. The publisher rises, leans over, and whispers to Max.

JENNY (*heard singing*).
The smiles you'll gather will look well on you.

We again see Jenny and the boys.

JENNY.
Oh, I hope you're
Going My Way,
too.

We see the entire group, with part of the orchestra in the foreground. Bozzanni comes forward to the front of the stage.

BOYS (*singing*).
Round the bend you'll see a sign.

JENNY (*singing*). Ahhhhhh.

We again see only Jenny and the boys.

JENNY.
Dreamers' Highway.

BOYS.
Happiness is just ahead.

JENNY. Ahhhhh.
Going My Way?
The smiles you'll gather will look well on you.

We see the entire group—O'Dowd, Max and the publishers in the foreground.

JENNY.
Oh, I hope you're
Going My Way, too.

BOYS.
Oh, I hope you're
Going My Way
Ahhh-mmmmm. (*The music stops.*)

And now O'Malley turns, smiling hopefully toward the publishers. Jenny also smiles expectantly toward them. Then we see the entire group as Max hesitates, looking uncomfortable, then rises, and comes forward to them.

MAX. Well, that's very good—wonderful! You sang it great, Miss Linden.

JENNY. Thank you.

MAX. That's a pretty good song you've got there, Father.

O'MALLEY. Thank you. I guess you ought to know.

O'DOWD (*rising and coming forward to Max*). Oh, you bet he does. (*Putting his arm around Max's shoulder*) They say he's the sharpest little man in town. (*He laughs.*)

MAX. Well, now I'm embarrassed.

O'DOWD. You mean to talk business—the money? Oh, don't let that embarrass you. We love it. (*And he laughs.*)

MAX. Well, what I wanted to say is, although it's great, it's just as I told you, Father. It's too good for us. It's way over our head. You see, it's not just the type song that a guy would —pardon me, Father—that a—a gentleman would croon to his babe, if you know what I mean. It—it doesn't say enough. It hasn't got that —uh— (*He snaps his fingers.*) Well, it's just not for me. (*The publishers rise and come forward to the group.*) I think you ought to try it out on someone who publishes higher class stuff. (*One of the publishers hands Max his hat, then goes out with his associates.*) (*To the publisher*) Oh, thanks. (*To the group*) Well, I guess we'd better get back to the office. You know, Father, I could be wrong. I hope I am. Good-bye. (*He goes out.*)

O'MALLEY (*downhearted*). Good-bye.

JENNY. Oh, I'm sorry.

O'MALLEY. Well, we tried. You sang it beautifully, Jenny. And, boys, you did fine. Not a single mistake.

BOYS (*off scene*). Thank you, Father.

O'DOWD. If that isn't good, I'll go into the real estate business.

BOZZANNI (*who has come over to them*). I was going to ask you and the boys to sing a little more, but maybe you don't feel like it now. They sing divinely, and they look like Botticelli's angels.

JENNY. Hmm.

BOZZANNI (*As O'Malley goes around to the piano*). Maybe a little something, huh?

We then see O'Malley seated at the piano, with the boys grouped around him.

O'MALLEY. What do you think they'd like to hear, boys?

BOY. The Mule.

O'MALLEY. Huh?

BOY. The Mule.

O'MALLEY. The Mule?

BOYS (*calling out*). Yeah.

O'MALLEY (*starting to play*). Is that all right with you? (*Singing as the boys sing the obbligato*)
Oh, would you like to swing on a star,
Carry moonbeams home in a jar,
And be better off than you are,
Or would you rather be a mule?

We get a close view of O'Malley and the boys.

O'MALLEY.
A mule is an animal with long funny ears,
He kicks up at anything he hears.

There is a closeup of one boy, while the others sing the obbligato.

BOY (*pattering*).
His back is brawny and his brain is weak,
He's just plain stupid with a stubborn streak.

As we see O'Malley and the boys:

O'MALLEY.
And by the way, if you hate to go to school,
You may grow up to be a mule.

There is a closeup of O'Dowd listening and smiling.

BOYS (*heard singing*).
Oh, would you like to swing on a star,
Carry . . .

There is a closeup of Jenny listening and smiling.

BOYS (*heard singing*).
. . . moonbeams home in a jar.

There is a closeup of Bozzanni listening, pleased.

BOYS (*heard singing*).
And be better off than you are,
Mmmmmm.

We see O'Malley and the boys again.

O'MALLEY (*singing*).
Or would you rather be a pig?

There is a closeup of the second boy as the others hum.

SECOND BOY (*pattering*).
A pig is an animal with dirt on his face,
His shoes are a terrible disgrace,
He has no manners when he eats his food—

There is a closeup of a third boy while the others are heard humming.

THIRD BOY.
'N' he's fat'n lazy 'n extremely rude!

We see O'Malley and the boys again as the latter sing obbligato.

O'MALLEY (*singing*).
But if you don't care a feather or a fig,
You may grow up to be a pig.

We see the entire group.

BOYS (*singing*).
Oh, would you like to swing on a star?

A closeup shows Jenny listening raptly.

BOYS (*heard singing*).
Carry moonbeams home in a jar,
And be better off than you are—

We again see O'Malley and the boys, who hum.

O'MALLEY (*singing*).
Or would you rather be a fish?

There is a closeup of a Negro boy, while the other boys are heard singing "Ooooh."

NEGRO BOY.
A fish won't do anything but swim in a brook,
He can't write his name or read a book.
To fool the people is his only thought—

The view moves over to another boy.

FIFTH BOY.
Yeah, but even though he's slippery, he still gets caught.

We again see O'Malley and boys.

O'MALLEY (*singing*).
But then if that sort of life is what you wish,
You may grow up to be a fish.

O'MALLEY AND THE BOYS (*singing*).
And all the monkeys aren't in the zoo,
Every day you meet quite a few.

O'MALLEY (*singing*).
So you see it's all up to you,
You can be better than you are.
(*As the boys hum*)
You could be swinging on a star.

There is a closeup of a boy moving his eyebrows up and down as the boys sing "Doo-ooh-doo-doo-doo-doo-ooh," then the music stops.

And now Max enters from behind the curtains, followed by the other publishers. They have been listening unseen.

MAX. Is that your song, Father?

O'MALLEY. Yes.

MAX. Well, we'll take a flier on that!

O'MALLEY. Did you hear that, Timmy?

O'Dowd rushes in and pumps Max's hand up and down.

O'DOWD. Max! (*Laughing*) You're a grand lad! I knew your name wasn't Dolan for nothin'!

And as Max and O'Dowd laugh, the scene wipes out and we see a TAXICAB with O'Dowd, Max and a publisher in the rear seat—another publisher seated on the jump seat.

O'DOWD. Look, fellas, if you'll come to St. Dominic's tomorrow morning at ten-thirty—

MAX (*alarmed*). Church?

O'DOWD. Oh, now, Max, a day in church isn't going to hurt you that much! Be there—and bring the cash with you. Father O'Malley will tell you how he wants it paid. An old man, a very dear friend of Father O'Malley's, is involved in this—Father Fitzgibbon. It'd make Father O'Malley very happy if you fellows would—you know, just kinda do this his way.

MAX (*still hesitant*). Church!

O'DOWD (*firmly*) Church!

The scene dissolves to the interior of the ST. DOMINIC'S CHURCH, first revealing FATHER FITZGIBBON in the pulpit. He seems very old, very feeble, very worried.

FITZGIBBON (*tremulously*). . . . A you know, I've been here forty-fiv years . . . forty-six in October . . . and during that time I've always had my hand out . . . always asking for something. (*With a little sigh*) And now I have to ask you again. You all know how I feel about St. Dominic's . . . well, we're about to lose it, and I wouldn't like to see that happen . . . (*He pauses, then speaks, right from his heart.*) So give what you can.

The view has been drawing back to show the first three or four rows filled with the St. Dominic's parishioners. The old priest turns and slowly descends from the pulpit. The organ commences to play and the voices of the choir are heard singing "Ave Vernum." The sidesmen or ushers are moving down the aisles with their collection baskets.

The scene moves to a PEW, and a sidesman enters and passes his basket. We see Jenny, Father Timothy, Bozzanni, and, perched stiffly on the edge of the pew, the firm of music publishers. Jenny and Bozzanni contribute generously, but as the basket passes Max and his associates, they stuff in great handfuls of currency—the advance royalties on O'Malley's song. We see O'Dowd standing in the rear of the church, smiling. Slowly and importantly, he drops a coin into the collection box by the door. At the clatter of the coin, people turn around and stare at him. He makes an embarrassed apologetic gesture.

The scene dissolves to FATHER FITZGIBBON'S STUDY. Standing at his desk, with his back to Father O'Malley and Father O'Dowd, Father Fitzgibbon is putting bundles of currency and silver into a canvas bag. He is in great spirits, enormously flattered by what he thinks the pay-off on his oratory. O'Dowd and O'Malley beam on him a moment, exchange a glance of complete satisfaction and shake hands, and the gesture says: "We put it over!" Tying the mouth of the canvas bag, the old man turns with it in his hand.

FITZGIBBON (*patting the bag*). Gratifying. Very gratifying. (*He pats the bag and chuckles.*) And the Bishop thought I couldn't preach. Well, he should have been here.

The old man crosses to the safe and starts to put in the bagful of money.

O'MALLEY. Now that you're wallowing in wealth, Father, how about letting me have a half-a-dollar?

FITZGIBBON. What for? What for?

O'MALLEY. Well, Father O'Dowd and I thought, with your permission, we'd play a little golf tomorrow. I need a new golf ball. If I lose it, I'll swear off—I'll quit.

FITZGIBBON (*eying him over his glasses*). Take fifty cents. (*As O'Malley reaches for the money*) No, no, no! Take it out of the ladies' sodality. They never keep any books.

O'MALLEY. Do you suppose I could buy Father O'Dowd one, too?

FITZGIBBON (*hesitant*). Must we?

O'DOWD. I can get two nice repaints for fifty cents.

FITZGIBBON (*magnanimously*). Give him fifty cents.

O'MALLEY. You ought to come along with us, Father.

O'DOWD. You don't have to play, Father—just come along. The fresh air'll do you good.

O'MALLEY (*nodding*). Just walk around with us. Be a kibitzer.

FITZGIBBON (*puzzled*). A what?

O'MALLEY. Kibitzer.

FITZGIBBON. What's — what's a kibitzer.

O'MALLEY. Sort of an over-the-shoulder quarterback. (*O'Dowd laughs.*) (*To the old man*) Will you come?

FITZGIBBON. Well, now, maybe a little nice fresh air might do me . . .

O'DOWD (*laughing*). Sure.

O'MALLEY. Well, we'll get a ball for you too. (*He takes another coin out of the box.*)

This dissolves to the GOLF COURSE, where under the skeptical eye of Father Fitzgibbon, Father O'Dowd tees off.

FITZGIBBON (*looking around*). Plenty of mushrooms around here.

At this O'Dowd swings clear around, and O'Malley shushes the old man. Then O'Dowd again addresses the ball, swings, and knocks it out of sight.

FITZGIBBON (*wondering*). Where— where did it go?

O'MALLEY. Right there.

The old man shakes his head: a fool's game if ever there was one. Led by Father O'Dowd, the three priests start down the fairway. This dissolves to a SAND TRAP as O'Dowd goes into it, disappearing from view. Followed by Father Fitzgibbon, O'Malley approaches from the rear. He stops, as a little geyser of sand, shooting up above the edge of the trap, indicates that O'Dowd has flunked his first shot. Four more spurts of sand follow in rapid succession. O'Malley, grinning at Father Fitzgibbon, checks them off on his fingers: one, two, three, four, five.

FITZGIBBON. Now let me understand. If you get the ball in the hole in less hits than Father O'Dowd—

O'MALLEY. I win.

FITZGIBBON. Yes. So you've got to count the number of blows?

O'MALLEY. That's right, Father. Step aside. He's going to play now. Careful.

Fitzgibbon steps aside, and on the sixth shot, the ball "arcs" up out of the trap and falls onto the green beyond. The ball is followed by Father O'Dowd.

O'MALLEY (*to O'Dowd*). How many did you have?

O'Dowd holds up three fingers.

O'MALLEY. Three, huh?

FITZGIBBON (*wondering*). How many?

Two more of O'Dowd's fingers flip up sheepishly. Followed by Fitzgibbon O'Malley goes down into the trap O'Dowd continues onto the green to hole-out. O'Malley finds his ball and selects a niblick. Under Father Fitzgibbon's watchful eye, O'Malley takes his stance. By the old man's expression we know that the hypnosis of the game is getting hold of him. O'Malley makes a perfect "chip" shot. The ball "arcs" up onto the green. We see the ball land on the green and roll slowly into the cup. A moment later Fitzgibbon follows O'Malley out of the trap toward the cup. The old man is astonished to discover that the ball is now in the cup.

FITZGIBBON. Remarkable, remarkable . . . (*To O'Malley*) Can you do that all the time?

O'MALLEY (*gravely, with a look at O'Dowd*). Oh, I have been known to miss, Father—you know, a strong cross wind or something.

FITZGIBBON. I must admit that this is a game requiring great skill. (*Taking the niblick from O'Malley's hand*) Here, give me—give me—give me a-holt of that.

O'MALLEY. You want to try it?

FITZGIBBON. Yeh.

O'Malley tosses a ball into the sand trap. The old man starts after it. The two young priests stay on the green.

The old priest addresses himself to the ball, swings at it with his niblick. The ball and a hatful of sand fly up onto the green.

On the GREEN. The ball appears and rolls along, past Father O'Dowd. O'Dowd picks it up and drops it in the cup. Then we see O'Malley helping Fitzgibbon up the slope to the top of the sand trap. They look toward the cup.

O'MALLEY. Father, you holed out!

FITZGIBBON. Not bad for a beginner, huh?

O'MALLEY. Begin— Oh, you've played before? (*He wags his finger at Fitzgibbon.*)

FITZGIBBON (*earnestly*). Oh, no, no—believe me— (*He indicates the niblick in his hand.*) This is the first time I've ever had a—(*floundering*) had a caddy in my hand.

O'MALLEY. Well, you—you better play, and I'll watch then.

O'Malley pats him on the back, and Fitzgibbon beams with pride. Then the scene dissolves to FATHER FITZGIBBON'S STUDY: Facing each other across a small table, O'Malley and Fitzgibbon are playing checkers. Father O'Dowd is standing immediately behind O'Malley's chair. It's Fitzgibbon's move. He starts to move a checker, hesitates, looks up at O'Dowd. O'Dowd shakes his head "no." Fitzgibbon starts another move, again looks up at O'Dowd. O'Dowd nods "yes." The old priest makes the move, whereupon O'Malley, in a series of jumps, clears the board and wins the game. Sizzling gently, Fitzgibbon gives O'Dowd a reproachful look.

O'DOWD. Well, I'd better be going. (*Wagging his finger at Fitzgibbon*) Let that be a lesson to you, Father . . . Don't trust anybody. (*He rises and goes out.*)

FITZGIBBON (*looking after him*). What an extraordinary person!

O'MALLEY. Isn't he?

FITZGIBBON (*yawning prodigiously, covering his mouth*). Well, I'll—I'll sleep well tonight, anyway. . . . Must be that golf . . . Ah, it's fine exercise indeed. Never felt so relaxed in all my life. (*He flexes his arms.*) Never felt any better. Shades of me childhood—You know, I—I feel ten years younger.

He starts to whistle and, folding his arms, gives out with a few steps of a restrained little dance.

O'MALLEY (*patting Fitzgibbon's shoulder*). You know I was thinking, Father—now that everything is going so right—before something goes wrong—you ought to take a little time off.

FITZGIBBON (*starting upstairs*). To do what, for instance?

O'MALLEY. Well, like, for instance, take a trip home and see your mother. The interest is all paid up to date, and unless something goes wrong, I have plans that'll take care of the next payment.

FITZGIBBON (*keenly interested*). Do you really think it would be all right? I mean it would—

But just then the door bursts open and O'Dowd leans in as a fire gong is heard ringing.

O'DOWD. Father Fitzgibbon—Chuck! The church is on fire.

This dissolves into a view of the STREET showing people hurrying to the fire. Fire trucks pull up, firemen run to a fire hydrant and start attaching hose, while fire gongs are ringing. This dissolves to the CHURCH GARDEN showing the church going up in flames, while firemen are standing on ladders playing their hoses on the building, with O'Dowd, O'Malley, Fitzgibbon and Mrs. Carmody standing in the foreground watching.—O'Malley puts his arm around Fitzgibbon's shoulders in sympathy as we hear the roar of the fire. Finally there is a closeup of Fitzgibbon and of O'Malley trying to console the old man.

O'MALLEY. Don't worry, Father. We'll build again.

Fitzgibbon shakes his head hopelessly, then bows it. O'Malley pats his shoulder sympathetically, and the scene fades out.

PART ELEVEN

[We see the ruins of ST. DOMINIC'S as the church fades in next morning, and we see a slickered, helmeted fireman. He is playing a hose on the smoldering ruins. Mrs. Quimp, her head tied up in a bandanna-handkerchief, her nose peaked, moist and inquisitive, is talking to him.

MRS. QUIMP. Quite a fire, eh? (*Intent on the hose, and without looking at her, the fireman nods.*) (*With enthusiasm*) Did you ever see such a sight?

The fireman turns his head deliberately and scans her from head to foot. His expression gets over that he is looking at a sight now. The Quimp shoots a furtive look around her, and lowers her voice.

MRS. QUIMP. Have you got any ideas as to how it started?

FIREMAN. No, lady—we just put 'em out.

MRS. QUIMP. Mighty funny to me . . . All I know is, where there's smoke there's fire.

FIREMAN (*with a sidelong look*). Where were *you* when it happened?

Mrs. Quimp bridles, sniffs and moves away, and the expanding scene shows the devastation, the gutted church— walls still standing, but the roof gone— shows Tony and his gang, soot blackened and grimy, salvaging odds and ends from the debris and ruins piling them neatly in what is left of the cloister. Three or four firemen on the sidelines are still hosing down the smoldering debris. Over in one corner a derrick, with a huge iron ball at the end of a cable, is demolishing a condemned wall.—Then a further movement of the scene brings us to O'Malley, Jenny, and O'Dowd. They are sitting on a bench near the fountain, now smoke-blackened, its basin and bird bath bone-dry. Haines, Sr., is talking to O'Malley.

HAINES (*indicating the ruins*). Looks like I got my money out just in time.

O'MALLEY (*tongue-in-cheek*). You wouldn't be interested in another mortgage, would you?

O'DOWD. Six percent and safety?

HAINES (*emphatically*). No. (*Then eagerly*) But I'll take the property off your hands.

O'MALLEY (*shaking his head*). We're going to rebuild.

HAINES. How're you going to finance it?

O'MALLEY. We have plans . . . (*Indicating Jenny and O'Dowd*) We're working on them now.

HAINES. Well, if you change your mind, my offer for the property stands.

With a mumbled "Well, I'll be getting along," and tipping his hat to Jenny, Haines goes out, following which we get a close view of O'MALLEY, JENNY, and O'DOWD.

O'DOWD. I just figured it out, Chuck . . . if you wrote ten more hits, you might be able to buy a new organ.

O'MALLEY. You'd still have to build a church around it.

JENNY. At least my idea would put a roof over it.]

We see the CHURCH GARDEN: Fitzgibbon is coming up the path, carrying a bucket of water. O'Malley goes over to him.

O'MALLEY (*stepping forward*). Can I help you, Father?

FITZGIBBON. No, no, it's all right. (*Out of breath*) I—I can manage. (*Indicating the fountain*) It's—it's for the birds.

The view moves with them to Jenny and O'Dowd standing by the fountain. Fitzgibbon pours the water into the fountain basin.

FITZGIBBON. They're used to coming here. I don't want them to go away.

O'MALLEY. No.

Attracted by the water, a small bird flutters in and starts to drink. O'Malley draws Fitzgibbon's attention to the bird.

O'MALLEY. Oh, you see, Father? The birds are not leaving—nobody's leaving you. And when we rebuild again, they'll all be back.

[This pleases the old man. He takes O'Malley's arm.

FITZGIBBON. Come, my son . . . I want to show you something. (*To the others*) And you, too.

The view moves with them to the pear tree. It is badly fire-scarred, but still alive. There is even one solitary spray of pear-blossoms.

FITZGIBBON (*taking a twig between his finger and thumb*). You see— there's still life in it. It can be saved.

Jenny bends down the spray of pear blossoms and smells it.

JENNY (*encouragingly to Fitzgibbon*). It'll bloom again. (*Pausing*) Like St. Dominic's, Father.]

O'DOWD (*jovially*). In the meantime, you can send your congregation over to my parish. I'll split the collection with you fifty-fifty.

O'MALLEY (*laughing*). Take it, Father!

FITZGIBBON (*turning to O'Malley*). Now, what makes you all so hopeful that the church will ever be rebuilt. (*He looks off and as they follow his gaze, we see the blackened ruins of the church.*)

FITZGIBBON'S BEDROOM fades in. We see Fitzgibbon propped up against pillows in bed, O'Malley standing by the bed and holding out a spoonful of medicine.

O'MALLEY. Come on, you're supposed to take this.

FITZGIBBON. No, no, no, no.

O'MALLEY. Come on, please, Father—take it. I'll tell you what. If you'll take it, I'll take some, too.

O'Malley puts a spoonful of medicine in Fitzgibbon's mouth. Fitzgibbon swallows and makes a wry face.

O'MALLEY. There, now, that wasn't so bad.

FITZGIBBON. Ooooh! Don't you try it! Doctors! Medicine! Pah! What I need is to be up and about.

O'MALLEY. Being up and about's what got you down. Tramping all over the parish trying to raise funds! And how much did you collect?

FITZGIBBON. There's no need for ye to rub it in! Thirty-five dollars and eighty-five cents.

O'MALLEY. Yeah.

FITZGIBBON. How much was the doctor's bill?

O'MALLEY. Forty! It says here to take two. Now we want to get our money's worth. Here.

FITZGIBBON. Now, listen, there's nothin' in that bottle that's goin' to do me any good.

O'MALLEY. Oh, Father, now you're not going to lose hope, are you?

FITZGIBBON (*seen close; sadly*). Hope? Ye know, Chuck, when ye're young it's easy to keep the fires of hope burning bright, but at my age ye're lucky if the pilot light doesn't go out.

O'MALLEY. I know, Father. Forty-five years of your efforts in ashes. (*Pouring medicine into the spoon*) Here, take this. (*Feeding the medicine to him*) That'll keep the pilot light burning.

FITZGIBBON (*making a wry face*). Yes, it ought to. It tastes like it had kerosene in it! (*As O'Malley laughs*) Well, did ye make your parish calls?

O'MALLEY (*placing the bottle and spoon on the table*). Oh, yes. Mrs. McGonigle's rheumatism is kicking up again. I told her to bury a potato out in the backyard.

FITZGIBBON. That's for warts.

O'MALLEY. That's what she said. And I heard Mrs. Quimp's new gossip.

FITZGIBBON. Oh. What else?

O'MALLEY. And then I went to see Carol and Mr. Haines.

FITZGIBBON. Oh, did they hear from young Ted?

O'MALLEY. Oh, young Ted has been wounded in Africa.

FITZGIBBON. Oh, too bad.

O'MALLEY. They're shipping him home.

FITZGIBBON. A fine, upstanding young fellow. Maybe they'll decorate him?

O'MALLEY. No, I doubt it. Some friend of his ran over him in a jeep! Oh, I've got some good news. (*Taking a letter out of his pocket*) I have a letter from Miss Linden.

FITZGIBBON. Miss Linden!

O'MALLEY (*smiling*). Um-hmm.

FITZGIBBON. Well, now, that's very nice. And where is she?

O'MALLEY. She's in St. Louis. And here it comes, Father. I gave you that medicine to quiet your nerves. Tony and the boys are with her. They're on a concert tour.

FITZGIBBON. They're on a what?!

O'MALLEY. Now, I have their parents' consent, and they'll be back in time for school.

FITZGIBBON. But you—

O'MALLEY. Besides, travel's a great education. If they make enough money, it's going to build you a new church.

FITZGIBBON (*skeptical*). Yeah.

O'MALLEY. Not much of a one, maybe, but something to go on with. And Miss Linden sent you a check —with her love.

O'Malley hands the check to him, and sits down on the edge of the bed.

FITZGIBBON (*pleased*). Thirty-five hundred dollars!

O'MALLEY. How's the pilot light burning now?

FITZGIBBON. It's burning brighter, Chuck.

O'MALLEY. It's a long road back, but we've started, huh?

FITZGIBBON. You know, I've a feeling that St. Dominic's may rise again. (*Fitzgibbon rubs his hands together gleefully.*)

O'MALLEY. Sure, it'll rise again.

FITZGIBBON (*cheerfully*). You know, I—I think I'll get up meself! (*He tries to rise and O'Malley attempts to check him.*)

O'MALLEY. Now, now, you better stay there and get some rest. Rest'll do you good. You need that, you know.

FITZGIBBON. I feel—I feel better. I feel a great deal better.

The scene fades out, and the interior of the TEMPORARY CHURCH fades in. Boys are playing on the scaffolding, the sawhorse, etc. Fitzgibbon enters from the garden.

FITZGIBBON. Here now, boys, boys, boys, boys! Now, go on—go on home. Go on, away with you now. Your dinner's ready. Go on home. Go on, go on.

O'Malley enters in the background from the garden and passes the boys as they go into the garden. Fitzgibbon crosses to O'Malley who stops by the organ.

BOYS. Good-bye, Father.

O'MALLEY. Good night, boys.

FITZGIBBON. Fine girl, Miss Linden. Very thoughtful—very generous.

O'MALLEY (*to the boys*). Close this up. Keep the sawdust out of it, huh? (*They close the organ cover.*)

FITZGIBBON. That will lend beauty to the dedication, and at Christmas you and the choir will be—

O'MALLEY (*coming forward, sitting down on a sawhorse*). Father, I won't be here at Christmas. (*It takes the old man a moment to grasp the significance of this.*)

FITZGIBBON. Huh?

O'MALLEY. Well, I was with the Bishop this afternoon and he's transferring me to another parish.

FITZGIBBON (*coming forward to him, in great alarm*). Oh, you're leaving me? Why, now, it never occurred to me that some day you might. But, me boy, what am I going to do without you? You didn't ask to?

O'MALLEY (*smiling*). Oh, no, no, Father! As a matter of fact, I asked to stay with you, but (*a little embarrassed*) the Bishop asked me to help him out and I—

FITZGIBBON (*worried*). But St. Dominic's—what's going to happen?

O'MALLEY (*calmingly*). Oh, you'll be all right, Father. I wish you could have heard some of the things the Bishop said about you—it would have done you good. He says you're looking ten years younger. He has all the confidence in the world in you. Now, don't worry, you'll have a new assistant.

Fitzgibbon comes around the sawhorse and sits down by O'Malley.

FITZGIBBON. Well, now, I want to wish you all the success in the world, which I know you'll have. (*Hopefully*) Is it a parish of your own?

O'MALLEY. Well, no, not—not exactly, Father. You see, this—this church, St. Charles, it's—uh—well, the pastor is getting along in years and things aren't—

FITZGIBBON (*cocking his head at him*). You mean they're in trouble?

O'MALLEY. Yes. And I'm supposed to go in there and try and help them.

FITZGIBBON. You mean without the old fellow knowing it?

O'MALLEY (*smiling*). Uh-huh.

FITZGIBBON (*innocently, reassuring O'Malley*). Well, now, that's a difficult assignment. But it'll work out. You may have trouble with the old man at first. He may be runnin' off to the Bishop every few minutes, but don't let that bother you. Ah, you'll bring him around to your way of thinkin'.

O'MALLEY (*as the dinner bell is heard*). Well, there's dinner.

FITZGIBBON (*as they rise and start toward the garden*). You'll know how to manage these old fussbudgets. (*Pounding his chest*) Take him out on the golf course—get him out in the fresh air.

O'MALLEY. Yeah, we'll get along. Just—just so he—so he—

FITZGIBBON. Knows enough to come in out of the rain.

O'MALLEY (*smiling*). That's it—that's it, Father. That's it exactly.

O'Malley links his arm in Fitzgibbon's and they go out together as the scene fades out.

We see FATHER O'MALLEY'S BEDROOM, where O'Malley is packing a suitcase. There is a knock on the door.

O'MALLEY. Come in.

Mrs. Carmody enters, closes the door behind her, and remains there.

MRS. CARMODY. Tony Scaponi is here

to see you, Father—he wants to say good-bye.

o'malley. All right, Mrs. Carmody—I want to see him, too.

Mrs. Carmody turns to go, then hesitates. We see that she is visibly affected by Father O'Malley's departure. She turns.

mrs. carmody (*with emotion*). Father O'Malley, I'd like to say good-bye, too. I suppose you must know we're all going to miss you—it's too bad you won't even be here for Christmas . . . You've been just what this place needed. St. Dominic's is very old, and after you've gone I sometimes wonder— (*She starts to break up, struggling for words.*) I hope your stay here has been—pleasant.

o'malley (*in an attempt to relieve the situation*). It most certainly has, Mrs. Carmody—and you've helped to make it so.

mrs. carmody. Thank you for saying that, Father, but you know yourself that at first I—

o'malley. You're a very loyal woman, Mrs. Carmody, and loyalty is a very beautiful thing.

mrs. carmody. Thank you, Father. (*She stands there, inarticulate. In an effort to get off*) I'll send Tony up . . . Good-bye, Father.

o'malley. Good-bye, Mrs. Carmody.

She goes out. There is a pause, and Tony enters.

tony. Hyah, Fadder! So you're really leavin' us, huh?

o'malley. Yes. I've got my orders.

tony. I guess when the Bishop says you gotta go, you gotta go and that ain't hay, huh?

o'malley. That's right, Tony.

tony (*glumly*). Well, you know, sometimes I think I don't like Bishops.

o'malley (*smiling*). Oh, Tony, Bishops are like umpires. You have to have 'em to call the close decisions.

tony. Oh, really?

o'malley. Say, I have a little Christmas present for you. (*He goes to a closet.*) I want you to take my place with the choir, Tony. From now on you're in charge.

He brings out the St. Louis jacket and cap, and puts them on Tony.

tony. That's swell of you, Fadder.

They're much too big for Tony. They both laugh at his appearance.

tony. Great present—I always had my eye on it.

o'malley. I thought so.

tony. Say, when you gonna give Father Fitzgibbon *his* present?

o'malley. Not so loud . . . when we get to the church. You and the gang haven't told—

tony. No, Father—not a word. If they did I'd kick their—I mean, I'd be disappointed in 'em. (*He laughs.*) Well, I'll get goin', Father. I know there's a lot on your mind you wanted to tell me about taking your place with the gang—(*indicating the sweater*) and everything, but I'll make it easy for you. I'll be everything you want me to be—just like you was here checkin' up on me.

O'MALLEY. And if you don't, I'll drop you like a hot potato.

TONY. Okay, Fadder. That's a deal. Good luck to you.

O'MALLEY (*shaking hands*). Good luck to you.

TONY. So long, Fadder.

O'MALLEY. So long.

Tony leaves. O'Malley closes his bag and takes a last look at his quarters. As he is doing this, we hear the tinkling of a music-box that is playing "Too-ra-loo-laroo." Father Fitzgibbon appears in the doorway. He crosses to O'Malley and puts the music-box on the table. He brings out his two glasses and pours them, and repeats the business of giving O'Malley an extra drop. The two men take their glasses. Father Fitzgibbon has great difficulty in speaking. He looks with deep affection at Father O'Malley.

FITZGIBBON. I'm sure that the way to say what I'd like to say will occur to me after you've gone. (*Very haltingly*) We are separated by many years, Father O'Malley, which could be the reason why we haven't seen eye to eye in many instances, but though we've had many differences, we never differed in fundamentals—it was only in method.

O'MALLEY (*touched*). But never in our hearts.

They look at each other, and their looks prove the thought. They raise their glasses to drink to that, and as they do—

FITZGIBBON (*drinking*). Good stuff, huh?

O'MALLEY. Oh, yes.

This dissolves to the LIVING ROOM of the PARISH HOUSE as O'Malley is saying good-bye to Ted, Haines, Sr., and Carol.

O'MALLEY (*shaking hands*). Good-bye, Ted. Good-bye Carol— (*Looking at Ted*) The right man did come along, you see?

CAROL. Yes, but not past our house.

O'MALLEY (*laughing*). Stubborn, huh?

At this, Father O'Dowd rushes in and calls O'Malley aside, and we see them close.

O'DOWD. This is the end—I've just left the Bishop. He told me to report to Father Fitzgibbon. I'm taking your place.

O'MALLEY (*astonished*). What!

O'DOWD. I'm the new curate! (*They laugh.*)

Before they can get any further, they are interrupted by the entrance of Father Fitzgibbon, who almost bumps into Father O'Dowd and scowls at him, then turns to O'Malley.

FITZGIBBON. Come on, come on, Father O'Malley—you have very little time. They're waiting at the church to say good-bye.

O'MALLEY. All right, all right, Father, but I've been doing you a lot of good. You're going to have a new church after the war.

FITZGIBBON. Yes, but we didn't raise enough money.

O'MALLEY (*putting his arm around Haines, Sr.*). That's just it . . . Mr Haines is going to give us a mortgage to take care of the difference.

HAINES (*grinning sheepishly*). That's right, Father. He convinced me tha

O'Malley and Timothy: "Hail, Alma Mater."

O'Malley: Can you imagine "Beat Me Eight to the Bar" — by Daddy O'Malley?

O'Malley: You see, Father? The birds are not leaving — nobody's leaving you.

O'Malley: The right man did come along, you see?

I have a heart of gold. And, after all, it wouldn't be a church without a mortgage.

FITZGIBBON (*happily*). That's right, that's right.

HAINES (*pointing to O'Malley*). He's a wonder.

FITZGIBBON. I don't know what I'm going to do without him. I have no idea who the Bishop is sending to take his place, but whoever it is, believe me—

O'MALLEY (*whispering to him*). Oh, Father—

Father O'Malley has an expression on his face that bothers Fitzgibbon, and he follows O'Malley's gaze. His eyes meet Father O'Dowd's. Father O'Dowd gives him the same grin that disturbed him so much throughout their association. Father O'Malley takes Father Fitzgibbon's arm in mock sympathy and they start out, Father Fitzgibbon looking apprehensively over his shoulder at Father O'Dowd.

O'DOWD. Congratulations to you. (*He laughs as he shakes Fitzgibbon's hand.*)

FITZGIBBON (*pathetically, to Father O'Malley*). Oh, no! Oh, the Bishop wouldn't do that to me again.

O'MALLEY (*laughing*). Yes, he's done it.

They go out into the hall, leaving O'Dowd behind. Then Haines comes in.

O'DOWD (*cheerfully*). Mr. Haines, it's nice of you to give that mortgage to the church.

HAINES. Oh, not at all, not at all.

O'DOWD. Can't tell you how much we appreciate it.

The scene dissolves to the interior of the TEMPORARY CHURCH, and we see Fitzgibbon crossing to the platform, O'Dowd entering and following him. Fitzgibbon steps up onto the platform and looks into the auditorium.—Next we see Tony, the organist and the choir at the rear of the church—the congregation seated in the foreground. —Then we see Fitzgibbon with O'Dowd beside him.

FITZGIBBON. As you know, we're all goin' to miss Father O'Malley. He was a fine man.

We see O'Malley crossing the GARDEN. Then the view moves with him, including Jenny and an extremely ancient-looking woman, who has a lovely wrinkled face and steps haltingly (Mrs. Fitzgibbon), coming forward from the parish house.

JENNY. This is Father O'Malley, the man who sent for you.

O'MALLEY (*shaking Mrs. Fitzgibbon's hand*). How do you do, Mrs. Fitzgibbon. I've heard so much about you, now it's good to see you.

This cuts to the TEMPORARY CHURCH, with Ted, Haines and Carol in the front row, and other people behind them.

FITZGIBBON (*heard speaking*). I think you'll agree with me that we're all a little better for havin' known him.

We again see FATHER FITZGIBBON as he continues.

FITZGIBBON. He was always thinking of others, and that, you know, can make life very beautiful. Believe me, it's what we do for others—(*suddenly the organ starts playing*) that— (*He tries to go on, but cannot be-*

cause at this point the choir begins to sing the Irish lullaby of the music-box, "Too-ra-loo-laroo.")

FATHER FITZGIBBON looks up, pleased, and we see Tony leading the choir. The singing continues, and FITZGIBBON is seen looking up, listening and smiling contentedly. But he suddenly reacts as he sees something, and we see Jenny and Mrs. Fitzgibbon standing at the door. The old woman is crying as she toddles forward. Then we see Father Fitzgibbon leaving his platform and going to meet her. She comes to him and takes him in her arms.

And now the scene cuts to the exterior of the TEMPORARY CHURCH and we find O'MALLEY standing outside the partly open door, as the singing comes out, beautiful and clear. He closes the door, smiling contentedly. Then we watch him, holding his light luggage and walking across the snow-covered garden to the dim background—as the scene fades out along with the last strains of the song.

THE MIRACLE OF MORGAN'S CREEK

(*A Paramount Picture*)

Written and Directed by
Preston Sturges

The Cast

NORVAL JONES	Eddie Bracken
TRUDY KOCKENLOCKER	Betty Hutton
EMMY KOCKENLOCKER	Diana Lynn
OFFICER KOCKENLOCKER	William Demarest
JUSTICE OF THE PEACE	Porter Hall
MR. TUERCK	Emory Parnell
MR. JOHNSON	Alan Bridge
MR. RAFFERTY	Julius Tannen
NEWSPAPER EDITOR "McGINTY" and "THE BOSS"	Victor Potel
WIFE OF JUSTICE OF PEACE	Almira Sessions
SALLY	Esther Howard
SHERIFF	J. Farrell MacDonald
FIRST M.P.	Frank Moran
CECILIA	Connie Tompkins
MRS. JOHNSON	Georgia Caine
DOCTOR	Torben Meyer
U.S. MARSHAL	George Melford

Film Editor—Stuart Gilmore

Screenplay of the Paramount photoplay "The Miracle of Morgan's Creek," copyright 1943 by Paramount Pictures Inc. By permission of Paramount Pictures Inc.

THE MIRACLE OF MORGAN'S CREEK

PROLOGUE

THE MAIN STREET OF MORGAN'S CREEK—seen through the glass door of the Bugle Building: About one hundred and fifty people are milling around talking excitedly. Suddenly they move back and look toward the door of the Morgan Memorial Hospital as it bursts open and the Editor of the *Bugle* and Mr. Rafferty come flying out. They take a wide turn, then hot-foot it toward us, knocking people right and left. As they get near the door of the Bugle Building, the view draws back to allow for their entrance.

EDITOR (*coming to a Tom Mix stop*). Hold the presses!

MR. RAFFERTY. Hold everything.

EDITOR. What'll we do next?

MR. RAFFERTY. Call the President.

EDITOR. Wouldn't he be a little hard to get?

MR. RAFFERTY. All right, then the Governor of the State. What are you standing there? This is a matter of National veal . . . weal . . . whatever it is.

EDITOR (*nervously*). You think it's all right to call the Governor?

MR. RAFFERTY. All right? What do you mean all right? *I* voted for him . . . call him! (*They hurry to a phone.*)

EDITOR (*into a telephone*). Get me the State Capitol . . . I've got to talk to the Governor immediately . . . It's a matter of life and death.

MR. RAFFERTY (*correcting him*). No death . . . LIFE!

EDITOR. All right, it's a matter of life and–and . . .

MR. RAFFERTY. Life, State honor and national pride.

EDITOR (*into the telephone*). That's right, that's right, the Governor of the State. This is the Editor of the *Bugle* . . . It's very important. I've got to talk to him about . . .

Music drowns out his voice and superimposed on the screen we read: THE MIRACLE OF MORGAN'S CREEK. The Editor waits for his connection during the rest of the titles and Mr. Rafferty walks up and down nervously. After the last title, the music dies down.

MR. RAFFERTY. What soivice!

EDITOR (*excitedly*). Hello . . . Mr. Governor? *

Copyright 1943, by Paramount Pictures Inc.

* The film on the screen opens somewhat differently. Omitting film credits, it would read as follows:

THE INTERIOR OF A NEWSPAPER OFFICE (Long shot—shooting through the door.)

THE EDITOR and RAFFERTY are running forward through a crowd in front of a hospital. An intern is running after them.

INTERN. Hey, Doctor!

RAFFERTY. I'm not a doctor. He's upstairs.

The GOVERNOR: Three-quarters back to us. He leans on a great desk, telephone in hand. Beyond him we see the large Gubernatorial office, its walls hung with paintings of former governors. The afternoon sun slants in through the high windows.

GOVERNOR. Yeah . . . the editor of what? . . . Oh, the *Bugle,* yeah . . . What was that town again? . . . Morgan's Creek, yeah. Is it in my State? I never heard of it.

He turns toward us and lights a cigarette with a match from the rear or console desk, whereupon the scene cuts to the EDITOR, and MR. RAFFERTY, in the *Bugle* office. The editor is seated at the desk talking into the phone; Rafferty is standing by him.

EDITOR (*indignantly*). You never heard of it, hunh? By tomorrow morning Morgan's Creek will be the most famous town in America.

MR. RAFFERTY (*indignantly*). The world, what are you talking?

EDITOR. This is the last free phone in the town . . . Every room has been reserved for fifteen miles around. A hundred newspapermen are here already and five hundred more are expected in the morning.

MR. RAFFERTY. A thousand.

EDITOR. There's a shortage of food, telephones.

MR. RAFFERTY. Milk.

EDITOR. Telegraph wires.

MR. RAFFERTY. Liquor.

EDITOR. Transportation.

RAFFERTY. Tents.

EDITOR. Policemen and everything else. We need a lot of help or they're going to tear this town up by the roots.

MR. RAFFERTY. And that's only the half of it.

EDITOR. We need State Police, food, water, beds, blankets.

MR. RAFFERTY. Plumbing.

This cuts to the GOVERNOR—at his desk.

GOVERNOR. Wait a minute. Take it easy, will you? . . . What happened down there? . . . You got a flood or did you strike oil, or something?

This cuts to the EDITOR *and* MR. RAFFERTY.

EDITOR. Did we strike oil or something!

MR. RAFFERTY. Tell him!

The Editor and Rafferty run forward to the newspaper office, open the door, and come inside. The moving view brings them to the desk.

EDITOR (*into a telephone*). Hold the presses!

We see the men in THE PRESS ROOM, as Rafferty's voice is heard calling out, "Hold everything!"

EDITOR'S VOICE (*as heard in the room through the telephone*). Flo!

We see THE EDITOR again at his desk, Rafferty standing by him.

EDITOR (*into the phone*). Get me the State Capital. I've got to talk to the Governor immediately! It's a matter of life and death.

Here follows a list of screen credits, and when the title dissolves out, the scene continues.

EDITOR (*into the phone*). Hello, Mr. Governor?

EDITOR. No, Mr. Governor, we did *not* strike oil!

MR. RAFFERTY. Anybody can strike oil.

EDITOR. We have not got a flood . . .

MR. RAFFERTY. Anybody can have a flood.

EDITOR. What *we've* got, Mr. Governor, is . . .

This cuts to the GOVERNOR at his desk. A secretary enters from the background.

GOVERNOR (*suddenly electrified*). You got *what!*

SECRETARY. Yes, Mr. Governor.

GOVERNOR. Shut up! (*Into the phone*) Not you! Now, are you sure of your facts? (*He drops his cigarette.*) This is terribly important . . . (*He presses all the buttons on his desk.*) I wish I could be there myself. This is a matter of State policy, State pride . . . National pride . . . hold the wire a minute. (*He rises, brushes at his trousers, trying to put out the cigarette burn. He pours a glass of water on his trousers. As he does so, he addresses the secretary.*) Get on this line and take everything down in shorthand. (*A second secretary enters. The first secretary gets notebook and pencil, and picks up another phone.*) Get a map of the State and make sure Morgan's Creek is in it . . . if it isn't we might be able to . . . persuade them to move over or something—oh, boy!

SECOND SECRETARY. Yes, Mr. Governor.

GOVERNOR. Shut up! (*Into the phone*) Not you. (*Into the dictograph*) Get me all the newspaper boys . . . and I want to speak to the radio stations . . . things like this have to be guided.

This cuts to a DOOR TO AN ADJOINING OFFICE. It has just opened and the political boss of the State stands there, worried.

BOSS. What happened?

GOVERNOR. Shut up!

BOSS. What?

This cuts to the GOVERNOR at his desk as the Boss walks into the scene.

GOVERNOR. You better get down to Morgan's Creek and buy up a few choice corners—some hotel sites maybe. They need some, and the bus franchises will be very valuable . . .

BOSS. Morgan's what?

GOVERNOR (*impatiently*). Morgan's Creek . . . Creek—like a little river.

BOSS. A little river should have a big dam.

GOVERNOR. Why not? (*He turns to the telephone.*) All right, now give me all the facts. (*Then to the Boss*) This is the biggest thing that's happened to this State since we stole it from the Indians.

BOSS. Borrowed.

Without asking permission the Boss picks up the phone and listens in, and as he does so the scene cuts to the EDITOR and MR. RAFFERTY in the NEWSPAPER OFFICE.

MR. RAFFERTY (*sharing the earpiece*). Who's excited now?

EDITOR (*into the phone*). I'll tell you all I know, Mister Governor. As a matter of fact I started the whole thing.

MR. RAFFERTY (*indignantly*). You started it.

EDITOR (*ignoring him*). I was writing my midweek editorial, that is to say I was looking for a subject for it . . .

This again cuts to the GOVERNOR and the BOSS, who are listening over the phones in the GOVERNOR'S OFFICE.

EDITOR'S VOICE. I'm rather famous for my editorials in this part of the State . . .

BOSS (*putting his hand over the mouthpiece*). He's going to tell us his life story?

GOVERNOR. Shhh.

The scene cuts back to the EDITOR and MR. RAFFERTY.

EDITOR. And I noticed that there were quite a few soldiers in the town . . .

MR. RAFFERTY. What an eye!

The scene cuts to the GOVERNOR'S OFFICE.

BOSS. What a bore!

EDITOR'S VOICE (*heard as the scene changes*). And it occurred to me that the girls *in* the towns—

This cuts to the NEWSPAPER OFFICE.

EDITOR. . . . and the soldiers *around* the towns would make an excellent subject for my editorial. (*He reaches for it.*) I'll be glad to read it to you, Mister Governor.

This scene cuts to the GOVERNOR and the BOSS.

BOSS (*automatically into the phone*). No.

GOVERNOR (*looking up at him*). No.

The scene cuts back to the EDITOR and MR. RAFFERTY.

MR. RAFFERTY. No.

EDITOR (*hurt*). Just as you say, Mister Governor. Anyway, that was nine months, four hours and twenty-one minutes ago.

This cuts to the GOVERNOR and the BOSS.

BOSS (*looking to high heaven*). What a bore!

EDITOR. I was looking out the window . . . *

EDITOR. And there I saw Officer Kockenlocker, our town constable, directing traffic as usual. As I said before, there was a noticeable number of soldiers in the town . . . **

PART ONE

The MAIN INTERSECTION OF A SMALL TOWN fades in. A TRAFFIC COP directs the traffic expertly and importantly. He is a man of forty-eight, roughly speaking. Some truckloads of soldiers are in evidence and there are quite a few on the sidewalks. A jeep with some M.P.'s is cruising around.

OFFICER KOCKENLOCKER. Evening, Henry . . . Evening, Mr. Dunbar . . . Watch your step, Madam; stick between them white lines or you won't get your insurance when you get run over . . . Who gimme that horn? . . . Hold your horses you . . . What was that? (*He crosses to an Army truck.*)

---

* An eight-foot DISSOLVE starts here.
** The DISSOLVE is now complete.

SOLDIER AT WHEEL. Which church is giving the dance tonight?

KOCKENLOCKER. How many churches you think we got? . . . It's right behind you and no U turns.

SOLDIER AT WHEEL. O.K., Sarge.

KOCKENLOCKER. And you ain't kiddin'. (*Now he resumes his business.*) Watch your step now . . . and keep under thirty-five, you. What was that? (*This last to a delegation of soldiers who have come out in the middle of the street.*)

A SOLDIER. Say, we got to round up some more girls for the dance tonight. You know any numbers?

KOCKENLOCKER. Try the telephone company . . . what do you think I am?

FIRST SOLDIER. Oh, a tough guy, hunh?

KOCKENLOCKER (*threateningly*). Tough enough, rookie.

SECOND SOLDIER. Where do you get that rookie stuff?

KOCKENLOCKER. Listen, cookie, I was in France before you was housebroken . . . now get off the street and behave yourself.

FIRST SOLDIER. What have we done?

An M.P. rolls up in a jeep.

M.P. Hey! What's all the trouble?

KOCKENLOCKER. There's no trouble. I just don't like to be talked to by rookies.

M.P. (*with exaggerated courtesy*). This is Mr. Kockenlocker, gentlemen; he was a sergeant in the other war. (*Then to Kockenlocker*) We do it different now, Ed. It's all done with kindness. (*Now he turns to the three soldiers.*) Come on, get off the street, quit blocking the traffic . . . please. (*The soldiers hurry away.*) (*To Kockenlocker*) You get the idea? It's more psychological. (*He raises his cap.*) Good afternoon.

He drives away in his jeep. Kockenlocker laughs after him. Two other soldiers approach him. One is very innocent-looking and has a paper in his hand.

INNOCENT ONE. I beg your pardon, could you direct me to a family called Issippi . . . they have a daughter, I believe.

KOCKENLOCKER (*suspicious of all rookies*). A family called Issippi?

INNOCENT ONE. Yes, we're looking for a Miss Issippi.

KOCKENLOCKER. A Miss Issippi? (*Then getting it suddenly*) Will you get outta here? (*The boys jump. He calls after them.*) Please.

The scene cuts to the THREE SOLDIERS and CECELIA, a tall blond girl in spectacles.

CECELIA. Oh, ecthuthe me, were you looking for thome girlth?

FIRST SOLDIER. We thertainly were.

CECELIA. Well, I know of *one*.

FIRST SOLDIER. I'll bet you do, sugar.

CECELIA (*pointing at Kockenlocker*). Ith hith daughter. The'th one of the prettieth girlth in town.

SECOND SOLDIER. That crab?

CECELIA. The don't look anything like him. The workth in Rafferty'th Muthic Thore.

FIRST SOLDIER. For heaven'th thake.

THIRD SOLDIER (*to Cecelia*). How about yourself, babe?

CECELIA. I'll be there anyway. (*She flips a badge at him.*) I'm one of the Thivilian Thervith Thithterth . . . but it'th tho hard to thay.

THIRD SOLDIER. You thaid it.

This dissolves to a bunch of soldiers leaning over the record counter of RAFFERTY'S MUSIC STORE.* They are listening enthusiastically and keeping time to a Crosby record. This cuts to TRUDY KOCKENLOCKER—from the boys' point of view. Behind her we see the record cases and a playing phonograph. It is she, however, who seems to be singing the Crosby record. Her lips are in perfect synchronization with the record and she seems to be doing the whole thing. She finishes in a blaze of glory.

SOME VOICES. Now do the opera again.

Trudy takes the Crosby record off the machine, substitutes an opera record and proceeds to sing all by herself a quartet from *Rigoletto* or the sextet from *Lucia*. She finishes up her performance by a basso profundo rendition of "The Bell in the Bay," then gives her friends the brush.

TRUDY. Come on now. You gotta beat it or buy something before Mr. Rafferty gets after me.

A SOLDIER. Will you come tonight?

TRUDY. Sure, I'll be there.

ONE SOLDIER. All right. So long, Trudy.

A SECOND SOLDIER. Save the first dance for me, will you?

A THIRD SOLDIER. I'll flip you for it.

A FOURTH SOLDIER. Save me the last dance.

FIFTH. Goodbye.

This cuts to the DEPARTING SOLDIERS. As they leave with, "So long, Trudy," and "Save the first one for me," NORVAL, a young man in civilian clothes, is revealed standing behind them. One of them bumps him and another one steps on his foot, which he forgives in polite pantomime. As he comes forward the view moves to include Trudy.

NORVAL. Hello, Trudy.

TRUDY. Oh, hello, Norval.

NORVAL. I'd like a package of phonograph needles, please.

TRUDY. Three indestructos or thirty-six Ragons?

NORVAL. It doesn't really matter, Trudy—

TRUDY. Well, I think the indestructos are— (*She hands him a package.*)

---

* Alternative scene, as used on the screen: Dissolve into the INTERIOR OF RAFFERTY'S MUSIC STORE as Rafferty is waiting on two women, while phonograph music is heard, a man's voice singing throughout, "Boom, boom, tolled the bell in the bay, As the wind sang a dirge overhe-e-e-e-ad. And the roll of the waves Marked their watery graves, While the bell chimed the toll of the dead." Soldiers can be seen on the sidewalk, through the window of the store; people and traffic passing on the street. Some soldiers come inside the store. A close view of TRUDY shows her standing by the counter mouthing the words as though singing. A closeup shows the record playing. We again see TRUDY, then the soldiers at the counter looking in her direction while another group of soldiers enters. Next, Norval, a young man, comes forward across the store, stops at the steps, and looks in her direction. A medium shot shows the soldiers crouching down as the bass voice goes lower and lower. A close shot shows TRUDY stooping down as though singing the low bass note; then she jumps up laughing while the soldiers are heard laughing and applauding; and "the camera pans" as she turns to the phonograph and takes off the record.

This cuts to the EXTERIOR OF THE MUSIC SHOP. A jeep crunches back over a scooter and pulls ahead gaily. Now another jeep drives into the scene and parks over the fallen scooter. Then the scene cuts back to NORVAL receiving the package of needles.

NORVAL. Thank you, Trudy. . . . Say, I just looked in the lobby and they've got three pretty good pictures at the Regent tonight and it occurred to me that if you weren't doing anything . . . considering that I was also free . . .

TRUDY. Well, I'm awfully sorry, Norval, but I wouldn't be able to make it tonight. You see, I promised to go to the dance for the boys who are going away.

NORVAL (as Trudy's back is turned). Oh, for the soldiers.

TRUDY. That's right, Norval. I'm awful sorry.

NORVAL. You'd think they'd give a party sometime for those who have to stay behind. They also serve, you know, who only sit and—Well, whatever they do, I forget.

TRUDY. I'm sure they do, Norval.

NORVAL. I don't get to see you quite as much as I used to—or as I'd like to, Trudy.

TRUDY (as Norval's back is now turned). I'm awful sorry, Norval. Naturally, the camps and the canteens and everything take up quite a lot of your spare time.

NORVAL. Naturally.

TRUDY. Why don't you come tonight? The tickets are only fifty cents.

NORVAL. Oh, it isn't the fifty cents. I just wouldn't feel right not being in uniform.

TRUDY. I guess nobody feels very good about that.

NORVAL. It isn't as if I hadn't tried. But every time they start to examine me, I—I—I—

TRUDY. I know.

NORVAL. And then—

TRUDY. I know.

NORVAL AND TRUDY. The spots.

There is a closeup of NORVAL, saying, "Well, maybe some other time, Trudy." Then we see TRUDY, with Norval's back turned.

TRUDY. I'd be glad to, Norval.

NORVAL. Good night, Trudy.

TRUDY (as Norval leaves). You forgot your needles.

We see NORVAL going to the steps, while RAFFERTY stands in the background.

NORVAL (turning). Oh, it doesn't really matter. I haven't got a phonograph, anyway. (Norval turns his back, and starts down the steps.)

As TRUDY looks after him pitifully and puts the package of needles away, the scene dissolves into a closeup of a newspaper editorial:

MIDWEEK EDITORIAL
By Ye Ed

ARE MILITARY MARRIAGES A MENACE?

This is war. Our homes, full of lonely young women, are surrounded by camps, full of lonely young men. This is war. Death may be just around the corner and life moves at a desperate pace. Forgotten are caution and circumspection. Haste is the by-word. Factories, villages, cities are built overnight and decisions are made in a moment which formerly took years of thought. Marriages made in a moment....

[The scene dissolves to the EDITOR and MR. RAFFERTY.

EDITOR (*editorial in hand*). Just let me read you the end of it, Mister Governor. (*He wets his lips.*)

This scene cuts to the GOVERNOR and the BOSS.

BOSS (*into the phone*). All right, let's have it.... We're gonna get it anyway.

EDITOR'S VOICE (*heard faintly*). War time is a dangerous time ... not only for the brave young men who sally forth to battle but also for their sisters ... who remain at home. Let me be the last to urge a lack of hospitality, but let me be the first to remind you that all is not gold that glitters.

BOSS. A politician.

GOVERNOR. It ain't bad. I may use some of it.

EDITOR'S VOICE (*faintly*). That the young are scornful of danger, that wartime is an impetuous time.

BOSS. So what?

This cuts to the EDITOR and MR. RAFFERTY.

EDITOR (*ringingly*).... And that in any large group of good men, there are, by necessity of the laws of average, some scoundrels and some fools.... It is against these that I warn you. Beware, young woman, the spell of the jingling spur ... the spell of flags and martial music, of brass buttons, and short romances, of the hasty act repented at long leisure, of promiscuity confused with patriotism ... or loyalty with laxity ... *Beware!*

A NEWSPAPER INSERT fades in: "MILITARY MARRIAGES MENACE, SAYS MINISTER." "In an informal talk yesterday at the Ladies' Friday Luncheon Club the Rev. Doctor Thorndyke, local pastor, warned against hasty marriages. 'Act in haste,' he said, 'and repent at leisure.'"]

This cuts to OFFICER KOCKENLOCKER reading the paper in his PARLOR. He looks up, considers what he has just read, then bends a suspicious look across the room, and the scene moves with it toward EMMY, who is playing the piano. As he stares at her, she looks up. She reacts to her father's scowl and looks at him suspiciously.

EMMY. What are you looking at?

KOCKENLOCKER. You wasn't thinking of getting married, was you?

EMMY. At fourteen? I was thinking of going down to the corner and having a soda.

KOCKENLOCKER (*irritably*). I didn't mean what you was thinkin' about right now ... I mean generally.

EMMY. Generally, yes.

KOCKENLOCKER. Generally, yes what?

EMMY (*seen close*). Generally, yes, I think about marriage ... what else do you think I think about?

KOCKENLOCKER. Oh, you do, do you?

EMMY. Anybody can think about it, can't they? ... It doesn't cost anything to think about it.... It's only when you do it that it costs two dollars.

KOCKENLOCKER. *What* costs two dollars? You seem to know a great deal about a subject far beyond your years . . . like it says here in the paper . . .

EMMY (*placidly*). Well, it's your subject, Papa. . . . You introduced it; if you don't like it . . . ignore it. (*She goes back to her piano playing.*)

Mr. Kockenlocker looks around hopelessly, then up at the ceiling, and the scene cuts to TRUDY'S BEDROOM, with a close view of TRUDY'S FEET doing a little dance, following which the view moves upward, revealing Trudy as she rises from the bed and dances around the room, calling out, "Yip-yip!" Then we see MR. KOCKENLOCKER and EMMY in the PARLOR. (He is still looking straight up and now receives a small piece of plaster in his eye.)

KOCKENLOCKER. Tell your sister the house ain't paid for, will you?

EMMY (*still playing the piano*). She knows that, Papa, you tell her every day.

KOCKENLOCKER. Every day ain't enough. . . . What's she doing up there anyway?

EMMY. Getting ready for the party.

KOCKENLOCKER. Getting ready for *what* party?

EMMY (*stopping her playing*). The dance, Papa. . . . You've got to kiss the boys goodbye . . . it's a farewell party . . . a military affair.

KOCKENLOCKER. Again? . . . Where is this affair to be unfurled?

EMMY. I don't know, Papa . . . I'm only fourteen.

KOCKENLOCKER. What kind of an answer is that?

The scene cuts to TRUDY'S BEDROOM as Trudy dances to the bed, picks up her coat, dances to the door, opens it, and goes out into the hall, humming all the time, following which she appears on the stairs, dancing down them, and running into the PARLOR.

TRUDY. Good night, Papa.

KOCKENLOCKER (*rising and coming forward*). Just a moment. . . . What is this military kiss-the-boys-goodbye business and where is it to be transacted?

TRUDY. Oh, just like they always do . . . in the church basement, and then at the country club and then kinda . . . like that. (*She laughs.*)

KOCKENLOCKER. Like what?

TRUDY (*edging away*). That's all. Good night, Papa.

KOCKENLOCKER. Just a moment. What happens after the country club?

TRUDY (*on the defensive*). Well, then they bring you home.

KOCKENLOCKER. Yeh . . . by way of Cincinnati . . . with a side trip through Detroit. I was a soldier too, you know . . . in the last war.

TRUDY. But, Papa . . . I've already promised, and I'm already dressed up . . .

KOCKENLOCKER (*a little bit lost*). Yeh . . . well . . . you can get undressed . . . it says here in the paper—

TRUDY (*pointing to her dress*). But, Papa . . .

EMMY. People aren't as evil-minded as they used to be when you were a soldier, Papa.

KOCKENLOCKER (*threateningly*). When I want any advice out of you, I'll ask for it.

EMMY. And you'll get it.

KOCKENLOCKER (*advancing*). Oh, yeah!

TRUDY (*almost crying*). I wish Mama was here.

KOCKENLOCKER (*stopping*). So do I . . . believe me, but she ain't. Daughters! So as your father and mother combined, I'm here to tell you that you are not going on no more military parties. Read what it says in the paper.

Trudy turns away and starts slowly for the stairs. Emmy follows her.

EMMY (*looking back*). If you don't mind my mentioning it, Father, I think you have a mind like a swamp.

KOCKENLOCKER (*whirling*). What!

He takes a flying kick at his youngest's southern exposure, but unfortunately flies off his feet and falls out of the scene with a thud.

The scene dissolves to the FRONT PORCH of the JOHNSON HOUSE. NORVAL is sitting on the steps. MRS. JOHNSON is in a rocking-chair behind him, knitting. In a window we see a sign: "Room To Let."

MRS. JOHNSON. Aren't you going out, Norval?

NORVAL. No, ma'am.

MRS. JOHNSON. I thought you were going to the picture.

NORVAL. I thought I would . . . and then I figured I wouldn't.

MRS. JOHNSON. Oh. (*Then, after a pause*) Isn't there a dance or something tonight?

NORVAL. For the soldiers.

MRS. JOHNSON. Oh. (*Then, after a pause*) I'm sorry, Norval . . .

NORVAL. If they don't want me . . . they don't want me.

MRS. JOHNSON. Couldn't the doctor give you something to calm you just long enough for the examination . . . like some whiskey or something?

NORVAL. I'm perfectly calm . . . I'm as cool as ice, then I start to figure maybe they won't take me and some cold sweat runs down the middle of my back and my head begins to buzz, then everything in the middle of the room begins to swim and I get black spots in front of my eyes, and they say I've got high blood pressure again and all the time I'm as cool as ice.

The phone rings inside the house and he jumps four feet straight up in the air, nearly misses the step and rushes into the house.

MRS. JOHNSON. Don't get so excited, Norval.

NORVAL. Who's excited? (*At the wall phone*) Hello—Yes, yes . . . oh, gee, that's swell, Trudy . . . kind of lucky break, huh? Well, I certainly appreciate your calling me right away . . . I'll be right over. Goodbye.

He hangs up and hurries out.

NORVAL. Oh, boy! (*He starts for the door.*)

MRS. JOHNSON. Have you got any money?

NORVAL. Oh, money. . . . What for? Oh, yeah . . . I've got plenty. Good bye. Goodbye.

MRS. JOHNSON. Norval, your coat!

NORVAL. Oh, my coat. My coat.

He hurries up the steps, walks right through the screen door, gets his coat, runs down the steps and goes out.

MRS. JOHNSON. Don't get so excited!

THE KOCKENLOCKER HALL: Norval opens the screen door and comes inside. The scene moves with him as he runs to the parlor archway, where we see Kockenlocker, Trudy and Emmy.

NORVAL (*the door banging*). Hello, Trudy; hello, Emmy. . . . Good evening, Mr. Kockenlocker. Well, I'm certainly glad you're going to the picture show with me tonight.

KOCKENLOCKER. Who—me?

TRUDY. I'm very glad to go with you, Norval.

NORVAL. Oh, fine. I don't want to sound unpatriotic or anything like that, but I'm almost glad they called that dance off . . . for my sake, I mean.

EMMY. It wasn't exactly for your sake. (*At this Trudy nudges her.*)

NORVAL. Oh, I didn't mean that.

KOCKENLOCKER. It was just called off.

NORVAL (*pointing to Trudy's outfit*). Maybe I should have put on my tuxedo.

TRUDY. You look fine, Norval. (*She takes his arm.*) Come on, Norval. Good night, Emmy; good night, Papa.

EMMY. Don't do anything I wouldn't do.

KOCKENLOCKER (*to Emmy*). What kind of a joke is that? (*Then to Trudy*) And be home right after the picture.

TRUDY (*with feigned indignation*). Where else could I go?

KOCKENLOCKER. I didn't ask you where else you could go; I said . . .

EMMY (*pointing into the distance*). There's a new little boogie-woogie joint about . . .

KOCKENLOCKER (*grabbing her by the back of the neck*). Listen, you.

TRUDY. Come on, Norval.

KOCKENLOCKER. And be home right after the picture.

TRUDY. Yes, Papa.

NORVAL. Yes, *sir*. (*They go out of the scene.*)

KOCKENLOCKER. Now what do you know about this little boogie-woogie joint?

EMMY (*innocently*). Nothing. I just heard you were there . . . digging quite a trench. (*She turns and starts to go out as her father is startled.*)

TRUDY and NORVAL are now going down the path and are coming through the gate, following which they are seen walking along the street.

TRUDY (*with a tinge of nervousness*). It was certainly very sweet of you to come and get me right away, Norval.

NORVAL. What are you talking about, Trudy? The pleasure is all mine. Except to get into the Army I can't hardly think of anything that gives me as much pleasure as taking *you* out.

TRUDY. That's certainly nice to hear, Norval. You certainly helped me out by taking me out tonight . . . when I was all dressed up like a horse and everything.

NORVAL. The pleasure's all mine, Trudy. . . . Not that you look anything like a horse.

TRUDY. Thank you, Norval. . . . You certainly helped me out.

NORVAL. Any time.

TRUDY. You really mean that, Norval?

NORVAL. Really mean what?

TRUDY. You'd help me out any time?

NORVAL. Why, Trudy, that's almost all I live for. Except maybe getting into the Army, nothing could make me happier than helping you out. I almost wish you'd be in a lot of trouble sometime so I could prove it to you.

TRUDY. You can prove it tonight.

NORVAL. Hunh?

TRUDY. I am in a lot of trouble, Norval. . . . They didn't call off the military dance. Papa just called it off as far as I was concerned.

NORVAL. Oh . . . he did? Well, he probably had pretty good reasons then. . . . That's what parents are for . . . to listen to their advice. . . . That's why I always missed losing my parents so much.

TRUDY. I know, Norval . . . but he didn't have a good reason. He's just old-fashioned. . . . Soldiers aren't like they used to be when he was a soldier. . . . You know, all in France and like that.

NORVAL. Oh, aren't they?

TRUDY. Of course they're not. They're fine, clean young boys from good homes and we can't send them off maybe to be killed in the rockets' red glare . . . bombs bursting in air . . . without anybody even to say goodbye to them, can we?

NORVAL. They've probably got their families.

TRUDY. Well, even if they have, they ought to have girls and dancing and . . . how about those who haven't got any families? How about the orphans? Who says goodbye to them? You ought to know about them.

NORVAL. The superintendent probably comes down from the asylum . . . for old times' sake.

TRUDY. Norval, I think you're perfectly heartless . . . I just hope you get into the Army some day and the last thing that happens to you, the last thing you get before you sail away, the last thing you have to treasure while fighting beneath foreign skies is a kiss from the superintendent.

NORVAL (*depressed*). Well . . . what do you want me to say?

TRUDY. I want you to say: "Trudy, it's your bounden duty to say goodbye to our boys, to dance with them, and give them something to remember and something to fight for! I won't take no for an answer, so I'll drop you off at the church basement, take in a movie, then pick you up and take you home like a chivalrous gentleman, so you don't get in wrong with Papa." That's what I want you to say.

NORVAL (*after a slight pause*). I won't say it.

TRUDY (*pathetically*). Oh, please, Norval.

NORVAL. I won't do it! I won't sit through three features by myself.

TRUDY. Couldn't you sleep through a couple of them? (*They stop outside the movie theatre.*)

NORVAL. Suppose you get caught, where does that put me with your father?

TRUDY. Why should I get caught? ... Anyway, I'm not doing anything wrong ...

NORVAL. Well, the whole idea sounds very cheesy to me, Trudy. I don't want to be di-di-disagreeable, but if all you want me for is a kind of a f-f-false front, a kind of d-d-decoy ... I'd just as soon take you home right now, Trudy, and ... say goodbye to you. (*Trudy starts sniffling, and he notices it.*) That doesn't cut any ice with me. (*Trudy is sobbing now.*) Go ahead ... cry all you like ... I've seen you cry before. (*Trudy snuffles.*) Oh, s-s-stop it, will you?

TRUDY. I'm not c-c-crying for me ... I'm just thinking of those p-p-poor boys going away like p-p-poor little orphans.

NORVAL. Well, you're not the only ... dame in town, are you?

TRUDY. That's right, insult me.

NORVAL. I'm not insulting you, Trudy, I ... Oh, where would I meet you?

TRUDY. It doesn't matter now that you spoiled everything.

NORVAL (*quickly*). Doesn't it?

TRUDY (*with snuffles*). What time is the third feature over?

NORVAL (*gruesomely*). About 1:10 ... if my seat holds out.

TRUDY. All right, I'll pick you up at 1:10.

NORVAL (*indignantly*). Pick me up! What do you mean, pick me up?

TRUDY. Don't you think I'd better take your car? The boys mightn't have any.

NORVAL (*outraged*). Take my car! First you get me out under false pre-pre-pre ... tenses, which you never even had the sl-slightest intentions of, of, of ... then you want me to sit through three f-f-features all by myself, and now you want to take my car into the bargain for a bunch of, of—Of all the confounded nerve I ever, I ever, I ever ...

Trudy bursts into sobs, whereupon he gets the key from his pocket, and hands it to her.

NORVAL. All right ... all right! Here! The car's in front of my house. Is there anything else you want? How about my gas card? My money? My watch? Maybe one of the boys could use it. (*Hitting his hands together*) What a war!

He goes to the ticket window, as Trudy turns and goes away. He buys the ticket, and starts into the theatre.

The scene dissolves to the EXTERIOR OF THE CHURCH BASEMENT, an M.P. standing at the side of the steps, soldiers and girls entering, going down the steps, and going inside. Trudy appears and goes inside; and the view moving around to a window, showing the crowd outside, we see couples dancing. Trudy takes off her coat and starts dancing with a soldier. Amid much laughter and the confused sound of voices, women are seen playing a harp and a piano, and a fat soldier cuts in, dances with Trudy, and sings to her as they dance. Next a fat woman is seen playing a trombone on the stage. A tall soldier cuts in to dance with Trudy and the fat soldier leaves.

A SOLDIER. Say, I've got a wonderful idea.

A GIRL. What?

A SOLDIER. Let's all get married. (*His words are greeted with laughter.*)

A short soldier cuts in: then the scene dissolves into a close-up of HANDS ladling up lemonade into cups held by other hands, the view then moving up to TRUDY, the short soldier, and other people at the table. Trudy takes a taste of the lemonade and grimaces.

The scene dissolves to a street. TRUDY is driving Norval's car which is full of soldiers and girls. They are singing amid the honking of horns: "Merrily, merrily, merrily, merrily, Life is but a dream. Row, row"—And this dissolves to the COUNTRY CLUB, where couples are dancing, people are seated at the bar in the foreground, and an orchestra is playing far in the background. The view then moves around to include a man and his wife seated at a table. He rises. She tries to stop him but does not succeed, and he moves to the bar.

MAN (*to the bartender*). The finest bunch of boys I've ever seen. I want champagne for everybody in the house. (*To a woman at the bar as he swings his hands and nearly hits her*) I am so sorry. (*To the bartender*) The whole house.

This dissolves into a view of TRUDY dancing with a soldier, while others are dancing too and different soldiers cut in, and a close view shows one soldier and a girl seated at the bar.

SOLDIER. I've got a wunnerful idea.

This dissolves to a ROAD, TRUDY driving Norval's car which is jammed with soldiers and girls again singing, "Merrily, merrily, merrily, merrily, Life is but a dream."

This dissolves to a PARTY in full swing at the ROADHOUSE. Some jitterbug dancing begins. Trudy does a high one over her partner's head, bumps her own head on the ceiling and lands on the floor in a sitting position. When picked up she says she is all right. A boy says, "That's the spirit that wins . . . we don't know when we're licked. What's your name, sweetheart?" Trudy looks at him vaguely, and rubs her head.

A GIRL (*slightly squiffed*). Don't give your right name.

The same SOLDIER approaches.

SOLDIER (*to a girl*). Shay, I've got a wunnerful idea.

THE GIRL. Well, don't keep it bottled up; pour it out.

SOLDIER. Lesh all get married.

TRUDY. 'Sa funny idea.

As they crowd around, the scene fades out.

PART TWO

THE EXTERIOR OF THE PICTURE THEATRE fades in, with NORVAL standing in front of the theatre, stretching his cramped legs. He looks off and suddenly reacts to what he sees:

He sees a MILKWAGON driving up. NORVAL looks at his wrist watch; looks up and down the street; then he goes to a stone bench in the lobby, sits down, jumps up, then gingerly eases himself down and stamps his foot to wake it up. This, then, dissolves to a close view of NORVAL huddled up on the bench, asleep, and this in turn dissolves to the DESERTED STREET as Trudy drives up. She turns the car and runs into the curb, whereupon we see NORVAL leaping up in the air and whirling around.

TRUDY'S VOICE. Hello, Norval.

TRUDY is next seen hanging out the window of the car.

TRUDY (*strangely excited*). Gee, it's nice to see you. . . . Did you enjoy the picture. . . . How long have you been waiting?

NORVAL is approaching.

NORVAL (*looking at the daylight*). Well, what do *you* think? (*Now he looks at his watch and sneezes.*) Holy mackerel, you know what time it is? (*He looks from his watch to her and back again.*) What have you been doing until this hour?

TRUDY. We had a wonderful time, Norval. We sang and then we danced and then we had some lemonade, and then we sang some more, and then we danced some more and then we had some more lemonade and then we sang still some more and then we danced some more . . . and then I don't remember . . . Isn't that funny: the next thing I remember I was driving down the street here and all of a sudden I said, "Norval! Norval must be waiting for me . . . I bet I'm a couple of minutes late!"

NORVAL. You win.

TRUDY. I'm awfully sorry, Norval. If there's one thing I despise it's people who—I mean if there's one thing I love it's punctual . . . punctuality . . . people who are on time . . . and to think that I let my little Norval wait in . .

NORVAL. You've been drinking.

TRUDY (*indignantly*). Who's been drinking? I never had a drink in my life! How dare you insinuate I've been drinking?

NORVAL. Well, you certainly didn't get what you've got on lemonade.

TRUDY. Well . . . I certainly did . . .

NORVAL. All right . . . what have you been using on my car, a pickaxe?

He tries to straighten a fender.

TRUDY (*happily*). Oh, is this your car? I just grabbed the first jalopy I could find. . . . Where do you suppose I've been?

NORVAL. I don't know.

TRUDY. S' funny, I remember everything perfectly up to . . . some place . . . and then I don't remember anything.

NORVAL. What am I supposed to do now, take you home?

TRUDY (*innocently*). Naturally, Norval, since I'm out with you.

NORVAL. What's your father going to say?

TRUDY. He's asleep; we don't have to worry about him.

NORVAL. I suppose you realize it's eight o'clock in the morning.

TRUDY (*with big eyes*). Eight o'clock Oh, Norval. . . . You shouldn't have kept me out so late. . . . Papa vill be sorer than a boil.

NORVAL (*crossly*). *I* shouldn't have kept you out so late!

TRUDY. Papa will be very cross with you, Norval. He doesn't like me to be kept out so late. . . . He'll sa

Norval, you're a naughty-naughty boy . . . whambo! (*She pretends to punch herself on the nose and reacts.*)

NORVAL. Oh, he will, will he! Suppose I just tell him I been waiting in a picture lobby for you all night.

TRUDY (*hurt*). That doesn't sound like you, Norval . . . I've heard lots of things against you, but I never heard anybody say you were a heel . . .

NORVAL (*getting into the car*). Thanks . . . well . . . maybe we could tell him we had an accident or something.

TRUDY. We'd have to wreck the car a little more.

NORVAL. It could pass the way it is. . . . Maybe we just went for a ride after the movie and had a flat tire. . . . That's old but it's reliable.

TRUDY. I don't think Papa goes for that one. . . . He makes you show the patch.

NORVAL. Oh, he does?

TRUDY. Yes. . . . We might have fallen asleep in the movie and not waked up but the best thing I can think of is that Papa had better be asleep when we get there.

NORVAL. You said it.

TRUDY. Now, just tell me what the pictures were about and everything will be jake.

NORVAL. All three of them and the Newsreel, and the travelogue and the Popeye?

TRUDY. Well, it isn't going to be any harder on you than it is on me, Norval.

NORVAL. What a war!

The car backs into the street and, as it pulls away we read, scrawled across the back of it: "JUST MARRIED."

This dissolves to MR. KOCKENLOCKER snoring in his bed. Suddenly his alarm goes off. He makes a dive for it, misses it and falls out of bed. This dissolves to the STREET in front of the KOCKENLOCKER RESIDENCE early in the morning. Norval's car arrives and Trudy descends.

TRUDY. Thanks a million, Norval. I'll never forget your kindness tonight . . . I had a wunnerful time. (*In a whisper*) Even if I can't remember anything about it. And the pictures were just . . . lowvly.

NORVAL (*slightly worried*). Can you get in all right?

TRUDY (*striking a dignified attitude*). Can I get in all right? . . . What's the matter with you, Norval? . . . I never had a drink in my life and you talk as if I was . . . swaffled or something. Good night.

She catches her coat on the gate, falls the length of it and lands flat, lying on the ground twisted up in her long evening dress. Norval scrambles out of his car and tries to help her to her feet.

NORVAL. Are you hurt, Trudy? Are you all right?

TRUDY (*striking at him*). You stop that!

NORVAL (*dismayed*). Oh! I—

TRUDY. Norval, you stop! You're playing too rough.

And now KOCKENLOCKER appears on the front porch. Mr. Kockenlocker stands there in his nightgown. His face is covered with lather, and he holds the badger brush in his hand.

KOCKENLOCKER. . . . And what kind of a game is this?

This cuts back to TRUDY and NORVAL on the ground. They look off and react to his appearance.

TRUDY (*very amiably*). Oh, hello, Papa. We were just kidding around a little before saying good night.

KOCKENLOCKER (*as he comes down the steps*). I see . . . (*frigidly*) And what time do you say good night as a rule?

NORVAL (*scrambling to his feet*). Good night. Good night. (*He backs away.*)

TRUDY (*helping herself up by hanging onto him*). Good night, Norval dear. (*She kisses him on the cheek.*) Thank you very much for taking me to all those movies and everything. . . . Good night, Norval. (*She gives him a little push.*)

KOCKENLOCKER (*grabbing him by the necktie*). Just a minute, Mr. Jones, where have you been with my daughter till this hour of the morning and I don't want to hear the one about the little accident on the way home, or the flat tire, or falling asleep in the movies.

Trudy has been shushing Norval, and he opens his mouth but no sound issues therefrom.

TRUDY. But it's not so late, Papa. Good night, Norval.

She tries to push him away from Kockenlocker, who holds onto him.

KOCKENLOCKER (*with heavy sarcasm*). It may not be late where you come from, but where I come from . . .

TRUDY. We come from the same place, Papa.

KOCKENLOCKER (*loudly*). Shut up! We call eight o'clock in the morning kinda late to be bringing a young lady home. (*To which Norval gestures no, no, no.*)

TRUDY. We were just fooling around a little down the road a piece.

KOCKENLOCKER (*at the top of his lungs*). For eight hours?

Norval opens his mouth and waves no, no, no.

KOCKENLOCKER (*at the top of his lungs*). Why don't you say something instead of standing there like a stuffed ninny?

EMMY (*hurrying out of the house*). Papa, don't make so much noise . . . you're waking up the whole neighborhood.

KOCKENLOCKER (*to Emmy*). Will you get back in the house? (*Then to Norval*) Now I'll give you one more chance . . .

Norval feels of his temples, presses his cheeks with both hands and tries unsuccessfully to speak.

TRUDY. He's going to explode.

NORVAL (*in a husky whisper*). Flat tire.

TRUDY (*quickly*). We fell asleep in the movie.

NORVAL (*gesturing no, no, no*). Flat tire.

TRUDY (*gesturing no, no, no*). We fell asleep in the movie.

KOCKENLOCKER (*menacingly*). That's all I wanted to know. (*He grabs Norval by the throat.*) I'll flat tire you, you . . . flat tire.

Trudy and Emmy now go to work to save Norval.

TRUDY. Stop it, Papa. Beat it, Norval. Trip him up, Emmy.

Norval is tripped flat on his face.

TRUDY. Not Norval. . . . Help me with Papa. Now you stop it, Papa. (*She leaps on him.*) Beat it, Norval. Trip him, Emmy.

Emmy rubber-legs her father from the rear, and the family falls to the ground.

TRUDY (*from the ground*). Now hang onto him, and beat it, Norval.

KOCKENLOCKER (*muffled*). Will you let go of me?

EMMY (*triumphantly*). I've got a toe-hold.

KOCKENLOCKER (*roaring like a lion*). Wow!

[This cuts to a NEIGHBORING BEDROOM, where Cecelia in curlpapers is looking out of the window. Her mother is sitting up in bed.

MOTHER. What is it?

CECELIA (*relishing the words*). Norval Jones just brought Trudy Kockenlocker home and her father tried to beat him up.

MOTHER. You'd never think that of Norval to look at him.

CECELIA. Still waters run deep . . . as I always say. (*She picks up a phone.*)

MOTHER. What are you doing at this hour?

CECELIA (*putting the phone down*). Oh, nothing . . . I can always do it later.]

The scene dissolves to a view of Norval pulling up by the gate of the JOHNSON HOUSE. The neighbors, MR. AND MRS. SHOTTISH, and their son, are then seen standing by their house and looking in his direction, following which we see NORVAL getting out of the car and looking in their direction.

NORVAL. Oh. 'Morning, Mr. Shottish.

The scene moves with the SHOTTISH FAMILY, bringing them to Norval by the car.

SHOTTISH. Good morning, Norval. Been out on a little party?

NORVAL. Uh-huh? Oh—uh—yes, sir. You know how it is. (*The car door closes.*)

SHOTTISH. I certainly do!

At this Norval comes through the gate, and the scene dissolves to a ROAD. Army trucks are coming forward, as other trucks, loaded with soldiers, are lined up along the other side of the road. And this scene dissolves to ARMY GROUNDS, showing soldiers in the back end of an army truck, with other soldiers below, throwing bags up to them. A bugle is heard. An officer then appears and the scene moves with him as he goes around a truck, while a sergeant is standing by the building and other soldiers are coming forward and going out of sight.

OFFICER. All right, step lively. Get those bags up there. That's it.

And now there appear THREE SOLDIERS, two of whom had been dancing with Trudy, and they approach the sergeant.

ONE SOLDIER (*to the sergeant*). Well, so long, Lefty. It's a swell town you got here.

SERGEANT. Take care of yourselves.

SECOND SOLDIER. Swell girl.

THIRD SOLDIER. Swell party.

SERGEANT. How can you feel so good this morning?

FIRST SOLDIER. What do you mean? I never felt better in my life.

THIRD SOLDIER. Why shouldn't we feel good?

SERGEANT. If I drunk that much lemonade, I'd be sour for a week. (*The soldiers laugh at this.*) Puts my teeth on edge to think of it.

OFFICER (*approaching*). Any prisoners, sergeant?

SERGEANT. Nothing, sir. Sunday morning and not a stiff in the guardhouse.

OFFICER (*leaving*). Fine.

SERGEANT (*calling after him*). Psychology!

The scene dissolves to EMMY and TRUDY in the latter's bedroom. Trudy is in bed, Emmy on the edge of it. A tray of bread, butter, jam, tea and milk sits between them.

EMMY. But I still can't understand how you could stay out so late . . . no matter how much fun you had.

TRUDY. I can't figure that out either. . . . I remember everything up to some place we were dancing . . . and the next thing I remember I was driving down Main Street . . . and Norval was waiting.

EMMY. You didn't go to sleep somewhere or something?

TRUDY. I don't think so. . . . You know me; I never get tired. . . . Did somebody say something about "let's all get married," or something?

EMMY. No!

TRUDY. Or did I dream it? Yes, they did! And some of those poor dumb kids thought that would be a wonderful idea.

EMMY (*aghast*). No!

TRUDY (*shaking her head in horror*). Can you imagine getting hitched in the middle of the night with a curtain ring to somebody that's going away, that you might never even see again, Emmy?

TRUDY sets her teacup down, sees the ring on her finger, and stares at it, horrified.

EMMY. You don't suppose any of them . . . (*Now her expression becomes horrified as she sees the ring.*) Trudy! (*Shaken*) What's that on your third finger? You didn't—you didn't—!

A closeup of TRUDY's HANDS shows the curtain ring on her finger, as Emmy's voice is heard calling out, "Oh, Trudy!"

[This dissolves to TRUDY and EMMY in her bedroom.

TRUDY. But I *can't* be!

EMMY. Then what does that mean?

TRUDY. Well, if I'm married, I'm married. I guess I shouldn't of, but if I did, I did, and maybe it will work out just as well as if I spent nine years picking him out. You talk like Aunt Wilhelmina who thought it over for sixteen years and sewed enough hope chests to fill two box cars and then tried it for one day. (*She makes a gesture.*) She didn' like it.

EMMY. Do you think he'll come and find you?

TRUDY (*indignantly*). Why shouldn' he?

EMMY. Well, maybe he didn't war to get married; maybe he's just wal ing up in some Army camp right now and saying "Holy Moses . . . it's a good thing I didn't give my right name!" . . . Was it a Marine?

TRUDY. How do I know . . . and why do you have to dream up things like that . . . why should he be such a heel?

EMMY. How about Uncle Roscoe?

TRUDY. He isn't in the army, is he?]

EMMY. Are you sure you can't remember his name?

TRUDY (*almost crossly*). How can I even remember— Wait a minute . . .

EMMY (*rigidly*). What?

TRUDY (*as she rises and moves behind Emmy*). I remember I danced with a tall dark boy with curly hair, and a little short one with freckles, and a big, fat blond—one who sang in my ears, and . . . But if I married any of those, it would have been the tall dark one with curly hair, don't you think?

EMMY (*as Trudy sits down on the bed*). That's a big help. Now, all we've gotta do is line up all the curly-haired men in the Army and the Navy and the Marine Corps—

TRUDY (*triumphantly*). I think it had a "Z" in it.

EMMY. His hair?

TRUDY. His name, foolish . . . like Ratziwatski . . . Private Ratziwatski, or was it . . . Zitzikiwitzki?

EMMY. With a name like that I'd forget him.

TRUDY. Oh, now you knocked it out of my head.

EMMY. Wait a minute, what's the matter with us? . . . If you got married you musta given your name . . . All we've got to do is find out where you got the license and there you have your name and his name and the date and everything and there you are.

TRUDY (*in a small voice*). I've just remembered something else.

EMMY. What?

TRUDY (*avoiding her sister's eye*). Somebody said, don't give your right name.

EMMY (*in an icy voice*). But you didn't fall for it? . . . You told them to go suck a lemon . . . you weren't such a corn-fed dope as to . . . (*Her voice trailing off*) What name did you give?

TRUDY. I don't remember.

EMMY (*after a pause*). Then the guy can't ever find you! . . . Even if he comes looking for you. (*Trudy looks at her then looks away.*) Then we'll never even know if you *got* married.

TRUDY. I . . . hope not.

Emmy looks at her vaguely, then away, then looks back at her violently. She puts her hand on her sister's wrist.

[The scene dissolves to the STEEPLE OF A SMALL TOWN CHURCH, and we hear the wailing of many babies and the voice of the sexton.

SEXTON'S VOICE. Here, here, here, now, now, now. Shut up, will you? There's a service going on inside.

The view thereupon moves down onto the sweating sexton in a rusty frock coat in a sea of baby carriages.

SEXTON (*picking up a milk bottle*). Look. Nice milky-wilky . . . good.

He pretends to drink, rubs his stomach

and smacks his lips. The wails increase. He looks toward another crib, spills milk down the front of his coat, and pretends to laugh it off. This then dissolves to the INTERIOR OF THE SMALL CHURCH, where the REVEREND DOCTOR UPPERMAN is heard through the wailing of the infants.

DOCTOR UPPERMAN. . . . From the Book of Moses, called Genesis. (*He listens to the wail of the infants for a moment.*) If some of the young mothers would be so kind as to rise and lay soothing hands on their offspring. (*Now in his other voice he proceeds.*) When the abominations we have committed seem at last to have filled the cup till it overfloweth, when the world is being destroyed, when God seems to have abandoned us to our own miserable devices and the race of men is rapidly vanishing from this earth . . . it may be particularly appropriate to talk about creation, and particularly creation in wartime when it is so needful . . . for future wars . . . (*He looks down at the pulpit and reads.*) And God blessed them and God said unto them, "Be fruitful and multiply and replenish the earth . . . and subdue it." (*Now he looks up and removes his spectacles.*) Wartime is a dangerous time . . . not only for the brave young men who sally forth to battle . . . but also for their fathers and mothers . . . and for their sisters . . . particularly for their sisters. It is to these I speak today . . . to these and to their parents. God said, "Be fruitful and multiply and replenish the earth," and it is a fact that during war the earth is more fruitfully replenished than during peace. The uniforms, the brass buttons, the bright colors, the helmets with plumes and horses' tails, the music, all of these have so captured the imagination, electrified the emotions of all young women from the beginning until now, that more little children, little boys especially, are born in wartime than any other time . . . which is excellent in itself, but attended, as are so many excellent things, with dangers. Our homes are surrounded by camps . . . the camps are full of lonely young men . . . let me be the last to speak against them or urge a lack of hospitality . . . but let me be the first to remind you that all is not gold that glitters, that the young are impetuous, that wartime is a thoughtless time and that in any large group of good men there are of necessity some fools and scoundrels . . . and against these I warn you. Beware of the spell cast by jingling spurs . . . of the hasty act repented at leisure . . . of confusing patriotism with promiscuity, of interpreting loyalty as laxity . . . beware, young women.

He turns abruptly and the organ starts to play, following which we see TRUDY and EMMY in their Sunday best, looking around a little nervously. Then Trudy leans close to Emmy.

TRUDY (*emotionally*). We ought to come here more often.

EMMY (*icily*). And sooner.]

The scene dissolves to the OFFICE OF A SMALL TOWN DOCTOR, who is seated at his desk.

DOCTOR. If you will just follow these instructions and come in again in about a month.

TRUDY (*sitting in a chair crying, then rising*). Thank you, Doctor.

DOCTOR (*coming to her as she puts on her coat*). There, there, there . . you'll find your husband, I'm sur of it . . . and if you shouldn't find him . . . You *will* find him!

TRUDY. Thank you, Doctor. (*She sobs.*) You don't have to tell anybody —I mean you won't tell anybody until I do find him?

DOCTOR (*handing her a sheet of instructions*). Of course I won't, Trudy —I'm a doctor, not a gossip smearer.

TRUDY (*folding up the instructions*). Thank you, Doctor. (*They walk to the office door together. He opens it, and she starts out.*)

In the OUTER OFFICE, Emmy, seated in a chair, rises and goes to her sister, who is coming out of the office crying.

EMMY. Well?

TRUDY (*almost resentfully*). Well, what?

EMMY. How are we doing?

TRUDY. Great!

EMMY (*sympathetically*). . . . Then we're really in a mess.

TRUDY (*sniffling*). Not you . . . just me.

EMMY. . . . So what? You don't have to cry about it . . . (*She snuffles herself.*) You're not the first dumb cluck who couldn't find her husband. . . . What with the war and all, there'll probably be millions of them. (*She snuffles.*) They say they have much the prettiest babies, too.

TRUDY. He'll come back. . . . He has to come back . . . (*As Emmy giggles*) What are you laughing about?

EMMY. I was just wondering if I'm going to be an aunt or an uncle.

TRUDY (*getting ready to cry again*). Aw, stop it, will you?

EMMY (*apologetically, as they start across the office*). I'm only trying to make you smile, Trudy. Come on, we'll see Mr. Johnson, the lawyer.

TRUDY (*frightened, stopping*). What for?

EMMY. To find out if you're really married.

TRUDY (*indignantly*). You're kind of hard to convince, aren't you?

This dissolves to JOHNSON'S OFFICE, where we see MR. JOHNSON, the lawyer, sitting. He rises, and the scene moves with him to TRUDY seated in a chair with EMMY perched on the chair arm.

MR. JOHNSON (*scowling*). Certainly she's married.

EMMY. Even with a phony name, Mr. Johnson?

JOHNSON. What's the name got to do with it? Marriage is a matter of fact, not of names. The marriage was celebrated, I presume. . . . They usually are.

Emmy looks blankly at Mr. Johnson, then at her sister, who nods in the affirmative.

TRUDY. I think so.

MR. JOHNSON. Well, since you are here on behalf of a friend who does not wish to appear, all I can say is that your friend ought to be ashamed of herself.

EMMY (*cutting in*). She's a *very* nice girl. . . . It just happened, that's all.

JOHNSON. I mean because of her carelessness. The responsibility of recording a marriage has always been up to the woman; if it weren't for them marriage would have disappeared long since. No man is going to jeopardize his present or poison his future with a lot of little brats hollering around the house unless he is forced to. It is up to the woman to knock him down and hog-tie him and drag him in front of two witnesses immediately if not sooner. Any time after that is too late. Your friend doesn't remember the bridegroom's name?

TRUDY. No, sir.

JOHNSON. And she used an assumed name. . . . Perfect . . . that's really air-tight.

TRUDY. Couldn't you do *anything*, Mr. Johnson?

JOHNSON. What, for instance?

TRUDY. Divorce him . . . or annul him?

EMMY. Or sue him for alimony?

JOHNSON. Sue who—annul who? Look! I practice the law. I am not only willing but anxious to sue anybody for anything, any time, but they've got to be real people . . . with names and corpuses and meat on their bones . . . I can't work with spooks. Your friend doesn't need a lawyer; she needs a medium.

TRUDY (*as the girls rise and start to leave*). Thank you, Mr. Johnson.

JOHNSON. That will be five dollars . . .

TRUDY (*stopping and reaching into her pocket*). Oh.

JOHNSON. . . . which you will kindly hang on to and buy flowers with on the happy day . . . for your friend, of course.

EMMY. You don't have to tell anybody, do you . . . about our friend?

JOHNSON. How could I when I don't even know who she is?

TRUDY. Thank you, Mr. Johnson. (*The girls leave and Johnson goes back to his desk.*)

And now the girls come down the stairs and start walking along the sidewalk, passing people.

TRUDY (*after a moment*). Well, I've got to get back to the store now, Emmy. Could you get me a sandwich and bring it to me—a Swiss on rye?

EMMY. Sure . . . but the way I look at it: It was a man got our friend in the soup . . . let a man get her out of it.

TRUDY. How?

EMMY (*avoiding her sister's eye*). Well . . . she could always get married, couldn't she?

TRUDY. How can I get married when I'm already married?

EMMY (*as they turn a corner*). Don't talk about yourself; we're talking about our friend. It's all very well to *say* she's married but when the time comes to *prove* it—

TRUDY. Are you trying to call our friend a liar?

EMMY. Don't talk so loud.

TRUDY. Well, you'd better not.

EMMY. Look: I'm only fourteen . . my ideas probably aren't any good . . . anyway. I was only trying to be helpful. Our friend could just marry somebody and then one day—could say: "Oh, by the way . . ."

TRUDY. Oh, sure! And then one day she could say, "Oh, by the way there's something I forgot to men tion." Only I'm already married, Emmy. Mr. Johnson said so.

EMMY. What does he know? He takes in roomers. Nobody's going to believe it, nobody believes good unless they have to, if they've got a chance to believe something bad.

TRUDY. But that would be bigamy!

EMMY. How could it be bigamy if you didn't have your right name . . . *you* never got married. That was somebody else.

TRUDY. Maybe I could ask some of the other girls who were on the party.

EMMY. If they knew, we would have heard about it . . . you can bet your life. You must have slipped away somewhere and done it quietly like a couple of movie stars.

TRUDY (*after a pause*). I wonder what Papa's going to say.

EMMY. He probably won't say much; he'll just haul off and shoot Norval so full of holes he'll look like a Swiss cheese. . . . That was Swiss on rye you wanted, wasn't it?

TRUDY. Norval! Where does he fit in?

EMMY. He took you out, didn't he? He brought you home, didn't he? At eight o'clock in the morning, didn't he? He fits like the skin on a wienie.

TRUDY. Oh, poor Norval. . . . We'd better warn him.

EMMY. We'd better marry him . . .

TRUDY. Marry him! How can you say such things, Emmy?

EMMY (*coldly*). What's the matter with you? He was *made* for it. . . . Like the ox was made to eat . . . and the grape was made to drink. (*She turns back toward a restaurant.*) I'll get you the Swiss on rye. (*Emmy turns and goes back the way they came, and Trudy walks on.*)

The scene dissolves to the KOCKENLOCKER KITCHEN at night. NORVAL is seated at the table eating and smiling in Trudy's direction. He swallows his tapioca and sips his coffee.

NORVAL. I'm certainly very glad to see you all again. (*As the whole family is seen seated at the table*) For a while I thought you were kinda sore at me, Mr. Kockenlocker.

TRUDY (*quickly*). Oh, Papa's bite is worse than his bark. (*She laughs.*)

EMMY. You said it.

KOCKENLOCKER. Well, wait till you get married and have half a dozen daughters, and see how *you* feel when some mugg brings them home at eight o'clock in the morning.

TRUDY. Oh, but, Papa, you've only got two daughters.

KOCKENLOCKER. That's plenty. . . . They're a mess no matter how you look at 'em . . . a headache till they get married . . . (*His voice continues as we get a close view of Norval starting to take a spoonful of tapioca pudding, then stopping suddenly, reacting . . .*) If they get married and after that they get worse . . . (*We see the family group again, and Trudy offers him a spoonful of pudding, saying, "Pudding?"*) Either they leave their husbands and come back with four children and move into your guest room, or their husband loses his job and the whole *caboodle* comes back. . . . Or else they're so homely you can't get rid of them at all and they hang around the house like Spanish Moss and shame you into an early grave.

EMMY. How about sons? They're no bargain either.

KOCKENLOCKER. That's right, but there's *one thing* don't happen to them. . . . They never turn into old maids. (*He laughs meanly.*)

His daughters exchange porcelain smiles.

NORVAL. You don't make out much of a case for marriage.

KOCKENLOCKER. Wait till you try it. You'll settle for half a case.

EMMY. Why don't you and Trudy go out on the front porch. . . . We'll do the dishes, won't we, Papa?

KOCKENLOCKER (*vulgarly*). In a pig's nose. . . . What? . . . Oh, sure.

The scene dissolves to the KOCKENLOCKER PORCH, with TRUDY and NORVAL standing at the porch rail.

TRUDY. I guess it's a good thing I didn't have any designs on you or anything . . . I mean, the way Papa talked about marriage and all.

NORVAL. If you had designs, they wouldn't be on me much, anyway . . . I guess.

TRUDY (*with feigned indignation*). Well, I guess they would be . . . if I had any.

NORVAL (*as she sits on the rail*). Yes, but you haven't, that's what I mean. . . . Like that night of the party . . . you could have stayed and gone to the show with me, but instead you didn't.

TRUDY. I'm sorry I didn't, Norval.

NORVAL. No foolin'?

TRUDY. No foolin' . . . I wouldn't have got your car nicked up or . . . anything. . . . It was only for the boys.

NORVAL. I know . . . you can't expect a girl to see much in a civilian these days . . . even an unwilling civilian. . . . If they had uniforms for them it might be a little different.

TRUDY. I'm not so crazy about uniforms.

NORVAL (*surprised*). You're not! Gee, I'd give anything to wear one.

TRUDY. That's because you're a man.

NORVAL. Oh, lots of women wear them too, like those Whackos.

TRUDY. Woman's place is in the home.

NORVAL. That sounds kinda old-fashioned and domestic coming from you, Trudy.

TRUDY. Sometimes you just naturally feel old-fashioned and domestic, Norval . . . I guess no girl ever gets away from it really. . . . She thinks she's away from it and then one day something happens and she finds out she isn't. Hmm.

NORVAL. Something like—like what, Trudy?

TRUDY (*her chin trembling*). Something like . . . falling in love, maybe . . . or something.

NORVAL (*after a long pause*). Why, why . . . Trudy (*He starts to get excited.*) If I didn't know you so well and know that nothing could be further from your mind, a fellow would almost swear you were pro, pro . . . pro, pro . . . giving him a hint.

TRUDY (*lowering her eyes*). Well, would that be . . . so terrible?

NORVAL. Terrible! It would be marvelous.

TRUDY. Well, how much of a hint would you need?

NORVAL (*getting wildly excited*). Why, Trudy, I, I, I . . . (*He gets to his feet*) I, I, Yi, I, I, I, I . . .

TRUDY (*rising and seizing his wrist*). Norval! Remember your blood pressure! I wouldn't want anything to happen to you just before you said whatever you were getting ready to say.

NORVAL. Oh, don't worry about me. I—it's just only the surprise of realizing that . . . that what you've been thinking about . . . I—I mean, you've been thinking about all these—is not only not—not impossible, but—but even totally p-pos . . . p-p-posp-pposposp-pos— (*He hits the rail.*) Trudy, will you marry me?

TRUDY. Oh, Norval, this is so sudden!

NORVAL. Oh, Trudy!

He topples off the porch rail, grabs a vine and falls out of sight. Then NORVAL is seen falling to the ground, clinging to a piece of vine as Trudy is heard calling, "Norval!" The gutter falls, hitting him on the head. TRUDY runs up to him, kneeling by him, crying, "Are you all right?" And now KOCKENLOCKER and EMMY come running forward along the hall, open the door, stop and look outside.

KOCKENLOCKER. What happened this time?

We see TRUDY and NORVAL are on the ground.

TRUDY. Oh, nothing, Papa. Norval just took a little fall.

KOCKENLOCKER. Well, don't tear the house down. It ain't paid for.

EMMY. She knows that, Papa. You tell her twice a day!

KOCKENLOCKER (*as Emmy drags him back into the hall*). Well, twice today ain't enough.

TRUDY is seen helping NORVAL up.

NORVAL. I'm sorry I was so clumsy.

TRUDY. That's all right. (*She helps him to the steps and sits down beside him.*) There. Are you comfortable?

NORVAL. Fine, thanks. (*He gets a sudden thought, and turns to her.*) Say, did I just p-p-propose to you or something?

TRUDY. Yes, you did, Norval.

NORVAL. How did I come out?

TRUDY. Well, it was so sudden.

NORVAL (*now seen close with Trudy*). So sudden? What do you mean it was so sudden? How can anything be sudden that's gone on since we were little kids together—almost since I can remember. I can tell you what you wore almost at the first Fourth of July party and you weren't hardly any bigger than the firecrackers . . . then you remember the church lawn party when you sat in the apple-butter and they blamed me for it and then later at high school when I took all kinds of subjects I didn't give a hoot about just to be near you, Trudy . . . the cooking wasn't so bad, but the sewing! . . . and then the older I got the uglier I got . . . when I was a kid they said, "He'll grow out of it" . . . but I guess a face like mine you can't grow out of so easy . . . it's like it's cast in iron . . . so I didn't really blame you when you began looking at the personality kids . . . with the Greek profiles and the curly haircuts.

TRUDY. I did not.

NORVAL. I didn't blame ya . . . I even bought a thing once for my nose . . . but it kept me awake at night except once when I nearly smothered. (*As Trudy pats his hand*) It was only for you . . . it's always been for you and nobody but you . . . that's what I went into the bank for . . . to get rich and buy you things some day . . . any little thing your heart desired . . . and then it began to look as if everything I'd always hoped for wasn't going to be . . . and you had less and less time for me . . . and then not having a uniform and all . . . but now, Trudy . . . now that everything in the world is right here beside me . . . everything I've dreamed of all my life . . . to have and to hold . . . to cherish . . . to protect . . . how can you say it's so sudden? (*In reply, Trudy, who has been sniffling for some time, bursts into tears.*)

TRUDY. Oh, Norval!

NORVAL. Why, Trudy, what's the matter?

He goes over to her, but Trudy renews her sobs and bellows from now on.

NORVAL. Trudy, if I said anything to hurt your feelings . . .

At this point we again see KOCKENLOCKER and EMMY running forward in the hall, and coming out onto the porch, listening to Trudy's sobbing and the conversation.

NORVAL'S VOICE. You know I wouldn't hurt your feelings for anything in the world.

TRUDY'S VOICE. I can't do it to you, Norval!

NORVAL'S VOICE. You can't do what—what to me, Trudy?

At this Kockenlocker throws down his dishmop. The father and Emmy move toward Trudy and Norval on the steps. Kockenlocker grabs Norval by the collar and pulls him to his feet. Trudy rises and grabs Norval's lapels. They pull him back and forth between them.

KOCKENLOCKER. What have you done to my daughter now?

TRUDY. Papa!

EMMY. Please—the neighbors!

KOCKENLOCKER. What have you done to her?

EMMY. Ssssh!

TRUDY. Papa, please. It wasn't his fault!

KOCKENLOCKER. Oh, it wasn't? Then what're you crying about?

EMMY (*simultaneously*). Stop! You're making so much noise.

TRUDY. I can cry if I want to!

KOCKENLOCKER. I'm gonna give you one more chance!

TRUDY. Papa, please! Norval, take me for a soda.

NORVAL. Soda!

EMMY (*as Trudy pulls Norval out of the scene*). Papa! Can't you learn to be a little more refined?

KOCKENLOCKER. Refined!

Emmy turns, goes to the door, opens it and goes inside just as Kockenlocker starts to kick her. He falls on his back. She runs down the hall.

The scene cuts to the STREET as Trudy and Norval are standing at the gate. Then the scene moves with them as they walk forward along the sidewalk.

NORVAL. How do you feel?

TRUDY. How do you feel?

NORVAL. It doesn't matter about me.

TRUDY. Thank you, Norval.

NORVAL. What made you cry? (*As she sobs in reply*) I'm sorry. Was it the thought of marrying me?

TRUDY. Yes, but not the way you think.

NORVAL (*perplexed*). Oh.

TRUDY (*as they stop*). I'm in terrible trouble, Norval, and somehow I just naturally turned to you. Like you said that night, you remember, you almost wished I'd be in terrible trouble so you could help me out of it?

NORVAL. That's right.

TRUDY (*as they resume walking*). Well, you certainly got your wish. I don't suppose you'd want to help me out again. I mean, the idea might not appeal to you entirely. (*Her lips begin to tremble.*)

NORVAL (*sourly*). Where's the party tonight?

TRUDY. What? Oh, no. That party I went to was enough of a party for me for quite a while. (*Trudy is now seen in a closeup.*) That was kind of a party to end all parties, if you get what I mean.

NORVAL (*again seen walking with her*). But, Trudy, you said you had such a wonderful time.

TRUDY. I did, in a way, but some kind of fun lasts longer than others, if you get what I mean.

NORVAL (*blankly*). I'm not sure that I do, Trudy. (*They pause at the curb and then cross the street.*)

TRUDY. Well, maybe I can find a better way to explain it to you.

NORVAL. Maybe you can.

TRUDY. When you asked me to marry you, Norval, did you really mean it?

NORVAL. Of course I did.

TRUDY. Could you think of any reason, maybe, why you wouldn't want to marry me?

NORVAL. What would I do with such a reason? I do want to marry you.

He pulls her back just as a horse and buggy pass through the scene; then they continue forward.

TRUDY. Oh! (*Starting to cry*) I can't do it to you, Norval!

NORVAL. Well, now we're right back where we started.

TRUDY. Norval, can you keep a secret?

NORVAL. Of course I can.

TRUDY. Cross your heart and hope to die, boil in oil and stew in lye?

NORVAL. Cross my heart and hope to die.

TRUDY. Boil in oil and stew in lye?

NORVAL. Sure.

TRUDY (*slurring the word*). I'm married.

NORVAL. You're married. Well, that's—*you're what?!*

He stops, grabs her, and whirls her around.

TRUDY. Sssh. Norval! Don't get so excited!

NORVAL. Well, what you said—

TRUDY. Sssh!

NORVAL (*as they continue walking*). Oh, excuse me. I—I thought for a minute there you said you were married.

TRUDY. I did say I was married.

NORVAL (*as he backs up against a lamp post*). You did say you were married? *You did say you were married!*

TRUDY. Ssssh!

NORVAL. Trudy, you—the spots—said you were married.

TRUDY. It happened that night.

NORVAL. It happened that night? You mean the night you were out with me?!

TRUDY (*looking away*). That's right.

NORVAL (*excitedly*). Trudy, that's the terriblest thing I ever— How could you do it—the spots!—to me, Trudy?

TRUDY. That isn't even the worst of it.

NORVAL (*electrified*). That isn't even the worst—that isn't even the w-w— What could be worse than that?

TRUDY. You're going to make me cry. (*And she sobs.*)

NORVAL. Well, go ahead, cry—cry all you like—see if I care! The spots! Who did you marry?

TRUDY. I don't know.

NORVAL. You don't know. *You don't know!* What do you mean you don't know? That's the most ridiculous statement I ever—I've—I've . . .

They stop.

NORVAL (*walking forward with her again*). . . . I've—I've ever—

TRUDY. It has a "Z" in it. His name had a "Z" in it, I think. I don't know. I've thought so much about it, and the more I think about it, the less I can remember—

NORVAL. But—

TRUDY. And don't tell me to find the name on the marriage license because I haven't got any. (*Sobbing*) And don't ask me if I'm sure I'm married, because I am sure.

NORVAL. How can you be if there's no name on the r-r-r-record? How can you pos-pos-possibly be su— Trudy, you don't mean—? (*They stop.*)

TRUDY. That's right.

Norval staggers to a bench and collapses on it. Trudy sits down by him.

NORVAL (*suddenly pointing to himself*). The spots! Oh, that's terrible! I—I feel terrible.

TRUDY. How do you suppose I feel?

NORVAL. Oh, that's the terriblest thing I ever— What's your father going to say when he finds out and you c-can't —I mean, you haven't any husband —I—I mean any proof—I—I mean any— Who's—who's he going— (*He breaks off as Trudy looks at him. He points to himself.*) The spots!

TRUDY. I can almost see them myself.

NORVAL (*rising*). Oh, how can—how can you—

TRUDY (*rising with him*). Norval, take it easy.

NORVAL. I'm the last person—I tried —I tried—

TRUDY. Norval, try to concentrate! Try to focus.

NORVAL. F-f-f-f-focus.

Trudy: Stop it, Papa. Beat it, Norval.

Kockenlocker: I wanta have a little talk with you.

Norval: With this ring I thee wed.

Kockenlocker: What are all you coppers doing in my town?

TRUDY. You better take me home, Norval.

NORVAL. F-f-f-f-focus.

TRUDY. No, home.

NORVAL. H-h-h-hocus.

The scene dissolves to the KOCKENLOCKER HALL, with Trudy coming in and closing the door. Then she comes forward to the stairs.

KOCKENLOCKER'S VOICE (*heard calling out*). Hey! (*Whereupon Trudy stops and looks up.*)

Next we see KOCKENLOCKER in the doorway of the parlor, and the scene moves with him to Trudy at the foot of the stairs.

KOCKENLOCKER. Just a minute! Now, what was all that clowning around on the front porch?

TRUDY (*with a strange dignity*). Don't you know there are times when a woman doesn't care to talk?

KOCKENLOCKER (*indignantly*). A woman doesn't care to talk? Only time a woman doesn't care to talk is when she's dead. And where do you get that woman stuff?

TRUDY (*with a faraway look, as she starts up the steps*). Or to be questioned?

KOCKENLOCKER (*leaping forward*). Or be what?

Trudy sheds her dignity, screams, runs up the steps, and disappears as he starts in pursuit and falls.

KOCKENLOCKER. Why, you fresh little—

THE UPPER HALL: Trudy comes up the stairs, runs along the hall to her door, opens it, and goes inside just as Kockenlocker appears in pursuit. Trudy exclaims, "Papa, don't," and the door slams shut in his face, so that he bumps into it. Then we see the BEDROOM with Emmy standing by the dressing table.

EMMY. What happened?

Trudy appears at the door, and goes to Emmy.

TRUDY. Oh, nothing. Just Papa pulling his usual stuff.

EMMY. No. I mean with Norval.

TRUDY (*avoiding her sister's eye*). Oh! I couldn't do it to him, Emmy. He was so sweet, honey. He said he loved me ever since I wasn't any bigger than a fire hydrant or something, and how he didn't blame me for not loving him because he was so homely in the face, and how he went to cooking class and sewing class just to be near me, Emmy.

EMMY. But he's perfect. He could do all the housework.

TRUDY (*sobbing as she goes to the bed and sits down on it*). I couldn't do it to him, Emmy.

EMMY (*sitting down on the bed beside Trudy*). Why don't you give yourself up! You ought to have your brains counted.

TRUDY. I couldn't do it to him. We'll just have to find something else.

EMMY. Where are you going to find another clunk like that one?

TRUDY. Well, there's nothing says you got to have a husband on the happy day. You take like a widow.

EMMY. Yes, but a widow *had* one.

TRUDY (*belligerently*). Well, I *had* one.

EMMY. You don't have to convince me, Trudy. I love you. I know you wouldn't do anything wrong, except you take after Papa's side of the family a little. It would hurt me just as much as it would you to have you hurt and miserable and ashamed and everything. That's the only reason I want you to get married. You can't tell how a town's going to take things —a town that can produce schnooks like Papa—all suspicious and suspecting the worst in everything. There are very few dopes like Norval, honey. You can't use anybody too snoopy.

TRUDY (*through her tears*). Then maybe I shouldn't of told him.

EMMY (*her eyes popping out of her head*). You didn't tell him! Oh, murder!

TRUDY (*weeping*). Oh, Emmy!

They throw their arms around each other, and both howl in unison.

The scene cuts to the UPPER HALL, with Kockenlocker standing by the bathroom door, startled by the sound of Trudy's and Emmy's sobbing. At this he crosses to the bedroom door and pounds on it.

KOCKENLOCKER. Hey! What's going on in there, anyway? How about a little quiet? Daughters! Phooey!

As he tries the door the scene fades out.

PART THREE

THE INTERIOR OF THE BANK fades in. Norval is in the teller's cage, stamping papers. Then we see the dignified-looking MR. TUERCK getting his hat from a rack. He goes to the gate and looks out.

TUERCK. Going to lunch.

NORVAL'S VOICE. Yes, sir.

Mr. Tuerck starts towards the door, then turns and goes toward Norval.

TUERCK. Funny thing happened this morning, Norval.

NORVAL. Yes, sir?

TUERCK. Mr. Shottish asked me if you had announced your engagement yet.

NORVAL. My enga—my enga-enga—

TUERCK. Yes. He kinda had a wild idea that maybe you'd eloped or something.

NORVAL. Oh, wh-wh-what would I—w-what would I elope for?

TUERCK. What are you so nervous about?

NORVAL. Who—who's nervous? I mean, w-w-who's nervous?

TUERCK. All I mean, Norval, is this: It isn't any of my business what time you get home in the morning or how drunk you are when you do get home, but it is the bank's business.

NORVAL. T-t-t-the bank.

TUERCK. That's right. A man in a bank is like a fellow crossing Niagara Falls on a tight rope. He cannot be too careful.

NORVAL. Oh, yes, I—I get what you mean, Mr. Tuerck.

TUERCK. Fathers taking pokes at you and all that sort of stuff. Very bad for a banker.

NORVAL. Oh, you sa—you said it, Mr. Tuerck, Y-y-you—you said it.

TUERCK. Remember it.

NORVAL. Yes, sir.

Tuerck goes out, and Norval, in his excitement, knocks over a tray of change. Tuerck, seen walking away, stops, looks back, reacting to the crash, then turns and continues on his way. A close view of NORVAL next shows him stooping behind the counter, peeking up over it. Then he kneels and collects the scattered money on the floor.

This dissolves to the STREET, with Kockenlocker in the center, as people appear on the curb. Tuerck comes forward with the people. He stops by Kockenlocker.

KOCKENLOCKER (*having his usual troubles directing traffic*). Come on, step lively. Step lively here.—Hiya, Mr. Tuerck.

TUERCK (*jovially*). Hello, Edmund. I'm glad to see they haven't run you down yet.

KOCKENLOCKER. I'll probably get it from a horse when I get it.

TUERCK (*after a polite laugh*). I heard a rumor that one of your daughters is getting married. Any truth in it?

KOCKENLOCKER. One of my daughters! Who told you?

TUERCK. A little bird. We bankers, you know. Heh, heh, heh. We have our own little channels of information. (*As he leaves*) Well, congratulations, Edmund.

[This dissolves to RAFFERTY'S MUSIC STORE. Trudy's hand comes into view and puts a record on the turntable. The machine begins to play "Chopin's Funeral March." The view moves over to Trudy and we see her sitting dejectedly, listening lugubriously to the music. She reaches for a knob and turns the music up a little higher. This cuts to MR. RAFFERTY at his desk near the cash register. He looks indignantly in Trudy's direction, tries to write in his journal, then slaps it closed and hurries toward Trudy.

MR. RAFFERTY (*indignantly*). For heaven's sake, Trudy, what's the matter with you? "Chopin's Funeral March" again . . . "Gloomy Sunday" all day. "A Violet From Mother's Grave" yet . . . what are you trying to do . . . drive me into 77B?

TRUDY (*dejectedly*). I'm sorry.

MR. RAFFERTY. What's the matter with you? You'd give the heebie-jeebies to a horse! You got the melancholic . . . maybe it's your toots . . . nothing gives so much trouble like the toots . . . now you take me till I had mine hex-rayed did I . . . *Will you turn that thing off and play something jolleh?*

TRUDY. Yes, sir.

RAFFERTY. You know what it showed in the hex-ray? . . . I won't cut your appetite. Anyway . . . now . . . (*He pushes his uppers firmly into place.*) . . . a pleasure.

TRUDY (*turning from putting on another record*). I'm all right—I'm just a little bit blue.

The machine starts to play a sentimental Paramount number.

RAFFERTY. Your gallbladder! . . . now take me till I had my gallbladder hex-rayed, was I nauseous!

TRUDY (*cutting in*). There's nothing the matter with me, Mr. Rafferty.

Mr. Rafferty is nonplussed for a second—but only for a second.

RAFFERTY (*triumphantly*). I got it: your feet! Till I had my feet hexrayed did I suffer from back pains . . . shooting through here. (*Now he demonstrates with his hands.*) My arches was pressing on my nerves and shooting pains up my . . . sometimes it would catch me . . . (*He clutches the back of his neck.*)

TRUDY. It isn't my feet.

RAFFERTY. Then you're in love. (*Now he leaps on this theory with joy.*) Trudy, you little monkey, you're in love, that's wonderful . . . who is it . . . don't tell me, let me guess: a soldier . . . one of them lieutenants maybe . . . all right he isn't a lieutenant . . . he'll be a lieutenant.

TRUDY. Mr. Rafferty, please. (*She starts to cry.*)

RAFFERTY (*desolated—putting his arm on her shoulder*). Trudy, did I say something . . . would I try to hurt you, Trudy?

The automatic phonograph takes off the record and starts playing "Chopin's Funeral March" underneath it.

RAFFERTY. Trudy, please will you take that thing off . . . and break it . . . or put it back in the files. Now tell me . . . what's the matter?

We hear the shop door open and they both turn, and the scene cuts to NORVAL coming in with a little bunch of flowers in his hand.

RAFFERTY. Oh, ho . . . aha, enough said, two and two is four, plus ten percent amusement tax, plus five percent federal and three percent unemployment. (*He laughs at his lousy little joke.*) Come on now, smile for him when he comes in . . . smile kitsy-kitsy. (*He tickles her.*) And no more funeral marches . . . wedding marches . . . I'll take a powder. (*He starts toward Norval.*)

Norval comes forward.

RAFFERTY (*crossing to him*). Good evening, Norval. (*He takes his hand and shakes it significantly.*) I know from nothing. (*He gives Norval a wise wink, and hurries to his desk.*)

Norval goes to Trudy.

TRUDY. Hello, Norval.

NORVAL. Hello, Trudy. (*Then jerking a thumb toward Rafferty*) What's he talking about?

TRUDY. I don't know.

NORVAL. The whole town seems to know something.

TRUDY. H-h-how could they?

NORVAL. I don't know . . . but Mr. Tuerck was saying I'd better watch my step and . . . and . . .

TRUDY. Why should *you* watch your step?

NORVAL. I don't know. And then your father came in and kind of threatened me.

TRUDY. You didn't tell him anything?

NORVAL. Trudy, how can you say such a thing? I mean the way I feel . . . I couldn't sleep all last night, Trudy.

TRUDY. I'm sorry, Norval . . . I wouldn't want to upset you for anything.

NORVAL. You wouldn't want to upset *me*, Trudy! How can you be so brave in the most terrible situation I ever, I ever, I ever . . .

TRUDY. Norval, relax . . . don't start again . . . and be careful what you say—I'll play something to soothe you.

She takes a record at random, puts it on the turntable. It turns out to be "I Don't Want to Walk Without You."

TRUDY (*returning to Norval*). You better buy some needles.

NORVAL. S-s-sure. (*He reaches into his pocket.*) I didn't sleep all last night and I don't think I'm ever gonna sleep again until I know you're fixed up.

TRUDY. You can take my word for it, Norval.

NORVAL. I mean you've given me something to live for, Trudy. Don't be downhearted, don't be blue . . . don't give up the ship . . . we'll see it through . . . it used to be that all I could think of was to get into uniform but now all I can think of is to get you out of trouble. I can't think of anything else . . .

TRUDY. I don't know how to thank you, Norval.

NORVAL. That's all right. I'll tell you what I figured: We'll take an ad in every camp paper in the country—they make a club rate—and we'll say . . .

TRUDY. But that'll cost you a fortune, Norval.

NORVAL. What does that matter? I've got nine hundred dollars saved up, and to spend it on you would be my dearest wish, Trudy. We'll say: "Party wishing to locate missing Ratzkiwatzki. Will pay liberal reward for information leading to his return" . . . something like that.

TRUDY. You don't suppose they'll think it is a dog, do you?

We then see NORVAL and TRUDY in the local NEWSPAPER OFFICE: Norval is going through a handful of mail. The envelopes are stamped with dog food ads, bargains in orange groves, electric vitality belts, a million ways to make a million dollars, the personality that punches, etc. We hear the SOUND of the PRESSES.

NORVAL (*disgustedly*). We will give you back your vitality with dividends. . . Do you want a body like a Greek god? . . . Flat-o for flat feet. . . . Do you want to retire in thirty-eight years? . . . The Naughty Novelty Company. . . . A million ways to make a million dollars. . . . (*He tosses the envelope on the counter.*) But no Ratzkiwatzki.

TRUDY. Maybe he doesn't read the papers!

NORVAL. Maybe he doesn't read at all.

TRUDY. You mustn't speak that way about the Armed Forces, Norval.

NORVAL. Well, what good is he to you? All *he's* doing is stopping people who want to do you some good from doing it . . . the rat.

TRUDY (*reprovingly*). Norval!

NORVAL. I'm sorry, but any husband you have to advertise for, I don't think is worth the paper you print him on.

TRUDY. Talking against him isn't going to help anything.

THE EDITOR (*coming in brightly*). Say, Norval, did you ever find that . . . whatever it was you lost?

NORVAL. No. (*He turns away.*)

THE EDITOR. By the way, what *is* a ... Ratzkiwatzki?

NORVAL. You can search me.

Leaving the editor somewhat surprised, Trudy and Norval exit and the scene cuts to a view of TRUDY and NORVAL coming out of the newspaper office and starting to move on.

NORVAL. You don't remember anything about him except that he had curly hair? (*As Trudy merely shrugs*) Did he wear glasses?

TRUDY. Where?

NORVAL. Well, where do you usually wear glasses? Not on your ...

TRUDY. I don't know.

NORVAL. Was he tall?

TRUDY. Probably ... I don't know. ... All I know is that I was dancing with a tall dark boy with curly hair ... at least you imagine he must have been tall and dark.

NORVAL (*slightly indignant*). Oh, you do? You think a medium-sized man with red hair or even a little short guy as bald as an eagle ...

TRUDY. Don't be vulgar, Norval.

NORVAL. I'm not vulgar. Why do you just naturally conclude that anybody you dance with would have to be ... (*holding his hand eight feet in the air*) ... this high with black oily hair?

TRUDY. You're just jealous.

NORVAL (*subsiding*). I guess I am ...

TRUDY. Do you think maybe I could divorce him?

NORVAL. Not unless you could prove you were married to him first. ... That's the foundation of divorce ... unless there's such a thing as a John Doe divorce ... like they have those John Doe indictments. ... If you can indict a John Doe ... you might be able to divorce him.

TRUDY. His name wasn't John Doe; it was Ratzki ...]

This dissolves to a STREET, on which Trudy and Norval are walking.

NORVAL. Maybe you oughta just marry me and forget the whole thing.

TRUDY (*as they stop*). I couldn't do that to you, Norval. I couldn't let you take the risk of going to jail for twenty years for bigamy.

NORVAL (*as they resume walking*). Well, you were going to on the front porch, and you didn't mention anything about the twenty years w-w-when I started to pr-pr-propose to you.

TRUDY (*as they stop again*). I wasn't in love with you then, Norval.

NORVAL. Do you really mean that, Trudy?

TRUDY. I feel very much ashamed of myself for what I almost did to you, Norval.

NORVAL (*as they resume walking*). What are you talking about? All you did was give me the chance I've always wanted—that I've been waiting for—to show you how much I love you, and the kind of love I have for you. You've got to marry me, Trudy.

TRUDY (*stopping again*). I can't do it to you, Norval. But I want you to know how much I appreciate your offer, and how much I wish I'd known how sweet you are a little sooner. I want you to know that, and to remember it always. It will be my dying wish. (*She starts running ahead.*) And when they fish me out, I want you to know that my last thought was of you.

NORVAL (*rushing forward and stopping her*). F-f-f-f-fish you out? You mean of t-the c-c-c-creek?

TRUDY. It may be the only way.

NORVAL. What are you talking about, Trudy! That's the last way, when everything else has failed. Before I tried that, I'd try b-b-bigamy, f-f-forgery, b-b-b-burglary—anything.

TRUDY. The only awful part about it is that Papa'd be sure to shoot you then.

NORVAL (*as they walk on*). Well— Oh! Of course, without you, it wouldn't matter, anyway.

TRUDY (*stopping*). Thank you, dear. Maybe we could jump in together.

NORVAL. There's not much water this time of year, Trudy.

TRUDY. Well, isn't there a swimming hole about ten miles away?

NORVAL. You're not supposed to use your tires for anything like that, Trudy. (*They are crossing the street now.*) Besides, I'm a very good swimmer, and being a very good swimmer, they say that whenever they get in a situation like that, they —they just naturally sw-sw-swim right out.

TRUDY. I'm a very good swimmer, too—I hadn't thought of that.

NORVAL. Well, then let's forget the creek.

TRUDY. Maybe we could tie rocks around our necks.

NORVAL. Never!

TRUDY (*stopping at the Kockenlocker gate*). What's the matter with gas?

NORVAL. What's the matter with bigamy?

KOCKENLOCKER'S VOICE (*heard calling*). Hey!

At the KOCKENLOCKER PORCH, Kockenlocker is seen holding a revolver. He beckons with it.

KOCKENLOCKER. Come here.

Trudy and Norval, at the gate, react apprehensively. She opens the gate and takes his hand. Then they go on and go up the steps to the porch.

KOCKENLOCKER. I wanta have a little talk with you.

TRUDY (*nervously*). With me, Papa?

KOCKENLOCKER. No, with your gentleman friend there. You go in the house.

TRUDY. Yes, sir.

KOCKENLOCKER. Go on! (*To Norval, barking*) Sit down!

Trudy goes in, and Norval goes to a stool, sits down but jumps up and removes an oil can from under him. Kockenlocker sits down, too.

KOCKENLOCKER. What are you so nervous about?

NORVAL. Who's n-nervous?

Norval pulls a brush out from beneath him. Then there is a close view of Norval and Kockenlocker. Kockenlocker grabs the brush, and puts it on the table.

KOCKENLOCKER. There's getting to be quite a little talk in the town.

NORVAL. Oh.

KOCKENLOCKER. Where I came from we don't skulk around in the bushes, you get me?

NORVAL (*inaudibly*). Yes, sir.

KOCKENLOCKER. When we gotta cross the street, we don't crawl through the sewer to get there.

NORVAL. Y-y-y-yes, sir.

KOCKENLOCKER (*shouting*). When we've got something to say, we say it!

NORVAL. Yes, *sir*.

KOCKENLOCKER. When is the happy event?

NORVAL (*slipping off the edge of the chair*). I didn't hear e-e-exactly what you said.

KOCKENLOCKER. When are you and Trudy getting hitched?

NORVAL. Oh! (*He laughs idiotically*.)

KOCKENLOCKER. What are you laughing about?

NORVAL. Who—me? I'm not laughing. (*He laughs*.) Just something I heard at the bank today. (*He laughs again*.)

KOCKENLOCKER. You haven't answered my question.

Kockenlocker picks up a larger gun, and a closeup shows NORVAL looking up at the gun nervously.

NORVAL. Oh. (*He laughs nervously*.)

KOCKENLOCKER (*seen close with Norval*). There isn't any idiocy in your family, is there?

NORVAL. She won't have me.

KOCKENLOCKER. Oh, she won't?

NORVAL. I already asked her.

KOCKENLOCKER. You didn't ask her right. You gotta be more forceful in these matters. Dames like to be bossed. Now, you take me—

NORVAL. I did my best.

KOCKENLOCKER. You can do better. You better do better!

NORVAL. Well, all you can do is ask.

KOCKENLOCKER. We accept! You're in!

Kockenlocker shakes hands with Norval.

NORVAL. N-n-now, w-w-wait a minute. T-there might be a couple of reasons—a couple of d-d-details—

KOCKENLOCKER. You can settle the details up between youse. All I'm interested in is results. I'm a man who looks at things broadly, see? I'm a man who—

NORVAL. Now, wait—

Kockenlocker fires the gun accidentally. The scene thereupon cuts to the KITCHEN, and we see Trudy reacting to the shot nervously.

On THE PORCH, the intimidated Norval rises, goes to the door, and fumbles with the knob.

NORVAL. I—I—I'll go!

KOCKENLOCKER. I almost forgot. Congratulations! (*Kockenlocker shakes hands with him*.)

NORVAL. Th-th-thank you.

Norval turns, steps right through the screen door, and goes inside. Kockenlocker jumps up, looks after him, reacting to the tearing of the screen.

Next Norval appears staggering up the HALL—Kockenlocker standing in the doorway, looking after him. Norval stops and leans on a newel post weakly. Then he comes forward and stops in the kitchen doorway. His mouth moves, but no words come out.

In the KOCKENLOCKER KITCHEN, Trudy is standing by the sink nervously. Noticing Norval leaning weakly against the door jamb, she goes to him.

TRUDY. What was that shooting?!

NORVAL. (*"rubber-legged"*). Oh, n-nothing. He was just p-p-p-prac-prac-practicing.

TRUDY. Oh, it frightened me! (*She assists him across the room to the sink.*)

NORVAL. Oh, there's nothing to be f-f-f-f-frightened about—only he wants us to get married r-r-r-right away, Trudy, and he was very f-f-f-f-firm about it.

TRUDY (*indignantly*). Why? Oh, you mean because you brought me home the other morning.

NORVAL. Oh, you mustn't start arguing, Trudy. The whole town's t-t-talking. You're in a t-t-terrible spot, Trudy. You've either got to marry me r-r-right away or—or—or tell him the whole t-t-truth, which would be t-t-terrible.

TRUDY. I can't do it to you, Norval.

NORVAL. What are you talking about, Trudy? It's just a lucky break for me. I tried to tell you that. You're just giving me an opportunity.

TRUDY. But that's bigamy! I'm already married to Ratzkiwatzki. I can't keep on marrying people, no matter how sweet they are.

NORVAL. I've got it! (*He snaps his fingers.*)

Trudy clasps her hand over his mouth, and leads him to the door. They go out and down the steps into the back yard.

TRUDY. Ssssh!

NORVAL. (*All we hear is his muffled talking.*)

TRUDY. Norval! Don't get so excited! Sssh!

THE BACK YARD:

NORVAL (*dynamically*). Wait a minute, Trudy, wait a minute. I've got it!

TRUDY. Don't get so excited, Norval.

NORVAL. Who's excited? This is air-tight and water-tight. It's fool-proof and almost legal, Trudy. And when we get through, you can divorce that g-g-gink and m-marry me.

TRUDY. Norval, take it easy.

NORVAL. It's a cinch! It's almost an insp-insp-inspiration! Now, will you go to the movies with me tomorrow night—the early show?

TRUDY. Of course. I'll be glad to, dear.

NORVAL. All right; that's all there is to it. Now, look, I'll get everything ready and I'll go this way. I don't—I don't want to meet your father just yet.

TRUDY. Well, Norval, wait a minute.

NORVAL. Now, don't worry about a thing. It's—it's just as easy as falling off a log.

TRUDY. But, Norval—!

He turns, walks away, runs into a tree limb, and falls to the ground on his back. Trudy runs, kneels by him and raises his head.

TRUDY. Oh! Oh, darling! Did you break anything, dear?

NORVAL. Nothing but my b-b-back.

The scene dissolves to a STORE. There are gardenia corsages in the glass case—and Norval's hand is pointing to one. The clerk's hand takes it from the case. This then dissolves to a JEWELRY STORE, with Norval standing in front of a counter examining a wedding ring; the jeweler has his back turned in the foreground.

NORVAL. Who, me? Oh, no, no, no. It's—uh—it's—it's for my—my aunt in the East. She dropped hers down a r-r-rat hole—a c-c-c-crack in the floor, so I'm getting this as a s-surprise for her. Her fin-finger—finger felt kinda n-n-naked.

This dissolves to a CLOTHING STORE, where Norval and Swartz come forward.

SWARTZ. I can't do it, Norval!

NORVAL. But, Mr. Swartz—

SWARTZ. They wrote me a letter.

Swartz opens the cash register, and takes out a letter.

NORVAL. But it's j-just to wear around—

SWARTZ. Wool is very scarce. We've got to save it for the soldiers.

NORVAL. Well, how about c-c-cotton?

SWARTZ. Cotton is very scarce. It says so in the next paragraph somewhere. What for do you want a uniform for, anyhow?

NORVAL. I—I wouldn't want—I wouldn't want you to tell anybody.

SWARTZ (*hurt*). Norval!

NORVAL. Well, i-i-it's just to put—uh—uh—I mean to wear—to wear around the house, you know, when you've always wanted—

Swartz pushes him over to an Indian figure.

SWARTZ (*pointing to it*). How about an Indian suit with feathers?

NORVAL. Oh, that? Oh, no, no, no, thank you.

SWARTZ (*electrified, grabbing Norval*). Vait! Just to vear around the house?

NORVAL. Well, in—in the yard, maybe.

SWARTZ. I got it!

NORVAL. Y-you have?

There is a close view of a CUPBOARD.

NORVAL'S VOICE. You got it?

SWARTZ'S VOICE. It ain't the latest.

NORVAL'S VOICE. Well, w-what does that matter? You got the shoes, too?

Swartz leans into the scene, opens the door, and gets out a dusty package and an old 1918 campaign hat. The view moves up with Swartz' hands as they place the package and hat on the table.

SWARTZ. I'll even t'row in the gun. For five dollars you got the whole voiks, and you can play soldier till your feet wear out.

NORVAL'S VOICE. Oh, that's very kind of you, Mr. Swartz.

SWARTZ'S VOICE. Very kind of you, Norval. You can have the steel helmet, too.

The scene dissolves to KOCKENLOCKER's KITCHEN. Trudy and Emmy are at the sink, Emmy scraping dishes, and Trudy washing them.

TRUDY. And then we get married. ... And then I get the certificate. ... And then everything is legal. ... It just makes the first time *more* legal.

EMMY. But that's bigamy—just as much as if you married him as Norval Jones.

TRUDY. No, it isn't. They do it all the time. Like when a king wants to get married, only he's too busy in his own kingdom, and he can't get over to the other kingdom, and the other king won't send the princess over C.O.D. because he doesn't trust the first king. So they send a kind of a phony bridegroom over and he marries the princess—except he doesn't really marry her. It's what they call marriage by prexy.

EMMY. I didn't know prexies could perform marriages.

TRUDY. I didn't either.

EMMY. Well, it's bigamy.

TRUDY. It is not! Because I'm not marrying two different people, don't you see? I'm just marrying Ratzkiwatzki again ... it's like you send a check to somebody and it gets lost so you write out another one. That's all we're doing ... it's still the same check to the same person, see ... for the same amount. It isn't like you wrote *two* checks to *two* different people, see? That would be bigamy.

EMMY. What happens if the first check shows up?

TRUDY. Why do you have to go and think up things like that? ... He's fixed everything up very cleverly! Like how he got the ring and uniform without anybody suspecting anything.

EMMY. How can a dope do anything clever?

TRUDY. You mustn't talk about him that way, Emmy. He's one of the most noblest men who ever drew the breath of life.

EMMY. They're always noble.

TRUDY. Well, he *isn't* a dope, and even if he was, it wouldn't be his fault, would it?

EMMY. I didn't say it was his fault. I just said he was a dope.

TRUDY (*on the verge of tears*). But he's got everything figured out! ... He says it's going to be like falling off a log.

EMMY. You know how high you can fall off a log?

TRUDY. Oh.

She relaxes disgustedly and lets the dish she is wiping fall on the floor.

[TRUDY and EMMY in the KITCHEN:

EMMY (*picking up the broken dish*). Is he coming here in the uniform?

TRUDY. Of course not, stoopid. He only puts that on when we get way out in the country ... in a field or something.

EMMY. He'll probably get chased by a bull.

TRUDY (*dissolving in tears*). Don't be so mean and sour about everything, Emmy. ... Here it was almost like going on a picnic and now ...

EMMY (*putting her arms around her sister*). It's only because I'm worried about you, honey ... if only I could go along and keep you out of trouble.

TRUDY (*desperately*). But, he's got everything figured out.

EMMY. How can a *schnook* figure anything out?

TRUDY. Oh, Emmy. (*And she starts to cry.*)

EMMY (*taking her in her arms*). I'm sorry.

A platter crashes to the floor between them.]

As the plate smashes, the scene cuts to the PORCH, where Kockenlocker is reading a newspaper. He jumps, and looks around, reacting to the crash of the dish. Then Kockenlocker looks off and sees Norval opening the gate in the YARD. The scene then cuts back to the PORCH as Norval enters and goes up to the porch.

NORVAL. Good evening. (*Laughing*) I've come to take Trudy to the m-m-movies. (*He laughs again.*)

KOCKENLOCKER (*rising*). What's so funny about that?

NORVAL. Oh, n-n-nothing. Shall I tell her I'm—I'm here or—(*laughing*)—or will you?

KOCKENLOCKER. What do you want me to do—fire a salute?

NORVAL (*laughing*). Very f-f-funny.

KOCKENLOCKER. You remember what I told you last night?

NORVAL. Yes, sir.

KOCKENLOCKER. Keep thinking about it.

NORVAL. Yes, sir.

KOCKENLOCKER. Movies is a very good place.

NORVAL. Yes, sir.

KOCKENLOCKER. You can hold hands.

NORVAL. S-s-sure.

KOCKENLOCKER. Snuggle up.

NORVAL. Fine.

KOCKENLOCKER. You get the idea?

NORVAL. Oh, p-p-per-per-per-fectly.

KOCKENLOCKER. Do you want me to come and sit behind you?

NORVAL. Oh, n-n-n-n-n—

KOCKENLOCKER. Okay. Then I guess that's about all. (*He calls out loudly.*) Trudy!

There is a crash of dishes, and Norval jumps, and almost collapses.

KOCKENLOCKER. They ain't giving away a set of dishes tonight, are they?!

In the KOCKENLOCKER KITCHEN Trudy grabs up her purse and Emmy gets her coat.

TRUDY. That must be him! Emmy, get my coat!

EMMY. Keep cool, Trudy—keep cool.

TRUDY. I'm cool! I'm not excited!

They run out, and the scene cuts to the PORCH, with Norval and Kockenlocker standing in the foreground as Trudy and Emmy come down the hall from the background.

TRUDY. Hello, Norval.

Norval opens the screen door. Trudy and Emmy come out onto the porch.

NORVAL. Hello, Trudy. We're going to see some pretty good m-m-m-movies tonight.

TRUDY. You s-s-s-said it, Norval.

KOCKENLOCKER (*sourly, as the door bangs*). Are you gonna start that stuff now?

Trudy hugs and kisses Kockenlocker.

TRUDY. Well, goodbye, Papa!

NORVAL. Goodbye, Mr. Kockenlocker.

TRUDY (*sobbing*). Goodbye, Emmy.

Trudy and Emmy embrace and kiss.

NORVAL. Goodbye, Emmy.

EMMY. Goodbye, honey.

KOCKENLOCKER. What's all the goodbyeing for to see a couple of bum features?

NORVAL. Oh, th-th-three features.

TRUDY. "The Bride Wore Purple," "The Road to Reno"—(*sniffling*) and "Are Husbands Necessary?"

KOCKENLOCKER (*as they depart*). And then home! No boogie-woogie!

EMMY. Papa, can't you be more refined? (*Calling after them*) Goodbye—and watch your step!

Emmy, bursting into tears, throws her arms around Kockenlocker's neck.

EMMY. Oh, Papa!

KOCKENLOCKER (*stupefied*). What's going on around here, anyway?! (*He sits heavily in his chair, and takes Emmy in his lap. The chair collapses into kindling wood.*)

The scene dissolves to a ROAD, on which Norval is driving his car, Trudy seated beside him.

NORVAL. It's a-about t-t-twenty-five miles.

TRUDY. I'm going to die before we get there.

NORVAL. T-t-there's nothing to be nervous about. T-there's a Justice of the P-Peace.

TRUDY. You got the uniform?

NORVAL. It's—it's in the back.

TRUDY. And the ring?

NORVAL. It's—it's—it's in the uniform.

TRUDY. How do you look in it?

NORVAL. I—I don't know. I—I haven't tried it on yet. Now—n-now, look. T-there's one thing we—we've got to settle on. W-what was his first name?

TRUDY. Oh, you mean R-Ratzkiwatzki?

NORVAL. N-n-naturally.

TRUDY. Does he have to have a f-f-first name?

NORVAL. Of course he has to have a f-first name. Everybody has a first name. Ev-even dogs have first names, even if he hasn't got any last name.

TRUDY. Well, I don't know. I had an uncle named R-Roscoe.

NORVAL (*not liking it from the start*). Ros-Roscoe! "He eats 'em alive!"

TRUDY. What?

NORVAL. T-t-that's a snake eater's name!

TRUDY (*resentfully*). Well, it was my uncle's name.

NORVAL. Well, h-how about Hugo?

TRUDY. Oh, phooey.

NORVAL. Well, how about—uh—Otis? That was—

TRUDY. Oh, phooey!

NORVAL. That was my father's name!

TRUDY. Oh, I'm sorry.

NORVAL. Well, it doesn't matter. You can call him Montmorency for all I care.

TRUDY. Oh, phooey.

NORVAL. Well, what goes good with Ratzkiwatzki?

TRUDY. Nothing!

NORVAL (*after a pause*). How about—uh—Ignatz?

TRUDY (*as they both laugh*). Ignatz! You'd have to take b-b-bicarbonate with that one.

NORVAL. Ignatz R-R-Ratzkiwatzki. Yeah, that—that fits all right.

TRUDY. Oh, p-p-phooey.

NORVAL. Oh, it's all very well to sit there and say, "Oh, phooey!" But I've got to f-find a f-first name before we g-get there.

TRUDY (*laughing*). All right—I—Ignatz.

NORVAL (*also laughing*). It's funny having almost our first fight on the way to the altar.

TRUDY. Well, it isn't like having a bad fight. It's more like p-people have when they're picking out a name for their— (*Suddenly she breaks off in embarrassment.*)

NORVAL. You mustn't think about that, Trudy. Remember what it says in the Bible: "Sufficient unto the day is the evil thereof"—and there isn't going to be any evil, Trudy—never for you.

TRUDY (*blinking her eyes*). Thank you, Norval.

NORVAL (*handing her the corsage*). I—I bought you something.

TRUDY. Oh, thank you, Norval! (*And she starts to snuffle.*)

NORVAL. Oh, please don't do that. It's just that I feel almost as if it was me marrying you.

TRUDY. I wish it were, Norval—so much.

NORVAL (*exultantly*). You really mean that, Trudy?

TRUDY. Of course I do.

NORVAL. Oh, Trudy!

He lets go of the wheel, starts to put his arms around her. A horn sounds a warning, and he grabs the wheel, Trudy calling out, "Look out!" Norval regains control of the car and looks ahead happily with a big lip-print across his mouth.

[We see NORVAL and TRUDY in a slowly moving car.

NORVAL. There it is.

TRUDY (*clutching her heart*). Gee whiz.

NORVAL. Now, just keep cool; there's nothing to . . . (*clearing his throat*) worry about . . . we'll just go some place and I'll . . . (*clearing his throat again*) put on the uniform.

TRUDY. Where're you going to go?

NORVAL. Well, I figured some b-b-b-bushes somewhere . . . so nobody will see me come out. I mean, instead of a m-m-m-motel or anything.

TRUDY. I think the b-b-b-bushes are b-b-better.

NORVAL. Don't get exc-exc-cited.

TRUDY. I w-w-won't.

This dissolves to SOME BUSHES, and the car pulls into view and Norval gets out.

NORVAL (*getting the uniform out of the back*). Just k-k-keep c-c-cool. Don't be n-n-nervous about anything . . . thing.

TRUDY. I'll keep a lookout.

NORVAL. F-f-fine. If you hear anybody c-c-coming just wh-wh-whistle like a wh-whi-whippoorwill.

TRUDY. H-h-how does it go?

Norval tries to whistle like a whippoorwill but his nervousness makes it come out like the laugh of a hyena.

TRUDY (*after a couple of his efforts*). Doesn't that sound more like a hyena?

NORVAL. No, a hyena goes more like this. (*He continues to make the same sound.*)

TRUDY. I can make a noise like a dog: ooup, owoop . . .

NORVAL. All right, anything will do.

He goes behind the bushes. Trudy pins the flowers on herself and starts to repair her make-up. Unable to see very well, she gets out of the car and stands in front of the headlights.

This cuts to a MIDDLE-AGED MAN approaching and looking at Trudy in surprise; then to TRUDY as she hears the man's footsteps, and then looks at him as he comes into view. At this, she barks like a dog, and the man stops in his tracks and looks back at her.

THE MAN. Did you say something?

TRUDY. Who? Me? . . . Oh, no.

THE MAN. I'm sorry, I thought you said something.

He turns to go, and looks toward the bush which conceals Norval.

TRUDY. Owoop.

THE MAN (*turning*). Must be a dog around here.

TRUDY (*nervously*). I didn't see any.

THE MAN. I said there must be a dog around here. I love dogs.

He whistles for a dog, whereupon Norval answers with his imitation of a whippoorwill from behind the bushes.

THE MAN. It's a jackal!

TRUDY. N-n-no, it isn't.

THE MAN. I said, it's a jackal. (*And he starts cautiously for the bushes.*)

TRUDY (*desperately*). Owoop . . . owoop . . .

THE MAN (*turning to Trudy*). There's two dogs.

He whistles for it and Norval answers with his imitation.

THE MAN (*turning*). He's coming closer.

At this TRUDY barks desperately.

THE MAN. I love any kind of a dog: big dogs, little dogs, long dogs, short dogs.

TRUDY. Is that so?

THE MAN. I even like those little naked ones with the poppy eyes.

TRUDY. That's very interesting.

THE MAN. If there were more dogs in the world and less people it would be a better world—much better.

TRUDY (*desperately*). That's very interesting.

THE MAN. Did you know there's no insanity amongst dogs?

TRUDY. Is that a fact?

THE MAN. Well, bow-wow. (*And he leaves.*)

TRUDY (*to the bushes*). He's gone.

NORVAL'S VOICE. All right.

TRUDY. Are you dressed?

NORVAL'S VOICE. Almost. (*Then appearing*) Maybe you can help me a little.

He appears in the lights of the car and now we see for the first time his uniform in its full glory. The campaign hat is a size too big and the chin strap gets in his mouth. The tunic is a little too small and ducks up behind. The breeches are too big and droop terribly in the seat. The shoes are enormous and studded with hobnails. One spiral puttee hangs around his knee like a concertina and the other one is dragging behind him. He carries his street clothes over his arm.]

This dissolves to a HIGHWAY IN THE COUNTRY, beginning with a closeup of Norval's and Trudy's feet and legs.

NORVAL'S VOICE. It doesn't seem to be such a very good fit.

TRUDY'S VOICE. There s-s-seems to be something wrong with it, Norval.

The view moves up and draws back, revealing Norval and Trudy standing by the car—Norval clad in a badly fitting First World War uniform.

NORVAL'S VOICE. Well, this must be the Cavalry—(*now visible*)—or something. I haven't seen anything like this around here.

TRUDY (*indicating the leggings*). Well, what are those things?

NORVAL. Well, I guess they go around your legs or something—I don't know.

TRUDY. Maybe it's a tropical uniform, like General MacArthur wears.

NORVAL. Well, I never saw any pictures of General MacArthur looking like this.

He pulls at the seat of his trousers, and the result is a ripping sound.

TRUDY. What happened?!

NORVAL. I'm afraid to find out.

He pulls a patch off the trousers.

TRUDY. Norval!

NORVAL (*feeling*). Well, there seems to be another seat left, anyway.

TRUDY. Couldn't you hoist them up a little?

She pulls him up by the seat of the trousers, and there is another ripping sound.

NORVAL (*desperately*). B-b-be careful! How many seats do you think these pants have, anyway?!

TRUDY. I'm sorry.

NORVAL (*turning around*). Well, how do I look?

TRUDY. Well, you don't look like General MacArthur.

After giving her a queer look, Norval puts one foot on the bumper and starts to work on the spiral puttee. As he works with it, not rolled up but at its full length, this is a very difficult job. There are yards and yards of it.

TRUDY. Let me help you.

NORVAL (*pettishly*). Not around both legs.... Look out what you're doing.

Trudy squats down and passes the puttee back and forth to him.

TRUDY (*after a while*). Now put the other foot up.

NORVAL (*beginning to lose his balance*). Hey! You wrapped me to the bumper.

TRUDY. Look out! (*And as she tries to save him they both fall in a heap.*)

The scene dissolves to a MOTEL, the entrance bearing a sign:

    HONEYMOON MOTEL
    JACOB WOODSON
    PROPRIETOR
    JUSTICE OF THE PEACE
    HOT AND COLD WATER
    MARRIAGES PERFORMED

The exterior of the "Motel" dissolves to the INTERIOR OF THE JUSTICE'S SITTING ROOM, the Justice seated at a desk, and looking at stereoscopic slides. The lower part of his wife's body is seen in the background as she opens the door.

TRUDY'S VOICE. Good evening.

NORVAL'S VOICE. We'd like to be m-m-m-married.

WIFE'S VOICE. Straight ahead, please.

Trudy's and Norval's feet and legs enter through the door. The wife closes the door, then her lower body comes forward.

WIFE'S VOICE. Another army couple, Jake.

The OFFICE, with Norval and Trudy standing nervously in front of the counter:

NORVAL. J-j-j-just t-t-t-take it easy. It'll —it'll all be over in a m-m-m-minute.

TRUDY. I wish it were all o-o-over now.

NORVAL. Well, there's nothing to be n-n-n-nervous about.

JUSTICE'S VOICE (*suddenly heard*). Good evening.

Startled, they leap forward to the counter as the Justice comes forward.

JUSTICE. Thinking of getting married? Good idea. The names, please.

TRUDY (*with an effort*). G-G-Gertrude K-K-K-K-Kockenlo—

JUSTICE. How was that again?

TRUDY. G-G-Gertrude K-K-K-K-K—

JUSTICE. Now, take it easy. There's nothing to be scared of. People do it every day. The bad part comes later.

TRUDY. G-G-Gertrude K-K-K-K-Kockenlocker. K-o-c-k-e-n-l-o-c-k-e-r.

JUSTICE. —l-o-c-k-e-r?

TRUDY. Y-yes . . . sir.

In the group, we see Norval's legs sagging under him and letting him down to the floor. Trudy grabs him, and starts to pull him up.

JUSTICE. That's better. And yours, young man?

TRUDY. Ignatz!

NORVAL. Igna-Igna-Igna-Ignatz Ra-Ra-Ra-Ratzki-watz-watz-watz—

JUSTICE. How was that again?

NORVAL. Ignatz Ra-Ra-Ra-Ra—

JUSTICE. Now, take it easy, will you?

TRUDY (*simultaneously with Norval*). N-N-N-Norval—Ignatz!

NORVAL. `Ignatz. I-g-n-a-n-a-t-t-z.

TRUDY. R-a-t-z-w-i-z-k-i-w-z.

JUSTICE. K-z what?

TRUDY AND NORVAL. Ra-Ra-Ratzkiwatzki.

JUSTICE. Well, that's close enough. Bride's residence?

TRUDY. Seventeen Genessee Street, M-Morgan's Creek.

JUSTICE (*writing*). Morgan's Creek. Ever been married before?

Trudy and Norval exchange frightened looks.

JUSTICE (*looking up*). I said, you ever been married before? That's a simple question.

TRUDY. No, sir.

JUSTICE. Groom's residence.

At this, Norval's shaking legs sag beneath him, and he sinks toward the floor.

JUSTICE. What are you doing down there?

TRUDY (*pulling him up*). Oh!

JUSTICE. What is the groom's residence? Where do you live—in a tree?!

TRUDY. Your camp—camp.

NORVAL (*slurring the name of the camp totally*). Oh. C-c-c-camp—uh—Camp Sm-Smum.

JUSTICE. Camp what?

NORVAL. S-S-S-Smum.

JUSTICE. Where is it located?

NORVAL. It's located in—in—S-S-Smum—Smum County.

JUSTICE. Suppose I just put U.S. Army?

NORVAL. Oh, f-f-f-fine.

JUSTICE. Fine.

TRUDY. F-fine.

THE ENTRANCE HALL OF THE MOTEL. We see a woman who is to act as witness, Sally Blair, outside the front door. The Justice's wife opens the door and Sally comes in.

SALLY. Is there still time?

WIFE. Plenty.

In the JUSTICE'S OFFICE:

JUSTICE. Now, if the witnesses will ever get here— (*Sally's giggles are heard.*) Oh, Miss Sally Blair and my wife who'll act as witnesses for you.

SALLY (*entering, followed by the Justice's wife.*) How do you do? How do you do? (*She giggles.*)

JUSTICE. Miss Gertrude Kockenlocker and Mr. Ignatz Ratastki Watastki.

NORVAL. Ratzkiwatzki.

SALLY (*impulsively*). Oh, I do hope you'll be happy. So many of these marriages go on the rocks.

JUSTICE. Something like that. Or should that be Private Ignatz and the rest of it?

NORVAL. Mister will be all right.

SALLY. Are you certain sure that you love each other?

JUSTICE. What do you think they came here for?

SALLY. Oh, I know—but are they sure?

NORVAL. S-s-sure.

JUSTICE (*to Sally*). What more do you want?

SALLY (*to the couple*). And do you want lots and lots of little babies? Do you long for the patter of little footsie-wootsies?

WIFE. Of course they do, Sally.

JUSTICE. You better lay off or I won't let you be witness any more.

SALLY. I always say a childless home is like a tomb.

JUSTICE (*striking the counter*). Now, let's get down to business!

SALLY. Oh, let's!

JUSTICE. Take off your hat. (*Norval removes his hat.*) Ignatz Razly-Wazly, do you take this woman, Gertrude Sockenbocker, for your lawful wedded wife, to have and to hold, to cherish and to keep forever till death do you part?

NORVAL. I do.

JUSTICE. Gertrude Krockendocker, do you take Ignatz Razzby-Wadsby for your lawful wedded husband, to have and to hold, in sickness or in health, to love, cherish and keep forever till death do you part?

TRUDY. I do.

JUSTICE. Then give me the ring.

Norval takes out the ring box, hands it to the Justice who removes the ring and gives it to Norval.

JUSTICE. Place it on her third finger and repeat after me: With this ring I thee wed.

NORVAL (*placing the ring on Trudy's finger*). With this ring I thee wed.

JUSTICE. Then with the authority vested in me by our sovereign state, I now pronounce you man and wife.

Trudy and Norval kiss. Then the Justice turns the register around.

JUSTICE. That'll be two dollars, please, and that's all there is to it. Sign here.

NORVAL. Oh, that certainly made me n-n-nervous. (*Norval feels in his pockets for money.*)

JUSTICE. If you knew what it was like, it would make you still nervouser.

WIFE. Jake!

TRUDY. I've got it, dear. (*Trudy gets money out of her purse and hands it to the Justice.*)

SALLY (*to the Justice's wife*). She shouldn't start paying her way so soon!

JUSTICE. Oh. Fine. Now, sign there.

NORVAL (*signing the register*). It certainly makes me feel much b-b-better.

JUSTICE (*placing the certificate in an envelope*). There you are. And a little cookbook goes with it, with best wishes from those who may have to eat the cooking. (*Trudy laughs, and the Justice hands the envelope to her.*)

SALLY. And don't forget the pitty-patter.

JUSTICE (*jokingly*). Call again.

SALLY. As I always say, a childless home is like a homeless child.

Norval, Trudy, Sally and the Justice's wife turn to go. The Justice looks at the register.

JUSTICE. Just a minute! (*They stop.*) Who's Norval Jones?

TRUDY. Norval!

The Justice gets his gun from under the counter, and points it at Norval. Norval sinks down helplessly as the Justice picks up the phone.

JUSTICE. Lock the door, Maria! This man is an abductor!

[Sally starts to attack Norval. She grabs a double fistful of his tunic (which doesn't do it any good) and shakes him.

SALLY (*hysterically*). You double-dyed deceiver. You wolf in cheap clothing . . . leading this poor lamb astray for your own vile ends . . . and a fate worse than death.

She starts to slap him with one hand after the other. While Norval is defending himself as best he can, Trudy, runs forward to protect Norval.

TRUDY. You leave him alone. . . . He didn't mean me any harm.

SALLY. I can read his intentions like a book, and each one is viler than the other. . . . You leper. (*And she attacks Norval again.*)

TRUDY (*defending him*). You leave him alone.

JUSTICE'S WIFE (*pulling on Sally*). Stop it, Sally. It isn't any of your business.

SALLY (*turning on her*). Well, I just guess it is. I guess I know my bounden duty when I see it! I just guess . . .

JUSTICE (*with one hand over the phone*). Shut up! (*Then into the phone*) Get me the military police. (*Then to the others in the room*) Now shut up. . . . That goes for you too, Sally. Don't let them talk to each other, Maria. (*Then into the telephone*) I said: Get me the military police . . . the M.P.'s.

TRUDY (*desperately*). But he isn't a soldier.

NORVAL (*aghast*). T-T-Trudy.

JUSTICE. Oh, he isn't, hunh? (*Then into the phone*) Get the Sheriff over here. (*Then to Norval*) Then what are you doing in that uniform . . . Wait a minute . . . (*Then into the phone*) Get me the Secret Service . . . in the U.S. Marshal's office . . . and the Marshal too, while you're at it . . . and the State Police. (*Then to Norval*) Trying to pull a fast one, hunh . . . on a poor old country hick?

This dissolves to the COUNTY SHERIFF'S OFFICE, plainly and appropriately marked on the window. The Sheriff and his deputy come out and hop into a car, and it zooms away. And this dissolves to the U.S. MARSHAL'S OFFICE, the window mentioning something about this being the local branch of the Secret Service. Two young men hurry out and hop into a car.

Then we are back in the JUSTICE OF THE PEACE'S OFFICE. Trudy and Norval sit miserably in the corner. The Justice's wife and Sally wait meanly.

TRUDY (*in tears*). He didn't want to do me any harm. . . . He wanted to do me some good.

SALLY. The law has another name for it.

JUSTICE. With different degrees . . . first degree, second degree, third degree . . . like that.

TRUDY. Well . . . if we did anything wrong, I did half of it. (*Norval gestures no, no, no.*)

SALLY. You poor misguided little lamb.

TRUDY. Oh, phooey on you. . . . Why don't you give yourself up?

SALLY (*to the Justice's wife*). Gratitude.

JUSTICE'S WIFE. They never want to be saved . . . I've seen it time and time again.

We hear the roar of the jeep outside and a distant siren.

JUSTICE. Here they are.

He crosses toward the door, and Trudy and Norval back into the corner. Then we get a close view of TRUDY and NORVAL as she points to the electric light switch which is near them and the window beside it.

TRUDY (*in a whisper*). Norval.

She reaches for the switch and all the lights go out. Sally and the Justice's wife scream.

JUSTICE'S VOICE. Stop that . . . help. (*And he starts firing his revolver in the air.*)]

The scene dissolves to the EXTERIOR OF THE KOCKENLOCKER HOUSE. Emmy is standing by the porch rail, looking off anxiously. Then she goes over to Kockenlocker, asleep in a chair. She sits down on his lap, and he awakens. The faint sound of a siren is heard.

KOCKENLOCKER. Git off my lap! What's the matter with you?

EMMY. I've got a right to sit on your lap, haven't I? I'm your daughter, aren't I?

KOCKENLOCKER. That's what they told me.

EMMY. I'm nervous.

KOCKENLOCKER. What about?

EMMY. You don't hear a police siren, do you?

KOCKENLOCKER. A police siren! That's a tree toad.

EMMY. I keep feeling I hear a police siren.

KOCKENLOCKER. How could you hear a police siren when there ain't one in town?

EMMY. I don't know. (*She rises, and comes forward to the steps.*) I thought I heard it again then.

KOCKENLOCKER. How could you hear a police siren when—(*reacting, as he too hears the siren; rising and going to her*)—there ain't one in town?

EMMY. What's that—a hoot owl?

KOCKENLOCKER. That's a—

Now they also hear the sound of cars coming closer, as well as the sirens. They look out toward the street, following which we get a long view of motorcycle cops coming down the street followed by Trudy, Norval, the Justice and others in a car—a jeep and other cars follow. Next we see them pulling up in front of Kockenlocker's house. The Justice, an M.P., Trudy and Norval get out of the car. A Sheriff and others appear and follow the group as they come in through the gate.

JUSTICE. Make way, please—make way.

TRUDY (*seeing her father*). Hello, Papa.

This cuts to Emmy and Kockenlocker standing on the porch, looking off at the arrivals and reacting with astonishment.

EMMY (*calling out*). Oh, Trudy! (*And she runs down the steps.*)

KOCKENLOCKER. What's all this? What are all you . . .

We see Trudy, Emmy, Norval, the Justice and the group—Emmy and Trudy embracing.

KOCKENLOCKER'S VOICE. . . . coppers doing in my town?

JUSTICE (*pointing to Norval*). Did you ever see this man before?

KOCKENLOCKER (*approaching the group*). Certainly I've seen him before! (*To Norval*) What're you doing in that outfit, Norval?

JUSTICE (*triumphantly to all*). All please take notice his name is Norval, not Ignatz, and that that is not his regular outfit.

KOCKENLOCKER. Well, who said it was! What're they supposed to have done, anyway?

THE M.P. You'll find out!

KOCKENLOCKER. Go on in the house! Go on! (*To the crowd*) Clear outta here, folks. G'wan! G'wan home before I pinch you for loitering! Get outta here!

Trudy, Norval, Emmy, the Justice and the group move into the house. Kockenlocker follows them, but the crowd starts out after him. The scene dissolves to the HALL OF MR. JOHNSON, the lawyer. Johnson is standing at the wall phone, and Mrs. Johnson enters from the parlor.

JOHNSON (*into the phone*). He did what? What?! In a fake uniform.... All right, Edmund, I'll be right over. (*He hangs up.*) Norval is in some kind of a mess with the Kockenlocker girl.

MRS. JOHNSON. I don't believe it!

JOHNSON. Nobody asked you to!

He reaches for his hat, and runs out. The scene dissolves to KOCKENLOCKER'S PARLOR, which is buzzing with excited voices. Present are Kockenlocker, Trudy, Emmy, Norval, the Justice, two M.P.'s, and the group; a crowd of people stand in the hall in the background.

KOCKENLOCKER (*to Norval*). Are you nuts or something? What's the idea of the get-up?

JUSTICE. Please take notice—

FIRST M.P. What war do you think you're in, Buddy?

SECOND M.P. The ghost of the A.E.F.!

FIRST M.P. Let's see your dog tags, General. (*He rips Norval's collar open.*) No more dog tags than feathers on a fish!

SECOND M.P. What camp you from, soldier?

NORVAL. Camp Sm-Sm—

The First M.P. looks at the insignias on Norval's collar.

FIRST M.P. U. S. Marines on one side and Cavalry on the other!

SECOND M.P. A horse marine! I always wanted to see one.

SHERIFF (*stepping forward*). Do you mind if I examine the evidence, Corporal?

FIRST M.P. Sergeant, if it's all the same to you.

SHERIFF. Well—

TRUDY (*stepping in front of Norval*). Why don't you leave him alone! I can explain everything to my father!

JUSTICE (*stepping forward*). Yes, but can you explain it to the Judge?!

KOCKENLOCKER (*pushing him aside*). What judge! What's the charge?

AN F.B.I. MAN. I fear there may be several.

KOCKENLOCKER. All right, what are they?

SHERIFF. If it's all the same to you, I'm the Sheriff of this County and will conduct the investigation.

KOCKENLOCKER. Yeah?! Well, you happen to be in the Township of Morgan's Creek and I happen to be the Town Constable—so if anybody's going to conduct an investigation—

THE MIRACLE OF MORGAN'S CREEK

MARSHAL (*stepping forward*). As a matter of fact, it's a Federal matter, as a matter of fact, so if it's all the same to you gentlemen— (*He starts to lay a heavy hand on Norval's shoulder, but the First M.P. catches his hand.*)

FIRST M.P. The way I learned it, any guy in a uniform is in the army till proved different, so we'll just take him over to camp.

The M.P.'s grab Norval, while Trudy clings to him.

SHERIFF. Take your hands offa my prisoner! (*At this point the Editor's voice is heard.*)

EDITOR'S VOICE. Good evening, all. Good evening, all. (*Now entering*) Who did what to who and where, and any little colorful sidelights and stories of general interest. (*At this point Johnson's voice is heard.*)

JOHNSON (*pushing his way through the crowd*). I'm Mr. Johnson, the lawyer. I represent—Norval Jones. Why, Norval! What are you doing in your Boy Scout outfit?

SHERIFF (*shrewdly*). Boy Scout outfit!

There is a close view of Trudy, Norval, Johnson, the First M.P. and Kockenlocker; the others appear in the background.

FIRST M.P. He's a mouthpiece! He knows it's a U.S. uniform. Don't fall for that stuff!

JOHNSON. What are you talking about? That's a Boy Scout outfit if ever I saw one. I remember very well when you joined the Scouts. I said to Mrs. Johnson only the other day—

NORVAL. Oh, no, no.

JOHNSON. It isn't? (*He glares at Norval, and giving the others a quick look, attacks again.*) Of course it isn't! I remember now. The Woodsmen of the World. I remember when your axe came. I said to Mrs. Johnson: "I hope he's not going to chop—"

NORVAL. No, no, no, no.

JOHNSON. No? Very well, Norval. What's the alleged charge—it being understood that we admit nothing!

All start talking together, mentioning the various charges—a babel of voices.

[This cuts to a view of FRIENDS AND NEIGHBORS on the FRONT PORCH. From inside the house we hear the angry abadaba as we see quick views of these people.

A LADY NEXT DOOR. He took Trudy to a motel . . . with a false name.

A NEIGHBOR. What was its real name?

AN OLD MAID. They ought to shoot him.

SECOND OLD MAID. Maybe they will . . .

This cuts to the NEIGHBOR'S HUSBAND.

NEIGHBOR'S HUSBAND. I can understand everything but the uniform. Why did he put on a uniform?

THE OLD MAID. So she'd run off with him, of course.

A MAN (*happily*). This should be in all the papers. . . . It's the biggest thing since the mad dog on Fourth of July.

A NERVOUS WOMAN. You say there's a mad dog?

This cuts to MR. JOHNSON in the middle of the mess, in the Kockenlocker home.

MR. JOHNSON. Gentlemen, gentlemen, just a minute . . . one at a time, please.]

RAFFERTY (*enters*). Trudy! Trudy!— Vot happened?

TRUDY. I don't know, Mr. Rafferty. Papa, he didn't do anything!

Kockenlocker pushes Trudy forward and goes out with her. The M.P.'s shove Norval around, amid much yelling.

JOHNSON. Quiet! Quiet! One at a time!

THE KITCHEN, with Trudy, Emmy and Kockenlocker.

TRUDY (*sobbing*). Oh, Papa!

KOCKENLOCKER. Never mind the "Oh, Papa!" What happened?

Trudy throws her arms around him. He falls into a chair and Trudy sits on his lap. Emmy goes around behind them.

TRUDY. Oh, Papa!

KOCKENLOCKER. Now, what happened?

EMMY. Everything!

KOCKENLOCKER. You go upstairs to bed. This ain't for fourteen-year-olds. Go on now.

Instead of going, Emmy sits down on his knee.

EMMY. Oh, piffle!

KOCKENLOCKER. Will you get off my lap and get out of here?!

TRUDY. She knows all about it, Papa.

KOCKENLOCKER. Oh, she does, does she?! Well, how about letting your old man in on some of the dirt? Or am I being too snoopy!

EMMY (*to Trudy*). You think it's wise? He'll blab it all over town.

KOCKENLOCKER. Listen, ladder legs!

TRUDY. It'll be all over town anyway, now.

EMMY. Even the secret?!

KOCKENLOCKER (*pointing toward the people in the parlor*). The secret! This is some secret!

THE PARLOR, with Johnson, Norval, the M.P.'s, and the group, amid a babel of voices.

JOHNSON (*to the M.P.'s, acidly*). Will you kindly keep your nose out of this! It's already been established this matter is not military!

THE KITCHEN, Trudy and Emmy sitting on Kockenlocker's lap:

EMMY. I told you what you could expect from that picklehead!

KOCKENLOCKER. Pickle—!

TRUDY. You mustn't talk about him that way, Emmy. He was only trying his best.

EMMY. Imagine if he hadn't been really trying!

KOCKENLOCKER. Who signed what? Who's Katzenjammer and where does he tend bar?

EMMY. It was Norval, Papa. You wouldn't understand anything about it.

KOCKENLOCKER. Understand it!

EMMY. But you got the certificate? You didn't muff that!

TRUDY. I haven't got it.

KOCKENLOCKER. What certificate?

EMMY. Her marriage certificate! Why didn't you get it?

TRUDY. He pulled a gun, and then he telephoned—

KOCKENLOCKER. Who pulled a gun— that Norval?

EMMY. Don't try to understand, Papa!

TRUDY. And then all those policemen came, and that's all.

EMMY. Who's got the certificate?

TRUDY. I don't know—the Justice, I guess.

KOCKENLOCKER. What certificate?

EMMY. Her marriage certificate!

TRUDY. To Ratzkiwatzki.

KOCKENLOCKER. To Ratzkiwatzki?! I told Jones to marry you!

EMMY. She's already married, Papa, perfectly respectably, to a gentleman called Ratzkiwatzki, only she can't prove it. She hasn't got the certificate. It's just one of those things.

TRUDY. So tonight I married him again.

EMMY. Just to get the certificate, don't you see?

KOCKENLOCKER (*firmly*). No.

TRUDY (*as to a child*). You have to have a certificate.

EMMY. So she married Norval.

KOCKENLOCKER. She married Norval.

TRUDY. To prove I was married to Ratzkiwatzki. But then he signed the wrong name and now they've got him and we're in the soup.

KOCKENLOCKER. I'll shoot him!

TRUDY. He didn't sign the wrong name on purpose, Papa.

He tries to rise. They hold him down.

KOCKENLOCKER. I'll shoot him, anyway!

EMMY. The one you'd want to shoot is Ratzkiwatzki, Papa.

KOCKENLOCKER. Well, isn't he Ratzkiwatzki?

TRUDY. No, I married him a long time ago.

KOCKENLOCKER. When?

TRUDY. The night I was out with Norval. (*Kockenlocker grabs his head to keep it from exploding.*)

EMMY. Can't you understand anything?!

Now we see JOHNSON entering through the doorway, stopping, and calling out:

JOHNSON. They can't agree on anything, Edmund. Each one wants to put him in his own jail . . . and if they do, we won't even be able to find him again, let alone get him out! Now, have you got anything against him?

KOCKENLOCKER (*rising with Trudy and Emmy*). Nothing except a good kick in the pants.

JOHNSON (*moving to them*). I'll tell you what you do. You take him down and lock him in your jail and then they can draw lots for him tomorrow. In the meantime, we'll sift the whole thing down. It's perfectly ridiculous. They've got about nineteen charges against that boy!

TRUDY. But he didn't do any of those things, Mr. Johnson.

JOHNSON (*mimicking her*). He didn't do any of those things?! He did all of those things in the eyes of the law! (*Turning to Kockenlocker*) Will you do that for me, Ed?

KOCKENLOCKER. All right. And what you two ought to have is a good shellacking! Daughters! Phooey!

THE PARLOR: Kockenlocker comes forward, goes toward Norval and the group, and grabs Norval.

KOCKENLOCKER. You're under arrest! Follow me.

CROWD. You can't do that!

KOCKENLOCKER. Quiet! One more crack out of you guys and I'll lock youse all up! (*To Norval*) Come on, Ox-Brains!

TRUDY (*going to Norval and hugging him*). Oh, Norval!

NORVAL. Don't worry, Trudy. I'll be —I'll be—I'll be—

TRUDY. I'll knit you something, darling.

JUSTICE (*dryly*). You'll have lots of time.

RAFFERTY (*angrily, to the Justice*). Who asked you something?! Put away that gun before you shoot somebody!

JUSTICE. Who are you?!

KOCKENLOCKER (*to Norval*). Come on! (*To Trudy*) You get back in the kitchen. I ain't finished with you.

Trudy goes out and the scene moves with Norval, Kockenlocker and the group as they go out into the hall amid the crowd.

SHOTTISH (*a townsman*). Shame on you, Norval Jones!

WOMAN. Shame on you!

CECELIA. That'll teach you to bethmirch the name of our fair thity.

KOCKENLOCKER (*shouting*). Quiet!

The scene dissolves to the EXTERIOR OF THE JAIL, with Norval looking out the window, while we hear a great deal of shouting. He is looking at something, whereupon the scene cuts to the FIRE ENGINE ROOM, with Kockenlocker standing in the doorway, surrounded by the Sheriff, the M.P.'s, the Marshal and a group—people crowded around. Kockenlocker is signing receipts.

FIRST M.P. I'll take one of those, too.

MARSHAL AND F.B.I. MAN. Me, too.

KOCKENLOCKER (*to the crowd*). Go on home, folks. (*To the others*) There you are. There you are. (*To the others*) Go on. Go on before . . .

Now we see the JUSTICE beckoning.

KOCKENLOCKER'S VOICE. . . . I pinch some—

We see Kockenlocker and the group as the crowd starts dispersing. The scene then moves with Kockenlocker to the Justice standing in the doorway.

KOCKENLOCKER. Yeah?

JUSTICE (*mysteriously*). I wouldn't want this to go no further, see? But I figure you and your daughter are in enough trouble without having to annul this marriage and go through all that rigamarole. You get me?

KOCKENLOCKER. No. (*To the crowd*) Go on home now!

JUSTICE. I could of called the cops in before the ceremony instead of after, couldn't I? If I don't write it on the books, it ain't a marriage, is it?

KOCKENLOCKER (*getting the idea*). That's certainly mighty white of you, brother.

The Justice takes out money and hands it to Kockenlocker.

JUSTICE. That's all right. I may call on you some day. Here's your two dollars. There was no marriage. She was saved in the nick of time.

KOCKENLOCKER (*genuinely touched*). That's mighty white of you, brother—mighty white!

The Justice takes the license from his pocket.

JUSTICE. And here's the last evidence—the certificate. Now you see it—(*tearing it up*)—now you don't. Not a trace.

KOCKENLOCKER (*gripping his hand*). Thank you, brother!

JUSTICE (*starting out*). Forget it. I might call on you some day. (*Kockenlocker looks after him and shakes his head—his faith in man restored.*)

The scene dissolves to the KOCKENLOCKER PARLOR, with Trudy sitting on a chair arm, Emmy standing by her.

EMMY. I wonder who else you could marry.

TRUDY. Emmy! How can you be so heartless! I'll love Norval to my dying day. How could I even look at another man? I think he's the most wonderful man that ever lived.

EMMY. Yes, but he's going to be in jail, Trudy, for a long time. He can't do you any good in stripes, honey. You can't be so choosey.

TRUDY (*sobbing*). Oh, Emmy! (*They look around as they hear the door bang.*)

Kockenlocker enters the hall, hangs up his hat, and goes toward the girls.

KOCKENLOCKER. Well, you fixed *him*—and you certainly give us a good name in the town! You spend all your life behaving yourself, then they find your daughter in a—in a lovely mess.

EMMY. Don't take it that way, Papa.

KOCKENLOCKER (*glaring at her*). "Don't take it that way, Papa!" Don't take it what way, Papa? You're just a kid. You can duck down the alleys. Me, I gotta stand out in the middle of the street and take it—from every rat in town!

TRUDY. I'm sorry, Papa. (*She starts to cry.*) You told me not to go out that night.

KOCKENLOCKER (*walking away from them, troubled*). Yeah. Well, I could be wrong, too, you know, but why don't you come to me if you're worried about something? The trouble with kids is they always figure they're smarter than their parents. (*Moving back to them*) Never stop to think if their old man could get by for fifty years and feed 'em and clothe 'em, he maybe had something up here to get by with. Things that seem like brain-twisters to you might be very simple for him—like this, for instance. (*He takes out the money and tosses it on the table.*) There's your two bucks. You never got married tonight. You got nothing to worry about.

TRUDY (*palely*). What?

KOCKENLOCKER. I got the guy to tear up the certificate. Just a little politics. And if you'd-a come to me in the first place—

EMMY. You got the guy to tear up the certificate?

TRUDY (*collapsing on her sister's shoulder*). Oh, no!

KOCKENLOCKER (*irritated*). What's the matter with you? If nobody knows you're married to this Katzenjammer and it was all by mistake anyway, with false names a corpse couldn't dig up, why do you have to go around proving things? Why can't you be practical?

EMMY (*to Trudy*). Shall we tell him or let him linger?

KOCKENLOCKER. Tell him what?

TRUDY (*very simply*). I'm going to have a baby.

KOCKENLOCKER. You're going to have a baby . . .

As he starts to walk, he suddenly realizes what has been said, turns, and grabs them.

KOCKENLOCKER. *What do you mean you're going to have a baby!*

EMMY (*quietly*). I told you he'd blab it all over town!

TRUDY. That's why we wanted the certificate.

EMMY. The one you got the guy to tear up!

KOCKENLOCKER (*looking at them like a stricken man*). The one I got the guy to tear up.

Kockenlocker walks away, then stops and looks back.

KOCKENLOCKER. Did Norval know about this when he asked you to marry him?

TRUDY. Yes, Papa.

KOCKENLOCKER. So he gets charged with abduction, imitating a soldier, repairing the morals of a minor, resisting arrest, perjury! He'll be lucky if he gets life! Then when your little surprise package happens, he'll probably get some more!

TRUDY. You've got to let him escape, Papa.

KOCKENLOCKER. Oh, sure! And take my pension right along with him, that I've been working seventeen years for, and land in the hoosegow besides!

EMMY. Couldn't you think of some bright way of doing it? You're always having bright ideas!

KOCKENLOCKER. Listen, zipper-puss! Some day they're just gonna find your hair ribbon and an axe some place—nothing else! The mystery of Morgan's Creek!

TRUDY. Papa, that's really not being very helpful.

KOCKENLOCKER (*bitterly*). Well, what do you want me to do—learn to knit?! I'm going out for a walk! (*He goes into the hall, puts on his cap and goes out.*)

The scene dissolves to the CELL, in which Norval is seated dejectedly on his cot. He looks up as he hears a door open. Next we see Kockenlocker coming in through the jail door. He comes forward to the cell, unlocks and opens the door, and stops in the doorway, looking off at Norval.

KOCKENLOCKER. Trudy told me what you done for her—at least, what you tried to do.

He comes forward and sits down beside Norval.

KOCKENLOCKER. I didn't understand

NORVAL. Oh, that's all right. I'd just as soon she hadn't told you, though. The less people know about it, the better it's going to be for her.

KOCKENLOCKER. It's too bad it had to turn out like this.

NORVAL. Oh, I'll be all right.

KOCKENLOCKER. What do you mean you'll be all right! You know what they got lined up against you? What'd you have to take a minor to a "motel" for, anyway? That's no place to take a minor.

NORVAL. I'm not even thinking about that. I'm so worried about Trudy.

KOCKENLOCKER. Well, all she's worried about is you.

NORVAL. Poor Trudy! To think that I've got to be locked up in here at the very time she n-n-needs me most. If I could just get out of here for a while, I—I betcha I could find that s-s-skunk. I betcha I could.

KOCKENLOCKER. I couldn't do it, Norval. It would cost me my job. Why, if I conspired in any way to—

NORVAL. Oh, I didn't mean anything like that, Mr. Kockenlocker. I wouldn't do anything to get you in trouble—just when Trudy needs you so much.

KOCKENLOCKER. If you got out, it would have to be without any help from me in any shape or form whatsoever. You'd have to do it all by yourself.

NORVAL. I wasn't even thinking about anything like that.

KOCKENLOCKER. Of course, if I was to turn my back . . .

Kockenlocker rises, goes to the basin, and stands with his back to Norval, following which a closeup shows Norval pondering as Kockenlocker continues. (We also see Kockenlocker's lower body, the keys, blackjack and gun hanging from his belt.)

KOCKENLOCKER'S VOICE. . . . on you, carelessly like—

Kockenlocker's hand wiggles the thong on the blackjack. Norval touches the blackjack, then pulls his hand away.

KOCKENLOCKER'S VOICE. —and you happened to grab my blackjack and konk me over the dome with it—

A closeup shows Kockenlocker looking around over his shoulder, then closing his eyes, removing his cap and bending his knees.

KOCKENLOCKER. —that would be something else.

NORVAL (*next seen in a closeup*). As if I'd do anything like that, Mr. Kockenlocker!

A closeup of Kockenlocker shows him opening his eyes, reacting, jamming his cap on his head, and slamming the cup down.

KOCKENLOCKER. Or if you made a sudden dive for me, grabbed me around the neck, spun me, hit me on the jaw—

Then Kockenlocker grabs himself by the neck, wrestles with himself, and hits himself on the jaw. He falls on the cot, and bumps his head.

KOCKENLOCKER. —and while I lie here helplessly, you beat it.

NORVAL. As if I'd do anything like that, either!

KOCKENLOCKER. How did you do in school?

NORVAL. Who, me? Fine.

KOCKENLOCKER (*sitting up*). Is that so?! (*Trying again*) Kinda stuffy in here, ain't it?

NORVAL. I hadn't noticed it.

KOCKENLOCKER (*rudely*). Oh, yes, you had!

NORVAL. Huh?

KOCKENLOCKER. I'll go around the back and open the window. It works from the outside.

NORVAL. Yes, sir.

KOCKENLOCKER. You get me?

NORVAL. Yes, sir.

KOCKENLOCKER. Way around in the back.

NORVAL (*occupied with his troubles*). Thanks very much.

Kockenlocker rises and exits. Then he is seen reappearing, stopping in the cell doorway, looking back, and pushing the door open.

KOCKENLOCKER. You get me?

He turns and starts out. And this dissolves to a scene in which Norval is seen standing at the window while Kockenlocker appears on the branch of a tree outside the window.

NORVAL (*calling out anxiously*). Oh, b-b-be careful, Mr. Kockenlocker!

Kockenlocker reaches over, unlocks and opens the window.

KOCKENLOCKER. It's a good thing you didn't try to run away just now. I forgot to lock the doors and it would take me five minutes to get down out of this tree. You get me?

NORVAL. Don't you worry, Mr. Kockenlocker. I'll be right here.

But now the branch breaks and Kockenlocker falls out of sight with a crash, following which the scene cuts to the BACKYARD OF THE JAIL. Kockenlocker is lying on the ground tangled up in a tree branch. He extricates himself, and sits up when Norval hurries over to him and kneels by him.

NORVAL. Are you hurt, Mr. Kockenlocker?

KOCKENLOCKER. I'm all right. (*Coughing*) It just knocked the wind out of me. Only I ain't going to do any running for the next hour or so, not if you give me a million dollars. You get me?

NORVAL. Yes, sir.

KOCKENLOCKER. And my gun is way over there some place. I'm defenseless.

NORVAL. I'll go get it for you.

Norval rises, and goes to pick up the gun. At this Kockenlocker rises, holding his hands in the air. As Norval approaches with the gun, Kockenlocker backs away and Norval follows, until Kockenlocker backs up the steps.

KOCKENLOCKER. All right, you got me, pal! Don't you shoot! I know when I'm licked. Just lock me in the jail. The key is in the door.

NORVAL (*protesting*). Oh, no, no, no, Mr. Kockenlocker!

KOCKENLOCKER (*insistent*). Shut up! I know you're going to escape, but I can't help it. I can't do anything about it. My car is right down in front of my house, and if you need any gas there's a can with five gallons in my woodshed. But you wouldn't take that from me, would you, pal?

NORVAL. Of course I wouldn't, Mr. Kockenlocker.

KOCKENLOCKER (*lowering his hands*). Maybe I can make things clearer, Norval!

The scene cuts to the FIRE ENGINE ROOM, and we see Trudy and Emmy getting out of a car parked outside.

There is a clatter of tools.—Then we again see the BACKYARD OF THE JAIL, with Kockenlocker looking toward the car.

KOCKENLOCKER. Jiggers! There's somebody in there! (*They run into the door.*)

Trudy and Emmy are now seen getting tools out of the car.

EMMY. Ssssh!

Kockenlocker and Norval tiptoe forward. Trudy and Emmy are again seen getting tools from the car. Kockenlocker and Norval are seen watching. Now Trudy and Emmy tiptoe forward, look off, start with terror, scream, and drop the tools with a crash as they hear their father's voice.

KOCKENLOCKER'S VOICE. You get back to bed!

They run forward to Norval and Kockenlocker.

TRUDY. Papa, he isn't guilty of anything!

EMMY. Why isn't he in his cell?

KOCKENLOCKER. How about keeping your trap shut! He escaped. (*Kockenlocker raises his hands.*) Can't you see he's got me covered? Don't shoot, Norval.

NORVAL (*protesting*). Oh, no, no, no.

TRUDY (*understanding what her father has been trying to do*). Oh, Papa! (*Trudy hugs Kockenlocker.*) You don't think they'll fire you, do you?

NORVAL. Of course they won't. I just picked this gun up for him. I'm not going any place.

KOCKENLOCKER. All right, I give up! See if you can do anything with him!

TRUDY (*as she leads Norval to one side*). I want you to go away, Norval. Don't you understand that, dear? I couldn't bear to have you in trouble on top of everything else.

NORVAL. But that would only make matters worse . . .

Emmy and Kockenlocker are seen watching and listening with dismay.

NORVAL'S VOICE. . . . Trudy. They can't send me up for very long.

This cuts to Trudy and Norval as they stand together.

NORVAL. And, anyway, I'll be happy about it, because I'll be doing it for you, Trudy. Every day I'll think—well, this is for Trudy—and as soon as I get out we'll straighten it out somehow and we'll be married again —but really, Trudy, for always and always.

Trudy goes to Kockenlocker, and Emmy and Norval follow her.

TRUDY (*sobbing*). You're just making me cry, but you're not helping anything.

NORVAL. Don't cry, Trudy!

TRUDY. Oh, Norval!

KOCKENLOCKER (*after exchanging a disgusted look with his youngest*). What about that guy you was gonna find if you could just get out for a little while?

TRUDY (*seizing at straws*). That's right! Maybe you can find Ratzkiwatzki. Of course you can. Anyway, it's worth trying.

EMMY. Sure.

NORVAL. Do you really think so?

EMMY. Yes.

NORVAL. If I really thought so I'd track him to the ends of the earth.

TRUDY. Of course you can.

NORVAL. But I haven't any car.

KOCKENLOCKER. Steal mine.

EMMY. It's insured.

KOCKENLOCKER. Shut up!

NORVAL (*vacillating*). If I was really sure it was for you, Trudy, and not for selfish reasons— I'd need a little money. I've got nine hundred dollars in the bank only it's in bonds. Do you think it'd be wrong if I took nine hundred dollars in cash and left my bonds? I've got a key at the house.

EMMY. It might be wrong, but it would be very handy!

This scene dissolves to the BANK, and we see Norval coming in, followed by Kockenlocker—while Trudy and Emmy are in the car outside in the background.

KOCKENLOCKER. All we needed was a little bank robbery!

Now, Norval and Kockenlocker start forward. Trudy and Emmy get out of the car and start to go inside. Trudy accidentally kicks the door and Kockenlocker jumps and whirls around, but Norval continues forward and disappears.

KOCKENLOCKER. Will you get out of here!

TRUDY (*whispering*). I'll be all right, Papa.

Kockenlocker comes forward to the teller's window. Norval re-enters, stumbles and falls out of sight. Trudy and Emmy run forward to the window. Kockenlocker turns a flashlight on him.

KOCKENLOCKER. Are you hurt?

NORVAL. No, no, I'm—I'm all right.

KOCKENLOCKER. Why don't you look where you're going!

Kockenlocker helps him, and they go to the safe. Norval starts working the combination.

NORVAL. I'll leave a note the minute I get through. You have to be very careful with this. You have to know exactly what to do or else it'll set off the alarm.

KOCKENLOCKER. Can you do it?

NORVAL. Oh, yes.

Norval swings the safe door open, but at that moment an alarm gong rings, startling them. As the alarm continues ringing, Trudy and Emmy at the teller's window become frightened and back away, screaming.

KOCKENLOCKER'S VOICE. Forget the money!

We next see Norval and Kockenlocker, Norval counting the money with the speed of a magician. Kockenlocker rises and goes out. Norval rises, and runs after Kockenlocker, Trudy and Emmy. All go out and run to the car.

KOCKENLOCKER. Go on, beat it! Come on, get goin'! Go on!

This scene dissolves to a view, as seen through the open door of the FIRE ENGINE ROOM, of a car approaching and stopping. Norval and Kockenlocker get out and Kockenlocker goes behind the car while Norval helps Emmy out.

NORVAL. Come on, Emmy. Goodbye.

Emmy leaves, and Trudy and Norval kiss.

EMMY. Goodbye, Norval.

NORVAL. Goodbye, Trudy.

Now Kockenlocker reappears from behind the car and joins the three youngsters.

KOCKENLOCKER. Beat it, Norval—beat it!

TRUDY. Norval, you've got to hurry!

Norval gets into the car, and Kockenlocker picks up a rope.

TRUDY. Goodbye.

KOCKENLOCKER. Come on, come on!

TRUDY. Goodbye, Norval!

KOCKENLOCKER. Go on, Norval!

Norval drives away, and Kockenlocker runs forward to the door, followed by Trudy and Emmy.

KOCKENLOCKER. Come on in here!

This cuts to the JAIL CELL, with Kockenlocker running in through the jail door. Trudy and Emmy come running after him into the cell.

KOCKENLOCKER. Come on!

TRUDY. Be careful, Papa. I wouldn't want you to get into any trouble.

KOCKENLOCKER. Tie me up, quick! Come on! Around here. Tie it tight. Come on!

Trudy starts to tie him up. He puts handcuffs on his wrists.

TRUDY. Yes, Papa. Here, Emmy—swing him.

Trudy and Emmy whirl him around, winding the rope around him. Trudy ties the rope around his neck.

KOCKENLOCKER (*in a close view of the little family group*). All right, not so hard! What are you trying to do—strangle me?!

TRUDY. Oh, I'm sorry.

KOCKENLOCKER. All right, that's tight enough. Now, a little klunk on the head. Take the blackjack out of my pocket, lock the door and beat it home and hide the keys.

TRUDY. All right, Papa. Which side?

KOCKENLOCKER. Any side!

Trudy taps him lightly on the head with the blackjack.

KOCKENLOCKER (*disgusted*). Harder! But not too hard! (*She taps him again.*) Harder! How could that knock anybody out! (*She gives him another gentle tap.*) Is that all the harder you can hit?! For heaven's sake, will you try to do one thing right?!

EMMY. Oh, here! (*She grabs the blackjack, and hits him hard on the head.*)

Kockenlocker starts to fall, with a grunt, whereupon Trudy cries out with distress: "Oh, Papa!" We then see Trudy and Emmy trying to catch Kockenlocker as he falls to the floor.

TRUDY. Papa! Oh! Oh, Emmy! Oh, Papa, did we hurt you?!

They grab his feet and start to drag him forward to the cot, as the scene fades out.

The scene dissolves to the GOVERNOR's OFFICE, with the Governor seated at his desk; the Boss, perched on the desk, listening on the other phone—a cop, secretaries, stenographers and people in the background.

GOVERNOR (*into the phone*). Wait a minute! Never mind the details. Is the girl married or isn't she married?

BOSS (*into another phone*). Yes!

GOVERNOR. It's a matter of State honor —a matter of public weal!

This cuts to the NEWSPAPER OFFICE, with the Editor and Rafferty.

EDITOR (*into the phone*). I'm very sorry, Mr. Governor, but nobody knows whether she's married or not.

The scene cuts to the GOVERNOR'S OFFICE.

GOVERNOR (*into the phone*). Well, she's got to be married, that's all there is to it! We can't have a thing like that hanging over our fair State —besmirching our fair name.

The scene cuts back to the NEWSPAPER OFFICE.

GOVERNOR'S VOICE. Where is the father now?

EDITOR (*into the phone*). In jail!

This cuts to the GOVERNOR'S OFFICE.

GOVERNOR (*into the phone*). What do you mean he's in jail! Don't you realize he's one of the most famous men in the world?! I thought you said he escaped.

BOSS. He did say he escaped!

The scene again cuts to the NEWSPAPER OFFICE.

EDITOR (*into the phone*). Yes, but he came back and got caught again.

This cuts to the GOVERNOR'S OFFICE.

GOVERNOR (*into the phone*). When?

BOSS (*into the other phone*). Yes.

EDITOR'S VOICE. Yesterday. It must have been around six o'clock, I guess . . .

This dissolves to the EXTERIOR OF THE KOCKENLOCKER HOUSE as the Editor's voice and Rafferty's are heard continuing the telephone conversation. We see Norval getting out of the car, going to the broken gate, stopping in amazement and looking with surprise at it; then going up the path to the abandoned house.

EDITOR'S VOICE. . . . because Mr. Tuerck was still in the bank for the Christmas Club and Mr. Rafferty was still in his store.

RAFFERTY'S VOICE. It was closer to seven.

We get a close view of a loosely nailed "FOR SALE" sign on the front porch, and this cuts to Norval, who seems quite lost, turning and starting back down the path which is covered with drifting leaves, for it is Christmas time now. This dissolves to the JOHNSON PARLOR, in which Mrs. Johnson is seated in a chair, knitting.

MRS. JOHNSON. They left about six months ago.

NORVAL'S VOICE (*calling out while approaching*). Six months ago!

We get a close view of Johnson and Norval standing.

JOHNSON. They left kind of hurriedly, Norval, right after he was discharged by the Town Council.

NORVAL (*horrified*). Discharged! What for?

JOHNSON (*as Mrs. Johnson looks away*). It had something to do with the escape of a prisoner. They didn't quite believe it.

NORVAL (*pointing to himself*). You mean me?

JOHNSON. I guess so, Norval.

NORVAL. Oh, but that's terrible! I was just trying to help Trudy—looking for someone I—I never found. But you wouldn't know about that—or would you?

JOHNSON (*in a dead legal voice*). I don't know what you're talking about, Norval.

NORVAL. Well, anyway, now that I'm back and ready to give myself up, I guess they'll take Mr. Kockenlocker back on the job all right, won't they?

JOHNSON. I hardly think so, Norval. Besides, you know what Mr. Kockenlocker is like. He didn't exactly take it lying down when they fired him. He left on very bad terms. They had to take six stitches in Mr. Tuerck alone.

NORVAL. Poor Trudy.

JOHNSON. Poor Mr. Tuerck.

MRS. JOHNSON. It was ghastly.

JOHNSON. You haven't asked my advice, Norval, and it certainly isn't up to me to advise you to evade the law, but since you were kind of dragged into this situation, and it's practically forgotten now anyway, and the Kockenlockers have gone, probably taken root some place else—they may even have changed their name—why don't you do the same?

MRS. JOHNSON (*rising and stepping up to them*). I'm sure it would be wiser, Norval.

NORVAL. But I couldn't do that, Mrs. Johnson. I've just got to find Trudy. She must be in terrible trouble now.

JOHNSON. I've given you my very best advice, Norval. It's up to you to act as your conscience dictates, but if there were that many charges pending over me, you wouldn't see my coattail for the dust. Even if they didn't press the Kockenlocker charges, there's the uniform, the jail break, the bank robbery—

NORVAL (*horrified*). The bank robbery! But I took my own money!

MRS. JOHNSON. Oh, Norval, I'm so glad.

JOHNSON. So am I, but that isn't exactly what Mr. Tuerck allowed us to understand.

NORVAL (*backing away*). Holy mackerel! Goodbye, Mrs. Johnson. Goodbye, Mr. Johnson. (*Norval shakes hands with them.*)

JOHNSON. Goodbye, Norval.

NORVAL. Thank you. Goodbye. (*Norval kisses her cheek.*)

MRS. JOHNSON (*impulsively, putting her arms around him*). Norval, wouldn't you like to take some fruit cake with you?

NORVAL. No, thank you, Mrs. Johnson. I'm afraid I couldn't swallow it.

MRS. JOHNSON (*in tears*). Merry Christmas, dear.

NORVAL. Merry Christmas to you.

He looks at them one last time, then departs like a thief in the night. Mrs. Johnson falls into her husband's arms and cries softly. Then we see Norval coming out the front door. He closes it, and starts across the porch.

This dissolves to the EXTERIOR OF RAFFERTY'S MUSIC STORE, with Rafferty and Mr. and Mrs. Shottish going to the door. Rafferty opens it, and Mr. and Mrs. Shottish come out.

RAFFERTY. Merry Christmas, Mr. and Mrs. Shottish.

MRS. SHOTTISH. And a merry Christmas to you, Mr. Rafferty.

SHOTTISH. Merry Christmas, Mr. Rafferty.

RAFFERTY. Many happy returns. (*After returning to the door, he suddenly does a double-take at something he sees, and exclaims.*) Norval! Gott tsu donken!

NORVAL (*coming forward slowly*). Hello, Mr. Rafferty.

RAFFERTY. What are you doing here?! Don't tell me! You're just in time.

NORVAL. Do you know where Trudy is?

RAFFERTY. I know from nothing. Wait a minute. I'm just going to see her. We'll take her around a toikey.

He turns, and goes into the store. This dissolves to the EXTERIOR OF THE BANK with Tuerck inside the glass doors. He switches out the light, comes out through the door, turns to lock it, glances out, narrows his eyes as he sees something, and runs back into the bank.

Now on the STREET outside the bank, we see Norval pacing up and down in front of the music store. Rafferty appears with the turkey, hands it to Norval and starts towards the door of the music store.

RAFFERTY. Sssssh!

At this, Mr. Tuerck comes out from the bank, holding an automatic, and starts down the street.

On the STREET, Norval and Rafferty are now crossing to the car, and get in, closing the door.

RAFFERTY. We'll buy at the bakery a plum pudding. Nothing gives so much indigestion but at the same time so much pleasure like a plum pudding, except a fruit cake. One time when I was a boy—

Tuerck's hand pushes the automatic forward, startling Rafferty. Norval turns, sees the gun, and is startled.

TUERCK. Good evening, Mr. Rafferty —and you, Mr. Jones! I wondered if you'd come back. (*He puts a police whistle to his lips and blows stridently.*)

This dissolves to a little FARMHOUSE IN THE SNOW at night. The strains of a harmonium or organ are heard from the house. This dissolves to the FRONT ROOM where Emmy is seated at an organ, playing. Noises from the outside cause her to stop and look up. As the scene moves, it reveals Kockenlocker standing on a ladder by a Christmas tree, hammering an ornament to the top of the tree. He hits his thumb.

KOCKENLOCKER. Well, anyway, we're going to have a white Christmas. (*He looks up.*) Why don't you say something?

He steps down from the ladder, and comes forward. The scene moves with him to Trudy lying on a chaise longue in the foreground. He sits down beside her, and pats her hand.

KOCKENLOCKER. How about a little smile, huh?

As Emmy is heard playing again and Trudy smiles up at her father but not very gaily, he continues huskily.

KOCKENLOCKER. You gotta have more confidence in the Almighty, or whatever it is that makes the wheels go 'round. All right, it's almost Christmas. Where was He born? In a cow shed. You might be waiting for the President of the United States. You got to have more confidence.

EMMY'S VOICE (*as her playing stops*). Speaking of cow sheds . . .

We see EMMY looking around at her father, then around a little further, then back at her father.

EMMY. ... did you remember to milk Bessie tonight, Papa?

KOCKENLOCKER (*mimicking her*). Yes, I remembered to milk Bessie tonight, Papa.

EMMY. Then what's she doing in the kitchen?

KOCKENLOCKER. What! (*He rises and starts for the kitchen, calling out*) Will you get outta . . . here.

We see the cow coming through the kitchen door. Kockenlocker appears, pushes the cow back into the kitchen, and wrestles with her.

KOCKENLOCKER. Come on, get out of here! (*In reply the cow moos, and this is overlapped by noises from the outside.*) Come on!

At the noise, we see Emmy and Trudy listening and laughing, Trudy calling out, "Poor Papa!" This cuts to the EXTERIOR OF THE FARMHOUSE, and we see the lower part of Rafferty's body—the turkey in his arms. He rings the doorbell. This cuts to the PARLOR, with Emmy seated at the organ. She rises, and moves past Trudy as she goes into the hall. Emmy opens the door a crack, peeks out, then opens it wide, and Rafferty enters.

EMMY. Hello, Mr. Rafferty. It's so good to see you.

RAFFERTY (*handing her the turkey*). I've brought you a toikey.

EMMY. Thank you, Mr. Rafferty.

TRUDY. Hello, Mr. Rafferty.

She closes the door, and they come forward to Trudy.

RAFFERTY (*sitting down beside her on the chaise longue*). Trudy! Feeling good, huh? It's natural.

TRUDY. Thank you, Mr. Rafferty— and for all your kindness. I don't know where we would have been without you.

RAFFERTY. What are you talking? It's a privilege. The doctor vill come from the next town, then he'll go back to his town and forget it. You got nothing to worry about. It'll be as quiet as a buttered eagle. (*He squeezes her hand and smiles nervously.*)

EMMY. Would you have a cup of tea, Mr. Rafferty?

RAFFERTY. Oh, thank you.

EMMY. Yes, sir.

RAFFERTY. How's Papa?

TRUDY. Fine, thank you. He's out with Bessie.

RAFFERTY. Dat Bessie, I remember her. Never satisfied. I brought Papa back his car. (*He looks at Trudy uneasily.*)

TRUDY. But Norval had it! You mean he came back? Where is he? Why didn't he come out with you?

RAFFERTY (*still more uneasily*). He didn't find anybody while he was away, Trudy.

TRUDY (*indignantly*). Well, that's no reason for him not to come out to see me. He ought to know better than that, when I've been waiting so long, so anxiously to see him.

RAFFERTY (*avoiding Trudy's eyes*). That ain't why he didn't come back. They caught him again. He's in jail.

TRUDY (*starting to cry*). Oh, Mr. Rafferty!

RAFFERTY (*holding her back on the chaise longue*). Now, now, now, what good is this? You've got something else to think about. So he's in jail, so he'll get out—some day.

TRUDY. All right. I'll go back to Morgan's Creek and I'll tell them everything.

RAFFERTY (*starting to get furious*). Trudy!

TRUDY. They'll have to drop the charges when I tell them what he did and why.

RAFFERTY. What are you talking? How about your reputation? We spend six months planning—fixing everything—building up a secret—now you got to built it down over night?

TRUDY. I've got to.

RAFFERTY. All right, you don't care about yourself. How about your father? Ain't he got enough trouble? How about your sister? How about me? How about— Anyway, they wouldn't believe you.

TRUDY. They will when they see me.

RAFFERTY. Trudy, vill you listen to— Vhat's the use. I love you for it. (*As Trudy sobs, he pats her.*) There, there.

This dissolves to the STREET, where Kockenlocker is getting out of the car with Trudy and Emmy in the back seat. Rafferty comes around the back of the car. Kockenlocker closes the door, and looks back in at Trudy.

KOCKENLOCKER. You still have time to change your mind.

RAFFERTY. Why don't you, Trudy? I'll get him out on bail and—and— (*His voice trails off.*)

But Trudy shakes her head, and Kockenlocker and Rafferty turn, and start across the street, whereupon the scene moves up to the firehouse sign: MORGAN'S CREEK FIRE DEPT., where the Town Council room is located.

This dissolves to the TOWN COUNCIL ROOM. The Mayor is sitting at the head of the table. The Editor, Mr. Johnson and the Justice are standing beside him. The Marshal, the F.B.I. men, Tuerck, Swartz, the Sheriff, the Doctor, and others are seated around the table.

MR. JOHNSON. I just want to be fair about this, Mr. Mayor. . . . It isn't because I represent Norval . . . but the Kockenlockers have gone . . . in disgrace . . . where . . . deponent sayeth not . . . Norval has lost his job. . . . We'll never hear from him again. . . . It's the day before Christmas . . . let us show a little of the yuletide spirit . . . withdraw the charges . . . wipe the slate clean and forget the whole thing.

TUERCK (*slapping the table*). Either we make an example of this man or we're opening the doors and inviting crime in to dinner!

JOHNSON. Piffle!

TUERCK. It may be piffle in your book, but I say that breaking and entering, theft, perjury, impersonating a soldier, impairing the morals of a minor, jailbreak—with or without conspiracy . . .

A close shot of the GROUP shows Tuerck still talking vehemently.

TUERCK. . . . et cetera, et cetera— (*banging the table*)—are not piffle!

JOHNSON. Piffle!

TUERCK (*belligerently*). You say that once more, Johnson, and I'll—

JOHNSON. Piffle!

At this, Tuerck rises threateningly. But the Mayor rises, and he and the Editor push Tuerck back into the chair.

MAYOR. Gentlemen! Gentlemen, please! There's a great . . .

Now we see Kockenlocker standing at the top of the circular staircase.

MAYOR'S VOICE (*continuing*) . . . deal to be said for both sides.

KOCKENLOCKER (*calling out*). Hey!

The Mayor and the group all turn to look. Then we see Kockenlocker joined by Rafferty, who comes up the stairs. They go up to the Mayor and the group at the table.

KOCKENLOCKER. My daughter wants to see you.

RAFFERTY. Right away.

TUERCK (*angrily*). What are you doing in Morgan's Creek? I warned you that if you ever showed up in this town again—

At this, Kockenlocker makes a move to hit Tuerck, but Rafferty grabs him.

KOCKENLOCKER. Oh, yeah?!

MAYOR. Gentlemen, gentlemen, is this the Christmas spirit? What is it that you want, Mr. Kockenlocker?

KOCKENLOCKER. My daughter wants to tell you about Norval—why he done what he done. She says when you hear what she has to say, you'll never prosecute him.

RAFFERTY. Impossible.

JOHNSON. You see?

MAYOR (*after looking around*). Well, bring her up. We must hear both sides—always.

TUERCK. That is strictly the bunk! Women are always trying to take the blame for men. It's what you call the mother instinct.

KOCKENLOCKER (*furiously*). Well, you can listen to her, can't you, you dumb—

Kockenlocker starts for Tuerck, but Rafferty and the Mayor grab him.

RAFFERTY (*shaking a finger under Mr. Tuerck's nose*). Or I'll take my business out of your bank so quick it will make your hair sizzle!

MAYOR. Gentlemen! Gentlemen! Bring her up.

KOCKENLOCKER. I'm afraid you'll have to come down. She don't feel very good.

MAYOR. Really?

TUERCK. Oh, is that so? Well, well, well!

KOCKENLOCKER. Yes! What about it, you dumb—

RAFFERTY. Gentlemen!

Kockenlocker lunges at Tuerck, and again Rafferty and the Mayor hold him back. And at this moment Emmy's voice is heard calling, "Papa! Papa!"

EMMY, calling out, "Papa!," is running up the circular staircase. This cuts to the COUNCIL ROOM, Emmy appearing on top of the stairs and running up to Kockenlocker, Rafferty, the Mayor and the group at the end of the table.

EMMY. Papa! Papa! Papa! Trudy! Trudy is—

KOCKENLOCKER. Trudy!

RAFFERTY. Well, what are you standing there? Doctor! Doctor! Come quick!

There is excited yelling as they all run to the stairway. Kockenlocker again tries to grab Tuerck, and the Editor and the others hold him back. Tuerck runs down the stairs, and Kockenlocker runs forward, slides down the fire pole, and disappears. Then the scene moves with Kockenlocker as he reaches the floor. He waits as Emmy, the Justice, the Editor and the F.B.I. men come down the stairs and go out. Finally, Tuerck comes down the stairs. Kockenlocker sees him, and seizing this opportunity, he hits him, knocking him down, brushes his hands off, turns and starts out.

The scene dissolves to a HOSPITAL CORRIDOR, where Emmy and Rafferty are sitting on a bench, and Kockenlocker is pacing forward while a nurse moves past them in the background. Emmy rises, goes to Kockenlocker, and puts her arms around him. He pats her shoulder, then resumes pacing, and she returns to the bench and sits down. Kockenlocker turns, starts forward, then looks up a side passage, turns and goes up.

Next we see Kockenlocker appearing at the second floor window, and looking down, following which we see Tuerck, the Editor, the Mayor, the Marshal, the Sheriff, the Justice, Swartz, the F.B.I. men and a crowd gathered IN FRONT OF THE HOSPITAL. Tuerck is holding a handkerchief to his black eye as he looks up and gestures threateningly toward Kockenlocker. The Editor leaves the group and starts toward the hospital building. Then Kockenlocker is again seen looking out the window. He raises his arm in a gesture of defiance, and turns away.

[We see DOCTOR MEYER in the CORNER OF THE DELIVERY ROOM. He is adjusting his gloves. Behind him a shadow is going through the usual scooping motions. The view moves with Doctor Meyer across the room, a nurse puts a mask over his nose and hands him a stethoscope. Now he comes straight forward. He raises his gloved hand to beat the pulse.

DOCTOR MEYER. Ready.

He places the end of the stethoscope just under the CAMERA and starts to beat time. Now his eyes blink in surprise. His finger comes to a stop. He looks around at someone then starts again. He seems to have trouble catching the beat like a rookie trying to get in step with a column. He looks around again, unsanitarily twirls his finger in his ear, replaces the stethoscope, then listens. The view moves to a closeup including his eyes and his nose. As it does so we hear the deafening beat of the war drums in an African jungle. The doctor's eyes bug out in surprise.

This cuts to the UPPER HOSPITAL CORRIDOR. Here we see Rafferty, Kockenlocker and Emmy. Kockenlocker nurses his right knuckles vaguely then wanders over to a window and looks down. He reacts unpleasantly to what he sees. And this cuts to a view down the STREET. Here we see a group comprising the Mayor, Mr. Ziegler, the jeweler, Justice Meade Woodson, Mr. Shottish, Mr. Swartz, Mr. McNanny, Mr. Glumpf, the other members of the council plus two women, Mr. Johnson, the Sheriff, Pete, the Secret Service men, the U.S. Marshal, the two M.P.'s, and the newspaper Editor. Now Mr. Tuerck walks out of the drug store across the street and joins them. He is slightly bandaged and very indignant. He points up to the hospital and shakes a warning finger. The newspaper Editor takes down his threats, then starts for the hospital. While this has been going on quite a few gossips, including

Cecelia and her mother, have joined the group.]

The HOSPITAL CORRIDOR: Rafferty and Emmy are seated on the bench as Kockenlocker comes toward them from the window embrasure.

KOCKENLOCKER. Some secret!

RAFFERTY. So they know. So what do they know?

At this moment, footsteps are heard and Kockenlocker stops, and glares toward the stairs. The Editor appears, runs down the hall past him, then turns and comes back.

EDITOR. Have you any statement to make? Any little item of general interest?

KOCKENLOCKER. How would you like a punch in the nose?!

EDITOR. Mr. Kockenlocker!

Rafferty rises, and goes to them as a nurse enters from the delivery room in the background.

RAFFERTY. Now, let me handle this. (*To the Editor, confidentially*). How much would it take to keep this quiet?

EDITOR. Mr. Rafferty!

The nurse comes forward. Emmy sees her and rises. All watch the nurse.

NURSE. It's a boy.

RAFFERTY (*exultantly, shaking Kockenlocker's hand*). A boy! Trudy! That's wonderful! Muzzeltoff!

The nurse starts to go back but a door opens and a doctor comes out, and talks to her.

EDITOR. Congratulations, Edmund.

KOCKENLOCKER (*sourly*). For what?!

RAFFERTY (*philosophically*). A boy is a boy! No matter how you look at it, it's—

But Rafferty breaks off as they see the nurse coming forward. She passes them, goes to a linen closet and gets out a bundle. Now as the nurse and the doctor go into the delivery room, the head nurse comes through the door of the ward room.

NURSE (*as she passes them*). Twins.

RAFFERTY. Twins! That's wonderful! (*Looking at Emmy and noticing that she is crying*) What are you crying?

KOCKENLOCKER. What are you laughing?

EDITOR. Congratulations again, Edmund.

HEAD NURSE. Ssssh! Please be quiet Kindly remember this is a hospital (*She goes back into the ward.*)

EDITOR. I'd like to get a few more facts.

KOCKENLOCKER. Will you get out of here!

RAFFERTY. Ssssh!

EDITOR (*to Emmy, sitting down by her, as Kockenlocker starts pacing again*). Now, where have you been living for the last six months?

The scene dissolves and we again see Rafferty, Emmy and the Editor seated on a bench, and Kockenlocker pacing up and down.

EDITOR (*rising*). Thank you very much. I have all I need. I'll be getting back to the office.

But at this point, the delivery room door opens, and the nurse enters, followed by the doctor. He stops in the doorway as Rafferty and Emmy rise.

All watch as the nurse rushes forward to the linen room, gets two bundles hastily, and gives them to the doctor, following which they both go into the delivery room. Kockenlocker and the others exchange startled looks. But they have hardly had time to consider this strange behavior when the nurse re-enters from the delivery room, runs past them, goes into the linen closet, and comes back with an oxygen tank. She runs back to the doctor, who has appeared in the doorway, and they both go back into the delivery room.

> EDITOR (*pondering this*). If you don't mind, I guess I'll stick around a minute or two!

The Editor and Rafferty sit down, and Emmy goes over to Kockenlocker and puts her arms around him.

The scene dissolves to the DELIVERY ROOM, affording a closeup of Dr. Meyer, with the head nurse and two nurses in the background. He straightens up, turns to them, gestures and goes out. They are startled and begin to run out. Next we see Dr. Meyer coming into the CORRIDOR, running across the hall, and going into another room, followed by a nurse. He comes out of the room with a baby basket, runs to the delivery room and goes inside. Kockenlocker, Emmy, Rafferty and the Editor rise and watch tensely. The nurse gets another baby basket from the room. Another nurse enters from the delivery room, and as she passes the group, she holds up four fingers.

> RAFFERTY (*holding up four fingers, bewildered*). Did she do that? My eyes ain't so good.
>
> KOCKENLOCKER (*puzzled*). Did she do what?
>
> RAFFERTY (*holding up four fingers again*). That!

The head nurse enters and runs past them into the linen room, and gets the bundles. Kockenlocker sinks down on the bench.

> EMMY. You don't suppose that—
>
> HEAD NURSE. Whoopee!
>
> RAFFERTY. Emmy!
>
> HEAD NURSE. Whoopee!
>
> EDITOR. Everybody just keep calm.
>
> KOCKENLOCKER (*rising*). What?!
>
> RAFFERTY (*excited*). Gott tsu helfen! (God help us!)
>
> EMMY (*throwing her arms around her father*). Papa!
>
> KOCKENLOCKER. Will you get off my neck!
>
> DR. MEYER (*running in from the delivery room*). Hooray!
>
> EDITOR (*just as excited*). Everybody keep calm!

Dr. Meyer runs into the linen room and gets a tray.

> KOCKENLOCKER (*anxiously*). How is she, Doctor?
>
> DR. MEYER. Hooray!
>
> KOCKENLOCKER. How is she?
>
> DR. MEYER (*running out, breathlessly*). Wonderful! Wonderful! Hooray! Hooray!
>
> HEAD NURSE (*entering and throwing her arms in the air.*) Six! All boys!

Kockenlocker faints and falls to the floor. Emmy tries to revive him. The Editor and Rafferty dance around, shouting madly.

This dissolves into a composite picture of newspaper presses, and of news papers coming off the press. One paper stops, showing the headline: "SIX BOYS!!"—This dissolves into a composite picture of a newsboy selling papers to people on a corner, the newspaper bearing the headline: "SEXTUPLETS BORN IN MIDWEST."—This dissolves into a composite picture of a newspaper press, and of a newspaper with the headline: "SIX! ALL BOYS! SIX!"—This dissolves into a composite picture of hands typing—and a newspaper with the headline:

CANADA PROTESTS
"POSSIBLE BUT NOT PROBABLE,"
SAYS PREMIER

This dissolves into the GOVERNOR'S OFFICE, with the Governor and the Boss holding telephones and a crowd appearing in the background.

GOVERNOR (*into the phone*). You mean he's still in jail, you dumb blockhead?!

This cuts to the NEWSPAPER OFFICE, with the Editor and Rafferty.

RAFFERTY (*into the phone*). Yes!

The scene cuts to the GOVERNOR'S OFFICE.

GOVERNOR. Well, get him out!

This cuts back to the NEWSPAPER OFFICE.

EDITOR. But how can I, Mr. Governor, with all those charges against him?

This again cuts to the GOVERNOR'S OFFICE.

GOVERNOR. By dropping the charges, you dumb cluck!

BOSS (*also into the phone*). You vealhead!

GOVERNOR. Now, get me that banker on the phone.

BOSS. His charter is cancelled!

GOVERNOR. And the Justice of the Peace!

BOSS. His license is revoked and his "motel" is condemned!

The scene cuts back to the NEWSPAPER OFFICE.

EDITOR (*into the phone*). Do you want the M.P.'s and U.S. men, too?

This cuts to the GOVERNOR'S OFFICE, the Governor and the Boss speaking into the telephones.

GOVERNOR. What've they got to do with it? That was a State Guard uniform!

BOSS. I can see it from here!

GOVERNOR. As a matter of fact, he's a Colonel in it. I'm bringing him his commission tomorrow.

BOSS. Retroactive as of last year!

GOVERNOR. Go out and get him a uniform!

This dissolves into a composite picture of newspapers coming from the press—the newspaper bearing the headline: "NATURE ANSWERS TOTAL WAR."—This dissolves into a composite picture of newspapers coming off the press—the newspaper heading reading: "PLATOON BORN IN MIDWEST." And there follow in quick succession pictures of a Russian newspaper; a world globe and a Chinese newspaper; other papers coming from the press—an Italian newspaper carrying the headline:

STATI UNITA BURLA MONDO
ANNUNCIANDO NASCITA
SESTUPLI.

And this dissolves into an OFFICE, with "Mussolini" seated at a desk, an officer standing beside him. A second officer enters, runs to the desk, slips and falls to the floor. Then we see "Mussolini" reacting to the news—rising, going into a tantrum, and yelling some gibberish. And this dissolves to the picture of a hand tapping out a message on the telegraph key—a newspaper bearing the headline:

> MUSSOLINI RESIGNS
> "ENOUGH IS SUFFICIENCY"
> SCREAMS IL DUCE

This dissolves to the EDITOR'S OFFICE.

EDITOR (*into the phone*). There's only one thing more, Mr. Governor—the marriage.

The scene cuts to the GOVERNOR'S OFFICE.

GOVERNOR. What's the matter with her marriage?

BOSS. Yeah!

GOVERNOR. She's married to Norval Jones.

BOSS. Huh!

GOVERNOR. She always has been. The guy married them, didn't he? The boy signed his right name, didn't he?

BOSS. Sure!

This cuts to the NEWSPAPER OFFICE.

EDITOR. But he gave his name as Ratzkiwatkzi.

The scene cuts back to the GOVERNOR'S OFFICE.

GOVERNOR. He was trying to say Jones. He stuttered!

BOSS. What are you looking for— needles in a haystack?!

This cuts back to the EDITOR'S OFFICE.

EDITOR. Then how about the first Ratzki— . . .

Again the scene cuts to the GOVERNOR'S OFFICE.

EDITOR'S VOICE. . . . —watzki?

GOVERNOR. He's annulled!

BOSS. Schnook!

This cuts to the EDITOR'S OFFICE.

EDITOR. Who annulled him?

The scene cuts back to the GOVERNOR'S OFFICE.

BOSS. Get me Mendoza.

GOVERNOR. The Judge—who do you suppose?!

BOSS. Retroactive!

GOVERNOR. Get Judge Mendoza on the phone.

BOSS. I'm getting it.

GOVERNOR. He's out of the picture.

BOSS. He was never in it!

GOVERNOR. Now, get me those guys on the phone.

BOSS. Who do they think they are, anyway?! (*Into second phone*) Oh, hello, Mendoza. (*Into first phone*) They'll find out!

GOVERNOR. Fooling with the honor of our fair State!

This dissolves to the picture of a hand sending a message on a telegraph instrument, and a hand turning a mimeograph machine—with a German newspaper superimposed. And this in turn dissolves to HITLER'S TENT IN RUSSIA. It is very cold, and "Hitler" with some generals is poring over some maps. A colonel comes running in past some guards and goes to the table.

COLONEL (*in German*). A woman in America has had six children!

At this "Hitler" goes into a tantrum, rising and pounding on the table, and yelling some gibberish. And this dissolves to a picture of newsboys running forward, carrying a newspaper with the headline:

HITLER DEMANDS RECOUNT

This dissolves to the JAIL, where Kockenlocker is seen opening the cell door. We see him now in the full magnificence of his Chief of Police uniform.

NORVAL. Hello, Mr. Kockenlocker. (*As Kockenlocker merely laughs in reply*) How's Trudy?

KOCKENLOCKER (*grabbing Norval, who hangs back*). She's sleeping, but she'll be ready to see you in a few minutes. Come on!

NORVAL. But I wouldn't want to get you in wrong again.

KOCKENLOCKER (*astonished*). Get me in wrong! I'm the Chief. (*He laughs out loud.*) Where have you been?

NORVAL. R-r-r-right here.

KOCKENLOCKER. Haven't you heard about—about—

NORVAL. About what?

Kockenlocker's mouth moves but no words come out.

NORVAL. You mean she's had it?

KOCKENLOCKER. Has she had it! You'd better come and see your wife.

NORVAL. My wife? B-b-but I'm not m-m-m-marr—

KOCKENLOCKER. Oh, yes, you are, my boy!

And Kockenlocker pulls him to the door just as the Editor, Swartz, Rafferty, and Mr. and Mrs. Johnson enter. The Editor puts a clothes box in Norval's hands as they surge in and push Norval and Kockenlocker back into the cell. Swartz takes a uniform from the box, and Johnson puts a colonel's cap on Norval's head.

This scene dissolves to the HOSPITAL CORRIDOR, with Norval and Kockenlocker coming up the steps through the crowd, followed by the Editor, Swartz and others. The scene moves with them as the group comes forward down the hall through a milling and shouting crowd of reporters, cameramen and people who almost mob Norval.

Next we see Dr. Meyer, the head nurse and a nurse standing in front of Trudy's door, holding the crowd back. Norval, resplendent in a State Militia Colonel's uniform, Kockenlocker and their group pushing their way through the crowd to the doctor and the nurses, as Kockenlocker yells in his familiar traffic-cop manner, "Come on—quiet! *Quiet!*" The head nurse embraces Norval, who then backs into Trudy's room. A cameraman's voice is calling out: "Hold it just a second." There is a flash of light from a picture being taken, and Norval shuts his eyes. Then he closes the door, opens his eyes, turns, and removes his hat. Following this he comes forward into the room, where Emmy is standing at the foot of the bed. He joins her. His sword, attached to his colonel's uniform, clatters against the bed.

EMMY (*putting her fingers to her mouth*). Sssssh!

Thereupon a closeup shows Trudy in bed, asleep.—Norval and Emmy stand looking at her, and Emmy kisses his cheek.—Trudy is seen smiling in her sleep as Norval kneels beside the bed. She opens her eyes, sees him, and pats his face gently.

TRUDY. Oh, Norval!

NORVAL (*whispering tenderly*). Trudy.

TRUDY (*noticing his uniform and admiring it*). You look so beautiful. Where did you get—

NORVAL (*as she points to his uniform*). I don't know. T-t-the Governor sent it. You look so beautiful.

TRUDY. I love you.

NORVAL. Your father said—I don't understand exactly how—I—I—I don't understand a lot of things but —well, I'm out of jail now and— and we're really married, Trudy— for always and always.

TRUDY (*in a whisper*). I'm so happy.

NORVAL. I love you.

TRUDY. You're a papa now.

NORVAL. I feel like one, anyway.

TRUDY. You are one. The papa gives love and protection—

NORVAL. I'll do the best I can, Trudy, for always and always.

TRUDY. We'll have to pick out a name for it. Was it a boy or a girl?

NORVAL. I'll find out.

TRUDY. I'm so happy. (*She closes her eyes with exhaustion*).

The scene cuts to Emmy, who is looking in their direction with a long fishy stare, following which we see Norval rising from beside the bed and going toward Emmy, who beckons to him with her finger, takes his hand, and leads him to the door, leaving Trudy asleep.

NORVAL (*whispering to Emmy*). Was it a boy or a girl?

The scene cuts to the NURSERY as Norval and Emmy are coming forward down the corridor. The view, moving closer, reveals a row of bassinets lined up in front of a window. Norval and Emmy stop outside the window and look at the babies. Norval moves along in front of the window, looking at all six babies, smiling and waving at them. Then he returns to Emmy, and evidently asks her which baby is Trudy's. Emmy indicates all of them, whereupon he lets out an ear-piercing yell and runs to the door, Emmy chasing after him.

This scene cuts to TRUDY'S HOSPITAL ROOM, showing Trudy sitting up in bed. Norval runs in through the door, slips, and falls to the floor. He slides across the room, crashes into the table, knocking over flower vases. Then as Emmy runs in he rises and staggers forward to Trudy, babbling incoherently. Dr. Meyer, Kockenlocker and the crowd rush in. Trudy is frightened and addresses him indistinctly. And now everybody is talking all at once.

NORVAL (*calling out*). The spots! (*And he babbles incoherently. Then he collapses across the bed.*)

TRUDY (*crying out*). Emmy! Do something!

Emmy picks up the water carafe and pours water on Norval's head.

The scene dissolves and we see Norval recovered. He becomes increasingly happy for, as Shakespeare said: "Some are *born* great, some *achieve* greatness, and some have greatness *thrust upon* them." The scene fades out.

WATCH ON THE RHINE

(A Warner Brothers Production)

Screenplay by DASHIELL HAMMETT

Based on the Play by LILLIAN HELLMAN

Additional Scenes and Dialogue by LILLIAN HELLMAN

Produced by HAL B. WALLIS

Directed by HERMAN SHUMLIN

The Cast

SARA MULLER	Bette Davis
KURT MULLER	Paul Lukas
MARTHE DE BRANCOVIS	Geraldine Fitzgerald
FANNY FARRELLY	Lucile Watson
ANISE	Beulah Bondi
TECK DE BRANCOVIS	George Coulouris
DAVID FARRELLY	Donald Woods
PHILI VON RAMME	Henry Daniell
JOSHUA	Donald Buka
BODO	Eric Roberts
BABETTE	Janis Wilson
MRS. MELLIE SEWELL	Mary Young
HERR BLECHER	Kurt Katch
DR. KLAUBER	Erwin Kalser
OBERDORFF	Robert O. Davis
SAM CHANDLER	Clyde Fillmore
JOSEPH	Frank Wilson
HORACE	Clarence Muse

Film Editor—RUDI FEHR

Dialogue Director—EDWARD BLATT

WATCH ON THE RHINE. Copyright 1943 by Warner Brothers Pictures, Inc. Screenplay of the Warner Brothers photoplay "Watch on the Rhine," copyright 1943 by Warner Brothers Pictures, Inc. By permission of Warner Brothers Pictures, Inc., Random House, publishers of the stage play, and Lillian Hellman, author of the original stage play.

WATCH ON THE RHINE

PART ONE

The U. S. border, as seen from the Mexican side: As the scene fades in, a man, a woman, a girl and two boys are walking toward a small clapboard U. S. Immigration Station on the boundary line. They walk abreast. KURT MULLER is in the middle of the group. He is a German of about forty-seven with a strong handsome face and the physique of an athlete, but there are lines of weariness in his face, and he moves with the obvious carefulness of a man who is not well. SARA, Kurt's American-born wife, walks on his right. She is a good-looking woman with a well-bred, serious face. On her right is the oldest of the Muller children, JOSHUA, a sturdy boy of fourteen. On Kurt's left are his daughter, BABETTE, a pretty little girl of twelve, and BODO, a boy of nine. Their clothes are neat and clean, but somewhat dowdy and much too warm for this country in spring. They carry three shabby valises, a briefcase, a large paper bundle and extra coats.

The early morning sun casts their shadows out in long diagonal lines behind them to the left. The ground over which they are walking is absolutely flat, without vegetation of any sort. Behind the Immigration Station the land rises in gentle hills bearing sufficient grass, bushes and trees to make marked contrast with the foreground—though not enough to give a Garden of Eden effect.

As they approach the Station the view draws closer and, as they pause, we get a closeup of the station signs and then a close view of the MULLERS: Their faces are strained and nervous. They are walking stiffly. Kurt looks at the building and stops. There is a pause; then he wets his lips and slowly puts his hands over the pocket containing the papers. All the Mullers are looking up at him. Finally, he turns.

KURT (*with a German accent, quietly —tensely*). And so the moment has come. This time it is of the utmost importance. Please do not talk. Please do not seem nervous.

All of them stare at him. Only Sara nods. The children take a firmer grip on the things they are carrying and as Kurt moves toward the door, the view moves with them as they pass in.

The scene dissolves to the OTHER SIDE of the IMMIGRATION STATION. It is a few minutes later. All the Mullers are out of the station, all of them looking toward the door. Kurt comes out immediately. As he does, all of them smile and look up to him.

SARA (*as Kurt moves toward her*). I can't believe it, darling.

KURT. I give you orders to believe it. And now you are in your own land, Sara, and that is good.

Bodo is straddling an imaginary line: one foot in Mexico, one in the United States.

BODO (*first speaking in German*) Whenever we cross a border, I do this. It is good luck.

Copyright 1943, by *Warner Bros. Pictures, Inc.*

BABETTE. Papa told you it is good manners to speak the language of the country you visit. Therefore speak in English.

BODO (*in English*). I said that whenever we have crossed a border, I so fix my feet from one country to the other. I have found it to be of good luck and so I advise all of you—

JOSHUA (*pleasantly*). Yes. You are one of the many people of the world who are so pleased with what they say that the tenth time they have said it, it is as fresh to them as the first.—Spare us.

KURT (*to Sara, as they pick up the valises, smiling at her*). Your face is most happy, Sara, and most pretty.

As she smiles, delighted, and as they move off, followed by the children, the scene dissolves to a CROWDED DAY-COACH. The Mullers sit in facing seats, the children riding backward, Kurt and Sara facing the engine. The scene is filled with the clacking of car wheels and the creaking of the car, the crying of a baby, the rattling of paper, and the sound of passengers' voices.

SARA (*to the children*). Are you comfortable?

BABETTE (*bouncing a little on the seat between her brothers*). Oh yes, Mama. This is most luxurious.

Bodo flattens his nose against the window, looking out, whereupon we see the WESTERN LANDSCAPE through which the train is moving. It is arid country of sand, sagebrush and scrub-oak under a strong sun. Then we see the MULLERS in the DAY-COACH as Bodo turns from the window.

BODO (*abruptly*). I am surprised! The United States of America is a sun-lighted dusty country with vegetation of no great height and—

JOSHUA. You are ready to write a book about it?

SARA. This part of it is. But this part of the country is strange to me, too. (*With feeling*) Perhaps it will all be strange to me. It's been seventeen years—

Kurt, resting with his head against the back of the seat, his eyes closed, smiles without opening his eyes and puts a hand on Sara's. Joshua, sitting on the aisle, has twisted his head around to look up toward the other end of the coach, following which there are FLASHES of the OTHER PASSENGERS: Two Mexican laborers sleeping; an Italian woman nursing a baby behind an open newspaper while her husband sits reading another sheet of the paper beside her; a boy and a girl of six or seven playing tag in the aisle; a woman wolfing chocolate bars; a man trying to reclose an over-packed suitcase; a trainman opening the door to bawl the name of the next stop. (These people are of various types, but there should be no attempt to make this day-coach look like the American Melting Pot.) Then we return to the MULLERS, who are seen close.

BABETTE. There are, I think, others here who are not Americans.

BODO (*in a superior tone*). You do not know that people from the utmost different parts of the world have found refuge in the United States of America?

JOSHUA (*impatiently*). We know that.

Bodo again turns to the window, and there appear (*over Bodo's shoulder*) widely spaced RAMSHACKLE HOVELS along the railroad as seen from the car window, following which the view shifts back to the MULLERS. Bodo is speaking in a whisper so as not to wake Kurt, who has his eyes shut, and to keep his mother from hearing.

BODO. I did not imagine houses in America to be as those I have seen from this train. Do you think the house of Mama's Mother is one such?

BABETTE (*in a whisper*). I do not know. Is it that you have been accustomed to palaces?

BODO (*in a whisper*). I do not complain. I only ask. I live where Mama and Papa take us. But it is only natural that I have curiosity for our relatives.

The scene dissolves to an exterior view of the FARRELLY HOUSE. The house—a large red brick one not far from Washington—was built in 1760 and is a good example of the best mid-Eighteenth century architecture. Few changes have been made in its exterior since then, though the interior has been modernized from time to time. There are four tall brick chimneys—two at either end—and a high-pitched roof with peaked dormers. On one side there is a terraced pavilion looking down on a sunken garden. The wide grounds are well tended, but not too formal. It is now the first week in April, so only the earliest flowers are in bloom—perhaps a few magnolia and dogwood trees. A Negro gardener, HORACE, and his fifteen-year-old son, DOC, are working on a flower bed. Birds are singing.

On the TERRACE, a breakfast table is set for six people. Beside it stands ANISE, a Frenchwoman of sixty, in a dark housekeeper's dress, sorting the morning mail. She takes the mail from a small basket, holds each letter up to the light in search of clues to its contents, carefully reads each postcard, then puts them in little piles beside the plates on the table. JOSEPH, a tall middle-aged Negro butler, is seen putting pats of butter on the table, and as Joseph goes out of sight, FANNY FARRELLY appears in the French doorway behind Anise. Fanny is a handsome woman of sixty-three; head-strong, violent, generous, vain, witty and spoiled, and she has a very good time being all these things. She is wearing an attractive fancy dressing-gown.

For a moment Fanny watches with amusement Anise's examination of the mail. Then she turns her head in the direction Joseph has gone.

FANNY. Joseph! (*To Anise*) Morning.

ANISE (*continuing to examine the mail*). Good morning, Madame.

The scene expands to include Joseph as he turns back.

JOSEPH. Yes'm?

FANNY. Everybody down?

JOSEPH. No'm. Nobody down. I'll get your tea.

FANNY (*with emphasis*). Breakfast is at nine o'clock in this house and will be until the day after I die. Ring the bell.

JOSEPH (*patiently*). It ain't nine yet, Miss Fanny. It's eight-thirty.

FANNY. Well, put the clocks up to nine and ring the bell.

JOSEPH (*going out*). Yes'm.

FANNY and ANISE at the TABLE: Fanny sits down at her place, Anise finishes examining and sorting the mail.

FANNY. I couldn't sleep. I kept thinking of Sara coming home. But you slept well, Anise. You were asleep before I could dismantle myself.

ANISE. I woke several times during the night.

FANNY (*picking up her mail and opening a letter, reading it while speaking*). You did? Then you were careful not to stop snoring. Now that Sara and her family are coming, we must finally get around to moving your room. Jenny's daughter is still going with that actor. An actor... Well, fashions in sin change. In my day it was Englishmen. My mail is dull. Anything in anybody else's mail?

ANISE. Advertisements for Mr. David. For the Count and Countess de Brancovis there is nothing but what seems to be an invitation to a lower-class embassy tea and some letters asking for bills to get paid.

FANNY. That's every morning. (*Thoughtfully*) In the six weeks Marthe and her husband have been visiting us they seem to have run up a great many bills. Why in the world do you suppose anyone would give charge accounts to Roumanian nobility?

ANISE (*knowingly — pointing to Fanny*). Perhaps because they are guests of Madame Joshua Farrelly.

FANNY (*dismissing the subject*). Perhaps. How does David's flirtation with Marthe get on? Anything happen?

ANISE. Happen? I don't know what you mean.

FANNY. You know what I mean.

ANISE. Oh, *that!* No, I don't think that.

FANNY. I must—(*She breaks off as she remembers the bell, and turns her head to scream.*) Joseph!

We see JOSEPH at the END of the PAVILION. A large old-fashioned bell hangs there, with a cord dangling from it.

JOSEPH. Yes'm.

Joseph takes hold of the bell-cord, winces, shuts his eyes, and yanks. With the sound of the bell a flock of small birds (which had been singing throughout the scenes) rises from the bushes and flies off.

JOSEPH (*softly—between yanks*). Little birds, I don't blame you.

At this, DAVID FARRELLY comes on to the terrace. He is Fanny's son, an amiable man of thirty-nine.

DAVID (*calling*). Joseph! Stop that!

JOSEPH. Ain't me, Mr. David. I don't like *any* noise. Miss Fanny told me.

DAVID. She didn't tell you to hang yourself with it.

JOSEPH (*as he moves off*). I ain't hung.

We see an UPSTAIRS WINDOW and MARTHE DE BRANCOVIS leaning on the sill. She is fully dressed in smart country clothes.

MARTHE. Good morning, David.

DAVID (*looking up from the pavilion*). Good morning, Marthe. I'm going to have the chicken-house fixed up as a playroom for my mother. I'll hang it with bells and she can go into her second childhood in the proper privacy.

MARTHE (*from the upstairs window, laughing*). She'll only make us have breakfast there.

FANNY'S VOICE (*heard screaming*). David! Come to breakfast!

Marthe smiles toward David and withdraws from the window, whereupon the scene cuts to MARTHE'S BEDROOM. As she turns from the window, TECK DE BRANCOVIS, her husband, is seen standing in the doorway. He is a good-looking Roumanian aristocrat of about forty-five.

TECK. Shall we go down together? (*He motions to the window.*) Couldn't you ask your admirer if perhaps it would be possible to have breakfast a little later than nine o'clock?

Marthe looks at him, then shrugs, smiles, and begins to move to the door.

MARTHE. I don't mind that as much as having to eat it on the terrace any morning it's not positively snowing.

Next TECK and MARTHE are seen moving down the hall.

TECK. Anything Madame Fanny's long dead husband did, she thinks God intended everybody else to do. It is unfortunate that early American liberals were such a hardy people. Breakfast promptly at nine, outdoors, dinner promptly at eight. . . . I won't be in tonight for dinner. Does that please you? You might have it with David.

MARTHE. I might. With whom are you dining? (*By this time they are moving down the stairs.*)

TECK. You will not bump into me. I'll be at the German Embassy.

MARTHE (*looking up at him, annoyed*). Teck. . . . I've asked you—

As he moves down the steps, away from her, the scene cuts back to the PAVILION where FANNY, DAVID and ANISE are at the BREAKFAST TABLE. Fanny is drinking tea.

FANNY. Did you phone the upholsterer?

ANISE (*looking at the watch pinned on her bosom*). It is not yet nine o'clock. Nobody in Washington, D.C. is anywhere at such an hour.

FANNY. Phone him at home. His name is Cobey or something. No, that's the architect. (*To David, who is eating*) You slept well. It does not seem to matter to you that your sister whom you have not seen for so many years is coming home.

DAVID. They aren't coming until tomorrow, Mama.

FANNY (*to David*). I lay awake most of the night, thinking of Sara and o your father, wondering what h would have thought of her comin home with her husband and chi dren . . . Three grandchildren. H would have liked that. (*Coming bac to earth*) I hope I shall.

DAVID (*laughing*). You will. (*T Anise*) Anything in my mail?

ANISE. Advertisements only.

DAVID (*pushing aside his mail*) Thanks. You and Mama save m a lot of time reading.

ANISE (*rising—haughtily*). I canno of course, speak for Madame Fann but I have never opened a letter i my life.

DAVID (*teasing*). You don't have t For you, they fly open.

As Anise marches out of sight an Fanny laughs merrily, the sce changes to the FRENCH DOOR leading from the terrace to the living room. Anise, her indignant nose in the air, almost collides with Marthe and Teck, who are coming out.

MARTHE (*in French*). Oh! Good morning, Ma'mselle Anise.

ANISE (*in French—sharply*). Good morning.

Anise goes out through the door, while the scene moves with Marthe and Teck as they join Fanny and David at the table. Then we see the group.

FANNY (*briskly*). Oh, there you are! Don't people ever get out of bed in Roumania?

Fanny makes a lot of noise with a small silver bell on the table. Joseph, immediately behind her with the breakfast wagon, leans over, and gently takes the bell from her hand. David looks up, grinning.

TECK. Not if they can help it. But my apologies.

DAVID (*pointing to the bell—to Marthe*). Has science a name for women who enjoy noise?

A closer shot at the BREAKFAST TABLE:

MARTHE (*laughing*). Fanny's excited. You're excited, too. One more day and your Sara will be home.

At the words "your Sara," Fanny looks up from her food as if about to say that Sara is hers too, but Marthe's and David's inability to hide their interest in one another amuses her and she slyly watches them and Teck. Teck, enjoying his breakfast, gives no signs that he notices anything. Marthe and David talk about Sara as if they do not know they are playing a love scene.

DAVID (*nodding*). I am excited and I'm afraid, too.

MARTHE. Why?

DAVID. I don't know. It's been so many years. Afraid she won't like me any more, I guess.

MARTHE (*emphatically*). Oh, but she will!

Fanny lowers her head a little to hide her amusement. Teck looks up, but his face and voice are politely expressionless.

TECK. Of course.

MARTHE (*hastily*). I remember Sara. Mama brought me one day when your father was stationed in Paris. I was about six and Sara was about fifteen and you were—

DAVID. You were a pretty little girl.

MARTHE. Do you really remember me? You never told me. I wanted you to remember me, but—

Fanny puts down her napkin and looks toward the French door, as we hear Anise speaking.

ANISE appears in the DOORWAY. Her still-offended dignity will not let her come further out on the terrace.

ANISE. Monsieur Chabeuf, the upholsterer, says not a pincushion, even so much as, could he re-upholster in two days, and in the matter of four chairs, a chaise longue, a footstool, two—

The scene expands to include Fanny.

FANNY. Nonsense. Your Monsieur Chabeuf is lazy. Is he on the phone? (*As she sweeps by Anise*) Everybody is lazy . . . except me.

ANISE (*following Fanny into the house*). Indeed. . . .

At the BREAKFAST TABLE, with DAVID, MARTHE and TECK:

TECK. Madame Fanny has energy. I find it most attractive.

DAVID (*smiling*). Perhaps because you're not related to it. But it works wonders.

TECK. What sort of man is the husband of your sister?

DAVID. I've never met him. My mother did once—in Munich. The day Sara met him, I think.

MARTHE. I remember my mother telling me about it. It was rather a scandal, wasn't it? The Farrelly daughter marrying a German who was poor and unknown—

DAVID. Oh, Mama wouldn't have minded that. If only they had come home and allowed her to arrange their lives for them—but Sara didn't want it that way, and that made her angry—(*He smiles.*) But all was forgiven a long time ago. And now that they *are* coming home. . . .

MARTHE. They're fortunate to be able to get out of Germany now.

DAVID. They've been out of Germany since the early thirties.

TECK. Oh. Where have they been living?

DAVID. They've moved around a great deal since then. Sara's letters have come from all kinds of places—Czechoslovakia, Denmark, France, Switzerland . . . (*As if he were a little puzzled*) Kurt is an engineer. But I'm not sure—

TECK. Well, you will have a house full of refugees now—us and—

DAVID (*too casually*). Are you a refugee? I'm not sure I know what you're a refugee from.

TECK (*casually*). From Europe.

DAVID (*rising, looking at his watch—carefully*). From what Europe?

TECK (*too casually*). Just Europe. (*And he smiles.*)

FANNY'S VOICE (*heard screaming*). David! David!

DAVID. This is one of Mama's screaming days. I'm going to the office before she finds any more errands for me to do. (*He smiles at Marthe as he leaves, counting on his fingers, while the scene moves with him.*) Ask Penfield about best school for twelve-year-old girl. Ask Walton about school for boys. Buy boy's books. Buy girl's books. Buy bicycles. Three puppies—

Back at the BREAKFAST TABLE with MARTHE and TECK: Marthe looks off after David. Teck picks up his and Marthe's mail and looks at the envelopes.

MARTHE (*after a second's silence, as if to herself*). From what Europe? I'm not sure what we're refugees from, either.

TECK (*looking at her*). Aren't you? (*Looking at the letters*) A great many mistaken people seem to have given you a great many charge accounts.

MARTHE. It would be nice to be able to pay bills again.

TECK. Do not act as if 'I refuse to pay them. I did not sleep well last night. I was worried. We have eighty-five dollars in American Express checks. (*Pleasantly—looking at her*) That's all we have, Marthe.

MARTHE (*shrugging*). Maybe something will turn up. It's due.

TECK. David? (*As Marthe merely stares at him*) Money does not worry you?

MARTHE. It worries me very much. But I just lie still now and hope. I'm glad to be here. (*She shrugs again.*) We've come to the end of a road. That's been true for a long time. Things will have to go one way or the other. Maybe they'll go well for a change.

TECK. I have not come to the end of any road.

MARTHE. No? I admire you. (*She leans forward.*) Perhaps because you think the road is going to lead you back to Europe? (*Shaking her head slowly*) You can't give up that dream, can you, Teck? That you can get back into their good graces again? That they'll let you come back and play with them? (*Sharply*) You ought to stay away from them.

TECK (*smiling*). You have political convictions now?

MARTHE. I don't know what I have. But I've never liked Nazis and you should have had enough of them. They seem to have had enough of you. They are smarter than you are and it's time you let them alone.

Teck looks carefully at her for a moment before he speaks.

TECK. I think you are trying to say something to me. What is it?

MARTHE. That you ought not to be seen at the German Embassy and that it is insane to go on playing poker there with eighty-five dollars left. Suppose you lose this time? I don't think they'd like your not being able to pay up.

TECK. I shall try not to lose tonight.

MARTHE. But suppose you do and you can't pay? Everybody in Washington will know it in an hour—and we'll be out of here.

TECK (*carefully*). I think I want to be out of here. I find that I do not like the picture of you and our host.

MARTHE (*carefully*). There is no picture, as you put it, to like or dislike.

TECK. Not yet? I'm glad to hear that. (*Leaning slowly toward her*) Marthe, you understand that I am really not a fool? You understand that it is unwise to calculate me in that way?

MARTHE (*slowly, as if with an effort*). Yes, I understand that. And I understand that I'm getting tired—just plain tired. The whole thing's too much for me. I've always wanted to ask you, since you play on so many sides, why we don't come out any better. I've always wanted to ask you how it happened. (*Sharply*) I'm tired, see? And I just want to sit down. Just sit down in a chair and stay.

TECK (*carefully*). Here?

MARTHE. I don't know. Any place.

TECK. You have thus arranged it with David?

MARTHE. I have arranged nothing.

TECK. But you are trying, eh? (*He rises.*) I think not. I would not like that. (*He smiles again.*) I would not like that at all.

He smiles and moves off. She does not look at him, but sits quietly staring at her hands.

The scene dissolves to the MULLERS' SEAT in the DAY-COACH at night. Babette is holding the Italian woman's baby on her knees. Sara, sitting beside Babette, is playing with the baby. Kurt and Joshua are on the facing seat, Kurt looking out the window, Joshua reading a newspaper. Bodo is not present.

JOSHUA (*looking up from the paper*). Papa, do you know the science of the game of baseball? And could you tell me what this means? (*He reads.*) "Augusta, Georgia, April 4.—Those two great rivals of the barn-storming trail, Carl Owen Hubbell and Bob Feller, carried their duel into this sector of the minor league terrain to-day and, in the contest between the strong arm of the youthful Feller and the wizardry of Hubbell's experienced soup bone, the Giants swallowed their first shut-out of the year, and the Indians squared the exhibition series at three all."

KURT. Translate it, Sara.

SARA (*smiling*). I can't.

JOSHUA. Well, I am going to learn baseball while we are here. That would not take too much time, would it, Papa?

SARA. Your Uncle David will teach you. (*She then smiles ruefully.*) My goodness! I keep forgetting he's only a few years younger than I. He was eighteen the last time I saw him. That's a long time ago.

KURT (*looking affectionately at her*). I do not think he will be on crutches.

SARA. I was twenty-one. . . .

At this Bodo comes into the scene and squeezes past Sara and Babette to his seat by the window.

BODO. At twenty-one years of agedness George Washington, the first President of the United States of America, was a Lieutenant-Colonel. A man in the car where smoking is allowable told me that. His name is Parker and he lives in Vermont. Vermont is a French name, but it is situated in the United States of America. I like to talk to foreigners.

BABETTE. It is not polite to speak of people in a country you are visiting as foreigners.

The view draws back as the Italian man and woman come into sight, both beaming on the Mullers. They are a few years younger than Kurt and Sara —a pleasant couple in American clothes that are just a little loud in pattern. Each wears some jewelry. They have very slight accents. Bodo stares at them with great interest.

ITALIAN WOMAN (*to Sara*). Thank you. (*To Babette*) Thank you. (*To Kurt*) Thank you.

ITALIAN MAN (*raising his hat—indicating the baby*). It was swell of you to take him off our hands for a while.

The Italian woman reaches for the baby, which clutches Babette's dress and tries to bury itself in her lap. The woman turns her head to smile at her husband.

ITALIAN WOMAN. That little Joe—he knows when he is with nice people. (*She picks up the baby.*)

BABETTE. May I borrow him again?

SARA. He is a fine baby. (*At this, the Italian man lifts his hat again.*)

ITALIAN WOMAN. And *you* have fine children.

BODO (*who has been quiet too long*). Thank you. You are Italian?

ITALIAN. Italian, yes, but American.

BODO (*as the Italian woman carries the baby away*). Do you know a Tullio Tipaldi who fought in Spain with Papa? (*The Italian man shakes his head doubtfully.*) You ought to. He was a soldier of much excellence in Spain. So was Papa. Papa was brave, he was calm, he was expert, he was resourceful, he was—

KURT (*to the Italian*). My biographer. And as accurate as most.

The Italian is troubled—divided between his liking for the Mullers and the suspicion that Bodo's words have aroused.

ITALIAN. You are German? (*Slowly*) What side did you fight on in Spain? (*At this Bodo and Joshua rise.*)

BODO. I beg your pardon? (*But Kurt shakes his head slightly.*)

JOSHUA (*to Bodo*). Be still, Papa says. (*And he sits down.*)

KURT (*smiling*). I fought with the Army of the Republic. I am not a Nazi or a Fascist.

The Italian's face lights up and he moves closer to Kurt. Then he scowls ferociously.

ITALIAN (*to Bodo*). I'm a big fool. I beg *your* pardon. (*To Kurt*) Don't forgive me. I might have known which side a man like you would be on. (*Very friendly*) Used to make me feel good that Italians and Germans went to fight against the Fascists in Spain. Kind of showed people that all Germans and Italians weren't—(*Stopping, he looks at Kurt, thoughtfully.*) Did you just come from Europe?

KURT. Yes.

ITALIAN. What's happening over there? I can't make any sense outa what I read. Nobody seems to be doing anything . . . no fighting, I mean.

KURT (*slowly*). It will come soon now, I think.

ITALIAN. Good, good. Then that fat Musso and his boss, Hitler, will be finished and through. Boy, will that be. . . .

KURT (*looking at him*). We have just come from France.

ITALIAN (*sensing the meaning*). Well, the French will fight fine. My aunt's married to a Frenchman. They're good soldiers. Always been.

KURT (*slowly*). All men are good soldiers when they know for what they fight . . . and are not betrayed. But the French have their bad men. Too many of them, now, I think. Like your people . . . and like my people.

ITALIAN (*laughing*). I hope they ain't got as many. (*He stops laughing.*) That's bad news, what you say. But ain't there some chance the German people themselves will kick Hitler out?

KURT. Hitler alone is not what is wrong: let us not make too much of him. And not alone Nazism, either. But all fascist doing and thinking, by whatever name you wish to call it, and all that brings it about.

ITALIAN. Yeah, I know that. But kicking him out would be a good start.

KURT. Yes. But it is not done with such ease.

ITALIAN. But you read about men in underground organizations. Is that just talk?

Sara and the children look up. Kurt hesitates for a second.

KURT. No. It is not talk. These men, in what you call underground organizations, work most hard and in great danger.

ITALIAN (*shaking his head*). But—well, it looks bad to me.

KURT. It is not all black. Take my word: there are men in your country and in mine who fight on. (*Slowly*) I know! I have friends among them.

ITALIAN. What do you do? I mean, what's your trade?

KURT (*rising*). I? I fight against Fascism. That is my trade. (*He smiles, wipes his brow, and begins to move down the aisle.*) It is most warm.

The scene dissolves to the FARRELLY LIVING ROOM: The room has size, simplicity and style. Four or five generations have furnished this room and they have all been people of taste. It has no one style, no period; the room has never been "completely refurnished." Each careless aristocrat has thrown into the room what he or she liked as a child and what he or she brought home from abroad when grown up. Hence the furniture is of many periods: the desk is English, the sofa Victorian, the piano something else; some of the pictures are modern, some of the numerous ornaments French. Though the room has too many things in it—vases, clocks, miniatures, boxes, china animals, etc., it is nevertheless, in normal circumstances, cool and clean and comfortable, and the soft colors of its fabrics and woods do not clash. Prominent on one wall is a rather formal oil painting of Fanny's dead husband, Joshua—a big kindfaced man in the evening clothes of 1900. At the moment the room is all upside-down, furniture out of place everywhere.

MRS. MELLIE SEWELL is sitting on the far side of the room. She is a woman of about Fanny's age; small, very proud of her tiny hands and feet, ostentatiously feminine, still hanging on to her life-time role as the helpless little woman-thing. Underneath this, and in her own way, she is probably at least as tough as Fanny. She is the widow of a Southern Senator and talks with a Southern accent. She and Fanny have been close friends—if you can call it that—since childhood. She wears a good many ribbons, bangles and furbelows, and a hat with flowers on it. Her face is small and somewhat wizened; cuteness-and-pertness-gone-toseed.

MR. CHABEUF, the upholsterer, is measuring a chair. He is a small man with a nervous manner and a thin self-important face almost hidden by spectacles and moustache.

Joseph is vacuuming drapes inside the French windows. The vacuum cleaner is a fairly noisy one.

Belle is standing on a ladder washing the glass over a picture. She is a plump middle-aged Negro maid with a towel tied on her head.

Horace, the gardener, and his son, Doc, are standing in the center of the floor holding a large sofa, waiting for Fanny to tell them where to put it. Horace looks like a Negro deacon, which he is. Doc is a loose-jointed boy of fifteen with a soft voice and a shy smile.

Fanny, dressed for the day now, looks

around the room, squinting a little. Then she points at a space between one side of the fireplace and a large chair.— We see FANNY, HORACE and DOC.

FANNY. Try it there, Horace.

HORACE. It won't fit in there, Miss Fanny.

FANNY. Nonsense. . . . Try it.

The scene moves with Horace and Doc as they carry the sofa to the indicated space, Fanny following them. The space is too small, but Horace does not look as if he had told her so.

FANNY. No, that's awful. Looks like a dentist's waiting room. Take it out of there.

MELLIE (*tapping her foot*). Fanny . . . Really . . . I've been sitting here for an hour waiting to drive you to Washington. All you're doing is messing up this lovely room. . . .

Fanny looks at her, ignores her, and turns back. Horace and Doc pick up the sofa and stand awaiting orders.

FANNY. Joseph! (*Then louder*) Joseph!

The view moves to Joseph at the French window. He turns his head and switches off the vacuum cleaner so he can hear.

FANNY. Find a place to put this sofa.

JOSEPH (*to Horace and Doc*). Yes'm. Put it back where it's been doing all right for fifteen years.

We see FANNY and MR. CHABEUF: Mr. Chabeuf, kneeling, holding a length of tape-measure against one side of the small sofa, is looking up at Fanny.

FANNY. There will be children—*my* grandchildren. They will climb on furniture—I always did. My grandchildren will be *healthy* children. So don't cover them with any of your dainty, sleazy materials. (*She points to Mellie.*) This isn't Mrs. Sewell's house.

Horace and Doc, having placed the sofa, leave.

MELLIE (*with dignity*). I had no children, therefore it is impossible for me to have grandchildren. If I'd've had a daughter, I would have named her Emmeline Lou.

Fanny looks Mellie up and down, studying her critically, then smiles as if satisfied.

FANNY. Well, everything works out for the best.

Anise comes into view trailing a length of curtain material behind her. She holds scissors and tape-measure in her other hand, and pins between her lips. The pins do not in any way interfere with her talking. The watch on her breast goes up and down rapidly with her breathing.

FANNY. We're going into Washington. Where's that list of things?

Anise transfers the tape-measure and scissors to her mouth and with the hand thus freed brings a long roll of paper out of a skirt pocket. Fanny unrolls the list to glance at it.

MELLIE (*rising, and staring at the list*). You'll never have time to get all that. I've got to have a fitting on my evening dresses.

The scene moves with Fanny and Mellie as they go out.

FANNY. I never understand why you need so many evening dresses. Do you lead a secret life—at your age?

The scene dissolves to a view of MELLIE'S LIMOUSINE, with FANNY and MELLIE in it, as it rolls out of the grounds. This cuts to a view of MARTHE, her arms full of flowers, going up to the house, as the car passes her. She waves at the car. Thereupon the scene cuts back to MELLIE'S LIMOUSINE as MELLIE turns, very sharply, very curiously, to stare at Marthe. She waves to her. Marthe waves back.

FANNY. You'll break your neck, Mellie.

MELLIE (*looking curiously at Fanny*). She's a pretty girl.

FANNY. All the Randolphs were good-looking, no matter what else they weren't.

MELLIE (*too casually*). I reckon men find her most attractive.

Fanny does not look at her. She is inspecting her shopping list.

MELLIE. Don't you think so, Fanny? Don't you think she is most attractive to men?

FANNY (*too bored*). I'm sure I don't know. I'm not a man.

MELLIE. Of course, Jennie Randolph wanted her to marry nobility. It was a brilliant wedding, remember, Fanny, in Paris? . . . Now doesn't it seem strange that she's back here and the circle is completed, as they say. Right in your house and. . . .

FANNY. What circle? What are you talking about? . . . Candy—I'll buy messy candy. That's what my grandchildren will like—messy candy. Now if you'd had grandchildren, Mellie—heavens forbid!—they'd have been the kind of children who never ate between meals and were sickly. All your family were sickly, Mellie, although I, myself, think you've made up a good deal of it—Licorice —that's what I'll buy. . . .

This dissolves to a STREET in the center of WASHINGTON as the car comes along, followed by a closeup of a BOX OF LICORICE on Mellie's lap. Then we again see FANNY and MELLIE: Fanny is eating a large piece of licorice. There is no free space around Mellie; her feet, on the other side of her, are surrounded with Fanny's purchases. There are a tricycle, a globe of the world, a croquet set, small packages, etc. Mellie is thoroughly hemmed in. Fanny sits comfortably, no packages near her.

MELLIE (*angrily*). Really, Fanny You've wasted all afternoon for me Now it's too late to try on my dresses. . . .

FANNY (*as the car turns a corner*) Do be careful of the candy, Mellie Close up the box.

MELLIE. You're acting like a six-year old about Sara's homecoming. Migh be better if you spent your time worrying a little about David. I isn't that I believe everything Cora says, but she says *everybody* is talking, especially after he took her to the Colonel's dinner party and a lot of people said—

FANNY. What are you chatterin about? You *must* get new uppe teeth, Mellie. Nobody can unde stand a word you say any more. Yo used to have lovely teeth when yo were young. . . .

Mellie is shrill with anger. As sh moves, the tricycle moves. During he speech Fanny leans down and picks u the tricycle.

MELLIE. *You* can't understand m But then *you* can't even understan that all of Washington is talking about your son and the Countess de Brancovis. Everybody is saying that it's serious, too, not just . . . you know. If it was just . . . you know . . . people would gossip a little and then stop.

FANNY (*giggling*). What is "just you know"? Really, Mellie, you're old enough to say what you mean. (*To the chauffeur*) Let me out at the next block.

She adjusts the tricycle on Mellie's lap, deliberately fixing it so that the handle bars are dangerously near Mellie's face.

FANNY. I promised to fetch David. You take this stuff home for me, darling, and thanks for the car.

The scene cuts to a BROWNSTONE STREET as Mellie's car drives in and stops at the curb. Fanny gets out and shouts back in.

FANNY. Do be careful of the packages. Don't let them bump around. And be very careful when you take them out and give them to Joseph himself. Goodbye, dear.

The scene moves with FANNY as she goes up the steps of an old-fashioned brownstone house, and then cuts to the ENTRANCE of this house. On one side of the steps is a sign: PENFIELD, BROADHOUSE, WELTON AND FARRELLY, Attorneys. On the other side of the steps is a small plaque:

THIS PLAQUE IN MEMORY OF
SUPREME COURT JUSTICE JOSHUA
FARRELLY, DISTINGUISHED
AMERICAN JURIST.
1868–1915

A close view of FANNY shows her touching Joshua Farrelly's name, smiling slightly, with the pleasure and affection she always feels upon seeing it. Then he opens the door and the scene follows her in. She passes a Gibson-girl middle-aged lady at a desk.

FANNY. Hello, Miss Drake.

MISS DRAKE (*rising, delighted*). Hello, Mrs. Farrelly.

We see an OLD-FASHIONED HALL as Fanny sweeps down its length, knocks on the first door marked: "Mr. David Farrelly," and throws it open before the knock can be answered.

DAVID FARRELLY'S OFFICE, where David is at his desk as Fanny enters:

FANNY. Come. . . . Take me home. (*She looks at a picture of Joshua Farrelly on the wall, and points to it.*) I don't like that picture of your father. I've told you before. It's not big enough. Get a bigger one. Goodness! My Joshua was handsome, wasn't he?

Without waiting for an answer, she sweeps out of the room and we follow her down the hall to the next door marked: "Mr. Cyrus Penfield."

CYRUS PENFIELD'S OFFICE: PENFIELD is a man of seventy, dressed like the popular picture of a Kentucky colonel. He is seated at his desk, dictating to another elderly lady.

PENFIELD (*dictating*). Whereas the purchaser relies upon the warranties and representations hereinabove and. . . .

FANNY (*in the doorway*). Cyrus . . . Hello, Miss Hall . . . Cyrus, my German son-in-law is coming tomorrow. He's an engineer.

CYRUS (*booming—rising*). Fanny!

FANNY. The Government or somebody must have use for engineers. Find him something very good, Cyrus. How's Marjorie?

CYRUS (*bewildered—coming toward her*). Looking her age, Fanny. . . . Which you never do. It's remarkable.

FANNY. Not very remarkable. I was a great beauty, Cyrus—you remember.

CYRUS. We all of us remember. When Joshua snapped you up, I was heartbroken.

FANNY (*correcting him*). All of Washington was heartbroken. Most of it, anyway. (*She starts to move out of the door, but meets David, who has just come up to it.*) Goodbye, Cyrus. Thank you so much for arranging the fine job for my son-in-law.

CYRUS. Er . . . Er . . . Fanny. What kind of engineer is he?

FANNY. What kind? Any kind. (*To David*) What *does* Cyrus mean?

DAVID (*patiently*). There are kinds of engineers . . . civil, mining, electrical . . . (*To Cyrus*) He used to work for Dornier. I guess that would make him a. . . .

FANNY. Oh, never mind. He's all kinds of an engineer, I'm sure. (*Cyrus starts to protest, but David winks and takes his mother's arm.*)

FANNY. Goodbye, Cyrus. Bring **Marjorie** for dinner. . . .

We follow DAVID and FANNY as they leave the office and go down the hall.

FANNY (*continuing—giggling*) . . . but not soon. In about five or six years.

As David laughs, the scene dissolves to a close view of DAVID and FANNY in the AUTOMOBILE as they drive through Washington streets out toward the country.

FANNY. I like this car. Mellie's car had so many packages in it, I had to get out. (*She looks out of the car again, then lightly, as if merely making conversation*) How much longer do you think the de Brancovises are going to be with us?

DAVID (*starting to look at her, then holding his eyes front*). I don't know.

FANNY. Now that Sara and Kurt and the children are coming, even our house might be a little crowded. I feel sorry for Marthe. I suppose—after all, her mother was my good friend—(*watching him out of the corner of her eyes*)—and Teck rather amuses me. He plays good cribbage and tells good jokes. But that's not enough for a life-time guest. And they've been here six weeks. Have they borrowed much money from you?

DAVID (*looking sharply at her*). None!

FANNY (*laughing*). Don't bite me. I didn't know. I hope *you* haven't been urging them to stay.

DAVID. You invited them, Mama. They're your guests.

FANNY. Ah, they were mine, but that was before you became enamoured of Marthe. (*Thoughtfully*) She was such a pretty young girl.

DAVID (*after a pause*). I think she's still pretty.

FANNY (*tolerantly*). Naturally—or you wouldn't be so ardent. Though I don't know why I say that. You were certainly ardent enough with that Carter girl and you *couldn't* have thought her pretty.

DAVID (*grinning uncomfortably at Fanny*). She had a nice disposition.

FANNY. Why not? Who would have spoiled her? Look here, David . . . What's going on between you and Marthe?

DAVID (*a little sharply*). I don't like that question, Mama. Nothing's "going on." I like her very much. I hope she likes me.

FANNY. I can assure you she does. So can all of Washington. There's a good deal of gossip about both of you.

DAVID (*slowly—disturbed*). Gossip?

FANNY. Nothing serious, most of it rather amusing.

DAVID. *There is nothing to gossip about.*

FANNY. That's never stopped anybody from gossiping. You and Marthe haven't been very good at hiding whatever there is to hide. (*Quietly—seriously*) You know, I wonder whether it's reached Teck.

DAVID (*protesting*). Mama, I—

FANNY (*slowly—softly*). I only wanted to say, David, that I have a feeling he isn't really a very good-natured man. Underneath the manners and the calmness, I have a feeling that he isn't good-natured at all.

The scene fades out.

PART TWO

The FOYER of the GERMAN EMBASSY fades in, and a middle-aged man in a German admiral's dress uniform is standing near the foot of a broad stairway saying good night to departing guests. He is a compactly built man whose face, eyes, hair, clothes, decorations and manner wear a hard, smooth polish. The departing male guests are of various nationalities—except that there are no British, French or Poles—and wear various military, naval and diplomatic uniforms and formal civilian evening clothes with and without decorations. The women are in evening clothes and a good deal of jewelry is in sight. There is a hum of conversation from foyer and stairs.

GENERAL (*in Spanish—to two men and a woman*). Good night. (*In German—to a man and woman*) Good night, good night (*In English—to three men—very American men*) Good night.

ONE OF THE AMERICAN MEN. It was an excellent party.

GENERAL (*in English*). Thank you. Good night.

The SECOND FLOOR HALLWAY: Cloakrooms are on the left, doorway to the large reception room further down. A man stands at the top of the stairs bowing to departing guests. He is PHILI VON RAMME. Phili is a tall blond man of forty in a German army officer's dress uniform. He wears a monocle and is very "English" in appearance, in the manner popular with pre-Hitler German officers. His face is handsome, aristocratic, but rather cold and bored. TECK is standing talking to DR. KLAUBER, a man of sixty with the benign appearance of an old-time country doctor—although he is actually a German-language newspaper publisher. He wears a fluffy white beard, and rather baggy dinner clothes. TECK wears white tie and tails. Both men talk as if they were merely killing time. People move past and around them. They are near Phili and are watching him.

TECK. I do not think I envy you, Dr. Klauber.

KLAUBER (*complacently—he has no accent*). Envy me? Of course not. Perhaps publishing a pro-Nazi paper in the United States isn't the best of all occupations. (*He makes a mild joke.*) There may be no future in it. But it pays.

As the last guests go, Phili turns to the balcony railing, and looks down. Klauber and Teck join him at the railing.

KLAUBER. Well, that should be enough of the hand-shaking. Are we ready?

PHILI (*looking at the people below, a little unpleasantly*). How many of them come here! Our Herr Hitler violates their morality in the morning, but by evening they have recovered and are here in the Embassy for dinner. And so it has gone, in most places in the world, for seven years.

The scene moves with him as he begins to move down the hall. The others walk with him.

PHILI (*continuing*). One might almost suspect their morality.

KLAUBER (*jovially*). That would be cynical. (*Teck laughs.*)

PHILI (*smiling*). I daresay.

Halfway down the hall Teck pauses to catch the attention of SAM CHANDLER, who is standing in a group of six or eight men, all of whom seem to be talking at once. Chandler is a big, opulent man of fifty, who looks like what he is—a successful promoter of dubious but profitable enterprises.

Teck makes small, rapid motions with his hands, as if dealing cards. Chandler gives no indication that he has seen the signal. Thereupon Teck goes on down the room, following Phili and Klauber.

Near the far end, OBERDORFF appears beside him. Oberdorff is a smallish man of thirty-four, completely colorless and non-committal. His rather large forehead and his rimless spectacles give him a slightly studious look, but otherwise his face is a pale blank mask. Oberdorff nods good evening, Teck nods back. They turn into a room immediately after Phili and Klauber.

The scene cuts to a SMALL ROOM in the EMBASSY as Teck and the others enter. A poker table is in the center of the floor. A man is sitting at the table playing solitaire. He is BLECHER, a swarthy man of thirty, built like a wrestler—barrel-chested and big hairy hands. His nose has been broken, there are ridges of scar-tissue above his little piggish eyes, and his close-shaven skull is ridged and dented. He wears a white shirt with a soft collar open at the neck, gray flannel slacks and white sneakers. There is nothing clownish about him. He is a complete savage but too sure of himself and the Nazi Party to be disturbed by either opposition or ridicule. He is phlegmatic, but not stupid; uneducated, but shrewd the harshness of his voice and the rudeness of his manners have an impersonal quality.

BLECHER (*looking up, contemptuously*). How was the tea-party?

All of the men begin to arrange themselves around the table. The servan comes to them, and leans down to find out what they wish to drink.

PHILI. It was a distinguished gathering. A tribute to the diplomacy of the Fatherland.

He sits down and as he speaks, the game begins. Oberdorff gets the high card, puts one deck in front of Phili for the cut, and then deals stud hands from it. Phili gathers up the other cards and shuffles them for the next dealer. The game goes on swiftly and expertly, with no talk about the cards or the bets. The players let their chips speak for them when betting, check by tapping the table, drop out by turning down their exposed cards, and show their hole-cards when called. Such conversation as takes place does not slow up the game and draws none of their attention away from it. They play very rapidly, as if anxious to get in as many hands as possible in their allotted time. Klauber goes into comparatively few pots, but usually wins when he does, and his stack of chips steadily grows. *Teck is losing*. The others win or lose moderately.

PHILI. Don't put it in your paper, Klauber, but His Excellency acts the host as if he were on a beer party in a cellar. He is a dull man.

BLECHER. Ribbentrop did not send him here to amuse people.

PHILI (*mockingly*). Then he is doing very well.

KLAUBER. In my paper he is all things to all men.

BLECHER (*to Klauber*). Tomorrow we will have a little talk about your paper—you and I.

KLAUBER. Gladly. The cost of everything rises—paper, ink, wages.

BLECHER. That is not what we will talk about.

Chandler is attentively observing this exchange between Blecher and Klauber.

PHILI (*to Chandler*). It is generally supposed that these "little talks" of . . . (*pouting*) . . . Blecher's are most instructive and unpleasant.

BLECHER. Baron von Ramme, too much may be generally supposed.

PHILI (*leaning forward a little to stare coldly at Blecher*). A threat, Butcher Boy?

BLECHER (*undisturbed by Phili's challenge, scornfully, but without heat*). Butcher Boy. That is funny, yes. We Nazis are always funny. And we have a funny Leader with a funny mustache. His name used to be Schickelgruber and he was a paperhanger. That, too, is funny, yes. And so we have divided the world into two parts. Those like you . . . (*indicating all three*) . . . who want to work for us or with us. And those others who lie awake trembling and hating us because they are afraid of us. Tell me, is not that also funny? (*After a pause*) No. I wouldn't threaten you, Phili. You could not be handled that way.

PHILI. With all your other duties you still have had time to make a study of me.

BLECHER. You are not complicated.

PHILI. No?

BLECHER. No. Aristocrat. Bred to government service—military or diplomatic. Contemptuous of us and our methods, but chiefly because we are not gentlemen. Would be satisfied enough doing the same things, or worse, under some dim-witted Hohenzollern. (*Smiling*) You are too cynical to be really dangerous, Baron von Ramme.

PHILI (*half-seriously*). Bravo! You make me ashamed of being so simple. Do Klauber for us.

BLECHER (*scowling a little*). Money. That is all. Nothing else. He becomes too expensive—but he will remedy that before it is too late.

KLAUBER (*undisturbed*). One makes a living.

PHILI. Mr. Chandler?

BLECHER. A man who wishes to sell us quantities of oil he has by some means come into control of. Later—and always—he will have other things to sell—They always do.

CHANDLER (*starting a weak protest*). Look here! I—

PHILI (*interrupting*). And Oberdorff?

BLECHER (*shaking his head*). Oberdorff I do not know. I have tried. A pale lump of a man. He sits. He observes. He says nothing. He writes no letters. He gets none. Perhaps he is of the secret police. Perhaps he's even writing a book. I do not give up, but I do not know.

PHILI (*pleased*). He may be a spy, an anti-Nazi.

BLECHER. I know nothing. His credentials are of the best.

PHILI. Herr Oberdorff, we must see more of one another. You have stumped Blecher—your credentials *are* of the best.

Oberdorff smiles briefly, seemingly uninterested in what is being said.

PHILI (*to Blecher*). Perhaps he is a member of the underground anti-Nazi movement. It would be very amusing.

KLAUBER (*giggling*). Perhaps he is even Max Freidank.

PHILI. No. Oberdorff isn't Max Freidank. I know Freidank.

KLAUBER (*playfully, as if he were quoting*). You know the legendary hero of the Underground Movement?

PHILI. He's no legend. We were in school together.

BLECHER. Yes. And you and he met, by accident, on a street in Prague in 1936. He had with him a man called Gotter.

PHILI (*to Oberdorff*). I admire you more and more. (*Oberdorff smiles. Then there is silence for a minute.*)

TECK. I feel slighted, Herr Blecher. You have not spoken of me.

BLECHER. Because it has not been necessary to consider you, Count de Brancovis. One knows, of course, the routine things: Roumanian, former diplomat . . . (*Blecher used the word "diplomat" with contempt and Teck laughs.*) . . . a gambler. Like Phili, an aristocrat who would rather be with his own class, but the career goes a little wrong—I do not know how, or why, but I make the guess. Also, I make the guess that you, like Mr. Chandler, are a man who sells things. But I would guess, also, that at the moment you are a man who has nothing to sell.

TECK (*unpleasantly*). I will call on you—when I have.

BLECHER. Good. That is why I am here.

The scene dissolves to a RAILROAD STATION LUNCH COUNTER. The Mullers sit with their backs turned at the counter in a row—Joshua, Babette, Sara, Kurt and then Bodo—facing a long mirror behind the counter. On the mirror are pasted breakfast menus—HAM & EGGS—25¢; CLUB BREAKFAST—40¢; BREAKFAST STEAK—35¢; HOT CAKES & SAUSAGE—20¢; etc. Reflected in the mirror are the faces of the Mullers and other breakfasters and the train behind them, while we hear the locomotive, baggage trucks, and other noises. Next to Bodo sits a husky boy of twenty in a pullover sweater with an "L" on it, finishing up a double orange juice and starting in on a bowl of hot cereal. The counterman puts in front of each of the Mullers a small plate holding two doughnuts. The children have milk, Kurt and Sara coffee. Kurt pays the counterman in silver, counting out the exact change.

BODO (*his mouth full*). Gwug awrm braw mawug, etc.

KURT (*teasing*). Speak in English, Bodo.

JOSHUA. Bodo has learned a new language. It is doughnutian.

BABETTE. Doughnuts are most delicious, Mama. Are they a characteristic American food?

SARA. Yes, Babby.

BODO (*having washed down his mouthful with milk*). I said I like foodstufferies which have to them a solidarity like these.

Bodo fills his mouth again. Babette and Joshua eat with as much enjoyment as he, though not so rapidly. The boy beside Bodo has finished his cereal. The counterman brings him ham and eggs, waffles with strawberry jam on them, and coffee.

JOSHUA (*as if asking an often-repeated question*). How long now is it before we will be in Washington?

SARA (*looking at the lunch counter clock*). Exactly two hours and five minutes, Joshua.

BABETTE (*to Sara*). When we are on the train again I shall brush your hair and you will be very pretty for our grandmother.

SARA (*smiling, putting up a hand to her hair*). Thank you, darling.

Bodo has finished his second doughnut and is staring intently at the boy beside him, who is eating his ham and eggs and waffles. Bodo's jaws move a little in unison with the boy's. Kurt looks at Bodo, smiles a little sadly, and puts his own second doughnut on Bodo's plate, then touches Bodo's shoulder and points to the doughnut. Bodo looks up at Kurt in protest. Kurt nods.

BODO (*grinning at him—then, softly—in German*). Thank you.

Bodo picks up the doughnut and begins to wolf it. The boy beside Bodo turns to look at him, then, still chewing, calls to the counterman.

BOY. Hey, Curly! Give me a couple of doughnuts too, will you?

The sound of the engine becomes louder. The reflection of a uniformed trainman appears in the mirror.

TRAINMAN. All aboard Washington train. All aboard!

The Mullers drink the last of their coffee and milk as they rise from the counter, and they begin to move quickly toward the door.

The scene dissolves to the PLATFORM BESIDE AN EMPTY TRACK IN WASHINGTON'S UNION STATION, where DAVID is looking at a watch, and impatiently looking down the track. This is not an important train. Nobody else has come through the gates to meet it. On the platform, beside David, there are two baggage trucks drawn by a motor and perhaps two red-caps.

We see the TRAIN coming into the station. As it comes in, David walks down the platform, watching passengers getting off, looking in car windows, turning his head to see if the Mullers have got off the train. Then he sees them, is not really sure it is they, and puts his hand tentatively in the air.

Next the MULLERS are seen alighting on the COACH STEPS, carrying bags, coats, and packages, as when we first saw them. Sara sees David, starts to smile and wave, but hesitates, her face frightened and shy.—A close view of DAVID shows him walking toward the Mullers, his face changing as if he were alternately saying to himself, "That can't be Sara," and "That must be Sara."—Then a close view of SARA shows her making up her mind, and she holds out her hands.

SARA. David!

The scene expands to include Kurt and the children as David comes to them.

DAVID (*smiling self-consciously*). Sara! (*He breaks off awkwardly but by this time they have clasped hands; his awkwardness leaves him and he calls out.*) Sara!

He puts his arms around her and kisses her. She clings to him, laughing and crying. The Muller children exchange smiles and nods, as if to say, "This is the way it should be."

DAVID (*softly*). It's been such a long, long time. I got to thinking it would never happen.

SARA (*excited*). David! David, darling! Isn't it strange? To see each other. . . . (*She turns awkwardly, clinging to David.*) This is Kurt.

DAVID (*holding out his hand*). I am happy to meet you, sir, and to have you here.

KURT. Thank you. Sara has told me so much of you for so many years.

SARA. And these are my children—Babette, Joshua, Bodo.

The three children range themselves in line to shake hands.

BODO. How do you do, Uncle David?

DAVID (*shaking hands with Bodo and Joshua*). How do you do? Boys can shake hands, but so pretty a girl must be kissed.

David kisses Babette, who smiles, very pleased, and moves over to adjust Sara's sash.

BABETTE. Thank you, sir.

David then puts a hand on Sara's arm and on Kurt's arm.

DAVID. And now you must come home very quickly or they'll have to tie Mama with ropes.

He motions to the porters. They pick up the bags. David, his arms around Sara and Kurt, starts down the platform. Joshua follows, then Babette and Bodo.

BODO (*to Babette*). To tie with a rope?

BABETTE. It is most probably an idiom of the language.

BODO. It sounds of interest.

BABETTE (*speaking from experience*). And it would be most wise for you not to make use of it until we find out what it means. You do not have to learn every language in the space of one day.

This dissolves to the FARRELLY HOUSE and LAWN as David's car draws up. Sara gets out first, and stands staring, her face still but intensely excited. As the others begin to get out, dragging bags, she suddenly starts to run. They turn and stare as the view follows her running over the lawn, onto the terrace and into the house.

We see the LIVING ROOM as Sara runs in from the terrace. She stands staring at the room, then slowly, closing her eyes, she begins to move around the room touching things, as if trying to find out how well she remembers. As she moves, David, Kurt and the children come through the doors carrying bags, coats, and packages. Kurt stands looking at Sara, smiling.

DAVID (*with good-natured exasperation*). Where is everybody? That's Mama! For days she's expected you every minute—though she knew when you were coming—and now that the time's here, she's off some place else.

Joshua puts the bag he carries in a corner, and moves the two David dropped over beside it. Babette puts her bundle on one of the bags and takes the coats Bodo is carrying and folds them before putting them on the bags. David goes over to the bell and rings.

DAVID (*heard calling*). Mama!

Kurt sits down slowly, obviously very tired. Joshua takes the briefcase from Kurt and puts it with the other things in the corner. David rings the bell impatiently again, then goes out of sight. Kurt and the children all watch Sara.

KURT (*softly*). I have always known you must have grown up in a lovely house like this.

She smiles and touches his hair, and moves away.

SARA (*to the children, but not looking at them*). Sit down. Be comfortable.

BABETTE (*pointing to the couch*). Is it allowed?

KURT (*smiling*). Yes, it is allowed.

JOSHUA (*softly—puzzled*). The door of the home was not locked. We just came in.

KURT. You'll find it curious there are people who live and do not need to watch, eh, Joshua?

JOSHUA. It is strange. But it must be good, I think.

KURT (*smiling*). Yes.

SARA (*very softly*). Isn't it a lovely house? I'd almost forgotten. (*Then she looks up at the portrait of Joshua Farrelly.*)

There is a closeup of the PORTRAIT of JOSHUA FARRELLY as Sara's voice is heard continuing:

SARA. That was my father when he was the famous Joshua Farrelly. We were very proud of him.

The MULLERS are then seen again as Sara smiles and turns to a table and picks up an old-fashioned photograph which she regards in her continued mood of remembrance.

SARA. And this was my grandmother.

And we see an OLD-FASHIONED PHOTO of a STATELY WOMAN in the costume of the 1890's as Sara is heard continuing.

SARA'S VOICE. She believed in nothing except William Jennings Bryan and sulphur and molasses.

A close view of SARA shows her putting down the photograph and the scene moves with her to the piano. She picks up another picture.

SARA (*reading*). "To Joshua and Fanny Farrelly. With admiration. Alfonso. May 7, 1910." (*Looking up from the photo—dreamily*) I had an ermine boa and a pink dress. Alfonso gave a great party at the palace and I had cakes and a glass of champagne. I was ten, I guess. (*She puts the picture down and moves over toward the French door.*) Later that day a dreadful thing happened. Somebody tried to shoot Alfonso. He was always getting shot at or bombed.

Next we see the GROUP consisting of KURT, BODO, JOSHUA and BABETTE.

BODO. *Certainement.*

BABETTE. Speak in English, please.

JOSHUA. Since when do you think it is right to shoot upon people?

BODO. Do not give me lessons. It is not right to shoot upon people. I know that. Nor is it right to grow fat on the poor people and give pictures of the face. Alfonso seemed always to give his photograph. That is a bad flag on a man.

We get a close view of SARA at the FRENCH DOOR, looking out.

SARA (*still remembering*). An ermine boa. (*Turning*) A boa is a scarf. I should like to have one for you, Babbie. Once in Prague I saw a pretty one. I wanted to buy it for you. But we had to pay our rent. (*She laughs.*) But I almost bought it.

KURT, BODO, JOSHUA and BABETTE are seen again.

BABETTE. Yes, Mama. Thank you.

SARA is looking around the room.

SARA (*softly*). Almost eighteen years—

BODO (*seen with the others*). You were born here, Mama?

SARA (*seen close*). Upstairs. (*Going to the door*) David and I used to have our own garden, across the pond. I like a garden. I've always hoped we'd have a home some day and settle down—(*Breaking off, smiling apologetically*) I am talking so foolishly. Sentimental. At my age. Gardens and ermine boas. I haven't wanted anything.

Kurt comes into view, and takes her hands.

KURT. This is a fine room, a fine place to be. Everything is so pleasant and full of comfort. This will be a good piano on which to play again. And it is all so clean. I like that. You must enjoy your house, Sara, and you shall not be a baby. You shall not be afraid you will hurt me because I have not given you a house like this. Yes?

SARA. Yes, of course. It's strange, that's all. We've never been together in a place like this.

KURT. That does not mean, and should not mean, that we do not remember how to enjoy what comes our way. We are on a holiday.

ANISE (*heard screaming at this point*). Miss Sara! Miss Sara!

The scene cuts to ANISE in the DOORWAY and moves with her as she hurries toward Sara.

ANISE. I would have known you. Yes, I would. I would have—(*Anise reaches Sara.*)

SARA (*softly*). Anise.

Both laugh happily. Sara kisses her. Anise, excited, bewildered, nervous, looks at Kurt as the view expands to include all the Mullers in the scene. The children rise.

ANISE (*to Kurt*). How do you do, sir? How do you do? (*To the children*) How do you do?

SARA (*very happy*). You look the same. I think you look the same. Just the way I've always remembered. (*To Kurt and the children*) This is the Anise I've told you so much about. She was here long before I was born.

ANISE (*nervous—rattled*). But Madame Fanny will have a fit. Where is she?

BODO (*conversationally*). You are French, Madame Anise?

ANISE. Yes. I am from the Bas Rhin. (*Looking at Kurt, bobbing her head idiotically*) Sara's husband. That's nice. That is nice.

BODO. Yes. Your accent is from the North. That is fine country. We were in hiding there once. (*At this Babette steps on Bodo's foot.*)

ANISE. Hiding! You were, er—

She breaks off as Fanny comes into view, and stands for a second in the doorway.

SARA (*softly*). Hello, Mama.

They quickly move toward each other. Fanny speaks softly.

FANNY. Sara . . . Sara, darling! You're here! You're really here! (*She takes Sara's arm, staring at her —and smiles.*) Welcome! . . . Welcome! Welcome to your house, Sara. (*Then, slowly*) You're not young, Sara.

SARA (*smiling*). No, Mama. I'm thirty-eight.

FANNY. Thirty-eight. Of course— (*Then quickly*) You look more like your Father now. That's good. The years have helped you. (*She turns to Kurt.*) Welcome to this house, sir.

KURT (*warmly*). Thank you, Madame.

Fanny looks at Sara again, and nervously pats her arm; nods, and turns back to Kurt—nervous and chatty.

FANNY. You are a good-looking man, for a German. I like a good-looking man. I always have.

KURT (*bowing*). And I like a good-looking woman. I always have.

BODO (*to Sara*). Ist das Grossmama?

FANNY. Yes. I am your Grandmother. Also, I speak German, so do not talk about me. I speak languages very well. But there is no longer anybody to speak with. Anise has half-forgotten her French. (*To Sara*) Oh, it's good to have you home again. I'm chattering away, I—

JOSHUA. Now you have us, Madame. We speak ignorantly, but fluently, in German, French, Italian, Spanish—

KURT. And sometimes boastfully in English.

BODO. There is never a need of boasting. If we are to fight for the good of all men, it is to be accepted that we must be among the most advanced.

ANISE (*amazed*). My goodness!

FANNY. Are these your *children*? Or are they dressed-up midgets?

SARA (*laughing*). These are my children, Mama. This, Babette. This, Joshua. This is Bodo.

Babette curtsies, and Joshua and Bodo bow. David comes into view.

FANNY (*to Joshua—approvingly*). You were named for your grandfather. (*She points to the portrait.*) You bear a great name.

JOSHUA (*politely but firmly*). Two great names. (*And he looks at Kurt.*) My last name is Muller. (*At this, David pats Joshua's shoulder approvingly.*)

FANNY (*turning to Babette*). You are a nice-looking girl. That's good. (*To Bodo*) You look like nobody.

BODO (*proudly*). I am not beautiful.

FANNY (*laughing*). Well, Sara, well. Three children. You have done well. (*To Kurt*) You, too, of course, sir. (*She looks more sharply at him.*) You do not look well.

KURT. It is only that I am a little tired. In a little while I will. . . .

FANNY. You look more than tired. We must take good care of you. (*At this, Kurt smiles, and sits down.*)

FANNY (*pointing to the picture over Kurt's head*). That was my Joshua. We were very much in love. Hard to believe of people nowadays, isn't it?

SARA. No. Kurt and I love each other.

FANNY. I daresay. But there are ways and ways—

SARA. How dare you, Mama . . . ?

DAVID (*laughing*). Ladies! Ladies!

SARA (*giggling*). I almost got mad then. You know, I don't think I've been mad since I last saw you.

BODO. You must not get angry. Anger is protest and should only be used for the good of one's fellow-men. That is correct, Papa?

FANNY (*peering down at him*). If you grow up to talk like that, and stay as ugly as you are, you are going to have one of those successful careers on the lecture platform.

JOSHUA. It is a great pleasure to hear Grandma talk with you.

ANISE (*beaming at the children*). I think I shall wash you . . . Come.

JOSHUA (*amazed*). Wash us? Do people wash each other?

SARA. No . . . but the washing good idea. Go along now and change your clothes, and then we'll all have a fine big lunch again. (*The children and Anise go out.*)

FANNY. Again? Don't you usually have a good lunch?

KURT (*smiling*). Only sometimes.

SARA (*lightly*). Oh, we do all right usually. (*Looking around very happily*) It's good to be here! I want to see everything, my old room and the lake—Haven't I fine children?

DAVID (*smiling down at her and putting an arm around her*). Very fine. You're lucky. I wish I had them.

FANNY. How could you? All the women you like are so draughty, if you know what I mean. I'm sure none of them could have children which is as God, in his wisdom would have it.

SARA (*laughing*). Mama hasn't changed. And that's good, too.

FANNY (*to Kurt*). I hope you'll like me.

KURT. I hope so.

FANNY. I have fine plans. I'm having the wing done over for you, walls taken out—

SARA (*quickly*). That's kind of you, Mama. But—but—we won't make any plans for a while. A good long vacation for Kurt and—

FANNY. Vacation? You're staying, of course. David is already seeing about schools for the children and Cyrus Penfield has promised to find an engineering post for Kurt.

KURT. I have not worked as an engineer since many years, Madame.

DAVID (*puzzled*). Haven't you? I thought—Didn't you work for Dornier?

KURT. Yes—before '33.

FANNY. But you must have worked in other places. A great many other places, I should say. Every letter of Sara's seemed to have a new postmark.

KURT (*smiling*). We moved most often.

DAVID. You gave up engineering?

KURT. I gave it up? (*He nods.*) One could say it that way.

FANNY (*bluntly*). What do you do?

SARA. Mama, we—

KURT. It is difficult to explain.

DAVID (*uncomfortably*). If you'd rather not.

FANNY (*to David*). No. I'm trying to find out something. (*To Kurt*) May I ask it right out?

KURT. Let me help you, Madame. You wish to know whether or not being an engineer buys adequate lunches for my family. It does not. I have no wish to make a mystery of what I have been doing. It is only that it is awkward to place neatly. It sounds so big. It is so small. (*He smiles, and motions with his hand.*) I am an anti-Fascist. And—to answer your question—that does not pay well.

FANNY. But we're all anti-Fascists!

SARA. Yes, but Kurt works at it.

FANNY. What *kind* of work?

KURT (*simply*). Any kind. Anywhere.

FANNY (*displeased*). I will stop asking questions.

SARA (*sharply*). That would be sensible.

DAVID (*to Sara*). Darling, don't be angry. We've been worried about you, naturally. We knew so little except that you were having a hard time.

SARA. I didn't have a hard time. We never . . .

KURT. Do not lie for me, Sara.

SARA. I'm not lying. I didn't have a hard time—the way they mean—not ever. (*To Fanny*) For almost twelve years Kurt went to work every morning and came home to me every night and we lived modestly and happily. (*Sharply*) As happily as people could live in a starved Germany that was going to pieces.

KURT. Sara, please. I do not like you to be angry. Let me try to find a way to tell it with quickness. Yes. (*Sara starts to speak, but stops.*)

KURT (*to Fanny*). I was born in a town called Furth. There is a holiday in my town. We call it Kirchweih. It was a gay holiday with games and music and hot white sausage to eat with the wine. I grow up, I move away—to school, to work. I get married—but always I come back for Kirchweih. It is for me the great day of the year. (*Slowly*) But after the war—the first world war—that day begins to change. The sausage begins to be made of bad stuff. The country people come in without shoes. The children are too sick—(*Carefully*) It is bad for my people, those years. But always I have hope. In the festival of August, 1931, more than a year before the Nazi storm, I am taught that hope by itself is not enough. On that day I see twenty-seven men murdered in a Nazi street fight. I cannot longer just only look on. My time has come to do more. I say with the great Luther, "I must make my stand. I can do nothing else. God help me. Amen."

SARA (*after a slight pause—slowly*). We had seen the evil coming, every day more and more—but that festival was the symbol of the end. It hit Kurt hard—(*She stops, less tensely, sadly.*) It doesn't pay in money to fight for what we believe in. But I wanted it the way Kurt wanted it. I always will. (*She shrugs.*) Kurt is not very well. There aren't many parts of Europe any more where he could—could rest. You've always said you wanted us. So Kurt brought us home. If you don't want us, we will understand.

DAVID (*angrily*). We want you very much . . . Forever, or however long *you* want.

FANNY. I am old and made of dry cork. And bad-mannered. Forgive me.

SARA (*going quickly to Fanny*). Be still, Mama. We're all being foolish. (*She kisses her.*) And I only want to be foolishly happy. (*She turns to David.*) Is our old garden still there?

DAVID (*shaking his head*). But we've made the pond larger, and put blackberries on the island.

SARA. Let's—(*She breaks off, and looks at Kurt.*)

KURT. Go on. (*To Fanny*) You are a kind woman, Madame.

The scene moves with David as he goes toward the French door with Sara.

DAVID. That's what she's always said.

FANNY (*as David and Sara go out*). I have disrespectful children.

Looking after David and Sara, her face softens. Unconsciously she puts a hand on Kurt's arm.

FANNY. My children are together again. That makes me feel good . . . Come now. You shall have a rest before lunch. And I shall send you up a sherry and some biscuits and perhaps an eggnog, too. I'm a great believer in eggnogs if they have enough liquor in them. . . .

The scene moves with them as they begin to go out of the room. And just then TECK comes in from the hall.

TECK (*warmly*). How do you do?

FANNY. This is the Count de Brancovis. He and his wife are staying with us for a while. This is my son-in-law, Kurt Muller.

KURT (*as they bow to each other*). How do you do?

TECK. Would it be impertinent for one European to make welcome another?

KURT. Thank you, sir.

TECK. Have we met before, Mr. Muller? Did you live in Paris? I was in the legation there and I think, perhaps. . . .

KURT. No—We have not met before. (*He smiles.*) If it is possible to believe, I am the exile who is not famous.

TECK. Strange. I have a feeling— (*He smiles.*) It is interesting. I have always had a good ear for the accents of your country, but yours is most difficult to place. Is it South German or. . . . ?

KURT (*a little slowly*). It is difficult to place my accent, Count de Brancovis, because I speak other languages. Yours would be Roumanian?

FANNY (*interested*). Goodness! Is it that bad?

At this Fanny takes Kurt's arm, and begins to move him up the stairs.

FANNY (*to Teck as they move up the stairs*). My grandchildren are charming. You will see them at lunch.

Teck is watching Kurt, who holds to the banister as he moves up the stairs.

TECK (*to Fanny*). Your grandchildren would have to be charming.

Fanny turns her head, and nods approval at this excellent sense.

FANNY. Of course.

The UPSTAIRS BATHROOM: Joshua is under the shower. Bodo, naked except for a towel around his hips, is examining the contents of a medicine cabinet. He picks up a bottle. At close view, it is seen to be labeled:

MILORD
AFTER SHAVING LOTION

A close view of BODO shows him considering the bottle for a moment, pouring lotion on his hands and patting it barber-fashion on his cheeks, chin and throat, then looking approvingly at himself in the mirror. He turns quickly toward the door. Then at the OPEN BATHROOM DOOR we see FANNY and KURT standing there, but they do not come into the room. Bodo comes out, facing them.

BODO (*with feeling*). Papa, this is a house of great wonders. Each has his bed. Each has his bathroom. The arrangement of it, that is splendorous.

FANNY (*laughing*). You are a fancy talker, Bodo.

JOSHUA (*sticking his head out from the shower*). Oh, yes . . . In many languages.

BODO (*gravely—to Fanny*). Please to correct me when I am wrong. (*To Kurt*) Papa, the plumbing is such as you have never seen. (*Turning to point*) Here each implement is placed on the floor, and are all simultaneous in the same room. You will therefore see that being placed solidly on the floor allow of no rats, rodents or crawlers, and is most sanitary. (*To Fanny*) Papa likes to know how each thing is put together. And he is so fond of being clean.

KURT (*to Fanny*). I am a hero to my children. It bores everybody but me. (*To Bodo*) It is a fine bathroom. Better than Brussels, eh?

BODO (*seriously*). Trapping the mice there was most interesting.

FANNY. Goodness! (*To Kurt*) And now you shall rest before your lunch.

In the DRAWING ROOM, TECK is sitting on the arm of a chair watching Joseph pick up two of the suitcases and some coats. Joseph disappears as Marthe comes in from the terrace. Then there is a close view of MARTHE and TECK.

MARTHE. I hear they've arrived. Have you met them?

TECK. What has David told you about Herr Muller? (*He gets up, moves to the baggage, and stands staring at it.*)

MARTHE. What has David told me? Nothing more than he's told you. What is there to tell?

TECK. I do not know. But I would like to. David said they had been in Czechoslovakia, Denmark, Poland, France and Switzerland. These are all countries that Germany has either gone into or threatens. It is the German practice to send into such countries men to prepare the way. I had thought Herr Muller might be such a man. I do not think so now.

He has leaned down and pressed the lock of one of the valises. It opens. He closes it again. Then he picks up the briefcase.

MARTHE. What are you doing?

TECK. Wondering why luggage is unlocked and a shabby briefcase is so carefully locked.

MARTHE. You're very curious about Mr. Muller.

TECK. I am curious about a daughter of the Farrellys who marries a German who has bullet scars on his face and broken bones in his hands.

MARTHE (*as she sees him put down the briefcase*). Is he any business of yours?

TECK. Anything might be my business now.

MARTHE. Yes, unfortunately.

TECK. You sound bitter about me, Marthe. Are you in love with David?

MARTHE. What kind of talk is this. . . . ?

TECK. Answer me.

MARTHE (*tensely*). I like him.

TECK. Yes . . . And he likes you. (*After a second—sharply*) Please find out from him about Herr Muller.

MARTHE (*angrily*). I will certainly do no such thing. Ask your friends at the Embassy. They always know their nationals.

TECK. Yes. But I do not like to ask questions without knowing the value of the answers.

MARTHE (*coming to him—tense and frightened*). Teck! (*She points to the baggage.*) Let these people alone. They've evidently had a tough enough time. I won't let you interfere.

TECK. You won't *let* me interfere—? You are in love with David. Well, do not make any plans, Marthe. You will go with me when I am ready to go.

He takes her arm, as she is about to speak and presses it tightly. Joseph comes back in to pick up the rest of the luggage. Teck goes out on the terrace, Marthe stands as she is, Joseph picks up the luggage and moves off.

A close view of KURT in the BEDROOM: He is standing at the open French windows of his charming bedroom. He is in his shirt sleeves, looking down at the lawn. This cuts to the LAWN, as seen from Kurt's angle, and we see what he sees: In the distance Sara and David, their arms around each other, are coming toward the house. After a second, Teck also appears, walking down the lawn. Then we again see KURT standing in the FRENCH WINDOWS. He stares at Teck and sighs very slightly, as the scene fades out.

PART THREE

A SMALL SEWING ROOM fades in. There is a sewing machine, a form, triple mirror, etc. Sara has her back to the mirror. Her hair is very well arranged. Anise is standing before her, pinning the hem of a very acceptable, plain dress. She rises, repins the waist, goes to the other side, unpins the waist, and alters the line.

ANISE. I could not see you eat another dinner in that dress you have been attiring yourself in. I am a woman of the most immaculate morality but I say there are clothes that are no better than nakedness. I am beginning to talk like your son.

SARA (*laughing*). It is the only dress I have.

ANISE (*pointing to the dress she is pinning*). This will do very well for a few days. Until the good clothes arrive.

SARA. What do you mean, until the good clothes arrive?

Anise shakes her head, stands aside to look at the dress, and nods with admiration.

ANISE. No. I cannot tell you about the new clothes. I have given my word.

Sara looks at her and says nothing. Anise goes back to the pinning. When Sara does not urge her, she can no longer stand it.

ANISE. Very well. Since you are so anxious to know, I take back my words. (*Very importantly*) On Saturday, Madame Fanny and I arrive at Savitt's. Before that I have taken all measurements in secret. First, Madame Fanny delivers a most sharp ultimatum that all must be finished in a week . . .

SARA. Savitt's? *What* must be finished in a week?

ANISE. Clothes . . . For all of you. In an amount you have not previously considered. Dresses, suits, summer clothes, stockings—all must be done with the hand sewing . . .

SARA (*softly—very touched*). How nice of Mama! How very, very nice . . .

Fanny appears in the open door, followed by Joshua, who is carrying a stack of small notebooks.

FANNY. What is so nice of Mama?

ANISE (*softly, but sharply to Sara*). You are to say nothing. I gave my word.

SARA (*laughing*). Everything is nice of Mama. Mama is a great darling.

FANNY. Certainly. (*She points to the books Joshua is carrying.*) We've been in the attic looking over old books. You know, I find that Joshua is an educated boy. Your father would have liked that. (*She sees the dress and hair arrangement.*) Goodness! You *are* a handsome woman, Sara. Where did the dress come from?

ANISE. From me. I make it.

SARA (*smiling—to Anise*). Remember when I was a little girl and you taught me to sew? It came in handy, years later. (*Proudly*) Often when Kurt—when Kurt had to be away for a long time—I made dresses and earned enough to pay the rent and the food and send the children to school. . . .

Anise has been staring at Sara. Fanny speaks slowly, carefully.

FANNY. You sewed for a living? (*Then sharply*) Really, Sara. Were these things necessary? Why couldn't you have written to us and told us . . . ?

SARA (*laughing—but a little tartly*). Mama, you've asked me that twenty times in the four days we've been here.

JOSHUA (*gently*). I think it is only that Grandma feels sorry for us. Grandma has not seen much of the world and she does not understand that a great many work most hard in order that they eat.

FANNY. Come along. Don't you start giving me lectures. I get enough from Bodo.

Fanny and Joshua turn and start down the hall.—We then see the HALL outside the door to the sewing room as Anise comes quickly to Fanny, outside the door, and beyond Sara's hearing.

ANISE (*in a stage whisper*). Ask Herr Muller to come up here.

Fanny stops, but Joshua continues down the hall and goes out of sight.

FANNY. Why?

ANISE (*in a whispered half-shriek of impatience*). Why? Why? Because he is a man in love with his wife and because his wife looks most beautiful. You are getting so old you no longer understand matters of delicacy between the men and the women.

As Fanny giggles, the scene dissolves to a closeup of SARA in the SEWING ROOM looking at herself in the mirror. Anise is standing proudly by. After a second, Sara puts out her hand and touches her reflection in the mirror.

SARA (*softly*). Me! I had forgotten.

As tears come into her eyes, the scene expands including the door: KURT is in the doorway and stands watching her, spellbound.

KURT. *Liebe Sara!* You are beautiful! (*His face clouds—softly.*) How many years have I kept you from looking like that. It makes you have tears. It also makes me have tears.

As Anise, delighted with the whole affair, goes out, shutting the door, KURT and SARA are seen closer.

SARA (*putting a hand to the neck of her gown; genuinely angry*). If you say that, I'll tear it off!

KURT. No, no. Then I do not say it. (*He goes to her.*) I do not think it. I think only with pride how beautiful is my Sara.

Kurt puts his arms around her, jerks one hand away, then puts it back elsewhere.

SARA (*laughing*). Anise has put me together with pins. I'm a porcupine

KURT (*holding her*). If you had not married me so many years ago, would you have married me today? I am so tired and so shabby and you are so. . . .

SARA (*softly*). I would have married you any day in my life.

As he leans down to kiss her, with great feeling, the scene dissolves to JOSHUA standing on a LAWN; he wears a torn first-baseman's mitt on his left hand. The view moves with him as he runs headlong to one side. His face is desperately earnest. He stops a grounder with the mitt, quickly picks up the ball and throws it.

JOSHUA. Was not that better, Doc?

We see DOC in the FIELD as he holds a baseball bat in his right hand. With his bare left hand he nonchalantly catches the ball Joshua throws him.

DOC. Sure. You're doing first-rate. Just take it easy and don't fight with the ball.

We see BODO and ANISE in the FIELD. They are sitting not far from the baseball players, in a section of the lawn where there are benches, tables, an umbrella, etc. Bodo is lying on the ground, working on a mangled, ripped-apart electric pad. Anise is sitting on a bench, sewing.

BODO (*looking at the bag*). It is most remarkable . . . the scientific advances that man has made! How much did this heating pad cost you?

ANISE. It cost me ten dollars and you have made a ruin of it.

BODO. That is not as yet completely true. Now as I was wishing to point out to you: man has learned to make man comfortable. Comfort and plenty exist. Yet all cannot have them. Why?

ANISE. How do I know? It has worried many people. Why?

Bodo takes a deep breath and raises his finger as if about to lecture.

BODO. Why? (*He considers a minute, then deflates himself.*) I am not as yet sure.

ANISE. I thought not.

Bodo looks up to see Kurt. Kurt is in his shirt sleeves and is pushing an electric lawn mower.

KURT (*to Bodo*). What are you doing?

BODO. What are *you* doing?

KURT. I am the new assistant farmer and I like it.

BODO. Well, I am repairing an elderly electric pad for Miss Anise.

ANISE (*angrily*). He has made a pudding of it.

BODO. I am confused about it. Something has gone wrong with the principle on which I have been working. It is probably I will ask your assistance.

Kurt, in cutting the grass, pushes the lawn mower a little too close to Bodo.

KURT. Thank you, whenever you are ready.

There is a long view of DOC and JOSHUA: Doc's back is turned, and Joshua is facing him some sixty or seventy yards away. Doc tosses the ball in the air and hits a looping fly to Joshua. A close view of JOSHUA shows him catching the ball, and his face lights up with satisfaction.

BODO (*seen close, as he watches this*). Baseball players are among the most exploited people in this country. I read about it.

We see JOSHUA watching him.

JOSHUA (*to Bodo*). Sometimes I think you never should have learned to read.

Next DAVID and SARA are seen in a BOAT on the lake. The boat is a small flat-bottomed one, which David propels by sculling with a single oar. The pond covers some three or four acres, with a small, flat bushy island near the center.

SARA (*laughing*). With Mama, what you need is not to be afraid of making a fool of yourself. Anything she doesn't like she makes seem silly.

DAVID (*smiling*). Yes. And it's worked for a good many years. She thinks of me only as a monument to Papa—and a not very well-made monument at that.

SARA. Yes. And since you're worth a good deal on your own, do what you want and—(*turning to look at Marthe on shore*)—Marthe's a nice girl, I think. Kurt thinks so, too, and Kurt is smart about people.

DAVID (*nodding—very pleased*). You are very much in love with Kurt.

SARA. Oh, yes. I've been a happy woman. (*Suddenly*) David, Kurt is a sick man. Sicker than he knows. The wound he got in Spain has never healed right and then again—about six months ago—over there—(*as if she were changing the subject*)—he's better—even this week here has done him good, but he'll never be able to go back and do the kind of work—

DAVID. You know, darling, I don't think I understand what kind of work he was doing.

Sara looks away, then looks again at David.

SARA. How long has Marthe been married to the Count?

DAVID. I don't know. When she was very young.

SARA (*shaking her head—then laughing*). You know, the Count de Brancovis scares me a little.

They have now reached shore—beyond Babette and Marthe—who are lying on the grass at the edge of the water. Babette has been gathering flowers, is finishing a bouquet. David is pulling up the boat.

DAVID and SARA appear on the SHORE with MARTHE and BABETTE in the background.

DAVID. *Scares* you?

Sara looks at him as he hands her out. She pats his shoulder.

SARA. You, Mama—(*moving her hand*)—most people here, I guess. ... You don't know what it is to be frightened. Unfortunately, I think you will have to learn. (*She calls to Babette.*) Come, darling.

Babette and Marthe rise, and we see the GROUP with BABETTE and SARA in the foreground. Babette turns to look at David and Marthe, who are walking behind her and Sara.

BABETTE (*to David*). Uncle David, have invited the Countess Marthe to join our sightseeing trip. I hope you will find that agreeable?

DAVID. Very, very agreeable.

He smiles at Marthe. She looks very happy. He takes her arm.

SARA (*looking down, smiling at Babette—softly*). You're a wise girl, Babbie.

BABETTE (*too innocently*). Am I, Mama?

The scene dissolves to a view of THE WHITE HOUSE from the street, with DAVID, MARTHE and the CHILDREN.

(NOTE: In this series of short shots David and Marthe are placed closer together physically in successive scenes.)

BABETTE. It is the most beautiful house I have ever seen.

This dissolves to a view of the TREASURY BUILDING, with the group looking at it.

BODO (*muttering*). Dinosaur diplodocus. I shall go back to the National Museum and see it again. It is as big as ten horses.

The MAIN ENTRANCE of the SUPREME COURT BUILDING appears next. The group is looking up at the pediment.

DAVID. This is the Supreme Court.

There is a closeup of the CARVED INSCRIPTION: "EQUAL JUSTICE UNDER LAW," followed by a closeup of the GROUP.

BODO. That is a fine saying.

JOSHUA. I am certain they will be glad to have your approval.

BABETTE. This is where you work, Uncle David?

DAVID. No, but thank you, Babbie.

This dissolves to the LINCOLN MEMORIAL, then the WASHINGTON MONUMENT as David, Marthe and the children go in, then to the TOP of the MONUMENT, with the children appearing at the windows, following which we see WASHINGTON and the vicinity as seen from the monument. Babette's and David's voices are heard over this scene.

BABETTE. Where is our house?

DAVID. See where that road bends away from the river through the trees? Back of that.

We see the DISTANT ROAD and then a large old-fashioned BUTLER'S PANTRY as Fanny is sitting at a kitchen table looking at silver, knives, forks, and dishes. Anise is standing next to her. Joseph is standing over the table, looking down at Fanny.

JOSEPH. But, Miss Fanny, you know I always been a good silver cleaner.

FANNY. You're getting out of practice.

ANISE. I have given it careful thought. Miss Sara is better looking. Don't you think so, Joseph? Don't you think Miss Sara is better looking than Miss Fanny?

FANNY (*very irritated—to Joseph—pointing to some of the table service he has put in front of her*). You call that good cleaning? (*Joseph starts to agree with Anise, but quickly changes his mind.*) That silver's lasted for two hundred years and it's going to last for two hundred more.

JOSEPH. Not the way you treat it, Miss Fanny. Sometimes *you* scratch it. I watch you at the table and I say to myself there's Miss Fanny doing it to the knife again. . . .

FANNY (*screaming*). I was using a knife and fork before you arrived to teach me how.

JOSEPH. You told me the next time you screamed at me, I should remind you to ask my pardon.

FANNY. You call that screaming?

JOSEPH. Yes'm.

FANNY. Very well. . . . I ask your pardon.

TECK appears in the pantry door. He is in street clothes, as if he had just come in.

TECK. Oh . . . It's very warm in Washington today. You will forgive us, Madame Fanny. We are dining in town tonight.

FANNY (*too warmly*). I will forgive you.

TECK. Have you seen Marthe?

FANNY. She went on the sightseeing trip. . . . With the children . . . (*an almost imperceptible pause*) . . . and David.

TECK (*looking at her*). Ah . . . Well, I daresay she'll be back in plenty of time to dress for dinner.

FANNY. I hope so.

She does not look at him. He looks at her for a minute. Then the view follows him as he moves out of the pantry, and this dissolves to a view of TECK as he comes up the stairs. He is thinking and as he passes the hall window, he stops.

Through the WINDOW, from Teck's angle, in the distance we see Sara, Kurt, Horace and Doc. Kurt, Horace and Doc are spraying trees. Sara is kneeling on the ground tying bushes. TECK watches them for a second, then, as if he had made up his mind, he goes quickly down the hall, and into Sara's and Kurt's room.

SARA's and KURT's ROOM as Teck enters: He looks around and begins to open drawers. He is quick and efficient, but unworried. When he comes to the third drawer, he finds that it contains handkerchiefs, stockings, hairpins, etc. He moves them aside. Under them is the briefcase. He picks it up and tries the lock. Unable to open it, he goes to work with hairpins and a small blade of a penknife. He opens the case flat on the dresser, and bends over it to look at its contents.

A closeup of the BRIEFCASE shows its contents: a package, tied carefully, with rubber bands; a Luger pistol, passports, a wadded silk handkerchief.

There is a closeup of TECK as he looks at the pistol, goes through the passports—which are for Sara and the children, none for Kurt—and opens the handkerchief. In it is a gold signet ring that has been roughly mashed flat. On it are the initials M.F. Teck looks thoughtfully at the mashed ring and rewraps it. Then he begins to undo the package. In it is a large amount of money in large bills. He stares at it. Then quickly runs through it. When it has been counted, he rewraps it, puts everything back, shuts the briefcase and tries to lock it and cannot. He shrugs, returns it to the drawer, covers it as it was before, then he leaves the room.

We follow TECK as he goes down the hall and into his own room, and then see him in his ROOM as he enters. On a small table there is a phone. He dials, waits.

TECK (*into the phone*). The Baron von Ramme, please. The Count de Brancovis is calling him. (*After a pause*) Phili? . . . How are you? . . . Last week in the poker game you mentioned a man called Freidank ... Max ... wasn't that his name?

A closeup of PHILI at the PHONE:

PHILI. Yes . . . Max Freidank.

A closeup of TECK at the PHONE:

TECK. I think you said you went to school with him. . . . What does he look like?

A closeup of PHILI at the PHONE:

PHILI (*very softly*). That is not my department. *That* I have not as yet reached. Blecher, the bloody butcher boy, is perhaps your man. (*With bitterness*) If you're up to what I think you are, you're wasting your time. Max Freidank—more dead than alive from bullet wounds—was arrested in Frankfort a few days ago. It is in the Washington papers this afternoon. (*Nastily*) You've come a long way, haven't you, Teck? (*He hangs up the phone.*)

A closeup of TECK at the PHONE:

TECK. Hello! . . . I . . . Hello! . . . (*He puts down the phone, and scowls at it.*)

This dissolves to the DRIVEWAY as David's car drives up. Marthe, David and the children climb out of David's car. It is now late afternoon, about 6:30, and the light is dimming. The children have happy, excited faces as they come toward the house. David takes Marthe's arm as they come up the walk. They are intimate, happy people.

There is a close view of TECK at the WINDOW. He has on dinner clothes and is fixing his tie. He stands watching Marthe and David with great interest. We see the DRIVEWAY and the GROUP, seen from Teck's angle, Teck in the foreground. In the FARRELLY LIVING ROOM, FANNY in dinner clothes, is fixing a cribbage board. In the HALL of the FARRELLY HOME, ANISE carrying a tray of liquor, siphons, etc., is on her way into the living room. The children come into the hall.

BABETTE. We had a splendid time.

ANISE. It is time for you to clean and dress for dinner. Clean well. You have on you the dirt of Washington.

JOSHUA (*as he runs up the steps laughing*). That sounds most unpleasant, Anise.

FANNY (*coming into the hallway, calling up to them*). I'll come with you the next time. It's shocking how ignorant I am about Washington.

BODO. I will conduct you on the tour, Grandma. One need not be ashamed of ignorance unless it is unaccompanied by a wish to learn.

JOSHUA (*irritated*). Oh, come along.

Fanny laughs.

SARA and KURT'S ROOM: Kurt is in his shirt sleeves brushing his hair. He picks up his coat, puts it on, and calls into the bathroom.

KURT. Shall I wait for you, Sara?

Sara, her hair down, in a silk slip, appears from the bathroom.

SARA. No . . . go along downstairs. I find I'm becoming very vain and it takes me a long time to dress. Each night, now, I wait for you to tell me if I look nice.

He smiles, and goes toward the door. Then the scene dissolves to the FARRELLY LIVING ROOM as Kurt enters. Fanny and Teck are playing cribbage. On the table behind them is an afternoon paper. Anise is sitting in a chair. She rises to make Kurt a drink.

FANNY (*playing a card*). One.

Kurt goes to the piano, and begins to look through the music. Anise brings him a whiskey and soda, and places it near him.

ANISE (*as she moves*). All day the discussion has been raging. You shall settle it, Herr Muller—who is the better looking? Miss Sara or Madame Fanny—many years away, of course?

FANNY. I don't consider him an impartial judge.

KURT (*laughing*). Both are of a great beauty. I am not a man who walks himself into trouble.

TECK (*casually playing*). No . . . I should not think you were.

ANISE. It is a belief of mine that the disposition shows in the face. Miss Sara's is like the angels. But Mr. Joshua used to say Madame Fanny was a woman of most peculiar disposition.

FANNY. What are you talking about? He never said any such thing.

ANISE (*delighted she has annoyed Fanny*). Well, I remember it. (*To Teck and Kurt; Kurt has begun to play the piano very softly.*) Once a large ball was given here in honor of an English beauty whose name— (*She stops a second to think.*)

FANNY. Oh, do stop chattering.

ANISE. Mr. Joshua, as was fit, had *two* waltzes with the English beauty. Immediately Miss Fanny was seized with a great illness and retired to her bed for a week. She would lie up there, claiming severe pains in the body, and stealing candy from herself.

FANNY. How you invent!

ANISE. Do not call to me that I am a liar. Every time Mr. Joshua would rest himself for a minute, a scream would dismantle the house. It was revolting. And now that the years have passed, I may disclose to you that Mr. Joshua knew you were going through the play acting.

FANNY (*rising*). He did not! You are. . . .

ANISE. Once he said to me, "Anise, it is well that I am in love. This is of a great strain. Her great-uncle Freddie was not right in the head, neither."

FANNY (*screaming*). You are a liar A woman of . . .

TECK (*amused*). I find you both mos charming. You are like children.

KURT (*laughing*). You are insultin; my children.

Fanny turns to look at him. Then wha he has said amuses her and she giggle: Then she turns to find Anise sailin; from the room, very angry.

FANNY. All right. I beg your pardor

Anise stops, then turns, most graciously

ANISE. I accept your apology. Sea yourself.

Graciously, in high good humor, sh leaves the room. She stops at the doo

ANISE. It would be of a great foolisl ness to deny that you were han« some. (*Teck and Kurt laugh.*)

A close view of SARA in the BEDROO* She has finished arranging her ha rises from the dressing table, goes the drawer in the bureau that contai* the briefcase, takes a handkerchief, few hairpins, and in the movemen* sees the briefcase. She stares at it, fin it unlocked, then slowly, her face frightened but calm, she takes it out and immediately opens the packet of money.

The LIVING ROOM with FANNY, KURT and TECK: David is now in the room and is mixing himself a drink. Fanny and Teck are still at the cribbage board, Kurt still at the piano.

FANNY. Mellie Sewell called this afternoon.

DAVID (*sharply*). With more gossip? (*To Kurt*) Mrs. Sewell brings Mama all the news of Washington. She gets it all wrong but that doesn't worry either Mama or her. Mama fixes it, wits it up, Papa used to say. . . .

FANNY. Certainly. I sharpen it a little. Mellie has no sense of humor. (*To Teck*) Did you know the old Baron Ramme? (*Kurt looks up at the name.*)

TECK (*nodding*). He was stationed in Paris when I was there.

FANNY. Of course. I always forget you were a diplomat.

TECK. It is just as well.

FANNY. There's something insane about a Roumanian diplomat. Pure insane. Well, I could have married old Baron von Ramme. Any American, not crippled, whose father had money. . . . He was crazy about me. Most men were in those days. Anyway, later when he was ambassador and had married the rich and hideous Calloway girl, somebody asked me if I didn't regret not marrying him. I said I regret it every day and I am happy about it every night. You understand what I meant by *night?* Styles in wit change so.

DAVID (*as Teck and Kurt laugh*). We understood.

Fanny and Teck go back to playing cribbage as Sara comes into the room. Sara goes swiftly to Kurt, and sits with him.

A close view of KURT and SARA seated at the piano:

SARA (*very softly*). The briefcase has been opened.

His fingers trail off the piano. To cover the interruption in sound, she begins to play.

SARA. There's no money missing, but the case has been examined—the gun was put back in a different place.

After a second, in which he sighs, he nods at Teck's back. She nods. Then he takes her hand, holds it for a second, and nods as if to say he is all right. Then he motions to the couch. She rises, and moves toward it. Then we get a larger scene, including FANNY, TECK and DAVID.

FANNY. Oh. . . . As I was saying. Mellie Sewell told me that you were playing in a large gambling game at the German Embassy with the *young* Phili von Ramme and with Sam Chandler, who is related to me and has always been a scandal.

There is a pause. Kurt very suddenly stops playing; Sara looks down at her hands as if she were trying not to look at Kurt.

DAVID. Nazis and Sam Chandler must make an unpleasant game.

TECK. I do not gamble to be amused.

FANNY (*sharply*). No? Well, then we'll certainly stop. I owe you eight dollars and fifty cents.

TECK (*getting up, turning to Kurt*). The young Baron von Ramme, Herr Muller, was your government military attaché in Spain.

KURT. My government attaché? He was the *German* government attaché. (*Carefully*) He was not attached to the side on which I fought.

TECK. I thought you might have known him.

SARA. We do not "know" Nazis, Count de Brancovis.

TECK. No? I should have known that. (*As if he had not heard her—smiling*) You are people who have lived close to the borders of Germany. You, therefore, must have had hopes that National Socialism would be overthrown on every tomorrow.

SARA. We have not given up that hope. Have you?

TECK. I never had it.

SARA. Then it must be most difficult for you to sleep.

Fanny and David have been listening. For the last minute Kurt has again been softly playing the piano. She turns to him.

FANNY (*to Kurt*). What is that?

TECK. It was a German Soldiers' song. They sang it as they straggled back in '18. I remember hearing it in Berlin. Were you there then, Herr Muller?

KURT. I was not in Berlin.

TECK. But you were in the war, of course?

KURT. Yes, I was in the war.

FANNY. You didn't think then we'd live to see another war.

SARA. Many of us were afraid we would. (*Sadly*) All of us have not been so isolated as you seem to have been in this house.

DAVID (*quickly—to Kurt*). What are the words?

A closeup of KURT at the PIANO:

KURT. This is what you heard in 1918, in Berlin. (*He begins to sing.*)
Wir zieh'n Heim, wir zieh'n Heim,
Mancher kommt nicht mit,
Mancher ging verschütt',
Aber Freunde sind wir stets.
   (*Then in English*)
We come home. We come home.
Some of us are gone, and some of us are lost, but we are friends;
Our blood is on the earth together.
Some day. Some day we shall meet again.
Farewell.
(*To Teck*) At six o'clock on the morning of November 7th, 1936, eighteen years later, five hundred of us Germans were walking through Madrid streets on our way to fight the fascist swine along the Manzanares River. We felt good that morning. You know how it is to feel you are good when it is needed to be good? We were like that. So we had need of new words to say that to ourselves. I translate with awkwardness, you understand. (*He turns back to the piano, sings and plays.*)
And so we have met again.
The blood did not have time to dry.
We lived to stand and fight again
This time we fight for people.
This time the—
   (*loud notes—indicating he is leaving out a word*)
—will keep their hands away.
Those who sell the blood of other men, this time,
They keep their hands away.

For us to stand.
For us to fight.
This time, no farewell, no farewell.
(*He stops playing and is silent for a moment.*) We did not win. (*He looks up, gently.*) It would have been a different world if we had.

The scene expands.

TECK (*after a pause*). You know, Herr Muller, it does not seem natural to me that you should settle yourself into this quiet country life.

KURT (*then, as if he had come to a decision*). Perhaps. When did you leave the diplomatic service, Count de Brancovis?

TECK. In 1931.

KURT (*nodding*). After the Budapest oil deal? That must have been a thing of high comedy, that conference. (*He turns deliberately to Fanny and David.*) Fritz Thyssen, the millionaire who made available the money for Hitler, was buying oil. Everybody was trying to guess whether this talk of National Socialism was a smart blind of Thyssen's, or whether his rivals were—(*To Teck*) It is too bad—you guessed an inch off, eh?

TECK (*slowly—watching Kurt carefully*). More than that.

KURT. And Nazis have good memories.

TECK (*smiling*). Most uncomfortable memories. (*Carefully*) You know more about me than I do about you. And yet—I still have a feeling that I have seen you, or heard about you. That feeling has been so insistent that I make guesses. (*He goes to the newspaper on the table but does not touch it.*) But bad guesses—I thought you might be Max Freidank.

At this, Sara rises. Kurt comes toward him, then stops.

KURT. Freidank is a hero to my people. You do me too much honor.

TECK. Yes. I found that out. (*He picks up the paper.*) "Zurich, Switzerland: The Zurich papers reprinted today a dispatch from the *Berliner Tageblatt* on the capture of Colonel Max Freidank. 'Freidank is said to be the Chief of the Anti-Nazi Underground Movement. The son of the famous General Freidank, he was a World War Officer and a distinguished physicist before the advent of Hitler.'"

Kurt makes a slight movement. Sara sighs, very deeply, as if something hurt her. Kurt is near her. He puts a hand on her arm. Teck watches them, then, pleasantly, as if the effect was what he wanted:

TECK. Ah . . . That is bad news for you, Mrs. Muller. I am most sorry. He was a friend of yours?

SARA (*carefully*). He was a friend to all decent Germans. (*Sharply—as if she meant to tell him something*) A friend to all decent *people,* Count de Brancovis.

TECK (*sighing*). Well, it's what often happens to heroes, unfortunately. (*He looks at his watch.*) Marthe must be ready by now. (*A little too slowly*) We will be back early. I do not like long dinner parties. (*He turns and looks at Kurt.*) Your hands are shaking, Herr Muller.

KURT. My hands were broken. They are bad when I have fear.

TECK (*nodding*). Fear for Freidank, you mean?

KURT (*coming to him—slowly*). I am a man who has *many* kinds of fears. I do not think you would understand that.

TECK (*thinking*). No. I do not think I have ever been very frightened.

KURT (*shaking his head, sympathetically*). That is bad. It is sometimes the road to trouble.

TECK (*laughing*). I daresay. (*Very pleasantly—to everybody*) Good night.

He goes out. Sara moves toward Kurt swiftly.

SARA. Kurt . . . Kurt! . . .

KURT (*pressing her arms*). It may not be true. (*Quickly—to Fanny*) I am going to use your phone—for a long distance call. (*Quickly he moves out of the room.*)

DAVID (*coming to Sara*). What is it, darling? . . . What . . . ?

FANNY. What has all this been about, Sara?

SARA (*sharply*). I don't know all of it yet. I do know that . . . (*pointing to the door*) . . . he broke open Kurt's briefcase. And he saw what we carry with us, and he knows about Freidank, which probably means he is guessing about Kurt.

DAVID. What do you mean, what you carry with you, and guessing about Kurt? I . . .

SARA (*as if she were thinking of something else*). Kurt works in an illegal organization. He has, for seven years. We are carrying with us twenty-three thousand dollars. It's been collected here and in Mexico from the pennies and the nickels of poor people who don't like Fascism and believe in the work we do. It was to be picked up and taken back by the first man going . . .

She stops and stares, as if something had just occurred to her. Then slowly, drawing her breath as if she were going to cry:

SARA (*continuing*). Max and Kurt . . . they loved each other. They were in the war together and in Spain together. Once in Spain, after Kurt brought his brigade through, Max made a medal from a ring. "I make you a medal because you are a fine soldier," he said. And once six months ago, he rescued Kurt from the Gestapo on a train, and Kurt was badly hurt. Max carried him on his back for seven miles across the border. He is quite a man. But they caught him in the end. Nobody's got much of a chance any more . . . Nobody.

David moves toward her sympathetically.

FANNY. Wasn't it careless to have twenty-three thousand dollars lying around to be seen?

SARA. No. It wasn't careless. We've carried money that way for years (*Sharply*) There didn't seem any safer place than my house. It was careless of you and David to have a man like that in this house.

DAVID. Yes . . . It was very careless

FANNY. But how could we know . . .

SARA. The world has changed, Mama, and some of the people in it are dangerous. It's time you knew about that.

Kurt comes in quickly, goes to Sara and nods.

KURT. It is true. But he is not dead. Hans and Ernst were taken with him. (*He smiles.*) Max is not an easy man to kill. (*He stops smiling.*) But most of his face and one arm . . . (*He puts his arms around Sara, then smooths her hair.*) It is not nice when it comes. (*He starts to speak, clears his throat, then gently*) Well, Sara . . . (*Sara raises her head and looks at him.*)

SARA (*harshly*). No.

KURT (*very gently*). It must be yes.

SARA. But Max knows you are not well enough. He sent you here . . .

KURT. But now I am more well than he is.

SARA (*turning from him*). When?

KURT. I think tonight, Sara, darling. But I do not know. It will depend upon the Count de Brancovis.

FANNY. *What* will depend upon him? (*Slowly—horrified*) Did he steal the money?

KURT. No. Of course not. He is not a man who steals. It will come another way.

DAVID. But why are you afraid of him? You're in this country now. There's nothing he can do.

KURT. We will see. We will wait, and we will see.

SARA. Kurt's not going to be in this country. He's going back to get them out. (*Carefully—to Kurt*) Is that right, Kurt?

KURT (*nodding*). Yes, Sara. They were taken to Sonnenburg. Guards can be bribed in Sonnenburg. I will try for it that way, Sara.

Without thinking, he puts his hand to his mouth, sighs and sits down as if he were very tired. Immediately she comes to him.

SARA. All right, Kurt. (*She leans over and puts her arms around him.*) You'll do it. You'll get them out. (*Childishly, breathing hard, to Fanny and David*) Kurt will do it. You'll see. (*She is crying now and trying not to.*) Don't be afraid, darling. You'll get back. You'll get Max out and then you'll do his work, won't you? (*She gasps.*) You'll do a good job. The way you've always done. Kurt doesn't feel well. Don't be afraid, darling. You'll get home. Yes, you will . . .

She is crying as the children come into the room. All three stop at the door.

JOSHUA (*slowly*). What is it, Mama?

SARA (*raising her head*). You will be told . . . Later . . . Don't worry now. (*To Fanny and David*) Go in to dinner, please. We will come in a minute.

She puts her head on his and holds him, as the scene dissolves to a TAXICAB with MARTHE and TECK at night. The cab is driving through Washington, D.C.

TECK. Much has been going wrong—with us and between us. But suppose, Marthe, suppose we could go back to Europe again, and with a little money? Do you think we might . . . (*He gestures.*) . . . pick up again what we have lost?

Marthe thinks for a moment, then slowly shakes her head.

MARTHE (*simply—without emphasis*). What we lost? I don't think there was ever much to lose and I left nothing in Europe that I'd want to go back to.

TECK (*with cold anger*). You have other plans? (*He takes her roughly by the shoulders and twists her around to face him.*) If so, you are wasting your time. I will tell you what you are going to do and you will do it. We are leaving the Farrelly house perhaps tomorrow—you and I—understand? (*Her face becomes cold and angry, but she does not answer.*)

The TAXI DRIVER turns his head. His voice is tough and cheerful.

TAXI DRIVER. Anything going wrong back there?

MARTHE and TECK in the TAXICAB:

TECK. Drop me at the corner.

DRIVER (*his voice heard*). Like a hot potato, boss.

TECK (*to Marthe*). You will go on to dinner. I will pick you up later.

Teck opens the door as the taxi draws up to the curb. Then the scene dissolves to a SMALL OFFICE in the GERMAN EMBASSY. It is meagerly furnished with simple metal furniture. Blecher sits at the desk looking at some papers. He wears slippers, pajamas and a thin robe that bulges over his muscles. Teck is sitting opposite him.

TECK. How did you manage in the game the other night?

BLECHER. Count de Brancovis, in this room I work.

TECK (*grimacing*). That is commendable. Your people caught Max Freidank. Are there any others—close to Freidank perhaps—that you want?

Blecher stares at Teck, studying his face before replying.

BLECHER (*after a pause*). We want them all. (*He goes to a filing cabinet and takes out a sheaf of papers.*) Here are the lists.

TECK (*folding the papers and pocketing them*). If I should know where one—or more—of these men could be found, what would that information be worth to your government?

BLECHER. It would depend on who they were or where they were. In the United States, they would be worth very little—nothing.

TECK. Nothing at all?

BLECHER. What are we to do here? Have them assassinated in an alley? Kidnap them? Follow them for months hoping we'll know when they go back to Germany? With such men as these, that is not easy. (*He leans forward.*) But show us where we can put our hands on one of them in the Fatherland—or in any of the countries where we have influence—that is another matter. You could name your own price—in reason. (*He nods—then*) We might also manage a visa for you. I am sure you are homesick for shabby palaces and gaudy cafés and the rest of the decaying things that represent Europe to you.

TECK (*pleasantly*). We do not like each other, Blecher.

BLECHER (*pleasantly—surprised*). But that will not stand in the way of our doing business.

Teck smiles as he rises and the scene dissolves to the FARRELLY LIVING ROOM with KURT, SARA, FANNY, DAVID and the CHILDREN. They are around a table on which there is a coffee service, brandy etc. Kurt is sitting on the couch as if he were resting. Fanny is fidgeting. David is pacing about the room, Sara is sitting next to Kurt. The children are watching everybody with great interest.

FANNY (*after a second—to David*). Would you stop that pacing about, please.

Again there is a silence. Then she speaks as if for the benefit of the children.

FANNY. And tomorrow, because it's Babbie's birthday, I shall go and buy presents for everybody. We always do that here. It started because I didn't like not getting a present on other people's birthdays. And we'll have music in the evening. (*She sighs, exhausted with this chattery social effort. She looks to David.*)

DAVID (*hurriedly, flatly*). Yes. We'll have a fine time.

BODO. You think you fool us, eh?

FANNY. What?

BABETTE (*very kindly*). Something has gone wrong. Always Mama and Papa look like that when it happens so.

Kurt rises and turns his back. Joshua, silent, is wide awake and watching Kurt.

BABETTE. You must not be nervous for our sake, Grandma. (*As if she were older than Fanny, she pats her hand.*)

BODO. We will do whatever it is Mama and Papa will ask of us.

KURT (*softly*). Yes, you always have. And now would you go upstairs? Later I will come and say good night.

All three rise. Joshua hangs back. They go to the door.

BABETTE AND BODO (*with quiet dignity*). Good night.

When they have disappeared, Kurt moves his head toward the terrace. Joshua follows him out, and as he does so the scene dissolves to the TERRACE with KURT and JOSHUA: Kurt is speaking simply as if talking to a colleague. Joshua speaks tensely, earnestly, his fists clenched in a desire to convince Kurt.

JOSHUA. You must let me come along, Papa. I will help in small ways. I will learn. You will teach me . . . I am not as yet a man and it would not be of such importance if anything happened to me.

KURT (*looking at him*). Now I give you some rules. (*Sharply*) Please remember them, Joshua, and never to disobey them. (*Solemnly, Joshua nods.*) Our forces are small. (*He holds up one finger as he speaks to the boy.*) Therefore we must risk no more men on any enterprise than are needed to carry it out. (*He holds up a second finger.*) Always in our work, a man will wish to go with you. That is wrong. We are not here to show we are brave, and not to be modest, either, and say, "I am not important, let me take the risk." He takes the risk who is entitled to it. (*He leans forward.*) Soon you will be a man. Never have I doubted that for you, also, this will be what a man should most do. I am right?

JOSHUA (*surprised that he should be asked*). Of course, Papa.

KURT. You are young, you are smart, you are strong. You are a fine investment for our work . . . when the time comes. In the meantime, I give you orders: You think, you train yourself, in mind and body. (*Quickly*) Your day is not so distant. If it should come and I have not as yet returned . . . (*Too casually*) It is not wise, perhaps, to speak so far in the future, but the world goes bad, and who knows how long that will last. Therefore, with delicacy and care, I wish you also to prepare Bodo when his time, too, shall come, God help us. (*Without rising*) Go upstairs now and say nothing to the others. I will come later. (*He stays where he is. Joshua rises, and goes off.*)

The LIVING ROOM with FANNY, SARA, and DAVID.

FANNY. Does Kurt intend to *bribe* his friends out of prison? Is that what he said?

SARA. Yes.

FANNY. It's all very strange to me. I thought things were so well run . . .

SARA (*smiling—shaking her head*). What wonderful work Fascists have done in convincing people they are men from legends.

DAVID. They've done very well for themselves . . . unfortunately.

SARA. But not by themselves. We don't like to remember, do we, that they came in on the shoulders of some of the most powerful men in the world? That makes us feel guilty and so we prefer to believe that they're mysterious men from the planets. Well, they aren't. They're smart and slick and cruel. But given men who know what they fight for, and will fight hard. . . .

We see KURT in the DOORWAY of the terrace. He comes into the room and sits down.

KURT. Yes. Given men who know what they fight for . . . I will console you. A year ago last month, at three o'clock in the morning, Freidank and I, with two elderly pistols, raided the home of the Gestapo chief in Konstanz, got what we wanted and the following morning Freidank was eating his breakfast three blocks away and I was over the Swiss border.

FANNY (*slowly*). You are brave men.

KURT. I do not tell you the story to prove that we are remarkable but to prove that they are *not*.

DAVID. Would you like a drink? You look . . . you look very tired. (*Kurt nods, and David moves to get him a drink.*)

KURT. Waiting. It is waiting that is bad for me.

FANNY (*after a slight pause*). I don't really understand what you're waiting for. Now, I mean.

KURT. I think the Count de Brancovis will try tonight to find out who I am. I wait now to see if he has so found me out. Beyond that, I myself do not understand.

FANNY. But there's nothing he can do . . .

KURT (*as if he had not heard*). Once in Spain I waited two days for the Fascist planes to exhaust themselves. I say finally to myself, if I must reach up with naked hands, I will stop them . . . it is such waiting for which I am not fit.

SARA. You will not think that when the time comes. It will go.

KURT. Of a certainty.

FANNY. But must it always be your hands?

KURT. For each man his own hand. He has to sleep with them.

DAVID. That's right. I guess it's the way we should all feel. But you have a family. Isn't there somebody else who hasn't a wife and children . . .

KURT. Each could have his own excuse. Some have bullet holes, some have fear of the camps, and many are getting older. Each could find an excuse. (*Softly*) And my children are not the only children in the world, even to me.

FANNY. That's noble of course, but . . .

KURT. One means always in English to insult with that word noble?

FANNY. Of course not. I—I was thinking of Sara. . . .

SARA. I want it this way, Mama, the way Kurt wants it. You wanted a good life for your children: we want it for ours, too. This is Kurt's way of trying to get it for them.

As Kurt smiles, there is the sound of the front door closing. Sara rises, David rises, but Kurt does not move. MARTHE and TECK appear in the DOORWAY. Marthe looks puzzled and angry.

MARTHE. Good evening.

TECK. I have been to the German Embassy tonight, Herr Muller.

KURT (*nodding*). It is where I thought you would go.

MARTHE (*very tense—to all of them*). I don't know what this is all about, but I'm guessing, because I know Teck. I have nothing to do with any of it. I have nothing to do with Teck any more.

At this, Teck turns to her and speaks softly, surprised at the tone of her voice.

TECK (*to Marthe*). If you do not fully mean what you are saying, Marthe, or if you might change your mind, you are talking most unwisely.

MARTHE. You are trying to frighten me. But you are not going to frighten me any more. I am not going away with you this time. I am never going away with you again.

TECK. Shall we talk about this alone?

MARTHE. You can't make me stay with you, can you, Teck? You can't make me stay now that I'm not frightened any more?

TECK (*slowly*). No. Perhaps not.

MARTHE. Then there is nothing to talk about.

TECK (*indicating David*). You are in love with him?

At this, David moves toward Teck, but Marthe puts up a hand.

MARTHE. You never can understand anything that hasn't got tricks to it. I don't like you, Teck. I never have.

TECK. That makes me sad, Marthe. But I think I have always known it.

MARTHE. There is nothing you can do, Teck. We will not leave here together and we will not meet again.

TECK (*softly—as she passes him*). You will not believe me, but I tried my best and am now most sorry to lose you.

MARTHE. I believe you.

David moves toward her. She smiles at him, but shakes her head.

MARTHE (*to David*). Not now. (*To the others*) Good night.

FANNY (*looking at David, then exhaling sharply*). Well. A great many things have been said in the last few minutes. Am I to understand . . . ?

DAVID (*firmly—but pleasantly*). You are to understand anything you like.

TECK (*smiling unpleasantly at them*). Without Marthe I shall be a very lonely man. Already I am a very poor one. Before I go tonight I should like to have ten thousand dollars.

DAVID (*furiously*). You—Blackmailing with your wife—

David moves toward Teck. Quickly Kurt steps forward, and takes David's arm.

KURT. The Count de Brancovis is not bargaining with you and Marthe. He is talking to me.

TECK. I got from the Embassy a list and a description without, of course, saying why I wanted them. (*Very sharply*) But if I have to take any more of that, I shall go immediately back to them.

KURT. You will not again be interrupted.

Teck sits down, and Kurt comes to sit opposite him.

TECK. Some of these papers have to do with a man we shall call Gotter because that is the name he has most often used.

Sara moves toward them. Kurt looks at her and shakes his head. Teck begins to read.

TECK (*reading*). Age, forty to forty-five. About six feet. One hundred seventy pounds. Birthplace unknown. Original occupation unknown. Family unknown. No known political connections. No known trade-union connections. Many descriptions, all of them unreliable. Equally unreliable were Paris, Copenhagen and Brussels police descriptions. Only points on which there is general agreement; married to a foreign woman, either English or American; three children; has used the names of Gotter, Thomas Bodmer, Karl Francis. Thought to have left Germany in 1933 and to have joined the notorious Max Freidank. Known to have crossed border in 1934—February, May, June, October. Known to have again crossed border with Freidank in 1935—August, twice in October, November, 1936 (*He looks up, smiling.*) An active man, this Gotter.

KURT (*laughing*). Indeed—and with a bicycle.

TECK (*resuming his reading*). In 1934 outlaw radio station announcing itself as Radio European begins to operate. Gotter was known to have crossed border immediately before and after three of the broadcasts. Radio again active in early part of 1936. Active attempt made to locate Freidank. Gotter believed to have then appeared in Spain with Madrid Government Army, and to have been a brigade Commander under previously used name of Bodmer. Known to have lived in France the first months of 1938. Again crossed border some time during week when Hitler's Hamburg radio speech was interrupted off the air. (*He looks up.*) That was a daring deed, Herr Muller. I remember it well. It amused me.

KURT (*blandly*). It was not done for that reason.

TECK (*reading again*). Early in 1939 an informer in Konstanz reported Gotter's arrival carrying money which had been exchanged in Paris and Brussels. Following day home of Konstanz Gestapo chief was raided by two men who took spy list and—Herr Muller, that job took two good men.

SARA. Even you admire them.

TECK. Even I. I think you are Gotter, Karl Francis—

KURT. Please do not describe me to myself again.

TECK. And I think that because Freidank has been taken, you will soon be traveling home. If I am wrong, you will not be going back, the German Embassy will—

KURT. I am going back. I am starting tonight.

TECK (*looking pleased, then puzzled*). So? You tell me free of charge? I will tell you free of charge: I do not believe they have forced any information from Freidank or the others.

KURT. Thank you. I am sure they would not. I know all three most well.

SARA (*very tensely*). They will be able to stand up under—under whatever will be given them.

TECK (*looking at her, nodding—softly*). Yes. There is a deep sickness in the German character. A love of death, a love of pain . . .

DAVID (*very angrily*). Spare us your moral judgments.

FANNY. Yes. They are sickening coming from you. Get on with your dirty business.

KURT (*to Teck*). Fanny and David are Americans. They do not understand our world. If they are fortunate, they never will. (*He turns to Fanny.*) All Fascists are not of one mind, one stripe. There are those who give the orders—(*slowly to Teck*)—and those who take them: *They* came late. Some of them were—up to a point—fastidious men. For these we may some day have pity. They are lost men, their spoils are small, and their day is gone. (*To Teck*) Yes?

TECK (*slowly*). You have the understanding heart. Some day it will get in your way.

KURT. I will watch it.

TECK. We are both men in trouble, Herr Muller. The world, perhaps ungratefully, seems to like your kind even less than it does mine. (*He leans forward.*) Now—Let us do business. You will not get back if I inform the Embassy you are going. They will see that you are killed before you get there.

KURT. You are wrong. I would get back. There are many men they would like to have besides me. I would be allowed to walk directly to them until they had all the names and all the addresses. Roumanians would pick me up beforehand. . . . The Germans would not.

TECK (*smiling*). Still the national pride?

KURT. Why not? For that which is good?

FANNY (*advancing angrily*). I have not often felt in my life what I feel now. Whatever you are, and however you came to it, the picture of a man selling other men's lives—

TECK. Is very ugly, Madame Fanny. I do not do it without some shame—

and therefore I must sink my shame in large money. (*To Kurt—pointing upstairs*) You have twenty-three thousand dollars in your briefcase.

KURT. Yes. You are an expert with locks.

TECK (*smiling, continuing*). For ten thousand dollars you can go back to —wherever you go. Nobody will know that you go and I will give you my good wishes.

Slowly, deliberately, Kurt begins to shake his head. Teck waits, then, carefully:

TECK. What?

KURT. That money is going home with me. It was not given to me to save my life, and I shall not so use it. It is to save the lives and further the work of more than I. (*Very sharply*) Count de Brancovis, the first morning we arrived in this country, my children were hungry; that is because we were not able to buy for them sufficient breakfast. If I would not touch that money for them, I would not touch it for you. It goes back with me, the way it is. And if it does not get back, it is because I will not get back. (*There is a pause, and Sara gets up, turns away.*)

TECK. Then I do not think you will get back. You are a brave one, Herr Muller, but you will not get back.

KURT. I will send to you a postal card and tell you about my bravery.

DAVID (*coming toward Kurt*). Is it true that if this swine talks, you and the others . . . ?

SARA. Will be caught and killed. If they are lucky enough to get killed quickly.

FANNY (*violently*). All right. We'll give him the money. Let's give it to him and get him out of here.

DAVID (*to Teck*). And what is to keep you from also selling to the Embassy?

TECK. I do not like your thinking I would do that.

DAVID (*furiously*). Look here. I'm sick of what you'd like or wouldn't like. We'll get this over without any more fancy talk from you. I can't take much more of you at any cost.

TECK (*smiling*). It is your anger which delays us. I suggest that you give me a small amount of cash now and the rest in a check dated a month from now. In a month, Herr Muller should be home, and he can let you know that he is safe and I have kept my bargain. (*He shrugs.*) We are taking chances on each other. Of course. I suppose one always does —(*smiling*)—in a deal of such delicacy as ours.

Kurt is leaning back on the couch, as if he were disinterested now.

DAVID (*to Kurt*). Is a month all right?

KURT. What? I do not know.

DAVID (*to Teck*). Two months from today. How do you want the cash and how do you want the check?

TECK. One month. That I will not discuss. One month. Please decide now.

DAVID (*sharply*). All right. Leave your address. I'll send the money in the morning.

TECK (*bitterly*). Address? I have no address. And I wish it now.

DAVID. I have only a couple of hundred in cash . . .

Blecher: How was the tea-party?

David: Where is everybody?

Kurt: We did not win. It would have been a different world if we had.

Teck: That is bad news for you, Mrs. Muller. I am most sorry.

FANNY. I have fifteen or sixteen hundred in the sitting room safe.

TECK. Very well. That will do. Make the rest in a check.

David starts for the library door. Fanny goes out toward the hall. When they have left, Kurt does not look up, and Sara does not move

TECK (*awkwardly*). The new world has left the room. (*He looks up at them.*) I feel less discomfort with you. We are Europeans, born to trouble and understanding it. (*He points upstairs.*) They are young. The world has gone well for them. For us . . . (*He smiles.*) The three of us—we are like peasants watching the big frost. Work, trouble, ruin . . . (*He shrugs.*) But no need to call curses at the frost. There it is, it will be again, always . . . for us.

SARA. You mean my husband and I do not have angry words for you? It goes deeper than that with us. We know how many there are of you. They don't yet. My mother and brother feel shocked that you are in their house. But we have seen you in so many houses.

TECK. I do not say you want to understand me, Mrs. Muller. I say only that you do.

SARA. Yes. You are not difficult to understand.

Kurt gets up and stands stiffly. Then he moves toward the decanter table.

KURT (*slowly*). A whiskey?

TECK. No, thank you.

He turns his head to watch Kurt move. He turns back.

KURT. A brandy?

TECK (*nodding*). Thank you, I will.

Kurt is fixing the drinks. Sara is watching him now.

KURT. You, too, wish to go back to Europe.

TECK. Yes.

KURT. You know, I do not think the Embassy would pay you for a description of a man who has a month to travel. But I think they might pay you in a visa. I think you want a visa almost as much as you want money.

Bringing the drinks, Kurt passes Sara, looks toward the doors, and makes a motion to tell her to move out of the way. Staring at him, she moves back.

KURT (*continuing*). Therefore I conclude you will try for the money here, and the visa from the Embassy. (*He is about to place the glasses on the table.*) Did you think I would allow this fantasy with the money? Unlike you, I do not take chances . . . I am not a gambler.

Teck has half risen. As he does so, Kurt drops the glass, and hits Teck. It is a violent blow; the blow of a sick man who knows he must hit once and do it well. As Teck begins to rise, Kurt takes the Luger from his pocket.

KURT. Get up, please.

Teck rises, staring at him. Kurt motions him to the door.

KURT (*to Sara*). Mach die Tür auf. (*As she opens the door*) Mach die Tür zu! I wish nobody to come outside.

SARA, seen close, nods, and quickly closes the door. She stands for a minute, trembling. Then she moves to fix the overturned chair and to pick up the fallen glass. Then she moves to the telephone, looks at the telephone book, and begins to dial a number. After a second, there is a closeup of SARA at the TELEPHONE.

SARA. Hello . . . What time is your next plane? . . . Oh . . . To . . . South . . . To El Paso or Brownsville. . . . Yes.

The scene expands as David comes into the room. After a second he looks around, puzzled at the absence of Kurt and Teck. A second later Fanny comes in from the hall entrance. They both stare at Sara at the phone.

DAVID. Where is he? Upstairs?

SARA. They went out . . . outside.

FANNY (*bewildered*). They went outside?

David moves toward the door.

SARA. No, David. *Don't go out.*

He draws back and stares at her. She speaks again into the phone.

SARA (*in a closeup, at the phone*). Yes. . . . That's all right. . . . No. . . . The ticket will be picked up at the airport. . . . Er, Ritter. . . . R-i-t-t-e-r. . . . From Chicago. . . . Yes.

The scene including DAVID and FANNY:

DAVID. Sara! What is this? . . . What is happening. . . . ? (*He moves again toward the door.*)

SARA (*very sharply—very much in command*). No. Do not interfere now. Either of you.

As their frightened, puzzled faces express their reaction, the scene dissolves to a view of KURT and TECK standing near a tree, a few feet from a large garage. One of the garage doors is open. Kurt has Teck close to him, the gun touching Teck.

TECK (*whispering—passionately*). I know when I am a loser. I give you my word—

KURT. Your word? What guarantees, what bonds, could hold such a man as you? There's no substance to you —nothing that could be held to anything. You are not even a coward. If I tried to frighten you into silence, by tomorrow you would have forgotten your fear. (*Angrily*) You are a fool. You play with men's lives in order to have money to live in worthlessness. You and all your shabby kind. (*Very angrily*) When you kill in a war, it is not so lonely. Tonight, before you come home, I pray for you. I pray that you will have done nothing, that I will not have to touch you. I do not like to kill this way. But I have done it before, and I will do it again. Whenever it must be done. (*His voice drops.*)

TECK (*desperately—whispering*). Listen to me. I. . . .

KURT (*very quietly—very sadly*). I have seen many men die. I give you advice. It is easier without words. They will not now do you good. You will be better without them.

On "They will not now . . ." he begins to move Teck backward. They are now out of the light and only the words are heard as they move into the garage. A second later the garage door closes; a second after, there is the muffled sound of a shot.

The scene cuts back to the LIVING ROOM where DAVID and FANNY are standing. Sara is sitting.

SARA (*softly*). For seven years now, day in, day out, men have crossed the German border. They always may be going in to die. Did you ever see the face of a man who never knows if this day will be the last day. It is a strange face, unlike any other. Some day, when it's all over, maybe there'll be a few of them left. There aren't many of Kurt's age any more. He couldn't have taken a chance on them. They wouldn't have liked it. (*Violently*) He'd have had a bad time trying to explain that because of this house and this nice town and my mother and my brother, he took chances with their work and with their lives. (*Softly*) I think it's all over now. There's nothing you can do about it. It's the way it had to be.

FANNY. Do you mean . . . ? (*Slowly she sits down.*)

SARA. He's going away now. I do not think he will come back. . . . Never, never, never. I don't like to be alone at night. I guess everybody in the world's got a time they don't like. Me, it's right before I go to sleep. And now it's going to be for always. All the rest of my life. (*She looks up as Kurt comes in and addresses herself to him.*) I've told them. I've made you a reservation on a midnight plane to Brownsville.

KURT (*looking at her*). Liebe Sara. (*To Fanny—going toward her—gently*) It is hard for you, eh?

FANNY. Hard? I don't know. I . . . don't . . .

KURT. Before I come in, I stand and think. I say I will try to make Fanny and David understand. I say how can I. Does one understand a killing? No. So, in the end, what is there to say? Then do not try to explain. I say I do what must be done. I have long sickened of words when I see the men who live by them. I have stopped a man's life. I want only for you to know that I pray that it will not have to be, but I know I will have to kill him. I know that if I do not it is only that I pamper myself and risk the lives of others as well as myself. So I want you from the room. I know what I must do. All right! Do I now pretend sorrow? Do I now pretend it is not I who act thus? No. I do it. I have done it before. And I will do it again. And I will keep my hope that we may make a world in which all men can die in bed. I have a great hate for the violent. They are the sick of the world. Maybe I am sick now, too.

SARA. You are not sick. Stop it, Kurt. It's late. You must go soon.

He puts out his hand and touches her. Then he moves to David and Fanny.

KURT. I am going to take your car. I will take him with me. After that, it is up to you. Two ways: You can let me go and keep silent. I believe I can hide him and the car. At the end of two days, if they have not been found, you will tell as much of the truth as it is safe for you to say. I will have left the gun. There will be no doubt who did the killing. If you will give me those two days, I think I will be far enough away from here. If the car is found before then . . . (*He shrugs.*) I will try to move with speed. (*He pauses.*) I do not think, for the world, you will be in bad trouble. Inside yourselves, that is for you to decide. You may take the other way. I am going to say goodbye to my children. That will give you time to call the police. I will still leave: but I will not get home.

Swiftly, he moves out of the room. There is silence for a minute. Then Sara moves quickly to Fanny and David.

SARA (*tensely—with force*). Papa wrote it years ago. Papa said the only men on earth worth their time on earth are the men who will fight for other men. Papa said: "We have struggled through from darkness. But man moves forward with each day and each hour to a better, freer life. That desire to go forward, that willingness to fight for it, cannot be put in a man. But when it is there...." (*She stops—choking.*) Please. Let him go back.

DAVID (*softly—gently*). Of course, darling. He'll have his two days. We'll take care of things.

FANNY (*putting out her hand, touching Sara*). It is a fine thing to have you for a daughter. I would like to have been like you.

As Sara leans over and kisses her hand, the scene cuts to the UPSTAIRS HALL. KURT is carrying his coat and briefcase, coming out of his room. He goes down the hall, stands in front of the door of Joshua's room, takes a deep breath; then he opens the door.

In JOSHUA'S BEDROOM, all three children are sitting quietly, stiffly, as if waiting for him. They rise as he comes in. He stands looking at them.

KURT. We have said many goodbyes to each other, eh? Well, we must now say another. (*Smiling slowly—with difficulty*) But this time I leave you with good people to whom I believe you also will be good. (*He sits down. They come to him playfully.*) Would you allow me to give away my share in you until I come back?

BABETTE. If you would like it.

KURT. Good. To your Mother, her share. My share to Fanny and David. It is all and it is the most I have to give. (*He laughs.*) There. I have made a will, eh? Now, we will not joke. I have something to say to you. It is important for me to say it.

BABETTE. You are talking to us as if we were children.

KURT. Am I, Babbie? I wish you were children. I wish I could say, love your Mother, do not eat too many sweets, clean your teeth— (*As he draws Bodo closer*) I cannot say these things. You are not children. I took your childhood away from you.

BABETTE. We have had a most enjoyable life, Papa.

KURT (*smiling*). You are a gallant little liar and I thank you for it. I have done something bad tonight.

BODO. You could not do a bad thing.

BABETTE (*proudly*). You could not.

KURT (*shaking his head at them*). Now let us get straight together. The four of us. Do you remember when we read "Les Miserables"? Do you remember that we talked about it afterwards and Bodo got candy on Mama's bed?

BODO. I remember.

KURT. Well. The man in the book stole bread. The world is out of shape, we said, when there are hungry men. And until it gets in shape, men will steal and lie and ... (*a little more slowly*) ... kill. But for whatever reason it is done, and whoever does it—you understand me —it is all bad. I want you to remember that. Whoever does it, it is bad. (*Very gaily*) But you will live to see the day when it will not have to be. All over the world in every place and every town, there are men who are going to make sure it will not have to be. They want what I want: a childhood for every child. For my children, and I for theirs. (*He picks Bodo up—and rises.*) Think of that. It will make you happy. In every town and every village and every mud hut in the world, there is always a man who loves children and who will fight to make a good world for them. And now goodbye. Wait for me: I shall try to come back for you.

The view moves with him toward the door. He is followed by Babette, and more slowly, by Joshua.

KURT. Or you shall come to me. The boat will come in. I will be waiting on the dock. There will be the three of you and Mama and Fanny and David. And I will have ordered an extra big dinner and we will show them what our country can be like . . .

He puts Bodo down. He leans down and presses his face in Babette's hair. Tenderly she touches his hair.

JOSHUA. Of course. That is the way it will be. Of course.

KURT (*kissing Babette*). Gute Nacht, Liebling!

BABETTE. Gute Nacht, Papa. Do it well! Mach's gut!

KURT (*leaning to kiss Bodo*). Good night, baby.

BODO. Good night, Papa. Mach's gut!

KURT (*kissing Joshua*). Good night, son.

JOSHUA. Goodnight, Papa. Mach's gut!

They stand side by side as Kurt goes. Then the scene dissolves to the DRAWING ROOM as Kurt comes in. Sara is standing immediately outside the door, on the terrace.

FANNY (*after a second*). You go with our blessing. We will take care of things here. David and I would like to give you this money to use for your friends.

She hands him the money. He leans down and kisses her hand.

KURT. A thank you is too small. I . . . Goodbye.

He moves toward David. David holds out his hand.

DAVID (*very warmly*). Good luck.

Kurt nods, smiles, and moves out of the door to the terrace to Sara, following which there is a closeup of SARA and KURT on the TERRACE. She turns to him.

KURT. Men who wish to live have the best chance to live. I wish to live. I wish to live with you.

SARA (*taking his arms*). For seventeen years. It is as much for me today . . . I have loved just once and for all my life. Come back for me, darling. If you can. (*He kisses her.*)

KURT (*simply*). I will try. (*He turns.*)

Fanny and David are standing in the room.

KURT. Goodbye to you all.

He goes out. After a second there is the sound of a car. Slowly Sara turns and moves back into the room. Gradually the noise begins to go off into the distance. A second later, Joshua appears.

JOSHUA. Bodo cries. Babette looks very queer. I think you should come, Mama.

Sara nods. Joshua speaks to Fanny and David.

JOSHUA. Bodo talks so fancy we forget sometimes he is a baby.

As Sara reaches him, he takes her arm and they disappear. Fanny looks at Sara with great admiration.

FANNY (*after a second*). Well, we've been shaken out of the magnolias, eh?

DAVID. Yes. . . . So we have.

FANNY. Yes. (*She sighs.*) Well, tomorrow will be a hard day. But we'll have Babbie's birthday dinner and we'll have music afterwards. I think you'd better go up to Marthe now. In the end, she will have to know. Be as careful as you can. (*She begins to put out the lights.*) I think I shall go and talk to Anise. I like Anise best when I don't feel well.

DAVID. Mama. (*She turns.*) We're going to be in for trouble. You understand that?

FANNY. I understand it very well. We'll manage. I'm not put together with flour paste. And neither are you—I'm happy to learn.

As the last light goes out, he presses her arms and the scene fades out.

PART FOUR

A FOREIGN CITY fades in, then the scene cuts to a ROOM in a GERMAN CITY—a shabbily furnished room that might be in a rooming house or a small hotel. Kurt, worn and gaunt, sits at a plain deal table straightening out a pile of German paper money. Beside him stands a thin-faced, shabbily dressed young man. The young man's attitude towards Kurt is one of great respect. Kurt finishes straightening out the money, puts it in the table drawer, then takes the Luger pistol from his pocket and puts it on top of the money. He looks at a small clock across the room.

KURT. Well. . . . Soon we will know whether we can buy them out of prison.

YOUNG MAN (*hesitantly*). There are rumors that the Herr Direktor of Sonnenburg Prison grew more honest with his promotion.

KURT. Perhaps he only grew more expensive. With them it has nothing to do with honesty. One day you can bribe them, the next day they have set a trap for you.

YOUNG MAN. There is still time to go, Herr Muller. Perhaps in a few days we could find out whether the bribe will be taken. . . .

KURT (*smiling*). With the Herr Direktor, there would never be any certainty. No. It will be tonight.

Without thinking, he touches the gun. The young man sees the movement and quickly Kurt takes his hand away.

YOUNG MAN (*very tensely*). Herr Muller, please allow *me* to see them. It means too much to us to have you here. . . .

KURT (*shaking his head*). No. Whatever happens, I wish no one else to be involved. You understand? (*The young man nods.*) Are you married, Hans? (*Hans nods.*) Children?

YOUNG MAN. Yes. . . . Two.

KURT (*after a second*). I have three children—good children. My oldest boy will, perhaps, be coming some day. He will find his way. (*He smiles.*) In our work it makes one feel better to have children, eh? It is not then so bad to grow old or to die. They will be there to go on. (*Slowly*) If you should ever meet my boy, and I—(*carefully, with not too much emphasis*)—am not around at the time, will you. . . . ? (*He stops as if he has heard a noise.*) Go now, quickly, please. Do not worry.

The boy grabs his hand, and runs for the back door. Kurt is smiling. He stops smiling when, after a minute, heavy boots are heard on the stairs. The door opens and two men appear. Kurt puts one hand on the money, one hand on the gun.

KURT. So, Herr Direktor, we meet again.

This scene dissolves to the DRAWING ROOM of the FARRELLY HOME: It is winter and there is a fire in the fireplace. Fanny is looking at a fashion magazine. Bodo is lying on the floor, in a warm bathrobe, reading. Babette is knitting. After a second Joseph comes in with some logs.

BODO (*to Joseph*). Did you have much trouble dorbulating on the carpul with those logs down fallamy?

JOSEPH. Not much. Because I used ackingless pawning on them. (*He goes out.*)

FANNY. *What?* What are you talking about?

BABETTE. Don't pay any attention, Grandma. He's learning what they call double talk here. He likes it very much because he can now use long words without even trying to know what they mean.

FANNY (*holding up the magazine*). That's a pretty dress but it isn't—it isn't regal enough for me.

BODO. Now, Grandma. One must not have illusions about one's self. (*He gets up, looks at the magazine, looks at Fanny, and shakes his head.*) It leads one away from reality, and to be led away from reality is not to find the truthfulness inherent in. . . .

FANNY. It's a wonder somebody at school hasn't beaten you up for talking that way.

BABETTE (*pleasantly*). Somebody will.

In JOSHUA'S ROOM with SARA and JOSHUA: Sara is holding a book. Joshua is sitting at a table looking at a map. He has a pencil in his hand and is drawing lines on it. His school books are closed behind him.

SARA (*idly, after a minute*). Maybe we'll have a letter soon. You can't tell. (*She turns to Joshua as if she were convincing herself.*) After all, it isn't so easy to send word. There have been long times before. Don't you think so, Joshua? Don't you think—maybe?

JOSHUA (*gently*). Maybe.

SARA (*after a minute, pointing to the map*). But you can't find Papa on a map.

JOSHUA. No.

SARA (*carefully*). Are you using the map for your lessons?

JOSHUA. No.

SARA (*after a minute—carefully*). What do you mean "no"? What are you doing with that map? (*He looks up, but merely shakes his head.*) Answer me, Joshua!

Joshua closes the map and gets up.

JOSHUA (*gently*). I was thinking about ways to get home.

SARA (*as she rises*). *What are you talking about?*

JOSHUA. In five months, I will have a birthday. If by then we have not yet had word from Papa. . . . (*He turns to her—with emotion.*) I shall be going, Mama. You have known it. And I have known it. But we have not wanted to speak of it.

SARA (*fiercely*). What kind of talk is that? *You will not go.* You are only a child—I will not let you. Do you hear me, Joshua? *I will not let you—*

JOSHUA (*turning to her*). I do not believe that. I believe that you will let me go. I believe when my time will come, you will want me to go. I believe, too, and I will say it now, that you will tell Bodo the things he needs to know and if the world stays bad so long, you will send him after me—when his time comes. You are a brave lady, Mama, and that's the way you will want things to be.

Sara has turned her back to him. Then a closeup of SARA shows that there are tears in her eyes.

SARA (*softly*). Thank you, son, that was a nice thing to say. I am not brave: it isn't like that at all. (*She lowers her head.*) When the time comes—when it comes I will do my best.

The scene fades out.

DRAGON SEED

(A Metro-Goldwyn-Mayer Production)

Screenplay by MARGUERITE ROBERTS and JANE MURFIN

Based on the Novel by PEARL S. BUCK

Produced by PANDRO S. BERMAN

Directed by JACK CONWAY and HAROLD S. BUCQUET

The Cast

JADE	Katharine Hepburn
LING TAN	Walter Huston
LING'S WIFE	Aline MacMahon
WU LIEN	Akim Tamiroff
LAO ER	Turhan Bey
LAO SAN	Hurd Hatfield
JAP KITCHEN OVERSEER	J. Carrol Naish
THIRD COUSIN'S WIFE	Agnes Moorehead
THIRD COUSIN	Henry Travers
LAO TA	Robert Bice
CAPTAIN SATO	Robert Lewis
ORCHID	Frances Rafferty
WIFE OF WU LIEN	Jacqueline De Wit
FOURTH COUSIN	Clarence Lung
NEIGHBOR SHEN	Paul E. Burns

Film Editor—HAROLD F. KRESS

Screenplay of the Metro-Goldwyn-Mayer Studios photoplay "Dragon Seed," copyright 1944 by Loews' Incorporated. By permission of Metro-Goldwyn-Mayer and Miss Pearl S. Buck, author of the novel *Dragon Seed*, published by the John Day Company (also published by Macmillan Company of London). Copyright 1941, 1942 by Pearl S. Buck.

DRAGON SEED
PART ONE

A long view of a pleasant valley fades in. The valley is set under hills from which the water runs down even in dry weather. A river flows through this valley, past the small village of Ling, and southwest toward the walls of a city. Surrounding the village can be seen the scattered, low-roofed houses of the small farmers, set amid their grain fields and flooded rice paddies.

NARRATOR'S VOICE (*simultaneously*). This is the village of Ling as it was in the early summer of 1937. The people who lived here were farmers. They had heard there was a world beyond the hills that bounded their little valley, but as yet no one had climbed those hills to see for himself. Perhaps it was because they were more fortunate than most. Their land was rich and their bellies were full.

This dissolves into a moving view of the house and farm of Ling Tan: The walls of this house are of ancient brick, and the roofs are tiled. There is a courtyard paved with smooth stones, over which is a canopy of matting, for protection from the wind and rain, and a wall with a barred gate. A bamboo thicket grows just beyond the courtyard. On the other side of the house (but giving to the courtyard through an arch) is a walled compound with a shed for the ox, a chicken house, a pig sty and a pond from which Ling's family gets fish. Beyond the house are seen the fields, where three men labor under the hot sun as they plant the rice seedlings in the flooded earth.

NARRATOR'S VOICE (*simultaneously*). On this farm lived Ling Tan and his family, and they were among the most fortunate. They were neither too wealthy nor too poor, and they were greatly respected in the village. They owned the strong house and tilled the soil that had belonged to their ancestors. They were both good and bad, both wise and foolish, and sometimes all these things at the same moment—and, therefore, they were very much like such families in any other land.

We now see the THREE MEN who are LING TAN, LAO TA, LAO ER: They are knee deep in water, and clad only in cotton trousers rolled above their knees, and wide-woven hats. Ling Tan works a little apart from the two younger men, who are his sons.

NARRATOR'S VOICE (*simultaneously*). It was time for the rice seedlings to be planted—

A closer view of LING TAN working steadily, like a machine: He is a man past fifty, but still hard and thin and brown. He looks up; his eyes light with pride and pleasure as he looks toward his sons, but he does not miss a movement in his work.

NARRATOR'S VOICE (*continuing*). —and Ling Tan was eager for but one thing —to finish as much of the work as could be done before the sun was gone from the sky.

LAO TA and LAO ER (as seen from Ling's angle): Rhythmically they plant the seedlings, their right arms thrusting to-

Copyright 1944, *by Loews' Incorporated.*

gether like the arms of one man. They are both in their early twenties. Lao Ta, a year or so the elder, has a smooth and untroubled face, touched with smugness. Lao Er is lean and restless.

NARRATOR'S VOICE. But Ling's first and second sons were eager for many other things as well, for they were young. . . .

This dissolves to a long view of THE FIELD—with LING'S HOUSE in the background. It is now sundown and long shadows streak across the earth. It is evident that a great deal of work has been done in Ling Tan's field, and the three men are near the end of a row of planting.

NARRATOR'S VOICE. But this day ended at last, as all days must. . . .

The figure of a woman (LING'S WIFE) appears at the gate of the compound, and her call blends with, and drowns out, the last words of the narrator.

LING'S WIFE (*calling—long-drawn and shrill*). Haiiiiiii!

A closer view of the THREE MEN:

VOICE OF LING'S WIFE. Haiiiii!

LING TAN (*without looking up*). Is that your mother?

LAO TA. It is, my father.

LING TAN (*working on*). Do not answer her. Time enough to speak with women when there is no light to work by.

The boys exchange a knowing, amused look, but continue to work.

This is followed by a close view of Ling's Wife at the COMPOUND GATE as she calls again.

LING' WIFE (*frowning, bellowing now*). Old Man! Do you hear? The evening meal is ready!

We again see the MEN in the FIELD.

LING TAN (*firmly*). We will finish this row, at least!

VOICE OF LING'S WIFE (*insistently*). Are you deaf and dumb!

Ling Tan continues to work, as if not hearing, but the boys are aware that he does hear and is uneasy.

VOICE OF LING'S WIFE. Hurry! You old turnip!

Lao Ta gives Lao Er a meaningful look, unseen by Ling Tan.

LAO TA (*to Lao Er*). I am weary, brother. Are you?

LAO ER (*nodding*). I am. My back is very tired.

VOICE OF LING'S WIFE. Come! Or shall I come there to you!

Ling Tan straightens up, still pretending not to hear his wife. He looks at his sons, and shakes his head sorrowfully.

LING TAN. Well then, since you are not men enough to go on—we will stop.

LAO TA (*with a straight face*). Yes, my father.

LAO ER (*equally respectful*). Thank you, father.

Ling Tan, his dignity intact, starts for the house. The two boys stop work, and start to pick up their tools, smiling a little at each other.

This dissolves to a moving view of the exterior of the COMPOUND (near the gate) as LING TAN joins his wife. Ling's Wife is a strong, managing mother. She is no longer young, but her body is straight and her eyes snap with fire. In the twisted knot of her hair she wears a long silver pin with enameled ends and an earpick with a toothpick on the other end which she uses a great deal.

LING'S WIFE. Do you grow old and deaf? Must I bawl like an ox to make you hear?

She goes through the gate. He follows, and the view moves with them into the compound. The ox's stall is in sight, a few chickens wander to and fro beneath their feet, and a dog jumps up and runs to Ling Tan to greet him. Ling's Wife guides him toward a tub of water which stands near a bench where she has evidently been plucking ducks.

LING TAN. Now what? There is work to be done and you call me from the fields!

LING'S WIFE. You work too hard and too long. You have sons to labor for you.

LING TAN (*indignantly*). What nonsense is this! I am not yet so feeble—

LING'S WIFE (*calmly*). You are no longer young and you must not strain yourself.

LING TAN. I do not strain myself! I am as much a man as I ever was!

But it is obvious that he is very weary, and his wife firmly indicates the tub.

LING'S WIFE (*with a twinkle*). Come. Wash your legs. The very weight of the mud can tire a man of your great age.

Ling Tan allows himself to be bullied into the tub, where he stands meekly. His wife kneels and begins to wash the mud from his legs.

LING TAN (*thoughtfully*). Perhaps a younger wife—with a softer will—might be added to a man's household.

LING'S WIFE (*snorting*). Bring her on, old man. I shall have someone to help me with my work, and you shall be in your grave before your time.

LING TAN. I think I would survive, and I may try it to see.

LING'S WIFE (*as if idly, looking up*). What are those teeth marks on your left ear, old turnip?

LING TAN. A hill tiger bit me. It was a long time ago.

LING'S WIFE. Yes. I was a hill tiger. And you made the mistake of treating me as a tame house cat. It could happen again.

LING TAN. Not so long as the scars remain to remind me.

They smile at each other. These two are very close.

LING'S WIFE. Is it not good here with me in the shade?

The washing is finished and Ling Tan steps out of the tub, and begins to dry his legs.

LING TAN (*sitting down and yawning*). It is. But a man with his juices still in him should not so indulge himself. (*Without moving*) I should go back to the field.

LING'S WIFE. It will be finished without you. And if you must be useful —here—help me make these ducks ready for market. (*She thrusts the half-plucked duck at him.*)

LING TAN. That is woman's work.

LING'S WIFE. If Heaven sends a woman too much work, Heaven will also send the help to do it.

LING TAN (*grinning, starting to work*). How is it, old one, that Heaven's will and your own are always the same?

LING TAN'S RICE FIELD is now seen at sundown; long shadows streak across the earth. Lao Er and Lao Ta have finished their work and are moving leisurely down the rutted path toward the compound gate. Then LAO ER and LAO TA appear at close range, moving along.

LAO ER (*looking off*). The grass is good in the hills. The ox grows fat.

Next Lao San, Ling's third son, appears (as seen from their angle) riding an ox down a slope toward his brothers on the path. He is playing a flute; music is heard.

LAO TA (*grinning*). Which is the ox, and which is our brother?

A close moving view of LAO SAN as he rides along: He is a slim, sensitive, intense boy—a strange one in this family of sturdy farmers. The view widens as the ox reaches the path, and falls in behind Lao Er and Lao Ta.

LAO TA (*grinning*). Is our brother dreaming?

LAO ER. No. That vacant look is his usual expression.

LAO SAN (*giving them a lofty look*). You are very dirty. Have you been playing in the mud again?

LAO TA (*winking at Lao Er*). We have. And it was very pleasant. Why do you not join us tomorrow?

LAO ER. You ask too much. Where you find hard work, you will *not* find our brother.

LAO SAN (*calmly*). There is work for all—for those with strong backs, and for those with strong minds. (*Smiling*) If the mind is strong enough, the back need not bend, nor need the feet get muddy.

Still smiling, he urges the ox on through the gate and his two brothers are forced to leap nimbly aside, into the ditch. Then we again get a close moving shot of LAO ER and LAO TA as they regain the path.

LAO TA (*jerking his head after Lao San*). He speaks of his mind, but I say he has none at all—only a temper!

He turns to Lao Er for agreement, but Lao Er has lost interest in teasing Lao San, and is walking along thoughtfully.

LAO TA (*giving him a sidelong look*). Brother, *your* mind is absent these days. Why is this?

LAO ER (*after a pause, then reluctantly*). I think—and my thoughts trouble me.

LAO TA (*affectionately*). What is a brother for, if not to share your troubles?

LAO ER. Well, then . . . . here is one of the things . . . (*He hesitates, then blurts out.*) Women are not the same as we are.

LAO TA (*laughing*). Married four months, and you have just found this out!

LAO ER (*embarrassed, but dogged*). And here is another thing: Women do not think as men do.

LAO TA. Women should not think at all—they are not equal to it. (*By now they have entered the compound, and go to put away their tools.*)

LAO ER. My wife Jade is equal to it.

LAO TA. You worry too much about that one of yours. When she has a son, the son will be more important than the mother is.

LAO ER. Son! I have not yet a wife—as I would have her. She is like a western wind. When I reach for her, she is gone. . . .

LAO TA. Even a western wind can be caught and tamed. (*They now pass Lao San, who is bedding down and feeding the ox.*)

LAO ER. I do not want her tame! Only . . . . I do not understand her . . . . she is mine, yet not mine . . . . when I touch her, it is as if her spirit goes, and only her body is left there.

LAO TA. If she is beautiful and sweet-smelling, is that not enough? (*They reach the pond, step in, and start to wash their legs.*) It is your fault. I have watched you. At night when the men sit and smoke you are the first to leave.

LAO ER (*a little sheepishly*). Can I help it if the desire for sleep overcomes me?

LAO TA. Do you not know that with a woman eagerness passes for weakness? Tonight sit with the old men until the last, as I do.

LAO ER. That is easy for you. But I have never found Jade in the same place twice, and never waiting for me. . . . (*Then, suddenly*) Do you think that is the answer to what troubles me? (*As Lao Ta nods sagely*) Then I will not go to her until dawn and perhaps not even then!

This cuts to the main ROOM of LING'S HOUSE. This is a large room with a stove and a long table, benches and chairs, a chest or two and a few ornaments, including the ancestral tablet. Three doors lead from it to the sleeping quarters of Ling Tan and his wife; Jade and Lao Er; and Lao Ta and Orchid. Lao San sleeps on a bamboo couch in a corner. Ling's Wife enters, carrying an armful of fuel, which she throws down.

LING'S WIFE. Where are the women my sons married? (*She sniffs the rice in a cauldron on the stove.*) Orchid! You good-for-nothing! Your husband comes! Jade! Jade! (*She takes up a pile of clean towels from the table, goes to Lao Ta's door, and pounds on it.*) Orchid! You lazy one!

The door opens and Orchid, Lao Ta's wife, appears. She carries a baby girl, a year-and-a-half old, in her arms, and a boy-child of four or five tugs at her trouser legs. Orchid is a pretty, soft, stupid and kindly creature.

ORCHID (*breathlessly*). I must tell you about my youngest child.

LING'S WIFE (*alarmed*). My grandchild? What about her?

ORCHID. She was lying there . . . . and all at once she opened her mouth and I thought—I thought she was going to speak!

LING'S WIFE (*exasperated*). Now then! You are surely one of those who has given birth and remains in a daze at what you have done! (*She shoves her toward the courtyard.*) Your husband waits! Attend him!

ORCHID (*meekly, starting out*). I go, mother.

LING'S WIFE (*snorting, she flings the towel over Orchid's arm*). Then take this clean towel I have made ready (*Orchid goes, and Ling's Wife hammers on the door of Lao Er's room.*) Jade! Jade! The men of the house are at home!

The scene cuts to the POND at which Lao San is sitting on a rock, idly playing the flute, following which we see LING TAN, who is standing a little apart watching him with indulgent eyes

Ling's Wife, carrying two towels, comes to Ling Tan. He turns, conscious that she has caught him watching his third son.

> LING TAN. It is a pleasing tune our third son plays.
>
> LING'S WIFE (*snorting*). I would take that squealing thing from him and get him a wife. It is time he brought grandsons into this house!
>
> LING TAN (*mildly*). In time .... in time....

They start toward the pond, the scene moving with them

> LING'S WIFE. If you told him to marry you are not sure he would obey. So you spare yourself the need of dealing with him.

As Ling Tan frowns, but does not answer, the scene cuts to a view at the pond (as seen by them): Lao San runs a little trill on the flute and Lao Ta makes a sour face, grabs the instrument and tosses it into the pond. Lao San, his face suddenly furious, whirls on Lao Ta and knocks him into the water after the flute. Lao Ta lands with a great splash, drenching Orchid, who stands waiting with her towel. Then we again see LING TAN and his WIFE, who have been watching this scene.

> LING TAN. He plays a squealing thing perhaps, but he takes care of himself also.
>
> LING'S WIFE. Shall I tell you a secret thing that is in your heart, old man?
>
> LING TAN (*hastily*). No.
>
> LING'S WIFE. Our third son is the son you love best, but most uneasily. He is different from the others, and you fear that difference. That is why you ever go on the far side of an argument with him.
>
> LING TAN (*loudly, ignoring her remark*). Our sons wait for their towels!

Ling's Wife laughs at him, and goes on toward the pond. Ling Tan takes a seat on the bench to watch.

LAO TA now has climbed out of the pond and is washing his own head and shoulders. He comes up, spluttering, as he reaches for the towel.

> ORCHID (*dreamily*). This day our youngest child did a wondrous thing. She was there on the floor and as if by magic she—

Lao Ta grabs the towel and plunges his face in it.

> LAO TA (*breathing deeply of the towel*). It is clean. I can smell it. (*He smiles at her proudly.*) You washed it.

Orchid smiles and drops her eyes, accepting the unearned compliment. At this moment Ling's Wife passes, and gives her a hard look...

A fuller view at the POND discloses Ling Tan sitting down as he watches his sons. Lao San is now standing in the pond, washing. As Ling's Wife passes him, she tosses him a towel. Lao Er, who has just finished washing his head and shoulders, is blinded by the water in his eyes and gropes out for his towel.

> LAO ER. Jade! Jade! Where is my towel! (*He finds the towel in his mother's hand and reacts in relief.*) Thank you, Jade. (*He wipes the water from his eyes and sees, not Jade, but his mother, who regards him ironically.*)
>
> LING'S WIFE (*sniffing*). Jade! I have not seen her since the sun was in the middle of the sky. The matchmaker cheated us on that one.

Lao Er is appalled and ashamed. Even Jade has never flouted family custom like this before. He is very conscious that the others are watching him, with badly-concealed amusement.

    LAO ER (*trying to bluster*). What? My wife is not in the house?

    LING'S WIFE. I could not find her. It comes of women having their feet free. Nowadays they run around like goats.

To cover his almost overpowering discomfiture, Lao Er suddenly becomes very intent on toweling his body. By this time Lao Ta and Lao San have finished washing, and, wrapping their big towels around their middles, they kick off their trousers. Ling's Wife picks up the muddy garments, and begins to rinse them in the pond.

    ORCHID (*without moving*). May I help you, mother?

    LING'S WIFE (*with a mirthless laugh*). Have you ever done so? (*To Lao Er*) Or has *your* worthless one? All that is done in this house—*I* do!

Lao Er looks even more unhappy, but Lao Ta grins wickedly.

    LAO TA (*pointedly*). At least *my* wife stays at home.

    LAO SAN (*chiming in*). But Jade has a *reason* to go to the village. (*Wisely*) When a woman knows a man wants her—she will ever display herself before him. (*At this, Lao Er's face darkens with anger and jealousy.*)

    LAO TA (*playing it up*). That is true! Have you not seen our fourth cousin look at Jade? He resembles a sick cat. (*He imitates the fourth cousin.*)

    LAO SAN. If *I* had such a wife I would beat her until she was not so good to look upon.

    LING TAN (*laughing*). If more of that were done—there would be less trouble with wives.

    LING'S WIFE (*drily*). Only men should make sure first they are able! These new-fashioned women are not so easily beaten!

Lao Er abruptly kicks off his trousers and wraps his towel around his middle.

    LAO ER. I will dress and go find her, and then we will see who is able! (*He climbs out of the pond, and stamps majestically toward the house while the others grin after him.*)

    LING TAN (*after him*). Eat first, my son, and your arm will be stronger for all this beating!

LAO ER, seen close, disappears into the house, with his towel flapping, while laughter is heard from the family. This dissolves to the COMPOUND GATE as Lao Er, now dressed in fresh clothes, comes out. He quickly cuts a bamboo switch, tries it smartly against his leg, then, frowning, he starts off. And this dissolves to a BRIDGE, IN MOONLIGHT, as Lao Er walks purposefully along and without seeming to do so, keeps an eye peeled for Jade. He carries the bamboo switch. As he crosses the bridge, a family at dinner on the deck of a sampan, looks up and greets him. He passes on without stopping.

    FAMILY (*chattering*). He hurries. Perhaps someone is sick in his house. A man does not look for a doctor with a switch in his hand. He goes toward his cousin's house. The only sickness there is laziness.

A closer moving view shows Lao Er coming to the Third Cousin's house a poor and dirty place. He hesitates then steals around to the window, and looks in.

VOICE OF THIRD COUSIN'S WIFE (*sharply*). Who tries to see within our house without himself being seen?

The FRONT DOOR OF THIRD COUSIN'S HOUSE: Standing in the doorway is Third Cousin's Wife, a large, pig-shaped woman, holding a bowl of rice to her face and supping out of it loudly. Lao Er enters, a little sheepishly.

LAO ER (*politely*). Are you eating, wife of my Third Cousin?

COUSIN'S WIFE (*whining voice, still gobbling*). Our rice is poor and scanty and we have no pork at all, but will you share it with us?

LAO ER. Thank you but I cannot. (*Peering around*) Are you alone, then? Is my Fourth Cousin not here?

COUSIN'S WIFE. My son is not home yet. (*Scornfully*) But your Third Cousin, my honored husband, is here.

She steps inside, revealing her husband, the Third Cousin. He sits just inside the door, bent over a book. He is a thin old man with a scholar's cap and spectacles.

LAO ER (*bowing*). How are you, sir? What new thing have you found in your books? (*The Third Cousin smiles, but before he can answer, his wife cuts in.*)

COUSIN'S WIFE (*sneering*). Nothing his family can chew and swallow and grow fat on, I can tell you!

LAO ER (*trying to keep suspicion out of his voice*). My Fourth Cousin is in the city, perhaps?

COUSIN'S WIFE. I do not know. My son has been gone since the noon-meal.

Lao Er's face darkens, but Third Cousin goes peacefully back to his book.

LAO ER (*turning away*). I must get on. I have business in the village.

Cousin's Wife looks after him as he leaves. Then she turns and nudges her husband with her foot.

COUSIN'S WIFE. He lies. He has no business in the village at this hour.

THIRD COUSIN (*immersed in his book*). Eh?

COUSIN'S WIFE. He looks for his wife, Jade. (*She draws in her breath sharply.*) And if he finds her with our son, as he well may—

THIRD COUSIN (*mildly*). Jade is married to Lao Er. The thing my son felt for her is ended.

COUSIN'S WIFE. It will never be ended until one of them is dead. (*Bitterly, as Third Cousin sighs and goes back to his book*) You old book fool! It is your fault. It is your fault that we starve. It is your fault we did not get Jade for our son!

THIRD COUSIN. Can I control a woman's choice?

COUSIN'S WIFE. A woman's choice! Did not your cousin Ling Tan give you thirty silver dollars and then did you not tell our son he could not have the girl?

THIRD COUSIN. Quiet, woman, I read.

COUSIN'S WIFE (*shrilly*). Aiiii! Out of all this something terrible will happen!

This scene dissolves to LAO ER as he nears the teahouse in the center of the town. His eyes are hot with jealousy, and he looks fully capable of causing "something terrible" to happen. He stops, looks off, then strikes his switch against his leg. This cuts to the SQUARE before the teahouse, where a number of people are gathered to see some magic pictures on a sheet of white cloth hung between two bamboos. Four or five young men and women, city people, are in charge of the event and one of the young men is making a speech, following which we get a close view of the SPEAKER with the screen behind him.

> SPEAKER. We are students and we have come from the University to travel through the country and tell you and others like you news of the war in the North. The Japanese march toward us. . .

On the screen we see a motion picture of many Japanese marching, then quick scenes of the Japanese investing a city.

The VILLAGERS are looking intently at the scenes and are disturbed by them. A close view of LAO ER then shows him reaching the edge of the crowd and looking about.

> SPEAKER'S VOICE. These are true pictures of what the Japanese are doing! They are doing it *now!* While you sit here and watch, these very things are happening!
>
> LAO ER (*to a man in the audience*). Have you seen my Fourth Cousin, Neighbor Shen?

Neighbor Shen nods and points off. Lao Er looks, and frowns, and FOURTH COUSIN comes into view. He is a good-looking young man. He is listening to the speaker. A woman sits beside him, her face hidden by a hat.

> SPEAKER'S VOICE. These are your people they are murdering—and mine! This is *our* country they are looting. . . !

LAO ER moves forward, suspicious at the sight of the woman beside his cousin. He is so angry and jealous that he does not listen to the Speaker, but as he passes the villagers it is obvious that they are concerned by both the pictures and the words.

> SPEAKER'S VOICE. The enemy is ruthless, and he is savage! He regards us only as slaves! We cannot deal with him! We must resist him.

Lao Er now reaches Fourth Cousin.

> FOURTH COUSIN (*looking up, disagreeably*). Seeking someone, perhaps?

The woman turns and Lao Er sees she is an elderly woman. His scowl changes to a grin.

> LAO ER (*loftily*). Not one who would sit near you, my cousin.
>
> FOURTH COUSIN (*acidly*). If my father had been rich enough to give me the wife of my desire, I would see to it that I could put my hands on her at all times.
>
> LAO ER (*blandly now*). It is with pleasure I leave you.

He moves off. During this the voice of the Speaker has been silent. Lao Er passes the stereopticon machine and its operator. He looks at it, then off toward the screen.

We see the SCREEN and the SPEAKER at the screen shows Japanese machine gunning civilians, killed and wounded Chinese, burning houses, Chinese women mourning their dead, the bodies of dead children, and Japanese soldiers looting a shop. Lao Er stands to one side, watching the screen. He, too, for the moment is caught up.

> SPEAKER. When the Japanese reach your village, and they will come here

be sure of that—you must resist them! They will come with lies in their mouths and death in their hands and you must resist them to your own deaths and beyond! Are you able to do this?

JADE now comes into view: she is sitting in the crowd. She is young, slim, and just now caught up with what the Speaker has been saying. She looks at the people around her, obviously eager for them to reassure the student.

SPEAKER. All of you—rise and tell me you are able!

JADE (*suddenly, impulsively, jumping to her feet*). Yes .... we are able!

The people around her merely turn to stare, and appalled at finding herself standing alone, she starts to sit down.

SPEAKER. See! There is one who speaks! Are there not others? Tell me! Come!

JADE (*carried away*). Yes! Come!

LAO ER has now seen Jade and is angry that she should cry out so before everyone.

LAO ER (*to Jade*). You come! I am hungry! (*As he starts for Jade he passes Fourth Cousin, who lifts an ironic eyebrow.*)

We see the CROWD (including JADE and LAO ER): The crowd, in spite of its concern at the pictures, is amused by this. Jade turns and stares unseeingly at Lao Er for a moment.

CROWD (*laughing*). The boy is right! A woman should have food ready when her man is hungry! *My* wife is at home and where she should be!

At this Jade turns, and goes meekly toward Lao Er.

SPEAKER (*continuing*). Am I speaking into the wind? Have you not understood what you have seen and heard? I know you have! Tell me you will resist the enemy when he comes! There was one brave enough to stand and speak! Let me hear the voices of you all! And let your words swell into a mighty roar that the enemy will hear and tremble before!

The crowd turns back to him, forgetting the diverting incident.

CROWD. How then can we resist? Can we fight machines with our hands? I do not know what *I* can do! Nor do I! The enemy is evil—yes—but what can lone men do against him? Your words are strong, but we are weak—

LAO ER and JADE are again seen as she reaches his side, smiling tentatively at him; but his face is ashamed and he keeps his eyes from her. He turns and walks stiffly off, first making sure, from the corner of his eye, that she is following him, albeit a little resentfully. The scene following them, they move out of the square, Lao Er striding purposefully, Jade following behind. They pass Fourth Cousin, who looks at Jade hungrily. Lao Er tightens his lips, and slaps his leg again with the bamboo switch.

Approaching the BRIDGE Lao Er, still slapping his thigh with the switch, walks along rapidly.—He is frowning and steely-eyed.—Jade watches him speculatively.—As they approach the VIADUCT Lao Er is still walking ahead of Jade. Then we see them closer: Lao Er (still carrying the switch) is very conscious that Jade is there behind him. She leans forward and tries to see his face. Her own face is now alive with both defiance and mischief.

LAO ER (*finally, in a surly voice*). Why do you shame me by showing yourself off to everybody? (*Receiving no answer*) I come home, my belly roaring like a hungry lion. . . .

JADE. Why did you not eat then and silence it?

LAO ER. How can I eat when you are not in your proper place? I am ashamed before my own parents. (*Receiving no answer—sternly*) I wish you would not go on the street alone.

JADE (*challengingly*). Why?

LAO ER. Other men will see you.

JADE (*shrugging*). I do not look at them.

LAO ER. I do not want them to look at you. You are pretty and you are my wife.

JADE (*with more than a tinge of rebellion now*). But how can I stay always in the courtyard? These are not ancient times.

LAO ER. I wish it were those times. I would like to lock you up.

JADE. If you locked me up, I would not eat, and then I should die.

LAO ER. I would not let you die.

JADE. But these are the new times and I will come and go.

LAO ER. I should beat you.

JADE (*lifting her chin*). I have done nothing.

LAO ER. But you were not where a woman *should* be . . . . at home and waiting for her husband. (*He strides on, and she follows.*)

As they come near the GRAVEYARD Lao Er starts walking slower and slower, and as they are seen near the willow tree he goes even more slowly.

LAO ER. . . . . And there is this thing —before we were wed, when the choice was put to you, why did you choose me above my fourth cousin? (*Jade is stubbornly erect and silent. He goes on, more loudly.*) If you could choose now, which would it be?

JADE (*flatly*). You both have two legs and two arms and all your fingers and toes and you are neither of you cross-eyed nor scabby-headed, so what is the difference between you?

LAO ER (*unhappily*). You use me very ill.

JADE (*laughing*). Oh, you look so pale and so thin! Oh, you are so to be pitied, you big turnip!

But he does not want her laughter. He stops, and draws her to a halt directly beneath the great willow. The frogs croak nearby in the rice-fields.

LAO ER (*wistfully now*). I wish I were a man of learning. I wish I knew the words to ease myself so I could tell you what I feel.

JADE (*watching him, her own eyes inscrutable*). What do you feel?

LAO ER (*helplessly*). I know—but I do not have the words.

JADE. I, too, am not very learned.

LAO ER. Is that why you do not often speak to me?

JADE. Two must speak for understanding.

LAO ER. Will you tell me everything that is in you if I tell you all that is in me?

Jade continues to study him for a moment, her eyes still remote.

JADE (*slowly*). Yes. . . .

LAO ER (*eagerly*). Then tonight we will speak together?

JADE. Yes.

Lao Er looks at her, hopeful that this will lead to an understanding between them. As he starts off, he almost shyly reaches to take her hand and realizes he still holds the switch. A little sheepishly, he drops it. She laughs, and takes her place beside him, as an equal, not a woman. The gesture has a kind of bold comradeship in it, but nothing of the love and desire he craves from her.

This scene dissolves to the exterior of LING TAN'S FRONT GATE in the MOONLIGHT: Lao Er and Jade approach the gate, still side by side. Lao Er stops and looks at Jade, then toward the house and back at her. Jade laughs, shrugs and steps back, indicating she will save his face if he so wishes. She demurely follows him and relieved, he strides masterfully through the gate, as the scene wipes to the INNER COURTYARD.

The courtyard is a pleasant place. There is a small pool in the center of the yard and a lotus with six blossoms blooming in a jar. There is a table, a bench, some stools, and a jar of water with a bowl for dipping. Herbs and fish are spread out to dry. Fuel for the stove inside is piled near the door.

The men have finished their food and Ling's Wife (with Orchid's baby on her lap) and Orchid are eating at the table as Lao Er and Jade come in. The dog is eating too.

LING'S WIFE (*chewing rice*). We could wait no longer. (*She takes some of the softened rice from her own mouth and feeds the baby.*)

LAO ER. I want no waiting. (*Then, roughly to Jade*) Fetch me my food. I will eat where my father and brothers are. (*He sits near Ling Tan and Lao Ta.*)

JADE (*meekly*). Yes, my husband.

LAO ER (*crowding his luck*). Since you did not cook the meal, you may clean up after it!

JADE. I will, my husband.

Orchid looks surprised at Jade's sudden meekness. Jade takes a bowl of rice to Lao Er.

LING'S WIFE (*aloud, to herself*). He *must* have beaten her!

Then, seeing Orchid smile, she frowns and Orchid hastily straightens her face.

This dissolves to the COURTYARD at night: It is nearly bedtime. Ling Tan and Third Cousin sit talking and smoking. Lao Er and Lao Ta sit nearby, as does Lao San. Through the open doorway the women can be seen as they finish the tasks of the day. Lao Er keeps one eye on Jade as she works.

THIRD COUSIN (*mellowly*). . . . . . I do not take too much credit to myself that I am the only man in these parts who can read and write. How would I find the time for my books if you did not send me rice, and a new coat now and then, and sometimes even meat?

LING TAN (*warmly*). You are a scholar, and my honored cousin. It is only proper that your needs and comforts be supplied. And my land yields enough for all. . . .

Third Cousin bows. It is obvious there is a strong tie of affection as well as blood between these two.

LING'S WIFE. Orchid, it is time for your children to be in their bed.

Orchid nods and goes toward the bedroom with her children. Jade starts to move toward a part of the room no longer visible from the court.

We then see LAO ER and LAO TA: Lao Er is watching Jade hungrily as she disappears from sight, and half rises.

> LAO TA (*touching his arm*). You have made a good beginning. Do not spoil it.

With dignity, Lao Er re-seats himself, and the scene expands to include the others.

> THIRD COUSIN (*thoughtfully, to Ling*). But, cousin, have you ever thought of this? When your time comes to go into the earth yourself, shall you divide your land among your sons? (*As Ling Tan nods*) And will there *still* be enough for all—or will they quarrel because their bellies are not full?
>
> LING TAN (*to Lao Ta, easily*). As my eldest son, you must answer our cousin. Can this land feed three men and their wives and children after I am gone?
>
> LAO TA. It can. For I will eat less meat, if my brothers will, and live in peace with them.

Lao Er and Lao San nod and smile. Ling Tan also smiles contentedly. He was sure of this answer.

> LING TAN. If I have taught my sons that peace is good I am content.
>
> JADE'S VOICE (*suddenly heard*). If you had been with me today you would not talk so easily of peace, father!

Amazed, they all turn, and the scene expands to include Jade, who stands in the doorway. Again, as before the teahouse, it is as if she has spoken from an inner compulsion and in spite of her natural shyness.

> LING TAN (*mildly, to the men*). If it were proper for a man to speak directly to his daughter-in-law, I would ask her why should not peaceful men speak of peace.

At this, Lao Er gives Jade a warning look, and she drops her eyes, then steps back.

> LAO ER (*uncomfortably*). Forgive my wife, father, if she speaks too boldly, but today at the teahouse students came and showed the magic pictures and talked. They told of the war in the North, and how the little dwarfs from the East Ocean Islands burn our cities and kill our people!

Ling Tan turns and looks at Jade, and it is plain he sees in her only a woman who must be soothed and comforted.

> LING TAN. I wonder if my daughter remembers when other students brought to us the pictures of the flies?
>
> LAO SAN (*before she can speak*). I remember! Flies as large as water buffalo!
>
> LING TAN (*nodding*). And they told us they were more dangerous than tigers. Now, everyone knows *our* flies are as small as a grain of rice, and as harmless. (*Proving his point*) And so, does it not follow that today also perhaps both pictures and words were made too large to be life or truth, and does that not quiet the woman's fear of my daughter?
>
> LING'S WIFE (*appearing beside Jade*). Of course it does, and it is time she was in her bed.

Jade stands for a moment, irresolute, then she turns and goes toward her bedroom. Lao Er's eyes follow her longingly.

LING TAN (*to the others*). But we, who are men, know there is killing and suffering in the North.

LAO SAN. And do you not believe it will come here, father?

LING TAN (*slowly*). I believe something else: If a man lives his life in decency and as he should and then evil comes to him, it cannot harm him and he will conquer and overcome it. I live by this and I think so do all our kinsmen in this village. We are men of peace.

THIRD COUSIN (*rising*). True. True. Also, the North is a long way from here. (*Yawning*) And so is my bed and I must get to it.

Ling Tan also rises, to see him to the gate, and then a close view of LAO ER and LAO TA shows Lao Er looking longingly after Jade as he makes a move to follow her.

LAO TA (*warningly*). She still is not cured. Wait five hundred heartbeats and then go to her. (*Reluctantly, at this, Lao Er nods, and sits back.*)

A larger scene includes the COURTYARD as Ling Tan escorts Third Cousin toward the gate. Lao Ta rises, goes into the big room and to his sleeping room. Lao San, yawning, follows him.

At the gate, Ling Tan takes a deep breath, and looks up: The moon is round tonight, and the color of a ripe peach.

THIRD COUSIN. I have read that the earth too is round.

LING TAN. Yes, you have told me that. But one thing troubles me. How is it then, if the world is round, that men on the bottom side can walk?

THIRD COUSIN. Everything is opposite there. Children are born with white hair and blue eyes. Scholars begin to write from the wrong side of the page. Youth is admired instead of age. So—why can we not believe they walk with their heads hanging down and enjoy it?

They chuckle briefly together and Third Cousin bows and departs. Ling Tan turns back into the courtyard, and meets his wife, who has come to meet him. She takes the pin from her hair and picks her teeth.

LING TAN. Old woman, have you thought that somewhere very far below the spot where we stand our land goes on and on until at last a stranger stands on it?

LING'S WIFE (*startled*). And plants seed and takes his harvest from it as though it were his own? (*As Ling nods whimsically*) But it is not. It is ours. And our sons after us.

LING TAN (*softly*). Yes. The land is ours as deep as it goes beneath our feet—and the stars above our heads belong to us and whatever there is beyond them. . . .

LING'S WIFE (*frowning*). But I am troubled about this stranger on our land. Somewhere he reaps his grain without asking you. You should ask him for rent!

LING TAN (*laughing aloud*). That I would do, old woman. I would have the law on him if I knew how to tell him so.

Still smiling, he starts for the big room. She looks after him, then follows. She passes Lao Er, who sits, grimly waiting for time to pass.

LING'S WIFE (*softly—noticing him*). Do not be troubled, my son. It is often *good* to beat a woman.

LAO ER. Mmmmm? Oh, yes . . . .

yes, my mother. (*She nods wisely, and goes on toward the door.*)

The BIG ROOM as Ling's Wife enters: Ling Tan blows out the lamp and the two of them cross the room toward their sleeping quarters. As they pass the couch where Lao San is already sleeping Ling's Wife pulls the cover over him.

LING TAN (*with a twinkle*). Can it be you have a soft spot for our third son also?

LING'S WIFE (*her face softening*). I will not deny it. When I look at him like this I do not see a quarrelsome boy, but the child he was—thin and sick and always crying . . . . when each day seemed to be his last. (*They stand looking down at Lao San.*)

LING TAN (*also sober now*). Can it be the gods have punished him for a thing *I* did—or did not do? The thought is ever with me.

LING'S WIFE (*brisk again*). It is folly to worry about what is past. (*She starts for the room; Ling Tan follows.*) It is something here and now that troubles me. It is Jade. Orchid is stupid—but she does what I tell her to do. While Jade—no, I do not think I like her.

LING TAN. Do you know why, old woman? Because she is the same as you are yourself. No man can tell what will come out of her. (*He chuckles tenderly.*) And here is another thing. Our second son will never tire of her, as I have never tired of you. . . . (*They go into the room together.*)

At the DOORWAY to the COURTYARD, Lao Er pops in, and fairly flies across to his own doorway.—Lao Er enters his SLEEPING ROOM, and reacts at what he sees: The room, as seen from his angle, is lighted by the moonlight which streams through the window. Jade is lying on the double mat. Then we get a fuller view of the ROOM.

LAO ER (*tentatively*). This is the first time I have found you waiting for me. (*Suddenly shy*) Who will speak first then?

JADE (*quietly, almost casually*). You. Ask me what you will.

Lao Er goes to the bed, and sits on the stool beside it. Then we see husband and wife closer. There is silence for a second, then Lao Er speaks, almost stammering in his excitement at this moment.

LAO ER. Well then. What are you thinking all day?

JADE (*frowning thoughtfully*). I think of twenty and thirty things at a time. My thoughts are like a chain and one is fast to the other.

LAO ER. But what are they?

JADE. I think of a bird and how it flies . . . and why I am not able to lift myself above the earth. . .

LAO ER (*eagerly*). But now. What are you thinking *now?*

Jade looks at him for a moment. The devil rises in her.

JADE. Now? I think of nothing at all.

LAO ER (*hesitating, trying again*). Well, then. What did you think of me the first time you saw me?

JADE (*promptly*). I cannot remember.

LAO ER (*let down, but persisting*). No, I mean when—after we were married.

JADE. I was glad you are taller than I am. For a woman I am too tall.

LAO ER (*gazing at her hungrily*). No, you are not. (*He touches her hand.*) And then what did you think?

JADE (*giving him a side-long look*). Then? Then I wondered what you thought about me.

LAO ER (*ardently*). But you knew that I wanted you.

Jade looks at him for a moment; it is as if she is on the verge of telling him what is really in her heart.

JADE. And then I wondered. . . .

LAO ER (*hardly breathing*). Yes. . . .

JADE. And I wondered if you would . . . (*meeting his eyes*) . . . . if you would give me the thing I would have.

LAO ER. Tell me. I will buy it for you.

Jade looks at him for a moment, then rises, moves to the window, and stands looking out.

JADE. Buy? Perhaps all the things I want cannot be bought.

LAO ER (*following her*). All women like presents. Tell me what it is.

JADE. I want . . . . (*her eyes hardening a little, shrugging*) . . . . earrings. Yes, that is it. A pair of earrings.

LAO ER. I will buy them for you tomorrow. (*Softly*) Now. Have I made you happy?

JADE (*indifferently*). Yes. (*Then, impulsively*) No. You have not. I do not want earrings, but there is something that can be bought I would have. Buy me a book.

LAO ER (*genuinely startled*). But you cannot read.

JADE. I can read.

LAO ER. Women like you never read!

JADE. I learned. A word or two at a time. My brother could read and I learned from him. A little every day. But I have no book of my own.

Lao Er stands silently for a moment. This is a strange and disturbing thing she has asked.

LAO ER. I never thought to see a *woman* read in this house. (*Looking down at her, melting*) I will give the book to you. But one more thing you must tell me. (*In a low voice, as if afraid to ask*) Do you ever think of my cousin who wanted you too?

JADE (*looking at him for a moment, then shrugging and laughing*). Is that what has been curdling in you? Then no—no—no—however you ask me I will say no. . . .

LAO ER (*moving very close to her*). And you are my wife, are you not?

JADE (*looking at him swiftly, her smile fading*). I am your wife.

LAO ER. And you belong to me, do you not?

JADE (*in a low voice*). I belong to you.

LAO ER. And you will belong to me all of your life?

JADE. Yes.

LAO ER. Then why do you not turn to me of your own will?

Jade does not meet his eyes. She turns, and goes to bed.

JADE. We must sleep. Tomorrow's work must be done. (*She gets into the bed, and pulls the covers over her.*)

LAO ER. You have not answered me.

JADE (*closing her eyes*). And if you

are to go to the city for the book you must rest now.

LAO ER (*with a despairing gesture*).

What man knows how a woman's heart is made?

The scene fades out.

PART TWO

A ROAD leading to the city fades in. It is early morning. Lao Er, carrying a basket, walks briskly toward the city walls which can be seen in the far distance.— This dissolves to a closeup of a SIGN IN CHINESE in front of the SHOP OF WU LIEN. Then the view draws back to disclose the STREET and Wu Lien's shop for the sale of things foreign. It is a prosperous little business. Lao Er approaches, looks in the windows with appreciation, smiles, and enters.

In WU LIEN'S SHOP: The place is filled with foreign wares: flashlights, rubber shoes, knitted garments, pens, pencils, dishes, pictures in frames, etc. There are several customers. The two clerks, (one old, one young) who know Lao Er, bow politely as he enters.

OLD CLERK. Ten thousand greetings, young sir.

LAO ER (*bowing*). Where is my brother-in-law, Wu Lien?

OLD CLERK (*indicating the rear of the shop*). He is within—and takes his morning rest.

We see the COURT of the shop as Lao Er comes out and goes to the house of Wu Lien. The house is snug and comfortable, even a little luxurious.

In WU LIEN'S LARGE ROOM: Wu Lien sits in a bamboo chair taking his ease while his five-year-old daughter fans him. Wu Lien is very fat, and as he sits now, naked to the waist, his body is revealed as soft and pale as a woman's. Around his lax, smooth wrists are rings of flesh and his fingers are fat and pointed. Wu Lien's mother, huge and old and stupid, sits in a corner of the room, and his seven-year-old son plays nearby. Lao Er enters, bows respectfully first to Wu Lien, then to Wu Lien's mother.

LAO ER. I greet you. And you, honored mother of my sister's husband.

The old lady can only manage a bow and a wheeze.

WU LIEN. Ah! Sit down! Sit down! (*He raises himself a little, but not more than is needed for the younger brother of a wife, then bawls out.*) Here is your second brother, mother of my children! (*To Lao Er, chuckling*) Well, then! You are a farmer and one who looks it! The dirt is still beneath your fingernails!

Wu Lien's Wife comes running out of an inner room, her coat loose at the neck. She is a round-faced, hearty country woman with bad teeth and a full red mouth. She carries a third child, a baby boy, in her arms.

WU LIEN'S WIFE (*shouting*). And how are the old ones and all the others? Is my sister-in-law Jade with child yet? (*She laughs and puts her hand over her mouth to conceal her teeth.*) Why, what a puny man you are! Can it be you take no interest

WU LIEN (*drily*). It would seem you take interest enough for both.

WU LIEN'S WIFE. My interest will never make him a father. (*She turns, and beams at Lao Er.*) Ah, you are hungry. I can tell it. (*She laughs again, and runs out.*)

WU LIEN (*good-naturedly, looking after her*). In each generation a city man should do as I have done. Take for wife a woman from the country. Thus the line is kept strong and hard. (*He slaps his own jelly-like belly.*)

Lao Er reaches out, and draws Wu Lien's son to him.

LAO ER (*admiring the child*). And here is the proof of your wisdom. (*Hesitating, then*) Brother, will you dip into your wisdom and tell me a thing? (*Wu Lien nods.*) I know that you are a man who reads. . . .

WU LIEN. Yes. Yes. I read. Often in the winter to warm my blood . . . . sometimes in the summer to cool it.

LAO ER. If you were to buy a book, what book would it be?

WU LIEN (*puckering his lips, considering*). There are books for every need. If a man wishes to read secretly and for his own private pleasure there are books for that. . . . (*He looks at Lao Er expectantly, but Lao Er shakes his head.*) Well then. For what is your book wanted?

LAO ER (*grinning nervously*). I married my woman thinking her like any other one, and now I find she can read and wants a book.

Wu Lien's Wife enters with tea and cakes, places them on the table, and stands listening, her mouth open.

WU LIEN (*to his wife*). You are only a woman, mother of my sons, but if you could read, what would you like to read? (*Wu Lien's Wife laughs, and again hides her mouth.*)

WU LIEN'S WIFE. I never thought of it. . . . I . . . .

WU LIEN (*cutting in*). *I* have thought of the one! (*To Lao Er*) It has everything in it. The good prosper and the wicked are punished. The name of the book is *All Men Are Brothers*.

LAO ER (*relieved, bowing*). Thank you. I will remember what you have told me.

At this moment there is a knocking on the door and one of Wu Lien's clerks enters.

CLERK (*nervously*). Sir, there is something.

WU LIEN (*frowning*). As before?

CLERK. Worse than before. And much louder, sir. They say they have warned you many times and their patience is at an end.

Wu Lien's face goes taut under all the fat. He hoists himself up with difficulty.

WU LIEN. These students cause trouble! An honest merchant cannot live in peace these times. . . . (*He goes out, following the clerk.*)

LAO ER. Is there evil in this for Wu Lien?

WU LIEN'S WIFE (*shrugging and laughing*). I think not. Students talk and argue, but that is all.

LAO ER (*playing with the child for a moment*). Well then. Our mother would have me ask some questions of you. (*He grins, slightly embarrassed.*) She would know if your husband likes you as well as ever.

WU LIEN'S WIFE. If anything, more.

He calls me whenever he wants anything.

LAO ER (*after a pause, delicately*). She would know—does your husband go out at night?

WU LIEN'S WIFE. Never. He tells me he is content with me.

LAO ER. Our mother also charged me to tell you that if a man speaks too well to his wife, she must take care also, lest he praise her to make amends.

WU LIEN'S WIFE. Our old one never leaves go of a child—even a daughter who is married well.

She and Lao Er laugh together. At this moment there is a terrific uproar of talk from the direction of the shop. Lao Er and Wu Lien's Wife jump up, and Lao Er runs toward the door.

In WU LIEN'S SHOP: Wu Lien is facing a student, a tall, thin young man. Outside, other such men watch through the window. The voices of both the student and Wu Lien are raised in anger.

STUDENT. We ask you once more, Wu Lien! Do not deal with the Japanese! We are at war with them! You cannot buy and sell their goods and call yourself a patriot!

Lao Er enters, and stands staring.

WU LIEN. Do you ask me to stop breathing in and out? There is a call for these things and a profit in them! Save your breath for arguments you can win!

STUDENT. Then we must speak to you in words you *can* hear.

Turning, he gives a signal. One of the young men outside the window hurls a stone through the glass. Lao Er stands aghast, as do the two clerks. The student inside the shop scoops up some goods and throws them into the street.

In the STREET other young men run forward and start to tear goods out of the window.

YOUNG MEN.
Destroy them!
Break them into pieces!
Do not let them be sold!

WU LIEN (*wildly, from within*). Stop! You are vandals!

The students pile up the goods, and set fire to them. Other merchants, from near-by shops, join the crowd and stand watching, their eyes grave. In the SHOP, now, the student, his arms full of the last of the goods, makes for the door.

STUDENT (*shouting, as he goes*). What happens here shall happen to every like house that sells Japanese goods! (*And he runs out.*)

Both Wu Lien and Lao Er dash after him. The two clerks stand shivering and afraid.

Out in the STREET the student who has led the demonstration shouts to the crowd.

STUDENT (*jumping up on the stoop, waving his hands at the crowd*). The merchant Wu Lien walks hand in hand with those who deal in your blood! He pays for Japanese goods in money that will come back to us in pain and death!

WU LIEN (*wildly to the crowd*). I deal only in innocent things that harm no one!

He tries to retrieve some of the goods, as does Lao Er. They, too, are thrust back.

STUDENT. This man Wu Lien loves his cash box above his country!

WU LIEN. That is not true!

STUDENT. Turn from this traitor as you would turn from the Japanese!

He gives a signal to the other students, jumps down from the stoop and runs off up the street, followed by the others. —Then we see Wu Lien turning appealingly to the group, including the merchants who are watching silently.

WU LIEN. Can it be that a thing I have done all my life is now held against me as a crime?

Slowly a couple of the men (obviously the merchants) turn away and go quietly into their shops. WU LIEN and LAO ER are then seen closer.

WU LIEN (*almost weeping*). Did you see those merchants turn away from me as from a bad odor? They are of my own kind!

Lao Er shuffles his feet; this is all out of his ken. He is alarmed and mystified by what has happened and he wants nothing better than to get away from this noise and uproar.

LAO ER (*lamely*). Be of stout heart, brother, it will pass. . . .

WU LIEN (*sadly*). I do not think it will and I am not a stupid man. I must turn this thing over in my mind, and decide what to do in the evil days I see ahead. . . . (*He breaks off, and sighs.*) I must think . . . . and weigh what comes out . . . . and think again. . . .

Lao Er looks after him, hesitates, then shrugs his shoulders, turns, and goes off down the street.

This dissolves to the SLEEPING ROOM of JADE and LAO ER at night: A book, wrapped in a piece of blue cotton, lies on the table. Jade stands before it, staring at it with delight and anticipation. Slowly she touches the wrapping, then as slowly loosens it and lifts out the book. She strokes it gently, then looks toward the door to the big room as she hears laughter and talk.

In the BIG ROOM Lao Er is seated at the table, eating a late supper, and telling Ling Tan, Lao Ta and Lao San what happened in the town. Ling's Wife and Orchid sit in the background, weaving sandals.

LAO ER. . . . . and then this strange young man jumped down and ran away and was gone!

LAO SAN. Was he a bandit then?

LAO ER. No. It was said he was a student.

LING'S WIFE (*snorting*). First you encounter this trouble and then you buy a book!

ORCHID (*timidly*). This book Jade now has . . . . what is it? Books have names. . . .

LAO ER. So has this one. It is called *All Men Are Brothers*.

LING TAN (*laughing*). All men are brothers! What of that stranger who lives on the other side of the earth and reaps his grain on my land? Is *he* my brother? I think not.

LAO TA (*also grinning*). Today I pulled a turnip. They grow small this year. Can it be our brother is pulling at the roots to plague us?

LING TAN. It is good to have him to blame.

ORCHID (*murmuring*). A book . . . . and Jade can read in it?

LING'S WIFE (*frowning*). You see. An idea spreads. A book! I have said and say again it is wrong to give a woman such a dangerous thing.

LAO TA. It is unnatural and mine will never have one!

LING'S WIFE (*to Lao Er*). What if a child comes, what will your woman do if she has not finished the book? Will she read on and let the child be born anyhow?

LAO ER (*embarrassed—laughs*). She will manage. (*His eyes wander toward his sleeping room. He yawns somewhat ostentatiously.*) The day has been full and there is work tomorrow.

LING TAN (*taking pity on him*). Yes, my son. Your eyes are heavy with weariness. . . . (*At this opportunity to go in to Jade, Lao Er rises with alacrity.*)

LAO TA (*grinning*). And your wife waits for you, brother, with a book in her hand.

LAO ER (*loftily*). Even a book can be closed and put away. (*He goes into the sleeping room.*)

A bean oil lamp is burning in the SLEEPING ROOM, and Jade is crouched on a stool near the bed, reading her book. Her face is intent as Lao Er enters, and stands looking at her.

LAO ER (*jealously*). It is but a book. And yet it keeps your eyes from me.

JADE (*looking up and smiling*). Come, sit beside me.

He quickly goes to her and the two are seen closer. Lao Er's eyes are on her caressingly, and at first her thoughts are only for what she has been reading.

JADE (*looking at the book*). And I will tell you what I have read.

Lao Er frowns again. He plainly wishes the book were far away.

LAO ER. How shall I know if you read truly?

He lies down on the mat within reach of her as she sits beside him on the stool.

JADE. You will know I could not make such things up. (*Her finger moves down the page.*) In this place it tells what happens when men know only greed . . . . it tells how peace is then lost . . . . and what men may do to each other. . . . (*At this, Lao Er reaches out, and touches her free hand.*)

LAO ER (*dreamily, ardently*). It is magic . . . . your eyes pick up those bird tracks . . . . and your eyes give them to your voice and your voice gives them to my ears. . . . (*He lifts her hand, and looks at it, but she, intent on the book, pulls it away.*)

JADE. And here it tells how then there is fighting. . . . (*He takes her hand again; she is suddenly aware of his nearness and although she keeps her eyes on the book, her voice trails off a little.*) . . . . and killing and even torture. . . .

LAO ER. It is wrong to torture. . . .

JADE. That is what it says.

LAO ER (*lifting her hand, and touching his face*). It is magic.

JADE (*trying to be stern*). But you do not listen.

LAO ER. I try. But my mind is gone from my body. That is because my flesh touches yours.

JADE (*with mock severity*). You must try harder. Money was spent for this book. We must not waste it.

LAO ER (*impishly*). We must waste nothing that is given us. Neither money, nor . . . . (*His hand strokes hers.*) . . . . the hours we have together.

JADE (*struggling to return to her book*). I cannot read when you keep watching me.

LAO ER (*reasonably*). Since I cannot look at the book and know what it means, I must look at you . . . . so the money will not be wasted . . . . (*His fingers go out, as if casually, and close the book.*) . . . . and nothing else.

JADE. Then I will teach you to read. (*She opens the book again, but this time with hardly the same overpowering interest.*) There is word here of how men must rise up and resist the things that make them weak. . . . (*She takes a breath; she herself feels a little weak.*)

LAO ER. That is advice *I* cannot take. Can you?

JADE (*desperately*). You will not listen!

Lao Er's free hand casually shoves the book a little to one side.

JADE (*in a last try for firmness*). And now you place the book where my hand cannot reach it.

LAO ER (*capturing both her hands now*). Shall I put it back within your grasp?

JADE. Yes. . . . (*Then, quickly, capitulating*) No. . . . (*As he smiles at her triumphantly, she makes one last effort for dignity.*) I will rest my eyes now. And I will teach you to read another time.

LAO ER (*smiling*). I will remind you . . . . when I am ready for reading. (*His eyes are on her, suddenly they go a little sober as she turns to him; he rises and kneels before her.*) I hope no evil lies ahead of me.

JADE. Evil?

LAO ER (*slowly*). There may well be. For I am wicked. I love you more than I love my father and my mother.

Jade draws in her breath sharply. Then she lifts both his hands, holding hers, and places them against the hollow of her throat. Lao Er does not move, he scarcely dares to breathe for fear of destroying this moment. And, when she speaks, he can hardly believe his ears, for her voice is gentler than he has ever heard it.

JADE (*softly*). I am more wicked than you. I *want* to hear you tell me this.

LAO ER. If there were food enough only for them or for you, I would give it to you and let them starve . . . . (*His voice shakes.*) . . . . And let the gods forgive me if they can, for it is the truth. (*Jade's arms reach down to him, and go around his neck.*) You turn to me . . . . of your own will . . . . and it is the first time this has been so. . . .

JADE (*almost shyly*). Yes. For this night you have said the thing my heart needed to hear. . . . (*In a whisper*) Now I know that you will care what I think and feel and what I *am*, and not only that I give you children and make your food. . . . I know that I am not only to belong to your house, but that I am to be yours . . . . and I am content. . . .

And she draws him close, as the scene fades out.

PART THREE

A view of freshly planted rice seedlings fades in. This dissolves to a patch of green, half-grown rice fields (perhaps a month later). This in turn dissolves to the FIELD in the MORNING. Ling Tan and his three sons (Lao San with the ox) are working in a field.

A close view of LAO ER shows him looking up at the sun. Then he makes a great show of licking his dry lips, and the view follows him as he goes to the side of the field and drinks from a water bottle. He glances around to see if he is being watched.—The others, as seen by him, are working, not noticing him at all.—LAO ER, satisfied, smiles, and moves off silently and quickly.

This dissolves to a WILLOW TREE as Lao Er lifts the trailing branches and comes beneath them expectantly, then reacts in disappointment. Suddenly there is the sound of Jade's teasing laugh, and he turns. The scene expands as she approaches him.

LAO ER (*smiling*). You are late today. Did you once more have trouble escaping my mother's eyes?

JADE (*tossing her head*). From this day on I will come to you openly—and she will say nothing!

LAO ER. I cannot believe my mother will change that much.

JADE (*as if willfully*). No. But *I* have changed. Do you not see it?

Lao Er cups her chin in his hand, and we hear the faint hum of airplane motors. They do not hear.

LAO ER (*studying her face*). Your eyes are as soft.... (*He touches her hair.*) .... Your hair as pleasant to my touch. No. I do not see this change and I do not *wish* a change.

JADE. It is within me but it is so great I thought it must show in my face.

LAO ER (*indulgently*). What is the cause of this great difference and when did it begin? (*And at this, Jade drops her eyes, suddenly shy before him.*)

JADE (*softly*). On the night we first opened our hearts to each other, my husband. . . . (*She meets his eyes again, her own aglow.*) I am very happy. Even if it is only a girl I shall be very happy.

Lao Er stares at her for a moment, then his face lights up with wonder and happiness. The airplane motors are louder now, but so engrossed in themselves are they that they still do not hear.

LAO ER (*exultantly*). We shall be ancestors. It will be a son!

JADE (*quickly*). I shall ask the gods for one, but if it is only a girl she still will be welcome.

LAO ER (*tenderly*). She will be welcome. If you are her mother she will be welcome.

JADE (*pressing her advantage*). And she will be taught to read. (*She smiles at him with mock severity.*) Even if her father himself is always too busy with lesser things to learn.

Lao Er tilts back his head and laughs, long and loud.

LAO ER. And where would this up-

City Man: This is not iron, my wise country friend — this is a factory that we carry on our backs, piece by piece.

Ling Tan and his wife plough, after the Japanese have plundered their ox and their tools.

Old Man: The great power of this is that a grain kills in a second and is as tasteless as flour.

Lao Er: You must burn what you have and leave only the ashes behind you.

start daughter be if I did not busy myself with those lesser things? (*Then he takes her hand, draws her closer to him. His mood changes abruptly to one of extreme tenderness.*) This is a good moment .... the best in my life so far. ...

The roar of airplanes is very loud now and they are suddenly aware of them. They look at each other, startled.

JADE. Listen! It is like the growl of a thousand savage dogs! (*They move out from under the tree.*)

We see the PATH as Lao Er and Jade, still hand in hand, look up. A flight of bombing planes is approaching them. This cuts to the FIELDS near by as the farmers, including Ling Tan, Lao Ta, and Lao San, also are looking up, followed by a closer view as they are watching the planes, and are frightened.

LAO SAN (*softly—in spite of his fear*). They are very beautiful—but they have an ugly sound.

We see FIVE PLANES on which the Japanese insignia is clearly marked; then a NEIGHBOR and his SON, in their rice fields, also gazing fearfully upward; then a distant view of the FIVE PLANES as they move swiftly across the sky. A silver fragment comes out of the last plane and drops slanting westward toward the rice field of Ling Tan's neighbor. Then we again see LING TAN, LAO SAN, and LAO TA in their field.

LING TAN. Something falls!

LAO TA. It shines like a piece of silver!

LAO SAN. Look at the earth! It is a black fountain!

We see the RICE FIELD, as viewed by them, as a spray of dark earth is rising from the spot the bomb has hit; then the other FIELD where Ling Tan, Lao Ta and Lao San look at each other, and start off on the run; then the NEIGHBOR'S RICE FIELD again. A dozen farmers have already gathered about a deep hole in the field, among them the neighbor and his son. Ling Tan, Lao Ta, and Lao San run up, as does Third Cousin, puffing and panting.

Next, LAO ER and JADE are seen running toward the hole.

LAO ER (*anxiously*). Perhaps you hurry more than you should.

JADE. I run strongly enough for two! (*She points toward the hole.*) See! A hole big enough to bury fifty men!

Then we get a closer view of the GROUP around the owner of the field as Jade and Lao Er enter to them.

LING TAN (*peering into the hole, gravely*). If one of us had stood near here, he would no longer live!

NEIGHBOR SHEN (*wryly*). Well then! I have wanted a pond on my land for ten years and never had time to dig it—and here it is!

SECOND FARMER (*also with grim humor*). It would be better if the barbarians did use the sky ships to dig ponds and wells!

FARMERS: That would be a better purpose than the one they now have! Perhaps it is an idea and we should tell them of it! Or perhaps we should say nothing, or they will make us pay for the digging!

But at this point Jade, who is looking off after the planes, points.

JADE. Look! Look! Rolling smoke!

And as everyone turns and looks, we see (as viewed by them) distant smoke rising over the city as though from fires.

The GROUP at the hole:

LAO ER (*excitedly*). There are eight

fires over the city wall and a small one to the side!

JADE. The flying ships come out of the smoke!

We hear the distant sound of bombing. The villagers all look at each other.

LAO SAN (*to Ling Tan*). What shall we do, father?

JADE (*before Ling can answer*). Some one of us should go to the city! (*Then she steps back, realizing she has been bold.*)

LAO ER (*quickly, to his father*). My wife thinks of our elder sister and what happens to her.

LING TAN (*as everyone looks at him for a decision*). We should all think of that. I will go.

THIRD COUSIN. I would not be hasty, cousin. If it is good news it will not spoil, and the more slowly one hears bad news the better.

LING TAN. My old woman would not let me rest if I did not go, nor could I.

LAO TA (*stepping forward*). Let me go in your place, father. If danger should come here, the household would need you, before me.

LAO ER. He is right.

LING TAN (*hesitating, then nodding*). Go quickly, then, and do what you can. The rest of us will get back to our work....

The farmers agree, and turn away. Jade moves off, Lao Er following, after which we see them moving along.

JADE (*slowly*). The end of our good moment has commenced. I feel it.

LAO ER (*trying to rally her*). That is like saying that from the day of our birth we begin to die.

JADE (*looking toward the city*). This is death, perhaps, but one we do not wait for....

LAO ER (*tenderly—protectively*). You are afraid. You who never have been afraid.

JADE. I can think only of the child .... and who can care for us now but you? (*She turns to him instinctively.*)

LAO ER (*in spite of his worry, smiling*). When you turn to me like this —I grow two feet in height. (*He struts a little.*) And there is nothing I cannot do!

The scene dissolves to LING TAN'S COMPOUND GATE at night, affording a close view of a DOG, which stands, backed against the gate, barking savagely at someone who approaches. Then we see Ling Tan, Ling's Wife and Lao Er coming toward the gate.

LING'S WIFE. Can it be our son at last —I am afraid to believe it is!

The dog stops barking suddenly, and there is the sound of knocking on the gate.

LAO TA'S VOICE. Father! Mother!

Ling Tan flings open the gate, revealing Lao Ta, and behind him Wu Lien and his entire household in a pitiful state of exhaustion and agitation. Wu Lien is between the shafts of a ricksha in which has ridden his fat old mother and his youngest son. He helps the old lady down, and then, carrying the baby, comes toward the gate, followed by his wife, the other two children, and his mother. They all carry a few belongings. Wu Lien's face is slack and his eyes are staring. He has obviously had a great shock. His wife is near hysteria, and the old lady is at the point of complete collapse.

LAO TA. Here we are—all of us!

LING TAN. You are safe! We are thankful for that!

WU LIEN. We are all but dead!

LING'S WIFE. Are the children unhurt? (*She starts to lead them toward the house.*) Come inside so I may see for myself!

WU LIEN'S WIFE (*wailing*). We might have been dead had we been ten feet nearer the street!

WU LIEN'S MOTHER (*piteously*). It was too much noise . . . . there was such a noise. . . .

The scene wipes to the BIG ROOM where Jade, Orchid and Lao San are waiting. As the others enter from the compound, Wu Lien's Mother immediately collapses into a chair, sobbing.

WU LIEN (*slowly, dully, a man without hope*). The shop is half gone! We have nothing but our bare lives in our hands! We are lost! All is lost! Everywhere the silver eggs dropped they burst the buildings into dust . . . . and the shops . . . . and all the goods within are waste. . . . !

LING TAN. But what of the people?

Ling's Wife gets wine, and pours out portions.

WU LIEN'S WIFE. Into pieces, as though they too were made of clay. Here an arm, there a head, there a piece of foot . . . (*She breaks off, shuddering.*)

LING TAN (*sadly*). But why? How can men do this to other men? The sky is over us all.

WU LIEN'S WIFE (*mourning*). Our own servants and the two clerks are dead, and one such an honest young man that where shall we find one like him again?

Ling's Wife offers wine to Wu Lien.

WU LIEN (*groaning*). What is the use even of . . . . (*He takes the wine from Ling's Wife, drinks, and revives.*) . . . . an honest man if there is no shop to put him in? Our shops . . . . our goods . . . . all gone! And I am a man who can prosper only in peace!

LAO ER. Can it be those students who cried out against the enemy spoke the truth?

WU LIEN. The truth? What is the truth? Each man sees it differently. The truth I see is that the East Ocean people will come and enter the city and the city will fall and so will the nation.

LING'S WIFE. Can that be? The nation is only the people and we are the people. And while we remain so does the nation.

WU LIEN. We are not strong enough.

LAO SAN. Why are we not strong enough? Why do we not have things to kill with, too?

LAO TA. They are of no use to people like us who love only to live.

JADE. Then we will die!

LING TAN (*slowly—as if bewildered*). Death is each man's natural end and that I know . . . . but not this kind . . . . this is beyond the mind of man unless he sees it for himself . . . . and that I must do. . . .

This dissolves to a CITY STREET near Wu Lien's Shop next day. Ling Tan and Lao San walk along, looking around. The people are coming and going much the same as always, except that their faces are graver, and some are wounded a little. There is evidence of bombing in a shattered building, a small crater, and some debris in the street, which people are trying to clean up. Lao San looks around, appalled.

LAO SAN. I would not know the street. It is so changed!

LING TAN (*nodding*). Here is the shop of Wu Lien. (*They stop to look at the building. One wall is out.*) Come, we will see what has become of his goods. (*And they go into the shop.*)

In WU LIEN'S SHOP, there is great disorder, but the Old Clerk is straightening up what he can.

LING TAN (*recognizing him*). What then? We heard you had perished.

OLD CLERK (*shrugging*). When I dug myself out I found I was alive.

LING TAN (*warmly*). It is good to find you here. (*He looks around.*) What waste! What ruin!

OLD CLERK (*bitterly*). If you wish to see what the pygmies can really do, go to my street. I had a little house of earth and straw, and it is gone and all in it are gone.... (*He chokes, unable to go on.*)

LING TAN (*gently*). I share your sorrow, brother.

OLD CLERK. Thank you. I would have been with them had I not been here. And I wish I were with them. I had two little sons, born in two years.

LING TAN. It is indeed worse than I thought.

OLD CLERK (*dully—as if stunned*). For many years I hated this shop because it kept me from my family ... but now it is all I have left to care for....

Suddenly, there is the sound of approaching planes. From outside come shouts, and through the broken windows people can be seen as they run for cover, and Ling Tan and Lao San go to look out.

THE PEOPLE OUTSIDE. The ships! The flying ships! They have returned!

All the people in the street have vanished by now, and Ling Tan and Lao San stare helplessly.

OLD CLERK (*sighing*). You had better hide yourself. (*He indicates a stout table.*)

LING TAN. Where can men hide from such as this?

The hateful roar comes closer. The Old Clerk, as if not hearing the planes, continues his work. There is a terrific whine and a crash as a bomb falls somewhere near. The Old Clerk again motions them to creep under the table. This time they obey, but the Old Clerk continues to go about his work.

LING TAN. Why do *you* not hide, friend?

OLD CLERK. I have no need.... I have lost everything but myself....

We see LING TAN and LAO SAN crouching under the table. Ling Tan tries to speak to Lao San and reassure him, but his voice is drowned out by the roar of planes and the exploding of bombs. Seeing the look of horror on the boy's face, he puts a hand on his arm. The din is deafening. Lao San is bent down with his head between his legs and his knees pressed against his ears and his arms wrapped about himself. The scene expands a little as the uproar increases, and the boy raises his head, his eyes almost insane with fear. Ling Tan pretends not to see this.

Then the OLD CLERK is seen going about his work, his old face like a mask. The uproar now subsides and the Old Clerk looks out the window, then moves back to Lao San and Ling Tan.

OLD CLERK. The evil has passed over.

Ling Tan and Lao San scramble out of their shelter. Lao San sways on his feet, trying desperately to regain his composure. Ling Tan turns his back to spare his son.

LING TAN (*to the Old Clerk*). You are brave, as all must be brave in your place, and I doubt if I could be. . . .

OLD CLERK (*shrugging*). Men do what they must, and, when the time comes, they find courage they did not know they had.

LING TAN (*pressing his hand*). Keep yourself safe until Wu Lien's return. (*He turns to Lao San.*) Come, my son. Let us go out into the street now. (*He stops, and listens.*) What is that new noise?

OLD CLERK. That is fire. It finishes what the devils have started.

Ling Tan and Lao San go toward the street, following which we see them outside WU LIEN'S SHOP. Other people are appearing cautiously. Some of the bombs have hit very near the shop. Ling Tan and Lao San look off with horrified eyes and see:

The DEVASTATED AREA, now burning as people are trying with pathetic impotence to put out the raging fires with inadequate hose and buckets of water.

Next, LING TAN and LAO SAN appear moving toward a heap of bricks and mortar and beams and dust where people are already digging frantically with their hands and what tools they can find.

WOMAN'S VOICE (*uttering a terrible scream*). Haiiiii!

And they turn to look, whereupon the scene cuts to a WOMAN at a heap of rubble: She has been digging with her hands and has found something.

WOMAN (*wailing horribly*). It is my husband! He is here . . . . beneath this rubbish!

Men run to help her, and uncover more.—A close view of LING TAN and LAO SAN shows them watching the scene, and the boy's face is white. Then we see the WOMAN and the DIGGERS as they uncover the arm of a man.

WOMAN. Yes . . . . it is his hand! I would know it anywhere!

She tries to pass through the group which quickly covers the object they have brought to light. They try to hold her back but she claws her way past and looks down. She sinks to her knees. Then we again see LING TAN and LAO SAN as the Woman's Voice screams, "Haiiiiii! Haiiiiiiii!"

LING TAN (*shaken, as if to himself*). There is only an arm . . . . no more.

Lao San turns away suddenly and Ling Tan sees he is vomiting. He goes to him.

LING TAN (*gently*). It is too much to bear . . . . and I do not blame you. (*Then, as the boy straightens up and turns to face him, ashamed of his weakness, and the sound of the woman's wailing rises*) Come. We must see what can be done here.

The scene expands as he grimly falls to, helping with the rubbish. Lao San hesitates, then, clenching his teeth against his nausea, forces himself to do likewise.

The scene dissolves to a ROAD near Ling Tan's at night as the first refugees from the city are straggling along the road. Men, women, boys, girls, young children, babies and grandparents . . . . a few in old cars, some in wagons and carts, some with children in wheel barrows. An aged woman rides on the back of an ox. Many are walking and all are carrying bundles. Mules are saddled with a few sticks of household furniture. An old man carries his wife on his back. (Note: This should give the feeling of being the beginning of the exodus from the city.)

Lao San and Lao Ta stand at the wall of the compound, looking out at the refugees.

> LAO TA (*softly*). Our village has become an island in a river of fleeing people. . . .
>
> LAO SAN (*shuddering, still shaken by what he has seen in the city*). But they cannot run fast enough to forget the horror behind them.

At this point, Wu Lien's eldest son approaches them.

> WU LIEN'S SON. My grandfather would speak to you now.

Lao Ta and Lao San nod and follow him toward the big room, following which we see the BIG ROOM as Ling Tan, his face drawn and weary, his clothes dirty, stands facing his wife, Orchid, Wu Lien, Wu Lien's Wife, and Wu Lien's Mother, who are already seated. Jade and Lao Er come out of their room, and take their places. They are grave and thoughtful, as if they have reached a decision. Lao Ta and Lao San, with Wu Lien's son, enter from the compound and sit near the others. (Note: Over the ensuing scene comes the sound of the refugees passing outside—the tramp of feet—the creak of vehicles—the occasional murmur of voices.)

> LING TAN (*slowly*). I know you are looking to me to save you from this great trouble. I have been trying to find a way . . . . (*He shakes his head.*) . . . . But I cannot—for I cannot save myself. I know that what today was will be again tomorrow (*He looks at each as he goes on.*) You, my three sons, are men, and you Wu Lien, are older than they. If you have anything to say, then say it. (*The three sons look at Wu Lien to speak first.*)
>
> WU LIEN (*coughing*). I have not yet thought of any way to save any of us. I am a man who only knows how to do business with others. In times of war, such men as I must live as we can and where we can and hope and work for peace.

At this, Ling Tan nods, and turns to Lao Ta.

> LAO TA (*hesitantly*). There are two things which can be done. One is to escape the evil by running away and the other is to let it come and bear it. In this, my father, I ask what you will do yourself.
>
> LING TAN. I stay here where I was born and where I have lived.
>
> LAO TA. Then I say I will do what you do.
>
> LAO SAN. I, too, will stay.
>
> LAO ER (*suddenly, with firmness*). But I, my father, I will escape it!

There is a sharp movement of surprise at this and Jade moves closer to Lao Er, her face alight with pride and trust in him.

> LING TAN (*quietly, after a moment*). I will say nothing to any who do go. Let those who will, stay with me— and those who would go, let them go.
>
> LAO ER. You blame me, my father?
>
> LING TAN. No, I do not blame you.

LAO ER. Then do as I will do. Leave this place.

LING TAN (*thoughtfully*). If I could roll up my land like a cloth and take it with me.... (*He breaks off, and shakes his head.*) But that is impossible. I stay, my son. You are free to go.

LAO ER (*after a pause*). I do not run away because *I* am afraid. I fear for my coming child.

LING'S WIFE (*joyously*). Ah-h! A grandchild!

She nods approvingly at Jade and Jade smiles back. Orchid tries to look pleased, but isn't altogether. Lao Er and Lao Ta exchange looks of affection tinged with laughter.

LING TAN. That is good news, my son, and I think it well that you go.

LAO TA (*softly*). When will you leave us, brother?

LAO ER. We have yet time. We will wait until we find those we would go with.

LING'S WIFE (*suddenly*). I do not like this talk! I do not see why Jade should be taken away.

JADE (*quickly*). It is only that I may finish what I was made to do, my mother.

LING'S WIFE. But who will look after you when your time comes?

LING TAN (*soberly*). It may be better if they go. We do not know what lies ahead. Strange feet may enter our gate.

LING'S WIFE. If our son wants to go he will go, but let Jade stay. Her duty to you comes first!

LING TAN (*quietly—settling it*). I think it does not. A woman should go with her man.

There is silence for a moment, and the constant tread outside is heard more plainly.

This dissolves to a full view of the ROAD from the city at sundown about three weeks later. The refugees continue to pour from the city. The roads are now packed. Next we see the ROAD near Ling Tan's CABBAGE PATCH: In the foreground Ling's family (all the men except Wu Lien) are seen at work. Third Cousin lounges lazily beside the field. In the background is a group of refugees. They seem different from those seen before in that they are marching with some semblance of order and appear to be more or less of a unit. A wind is blowing.

A STREAM near the road: Jade and Orchid are washing clothes in the stream. The children play near by. Jade looks up, then rises to get a better look.

JADE. There are so many who flee. The very face of the earth has changed these past weeks.

A CABBAGE PATCH: the men work on, taking the refugees for granted.

THIRD COUSIN (*staring at the refugees, then, turning to Ling Tan*). Ling! What comes now! These carry different burdens!

Ling looks up, reacts in wonder, as do the others, and we see, from their angle, the procession drawing near. The men do bear strange burdens. JADE and ORCHID with the CHILDREN are then seen as Jade, her interest also caught by the refugees, leaves the stream, and goes toward the cabbage patch.

The procession draws near Ling's group, and other farmers are seen to come to the edge of the road to watch.

At the head of the procession marches a tall, thin man of middle-age.

> LEADER (*calling back*). Keep to the road! Do not destroy good food! We are not vandals!

Now as the stream of people begins to pass the farmers it is seen they *do* bear strange burdens. A score of sweating men push a gasless truck laden with what looks like an assortment of scrap iron—wheels, axles, pulleys, piston rods, etc. A dozen other men plod along bearing on their shoulders a long, steel rail, staggering under its weight. Others, singly or in pairs, are bowed beneath leather machine belting, wheels, gears and miscellaneous pieces of machinery. Women and children, apparently the families of the men, carry smaller burdens, but they, too, move in an almost military fashion. Their passing causes even more dust to fill the air.

We get another view of the ROAD and the FIELDS near LING'S GROUP as the farmers are mystified and somewhat amused by what they see.

> NEIGHBOR SHEN (*good-humoredly*). What foolishness is this? Only a city man would break his back under an iron rail when he might carry a bag of rice!

> LAO ER (*laughing, to a man with a wheel*). Why did you not take two wheels and make a cart and ride?

The man merely shrugs, smiles, and goes on. Jade enters, and stands by Lao Er.

> LAO SAN (*to a man with a machine belt*). What is that? A belt to gird a giant? You must expect to grow fat where you are going.

> CITY MAN (*from the road*). You will never grow fat here when the dwarfs come, young farmer, and remember I have said it.

The foregoing exchange remains good-natured, but is obviously between men who do not understand each other very well. The farmers wipe dust from their eyes.

> LAO TA. Look at those fools. They will eat iron—if they eat at all.

> CITY MAN (*from the road*). This is not iron, my wise country friend—this is a factory that we carry on our backs, piece by piece.

> SECOND CITY MAN. And you may as well grow used to seeing such things, for a whole city walks behind us! (*At this, the Leader comes swiftly back down the line of the march.*)

> LEADER (*noticing that the men near him are staggering with fatigue*). We will rest now for a little. (*He turns, and shouts out a command.*) Halt! Rest!

The words "halt" and "rest" echo and re-echo down the line of march, following which the MARCHERS lay down their burdens and gratefully sink to the ground and sprawl there.

LING TAN and the GROUP observe this.

> JADE (*to Lao Er*). These are not as the others were. They seem to have a plan.

Ling Tan hearing this, reacts, and goes toward the LEADER, who is then seen close.

> LING TAN (*approaching*). You are weary and the road ahead of you is steep and hard.

> LEADER (*nodding and sighing*). We had hoped to pass over those hills before night, but we cannot.

> LING TAN. Why do you not sleep here

on our land? There is water and we will share what we have with you.

There are murmurs of welcome from the farmers.

LEADER (*gratefully*). You are good to us, as all of our own have been, or we could not have come this far. (*He turns and shouts out.*) We will rest here tonight with these, our friends. Everyone find a place, and do not trample the grain! (*At his words, the marchers look up thankfully; and there is a murmur of approval.*)

This dissolves to a long view of the FIELDS and the VILLAGE at night: The city people have made camp. A group has been taken to the land of each farmer, and from the camps can be seen fires and an occasional burst of song and talk can be heard. The wind has died down a little and the sky is thick with rain clouds.

We see LING'S COMPOUND: The Leader of the City People is camped here with some of the others. They sit and smoke. —At the ARCHWAY to the inner courtyard, Ling Tan and Wu Lien stand looking out at the travelers. They are joined by Jade and Lao Er.

LAO ER (*quietly*). These are the people we would join, father. (*At this, Ling Tan looks questioningly at Jade.*)

JADE. Yes. These are the ones we have waited for. They are strong and full of courage.

At this, Ling Tan nods, and leads the way toward the encampment by the pond, followed by the others. Then at the POND, the Leader rises, smiling, as Ling Tan and the others enter to him.

LING TAN. I would ask you, where do you go?

LEADER. Our eyes are on the mountains a thousand miles from here.

LAO ER (*eagerly*). What will you do there, sir?

LEADER. We will set up these machines we carry, and they will be a factory. Then we will make bullets and guns for our army.

WU LIEN (*slightly acid*). Where is our brave army now?

LEADER (*giving him a cool look*). They fight between you and the Japanese. Many thousands of them have already died to delay the evil dwarfs from coming here.

WU LIEN. But they do not stop them, nor can they.

LEADER (*briefly, but courteously*). They only do what they can, and perhaps they would do better if *you* helped them. (*But Wu Lien merely shrugs, and steps back.*)

LING TAN. My son would join you in your journey, if he is welcome.

LEADER (*bowing in acceptance*). We would be happy to take something of yours with us.

LING TAN. And what is a man without his wife? (*He looks at Jade, who steps forward.*)

JADE. I, too, am strong and can be of help.

LEADER (*smiling*). You are welcome also.

As Jade and Lao Er turn away, the view moves closer to Ling Tan and the Leader. A gentle rain begins to fall.

LING TAN (*holding out his hand*). The wind has brought rain. (*To the Leader*) It is good for our land, but is it not bad for travelers?

LEADER. If it helps you, then it must help us.

This dissolves to a scene near the WILLOW TREE at night: The rain is coming down more steadily now and Jade and Lao Er, laughing, run under the branches of the tree for shelter. They stand for a moment, trying to regain their breath, and then Lao Er takes Jade's hand.

LAO ER. Now that we are to go, I wonder if it is not too far for you?

JADE (*head up*). I will be on my feet when others drop.

LAO ER. I wish I could carry the child for you.

JADE (*laughing*). One of these days, you shall.

LAO ER (*looking around, a little wistfully*). I never thought a child of mine would be born anywhere except on this land where I was born.

JADE. He will find a place of his own to be born in.

LAO ER. It is very meaningful to a man where he is born. We must mark the place.

JADE. What better place to mark for him than our tree? (*She takes a pin from her hair, and starts to scratch a mark on the tree.*) And now it will be his also. . . . (*As she works, Lao Er reaches out, and puts an arm around her.*)

The scene dissolves to the COUNTRYSIDE early in the morning as the people who carry the factory pick up their burdens and take their places. The rain of the night before has stopped, but it has made the road slippery and hard to walk upon.—In the COMPOUND, the whole family (with the exception of Ling's Wife and Jade, and including Wu Lien and his family) have gathered to say good-bye. Lao Er is holding Lao Ta's youngest in his arms. He touches the baby's cheek with his own cheek and hands it back to Orchid, who receives it proudly.

LAO ER (*to Lao Ta's son*). You must care for this house while I am gone. (*Then, looking from one to the other*) I will carry your faces with me.

LAO SAN (*sincerely*). And our good wishes also, brother.

LAO TA (*soberly, to Lao Er*). I hope that this way is the best, and you have chosen wisely.

WU LIEN. How can it be wise for a man to leave what is his, and what belongs to him?

Lao Er turns to his father, as Jade hurries in from the courtyard. She, like Lao Er, is dressed in strong, plain clothes and straw sandals.

JADE. I have looked everywhere, but I cannot find our mother to say goodbye.

LAO ER (*to Ling Tan*). Tell her it is our sorrow we could not find her.

LING TAN. I will tell her. (*But he looks off and reminds them.*) You must not keep your friends waiting.

And Ling Tan, Jade and Lao Er move to the gate.—Here, next, we see the travelers, now almost ready to start the march. Ling Tan turns to the young people.

LING TAN (*quietly*). Send me word somehow when the child is born. If it is a boy, send me a red cord in the envelope and if it is a girl, let it be a blue one. (*To Jade, gently*) My child, remember the woman is the root and the man the tree. The tree grows only as high as the root is strong.

JADE. I will remember, father.

Ling Tan would say more, but he cannot trust himself. He makes a gesture for them to go, and with a last look at him, they do so. Ling Tan watches them.

Jade and Lao Er, as seen from Ling Tan's angle, fall into line, and take up their appointed burdens.

LEADER. We must cross those hills before the mid-day rest. (*He calls out.*) March!

He raises his hand—and the procession starts, slipping, sliding, struggling for a foothold in the mud. Jade and Lao Er also slip and slide in the mud, and then turn and laugh at each other and at the people around them, who laugh in return.

LING TAN goes outside the wall, and stands there, watching. His face shows the great emotion he feels. And from his angle, the people are now seen marching past and away, and as they do so, they start to sing a marching song (perhaps "Chee Lai"). Lao Er and Jade join in the song—at first haltingly, then lustily. And now farmers can be seen as they come to the edge of the fields and wave goodbye to the city people. Among them are: ORCHID and LAO TA, the latter's face showing great sadness; WU LIEN, his WIFE and his CHILDREN as they, too, watch the departure; LAO SAN as he climbs a wall to watch; and LING TAN straining his eyes after Lao Er and Jade.

And now the procession, as seen by him, starts to climb the hill. The song comes drifting back to Ling Tan. This cuts again to LING TAN standing very quietly, and then to another view of the PROCESSION as the first of the people reach the crest of the hill and start over. The others, like a long, black snake, are stretched out behind them.

LING TAN's eyes are wet with tears. He turns blindly, as if seeking someone who is not at his hand. He feels, as never before, the need of his wife's presence, and he starts toward the stream.

The STREAM near the house: Ling's Wife is on her knees beside the stream, beating the dirt out of a pair of Ling's trousers with a stick. She seems to beat more strongly than is necessary, and her head is bowed over her work when Ling Tan approaches her. The sound of the singing marchers is now diminishing.

LING TAN (*looking down at her*). Where were you? They looked for you.

LING'S WIFE (*not looking up*). I would not come to see him go. Pulling and straining like an ox .... and bawling like one.

Ling Tan crouches beside her. He lifts her face. There are tears in her eyes.

LING TAN (*gently*). You have been weeping.

LING'S WIFE (*loudly*). I have not. I have splashed water in my face. (*And she beats the luckless trousers again, more violently than ever.*)

LING TAN. He looked so small beside the others.

LING'S WIFE (*quickly, fiercely*). He did not. He was the largest by far— (*She breaks off as she realizes she has revealed she* did *watch Lao Er go.*)

LING TAN. You are the best mother in the province, and where is there one beyond the seas?

LING'S WIFE (*sitting back on her heels*). Curse me for a fool! I miss them already. Even Jade!

LING TAN. Yes. Some sort of strength has left the house with their going.

LING'S WIFE (*going back to pounding the trousers*). And yet, I would not say I want them back! They want to go—they go!

LING TAN (*laughing*). I would not have you a cool, thin soul. I like you hot-tempered and gusty.

LING'S WIFE (*pleased, scowling to cover it*). You old turnip! (*She spreads out the trousers, sees they are beaten into holes. He laughs again. She grins reluctantly, then turns to him and looks into his face.*) Come here, old man, and let me see that spot on your cheek and see if you are to have a boil after all these years.

LING TAN (*bending forward so that she can look*). It is only where a mosquito bit me.

LING'S WIFE. Do not tell me what it is. I can see for myself. (*She gives him a small blow on the shoulder.*) And can you not catch a mosquito any more, and must you be bitten like a child, you clumsy?

LING TAN. I like your quick tongue even when it is turned on me. (*He looks down at her.*) Old Woman, I will tell you this. If you should die before I die, even then I will not marry another, for after you any would be like a carrot dried without salt.

He draws her to him and for a moment, they stay there, very close to each other, and are comforted as the scene fades out.

PART FOUR

A moving view of the REFUGEES fades in as the Narrator's Voice begins:

NARRATOR'S VOICE. Those who fled dared pause neither to rest nor to eat for the enemy came ever closer. Already he had taken the land a hundred miles deep from the sea, and the people of the village of Ling, who had stayed behind, knew they stood within the second hundred miles, and they were afraid.

This cuts to a view of Lao Ta and Lao San cutting grain, and Ling Tan tying bundles.

NARRATOR'S VOICE. But the harvest was at hand, and they went into the fields to. . . .

WU LIEN and his young SONS are seen tying bundles. Wu Lien is clumsy. His little sons are more skillful.

NARRATOR'S VOICE. . . . reap the grain, and each man helped his neighbor. For they were farmers, and war or no. . . .

We get closeups of LING TAN and LAO TA cutting grain, with clouds overhead.

NARRATOR'S VOICE. . . . war they knew they must bring their food from the earth so . . . . that whatever came they could feed their families, and they . . .

LING'S WIFE, WU LIEN'S WIFE, ORCHID and the CHILDREN are tying grain.

NARRATOR'S VOICE. . . . worked faster than ever before, because time too had become their enemy.

There follow pictures of a FARMER

drinking; REFUGEES streaming past; LING'S WIFE, WU LIEN'S WIFE, ORCHID and the CHILDREN loading grain and taking it away; WAGONS and PEOPLE carrying grain to houses; LING'S COMPOUND, with the family flailing grain, while Third Cousin is watching. But suddenly we hear the sound of planes, and they all look up, whereupon we see JAPANESE PLANES, followed by more scenes of people looking up, Japanese planes flying, Ling's entire family flailing while the wind starts blowing, scattering the grain, and people rushing to load grain and take to shelter in the rising storm.—Then there is another view of the bombing of a city while the Narrator speaks.

NARRATOR'S VOICE. And then the day came—the day that Ling Tan and his kinsmen dreaded above all others. The guns were silent, and the flying ships were gone from the air.

This dissolves to a TEAHOUSE, beginning with a close view of the BELLOWS of a STOVE as Ling Tan is heard speaking.

LING TAN'S VOICE (*somberly*). I fear this quiet more than the noise of battle. . . .

The view moves to Ling Tan's tense face as he continues to speak.

LING TAN. It does not mean peace. It can mean but one thing and we must face it.

Then we see the ROOM, revealing that the responsible men of the village have gathered together. Near Ling Tan sit Third Cousin, Wu Lien, and Lao Ta. The atmosphere is one of fear and indecision.

LING TAN. Those who defended the city have been overcome, and even as we speak the enemy is at the gates. In a few hours he will be upon us.

THIRD COUSIN (*in a quavering voice*). That is true. The enemy comes swiftly, and we have no arms.

THE VILLAGERS.
What shall we do?
Are we then lost?
I am afraid of this enemy.

WU LIEN (*slowly—rising*). I speak for myself, but you are welcome to listen. We cannot stop the Japanese, and as soon as they have occupied the city, I believe we shall be able to deal with them. (*The others stare at him.*)

LING TAN. How can you say this?

WU LIEN. I bought and sold their goods, as did my father before me, and I found no great evil in the face they turned to me. I *did* find evil in my own people—green boys who burned my goods without reason.

LING TAN. I do not agree with you. I think there are days of great misery ahead of us.

WU LIEN. I think not. The Japanese have sent down writings from their flying ships in the past few days telling us not to be afraid, because they bring only peace and order.

The men are silent. His words have weight, but not quite enough. Slowly Ling Tan rises, and they turn to him with respect and trust.

LING TAN. Wu Lien, if, when they come, you are right, I will say you are. But, even if you are not, what can we do but take their rule for ours, also? We want only peace and to be left alone to live.

There is a murmur of agreement. If Ling Tan says this, it must be true, for he is honorable and wise.

OLD FARMER. Our time is short. What is the plan?

VILLAGERS. How shall we meet them? How shall we show them what is in our hearts?

LING TAN. What ways do we know but our own? Let us do what we would do for any new ruler coming to our village, but, let us keep our pride.

VILLAGERS (*with growing approval*). Good. . . . That is the right thing. . . . He speaks the truth. . . .

Third Cousin clears his throat. After all he is the scholar of the village and he must be heard.

THIRD COUSIN (*pompously*). My cousin took the words from my mind and spoke them as his own. I was about to say the same thing.

LING TAN (*affectionately*). And you shall speak to the enemy for us, respected cousin.

THIRD COUSIN (*pleased*). Yes. It is only fitting that I speak for you. I am the scholar.

FARMER. What will you say?

THIRD COUSIN (*very positively*). I will say—(*Looking blank, turning to Ling Tan*) Let us hear your ideas, cousin, and then I will tell you mine.

Then we see the ROAD LEADING TO THE CITY as a group of representative men of the village dressed in their best are gathered beside the road. Third Cousin and Ling Tan are at the head of the group. Wu Lien is not present. To one side of the elders are several young men (not dressed in their best), Lao Ta and Fourth Cousin among them.

LING TAN. They come.

We see, from the viewpoint of the villagers, strange, huge gray shapes through the afternoon shadows. These machines are coming forward.

THIRD COUSIN (*seen closer, with the villagers—despairingly*). But they are machines! How can you speak to machines—and them belching smoke?

The huge shapes now come closer, their noise and dust polluting the air. And next the tanks bear down upon the villagers, and they jump aside, gaping, the tanks moving on. Overhead roars an umbrella of planes.

NEIGHBOR SHEN. Is this then the enemy!

LING TAN (*pointing*). There! There is the enemy!

THIRD COUSIN (*nervously plucking his sleeve*). But do not use that word—at least so loudly.

Now trucks come briskly toward them, loaded with Japanese soldiers.—The VILLAGERS draw closer together. The trucks begin to go by. The men in the trucks have dark, savage faces, and the villagers shrink back. Third Cousin opens his mouth to speak, but his voice is lost in the sound and rattle of equipment. A staff car stops and an officer and several soldiers get out. Then the VILLAGERS are seen closer.

THIRD COUSIN. Are these, then, the ones to address?

The others nod, and shove him forward. The scene expanding, the Japanese move toward them. Their commanding officer halts them, steps forward. Behind him are his men, and again the villagers are sharply conscious of the wild, fierce faces of these strangers.

THIRD COUSIN (*doffing his cap*). Sirs . . . . sirs . . . . I am come . . I am here . . . we are here, sirs. . . . (*But his voices trails off in a squeak, as he looks at the soldiers. He looks at Ling Tan, panicky.*)

LING TAN (*stepping forward, quickly*). Sirs, we are only farmers and a small merchant or two, and my cousin here the scholar. We are men of peace and reason...

OFFICER (*brusquely*). Where is your inn, farmer? (*As Ling Tan, taken aback, stares*) Lead us there.

The villagers look at each other. There is nothing to do but obey and they start off, leading the way. Third Cousin, trembling and afraid, has trouble keeping up. The young men are caught up in the march and swept along with it.

Third Cousin moves as fast as he can but he is not fast enough and one of the soldiers prods him with his bayonet.

THIRD COUSIN. I am hurt.

Ling Tan turns to protest but his mouth goes dry as he sees the unnatural smiles of the enemy, and he helps the old man keep ahead of the bayonets.

The scene dissolves to the TEAHOUSE: The soldiers are seated. The villagers are huddled near the rear door, watching anxiously. Then we get a close view of THIRD COUSIN as Ling Tan helps him to a seat and Fourth Cousin enters anxiously.

FOURTH COUSIN. You are ill, my father?

THIRD COUSIN (*whispering, fearfully*). No. No. It is nothing.

The Innkeeper and two sons enter with bowls of tea, and start serving it.—The CHINESE are watching—hoping for the best.—One of the Japanese soldiers tastes his tea, and spits it out.

JAPANESE SOLDIER (*roaring*). Wine! We want wine, not tea!

THIRD COUSIN (*falteringly*). We have no wine. We have that only on feast days.

At this, the soldiers mutter and hurl the bowls of tea to the floor.

OFFICER. Then where are your women? (*He smiles.*) There are other things than wine.

The villagers look at each other with dawning horror. Suddenly Fourth Cousin turns, and starts to run wildly toward the door. The officer raises his gun, and shoots, following which we see FOURTH COUSIN spinning around once, dropping and lying still. He is dead.

THIRD COUSIN starts for his son, but LING TAN grips his arm and restrains him.

LING TAN (*finding his voice*). We have wine in our homes. Good wine. We .... we will have the women bring it to you.

He turns, and walks toward the door, not too hurriedly. The others follow him. The officer looks after them, frowns, then shrugs. Apparently he believes they will do what they say.

OFFICER. Make haste then.

Ling Tan, Third Cousin and Lao Ta come to the doorway where Fourth Cousin lies dead.

LING TAN (*to Third Cousin*). Do not stop. (*The men know what he means and keep going through the door.*)

The instant Ling Tan comes through the door he starts running, the others after him, each going toward his own house.

This dissolves to the GATE of LING TAN's HOUSE as Ling Tan comes running to the gate and dashes through, followed by Lao Ta.

In the COMPOUND, Lao Ta bars the gate, then goes to watch over the wall. Ling's Wife, who is tending the horse turning the stone mill, runs up.

> LING TAN. Get the household together inside! Quick! The enemy comes!
>
> LING'S WIFE (*as she runs toward the house*). Orchid! Eldest daughter! All of you! Bring the children!

Lao San runs from the stall where he has been working and Wu Lien appears from a spot where he has been sitting and smoking.

> WU LIEN (*anxiously*). But what of the speech?
>
> LING TAN (*bitterly*). Our mouths spoke into the mouths of guns.

The scene wipes to the BIG ROOM where Ling's Wife has now gathered the women and children together. The children are whimpering, and the women try to quiet them. Ling Tan runs in, followed by Lao San and Wu Lien.

> LING TAN. You must scatter over the land . . . . each man is to look after his own and my third son his mother. (*He meets his wife's questioning eyes.*) I will stay here with the house.
>
> LING'S WIFE. I stay by you.
>
> LING TAN. You cannot. I will climb into the rafters and hide there.
>
> LING'S WIFE. Can I not climb also?

Outside the COMPOUND, the view extending over the wall toward the valley, Lao Ta, at the wall, sees the Japanese appear on the road. He whirls, and runs toward the house. This cuts to the BIG ROOM as Lao Ta runs in.

> LAO TA. They come by the road!

In panic, upon hearing this, Wu Lien starts toward the side gate of the compound.

> LING TAN (*calling out*). No! They will see us there! (*He leads them toward the inner courtyard.*) This way! The hole in the wall!

We see the INNER COURTYARD as Ling Tan herds them all toward a hole in the rear wall. Vines hang over this opening and conceal it. Ling Tan pulls the vines aside, and Wu Lien starts to help his mother through the hole, but she collapses and falls to the ground. She is gasping with exhaustion and fear.

> WU LIEN'S MOTHER. No! I can walk no further!
>
> WU LIEN (*looking at Ling Tan in sudden terror*). But we cannot carry her!
>
> LING TAN. Let the others through first.

Wu Lien helps his wife and children through, and follows them.

> WU LIEN (*groaning*). My mother! She is lost!
>
> LAO TA (*to Orchid*). Come. . . . (*To a crying child*) Be brave, my son . . . . you will soon be safe.
>
> WU LIEN'S WIFE (*wailing*). Safety! Where is safety!

They are all through now.

> LING TAN (*to Wu Lien*). Go with the others. I will do my best for your mother. (*To Lao Ta and Lao San*) Let each look out for those in his charge and pay no heed to the other.

They nod and Ling Tan lets the vine drop over the opening. Wu Lien's mother leans against the wall, weeping. Quickly Ling Tan covers her with the vines. We hear the sound of running feet outside the compound. Ling Ta grasps his wife's hand and they run into the house.

Ling Tan and his wife appear in the BIG ROOM and hear the soldiers yelling triumphantly as they reach the gate. The dog starts to bark savagely.

LING'S WIFE. Our old dog! They will kill him!

At this second the dog yelps once, howls, then grows still. They look at each other, knowing what has happened, then Ling Tan climbs up on a table and swings up to a big beam above it and behind him comes his wife like an old cat. He gives her his hand to help.

We see Japanese soldiers at the GATE of the COMPOUND. They are forcing the gate with savage threats and curses.

As the sound of the gate giving way is heard, Ling Tan burrows a hole into the thatch and helps his wife into it. There they cling, suffocated by dust and straw but unseen from below. They are no more than secure when they hear the soldiers outside.

The soldiers surge into the BIG ROOM (as seen from the thatch ceiling) and bellow with rage as they see the room is empty. Some open doors and look into each of the sleeping rooms while others break up the furniture, slash the chests, throw the dishes onto the floor, cut the bedding on Lao San's couch with their bayonets, and wreck whatever they touch.

JAPANESE SOLDIERS (*everybody shouting at once*). They have escaped! No, they are hiding! Here is rice! Take all the food you find!

We get close views of Ling Tan and his wife as they cling together and listen to the havoc below, Ling Tan moving a little to see and shaking down some dust; and of the dust falling onto the TABLE.

A soldier, near the table, has just jerked a string of dried garlic from the wall. He stares at the dust settling on the table, then looks at the string of garlic in his hand, apparently satisfied that he, himself, caused the dust to fall.

JAPANESE OFFICER (*sharply, to the men*). Come, do not waste time on this rubble! Find the farmers!

And at this the soldiers run out, toward the courtyard. Then a close view shows LING TAN and his WIFE clinging together while the Japanese are heard outside in the courtyard.

JAPANESE VOICES (*from the courtyard*). Where did they go? We will find them and burn them alive! Is there a way out of this courtyard? Here! Here is a hole! (*Ling Tan and his wife look at each other fearfully, thinking of Wu Lien's mother.*) Pull aside the vines! Yes—someone has crawled through here! (*There is a yell of triumph from one of the soldiers.*) Come and see what we find! A woman? Is this a pig or a woman? Whatever it is, it could not run!

As Ling Tan and his wife exchange looks of rising horror, the scene cuts to the COURTYARD where the soldiers have found Wu Lien's mother and are dragging her out from under the vines. They crowd around, hiding her from view.

Raucous laughter bursts in from the courtyard as the scene cuts back to the BIG ROOM. Suddenly Wu Lien's mother screams, but the scream ends in a kind of gasp. Ling Tan and his wife shudder as they realize what is happening, and Ling Tan moves to go to the old woman's aid.

LING'S WIFE (*holding him*). No. She

is old. There are the young to think of.

He knows she is right, and although it is the most difficult thing he has done in his life, he does not move.

Then we see the LAND BACK OF THE HOUSE. It is dotted with little bamboo thickets and rushes and a hillock now and then. Wu Lien, Lao Ta and Lao San herd the women and children along swiftly. Behind them is heard the shouts of the soldiers.

> LAO TA (*looking back*). We must hide singly, and each group to itself.
>
> WU LIEN. You are right. Then if one is found, all need not perish.

They separate into three groups. Wu Lien takes his wife and two of his children. Lao San takes Wu Lien's second child. Lao Ta moves off with Orchid and his children, following which we see each little group separately, moving along.

LAO SAN and WU LIEN'S CHILD:

> LAO SAN (*whispering*). Here. Make yourself small against the ground. (*He indicates a small ravine and they crouch in it.*)

WU LIEN, his WIFE and CHILDREN as they reach a spot he considers a good one: He indicates for his wife to crouch down behind a small hillock. She does so.

> WU LIEN. For once I grieve that we have so much flesh on us. . . . We make the better targets for it.

LAO TA and FAMILY, who have gone the greatest distance from the house: As they come to a tiny bamboo thicket Lao Ta stops, and puts his older child in a clump by himself. The child looks at him fearfully.

> LAO TA (*calmly, encouragingly*). You will stay here, my eldest son, like a man and by yourself.

The little boy obediently crouches down, without speaking, and watches with round eyes as his father takes Orchid and the other child a little distance from him.

> LAO TA. And you here, my wife. Do not move for anything. (*He starts to crawl away on his belly.*)
>
> ORCHID (*her hand to her throat*). Where will you go?
>
> LAO TA (*looking toward the house, where sounds of looting can be heard*). Back a little. I will stay between you and the evil thing there.
>
> ORCHID (*hardly able to whisper*). Yes, my husband.
>
> LAO TA (*tenderly*). You tremble, and your nose twitches . . . . like a little rabbit. . . . (*He touches her once, and goes.*)

On the other side of the high wall, behind which is the courtyard, can be heard the sound of the soldiers as they disport themselves with the mother of Wu Lien. Then we see ORCHID as the sounds from the house seem unbearably loud to her ears. She looks down anxiously at the sleeping child in her arms, then raises herself, and peers cautiously out from her hiding place.

> ORCHID (*whispering*). My husband . . . . the noise . . . . should we not leave it behind us?

She can see no one. She waits a second but there is no answer to her call. She reacts in panic, and starts to crawl toward her son. We then see ORCHID' ELDER SON as she crawls close to him carrying the baby, who still sleeps.

> ORCHID (*fearfully*). Come, my son We will be safer in another place...

She starts to crawl on, away from Ling Tan's house, and her son follows, also flat on his belly. This dissolves to a view of ORCHID and the CHILDREN moving across a clearing to a thicket, the sounds from the house fainter now. She stops in the thicket and relaxes in relief, but instantly stiffens as she hears a sound in the bamboo grove just ahead of her.—A group of Japanese soldiers (in the BAMBOO GROVE) who have just looted another farm are coming toward Orchid's hiding place. Their fixed bayonets glitter cruelly in the sunlight.—ORCHID is seen close. She is frozen in terror. And just then the baby in her arms opens her eyes, smiles up at her, and starts to whimper.

The JAPANESE SOLDIERS in the bamboo grove hear the child, stop, and look at each other with evil smiles. But the whimpering ceases, and they frown, wondering if their ears have deceived them.

ORCHID has her hand over the baby's mouth, stifling its cry. Then realizing she will smother it, helplessly takes her hand away, and the baby wails again. The JAPANESE SOLDIERS hear the second cry, and start to move toward it, one of them calling out "I heard a child crying. Where there is a child, there is a woman."

ORCHID, crouching low with the whimpering child, looks off, and seems to stop breathing.—The Japanese, as seen from her angle, have come out of the grove and look around.—The baby is quiet now. Desperately ORCHID thrusts it deeper into a thick growth of rushes, and pushes the older boy back beside it.

ORCHID (*fiercely, to the boy*). Remember, a little man does not cry out—no matter what he sees! (*She crawls a little way from them.*)

The JAPANESE SOLDIERS are next seen starting for the sound they have heard. —ORCHID sees that they will come upon the children. Deliberately, therefore, she rises, and stands there, fully revealed to them.—The leader of the JAPANESE SOLDIERS draws in his breath sharply as he sees her.

ORCHID, as seen by the soldiers, stands very quietly, looking toward them. She is waiting to see if they will veer away from the children.—The JAPANESE SOLDIERS start for her, passing near, but not seeing the children.—Orchid stands her ground for another moment, then she turns and starts to run—*away from the spot where her children are hidden.* Her action is as instinctive and natural as that of an animal leading the enemy away from its young.

We see ORCHID continue running desperately, but she stumbles and falls, her leg twisting under her. She tries to rise, but cannot—her leg dangles helplessly, as it is broken. She crouches there, her breath coming in long, tearing gasps. There is a sound of running feet as the soldiers come upon her, and she looks up. The scene expands to reveal the heavy shoes of the soldiers as they surround her. One of the Japanese draws back his foot, and kicks her as she lies there.

This cuts to a close view of the CHILDREN in the THICKET: The little boy, his eyes staring, is watching. There comes a faint cry from Orchid, and the boy soundlessly hides his eyes. The view moves past the boy to the baby. The baby is smiling now, chuckling and playing with its toes. Again the faint cry comes, then there is silence.

The scene dissolves to LAO SAN, crouched in the thicket with Wu Lien's child, at night. He hears something approaching, and tenses. He relaxes a little as Wu Lien crawls in to him.

LAO SAN. Where is my eldest brother?

WU LIEN. I have not seen him. (*He pulls at Lao San's arm.*) Come. The soldiers are no longer between us and the city.

LAO SAN. The city? You would not go there?

WU LIEN (*drawing his son to him*). Why should I not? I was a fool to come here. Everything I live for is there—not here! (*And he starts to crawl out with the child.*)

LAO SAN. But the enemy is there!

WU LIEN (*muttering*). Is he not here also? He is everywhere. And a man is safer on his own ground!

Lao San hesitates, then follows, and the scene dissolves to a view of LING TAN'S FARM at night, as seen from above. It is very quiet. The enemy has gone. This cuts to the BIG ROOM, the moonlight revealing that the place has been wrecked. For a moment there is no sign of life anywhere, then some dust and straw float downward. And next Ling Tan and his wife are seen moving cautiously from their hiding place in the ROOF. There is no word spoken between them as Ling Tan creeps down noiselessly and helps his wife to follow. The distant sound of artillery is heard. They stop, then breathe again.

LING TAN. The sounds of death are far away now.

We see the BIG ROOM as they gain the floor and look about. The eyes of Ling's Wife widen with hysteria.

LING'S WIFE (*moaning*). Oh, my good red pigskin boxes that I brought here as a bride! (*She flings herself on the boxes, examines them; they are ruined. She gets up, looks around.*) And my little pair of side tables! Oh, how can I keep house! Where is all I had!

LING TAN (*soberly*). There is worse to see in the courtyard.

LING'S WIFE (*quieting*). Yes. (*Resolutely, moving toward the door*) And we must be the first to see it. We must not let any of the children come on it before us. . . .

Together, they go out, and the scene cuts to the COURTYARD as Ling Tan and his wife come from the house and go quickly toward the hole in the wall. Suddenly they stop and Ling Tan thrusts his wife behind him so that she cannot see what he sees. She stands, trembling, for a moment, then she moves forward again.

LING'S WIFE. Do not spare me what you must see.

They reach the body of Wu Lien's Mother and Ling's Wife, bending down, sees that she is past help. Then, very tenderly, she allows the vines to drop and cover the broken old body while Ling Tan watches her silently. At this point, suddenly, there is a sound from within the house, and Ling Tan and his wife tense and start to creep backward toward the big room.

LAO SAN'S VOICE (*from within, a shaken whisper*). Is anyone here?

LING TAN (*with almost unbearable relief*). It is our third son.

A dark figure emerges from the house, and reaches out to them with shaking arms.

LAO SAN. Father . . . . mother . . . you are safe! (*Ling's Wife puts her arms around him.*)

LING'S WIFE (*soothingly*). Yes, yes we are safe. . . .

LING TAN. Where are the others?

LAO SAN (*shuddering but pulling himself together a little*). We met people who told us there was safety in the foreign school in the city. My sister and her children are there. . .

LING'S WIFE (*anxiously*). Where is your eldest brother and his household?

LAO SAN. I do not know. We lost each other and did not come together again.

LING TAN. Where then is Wu Lien?

LING'S WIFE (*a bit tartly*). Perhaps he donned a woman's robe and stayed in safety with our daughter.

LAO SAN. No. He is not afraid now. He went back to his shop and he will stay there, he said. (*His voice rising*) But how he can I do not know . . . . the women . . . . and little children . . . . the streets run with their blood. . . . (*Beginning to break once more*) In the village seven young girls are dead . . . . and four women . . . . and no one knows how many others still live but would be better dead. . . . (*Near hysteria*) What I have seen this night . . . . I cannot—(*He chokes and cannot go on.*)

Ling's Wife again puts an arm around him to comfort him, but Ling Tan, who has been looking off, touches her arm, and she, too, looks. Thereupon we see the ARCHWAY to the COMPOUND, as seen by them, and the moonlight reveals Lao Ta as he appears, carrying Orchid's body in his arms. His face is terrible with grief and shock. As he steps inside the courtyard, his son is seen behind him. The little boy, although his face is streaked with tears, walks manfully, carrying his little sister.

The COURTYARD as Lao Ta carefully lowers the body of his wife to the ground: The others stare down at her, then Lao San, with a stifled groan, turns away. He can look no more.— We see ORCHID'S BODY, her clothes torn, her face bruised. Then the view expands to include the others as Ling Tan puts a hand on Lao Ta's arm.

LAO TA (*looking at his father unseeingly*). She was ever a poor foolish little thing . . . without courage . . . but she was my wife . . . . and the mother of my children . . . . (*He breaks, unable to go on, then drops to his knees beside the boy.*)

ORCHID'S BABY (*wailing*). M'ma. . . .

With a cry, Ling's Wife gathers both children into her arms, to shield them from more of the sight.

LING'S WIFE. There . . . . there . . . . my meat dumplings.

LAO SAN (*suddenly, hoarsely*). I cannot stay here! I cannot!

LING TAN (*glancing swiftly at him; to Lao San*). Quiet, my son! (*In a low voice, trying to hush him*) This is your home.

LAO SAN (*beyond restraint*). No longer! I hate it! I do not care where I go, but I cannot stay here . . . . I will go. . . . (*Then, grasping at anything*) To the volunteers in the hills! Yes, that is it! They fight this horror. I will join the volunteers.

Ling Tan and his wife exchange a helpless look. They know they cannot keep this boy if he does not wish to stay.

LING'S WIFE. Rest a day first . . . . do not think of it now. . . .

LAO SAN. I cannot rest! I cannot! (*And he brushes past them, into the house.*)

LING TAN (*sadly, to his wife*). Help our third son make ready for his journey.

She gives him a distracted, brokenhearted look, then bows her head and goes, with the children. Then we see the grieving Lao Ta still bent over Orchid's body, and Ling Tan goes over to him.

LING TAN (*gently*). Remember, my son, all weeping ceases at last.

The scene dissolves to the area outside the COMPOUND. It is almost dawn.— Two graves (one for Orchid and one for the mother of Wu Lien) have been dug and Ling Tan and Third Cousin are just putting the last touches to the smaller mound (Orchid's). Lao Ta is crouched silently beside the grave of his wife, his face set in lines of grief, his hand automatically reaching out and crushing the clods of earth. Third Cousin looks at Lao Ta compassionately, then meaningfully at Ling Tan. Ling Tan nods, and approaches Lao Ta.

LING TAN (*quietly*). Your brother is rash, and foolish. I would have a finger on him. If not my own—then one I can trust. And I trust you. (*As Lao Ta looks up*) I would have you follow him to the hills, and watch over him for me.

LAO TA (*flatly*). Do you so command me?

LING TAN. I do.

Lao Ta lifts his head, and as he begins to speak, his eyes kindle a little.

LAO TA. The hills? There I—I, too could fight. . . . (*He crushes a clod of earth; suddenly*) Yes! I could pay these dwarfs some of what I owe them! I could kill them like lice in a winter coat!

He rises, his eyes hard now, and determined. He turns and looks at the grave for a brief moment, then strides toward the house. The view moves closer to Ling Tan and Third Cousin, as they watch him go.

THIRD COUSIN. Since this time yesterday, cousin, we have both lost sons.

Now daylight streaks the sky, as we hear a cock crowing.

LING TAN (*in wonder*). Can a cock still crow?

THIRD COUSIN. It does not seem one should. I feel there is no tomorrow.

Slowly they turn, and together, go toward the house as the scene fades out.

PART FIVE

The STREET NEAR WU LIEN'S SHOP fades in. Some of the buildings are now only heaps of rubble, and all of them have been damaged. There is no sign of life, but from an alley there is a rattle of machine-gun fire as a Chinese faces the execution squad. Suddenly, from around a corner appears a Japanese staff car, containing an officer and several soldiers.

A closer view in front of Wu Lien's Shop shows the staff car slowing down and the officer directing the driver to stop. The front window of Wu Lien's shop is broken and patched, as are the walls near it. A hand is seen to pull aside the blind, and eyes peer out, hardly visible in the shadows. The blind is quickly dropped as the Japanese Officer (a Captain Sato) gets out of the car, followed by three soldiers.

Sato opens the DOOR of Wu Lien's Shop and enters. Then we see the interior of the shop as Wu Lien, bowing and smiling, but with a flickering fear in his eyes, comes forward to meet the officer. In the background can be seen the Old Clerk, who has been helping Wu Lien put his shop in order.

WU LIEN (*to the Japanese*). Come in. Come in, sirs.

The Old Clerk watches unblinkingly, then moves to work near the rear door.

CAPTAIN SATO (*looking around*). Salted fish?

WU LIEN (*grasping a tin of fish*). Fish. Here is fish. (*Then, humbly*) But I am of all creatures the most unfortunate. These fish are not salty. They are only soaked in oil.

CAPTAIN SATO. I will take them

WU LIEN. Then take them as a gift. I bought them from your country and now I return them to you.

CAPTAIN SATO (*pleased, accepting the fish*). Ah. You do not hate us?

WU LIEN (*earnestly*). I hate no one. (*At this Captain Sato smiles, and his soldiers smile also.*)

CAPTAIN SATO (*indicating the ruined street outside*). For all this—we are sorry. Our soldiers very brave . . . . angry. . . .

WU LIEN (*hastily*). I know how soldiers are. But now—let us hope for peace. Only in peace can we do business. (*He gets a package of sweets, and hands them to the soldiers.*)

Suddenly, and crashingly, from the street outside comes the sound of a woman's prolonged scream—then there is silence. Captain Sato looks full into Wu Lien's eyes.

CAPTAIN SATO. I am glad to meet a man who hates no one.

WU LIEN (*as if the scream had not been*). What can I say except that whatever you want me to do I will do.

CAPTAIN SATO (*smiling*). You may be useful to us, if you will.

WU LIEN (*fervently*). Will I not be?

CAPTAIN SATO. We shall set up a people's government here, and those who rule will rule for us. Can you read? And write?

WU LIEN (*with dignity*). I? Certainly. I am a man of culture.

Captain Sato looks at him, then, satisfied, takes a card from his pocket, and hands it to Wu Lien.

CAPTAIN SATO. You know the address written here?

WU LIEN. Yes. I have delivered goods there. It is the house of a very rich man.

CAPTAIN SATO (*smoothly*). And now he shares it with us—his friends. You will come there tomorrow—and live there. (*He gives the card to Wu Lien.*) You see how merciful we are to those who do not resist us.

He gives a signal to one of the soldiers, who salutes, takes a Japanese flag from a pack, goes to the door, and starts to tack it up outside.—The OLD CLERK is seen close as the sound of the pounding is heard. The muscles of his cheek move a little, but that is all. Then we again see the SHOP with the OLD CLERK in the background.

CAPTAIN SATO. Our flag above your

door will protect you until you come to us. (*He starts out.*)

WU LIEN (*bowing repeatedly*). All my thanks, great one, even to ten thousand thousand.

Captain Sato exits, and closes the door behind him. The sound of the departing car is heard. Wu Lien stands, supporting himself against a table as if in weakness and relief.

WU LIEN (*to the Old Clerk*). I am more cheered than I have been for months. Now I can be with my household again! How wise am I to arrange my own affairs so well!

The Old Clerk stares at him unblinkingly, but does not reply. At this moment from outside comes a clatter of machine-gun fire, a hoarse, shouted defiance, then more gunfire. The old man stops work, and listens. His face is impassive. Wu Lien also listens.

OLD CLERK. Another patriot has died.

WU LIEN (*sharply*). Patriot? What then is a patriot? To be one must a man die and let the worms eat his flesh? No! I think not!

The old man does not answer, but he puts down what he is doing.—WU LIEN, seen close, now starts to putter with his goods.

WU LIEN (*over his shoulder*). These things that happen are not my affair. Whatever comes, I am a man of peace. And whatever Heaven sends I will take and go on with my business. If this foolish resistance would stop—there would be peace for all. Do you not agree?

Receiving no answer, he turns, and the expanding view then includes the spot where the Old Clerk was standing. He is gone, but the rear door is still swinging. There is a sudden noise at the front door and Wu Lien whirls to face it, listening. The noise comes again—then silence. Wu Lien, stiff with fear, forces himself to go to the door.

WU LIEN opens the door, and we observe that the Japanese flag, which was to have been his protection, is gone; only shreds of it are still hanging there. Frightened, he glances up and down the street.—No one is in sight.

WU LIEN (*again seen at the door; in panic*). I have an enemy near me. An enemy among my own people!

Hastily he closes the door and draws the shade, and the scene dissolves to LING'S POND where several Japanese soldiers are seining the pond. The first haul or so nets them many baskets of fish, the last one almost nothing. A stiff wind is blowing.

JAPANESE OFFICIAL'S VOICE (*suddenly heard*). "Farmer! This country now belongs to us, your conquerors. You must produce on your land as we say and the harvest is to come to us at the price we tell you it shall be."

And on his lines, the view swings to the COMPOUND where the Japanese Official (a pompous little man) is reading his proclamation to Ling Tan and Ling's Wife, who, hardly listening to him, are staring in horror at the soldiers who are robbing them of their fish. Lao Ta's children are huddled near Ling's Wife.

JAPANESE OFFICIAL (*significantly, watching them*). *And* those who disobey us will need their land no longer.

LING TAN (*bursting out*). But they take all the fish! The pond is mine!

JAPANESE OFFICIAL (*glaring*). Nothing is yours! Will you village men never learn that you are conquered!

Ling Tan lifts his head and his eyes glitter with defiance and hatred. In the background several other soldiers can be seen as they systematically loot the farm. They carry out bamboo baskets of rice and other stores of food.

LING'S WIFE (*seeing the soldiers*). But they take all the rice! How then can we live—and plant our fields in the spring?

JAPANESE OFFICIAL. You can live off your own fat and you will be given seed when the time comes.

Ling Tan turns, and sees the soldiers crating and carrying out his chickens, ducks, and pigs.

LING TAN. You do not leave us even breeding stock?

JAPANESE OFFICIAL. We will raise the animals henceforth—and also eat them. (*To the soldiers*) Do not forget the ox.

And at this, one of the soldiers goes to the ox, unties it, and leads it away.

LING TAN. My ox! Who will pull the plow?

JAPANESE OFFICIAL (*smiling unpleasantly*). Your own back looks strong. (*Seeing that the soldiers are finished, he turns on his heel and follows them.*)

The view then moves closer to Ling Tan and his wife as they look after the Japanese, quivering with impotent rage.

LING'S WIFE (*holding the children to her*). How will we feed our grandchildren now? Why did you not defy him?

LING TAN (*softly—through his teeth*). Why? Because . . . . alive I can hold all my land . . . . and dead . . . . I can hold only so much as I am buried in. . . .

The scene fades out.

PART SIX

The valley of Ling fades in. The first chill winds of autumn rise and whistle over the barren fields.

NARRATOR'S VOICE. And, while Ling Tan and others like him clung to their land—their land which, like a sick man, could not be moved to a safe place—

Another valley dissolves in—far in the interior. Crossing this valley can be seen the people who carry the factory.

NARRATOR'S VOICE. . . . those who had taken machines apart with their hands so that they could be carried piece by piece on their backs, were making their way forward. . . .

A DESERT dissolves in as the column of people is seen sweating and straining, but moving forward under the burning sun.

NARRATOR'S VOICE. . . . . they were stopped neither by the sun nor the lands burned to death by the sun, neither by the hot sky overhead nor the hot sand underfoot.

We see the column (Jade and Lao Er in the foreground), as some of them labor to push a truck out of a muddy bog. The rain is pouring down on them but they pay no attention to it and work on. Lao Er looks worriedly at Jade, but she smiles at him, and keeps tugging at the wheel.

NARRATOR'S VOICE. They were stopped neither by the mud nor the rain—mud that set like plaster-casts, rain that so filled the air that fish could have lived in it.

We see a high and snowy mountain pass. Jade and Lao Er, tied to the others with ropes, make their way up a tortuous slope.

NARRATOR'S VOICE. Nor were they stopped by the high mountain passes where breath froze and feet left blood on the snow.

The column is crossing a swift river on an improvised bridge. Jade is not helping now, but simply moving along with the others. The cart Lao Er is dragging gets stuck and Jade moves to him, tries to add her strength to his. He motions her away, but she stays at his side.

NARRATOR'S VOICE. Water was made to cross, and it was crossed many times. And, when it could not be walked in, it was walked over—on bridges made of rags, belts and rope. And then, when the people had passed on, the bridges were taken apart and worn again.

A broad plain near a city in the interior dissolves in. The people who carried the factory are busy setting it up. They are thin and drawn as a result of the march but they are happy.

NARRATOR'S VOICE. Nothing stopped them, except their own will. Their march was over only when they wanted it to be over and they had reached the spot they had chosen. All rejoiced when the march was done. . . .

We see JADE and LAO ER as Jade, her face contorted with pain, lies beneath a tree. Lao Er bends anxiously over her.

NARRATOR'S VOICE. . . . . but none more so than Jade, for she knew that her time was near.

This fades to a STREET in the VILLAGE of LING. It is a winter day. A squad of Japanese soldiers tramps through the desolate streets.

NARRATOR'S VOICE. But there was no rejoicing in the village of Ling. The enemy was everywhere, leaving footprints on the sick earth—

A series of quick, impressionistic views follows: The farmers and their families, (Ling Tan and his wife among them) grub in the fields for roots.

NARRATOR'S VOICE. —and the starving people were everywhere, looking for a sign of life—

Pitifully haggard children peer into empty shop windows.

NARRATOR'S VOICE. —and many died, while they were looking for it.

Men, women and children dig in rubbish heaps for scraps of food. A man collapses.

NARRATOR'S VOICE. Some were driven mad, and became as animals.

Some starving farmers find a dead dog, and fall on it ravenously. Then the scene dissolves to a view of the SKY above the City and Village. A Japanese plane soars over. It drops, not bombs, but sheets of paper. The paper flutters down to earth.

NARRATOR'S VOICE. And then came still another way to die.

We see a CANAL leading from the city to the village. Bloated corpses float, face downward, and the leaflets drift softly down upon them. The view moves closer to a dead swollen hand. Near it is a watersoaked leaflet. The leaflet reads:

"CHINESE!
Do not resist your liberators!
The Japanese bring you new life!"

NARRATOR'S VOICE. Not bombs nor machine-gun bullets—for those were quick and final. Not iron from the sky—but irony! It takes a long time, and it hurts very much, to laugh yourself to death!

This dissolves to LING'S FARM at dawn, early in March. A skiff of snow, a slight wind—bare fields. Ling Tan walks slowly across the field toward the house. He carries a snake, and fishing pole.

NARRATOR'S VOICE. —But not even the enemy could change the seasons, and now the winter was coming to an end, and Ling Tan was still there, on his land. . . .

This wipes to LING TAN'S SLEEPING ROOM where Ling's Wife crouches over the little girl who lies motionless. Slowly Ling's Wife covers the child's head, and smoothes her hair.

BOY'S VOICE (*weakly*). M'ma.

Ling's Wife rises, and goes toward the boy. The view widens to include the bed where he lies as she sits beside him.

BOY (*raising his hand*). M'ma. . . .

LING'S WIFE (*brokenly*). You will not be long apart. I promise you.

As the boy lets his hand drop, the scene cuts to the BIG ROOM showing Ling Tan entering eagerly, tossing the snake near the stove, and going to the sleeping room, then back to the bedroom as Ling Tan enters. He looks at the little girl, then swiftly toward the boy.

LING TAN. I have food for them!

At this, Ling's Wife, her face bleak with despair, slowly straightens.

LING'S WIFE (*dully*). The girl is dead.

Ling Tan goes to her swiftly, his eyes darting fearfully to the boy.

LING TAN. But the boy . . . . he was stronger. . . .

LING'S WIFE (*shaking her head*). No. He will follow her soon.

And as Ling Tan moves quickly to her, we get a close view of the BOY'S BED and see his life ebbing swiftly.

LING TAN. That I should go on living while my grandchildren die. . . .

Even as he looks, the boy shudders and is still; and Ling's Wife touching his face, realizes he is dead.

LING'S WIFE (*agonized*). What is a house where no children are? (*Her voice breaks.*) They were so small . . . . and helpless . . . . what need could the gods have of them. . . . . ? (*She begins to cry.*)

Slowly Ling Tan rises. He clenches his fists and begins to curse, softly and bitterly.

LING TAN. Curse all these men who make wars. Curse all women who give birth to these men and curse their grandmothers and all who are their kin. (*His voice rising*) Why do not men of peace and sense band together and forbid life to all who would make wars? (*Then his shoulders slump, and the fire goes out of him.*) And yet, what can I do—one man upon my land.

His wife, seeing his need of her, rises, puts a hand on his arm, and they stand there for a moment, sorrowing. Suddenly a voice calls out to them.

VOICE OF THIRD COUSIN. Cousin . . . . are you here then?

They turn unseeingly toward the door and the scene cuts to the BIG ROOM which has been entered by Third Cousin and his wife, wrapped also in rags against the cold. Third Cousin's Wife's face is a mask of malice and hate.

> THIRD COUSIN. Cousin! Cousin! Where is the man? I come with big news in my mouth!
>
> THIRD COUSIN'S WIFE (*seeing the snake*). See! *They* have food! And do not share it!

She snatches up the snake and hides it in her coat as Ling Tan and his wife enter from the sleeping room. They move mechanically, as if stunned.

> THIRD COUSIN (*excitedly, waving an envelope*). This is from your second son! A messenger brought it to the teahouse!

Ling Tan and his wife look at each other with wonder, hardly taking this in.

> THIRD COUSIN'S WIFE (*bitterly*). A letter from a son is something *I* will never have now.
>
> LING'S WIFE (*gently*). We have all lost much.
>
> THIRD COUSIN (*to Ling Tan, who stands, holding the envelope*). Well then, open it!

Ling Tan opens the letter, and a cord falls out. Slowly joy dawns in his eyes, in spite of his despair.

> LING TAN (*in a hushed voice*). The cord is *red*. It is a son.
>
> LING'S WIFE (*hardly able to speak*). We have a grandson! (*Tears start in her eyes.*)
>
> THIRD COUSIN. But you weep! This is a time for joy!
>
> LING'S WIFE (*brokenly*). Two grandchildren lie dead in our house. Can I thank Heaven for sending us back but one!
>
> LING TAN (*quickly, looking upward*). Quiet, woman, or Heaven will hear you and take even him away! (*Then, to Third Cousin*) Thank you, cousin . . . . this news lightens our heavy hearts. A grandson is no small thing.
>
> THIRD COUSIN'S WIFE (*venomously*). By rights this child of Jade's is not yours!
>
> THIRD COUSIN (*angrily, to his wife*). You talk with no thought. (*To Ling Tan*) Pray excuse her, bitterness has turned her words to gall.
>
> THIRD COUSIN'S WIFE (*spitting it out*). Had Jade married my son, as she ought, he would be alive today and safe there with her . . . . and so, before the gods, her child is *our* grandchild!

Ling's Wife turns to her as if to strike her down. But her grief at the loss of Lao Ta's children and the reaction to this news on top of it has robbed her of her old fire.

> LING'S WIFE (*with great dignity*). I should drive you from my house, but it would soil this moment . . . . (*her eyes glittering with tears, but she goes on bravely*) . . . . this joyful moment.

Third Cousin, not too gently, leads his wife away, and the view moves closer to Ling Tan and his wife as they look down at the red cord, and the tears of both fall upon it. The scene fades out to indicate the passing of much time, and then a village street fades in as an evil-looking Japanese Official is measuring out rice plants and other seed to farmers, Ling Tan among them.

This dissolves to a close view of the LAND as it is turned by a plow. The view pulls back to reveal Ling Tan, harnessed to the plow in place of the ox. His wife guides it behind him. They wear fewer rags now, for it is warmer. As they pass a tree that is just beginning to put forth leaves, a bird trills shrilly. They look at it, and listen for a moment, and then they smile. The smile sits strangely on their faces, as if it were the first for a long while.

This dissolves to a FLOODED FIELD as Ling Tan and his wife plant the seedlings, and then to the same field later in the year when the shoots have grown and the soft green masks the dark earth.

This dissolves to Ling Tan's BIG ROOM at night. Ling's Wife, on her knees behind the stove is digging a hole, using a broken hoe as a tool. Ling Tan comes to her. The earth is very hard, and she makes slight progress.

LING TAN (*staring*). Has the enemy not done enough damage to my house? Must you dig up the foundations?

LING'S WIFE (*still digging*). We will keep what we can of our seed and the vegetables we grow and hide them in this hole. I will make it big enough to hold a pig.

LING TAN. What pig?

LING'S WIFE (*tartly*). The one you will steal from the enemy's breeding farm.

LING TAN (*considering the hole*). But how can you dig so large a thing without help? The earth is stubborn.

LING'S WIFE (*drily*). Heaven gave me the thought—Heaven will provide the help. (*She indicates a shovel near the stove.*) The shovel is there.

This is one of her favorite quips and her first joke in a long time.

LING TAN (*chuckling*). I am too just a man to deny sense even to a woman when I hear it from her. (*He starts to work.*) We will steal food from ourselves and eat it.

LING'S WIFE (*digging*). If all in the village do this we will harry the enemy like fleas in a dog's tail.

LING TAN (*nodding*). And it may be he will make little headway for stopping to gnaw at his rear.

Suddenly a noise is heard in the compound outside, and they stiffen.

In the COMPOUND two muffled figures, their identities impossible to distinguish in the darkness, are nearing the door.

Ling Tan and his wife in the BIG ROOM are tense, listening.

LING TAN (*in a whisper*). Cover the hole.

She throws a cloth over the hole, then follows him as he moves toward the door. The door swings open, and two figures appear in the opening. Ling Tan picks up a lamp, and holds it to illuminate the figures. Jade and Lao Er stand blinking in the light. Ling Tan and his wife are transfixed.

LAO ER. My father! My mother! (*Clasping them*)

LING TAN (*joyfully*). What gladness!

LING'S WIFE (*finding her voice*). Have I no grandson? Where is he? (*Jade laughs softly.*) Where is he?

LING TAN. Quiet, woman, before you burst and the enemy hears the sound you make!

He hands his wife the light, and closes the door. As Jade and Lao Er come into the room, Ling's Wife holds the lamp full on them, and they are revealed more clearly. They look like two slim young farmers. Jade has her hair cut short and is dressed in the same clothes that Lao Er is wearing—plain, strong blue trousers and jacket and stout straw sandals. The faces of both are thin and brown, and they have packs strapped to their backs like peddlers.

LAO ER. Shade the light. We should not be seen.

LING'S WIFE (*shading the light, then, eagerly*). Well, then! Where have you left my little meat dumpling?

Jade smilingly lifts the cover of the pack on her back and there is hidden a boy baby.

JADE. Here he is. And he has been fed and is ready to greet you.

LING'S WIFE. Give him to me! (*Reaching out her demanding arms*)

Jade unstraps the child, removing several books that are packed beside him.

LING'S WIFE (*impatiently*). Books! Still books! You have crushed him beneath them! You seem to love them more than your child! (*Grabbing the child, beside herself*) Ah! How sweet his flesh smells! (*She sniffs him hungrily, then sinks into a chair, and unwraps him.*) Bring the light close so I can see him! My little meat dumpling! How firm he is of body—and his hair like black silk! He is exactly as I thought he would be! (*She begins to rock back and forth, crying and laughing.*) Oh, how it eases me! How I am comforted to hold him like this! I knew you would bring him back to me, else I could not have lived! (*Her face is broken with emotion.*) Night after night I have dreamed . . . . of holding him so. . . . (*She breaks off, near hysteria.*)

LING TAN (*alarmed*). Guard your heart, old woman!

LAO ER. Yes, mother. Too much joy is as bad as too much sorrow.

Ling's Wife tries to speak, but cannot. Ling Tan takes the child from her and Jade quickly pours some cold tea into a cup for her.

JADE. Here, my mother. Drink down this cold tea and then the words can come up!

LING'S WIFE (*drinking and sighing*). Ah. That brought my heart back again into its place.

She reaches for the child again, but Ling Tan has now seated himself and is looking at the baby pridefully.

LING TAN. This is no usual child. Look at his face, how square it is, and he has a square mouth.

LING'S WIFE (*impatiently*). Give him back to me. (*At this, Jade and Lao Er exchange a warm, amused look.*)

LING TAN (*with dignity*). In a moment, old woman. In a moment. (*He examines the child again.*) What can the enemy do to us, when our family goes on like this?

And then he sees the look in his wife's eyes and her arms outstretched and he gives the child back to her. She smiles at the baby, engrossed in him, takes a bit of cold rice from a bowl on the table. She chews it first herself and starts to feed it to the baby.

LING'S WIFE. There now! You are in your home and you must eat!

JADE (*quickly, catching her arm*). I beg you not to be angry with me, mother, but do not put food from your mouth into the child's.

LING'S WIFE (*looking up—outraged*).

Why, I fed my sons so, and it did no harm to them.

Lao Er and Ling Tan exchange a helpless look at this woman's quarrel, but say nothing. Jade smiles at Ling's Wife. This is a Jade who has gained in dignity and authority.

JADE (*firmly, but pleasantly*). But it is not thought good now, mother. I bought a book—(*Ling's Wife sniffs scornfully at this.*)—and it told how to care for children, and it spoke against such things.

LING'S WIFE (*stiffly*). You had better take your child. Doubtless I pollute him when I hold him. (*She holds out the child, albeit reluctantly.*)

JADE (*gently, not taking the baby*). Oh, mother. It was for you I brought him home!

LING TAN (*who has had enough of this foolishness*). Cool your anger, both of you. Shall we quarrel this night of all nights and over the child who is the center of all our hearts?

LING'S WIFE (*with spirit*). Did I ever have a book to feed my children and did I ever lose a son?

But the anger is gone from her and she turns again to the child, smiling at him and holding him close. Then she begins to feed him, but with the chopsticks and not from her own mouth. This cuts to a scene in which LING TAN, LAO ER and JADE appear together.

LING TAN (*softly*). Indulge her with the child. It will heal her for everything. (*They nod and he goes toward his wife.*)

We see LING'S WIFE and the CHILD she is holding, and as Ling Tan enters she looks up.

LING'S WIFE (*eyes aglitter with tears*).

Our house has come alive again, old man.

He nods as the scene fades out, and then a VILLAGE STREET fades in: Lao Er and Ling Tan move softly along in the night. They come upon Neighbor Shen, who stops and looks in amazement at Lao Er.

LING TAN (*softly*). Here is my son back again. He has seen and learned many things and if you are willing, he will tell you of them.

LAO ER (*respectfully*). Not because I have any merit in knowing them, neighbor, but to hear will give you heart.

This dissolves to a WATER WHEEL as two farmers are treading the wheel and listening to Lao Er. Ling Tan, as lookout, is in the background.

LAO ER. I come from the high command, the government in the free land. And there are many like me and they spread among the villages to tell such men as you what we must do. . . .

This dissolves to the TEAHOUSE at night as Lao Er and Ling Tan are being served tea and Lao Er is speaking to the proprietor and his sons.

LAO ER. Shade the window. I would not be seen.

LING TAN. We are lucky in one way. The enemy does not live here in our village, but in the city, and comes here only now and then to loot and spy and prowl.

LAO ER. This enemy must be resisted —openly where the land is free—and secretly where the land is lost. We who must resist secretly have a harder task than the others. . . .

This dissolves to a close view of THREE FARMERS sharpening a scythe, with Lao

Er (Ling Tan in the background) talking to them.

> LAO ER. We must act together, as the fingers on one hand. (*Quietly, with emphasis*) *We must track down this enemy—and kill him.*

At this a farmer looks up, and draws the sharpening tool across the scythe with a harsh noise.

This dissolves to THIRD COUSIN'S HOUSE, at night, where Third Cousin, a book before him, is scratching his beard dubiously as he faces Lao Er. Ling Tan, as lookout, stands in the doorway.

> THIRD COUSIN. Join with the hillmen! Are you inviting us to be ready to die?
>
> LAO ER (*hotly*). Yes! But to die like men—not sheep on the butchering block!
>
> LING TAN (*gently, from the door*). Do not blame your cousin. A learned man can never be as brave as one unlettered.
>
> LAO ER (*more quietly*). We must build the hole under my father's house into a strong room. And there we will hide men who must hide.

This dissolves to LING TAN'S BIG ROOM at night: Ling's Wife is busy at the stove. Farmer Shen passes her, carrying an empty basket and goes behind the stove. The hole is now obviously an opening into a cave. She hands the empty basket down and receives another basket full of earth from the men who are digging the hole.

In the HOLE, Ling Tan, Lao Er, and several of the farmers previously identified as listening to Lao Er are working steadily, enlarging the hole.

> LAO ER (*as he works*). As often as can be done an enemy, or a few enemies, must die from unseen guns in our hands.
>
> FARMER (*as he works*). Guns! We have no guns.
>
> LAO ER. Every man will have one. I promise it.
>
> SECOND FARMER. How then will this be done?
>
> LAO ER. It is already arranged. As I came here I passed through the hills and saw my brothers there. The guns will be brought to you by those who feel as we do. . . .

This dissolves to the HOLE when it is much larger and has been made into a room, braced with poles and brick and tile. Provisions are now stored here, also some live animals. Several farmers (not including Shen this time) are at work storing away guns and ammunition. Lao Er puts down an armful of guns, turns, and goes toward the ladder leading into the big room.

> FARMER (*grinning, after Lao Er*). Where did you find these guns? Some of them have foreign writing on them!

LAO ER in a close moving view:

> LAO ER (*laughing, starting up the ladder*). A wise man does not question a gift too closely.

The view moves with Lao Er as he enters the Big Room, passing another farmer who climbs down into the hole, carrying guns. Lao Er goes to Jade, who stands at the window looking out.

> LAO ER. I will take the guard now.
>
> JADE. No. Eat first. I am not weary.

Lao Er touches her arm and turns away. She looks after him for a moment, her eyes soft, then goes back to her watching.

Then we see Lao San and Lao Ta sitting at the table, eating. They are brown and hard and fierce looking and eat hungrily, with small manners. Ling Tan and his wife sit near, watching their sons as if they were starved for the sight of them. Ling Tan holds Jade's son.

LAO ER (*crossing to the table*). Our kinsman wants to know where you found the guns! (*He seats himself.*)

LAO SAN (*laughing*). Tell him they are easiest found by sticking a knife into the belly of an enemy soldier. Thus—(*He makes a gesture of disemboweling a man.*)—and there is the gun for you as if from his insides!

Ling Tan looks at him quickly. It is obvious that this talk from his third son both surprises and disturbs him. Ling's Wife, however, is oblivious to all but her joy.

LING'S WIFE. My sons! All my sons! What more can I ask, who am only a woman!

LING TAN (*soberly*). To hear our third son speak one would think he *liked* to kill.

LING'S WIFE (*patting Lao San*). How well you look and not on my cooking! I cannot understand it!

LAO ER. You should see the women admire him now! And still he has yet to choose one!

LAO SAN (*sneering*). Women!

LING'S WIFE (*sharply*). Do not turn your nose toward Heaven! It is time you brought home a daughter-in-law! See that you do!

Everyone smiles. It is good to be together again if only for a little while and have the mother ordering them about. Even Ling Tan, disturbed as he is by Lao San, smiles.

LING TAN. What would come to us if we did not have the women to keep at us?

LING'S WIFE (*with spirit*). If you had no women none of you would be born at all! I want grandsons from all of you before I die!

LAO SAN. Let fat men like Wu Lien bother with such nonsense. I am lean enough to fight, and that is what I will do.

LAO TA (*suddenly—thoughtfully*). I have wanted to ask—what news of Wu Lien?

LING TAN. He and his family live in the city and in safety and are protected, I have heard.

LING'S WIFE (*sniffing*). Yes, we have *heard*. But they have not come near to tell us so themselves! Nor has Wu Lien been here to see his mother's grave! (*At this, Lao Ta, Lao San and Lao Er exchange a meaningful look.*)

LAO TA (*troubled*). I have known of others who are "protected." Could this word of Wu Lien mean he deals with the enemy?

LING TAN (*sharply*). I will not believe that until I know it is so!

LING'S WIFE. Nor will I.

JADE (*sharply*). Someone comes!

Everyone tenses, and turns to look toward Jade, who strains her eyes to see out the window.

JADE (*relaxing a little*). It is Neighbor Shen, the lookout.

There comes the sound of running feet and Neighbor Shen enters quickly.

NEIGHBOR SHEN. Enemy soldiers are in the village. They look for young men to slave for them.

LAO SAN (*rising—grinning*). Well, then—let us help them find what they seek.

LAO ER (*to Shen*). How many of the enemy?

NEIGHBOR SHEN. A line from here to the door.

LAO ER (*to the men in the hole*). Come out, and bring enough guns for the others who will act with us.

The farmers climb up out of the hole, bringing several guns. Lao San calmly takes a last bite of food and Lao Ta picks up his gun.

LING TAN (*slowly*). This is the beginning of it, then. (*He looks at his gun.*)

LAO SAN (*laughing—striding toward the door*). You will have to hurry to equal my record, father.

We get a close view of JADE and LAO ER as they take silent leave of each other, and he turns toward the door.—Then as Lao Er goes out, Ling Tan looks at his wife before leaving her.

LING TAN (*to his wife*). You will be safe?

LING'S WIFE (*with bravado*). Let them come—the bandylegs! (*And she pats the gun beside her.*)

Ling Tan looks at her, then walks to the door, and goes out, following which we see the ROOM, very empty now with only Jade and Ling's Wife and Jade's son. The women stand motionless for a moment, listening to the faint sounds made by the departure of their men. Then Jade looks at Ling's Wife who sits down as if the false courage has suddenly drained from her. Jade realizes that the older woman is deeply disturbed, although she would die before admitting it. Jade goes calmly to the table, and sits down, putting the gun beside her. She starts to feed the baby; after a bite or two she takes up a book, and reads as she spoons the rice into the eager little mouth. Ling's Wife watches her, forgetting her own concern a little in her indignation at what she is seeing.

LING'S WIFE (*bursting out*). You read a book and feed your child at the same time!

JADE. Yes, mother.

LING'S WIFE (*acidly*). It seems to me a danger to do two such opposite things when you are but a woman. (*She sits near Jade, watching the child hungrily.*)

JADE. Is not the child fat and well?

LING'S WIFE (*tartly*). Then he thrives in spite of it.

Jade smiles at her. She knows the older woman is suffering under a strain and seeks for a way to ease it.

JADE. Here. Hold your grandson and feed him.

LING'S WIFE. It is your child. I would not rob you. (*But even as she speaks her arms reach out for the baby.*)

JADE. Neither of us can rob the other. He belongs to both of us—and to all who have gone before in this house and all who will come after.

Ling's Wife starts to feed the child. Slowly she relaxes, forgetting her fears in her joy in him. Jade watches her affectionately. She, too, is worried about the men, but she knows the attitude she must maintain for the good of all.

The scene dissolves to a VILLAGE STREET where nine or ten Japanese soldiers are loading several young men and boys taken from village houses onto a horse-drawn cart. The Japanese are relaxed and a little careless, and laugh and talk as they work. The village street seems empty. This is followed by quickly successive views of:

LING TAN, at his hiding place between two houses. He is frowning, as if something eats at his mind.—

LAO ER, calm and sure, crouched behind a wall.—

LAO TA, at his post. He is stolid and expressionless.—

LAO SAN, his eyes glowing with anticipation.—

NEIGHBOR SHEN, nervous, but determined.—

OTHER FARMERS, also nervous and tense and a little uncertain, who have been deployed in strategic places of ambush.—

We see the JAPANESE as they herd the Chinese into the cart. Their officer lounges against the wall, smoking. A close view of LAO ER then shows him giving the signal to fire, and we see the JAPANESE again as they are struck by the volley of gunfire and six of them fall. The others scramble for their guns, but all except one (who is in the wagon) fall before a second burst from the hidden villagers. The Chinese in the wagon, at the first volley, leap out and run to cover.

Successive quick views then show:

LAO TA, who has killed with skill and precision and no feeling at all.—

LAO ER, who has also acted almost mechanically.—

LING TAN, who, as if stunned, stares at the Japanese he has killed, then at his gun.—And

LAO SAN, whose lips are curled back from his teeth in a savage grin of fulfillment.

And now at the WOODPILE, the one remaining Japanese in the wagon lashes the horses away and down the street. A farmer who tries to stop him is run down and screams horribly. At the moment it appears the Japanese will escape, but Lao San leaps from his hiding place and drags the horses to a halt. We then see LAO SAN and the JAPANESE.

JAPANESE (*raising his hands*). Do not shoot me.

LAO SAN (*softly, grinning*). Do not be afraid. I will not *shoot* you.

Then, with one quick, violent motion he hauls the Japanese down from the wagon. And as he lifts his knife and brings it down, the scene cuts quickly to a close view of LING TAN watching, in horror. The Japanese soldier's death scream is heard, and Ling Tan turns away, sickened.

The view moves to LAO ER as he runs across the street, and speaks to frightened villagers who have begun to pour out of their houses.

LAO ER (*shouting*). Bury these men and leave no trace! If anything is found all of us will die! We are in this together!

As the villagers speak in agreement, the scene fades out.

PART SEVEN

The COMPOUND fades in. It is day. Jade and Ling's Wife are bathing the baby in a small tub. The baby laughs and plays in the water. Ling Tan and Lao Er are at work repairing a plow. From time to time they look toward the women and child and smile. It is very peaceful. Suddenly Lao Er looks off over the wall, and stiffens.

LAO ER. Someone comes.

Jade grabs up the baby, all dripping and shiny with water, and holds him to her as they all go to look over the gate. Then, as viewed by them, we see the ROAD on which two rickshas, with Wu Lien and his household in the first one, are approaching.

LING'S WIFE (*as the scene cuts back to the* COMPOUND—*relieved*). It is only your elder sister.

JADE (*swiftly*). Mother, you are not to say that we are here.

LAO ER. Tell nothing. We will go to the hidden room. (*He and Jade disappear quickly into the house.*)

LING'S WIFE (*to Ling*). This is a strange day when brothers and sisters must hide from each other.

LING TAN. All days are strange now.

Together they go to the gate, and peer through the crack. Then we see as viewed by them the OUTSIDE GATE as Wu Lien and his wife and children get out of the first ricksha. They are fat and dressed in fine clothes. Two sullen and bored enemy guards appear behind them.

This cuts to LING TAN and WIFE reacting to what they have seen.

LING TAN. Soldiers!

They look at each other and their eyes harden, then they look back at the visitors.

LING TAN. Were Wu Lien and his household always so fat?

LING'S WIFE. Perhaps our eyes have grown used to people afraid and hungry and wounded. . . .

She flings open the gate as Wu Lien and his wife come toward them, beaming, followed by guards.

WU LIEN'S WIFE. Ah! My old ones! Here we are to see you!

WU LIEN (*bowing*). A thousand fortunes! (*As Ling Tan does not bid them enter*) Are we then welcome to come within?

LING TAN (*quietly*). You and your family are welcome, but I cannot let others into my house. (*He looks hard at the guards.*)

WU LIEN (*quickly—smoothly*). You need not fear. These two only came to guard me.

LING TAN (*stiffly*). What guard do you need in my house? (*He steps aside, allowing Wu Lien's Wife and children inside.*)

WU LIEN (*apologetically, to the guards*). My father-in-law is old, and afraid.

LING TAN (*loudly*). I am not afraid of them, but I will not have them in my house. (*At this, Wu Lien looks helpless; then he hits upon an idea.*)

WU LIEN. Then we must wait here

with the guards. Will you bring stools to sit upon?

LING TAN (*hesitating, then*). I will. (*He goes into the compound, shutting the gate.*)

Wu Lien smiles at the guards to soothe their feelings.

WU LIEN. Country people have no manners. (*The guards grunt in response.*)

INSIDE the COMPOUND Ling's Wife, Wu Lien's Wife and children now find seats in the shade. Ling gathers up stools. We see the two women moving together.

WU LIEN'S WIFE. Where then are my brothers?

LING'S WIFE (*quickly*). They are gone, and we are alone. Even your elder brother's children are dead. (*She looks at Wu Lien's fat children.*) They died of sickness . . . . and starvation.

WU LIEN'S WIFE. It is these times I grieve for my elder brother—and for you also. I weep for you.

LING'S WIFE (*repelling her sympathy*). Do not waste your tears. My own have dried.

They are now near the tub. They sit down.

WU LIEN'S WIFE (*noticing the tub*). But if there are no children, why do you put water in a child's small tub? Do you wash yourself in it now?

Ling's Wife looks panicky for a moment, then she shrugs, kicks off her sandals, sits and puts her feet in the tub.

LING'S WIFE (*shortly*). Only my feet. (*She looks at her fat daughter.*) But soon I will be thin enough to sit in it and have room to spare.

WU LIEN'S WIFE (*uncomfortably*). I do not understand. . . . I see no welcome in your eyes.

LING'S WIFE (*soberly*). I do not like anyone of my blood to look so fat when others are lean.

WU LIEN'S WIFE. I eat only what I am given.

LING'S WIFE. Who gives it to you?

WU LIEN'S WIFE. My husband. (*As Ling's Wife sniffs*) You cannot understand how good he is. The enemy rules, and somehow we must live under that rule.

LING'S WIFE. But not prosper too much under it.

Wu Lien's Wife is deeply troubled now. She pushes her children forward. They should soften her mother's heart if anything will.

WU LIEN'S WIFE (*pleading for approval*). These grandchildren are left to comfort you. Have they not grown?

LING'S WIFE. Yes. Your children have grown. (*She rises, and steps out of the tub. In spite of the action, she is dignified and aloof.*) If I had anything in the house to give you and your children, for courtesy I would prepare it for you. But we have nothing. I cannot treat you courteously, therefore.

Wu Lien's Wife stares at her incredulously. Then suddenly she starts to cry. Her mother watches her, but does not try to comfort her.

At the GATE: Ling Tan has brought out stools. The two guards squat a little way from where he and Wu Lien are seated in the shade of the wall.

WU LIEN. Why are you so stiff? (*He looks toward the guards, and lowers his voice.*) You must know that what I do is done only for the best.

LING TAN (*loudly*). I do not know what you do.

WU LIEN (*softly, nervous*). Times are times and the wise man takes his time as he finds it. Compromise is sometimes better than valor.

LING TAN (*looking at him coldly*). Where do you live now?

WU LIEN. At the tenth house of the North Gate Street.

LING TAN. That is a street of fine houses. How can you live there?

WU LIEN (*loudly, for the guard's benefit*). I am told to live there. I work for the new government. I am well paid and I am content. You see what I would say, my father-in-law?

LING TAN (*loudly*). I am a common man. I am so stupid I understand only when a thing is said to me and I hear it.

Wu Lien coughs, smiles apologetically at the guards, then moves close to Ling Tan.

WU LIEN (*very softly*). I am come here today to help you. If you do as I say, your life will be easier.

LING TAN. What must I do?

WU LIEN (*pleased, thinking he is impressing*). Do whatever is told you to do, and I will manage for you here and there as I am able.

LING TAN (*studying him*). And what have you to do, son-in-law?

WU LIEN. For one thing, I am a controller of all incoming goods. Rice and wheat, fish and salt, and opium—

LING TAN (*in a terrible voice*). Opium! That evil was driven out of this country by great pain and suffering and now you bring it back!

WU LIEN (*shrugging*). I am not my own master.

Ling Tan looks at him for a long moment, then slowly, deliberately he spits.

At the GATE, then, as Wu Lien's Wife comes out, sobbing, and leading her children:

WU LIEN (*to his wife*). You do well to leave. We are not wanted here. (*He helps her and the children into a ricksha; the guards get into the other.*)

WU LIEN'S WIFE (*sadly, to Ling Tan*). How can you be so hard when there are only you two old people left and we are all you have!

LING TAN (*quietly*). We can live.

Wu Lien's Wife sobs again, and the rickshas start away, following which we get a close view at the GATE as Ling's Wife joins him.

LING'S WIFE (*tears in her eyes*). Curse this enemy. He has made me quarrel with my daughter.

LING TAN (*slowly*). This makes the answer about Wu Lien that our son feared was true. . . .

Together they turn back into the gate. Then the scene dissolves to a VILLAGE STREET as the rickshas bearing Wu Lien and his party move smartly along, over the rough roads. They look very smooth and prosperous and sleek, in spite of the fact that Wu Lien's Wife is sobbing and blowing her nose. As they pass Third Cousin's house, the scene cuts to a view of THIRD COUSIN'S WIFE watching them, as they disappear, while Third Cousin sits dreaming over a book.

THIRD COUSIN'S WIFE. See! Silk coats and enemy soldiers to serve them! It is plain Wu Lien has got his fingers into the fat. (*Then, sharply, as he does not speak*) Of what value is a rich relative unless you can put him to use? (*As Third Cousin looks up, startled, she sneers.*) Can you find the answer to that in your cursed book? (*She grabs the book, and throws it into the dirt.*)

Thereupon the scene dissolves to a CITY STREET as Third Cousin and his wife (carrying a basket) come up to the gate of a fine house. A Japanese soldier is on guard.

THIRD COUSIN'S WIFE. We are his kinsmen and would see Wu Lien.

GUARD (*contemptuously*). Go in. Wu Lien sees anybody.

They enter, and the scene cuts to the COURTYARD as THIRD COUSIN and WIFE move through the courtyard and look around at the rich surroundings.

THIRD COUSIN'S WIFE (*awed, but covetous*). What a fine house! I have never seen a house like this. I did not know there were such places.

THIRD COUSIN (*peering sidewise at her*). Why do you take a fish to Wu Lien who has pork, when there is nothing in *my* belly but wrinkles?

THIRD COUSIN'S WIFE (*enigmatically*). I will always exchange one fish for a basketful.

THIRD COUSIN (*worried*). I have the feeling you often give me—that I am about to be crushed between two grindstones.

They are near the Archway now. A second guard is posted there.

THIRD COUSIN'S WIFE. Where are the rooms of Wu Lien, our rich relative?

GUARD (*jerking his thumb*). In there.

They enter the Archway, and the scene cuts to WU LIEN'S QUARTERS, where we first see WU LIEN, fat and bland and smiling and dressed in a fine silk robe; then the scene expands to reveal the well-furnished and comfortable room. Wu Lien's Wife is serving tea and cakes to Third Cousin and his wife. Third Cousin looks unhappy, but there is a determined glint in his wife's eye.

WU LIEN'S WIFE (*to Third Cousin*). It is good to see you looking so well, honored cousin.

She presses cakes on them. Third Cousin's Wife stuffs her mouth and gobbles greedily. Third Cousin tries to refuse food, but is hungry and cannot resist it. Wu Lien looks on, a little bored, but watchful.

WU LIEN. What greater pleasure is there than a *short* visit from relatives? (*Watching them eat*) Next time eat the fish—and do not bring it to us.

THIRD COUSIN'S WIFE (*studying him*). Wu Lien, you are a kind, good man. (*Wu Lien bows.*) A man does not grow so fat as you unless he has an easy heart and a liver without gall in it.

WU LIEN'S WIFE (*gratified*). That is true. (*Eagerly, a little wistfully*) Cousin, will you speak for my children's father to my parents? They do not give him his due.

THIRD COUSIN'S WIFE. The small of heart are ever unwilling to speak well of those who are large. (*To Wu Lien, cashing in on her promise*) Wu Lien, can you not find my old man a worthless little piece of work here in these walls to pay us something.

Wu Lien gives her a side-long look.

Third Cousin is startled, starts to protest, but chokes on the cake.

> WU LIEN (*watching her closely now*). But will my father-in-law let him come here?
>
> THIRD COUSIN'S WIFE (*waspishly*). My husband by rights should have more power than your father-in-law, because he is older, and it is time he took that power!

Third Cousin looks unhappy, and makes a self-demeaning gesture. Wu Lien looks from him to his wife, his own eyes suddenly intent.

> WU LIEN (*smoothly, to Third Cousin*). Do *you* think the same way, elder cousin?

Third Cousin starts to deny this, but his wife is too quick for him.

> THIRD COUSIN'S WIFE. My husband always thinks as I do.
>
> WU LIEN (*softly*). And how is that?

Third Cousin's Wife takes a long breath, and looks searchingly at Wu Lien. Something in his eyes reassures her and she decides to take the plunge.

> THIRD COUSIN'S WIFE. I think we must save ourselves at all cost . . . . (*significantly*) . . . . and bow before what is upon us and do what we can to make something of it.

There is a moment's silence as this sinks in. Wu Lien shows nothing on his face, but his eyes are bright and alive and calculating. His wife shrinks back into herself a little, as if dreading the turn the conversation has taken. Third Cousin looks sharply at his wife, growing apprehension in his face.

> WU LIEN (*smiling*). Perhaps you would be more content to remain in the village . . . . where you are known . . . . and know everybody. . . . But you are welcome to visit us here and we will give you food . . . . and money . . . . (*His voice is very bland.*) . . . . And then you can give us the news.
>
> THIRD COUSIN (*finding his voice*). We have very little to tell. Nothing happens in our village—
>
> THIRD COUSIN'S WIFE (*sharply, cutting in*). Quiet! Much has happened and more will! (*Then, as the old man subsides uneasily*) Wu Lien, my old man and I will be as one eye and one ear—and all that we see or hear you shall see and hear also.
>
> WU LIEN (*softly*). We always like to hear how you do, and my wife's father and her mother. . . .
>
> THIRD COUSIN'S WIFE (*insinuatingly*). And her brothers also?
>
> WU LIEN (*his eyes lighting, but cautiously*). Of course—they are also our kin. But since they are away there must be little news of them. . . .

Third Cousin's Wife starts to speak, but this time he is quicker than she.

> THIRD COUSIN (*loudly*). True! True! They are all in the free land and not at home!
>
> THIRD COUSIN'S WIFE (*glaring at him*). Then perhaps I saw Jade and her fat child in a dream?

Third Cousin looks panicky and gulps. Wu Lien, his eyes alert, but his face still smooth and smiling, leans forward.

> WU LIEN (*silkily*). Jade has a child then?
>
> THIRD COUSIN (*again trying to circumvent his wife*). Yes. Yes. The news came in a letter from the free land. But we have not seen the child.

THIRD COUSIN'S WIFE (*flatly*). The child is a fine boy. Too fine. Such an unusual child is certain to die young. Death sits on his eyebrows I say whenever I look at him . . . . *which is often.*

THIRD COUSIN (*trying wildly to change the subject*). You live well here, cousin. Your position must be good.

WU LIEN. It is smooth on the top but under it is another thing. (*Slowly, looking at Third Cousin's Wife*) Our conquerors feel a rising anger that may engulf us all.

THIRD COUSIN'S WIFE (*startled*). How then?

WU LIEN. Too many soldiers have gone forth from the city for food and goods and have not returned—not even their bodies have been found. . . . (*She casts a quick glance at her husband, who shakes his head, begging for her silence.*)—It is a great mystery and one that may destroy all of us—*even the innocent.*

Third Cousin's Wife draws in her breath sharply as fear rises in her.

THIRD COUSIN'S WIFE. Now I will speak—and fully! (*Third Cousin puts a pleading hand on her arm but she shakes it off.*) The enemy is sure to find out that the killing started in our village, and then what will our lives be worth? (*Fairly babbling, as Wu Lien, satisfied, sits back*) Wu Lien, *we* had nothing to do with it! It is Ling Tan! Ling Tan and his sons! They are all three returned and they work with the hillmen! I have seen them myself and they are the leaders!

THIRD COUSIN. The woman is blind as a mole and crazy!

THIRD COUSIN'S WIFE (*hysterically*). Not too blind to see the enemy dead piled in the street and then buried, and the hidden room beneath Ling Tan's house where men and guns are. (*Shaking with fury and fear*) Yes! Other young men have died, my son among them! But not the sons of Ling Tan! They still spit and stride about and boast!

Wu Lien sits motionless, smiling and listening. His wife, now plainly frightened at what has been revealed, looks from one to the other. Third Cousin rises slowly, and although he is a little, shrivelled man, he suddenly seems to tower.

THIRD COUSIN (*sternly, to his wife*). Woman, how can you utter such lies against Ling Tan? He has been good to us. He has fed us often. Can you forget this?

THIRD COUSIN'S WIFE (*shrilly*). I can forget it! He *likes* to give us small gifts. It makes him bigger in his own eyes! Shall we thank him for his own pride?

THIRD COUSIN (*quietly*). I am not concerned with *his* pride. I would rather have some of my own. (*And he starts for the door.*)

THIRD COUSIN'S WIFE. And you shall have! I will see to it! When you wear a silk coat over a full round belly you will have pride in yourself then!

Third Cousin, at the door, turns and looks at her.

THIRD COUSIN (*sadly*). What use to speak to you of pride when we use the same word but mean different things by it? (*He goes out.*)

THIRD COUSIN'S WIFE (*after him*). Of all men on earth you are least like a man! (*To Wu Lien*) Do not worry about *that* one. He will follow me or answer *to* me!

Wu Lien, his face still smooth and unruffled, rises. He bows to Third Cousin's Wife, and presses a few pieces of money into her hand.

WU LIEN. We will always be glad to see you, kinswoman. (*His gesture indicates the door.*) Another time—another quiet little talk such as this one has been. . . .

He smiles, not without a little sarcasm. It is plain he intends to hear everything this woman will tell, but he cannot approve her manners.

THIRD COUSIN'S WIFE (*bowing*). Yes. Yes. As soon as we have fresh news. (*She scurries out.*)

Wu Lien looks after her impassively, and starts to prepare his pipe. His wife watches him.

WU LIEN'S WIFE (*softly—anxiously*). My poor father and his household walk on a rope above a pit. . . . (*Then, tentatively, as Wu Lien does not answer*) I have forgotten the things we have heard. Have you, my husband?

WU LIEN (*narrowing his eyes, squinting at the smoke*). I have a mind that lets go of nothing.

She stares at him with rising alarm, torn between concern for her parents and love for him. A soldier jerks open the door and enters, without knocking.

SOLDIER (*bluntly*). Captain Sato calls for you. He says bring work you have finished.

WU LIEN (*jumping up quickly, putting down his pipe*). Yes. Yes. At once.

The soldier goes out, slamming the door with scant courtesy. Wu Lien hurries to where a rolled sheet of paper leans against the wall and picks it up carefully. As he bustles out his wife sits motionless, looking after him with anxious eyes.

The scene dissolves to CAPTAIN SATO's ROOM as Wu Lien, carrying the rolled paper, enters meekly. The room is large and airy and full of fine furniture and bric-a-brac taken from the wealthy houses of the city. There are three pianos and a pile of rich carpets, these latter being packed in boxes by Japanese soldiers in the background. Captain Sato, together with Major Yohagi and Captain Yasuda, two more polite and icily cold little Japanese officers, are seated at an elaborately carved table. (We observe that whereas Wu Lien, in the scene with Third Cousin and Third Cousin's Wife, was suave and the complete master of the situation, now it is reversed, and it is the Japanese who are in command and Wu Lien who feels his way forward with caution.)

CAPTAIN SATO (*indicating the poster*). It is finished?

WU LIEN. Yes, great one.

CAPTAIN SATO. Then let us hear what you have written at my order.

Wu Lien unrolls the poster, and we see it close: It shows a smiling Japanese soldier holding out food to kneeling and grateful Chinese. Beneath the picture is a legend in Chinese.

CAPTAIN YASUDA'S VOICE. The picture is good.

We see the GROUP again.

CAPTAIN SATO (*critically*). It is not too bad. But perhaps it needs more of a smile on the face of the soldier. (*To Wu Lien*) Do you hear?

WU LIEN. I hear, sir, and I will broaden the smile at once.

CAPTAIN SATO. Read then.

Wu Lien's eyelids flicker just a fraction, and he swallows.

CAPTAIN SATO. Your throat is dry?

WU LIEN (*hastily*). No, great one. (*He reads, pointing to the legend.*) "The Chinese people welcome their good neighbor, who gives them food, peace and safety!"

MAJOR YOHAGI (*approvingly*). Banzai!

Captain Sato bows to acknowledge the approval of his superior, then turns to Wu Lien.

CAPTAIN SATO. Why do you not also say Banzai to those noble words?

WU LIEN. Sir?

MAJOR YOHAGI. Does he know what Banzai means?

WU LIEN (*to Yohagi, politely*). Yes, great one. Banzai means "long live."

CAPTAIN SATO. Then say it.

WU LIEN (*a little flatly*). Banzai....

They look at him sharply, and he smiles ingratiatingly.

CAPTAIN SATO (*very softly*). I am not sure I like the *way* you say it.

WU LIEN (*quickly—meekly*). Could my pronunciation ever be as fine as yours, great one?

Captain Sato gives him another look, then shrugs, and lets it pass.

CAPTAIN YASUDA (*to Sato*). It is a clever work, and I believe it will help to put an end to these killings.

Wu Lien straightens suddenly, frozen with fear at the turn the conversation has taken.

WU LIEN (*hastily*). I will put the poster in all the usual places. (*He bows, and turns to go, anxious to be gone before there is more talk of the killings.*)

CAPTAIN SATO (*suddenly, sharply*). Chinaman!

Wu Lien stops as though a dagger had been driven through his heart. He turns reluctantly.

CAPTAIN SATO. Come here. (*Wu Lien moves back to him. In spite of his control a glint of fear is beginning to show in his eyes and a slight beading of sweat appears on his forehead.*) Did I not instruct you to obtain information for me about the disappearance of our soldiers?

WU LIEN (*taking a deep breath*). Sir.... (*hesitating, then going on*) .... I have found nothing .... (*quickly, as Sato frowns*) .... as yet.

CAPTAIN SATO (*leaning forward*). These things must be stopped.

Wu Lien looks helplessly from one to the other. It is as though they hold him personally responsible for every act committed by his countrymen.

WU LIEN (*murmuring*). Yes. Yes. They must be stopped.

MAJOR YOHAGI. How?

WU LIEN (*trapped*). I.... (*Then, blurting it out*) When these men are convinced you are here for their good, they will welcome you, great ones, and all evil will stop.

MAJOR YOHAGI (*looking straight at Wu Lien*). Do you think one village is the center of this rebellion? And if it is—how can we find it?

WU LIEN. There is always a queen flea on a dog's back—the question is how to tell one flea from another.

CAPTAIN SATO (*musing*). Perhaps we

should burn *all* the villages and shoot *all* the farmers. (*Sharply, to Wu Lien*) Would that stop this resistance?

WU LIEN (*stammering*). Perhaps, sirs. . . . But . . . . then who would plant and harvest the crop next year if you did that? And if there was no crop how could your army here be fed? And how would you yourselves eat?

CAPTAIN SATO (*drily*). We thought of that, Chinaman. We only wondered if you had also. And so now we are all agreed.

WU LIEN. Yes, great one.

MAJOR YOHAGI (*smiling thinly*). We are agreed that we must find the center and destroy it.

CAPTAIN SATO (*to Wu Lien*). And it will be your privilege to help us.

WU LIEN (*unhappily*). I will have information soon . . . . if it is possible . . . . very soon. . . .

Captain Sato jerks his head in dismissal, and Wu Lien, sweating visibly now, hurries thankfully toward the door, the scene moving with him as he reaches it and goes out. Two soldiers are working near the door, nailing up a box that is addressed to someone (name not legible) in Tokyo.

We get a close view of the JAPANESE OFFICERS at the table.

CAPTAIN SATO (*contemptuously, looking after Wu Lien*). How could we conquer a country without its traitors?

This cuts to WU LIEN'S QUARTERS as he enters, and stands leaning for a moment against the door.

WU LIEN (*sitting down weakly*). They order me to broaden the smile on the face of the soldier. (*He unrolls the poster, and looks at it.*) Do they not know a broader smile will only make him resemble a shark the more?

WU LIEN'S WIFE (*anxiously*). You did not speak of your new knowledge?

WU LIEN. I did not.

WU LIEN'S WIFE (*as if afraid to ask*). Will you ever speak of it?

WU LIEN. As long as I am able, I will not.

WU LIEN'S WIFE. But when you are no longer able—what then?

WU LIEN. How can I tell that, woman? How does a man know today what he must do tomorrow?

WU LIEN'S WIFE (*despairingly*). You are afraid. You are in danger here.

WU LIEN (*spreading his hands*). Where am I *not* in danger? In these times one chooses to live in the den of the tiger or the lion. There is no other place. (*Helplessly, as she looks at him*) I am a man in the middle! And can a man in the middle stay there without splitting himself? And if he does that he is only half a man—and can half a man still live?

This dissolves to LING TAN'S COMPOUND as Third Cousin, nervous and excited, walks rapidly across a field, then to the interior of the compound as Ling's Wife is cutting Ling's hair. Jade is plaiting straw sandals; the baby plays at her feet.

LING TAN (*good-naturedly, to his wife*). Do not cut my ear. I have use for it.

JADE (*looking up*). Here is our cousin.

The view expands at this point to include Third Cousin as he enters, obviously horribly disturbed.

LING TAN (*smiling*). How are you, cousin?

THIRD COUSIN (*wringing his hands*). I should have killed her even as she spoke. (*He strides up and down, torn by agitation.*)

LING TAN (*mildly*). Who would you kill then?

THIRD COUSIN. The female I call my wife!

LING'S WIFE (*amused*). Has that woman been snapping at your heels again?

THIRD COUSIN (*striding again*). Of course, had I killed her, I would myself have been killed. But at least our village would now be safe and all our kinsmen!

JADE (*alarmed*). What is this you say, cousin?

THIRD COUSIN (*more quietly now*). This is not easy for me to say, but I must. My wife is a traitor. She has told Wu Lien all that she knows of what happens here. Of the secret room, and your sons, and the resistance!

The effect of this on the others is immediate and electric. Ling Tan's face goes taut; his wife draws in her breath sharply; Jade moves quickly toward him.

JADE. Wu Lien—the running dog!

LING TAN. What shall be done!

JADE. He must be silenced!

LING TAN. But he may not speak!

JADE. There is another who has already spoken and may do so again! The wife of our cousin here!

They all look at Third Cousin. He seems to change before their very eyes from an uneasy old man into a personage of character and decision.

THIRD COUSIN (*with quiet conviction now*). I can say only this: she will speak no more.

LING'S WIFE. You have killed her?

THIRD COUSIN (*almost smiling*). No-o. I did not kill her, although there was a moment when I thought she no longer breathed. I beat her. I beat her until she leaned against the wall to keep from falling. (*Then, with dignity*) And I promise you: her mouth will remain closed—by a swelling if need be.

JADE. What then of Wu Lien?

LING TAN (*torn*). We must remember this: he is of our family.

LING'S WIFE. Our sons return from the hills tonight. They will know how to deal with him.

JADE (*very slowly*). There is but one way, and I know my husband will see it as I see it and be willing to do what is to be done!

LING TAN (*appalled, catching her meaning*). Would you have him kill his brother-in-law?

JADE. Rather than have his brother-in-law kill him!

LING TAN (*a little helplessly*). Can anything ever be the same again—even though peace comes? I cannot decide this alone. It concerns us all in the village. (*He starts for the gate.*)

THIRD COUSIN (*following, almost gaily*). Some small good has come of this. Out of it I am born a man again.

We get a close view of JADE and LING's WIFE.

JADE (*slowly*). I must go to the city.

LING's WIFE. I read what you would do in your eyes.

JADE (*turning to her*). Then you are with me in this, mother?

LING's WIFE (*firmly*). I am with you, daughter. Women ever must act while men waste time in talk.

They exchange a warm, close look, as the scene dissolves to a SMALL SHOP in the city: First we see a man's withered old hands measuring out a white powder. Jade's hands are also visible.

OLD MAN's VOICE (*quaveringly*). The great power of this is that a grain kills in a second and is as tasteless as flour. Many women buy this poison in these times. Some for themselves, and some for . . . . others. How much will you need?

JADE's VOICE (*slowly—calmly*). I may not need any at all and I hope I do not . . . . (*spreading money on the counter*) . . . . but I will take as much as I have money to buy.

This dissolves to WU LIEN's QUARTERS as Jade comes down the hall, and goes to Wu Lien's door; this wipes off to the DOOR leading to WU LIEN's QUARTERS as Jade is being greeted by Wu Lien's Wife.

WU LIEN's WIFE (*agog*). Jade! It cannot be!

JADE (*cool—composed*). How are you, sister? (*She enters.*) This house is well guarded, but when I told them I was your relative the gate opened like magic.

WU LIEN's WIFE (*unable to get over Jade's boldness*). Yes. They guard themselves, but not against my husband. (*She leads the way into the room.*)

JADE (*easily*). Why do you stare so at me? Are you not glad to see me?

WU LIEN's WIFE (*now in the room; hastily*). Yes, yes, I am glad. You look well, if not fat.

JADE (*watching her*). I have not rested yet. We returned from the free land only yesterday.

WU LIEN's WIFE (*involuntarily*). Only yesterday! But we—(*She breaks off as Wu Lien, partially dressed, appears in the alcove to the dressing room.*)

WU LIEN. Where is my silk coat, I— (*He stops in his tracks as he sees Jade.*)

WU LIEN's WIFE. Here is Jade to see us! And she tells me she returned but yesterday!

JADE (*smiling*). Together with my husband and son, and today they still sleep.

Wu Lien has regained his composure by now and gives his wife a warning look.

WU LIEN (*blandly*). Welcome, sister-in-law. We are glad you are home again. The old ones have been too long alone. (*To his wife*) And now, where is my coat?

Wu Lien's Wife picks up his coat from a chair, and hands it to him.

WU LIEN's WIFE. Here it is, ready for you to wear. (*To Jade, proudly*) My husband will be honored tonight at a banquet for the conquerors.

WU LIEN (*smiling*). And now I must dress for it.

He goes back into the alcove. (*During the ensuing scene, as Wu Lien finishes* dressing, he is at times visible to the women, and at times not.)

JADE (*ironically*). Will not our women's prattle disturb him?

WU LIEN (*smiling*). No. I will not hear it.

Jade seats herself, as does Wu Lien's Wife. During the following scene Jade's words are ostensibly addressed to the other woman, but they are really for Wu Lien's benefit, in a last hope of reaching and changing him.

JADE. As I came through the city I found many changes.

WU LIEN'S WIFE. My husband says the conqueror prides himself on the public improvements he has made.

JADE. Improvements? Today I saw enemy soldiers pasting up a picture which showed another enemy soldier smiling and giving food to our people, who knelt before him.

WU LIEN'S WIFE (*importantly*). That is my husband's handiwork. Is it not good to look upon?

JADE. Very. Beneath the picture and looking up at it stood hungry people. And they brought bowls and crept close and scooped up some of the paste that the soldiers were using and then they ran and hid and ate it.

WU LIEN'S WIFE (*horrified*). Ate the paste! But that is only flour and water!

JADE (*shrugging*). Even that is better than nothing.

Wu Lien's Wife looks at him nervously, hoping for guidance, but he pretends to be busy with his dressing, although he is very conscious of what is going on.

WU LIEN'S WIFE (*lamely*). But the conqueror *does* give food. He gives it to us and there must be others.

JADE. Yes, there are others. The enemy sometimes gives sweets—and often to children.

WU LIEN'S WIFE (*thinking she has scored*). Well then! You must admit that giving sweets to children is not evil.

JADE. Is it not? In the sweets is opium. So when the children once eat it they have the hunger that is fire in their veins, and so they are spoiled forever. (*In spite of her intention to speak of these things calmly, her voice breaks a little. She draws Wu Lien's son close to her.*) Your own children look well. . . . (*As the child looks up at her, smiles, and speaks a word of Japanese*) Ah! He has learned the tongue of the enemy very quickly! Who knows what he will grow up to say in it!

Wu Lien's Wife turns to her husband appealingly, wanting him to stop Jade, but he is arranging his coat, his face impassive.

WU LIEN'S WIFE (*blundering on*). We will remember our own things to tell him.

JADE (*smiling coldly*). Then do not forget to tell him of other children, and of the mothers and fathers of those children—all tied together and soaked with oil and burned alive while they cried for mercy.

WU LIEN'S WIFE (*who can stand no more*). I would hear no more of this! All the killing—

Wu Lien is in the doorway to the alcove; Jade looks full at him.

JADE. Tell your wife not to shudder, brother-in-law. People now take these as things that might happen to anyone and any day.

Wu Lien's Wife, bewildered and unhappy, rises. She wants to escape.

WU LIEN'S WIFE. I—I will get tea. (*She goes out.*)

Wu Lien goes over to Jade; he is now fully dressed.

JADE. I trust I did not disturb you.

WU LIEN. I heard very little.

JADE. Can it be you have trained your ears not to hear what you do not wish to hear?

WU LIEN (*shrugging, evading*). You must forgive my wife. She is but a woman—and not as we are. . . .

JADE. I do not think *we* are the same. (*Very directly now*) I think you are against me and all who are with me.

WU LIEN (*carefully*). I am against no one.

JADE. Are you for us, then?

Wu Lien moves silently and swiftly to the outer door, like a big, sleek cat. He opens the door quickly. Satisfied that no one is listening, he closes the door and sits near Jade. Jade watches him. Can this mean Wu Lien is against the enemy?

WU LIEN (*softly*). I am neither for nor against anyone or anything.

JADE (*disgusted—her brief hope gone*). What you are not for you are against.

WU LIEN. You have changed while you were away in the free land. (*He looks at her critically.*) I am not sure the change becomes you. (*With bite*) No, it does not. A woman should be soft—like the skin of a peach—and not hard like the stone which does no one any good.

JADE. Do you not forget that the tree itself grows from the stone? Certainly that is the beginning of everything.

Wu Lien shrugs, and makes a final adjustment of his collar at a mirror. Jade watches him. The door opens and Wu Lien's Wife enters, carrying tea and cakes. She is relieved to find they are silent.

WU LIEN'S WIFE (*wistfully, placing the tea things*). If I could see my parents sometimes, I would be content.

JADE (*sweetly now, as if somewhat subdued*). Your husband is content, and so you must be.

Wu Lien studies her, caught by this change on her part. Can it be possible she is wavering?

WU LIEN. I am what I am and so is my wife . . . . (*patting his wife's hand*) . . . . and *she* is one who has always known her place as a woman —and kept to it.

WU LIEN'S WIFE (*impulsively*). Will you tell my parents this for me— (*catching Wu Lien's eye, stopping, then going on*)—tell them that I think of them often, and—

WU LIEN (*interrupting, sharply*). She will tell them. And now, if you should feed your children, we will excuse you.

Wu Lien's Wife takes the hint. She rises, and bows to Jade, who bows in return. Then we get a close view of JADE as she smiles enigmatically and bends over the tea things. Her hand reaches into the pocket where the poison is.

JADE. Will you not share some tea with me, although I am only a woman? Come—I will pour it for you. (*She pours the tea.*)

The view then expands to include Wu Lien, who is staring at her. Does this mean that what he has said has swayed her?

WU LIEN (*smiling, regretfully*). No, although I thank you. I cannot eat when I have something on my mind to do. My stomach growls and takes offense.

JADE. But you are a man who should nourish yourself at every opportunity.

WU LIEN. Do not worry about me. I will eat myself full tonight. There is duck and I am very fond of duck.

Jade sits back, frustrated. At this moment there is a knock at the door.

WU LIEN. Enter.

The door opens and a Japanese Cook (the Kitchen Overseer) enters. He is a handsome and arrogant man.

WU LIEN. Well then, cook. I trust you are well.

KITCHEN OVERSEER (*bluntly*). You sent for me. I am here. (*His eyes slide past Wu Lien and rest on Jade. It is obvious he likes what he sees.*)

Jade is aware of the Kitchen Overseer's appraising eyes, and her own light up, as if with a daring and sudden thought. Then she quickly masks this emotion beneath a demure, side-long look at the Kitchen Overseer.

WU LIEN (*nervously—in a conciliatory tone*). Yes. Yes. I sent for you. But only to ask if the food will be prepared in the Chinese fashion, as I have ordered it. (*The Kitchen Overseer does not reply, and keeps his eyes fastened on Jade. Wu Lien ticks the menu off, with evident relish.*) The steamed duck, the pullets with Chinese herbs, the pigeon eggs in soup, the sharks' fins with crab meat—

KITCHEN OVERSEER (*rudely, still looking at Jade*). All will be ready. You have too many words.

WU LIEN (*with what dignity he can retain*). And, of course, the lobster fried with noodles. Be sure everything is ready at the hour I have set.

KITCHEN OVERSEER. Attend to your business.... (*He looks at Jade significantly.*) .... And I will attend to mine.

Another look at Jade and he turns on his heel, and goes out. Wu Lien coughs.

WU LIEN (*embarrassed*). You see we have plenty of food here—more than enough. Will you not take some of it home with you?

JADE (*curtly, anxious now to be gone*). No. (*She rises.*)

WU LIEN. But why? There is so much. It will only be thrown to the dogs. Why do you not take it?

JADE (*coldly*). Because, brother-in-law, we are not dogs.

Their eyes hold for a moment, and they both know it is war between them. Then Jade turns, and goes quickly out.

The scene wipes to the outside of the BANQUET ROOM in the courtyard as Jade enters from the door to Wu Lien's quarters. The Kitchen Overseer is just disappearing in the direction of the kitchen. Jade walks swiftly after him. —A close view of the KITCHEN OVERSEER shows him rounding the corner. He looks back, and sees Jade is following him. He reacts with pleasure. His ego is flattered.—This wipes to the LOWER HALLWAY, near the kitchen and the servants' quarters, where Jade is hurrying along after the Kitchen Overseer, who goes down the steps to the kitchen door.—JADE looks after him. Then we see, as viewed by her, the

Kitchen Overseer striding past the two Japanese guards posted at the kitchen door. As he enters, the door swings open and we get a glimpse of a huge bustle of preparation.—A close view of JADE shows her hesitating but only for a second. Then she gathers courage, touches the poison in her pocket to make sure it is there, and goes boldly down the steps.

This cuts to the DOOR of the KITCHEN as Jade enters. The Sentry bars her way.

SENTRY. You cannot enter! Strangers are not allowed in the kitchen!

She tries to brush past him and he grasps her arm brutally. She stumbles against the door and it swings open. The Kitchen Overseer appears, and stands, one arm on the door frame, blocking the entrance.

KITCHEN OVERSEER. What is this?

JADE (*boldly*). Did you not send for someone? A new cook, perhaps.

KITCHEN OVERSEER (*lifting an eyebrow*). I would not think that *cooking* is one of your talents.

JADE (*coolly*). How can you know that, until you have tried me?

She deliberately and insolently lifts his arm from the door frame and walks past him, into the kitchen. He stares at her, and for a moment, it appears he might strike her, or drag her back into the hallway, but, obviously intrigued by her impudence, he does not.

SENTRY (*starting after Jade*). I will throw her into the street.

The Kitchen Overseer restrains him. His eyes are thoughtful.

KITCHEN OVERSEER. I will do that myself .... but a little later, perhaps.

He follows Jade inside. The Sentry stares after him, then slowly an evil grin of understanding dawns on his face.

We get a full view of the KITCHEN where the Japanese cooks are working rapidly and skillfully. One is making soup, another shredding cocoanut, another arranging a great dish of tropical fruits, another preparing crabs and noodles, and still another baking pastries. Slowly, as they become aware that Jade has entered, they drop their tasks and look at her. In the eyes of some are lust, but others give her cold, hard looks of hate.

Jade stands waiting, as the Kitchen Overseer enters and slams the door behind him.

KITCHEN OVERSEER (*to the cooks*). Get on with your work!

A couple of the cooks give him black looks, but go on with their tasks.

We see the PASTRY COOK and his HELPER.

PASTRY COOK (*grumbling*). If there is so much to do, why does he bring a woman here?

We see the KITCHEN OVERSEER and JADE. (During this scene the Kitchen Overseer goes from stove to table, tasting dishes and supervising everything.)

KITCHEN OVERSEER (*abruptly*). How did you get into this house?

JADE. Is it not plain Wu Lien sent for me?

KITCHEN OVERSEER. Why? (*Then, as she shrugs*) You need not answer me. I have seen his wife. (*Then, narrowing his eyes at her*) Now—tell me why you came to the kitchen.

JADE. I am hungry. There is food here.

KITCHEN OVERSEER. Why did you not get food from Wu Lien?

JADE. I look to the future. Wu Lien will not last. He could not feed me for long.

We see the BANQUET ROOM: There are a number of small round tables seating thirty-five or forty people (including Wu Lien, Captain Sato, Captain Yasuda and Major Yohagi) who sit on stools, not chairs. They are now engrossed in eating their soup. The waiters are Japanese orderlies; Chinese are used to carry away soiled dishes, but not to handle the food.

YOHAGI. A toast to His Imperial Majesty—the Emperor!

OTHERS (*rising*). Banzai!

WU LIEN (*a little late*). Banzai! (*They all drink the toast.*)

A close view of JADE seated on a stool shows her looking around the kitchen, trying to formulate a plan. Then we see from her angle the Kitchen Overseer rushing back and forth—overseeing, tasting, testing. He goes to the noodle rack.

KITCHEN OVERSEER. The noodles!

The helper swings down the noodle rack, and hurries with it to another table.

KITCHEN OVERSEER (*pausing at the seafood table*). The sharks' fins! Are they tender? (*He tastes, nods, then turns and goes toward another table.*) Are the ducks ready?

JADE, at the mention of "ducks" turns, and rises a little from her stool to see.

At the TABLE, a helper is carving and arranging the ducks on individual platters. He starts to carve the last fowl as the Kitchen Overseer enters.

KITCHEN OVERSEER. Are you not finished yet? It is almost time to serve them! (*He turns, and bellows.*) Bring the gravy so I may season it!

A close view shows JADE sitting motionless, her eyes glued on the ducks. Then we see the TABLE covered with ducks as a helper hurries in with a large kettle of gravy. The Kitchen Overseer tastes it, grimaces, and starts to season it.

KITCHEN OVERSEER (*angrily, looking off*). Where are the mushrooms? Get them! (*As the helper looks confused, he reacts in disgust.*) Must I do everything myself?

He hurries out of sight to get mushrooms for the gravy. The helper trails along.

JADE rises quietly from her stool, and creeps over to the table where the ducks and gravy have been placed. She looks around swiftly.

We see the KITCHEN, from her angle. For the moment she is unnoticed; everyone is gathered around the Kitchen Overseer who is angrily finishing the chopping of the mushrooms.

KITCHEN OVERSEER. These are not fine enough!

JADE leans over the gravy kettle, and her hand comes quickly out of her pocket, holding the packet of poison. She sprinkles it into the gravy, then darts back to her place on the stool.

There is a fuller view of the KITCHEN as the Kitchen Overseer, carrying the dish of chopped mushrooms, comes back to the duck table. He dumps the mushrooms into the gravy, stirs it vigorously, then spoons some of it onto each platter of duck. Jade watches, fascinated. The Kitchen Overseer looks up, and sees her.

KITCHEN OVERSEER (*chidingly*). Ah, so you have eyes only for food and not for me! (*Then, as if in generos-*

ity) Well then, if you are so greedy, take some of the duck. (*As she looks at him, startled*) Go on. Take it. Eat it.

Slowly Jade rises and comes toward the table. He watches her, smiling. She reaches out a hand for the duck. If she must she will eat it and die, but she will not tell what she has done. As her fingers are almost on the duck, the Kitchen Overseer slaps her hand away and laughs sadistically.

> KITCHEN OVERSEER. No, little one. It would be my head if I let you have one of those. (*Jade almost faints with relief. He turns, and calls out.*) Take these and serve them while they are hot!

As two helpers enter and start carrying away the platters of duck, he lifts the kettle and pours the rest of the gravy into bowls, which are also carried away.

We see JADE as the ducks are carried past her and out of sight. Then the Kitchen Overseer's hand comes into view and grips her shoulder.

> KITCHEN OVERSEER'S VOICE. I have your own word for it, little one. The hungrier you are, the better it is for me.

This dissolves to the BANQUET ROOM as the soup is being taken away. Sato turns to a small, dry little man, a diplomat.

> SATO. You were saying, your Excellency?
>
> DIPLOMAT. I was suggesting that a Chinese be found to act as puppet ruler. (*Wu Lien pricks up his ears.*) Preferably someone of standing . . . . but more important, someone with great personal charm.
>
> YASUDA. A brilliant suggestion!
>
> YOHAGI. We must find such a one!
>
> SATO. Yes. We must search at once!
>
> DIPLOMAT (*spreading his hands*). But where can we find him? (*At this Wu Lien wriggles with anticipation.*)
>
> SATO (*abruptly, to Wu Lien*). Do you know of anyone who answers that description?
>
> WU LIEN (*as if pondering*). A person of standing . . . . and great personal charm . . . . ? (*Modestly*) Well then, perhaps—
>
> SATO (*cutting in, rudely*). No, of course you do not know of such a one. How could you? Such a one would not know you. (*To the others, leaving Wu Lien hanging in midair*) We will have to search long to find such a Chinaman.
>
> YOHAGI (*looking up*). Ah! Ducks. . . .

We see the DUCKS being placed on the table by a waiter.

> YOHAGI (*continuing*). Ducks . . . . and swimming in their own juices!
>
> WU LIEN. I went to great trouble to get them and have them cooked to your order, sir.
>
> SATO (*to Wu Lien*). The wine for the ducks. Where is it?
>
> WU LIEN. It will be served soon. I have ordered it.
>
> SATO (*sharply*). Order it again!

Wu Lien sighs, and rises. He goes out reluctantly. Sato smiles at the diplomat.

> DIPLOMAT. He sweats a great deal—even for a Chinaman.
>
> SATO. He will sweat even more tonight. We will amuse ourselves with him a little before we make him talk for us.

They all laugh. At this point Yohagi, who is the host, signals to the diplomat who helps himself to the duck, which is the signal for all of them to help themselves.

We see the KITCHEN as Jade, on her stool, looks anxiously toward the outer door. The Kitchen Overseer and his helpers are busy with the next course, which consists of shrimp, and there are preparations for further courses in evidence—vegetables, greens, etc.

   KITCHEN OVERSEER (*working with the shrimps, fuming*). They call these shrimp? I ask for fresh shrimp and what do I get? Thin and wrinkled things like worms!

   JADE, seen close, slips from the stool, and steals toward the door. As she reaches to open it—

   KITCHEN OVERSEER'S VOICE. Here now!

She stops and turns, as he comes to her and grabs her arm.

   KITCHEN OVERSEER (*mockingly*). You would not leave before you have eaten? I could not allow that. It would not be courteous.

   JADE (*trying to brazen it out*). I am weary of waiting. I will go elsewhere.

   KITCHEN OVERSEER (*suddenly menacing*). No. You will not. I, too, am weary of waiting.

Suddenly Jade's eyes widen with horror and she draws in her breath sharply. The Kitchen Overseer turns, and looks. This cuts to the BALCONY and we see Wu Lien, at the top of the stairs leading into the kitchen, staring down at Jade in amazement.—JADE, taking advantage of the fact that the Kitchen Overseer is turned from her, slips under his arm and out the door.—Wu Lien takes a couple of steps down the stairs to the KITCHEN.

   WU LIEN. That woman! Stop her!

We see the KITCHEN DOOR as Jade runs past the startled guard and disappears toward the street. The Kitchen Overseer appears at the door.

   GUARD (*highly amused at the Kitchen Overseer*). So *you* will throw her into the street? (*Furious, the Kitchen Overseer turns back into the kitchen.*)

This cuts to the KITCHEN.

   KITCHEN OVERSEER (*angrily, to Wu Lien*). You have frightened her away!

   WU LIEN (*hoarsely, with growing suspicion*). How long has she been in this kitchen?

   KITCHEN OVERSEER (*nastily, misinterpreting Wu Lien's emotion*). What is the difference? A woman like that is too good for you. And now neither of us will have her!

   WU LIEN (*lumbering downstairs*). Stop her! Stop—

Suddenly, Wu Lien stops in his tracks. It is obvious he is torn as to what to do, but only for a moment. He turns, and runs back up the stairs and along the balcony toward the banquet room.

   WU LIEN. Go after her! Find her!

He runs out. The Kitchen Overseer glares around at his helpers, who are pleased he has been left in the lurch.

   KITCHEN OVERSEER. I do not run after women! Get back to your work! (*They do so.*)

This cuts to the PASSAGEWAY as Wu Lien labors toward the banquet hall. A Japanese soldier runs past him.

   SOLDIER (*jabbering in terror*). We will all be burned alive for this!

Wu Lien, too panicky to question him,

runs on toward the banquet hall. Another Japanese runs out and past him.

JAPANESE. They have been poisoned! If they die, we all die! (*He runs on wildly.*)

Wu Lien goes toward the door, and as if automatically, the other Chinese helpers run past him and out.—A close view of WU LIEN as he reaches the doorway, shows him stopping, frozen in horror, and this cuts to a full view of the DINING HALL, as seen by Wu Lien: Of the diners, perhaps half of them have been stricken by the poison. Some are sprawled across the tables, others are huddled on the floor in their death agony. The men who have not eaten of the duck, together with the orderlies, are making futile, panicky efforts to aid the others.

A close view of WU LIEN follows: For a moment he is rooted to the spot in sheer terror. His eyes sweep around the hall. Then we get a moving view from his angle. It moves past the Diplomat, and it is seen that he is breathing in great gasps, with long intervals between breaths. A frightened orderly bends over him.

ORDERLY. Sir! Sir!

DIPLOMAT. A doctor . . . a do . . .

He collapses. The view moves on. As it passes the table where Yohagi was sitting, it reveals his face contorted with pain.

YOHAGI. Help me—! Help me—!

Another officer is trying to give him a drink of wine. Yohagi goes into a violent convulsion, and knocks the wine glass from the other man's hand. . . . The view moves on to Yasuda, who leans forward, his head sideways on the table at a horrible angle. He is motionless, already dead. The view moves on, and picks up the figure of Sato, who is dragging himself painfully along the floor, making for the door which leads to Wu Lien's rooms. He collapses against a pillar near the door, sweat beading his forehead.

We see WU LIEN again as two soldiers come up behind him. He shrinks back against the wall.

FIRST SOLDIER. A poisoner has been at work!

SECOND SOLDIER. Bring the guards! (*They rush out.*)

Now Wu Lien's thought is of escape for himself, and he realizes he cannot go back the way he has come. He looks around frantically, from door to door.—The view cuts to the DOORWAY leading to his quarters, as seen by him: this door is unguarded, and beyond it there seems to be no activity. It is the only avenue of escape. The scene then follows WU LIEN as he starts to move across the dining hall to the door. He moves slowly, afraid to accelerate his pace, expecting each step to be his last. As he moves we see more of the poisoned men, some in convulsions, some already unconscious. A man staggers forward, clutching his belly; in the background is visible an orderly helping another officer toward the window.

OFFICER (*gasping*). I cannot breathe!

As Wu Lien reaches the pillar where Sato has collapsed, the view rests on Sato. He opens his eyes. They are stary, with dilated pupils.—WU LIEN is next seen almost at the door, relief in his eyes. Now he has a chance to reach the door, and an opportunity to run to safety. Then a close view of SATO shows him fumbling, with a horrible effort, for his pistol.

SATO (*in a choked, whistling whisper*). Chinaman!

WU LIEN, seen close at the door, turns, involuntarily.—SATO, with his last strength, fires at Wu Lien.—We see WU LIEN: An expression of almost childlike distress crosses his face. He turns and goes out the door.

There is a full view of the DINING HALL as the door on the opposite side of the room from the one leading to Wu Lien's quarters bursts open and several soldiers run in. Sato tries to speak, but he cannot. He slumps down, the gun rattles to the floor. He is dead.

Outside the DINING HALL—near the door Wu Lien is seen leaning against the wall. Behind him in the banquet room is the sound of voices speaking excited Japanese. Wu Lien's eyes are glazed with pain and terror. He clutches his belly and slowly, agonizingly starts to make his way down the hall.

The scene wipes to WU LIEN'S QUARTERS: Wu Lien's wife startled by the growing noise outside, which has now increased to a bedlam as more and more Japanese are apprised of the incident, cowers in a corner with her children. Slowly the inner door opens and she presses a hand over her mouth in terror. As the door swings wide and she sees it is Wu Lien, her first reaction is one of relief, but it is replaced immediately by panic as he walks toward her, holding his belly in his two hands. She hurries to him, and helps him to a chair. His face is greasy with sweat and contorted with almost unendurable pain.

WU LIEN'S WIFE. Ai! Ai! What is it?

WU LIEN (*slowly—with tremendous effort*). The enemy .... was poisoned .... they blamed me. ...

(*He stops, unable to go on, then forces himself to speak.*) Take the children .... go to your father. ... (*He stops, and closes his eyes.*) I am dying .... go .... go now .... quickly. ...

WU LIEN'S WIFE (*wailing*). No. I cannot. (*Hysterically, as he takes his hands from his belly, she stares at the blood stains.*) Who did this thing?

Wu Lien opens his eyes. His mouth works feebly, whether to tell or to deny that he knows we cannot be sure. He topples over—dead—and slips to the floor. His wife bends over him, sobbing.

The scene dissolves to the SLEEPING ROOM of JADE and LAO ER at night. Jade is washing herself after her trip to town. The door is open and voices can be heard from the Big Room outside. Jade's face is strained and unsure.

LAO SAN'S VOICE. I say kill Wu Lien.

Inside the BIG ROOM we now see Ling Tan surrounded by his three sons, Lao San, Lao Ta and Lao Er. His wife works in the background, giving them food.

LAO SAN. Yes, kill him and let me do it! Heaven will lead me to the right place and time and Heaven will put power in my hand!

LING TAN (*turning on him*). Do not say Heaven this and Heaven that! If we must kill then let us not say it is Heaven who bids it! It is not Heaven's will that men kill each other!

LAO SAN (*contemptuously*). We who are young know better. You lie dead with your ancestors instead of living!

LING TAN (*sadly to his wife*). How could you have borne such a son?

LING'S WIFE. How could *you* have fathered him?

LAO ER (*slowly*). Wu Lien is of our family .... it is our one hope he cannot bring himself to destroy us .... we must be sure....

In JADE'S ROOM, JADE is listening. Can it be that her husband would have disapproved of what she tried to do? The scene cuts back to the BIG ROOM as the men fall to eating again. Suddenly, there comes a knocking at the outside gate of the little rear courtyard. The three sons of Ling rise and slip noiselessly behind the stove, ready to enter the secret room if there is danger.

VOICE OF WU LIEN'S WIFE. My mother! My father! It is your daughter!

They look at each other, then Ling's Wife goes silently toward the door. The scene wipes to a moving view of LING'S WIFE going to the courtyard to the gate, and opening it a crack. Wu Lien's Wife, her face streaked with tears, carrying and leading her children, is revealed.

LING'S WIFE (*cautiously*). Your husband is not with you?

WU LIEN'S WIFE. My husband is dead....

Ling's Wife, startled, makes the sign for silence and leads her toward the house, as the scene dissolves to the BIG ROOM, and now Wu Lien's Wife is seated in the midst of the family and is telling her story. Jade has come to stand in the doorway and listen.

WU LIEN'S WIFE. .... and so poison was put in the food of the high enemy officials by someone, and they blamed my husband for it and killed him.... (*She bursts into fresh tears.*)

LING'S WIFE (*with a quick significant look at Jade*). The enemy killed him?

WU LIEN'S WIFE (*brokenly*). They shot him and he came to me holding the last of his life inside him with his hands. . . . He lived only for his family, and now he is dead. He was so good, so—

LAO SAN (*disgusted*). I have been cheated of my pleasure!

His mother gives him a disapproving look, and puts her arms comfortingly around her daughter.

WU LIEN'S WIFE. It was at the feast I told you about when you were there today, Jade.

Everyone looks quickly at Jade, struck by this, and realizing what it means. But Wu Lien's Wife does not notice, she is sobbing again. No one speaks. Instead, they deliberately turn away from Jade.

WU LIEN'S WIFE. My poor husband with his last breath told me to come here .... there was great confusion or I would not have escaped. . . . (*Wailing*) Aiiiii. My husband is gone and I am a widow .... my poor self and my poor sons....

A close view of JADE at the door, shows her stunned by what she has heard, and Ling's Wife comes over to her.

LING'S WIFE (*very softly*). Then you did not fail, as you thought. (*Jade, unable to speak, shakes her head, then averts her face. Ling's Wife touches her arm reassuringly.*) And since it happened thus, we will not tell your sister-in-law.

Jade nods again, then turns, and hurries to the outer door and out.

This dissolves to JADE outside the COMPOUND at night: She sits by the pond, trailing her hand in the water, staring down unseeingly. Lao Er comes to her, but she does not look up.

LAO ER (*finally*). Poison is a woman's weapon.

JADE (*slowly*). It is and it was I who used it.

LAO ER. I thought so. I saw the look that passed between you and my mother.

JADE (*bursting out*). You said we must be sure. I *was* sure! He would have betrayed us! I would not have killed him had I thought he would not!

LAO ER (*shrugging*). You did not kill him. The enemy did.

JADE. No. I killed him as surely as I am now here. And he was one of ours. (*Her voice breaks a little.*)

LAO ER (*sitting beside her*). It was right that he should die. (*His voice is cold and analytical.*)

Jade stares again at the water, her eyes wide and troubled.

JADE (*in a whisper*). Do you hate me?

LAO ER (*reaching out—touching her face*). Why would I hate you?

JADE. I am so thin, my flesh is so hard. My face is dark and not like a woman's face.

LAO ER (*teasingly*). You do not look as you did when I married you, it is true.

JADE. Would you have married me then if I looked as I do now?

LAO ER. Doubtless I would not. (*She looks at him swiftly; and he laughs.*) But I myself was not the same man that I am now, and what pleased me then would not please me now.

JADE. And . . . . do I please you now . . . . ?

LAO ER. You do. (*He draws her closer, and puts his cheek to her hair.*) There is always this feeling between us we can return to from anything.

JADE. But will this feeling always be here? Will I always please you? (*A pause; then, she must say it*) Are you sure that you do not think me less a woman—because of what I did?

LAO ER. Of which thing you did? You are always doing something!

JADE (*slowly*). Will there come a day when you will look at me—perhaps long after peace comes—and say to your heart—"She could put poison into food, and kill one of our own," and then think me less a woman than you like?

LAO ER. You are brave. I wonder that a woman can be so brave . . . . and I love you.

JADE. And what do you love in me, my husband?

LAO ER. It is not a woman . . . . any woman . . . . not woman even . . . . but the creature that only you are. . . .

With a sigh, she closes her eyes, deeply content, and the scene fades out.

PART EIGHT

The FIELDS fade in. It is day. The fields are ready for harvest, and the ripened grain sways gently in the warm wind. Then we get quick glimpses of VILLAGERS as they sharpen and put their harvest tools in order. Perhaps some of them are even beginning to cut the grain. Then we see LING'S FIELD, at the edge of which Ling Tan and his wife are working. Ling Tan looks off, and touches his wife's arm.

LING TAN. It is our children—home from the hills.

Jade and Lao Er are seen coming down the road from the hills. Then they are seen closer as they move along. They are tired and dusty, but they walk swiftly, and with purpose. Suddenly Lao Er stops, drawing her to a halt with him. He looks out over the valley, as does she, and for a moment they are silent.

LAO ER (*finally, in a troubled voice*). Jade, how shall I tell them? It seemed so easy there in the hills when our leaders told us what we must do. But what words can I find to ask my father and his kinsmen to destroy their fields and their houses and all they have? (*Indicating the beauty before them*) When I look at this valley—I feel I cannot ask them. (*He makes a helpless gesture.*)

JADE (*putting a hand over his eyes*). Then do not look at this valley, but beyond it. Close your heart to your pity. See the end and not the moment. And then make our people strong as you are strong.

Lao Er reaches up, takes her hand from his eyes, and holds it.

LAO ER (*a little ruefully*). I am not strong. The greatest strength I have I take from you.

JADE. Then we two are indeed one, for your strength is mine also. (*They go forward together.*)

JADE (*softly, a little sadly*). Our valley . . . . it is so beautiful . . . . it has given us so much and so freely. It is hard to think it now must be destroyed.

LAO ER (*nodding*). With every step I take I have less stomach to ask this thing of our people. To burn their crops and houses, to leave all they have. . . .

JADE. As we understood it from our leaders in the hills, so our kinsmen must understand it from you.

LAO ER. Yes. We must not fail.

They move on for a moment or two and the scene expands as they come to Ling Tan and his wife, standing there in the grain.

LING'S WIFE. Well, then! You are back and in time to help us with the harvest!

LING TAN (*hefting a stalk*). The crop is good this year! The grain lies heavy in the hand. (*At this, Lao Er looks swiftly at Jade.*)

JADE (*quietly*). Yes. This field would feed many people.

LAO ER (*steadied by her quiet*). Father, will you call the heads of the village together? We have a task for them to do.

LING TAN. A meeting? There is danger in a meeting while there is light. Can you not wait until the darkness comes?

LAO ER. You are right. Tell them to gather at the first hour of the darkness. There is a thing we must do, and at once.

LING'S WIFE. What is it? What is all this mystery?

JADE (*taking her arm*). You will know soon enough, mother. (*As they start toward the house; to distract her*) Now tell me, did my son miss me? (*Then, quickly*) No. Do not tell me. I know he did not, for he was with you.

Ling's Wife laughs, her heart lifted, as the scene dissolves to the TEAHOUSE at night: It is filled with the heads of the village. Lao Er stands on the stairway, facing them. Jade sits a step or two above him. Ling Tan is in the foreground of the villagers, as is Third Cousin. Ling's face, like the faces of the other farmers, is full of incredulity and shock.

LAO ER. It is the only way! The enemy will never be defeated if we feed him! But without our food he will starve! (*His words are greeted by many voices.*)

NEIGHBOR SHEN: I will not destroy food, nor my house!

FIRST FARMER: No! It is too much!

SECOND FARMER: It is against the law of man to do this!

THIRD FARMER: To destroy food is evil!

LAO ER. But it is the task the High Command has set for you! You must burn what you have and leave only the ashes behind you!

LING TAN (*slowly, as if stunned*). Can it be that you, my son, ask this of me and our kinsmen?

LAO ER. I ask it that the enemy may be destroyed. Not only do we feed them, but while we stay here we are their work animals! (*Again his words are followed by many voices.*)

FOURTH FARMER: What we hear are the words of a young fool!

THIRD COUSIN: I, for one, will not listen to more!

FIFTH FARMER: I will not burn my house nor will I leave what I have!

LING TAN. We resist here. We keep what food we can from the enemy and kill him when and how we can. It is enough.

Lao Er looks helplessly back at Jade, until she rises slowly, and stands above him on the stair.

JADE (*to Ling Tan*). Do you not love your country?

LING TAN. Love my country? You say that to me? (*With great dignity*) Do I not love this earth, and is this earth not my country? Though I die I stay with it, and can a man love his country better than that?

JADE. But, my father, this earth is only your country in peace time—when there is freedom. (*Appealing to them all*) You are farmers, and the earth is more than earth to a farmer. It is the flower of this earth that he sweats for, and if the flower of your earth is in the belly of the enemy, then the earth no longer belongs to you—but to him!

LING TAN. I know only this: we must hold the land.

NEIGHBOR SHEN: Ling Tan is right, as always!

THIRD FARMER: I will ever follow what he says! It has truth and sense!

FIFTH FARMER: Yes! We will not leave our land—we will hold it!

JADE. Then you will hold only a handful of dead soil, and you will lose your whole country doing it! Your earth will not die if you leave it—it will wait for you to come back and you will have guarded its dignity. Could my husband be forced to give me over to the Japanese to bear their children—as your earth now bears fruit to feed the enemy? Would he not be stronger and love me more if he killed me and let my spirit live?

THIRD COUSIN (*impatiently—as one who knows*). When a man listens to a woman—he is lost indeed! I know this, and the cure for it! (*He raises his fist.*)

JADE (*as a farmer or two rise and start out*). Yes, I am a woman! But until the enemy is defeated and driven from this land *you* are not men—but slaves!

FIRST FARMER: I say again: we have done all we can!

SECOND FARMER: I will do no more! (*Now, in a body, the farmers rise and go out.*)

THIRD FARMER (*as he goes*). I have killed—that is enough.

FIFTH FARMER: I have starved and stolen from myself!

FOURTH FARMER: Can there be truth in what the young ones say?

SIXTH FARMER: No! No! There is neither truth nor good in it!

Now all the farmers are gone, leaving only Ling Tan and Third Cousin. Then they, too, rise slowly and go out. Jade reaches swiftly toward Lao Er, places her hands on his shoulders as if to comfort him, but her own eyes are despairing.

The scene dissolves to the BIG ROOM.—Lao San and Lao Ta are at the table, eating. Ling's Wife is bustling happily around, feeding them, assisted by Wu Lien's Wife. The children play on the floor. Jade's baby sits near the stove, trying his teeth on an empty cartridge. The door opens and Ling Tan enters, followed by Jade and Lao Er.

LAO SAN (*looking from one to the other*). Now what is wrong with all these long faces?

LAO ER (*despondently*). We have failed. Our kinsmen and our father among them have refused the plan.

LAO SAN (*looking at his father, and frowning*). You will not do as you are told to do?

LING TAN (*sharply*). I will not. Nor will the other kinsmen.

LAO SAN (*to Lao Er*). Then I know the answer to this. Hold a gun at their heads and make them do it.

JADE (*quietly*). No. It must be of their own will.

LAO SAN (*contemptuously*). The old should be allowed no will! (*He and Ling Tan glare at each other.*)

LING'S WIFE (*nervously*). Now then. Here is the old and the new again. There must be some meeting.

LAO SAN. There can be no meeting between what is dead and what is alive. (*He rises, and stands before his father.*) Our father and men like him grow too old, and have walked the earth too long! Others need the room they take!

Everyone gasps at this, and Ling Tan reaches out suddenly, and slaps Lao San.

LING TAN. You say that to me!

Lao San, his face livid with anger, lifts his hand as if to return the blow.

LAO SAN (*through his teeth*). You may not strike me.

LING TAN. I should beat you! Killing and love of killing—that is all you know!

LAO SAN. But I know it well! These are other times and I can kill you as well as any other!

Ling Tan's anger slowly goes out of him; his hands fall limply to his side.

LING TAN (*in a stricken whisper*). Yes .... you can kill me. ... I think you can kill anyone now. But I—I will kill no more.

He sits down, as if suddenly weak. Lao San looks challengingly at the others, and swaggers toward the door.

LING'S WIFE. Come back here.

LAO SAN. I will not. I have eaten enough foolishness in this house—and for the last time. (*He moves to the door and goes out.*)

For a moment no one speaks, then Lao Ta rises slowly.

LAO TA. I must go with him. (*He starts for the door, turning to Lao Er.*) You will find us in the hills, for you will follow us. (*Sadly*) Happiness in this family is over. (*And he leaves.*)

We see the ROOM as Ling Tan sits, staring before him. His wife is shocked and burningly angry, but helpless. Lao Er looks swiftly to Jade for guidance, but she is watching the old people, her eyes intent.

LING'S WIFE. Nothing is left to anyone if the old can no longer look to the young for obedience. . . . (*Her voice breaks on a sob.*)

LING TAN (*slowly*). I have come to this: I will not grieve the day they tell me my third son is dead. (*Even his wife recoils at this, but he goes on, steadily.*) He has become the sort of man I fear and hate most. Such men will not allow peace in the world. War springs from them as fire from tinder and is their pleasure and their life. Such men should die for the good of all.

But at this Jade suddenly springs to her feet. She seems suddenly very tall and her eyes flash with anger.

JADE. And you blame your *son* for what he is?

LING TAN. Who shall I blame then? It was his own arm he raised against me—and his own voice.

Ling's Wife moves to a post behind him. She is like a fierce old she-tiger, ready to support him in anything he will do.

JADE (*passionately*). You can not blame him! Has his life been as it should? Has he had peace to live, and find a wife, and have sons of his own? No! He has put the will he would have used for these into another thing—the will to kill!

LING TAN. He is so changed from the boy who retched at the sight of the first dead that he would strike down his own father!

JADE. Are we not *all* changed? And can we get our old selves back if the devils are not driven out soon? (*Challengingly, forcing his eyes to hers*) Can *you*? You hate to kill above all else, and yet you *have* killed! You have done the work of death as skillfully as you once tilled the land!

LING TAN. I would not hear this from a woman.

JADE. But you *shall* hear it! Our

mother here—is she not changed? Now she runs from her cooking to take up her hoe and bury the enemy as though the human flesh were animal! Can she go back to the old way? Can she ever forget what she has done?

Ling Tan turns slowly, and looks at his wife. She cannot meet his eyes, for she knows that Jade speaks the truth.

JADE. And your sons—they all kill! Your third son because he has come to love it—your eldest because it is the easiest thing to do—and your second son because he must! But they all kill and kill again! Can you deny this?

LING TAN. No. I cannot.

JADE (*indicating Wu Lien's Wife*). And your daughter! Can *she* forget what has come to her? And I—I have learned to hold a gun and fire it from a doorway and then go on and feed my son—and what does the child eat into himself with the food?

Ling Tan looks down at the child, playing with the empty cartridge, then quickly away. Jade sees the horror in his eyes, and at once knows his weakness. She sweeps the child up in her arms, and holds him before Ling Tan.

JADE. Look at him! Do not turn away! Even now your grandchild sharpens his little teeth on an empty shell and does not hate the taste of gunpowder! Yet he is young now and his mind at least is untouched! He can be saved and taught a good way to live if the enemy is driven from our country! But what is to become of him if this horror goes on? How can we teach him to be honest when he must lie and deceive to live? How can we teach him kindness when he must either kill first or be killed? How can we teach him mercy when he sees only cruelty? How can we teach him faith in mankind when he sees nothing but distrust and when even in our own family are traitors?

LING TAN (*unable to bear more*). But am I to blame for these things?

JADE. No! You are not! The Japanese who made the war are to blame and that is the greatest reason of all why they must be defeated and driven from the country and made powerless to do evil again!

LING TAN (*rising*). And you, with your words, how will you answer your son when he asks why did you leave our land?

JADE (*passionately*). I will say it was to save him, and his family, and his country!

LING TAN (*passing a hand over his eyes; wearily*). I—I do not know. I cannot. A cloud covers my mind. (*He turns, and moves slowly from the room.*)

Jade's shoulders slump hopelessly, as we get another view of the ROOM.

LING'S WIFE (*anxiously*). What will you do now, my son?

LAO ER (*slowly*). We will join our brothers in the hills where at least we can fight on. We will leave this house during the last hours of darkness before dawn. . . .

This dissolves to the SLEEPING ROOM of JADE and LAO ER at night. They have packed their few belongings and Jade is tying the baby's hood in place.

LAO ER (*looking around, sighing*). We have gone forth from this house before, but this time I know we will never see it nor my parents again.

JADE (*nodding*). I, too, will leave a piece of my heart here.

Together they go toward the door, Lao Er carrying the baby. Then we see the BIG ROOM as Jade and Lao Er enter. Ling's Wife turns from the table, where she is tying food in a bundle. Wu Lien's Wife is also present.

LING'S WIFE. Here is food for the journey.

At this moment the outer door opens and Ling Tan enters. He looks tired and drawn. There is a moment's silence as the eyes of Ling Tan and Jade meet.

JADE (*quietly*). We are glad you have come. It would be a bitter thing if you had not.

LING TAN (*with a faint and weary smile*). If you can wait, we will go with you.

Jade and Lao Er react in astonishment and joy. Ling's Wife stares, as does Wu Lien's Wife, her mouth agape.

JADE (*in a whisper*). Go with us....

LING TAN (*quietly*). Yes. I will burn my fields and my house and go with you.

Jade takes a quick step toward him, her eyes alight.

LING'S WIFE. Do my ears hear what you are saying, old man?

LING TAN. They hear what we must do, for the cloud is now gone from my mind. (*To Lao Er and Jade*) I have spoken to our kinsmen, and I have told them the things you told me. And I gave them the hour I would fire my house and asked them to do the same thing.

JADE. And will they?

LING TAN. I do not know. It is a great deal to ask of them and against their natures.

WU LIEN'S WIFE (*stepping up to them*). But what will become of me and my children?

LING TAN (*to Wu Lien's Wife*). You will go first and take your children to where my sons are in the hills.

LAO ER (*to Ling Tan*). The son of Neighbor Shen can guide her.

Ling Tan nods. Jade turns to Wu Lien's Wife.

JADE. And you will take my son too, sister.

LING TAN (*to Wu Lien's Wife*). We will meet you there.

The COURTYARD at night: Jade is just throwing the last bundle of straw against the walls of the stable. There is a great deal of straw already well prepared around the plow, thrasher, and other agricultural utensils as if she were just finishing her task. Lao Er comes over to her.

JADE. Is your sister gone then?

LAO ER. Yes, and the children with her.

JADE. Are you sure she will care for my son?

LAO ER (*smiling faintly*). Yes. She is skillful with children, if with nothing else.

JADE (*nodding, then looking around at the courtyard*). This is a hard thing to do.

LAO ER. If we find it hard what of the old ones?

JADE (*nodding*). The thought of them is part of my own grief. (*She looks toward the house.*)

In the BIG ROOM Ling's Wife, her face

fiercely controlled, is scattering straw in the corners and placing it carefully so that everything will catch fire almost at once. Ling Tan has removed several tiles from the floor and has dug a hole in which he is burying a few trinkets.

LING TAN. These things will mark our land, and when we come back we can prove it is ours and claim it.

He looks up. He sees the old woman has left off with her work and is staring around the room. Suddenly, impulsively, she goes to the table and straightens some of the things there. As she does so, she chokes back a sob.

LING TAN. What nonsense is this? In a little while those things will be ashes and so what matter how they look now?

LING'S WIFE (*with great dignity*). Would you bury a friend without first arranging him decently?

LING TAN. You are right.

LING'S WIFE (*looking around her, choking back another sob*). In these rooms your father and his father before him died and our children were born here and should die here.

LING TAN (*rallying her*). I helped you dig once, now you help me.

She hesitates for a moment, then kneels beside him. Together they place the trinkets in the hole. Suddenly, she looks up at him, and she, too, is smiling, although her eyes still glitter with tears.

LING'S WIFE (*in her old, sharp voice*). A worry has struck me!

LING TAN (*relieved that she has rallied*). What now, old woman?

LING'S WIFE. What if the stranger who walks head down on the other side of your land digs deep and finds these things and steals them?

LING TAN (*laughing*). He will not steal from us. (*He covers the hole, and together they replace the tiles.*)

LING'S WIFE. How can you know that?

LING TAN. I see clearly now—and for the first time.

We see JADE and LAO ER as they silently enter the door.

LING TAN'S VOICE. Third Cousin once said there is only one moon and one sun for all. If that is true and all share the sun and moon should we not also all share the earth?

Jade stops, and puts a hand on Lao Er's arm to halt him also. They exchange a look of pride and surprise at hearing this from Ling Tan.

We see LING TAN and LING'S WIFE.

LING TAN. This valley is not the world, but only part of the world, and there are others like me whose faces I have never seen. Elsewhere there are men who love peace and long for good and who will fight to get those things. And so the stranger is no longer a stranger to me, but a man like me.... (*With real longing*) If I could but know him.... if I could but see him....

LING'S WIFE (*practically*). What good to see him if you could not speak to each other?

JADE steps forward, unashamed tears in her eyes.

JADE (*softly*). You would not need speech.

We see the GROUP as Ling Tan and his wife look up at Jade and Lao Er.

JADE. If what you wish is the same,

there would be understanding between you.

LING TAN (*nodding*). Yes, that is true. Tonight I feel a circling power sweep around the world and bring all of us and that man who was a stranger together!

LAO ER. I, too, feel it.

LING'S WIFE (*with at least a shadow of her old spirit*). And so do I! Why am I left out of this?

LAO ER (*after a pause*). It is time now, father. Shall I fire the house?

LING TAN (*looking at his wife tenderly*). No. Your mother and I will do that.

JADE (*sensing their emotion*). We will fire the east field first then.

LING TAN. Leave the north fields to the last that we may escape that way.

Lao Er nods. Jade touches the arm of Ling's Wife for a moment, then turns away, followed by Lao Er. Then we see JADE and LAO ER in the COMPOUND: They take large bundles of torches from a cart and Lao Er picks up a sack full of spare torches and slings it over his shoulder. They move on out of the compound.

JADE. If there is trouble, care for yourself first.

LAO ER. I will. And you must do the same.

JADE (*smiling faintly*). We always say this—and yet we know we will not. (*They leave the compound.*)

Ling Tan and his wife come out, then go toward the compound gate. Ling lights the torch he is holding.

LING TAN (*turning her toward the house*). Look back once, old woman, then look back no more!

She nods speechlessly, then turns, takes a long, long look, storing up the memory of the place. Ling Tan looks at her for a moment, then turns, moves out of sight, toward the house. Ling's Wife continues to look at the house, and her almost unendurable grief shows in her face. And now we see Ling Tan going inside. He is seen to thrust his torch out toward a pile of straw near the wall.

A close view shows LING'S WIFE turning quickly, *away from the house,* and standing there rigidly. There is the sound of the first crackle of flame, then the noise grows swiftly. There are quick flashes of LING TAN touching his torch to: THE KITCHEN, BETWEEN THE TWO HOUSES, THE LIVING ROOM, THE SHED IN THE COMPOUND, and THE STABLES.

And now the whole house is afire, the flames being mirrored in the pond. Ling Tan runs to his wife, puts his arm protectingly around her, and the two old people go out of the gate for the last time.

Jade and Lao Er are seen lighting their torches near the WILLOW TREE. As they finish they turn and run out of sight, toward the viaduct. This cuts to the VIADUCT as the figures of Lao Er and Jade, carrying the torches, appear and start to run across. Jade flings a torch; it lands in a field. Lao Er also throws a torch.—We see the FIELD at the spot where the torches land: The dry grain bursts into flame.

We again see Jade and Lao Er running on the viaduct throwing torches right and left and occasionally pausing to light bundles of straw already prepared for this purpose on the viaduct, and we see the conflagration building up.—And now a close view of the VIADUCT shows the fire catching up with them.—They are silhouetted against the light as they run across the blazing structure.—Next, they are throwing torches into the surrounding grass fields. Then we see them reach the end of the viaduct and starting to set fire to the shed over the water well. And finally, we see them on the ROAD leading to the HILLS at the corner of the compound: Ling Tan and his wife hurry in as pre-arranged. They pick up their respective bundles. Ling's field, in the background, can be seen now entirely ablaze.

LING TAN. Keep to the hillroad!

And as they all turn and run out of sight, the scene dissolves to the TOP OF THE HILL as Ling Tan, Ling's Wife, Jade and Lao Er climb up, rounding a rock in the foreground. Jade looks off at the valley.

JADE. See! Look!

They all turn, and react in incredulous amazement. Seen very small, from their angle, there is a small fire visible near Shen's house; then a tongue of flame licks up into the night, and spreads.

A close view of the farmer SHEN shows him setting fire to the corner of his stable. The house behind him is already ablaze. Then we again see LING'S FAMILY.

LING TAN. Neighbor Shen is with us!

LAO ER (*pointing*). He is not the only one! There is even someone in the village!

Seen very small, from their angle, a house in the village is burning. Another catches flame. The dark sky is illuminated by the fires.

We see THIRD COUSIN'S HOUSE: The house is burning and Third Cousin's Wife staggers under the burdens Third Cousin is loading upon her—household possessions—books, etc. In the background, the village people can be seen firing their houses.

THIRD COUSIN'S WIFE (*piteously*). I am weary, my lord!

THIRD COUSIN (*loading on the last book*). But as you are not bruised—as yet.

He makes a threatening gesture and she scampers off.

At the TOP OF THE HILL, the valley behind them, Ling's family appears, looking down at the valley. This cuts to a view of the VALLEY seen very small by them, as another farm, as well as a field catches afire, burns like tinder, then another, and another. A house has a torch set to it; another field bursts into flames. Then we again see LING'S FAMILY, now joyous at what is happening—almost afraid to believe it.

JADE. Look, there is another!

LING TAN. And yet another!

LAO ER. They are all with us!

LING'S WIFE. The whole country is aflame!

There are quick flashes, then, of:

TWO FARMERS' WIVES, as they drive a team of oxen across a field. The oxen drag a burning plank between them and the field ignites over a large area.—

FARMERS as they run through a dry field with torches, shouting.—

AN OLD MAN pulling a burning cart across a field.—

THREE SAIL BOATS are moved under the bridge and now three men set fire to the sails which go up in a blaze and envelop the bridge.—

THE INNKEEPER runs out of his inn which is afire behind him.—

A GROUP OF YOUNG MEN set fire to a pile of oil drums.—

A STOREKEEPER sets fire to baskets of rice.—

This is followed by quick flashes of the faces of Ling's Family:

JADE, her head high, her eyes alight.—

LING TAN, reacting with pride.—

LING'S WIFE, her eyes full of tears.—

LAO ER, his eyes, too, alight with triumph.

Triumphant music starts over these glimpses. Then we get a PANORAMA, with LING'S FAMILY in the foreground, of the whole valley now in flames. The houses and the fields, the farm tools and the bridges are burning—everything these people have on earth. In the background, etched against the fire, can be seen the tiny figures of the villagers and farmers as they run before the fast-spreading flames, toward free China.

JADE. It was not too much to ask!

LING TAN (*humbly*). I have underestimated my own people. I have a great deal to learn.

As he turns, we see that his eyes are wet. He moves out of sight, followed by the others. The triumphant music rises as the view rests on the FIELD AND HOUSES.

This dissolves to the VALLEY: It is early morning. The field and farms lie in blackened desolation. The gate of the compound is burned out with one post standing and still smoking. A remaining part of the stone wall crumbles. The wind, a gentle wind, stirs the ashes and blows away the dust raised by the crumbling wall. There is utter desolation over the whole scene. And into the foreground of the scene creeps Lao San; he looks down at the waste. Then a close view of LAO SAN shows his amazement and satisfaction. The music rises to a crescendo.

This dissolves to a view of the GUERRILLA CAMP, as the music has dwindled to a spirited folk melody.—The Guerrilla Encampment is in a rock-sheltered spot high in the hills. This scene takes in a portion of the usual camp activity. Some of the guerrillas are seated around fires, eating and cooking. Others work on their guns. Still others sort ammunition, supplies, etc. As the view begins to move through the camp, one or two of the villagers, weary and smoke-begrimed, can be recognized, and, in the background, seated around a fire, can be seen Ling Tan, Ling's Wife, Lao Ta, Wu Lien's Wife and children, Jade, Lao Er and Jade's son. As the view draws close to LING'S GROUP, the music fades out.

We see LING'S GROUP as Ling Tan and his wife are re-packing their belongings, obviously for a further journey. The others watch them silently, and a little sadly. To one side, Jade is just finishing tying several things (which cannot be identified) into a small parcel. She hands the parcel to Lao Er who nods, and takes it.

LING'S WIFE (*to Wu Lien's Wife*). Why can you not come with us?

WU LIEN'S WIFE. No, mother. My place is here with my brothers.

LAO TA (*reassuringly*). The enemy fears to come here, mother. My sister will be safe and have food.

LING TAN (*nodding*). It is best. Our road will be hard, old woman, and our daughter is—

He breaks off suddenly, staring toward the path that leads toward the valley. The others, seeing this, also turn and stare.—And now, as viewed by them, we see Lao San, who has come from the valley and is moving toward the spot where Ling's family is seated. His face is immobile, and it is impossible to know what is in his mind.

There is a close view of LING TAN and HIS WIFE: Ling Tan sits motionless, waiting for his son. His wife moves closer to him, as if for support, but he seems unaware of her. And now the view expands to reveal the others. They, too, wait tensely for the meeting. —Then a close view shows LAO SAN reaching the group, and stopping.

LAO SAN. My father, I have seen what you have done, and the others also. (*Humbly*) I am ashamed.

LING TAN looks up at his son, and smiles.

LING TAN. No more than I, my son.

We see the GROUP.—The others relax, pleased that this has come about.

LAO SAN. Well then, I would have you take your place of command as head of our family once more.

LING TAN. I think there is now another command even above that. We have each been told what we must do and we will do it. You who are young will stay here and fight on.

LAO SAN. And you, father?

LING TAN. I would be where these hands can be used. I, and my old woman with me, will go into free China, and there raise food to fill your bellies while you fight.

Lao San nods. There is wisdom in this.

LING'S WIFE (*bursting out—overwrought*). Let us go then, while the strength is still in us.

Ling Tan rises, and helps his wife to her feet. They pick up their bundles. The others all rise, also, and stand waiting. It is a moment of deep emotion.

LING TAN. There is a thing. If one of us lives, he must go back one day to claim the land. I so charge you all. If you live, you must do this.

Each bows his head in obedience. Ling Tan and his wife take one last look at their children, and start to turn away. Jade casts a swift glance at Lao Er, who nods.

JADE. Your son and I will walk a little way with you. We would see you out of sight.

Ling Tan nods wordlessly, and Jade and Lao Er (Jade carrying her son) move off with them.

A close view shows Wu Lien's Wife and children, Lao Ta and Lao San as they watch their mother and father go Then we see LING TAN, LING'S WIFE, JADE carrying her son, and LAO ER as they walk toward the beginning of the path that leads off toward Free China. (This path is on the opposite side of the camp from the one where Lao San appeared.) As they reach the path, they stop and look at each other.

LING TAN. At this moment we part, we are closer than ever before. . . .

Ling's Wife looks at Jade's child, and her hand goes out involuntarily to touch his head.

LING'S WIFE (*gruffly—very near breaking*). When will this one begin to read?

JADE. As soon as he can be taught.

LING TAN. He will learn quickly— for he is the hope of us all. (*He smiles at the child.*) His eyes are open—make sure the one who teaches him has *his* eyes open, also.

Jade hesitates, but only for a moment, then she places her child in the arms of Ling Tan.

> JADE. I will do that, and I do it now. (*She smiles at him.*) Take your grandchild with you .... and care for him ... and teach him.

Ling Tan and his wife stare unbelievingly, first at Jade, who smiles at them steadily, then at Lao Er, who nods, and hands Ling's Wife the little packet, which it is now evident contains the baby's belongings. Ling Tan and his wife react with wonder and an almost overpowering joy.

> LING TAN (*softly*). He will be as our own.
>
> LING'S WIFE (*lifting her head, as with new hope and courage*). What else? For that is what he is!

Together the two old people turn and move forward on their journey.—We see Jade and Lao Er standing motionless, watching them go; then Ling Tan (carrying the baby) and his wife moving along. Then the view remains on the group for a moment, and moves in to the FACE of JADE'S SON as he smiles, and to JADE and LAO ER who are straining their eyes for a last glimpse of the old people and their son. Then the scene fades out.

THE MORE THE MERRIER
(A Columbia Picture)

Screenplay by ROBERT RUSSEL and FRANK ROSS;
RICHARD FLOURNOY and LEWIS FOSTER

Story by ROBERT RUSSEL and FRANK ROSS

Produced and Directed by GEORGE STEVENS

The Cast

CONNIE MILLIGAN	Jean Arthur
JOE CARTER	Joel McCrea
BENJAMIN DINGLE	Charles Coburn
CHARLES J. PENDERGAST	Richard Gaines
EVANS	Bruce Bennett
PIKE	Frank Sully
SENATOR NOONAN	Clyde Fillmore
MORTON RODAKIEWICZ	Stanley Clements
HARDING	Don Douglas

*Film Editor—*OTTO MEYER

The Torpedo Song by HENRY MYERS, EDWARD ELISCU
and JAY GORNEY

Copyright 1943 by Columbia Pictures Corporation. Screenplay of the Columbia Pictures photoplay "The More the Merrier," copyright 1943 by Columbia Pictures Corporation. By permission of Columbia Pictures Corporation, Robert Russel and Frank Ross, authors of the original story; Robert Russel, Lewis Foster and Richard Flournoy, authors of the screenplay.

THE MORE THE MERRIER
PART ONE

A long view of THE CAPITOL BUILDING, Washington, D.C., fades in; and the voice of the Commentator we hear is that of a corny travelogue lecturer of maybe ten years back, lush, soupy—a voice rising and falling with disgusting sonorousness.

> COMMENTATOR'S VOICE. Our vagabond camera takes us to beautiful Washington, D.C.

This dissolves to the LINCOLN MEMORIAL, Washington, D.C.

> COMMENTATOR'S VOICE. The National Capital of our United States—

The POTOMAC RIVER:

> COMMENTATOR'S VOICE. Situated on the broad banks of the Potomac River—

The WASHINGTON MONUMENT, Washington, D.C.:

> COMMENTATOR'S VOICE. Washington is one of the most important cities in the world—

This dissolves to a sizable OFFICE: Forty desks in a room made for twenty. Three people at a desk. Hectic activity. Pell mell madness. People are mouthing and grimacing at one another. If there was any sound in the scene, it would probably be deafening, but only the voice of the Commentator can be heard. And this is followed by a series of quick scenes paralleling the Commentator's remarks:—

The LOBBY of an APARTMENT HOUSE: Two harried clerks are gesturing apologetically and grimacing madly at a crowd of would-be guests in the small lobby. Everyone's mouth is moving. Everyone is pushing and shoving. Only the serene voice of the Commentator can be heard.

> COMMENTATOR'S VOICE. The dignified, old city has many spacious modern apartment buildings that welcome the visitors to the Nation's Capital with traditional hospitality—

A HOTEL BATHROOM: Three men shaving in the small bathroom, while a fourth man is in the tub.

> COMMENTATOR'S VOICE. Living is pleasant and leisurely—

A BEDROOM: A beautiful colonial room with a rare four-poster. In the four-poster are three people. In addition, there are three more people, each on a cot. Everybody is sleeping.

> COMMENTATOR'S VOICE. Washington's beautiful homes have the quiet dignity of another day—

The MALL: Eight girls pick up a sailor.

> COMMENTATOR'S VOICE. For it is a city of formality and custom—

A STREET: A taxicab drives up to a corner and stops. Ten people descend on it, five from one side, five from the other. All try to file in, pushing and shoving. The cab finally pulls out fully loaded with one man hanging on to the running board and a couple of people almost knocked down.

Copyright 1943, *by Columbia Pictures Corporation.*

COMMENTATOR'S VOICE. Manners and courtesy are responsible for the well-ordered conduct of its daily affairs—

A CROWDED HAMBURGER STAND: Most people are eating standing up. The types we see are unusual for a hamburger spot. We get the impression that they're here because they obviously couldn't get in any place else. Nothing in sight but hamburgers.

COMMENTATOR'S VOICE. The many fine restaurants of Washington are the delight of the epicurean and the gourmet—where one may enjoy to the full the rare dishes of the Old South—

A RESIDENTIAL STREET: People are milling and pushing on the sidewalk. In one window of a brownstone house there is a cardboard sign, reading: "NO VACANCY."

COMMENTATOR'S VOICE. Our trip would be incomplete if we neglected to visit the quiet, staid and dignified residential section—

A SECOND HOUSE: There is a sign on the door; it reads: "NO VACANCY."

COMMENTATOR'S VOICE. It is with pride that we view hospitable Washington—

ANOTHER DOORWAY: This, too, bears a sign: "NO VACANCY," prominently displayed.

COMMENTATOR'S VOICE. Friendly Washington—

We see ANOTHER SIGN which reads "NO VACANCY."

COMMENTATOR'S VOICE. Welcoming us to her doorstep—

Then we see the exterior of the WINTON JAMES HOTEL, with a PLATE reading "WINTON JAMES HOTEL"; and hanging beneath the plate is a placard, which also reads: "NO VACANCY."

COMMENTATOR'S VOICE. Eagerly throwing wide her doors.

This cuts to the crowded WINTON JAMES HOTEL LOBBY: A desk clerk is addressing a couple as an elderly, heavy-set gentleman, DINGLE, and a bellhop, carrying his luggage, approach.

DESK CLERK. Sorry. No vacancy. (*To Dingle*) Positively no vacancy.

DINGLE. I have a reservation.

DESK CLERK. Oh, pardon me. What was the name, sir?

DINGLE. Benjamin Dingle. Senator Noonan made the reservation.

DESK CLERK. Oh, Senator Noonan! Just a moment, Mr. Dingle. (*He gets out a card.*) We have the reservation, Mr. Dingle.

DINGLE. Good.

DESK CLERK. But Senator Noonan engaged a suite beginning the twenty-fourth. This is only the twenty-second. You're two days early.

DINGLE (*dryly*). Anything wrong with being two days early?

DESK CLERK. Why, no, sir, but—

DINGLE. Everybody ought to be two days early. When this Nation gets two days early, we'll be getting someplace.

DESK CLERK. Yes, sir—but unfortunately, the suite won't be vacated until day after tomorrow.

DINGLE. Can you connect me with Senator Noonan?

DESK CLERK. I can have the operator connect you with Mrs. Noonan. The Senator is out of town.

DINGLE. When will he be back?

DESK CLERK. He was due back day before yesterday, but he's—

DINGLE. Two days late.

DESK CLERK. Yes, sir.

DINGLE. Well, when Senator Noonan gets back late, tell him I was here early. (*And he goes out angrily.*)

The scene dissolving, we see the FARRAGUT STATUE. Dingle, with baggage, pauses to look at the statue and its inscription, and continues on his way. This dissolves to a NEWSPAPER BUILDING, where trucks are backed up to a loading platform, and workmen are loading and checking. A huge sign across the building reads: "THE WASHINGTON SUN."

Dingle appears, with luggage, takes a newspaper from the rear of the truck, and flips a coin to a man as the truck drives out. As he opens the newspaper, the scene dissolves into an ADVERTISEMENT in the NEWSPAPER which reads:

HALF OF SUNNY APARTMENT, Stone's throw from Supreme Court. Call after 5:00 P.M. only. Apt. 2B. 1708 "D" St.

Then we see 1708 "D" STREET, a small apartment building with an old-fashioned stoop, as Dingle arrives with baggage and makes his way through a crowd of waiting would-be renters, all unaware of him. He ascends the steps, removes the "Room For Rent" sign, and goes into the building, where he removes his coat and hat, leaves his overcoat and bags, and returns to face the crowd.—He lounges on the top of the steps as he addresses the group below.

DINGLE. Are all you people here about the ad in the paper; about the apartment?

MAN. I am.

WOMAN. I'll take it.

DINGLE. Just a moment, folks. I'm very sorry, but the apartment is all rented.

ANOTHER MAN. What do you mean, "rented"?

ANOTHER. It isn't even five o'clock yet.

FOURTH MAN. What's the idea putting an ad in the paper—

DINGLE. I'm very sorry, but the apartment is all rented. In case there's another vacancy, there'll be another ad.

A WOMAN. May I ask why you put all of us to the bother of coming here?

DINGLE. No, you may not. Good-day. (*And he goes brusquely into the building, shutting the door.*)

Dingle enters the DOWNSTAIRS HALL, dons his hat and coat, picks up the baggage, and goes upstairs, singing:

DINGLE.
"When Farragut sailed for Mobile Bay,
He heard torpedoes were in the way.
You know what Admiral Farragut said?
'Damn the torpedoes! Full speed ahead!'
The experts said, 'We'll meet our doom.
We'll never get through, there ain't no room.'
You know what Admiral Farragut said?
'Damn the torpedoes! Full speed ahead!'
'Damn the torpedoes! Full speed ahead!'
'Damn the torpedoes! Full speed ahead!' "

Then we again see the exterior of 1708

"D" STREET, as a pretty and tired-looking young girl, Connie, arrives in a Fiat car which is full of girls. She gets out and the Fiat rolls on while she goes into the building.

The UPPER HALL: Dingle ascends, looking at identifying cards on the doors, and finally arriving at 2B with a card beneath reading: "MILLIGAN."

At this, he drops his Gladstone bag and raises his hand to knock, but Connie reaches the door at the same time, ready to insert her key in the lock. He almost conks her, and silently they exchange looks. Connie goes into the apartment and the door closes. Instantly Dingle knocks and the door re-opens.

DINGLE (*tipping his hat*). How do you do?

CONNIE. How do you do?

DINGLE. I'm Benjamin Dingle.

CONNIE. You certainly are.

DINGLE. I'm about the apartment.

CONNIE. I've already rented it.

DINGLE. Just a moment, young lady. Do you think you know me well enough to lie to me?

CONNIE. Yes.

DINGLE. Even so, you shouldn't do it. Don't you realize that practically most of the trouble in the world comes from people lying to people? You take Hitler, for instance. There's the biggest . . .

CONNIE. I'm sorry, Mister, but I'd prefer—

DINGLE. Mister Dingle.

CONNIE. Mister Dingle. But I'd prefer sharing the apartment with a lady.

DINGLE. That's fine. So would I.

CONNIE. I'm sure you'll be happier someplace else.

DINGLE. I've been there.

CONNIE. Please try to understand my position, Mister . . . Mr. Dingle. I can't rent half my apartment to just anybody.

DINGLE. I'm not just anybody.

CONNIE. I'm only doing it on account of the housing congestion in Washington.

DINGLE. You said it!

CONNIE. I feel it's my patriotic duty to take in somebody—with everything so overcrowded.

DINGLE. I'm overcrowded.

CONNIE. Why don't you try the YMCA?

DINGLE. I'm too old.

CONNIE. Or the Veterans' Home.

DINGLE. I'm too young.

CONNIE. Well, I'm sure I don't know what—

DINGLE. Look. Sooner or later you're gonna rent me half of this apartment. Suppose I get a look at it, huh? (*He walks in, Connie following, as he glances into the living room.*)

We see the APARTMENT HALL as Connie walks in, followed by the undaunted Dingle.

CONNIE. Pretty sure of yourself, aren't you?

DINGLE. Once upon a time.

CONNIE. You wouldn't like it here.

DINGLE. Home is where you hang your hat. (*Suiting his words, he drops his on the settee.*) This way?

He precedes her into a spare bedroom.

CONNIE. Now, listen here—

DINGLE. Just looking. Just looking.

CONNIE. It's no use looking, Mr. Dingle, because I've made up my mind to rent only to a woman.

DINGLE. Let me ask you something. Would I ever want to wear your stockings?

CONNIE (*puzzled*). Of course not.

DINGLE. All right. Would I ever want to borrow your girdle or your red-and-yellow dancing slippers?

CONNIE. No.

DINGLE. Any woman, no matter who, would insist on borrowing that dress you're wearing right now. You know why? Because it's so pretty.

CONNIE (*pleased*). I made it myself.

DINGLE. Then how would you like it for her to spill a cocktail all over it at the party you couldn't go with her to, because she borrowed your dress to wear to it—in.

CONNIE (*amused*). She might have some clothes I could wear.

DINGLE. Not *her*.

CONNIE. Why not?

DINGLE (*poker-faced*). She's so dumpty looking! Never has a thing that's clean. Why do you suppose she's always borrowing your dresses? Runs in all her stockings. Never makes her bed. Lipstick on all your towels. She's sloppy.

CONNIE. How do I know you'd be any better?

DINGLE. Look at me. I'm neat like a pin. (*He turns around for her inspection. Then suddenly he pleads.*) Please let me stay.

CONNIE. Well, look—

DINGLE. Tell you what. Let's try it out for a week. End of the week comes and you're not happy, we'll flip a coin and see who moves out. Now about price?

The scene dissolves to the UPPER HALL, showing the DOOR of CONNIE'S APARTMENT as Connie's dainty fingers drop in a new card which reads: "MILLIGAN-DINGLE."

This dissolves to DINGLE'S ROOM: Dingle is in pajamas and smoking jacket, smoking a pipe and reading a Western magazine as he sits in an armchair. Then the scene moves to another room, showing Connie sitting at a desk in the living room, pigtails and pajamas, making an entry in a diary.

"Monday, June 15th: Rented half apartment to funny old man named Dingle. At least someone around to break the monotony."

She closes the book, and puts it in the desk drawer, picks up a schedule and a chart of the apartment, and goes to the hall.

Then we see DINGLE'S ROOM and the APARTMENT HALL as Connie knocks on his door.

DINGLE. Who is it?

CONNIE'S VOICE. It's me, of course!

DINGLE. Come in, of course.

CONNIE (*entering*). I brought you a copy—I didn't know you smoked, Mr. Dingle.

DINGLE (*dryly*). Worst thing a person can do. Tobacco's a real killer.

CONNIE. This is your copy of the morning schedule.

DINGLE. Hm?

CONNIE. The morning schedule.

DINGLE. Oh, the morning schedule.

He puts his magazine on the table, and

starts to rise to go to her as she stands by the doorway.

CONNIE. Yes. It's a matter of efficiency. You just follow this program and we won't have any trouble.

We see THE SCHEDULE, which reads:

MORNING SCHEDULE

MILLIGAN		DINGLE
7:00	Alarm goes off	7:00
7:01	Enter bathroom	
	Bring in milk	7:02
	Put coffee on	7:05
7:06	Leave bathroom	
	Enter bathroom	7:07
7:07	Start dressing	
7:10	Drink coffee	
	Leave bathroom	7:12
7:13	Put eggs on	
7:14	Finish dressing	
	Take eggs off	7:16
	Shave	7:17
7:18	Eat eggs	
7:21	Fix hair	
	Put eggs on	7:24
7:26	Make bed	7:25
	Eat eggs	7:27
7:28	Empty garbage	
	Wash dishes	7:29
7:30	All done	7:30

Over this unfolding schedule we hear Connie's voice; and as she starts speaking, this schedule dissolves to another insert, same size and shape. It is a floor plan of the apartment and looks something like this:

CONNIE'S		DINGLE'S
ROOM		ROOM
	HALL	BATH
KITCHEN		

CONNIE'S VOICE. Here, I'll show you. This is a floor plan. Here's my room; here's your room; here's the bathroom and here's the kitchen. We both get up when the alarm clock goes off. I enter the bathroom at 7:01; one minute later, you bring in the milk, and at 7:05 you put on the coffee. Minute later, I leave the bathroom, and a minute after that, you enter the bathroom, and that's when I'm starting to dress. In three minutes, I have my coffee, and just after that, 7:12, you leave the bathroom. 7:13 I put on my eggs and leave to finish dressing; minute after that you get on your shoes and take off my eggs at 7:16, and start to shave at 7:17. 7:18 I eat my eggs, and you finish dressing at 7:19. I'm back in the bathroom 7:21 fixing my hair, and you get back in the kitchen at 7:24 to put on your eggs, then you make your bed at 7:25 and I make mine at 7:26, and you go in to eat your eggs and I go to empty the papers and cans. You wash dishes at 7:29 and we're all done at 7:30. It's really very simple.

DINGLE (*amused*). Do we do all this railroad time or Eastern War Time?

CONNIE (*earnestly*). When you hear my alarm clock go off, you'll know it's seven o'clock.

DINGLE. You're a very systematic girl, aren't you?

CONNIE. I worked in the Office of Facts and Figures.

She turns back to the living room, and Dingle follows her to the doorway. Then we see the LIVING ROOM as Dingle follows Connie in, glancing around.

DINGLE. By the way, why aren't you married, Miss Milligan?

CONNIE. Well, really!

DINGLE. Some high-type, clean-cut, nice young fellow. You're very pretty, you know.

CONNIE. If you don't mind, Mr. Dingle—

DINGLE. Of course, there's not very many men around nowadays. But there's always one if you're out to get one.

CONNIE. Maybe I don't want to get married.

DINGLE. Well, don't you?

CONNIE. Well! !

DINGLE. Or maybe you do.

CONNIE. Well, I—

DINGLE. Come, come! Make up your mind, Miss Milligan!

CONNIE. Make up my mind? !

DINGLE. You know, "Damn the Torpedoes, Full Speed Ahead!" That's what Admiral Farragut said. Of all times, Miss Milligan, this is no time to be indecisive—in.

CONNIE. If you expect to get along here, Mr. Dingle, you'll have to mind your own business.

DINGLE. Well, in these times, everybody's business is everybody's business. War brings people closer together, you know.

The HALLWAY of the APARTMENT as she ushers him out resolutely:

CONNIE. Not me and you, Mr. Dingle. Good night. (*And she slams the door on him, muttering*) Mind your own business!

Dingle turns away toward his own room, tossing back his answer.

DINGLE. Who was in his own room minding his own business, when who else of course came in?

At this, Connie steps into the corridor, and stops him.

CONNIE. One more thing: we'd better not leave the apartment together in the morning.

DINGLE. You mean because people might think?

CONNIE. Well, not exactly, but people are so . . .

DINGLE (*amazed*). ME? !

CONNIE. Of course.

DINGLE (*really touched by the compliment*). Thank you, Miss Milligan. Thank you, indeed.

They go to their respective rooms.— Connie gets her diary from her desk, extinguishes the light there, raises the window, and sits on her bed to write in her diary. Dingle, meantime, prepares for bed, singing as he does so:

DINGLE.
"Now Jimmy Doolittle flew overseas,
Wanted to nip at the Nipponese,
Cleared a cloud and looked below,
And said, 'By golly! There's To-ki-o!'
Oh, Jimmy Doolittle he understood,
Dood his duty and he dood it good.
Somewhere Jimmy had heard it said,
'Damn the Torpedoes, Full Speed Ahead!' "

We then see both BEDROOMS, as a camera would catch them from the roof.

CONNIE (*calling*). Mr. Dingle! Mr. Dingle!

DINGLE. Yes, Miss Milligan?

CONNIE. Do you smoke in bed?

DINGLE. No, I sleep in bed!

CONNIE. Do I smell smoke?

DINGLE. Only the smoke of burning memories, Miss Milligan, rising from the smouldering embers of my romantic youth. . . Do you keep a diary, Miss Milligan?

Guiltily, she hides it—as though he could see it.

CONNIE. No, of course not; certainly not. What made you ask?

DINGLE. Well, there are two kinds of people: Those who don't do what they want to do, so they write down in a diary about what they haven't done. And those who haven't time to write about it, because they're out doing it. (*Singing*) "Damn the Torpedoes, Full Speed Ahead!"

Connie resurrects her diary, in decision.

CONNIE (*firmly*). Good night, Mr. Dingle.

DINGLE. Good night, Miss Milligan.

We then see CONNIE'S HAND making an entry in the diary:

"But at least he is someone to talk to. If this keeps up, I think I will join the Army—W.A.A.C.S. . . Maybe African Service."

The pen scratches out the words "I think"; then it scratches out the word "Maybe" as the scene fades out.

PART TWO

A view of the TWO BEDROOMS fades in; we see CONNIE'S ALARM CLOCK, on the shelf over her bed, just as it hits 7 A.M.; the alarm rings, and she shuts it off groggily. She goes into the living room, en route to the bathroom, as Dingle's alarm rings.

DINGLE (*startled*). Hello. Hello! (*He looks around the room and remembers.*) Oh!

He gets up to turn off the alarm as Connie returns to her own clock and turns it on as Dingle gets his silenced. Puzzled, she looks at the darned thing, and simultaneously with Dingle, realizes the mixup, and again turns off her alarm. Suddenly they remember the schedule and make a dash for the hallway—Dingle grabbing his schedule from the back of the door as he flies by with the alarm clock.

The APARTMENT HALL: Connie and Dingle dash in from their respective doors and skid to a stop within inches of a collision. She is grumpy with sleep, and growls her greeting.

CONNIE. Good morning.

DINGLE. You got a terrible disposition in the morning, haven't you? Good morning.

He rushes to the kitchen, Connie to the bathroom. Doors slam, then instantly reopen.

CONNIE. No!

DINGLE. No, what?

She points impatiently to the schedule in his hand and to the door which leads to the outer hall.

CONNIE. Bring in the milk!

Dingle goes to the outer hall to comply, and Connie crosses the hall to go into the KITCHEN. Here Connie puts a coffeepot on the stove, and starts back to the bathroom.

The OUTER and APARTMENT HALL: Dingle, returning with the milk, collides violently with Connie returning to the bathroom. Dingle goes into the kitchen to put the milk in the refrigerator while Connie goes to the bathroom and returns to see if he also brought the newspaper in. As she steps into the outer hall, Dingle reaches from the kitchen, and closes the door—locking her out.—Instantly the doorbell rings. He checks his alarm, runs into her room to check hers, and completely unravelled, rushes back to open the door to the outer hall. Connie stands at the doorjamb, fuming, but Dingle is too far gone by now to know what he's doing.

DINGLE. Good morning.

She starts in, but he closes the door in her face, sending her backwards. Dingle does a double take as he looks in the direction of the empty bathroom, realizing what he's seen, and re-opens the door.

DINGLE. Oh, it's you. What're you doing out there? Come in.

She shoves the newspaper at him, dancing in exasperation.

CONNIE (*going into the bathroom*). The paper!

Unaware he has taken it, Dingle goes into the outer hall, searching for the newspaper. Connie looks out, sees the door ajar, glares toward Dingle who she believes is in the kitchen, and kicks the door shut—locking Dingle outside. Then she slams into the bathroom. Dingle tries the doorknob, rings the bell, knocks, and finally calls out ingratiatingly.

DINGLE. Miss Milligan! Miss Milligan! Yoo Hoo! (*He goes down the hall to the window, through which he sees Connie in the bathroom.*) Yoo Hoo! Yoo Hoo! (*He opens the window, starts to throw the clock, and knocks at the window.*) Miss Milligan! It's me! Mr. Dingle! The paper! I'm locked out! Let me in!

Brushing her teeth, Connie is startled and shrieks. Then realizing the situation, she goes out to meet an apologetic, scraping Dingle in the hall as he offers his newspaper peace-offering.

DINGLE. Sorry. The paper. (*Then he looks at the schedule and remembers.*) The coffee. Coffee.

He scurries inside and goes into the kitchen, while Connie slams the door to the bathroom, and re-opens it only to fling the newspaper across the hall at him.

The scene dissolves to the KITCHEN where Dingle now has the table set, burnt toast and coffee on it, and is finishing squeezing orange juice. The second glass being only partially full, he fills it with water from the tap, sips, checks with the schedule, turns to pour coffee, and discovers only saucers on the table. As he opens what he thinks is the cabinet for cups, an ironing board falls out. And now Connie comes from the bathroom in a dressing jacket.

CONNIE. All right, Mr. Dingle. *Aprés moi.*

DINGLE. *Aprés moi, Mademoiselle.*

He takes the coffeepot with him to the bathroom unwittingly, while she puts eggs to boil, discards the burnt toast, and goes to her room to dress.

Next, in the BATHROOM, Dingle drops his clock and schedule, and turns on the "tub," only to be inundated by the shower. He adjusts the stream, and tries to remove his robe while retaining the coffeepot; the coffee pours from his sleeve into the tub.—Connie passes in the hall, and knocks.

CONNIE. Mr. Dingle! Hurry!

In the KITCHEN, Connie is finishing her egg, reading the newspaper by her plate, and again calls out to Dingle.

CONNIE. Mr. Dingle!

DINGLE'S VOICE. Yes, Miss Milligan I'm having a nice shower.

CONNIE. Mr. Dingle, do you have the coffee?

DINGLE. The coffee! Coffee! Coming! Coming!

He dog-trots from the bathroom, and starts to pour.

CONNIE. *Merci.*

The tiny trickle stops. She glances up at him questioningly. He shakes the pot for more, but to no avail, and dismisses it casually.

DINGLE. There's a war on, Miss Milligan.

CONNIE. Get dressed, Mr. Dingle. Stick to the schedule.

DINGLE. Oh, yes, get dressed, Mr. Dingle. (*He starts toward his room, repeating.*) Get dressed.

Connie grimaces as she tries to drink the coffee, and then returns to her room, stopping to turn off the bathtub faucet as she passes.

Then we see Dingle scurrying about in his room, and Connie entering hers, and starting to make her bed.

CONNIE. Mr. Dingle!

DINGLE. Yes, Miss Milligan?

CONNIE. Don't forget to make your bed!

DINGLE. Oh, yes, the bed! Make the bed!

As he throws the covers back, he inadvertently covers his trousers. Connie, however, makes her bed meticulously, does her hair, changes her dressing jacket—while Dingle dresses, looking for the trousers, barely missing being clunked by the falling wall bed.

DINGLE (*muttering to himself as he searches*). What did I do with those pants? I had them last night.

(*Singing*)
"Oh, Brian O'Flynn ain't got no britches to wear,
So took a sheepskin to make him a pair.
Skinny side out and woolly side in,
'Faith, they're a fine pair of britches,' said Brian O'Flynn!" (*He turns back the coverlet, then the blanket, then cries out inspirationally.*) The bathroom!

Cautiously, he opens the hall door, glances down at his pajama-trousered figure, and tiptoes toward the bathroom. Connie, in the meantime, gathers her gloves, handbag and briefcase, and then puts her diary away as she calls out to him.

CONNIE. Mr. Dingle, it's 7:30. If you're going downtown this morning, meet me downstairs at 7:32. I share a ride with Miss Hopkins. She picks me up at 7:32.

Dingle darts into the kitchen to hide as Connie steps into the HALL as she continues talking.

CONNIE. She picks me up at 7:32. We mustn't keep her waiting, because she picks up Miss Ledbetter at 7:34, and Miss Taylor and Miss Johannes at 7:37. (*She starts into the kitchen.*) Oh, my lunch!

The KITCHEN: Dingle squeezes behind the door as Connie enters, and the door knocks him through the swinging door into the living room where he falls face down over the screen, the conglomeration of stored articles tumbling down. Unaware of the catastrophe, Connie picks up her lunchbox, and continues.

CONNIE. Mr. Dingle!

DINGLE (*resting his face on his right hand, on the floor*). Yes, Miss Milligan?

CONNIE. Would you care to ride?

DINGLE. I have plenty of time. If you don't mind, I think I'll just roll downtown.

CONNIE. Have it your own way.

Upon hearing this, she slams the door, and runs downstairs humming nonchalantly—while Dingle struggles to his feet and straightens the kinks in his back.

The scene dissolves to the exterior of 1708 "D" STREET as Connie comes out of the building. She checks her watch as a Fiat with girls drives up. Connie gets in, and the car drives out.

This dissolves to DINGLE'S BEDROOM as Dingle rummages in the Gladstone for his navy-blue suit, having failed to find trousers to the suit he has on.—With his pajama trousers on, he sings:

DINGLE.
"Brian O'Lynn had no watch to put on,
He scraped out a turnip to make him a one.
He put a live cricket just under the skin,
'Faith! They'll think it's a-tickin',' said Brian O'Lynn!"

This dissolves to the exterior of 1708 "D" STREET as a good-looking young man, Joe Carter, saunters along the sidewalk carrying a huge airplane propeller while Dingle emerges from the apartment building. Oblivious to Dingle, Joe rests his bag on the steps while he checks the address against a newspaper he has taken from his coat pocket. Dingle sizes him up, decides on him favorably, and stands in front of the "No Vacancy" sign. He removes it, drops it into the mailbox behind him, removes his hat, and goes to work . . .

DINGLE. Are you here about the apartment?

JOE. Yeah, it says "Half an apartment." Is it rented?

DINGLE. You look like a high-type, clean-cut nice young fellow . . . No, come in. It's really only half of a half of an apartment, but it's not rented.

JOE (*going up the steps, carrying his propeller*). Good. (*The door closes after them.*)

The LOWER HALL: Joe starts up the steps ahead of Dingle, while the conversation resumes. It is evident that Joe is a man of few words, and he grows more laconic as Dingle becomes more inquisitive.

DINGLE. What's your name?

JOE. Carter.

DINGLE. Bill Carter?

JOE. Joe Carter.

DINGLE. Used to know a fellow name of Bill Carter.

JOE. Wasn't me.

DINGLE (*going up*). Don't you suppose I know that?

The UPPER STAIRWAY and HALL:

JOE. What didja ask for then?

DINGLE. I guess I know what Bill Carter looked like.

Joe stops to rest the propeller on the intermediate landing, permitting Dingle to pass him.

JOE. Not like me.

DINGLE. Then you know Bill Carter?

JOE (*picking up the propeller and starting up after Dingle*). No, I don't. But he sounds like a great guy.

DINGLE (*pushing the apartment door open*). Who?

JOE. Who? (*He leaves the propeller in the hall.*)

The APARTMENT HALL and BEDROOM:

DINGLE. In here.

JOE. Who's in here with me?

DINGLE. Me.

JOE. How much is it?

DINGLE. Six dollars a week.

JOE. I'll take it.

DINGLE. About time you made up your mind.

JOE (*counting currency*). Five, six.

DINGLE. How long are you going to be in town?

JOE. A week.

DINGLE. Oh, that's too bad.

JOE. Why?

DINGLE. Eight girls to every fella.

JOE. So they say.

DINGLE. So it is.

JOE. How long *you* been here?

DINGLE. Not long.

JOE. What do you do?

DINGLE. I'm a well-to-do retired millionaire. (*Looking at the propeller in the hall*) How about you?

JOE. Same.

DINGLE. What's that; part of an airplane?

JOE. It's a new type garden bench.

DINGLE. Looks like a propeller.

JOE. It does?

DINGLE. What brought you here, Mr. Carter?

JOE. Railroad.

DINGLE. I mean, what's your job?

JOE. Mechanic. I work in a baby carriage factory.

DINGLE. Where?

JOE. California.

DINGLE. San Francisco?

JOE. Burbank.

DINGLE. Baby carriage factory, eh?

JOE. Yep. Tokio Baby Carriage Corporation. Plain and fancy baby carriages for carrying babies to Tokio.

DINGLE (*"getting it"*). Oh, I suppose you think this is none of my business.

JOE. I suppose I do.

DINGLE. Probably your name isn't even Bill Carter.

JOE. Probably not. It's probably Joe Carter. (*He feels the bed.*) I'll take this one.

He turns back the sheet, picks up the trousers that Dingle mislaid and hands them to Dingle. Then he starts down the hallway.

DINGLE (*following*). Say, you got an alarm clock?

JOE. Yeah, how about a key?

DINGLE. Key?

The suspenders of the trousers catch on the doorknob. They snap back out of his hand, and fly through the open window, Joe watching this as Dingle turns back and looks around for the trousers helplessly.

The scene dissolves to the exterior of 1708 "D" STREET as Joe, with the propeller, emerges from the building, followed by Dingle. Joe turns to the left and Dingle to the right along the sidewalk. And this dissolves to an OFFICE where Joe's propeller lies on a desk, a Major Denton's desk, Joe standing with the Major and a couple of other officers around it. Joe leaves them a moment later, pauses in the corridor of the office to check his watch, and goes out.

This dissolves to the ELEVATOR and LOBBY of the WINTON-JAMES HOTEL, with Dingle emerging from the elevator into the busy lobby, stopping to check his watch, and hurrying out.—This dissolving, we see a TIME CLOCK and an ALLEY. Here Connie is in a long line of girls punching out. A lone boy traverses the length of the line and is greeted with whistles and calls. Connie watches a moment, and goes out as the boy, in growing alarm, breaks into a run and disappears around the corner in the distance.—This scene dissolving, we again see 1708 "D" STREET as Joe walks into view along the sidewalk and goes into the building; and as this dissolves, Dingle appears along the sidewalk, and hurries up the steps into the building. Then the Fiat drives up to the curb, Connie alights, waves the girls still in the car a "goodnight" and also goes into the building, while the Fiat drives off.

The UPPER HALL and STAIRS: Joe comes up the steps two at a time, pushes the doorbell, unlocks the door and starts inside, but pauses as he notices two names on the card under 2B. He takes out a pencil, writes his own name, and goes inside. Then Dingle hurries up the steps, pushes the doorbell, and knocks. Joe hurries back along the apartment hallway to admit him and returns to his bedroom, undressing.

JOE. Hello, Milligan.

DINGLE. I'm Dingle.

As Joe leaves him, Dingle spots the pencilled name on the card, and erases it industriously.

The APARTMENT HALL: Connie is now ascending the stairs, laden with packages. She looks up and sees Dingle erasing the card on the door. At this, Dingle steps inside, closes the door in her face, reopens it to say "Hello!" and closes it again. Again he opens the door, takes her keys from her as he says "Excuse me!" and closes the door on her again. He runs along the hall to slam the bedroom door where Joe is undressing. Then he runs back to again open the door for Connie, and hands her her keys.

DINGLE. Come in! (*As she passes him, glancing back at the card on the door, he adds, to explain his erasing.*) Only one "l" in "Dingle."

He gets in front of her, takes a position in front of the closed bedroom door, then reaches for her briefcase.

DINGLE. You must have been shopping. Let me help you, Miss Milligan. (*He opens the door to the living room, and she precedes him in, murmuring "Thank you."*)

The LIVING ROOM and ALCOVE-BEDROOM: Connie drops her packages, and starts to change into mules as they converse.

DINGLE. There you are.

CONNIE. Mr. Dingle, I—

DINGLE. Miss Milligan, I've got something to tell you. I don't know just how you'll take it.

CONNIE. Mr. Dingle, I've been thinking about it today, and—

DINGLE. Miss Milligan, I don't know just how to begin.

CONNIE (*going to him*). It just won

work, that's all. You'll have to give up your half of the apartment.

DINGLE. What's that, Miss Milligan?

CONNIE. I can't have a man around the house.

DINGLE. Well, as a matter of fact—

CONNIE. I'm sorry, but I've made up my mind. You'll have to move out in the morning.

DINGLE. Now, listen, Miss Milligan, I—

The APARTMENT HALL: Dingle dashes to precede her into the hall, almost bowling her over. He takes a stance in front of the closed bedroom door where Joe is undressing.

CONNIE. What's the matter with you, anyway?

DINGLE. Nothing. I'm a bit jumpy, that's all.

CONNIE. Well, calm down. You're making me jumpy, too.

Connie goes into the bathroom. From within the bedroom, Joe opens the door and Dingle falls backward against him.

JOE. Sorry.

DINGLE. It's all right. Nothing at all.

Joe starts down the hall, looking at the doors, and indicates the closed bathroom door.

JOE. This it?

DINGLE. Hey! Yes, but—

The JOE-DINGLE BEDROOM:

JOE. Be right with you.

At this, Dingle grabs at his heart, and feigns an attack.

DINGLE. Hey! Come here!

Joe returns, and as he steps into the room, Dingle closes the door.

JOE. What's the matter, Milligan?

DINGLE. Dingle. Listen, Bill.

JOE. Joe.

DINGLE. Listen, Joe.

JOE. What?

DINGLE. Something I gotta ask you.

JOE. Yeah?

DINGLE. You might think it a bit personal.

JOE (*sitting on the edge of the bed*). That's all right.

Dingle peeks into the hall, and sees Connie crossing from the bathroom to the living room, gloves in her hands, the back of her hair down.

DINGLE. Never mind. It's all right. I'll tell you later.

Joe goes into the bathroom, closes the door, and starts the shower instead of the tub. Instead of being annoyed, he turns his face up to it, gets under it and barks like a seal, squirting water from the palms of his hands at the mirror and the wash-basin.

In CONNIE'S ROOM: Connie removes her jacket, sits at the dressing table, and hears Dingle in his room yodeling to cover Joe's barking and showering. She goes back to the hall to talk to Dingle, who she supposes is in the bathroom—he, meantime, speaking from his bedroom through the crack of the door.

CONNIE. Mr. Dingle!

We see DINGLE'S BEDROOM as he talks through the crack of the door.

DINGLE. Yes?

CONNIE. Did I leave my comb in there?

DINGLE. No.

CONNIE. All right, never mind.

As she goes back into her room, she starts the phonograph, gets her robe from the clothes closet and rhumbas, Dingle steps into the hall and paces anxiously. The sound of the shower ceases, and Joe steps into the corridor.

Then we see the APARTMENT HALLWAY.

JOE. Did you say something?

DINGLE (*falsetto*). No, I— Water!

He plunges into the bathroom and Joe goes into his bedroom. Connie comes into the hall again, this time with her robe on her arm, and tries the bathroom door. Dingle calls out over the sound of the running taps.

DINGLE'S VOICE. Yes?

CONNIE. I'm sorry. I thought you were finished.

DINGLE. Be through in a minute!

CONNIE. It's all right. No hurry.

The BEDROOMS: Joe discovers Dingle's trousers on the window-boxes, tosses them to the bed, and picks up his shaving kit as Connie returns to her room. Each of them rhumbas. This cuts to the HALLWAY as Joe steps into the hall and rhumbas toward the bathroom, shaving kit in hands. Dingle starting from the bathroom, sees him.

DINGLE. Just a minute, please.

JOE. Okay, no hurry.

The KITCHEN: Joe enters, gets milk from the ice box, a hunk of cake from the cupboard, and starts to eat. Then we see the HALL as Connie comes from her room again as Dingle comes from the bathroom.

CONNIE. All right?

DINGLE (*louder*). All right.

She goes into the bathroom as Dingle rubs his head vigorously with a towel—even though we know he only put on an act with the water taps running. He looks in the bedroom, and instead of finding Joe, he finds his trousers again. —Then we see the BEDROOMS.

DINGLE. How did they get there?

Back he comes again, goes into the living room and Connie's bedroom searching for Joe as he calls out cautiously: "Bill! Bill!" Then he starts rhumba-ing, doing the "bumps" to phonograph music. And this cuts to the BATHROOM as Connie steps out of her skirt, and takes off her sweater. She brushes her hair, prepares the tub with bath salts, and turns on the water; the spray of the shower hits her. Angrily she rectifies the stream.—Now she coldcreams her face, and hearing the phonograph run down, she peeks out as Dingle comes from her quarters en route to his own bedroom. She ducks back, but sails out as she hears Dingle's door close. Simultaneously Joe dashes from the kitchen and Dingle, watching, almost swoons as they pass in the bathroom doorway—each unaware of the other. But as they reach their destinations and get full realization, both whirl and skid back into the hallway.—Connie and Joe stare silently at each other a moment.

JOE. You looking for somebody?

CONNIE. Who are you—how'd you get in here?

JOE. I live here.

At this point, Dingle steps into the bedroom for his hat.

CONNIE. Since when?

JOE. Since this morning.

Now Dingle, from the bedroom, starts along the hall to the outer door.

CONNIE. You don't by any chance happen to know a gentleman by the name of Mr. Benjamin Dingle, do you?

DINGLE (*turning, as he reaches the outer door*). You mean me, Miss Milligan?

CONNIE. Yes, I mean you. Have you anything to say for yourself?

DINGLE. Have you met my friend, Joe Carter?

CONNIE. I've met Joe Carter!

DINGLE. Oh, fine fella.

CONNIE. Mr. Dingle, answer me this: Who was it who located and leased this apartment? Who was it made the landlord repair and repaint it? Who was it bought draperies and furniture, and who was it knitted hand rugs, and who considers this apartment her home?

DINGLE. You.

CONNIE. Yeah. All right, then, answer me this: Who was it allowed you to sublet half of her apartment against her better judgment?

DINGLE. You.

CONNIE. Then why do you go behind my back and rent out my apartment to this—this—him?

DINGLE. But I only rented half of my half. Otherwise my friend, Joe here, woulda hadda sleep in the park.

CONNIE. Otherwise, your friend, Joe, here's gonna woulda hadda sleep in the park anyway. And you, too. Out! Both of you, out!

JOE (*stopping Dingle's move to leave*). Wait a minute. I'm paid up for a week. I gave him six bucks.

CONNIE. Give him back his six bucks!

DINGLE. Well, I hadda send some telegrams, and I had lunch, and—

JOE. And I don't move till I get my six bucks.

CONNIE. Give him a check.

JOE (*almost choking on a swallow of milk*). No checks!

CONNIE. Now look here, I don't owe you the six bucks. *HE* owes you the six bucks.

DINGLE. Just a minute, Miss Milligan. I gave you twelve dollars for a week's rent, and I've only been here one night. Give me back the difference and I'll have the money to pay him —with.

JOE. Yeah, that solves it.

Now Connie's in a spot, and she edges toward the living room doorway.

CONNIE. Yes, of course, only— Well— *I* bought a hat.

JOE. You bought a hat. Where's my money?

DINGLE. In her hat. (*He goes into the living room for it.*)

CONNIE. It is not. It's in his pocket, only he hasn't got it. (*As Dingle returns with her hat*) Now look here, what do you think you're doing?

DINGLE. Having a look at the hat. It's pretty, isn't it?

CONNIE. You've got a nerve!

DINGLE (*laying it atop her head*). Looks pretty on her, too, doesn't it?

CONNIE. It does not! (*Grabbing it off*) That isn't even the way it goes on. (*She takes the hat into the living room, drops it into its box, and returns.*) Now, where were we?

JOE. Looking for my six bucks. (*He turns from one to the other.*)

CONNIE. Well, I told you that I— How do you expect me to— *All right, stay!*

She goes into the living room, and slams the door. Joe and Dingle smile at each other conspiratorially, but as it develops, prematurely, for she immediately barges back in.

CONNIE. But just one week, remember!

And again she goes out, slamming the door. Resignedly, Dingle starts to lead Joe into their bedroom.

DINGLE. Come on. I'll show you the schedule.

JOE. What schedule?

DINGLE. For the steeple-chase tomorrow morning.

The scene fades out.

A montage of effects fades in. It is next morning, and we see Connie's clock reading 6:30 A.M., and then the alarm clock—7 A.M.—with the sound of Joe and Dingle awaking, and Connie's upset bed, her pajamas strewn about.

DINGLE'S VOICE. Bill! Bill!

JOE'S VOICE. Huh? Oh!—Joe.

DINGLE'S VOICE. Seven o'clock, Joe. Get up; get up!

JOE'S VOICE. Oh, thanks, Milligan.

DINGLE'S VOICE. Dingle. Get the schedule, Joe.

JOE'S VOICE. Schedule?

DINGLE'S VOICE. Yeah. Here it is. We're on time.

JOE'S VOICE (*making the sound of a train whistle*). Whoo-oo! Whoo-oo!

DINGLE'S VOICE. Shh!

Connie, dressed, crosses from the bathroom to the kitchen, spraying herself with perfume. Dingle peeks from his bedroom door, and opens it wider as he and Joe prepare to dash to the bathroom.

DINGLE. One, two, three, go!

They start out abreast, but get stuck in the door. Freeing themselves, they fall into single-file and play "train" down the corridor, "Choo-Chooing" as they go. From within the bathroom, their voices come over singing.

DINGLE. "Enter the bathroom seven 0 one."

JOE'S VOICE. "Wash your teeth, you son-of-a-gun."

DINGLE'S VOICE. "You know what Admiral Farragut said?"

BOTH VOICES. "'Damn the Torpedoes, Full Speed Ahead!'"

DINGLE'S VOICE. "Stick to the schedule, don't refrain."

JOE'S VOICE. "This joint's run like a railroad train."

DINGLE'S VOICE. "Back to the bedroom, the schedule said."

BOTH VOICES. "'Damn the Torpedoes, Full Speed Ahead!'" (*They re-enter from the bathroom, "choo-choo" back to the bedroom, and the door closes.*)

The scene dissolves to the UPPER HALL and KITCHEN. A colored porter is vacuuming the hall. Dingle and Joe pop their heads out, still playing "Train," and pop back in again. The scene moving over to the kitchen, we see Connie, groomed to a fault, breakfasting as Joe and Dingle "choo-choo" into the kitchen, and let off steam as they uncouple ...

JOE AND DINGLE. Good morning.

CONNIE. Good morning.

DINGLE. What's for breakfast?

CONNIE. You've had your breakfast.

DINGLE. When?

CONNIE. 7:07 A.M.

DINGLE. I guess we're kinda off schedule.

Joe sits watching Connie, fascinated, while Dingle pours his coffee.

CONNIE. What are you gawking at?

JOE. You. You look nice.

CONNIE. Oh!

JOE (*as Dingle pours his own coffee*). Hope I haven't upset your routine here.

CONNIE. Just stick to the schedule, is all I ask.

DINGLE (*pouring—significantly to Connie*). Well, it's rather nice to have a high-type, clean-cut, nice young fella at the table; better than nobody.

CONNIE (*feigning nonchalance*). I'm used to nobody.

DINGLE. You ought to have some high times around here, Joe. Young fellas don't come a dime a dozen in Washington. Eight girls to every fella, you know.

JOE. Yeah, well I haven't got time for that. Only gonna be in Washington for a week.

CONNIE (*interested*). Where're you going to? Where you came from?

JOE. Nope. Where they send me.

CONNIE. Who's they?

JOE. The Government.

CONNIE. Oh.

DINGLE. Too bad you're not going to be here regular. One less fella for the girls to look at. Like I told you, eight girls—

JOE. You're wasting conversation. I'm not interested.

DINGLE. But the girls are, eh, Miss Milligan?

CONNIE (*pointedly*). Those who haven't *got* any men friends are, I suppose. But in the case of a girl engaged to be married—

DINGLE. Engaged? You?

CONNIE (*primly*). Mr. Pendergast and I expect to be married in the very near future.

DINGLE. Mr. Pendergast?

CONNIE. Yes. Charles J. Pendergast.

JOE. Who's he?

DINGLE. Hasn't he something to do with the Housing Plan?

CONNIE (*proudly*). He certainly has. He just happens to be the Assistant Regional Coordinator of OPL.

JOE. Is that good or bad?

CONNIE. Eighty-six hundred dollars a year.

DINGLE. 'S good.

CONNIE. Furthermore, he's the youngest man to ever occupy the position of Assistant Regional Coordinator of OPL.

JOE. How old is he?

CONNIE. Only forty-two.

JOE (*startled*). Forty-two!

DINGLE. *Only* forty-two.

CONNIE. Forty-two is a good sane, safe age. When a man has reached forty-two, he knows a few things. Like Mr. Pendergast; he's an important man.

JOE. How long have you been engaged?

DINGLE. Two years, I bet.

CONNIE. Twenty-two months.

JOE. That's a long time for a girl to stick to one guy.

DINGLE. That depends on whether you're engaged to be married or just engaged. Why've you waited so long?

CONNIE. Mr. Pendergast—and I—felt it would be an unwise step to take in such times, with world conditions so unsettled.

DINGLE. World conditions *are* so unsettled, Miss Milligan, because people won't settle on things. They ought to stop pondering and start pushing. "Damn the Torpedoes, Full Speed Ahead!" (*Explanatorily to Joe*) That's what Admiral Farragut said.

JOE. He did, huh?

DINGLE. Yeah, at Mobile Bay.

CONNIE. You said that yesterday, Mr. Dingle.

DINGLE. And I meant it yesterday, Miss Milligan.

CONNIE (*loftily*). Well, Mr. Pendergast and I don't need your advice.

DINGLE. What did you say his first name was?

CONNIE. Charles J.

DINGLE. Don't you ever call him by it? Like Charlie or Chuck or something?

CONNIE. Call Mr. Pendergast Charlie?!

JOE. Why not?

CONNIE (*rising majestically*). Of course, you don't seem to realize that Mr. Pendergast is the type of man who has twice been to dinner at the White House.

DINGLE (*dryly*). Worst food in Washington.

JOE. You mean with the President?

CONNIE. Yes.

JOE. Well, I'll bet the President's wife calls him by his first name sometimes.

Being annoyed and unable to localize it, she tries personalities.

CONNIE. You—look—messy.

JOE. Huh?

CONNIE. Don'tcha ever brush your hair?

JOE. I suppose Mr. Pendergast brushes his hair every hour on the hour.

CONNIE. Mr. Pendergast *has* no hair.

She goes out, slamming the door, and Joe and Dingle resume their "train" game.

The scene dissolves to the KITCHEN and UPPER STAIRS, and we see Dingle and Joe at the breakfast table, resuming the "train" game as Connie descends the stairs—en route to work. This dissolves to the exterior of 1708 "D" STREET as Connie emerges from the apartment building. The Fiat with the girls drives up to the curb, Connie gets in, and the car drives out.

This dissolves to a PARK at a CONSTRUCTION SITE, and we see: Senator Noonan—a secretary taking notes—Dingle, Pendergast and a Housing Committee at a long table. There are also men and women getting trays at a tent canteen, sitting at picnic-like tables under trees. In the background huge structures are under construction. Dingle is discovered standing, addressing the body as the scene opens, gesturing toward the project.

DINGLE. This project illustrates my point. If the employees are housed near the plant in which they work, a full working day can be saved each week. (*His words are greeted with ad libs of agreement, "That's logical," etc.*) Time is one thing we cannot manufacture, but we can make speed. (*There is applause.*) If this Committee will cut out all the red tape and give us permission to go ahead, I'll get things done!

He takes his seat amid applause and ad libs of agreement. "That's the truth!" "That's what we wanted to hear, Dingle!" "Okay, Dingle, we're behind you!" etc. Pendergast leans forward to speak along the table to Senator Noonan.

PENDERGAST. Mr. Chairman! Mr. Chairman! Senator Noonan!

NOONAN. What is it?

PENDERGAST. What Mr. Dingle proposes is impossible. There are contractual obligations that have to be cleared up.

DINGLE (*jumping to his feet*). Then let whoever has to clear them up, clear them up while we're clearing up the ground around Defense Plants for building! (*The Committee applauds, but Dingle rides over the noise.*) We must do away with all forms and regulations. Cut all the red tape. Full speed ahead!

Again he sits down amid applause and cries of "Hear! Hear!"

PENDERGAST. Gentlemen, may I inquire the cost of the housing units you propose to erect?

DINGLE. *Cost!?* There's a war on, and you're asking about cost!

Ad libs of approval of Dingle's stand. "Who cares about the cost!" "Dingle's right. Time is everything." "Yes, sure." Pendergast finally gets to his feet.

PENDERGAST. I'm sorry, gentlemen, but as Assistant Regional Coordinator of OPL, it's my *duty* to inquire about the cost. Furthermore, I'd like to call to Mr. Dingle's attention, Article 845732, which states that the laws of a community must regulate the construction in that community. Now, that's a fact in Pennsylvania and New Jersey.

He sits down. Quietly Dingle leans forward, and speaks to him across the intervening Committeemen.

DINGLE. You said you represent the OPL, didn't you?

PENDERGAST. Precisely.

DINGLE. I don't think I caught your name.

PENDERGAST. Pendergast.

DINGLE. Not Charles J. Pendergast?

PENDERGAST. That's correct.

DINGLE. By golly! I should have known it!

As Pendergast glances sharply at him and Dingle puffs his cigar, smiling to himself, the scene fades out.

PART THREE

Connie's fingers are putting a card in the slot under 2B on the door of her apartment. It reads: "MILLIGAN-DINGLE-CARTER." This dissolves to CONNIE's BEDROOM at night. In pajamas, Connie lounges on her bed and writes an entry in her diary:

"Thurs. June 25—
Those two! Prying all the time! Questions about Mr. P. Wise-cracks. Very *un*funny. So mad today I could cry. Don't think I can stand them another day."

From their bedroom, Dingle's and Joe's singing comes over the scene:

BOTH VOICES.
"Now Jimmy Doolittle flew overseas,
Wanted to nip at the Nipponese.
Cleared a cloud and looked below,
And said, 'By Golly! There's To-ki-o!'
Oh, Jimmy Doolittle, he understood,
He dood his duty and he dood it good.
Somewhere Jimmy had heard it said,
'Damn the Torpedoes, Full Speed Ahead!'"

Two pages of the diary turn slowly. Connie is still writing:

"Sat. June 27—
Good fun! Beginning to like! Dingle cooked dinner. Wonderful. Joe turning out to be high-type clean-cut nice young fellow."

This scene fading out, the ROOF of the APARTMENT BUILDING fades in. It is Sunday. The view travels down the water tower to girls in bathing suits lined up to take showers beneath it. Residents and visitors are making a resort on the rooftop, children playing games, etc., while Joe's and Dingle's voices are heard as they read the funnies.

JOE'S VOICE. "Zzzzz! Chug—chug—chug. Dick Tracy's car streaks thru the night!"

DINGLE'S VOICE. "I am out to get the Leopard Lady single-handed."

JOE'S VOICE. "The old brownstone house looks harmless, but it is really the hideout of the Leopard Lady and her gang."

DINGLE'S VOICE. "This hallway is black as the night. Boards creak. Squeak—squeak."

JOE'S VOICE. "Bang! The door opens!"

DINGLE'S VOICE. "Face to face with the Leopard Lady, herself!"

JOE'S VOICE. "You have arrived as I expected, Mr. Tracy. Now I will make a bargain with you."

DINGLE'S VOICE. "What fiendish plan have you now?"

And now we see Joe and Dingle together, with Connie beyond in a sunsuit, knitting. All three are lying amid pillows, Victrola, etc., on blankets.

JOE. "With the Death Ray ours, we can conquer and rule the world, you and I, Dick Tracy."

DINGLE. "Count me out of your plan, Leopard Lady, for I mean to bring you to justice."

JOE. "Have you forgotten that I have the Death Ray?"

DINGLE. "Yes, but without my help, it is powerless!"

JOE. "Perhaps some boiling oil on

your back will persuade you to help me."

DINGLE. Gosh! That Dick Tracy is sure playing with dynamite!

JOE. He sure is.

CONNIE (*annoyed*). Is that the best you can do with your time?

JOE. Gotta keep up with what's going on.

DINGLE. Missed two Sundays with Superman once, and haven't felt right since.

CONNIE. Seems to me you'd read something beneficial.

JOE. Like what?

CONNIE. Like the Editorials or the columns. All well-informed people read the Columnists.

DINGLE. Such as Mr. Pendergast, I suppose.

CONNIE. You suppose right. Mr. Pendergast always reads the Columnists.

JOE. Are they funny?

DINGLE. Sometimes. But no pictures.

CONNIE (*dropping a stitch*). Oh! Darn it!

DINGLE (*to Joe*). Hand me that section, will you? (*As Joe hands it to him*) I want to see if anyone I know is being born today. Well, well, well. Listen to this. (*Pretending to read*) "Born today to Mr. and Mrs. Charles J. Pendergast, a son. Mrs. Pendergast, the former Constance Milligan, is doing nicely. Mr. Pendergast is doing all right, too. He gets eighty-six hundred dollars a year. The baby arrived three minutes ahead of schedule. Mr. Pendergast refused delivery."

CONNIE. Funny. (*Rising with her knitting bag*) Very, very funny.

JOE (*getting up*). Here, I'll help you.

CONNIE. This conversation is much too witty for me, so if you don't mind, I'll just leave you two up here to laugh at each other's jokes.

JOE. What did *I* say?

CONNIE. Any minute now, you may say something so funny that I might laugh myself to death.

JOE. But I didn't say a thing.

DINGLE. Maybe *I* said something.

CONNIE. If you're not too weak from laughing, bring these things with you when you come down.

Connie goes over the stile toward the exit, and Joe prepares to resume his sunbath.

JOE. What's she mad about?

DINGLE. Because you and the man she's engaged to are not anything alike, and he ought to be. (*Lighting a cigar as he gathers her blankets*) "Dorrie Miller was a colored gob,
Holding down a mess-boy's job.
But when the trouble with the Japs began,
Proved that he was a fighting man.
Dropped his ladle and he grabbed a gun,
Blazed away at the sons of the sun,
Said while he fed them red-hot lead,
'Damn the Torpedoes, Full Speed Ahead!'"

He discovers Connie's diary in the folds of the blanket, and abandons his task in order to look at it.

DINGLE. You were right, Mr. Dingle. A diary! (*He kneels, perusing it.*)

JOE. I wouldn't fool with that if I were you.

DINGLE. Hey, she's not mad at you. She likes you.

JOE. You're nuts.

DINGLE (*as he lies down again*). Says you're dumb but cute.

JOE. She's no bargain herself.

DINGLE. Smart enough to get you going.

JOE. I don't even know she's alive.

DINGLE. How come, then, last night you said her name in your sleep?

JOE. I did not! (*Then, unsure*) I did?

DINGLE. Take my word.

JOE. Well, a guy's apt to say anything in his sleep. Maybe I was really hollering at her.

DINGLE. No, you were cooing. Like this: (*Softly*) Con-nie!

JOE. You make me sick!

DINGLE. Con-nie!

JOE. All right; all right!

DINGLE. She says you are good company and nice to have around. She says you're good-looking, too, and she's going to try to make you . . . (*turning a page*) over.

JOE. No fooling, boy, I wouldn't read that if I were you.

DINGLE. She says you've turned out to be a high-type, clean-cut, nice young fellow.

JOE. She does? (*Glancing back over his shoulder, he sees Connie returning slowly, aware of their occupation, and calls out warningly, á la train.*) Whoo-oo! Whoo-oo!

Dingle offers her her diary as she steps between them.

DINGLE. Found your diary kicking about. (*As she snatches it*) You ought to be careful, Miss Milligan. You never know what kind of people are hanging around. (*She disdains him, and silently whirls around and leaves.*)

JOE. I told you you shouldn't have done it. (*As Dingle starts gathering their paraphernalia*) What're you going to do?

DINGLE. Find out what she's going to do.

Suddenly, as they start out, there is a deluge of rain, and people scatter in a hurry, in every direction.

The scene dissolving, we see the BEDROOMS and the APARTMENT HALL and find Connie sobbing on her bed as Dingle and Joe enter the hallway with the blankets. They stop by the living room doorway.

JOE. You'd better go in and square yourself. Go ahead. You remember that stuff about the torpedoes.

Aided by Joe's shove, Dingle steps into the living room calling her name softly, and we see both the LIVING ROOM and CONNIE'S BEDROOM.

DINGLE. Miss Milligan! Connie! Connie! (*As she approaches*) We brought your things down.

CONNIE. That was a miserable thing to do. If there's one thing that's cheap and—and—

DINGLE. Contemptible?

CONNIE. —contemptible, it's being caught reading someone else's diary!

DINGLE. If I caught anyone reading *my* diary—

CONNIE. In front of him, too.

JOE (*in the doorway*). Connie, I was hardly listening.

CONNIE. There's some things that are private, Mr. Dingle, and when people go sticking their noses into them, it's just too much, that's all! And yours is a very long nose, Mr. Dingle. I've tried to put up with you, but you've done nothing but meddle and pry ever since you came into this house. You'd just better pack up your stuff, and when I get home from work tomorrow, you'd better be gone, that's all. *Both of you!*

She whirls and goes out of the living room, and Dingle shoves Joe into the hall as they, too, go out and the scene fades out.

And now the SPARE BEDROOM fades in and we see Joe and Dingle packing as Dingle sings:

DINGLE.
"I'm Pierre de Ponton de Paris, de Paris,
I drink o' the win' o' the vee, of the vee,
I ride out each day in my little coupe,
And I tell you I'm something to see.
I care not what others may say,
I'm in love with Rosalee, charming Rose, Pretty Rose,
And my Rose is in love with me."

Joe adds a "Boom, Boom!" and Dingle starts a second song.

DINGLE.
"Now Doctor Wassell of the U.S.A.,
Was under fire down Java way.
Twelve wounded men were in his care,
And not an ambulance anywhere.
One by one he got 'em away,
Got 'em on a boat to Aus-tra-li-ay,
And every one of those wounded said,
'Damn the Torpedoes, Full Speed Ahead!' "

This dissolves to the UPPER HALL as Dingle descends the stairs with overcoat and baggage, and then Joe leaves the apartment, and descends the stairs, en route to headquarters office.

This dissolves to the UPPER HALL at night as Joe, documents in hand, ascends the stairs. Then we see him coming into the SPARE BEDROOM and finishing packing—including a uniform.

We again see the exterior of 1708 "D" STREET as the Fiat moves up to the curb. Connie alights, and waves after the rest of the girls in the car which drives away. Then Connie goes up the steps into the building, wearily, following which we see her in the UPPER HALLWAY: Connie coming up the stairs slowly and going into her apartment.

This cuts to a view of the entire APARTMENT, as it would be seen from the roof. Connie enters, and sits on the edge of the bed. She hangs her hat on the post of the bed. It drops, and simultaneously Joe slams the dresser drawer in the next room. Unaware that he is there, Connie pauses, puzzled. She removes first one shoe, then the other, getting an "echo" in each instance. She crosses to the windows, and opens one. —Joe hearing her, opens one of his windows. They look out, come face to face, and momentarily duck back. But they gather their forces, and lean out again.

CONNIE. Oh, it's you.

JOE. Uh-huh.

CONNIE. Well, I thought the arrangements were that you'd—

JOE. Yeah, yeah. Didn't have time to pack this morning. Had to get my orders, so just came back to pack now, and well, as long as I'm here, I might as well give you this.

He takes a letter from his coat pocket, which he hands to her around the windows, and Connie sits down at the end of her bed to read it aloud.

CONNIE. "I have moved out, but I wish to exonerate Joseph Carter, my former roommate, in the south half of 2B, of all implication of responsibility in being caught reading your diary. The fault is entirely mine, and Joseph Carter even protested my disgraceful action, as follows—quote—Oh, I would not do that if I were you—unquote. And wouldn't either because he's such a high-type, clean-cut, nice young fellow and—"

JOE. Yeah. Well, you can skip all that.

CONNIE. I am. "etcetera, etcetera. Signed, Benjamin Dingle."

JOE. I want that for my files. (*He reaches around the windows for it.*)

CONNIE. What's the fixed-up alibi for?

JOE. Are you kidding? Does that sound like me or Dingle?

CONNIE. How do I know you didn't write it?

JOE (*closing his bag*). You don't.

CONNIE. And even if he did write it, how do I know it's the truth?

JOE. You don't. Only it's the truth.

CONNIE. I don't know what to believe.

JOE. Well, I'm going to move out anyway—

And he goes to the hall. At this, Connie rushes back to meet him in the hall, and is nonplussed when he meets her as he enters the living room doorway.

JOE. So just to show you there's no hard feelings, I'd like to give you this.

He pushes a carton at her, sending her backwards into a chair with the carton on her lap.

CONNIE. Oh! . . . Why?

Joe is busy removing the carton, placing an overnight case on her lap.

JOE. Peace offering.

CONNIE. You didn't have to do that.

JOE. It's nothing much. Just a sort of genuine topgrain cowhide traveling bag with all the accessories here.

He sits on the end of the desk to lean close over her as he demonstrates the bag.

JOE. You have special gadgets back here. It has everything.

CONNIE. Be careful! It might break!

JOE. No, it has special eight-inch hinges. (*Joe lifts and drops the lid to demonstrate this feature.*) Can't hurt it, no matter what you do.

CONNIE. Are you sure?

JOE (*pulling out tissue*). Yeah. That shouldn't be there.

CONNIE. It's really beautiful. Smell. (*She lifts the container, and Joe's nose jams into the goo.*) Isn't that lovely? . . . Oh, but I couldn't take it. Mr. Pendergast would object, and he'd have a perfect right.

JOE. Well, then, just call it a wedding present. You can use it on your honeymoon.

CONNIE. Oh, I couldn't take one man's bag on another man's honeymoon.

JOE. Well, just keep it at home then. Look, Connie:—"C" for Constance.

CONNIE. You shouldn't have done it.

JOE. I didn't.—"C" stands for Carter, too. I got it for myself but the Government won't let me take it where I'm going. So you might as well keep it.

CONNIE. Oh. Well maybe you can take it back.

JOE. Look, Connie, I want to give it to you. Will it kill you to do me a favor and keep it? All I'm asking of you is to accept it as a gift—no strings attached—one genuine cowhide traveling bag. Will you, please?

CONNIE. I'm so embarrassed!

JOE. Please!

CONNIE. All right. It's so beautiful.

JOE (*rising*). No strings attached. (*He drops the keys into her palm.*) Oh, here are the keys.

CONNIE. Where are you going? California?

JOE. Uh-Uh. Africa.

She drops her bag to the floor and rises, startled. He raises a restraining hand.

JOE. Ask me no questions. Military secret. (*As they walk through the doorway into the apartment hall*) There are certain Government regulations and you can't tell people everything. I know there are a lot of things to be explained, but I'll write you about it.

CONNIE. When are you leaving?

JOE. In a couple of days.

CONNIE. To Africa in two days?

JOE. Sure.

CONNIE. You can't go looking like that.

She takes his handkerchief to remove a daub from his nose. He takes the handkerchief and finishes the job himself.

JOE. Oh, here.

CONNIE. Where are you going now?

JOE. Look for another place.

CONNIE. For just two days?

JOE. Sure. Can't sleep in the park.

CONNIE. Don't you think it's kinda silly to move for just two days?

JOE. You mean—? (*He looks off toward his room. She nods.*) Oh, boy, swell! Because when I get to Africa and the guys ask me what I did my last two days here, I'd sound like a dope saying I'd spent my last two days looking for a place.

CONNIE. Yes, I guess you would.

JOE. 'Cause you know guys like that, they'd expect you to kinda spend the last two days going places and seeing the town.

CONNIE. Sure. Well, thank you for the bag.

JOE. I mean, with somebody.

CONNIE. Oh, yeah. Well, thanks for the bag.

JOE. Say, do you think it would be all right if we went out and had dinner together?

CONNIE. You forget I'm engaged. And I don't think he'd like it.

JOE. No, he wouldn't.

CONNIE. And besides, I think I have a date with him tonight.

JOE. Oh. Well, that fixes that.

As he starts into his room, she comes forward and stops him.

CONNIE. Oh, Mr. Carter!

JOE (*eagerly*). Yes?

CONNIE. What time have you?

JOE. Oh. (*Disappointed*) Seven-thirty.

CONNIE. Well, he's supposed to call by eight o'clock. Of course, sometimes he gets tied up in a conference and can't even telephone, so if that happens, naturally the date's off. So I'll wait for him till eight o'clock and if he doesn't phone by then, I suppose it would be all right. After all, you're only going to be here a short time and you're working for the Government, and it's everyone's patriotic duty to do everything you can. (*At this point, the telephone rings.*)

JOE. Maybe it's the wrong number.

CONNIE (*picking up the phone*). Hello.

DINGLE'S VOICE. Can I speak to Carter?

CONNIE. Oh, it's you. What's the matter with you?

This cuts to DINGLE'S ROOM in the WINTON-JAMES HOTEL.

DINGLE. Gotta cold.

CONNIE'S VOICE. Oh, that's too bad. You ought to do something about that.

DINGLE. I am doing something. I'm sneezing!

CONNIE'S VOICE. Take care of yourself ... Just a minute. (*She hands the phone to Joe.*) It's for you. Mr. Dingle.

JOE'S VOICE. Hello.

DINGLE. Hello, Bill?

JOE. No, Joe. What's the matter with you?

This cuts to CONNIE'S APARTMENT.

DINGLE'S VOICE. I've got a cold.

JOE. Well, you sound awful. You better take something for that.

DINGLE'S VOICE. Yeah. How about going out with me for dinner tonight?

JOE. I don't know whether I can or not.

DINGLE'S VOICE. Well, when you find out, call me at the Winton-James Hotel.

JOE. I won't know until eight o'clock. I think I have a date.

DINGLE'S VOICE. Milligan?

JOE. Mm-hmm. If I don't, I'll meet you there.

DINGLE'S VOICE. Well, goodbye, Bill—Joe.

JOE. Goodbye, Mill—Dingle. (*Joe hangs up, and sits staring off abstractedly.*)

CONNIE. I guess I'd better get dressed.

JOE. O.K. (*Still lost in thought, and suddenly realizing*) Oh! Excuse me!

He jumps up, and goes to his own room, as the scene dissolves to a view of the CLOCK in the TOWER, against the SKYLINE at night: The clock reaches 8:00 P.M., as seen through a pair of binoculars.

This cuts to the BEDROOMS, and we see that Joe is standing in his windows watching the clock through binoculars. Blinds in Connie's room are raised and she, too, looks off at the clock. As it hits eight, each makes a dash for the APARTMENT HALL, and they stop in confusion as they come face to face.—She turns from his admiring gaze.

JOE. Boy, you look lovely!

CONNIE. Thank you.

JOE. It's eight o'clock.

CONNIE. It is?

JOE. Yeah, and our friend hasn't telephoned, has he?

CONNIE. No, he hasn't.

JOE. Well, in that case— (*He starts walking to the door.*)

CONNIE. Yes, in that case, I guess it would be all right to—

As they reach the outer door the doorbell sounds.

CONNIE. It can't be Mr. Pendergast. He always phones from downstairs.

JOE. He does?

CONNIE. Yes.

She opens the door, revealing a twelve-year-old Brooklynese boy. He snatches his cap from his head as he greets her eagerly, urgently. He is Morton Rodakiewicz.

MORTON. Hello, Miss Milligan.

CONNIE. Hello.

MORTON. Could I see you please, Miss Milligan, for a few minutes? It's very important; it's about a decision I have to make. Could I see you for a few minutes alone, please?

CONNIE. Well, couldn't it wait until tomorrow?

MORTON. No, it can't wait till tomorrow. It's important.

He barges in, and comes face to face with Joe. Ignoring him, he thumbs toward him only.

MORTON. Who's this?

CONNIE (*putting her arm around Morton, and addressing Joe*). This is my fella. He lives downstairs.

JOE. How do you do, Mr. Pendergast.

MORTON. My name's Morton Rodakiewicz! (*To Connie*) I gotta see you alone. (*Blithely, he crosses to the living room.*)

CONNIE. I'm sorry. I'll just be a minute.

She follows Morton into the living room. Joe crosses to open the door to his own room, and lounges against the jamb watching Connie and Morton in the living room across the hall.

The LIVING ROOM: When Connie enters, Morton is gazing off into space. She takes a position in front of the telephone on the table, and reaches behind her to remove the phone from its cradle before Morton snaps back to the present. He jumps to his feet, again pulling off his cap.

MORTON. Who's he?

CONNIE. He's a friend of mine.

MORTON. Where does he get that "Pendergast" stuff?

CONNIE. He was just joking, Morton. Now, what do you want, because I'm in a terrible hurry.

MORTON (*sitting down, speaking weightily*). Do I want to join the Boy Scouts? Or don't I?

CONNIE. Of course, you do.

MORTON. But I'm not the camp-craft type. So should I join the Boy Scouts because I don't like hunting and fishing and hiking and camp-craft and ought to? Or should I *not* join because I don't like hunting and fishing and hiking? And camp-craft.

CONNIE. Yes, definitely.

MORTON. It's some problem. A person should know is he the camp-craft type.

CONNIE. Morton, I think you ought to join the Boy Scouts right now.

MORTON. But Joe Thompson thought he was the camp-craft type and he didn't like it at all, and he never got to be a second-class Scout, even. Was I to go into it, I would want to be better than a tenderfoot Scout, only.

CONNIE. I'm sure you'd be better than Joe Carter.

MORTON. Who?

CONNIE. Joe Thompson.

MORTON (*jumping up*). You said Joe Carter.

CONNIE (*snapping him off*). I know it.

MORTON (*abashed, apologizingly*). Did I say something?

CONNIE. No, Morton, you didn't.

MORTON (*sitting down again*). On the other hand, isn't it my duty to my country to train myself for responsibility, first aid, citizenship, conservation, the putting out of incendiary bombs, rope-tying and all like that—by joining the Boy Scouts?

CONNIE. I'm going to be terribly disappointed if you don't join the Boy Scouts *tonight!*

MORTON (*jumping up*). I'll do it! Only I can't do it tonight because it's too late, but tomorrow I'll do it.

In her eagerness to get rid of him, Connie has started toward the hall door leadingly. But she's uncovered the table with the telephone off its cradle.

MORTON. Oh, your phone's off the hook. I'll fix it. (*He replaces it.*) There's my good deed for today. Already I'm a Boy Scout. (*He crosses to the door, and turns back.*) Will you be disappointed in me if I wait until tomorrow?

CONNIE. No. Morton.

MORTON. Oh, that's good.

As he starts down the hall, the telephone rings. He returns, and points to it.

MORTON. Phone's ringing there. There's your phone.

CONNIE. Thank you, Morton. Hello.

PENDERGAST'S VOICE. Constance?

CONNIE. Yes, Charles. How do you feel?

PENDERGAST'S VOICE. Oh, I feel wonderful.

CONNIE. Oh, you do?

PENDERGAST'S VOICE. Yes. I'm waiting downstairs.

CONNIE. Well, I'll be right down. (*She hangs up, and comes to the hall, to Joe.*) That's my date. I'm sorry.

JOE. Have a good time.

CONNIE. Thank you.

As she goes down the hall and passes Morton, he offers his bit.

MORTON. Have a good time.

CONNIE. Thank you, Morton.

She goes to the outer hall and descends the steps. Morton, too, starts down the steps, but watches Joe take a pair of binoculars and look down toward the street through the window.

MORTON. Hey, what're you looking at?

JOE (*without turning*). The Capitol Dome.

As Morton starts retracing his steps, the scene cuts to the exterior of 1708 "D" STREET, and we get a binocular shot of a sedan parked at the curb. Pendergast and Connie walk in from the right. He opens the car door, lifting but not removing his hat. Connie gets in, Pendergast closes the door, and goes around the rear of the car toward the driver's seat. Then we see JOE's BEDROOM and the APARTMENT HALL.

MORTON. You ought to not be looking out of those spy glasses.

JOE. Beat it.

MORTON. That's pretty suspicious activity.

JOE. Scram.

MORTON. You can get in awful serious trouble doing that.

JOE (*turning from the window*). Knock off.

MORTON. Everybody's giving their spy glasses to the Navy. I read it in the paper. Why don't you give your spy glasses to the Navy, too?

JOE (*turning from the window*).

And he bares his teeth in a Jappy smile, plunging toward Morton who shrieks and flees.

The scene dissolves to a TAPROOM at night. Here a girl entertainer, Sugar, and a chorus do a Military Revue, Sugar making forays into the audience to plant red greasy kisses atop various bald pates. She passes Pendergast as she eyes his obvious toupee, finishes the number, and the chorus files out. Joe and Dingle check their hats in the corridor outside the revolving door.

CHECK GIRL. Check your hat, please?

JOE. Oh!

Caught in the revolving door, he puts his hat on the rail and sends it around with the door, retrieving his stub in similar manner. The Head Waiter approaches.

DINGLE. Two.

HEAD WAITER. It'll be a couple of minutes before I'll have a table for you gentlemen. There's plenty of room at the bar.

This cuts to the CROWDED BAR where Dingle and Joe take stools vacated by a couple of women, and a girl bartender comes for their order. Another girl near Joe gives him the eye.

BARKEEP. Your order, gentlemen.

DINGLE. A beer.

JOE. Make it two.

BARKEEP. Two beers.

Goggle-eyed, she leaves for their order. Two girls reach from behind them to place glasses for refilling, declining Joe's and Dingle's seats.

GIRLS. No, just ordering. Thank you very much.

DINGLE. What'd I tell you? Eight girls to every fellow.

JOE. Yeah. What'd I tell you? Not interested.

DINGLE. Cheer up, Joe. We're out to have a good time. The only way to have a good time is to plunge right in. "Damn the Torpedoes, Full Speed Ahead!"

WAITER (*from the floor for orders*). Excuse me. Two beers!

DINGLE (*singing*).
"And so it is, and so it goes,
We've got to be up and on our toes,
We learn from what has gone before,
There ain't no other way to win a war.
The cowards have their ifs and buts,
But we've got plenty of Farraguts,
Are we gonna do what the Admiral said?" (*Joe joins in.*)

JOE AND DINGLE.
"Yes! Yes!
Damn the Torpedoes, Full Speed Ahead!
Damn the Torpedoes, Full Speed Ahead!

Damn the Torpedoes, Full Speed Ahead!

Damn the Torpedoes, Full Speed Ahead!"

WAITER (*taking the tray of beers, and leaving*).
"Damn the Torpedoes, Full Speed Ahead!"

JOE AND DINGLE.
"Damn the Torpedoes, Full Speed Ahead!

Damn the Torpedoes, Full Speed Ahead!

Damn the Torpedoes, Full Speed Ahead!"

HEADWAITER. I have your table for you now, gentlemen.

And now a close view shows CONNIE and PENDERGAST seated at a table. The waiter passes them with his tray of beers, still singing "Damn the Torpedoes, Full Speed Ahead!" whereupon Connie realizes at once that Joe or Dingle are somewhere and starts craning her neck to find them at the bar.

PENDERGAST. Constance. Constance!

CONNIE. Oh, yes, Charles.

PENDERGAST. I've been thinking lately. We've been shilly-shallying around too long. The time has come to stop pondering and start pushing. I've come to the conclusion that we ought to get married right away.

CONNIE. You have?

PENDERGAST. Yes. Yes, I have. We've put it off long enough. From now on, it's "Full Speed Ahead"—with reservations.

CONNIE. Well, I thought you said something about world conditions being so unsettled.

PENDERGAST. Exactly. No reason for us to be unsettled, too. How about Saturday afternoon? We have a half holiday.

The orchestra starts playing a number, and a Red, White and Blue Chorus files out and dances.

PENDERGAST. I'll apply for the license tomorrow. Why, we can be back at work bright and early Monday morning.

CONNIE. Don't you think we ought to make some plans and things?

PENDERGAST. Let me worry about the plans, my dear. Saturday's the day.

We see Joe and Dingle are stymied between the lines of the chorus. Joe finally escapes.—Pendergast moves his chair closer, encircles Connie and leans to kiss her just as Joe, passing, pauses interestedly behind her chair. Whereupon Pendergast looks up and Joe starts to move on.—Dingle, meantime, tears himself away from the fascinating chorus, and starts after Joe. Again Pendergast starts to kiss Connie and again Joe pauses to look; and the third time, Connie looks up and Joe sees her. He rushes off, but Dingle, passing, recognizes Pendergast and stops.

DINGLE. Pendergast!

PENDERGAST. How do you do, Mr. Dingle.

DINGLE. Well, well, this is a happy coincidence. Hey, Joe! Joe! Come here! (*Pendergast rises. Joe returns.*) Meet my friend, Joe Carter. Joe, this is Charles J. Pendergast.

JOE AND PENDERGAST. How do you do?

The chorus finishes the number, and starts filing out.

PENDERGAST. This is my fiancée, Miss Milligan. Mr. Dingle and Mr. Carter.

DINGLE. Delighted, Miss Milligan.

JOE. Hello.

CONNIE. Why, I— (*To Dingle*) How do you do? (*Sidewise up at Joe*) Mr. Carter?

PENDERGAST. Won't you sit down?

DINGLE. Yeah, sit down, Joe. Here, have a chair.

JOE. Thank you, Ben.

DINGLE. I have a feeling we've met before, Miss Milligan.

CONNIE. Hm?

DINGLE. But, no, I guess not.

CONNIE. I guess not, too.

PENDERGAST. Mr. Dingle is in Washington to discuss the Housing Plan.

CONNIE. Indeed.

PENDERGAST. Are you also interested in the Housing situation, Mr. Carter?

JOE. Well, yes, I was. But I'm not anymore.

PENDERGAST. You're not anymore? I don't understand.

JOE. I mean, I found a spot.

PENDERGAST. Oh.

DINGLE. And very nice, too.

PENDERGAST. You're very fortunate, Mr. Carter.

JOE. Yes, I'm downright lucky.

PENDERGAST. I suppose you're crowded like everyone else in Washington.

JOE. Huh, uh, I'm crowded like *nobody* else.

PENDERGAST. Then you realize what a problem we're up against.

JOE. Yes. I wish I had more time to look into it.

DINGLE. Joe's been working pretty hard. In a few days, he'll be working a lot harder. Tonight I want him to have a little fun. What do you say we have some fun?

PENDERGAST. It certainly *is* a problem.

JOE. You mean—having fun?

CONNIE. Mr. Pendergast is speaking of the Housing Problem.

JOE. Oh.

DINGLE. Yes, Joe. Do you know there are cases on record where two and three people are practically *forced* to live in the same room?

JOE. No!

PENDERGAST. Yes. I tell you the condition is deplorable.

JOE. Oh.

DINGLE. Kinda cozy, though, don't you think?

PENDERGAST. It's nothing to be facetious about, Mr. Dingle. It's the most crowded state any city has ever been in.

JOE. That's bad, huh?

PENDERGAST. Mr. Carter, I lie awake nights, worrying about the situation.

JOE. No!

DINGLE. And little do you know how much you've got to worry about, too.

PENDERGAST. Oh, yes, I do.

DINGLE. Oh, no, you don't.

PENDERGAST. Oh, yes, I do.

A rhumba starts. Joe and Connie "dance" in their chairs, as the scene continues.

DINGLE. Oh, no, you don't!

PENDERGAST. At the present time, at

least thirty thousand four-party units could be absorbed just by the incoming populace alone.

DINGLE. I wonder how many single-party units it would take to relieve the present situation. Make a guess.

PENDERGAST. I don't have to guess. I know. One hundred and eighty-seven thousand, six hundred and eighty-three.

DINGLE. My word, Pendergast, you're a wizard! I never dreamed you were so well informed.

PENDERGAST. After all, Mr. Dingle, it's my business. And I know my business.

DINGLE. Have you got facts and figures to substantiate—

PENDERGAST. I certainly have.

DINGLE. Well, well— Say, why don't you young people dance while Charlie and I talk this thing over?

Joe hops to it, and starts tugging Connie by the wrist.

CONNIE. I don't think I'd better. Charles—

PENDERGAST. Yes, yes, it's all right. Run along.

Joe and Connie go to the dance floor, and start to rhumba.

PENDERGAST. Let's see, now. Mr. Dingle, I'm delighted to see a man get a nice trim, single unit. These prefabricated jobs are much more solid than you think. You want to know the facts and figures?

DINGLE. Yes, I do.

PENDERGAST. Have you got something to write on?

DINGLE. How's that?

PENDERGAST. Yes, that's fine. Thank you. Now if you multiply the single unit costs by the total labor over all, you arrive at this figure.

DINGLE. That's right. Charlie, my boy, you astonish me.

PENDERGAST. You know, Mr. Dingle, sometimes I astonish myself. Now take the figure ten thousand. Break it down into its component parts and what have you got? You have a curve. We have this all charted at the office on charts and graphs.

DINGLE. How do you work out a three-party unit plan?

PENDERGAST. Three-party unit? Approximately the same thing. Watch this. There it is. Let's see. Oh, that music! I can't concentrate.

DINGLE. Charlie, my boy, you don't know how you've simplified this whole problem for everyone concerned. Come up to my suite where you *can* concentrate. With a little luck, we can have this whole plan ready to present to the Board tomorrow morning.

PENDERGAST. All right.

As Dingle drags him past the dance floor, where Pendergast ducks electric fans and reaches for his precious toupee, Dingle calls to Joe dancing with Connie.

DINGLE. Take good care of Miss Milligan.

JOE. Don't worry.

PENDERGAST. Constance! Constance! I'll be back!

Dingle drags him on again, and Pendergast checks his toupee as they duck under a palm. Pendergast goes through the revolving door to the checkroom while Dingle pauses to buy gum from a girl. This he hurriedly chews as he follows through the revolving door, puts it in the crown of a hat placed on the counter for another guest, and slams it onto Pendergast's head. Irately the man removes his hat from Pendergast's head, taking the toupee with it, puts it on his own head, and exits with his party to the elevators. Unaware of his misfortune, Pendergast dons his own derby and starts with Dingle to the elevators. But as the guest removes his hat in the elevator, taking the toupee with it, Pendergast realizes his plight, jumps into the elevator, and cowers in the corner.

In the taproom Connie and Joe dance on in their own little heaven.

JOE. Now we are alone.

CONNIE. At last. . . . You don't suppose Mr. Dingle will say anything to Mr. Pendergast that Mr. Pendergast won't understand, do you? . . . Joe? . . . Answer me, Joe.

JOE. I can't talk while I'm dancing.

CONNIE. Who taught you to rhumba? Some girl, I'll bet. Was she nice?

JOE. Not half as nice as you are.

The dance ends, and a couple of girls stare and then barge up.

MISS ALLEN. Connie! Hello!

MISS BILBY. How are you?

CONNIE. I'm fine, I guess. Miss Allen, Miss Bilby, Mr. Carter.

TWO GIRLS. How do you do, Mr. Carter?

MISS ALLEN. Have you been in Washington long, Mr. Carter?

JOE. Well, matter of fact—

MISS BILBY. Where are you from, Mr. Carter?

JOE. Well, I'm—

CONNIE. Mr. Carter is from California!

MISS BILBY. Hollywood?

JOE. No, Burbank.

MISS BILBY. You couldn't be in the P-38 Interceptor business?

JOE. Potatoes, that's my line.

CONNIE. Mr. Carter is only going to be here—

MISS ALLEN. You're a farmer?

JOE. Burbank potatoes.

Now four more girls enter.

MISS CHASEN. Hello, Betty!

MISS ALLEN. Miss Milligan, Mr. Carter, Miss Hopper, Miss Chasen, Miss Bilby, Miss Ewing, Miss Dalton.

As they ad lib "How do you do," two more enter, one the gal who sat next to Joe at the bar.

MISS FINCH. Hello, Stella. What are you doing here?

MISS EWING. What are you doing here?

MISS FINCH. This is Miss Geesekin.

MISS EWING. Miss Finch, Miss Geesekin, Miss Dalton, Mr. Carter.

There are more "How do you do's."

MISS DALTON. Miss Chasen, Miss Bilby, Miss Ewing, Miss Finch, Mr. Carter.

MISS BILBY. Miss Allen, Miss Finch, Miss Geesekin, Mr. Carter.

More ad libs of "How do you do." A waiter enters from the direction of the bar, and pauses.

CONNIE. I'm Miss Milligan.

GIRLS. How do you do?

WAITER. Miss Milligan?

CONNIE. Yes.

WAITER. You're wanted on the telephone.

CONNIE. Oh.

GIRLS. Oh!!

Connie starts to follow the waiter, but turns back to Joe.

CONNIE. Would you show me where the telephone is?

WAITER. Oh, right over here, Miss.

CONNIE. Oh. Thank you.

She goes reluctantly into the telephone booth. The girls now have a free field.

GEESEKIN. Have you been in Washington long, Mr. Carter?

JOE. Well, matter of fact—

BILBY. Say, Miss Geesekin, didn't you used to be at WPB?

GEESEKIN. Yes, I used to be, but I got transferred. (*Looking directly at Joe*) I'm in—the—OPL—now.

JOE. That's fine.

The entire group crosses the dance floor. As Joe starts to take his seat, two girls also start to sit down. Startled, Joe stands again, but is forced to issue the invitation.

JOE. Won't you sit down?

The girls scramble for chairs, ad libbing "Thank you so much."

ALLEN. Move over, Geeseky. Isn't this chummy? (*Stunned, Joe sits too.*)

At the TELEPHONE BOOTH, Connie tries to get the waiter to move so that she may be able to watch Joe with the girls at the table while she carries on her telephone conversation.

CONNIE. Hello.

PENDERGAST'S VOICE. Constance?

CONNIE. Yes, Charles. Where are you?

PENDERGAST'S VOICE. I'm up in Mr. Dingle's room.

CONNIE. In Mr. Dingle's— Does he live here?

PENDERGAST'S VOICE. Yes. It was so crowded and noisy at the table, we couldn't hear ourselves think, so we came up here to finish our discussion of the housing problem. You understand, don't you, Constance?

CONNIE. Of course I understand.

PENDERGAST'S VOICE. I hate to run away from you like this—but it's most important. I doubt if I'll be able to get back.

CONNIE. What did you say?

PENDERGAST'S VOICE. I said I doubt if I'll be able to get back.

This cuts to DINGLE'S ROOM in the WINTON-JAMES HOTEL and we see Pendergast, his derby still on, sitting at the desk, Dingle on a divan by the windows.—apparently busy with documents, but with an ear cocked to Pendy's conversation.

CONNIE'S VOICE. You mean you're not coming back at all?

PENDERGAST. Now, now, don't worry. Mr. Dingle says that Mr. Carter will be glad to take you home. Do you mind?

CONNIE'S VOICE. No, I don't mind going home with Mr. Carter.

PENDERGAST. Mr. Dingle says you won't be taking Mr. Carter very much out of his way.

CONNIE'S VOICE. No, it isn't out of his way at all.

PENDERGAST. I'm awfully sorry, Constance.

Connie leaves the telephone booth and starts back toward the table, and we again see Joe, seated at the table, surrounded by the girls. There are ad lib laughs.

GEESEKIN. You know your eyes are blue like the color of your necktie, aren't they?

ALLEN. Oh, they are not. They're gray like his shirt.

FINCH. Let's see, oh no, I think they're hazel.

BILBY. Oh, honey, they're blue!

AD LIBS. I say they're gray. They're blue.

Connie appears and stands beside Joe, who looks up and sees her.

JOE. Oh!

GIRLS (*looking up, disappointed*). Oh.

CONNIE. Oh . . . Mr. Pendergast phoned and said he would like to have you take me home.

JOE. Oh.

GIRLS. Oh.

CONNIE. Immediately.

GIRLS. Oh.

JOE. That means right now.

CONNIE. Of course you don't have to, because I can—

GIRLS (*eagerly*). Oh!

JOE. I couldn't let you go home alone.

At this Joe and Connie start toward the dance floor, but they pause.

CONNIE. Look, you can always come back later, you know, if you want to.

JOE (*looking at the man-eaters*). Oh . . . no.

Joe and Connie hurry out, the girls craning to look after them. As Joe turns to look backward, he and Connie collide, then continue out.

The scene dissolves to the exterior of 1708 "D" STREET at night.

Joe and Connie walk in around the corner and continue their conversation the length of the block, Connie fending off his reaching hands.

CONNIE. Who's we?

JOE. Oh, my mother and father and my sister.

CONNIE. Oh.

JOE. And on Sundays we generally go down to the beach.

CONNIE. What beach?

JOE. Pacific Ocean Beach.

CONNIE. Oh. Who's "we"?

JOE. Whole gang.

CONNIE. Like who—?

JOE. Oh, Bill Widmayer, Bob Rowe, Jeff York.

CONNIE. Don't you ever go with any girls?

JOE. Sure.

CONNIE. Who?

JOE. Helen Tuttle.

CONNIE. Oh. Is she your girl?

JOE. No. I just go with her.

CONNIE. Long time?

JOE. Just a girl I know.

CONNIE. Is she your girl?

JOE. I just go with her.

CONNIE. Is she attractive?

JOE. I guess so.

CONNIE. Who'd you go with before her?

JOE. Elsie.

CONNIE. How long?

JOE. Couple months.

CONNIE. Then what?

JOE. She wanted to get married.

CONNIE. And what happened?

JOE. She got married.

CONNIE. Who did you go with before Elsie?

JOE. Martha and Adele, I think.

CONNIE. What happened to them?

JOE. I still go with them.

Connie pauses by the steps for her final question.

CONNIE. Are you afraid to get married or something?

JOE. No. (*He pulls her down onto the steps.*) I just don't want to get involved.

CONNIE. They say that's what happens to a man when he gets married.

JOE. Marriage is okay, if you want to be.

CONNIE. I expect to be very happy.

JOE. You do?

CONNIE. Yes. I consider myself a very lucky little lady.

JOE. How's that?

CONNIE. Being engaged to Mr. Pendergast.

JOE. Oh, yeah. Eighty-six hundred dollars a year.

CONNIE. That's a lot of money.

JOE (*gradually managing an embrace*). Sure is.

CONNIE. Two can live very well on that. Especially if they are highly educated like Mr. Pendergast and know how to budget and plan.

JOE. Sure.

CONNIE. We're planning, very carefully.

JOE. Way to do, all right.

CONNIE. Take my engagement ring, for instance. Don't you think it's nice? Not gaudy, I mean.

JOE. You bet. (*He kisses her hand.*)

CONNIE. Well, we thought—Mr. Pendergast and I—that it would be better to get a conservative ring and put the extra money into our home.

JOE. Way to do, all right.

CONNIE. We've been looking at an awful nice—awfully nice house in Georgetown.

JOE. Must be swell. (*He kisses her neck.*)

CONNIE. For after the emergency, of course.

JOE. Sure.

CONNIE. But Mr. Pendergast is so busy now that we can't think of it.

JOE. Yeah, I can understand that.

CONNIE. Last week one night, he was at a dinner conference that Leon Henderson and Donald M. Nelson were at, and— (*Joe kisses her neck.*) Leon Henderson and Donald M. Nelson.

JOE. Must be a pretty important man.

CONNIE. And *so* considerate! When a cousin of mine used to have a stamp collection, he used to save all the foreign stamps from his office mail for me to give to her—my cousin.

JOE. Mm-hm. Is that so?

CONNIE. That's the way it is with those—(*He takes her face in his hands.*)—older men like Mr. Pendergast. A girl comes to appreciate their more—mature—(*He kisses her on the lips.*)—viewpoint!

Now Connie takes the initiative and kisses him, but at its conclusion she rises, sweeping up her fur wrap with her.

CONNIE. I guess I'd better go. (*She offers her hand.*) Good night, Mr. Carter.

JOE (*taking his hat off.*) Good night, Miss Milligan.

She goes up the steps into the hall, and shuts the door. Joe starts down the sidewalk, but remembers he, too, lives there, and turns back just as Connie also remembers and reopens the hall door, waiting for him self-consciously.

The LOWER HALL: As Connie goes to the steps, Joe enters the darkened hall, looking back half guiltily to the street as he closes the door. Then as he turns across the hall, he stumbles over a cot on which a man is sleeping. Startled, he scrambles to his feet and stumbles backwards over another cot on which an irate Westerner has been sleeping. He awakens thunderously, turning on the lights, disclosing three other men on cots and old-fashioned lounges, and all of them mumble imprecations as Joe sheepishly follows Connie up the stairs.

LON. What's the big idea?

VIC. Hold on there! Where you headin' for? Can't you see we're bedded down peaceful-like?

OTHERS. Trying to get a little rest. Waking people up in the middle of the night.
We have to work for a living.
Have important work to do for the government.

VIC. You ain't got the sense you was born with!

The lights are again extinguished as, still grumbling, they try to settle down to sleep again.

The UPPER HALL: Connie precedes Joe upstairs, and discovers that the door is locked.

CONNIE. You have my key.

JOE. Hm?

CONNIE. In my bag in your pocket.

JOE. Oh! Here, I have Dingle's key.

She starts by him as he unlocks the door, whirls as she hears him following close behind her, then relaxes as she sees the reason; the length of key chain carried him with the door.

CONNIE. Thank you. Good night.

The BEDROOMS: Connie and Joe enter their respective rooms, and turn on the lights. She pulls her shades, but Joe paces in and out of the scene as he undresses.

CONNIE. Goodnight, Mr. Carter.

JOE. Hadn't you better call me "Joe"? Sounds funny you calling me "Mr. Carter."

CONNIE. Good night—Joe.

JOE. Good night, Connie.

CONNIE. Oh, Joe.

JOE. Yeah?

CONNIE. I forgot to thank you. I had a wonderful evening.

JOE. It was all right.

CONNIE. I just didn't want you to think I was unappreciative.

JOE. No, I know . . . Connie.

CONNIE. Yes?

JOE. What time is it?

CONNIE. Twelve thirty-two.

JOE. Thanks.

As her lights are extinguished and the shades raised, Connie is discovered in a nightgown. They get into their respective beds.

JOE. Connie.

CONNIE. Yes?

JOE. Are you asleep?

CONNIE. No.

JOE. Me, neither. I've been thinking.

CONNIE. I've been thinking, too.

JOE. What about?

CONNIE. Mr. Dingle.

JOE. Oh.

CONNIE. People can't do like he says, can they?

JOE. You mean "Full Speed Ahead"?

CONNIE. A person can't just rush in.

JOE. No. No, they can't.

CONNIE. *He* can't.

JOE. Who can't?

CONNIE. A person. You say "he" instead of "they" when you're talking about one person.

JOE. Oh, yeah. Thanks a lot.

CONNIE. You know what I mean, don't you, Joe?

JOE. Sure.

CONNIE. It's all right for Dingle to talk. He hasn't any decisions to make. But for a person like us—

JOE. Huh?

CONNIE. *We* have to think things out very clearly, and be sure we're going in the right direction. For instance, Mr. Pendergast wants to get married right away—you know—our engagement.

JOE. Yeah, I know. Take my case, too. I've got to go across on special duty. I'm not supposed to talk about it, but under these circumstances, I guess it's all right. I might not come back. Whatever a fellow like me does, he's got to figure on that.

CONNIE. Yeah, he certainly has.

JOE (*after a long pause*). Connie.

CONNIE. Yes?

JOE. Are you asleep?

CONNIE. No.

JOE. Have you got an aspirin?

CONNIE. No, but I've got a headache.

JOE. Me, too. I can't sleep.

CONNIE. You can't?

JOE. No.

CONNIE. Why can't you?

JOE. I love you, Connie. (*After some silence*) Did you hear what I said?

CONNIE. Yes.

JOE. Well, if you feel the same way, would you tell me?

CONNIE. Would you stay right where you are?

JOE. Yes.

CONNIE. Promise?

JOE. Yes.

CONNIE. I love you more than anything in the world. (*She hears him sit up.*) You promised!

JOE. Oh, Connie!

CONNIE. You promised.

JOE. Connie . . . Connie.

CONNIE. Yes?

JOE. You asked me if I was afraid to get married. I'm not afraid.

CONNIE. Hm?

JOE. I mean, will you marry me? I want to marry you, Connie.

CONNIE. Oh, yes. Thank you. I'd love to. How? When? You said you'd be gone in a couple of days.

JOE. Yeah.

CONNIE. Then you'd go away and we may never even see each other again.

JOE. Yeah, but—

CONNIE. Well, don't you see?

JOE. Yeah. (*And he lies down again.*) I guess you're right.

CONNIE. It's an awful problem, isn't it—darling?

JOE. Sure is—dear. I'd be 'way over there and you'd be over here.

CONNIE. I'd be worrying about you, and you'd be worrying about me.

JOE. Yeah, it's no good at all . . . I guess not, huh?

CONNIE. I guess you'd better go to sleep—darling.

JOE. Will you write me a lot when I'm away?

CONNIE. You write me lots, too.

JOE. Good night—dear.

CONNIE. Goodnight, Mr. C—darling.

A doorbell rings. They jump up, Connie grabbing for a robe, Joe sitting on the edge of the bed to put on his bedroom slippers. The door to Joe's bedroom is flung open and two FBI men step inside.

EVANS. What's your name?

JOE. Joe Carter.

EVANS. My name's Evans. This is Mr. Pike. (*He shows his identification.*) Federal Bureau of Investigation.

JOE. FBI, huh?

EVANS. Yeah. Want to talk to you.

JOE. What about?

CONNIE (*in the hallway*). What's going on here?

EVANS (*both removing their hats*). Don't be alarmed. We're just going to have a look around, Mrs. Carter.

CONNIE. I'm not Mrs. Carter. My name is Milligan. (*As the FBI men replace their hats*) He's just a friend of mine—a very good friend. Look, he lives in there, and I live in here.

JOE. As a matter of fact, she's my landlady. I—

PIKE. That's just ducky.

JOE. Say, what do you fellows want here, anyway?

EVANS. We have a report that you've been having a peek at Washington.

JOE. Well, is there anything wrong with that?

EVANS. Depends on how you see it, Mr. Carter.

CONNIE. We just went to dinner—

JOE. And took a little walk.

EVANS (*sauntering to the windows, and looking out*). Nice view from here. Right into the Government Printing Office—with a pair of binoculars.

JOE. Ohhhh.

CONNIE. What are you "Ohhhing" about?

JOE. The binoculars. They think I was looking at stuff—buildings— through the binoculars. You know, your friend Morton Rodakiewicz.

CONNIE. Ohmigosh!

PIKE (*indicating Joe's uniform*). What's this?

JOE. My uniform.

EVANS. Why don't you wear it?

JOE. Oh, I always sleep in my pajamas.

EVANS. I mean earlier in the evening! Why didn't you have it on when you were looking out that window with the binoculars?

JOE. Oh, I can see all right without it on.

PIKE. You've got a mouth full of phony answers, haven't you?

EVANS. Better get dressed. Both of you.

CONNIE. Why do *I* have to get dressed?

PIKE. 'Cause—well, the traffic's jammed up enough as it is.

EVANS. Let's get going. Have to stop off for fingerprints.

JOE AND CONNIE. *Fingerprints!*

EVANS. Identification procedure.

Connie goes to her room, and Joe to the clothes closet. Pike moves closer to speak to Evans *sotto voce*.

PIKE. Somebody must've made a mistake down at headquarters. This guy doesn't look like a Jap!

The scene dissolves to SPECIAL AGENT HARDING'S OFFICE, FBI, at night. A stenographer sits by Harding at his desk, taking notes of the investigation. Joe is seated across the desk from Harding; Connie and Evans are in chairs by the hall door.

JOE. —so I said, "Listen, my outboard motor is worth more than your skiis anyway." So he says, "All right, tell you what I'll do with you: I'll throw in these binoculars." So I said, "Binoculars? What use have I got for binoculars?" So he says, "You want the skiis, don't you?" And I did, too. Well, lucky thing, I think of my Aunt Tess. So I said, "OK, it's a swap." So he got my outboard motor and I got his skiis and the binoculars.

HARDING (*bored*). I see.

JOE. Then I gave them away to my Aunt Tess. The binoculars, I mean. She's my Mother's sister. Because that's why I said, "OK, it's a swap." Because my Aunt Tess has been mad at my Father since three years ago. You're probably not interested in all this family stuff. But you asked me where I got the binoculars so I'm telling you.

HARDING. Go ahead.

JOE. Well, she's been mad at my Father since three years ago when he talked her into buying a second-hand car from a guy named Bargain Barney, that threw a rod the first day and had to be sold for junk. So I figured that with the binoculars—she lives across the street about a block away from us—she could see our house from her front porch, and see when my Father is going out, so as to come see my Mother—that's her sister—without running into my Father and getting into an argument about whether it wouldn't have thrown a rod if she'd remembered to check the oil.

HARDING. All this in California?

JOE. Yeah. Burbank.

HARDING. Go ahead.

JOE. Well, my Aunt Tess never learned how to focus the binoculars. She has a terrible temper, and she flies off the handle whenever you try to explain anything to her. So when I was leaving on this trip, she came down to the train and gave them to me to see the scenery with, and I said, "No, I didn't have room to take them," and I wish I didn't have. But she said, "Take them or she'd wrap them around my neck." Kidding, of course, but meaning I should take them. So I did.

HARDING (*standing up and stretching as he speaks*). You understand, it's no crime to own a pair of binoculars. (*And he sits down again.*)

JOE. Well, anyhow, that's how I came to have them.

HARDING. What about that uniform in your closet? I suppose you only wear that when you blow up bridges?

JOE. No, I'm attached to the Army Air Force, sent to Washington under special orders to clear an invention through the Patent Office. Mr. Evans has my papers.

Evans goes to Harding's desk, places the papers before Harding, and leans over to address him confidentially.

EVANS. Yeah, here they are. I checked these—bzz-bzz-bzz.

HARDING. Um-hm. Your papers seem to be in order. We did have reason to suspect you, but obviously your status in the Army is clear and you're OK. Now, the only thing we're concerned about is a telephone report that a Japanese at your address has been studying the Government Printing Office through binoculars.

JOE. Wasn't me.

CONNIE. Look, there's never been a Japanese near the place.

Pike enters.

HARDING. Can you think of anyone besides you and Carter that might have been seen around the apartment?

CONNIE. Yes, Mr. Dingle. I told you before.

HARDING. Oh, yes. What about Dingle, Pike?

PIKE. I phoned him. He said he'd be right over. (*Quietly*) He wanted to know if he could bring a friend.

HARDING. What does he think we're doing: serving tea?

PIKE. I don't know, sir.

Pike starts to go out again.

JOE (*rising*). Well, if he can substantiate our story, will you let us go?

HARDING. Probably.

Evans holds a whispered consultation with Harding as Joe takes the chair at the opposite side of room, following which the scene cuts to the FBI ELEVATOR and the CORRIDORS as Dingle and Pendergast come from the elevators talking. Pendergast's derby is jammed down in lieu of his missing toupee; his pockets bristle with scribbled papers.

PENDERGAST. I'd rather not give an opinion on the cost implied until the staff has the usual opportunity to weigh and analyze. Then my charts would—

DINGLE. Oh, blast your charts! How long will it take to get the material to the project?

PENDERGAST. Two days.

DINGLE. Make it one. How long to assemble labor?

PENDERGAST. Four days.

DINGLE. Make it two.

One cross-hall yielding no results, they swing back, and accost a policeman on duty.

DINGLE. Say, which way to room 42?

COP. At the end of the corridor, two doors to your left.

DINGLE. Thank you. Charlie, my boy, it was mighty nice of you to come traipsing over here with me in the middle of the night.

PENDERGAST. Well, I think you know me well enough by now to realize when things have to be done, *I* do not procrastinate.

DINGLE. I don't know what this is all about. There's no telling how long I'll be held up here.

PENDERGAST. Now, now! Everyone over here knows me. I'm sure my presence will speed things up. Then we can get on with our work.

DINGLE. That's the spirit! The average man would say "Let it go until tomorrow." Not you, Charlie. You're a go-getter; a go-getter.

PENDERGAST. I'm glad you think so, Mr. Dingle, because who knows? The opportunity may occur for you to—to put in a good word for me.

DINGLE. You mean Senator Noonan?

PENDERGAST. Well, I didn't mean to make any particular reference, but I suppose that—

DINGLE. Charlie, it's done! You don't overlook a trick, do you?

PENDERGAST. Well, I *do* know what's going on.

DINGLE. Every minute!

The scene cuts to the ANTE-OFFICE: Pike is just coming from Harding's office as Dingle and Pendergast enter. Pendergast greets Pike as a long lost brother, but Pike is puzzled, reaching in his memory for enlightenment.

PENDERGAST. Why, hello, there—uh—uh—

PIKE. Pike.

PENDERGAST. I'm Pendergast. This is my good friend, Benjamin Dingle.

PIKE. Oh yes, Mr. Dingle.

Dingle removes one of the scribbled papers from Pendergast's upper coat pocket.

PENDERGAST. Who's on duty?

PIKE. Harding.

PENDERGAST. Harding? I know Harding. Come on, Mr. Dingle. We'll get to the bottom of this in record time.

He opens the door and shoves by the astonished Pike; pokes his head inside and smiles at Harding.

PENDERGAST. Hello!

This cuts to the INNER OFFICE, as Harding is seated at his desk, Connie in a chair in the far corner of the room, Joe in another chair opposite. Evans is also present.

HARDING. Hello. Come in. (*At this Connie turns to peek, expectantly.*)

PENDERGAST. Harding, old man—

He goes directly to Harding's desk, unaware of the discomfited Joe and Connie.

PENDERGAST. How are you? Haven't seen you in weeks.

HARDING (*groping, politely*). Yes. I don't recall just where, when—

PENDERGAST. In the Chief Coordinator of the OPL's office. I'm Charles J. Pendergast. Surely you remember me?

HARDING (*only vaguely remembering*). Oh, of course, of course. Certainly.

Pendergast pushes on like a man taking charge. Dingle, enjoying the scene and taking stock of everyone in the room, moves to a chair beside Connie's, and buries himself in papers.

PENDERGAST. Want to ask a little favor, Mr. Harding. I'm a very busy man, you know. So, if you could just postpone whatever you're doing and give me a few minutes of your time—

HARDING (*a little annoyed*). I'd like to, but you see—

PENDERGAST. I knew you'd understand. You see, a very good friend of mine was requested to put in an appearance here tonight. He's working with me, as a matter of fact; and we're very busy. Oh, I forgot to introduce you to him. This is Mr. Dingle.

Ad lib "How do you do's." Dingle nods. Pendergast turns to gesture toward him, and sees Connie who is squeezing down in her chair, trying to remain out of his vision.

PENDERGAST. Mr. Dingle is— (*Doing a double-take*) Constance! What are *you* doing here?

CONNIE (*trying to talk, but no words come*). I—

PENDERGAST. Constance, what is it? What's the trouble? What's the matter? Speak to me!

CONNIE (*in a small voice*). Hello, Charles.

Dingle now takes a seat in the rear of the room, and pretends to study his papers, looking over them and gleefully taking in the scene.

PENDERGAST (*turning to Harding*). What's this all about? What's she done?

CONNIE. They think I was hiding a Jap.

PENDERGAST. Why would you hide a Jap?

CONNIE. If I had one, I'd certainly hide him, six feet deep!

HARDING. It's nothing to get alarmed about, Pendergast. Just a routine investigation. We received a wild report over the telephone.

PENDERGAST. Yes?

HARDING. We get hundreds of them. Usually nothing.

In his worried state, Pendergast almost removes his derby.

PENDERGAST. Well, I should hope so. I've known Miss Milligan for six years.

He turns about stiffly and indignantly. He catches sight of Joe, but continues back to Harding, continuing to speak before the impact hits him.

PENDERGAST. As a matter of fact, she's in my department, and we're eng— (*He breaks off and looks back at Joe.*) Carter!

JOE (*waving his hand airily*). How've you been?

Pendergast turns to Connie. He is getting really suspicious now.

PENDERGAST. What's *he* doing here?

JOE. I'm the Jap.

PENDERGAST. Really, Constance, I'm afraid I *don't* understand.

CONNIE (*pathetically*). And I'm afraid you're not *gonna* understand, Charles.

Harding and Evans exchange significant glances, and Evans can't resist a slight smile.

HARDING. We received a tip over the telephone that there was a Japanese with binoculars studying the Government Printing Office from the window of Miss Milligan's apartment.

PENDERGAST (*turning to Connie*). That's ridiculous!

CONNIE. Of course!

HARDING. Then you will vouch for Miss Milligan?

PENDERGAST. Certainly.

HARDING. Fine. Now as soon as we've made a written record of the case, you may leave, Miss Milligan.

CONNIE (*getting up, trying to explain*). The whole thing can be explained if you just let Mr. Dingle speak.

HARDING (*tersely*). Please, Miss Milligan.

CONNIE (*meekly*). Excuse me. (*She returns to her chair.*)

HARDING. Now, Carter—

JOE (*holding up his hand*). Present.

HARDING. Step over here, please.

Joe moves over, with a worried glance at Pendergast and a covert glance at Connie.

PENDERGAST (*to Connie*). Did you say Mr. Dingle could explain?

HARDING (*sharply*). You, Pendergast!

PENDERGAST (*turning to him*). Yes?

HARDING (*still sharply*). You can talk after Carter has been questioned!

PENDERGAST. What has Carter got to do with it?

HARDING (*exasperated*). Sit down!

Pendergast sits. Harding is pretty "burned."

HARDING. Carter was in Miss Milligan's apartment when we arrived, and he was in possession of these binoculars.

PENDERGAST (*getting to his feet and moving over to Connie*). What was he doing with his binoculars in your apartment?

CONNIE. Well—I—listen, Charles, it all started when Mr. Dingle—

HARDING (*shouting*). Pendergast! (*Pendergast whirls about as though he had been shot.*) Can you vouch for Carter, too?

PENDERGAST. Well—I—you see—Mr. Dingle, here—

JOE (*quickly*). It's all right. My commanding officer will be here later to identify me. (*To Harding*) Could she go now, sir?

CONNIE (*jumping to her feet*). Yes. Come on, Charles. It's getting late.

HARDING. Just a moment. (*She stops short.*) You may go as soon as we've heard from Mr. Dingle.

Connie turns and looks at Dingle pleadingly. Dingle smiles and nods reassuringly. Connie, still a little flustered, takes her seat.

PENDERGAST. What's Dingle got to do with it?

HARDING (*butting in*). Shut up! (*In complete tempo*) Sit down! (*Pendergast sits down.*)

HARDING (*confused*). Your address, Miss Milligan?

CONNIE. 1708 "D" Street—Apartment 2B.

HARDING. Beg pardon. I meant Carter.

Joe and Connie exchange worried looks. Evans, a bit sympathetic, tries to get the eye of Harding, shaking his head and pantomiming to Harding not to continue. He comes forward.

JOE. Burbank, California. 651 Sunnycrest Road—brown house on the corner.

Connie gives a little sigh of relief. Evans grins. Dingle takes it in with a wry smile.

HARDING (*tersely*). I mean—here in Washington.

Again Connie's heart is in her throat. Again Evans gestures, but to no avail.

JOE. Room 6310, Munitions Building. (*And Connie, for a moment, is relieved again.*)

HARDING (*looking up, slowly, a bit exasperated*). I mean your Washington address—where you sleep.

Evans gestures to Harding, but the latter merely looks at him, puzzled, then looks at Connie, who is ready to fall down.

JOE. Oh—over there on "D" Street—uh—not sure of the number—uh—1708, I think.

HARDING. Apartment?

JOE. Apartment?

HARDING. Apartment number! (*Evans turns back, defeated.*)

JOE (*making a futile gesture*). Oh. 2B.

Evans groans, and Harding looks up, startled. The stenographer laughs. Connie gives a little smothered moan. Pendergast rises with surprise, then sits down again, heavily. Dingle pretends to be extremely busy with his figures.

CONNIE. I told you I was afraid you wouldn't understand, Charles.

PENDERGAST (*weakly*). But how could it be? I only introduced you to him tonight.

CONNIE (*also weakly*). I forgot to say we'd met before.

Pendergast gets to his feet stumblingly.

PENDERGAST. I feel faint.

CONNIE (*jumping up, and going over to him*). Don't faint yet, Charles. It can all be explained. You see, I sublet half of my apartment to help relieve the housing shortage.

PENDERGAST (*angrily*). To Carter?!

CONNIE (*shouting*). No! To Mr. Dingle. Then Mr. Dingle sublet half of his half to Mr. Carter.

JOE. Yeah. How I came to rent it, I saw an ad in the paper, and I went around there and rented the place, half of it. It was all in the paper. Anybody might have rented it.

CONNIE (*quickly*). From Mr. Dingle —not me.

JOE. Yeah, Imagine my surprise after moving in, and there was this girl.

They look at each other and attempt a little smile over it, but nobody else smiles.

CONNIE. I was surprised myself— frankly.

PENDERGAST. Well, I'm surprised too —frankly.

CONNIE. You see, Charles, Mr. Dingle was there all the time until tonight, when we weren't there either, because we were here.

PENDERGAST. I'd like to believe you, Constance, but really—

JOE. You'll believe Dingle, won't you?

CONNIE. Yes. Ask Mr. Dingle. Mr. Dingle!

Dingle looks up from his figures with a faraway expression in his eye.

DINGLE. Beg pardon?

CONNIE. Mr. Dingle, you've got to help us out.

JOE. Yeah, Ben, you gotta.

DINGLE. Of course. Certainly. What is it?

CONNIE. Mr. Pendergast thinks that Joe and I—that we—

PENDERGAST. Really, Constance, I don't know what you expect to prove now.

JOE (*angrily*). That Dingle was in that apartment all the time, that I rented the apartment from Mr. Dingle!

DINGLE (*innocently*). What apartment?

HARDING. Miss Milligan's apartment.

DINGLE. Has Miss Milligan got an apartment?

JOE. Are you kidding?

CONNIE. You know I have. You lived there.

DINGLE. Very sorry, but I live at the Winton-James, don't I, Charles? You were up to see me tonight.

PENDERGAST (*completely flustered*). Of course I was. They know I was with you—

Connie and Joe are speechless with shock and anger.

JOE. But, Ben—!

CONNIE. Mr. Dingle, how could you?!

DINGLE. Sorry, like to help out you young folks, but after all, no use lying when the truth is staring you in the face.

PENDERGAST. There certainly isn't.

DINGLE. Thing to do is to be brave and bold. What's the sense of a lot of useless denials?

JOE (*bitterly*). If you were a younger man, Ben, I'd punch you right in the nose!

DINGLE. Yes, and if you were a smarter man, you'd use your brains instead of your fists.

Suddenly there is a knock on the door.

PENDERGAST (*shouting*). Come in! (*Harding "fries" at this.*)

PENDERGAST. I'm sorry. (*Apologetically*) I thought I was in my own office.

PIKE (*as the door opens and Pike enters with Major Denton*). Major Denton to identify Carter.

HARDING (*rising, while the others turn respectfully*). Come in, Major.

Denton strides across the room, coming up beside the desk.

DENTON (*to Harding*). Are you Mr. Harding?

HARDING. Yes, sir.

DENTON. Well, what's the charge, Sergeant. What's wrong?

JOE. They think I was looking at the Government Printing Office with these binoculars.

DENTON. Were you?

JOE. No, sir.

HARDING (*turning to Denton*). We discovered that. Now, Major, if you are willing to vouch for Carter—

DENTON. Certainly. He's here on special duty.

HARDING. Thank you, sir.

DENTON. Is that all?

HARDING (*nodding*). That's all. Good night.

DENTON (*shaking hands*). Good night. (*Turning to Joe*) You've got your orders, Sergeant?

JOE. Yes, sir.

DENTON. All right. (*To the others*) Good night. (*And he moves through the door to the outer office.*)

DINGLE (*to Harding*). Guess that about straightens everything out, doesn't it, Inspector?

HARDING. That's right. Show him out, Evans. (*Rising, politely*) Sorry if I've caused any of you embarrassment. (*Evans opens the corridor door through which Dingle and Connie exit.*)

PENDERGAST (*with rising inflection*). Embarrassment?

Pendergast exits to the outer office, while Evans stops Joe.

EVANS (*hurrying to the desk*). Oh, Mr. Carter! You may have your binoculars now.

JOE (*taking them*). Would you mind giving these glasses to the Navy for me, please? (*With a sympathetic smile, Harding takes the glasses.*) I hope they have better luck with them than I did.

Evans re-opens the corridor door for his exit, Joe donning his hat as he goes. Harding sits down at his desk again. Then the scene cuts to the CROSS-HALL as Dingle rushes from Harding's office, and scurries around the corner, Connie following after him. Pendergast emerges from the office, then Joe, and goes after the others. Then we see the trio appearing in the MAIN CORRIDOR, at the ELEVATOR. And now Connie overtakes Dingle as he is pushing the elevator button, and Major Denton is strolling to the corner of the cross-hall as he waits for the elevator.

CONNIE. Mr. Dingle! Mr. Dingle!

DINGLE. Beg pardon?

CONNIE. Did you, or did you not, live at 1708 "D" Street, Apartment 2B?

DINGLE. Shh! (*Now Pendergast is approaching them.*)

CONNIE. Come on, talk! (*Pointing to Pendergast*) Tell him!

PENDERGAST (*stopping by them*). Tell what?

Connie takes them, arm on each, walking with them across the hall a bit.

CONNIE. That he lived in my apartment. (*Denton strolls back.*)

PENDERGAST (*urgently*). Is that true? (*Dingle nods ponderously.*) You did? You lived in that apartment—

JOE (*hurrying toward the elevators, addressing them as he passes*). Hasn't anybody brains enough to push this little button? (*He looks up into Denton's unsmiling eyes—and gives a sickly smile.*)

CONNIE. Joe! Joe!—You!

JOE. Huh? (*Going to the trio*) What?

CONNIE. Our friend just broke down and told the truth.

JOE. Oh, he did!?

PENDERGAST. If that is true, Mr. Dingle, why didn't you say so in that room?

DINGLE (*weightily*). Scandal, my boy —scandal!

PENDERGAST (*fearfully*). Scandal!?

DINGLE. A thing like that gets around like—

He breaks off as a stranger comes around the corner reading a newspaper. Dingle strolls in the same direction, toward the elevators, perusing the documents in his hand. Connie follows him.

CONNIE (*furiously*). Of all the mean, contemptible, low—low—

The elevator doors open, and the colored elevator operator interjects matter-of-factly.

OPERATOR. Down!

DINGLE. Down! (*He rushes in with Denton and the stranger.*)

CONNIE. Yeah. Low-down—

She goes into the elevator, Pendergast following her, and Joe makes a dash for it, too.

JOE. Down!

The elevator doors close for the descent, and the scene cuts to the ELEVATOR, where as the doors close, Dingle removes his hat. Joe then doffs his, then the stranger. Pleadingly Pendergast looks toward the Major, straightens up, and clicks his heels with renewed confidence as he sees the Major making no move to remove his uniform cap. The Major, however, removes his hat a moment later and a deflated Pendergast reaches his hand up toward his derby, but drops it again.

PENDERGAST. I'm sorry. I—I think I'm catching a cold.

CONNIE. You should have stayed at home.

DINGLE. Probably caught it from me.

CONNIE. *You* should have stayed at home, too!

DINGLE. You're right, Miss Milligan. A man in my position can't afford to be mixed up in a thing like this.

PENDERGAST. Shh! (*He catches the stranger's eyes, and drops his own in embarrassment.*)

DENTON. Carter! (*Joe straightens to attention.*) Don't let this excitement make you forget your orders. (*He looks at his watch.*) You have exactly twenty-six hours. You report tomorrow morning at seven, ready to go. Understand?

JOE. Yes, sir.

The elevator doors open, and the scene cuts to the STREET FLOOR and we see a taxi parked at the curb in the background. Dingle sideswipes Connie with his hip, sending her into Joe's arms. Dingle scurries out donning his hat. Connie regains her composure, and starts after him.

CONNIE. Ladies first!

As Pendergast, Denton, Joe and the stranger go out, too, the scene cuts to the ENTRANCE of the DEPARTMENT of JUSTICE BUILDING.

A taxi is parked at the curb and is being approached by a man from the street as our group emerges.

MAN. Take me over to the Washington Sun Building. Let's go.

DRIVER. You'll have to wait. I've got to get a full load.

Dingle, Connie, Pendergast, Joe, Denton and the stranger come through the doors to the sidewalk.

DRIVER. Taxi!

Denton and the stranger go down the sidewalk, and the others continue forward to the parked taxicab.

PENDERGAST (*speaking as Dingle nears the taxi*). Mr. Dingle. Mr. Dingle, surely you really don't think there'll be any scandal?

At this, Dingle stops at the cab, opens the door, and turns back.

DINGLE. I don't dare think, Charlie.

PENDERGAST. But the FBI has a reputation for secrecy.

DINGLE. I know, but a lot of people saw these two come out of her apartment in the wee hours of the morning. That sort of thing can ruin a man.

CONNIE. Ruin a man! What about a lady?

JOE. Yeah. It won't do her any good, either.

DINGLE (*getting into the cab*). As far as I'm concerned, my boy, every man for himself.

PENDERGAST. Now wait a second, Mr. Dingle. You can't just— (*At this, Dingle slams the door shut, and turns to sit down.*)

DINGLE. I'll telephone you in the morning, Charlie. Goodnight, all. Winton-James Hotel. Go ahead.

PENDERGAST (*also getting into the cab*). Oh no, you don't. I want to have a talk with you. (*The door closes.*)

DINGLE. Go ahead, driver.

DRIVER. Gotta have a full load.

CONNIE (*getting in*). All right. I'm a full load.

DRIVER (*to Joe*). Taxi, bud?

DINGLE. Go ahead.

CONNIE. Wait! (*To Joe, on the sidewalk*) Stop gawking and get in. (*To the driver, as Joe starts to obey*) 1708 "D" Street.

The cab starts up with a mighty jerk, sending Joe and Pendergast backward into the laps of Dingle, Connie and the newspaperman. As the cab continues out, Connie continues.

CONNIE. You—you got to pick up your things, haven't you?

Next we see the interior of the CAB, where the newspaperman is now asleep in a corner. No one pays any attention to him, unaware of his calling.

PENDERGAST. Now see here, Mr. Dingle, if there's a scandal, you're responsible. You've put us all in a bad light.

DINGLE. I know. It was cowardly, but I can't afford to—

PENDERGAST. You can't afford! You're going to Michigan tomorrow. I have to stay right here. I'm engaged to Miss Milligan. Our engagement is widely known. You get off Scot-free by lying, and I'm right in the middle of things.

DINGLE. But you're a young man, Charlie.

PENDERGAST. I *am* a young man, yes, with a career just beginning.

CONNIE (*furiously*). Oh, let's by all means protect your career! Don't mind me! My position doesn't matter at all! It's only Charles J. Pendergast!

PENDERGAST. Shh! (*He indicates the man in the corner of the cab.*)

CONNIE (*in crescendo fury*). Don't you shush me! You've been shushing me for twenty-two months. Now you've shushed your last shush! For twenty-two months I've been engaged to a career, not a man!— (*She removes her ring and hands it to him.*) Maybe this'll relieve you of this embarrassing position! Now take your career—and run to cover!

PENDERGAST. Constance, this is unfair. Who involved me in the first place by harboring a Jap?

JOE (*"but definitely"*). Once and for all, I'm no Jap!

As he completes his sentence, he pushes Pendergast with his hand, and considering that he has put a period to the incident, turns his attention to the street on which they're traveling. Pendergast, however, returns the push, and Joe again pushes him. As Pendergast reaches to once more push him, Joe bares his teeth in a "Jap" smile, bulging his eyes at him as he did at Morton back in the apartment. Pendergast never completes his intent to push, and calls Connie's attention to Joe excitedly.

PENDERGAST (*returning all attention to her*). Maybe I was hasty, Constance.

CONNIE. You certainly were.

PENDERGAST. Then I apologize. Will you take back the ring?

CONNIE (*decisively*). No!

DINGLE (*hopping in, cautioningly*). Ah-ah-ah! I'd think twice if I were you, Miss Milligan.

CONNIE. About what?

DINGLE. In your position, you can't afford to burn your bridges behind you.

CONNIE. You mean if I'm engaged to Mr. Smug here, I can keep my respectability?

DINGLE. Not only engagement, my dear girl, but even a hasty marriage —before the story gets out.

CONNIE (*shouting*). Then let it get out!

JOE. You're making a five-alarm fire out of this, Ben. Nobody's going to hear the story unless you go shooting off your big mouth!

DINGLE (*blandly*). Me?

JOE. Yes.

DINGLE. You do me a great injustice. Better think twice, Miss Milligan. Charlie, here, is willing to do the right thing by you—and avoid a scandal.

JOE. He doesn't have to do the right thing by her. I'd do the right thing by her myself!

CONNIE. Oh, you would, would you? Do the right thing!

JOE. Oh, well, all right! Stay single!

The scene cuts to a HABERDASHERY STORE opposite the Washington Sun Building. The taxicab drives up to the curb, and stops. The driver calls to the little man apparently dozing in a corner of the back seat.

DRIVER. Hey, Mister! You—in the corner pocket!

MAN (*rousing himself*). Yeah?

DRIVER. You wanted the Washington Sun Building, didn't you?

MAN. Yeah.

DRIVER. Well, this is it.

MAN (*rising*). Pardon me.

Joe opens the cab door and steps to the curb to permit the man to squeeze by the others and get out.

MAN. Oh, me! It's been a dull night, but I finally got a good story . . . (*He turns back with pencil and paper in his hand.*) —thanks to you, Mr.—Mr.—Pendergast, isn't it?

PENDERGAST. Yes, Pendergast. Charles J., OPL.

MAN. Thanks. (*He hands a coin to the driver.*) There you are, driver. Got to make a deadline. Good morning. (*He turns to leave.*)

PENDERGAST. Good morning. (*But suddenly realization hits him, and he leaps up, yelling.*) Hey! A newspaperman! Let me out of here!

Joe, starting back into the cab, is forced to step back to the sidewalk to let the wild man emerge. And Pendergast not only emerges, but he hops up and down on the sidewalk to look over the top of the cab, following the direction taken by the newspaperman. Then he dashes around the rear of the cab in pursuit. Joe gets into the cab and it starts off again as he takes the rear seat.

This cuts to the SLIPPERY STREET in front of the WASHINGTON SUN BUILDING as the newspaperman hurries across the street, mounts the curb and starts into the building. Pendergast, racing after him, suddenly strikes a slick spot and slides across the street, his feet banking at the curbstone. The man turns and takes a snapshot.

The scene wiping off, we see the interior of the CAB as Joe is settling into his seat, slamming the cab door. Connie in the opposite corner, is trying to cover her sobs.

JOE. A million people in this town and it had to be a newspaperman in the corner pocket!

DINGLE. Tsk tsk—that's bad.

JOE (*noticing Connie's plight*). I'm sorry about this, Connie, but don't cry.

CONNIE (*dropping her hand*). Who's crying?

DINGLE. She is. She's got a perfect right to. Why not? Her name will be mud by morning.

JOE. Well, can't we—

CONNIE. Oh, don't bother about me, gentlemen. Every man for himself.

DINGLE. I warned her about burning Charlie behind her.

CONNIE. Look, just don't bother about me. I'll give up. I'll get out of town. I'll go back home and be miserable.

JOE. You started all this, Ben!

DINGLE. I know. It was cowardly of me.

JOE. Well, if I didn't have to leave in the morning, I'd do something about it—myself.

DINGLE. What would you do?

JOE. Well, I--

CONNIE. Don't be stupid! What *could* he do?

DINGLE. Telephone Charlie, get the ring, and use it himself.

CONNIE. Me be engaged to Joe Carter while he's away?

DINGLE. No, married! Kill the scandal.

CONNIE. That's preposterous!

DINGLE. Now, wait a minute. I mean one of these sort of in-name-only propositions. That's all.

JOE. Well—I'd be willing to cooperate.

Connie really "takes" that, and looks across at him, then at Dingle.

CONNIE. Cooperate! Oh, he would, would he? Well, that's mighty big of him!

JOE (*surprised, actually*). What's she getting so huffy about?

DINGLE. What're you getting huffy about?

CONNIE. He wouldn't even be happy that way, would he?

DINGLE. Would you?

JOE. If it's going to be that way, what's being happy got to do with it?

DINGLE. What's being happy got to do with it?

At this Joe peers behind Dingle to observe her reaction.

CONNIE. Nothing.

DINGLE. Right. All it needs is a little teamwork. You two cooperate on a quick ceremony for the sake of all of us. Then an annulment is a simple matter if you don't cooperate any further.

Joe and Connie peer around him, checking, catch each other's eye and subside. Dingle continues, blandly oblivious.

DINGLE. Miss Milligan stays right here at her war job, with her head high. Joe goes overseas with not a thing on his mind.

JOE (*as he "gets" the last supposition*). Hm?

CONNIE. Well—if he'd be willing to do it, I'd cooperate—that far.

JOE (*quickly, before she can change her mind*). Well, we'd have to do it quickly, because I have to leave here in the morning, you know—hot or cold.

CONNIE. Oh!

DINGLE. What's the matter?

CONNIE. Well, it just can't be done. It takes three days to get married.

DINGLE. It could be right now in South Carolina—hot or cold.

He puts a cigar into his mouth, and gets a time-table from his pocket while Connie answers.

CONNIE. South Carolina? That's hundreds of miles from here!

DINGLE. By plane, it's right next door. Here. I've got a little schedule. Take this down. (*He gives Connie his documents on which to write, and takes a pencil from his upper vest pocket as he continues.*) Schedules come in mighty handy at times, Miss Milligan. (*She takes the pencil. He pulls out his watch.*) Now, let's see.

It's now four twenty-one A.M. (*As Joe takes out his watch to check his time*) You could be at the airport by four-fifty. (*As Connie takes notes*) Your plane leaves at five forty-three—hot or cold.

CONNIE (*writing*). Cold.

DINGLE (*riding over her word*). I could be back at my hotel at six or six twenty-two at the latest, phoning Charleston and making all arrangements. You'd arrive at Charleston at eight forty-two—hot or cold. At nine thirty-five you get your license. At ten-fifteen you're standing in front of the minister, and at ten-thirty, you're married. At twelve o'clock, hot or cold—lunch.

This cuts to the CHARLESTON AIRPORT RESTAURANT at noon. We see a window opening into the kitchen. A colored chef's hands pass a fish plate over the counter to a white waiter's hands. The view then moves to behind the counter, where the plate is put down in front of Connie's hands.

WAITER. Here's your fifty-cent Blue Plate Special.

The view moves up to Connie, who is seen to be tearful. She looks up and howls.

JOE's VOICE. What kind of fish is this?

WAITER's VOICE. Cat-fish.

Connie looks at him, and bawls more vociferously, following which we see JOE and CONNIE together, with the airfield in the background. Joe tries to pick at the fish with his fork but doesn't get very far. The waiter enters from the kitchen with two dishes of boiled rice, which he places before them.

WAITER. Here's your boiled rice.

But now Connie, who has been crying forlornly, really goes to town . . .

JOE (*amazed*). Connie, what's the matter?

CONNIE. I never dreamed when the time came to throw rice at me, it would be boiled.

At this, the sound of a loud-speaker comes over the scene.

LOUD-SPEAKER. Flight Four to Washington in ten minutes.

JOE. We'd better eat our lunch in a hurry. (*As she only cries harder*) Come on, let's get out of here.

The scene moves to the ARCHWAY EXIT while Joe picks up the official and Dingle schedules, leaves a tip on the counter, and takes Connie by the wrist. He goes to the archway, the waiter hurrying along behind the counter to overtake them in the doorway.

WAITER. Is there anything wrong, Mister?

JOE. No, everything's just dandy.

Connie drops her head on Joe's shoulder for her sobbing.

WAITER. Then why is the young lady crying?

JOE (*viciously*). Because she's so happy!

WAITER (*inspirationally*). Oh, for goodness' sake! Newlyweds!

JOE (*"the topper to him"*). What's wrong with newlyweds?

He puts an arm around Connie, and leads her through the doorway beyond the arch as the waiter turns behind the counter again. Then the scene dissolves to the TAXICAB at night: Connie is asleep on Joe's shoulder, as he, too, sleeps. As he moves his head against her hair, he smiles, but awakens to find three men on the rear seat; the one sitting sidewise beside Connie is smiling. Thereupon Joe drops his eyes, and settles down again.—And now the man beside Connie looks at the girl driver, and turns to address the three men in the rear seat.

> MAN. Did you see who's driving this cab?
>
> SECOND MAN. Yep. Things ain't like they were in Grandpa's day.
>
> THIRD MAN. Imagine—at seven-thirty tonight I was four states away. In the old days, it would have taken me two days to get to Washington.
>
> SECOND MAN. Yep. Things ain't like they were in Grandpa's day.

The First Man says nothing but glances back to the happily-slumbering Joe and Connie.

The scene cuts to the exterior of 1708 "D" STREET as the taxicab swings in around the corner. The cab comes to a stop at the foot of the steps, and as it does so we get a close view of the driver at the wheel.

> DRIVER. I hate to do this, but here it is.

The view then expands to include the passengers in the cab.

> JOE (*looking at his watch*). Ten o'clock. Right on schedule.
>
> FIRST MAN. Schedule? What kind of schedule?
>
> JOE. Shall I tell 'em?
>
> CONNIE. Sure—go ahead.
>
> JOE. We just got married. (*Backing out of the cab*) Did it all in one day, on a schedule.

Joe reaches into the cab, helps Connie to alight, and stands at the open door.

> THIRD MAN. That so? What's next on the schedule?
>
> CONNIE (*reading*). "Mr. Carter goes upstairs, gets his baggage and leaves."
>
> SECOND MAN (*as Joe slams the cab door shut*). Well, things ain't what they were in Grandpa's day.
>
> DRIVER. One of you boys want to sit up here in front with me?

The men start to scramble from their seats, and the cab drives out while Joe and Connie walk to the foot of the steps.

The STEPS of 1708 "D" STREET: Joe reaches Connie, and offers her the document from his inside coat pocket.

> JOE. I'd better give you this marriage certificate, so if anyone asks if you're married, you can show them that.
>
> CONNIE. Thanks. And thanks for marrying me, Joe.
>
> JOE. It was a pleasure. Well, I gotta go up and pack my things so you can get your annulment and I can go to Africa with nothing on my mind.
>
> CONNIE. Yeah. Uh—where do you think you'll stay tonight?
>
> JOE (*turning, his hands going to his trouser pockets*). Oh, I'll just roam around town, I guess. I haven't seen much of Washington. I don't think I'd sleep much, anyway.
>
> CONNIE. That's kinda silly, isn't it? Your room is still vacant, and you're paid up until tomorrow, you know.
>
> JOE (*turning to her*). Do you think it would be all right?
>
> CONNIE. If the FBI comes, we can show them this, that's all.

She starts up the steps, and they continue their conversation while ascending the stairs.

JOE. I'd be quiet when I went out in the morning so's not to wake you up, because you're going to need a lot of sleep.

CONNIE. Don't worry about that. I'm a pretty sound sleeper.

They open the door, and he follows her into the lower hall, after a backward glance along the street.

The LOWER HALL, which now resembles a very crowded dormitory. Men are in sleeping togs, lounging about playing cards, etc. The Apollo Quartet and Dingle in a corner under the stairs are singing. Connie and Joe go up slowly, listening to the words, casting a glance or two at each other—and continue up the stairs.

JOE. I can sleep my head off when I get on the boat.

The men's song comes over.

SONG.
"Don't try to steal the sweetheart of a soldier,
It's up to you to play a manly part, etc."

Dingle joins in:

"They may not meet again to love each other, etc.
While he fights for you and me, to protect our liberty,
Don't try to steal his girl away."

Connie, humming, picks up the words again on: "They may not meet again to love each other—" Then we see Connie and Joe entering the UPPER HALL.

JOE (*handing her his key*). Well, here's your key. I won't be needing it any more.

CONNIE. Thank you. Will you write to me and let me know where you are?

They reach the top floor.

JOE. Yeah, when I know where I am.

CONNIE. Well, when I know where you are, I'll write you and tell you where I am.

She opens the door, and we next see them entering the APARTMENT HALL.

JOE. Yeah, do that, 'cause I'm gonna worry about you.

CONNIE. You mustn't do that. You ought to be going with nothing on your mind.

JOE. I know, but I won't be able to help worrying about you. (*He opens the door, and turns.*) Good night.

CONNIE. Goodbye.

Simultaneously they turn back into the hall. He kisses her cheek, then her lips. Then she goes into the living room, and turns back in the doorway.

The scene cuts to the LIVING ROOM, affording a close view at the DOORWAY.

JOE. Goodbye.

CONNIE. Goodbye.

She closes the door as Joe goes into his room. Connie sees the overnight case he gave her in time to provide an excuse for bursting into tears. And the scene cuts to JOE'S ROOM, affording a close view of JOE as he hears Connie sobbing softly.

JOE (*startled*). Connie, what is it?

CONNIE'S VOICE. I forgot to take it.

JOE. To take what?

CONNIE'S VOICE. I forgot to take my bag on my honeymoon.

JOE. Maybe you'll get to take it sometime—with somebody else. (*He listens intently for her answer.*)

The scene cuts to the LIVING ROOM where Connie continues to cry as though her heart were breaking.

CONNIE. I don't wanna go with somebody else.

JOE'S VOICE. Well, then, don't.

She continues to cry as she makes ready for a dreary bed.

The scene cuts to JOE'S ROOM where Joe, in semi-darkness, is getting ready for bed.

JOE. Another thing . . . don't take in any more roomers.

CONNIE'S VOICE. Why?

JOE. Why?! (*He is touchy on this subject.*) Because you pick up with a lot of riff-raff that way. Old guys and young guys. Just a lot of riff-raff.

Next we see BOTH BEDROOMS, as viewed through the windows. We perceive that the wall separating the rooms has been knocked out—obviously Dingle's machinations. This alteration, due to the dim light and their preoccupation, is unnoticed by both of them, for the time being.

CONNIE. I only did it to be patriotic.

JOE. You're sending a husband to Africa. That's patriotic enough! So don't take in any more roomers.

CONNIE. But, Joe—

JOE. Look what happened last time. It ought to be a lesson to you.

CONNIE (*always a girl of spirit*). What happened? Nothing! I'm not the kind of a person anything is going to *happen* to. I think *you* should know that.

JOE. Now, now! Wait a minute, Connie! As long as you're married to me, I said no more roomers.

CONNIE. Now you're acting like a real husband! You're only supposed to cooperate so far—you know.

JOE. I am a real husband until it's annulled. Ask anybody.

CONNIE (*more tears*). Annulled—annulled! That's all you'll talk about.

JOE. Oh, for gosh sake! All I said was no more roomers.

CONNIE. Suppose I don't get a job right away? Who's gonna pay the rent? At least a roomer would help.

JOE. I'm gonna sign my pay over to you. You don't need a job.

CONNIE. I don't want your pay.

JOE. You're gonna get it anyway. And I've saved some dough. You're gonna get that. And I'm gonna sign my insurance over to you, too. Then, if I get killed, you get ten thousand dollars.

CONNIE. If anything happened to you —I—I— (*She recovers and fights.*) I couldn't take that kind of money.

That's the last of Connie's fight. She's thinking of "If I get killed." She's crying.—And now Joe, having raised the window in her room from the outside, stands with his hands on it to hear her out, and whirls to her, shaking an angry forefinger.

JOE. I'd rather have you take that money than to take in roomers.

He turns, stalks angrily back to his own room, and gets beyond his own bed before he "gets it."

CONNIE (*her back to him, weeping*). You just be careful of yourself, that's all. (*Turning to him*) Just be careful—

Dingle: If you don't mind, I think I'll just roll downtown.

Connie: Just stick to the schedule, is all I ask.

Connie: Would you stay right where you are?

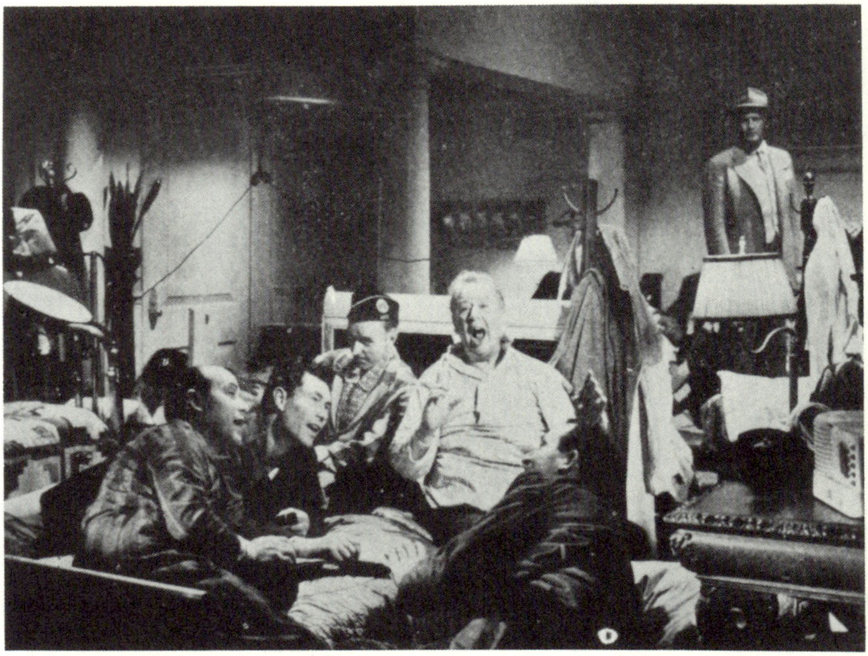

Dingle and Quartet: "They may not meet again to love each other . . ."

She sees him as he, too, turns, and yells as realization hits him. He smiles at her, loses his smile as he contemplates the missing walls, and goes to her smiling sheepishly.

JOE. Don't cry, baby!

He starts toward her around the foot of the beds as she wails, watching his progress—

The scene thereupon cuts to the UPPER HALL and we see Dingle ascending from the lower floor, in his bathrobe. He removes the "Milligan" card and substitutes a pencilled one reading "Mr. and Mrs. Sgt. Carter"—as he starts to sing:

DINGLE (*singing*).
"In love or war with people like us,
We've got to work fast or we miss the bus— (*Turning to the stairs*)
If you straddle the fence and you sit and wait—
You get too little and you get it too late, etc."

He reaches the foot of the stairs, and turns to find the men ranged behind him.

DINGLE (*continuing his song*).
"And our eighteen children will be glad we said— (*And the men join in lustily.*)
'Damn the torpedoes! Full Speed Ahead!'"

Dingle starts leading them to the lower floor as they keep repeating from:

"And our eighteen children will be glad we said,
'Damn the torpedoes, Full Speed Ahead!'"

The scene fades out.

THE OX-BOW INCIDENT

(*A Twentieth Century-Fox Picture*)

Screenplay by LAMAR TROTTI

From the Novel by WALTER VAN TILBURG CLARK

Produced by LAMAR TROTTI

Directed by WILLIAM A. WELLMAN

The Cast

GIL CARTER	Henry Fonda
MARTIN	Dana Andrews
ROSE MAPEN	Mary Beth Hughes
MEXICAN	Anthony Quinn
GERALD	William Eythe
ART CROFT	Henry Morgan
MA GRIER	Jane Darwell
JUDGE DANIEL TYLER	Matt Briggs
ARTHUR DAVIES	Harry Davenport
MAJOR TETLEY	Frank Conroy
FARNLEY	Marc Lawrence
MONTY SMITH	Paul Hurst
PANCHO	Chris-Pin Martin
SHERIFF	Willard Robertson
JOYCE	Ted North
MR. SWANSON	George Meeker
MRS. LARCH	Margaret Hamilton
MAPES	Dick Rich
OLD MAN	Francis Ford
BARTLETT	Stanley Andrews
GREENE	Billy Benedict
GABE HART	Rondo Hatton
WINDER	Paul Burns
SPARKS	Leigh Whipper
JIMMY CARNES	George Chandler
MOORE	George Lloyd

Film Editor—ALLEN MCNEIL

Screenplay of the Twentieth Century-Fox photoplay "The Ox-Bow Incident," copyright 1942 by Twentieth Century-Fox Film Corporation. By permission of Twentieth Century-Fox Film Corporation and Random House, publishers of the novel by Walter Van Tilburg Clark.

THE OX-BOW INCIDENT
PART ONE

The title: "NEVADA, 1885" fades in and out. Then a deserted STREET IN BRIDGER'S WELLS fades in as a very old dog, panting and weary, limps across the road. In the background two cowboys are riding into town. They are ART CROFT and GIL CARTER. Gil is a big, tough guy who loves nothing so much as a good fight. Art is a tall, thin, flat young rider. The little town, formerly a stagecoach stop, is developing into a cattleman's village. The houses—some built of logs or unpainted boards—stand back a bit from the road alongside a few brick or painted clapboards. Lilacs and other flowers bloom in the yards. The street itself is dry, with wagon ruts hardened in it, and the hoofs of the horses drum hard against it. Off to one side is a church, now boarded up—and beyond that the General Store, operated (as a sign discloses) by ARTHUR DAVIES. Next to the store is the Land and Mining Claims Office, across from the sagging BRIDGER'S WELLS INN with its double-decker porches.

The scene moves with GIL and ART.

GIL. It's sadder than a Piute's graveyard.

Art nods and smiles agreement as the moving scene brings them up to DARBY'S SALOON which bears the sign—"Darby's Saloon and Hotel." A few horses are hitched out front. Only one man is in sight—a big, dirty, soft-bellied man with gray matted hair down to his shoulders, named MONTY SMITH. Monty is the town's bum—a man with a nagging, conceited humor that makes people afraid of him. He is leaning against the post of the arcade in front of the saloon picking his teeth with a splinter and spitting. He looks Art and Gil over, nods, then looks away again, as if thinking of something else. Gil and Art pay no attention to him as they swing down, tie up, cross the narrow boardwalk, and go up the three steps to the high, narrow double door with its frosted panels—with Darby's name printed inside two wreaths.

We then see the inside of DARBY'S SALOON. It is cool and dark in here—sawdust on the floor. The bar runs along the full length of one side of the room. Down the other side are four green-covered tables. Four men are seated at a back table playing poker. They are hunched down to their work, quiet and businesslike, and look as if they've been playing for a long time. Darby himself is behind the bar—a tall, thin, "take-your-time" kind of man with gray hair combed to cover a bald spot, big knobby hands and wrists—and arms so long he can sit on the back counter and still mop the bar. Although the bar is spotless, Darby continues to mop it. There is no change of expression on his face—no greeting—as Gil and Art come in and step up to the bar.

Then a closer view of GIL and ART shows Gil pushing his hat back, folding his arms on the bar, and staring past Darby at a picture behind the bar.

Copyright 1942, *by Twentieth Century-Fox Film Corp.*

—This is followed by a close view of a big grimy OIL PAINTING known as the Woman With Parrot, and showing a heavily built woman stretched out on a couch pretending to play with a bird on her wrist, but really encouraging a man who is sneaking up on her from the background.—Then we again see GIL and ART as both stare at the painting.

DARBY (*still mopping the bar*). Well?

GIL. That guy's awful slow getting there.

DARBY (*without looking at the picture*). I feel sorry for him—always in reach and never able to do anything about it.

GIL. I got a feeling she could do better.

DARBY (*dryly*). You're boasting. (*After a slight pause*) Well?

GIL (*still studying the picture*). Don't rush me.

DARBY (*to Art*). What'll you have? Whiskey?

ART. What've you got?

DARBY. Whiskey.

GIL (*straightening up*). Did you ever see such a guy? All winter I been thinkin'—and all he's got is whiskey. (*Then to Darby*) And that's rotten, ain't it?

DARBY (*dead pan*). Rotten.

GIL (*grinning, feeling good*). Two glasses and a bottle.

Darby brings out a bottle and two glasses and Gil fills the glasses. As he and Art start to drink Monty Smith sidles up to the bar, a hopeful look on his face. Gil frowns, but Art nods and Darby pours Smith a drink. Gil and Art deliberately turn their backs on Smith.

DARBY. Well, what's on you boys' minds?

GIL (*setting down his glass*). Does something have to be on my mind?

SMITH (*lifting his glass*). Here's mud in your eye.

He tosses it off and ambles out, hitching his belt as he goes. The men ignore him.

DARBY (*to Art, indicating Gil*). Friendly cuss, ain't he?

ART (*grinning*). He's just getting around to asking if his girl is still in town.

DARBY (*refilling the glasses*). His girl? (*As Gil scowls at him heavily*) If you mean Rose Mapen—no. She went to Frisco the first stage out this spring.

Suddenly Gil reaches across the bar and seizes Darby by the throat and pulls him forward halfway across the bar.

GIL (*in a low, angry voice*). That's a lie! She said she'd wait!

For a moment he and Darby look into each other's eyes.

DARBY (*evenly*). It's a fact.

Gil holds him for another fraction of a moment, then releases him abruptly.

GIL (*furiously*). What a town! (*And he tosses off his drink hurriedly.*)

DARBY (*quietly—again mopping the bar*). It's my guess the married women ran her out. (*As Gil scowls even more fiercely*) Oh, no tar-and-feathers—no rails. They just righteously made her uncomfortable. (*His eyes twinkle ever so slightly as he looks at Gil.*) Not that she ever did anything. But they just couldn't get over being afraid she might.

Gil tosses off another drink. He is obviously going to get drunk in a hurry. He is sore, too.

GIL (*bitterly*). Say, what is there to do in this town, anyhow?

DARBY. Unless you want to get in line and woo Drew's daughter—

ART (*emphatically*). We don't!

DARBY. The only other unmarried woman I know of is eighty-two—blind—and a Piute. (*As they glare at him*) That leaves you five choices. (*Dead pan*) Eat, sleep, drink, play poker, or fight. (*As an afterthought*) Or you can shoot some pool. I've got a new table in the back room.

GIL (*with heavy sarcasm*). That's just great!

As Gil reaches for the bottle again, he looks off toward the door. Two men are just coming in. One is JEFF FARNLEY; the other a rider named MOORE. The latter is about forty and getting so fat that his belt hangs down under his belly. Farnley is a tall, thin rider with light blond hair and pale hostile eyes. Moore nods briefly. Farnley tosses a silver dollar out on the bar and leans forward without speaking.

DARBY (*as he sets out the drinks*). I see Risley's still around.

Moore jerks his head in assent but seems to resent the remark.

ART (*surprised*). The sheriff? (*As Darby nods*) I thought he never got closer than Reno—except on special calls.

Moore says nothing—just takes a couple of draws on his cigarette—glances at Farnley—then swallows half his whiskey.

ART. It wouldn't be that rustling folks were talking about last fall?

MOORE (*scowling, obviously not wanting to discuss it*). Could be.

Farnley picks up the bottle and he and Moore move along the bar—lean against it with their backs to Art and Gil, obviously avoiding Art and Gil. Gil scowls at them, resenting this treatment.

GIL. Getting to be a kinda touchy subject, huh?

DARBY (*in a low voice*). They don't like to talk about it—except with fellows they sleep with.

GIL (*belligerently*). Afraid they'll find it's somebody they know?

DARBY. Maybe.

ART (*in a low voice*). They lose some more this spring?

DARBY. Some.

ART (*leaning across the bar*). How many?

DARBY (*polishing the bar again*). About six hundred head.

ART. They got any leads?

DARBY (*in a low voice*). They picked up a small-herd trail and signs of shod horses down in the south draw.

GIL (*lifting his glass*). Wouldn't everybody know if there was strangers about?

DARBY (*nodding*). Sure—and there hasn't been—except you two.

Gil sets his drink down on the bar quietly—and glares at Darby.

GIL. That ain't funny.

DARBY (*grinning*). Now who's touchy?

GIL. You're talking about my business. Stick to my pleasures.

DARBY (*glancing from one to the other*). No offense, Carter. I just wanted to let you know where you two stand.

GIL (*resentfully*). Listen!

He seems ready to spring across the bar at Darby's throat, but Art catches his arm.

ART. Take it easy, Gil. (*To Darby, after a slight pause*) He's had five whiskies and he's sore about Rose Mapen.

GIL (*turning angrily on Art*). And you keep your mouth shut about Rose, see?

ART (*placatingly*). Okay, Gil. I was just joking. You can take a joke, can't you?

GIL. Sure I can take a joke... Some jokes. (*As he glares at Art, Moore looks around.*)

MOORE (*quietly, to Art*). Lost any over your way?

ART. No more than the winter and the coyotes could account for.

GIL (*turning toward Farnley, itching for a fight*). You haven't got any ideas, have you, Farnley?

FARNLEY (*evenly*). Except not to have ideas.

Darby, suspicious, starts around from behind the bar, ready for anything. He has a bottle in his hand.

GIL (*his eyes narrowing*). Make that clear. (*And at this Farnley's hand moves toward his gun.*)

FARNLEY (*softly*). There's a lot of things around here that ain't clear.

GIL. Still talking about rustling?

FARNLEY. And strangers.

Suddenly Gil leaps toward Farnley, swinging. Farnley ducks a right, but Gil swings a left that catches Farnley on the corner of the mouth. The latter spins around and folds up under the front window. Gil, laughing wildly, leaps at Farnley. Art tries to grab him but misses. Darby turns the trick, however, by rapping Gil neatly under the base of the skull. Gil's knees belly under him and he goes down in a heap and rolls over on his back, a silly, surprised grin on his face. Several men from the poker table hurry in, including ARTHUR DAVIES, the storekeeper, an old man with very white, silky hair; his young clerk, JOYCE; and BARTLETT, who is older than the others, and who wears a sombrero and frock coat.

DARBY (*admiringly*). Looks happy, don't he?

Art looks at Darby and laughs. The other men relax and laugh too. Art reaches down and lifts Gil into a chair.

ART (*grinning*). He just needed exercise. Whenever he gets low in spirits or confused in his mind, he doesn't feel right until he's had a fight. (*As Darby hands Art a pitcher of water from the bar*) It doesn't matter whether he wins or not. He feels fine again afterward.

And Art dashes the water into Gil's face. Gil comes to quickly and stares upward.—We see a closeup of the painting of the man and the woman, then Gil again as he sits up wondering.

GIL. Say, ain't that guy got there yet?

He shakes his head to clear it. Suddenly a queer, strangled look comes into his face. He claps his hand to his mouth, staggers to his feet, and makes a dash for the exit out the back way. There is a burst of laughter from the men as they watch Gil rushing off—obviously to lose his lunch.

This dissolves to the EXTERIOR OF DARBY'S SALOON, near the rubbish pile. Gil is bent over, hands on his knees, his back turned—now well emptied. Art stands beside him, back also to the camera.

GIL. Holy cow! Now I'm going to have to start all over again.

As Art laughs, the sound of a horse running on the hard ground is heard, and at this Art looks around. Then we see what he sees: A horse—running hard—is just rounding a corner into Main Street. The rider is bent over, his hat pulled back; he is pushing the horse to the limit. Gil is still bent over, uninterested in the horse.

ART (*still looking off*). Somebody's sure in a hurry.

GIL (*rubbing his head*). Say—Darby didn't use his fist, did he?

ART (*grinning*). No—a bottle.

Gil straightens up and a big grin comes over his face.

GIL. That's all right then.

Art laughs and the two start off, Gil still a bit wobbly.

ART (*as they go toward the rear entrance to the saloon*). Lay off Farnley, will you?

GIL (*belligerently*). Why should I?

ART. Because you hit him pretty hard—you made him look foolish. (*Instantly Gil grins, like a school boy.*)

GIL (*eagerly*). Did I really get him?

ART. I thought you'd busted his neck.

GIL (*vastly pleased*). No foolin'.

In the SALOON as Gil and Art come in: something obviously has gone wrong. Farnley stands near the front door facing a wild-eyed young man in his teens named GREENE, and surrounded by a group of riders. Moore has hold of one of Farnley's arms, Davies of the other.

FARNLEY (*furiously*). Why the no-good——!

Gil stops and stiffens up at this, but Art catches his arm.

GREENE (*excitedly—waving his arms*). Shot right through the head I tell you!

There's a low angry murmur from the men, and we see FARNLEY and the GROUP closer. The men all look quiet and angry. Greene's sombrero is pushed back off his forehead. He is out of breath, but feels his importance. Farnley reaches out and catches the two sides of the boy's vest in his hand, yanks him forward and speaks right in his face.

FARNLEY. Where'd it happen?

GREENE (*excitedly*). Down in the southeast corner of the valley—about eight miles from his ranch.

FARNLEY. You see him?

GREENE. No, sir, but Olsen did. He found him lying in the sun in a dry wash—shot right through the head.

FARNLEY. When?

GREENE. About two o'clock. But he must've been shot a lot earlier because they picked his horse up clear over at the ranch road.

FARNLEY. Any cattle missing?

GREENE. They couldn't tell—there've been so many working over that range down there.

DAVIES. Did Olsen send you to get us?

GREENE. No, sir, he was in such a big hurry he just yelled at me to go get the sheriff.

Suddenly Farnley lets the boy go, turns and pushes his way through the front door. The others turn and follow him—all except Darby who remains in the doorway, looking out, and Monty Smith, who sidles over to the bar and begins emptying glasses. Art and Gil step up behind Darby—look out past him after Farnley and the others.

ART. Rustlers?

DARBY. Looks that way.

GIL. Who was it they got?

DARBY (*without turning*). Kinkaid.

ART. Kinkaid? Farnley's buddy?

DARBY. Yes, they've been working together ever since they were kids—all the way from the Panhandle to Jackson's Hole.

GIL. Sure, I knew him. Little dark Irishman—didn't say much—liked to sing a lot. (*At this Darby turns and looks at Gil.*)

DARBY. These fellows'll go a long way to get that guy that killed Larry Kinkaid.

There is a slight pause, and Darby looks toward the street again.

ART (*quietly*). Lynchin'?

DARBY. I'd judge.

Gil and Art look at each other with the slightly guilty look of men who know they are not trusted. Then Gil pushes past Darby, with Art right behind him.

In the STREET Farnley is just climbing onto his horse, slowly and deliberately, like a man whose mind has been made up. Several other riders are unhitching their horses.

RIDER (*as he unhitches*). Hey, Farnley! Wait up! We'll get Tetley and form a posse!

FARNLEY (*harshly*). I can get 'em myself.

We get a close view of MOORE and DAVIES on the boardwalk looking off at Farnley, worried.

MOORE. He's crazy! He's got plenty of sand but when he's mad he's crazy.

He starts toward Farnley, but Davies rushes down the steps past him, and we follow Davies as he runs into the street and catches Farnley's bridle. The horse wheels. Farnley looks down at the old man as if about to hit him.

DAVIES. There's no rush, Jeff—even if they have got a five-hour start. It's a good five hundred miles to the first border. (*As Farnley glares at him*) Besides there might be a bunch of 'em. It won't help Kinkaid now to get killed yourself.

MOORE (*coming in alongside Farnley*). That fool kid Greene hasn't got any idea which way they went. Better wait till we know what we're doin'.

DAVIES (*laying a hand on Farnley's leg as Farnley still glowers; pleadingly*). We're all with you about Kinkaid. You know that, son. Only we ought to take our time and form this posse right.

MOORE. So if we go, we'll be sure to get what we go after.

FARNLEY (*looking down at them for a moment, considering this; then, brusquely*). Okay. Make your posse.

As Davies and Moore look up at him relieved, the scene cuts to the BOARDWALK. Darby still stands in the doorway, towel in hand. Monty Smith is behind him. There are several riders down in front unhitching their horses. Gil and Art are on the steps.

DARBY (*quietly*). Somebody better get the sheriff first thing. And Judge Tyler.

SMITH (*pushing past him, wiping his mouth*). What do we want with Tyler and his trials!

We get a close view of a rider named MARK as he looks across his horse and nods in emphatic agreement.

MARK. Yeh. One good fast job without no fiddling with legal papers, and that's all there is to it.

GREENE (*also seen close; excitedly*). Remember this ain't just rustling! It's murder!

A wider view, as the men around the boy nod grimly, shows Davies coming up the steps and facing the crowd.

DAVIES (*soberly*). Wait a minute, men. Let's not go off half-cocked and do something we'll be sorry for. We want to act in a reasoned and legitimate manner, not as a lawless mob.

SMITH (*with a twisted grin at Davies*). The trouble with you, Davies, is you've been keeping store too long. You can't see no profit in this. (*With a wink at the crowd*) Now if any of you fellows was to offer to buy the rope from him—

He grins broadly and is rewarded with a half-hearted laugh from some of the men. Davies looks at him, nettled for a moment, at a loss what to say. But Gil looks at Smith with quick dislike.

GIL (*evenly*). If we go, you're going too, Fat-gut!

SMITH (*emphatically*). Brother, I wouldn't miss it! In fact the only thing that'd get me out faster would be your necktie party. (*With a mocking grin*) And who knows? Maybe this is yours!

GIL (*his eyes narrowing dangerously*). I'll remember that. I'll see you handle the rope.

SMITH (*crossing toward the bar, grinning*). In that case I think I'll have a couple of drinks on the house. I want to be primed.

DARBY (*barring the way*). Not in here you don't. Two more and you'd have to be tied on.

As Smith laughs, Bartlett takes off his hat and steps forward in front of Davies.

BARTLETT (*addressing the crowd*). I don't know about the rest of you fellows, but me—I'm getting sick and tired of sweatin' to make a few honest dollars only to lose it all in one night because somebody like Davies here says we got to fold our hands and sit still and wait for eternal justice! I say stretch 'em!

RED is next seen, at close range. He is a big Texan with a slow, drawling voice.

RED. Down in Texas where I come from they just go out and get a man and string him up.

The GROUP: Bartlett is beginning to sweat and to roll his eyes. He is getting the mob excited too. The faces that look up at him are hard and angry with narrow, shining eyes. Bartlett wipes his face with the back of his sleeve.

BARTLETT. It's not just a rustler we're after—it's a murderer! Larry Kinkaid—one of the finest most God-fearing men that ever lived—is lying out there right now with a bullet hole in his head. You let that go and there won't be nothing safe—our cattle, our homes, even our womenfolks. (*Calling to Farnley*) I'm with you, Farnley! (*Starting down the steps*) I'm goin' to get me a rope and a gun, but I'll be back! And if nobody else'll do it, me and you'll do it ourselves!

There is a wild cheer from the men at this proposal, and at this the scene cuts to a close view of FARNLEY seated on his horse. He raises his hand carelessly in a kind of salute. His face is still tight and expressionless.—A wider scene on the STREET shows Bartlett pushing his way through the crowd, without even putting on his hat—the crowd calling out excitedly:

VOICES. Come on—let's get our guns! We'll be back, Farnley! Hey—you fellows, wait for me! Somebody go tell Tetley!

Several turn and rush off, a feverish sort of excitement now evident in the mob.

Next we see the BOARDWALK as several riders come hurrying down the steps, shouting and excited. Davies is standing, holding on to Joyce's arm, talking fast, and the boy nods. And now Davies turns to the crowd and holds up his hand for attention.

DAVIES. Listen, men! Listen to me! Don't lose your heads like this! (*Pleadingly*) You mustn't do this thing! You mustn't!

FARNLEY (*contemptuously*). Shut up, Grandma. Nobody expects *you* to go.

DAVIES. Remember justice has never been obtained in haste and strong feelings.

A close view shows GIL and ART watching Davies.

GIL (*in an aside to Art*). Fat chance he's got of changin' anybody's mind now—with that Farnley sitting here.

ART. Funny how worked up old Bartlett got 'em—especially when you think hardly any of 'em owns any cattle or land himself. I bet half of 'em didn't even know Kinkaid.

GIL (*nodding*). Yeh, and all that talk about their womenfolks. (*Grinning*) It ain't likely rustlers are goin' to change the kind of women they know.

Gil turns toward DAVIES and JOYCE.

GIL. Don't take it so hard, Mr. Davies. You did all you could.

Davies looks at him for a moment without replying, as if he were thinking of something else and hadn't heard.

DAVIES (*after a slight pause*). Will you do me a favor, Carter?

GIL (*cagily*). That depends.

DAVIES. I'm going to send Joyce here for the sheriff and Judge Tyler, and I want you to go with him to help explain.

GIL (*frowning*). You know how Art and I stand here. We came in at a bad time.

DAVIES (*nodding*). I've got to stay here and stop them, if I can, till they realize what they're doing. (*As Gil still hesitates*) If I can make this regular, that's all I ask.

GIL (*still not liking it*). All right. (*To Joyce*) Let's go.

As he turns away, Davies catches his arm.

DAVIES. Wait a minute. Do you know Mapes?

GIL (*pausing*). The one they call Butch?

DAVIES (*nodding*). The sheriff's made him deputy for times when he's out of town. And we don't want Mapes.

As Gil turns away, Monty Smith comes up the steps. He is now wearing a reefer jacket and two guns, and carries a coiled rope in his hand. Coming up to Davies he grins and holds out the rope. Gil hesitates for a moment, and watches.

SMITH. They said I'm to be the executioner, so I've come all fixed.

He holds the rope up to his neck and nudges it a couple of times as if tightening the knot against his ear. Then he jerks his head, lets it fall, sticks out his tongue and crosses his eyes.

SMITH. Don't tell me I don't know my trade.

Davies just looks at him sadly, without a word.

SMITH (*clucking his tongue against his teeth*). You don't look well, Mr. Davies. Maybe you'd better stay home and get rested up for the funeral. (*Grinning*) Maybe you could get the flowers. The boys won't begrudge a few flowers, even for a rustler—so long as he's a good, dead one.

As he roars with laughter at his own joke, Gil suddenly steps forward and grinds the heel of his boot into Smith's foot. As Smith lets out a yell of pain and looks around angrily, Gil looks at him with contempt and starts off, followed by Joyce. Smith wavers and turns away.

The scene dissolves to the SIDEWALK where GIL and JOYCE are hurrying along, Joyce half-running to keep up, and looking back toward the saloon all the time.

JOYCE (*anxiously*). Do you think Mr. Davies can hold 'em?

GIL (*lighting his cigarette by cupping a match in his hands*). I don't know. Most men are more afraid somebody'll think they're cowards than anything else. That's why nobody'll want to be first to back down.

JOYCE. Mr. Davies says lynchers always know they're wrong. That's why they never like to talk about it afterwards—and why they've always got to have a leader first—somebody they can ease their conscience by blaming it on.

Joyce looks off, frightened. They are now passing a big white-pillared house, built along Southern Colonial lines. Standing in the front yard, near the steps, looking off toward the saloon, are two men: MAJOR TETLEY and his son, GERALD. Major Tetley is a thin, aristocratic-looking man with sideburns and a gray mustache—the sort of man who is accustomed to leadership and who brooks no interference. He is a cold, hard, forceful man with an ironic expression who speaks quietly, yet everything he says seems important—perhaps because it is important to himself. Gerald, his son, is a thin, handsome young man, not too strong looking, with a gentle, almost feminine, soft manner and face. We get a close view of TETLEY and GERALD.

TETLEY (*turning toward the house*). Get your hat and gun.

GERALD (*steeling himself*). I'm not going, Father.

Tetley, as he goes up the steps, pauses and looks back at his son. His voice remains quiet—menacing.

TETLEY. I don't wish any argument. Do as I say. (*As Gerald looks at him helplessly*) Perhaps this will do what I've obviously failed to do—make a man of you.

As Tetley goes in, Gerald looks after him, a look of horror and shame in his eyes.

At the front door of JUDGE TYLER'S HOUSE: The house is built of brick, high and narrow with white painted stonework. Gil and Joyce come in and Gil pulls the fancy metal-knobbed bell. A jingly tinkle is heard inside. To one side of the door is a black shingle with gold letters reading: JUDGE DANIEL TYLER.

GIL (*grinning*). Scrape your boots, put your hat on your arm, and straighten your wig.

After a moment, the door is opened by a tall, raw-boned woman with a long yellow, mistrustful face, who wears gold-rimmed glasses and a frilly house cap. She stands in the doorway, hands on her hips, scowling. Her name is MRS. LARCH.

MRS. LARCH. Well?

GIL (*taking off his hat*). The Judge in, Ma'am?

MRS. LARCH (*tersely*). Yes.

GIL. Could we see him?

MRS. LARCH. You got business?

GIL (*getting a little sore*). No, we just dropped over to tea.

MRS. LARCH. Humph.

JOYCE. Mr. Davies sent us, Ma'am. It's awful important.

MRS. LARCH (*sniffing as she turns away*). It's not regular office hours.

As she disappears into a room off the hallway and closes the door behind her, Gil and Joyce step inside.—We then see them in the HALLWAY as they look around.

GIL (*in a low voice*). That the Judge's better half?

JOYCE. His housekeeper. His wife's dead.

GIL (*grinning*). Well, you can see why there's times when the Judge don't seem able to make up his own mind.

As he grins, the Judge's voice is heard booming from the adjacent room.

JUDGE'S VOICE. Come in! Come in!

Mrs. Larch reappears at the door.

MRS. LARCH. He says come in.

As they move toward the door, she comes out, still cold and unsmiling.

We see the JUDGE'S LIBRARY. JUDGE TYLER is just getting up from his roller-top desk and is coming forward, hand out as if conferring a great favor. Seated in a chair beside the door—his chair tilted back against the wall—is MAPES, the deputy sheriff, his gun belt and sombrero hung over a hook above him. Judge Tyler is a big, paunchy, typical politician. He wears a frock coat, big-collared shirt and black string tie. His hair is cut square at the collar like an old-time Senator's. He carries, in addition, a big watch-chain with charms with which he is constantly playing, and as he talks he teeters from heels to toes as if expecting to take off on a flight of oratory at any moment.

JUDGE (*in his best electioneering manner*). Well, well, Carter! How're things out in your neck of the woods?

GIL. All right, I guess, Judge.

JUDGE (*heartily*). You don't appear to have been pining away exactly since I last saw you. (*As he shakes hands*) And what can I do for you gentlemen?

JOYCE (*swallowing hard*). We're here for Mr. Davies.

JUDGE. So? And how is my friend Davies? Well, I trust.

GIL (*with a glance at Mapes*). Yes, sir, but could we see you alone for a minute, Judge?

Mapes lets his chair down heavily.

JUDGE (*grinning*). Ah! A matter of a private nature, eh?

GIL (*still looking at Mapes*). Yes, sir.

JOYCE. Mr. Davies said particularly just you and Sheriff Risley.

MAPES (*sharply*). Risley ain't here. He deppitized me.

GIL. Where'd the sheriff go?

MAPES. Down to Kinkaid's ranch early this morning.

GIL (*surprised*). Kinkaid's? When'll he be back?

MAPES. He didn't say. Couple of days maybe. (*Fingering the badge on his vest*) But anything you can tell him you can tell me. I'm acting sheriff.

GIL (*easily*). Sure, we know that Butch, but we're here for Mr. Davies. If the Judge thinks it's your job, he'll tell you.

JUDGE (*opening the door*). Certainly, Mapes—certainly!

Mapes stands there, his feet apart, staring at Gil. He has a big red fleshy face, and always looks angry and irritated and important.

MAPES. All right. (*To the Judge, as he goes out*) But if it's a sheriff's job, call me, see?

JUDGE. Naturally.

As Mapes leaves, the Judge closes the door then turns to Gil and Joyce.

Outside the JUDGE's HOUSE: the disgruntled Mapes comes out, an angry, sullen look on his face. He has his thumbs in his belt. Suddenly he looks off at the crowd down the street—a puzzled expression on his face—and yells:

MAPES. Hey—Red!

Then he starts off hurriedly,—and a different view of the STREET shows the rider known as Red going toward the saloon. He pulls up sharply and turns back toward the Judge's gate, as Mapes runs out into the street and up to him.

In the JUDGE's LIBRARY: The Judge has been told the news and he is very much concerned. He scowls—not so much with disapproval as with annoyance.

GIL. It's not so much that Mr. Davies doesn't want them to go. He just wants to make sure a posse's sworn in, to bring 'em in for a fair trial.

JOYCE. That's why he wanted you and the sheriff to hurry quick as you can.

JUDGE (*furiously*). But confound it, man! The sheriff's not here! Today of all days!

JOYCE. You could talk to them, Judge. They'll listen to you.

JUDGE (*even more angrily*). No, no! That's not my job! I haven't any police authority!

The door opens and Mapes comes back. All three turn and look at him. Mapes doesn't say anything, as he takes his gun belt and starts buckling it on.

JUDGE (*fuming*). Where are you going, Mapes?

MAPES (*quietly—enjoying it*). There's a posse forming, just in case you hadn't heard, Judge. That's sheriff's work, ain't it?

JUDGE (*roaring at him*). That's no posse! It's a lawless lynching mob!

MAPES (*as he starts out, pleased with himself and with his power*). It'll be a posse when I get there. I'll deppitize 'em all proper.

The Judge grabs Mapes' arms—stopping him in the doorway.

JUDGE (*bellowing*). You can't do that. Risley's the only one empowered to deputize.

Mapes looks at the Judge for a moment —starts to answer back, reconsiders— turns and deliberately spits past the Judge and over on the corner stove. Then he goes out. The Judge looks after him in helpless rage. Gil and Joyce start for the door.

GIL. Shall we tell Davies you're coming, Judge?

The Judge looks at Gil as if he'd like to murder him for dragging him into this mess.

JUDGE. Yes, yes, of course! I suppose I'll have to!

As Gil and Joyce leave, the Judge looks after them angrily.

JUDGE. But doggone it! This is the sheriff's job—not mine!

We then see the HALLWAY as Gil and Joyce start out at the front door. Mrs. Larch stands with her hand on the doorknob, still glaring. As Gil goes by he gives her a big, wicked wink. The moment they go, Mrs. Larch slams the door behind them, and the scene dissolves to the street in front of DARBY's SALOON: The mob has grown to about twenty now, and more people are coming in every minute. Farnley is still seated on his horse. WINDER and his stableman, GABE HART, are on mules. Winder is a short, stringy man, without beard or mustache. Gabe is a big, ape-like man, childish, mentally undeveloped. Darby stands in the doorway; Davies, Gil, and Joyce are off to one side engaged in earnest conversation. Art lounges on the boardwalk. Several women—some with children—stand around looking on. The men wear reefers or stiff cowhide coats, and some even have scarves tied down around their heads under their hats. Most of them have ropes tied to their saddles and carry carbines. They are quiet— ominously so—talking only in monotones.

We get a close view of MONTY SMITH as —weaving slightly—he crosses to the top of the steps and looks down and grins.

SMITH. Comin' along, Sparks?

Then another view of the mob includes SPARKS, a Negro, the handy man of the village. He is a tall, chocolate-colored man with a slow and careful speech, deep voice, and a nice, kind face. He wears dungarees and a blue shirt.

SPARKS (*embarrassed*). No suh, Mistah Smith, ah don't guess so.

SMITH. Better come along, Sparks. (*Grinning*) It ain't every day we get a hanging in a town as dead as this one.

Several of the men standing nearby look at Smith and frown, not caring for such joking about the matter, but Smith pays no attention to them. He is pleased with himself and his humor.

SMITH (*imitating Sparks*). You don't have to do anything. Th' real work is all signed up. But ah thought maybe we ought to have a reverend

along. There'll be some prayin' to do.
Several of the men laugh at this. But Sparks is deadly serious.

SPARKS. Maybe yu is right, Mistah Smith. Maybe somebody ought to go that feels the way ah do.

SMITH. Davies'll lend you his Bible so's we can have the right kind of reading at the burial.

SPARKS. Thank yu, suh, but ah knows mah text without the Book.

Gil steps over beside Smith.

GIL (*quietly*). They're kidding you, Sparks.

SPARKS. Ah knows that, suh, but ah think maybe Mistah Smith was accidentally right when he said ah ought to go.

There is a slight pause. Some of the men are a little ashamed of this sort of thing.

DAVIES (*quietly*). There's an old horse in my shed you can use.

SPARKS. Thank you, suh. Ah'll go get him. (*He turns away to go for the horse.*)

Suddenly Smith lets out a yell.

SMITH. Ye-ow! Here comes Ma!

The men all turn eagerly and look off toward the street, following which we see JENNY GRIER, known as MA, galloping toward the crowd; and a close moving view shows her to be a cheerful woman, strong as a wrestler, dressed like a man in jeans, shirt and vest, with a bandana around her neck and an old sombrero on her head. There is a coil of rope hanging from her saddle. She grins and waves a rifle over her head.

The GROUP in front of the saloon is grinning. Some men yell greetings to the woman.

VOICES. Hello, Ma! What's been holdin' you up? Come on—we're ready to go!

We see GIL and DAVIES observing the excitement.

GIL. You're going to have your hands full now they've got an audience to play up to.

DAVIES (*nodding sadly*). Yes, they're making quite a show of it. (*Looking off*) But here comes Tyler, too. Maybe if we can hold them off till dark they'll quit.

GIL. That ought to be easy—a powerful talker like the Judge.

And now Ma rides in and is instantly greeted with enthusiasm by the GROUP; Davies starts off past her to meet Judge Tyler who is to be seen hurrying forward, hat in hand, puffing and blowing from his fast walk.

MA (*grinning broadly*). Well, what are we waiting for now?

FARNLEY (*sourly*). Judge Tyler. Davies asked him to come over.

MA (*shaking her head and calling after Davies*). I declare, Davies, you're getting worse every day—drumming up business for Tyler and his fee-gorging justice!

And as several men laugh, the scene cuts to a close view of JUDGE TYLER, who comes hurrying up, puffing and blowing. Davies meets him.

DAVIES. Right up here, Judge.

Then the view moves with them as Davies leads Judge Tyler through the crowd and up the steps to the saloon. The Judge turns to face the crowd. The men turn, instinctively, to listen.

They don't think much of Tyler, but he represents the law.

JUDGE (*in his best platform manner*). I understand how it is, men! My old friend Larry Kinkaid, one of the finest and noblest—

FARNLEY (*cutting in quietly*). Cut the stumpin', Tyler! All we want is your blessing.

Tyler looks off at Farnley, displeased. Then he gets hold of himself and continues—but the wind seems to go out of him.

JUDGE (*weakly*). Of course you can't flinch from what you believe to be your duty, but certainly you don't want to act hastily in the very spirit of lawlessness that begot this foul crime.

SMITH (*shouting*). By the time you got ready to act, Judge, those rustlers would be over the Rio!

JUDGE (*turning angrily on Smith; loudly*). One more word out of you, Smith, and I'll have you up for impeding the course of justice!

MA (*grinning*). Judge, you can't impede what don't move anyway!

JUDGE (*turning on her, nettled*). And you, Jenny Grier—a woman! To lend yourself to this!

Ma laughs—coarsely—contemptuously. The Judge waves a hand at the crowd, choking with anger, unable to finish. Davies steps forward again.

DAVIES. Just a minute, men. I've just learned that Sheriff Risley's already down at Kinkaid's. (*Turning to Tyler*) That right, Judge?

JUDGE. Yes, he's been there all morning.

DAVIES (*smiling*). So you see, everything's probably being attended to right now—legally. All you'll get out of it is a long hard ride for nothing. It's going to be dark before long and mighty cold. My advice is to come inside. Have a drink and wait till we hear from the Sheriff.

The men look up at Davies. It is getting cold. The sun is shining very palely through the clouds. The idea of a drink, too, is tempting. The men rub their faces thoughtfully. One or two spit—each waiting for the next to take the initiative.

DARBY (*seen close*). Drinks on the house! (*Then turning, speaking over his shoulder*) But only one round. I'm not filling any bucket bellies.

Several of the men laugh at this, and Davies is quick to take advantage of the break.

DAVIES. I'll make it two!

DARBY. If any of you fellows wants to stay in town I can take six, if you don't mind sleeping double.

By now several of the men (not Farnley, however) are getting off their horses. They seem actually pleased to be getting out of it.

MA (*seen close, scowling*). I can take five, but any lazy puncher that holes up with me is going to pay for his grub. I'm no charity organization.

Several of the dismounted men are then seen coming up the steps to the saloon. Davies goes into the street urging the others to come in.

DAVIES. It's not like you were giving up, boys. It's just good sense.

Suddenly Farnley wheels and starts to ride off by himself. And at this Judge Tyler runs into the street.

JUDGE (*sharply*). Farnley, you come back here! (*Bellowing after him, as*

Farnley rides on) I'm not asking you, Farnley! I'm telling you!

Farnley reins in abruptly, turns and rides back to the Judge.

Then we see Farnley with Davies and Judge Tyler. He looks down at them, his face cold with anger. The mounted men form a circle around him. One look at Farnley's face and Judge Tyler deflates again.

JUDGE (*mealy-mouthed*). You don't need to worry, Jeff. This business is going to be taken care of.

FARNLEY (*coldly*). Yeh, and I know who's going to take care of it—me! I tell you now, whoever shot Larry Kinkaid ain't comin' in here for you to fuddle with your lawyer's tricks for six months and then be let off because Davies—or some other whining old woman—claims he ain't bad at heart. Kinkaid didn't have six months to decide if he wanted to die.

At this Davies steps up and again catches Farnley's knee.

DAVIES. Jeff, you know nobody in this country's going to let a thing like this go by. Sheriff Risley'll get 'em and there aren't twelve men in the West who wouldn't hang 'em. You can see that, can't you?

FARNLEY (*with cold hatred*). When I look at you, I can't see anything.

And he bends over and roughly pushes Davies' hand off his knee. There is a moment of silence. Then a cool, new voice speaks:

VOICE. Disbanding, men?

They all turn quickly and look at the speaker.—Unobserved by the others, MAJOR TETLEY, GERALD, and PANCHO, his Mexican hand, have ridden up—Tetley on a Palomino. Tetley wears a Confederate-grey field-coat without epaulettes, grey trousers tucked into cowboy boots, buckskin gloves, and a Confederate officer's hat. From his holster looms a pearl-handled Colt revolver. There is a moment's silence as Tetley looks the men over.

MA (*sarcastically*). Davies has just about convinced us, Major Tetley.

TETLEY (*quietly, to Davies*). Of what, Mr. Davies?

Davies looks up at Tetley and under the latter's cool gaze he wavers.

DAVIES (*stammering*). Why of—of—

TETLEY. I take it you were acting on the assumption that the raiders left by the South draw?

DAVIES. Why yes—of course.

TETLEY (*a thin smile on his face*). They didn't. They went east—by Bridger's Pass.

FARNLEY (*quickly—interested*). Through the mountains?

Men are now crowding around listening, interested.

TETLEY (*nodding*). Over the old stage road to Pike's Hole.

MOORE. But that's eight thousand feet up!

TETLEY. Approximately.

DAVIES (*in great distress*). But they'd be crazy to go that way.

TETLEY (*with maddening quietness*). Not so crazy perhaps, Mr. Davies, knowing how crazy it would look to us.

Now Ma pushes forward.

MA. How come you're so sure, Tetley?

TETLEY (*indicating the Mexican*).

Pancho saw them. (*The Mexican grins, and nods vigorously.*) He was coming back from Pike's and had trouble getting by them in the pass.

PANCHO (*nodding*). Si. (*He grins.*) Heem not see me, I theenk. Eet was low down where I can steel get out from the road. I take my horse into the hollow place so they can get by. At first I theenk I say hello. Then I theenk it funny to drive the cattle then.

FARNLEY (*sharply*). Cattle?

PANCHO (*grinning*). But sure. Why you theenk I have to get out of hees road?

FARNLEY. Go on.

PANCHO. When I see what marks those cattle have I be veree, veree quiet.

MAPES. What marks?

There is a close view of PANCHO.

PANCHO. On the throat three leetle what-you-call heems?

He holds up the thumb and forefinger of his right hand—with the second finger curving out and touching the forefinger at the nail—the finger of his left hand across the space between the thumb and forefinger of the right—making Kinkaid's dewlap.

A close view shows FARNLEY's face suffused with rage.

FARNLEY. Why that's Kinkaid's mark!

The men are getting worked up again —really angry this time. Several start to get back onto their horses. Davies seems helpless.

BARTLETT (*harshly*). The dirty rats! Kill a man and then risk a drive!

WINDER. Let 'em get away with it this time, and there's no telling what they'll try next!

FARNLEY. How many were there?

TETLEY. Forty head.

FARNLEY. I mean rustlers.

PANCHO. Three.

MA. You know any of them?

PANCHO (*the grin disappearing from his face; shaking his head*). I not evair see heem before—not any of heem.

Davies looks at the Judge. The latter is silent. The men are silently mounting, Art and Gil among them.

DAVIES (*pleadingly*). Major Tetley, it's late. You can't get them tonight.

TETLEY. If we can't, we can't get them at all! With cattle they'll have to move slowly. And in the pass there's no place for them to branch off.

DAVIES (*running his hand through his hair, puzzled*). Why were you so long bringing us this word, Major?

TETLEY (*turning and looking at Davies with that same dry smile*). I knew my son would want to go along. He was out on the range.

Davies looks at Gerald Tetley who is sitting on his horse, looking off as if he hadn't heard.

DAVIES (*pleadingly*). Major Tetley, you mustn't let this be a lynching!

TETLEY. It's scarcely what I choose, Davies.

DAVIES. Promise me you'll bring them in for a fair trial!

TETLEY. I promise that I'll abide by the majority will.

Davies looks around hopelessly—at a loss what to say.

JUDGE (*blustering*). Tetley, you know what's legal in this case as well as I do. (*Tetley bows ironically—as if accepting a compliment.*) All we ask is a posse to act under a properly constituted officer of the law.

MAPES (*swaggering forward*). That's where I come in. Risley made me deputy.

TETLEY (*turning to Mapes*). In that case, Mr. Mapes, suppose you deputize the rest of us.

JUDGE (*protesting*). That's not legal. No deputy has the right to deputize.

Mapes looks up at Tetley. The latter doesn't even nod. Just that thin little smile barely moves the corners of his mouth. Mapes looks around.

MAPES. How about it, boys?

SMITH (*riding up alongside Mapes*). It'll do for me, Butch. Go ahead and pray.

JUDGE (*bellowing*). Mapes, you're violating the law!

There is a slight pause. Nobody else voices a protest.

MAPES. Raise your right hands.

The men solemnly raise their hands. One or two are hesitant about it, but gradually, all except Davies, the Judge, Joyce and Sparks fall into line.

We get a close view of GIL and ART: They look at each other. Monty looks at them searchingly—suspiciously. Art gets this and raises his hand. Imperceptibly he indicates to Gil to do likewise and Gil raises his hand. Then we again see the GROUP as Mapes swears them in.

MAPES. I hereby solemnly swear that I am duly sworn in as a deputy in the case of the murder of Larry Kinkaid and am willing to abide by the decisions of the majority—so help me God. Say I do.

MEN (*as one*). I do.

There is a moment of silence. Then Farnley turns and rides off. The men swing into loose order behind him, leaving Davies, Joyce and the Judge standing in the road.

JUDGE (*yelling after them*). Tetley, you bring those men in alive or, as I'm Justice of this county, you'll pay for it—you and every jack-man of your gang!

Suddenly Davies starts running after the men, followed by Joyce. The view swings around and follows Davies as he overtakes Tetley and runs alongside, holding onto the saddle and talking earnestly. Tetley does not stop, nor does he, apparently, reply. Suddenly he rides off, leaving Davies behind. Davies continues to run forward for a few yards. Then he stops, and a close view shows DAVIES standing in the road. Joyce runs up beside him. Just then Gil rides by.

GIL (*as he passes*). Aren't you coming?

Davies looks up—doesn't say anything —then silently gestures for Gil to go on. Then he turns to Joyce.

DAVIES. Get my horse! I'm going with them. Then get on your horse—get down to Kinkaid's! Get the Sheriff!

As Joyce nods, Sparks lopes by on his broken-down old horse. He is riding without a saddle.

Finally we see the POSSE riding as several of the men turn and look back. And the next scene shows what they see back in the direction of the saloon: Davies and Joyce are running back toward the saloon. The Judge still stands in the street. Darby has come out—towel in hand—and stands beside him. They are looking after the riders, and the Judge is waving his arms in anger. In the sky the clouds are beginning to boil. The wind is rising. Afternoon is fading.—The scene fades out.

PART TWO

A long view of a RANCH LANE fades in, showing the cavalcade of twenty-eight men loping along—the riders strung out in pairs. It is now late afternoon and the sky is overcast.

This cuts to a head-on view of the CAVALCADE, showing Tetley and Mapes in the lead and close behind them, Farnley and Bartlett. Then the scene moves over to the SIDE OF THE LANE and we see the posse ride by. Ma Grier and Winder are riding side by side. Farther back are Gerald Tetley and Pancho. Gerald is silent—staring. Pancho puffs his cigarette and looks pleased. Still farther back—almost at the end of the cavalcade—are Gil and Art. Then, last of all, comes Sparks, hunched up on the saddleless horse, his trouser legs inching up, exposing his naked dark shanks. Sparks is singing the old spiritual "Deep River" as he rides.

Next we see down the long LANE, in the distance, a solitary horseman riding fast, following which the scene cuts to a close view of DAVIES pushing his horse to catch up with the cavalcade.

At the INTERSECTION OF TWO LANES we then see Tetley turning in his saddle and holding up his hand. He and Mapes pull up, and the other horses close in to make a half circle. Nobody speaks as Mapes and Tetley turn off from the lane, reconnoitering.—And now we follow TETLEY and MAPES as they go for about fifty feet, stop, and look down. The grass has been churned with sharp marks of cattle.

MAPES. Fresh tracks all right.

TETLEY. About forty I'd say.

MAPES. About.

They look at each other and Mapes smiles. Tetley, dead-pan, turns and the moving view follows the pair back to the lane. At this moment Davies catches up. Tetley and the others look at him, surprised and none too pleased, but nobody says anything. Tetley gives the signal and the cavalcade starts off again, the men stringing out in pairs as before.

GIL and DAVIES ride off side by side. Gil looks across at the old man and grins.

GIL. Still tryin' to reform us?

Davies looks at him and a slight, sad—almost whimsical—smile forms on his lips, but he says nothing. Offscene Sparks resumes his low singing again.

The scene dissolves to a long view of the CAVALCADE as the road begins to climb into the hills. The going is harder here, and the horses are forced to pick their way slowly through the heavy boulders. The wind is stronger and it's beginning to get dark. Sparks' singing continues soft and low; only now he has switched to "It's Me, O Lord, Standing in the Need of Prayer."

Next GIL and GERALD TETLEY are seen riding side by side. Gerald shivers and Gil pulls his own reefer tighter.

GIL. Wind's pretty cold.

GERALD (*looking at Gil with a strange*

stare). It's more than wind. A lot more. . . . You can't go hunting men —like coyotes after rabbits—and not feel anything about it.

GIL. We're not hunting rabbits tonight.

GERALD. No, our own kind. And in a pack! (*Scornfully*) Even a mangy coyote wouldn't do that. (*In bitter outburst*) Cocks of the dungheap! Bullies of the globe! Twenty-eight of us—trying to keep up a lot of cheap pretenses about our strength and courage and good fellowship!—lying about what we really think and feel! —pretending to be so noble and superior when all the time we're wishing we were somewhere else!— just because we're afraid somebody might think we're yellow!

GIL (*angry, because he knows the boy is right*). What do you want us to do—sit and play a harp and worry about how bad we are while some rustler kills a man and cleans out the country? . . . . You're crazy!

GERALD (*quietly*). Anybody who tells the truth is crazy.

GIL (*annoyed—bitingly*). I'm not wrong about you being here, am I?

GERALD (*after a slight pause, quietly —digging himself up by the roots to say it*). No, I'm here all right. I'm here because I'm weak—and my father's not.

Gil looks at the boy quickly. The latter is obviously suffering the pangs of the damned. Gil is silent, not knowing what to say.

GERALD. I'm not claiming to be superior to anybody. I'm not even fit to be alive. Because I know better than to do what I'm doing. (*In anguish*) And that's hell. Can you understand that that's hell?

GIL. You take it too hard. You didn't start this.

GERALD. If we get those men and hang them, I'll kill myself. I won't go on living—remembering that I saw this and was part of it myself. I couldn't! I'd really go crazy!

GIL (*impatiently*). We haven't hung anybody yet. You can still go home and keep your hands clean.

GERALD (*dully*). No, I can't. And even if I could it wouldn't matter. I don't count.

He looks at Gil for a moment, then suddenly digs his heels into his horse and rides off ahead. Gil looks after him, a puzzled look on his face, then he shrugs his shoulders. Davies rides in beside Gil.

GIL. Say, what's feeding on that Tetley kid anyhow? He don't sound right bright in the head to me.

DAVIES. How would you feel if you knew your own father hated you?

GIL (*surprised*). What? His own son?

DAVIES. I think he'd kill the boy if he didn't look so much like his mother. (*As Gil looks at him amazed*) Tetley's ashamed of him because the boy's been sick a lot—likes to stay by himself and read—despises everything his father stands for. As long as Mrs. Tetley was alive, she acted as a sort of shield for Gerald. She was a pretty little thing, very gentle and charming—probably the only thing that Tetley ever loved in his life. (*There is a slight pause. He looks up at the sky.*) It'll be dark before we're out of this pass.

There is another moment of silence, and then as Gil softly begins to hum "Buffalo Gal" the scene dissolves to a MOUNTAIN ROAD at night. It is a steep pitch—near the top of the pass. The road hangs on the face of a cliff, with a black terrifying drop on the other side. The horses are hugging the cliff side of the road—sometimes scraping against it. There is silence for a moment, broken only by the clop of the horses' hoofs and their breathing. The wind is cutting through here. Suddenly a voice from up front—unmistakably Tetley's—calls out.

> TETLEY. We'll stop here for a minute, gentlemen, and breathe our horses. (*Seen close after this, he turns to one man.*) Winder, take one man with you and go up the top of the ridge and see what you can see.

This cuts to a SMALL CLEARING near the top of the pass where the men are but faintly seen as they come out of the pass and pull up and climb down, following which we get a close view of ART as he gets off his horse and stands swinging his arms against his chest. Other men about him are doing likewise. Gil rides up, dismounts, and pulls out a bottle.

> GIL. Doing this in the middle of the night is crazy.
>
> ART. I thought you liked excitement.
>
> GIL. I got nothin' particular against hangin' a murderin' rustler. It's just that I don't like it in the dark. (*After taking a pull at the bottle*) There's always some fool to lose his head and start hangin' everybody in sight.
>
> ART. Us?
>
> GIL (*passing the bottle to Art*). Funnier things have happened.
>
> ART. We didn't have to come.
>
> GIL. It'd looked kind of funny if we hadn't, wouldn't it? (*Wiping his mouth on his sleeve*) Besides I like to pick my own bosses.
>
> ART. Whether we picked 'em or not, we sure got 'em.
>
> GIL. That's what I don't like. That Smith and Bartlett shooting off their mouths—Farnley—and that renegade Tetley strutting around in that uniform—pretending he's so *much*! He never even saw the South till after the war—and then only long enough to marry that kid's mother and get run out of the place by her folks.

We get a close view of ART looking off toward Tetley, puzzled.

> ART. I figured there was something fishy about him—dressing up like that.
>
> GIL (*seen close*). Sure—what do you suppose he'd be doin' living in this neck of the woods if he didn't have something to hide.

GIL and ART start to get on their horses, and then we see TETLEY, FARNLEY, and DAVIES together.

> DAVIES. Major Tetley, wherever these men are heading they'll have to go through Pike's Hole. Why don't we send a couple of men up there and ask them to pick them up.
>
> FARNLEY (*harshly*). Listen, Davies —I'd rather see those fellows hung than shot because it's a dirtier death, but if anybody's gettin' cold feet, let 'em say so and I'll bushwack all three of 'em myself.
>
> GIL (*stepping up into the group*). If you ask me, nobody but a horse-thief would bushwack any man—let alone three—especially when you didn't even see 'em do anything.
>
> FARNLEY (*turning, angrily*). Who said that?

GIL. Me. Here.

But as he faces Farnley, a voice calls out excitedly:

VOICE. Scatter, boys! There's horses comin'!

Instantly (in a new scene that includes the entire cavalcade) the men and horses scatter to both sides of the road. They are just shadows, dimly seen. A moment later there is silence complete, except for the wind roaring in the trees.

TETLEY. Stay where you are, all of you, till I tell you when. Then circle out slowly if it's anything we want. Don't do any shooting.

Then the scene cuts to a close view of GIL, a little way off the road, listening. The silence is broken at last by the dull thud of horses' hoofs on the thick pine needles near him. It is almost pitch dark here.

GIL. Who's that?

SPARKS. Just me—Sparks. Who are you, suh?

GIL. Gil Carter.

SPARKS. Yu don't mahnd if ah come ovah a bit closah, do yu, Mistah Carter?

GIL. No. Come on. I'm finding it kind of lonesome myself.

Sparks steps up out of the darkness.

SPARKS. Mortal cold, ain't it?

GIL. I've got a blanket if you want it.

SPARKS (*with a sad little chuckle*). Thank yu just the same, Mistah Carter. It takes all mah hands to keep on this ole horse.

GIL. There's some whiskey in my canteen. Better have a couple of shots.

SPARKS. Ah don't drink it, suh. There's devil enough in me by mahself. (*After a pause*) Ah sure wish we was well out of this business.

GIL. It's a way of spending time.

SPARKS. It's man taking upon himself the Lord's vengeance.

GIL (*amused*). Do you think the Lord cares much about what's happening up here tonight?

SPARKS (*with quiet faith*). He marks the sparrow's fall. (*After another slight pause*). Ah saw mah own brother lynched, Mistah Carter. Ah was just a little fella—but sometimes ah still wake up dreaming about it

GIL. Had he done what they—picked him up for?

SPARKS. Ah don't know. We didn't any of us ever know for sure.

GIL. They wouldn't lynch him without knowing.

SPARKS. Oh, they made him confess, but it wouldn't have done him any good not to, and confessin' made it shorter.

Both are silent for a moment.

GIL. Well, a drop or two more whiskey can't do my soul any harm.

Gil lifts his canteen to his lips, and takes a big swallow.

GIL. That Darby sure sells rotten liquor. (*After taking another drink*) Warms you up, though. Feels just like fire creeping in the short grass. I guess I'll just let her spread a minute.

He sticks a cigarette in his mouth, and lights a match, covering the flame.

FARNLEY'S VOICE (*from offscene—low and hostile*). Put out that light, you fool! Want to give us away?

GIL (*the cigarette bobbing in his lips*). Who to?

This cuts to a close view of FARNLEY. He has drawn his gun—faintly evident—and is covering Gil. The hammer clicks.

FARNLEY. Chuck that butt or I'll plug you.

This cuts to GIL and SPARKS. Gil is still smoking—the cigarette bobbing in his mouth.

GIL. Start something and for every hole you make I'll make two.

SPARKS. It looks like you'll have a lot of shootin' to do, Mistah Farnley.

FARNLEY looks around. All through the little grove men are lighting up cigarettes—matches flaring, cigarettes glowing.

ART (*disgruntled*). Let's get moving before we freeze to death—or else give it up.

MA. We'd be the laughing stock of the country if we went home now on account of a little cold.

SMITH. That's right. But I'm tellin' you, this rope's sure going to have to be thawed out before it's fit to use.

Mapes' voice calls out warningly.

MAPES. Listen! Something's coming.

And we get a long view of the ROAD as a STAGECOACH with four horses looms up coming around a curve. There is a lantern swinging off the seat.

MAPES (*calling out*). Stop him!

As the men yell to the driver to stop, the scene cuts to a moving view of the STAGECOACH. It is not going very fast. The driver—ALEC SMALL—starts to pull up. The lead horses rear and the brakes squeal. Then he changes his mind, stands up and lets his whip go over the horses, the whip exploding like a pistol shot. The horses yank and the coach gets under way on a breakneck run, the lantern banging back and forth.—Seated beside Small is JIMMY CARNES. He is trying to get himself laid over the top in order to shoot. As the coach swings along there is a glimpse of the passengers inside—two women and a man. The women scream and inside the flapping curtain the light goes out.

CARNES (*shouting to the people in the coach*). Keep down! It's a stickup! They'll shoot!

MAPES is seen running toward the road.

MAPES. Hey, Alec! Alec! You fool! (*And other voices shout to the driver to stop.*)

This cuts to the COACH: The horses are racing wildly along the dark road now, the lantern bobbing. Next CARNES is seen stretching out and firing at random in the darkness, following which we see ART in the saddle. He cries out in pain and slumps forward as the coach and horses are heard crashing along the road, in the darkness.

This cuts to the COACH racing downhill at breakneck speed. There is a screeching of brakes and the excited screams of the passengers.

We get a close view of ART: His horse wheels excitedly. Art hangs onto the horn of his saddle, sick. He feels his shoulder, making silly little chattering sounds to himself.

ART. What a fool way to die!

The coach dips onto the steep downgrade. One instant the lantern is there—then it is winked out—followed by a wailing of brakes as the coach disappears.—Then a wide view shows the coach tearing down the road in imminent danger of overturning. Small is standing up trying to stop the frightened horses. Near the foot of the first pitch he succeeds, the coach stopping on the level-off just before the first turn which would undoubtedly have sent it over the side of the ledge. The lantern is still burning.

We see ART again. He is hanging on as Gil rides up to him. The other riders are going by on their way to the coach.

GIL. What's the matter, Art?

ART. I'm shot.

GIL. Where?

ART. Left shoulder.

This cuts to the COACH on the LEVEL-OFF: Small, the driver, is still trembling with fright. He is a thin, blond little man with a droopy mustache. Carnes, the man on top, a big, black-bearded fellow, is already climbing down. Mapes runs in and goes straight to look at the horses.

MAPES (*shouting at Small as he passes*). You fool! You must be drunk! Nobody but a drunken idiot would start down a grade like that in the dark!

SMALL (*whining*). I thought it was a stickup!

MAPES (*examining the horses' ankles*). If these horses hadn't been a sight smarter than you that coach would have been piled up in the bottom of the crevice right now!

The riders come hurrying in, surrounding the coach.

And now the door opens, and the passengers climb out. First out is a tall, thin man with mutton chop whiskers—MR. SWANSON. He is followed by his sister, MISS SWANSON, an equally tall, thin woman in dark silk, and finally by a beautifully built and handsomely gowned young woman, wearing a lacy bonnet, from under which looks a pair of big black eyes, broad cheeks, and full-shaped mouth.

MA. Rose Mapen!

Rose smiles, and that smile alone is enough to explain the lack of enthusiasm on the part of the other women. Rose and Miss Swanson are busy straightening out their rumpled clothing. Swanson takes Rose's elbow, possessively.

We see ART and GIL riding toward the coach. Suddenly Gil pulls up short and looks off—in amazement and pleasure.

ROSE'S VOICE (*gayly*). Hello, everybody! This is my husband—Mr. Swanson of San Francisco—

The smile dies from Gil's face and is succeeded by a look of intense jealousy and hatred as he hears her.

ROSE'S VOICE. —and my sister-in-law, Miss Swanson.

We see the group around ROSE and HER HUSBAND, the men bowing and smiling, some with smirks on their faces. Swanson smiles and nods.

SMITH (*grinning*). Just get married, Rose?

ROSE. Today.

SMITH. No wonder you was in such a hurry!

There is a laugh at this. Rose, too, smiles as does her husband, but they obviously don't care for the joke, and Miss Swanson frowns. Tetley steps forward and extends his hand to Swanson.

TETLEY (*with a charming grace*). My name is Tetley, sir—and I can quite understand why Miss Rose was in such a hurry to show the other ladies what could be done in the way of matrimony.

SWANSON (*smiling*). Thank you, sir.

ROSE (*puzzled—looking around*). Say—what are all you doing up here this time of night?

There is a slight pause. Nobody wants to tell.

TETLEY (*in an awkward spot*). Why, er—

Then she sees something and a look of fright comes into her eyes.—Gil and Art are approaching. Gil slips from his horse. He is looking off at Rose. ROSE looks fearfully toward Gil. GIL now stands, motionless, looking at Rose. SWANSON is watching Gil and his wife through slightly narrowed eyes. Finally, we see the group of people, Gil and Rose still looking at each other, the others watching them, expecting trouble. Rose is fascinated by Gil's stare, her gaze held by his. There is a long suspenseful pause.

GIL (*quietly*). Art's shot.

Then he turns toward Art, who is still mounted. The tension is somewhat relaxed. Davies and several others quickly step over to Art.

ART. It's nothing.

The view moves close to ART as he is helped from the saddle. A circle forms about him and the lantern is brought forward. Art sits down and Davies starts to take off his shirt. Gil takes the lantern and holds it so Davies can see. At the same time Gil heats the barrel of his gun over the flame. Rose moves next to Gil, watching him out of the corner of her eye.

CARNES (*bending over toward Art*). Gee, I'm sorry.

ART. You couldn't tell.

CARNES. You hadn't ought to come bargin' out like that! In the dark especially. I couldn't see who it was—and everybody yelling like that.

GIL (*tersely*). Shut up!

Rose drops to her knees beside Art, to assist Davies.

ROSE. I'm good at this sort of thing.

ART (*in pain, and anger*). Look! Do women have to watch this?

Rose looks at him, then up at Gil. For the first time, Gil grins at her—a big, knowing grin. She quickly gets to her feet. Moore hands Davies a canteen of whiskey and he pours it over Art's wound.

GIL (*grinning*). That's a mighty poor way to waste good whiskey, if you ask me.

Someone puts a lighted cigarette in Art's mouth, and he takes a deep pull on it. Gil applies the heated barrel to the wound, and Art cries out in pain.—

A couple of bandannas are handed to Davies, and he starts to bind the wound. Gil and Rose are still looking at each other.

DAVIES. There's room for you in the coach.

GIL (*looking at Rose*). Yeh, I'd better get you on back to Darby's and get some hot food in you.

ART. I'm all right.

Rose withdraws her eyes from Gil and leans forward toward Art again, taking his elbow.

ROSE (*smiling, invitingly*). Now, come on, like a good boy. Don't be stubborn.

GIL. Yeh, don't be a fool!

ART (*sharply, to Gil*). Mind your own business!

Rose again glances at Gil, who is obviously disappointed. Suddenly Rose straightens up and moves off, obviously upset by this contact with Gil.

Rose goes straight for the coach, gets in, and slams the door, Gil looking after her.—This cuts to a close view of SWANSON standing near the back wheel of the coach, watching this by-play; and then to GIL and ART both looking off at Swanson.

ART (*in a low voice*). Red whiskers is measuring you for a coffin, my friend.

GIL. Yeh? What have I said?

ART. That's his wife now. And kind of new.

GIL (*loudly*). It does look that way, don't it?

At this Swanson steps up to them.

SWANSON (*quietly—with a smile*). I take it that you had the privilege of knowing Miss Mapen before she became my wife?

GIL. That's right.

SWANSON. And that possibly you imagined, at the time, that there was some understanding between you?

GIL (*grinning insolently*). Sure.

SWANSON (*unruffled*). My wife is a very impulsive woman.

GIL. That's what I'm saying.

Swanson continues to smile. Gil is watching him. Art and several of the other men are looking on expectantly.

SWANSON (*easily*). Needless to say I'm pleased to regard any friend of my wife's as a friend of my own. However, I don't have to remind you that the pleasure of such an acquaintance depends upon the recognition by all parties of the fact that Miss Mapen is now my wife.

Gil is suddenly speechless—confused. There is a slight pause.

SWANSON (*smiling*). She must be given a little time to become accustomed to her new responsibilities. As yet, I must confess, I'm jealous of her least attention. You'll forgive me, I know. A bridegroom is prone to be overly susceptible for a time. Later, when we've had time to get accustomed to our new relations, I'll be delighted to welcome you and others of my wife's friends at our home in San Francisco—if it's still her desire. (*Nodding pleasantly*) Until then—

And he turns and goes back toward the coach. Gil watches him helplessly, at a complete loss. At the COACH, next, Swanson opens the door and gets in. He ostentatiously takes Rose's hand in his, then closes the door. He is not smiling now.

ART and GIL:

GIL (*under his breath*). Why, the superior little—! (*He breaks off flabbergasted.*)

ART (*grinning*). Looks to me like Rose has caught herself a load of trouble.

GIL (*his eyes narrowing*). Yeh, and maybe she ain't the only one.

ART (*frowning*). Forget it.

GIL (*turning and swinging up into the saddle*). Sure . . . For now!

The scene dissolves to a ROAD near the summit of a range. The men are riding along, slowly. The night wind is blowing fiercely now. This cuts to a close view of ART and GIL. Art rides with his head down, half asleep. Suddenly Gil reaches out and touches Art's arm. Art looks up, quickly.

ART. Where are we?

GIL. The Ox-Bow.

TETLEY and MAPES are seen at the head of the cavalcade. They are just pulling up, looking off. Others fall in around them, looking off eagerly. Then we see what they see through the trees across the Ox-Bow: In the distance a camp fire is burning. A cabin is faintly seen. Sometimes the fire flattens out in the wind—almost disappears. Then it flares up again.

TETLEY. There they are, gentlemen.

The MEN are now looking off, silent and motionless. Faintly, on the wind comes the bellowing of steers. Tetley is dead-pan, Davies worried, anxious. Farnley's eyes are narrowed with hatred, Mapes is grinning, Gerald is frightened, in great mental anguish.

TETLEY. I suggest that we avoid any shooting or rough work until they have had an opportunity to tell it their way. Mr. Mapes and I will do the talking.

FARNLEY (*with quiet force*). The one that got Kinkaid is mine. Don't forget that.

TETLEY (*evenly*). He's yours when we're sure. (*To his son*) Gerald, you and Farnley come with me. The unarmed men will go with Mrs. Grier and come up from behind. Bartlett, take six men and work through the woods back of the cabin. We will close in simultaneously. (*To Davies*) Would you like a gun, Mr. Davies?

DAVIES. No, thanks.

TETLEY. Sparks?

SPARKS. No, suh, Cun'l Tetley—Thank you jus' the same.

TETLEY (*turning away*). As you choose. (*Motioning the men to proceed*) Let's go, boys—and good luck.

And the horsemen start off, Ma leading one contingent, Bartlett another, Tetley the third.

The scene dissolves to a moving view of the VALLEY at night. Tetley and his group appear, riding slowly, carefully forward. Suddenly Tetley pulls up and they all stop.

MAPES (*in a low voice*). Want us to spread out, Major?

TETLEY. No, we'll ride in on them in a bunch.

He rises in his stirrups and peers off. Then we see, from his view, through the trees: The campfire is dying down slightly. About it the forms of three men are seen lying in blankets. Beyond them on a little rise is what is left of a cabin, dark and unoccupied.

Mapes reaches under his armpit and gets a gun. Farnley moves his carbine across his saddle and the hammer clicks. Gerald is staring off, blindly. Gil's hand reaches across and touches him. The boy turns and looks at Gil as if he didn't understand. Gil indicates his gun. Gerald looks at him without seeming to understand. Tetley silently indicates that they are to advance. The scene moves with them as they ride forward slowly, stealthily.

And now we see a MEXICAN lying with his head on a saddle, his feet toward the camp fire, wrapped in a blanket. Two other figures are just shapes in blankets. Tetley rides in and stops at the Mexican's head. The others of Tetley's group circle to cover all three men, who are still sleeping soundly unaware of any danger.

TETLEY (*sharply and loudly*). Get up!

The Mexican wakes immediately and sits up, trailing one hand under the blanket as he comes up.

FARNLEY (*sharply—from beside Tetley*). Drop it!

He points his carbine at the Mexican who freezes, one hand still under the blanket. He has heavy black hair and a small black mustache, and his hair is done up in a club at the neck like an Indian's. He looks up at Farnley and Tetley, and suddenly he smiles as if he had just understood. As he does so, he brings his hand from under the blanket and drops a long-barrelled nickel-plated revolver onto the blanket.

FARNLEY. Now put 'em up.

The Mexican just stares and shrugs.

MEXICAN. No sabbey.

FARNLEY. That's all right, brother. You will. (*He punches at the Mexican with the barrel of his carbine.*)

We get a close view of an OLD MAN with tangled grey hair and a long drooping mustache and very thick eyebrows, looking up in bewilderment at Mapes, who has dismounted and is keeping him covered; then a close view of a young man, MARTIN, who has been sleeping with his gun on and his boots off. He starts to rise, but Gil, standing over him, covers him quickly.

GIL. Take it easy, Mister. Stay where you are and put your hands up.

Martin is a tall, thin, dark young man, with sensitive eyes and mouth. He stares at Gil, bewildered, not sure he isn't still dreaming.

This cuts to a wider view around the fire. The three men are covered now.

TETLEY (*dismounting; quietly*). Gerald—collect their guns.

MARTIN (*looking off at Tetley*). What are you trying to do? What do you want?

MAPES (*harshly, turning from the old man*). Shut up. We'll tell you when we want you to talk.

GIL. This is no stickup, brother. This is a posse, if that means anything to you.

MARTIN (*protesting earnestly*). But we haven't done anything!

Tetley looks at Gerald who is still mounted.

TETLEY (*sharply, his eyes narrowing*). Gerald!

Gerald dismounts dreamily, and picks up the Mexican's gun. Then like a sleepwalker he crosses toward Martin.

TETLEY (*sharply*). Behind him!

Gerald stops and looks at his father, puzzled.

GERALD. What?

TETLEY (*harshly*). Wake up! **Don't** get between him and Carter.

As Gerald starts to collect the guns, finding a carbine under Martin's blanket, Tetley turns to Martin.

TETLEY. Are there any more of you?

MARTIN (*angrily—starting to lower his arms*). I'd like to know what business it is—

MAPES (*prodding Martin with his gun*). Shut up—and keep them up!

TETLEY. It's all right, Mr. Mapes . . Tie their hands.

Several men instantly step forward with ropes, and start to tie the three men up.

MARTIN (*protesting*). At least you might tell us what we're being held for!

TETLEY (*with a quiet smile*). I'd rather you told us.

As the men are brought into the center and tied together—the Mexican stolid, the old man dazed, Martin angry and humiliated—Tetley walks over in front of the fire, stands with legs apart, warming his hands, a smile on his face. One of the men throws more wood on the fire and it blazes up. The Mexican's chin is down on his chest but he is watching everything. He looks smart and hard, expressionless. Suddenly sounds of others approaching are heard, and he looks around quickly.

We see with him: Ma Grier and her group coming out of the shadows toward the fire. Then a close view of MARTIN shows him looking off in the other direction, and he sees: Bartlett leading his group in toward the fire, silent and menacing. Finally, we see the entire GROUP as the rest of the posse come in.

MARTIN (*bitterly*). We must be pretty important—or else awfully dangerous.

MA (*getting off her horse*). It ain't that you're so dangerous, son. It's just that most of the boys has never seen a real triple hanging.

The other men are all getting off their horses, coming toward the fire with coils of rope.

MARTIN. Hanging? (*Looking around*) What have we done? (*After a moment of silence*) Aren't you even going to tell us what we're accused of?

MAPES (*importantly*). Rustlin'. Ever hear of it?

MARTIN. Rustling?

FARNLEY. And murder!

MARTIN (*looking at him foolishly*). Murder?

He runs his tongue over his lips for a moment—seems about to fold up. The old man begins to moan.

OLD MAN (*piteously*). Mr. Martin, what do we do?

MARTIN (*quietly*). It's all right, Dad. There's some mistake.

Martin looks around as if he were dreaming. And indeed there is something unreal about the scene—the firelight on the faces watching in a leaning ring—the big long heads of the horses peering from behind, the quiet men, some still sitting in their saddles.

We see the MEXICAN as Bartlett steps up to him.

BARTLETT. Remember me?

The Mexican looks at him as if he didn't hear or understand. Farnley wheels and slaps him in the belly with the back of his hand.

FARNLEY. He's talking to you, Mister.

MEXICAN (*looking bewildered*). No sabbey.

MAPES. He don't speak English.

BARTLETT. I got a different notion.

FARNLEY. I'll make him talk! (*And he prods the Mexican with his gun.*)

TETLEY (*sharply*). That will do, Farnley.

FARNLEY (*turning angrily on Tetley*). Listen, you! I've had enough of you playing God Almighty! Who picked you for this job anyhow? (*As Tetley *just looks at him coolly*) We got 'em! I say let's swing 'em—before we all freeze to death!

TETLEY (*quietly*). If you're cold— here's the fire. Warm yourself.

Farnley looks at Tetley murderously, as if ready to jump at him.

TETLEY (*coldly*). And I advise you to control your tongue, too, and we'll get along better.

Then he turns his back on Farnley, and we get another view of MARTIN and TETLEY.

TETLEY. Who's boss of this outfit?

MARTIN. I am.

TETLEY. And your name?

MARTIN. Donald Martin.

TETLEY. Where you from?

MARTIN. Pike's Hole.

At this one of the riders named Mark steps forward.

MARK. That's a lie!

Martin turns and looks at Mark. Tetley smiles.

TETLEY. This gentleman here is from Pike's Hole. Would you like to change your story?

MARTIN. I just moved in three days ago. I'm on Dave Baker's place up at the North end.

MARK (*to Tetley*). Dave Baker moved out four years ago. His place is a wreck—barns down, sagebrush stickin' up through the porch.

MARTIN. I bought the place from him for four thousand dollars in Los Angeles last month.

MARK (*laughing*). Then, mister, you been robbed.

MARTIN. Maybe. But you can't hang me just for being a sucker.

SMITH (*grinning*). Some folks has been hung for a whole lot less, brother.

MARTIN (*to Tetley*). Surely it's not so far to Pike's Hole that you can't go over there and find out. My wife's there right now—and my two kids.

SMITH (*clucking his tongue in old-maid sympathy*). Now that's really too bad. Just too, too bad!

MARTIN (*bursting out angrily*). Even in this Godforsaken country I've got a right to a trial!

TETLEY. You're getting a trial, with twenty-eight of the only kind of judges murderers and rustlers get— in what you call this "Godforsaken country."

WINDER. And so far the jury don't like your story.

Martin looks around; then his jaw sets defiantly.

MARTIN (*slowly*). I won't say another word without a proper hearing.

MA (*smiling*). Suit yourself, son. But this is all the hearing you're likely to get short of the last judgment.

We again see MARTIN and TETLEY together.

TETLEY. Have you any cattle up here with you?

Martin stares at him but doesn't reply. He shuts his mouth hard. Smith steps up to him with a rope making a hangman's noose. Martin looks at it, and sucks in his breath.

TETLEY (*quietly*). I'm not going to ask you again.

Davies: Wait a minute, men. Let's not go off half-cocked and do something we'll be sorry for.

Judge (*yelling after them*): Tetley, you bring those men in alive or, as I'm Justice of this county, you'll pay for it —

Martin is trying to write his letter.

Martin: I suppose it's no good telling you again that we're innocent?

MARTIN (*frightened—his eyes glued to the rope*). Yes, I have.

TETLEY. How many?

MARTIN (*watching the rope, fascinated*). Fifty head.

TETLEY. Where'd you get 'em?

MARTIN. From Mr. Kinkaid.

We see the GROUP: The men look at one another and nod, accepting this as proof. Tetley smiles briefly. Farnley glowers.

MA (*nodding*). That's what we figured, son.

MARTIN is seen close as he speaks earnestly, then looks around pleadingly.

MARTIN. I'm no rustler, though. I didn't steal them. I bought and paid cash for them.—My own were so bad I didn't dare risk bringing them up. So I sold them off in Salinas and I had to stock up again.

We get a larger view, including the others, as he sees that no one has accepted his story.

MARTIN. You can wait, can't you, till you see Mr. Kinkaid, or ask about me in Pike's Hole?

FARNLEY. That's a good one! He wants us to wait and ask Larry Kinkaid.

SMITH (*shaking his head*). I got to hand it to you, Martin. You're a cool one all right.

FARNLEY (*angrily, as Martin looks puzzled*). You know as well as we do that Larry Kinkaid can't tell us anything. He's dead.

MARTIN (*shocked—or pretending to be*). Dead?

SMITH. As a doornail.

FARNLEY. What do you think we're up here for?

MARTIN (*in sudden anger*). Well, how should I know? He was all right yesterday afternoon! (*Then yelling at them*) Listen! Why don't you stop this farce and take us in if you think we had anything to do with it?

FARNLEY (*with quiet menace*). Because the law's mighty slow and careless around here sometimes and we aim to see it's speeded up.

There is a slight pause, and Martin looks around wildly.

MARTIN. Who sent you up here?

TETLEY. The sheriff.

At this Davies steps closer to the fire.

DAVIES. That's not true.

SMITH (*groaning*). Oh, don't let's get started again! It's one o'clock now.

DAVIES. The sheriff didn't even know we were coming.

Tetley is watching Davies closely, a faint smile on his lips.

TETLEY. I beg your pardon—I should have said the deputy sheriff.

And he smiles at Mapes who grins, flattered and pleased.

DAVIES (*turning from Tetley—appealing to the group*). Listen, men, I'm not trying to obstruct justice, but as this young man says, this is a farce and it'll be murder if you carry it through. All he's asking is what any man's entitled to—a fair trial. (*Looking at Martin*) You say you're innocent, Martin, and I, for one, believe you.

MA (*dryly*). Then I guess you're the only one that does, Arthur.

Tetley jerks his head towards Mapes and the latter steps out and grabs Davies' arm and forces him back.— Then we see a moving view of DAVIES and MAPES as the deputy pushes Davies back, the latter struggling helplessly

DAVIES (*loudly*). If there's any justice in your proceedings, Tetley, it would only be after a confession. And they haven't confessed! They say they're innocent and you haven't proved they aren't.

TETLEY (*quietly, to Mapes*). Keep him there. (*Turning back to Martin*) Have you a bill-of-sale for those cattle?

MARTIN (*swallowing hard*). No, I haven't, but Kinkaid said it was all right. I couldn't find him at the ranch house. He was out on the range and didn't have a bill-of-sale with him. He said he'd mail it to me.

TETLEY (*without turning*). Moore.

MOORE (*stepping up behind Tetley*). Yes?

TETLEY (*still without turning toward Moore*). How long have you been riding for Kinkaid?

MOORE. Six years.

TETLEY. Did you ever know him to sell any cattle without a bill-of-sale?

MOORE (*unhappily*). No, I can't say I ever did. Of course I can't remember every head he sold in six years.

TETLEY. But it's customary for him to give a bill-of-sale?

MOORE. Yes.

TETLEY (*his eyes boring into Martin*). Did you ever know him to sell any cattle after Spring roundup? This year or any other year?

FARNLEY. I can answer that. I heard him say myself just a couple of days ago he wouldn't sell a head to nobody this Spring.

TETLEY (*to Martin*). Well?

MARTIN (*in a slow, tired voice*). I know it looks bad—giving a dead man for a witness—but it's the truth. (*After a pause*) You don't believe me?

TETLEY. Would you in my place?

MARTIN (*boldly*). I'd find out. I'd do a lot of finding out before I'd risk hanging three men who might be innocent.

TETLEY (*quietly*). If it were only rustling, maybe. But with murder, no.

There is a moment of silence. The faces of the men are serious, mouths hard, eyes bright and nervous. Farnley and Winder are knotting ropes. Martin's eyes go to them—he stares at them, fascinated.

We see FARNLEY'S HANDS KNOTTING ROPES. This cuts to MA, frowning.

MA. What are you trying to do, Tetley? Play cat and mouse with them?

This cuts to TETLEY, staring at Martin.

TETLEY. I would prefer a confession, Martin.

MARTIN seen close, swallows and wets his lips, but can't speak. Then he groans. The sweat breaks out on his face and his jaw is shaking. Then a more inclusive scene shows the old man mumbling to himself and the Mexican standing firmly, feet a little apart, saying nothing. Gil steps forward, scowling.

GIL. I don't see your game, Tetley. If you've got any doubts I say let's call off this party and take 'em in to the Judge like Davies wants.

TETLEY (*coldly*). This is only slightly any of your business, my friend. Remember that.

Gil drops his hand on his gun, and takes a step toward Tetley.

GIL (*hotly*). Hanging's any man's business who's around.

A couple of men reach out to stop Gil, but Tetley is as cool and unconcerned as ever.

TETLEY. If your stomach for justice is cooling, Carter, I suggest that you leave now before we proceed any further. Otherwise your interruptions will become very tiresome.

GIL (*still sore*). I still don't like it. Hanging murderers is one thing. To keep men you don't know for sure did it standing and sweating while you shoot off your mouth's another.

We see GIL and ART.

ART (*in a low voice*). Take it easy. This ain't our picnic. (*As Gil looks at him*) But if you keep on butting in, I've got a hunch it may be.

MARTIN and TETLEY:

TETLEY. You called this old man "Dad." Is he your father?

MARTIN (*in a very low voice*). No.

TETLEY (*sharply*). Speak up, man. You're taking it like a woman.

Martin lifts his head and faces them. Tears are running down his cheeks and his lips tremble.

MA (*cheerfully*). Keep your chin up, son. Everybody's got to die once.

MARTIN (*loudly*). No. He works for me.

OLD MAN (*blubbering*). But I didn't do it. I didn't even have no gun.

TETLEY (*quietly—turning to the old man*). Then who did?

OLD MAN (*pointing to the Mexican*). He done it. He told me so. (*His face lighting up with cunning*) No, he didn't. I saw him do it.

A close view shows FARNLEY looking at the Mexican, murderous hatred in his eyes, and then all the men are seen looking at the Mexican menacingly.

MARTIN. Juan couldn't have done anything. I was with him all the time.

OLD MAN (*who has been nodding; turning to Martin*). Yes he did, Mr. Martin. He was asleep. He didn't mean to tell me, but I was awake and I heard him talking about it.

MARTIN (*quietly*). The old man's feeble-minded. He doesn't know what he's talking about. He invents things. (*Then flaring up, as the men stare at him unbelieving*) Listen! If you've got to go through with this filthy comedy you can at least let him alone, can't you?

At this, Mapes takes a step closer to Martin.

MAPES (*quietly*). Shut up.

And suddenly he slaps Martin across the face—a stinging blow, so hard that if Martin were not tied he would be knocked over. Tears spring into Martin's eyes.

VOICES (*protesting—shamed*). Lay off, Mapes! You've got no call for that sort of thing!

MAPES (*scowling at Martin, angrier than ever because of the reproof*). First he won't talk—now he talks too much.

As Mapes sullenly moves aside, Tetley resumes his cross-examination as if he had never been interrupted.

TETLEY (*jerking his head toward the old man*). What's his name?

MARTIN. Alva Hardwick.

TETLEY (*indicating the Mexican*). And the other?

MARTIN. Juan Martinez.

BARTLETT. No, it ain't. (*And he steps up to the Mexican.*)

We get a close view of BARTLETT and the MEXICAN as Bartlett puts his face right in front of the prisoner.

BARTLETT. Still don't remember me?

The Mexican only stares at him as if he hadn't understood.

BARTLETT (*angrily*). I'm talking to you, mister.

MEXICAN (*with a shrug*). No sabbey.

BARTLETT. The devil you don't. Your name's Francisco Morez and the Vigilantes would like to get hold of you.

This cuts to a fuller scene as Bartlett turns to Tetley.

BARTLETT. He was a gambler. They want him for murder.

TETLEY (*to Martin*). How about that?

MARTIN (*hopelessly*). I don't know.

SMITH. They stick together nice, don't they?

MARTIN (*bitterly*). Why do you ask me all these questions when you don't believe anything I tell you?

TETLEY (*quietly*). There's truth in lies, too—if you get enough of them. (*After a pause*) What do you know about the old man?

MARTIN. He was in the army.

TETLEY. Confederate or Union?

MARTIN. I don't know. He's not clear about it, himself. Maybe both—at different times.

TETLEY (*smiling his disbelief*). A half-wit in the army?

We see TETLEY, MARTIN and the OLD MAN, as drawing himself up stiffly, Tetley clicks his heels.

TETLEY (*his voice ringing out*). Atten—tion!

The old man just looks at him vacantly. Tetley relaxes and smiles.

TETLEY. I don't think so.

MARTIN. He's forgotten.

TETLEY. Not that! (*After a slight pause*) I'll make a deal with you, Martin. Tell us which of you shot Kinkaid and the other two can wait.

Martin glances at the Mexican. There is a slight pause.

MARTIN (*quietly*). None of us killed anybody.

His eyes meet Tetley's. Tetley's eyes narrow.

TETLEY. Then that's all, I guess.

Thereupon the scene cuts to a more inclusive view of the others, and Tetley turns and motions toward a nearby tree.

MARTIN (*huskily*). You don't mean you're going to, really!

As Tetley merely smiles that thin smile, Martin suddenly starts to tug at his bonds, jerking the other two prisoners about. In the struggle the old man falls to his knees.

MARTIN. You can't!

TETLEY (*quietly*). Bring them along.

As he turns away, several men step forward and untie the three men. Then ropes are looped about the prisoners so that their arms are held flat against their sides.

MARTIN (*as he is being roped*). My kids!—One of them is just a baby! Just a baby! They haven't got a thing to go on—not a thing! They're alone!

But the men drag him off, and we next see him and the other two men being led across toward the tree, following Tetley and Farnley; Martin resisting—holding back—trying to dig his heels into the ground.

FARNLEY (*over his shoulder—at the Mexican*). The Mexican is mine. (*Tetley nods.*)

MARTIN (*as he is dragged along*). Give us some time! You've got to give us some time!

The old man's knees buckle under him and he stumbles, but the Mexican walks straight and steady, a wry smile on his face. As they come to the tree, they are lined up in a row.

OLD MAN (*moaning*). I don't want to die in the dark. I'm scared of the dark.

MARTIN (*pleadingly*). I've got to write a letter. If you're human you'll give me time for that anyway.

GIL. That's not asking much, Tetley.

MAPES. They're scared and they're trying to put it off, that's all.

FARNLEY. Yeh, do you want Tyler and the sheriff to get here and the job not done?

DAVIES (*sadly*). They won't come in this weather.

TETLEY (*smiling at Davies*). I believe you're right, Mr. Davies—though I doubt if you want to be. (*To Bartlett*) What time is it?

BARTLETT (*pulling out his watch and looking at it*). Five minutes after three.

TETLEY. All right. We don't want to give anyone cause for complaint. With your permission, gentlemen, we'll wait till daylight. (*He starts back toward the fire, smiling at Sparks as he goes.*) That'll give you time, Reverend, to settle your business at leisure.

FARNLEY (*grinning*). Sure. And them time to think it over.

We watch the men being led back to the fire, Tetley in the lead.

MARTIN (*indicating his tied hands*). I can't write like this.

TETLEY (*briefly*). Very well—untie them.

The ropes are quickly removed from the three prisoners. Martin stands rubbing his wrists. The Mexican turns to Pancho and speaks quickly in Spanish.

PANCHO (*translating*). He says he wants to eat. He is much hungry from so much much of the talk. (*The Mexican grins broadly.*)

This cuts to a close view of MARTIN and DAVIES as Davies offers Martin a pencil and a small leather-bound account book.

MARTIN. Thank you.

MA has been prowling around in Martin's saddle bag, and she pulls out a potato sack full of fresh beef rolled up in paper.

MA. Look! Fresh beef!

The men turn and look at Ma. Smith is taking a bottle from his pocket.

SMITH. Fix a spread for everybody, Ma! (*Looking around with a grin*) Can't nobody say it's robbery either, seeing by the time it's et it won't belong to anybody anyway. (*He takes a big drink.*)

MOORE (*turning away in disgust*). Nothing for me!

VOICES. Me neither. You can count me out.

SMITH (*grinning*). Queasy?

GIL (*scowling*). You don't eat a man's food in front of him—then hang him.

Smith just grins and takes another drink. Davies shakes his head sadly—Gerald turns quickly away, averting his eyes.

The scene dissolves to a view at the FIRE: Steaks are propped on forked sticks cooking; the grease falling into the fire sizzles. Then we see that several of the men, excepting those who eventually step out with Davies, have changed their minds and are now eating steaks. Ma is superintending the cooking.—The MEXICAN is eating big mouthfuls, taking his time and enjoying it. The OLD MAN is chewing and staring, apparently not even tasting the food.

MARTIN is trying to write his letter. He stares at the fire, his eyes glazed; he shivers, then puts the pencil to the paper, thinks, then stares again. Sparks steps up in front of him.

SPARKS (*kindly*). You better eat somethin' too, Mistah Martin.

Martin shakes his head absent-mindedly, writes something, then rubs it out.

We see ART and GIL stretched out on a blanket, smoking.

ART (*in a low voice*). What are you thinkin' about?

GIL. That sheriff. He's an awful long time gettin' anywhere.

ART. Suppose he don't get here at all?

GIL. That's what I'm wondering about. (*They look at each other for a moment then turn and look off-scene.*)

A close view shows GERALD picking up little sticks and digging hard in the ground. Suddenly the boy gets up and the scene moves with him as he crosses to the edge of the dark and stands with his back to the crowd. This cuts to a close view of TETLEY looking off at Gerald and frowning. Suddenly he, too, gets up. Then we see Tetley going over to Gerald and saying something in a low voice. Gerald turns and looks at him, then without a word, returns to the fire.

The scene dissolves to a close view of SPARKS and the OLD MAN. Sparks is down on his knees in front of him, singing softly "To the Promised Land I'm Bound to Go," but the old man is paying no attention—just staring at the fire. The wind has died down.

MARTIN sits hunched forward, his forehead in his hands. A giggle is heard and as he looks up he sees: MA and MONTY SMITH. Smith has one arm around Ma's thick middle and is holding the bottle up to her. She giggles and shakes her head. MARTIN draws his eyes away and bends his head, locking his hands behind it and pulling down hard as if stretching his neck. Suddenly Tetley's voice is heard.

TETLEY'S VOICE. I'm not disputing that fact, Mr. Davies. It may be a fine letter.

And at this Martin looks up quickly and frowns. Davies is seen holding Martin's letter out to Tetley—his back to Martin.

> TETLEY. But if it's an honest letter it's none of my business to read it, and if it isn't I don't want to.
>
> MARTIN (*in sudden, fierce anger*). Is that my letter you're showing?
>
> TETLEY (*smiling past Davies*). Yes. (*Davies turns to Martin.*)
>
> MARTIN (*angrily, to Davies—as he gets to his feet*). What are you doing, showing my letter?

Several of the other men sit up quickly and listen. Smith releases Ma and scrambles to his feet.

> SMITH (*threateningly—as he starts for Martin*). Don't go raisin' your voice like that, rustler.
>
> DAVIES (*stopping Smith*). Never mind, Smith. He's right. I told him I'd keep it for him.
>
> MARTIN (*starting for Davies*). All I asked you to do was make sure it was delivered.
>
> DAVIES. I'm sorry. I was just trying to prove—

Farnley steps in front of Martin, his gun out.

> FARNLEY. Sit down, you—and pipe down.

But Martin shows no sign of retreating. He is thoroughly aroused and indignant.

> MARTIN (*loudly*). It's enough to be hanged by a pack of bullying outlaws without having your private thoughts handed around to them for a joke.
>
> DAVIES. I said I'm sorry. I was merely—
>
> MARTIN (*cutting in*). I don't care what you were doing! I didn't write that letter to be passed around. It's none of these other murderers' business.
>
> FARNLEY (*warningly*). Easy on that talk!
>
> DAVIES (*earnestly*). I made no promise, son.
>
> MARTIN (*sick with scorn*). I thought there was one white man among you. Well, I was wrong. (*Brokenly*) Give me that letter.
>
> DAVIES (*holding the letter tightly*). I'll see that she gets it.
>
> MARTIN (*bitterly*). I wouldn't have her touch it now!
>
> TETLEY. In that case, give him his letter, Davies.

We get a close view of DAVIES and MARTIN.

> DAVIES (*quietly*). Your wife ought to hear from you, son. None of us could be as kind and understanding as this letter. She'll want to keep it—for your children.

Martin stares at him for a moment, then the wrath dies out of him.

> MARTIN (*quietly*). I'm sorry.

As Davies nods, Ma's voice cries out excitedly.

> MA'S VOICE. Hey! The Mex!

At this Martin and Davies turn quickly and look off, and we see Ma pointing off, excitedly, toward the woods where the horses are tied. In the background the Mexican can be seen working on a rope trying to release one of the horses. There are several yells and a wild scramble.

> BARTLETT (*warningly*). Spread out! He may have a gun!

A close view of MARTIN and DAVIES discloses Martin looking off, the old man seated on the ground at his feet whimpering like a scared child.

> TETLEY'S VOICE. Mapes—Winder—keep an eye on these two! (*Rushing past Davies*) If you're part of this trick, Davies—(*Several shots ring out.*)

The MEXICAN is seen working on the rope. As more shots go by him he yanks the horse around and shoots across it. The MEN drop, others scurry for safety behind trees and bushes. More shots are fired. The horse is rearing with fright. Suddenly the Mexican turns and makes a break for it on foot. FARNLEY jumps up, aims with his carbine, and fires. Then he dashes after the Mexican. The others jump up and follow him, several firing as they run.

We see the GROUP around the fire: The two prisoners, Davies, Gil, Art, Sparks, Gerald, Winder and Mapes stand frozen in their tracks, listening, watching. There is a long moment of silence. Then the quiet is broken by three short flat shots in quick succession, followed by a deeper one that echoes. Then there is quiet again, after which two more short flat shots are heard and a deeper one in reply. Again there is quiet. We see in successive close shots or closeups GERALD, listening, trembling; MARTIN, listening, keyed up; DAVIES staring into the darkness, tight-lipped.

Then the men come back toward the fire, half-carrying the Mexican. The MEXICAN is held up by Farnley and Bartlett. He is sweating and is obviously wounded.

> TETLEY. Where's he hit?

> FARNLEY. In the leg.

They move to the fire and the Mexican immediately sits down on a log. He is in considerable pain. Bartlett bends over and takes a pistol from the Mexican.

> BARTLETT. Here's his gun.

He hands the pistol to Tetley, who looks at it curiously. Then he smiles.

> TETLEY. Well, I guess we know now, don't we? (*He hands the gun to Farnley.*)

> FARNLEY (*staring at the gun*). Say! That's Larry Kinkaid's gun! (*Pointing to the butt*) Look!

A close view shows the name "Laurence Liam Kinkaid" inlaid in letters of gold in the ivory butt. Then we see Tetley turning to the Mexican—the other men looking on menacingly.

> TETLEY. Where'd you get this?

> MEXICAN (*in English; grinning savagely*). If somebody will take this bullet out of my leg, I'll tell you.

> MA. Oh! So he talks American!

> MEXICAN (*looking up at her*). And ten other languages, my dear. But I don't tell anything I don't want to in any of them. (*Indicating his leg*) My leg, please. I wish to stand upright when you come to your pleasure. (*Looking around*) If someone will lend me a knife, I'll take it out myself.

> BARTLETT (*quickly*). Don't give him no knife. He can throw a knife better than most men can shoot.

> MEXICAN (*smiling*). Better than any of you, no doubt. But if you're afraid —I promise to give the knife back—handle first.

> GERALD (*stepping up in front of the Mexican*). I'll do it.

As Tetley looks at his son in astonishment that quickly changes to a cold unspoken rage, Gerald kneels in front of the Mexican. There is a brief pause, then Farnley offers him a knife, but Gerald's hands shake so he can't use it. He puts his hand up as if to clear his eyes. The Mexican, amused, takes the knife away from him. Farnley's carbine turns on the Mexican. Several other guns are turned on him instantly, but he pays no attention. With one stroke he slashes through his chaps from thigh to boot top, exposing a wound just above the knee. Gerald gets to his feet, drunkenly, and turns away, unable to look at it.

MEXICAN (*grinning*). He is very polite but he has no stomach for blood, eh? (*As he looks at the wound*) Will somebody please make the fire better? There is not enough light.

A close view shows TETLEY looking at Gerald as the boy stumbles past him. His eyes narrow and at this moment you can believe he would kill Gerald.

At the FIRE, Mark throws on some more wood and the fire blazes up, lighting the faces of the men as they watch the Mexican, fascinated. There is no sound except the Mexican's panting. Then the Mexican begins to hum a Mexican dance tune, "Jorabe Tatatio."—A closeup of the MEXICAN shows him humming. He breaks off, grunts, then hums again.

GERALD, out on the edge of the dark, is hanging onto a tree limb with one hand, his back to the Mexican. He is weak and shaken. And this cuts to a closeup of TETLEY looking toward his son in a cold rage.

The MEXICAN looks at a slug which he has taken from his leg, then up at Farnley.

MEXICAN (*sarcastically*). That was fine shooting, my friend. (*Tossing it to Farnley, who scowls at him*) You should try again with that one.

Then he picks up the knife and, quick as a flash, tosses it so that it spins through the air and buries itself in the ground at Farnley's feet. Farnley automatically withdraws his foot. The Mexican grins up at him and winks. Then he starts to tie his neckerchief around the wound. Gil has lighted a cigarette and he reaches out and puts it in the Mexican's mouth. It is a gesture of respect for a brave man, and the Mexican takes a couple of deep puffs. Tetley steps up in front of him.

TETLEY. Now where'd you get that gun?

MEXICAN (*smoking*). I found it.

TETLEY. Where?

MEXICAN. Lying in the road.

TETLEY (*quietly*). You're a liar.

MEXICAN (*lazily exhaling smoke*). I thought we might find somebody to send it back by.

TETLEY (*his eyes narrowing*). You're a liar.

MEXICAN (*suddenly angry and stubborn looking*). And you're a blind fool!

TETLEY (*eyes narrowing*). I asked you where you got it.

MEXICAN (*shrugging*). No sabbey.

MARTIN. But that's the truth. He did find it.

Tetley looks at Martin, shrugs, and a faint smile crosses his face.

TETLEY (*ironically*). Undoubtedly.

Then he turns his back on Martin and the Mexican.

Near the edge of the dark, Davies is seen urgently trying to induce Art and

Gil to read Martin's letter. A couple of other men stand nearby.

DAVIES (*in a low voice*). Won't you even read it?

They both shake their heads. Davies holds it out to the other men. The others too shake their heads.

DAVIES. Is it because you've made up your minds? (*As they look at him without replying*) Or because you think everybody else has and you're afraid to stand up for what you feel is right?

GIL (*brusquely*). You heard what Martin said about showing his letter.

DAVIES (*sharp reproof in his voice*). Do you suppose it matters to him or his wife who sees this letter if it means his life? (*Pushing it toward them, pleadingly*) It's a beautiful letter. Read it and you'll know he's not the kind of man who could steal or kill.

ART (*stubbornly*). Maybe. But all that kind of argument in the world can't stand up against branded cattle, no bill-of-sale, and a dead man's gun.

At this Davies seems to shrink before their very eyes. His shoulders droop.

DAVIES. If we hang these men without a trial, we're due to be hanged ourselves.

ART. And who'll hang us?

DAVIES (*wearily*). Nobody maybe, and that's why we'll be worse than murderers. Their act puts them outside the law but keeps the law intact. Lynching weakens the very law itself.

ART. Yeh, but suppose the law don't work—and let's 'em go?

DAVIES. Better that—a thousand times —than commit a sin against society itself!

GIL (*annoyed because he doesn't want to think about such things*). Listen! Why pick on us? We're just a couple of the boys. We don't count.

DAVIES (*pleadingly*). Sometimes if only two or three people will listen—

GIL (*cutting in*). We've listened. What can we do?

Davies looks at the men, defeated. Then he looks down at the letter.

A closeup shows TETLEY looking toward Davies.

TETLEY (*impatiently*). Gentlemen, I suggest we act as a unit so there can be no question of mistaken reprisals. Mr. Davies, are you willing to abide by a majority decision?

DAVIES looks up and off at Tetley, and makes no reply. The men are now looking at Davies, waiting. He merely puts the letter in his pocket.

TETLEY. How about the rest of you people?

VOICES (*Mapes, Farnley, Winder taking the lead*). Sure. Go ahead. Majority rules.

TETLEY. Everybody who is with Mr. Davies for putting this thing off and turning it over to the courts, step over here.

And he points to a space in the center of the group. Davies immediately steps forward. There is a slight pause, then Sparks shambles out and joins Davies, smiling apologetically. After another slight pause, Moore also steps out beside Davies, followed by another man. Then Gil moves up beside Davies, followed after a moment by Art. We see

MARTIN watching, torn between hope and fear.

And now a closeup of TETLEY shows a faint, sardonic smile playing on his face. Then the smile fades and his face becomes a stern mask as he sees what his son is doing.—We see Gerald Tetley stepping out into the center beside Davies. His fists are clenched. Seven men in all comprise the group.

A closeup shows DAVIES looking around the circle of faces, a pleading look in his eyes. Then the moving view picks out the FACES of the men. They avert their eyes, but no one else responds. Farnley is scowling at the seven men who have dared vote for the law. Monty Smith is taking a drink. Gabe Hart grins stupidly. Ma Grier is looking off at the sky.

TETLEY is now self-possessed, showing no signs of weariness or excitement.

TETLEY. Seven. Not a majority, I believe, Mr. Davies.

MARTIN's last hope seems to drain out of him. He turns and looks off at the HORIZON: It is just beginning to get light. The cabin and trees can be seen clearly. There is no sunrise, just a slow leaking of light from all quarters.

This cuts to a view of the GROUP as Tetley steps over to Martin.

TETLEY. Any other message you'd like to leave, Martin?

Martin slowly turns and looks at him. Then he shakes his head. His mouth is trembling. The old man starts to jabber again, incoherently—something about not wanting to die. Sparks comes up to him and the old man clutches the Negro's arm.

MEXICAN (*abruptly*). I'd like to make a confession.

Tetley turns to him quickly, eagerly, as do the other men. A confession now would ease a lot of consciences.

TETLEY. At last!

MEXICAN (*his eyes meeting Tetley's*). To a priest.

Tetley looks at him and scowls, disappointed.

TETLEY. There's no priest here.

MEXICAN (*indicating Pancho*). This man can hear me and take it to a priest.

Tetley looks at Pancho, scowling. The latter nods.

TETLEY (*brusquely*). Very well. Get along with it.

Pancho steps up to the Mexican and helps him to his feet. Then he puts an arm around the Mexican and they move off, the Mexican in pain and limping badly. Tetley turns and nods to the other men and starts off for the tree. Several men take hold of Martin and the old man, and start off after Tetley.

At the TREE: Farnley and Mapes knot three ropes and throw them over the limb, with the nooses hanging down in a row. Several other men start to stake down the ends of the rope, Martin and the old man watching, the old man still whimpering. Sparks is beside him while Davies stands near Martin and it is difficult to say who is suffering more.

We see ART and GIL looking off.

GIL (*indicating with his head*). That must have been an awfully busy life!

We see what they see: The Mexican is trying to kneel but he can't make it. He hangs onto Pancho, obviously making his confession. Pancho is listening intently.

UNDER THE TREE the preparations are completed. The three horses have been brought up.

TETLEY. Farnley, you, Gabe Hart and Gerald will whip the horses out.

Gabe Hart shakes his head foolishly and turns to Winder, appealingly, for help.

WINDER. Gabe's not against us, Mr. Tetley. It's just that he can't stand to hurt anybody.

TETLEY (*looking around—scornfully*). Any volunteers?

There is a slight pause. The men look off, avoiding Tetley's eyes.

MA (*angrily*). All right, I'll do it if nobody else will.

She looks at Monty Smith, who deliberately shifts his gaze.

GERALD (*suddenly*). I won't do it!

TETLEY (*looking at his son with cold hatred; quietly*). You'll do it.

GERALD. I can't.

TETLEY. We'll see to it that you can.

Gerald shakes his head, trembling all over.

GIL. The kid's seen enough already. Why don't you leave him alone!

TETLEY (*in a cold rage*). This is not your affair, Carter. Thank you just the same.

Gil glares. Tetley's mouth is thin and hard. His eyes glimmer with restrained fury.

TETLEY (*to Gerald*). I'll have no female boys bearing my name. You'll do your part and say nothing more. (*He turns away, fighting to control himself.*)

The Mexican and Pancho are seen, past the tree, coming back, Pancho bearing the Mexican's weight. The Mexican is led in and put in place beside Martin and the old man under the tree. Davies steps up beside Pancho.

DAVIES (*clutching Pancho's arm*). What did he say?

Pancho looks at Davies, uncertain and confused.

PANCHO. I'm not a priest.

DAVIES (*shaking him*). But for God's sake, man, at least say whether we'd better wait!

PANCHO (*stubbornly, shaking his head*). I'm not a priest. I don't know.

The rider called Red has brought out a bottle of whiskey and the three prisoners are offered drinks. Martin and the old man shake their heads, but the Mexican takes a long pull on the bottle.

TETLEY. I'll give you two minutes to pray.

MARTIN looks around desperately. The MEN turn their faces or drop their eyes. MARTIN, now seen in the group, closes his own eyes, ducks his head, then drops to his knees. The Mexican remains standing but his eyes are closed and his lips are moving rapidly in prayer. The old man's knees again buckle and he grovels in the dirt with Sparks beside him. Moore takes off his hat. Several other men look at him, then follow his example.

DAVIES, seen close, drops to his knees. Several other men look around uneasily, then follow Davies' example. Those who don't kneel, bow their heads. Tetley is watching closely. There is a long pause.

TETLEY. Time's up.

This cuts to the THREE PRISONERS: The old man wails once. The Mexican opens his eyes, and glances up. There is a new expression on his face, almost of fear. Martin gets to his feet and looks around slowly. He is no longer desperate nor incoherent. Yet he is not resigned either. Instead there is only great bitterness in his face. But at the end he is taking it best of all. Davies steps up beside him.

MARTIN (*quietly, to Davies*). Will you find someone you can trust to look out for my wife and children?

Davies nods, his eyes full of tears.

MARTIN. You'd better take some older woman along. It's not going to be easy.

DAVIES (*hoarsely*). Don't worry. Your family will be all right.

MARTIN (*after a slight pause*). My parents are dead, but Miriam's live in Ohio. Kinkaid didn't want to sell those cattle. Maybe his wife'll buy them back for enough to cover their travel.

Davies nods, unable to speak. He puts his hand on Martin's shoulder, squeezes, then turns away, blinded.

We get a larger view of the men.

TETLEY. That all?

MARTIN (*as his hands are being tied*). I suppose it's no good telling you again that we're innocent?

TETLEY. No good.

MARTIN. It's not for myself I'm asking.

TETLEY. Other men with families have had to go for this sort of thing. It's too bad, but that's justice.

MARTIN (*suddenly flaring up*). Justice! What do you care about Justice? You don't even care whether you've got the right men or not. All you know is you've lost something and somebody's got to be punished. (*As Tetley waits, a smile on his thin lips*) I tell you there's nobody to take care of them. They're in a strange place. Can't you understand that, you butcher? (*His voice breaking*) You've got to let me go! If there's a spark of humanity in you, you've got to let me go! Send men with me if you want to! I'm not asking you to trust me. But at least let me see them —arrange for them to go somewhere —to get somebody to help them!

There is not the slightest response on Tetley's part to this plea and Martin looks around desperately. Old Hardwick begins to whimper again. His knees buckle and he falls forward. The Mexican just looks around and spits with contempt.

MEXICAN. This is fine company for a man to die with.

MARTIN (*turning on him, half-hysterically*). Shut up! You shut up!

Mapes steps up to Martin and suddenly slaps him across the face with the palm, then the back of his hand. A sob escapes Martin. Gil leaps straight at Mapes, swinging as he comes. He lands a terrific punch, and Mapes goes down. Gil leaps right on him, pummeling him.

TETLEY (*sharply*). Stop it, you fools!

Suddenly several men rush in and grab Gil. As they draw him to his feet he suddenly whips out his gun and turns on Tetley.

GIL. No, *you* stop it!

A close view shows FARNLEY whipping out his gun and firing. We see GIL as his gun is shot out of his hand and he is slightly wounded. Several men seize him and hold him.

Suddenly, in a larger scene, the Mexican begins to speak rapidly and incoherently as several of the men step forward and the three are lifted on horses and made to stand on them. Ma and Farnley get behind the horses with quirts in their hands. The three prisoners' feet and hands are now tied, and the noose around their necks. Gil continues to struggle but in vain.

TETLEY *(quietly).* Gerald. *(But Gerald doesn't move, and Tetley speaks more firmly.)* Gerald!

GERALD, like a sleepwalker, crosses behind the horses, and takes his stand. The men move back out of the way of the horses.—MAPES is then seen close. He has a pistol in his hand ready to give the signal. We get a closeup of DAVIES as he calls out frantically.

DAVIES. No—no!

But the sound of Mapes' pistol drowns out his cry, and this cuts to MA, FARNLEY and GERALD, with just the rear of the horses visible, as Ma and Farnley cut their horses sharply. Their horses leap forward. Gerald doesn't move and his horse merely walks out from under. As he stands motionless, Tetley steps up behind him and strikes him with the butt of his pistol. Gerald's knees slump and he falls to the ground unconscious.

TETLEY *(indicating Martin offscene).* Finish him.

Farnley raises his gun and fires. As he does so, Gil and Davies step over to Gerald and lift him.

The men are all starting toward their horses, silent, speechless. It is now getting bright. Tetley moves past them and goes to his Palomino, and a close view shows his face set, as he mounts his horse, turns and, without looking back, rides off.

Finally, we see the MEN GETTING ON THEIR HORSES. Some glance back, then turn quickly away. Davies and Gil come in among them, carrying the still unconscious Gerald. Gil looks back—then quickly shifts his eyes. Offscene comes Sparks' voice softly singing, "In Dat Great Gittin'-up Mawnin' " as the scene fades out.

PART THREE

A MOUNTAIN TRAIL fades in. It is dawn now. The cavalcade is riding home—a little faster now. Most of them are bunched together up front, with a second group of five trailing by a good 100 yards. . . The men up ahead take a turn in the down trail and disappear. Then we see the REAR GROUP—Gil, Art, Davies and Gerald—with Sparks jogging along in their wake. Art is half asleep; Gil dead pan, his thoughts a secret known only to himself. Davies keeps passing his hand over his face, rubbing his nose and mouth as if there were cobwebs on them. Gerald is not even looking where he is going. There are big circles under his eyes and he is obviously gnawing himself inside.

We see TWO MEN ride hurriedly into view on a hilltop and pull up under a tree. Then the two men are seen closer. One, as we shall later discover, is the Sheriff. The other is a rancher. They look off down the trail toward the valley, curious and excited, and the Sheriff half rises in his saddle, cups his hands and calls off:

SHERIFF. Hey there! What's all that shooting about?

We get a close view of several members of the posse, including MAPES, riding up the hill. There is a spirit of elation about Mapes as he calls back.

MAPES. We got 'em, Sheriff!

He kicks his heels into his horse, and they start off at a faster clip.

This cuts to the HILLTOP where the Sheriff and the rancher are looking off, puzzled, as the men of the posse gallop in and surround them.

MAPES (*pleased with himself*). It's all right, Sheriff! Everything's been attended to!

SHERIFF. What are you talking about?

FARNLEY. Kinkaid's murderers! We got all three of 'em!

SMITH. And hung 'em, too, Sheriff!

The Sheriff looks at the men—he is deeply shocked.

SHERIFF. What do you mean, Kinkaid's murderers? Larry Kinkaid ain't dead!

This is like a thunderbolt. The men stare at him, not believing.

FARNLEY (*stammering*). Not dead? !

MAPES (*bewildered*). But—we just—

He looks back over his shoulder toward the valley, and we get several close views of the men and their reactions: DAVIES, as he closes his eyes in horror; GIL, aghast; TETLEY, still cold, unyielding; MA, dazed. The Sheriff looks at Mapes, his face set, hard.

SHERIFF. I just left Larry Kinkaid with a doctor over at Pike's Hole. And I got the fellows that shot him, too.

MAPES (*pointing toward the Ox-Bow*). But Sheriff—these fellows—they had Larry's cattle down there. They even had his gun.

The Sheriff reaches out his hand.

SHERIFF (*grimly*). Give me that badge!

He takes the deputy's badge. He looks around again at the men. Farnley is confused; the men are dazed.

SHERIFF (*turning to Davies*). Mr. Davies, I know you well enough to know you didn't have anything to do with this. I'm depending on you to tell me who did.

DAVIES (*quietly*). All but seven.

The Sheriff looks around again at the men. They are all confused, shocked—all except Tetley, who shows no spark of feeling.

SHERIFF (*quietly*). God had better have mercy on you, because you ain't gonna get any from me!

And he kicks his heels and nods to the rancher. They start off toward the Ox-Bow. The men look after them, helpless. Then they turn and ride off, leaving Gil and Davies side by side.

GIL (*quietly*). If you haven't got any objections, Mr. Davies, I'd like to read Martin's letter.

Davies look at him and hesitates; then he thinks better of it, takes the letter from his pocket and hands it to Gil.

DAVIES (*quietly*). It might be a good idea if a lot of people read it.

He hands over Martin's letter, and as Gil opens it and starts to read the scene dissolves to a STREET IN BRIDGER'S WELLS as the men ride in, silent and ill-at-ease. A few people on the sidewalks turn and look at them, but no one speaks. Tetley is riding alone—the men avoiding him. We see TETLEY closer then, and he is really a man of iron. His face doesn't show anything, not even weariness. Monty Smith rides up alongside him, looks at him angrily, then rides away from him.

Outside DARBY'S SALOON as the cavalcade rides up: Darby stands in the doorway, towel in hand. Gil, Art and half a dozen others pull up. Tetley rides straight past the saloon, looking neither to the right nor the left, followed by Gerald and farther back by Sparks. Gerald still rides like one in a trance. Then we get a closer view as the men silently dismount and tie up in front of the saloon.

SMITH (*looking off after Tetley*). If you ask me, that Tetley's the one we ought to lynch!

GIL (*quietly*). You're a great one for hangin', ain't you, Smith?

He looks at Smith, and the latter's eyes waver and he turns away. Gil starts for the saloon, Art following.

We see DARBY in the doorway as the men file past him into the saloon. He is watching them curiously, but silently. The men brush by, eager to get drunk and to forget it.

This cuts to TETLEY'S DRIVEWAY as Tetley rides in, followed by Gerald; then to the FRONT STEPS of the Tetley home as he pulls up and dismounts. A yardman is waiting to take the horses. Without a word Tetley hands him the reins, goes up the steps and into the house, his face still frozen. Gerald dismounts and follows his father.

In the HALLWAY, Tetley deliberately turns the key in the lock. Then we get a close view of GERALD at the door. He tries the door—and finds it locked against him. He stares at it for a moment, then tries it again.

A close view of TETLEY shows him standing at the door, a look of cold hatred on his face, as Gerald attempts to open the door.

GERALD (*seen close; quietly—suddenly no longer afraid*). You loved it! That's why you kept them waiting so long. I saw your face. It was the face of a depraved, murderous beast.

We get a close view of TETLEY listening impassively.

GERALD'S VOICE. There are only two things that have ever meant anything to you—power and cruelty. You can't feel pity. You can't even feel guilt.

Tetley's eyes narrow and his hand trembles toward the doorknob. It is with difficulty that he restrains himself from throwing open the door and attacking Gerald.

A close view of GERALD shows him to be a new person now, speaking his mind for the first time as a free man.

GERALD. In your heart you knew those men were innocent, but you were cold crazy to see them hanged —and to make me watch it.

We see TETLEY again standing motionless, his face set, his body rigid.

GERALD'S VOICE. I could have stopped you with a gun—just as any other animal can be stopped—by fear— from a kill. But I couldn't do it because I'm a coward!

We see GERALD again as he suddenly laughs harshly.

GERALD. Aren't you glad you made me go, Father? Weren't you proud of me?

Suddenly Tetley, seen in the HALLWAY, can stand no more. He turns and starts off.

GERALD'S VOICE (*loudly*). How does it feel to have begot a weakling, Major Tetley? Does it make you afraid that there may be some weakness in you, too, that other men might discover and whisper about? Open the door, Major! I want to see your face. I want to know how you feel now.

Tetley goes into the library and slams the door behind him.

GERALD is no longer afraid. There is an almost exalted look on his face—the look of a man shriven of his sins. He looks at the door for a moment, smiling, then he turns away. We see him then as he starts off, head up, walking with the rapid gait of a man who knows where he is going and what he is going to do. Suddenly he breaks into a run as he goes down the steps and across the lawn toward the rear of the house.

This cuts to the TETLEY LIBRARY, a beautiful old room lined with books. A grate fire is burning. Tetley crosses to the window and looks out. We then see, from his view, through the window GERALD half running across the lawn toward the rear of the house. Another close view shows TETLEY looking out at his son, an inscrutable look on his face. Slowly he turns and looks off across the room at a PORTRAIT OF GERALD'S MOTHER, a lovely, delicate, charming woman, a faint smile on her lips—wearing a gown of the ante-bellum days.

This dissolves to the STREET outside the Tetley home at night. People are running toward Tetley's. A couple of men have lanterns in their hands. There is excitement in the air.—Outside the TETLEY BARN, next, we see a group of people looking into the barn through the window, all full of excitement. More people run in—press forward eagerly for a look. A group shocked—awed into silence. Davies is among them. Then there is a close view at the WINDOW: A woman looks in, then turns quickly away, shuddering and moaning. Her hand goes to her throat, clasping it. Gil and Art stare through the window.

GIL. I never believed he'd do it.

ART. Who found him?

DAVIES. The yardman.

ANOTHER MAN. And he was so scairt he couldn't hardly talk.

GIL. Anybody told his old man yet?

DAVIES. Sparks is in there now.

This cuts to the TETLEY LIBRARY, and we see Sparks in the doorway. No light is in the room except that which comes from the grate fire.

SPARKS (*softly—frightened*). Cunnel Tetley—

Tetley is not seen. He is seated in a deep chair in front of the fire.

TETLEY'S VOICE. Yes?

SPARKS (*hesitantly*). Mistah Gerald— he's done hung hisself.

TETLEY, now seen close, does not move. But somehow he seems to shrink, as if he realizes that he has lost his standing in the community, his son. everything.

TETLEY (*quietly, evenly*). Thank you, Sparks.

Just that—as if Sparks had delivered a package. There is a brief pause. The door is heard closing softly behind Sparks. Then Tetley gets to his feet and the view moves with him across to a big shelf above which rests his old army sabre in its scabbard. Tetley withdraws his sword and the moving scene brings him back to the fire. There he pauses and then deliberately places the point of the sword against his breast. As he leans against it the view moves up to the portrait of Mrs. Tetley above the mantel. Suddenly there is a heavy movement and Tetley's arms reach in and grab the sides of the frame. The picture is jerked from the wall—followed by a heavy thud of a falling body.

This dissolves to DARBY's SALOON: About a dozen men are lined up against the bar, hats on the back of their heads, drinking. Darby is behind the bar, silent as the men. This is followed by a moving view along the bar. The men are silent—drinking to forget. Farnley is there and beside him Moore. Next are Bartlett, Red, Mark, and Smith hanging on, licking his lips, hoping for a free drink. And down toward the end, Gil and Art. Gil is almost stiff by now. The view stops on GIL and ART, both of whom are leaning heavily on the bar.

GIL. They're making up a pot for Martin's wife. Even Mapes chipped in.

ART. I didn't know he was showin' his face.

GIL. He's not. He sent it by Sparks. (*After a slight pause*) That reminds me, I put in twenty-five bucks apiece for us.

ART. How much they got?

GIL. About five hundred.

ART (*after taking a drink*). Humph! Not bad for a husband who don't know any better than to buy cattle in the Spring without a bill-of-sale.

Suddenly Gil reaches in his pocket and brings out Martin's letter, unfolds it and lays it on the bar in front of him, then leans forward and studies it. After a moment he begins to read it aloud, as though to himself, and as if he had been puzzling over it all day.

GIL (*reading with slight difficulty*). "My dear Wife: Mr. Davies will tell you what is happening here tonight. He's a good man and has done everything he can for me. I suppose there are some other good men here too, only they don't seem to realize what they're doing. They're the ones I feel sorry for, because it'll be over for me in a little while, but they'll have to go on remembering for the rest of their lives."

Gil is absorbed in the letter. A strange thing is happening. The other men are listening, too. They drift in closer, silent, not drinking now.

GIL (*reading*).
"A man just naturally can't take the law into his own hands and hang people without hurting everybody in the world, because then he's not just breaking one law but all laws."

The view moves and picks out the faces of the men. They are silent, touched, and some of them faintly understand.

GIL (*reading*).
"Law is a lot more than words you put on a book, or judges or lawyers or sheriffs you hire to carry it out. It's everything people have ever found out about justice and what's right and wrong. It's the very conscience of humanity. There can't be any such thing as civilization unless people have got a conscience, because if people touch God anywhere, where is it except through their conscience? And what is anybody's conscience except a little piece of the conscience of all men that ever lived?"

This cuts to a view of the SALOON as Gil finishes reading the letter. There is a long moment of silence. Gil stuffs the letter in his pocket, turns and, without a word, goes toward the door. Art looks after him and follows. The men are stunned, speechless, helpless, repentant, but unable to do anything about it. One man fingers his glass of whiskey; another drums on the bar; another covers his eyes with his hand.

Outside the SALOON: Gil is just untying his horse. Art joins him.

ART. Where we going?

GIL (*as he swings into the saddle*). He said he wanted his wife to have this letter, didn't he? He said there wasn't anybody to look out for his kids.

Art swings onto his horse and they start off. The little town is deserted as the two men ride out just as they came in. Only the dog is there to watch them leave as the scene fades out.

ALTERNATIVE ENDING*

[There is a brief pause, and Gil folds the letter and returns it to his pocket. Again he fills his glass and starts to drink. Suddenly a burst of woman's laughter cuts in, followed by the deeper laugh of a man. Gil turns and looks toward the door.

Rose Mapen, dressed to kill, sweeps in, her head high, as if walking at the head of a parade. Just behind her are her new husband and his sister. Rose and Swanson are laughing gayly, but Miss Swanson is as sniffily disapproving as ever. Everybody has turned toward the door to watch. Instantly the room is charged with expectancy of trouble.

ROSE (*gayly*). Hello, everybody! Got room for one more? Or is this a private wake?

Some of the men look at her and smile weakly, as Rose leads her husband and sister-in-law across toward the bar. She is looking off at Gil, but covering up her feelings very well.

A close view shows GIL, with Art's head seen behind him, looking off at Rose and her husband. There is that same narrowing of the eyes that forebodes trouble. He takes a big drink. We then see ROSE and HER HUSBAND AT THE BAR looking off, at Gil. Rose continues to smile broadly, while Swanson has a forced, set smile on his lips. And this cuts to a view of the men silently watching the tableau. Darby is setting drinks in front of Rose and her husband. The sister-in-law shakes her head, disapprovingly.

ROSE. Just water for me.

GIL (*quietly—after a slight pause*). Miss Mapen is getting pretty proper these days—with her new attachment and duenna.

The smile dies on Swanson's lips. Rose, too, stops smiling, and lays a hand on his arm. They look off at Gil.

ART (*catching Gil's arm*). Come on —let's get out of here.

GIL (*quietly, looking at Rose's husband*). How do you start a decent fight with that kind of guy?

ART. Forget it and have a drink.

GIL. If I start a fight with him, I'll kill him. You know that, don't you?

As one, the men along the bar slowly drift out of the way, expecting the shooting to start at any moment.

---

* This is the original ending as of June 3, 1942. The ending printed above was substituted on August 17, 1942. It will be profitable for both the general reader and the student to compare.

This cuts to ROSE and SWANSON looking off at Gil. Rose continues to smile, not at all averse to being the woman in the argument. A close view of GIL shows him looking as if he were going to leap at Swanson's throat.—We see DARBY as his hand closes around a bottle. Then we see the tableau just one minute more, before Gil does leap—a big smile on his face. This is just what he has been needing—a fight! But as he springs toward Swanson, Darby again lets him have a bottle on the back of the skull and once more Gil's knees buckle under him and he folds up, a silly grin on his face. Rose looks down at him, then she takes her husband's arm and leads him off. Art comes over beside Gil, and the other men close in. Darby pours a glass of water in Gil's face. Gil quickly comes to and gets to his feet unsteadily and leans against the bar. Then he shakes his head and looks up at the suggestive picture on the wall behind the bar. A big, slow grin comes over his face.

GIL. Say—ain't that guy got there yet, either?]

HAIL THE CONQUERING HERO
(*A Paramount Picture*)

Written and Directed by
PRESTON STURGES

The Cast

WOODROW	Eddie Bracken
LIBBY	Ella Raines
MR. NOBLE	Raymond Walburn
SERGEANT	William Demarest
CHAIRMAN OF RECEPTION COMMITTEE	Franklin Pangborn
LIBBY'S AUNT	Elizabeth Patterson
MRS. TRUESMITH	Georgia Caine
POLITICAL BOSS	Al Bridge
BUGSY	Freddie Steele
FORREST NOBLE	Bill Edwards
DOC BISSELL	Harry Hayden
JUDGE DENNIS	Jimmy Conlin
CORPORAL	Jimmy Dundee

Film Editor—STUART GILMORE

Screenplay of the Paramount photoplay "Hail The Conquering Hero," copyright 1943 by Paramount Pictures Inc. By permission of Paramount Pictures Inc.

HAIL THE CONQUERING HERO

PART ONE

A WATERFRONT CAFE fades in, first revealing a TAP DANCER'S FEET. Then as the girl dances away the view moves up and we see the interior of the establishment: Service men, girls, Merchant Sailors and shipyard workers, behind them a little band. The girl finishes her number to great applause, the lights dim and a spotlight picks out another girl who starts to sing "Oh, How I Miss You Tonight . . . though I may roam, dear, Hard as the days may appear, etc." We now see different customers reacting to the song. Then we see the singing girl again, and the view starts drawing away from her. It leaves the dancing room, moves all the way down the bar and comes to rest on WOODROW, a depressed young man, dressed like a shipyard worker on Friday night. Four singing waiters now join the girl singer and re-enforce her with some close harmony.

BARTENDER. Fill her up?

WOODROW. Yeah.

BARTENDER (*filling the beer*). Why don't you grab yourself off a skirt and have yourself a time?

WOODROW. Your beer is running over.

The bartender shrugs, knocks the collar off the beer, and takes the money.

WOODROW. Why don't they sing something gay?

BARTENDER. Why don't you acquire a gay viewpoint? It's all mental . . . every bit of it . . . smile and the world smiles with you, frown and you frown alone.

WOODROW. Yes, well I'd just as soon be alone if it's just the same to you.

BARTENDER. Gratitude.

As he goes about his business, and Woodrow starts to drink his beer, the scene cuts to the SINGING GIRL and the SINGING WAITERS who finish the number to much applause, following which the girl starts "Jingle Jangle Jingle." And this cuts to the FOGGY SIDEWALK at night in front of the "joint" that has just been seen. Six Marines are approaching. We hear them before we see them.

SERGEANT. If you could shoot craps like you can shoot your mouth off, you'd be the biggest breeze shooter this side of Hong Kong.

JONESY. He's the *two* biggest.

CORPORAL (*defending himself*). I was *fading* the guy . . . how am I supposed to know the guy is going to pass eight times . . .

SERGEANT. You was fading the guy with our money. (*By now they are pretty well in view.*)

CORPORAL. Well it was my money too, wasn't it? We're partners, ain't we?

SERGEANT. 'Specially now.

JONESY. Partners in the soup.

BILL. No dough.

Copyright 1943, *by Paramount Pictures Inc.*

JUKE. Nothin' to do.

SERGEANT. And five days to do it in.

They come to a stop in front of the "joint" and look longingly toward the music which drifts out.

JONESY. If you wasn't so big, I'd take one poke at that dumb kisser of yours.

CORPORAL. Why don't you try it, Joe?

SERGEANT. Save it for the Japs.

BUGSY (*solemnly*). You shouldn't of faded so many times.

CORPORAL. You gonna start now? (*Then to the Sergeant*) Give me one last ten spot . . . I'll go back and . . .

SERGEANT (*sourly*). You had it, fancy fingers. (*Then mimicking him*) "Give me one last ten spot." Who do you think you're talking to—Morgenthau?

SERGEANT (*as Bugsy starts for the door*). Where you goin'?

BUGSY. I got fifteen cents. (*He laughs a little queerly.*) I held out on you.

The other Marines look at each other, then follow the moneyed man into the establishment. And this cuts to the interior of the CAFE as the Marines enter and are given a ringside table by a waiter. He passes around four large menus.

BUGSY (*clutching his fifteen cents*). One beer.

WAITER (*in astonishment*). One beer.

SERGEANT. One beer and no cracks. (*The waiter departs.*)

CORPORAL. You gonna share it or swill it all down yourself?

Bugsy laughs but says nothing.

SERGEANT (*to Jonesy*). Give me your Elk's tooth.

JONESY. Wait a minute, my old man gimme that . . .

SERGEANT. Come on.

Jonesy gives it to him reluctantly. The Sergeant motions to the manager.

SERGEANT. You the manager?

MANAGER. Yes, sir.

SERGEANT. We're just a little bit short of cash, see, or I'd never make you this proposition. I was gonna save it for the museum, see, but when you're out on a limb you gotta make sacrifices, that's all. I'm gonna let you in on the ground floor of something very rare.

MANAGER. Ahah.

SERGEANT (*with great secrecy*). You remember when General Yamatoho committed Harry Carey?

MANAGER. Possibly.

SERGEANT. I happened to be very close by, see?

MANAGER. Unhunh.

The Sergeant now goes through the motions of removing a tooth from his mouth then pops the Elk's tooth under the nose of the Manager who recoils visibly.

MANAGER (*looking at the tooth*). Big man, wasn't he?

SERGEANT. Immense. This is one of the rarest mementos . . .

MANAGER (*taking it out of his coat pocket and displaying its whole 4x6*). You wouldn't like to buy the flag they buried him in, would you? I could make it very reasonable. I have it in several sizes. (*He starts pulling more truck out of his pocket.*) MacArthur's suspenders, the first bullet to land in Pearl Harbor ... you can take your pick ... a piece of a Japanese submarine; if you look at it this way it becomes a German submarine, and this way it's a piece of shell that just missed Montgomery ... Here we have the seat of Rommel's pants and last but not least we have a button from Hitler's coat although that one I don't personally believe.

SERGEANT. Wise guy.

Now the waiter arrives with a heavy tray. On it there is a plate of sandwiches, pickles and six beers. The Marines exchange looks, then Bugsy takes one beer off the tray and puts down his fifteen cents.

WAITER (*waving back his money*). It's all paid for.

The Marines look at each other, then look around questioningly at the Manager.

MANAGER. Not by me, it wasn't. You don't have to give me any credit.

WAITER. A guy at the end of the bar.

The Marines each grab a sandwich and a beer, then start out of the room. Then the scene cuts to a view down the long bar. In the foreground we see WOODROW, the young unheroic-looking fellow. The Marines come through the beaded curtains in the background, look around, then spot Woodrow. He gives them a polite smile, then looks away. The Marines come closer.

SERGEANT. Was this from you?

WOODROW. That's all right. I just happened to hear the waiter say something about six Marines and one beer ... and to serve it with six straws or something.

SERGEANT. Oh, he did, did he?

CORPORAL. Where is he?

WOODROW. I already told him.

SERGEANT. Anyway that was a very nice gesture, Civilian.

WOODROW. Don't mention it.

SERGEANT (*holding it up*). You want General Yamatoho's tooth?

WOODROW. No, thanks.

BUGSY. You could send it to your mother ... if you got one.

WOODROW. No, thanks. I already sent her some souvenirs.

The Sergeant lifts his glass and the others do likewise.

SERGEANT. Well, then ... here's to you.

WOODROW (*lifting his glass*). Semper Fidelis.

THE MARINES (*somewhat surprised but gravely*). Semper Fidelis.

SERGEANT (*not making much of it*). You know our motto, hunh?

WOODROW (*quietly*). Yeh, I know the motto.

BUGSY. Was you in the Marine Corps, maybe?

WOODROW. Yeh, I was in the Marine Corps.

SERGEANT. That's too bad, Joe.

WOODROW. That's all right. Set 'em up again. ... Don't you want anything besides beer?

CORPORAL. Well, personally I never touch anything stronger than rye whiskey.

WOODROW. Seven ryes. . . . You can use the beer for chasers.

SERGEANT. Thanks. . . . You sure you ain't spendin' too fast like fancy Feelix, the Crap King, here? (*Indicating the Corporal*)

CORPORAL. Listen.

WOODROW. I just got paid tonight, besides I can't think of any way I'd rather spend my money than for Marines . . . from Guadalcanal.

BUGSY. It's a great place to be *from*. (*He laughs*.)

CORPORAL (*lifting the rye*). Well, Sukiyaki. (*They drink and Woodrow motions for another round*.)

SERGEANT. How long you out?

WOODROW. From the Marines?

SERGEANT. Yeh.

WOODROW. I was only *in* a month.

BUGSY. That's too bad.

CORPORAL. You hardly had time to get corns on your feet.

BILL. Were you wounded?

SERGEANT. How could he get wounded in Bootcamp?

JONESY. He could of fell off a roof.

SERGEANT. What would he be doing on a roof?

WOODROW. It was hay fever . . . Chronic hay fever.

JUKE (*sympathetically*). That's the worst kind, too.

CORPORAL. It's terrible . . . I had a girl once had it. Every time you'd get close to her she'd sneeze right in your kisser.

SERGEANT. She wasn't so dumb.

CORPORAL. It was the excitement.

BILL. Well, better luck next time.

WOODROW. Thanks.

SERGEANT. Did you try any of the other branches of the Service? . . . like the Army or the Navy . . . they'll take anything.

WOODROW. They wouldn't take me. I went into a shipyard.

JUKE. My grandmother is a WAC.

SERGEANT. What good is that gonna do him?

WOODROW. I don't know why hay fever is so terrible . . . (*He sniffles*.)

CORPORAL. It's because you never know when it's gonna hit you . . . I remember one night . . . this dame had a bowl of noodle soup in front of her and all of a sudden . . . (*Wiping the noodles out of his eyes*)

WOODROW. Anyway, I was kinda born to be a Marine . . . my father was killed in Belleau Wood the day I was born.

SERGEANT. Belleau Wood?

WOODROW. . . . Almost the same hour . . . All I ever thought about was being a Marine . . . I did exercises . . . I never drank or smoked . . . I studied about them . . . I can tell you every battle the Marines were in from 1775 down to now: New Providence, Fort Nassau, the second Battle of Trenton, the *Bonhomme Richard* and the *Serapis*, "I have not yet begun to fight" . . . (*As the view draws closer*) Tripoli in 1805, Nukuhive in 1812, The Battle of Hatchee-Lustee River, 1837, Vera Cruz in '46 . . . Chapultepec . . . The Halls of Montezuma

... Panama in '85, Guantanamo Bay in '98, then the Philippines, the Boxer Rebellion in China, Nicaragua, Coyotepe Hill, Fort Riviere in Haiti ... then Chateau-Thierry ... Belleau Wood ... Soissons ... Saint Mihiel ... and now Wake Island ... Guam ... Bataan ... Corregidor ... Guadalcanal ... they bled and died. ... They gave me a big send-off when I left home ... the band was playing and everybody hollering and all the dogs barking ... my mother crying ... everybody wondering if I'd come home a general or just a sergeant like my father. ... It's one thing to go home with things like that on your chest and another thing to go home with hay fever ... and a medical discharge.

BUGSY (*horrified*). You mean you ain't been home?

WOODROW. I wrote I was leaving for overseas.

BUGSY. You shouldn't do that to your mother.

WOODROW. I wrote a couple of letters to say I was all right, and asked a kid to mail them ... from overseas.

BUGSY. Suppose he didn't get a chance to mail them!

WOODROW. Well. ...

BUGSY (*indignantly*). That's a terrible thing to do to your mother ... you ought to be ashamed of yourself.

WOODROW (*quietly*). I am.

SERGEANT (*faintly suspicious*). You say your father was a sergeant at Belleau Wood?

WOODROW. That's right ... fill 'em up again ...

SERGEANT (*after exchanging a wise look with the others*). What was his name? I was at Belleau Wood.

WOODROW. Truesmith.

SERGEANT (*galvanized*). Truesmith! You mean Hinky Dinky Truesmith?

WOODROW. That's right.

SERGEANT. But he was my Sergeant ... I saw him fall.

WOODROW. Well, right then I was being born ... in Oakridge, California.

SERGEANT. Did you know your father got the Congressional Medal of Honor?

WOODROW. I grew up with it ... they hung it on me.

BUGSY (*a man of single purpose*). Is that where she lives? ... Oakridge?

WOODROW. Who?

BUGSY. Your mother.

WOODROW. Sure.

BUGSY. You ought to be ashamed of yourself.

He walks out of the scene.

SERGEANT (*with some embarrassment for Bugsy's rudeness*). It's an honor to meet you, kid. (*He takes him warmly by the hand.*) What's your name?

WOODROW (*bitterly*). Woodrow La-Fayette Pershing Truesmith ... go ahead and laugh.

SERGEANT. That ain't anything to laugh at ... to anybody who knows anything. ... Boys, I want you to shake hands with Hinky Dinky Truesmith's boy, Woodrow: Corporal Candida, Pfc.'s Jones, Gillette and Swenson. My name is Heffelfinger. Julius . . . and you can just call me Sarg . . . set 'em up . . . excuse me.

WOODROW (*to the Bartender*). Certainly.

SERGEANT (*happily*). I guess you never got to know your father very well, hunh?

WOODROW. Well not exactly . . . as he . . . fell the day I was born.

SERGEANT (*after a second's puzzlement*). That's right. It's . . . hard to realize . . . he was a fine lookin' fellow . . . he didn't look anything like you at all.

WOODROW. I know. We got a picture of him.

SERGEANT (*indicating Bugsy who comes back into the shot*). And this is Bugsy Walewski.

BUGSY (*sourly*). Pleased to meet you. (*He does not shake hands but looks at the change on the bar.*) Can I borrow fifty cents?

SERGEANT (*indignantly*). Listen, after a guy's bought you . . .

WOODROW (*to Bugsy*). Go ahead.

SERGEANT (*to Bugsy*). You ought to be ashamed of yourself.

BUGSY (*indicating Woodrow*). He ought to be ashamed of himself. . . . Treatin' his mother that way. (*He goes out of sight.*)

SERGEANT (*apologetically*). He never had any mother. . . . He's from a Home.

CORPORAL. He's a little bit screwy too.

SERGEANT. He's all right . . . he got a little shot up, that's all . . . nothing serious. (*He brushes the subject aside.*) So you're Hinky Dinky's boy . . . I travel one hundred thousand miles and run into Hinky Dinky's boy. . . . He was a brave kid . . . not quite as old as you are . . .

WOODROW. I know.

SERGEANT. They was sixteen of us, see, in this wood. . . . You couldn't see nothin'. . . . They'd be a German right there and you'd be right here and you couldn't see him and he couldn't see you.

WOODROW. I know.

SERGEANT. All of a sudden, almost right under our feet we hear the rat, tat, tat, tat . . .

This cuts to BUGSY in the PHONE BOOTH as he looks back, then puts two quarters in the telephone; then to a RURAL TELEPHONE EXCHANGE at night.

THE OPERATOR. Oakridge . . . sure I know her number, but isn't it kind of late to be calling somebody up in the middle of the night . . . Just a minute . . . yes, Doctor . . . I don't think she's home yet, the third feature don't let out till twelve-seventeen. . . . You're welcome. (*She flips another toggle switch.*) Are you sure it's important. . . . He did! Well, why didn't you say so in the first place . . . for Heaven's sake. (*She plugs a trunk in and starts ringing.*)

This dissolves to a view of WOODROW and the MARINES at the bar.

SERGEANT (*excitedly*). Somebody had to get 'em, see, the Looie is lyin' there holding his belly, one of the kids is cryin' and somebody says "let's draw lots" but Hinky says "I'm the Sergeant, see . . . I already won . . . you'll hear 'em when I get there

... then come in" and he starts through the bushes ... so there we are ... on your mark ... get set ... all of a sudden ...

BUGSY (*walking into sight*). Your mother's on the telephone. ... She wants to talk to you.

SERGEANT (*irritated at the interruption*). Just a minute ... WHAT?

WOODROW (*stunned*). You mean *my* mother?

BUGSY. That's right.

WOODROW. But how can I talk to her if I'm overseas?

SERGEANT (*to Bugsy*). You dumb clunk.

BUGSY. Because you ain't overseas ... you just come home with us ... from Guadalcanal ... you're goin' home tomorrow ...

WOODROW. Goin' home?

Thunderstruck, Woodrow looks toward the telephone, then starts for it.

CORPORAL. Are you nuts or something? This guy is tryin' to *keep* his mother from knowin' he ain't ...

BUGSY. You want to make somethin' of it?

SERGEANT. Pipe down.

This cuts to the TELEPHONE BOOTH as WOODROW comes into sight and enters the booth. He looks back at the Marines, then speaks.

WOODROW. Hello, is that you, Mama ... hello, Mama. ... Well, sure I'm all right. ... Of course I am ... never felt better in my life. How have you been, Mama?

This cuts to the MARINES who are now seen walking toward the phone booth on tiptoe.

BUGSY (*triumphantly*). See?

WOODROW (*seen in the booth*). Did you get my letters. ... You did, hunh? Well, that's fine ... I was afraid you might have been worried. ... Well, I don't know about that, Mama. ... It's very hard to get leave these days with the war and all. ... I just got up to Frisco for this evening, see. ... That I was wounded and honorably discharged from the service! Who told you I was wounded and discharged from the service? (*He turns and looks at Bugsy.*)

The view moves with him to the Marines who have come right up to the booth.

BUGSY (*to the Marines*). Then she won't have to worry no more.

This cuts to WOODROW in the BOOTH.

WOODROW. Now wait a minute, Mama ... You'd hardly call it a wound ... It was more like a scratch ... It was more like a fever ... Just a little fever, that's all ... Well, maybe it's called jungle fever, Mama. I don't know. ... No, I'm not being brave, but I just don't see how I'll be able to get home for quite some time, Mama. No I'm *not* seriously wounded. I wish I was ... I said I wished I could come home but I just can't make it. ... You can't do that, Mama. ... They don't allow visitors where I am. ... Well, then she must have known the Colonel ... or something ... I'm in wrong with him ... I can't tell you that, Mama ... that's military information. No, I'm not in jail. What would I be in jail for? ... I don't *know* why he said I was comin' home tomorrow, Mama. ...

HAIL THE CONQUERING HERO

He was probably talking about somebody else. . . . He had several calls to make, you know how it is. . . . Well, *of course* I want to come home, Mama. . . . Why wouldn't I . . . I'm crazy to see you and Libby and, and everybody . . . but this is war, Mama.

SERGEANT (*suddenly*). Wait a minute.

WOODROW. Hunh? (*He claps his hand over the phone.*)

SERGEANT. You can go home tomorrow. I figured it all out.

WOODROW (*struggling*). What are you talking about? How can I go home when I . . .

SERGEANT. Like rolling off a log. . . . Gimme that phone.

WOODROW (*resisting*). Now wait a minute.

SERGEANT (*snatching the phone away from him*). Hello, Mrs. Truesmith? This is Sergeant Heffelfinger . . . I guess you never heard of me, hunh? But I was a friend of Hinky Dink's . . . I certainly was. . . . Well, I got some good news for you. I fixed it up with the Colonel and your boy's comin' home tomorrow. . . . Yes ma'am . . . that sounds pretty good, hunh? Your boy is comin' home.

The scene fades out.

PART TWO

A LOCOMOTIVE—in the SAN FRANCISCO STATION—fades in. It pants pleasingly. We hear the strains of "Mademoiselle from Armentières." This dissolves to SEVEN PAIRS of MARINES' FEET, and the scene moves with them as they march down the platform past pretty girls' legs, a couple of babies and a dog. The three leading pairs and the three trailing pairs of feet are in perfect step. The pair in the middle seems reluctant. It drops back, then hops forward again as if it had been pushed.

This cuts to a CONDUCTOR and a BRAKEMAN, who stand in front of a Pullman car watching the approaching Marines.

CONDUCTOR. Guadalcanal.

BRAKEMAN. Gee!

Next we see the approaching MARINES; there are seven of them. They move to the entrance of the Pullman car. Bugsy carries one of Woodrow's suitcases and Jonesy the other. Woodrow's right hand covers a medal on his chest.

WOODROW. Look, it's bad enough to wear the uniform without wearing this on it. (*He uncovers an unusually small medal on his chest.*)

SERGEANT. What are you talking about? I don't even remember what I got it for. (*He points to a ribbon on the Corporal's chest.*) You know what he got this for? Some Japs was roasting a pig across the stream and the breeze was blowing it all right over in his kisser . . . so he went over and got it.

CORPORAL. Boy, that was some dish.

SERGEANT. Just a hog.

WOODROW (*pointing to his chest*). I know but . . .

JUKE. You gotta wear something.

JONESY. You can't come back from the Solomons without nothing.

BILL. Not the son of Sergeant Truesmith!

WOODROW. I can't help it! I don't like the whole idea.

BUGSY. You gotta think of your mother.

WOODROW (*wearily*). The regulations are very clear: you wear the uniform home but not longer than thirty days.

CORPORAL. Suppose you was paid off in South Africa?

SERGEANT. And you went home on foot?

CORPORAL. They can't tell you how to go home.

SERGEANT. You could go home on a pogo stick.

WOODROW. But the regulation distinctly says . . .

SERGEANT. That only applies to Marines. . . . You ain't really a Marine any more . . . Besides, regulations is very elastic. I was even a Colonel once for a couple of days . . . once.

CORPORAL. And a brig hound for a couple of months. (*Suddenly under his breath*) 'Shun.

As the Marines come to attention, the scene cuts to an approaching MARINE GENERAL. He is accompanied by his wife and a young daughter.

GENERAL (*answering the Marines' salute*). How are you, boys?

SERGEANT (*very basso*). Fine, sir, thank you, sir.

The Marines put their hands down but Woodrow keeps his up.

WOODROW (*his hand in salute and his knees in rubber*). Let's go back to my room and talk it over.

SERGEANT. Nonsense. (*He snatches Woodrow's hand down but it goes up again automatically.*) Keep your lip buttoned . . . keep your hand down and nobody will be the wiser.

WOODROW (*firmly*). No.

CONDUCTOR'S VOICE. All aboard.

SERGEANT. Come on, get on the train. (*The train starts to move.*)

WOODROW. No.

SERGEANT. Come on, will ya? Chuck his gear on.

WOODROW. No, no.

SERGEANT. Will you get on that train?

WOODROW. No.

SERGEANT. Hoist him on . . . After we went to all this trouble.

The four privates pull the struggling Woodrow on the train. They lose their balance a little. The Corporal and the Sergeant are now running alongside.

SERGEANT. All right now, get off there.

JONESY'S VOICE. He's sitting on me.

WOODROW'S VOICE. Let me off of here.

BUGSY'S VOICE. You gotta think of your mother.

CORPORAL. Why don't we go with him, seeing as how we ain't got any dough anyway.

SERGEANT (*beginning to puff*). Well, get on or get off or anything except running along here.

CORPORAL. Come on.

He hoists the Sergeant aboard. The music reprises "Mademoiselle from Armentières" as the scene cuts to a RAILROAD SEMAPHORE against the sky. It swings up to the all clear position or words to that effect. We next see a train passing under us and the smoke fills the screen, and this dissolves to a view of WOODROW and the MARINES—in the SMOKING ROOM of a PULLMAN CAR, with the scenery going by outside.

WOODROW. Look, I don't want to sound ungrateful . . . I know you mean it for the best and I don't mind the seven tickets or anything. I'ma, I'ma honored to have you go home with me . . . It's just the uniform . . . It makes me nervous.

BUGSY. Well, you can't go home without it.

WOODROW. I shouldn't go home with it . . . and this . . . (*He points to the medal.*)

BUGSY. You shouldn't have lied to your mother.

SERGEANT. I think it was for pulling a Frenchman out of a river or something.

JONESY (*pointing to his*). He ought to have the Battle Blaze . . . That don't look right.

WOODROW. Well, I'm not going to have the Battle Blaze. . . . It's bad enough like this.

SERGEANT. Who's gonna notice anything? . . . You slip off the train. . . . We'll kinda surround ya. . . . We slip up a side street. . . . Your mother is waiting on the front porch. . . . You put your arms around her . . .

BUGSY. That's right.

SERGEANT. You get outta your uniform . . . You salt it away in moth balls and there you are . . . *home*. She's happy . . . *you're* happy . . . everybody's happy . . . and nobody's hep to nothin'!

WOODROW. It isn't only my mother . . . I gotta girl too . . . I mean I did have . . .

SERGEANT. What'd you tell *her* . . . you was goin' in the Navy?

WOODROW. No . . . I told her I fell for somebody else . . . so she wouldn't wait for me.

SERGEANT. What are you gonna tell her now?

CORPORAL. Tell her you're married.

SERGEANT. What good does that do? Tell her you're divorced.

WOODROW. I'm no good at lying . . . Maybe she doesn't care anymore anyway. . . .

BUGSY. Is your ma a good cook?

WOODROW. Wonderful.

BUGSY. Gee, you're lucky.

WOODROW (*crossly*). Well, I don't *feel* lucky . . . I tell you the whole thing is . . . Suppose I see somebody I know at the station?

SERGEANT. We'll surround you . . . You got nothin' to worry about.

WOODROW. I hope not.

PORTER (*sticking his head through the curtain*). Oakridge.

Woodrow immediately salutes him and keeps his hand glued to his forehead.

SERGEANT. Don't do that . . . Keep cool will you . . . What can happen?

BUGSY. Does your ma put up preserves?

WOODROW (*barking at Bugsy*). Yes! (*Then to the Sergeant*) What can happen? . . . Anything can happen.

As the Sergeant shrugs his shoulders at

this childishness, the scene dissolves to a full view of the STATION AT OAKRIDGE, CALIFORNIA: Across the tracks a big banner reads "WELCOME WOODROW—HAIL OUR HERO" and that is only the beginning. The entire town seems to be here with music. The Progressive Party's band with a placard: "WELCOME WOODROW . . . VOTE FOR DOC BISSELL, YOU CLEANED UP GUADALCANAL, HELP HIM CLEAN UP OAKRIDGE." Then The Regular Party band with a placard: "WELCOME WOODROW, OAKRIDGE IS PROUD OF YOU . . . REELECT EVERETT J. NOBLE, VICTORY THROUGH VIGILANCE." Next a Junior Sheriffs' Auxiliary Band under a flag inscribed simply: "OUR HERO." Next is an American Legion band under a banner which says "WE DID IT BEFORE, WE'LL DO IT AGAIN . . . WELCOME, SON OF HINKY DINK" and a little old Western Union man with a sign which says "WELCOME FROM WESTERN UNION." Surrounding all of this are townspeople young and old; Mamie, a little girl in white with a bunch of flowers, loose children, squalling babies, barking dogs, an ice cream man with a tricycle, a few soldiers and sailors, a colored delegation from the Odd Fellows, a Chinese with welcome sign in Chinese, the village photographer with a tripod camera, and the cast: Woodrow's mother, Libby and her Aunt Martha, the Chairman of the Reception Committee, Mr. Noble, his wife, his son Forrest, the Political Boss, the Newspaper Editor, Judge Dennis, Doc Bissell, Schultz the grocer, and the Rev. Doctor Upperman . . . all wearing badges. A band starts to play. Then we see the CHAIRMAN.

CHAIRMAN. Not yet . . . not till I give the signal. (*He blows on a whistle which stops the music.*) Not till I give the signal. (*As the Western Union man comes into view*) Not here! Go stand some place else.

Next we see WOODROW'S MOTHER with a big bunch of flowers in her arms.

LIBBY'S AUNT (*coming into view*). I'm very happy for you, Sally.

WOODROW'S MOTHER. Isn't it wonderful . . . when he was away for so long . . . and only hearing from him twice . . . and *then* being his father's son . . . you can imagine the chances he would take . . . the risks he would run.

LIBBY'S AUNT. Do you suppose he knows about Libby?

WOODROW'S MOTHER. I don't know, Martha . . . I certainly didn't tell him.

LIBBY'S AUNT. Do you suppose he'll be broken-hearted?

WOODROW'S MOTHER. I . . . hope not.

LIBBY'S AUNT. Well . . . *he* broke off with her . . . *her* skirts are certainly clean.

WOODROW'S MOTHER. I don't know anything about it, Martha.

LIBBY'S AUNT. She would have waited till, till Judgment day . . .

WOODROW'S MOTHER. I'm sure she would have, Martha.

LIBBY'S AUNT (*looking away*). I wish she had.

WOODROW'S MOTHER. So do I, dear; but . . . (*Then forcing a smile*) Anyway my boy is coming.

As she takes Martha in her arms, the scene cuts to LIBBY and FORREST NOBLE, the latter a tall handsome young civilian. Libby is a pretty girl.

LIBBY. I don't know what to do.

FORREST (*faintly annoyed*). Well, it really isn't your *problem*, dear, you're engaged to me and that's all there is to it.

LIBBY (*looking at her engagement ring*). I know . . . but it's his homecoming. And homecoming means to find everything the way you left it . . . at least for a little while. I mean after all we *were* . . . sweethearts when he left . . . *whoever* he may have fallen in love with afterwards.

FORREST. I don't see that that has anything to do with it . . . If he'd waited a year longer there might have been three of us to welcome him . . . If he'd waited *two* years there might have been . . .

LIBBY. Oh, shut up.

FORREST. Well, that's what marriage is for, isn't it?

LIBBY. I suppose so if you look at it from a purely unromantic standpoint . . . like a breeding farm. (*She makes a hopeless gesture.*) I mean if you don't see anything soul-stirring in the return of a, a . . .

FORREST. Hero.

LIBBY. All right, a hero. If you don't find anything heart-warming . . .

FORREST. My dear girl, I tried to get into the Army by every possible means. I even lied about my condition.

LIBBY. I know you did.

FORREST. It is not my fault that I have . . .

LIBBY. . . . chronic hay fever. I know that, Forrest . . . I've heard it a thousand times . . . but since you bring it up I am forced to remind you that *Woodrow* also had hay fever.

Forrest opens his mouth helplessly.

LIBBY (*looking at someone out of sight*). Your father wants you.

Forrest hesitates, then leaves her, and now Libby crosses to Woodrow's mother.

LIBBY. I'm very happy for you, Mrs. Truesmith.

WOODROW'S MOTHER. Of course you are, dear.

LIBBY (*in some hesitation*). Will you tell him I'm going to be married to Forrest, please?

WOODROW'S MOTHER. No, I won't, Libby. I think that's up to you.

LIBBY. Will you tell him, Aunt Martha?

LIBBY'S AUNT. Who, me? Hah!

LIBBY. Well, you know it wasn't my fault . . . I would have waited for him . . . forever. (*She turns to Woodrow's mother.*) He *asked* me not to. (*She turns to her aunt.*) He *told* me to forget him. (*She turns to Woodrow's mother.*) He wrote me he didn't love me any more.

WOODROW'S MOTHER. Maybe you should have read between the lines a little.

LIBBY (*on the verge of tears*). Oh, I don't know what to do . . . I don't want to tell him I'm engaged to somebody else . . . I just want to take him in my arms and tell him I'm so glad he's safe and so proud of him. . . . After all, I grew up with him.

LIBBY'S AUNT. Then why don't you?

LIBBY (*tempted*). I don't know how Forrest would feel about it.

WOODROW'S MOTHER. I'm sure I don't know either, dear.

LIBBY'S AUNT. Why don't you ask him? If you can't handle a man the week before you marry him he'll have you carrying in the wood on the wedding night.

Libby hesitates a second, then goes out of sight. The two ladies exchange a significant look. . . . This cuts to MAYOR NOBLE, MRS. NOBLE, the POLITICAL BOSS, the CHAIRMAN and FORREST.

MAYOR (*indignantly*). What do you mean I don't speak first? If anybody speaks first it's the mayor . . . I mean to say if you think I'm going to stand around like a door post and, and . . .

CHAIRMAN. Very well, Mr. Mayor, I'm only the chairman of the Reception Committee but as I visualize it . . .

MAYOR (*to his son*). Did you bring the keys to the city?

FORREST. Yes, Father, right here.

He pulls them half out of his pocket and looks back toward Libby.

MAYOR. Because I don't want to pull out my fountain pen like I did that time General what-che-ma-call-it . . .

MRS. NOBLE. Why don't you let Mr. Pash arrange things?

MAYOR (*threateningly to his wife*). If it's all the same to you, my pearl . . .

BOSS. It's always better to talk last, Evvy.

As Mayor Noble turns to argue this:

CHAIRMAN. As *I* visualized it, the ceremony began with a little girl in white with a bunch of posies . . .

MAYOR. . . . in her grimy little mitts. I know, I've listened to her before.

CHAIRMAN. Whatever you say, Mr. Mayor.

MAYOR. She forgets her lines till rigor mortis sets in.

CHAIRMAN. Very well, Mr. Mayor, *you* arrange the reception.

He folds his arms and looks in the distance.

THE BOSS. I tell you it's better to talk *after* Bissell . . . Then you can give him the needle.

MAYOR. All right, have it your own way . . . after all, I'm only the Mayor.

CHAIRMAN (*departing*). Thank you very much, Mr. Mayor. (*Now to the Western Union man who has just come*) Not in front of the Mayor. . . . Out in the fringe somewhere. (*He leads him out.*)

MAYOR. You'd think this was a political campaign instead of a . . . Did you bring the keys to the city?

FORREST. Yes, Father.

LIBBY (*coming into sight*). Mrs. Noble.

MRS. NOBLE. Oh, call me mo . . . Myrtle, dear.

LIBBY. Do you think it would be all right if I didn't tell Woodrow I was engaged to Forrest right away?

THE MAYOR AND FORREST (*together*). WHAT!

MAYOR. Well, it most certainly would not be all right! Of all the confounded . . . what are you talking about?

LIBBY. I mean not to spoil his homecoming with, with . . . by striking a single sour note.

FORREST. Thanks.

LIBBY. I don't mean that, darling.

MRS. NOBLE (*putting her arm around her*). Why of course it would be all right . . . I understand perfectly.

FORREST (*coldly*). Well, I'm not sure that I do, Mother.

MRS. NOBLE. That's because you're not a woman, dear. (*Then to Libby*) It's *perfectly* all right. (*Then to Forrest*) Why, under similar circumstances I'd be perfectly willing to pretend I wasn't married to your father for several . . . *weeks* even.

MAYOR. You could make it several months as far as I'm concerned.

MRS. NOBLE. He talks that way in public . . . We understand perfectly . . . You go right down and take him in your arms and . . . kiss him all you like.

FORREST. Well, I may have something to say about that . . .

MAYOR. Oh, I suppose she could kiss him on the cheek.

MRS. NOBLE. Oh, kiss him wherever you like. Of all the nonsense—two men telling us how to welcome a hero.

LIBBY (*kissing her*). Thank you . . . Myrtle. (*At which Mrs. Noble winks at her.*)

LIBBY (*starting out*). And thank you, Mr. Mayor . . . and you, Forrest.

She pecks him on the cheek and goes happily out of the scene.

MRS. NOBLE (*to her son*). You're going to have her the rest of your life. . . . Let him have her for an hour.

MAYOR (*to his son*). This is war, you know.

THE BOSS (*to Forrest*). And you know what Sherman said about it.

This cuts to JUDGE DENNIS, DOC BISSELL, MR. SCHULTZ, the CHAIRMAN, the LEADER of the PROGRESSIVE BAND and some other characters.

DOC BISSELL. Then he talks first?

CHAIRMAN. No, no, no; it's just as I visualized it: little Mamie Reynolds, *then* the Mayor, then you.

JUDGE DENNIS. You can take him apart a little.

CHAIRMAN. Precisely. Now if I can ever get the music straight . . .

PROGRESSIVE BAND LEADER. I've got it straight. I start with "There'll Be a Hot Time in The Old Town Tonight."

CHAIRMAN. You start with "Home to the Arms of Mother." I've told you a thousand times.

PROGRESSIVE BAND LEADER. I thought Ed started with that.

CHAIRMAN. Well, aren't you Ed?

PROGRESSIVE BAND LEADER. No, I'm Ned. Ed is playing for the *Mayor*.

CHAIRMAN. Then where is *Ned*?

PROGRESSIVE BAND LEADER. I am . . . we'd better get together on this while there's still time.

CHAIRMAN (*shouting to somebody out of sight*). Oh, Ned . . . (*Then to the Western Union Man who has just come into the shot*) Not here. (*He drags him out with him.*) . . . Just a minute.

The Band Leader exchanges a helpless look with Judge Dennis and says to the Chairman:

PROGRESSIVE BAND LEADER. I'm Ned. (*He follows the Chairman.*)

JUDGE DENNIS. This boy Woodrow is going to be very popular in this town, Doc.

DOC BISSELL. He deserves to be.

JUDGE DENNIS. I wonder if the same thought has occurred to you that flashed through my mind?

DOC BISSELL. Probably.

This cuts to WOODROW'S MOTHER, LIBBY'S AUNT, and LIBBY.

LIBBY. Well, *that's* settled. I'm just going to hug him as if he'd never written to me at all.

WOODROW'S MOTHER. I think that is a very sweet thought, dear.

LIBBY'S AUNT. Do you want me to hold your engagement ring?

LIBBY. Oh. (*She looks around toward Forrest, then gives her ring to her Aunt, who puts it on her own finger.*)

CHAIRMAN (*hurrying into the shot with two band leaders*). If I could just move you over about six feet this way, Mrs. Truesmith, next to the band that plays "Home to the Arms of Mother."

WOODROW'S MOTHER. Certainly.

THE REGULAR BAND LEADER (*pointing in the opposite direction*). Well, *I'm* playing that over there.

CHAIRMAN (*putting the back of his hand to his forehead*). Are you Ned or Ed?

REGULAR BAND LEADER. I'm Ed.

CHAIRMAN. Very well, Mrs. Truesmith, then would you mind moving about twelve feet over *that* way?

WOODROW'S MOTHER. Surely.

REGULAR BAND LEADER. I begin with "Mademoiselle from Armentières" then go into "Hail, The Conquering Hero Comes."

CHAIRMAN (*stunned*). You begin with "Mademoiselle from Armentières"?

REGULAR BAND LEADER. That's right. (*To the Progressive Band Leader*) Then what do you play?

PROGRESSIVE BAND LEADER. "There'll Be a Hot Time in the Old Town Tonight."

CHAIRMAN. Then who plays "Home to the Arms of Mother"?

LEADER OF THE AMERICAN LEGION BAND (*coming into view*). I do.

CHAIRMAN (*looking at his sheet*). What's your name?

LEADER OF THE AMERICAN LEGION BAND. Eddie.

LEADER OF THE JUNIOR SHERIFFS' AUXILIARY BAND (*coming into view*). I thought I started with that.

CHAIRMAN. With what?

LEADER OF THE JUNIOR SHERIFFS' BAND. "Hail, The Conquering Hero Comes."

CHAIRMAN. Who's talking about "Hail, The Conquering Hero Comes"?

LEADER OF THE JUNIOR SHERIFFS' BAND. *I* am.

CHAIRMAN (*expiring*). No, no, no, you play . . . (*He puts the back of his hand to his forehead.*) Oh, death, where is thy sting?.

LEADER OF THE JUNIOR SHERIFFS' BAND. We don't know that . . . all we know is "Hail, The Conquering

Hero" and half of "Marching Through Georgia." We were only formed last week.

PROGRESSIVE BAND LEADER. Now wait a minute, Teddy . . . (*The Chairman reacts to this.*) I lead off with "A Hot Time in the Old Town Tonight," Ed follows with "Mademoiselle from Armentières" and modulates into "Hail, The Conquering Hero Comes." Eddie takes "Home to the Arms of Mother" and you play anything you know.

LIBBY. Can anybody play "Let Me Call You Sweetheart"?

PROGRESSIVE BAND LEADER. Sure, I can modulate into that from "There'll Be a Hot Time in the Old Town Tonight."

REGULAR BAND LEADER. Or I could take it after "Mademoiselle" and let Teddy take "Hail, The Conquering Hero."

CHAIRMAN. Certainly, if you want to upset all of my plans . . . After all I've only had one morning to whip this all together, you know.

LIBBY. I'm sorry.

CHAIRMAN. Play it! Play anything you like.

Now a large lady in white comes into view, and grabs the Leader of the American Legion Band.

LADY IN WHITE (*with an accent*). Mr. Pash.

CHAIRMAN. What?

LADY IN WHITE (*menacingly*). I am here to help . . . I do it for nothing . . . with joy . . . but I got to have cooperation: I sing the hymn in seven flats and *he* won't play it in seven flats.

LEADER OF THE LEGION BAND (*desperately*). We don't know *how* to play in seven flats . . . we're not musicians.

LADY IN WHITE. You don't have to tell me.

CHAIRMAN (*wearily*). Each work in your own key and do your best.

PROGRESSIVE BAND LEADER (*to the American Legion Band Leader*). Why don't *we* take it for her and you take "Mademoiselle from Armentières"?

LADY IN WHITE. I refuse to sing it.

PROGRESSIVE BAND LEADER. You don't understand, Madam.

CHAIRMAN (*at the top of his lungs*). Will you stop balling things up? . . . Everything was clear and simple and now (*Now he grabs a woman who is hurrying through the shot.*) Where is Mamie? She's always disappearing.

MAMIE'S MOTHER. She'll be back in a minute . . . It's the excitement.

A STENTORIAN VOICE. Here comes the train.

Two bands start playing immediately, and all the leaders rush out.

CHAIRMAN (*running in all directions at once*). Not yet! Not yet!

He blows his whistle, starts off in one direction, then stops and blows his whistle in the other direction. The Western Union Man comes into sight and settles himself for the Reception. After a moment he narrows his eyes and watches evilly as another little old man walks into view and stands beside him. The new arrival bears a placard which says simply: "POSTAL TELEGRAPH IS PROUD OF YOU."

This cuts to the JUNIOR SHERIFFS' AUX-ILIARY BAND as the boys start playing "Marching Through Georgia."

CHAIRMAN (*running into view*). No, no, no.

As he clutches his head and rushes out, the scene cuts to the BIG LADY IN WHITE with the AMERICAN LEGION BAND which is playing something we can't make out and she is singing likewise. The Chairman blows his whistle in her face. She looks at him indignantly and with one powerful shove shoots him out of sight. Then we see MAMIE and her bunch of flowers as the Chairman staggers into sight and sits on her. Mamie starts to holler and the Chairman is immediately spoken to very roughly by Mamie's Mother.

Now we see WOODROW and the MARINES in the SMOKING ROOM.

WOODROW (*frightened*). What's that music?

PORTER (*entering*). Brush you off, Gents? (*He locks the toilet.*) Fix you up for de reception?

WOODROW (*freezing*). The reception!

PORTER. I reckon it's for you all. . . . They's half a dozen bands and all de 'ficials . . .

WOODROW (*at bay*). Let me outta here.

SERGEANT. Now wait a minute . . . it's probably for somebody else. . . . We'll wait here till they get it over with and then slip off quietly on the other side when the train starts up again.

In the meanwhile Bill, Juke, Bugsy and Jonesy have stepped into the corridor to look. Now they start bringing back reports.

JONESY (*shouting above the music*). It ain't for anybody else. . . . It says "WELCOME WOODROW" . . .

BILL. "You cleaned up Guadalcanal . . ."

JUKE. ". . . help us clean up Oakridge."

JONESY. "Vote for Doc Bissell."

BILL. "Welcome Woodrow . . . Oakridge is proud of you."

JUKE. "Reelect Everett J. Noble."

WOODROW (*leaping to his feet*). Let me outta here. (*He starts unbuttoning his coat.*)

SERGEANT. You're just gonna make things worse.

WOODROW. Where's my suitcase?

PORTER. They's up ahead in the vestibule.

SERGEANT. Keep cool, will ya.

WOODROW (*pointing to the toilet*). Open that up . . . (*He sneezes.*) I'll hide in there . . . you can all get off and tell 'em I couldn't . . . (*sneezing again*) . . . come. Give them . . . (*sneezing*) my apologies. (*To the Porter*) Will you open that . . . (*He sneezes.*)

PORTER. Not while it's in the station, boss. . . . You'll have to wait.

WOODROW (*struggling out of his coat*). Then I'll get off in my underwear.

SERGEANT. Cut that out, we're just pullin' in the station.

JONESY. I told you he ought to have the Battle Blaze . . . with all those people.

CORPORAL (*forcing Woodrow back into his coat*). Be a Marine, will you?

JUKE. They got four bands. . . . That don't look good with only one medal.

SERGEANT (*nonplussed only for one second; decisively*). Come on, take that blouse off. (*He pulls it off Woodrow and while doing so says to the Corporal.*) Come on, gimme yours.

CORPORAL (*holding back*). What?

SERGEANT. It's gotta have the Blaze on it . . . with four bands . . . Come on, get outta that.

The Corporal sheds his blouse and helps force it on the struggling Woodrow.

WOODROW. Quit it, will you?

SERGEANT. Button him up.

They all go to work on Woodrow except the Corporal who struggles into Woodrow's blouse with considerable difficulty.

SERGEANT. It's a matter of honor . . . here.

He reaches into his breast pocket and starts pinning some additional medals on Woodrow. By now the music is deafening.

This dissolves to a moving view down the rails of the waiting populace while everybody starts hooraying, and this cuts to the VESTIBULE of the PULLMAN CAR as the struggling Woodrow appears covered with medals, supported by the Marines. The train comes to a stop. The front Marines get off and Woodrow's knees start to sag.

SERGEANT. Hurrah! Pick him up.

The Marines hoist Woodrow to their shoulders. The crowd goes wild. And as they carry Woodrow forward, the view pushes through the populace, ending in a close picture of WOODROW'S MOTHER, LIBBY and her AUNT.

WOODROW'S MOTHER (*opening her arms wide*). Woodrow.

The Marines take him down off their shoulders. As his feet hit the ground his knees give way and the Marines hoist him up again. He takes his mother in his arms, gets an eyeful of his medals while he does so and tucks them behind his arms. Now he sees the Battle Blaze; he puts his right hand over it.

LIBBY. Hello, Woodrow.

WOODROW. Hello, Libby.

LIBBY. We're so proud of you.

WOODROW. What did you say?

LIBBY (*shouting*). I said, we're so proud of you.

WOODROW. Thank you. (*He kisses her.*)

We see MAMIE at Woodrow's feet; she yanks on his blouse and starts talking in a voice like a bugle.

MAMIE. Welcome young warrior . . . Your natal city rejoices at your safe homecoming and takes great pleasure in presenting you with this beautiful bunch of chrys . . . chryszanthanamums. (*There is a spatter of applause.*)

CHAIRMAN (*coming into view*). And now, Woodrow, if you can spare a moment.

He drags Woodrow, his mother and Libby away, and the Marines follow.

CHAIRMAN. Mr. Noble has prepared a little speech.

MR. NOBLE (*seizing his hand*). Welcome home, Woodrow.

WOODROW. Thank you, Mr. Noble.

Mr. Noble now puts a cough drop in his mouth and starts hollering in Woodrow's ear so that his speech will carry to the ends of the station.

> MR. NOBLE. Friends, voters, returning hero and ex-employee of the Noble Chair Company, Seats of all Descriptions . . . home to the arms of your mother . . . It is with a sense of deep humility . . .

The AMERICAN LEGION BAND starts playing "Home to the Arms of Mother" with much force, following which we again see WOODROW, his MOTHER, LIBBY and the MAYOR: Having nothing else to do the Mayor shakes Woodrow's hand again, smiles wolfishly at the crowd and glares at the band which seems to be wound up. Now the photographer taps the Mayor on the shoulder and he looks at Woodrow again with a beautiful smile. A flash goes off; they all look back toward the band. The Chairman hurries out. We again see the AMERICAN LEGION BAND playing "Home to the Arms of Mother" as the Chairman hurries toward it and gestures for silence; then WOODROW, his MOTHER, LIBBY and the MAYOR:

> THE MAYOR. It is with a sense of deep humility that I hail this conquering hero! On what foreign shores has he not . . . (*Now he turns his head at the new interruption.*)

This cuts to the REGULAR PARTY BAND playing "Hail, The Conquering Hero Comes," then to the CHAIRMAN in front of the PROGRESSIVE PARTY BAND as he leaves hurriedly, then to MR. NOBLE, WOODROW'S MOTHER, LIBBY, and WOODROW and the OTHERS, all of them glaring at the Regular Band. The photographer taps Mr. Noble on the shoulder and gets another smiling picture. The Chairman tears out. We hear the band stop raggedly.

> MR. NOBLE. I say it is with a sense of deep humility that I welcome this young Marine. Actions speak louder than words. (*He points to the medals.*) Here are his words. From the Halls of Montezuma to the shores of Tripoli . . .

He turns and glares at the American Legion Band which picks up this cue in nothing flat. The Chairman hurries into view, mops his head with a handkerchief, and hurries out the other side.

> PHOTOGRAPHER (*coming into view*). Just once more, Mr. Mayor, and a *big* smile this time.

We see the AMERICAN LEGION BAND playing the Marine Hymn as the Chairman hurries toward it and gesticulates; but these are not men who take their eyes off their music. The Leader waves the Chairman away; as the latter stands there nonplussed the Lady in White comes into view, strikes an attitude and starts to sing. The Leader of the Junior Sheriffs' Band now comes into sight and hollers something to the Chairman.

> CHAIRMAN (*throwing his arms to the sky*). Go ahead, do anything you like.

This cuts to the PROGRESSIVE PARTY BAND as the Leader sees the Chairman's gesture and starts playing "Mademoiselle from Armentières"; to the CHAIRMAN in front of the American Legion Band as he turns wearily at the new music, then winces; to the REGULAR BAND as it is playing "There'll Be a Hot Time in the Old Town Tonight."

The CHAIRMAN, next seen, registers great frustration, then scowls to his left as the Junior Sheriffs' Band marches through playing "Marching Through Georgia." They are followed by the Western Union man who is followed

HAIL THE CONQUERING HERO

in turn by the Postal Telegraph man. This cuts to MR. NOBLE, WOODROW and the MARINES. Mr. Noble has his fingers in his ears. Now the Junior Sheriffs' Band comes into sight and Mr. Noble gives up. He gets the keys to the city from his son, presses them in Woodrow's hand and starts waving his hat goodbye. The Chairman rushes into view and apparently says: "But, Mr. Mayor." Mr. Noble threatens him with the back of his hand; Mrs. Noble smiles to show the Mayor doesn't mean it. Forrest looks at Libby who takes Woodrow's arm in reply. Now the Noble family departs. Woodrow, his mother and Libby move through the hooraying crowd, and the Western Union Man and the Postal Telegraph Man fall in behind them; the Marines bring up the rear and are followed in turn by all the bands. There is a scramble and the Junior Sheriffs' Band moves up ahead. Judge Dennis, Doc Bissell and Mr. Schultz shake Woodrow's hand. The Chairman goes mad trying to get up in front but is prevented from so doing by the crowd.

This dissolves to the SIDEWALK on the STREET SIDE of the STATION where some open cars decorated with bunting are waiting. The crowd comes through, eventually squeezing out Woodrow, his mother and Libby, and the Marines. Now Libby's Aunt joins them.

WOODROW (*shouting*). Goodbye, goodbye, thank you very much.

He shakes his hands high in the air like a fighter and exchanges a look with the Marine Sergeant, who pantomimes that it is really nothing.

WOODROW. Goodbye. Come on Mama. (*He starts down the sidewalk.*)

CHAIRMAN (*fighting his way through the crowd*). Where are you going?

WOODROW (*crossly*). I'm going home . . . Where do you suppose I'm going?

CHAIRMAN. Well, you certainly are not going home like that . . . What do you think these cars are for anyway? . . . You're going home with escort and besides you have to lay a wreath on General Zabriski's statue . . . Now if you'll just get in here. (*He tries to push Woodrow in the car.*)

WOODROW (*holding back*). Come on, Mama.

WOODROW'S MOTHER. You take Libby, dear . . . I've got to get some more food . . . I didn't know you were bringing quite so many friends . . . You ride with him, Libby.

LIBBY (*looking around nervously for Forrest*). Oh . . . well, I suppose it'll be all right.

WOODROW. What do I have to do at General Zabriski's statue?

CHAIRMAN. Oh, just say a few words: Unprepared as I am, it is with a sense of both reverence and admiration that I place this wreath, and so forth, and so forth, at the feet of, and so forth and so forth.

This cuts to the SERGEANT and LIBBY'S AUNT.

SERGEANT. What did *he* do?

LIBBY'S AUNT. Who?

SERGEANT. General Zablitski.

LIBBY'S AUNT. Oh . . . nobody can remember . . . but I think it was a battle or something.

SERGEANT. I get you.

LIBBY'S AUNT. You always start there.

SERGEANT. I get you.

Next we see WOODROW, LIBBY, the CHAIRMAN and the OTHERS as Libby is already in the car and Woodrow is getting in. The Chairman gets in on the far side and raises his whistle to his lips.

WOODROW. Wait a minute . . . How about the Marines?

CHAIRMAN. Oh . . . well, we hadn't exactly counted on so many Marines. (*Then with a generous wave*) Oh, put them in the third car . . . Make it the second. (*Now he "hollers" to somebody out of sight.*) Put the other Marines in the second car.

He blows his whistle and a Band starts playing "Praise the Lord and Pass the Ammunition." The car pulls out slowly. Then we see the Noble family getting into its car.

FORREST (*looking around*). Where's Libby? (*Now he sees her and takes a step forward.*) Say, wait a minute.

In pantomime his mother says "What does it matter?" Then the scene dissolves to WOODROW and LIBBY in the back seat of the CAR while the band music and the hooraying are quite loud. Woodrow is saluting to both sides of the street.

LIBBY. I have something to tell you, Woodrow.

WOODROW (*not hearing*). What?

LIBBY. I said I have something to tell you.

WOODROW (*saluting off scene*). What?

LIBBY. I'll tell you later.

WOODROW. What did you say?

Libby gives up, and the scene fades out.

PART THREE

We see a TURKEY BEING ROASTED BY WOODROW'S MOTHER in the KITCHEN, then Woodrow's Mother and Libby's Aunt preparing some "big eats."

WOODROW'S MOTHER. I do wish he'd told me he was bringing six friends . . . If everybody hadn't been so kind I just don't know what we'd have done.

The phone rings.

LIBBY'S AUNT. I'll get it.

She hurries toward the hall. There is a knock on the door.

WOODROW'S MOTHER. Come in . . . oh, dear.

We see a SMALL BOY and MR. SCHULTZ coming in the door:

MR. SCHULTZ. Just in case you was short I brought over a few little knicknacks.

WOODROW'S MOTHER. That's terribly kind of you, Mr. Schultz, but I haven't a single point left.

MR. SCHULTZ. Who asked you? It's all complimentary, including the points, with the compliments of Schultz' market.

TEDDY. Boy, I wished I was a Marine.

MR. SCHULTZ. You will be.

TEDDY. Aw, it'll probably be over by the time I'm big enough.

MR. SCHULTZ. From your mouth to Heaven's ear.

WOODROW'S MOTHER. Just put it here, Mr. Schultz . . . Everybody has been so kind.

Mr. Schultz deposits his merchandise on a table that is practically collapsing with its load of home canned and home smoked delicacies.

TEDDY. How many Nips did Woodrow get, Mrs. Truesmith?

WOODROW'S MOTHER. I'm sure I don't know, Alfie . . . I hope he wasn't too bloodthirsty.

MR. SCHULTZ (*as the little boy does the machine gun act*). Quiet! And if there is anything else . . . the slightest thing . . . when we're open or when we're closed . . . Teddy will be happy to run over.

TEDDY. I'm bow-legged now.

MR. SCHULTZ (*pointing to the door*). Raus. Goodbye, Mrs. Truesmith, and I'm very happy for you . . . One in the family is enough to lose. (*He goes out.*)

LIBBY'S AUNT (*hurrying in with a paper and pencil*). Well, that's done . . . You sleep the Sergeant and the one they call Bugsy . . . I'll take the tall blond one that looks so much like my brother, Charles. Madame Lebovska spoke for the big Corporal . . .

WOODROW'S MOTHER. Do you suppose he'll be safe with her? . . . I don't mean that to be unkind.

LIBBY'S AUNT. Let him look out for himself . . . Myra Winstead will take the Southern boy, so that's one left over and Madame Lebovska said she could really manage two in a pinch.

WOODROW'S MOTHER. It might be better at that.

LIBBY'S AUNT (*seeing the new arrival of food*). Good Gravy! When did that come?

WOODROW'S MOTHER. Just now. Mr. Schultz brought it.

LIBBY'S AUNT. What are we going to do with it? . . . Even seven Marines can't wolf away *that* much.

WOODROW'S MOTHER. We can always send it to the poor.

LIBBY'S AUNT. Where are you going to find any? There just aren't any. Why, down at the Assistance League we're getting desperate . . . Everything piling up . . . We have to keep dusting it and brushing it . . . and . . . here they are.

WOODROW'S MOTHER. Oh, dear, he'll just have time to wash for church. . . . Do I look all right, Martha?

LIBBY'S AUNT. Of course you look all right . . . I'll stay and get their dinner ready.

WOODROW'S MOTHER. Oh, would you? That's so very kind of you. (*She takes off her apron and starts fixing her hair.*)

This cuts to the FRONT DOOR of Woodrow's house from inside the corridor: Woodrow and Libby are coming through the screen door followed by the Marines. Woodrow has the keys to the city and a papyrus scroll, Libby has a bunch of flowers, the Marines have cigars, flowers and candy. They go back into the kitchen.

WOODROW (*starting to unbutton his uniform*). Well . . . that's that. (*Now he glares at the Sergeant.*) That was a great idea you had.

SERGEANT. What are you talking about . . . Everything was lovely.

LIBBY. I thought your speech at General Zabriski's monument was very moving.

WOODROW. Thanks. Now if you'll excuse me . . .

LIBBY. I have something to tell you, Woodrow.

WOODROW. Well, you'll just have to wait 'till I get out of these clothes.

LIBBY (*holding onto his arm*). Well, the sooner I tell you, Woodrow . . .

WOODROW. Yes. Well, the sooner I slip into something else . . . the better, too.

LIBBY. Aren't you going to wear your uniform for a few days anyway? You look so splendid in . . .

WOODROW (*fiercely*). *I am not.*

SERGEANT. You could wear it till tomorrow . . . the regulations is very elastic.

WOODROW (*fiercely*). Well, if it's all the same to you, I'm not going to stretch them any further . . . if it's all the same to you.

WOODROW'S MOTHER (*coming into sight*). Where are you going, dear?

WOODROW. To put on my blue suit.

WOODROW'S MOTHER (*holding on to him*). But we'll be late for church, dear.

WOODROW. *Then we'll be late for church.*

WOODROW'S MOTHER. But why can't you wear your uniform for a little while?

WOODROW. *I just finished explaining. It's against regulations.*

WOODROW'S MOTHER. Well, I think that's perfectly ridiculous. . . .

LIBBY. So do I.

WOODROW'S MOTHER. Your grandfather wore his Civil War uniform the rest of his life . . . He kept having new ones made.

WOODROW (*departing*). Well, his case was different.

WOODROW'S MOTHER. He said it helped to remind people that brother fought brother. *Hurry up, Woodrow.*

LIBBY (*looking after Woodrow*). He seems a little upset.

WOODROW'S MOTHER. I suppose that's natural after what he's been *through*, dear . . . He has jungle fever, you know.

LIBBY'S AUNT (*horrified*). Jungle fever!

LIBBY. Oh, the poor darling. . . . I thought he looked a little bit yellow.

LIBBY'S AUNT (*horrified*). They run through the woods without any clothes on with knives in their teeth.

SERGEANT. Oh, no they don't at all, lady . . You're thinkin' of Boksok . . . The Marines always dress very nice.

WOODROW'S MOTHER. Of course they do . . . You must be Sergeant Heffelfinger . . . who knew *my* Sergeant.

She takes his hand.

WOODROW'S MOTHER. I want you to see him . . . I want you all to see him.

HAIL THE CONQUERING HERO

She takes Bugsy's hand and the Sergeant's arm and leads the way toward the front room.

LIBBY'S AUNT (*after the others have left*). You'd better get back to the Royal family.

LIBBY. I will . . . I'll meet them at church.

LIBBY'S AUNT. How did Woodrow take the news?

LIBBY. I haven't had a chance to tell him yet . . . there was so much noise.

LIBBY'S AUNT. You sure you tried your best?

LIBBY (*indignantly*). Of course I did.

This cuts to the SMALL FRONT ROOM as Woodrow's mother comes in followed by the six Marines. She pulls up a curtain to get more light, then indicates a framed enlargement under which are suspended, also framed, the Medal of Honor above a great many other medals.

WOODROW'S MOTHER. There he is.

SERGEANT (*very gruffly*). 'Shun. (*The six Marines come to attention and salute in unison.*)

WOODROW'S MOTHER. Thank you. (*The Marines lower their hands.*) He looks so young . . . compared to me. (*Now she smiles.*) Now I have two heroes. (*She puts her arm around the Sergeant and Bugsy, then adds.*) I have eight heroes.

BUGSY. You can sure put me on your flag . . . I sure ain't got anybody else.

WOODROW'S MOTHER. I'll be very proud to. (*We hear a church bell.*) Oh, dear, we're going to be late . . . Woodrow. (*She hurries the Marines out of the room.*)

This cuts to WOODROW in his bedroom as the church bell is heard ringing. He is halfway into a blue serge suit, just putting on his tie. The room is decorated with baseball bats, pennants, pictures of American heroes, a beautifully framed "Semper Fidelis," an American flag and some movie stars.

WOODROW'S MOTHER'S VOICE. Hurry up, dear.

WOODROW. I'm doing the best I can, Mama . . . Boy, do I feel better!

This cuts to the HEAD of the STAIRS as the Corporal appears.

CORPORAL. Your ma says to hurry up . . . Gimme back my blouse, will ya?

WOODROW. And how. Here. . . . (*He hands it to him.*)

CORPORAL (*slipping into it*). Boy, does that feel better.

WOODROW. Where's the Sergeant? I'd like to have a little talk with him.

He slips into his coat and the scene moves with them to the stairs.

CORPORAL. He's talkin' to your ma. Everything went nice, didn't it?

WOODROW (*sarcastically*). Marvelous.

This cuts to the CHURCH STEEPLE AGAINST THE SKY as we hear the booming of the bell, then to the FRONT of WOODROW'S HOUSE as the door opens and Woodrow's Mother and Libby come out followed by Woodrow, the Sergeant and the Marines.

SERGEANT. You see . . . it's all over and everything went perfect.

WOODROW (*bitterly*). Sure . . . except I'm a haunted man for the rest of my life. What do I do from now . . .

SERGEANT. Boy, I wish that's all *I* ever had to worry about.

The view moves around after them and we see the little procession go up the street. One of the trailing Marines does a two-step to get into step. This dissolves to the CHURCH TOWER and the bell is seen still ringing. Then the view moves down to people standing in front of the church. In the background people are entering the doors. In the foreground we see the Mayor, Mrs. Noble and Forrest. Suddenly Forrest sees the approaching Libby, and the scene cuts to WOODROW, his MOTHER, LIBBY and the MARINES as they move into the group with the Nobles. Libby moves over next to Forrest and they all enter the church.

This dissolves to a view of DR. UPPERMAN beating time as the congregation finishes a hymn—"Saved from earthly taint and sin, etc." and then we see WOODROW, his MOTHER, the SERGEANT and BUGSY; behind them are the four other Marines, in the church. These latter finish the hymn in a fine barber shop chord with sliding half tones. The Sergeant turns and gives them an evil glance. Woodrow is too far gone to notice. Bugsy smiles at Woodrow's Mother, and now the congregation sits down. Then we get a close view of the REV. DR. UPPERMAN.

DR. UPPERMAN. And now, I have a very pleasant task to perform . . . (*There is a rustle from the audience.*)

We see part of the CONGREGATION and WOODROW'S GROUP as people turn and smile at Woodrow and his mother. Woodrow looks back in some alarm, and this makes the congregation laugh. Then we again see DR. UPPERMAN.

DR. UPPERMAN. Usually on Sundays I have to scold you a little because that is what I am paid to do and I try to earn my keep . . . but today is a day of rejoicing. (*There is a buzz of excitement and Dr. Upperman holds his hand aloft for silence.*) Home from the hills cometh the hunter . . . home from the wars . . . the hero.

This cuts to WOODROW'S GROUP as Woodrow sinks very low in the pew. His mother looks very happy. The Sergeant tries to look detached.

DR. UPPERMAN (*again seen*). Homecoming . . . what a beautiful word. Home to the arms of his mother, the widow of yet another hero . . . cut down in the bloom of young manhood.

We see WOODROW'S MOTHER, BUGSY and WOODROW: Woodrow's Mother's eyes are full of tears, and Bugsy pats her hand.

DR. UPPERMAN. The arms of a mother who struggled through poverty and privation to raise her son rightly and courageously, that he might follow in the honorable footsteps of his father.

We get a close view of WOODROW and his MOTHER as the latter lowers her eyes and Woodrow sits up a little during this part of the speech.

DR. UPPERMAN'S VOICE. The years were hard, not always was there work . . . and the winds of reality blew coldly against this frail woman protecting her infant son.

The scene moves to include Bugsy, who shakes his head sadly.

DR. UPPERMAN'S VOICE. She had one possession . . . her home, the little white house at the end of Oak Street . . . the home of heroes.

The scene moves to include the Sergeant. Woodrow sinks a little lower.

DR. UPPERMAN'S VOICE. She clung to it tenaciously but one day she reached the end of her rope and a mortgage was her only solution. (*The Sergeant sniffles.*)

DR. UPPERMAN (*again seen*). Mortgages have a way of growing . . . like beautiful trees . . . This one increased, then increased again and still again till the widow owned very little of the house she loved so well. (*He reaches calmly behind him and picks up a roll of paper tied with a ribbon.*) I have here the document in question, purchased by the grateful citizens of our township. . . .

This cuts to WOODROW and his GROUP as his mother looks ecstatic and Woodrow looks horrified. He waggles No, No, No and starts to rise. The Sergeant pushes him down in his seat.

DR. UPPERMAN'S VOICE. . . . purchased with deep respect by the grateful citizens of our township, who have asked me to perform the following ceremony.

Woodrow makes a sudden move and the Sergeant pulls him down again.

DR. UPPERMAN (*happily*). You will notice that I have nothing up my sleeve . . . (*He laughs at his little joke, then suddenly touches the rolled mortgage to the flame of a taper.*)

We hear a single organ note. Now Dr. Upperman holds the torch aloft and the flames increase as does the roar of the music. This then cuts to WOODROW and his GROUP as they start out of the church and are congratulated from all sides. Woodrow's hand is pumped up and down continuously.

This dissolves to the EXTERIOR of the CHURCH as the crowd is coming out. Woodrow's mother, her eyes full of tears, is congratulated from all sides.

WOODROW'S MOTHER. Thank you . . . thank you so very much . . . I don't know what to say.

LIBBY (*coming into view*). I'm so happy for you. (*She kisses her.*)

Next WOODROW is seen holding back from the crowd, waiting for the Sergeant, who appears a moment later but avoids his eye.

WOODROW. Everything went perfect, hunh?

SERGEANT. It was a very beautiful ceremony.

WOODROW. Yes, but how do I pay it back?

SERGEANT. They shoulda done it a long time ago on accounta your old man.

WOODROW. Wait till they find out.

SERGEANT. Who's gonna find out . . . (*He pauses as the Chairman hurries toward them.*)

CHAIRMAN. Oh, Woodrow, we want your opinion.

WOODROW (*suspiciously*). On what?

CHAIRMAN. On the location of the monument. Naturally General Zabriski has the choice spot . . . but then he's been there so long . . .

WOODROW (*fearful already*). What monument is that?

CHAIRMAN. Oh, didn't you know? But of course you didn't . . . We're raising you a little monument by public subscription. I always say it's better to do these things while they're hot.

WOODROW (*horrified*). Now wait a minute . . . (*He gives the Sergeant a fulminating look but the latter tries to avoid his eye.*)

CHAIRMAN. Oh, just something modest, in granite probably . . . bronze is simply impossible to get . . . It's just to our first hero of this present war.

WOODROW. Look, if anybody deserves a monument . . . it's my *father,* not me.

CHAIRMAN (*happily*). Oh, he's on it, too . . . you're *both* on it . . . shaking hands. It will be called: "Like Father, Like Son." (*Woodrow feels of his head*). Now I thought just in front of the station but there is much to be said for . . . (*He stands with his mouth open as Woodrow hurries out.*) Did I say something wrong?

This cuts to MR. NOBLE, the political BOSS, MRS. NOBLE, FORREST and LIBBY.

MR. NOBLE. A statue! (*He looks around from one to another.*) Wasn't General Zabriski enough of a pain . . . Now I suppose every function starts with laying two wreaths . . . going and coming. I certainly hope this war ends in a hurry . . . Holy Moses.

MRS. NOBLE. Maybe you could be standing in the middle, dear . . . introducing them.

MR. NOBLE. Really, Myrtle, there are times . . .

MRS. NOBLE. Well, I think he's cute . . . You're just hungry.

MR. NOBLE. Men, let's eat. (*He leads the way.*)

MRS. NOBLE. Come on, Libby.

LIBBY. Would you please excuse me for a few minutes . . . I have one more errand to do.

MRS. NOBLE. Oh . . . Oh, of course, darling.

She follows her husband out, leaving Forrest and Libby.

FORREST. What's the errand?

LIBBY. Oh, nothing. I just have to tell Woodrow something.

FORREST. What about?

LIBBY. About . . . us.

FORREST. You mean you haven't told him yet?

LIBBY. I didn't get a *chance* to, dear. Every time I started to a band started playing or they burned the mortgage on his house or, or . . .

FORREST. . . . raised him a statue.

LIBBY. Well, I can't help it.

FORREST. I suppose you're very proud of him now?

LIBBY. Why shouldn't I be? . . . I grew up with him.

FORREST. So did I, but I don't walk around starry-eyed . . .

LIBBY. Oh, you're just jealous.

FORREST. Well, make it snappy, will you?

LIBBY. Of course I will: I'll just say, Woodrow, I thought you'd like to know Forrest and I are going to be married next Sunday morning . . . I'm so glad you got back in time . . . to be there. That's all.

FORRSET. Well, you don't look glad.

LIBBY. Well, I *am* glad . . . I'm terribly glad.

FORREST. Well, you certainly conceal it beautifully.

LIBBY. Women have to conceal things beautifully, Forrest, that's their role in life.

She looks at him, then hurries away. Forrest looks after her a moment, then tightens his tie and goes after his father. The scene moves with him a little way so that we see the Noble Chair Company, Seats of All Descriptions, in the distance. Forrest looks back and the scene cuts to Woodrow's FRONT YARD as viewed from the porch: Woodrow and his mother lead the little procession. Way in the distance Libby is following. Woodrow opens the gate for his mother, who kisses him as she goes by.

WOODROW'S MOTHER. Now all wash your hands, dinner must be ready. . . All this lovely sentimental nonsense . . . and seven hungry men to feed.

CORPORAL. Oh, boy! (*They all file past except Woodrow.*)

WOODROW (*looking after the Sergeant*). Hey.

This cuts to the SERGEANT as he is about to enter the house.

SERGEANT. You talkin' to me?

We see WOODROW at the GATE: He comes in and closes the gate after him and walks up the steps until the Sergeant is included in the view.

WOODROW. What do I do now?

SERGEANT. Well . . . you just let it blow over.

WOODROW. Did you ever see a statue blow over?

SERGEANT. Maybe you could be sort of hard to please . . . They want it standing up, you want it sitting down . . . They want it shaking hands, you want it with the hands behind the back . . . They want it in front of the station, you want it where General Zablizki is, till one day they say: do you want it or don't you? And you say: in that case *no* . . . and there you are.

WOODROW. And what do I do about the mortgage?

SERGEANT. Well, you a . . . well you could kinda . . . look, I didn't get you into this. I just . . .

WOODROW. Oh, yes you did . . . I was gonna hide in the Gents' Room until . . .

SERGEANT. A Marine never hides in the Gents' Room . . . That's what Semper Fidelis means. It means face the music.

WOODROW. Yes, well it doesn't happen to mean that at all! . . . it means "always faithful."

SERGEANT. That's right . . . faithful to your mother . . . All right, you're . . .

WOODROW. It doesn't mean faithful to your mother . . . It means . . .

SERGEANT. What's the matter with you? You're home . . . your mother is happy. Did you see that look in her eyes? . . . Your girl still loves you, and the town give you a nice little reception.

WOODROW. I'll say they did, but in the first place . . .

SERGEANT. Boy, I wished *I* was in your shoes.

WOODROW. Boy, I wish you were too. Look: I don't want to sound ungrateful . . . I know you meant it for the best and I thank you for your good intentions . . .

SERGEANT. I tell ya it'll all blow over. Everything is perfect . . . except for a couple of details.

WOODROW. They hang people for a couple of details.

SERGEANT. What are you talking about? I been a hero, you could call it that, for twenty-five years and does anybody ever ask me what I *done?* If they did I could hardly tell 'em, I've told it so different . . . so many times . . . It ain't as if you done it on purpose . . . By *Tuesday* it'll be forgotten.

WOODROW. I hope you're right.

SERGEANT (*fortified as he sees Woodrow weakening*). I *know* I'm right. You take General Zabliski for instance . . .

WOODROW. Zabriski.

SERGEANT. All right, where did *he* tend bar?

WOODROW. That's a different case entirely . . . The town bought him from an iron works that was going out of business . . . He just happened to be a bargain.

SERGEANT. Well, you're the only guy that knows it . . . All everybody else knows is he's a *hero* . . . He's got a statue in the park . . . and the birds sit on it . . . and except I ain't got no birds on me I'm in the same boat.

WOODROW. Look . . .

LIBBY'S VOICE. Woodrow.

WOODROW (*turning*). Yes.

This cuts to LIBBY at the GATE.

LIBBY. Woodrow, could I see you for a moment, please?

She comes through the gate, and with some diffidence, up to the house.

WOODROW. Yes, Libby.

SERGEANT (*gallantly*). I'll leave youse two alone. (*He winks at Libby.*)

LIBBY. Thank you, Sergeant.

SERGEANT. It's a pleasure.

He opens the door to go into the house and Woodrow's mother pops out of it.

WOODROW'S MOTHER. Hurry up, dear, dinner is on the table . . . You can come too, Libby . . . We're glad to have you . . . After all your Aunt practically cooked it . . . Hurry up now while it's hot. (*She shoos them inside.*)

As the scene dissolves we see the CARCASS of the TURKEY; then Woodrow, Libby and the six Marines at the table, Woodrow's mother and Libby's aunt hovering behind them.

WOODROW'S MOTHER. Now just a little pie to fill in chinks.

CORPORAL. Yes, ma'm, I'll have to eat it in small pieces.

LIBBY. Aren't you hungry, Woodrow?

WOODROW. I guess the excitement kind of twisted my stomach a little.

LIBBY'S AUNT. It's the fever.

WOODROW. No, it isn't the fever . . . That never bothers me at all except . . . (*He sneezes.*)

LIBBY'S AUNT. You see.

WOODROW. Not at all . . . (*He sneezes again.*)

WOODROW'S MOTHER. Don't blow the house down, now that we own it. (*Woodrow faintly shakes, no, no, no.*)

LIBBY'S AUNT. Wasn't that a lovely gesture?

WOODROW'S MOTHER. This is the happiest day of my life.

LIBBY (*a little sadly*). If you're all finished, Woodrow, would you come outside with me a moment... There's something I want to...

WOODROW. Sure. (*He starts to get up.*)

At this point, there is a heavy knock on the screen door outside and Woodrow, caught in a jumping position, slowly sits down again.

WOODROW. Here it comes.

SERGEANT. Here *what* comes?

WOODROW'S MOTHER. I'll see what it is.

She goes out, and Woodrow drinks a glass of water with a shaking hand.

LIBBY. What's the matter, Woodrow?

LIBBY'S AUNT. Does he feel hot? Feel his head.

She comes over to do so.

WOODROW (*almost barking at her*). No I *don't* feel hot!... If I feel anything I feel... (*He sneezes, then looks up fearfully at his mother who is coming back in the room.*)

WOODROW'S MOTHER. Woodrow, Judge Dennis and the Sheriff and Doc Bissell and a lot of other men want to see you right away... They're in the parlor.

WOODROW (*having difficulty forming the words*). What about?

WOODROW'S MOTHER (*coming into view*). They didn't tell me, dear, they just said they wanted to see you right away.

WOODROW. Well... (*He starts to get up and makes it on the second try.*)

SERGEANT (*roughly*). They probably want to baptize a baby after ya.

WOODROW. I'll say.

He slips the knot of his tie so tight he nearly chokes himself.

WOODROW'S MOTHER. What's the matter, dear?

WOODROW (*smiling only with the teeth*). Oh... nothing.

The smile drops off his face like a dry mud pack. The Sergeant wiggles his finger over his head and whistles the proper bugle call—it may be Assembly. The Marines get to their feet instantly. As Woodrow starts out of the room, the Sergeant, in an unconcerned manner, picks a rolling pin off a side table. The Corporal picks up the whistling and seizes a potato masher. Woodrow and all the others start toward the front room.

This cuts to the SITTING ROOM of WOODROW'S HOUSE: Here we see Judge Dennis, Doc Bissell, the Sheriff, Mr. Schultz, the Rev. Dr. Upperman, the Chairman and about six other local businessmen. Judge Dennis is walking up and down gravely. Suddenly he turns.

JUDGE DENNIS. Ah, there you are, Woodrow.

We see WOODROW in the doorway; behind him stand his Mother, Libby and the six Marines.

WOODROW. Good afternoon, Judge... Dennis.

This cuts to the JUDGE and the OTHERS.

JUDGE (*severely*). Where are the medals?

This cuts to WOODROW and his GROUP.

WOODROW. Oh, the medals . . . (*He indicates them weakly.*) Oh, I just wore those to get off the train . . . I . . . suppose I shouldn't have but . . .

This cuts to the JUDGE and his GROUP.

DOC BISSELL. What do you mean you shouldn't have? If all good men wore medals it wouldn't be so hard to tell the good from the bad.

JUDGE. That's a good line, Doc. Make a note of it, Richard.

CHAIRMAN (*writing it down*). I have it.

We again see WOODROW and his GROUP.

WOODROW. I guess that's right all right . . . Well . . . I'm ready . . . Iya guess I deserve it all right.

MR. SCHULTZ. You certainly do.

DR. UPPERMAN. Beyond question.

WOODROW. Goodbye, Mama.

WOODROW'S MOTHER. Where are you going?

JUDGE DENNIS. Who told you about it?

WOODROW. I can put two and two together.

SERGEANT. Now, wait a minute.

WOODROW. Come on, let's go.

JUDGE. What are you talking about?

WOODROW. Aren't you taking me somewhere?

JUDGE. Not at all, we're going to do it here.

CORPORAL. Oh, yeh? (*At this all the Marines move up.*)

JUDGE. Woodrow, there is something rotten in this town . . .

WOODROW. I know it.

MR. SCHULTZ. That's why we're here.

WOODROW. I know it, but I don't see why you have to do it in front of my mother.

WOODROW'S MOTHER. What are you talking about, dear?

SHERIFF. Then let's get down to business . . . The trouble with our party is that everybody talks too long all the time.

JUDGE. All right . . . Woodrow, there is something rotten in this town . . .

WOODROW. You don't have to keep rubbing it in . . . ..I'm ready.

JUDGE. Nothing you can put your finger on exactly but a kind of something you can feel. It's like the town was selfish. . . . Everybody thinking about little *profits* and how *not* to pay the taxes and reasons for *not* buying bonds and *not* working too *hard,* and *not* working at night because it's nicer in the daytime . . . All things that are all right in peace time . . . things you used to call thrift and relaxation . . . that made many a fortune, but things that are plain dishonest in war time. The motto of this town is "Business as usual" but a lot of us feel war time ain't a usual time and that business as usual is dishonest. That's why we need an honest man for Mayor, an honest man who will wake us up and tell us the truth about something he knows all about.

SHERIFF. An honest man who will tell us the truth and who can win.

MR. SCHULTZ. We got an honest man who'll tell us the truth but he only pulls thirty-two votes outside of his brother and his wife.

DOC BISSELL. And I'm not even sure about her . . . I have everything but popularity.

JUDGE. In other words, Woodrow, we want you to take Doc Bissell's place.

DOC BISSELL. I will retire in your favor.

WOODROW. But I'm not a . . . veterinary . . . I hardly know one end of a horse from . . .

JUDGE (*gently*). We want you to run for Mayor, Woodrow . . . in the coming election.

DOC BISSELL. The good of the party comes first.

DOC UPPERMAN. The right shall prevail.

WOODROW (*looking around like a hunted animal*). You want me to run for m-m-mayor. (*He smiles idiotically and his knees give way.*)

The Marines grab him. He waggles no, no, no.

WOODROW'S MOTHER (*grabbing him around the neck*). But that's wonderful, Woodrow. Your father would be so proud of you.

Woodrow waggles a vehement no, no, no. Libby embraces him also and he is nearly strangled.

JUDGE. Three cheers for the new mayor.

DR. UPPERMAN. Hip, hip, hip. . . .

ALL. Hooray.

MR. SCHULTZ. Hip, hip, hip. . . .

ALL. Hooray.

CHAIRMAN. Hip, hip, hip. . . .

ALL. Hooray.

JUDGE (*leading the way*). Bring him out, boys!

DR. UPPERMAN (*with a magnificent gesture.*) Forward . . . (*The Chairman blows his whistle.*) . . . march.

The band outside starts to play, the Committee hurries out, and the scene cuts to the struggling Woodrow as the Marines start pushing him ahead. On seeing the crowd, Woodrow grabs the side of the door and hangs on desperately like a bum resisting a bum's rush.—We see the full CROWD trampling Woodrow's lawn and in the foreground, the band and the Committee.

THE CROWD. Hooray.

WOODROW is seen struggling to get back into the house, and is lifted out bodily by the Marines.—This cuts to the CHAIRMAN and the BAND as he blows his whistle for silence, and then to the JUDGE.

JUDGE. Ladies and gentlemen, I give you . . . *Our new Mayor.*

The band starts to play and the crowd goes wild.—WOODROW waggles "no-a-thousand-nevers" as he is dragged to the railing by the Marines. The Chairman whistles for silence, some voices scream "Speech."

JUDGE. First we'll have a few words from Doc Bissell.

CHAIRMAN (*with gestures*). A big hand please, a big hand.

DOC BISSELL. I'm gonna be even briefer than usual . . . You know what I stand for in this town . . . You know what I'm against. Our party is fortunate in having found a worthier standard bearer than I have ever been or ever could be . . . a man who fought for you overseas . . . a man who will fight for you here . . . AND WIN!

THE CROWD. Hooray.

DOC BISSELL. For the good of the party, for the good of the town and its war effort, for the good of the United States of America . . . I herewith retire in favor of, and ask you to vote for . . . Corporal Woodrow Lafayette Pershing Truesmith.

The crowd goes wild and the band plays "There'll Be a Hot Time in the Old Town Tonight." The Chairman stops the band after a moment.

> JUDGE. Before introducing the principal speaker I wish to point out that he appears before you NOT as a hero, NOT with decorations he so heroically won and so richly deserves . . . but as a simple citizen . . . a home town boy . . . back home. I need say no more of the character of this young man than that *he refused to wear his medals!* Ladies and Gentlemen, Mr. Truesmith.

The CROWD shouts with pleasure and the band starts to play. The Chairman stops it with difficulty.—WOODROW loosens his collar, reaches in his pocket, grins not too brightly, looks back at the Marines, laughs at the crowd and stops laughing as suddenly as he had begun.—The CROWD is enchanted with Woodrow's modesty and laughs happily.

> WOODROW. Ladies and Gentlemen, Iya . . . wished I was dead. (*The crowd laughs happily. Woodrow laughs and "unlaughs" suddenly.*) You're making a big mistake.

The crowd hoorays and the band starts to play. We hear the Chairman's whistle and the band stops.

> WOODROW. Iya . . . love my mother very much. (*The crowd hoorays and the band starts to play. Woodrow's mother kisses him.*) But she shouldn't have told you I was coming home and made all that fuss down at the station. (*There is a roar of laughter, and he shouts desperately.*) I really don't deserve it.

All the Committee burst out laughing and Woodrow now receives a kiss from Libby. The crowd hoorays and the band starts to play "Let Me Call You Sweetheart."—We see a GROUP in the crowd, an OLD MAN calling out "What a modest boy," then a GROUP OF WOMEN as an OLD LADY declares "Don't they make a handsome couple," and blinks away a tear.

This cuts to WOODROW on the porch

> WOODROW. There are many, many men . . . (*pointing to the Sergeant and the Marines*) any one of *these* young men for instance . . . far, far more deserving than myself. (*The Sergeant winks at the crowd, which roars back at him.*) The medals you saw on me you could practically say were . . . *pinned on by mistake.* (*The Sergeant winks at the crowd again. The crowd roars. Woodrow looks around a little nonplussed.*) I want you to believe me. (*There is a wild hooray from the crowd.*)

This cuts to the JUDGE and DR. UPPERMAN.

> JUDGE. He has a natural flair for politics.
>
> DR. UPPERMAN. A born speaker.
>
> WOODROW (*seen again, still addressing the crowd*). I've known you all, all my life . . . I've mowed your lawns and delivered milk . . . for your babies. (*There is a wild hooray, and Woodrow tries to stop it.*)

We again see the JUDGE and DR. UPPERMAN.

JUDGE. That milk and baby part is remarkable.

DR. UPPERMAN. After that he could be President.

WOODROW (*continuing his speech*). I even know the dogs and cats . . . (*He holds his hand up for silence as his words are greeted with laughter.*) Nothing would be dearer to my heart than to be worthy of the honor you offer me . . . I wish I could accept it. Iya . . . I'm no hero. Iya haven't Doctor Bissell's long experience with a . . . animals . . . (*The laughter starts again.*) Iya . . . there is the man for you . . . I thank you.

He waves and hurries into the house to a tremendous burst of music and hooraying.

We see the KITCHEN of Woodrow's house. Libby's Aunt is busy with more food as Woodrow staggers in.

LIBBY'S AUNT. Land sakes, what's all the noise this time? It's a good thing somebody keeps cool.

WOODROW. You said it. (*He goes to the sink and puts some cold water on his face.*) That was a close one. Boy!

WOODROW'S MOTHER (*hurrying in*). My boy.

She takes him in her arms and pats him on the back. Now the Judge, the Chairman, Mr. Schultz, Dr. Upperman and Doc Bissell come in.

JUDGE. Remarkable, Woodrow, remarkable.

MR. SCHULTZ. Wonderful.

DR. UPPERMAN. That's as good a political speech as I've heard since Bryan and the Crown of Thorns.

DOC BISSELL. You don't need any lessons from *me*.

JUDGE. If I might make *one* suggestion, Woodrow . . . I wouldn't play down the hero part quite so much hereafter, modesty notwithstanding . . . They like it, you know . . . Anyway the Sergeant is taking care of that part of it.

WOODROW (*astonished*). Hereafter? What are you talking about? What's the matter with him? What the . . . what's he doing?

He crosses to the hall where he can hear the Sergeant, who is next seen, with the other Marines, on the front porch, facing part of the crowd.

SERGEANT (*with some embarrassment*). I been asked to tell you a couple of things about Woodrow . . . I don't know just how he's gonna take this . . . In fact, he's so modest, I'm pretty sure he ain't gonna like it at all . . . In fact I may get quite a sock on the jaw before I'm through. (*This is greeted with laughter.*) Any way I'm gonna give ya just one sample . . . of his courage . . . and his resoursafullness . . . I'm gonna tell you how he saved my life. (*There is wild hurraying.*) We're on the beach, see, at Tenaru Bay. All of a sudden we hear "Here they come" . . . take cover and out of the jungle come two, maybe three hundred Japs preceded by a hail of bullets. I turn, and my foot catches in a . . . I didn't see exactly what it was. I was kinda in a hurry but I'm stuck, I'm lost, see? Now a voice says "Keep cool, pal" and beside me I see . . . Woodrow.

There is a wild hooray as the scene cuts to WOODROW and the OTHERS in the doorway of the kitchen.

WOODROW (*gesturing no, no, no*). What's the matter with him? He can't *do* that. (*He starts forward, but the others hold him.*)

DR. UPPERMAN. Relax, Woodrow, relax . . . Everything is all right.

JUDGE. That's doing you a lot of good.

WOODROW (*struggling*). But I tell you I'm not running for mayor.

JUDGE (*amused*). You're not running for mayor!

DOC BISSELL. Why, you couldn't stop from being mayor if you, if you . . .

DR. UPPERMAN. A miracle couldn't stop you.

Woodrow staggers to the kitchen table and tosses off a glass of wine.

WOODROW'S MOTHER. Don't drink that dear . . . it's cooking wine.

WOODROW. Well, *I'm* cooked.

We again see the SERGEANT and the other MARINES.

SERGEANT (*in full swing*). Zing, he got another one . . . zang another one hits the deck . . . zowie he clubs two of them with the butt end of his gun. We duck and run another little piece then drop, zing, zing, and two more brown brothers bite the dust. Now he picks up a machine gun . . . rat, tat, tat, tat, tat, tat . . .

The scene fades out.

PART FOUR

We see a bunting-draped banner which says: "VICTORY THROUGH VIGILANCE— Re-elect Mayor Everett J. Noble, Your Humble Servant." The view dips down onto the bunting-hung doorway of the Noble Chair Company, Seats of All Descriptions. Through this we see men walking in and out. Inside they stand around in groups. On the back wall there is an eight sheet picture of Mayor Noble.

The scene cuts to MAYOR NOBLE'S PRIVATE OFFICE, furnished with simple magnificence. The Mayor, toying with a twenty-dollar gold piece, is strutting up and down and dictating to his son, who is taking it down in long hand.

MR. NOBLE. Once again, fellow citizens, you have chosen me to be your mayor and once again I accept the charge— Make that responsibility— I accept the responsibility— Make that *deep* responsibility— No, just make that plain responsibility.

FORREST. I wish you'd make up your mind.

MR. NOBLE (*indignantly*). What?

FORREST. And don't go so fast . . . I don't know how to do this.

MR. NOBLE. Then why isn't Libby here?

FORREST. She'll be back.

MR. NOBLE. She's still getting paid as my secretary, you know, no matter who she marries.

FORREST. What do you mean "no matter who she marries"?

MR. NOBLE. I mean even if she is engaged to you. Now where was I?

FORREST (*reading*). I accept the charge— Make that responsibility. I accept the responsibility— Make that deep responsibility— No, just make that plain responsibility . . .

MR. NOBLE (*not believing his ears*). Are you simple-minded or something? (*Shouting*) I accept the responsibility with a sense of both humility, satisfaction and gratitude.

FORREST. You dictated "plain" responsibility.

MR. NOBLE. That's right, that means responsibility without adjectives. Now where was I . . . *Don't tell me*: I accept the responsibility with a sense of both humility, satisfaction and gratitude.

FORREST. You can't say both humility, satisfaction and gratitude. "Both" means two and you have humility, satisfaction and gratitude . . . that's three.

MR. NOBLE (*furiously*). I can't say it?

FORREST. You cannot.

MR. NOBLE. I've been saying it for years.

FORREST. It isn't correct grammar.

MR. NOBLE. I am not running on a platform of correct grammar . . . I even let my grammar slop over a little sometimes.

FORREST. You certainly do.

MR. NOBLE. *Purposely.*

FORREST. Unh-hunh.

MR. NOBLE. It gives that homey quality . . . horny hands and honest hearts. . . . Now where was I?

FORREST. With a sense of both humility, satisfaction and gratitude.

MR. NOBLE (*generously*). All right, take out humility.

FORREST (*shrugging*). Leave it in.

MR. NOBLE (*shouting*). Take it out! Will you do what I tell you? Instead of sitting there like a stuffed nincompoop trying to annoy me. (*Now he adds meanly.*) Just because your girl-friend is out with somebody else.

FORREST (*menacingly*). What?

MR. NOBLE. Now where was I?

FORREST. With a sense of both satisfaction and gratitude.

MR. NOBLE. *And* humility.

His son looks at him unbelievingly.

MR. NOBLE (*brushing off his vest*). What are you gaping at?

FORREST. Nothing.

MR. NOBLE Well . . . cut it out . . . now. . . . Well, it's about time . . .

And now we see LIBBY coming in the door.

LIBBY. I'm sorry. (*Then seeing what Forrest is doing*) I'll take it, Forrest.

MR. NOBLE. I trust the conquering hero is home and that's that.

LIBBY. Yes, sir.

FORREST. Have you been crying?

LIBBY. It's nothing.

MR. NOBLE. Now let's get this speech out of the way without further interruption. Dictating to my son is like dictating to a sponge.

LIBBY. Mr. Noble, before you go on with this there's one thing you might like to . . .

MR. NOBLE (*severely*). I said without further interruption, if you please.

LIBBY. Yes, sir.

MR. NOBLE. If it's all the same to you.

FORREST (*in a low voice*). What were you crying about?

MR. NOBLE. You can fight that out later. Now where was I?

LIBBY. With a sense of both humility, satisfaction and gratitude. . . . You can't say that; both means two and you have humility, gratitude . . .

MR. NOBLE (*slapping the desk*). Will you be so kind as to permit me to dictate my own speech, or do you just want to . . .

LIBBY. I'm sorry.

MR. NOBLE. As president and owner of the Noble Chair Company, Seats of All Descriptions, I am to most of you—make that many of you—make it some of you—your employer. But as mayor of our fair city, I am to *all* of you . . . your servant. That's a nice twist. *Mine* not to reason why, mine but to . . .

FORREST. Do or die.

MR. NOBLE. When I want your assistance I'll ask for it . . . *Mine* but to—don't keep looking at me—mine but to. . . . What's all that hollering down the street?

LIBBY. It's for Woodrow. That's what I thought you'd like to . . .

MR. NOBLE (*interrupting*). Statues! Well, I suppose that's natural so long as they don't overdo it. Now . . .

LIBBY. Mine not to reason why, mine but to . . .

MR. NOBLE (*pleased*). . . . harken and obey. Heaven knows I did not seek this distinction but since you force it upon me what alternative have I but to . . .

THE BOSS (*coming in*). Save your voice, Evvy.

MR. NOBLE. Huh?

THE BOSS. Bissell's just retired in favor of Woodrow, the local hero. . . . We got a fight on our hands.

MR. NOBLE (*repeating like a parrot*). In favor of Woodrow, the local hero. *That I welcomed at the station?*

THE BOSS. That's right.

MRS. NOBLE (*fluttering into the office*). Isn't it exciting, Evvy? . . . Now you have some *real* opposition . . . That boy made the loveliest speech . . . Wasn't it thrilling, Libby?

MR. NOBLE (*to his wife*). Will you kindly shut up for a minute? (*Then to the Boss*) You mean he's running for *Mayor?*

THE BOSS. That's right.

MRS. NOBLE. He was so shy and embarrassed . . . but at the same time so manly.

MR. NOBLE (*to his wife*). Will you kindly . . . (*Then to the Boss*) You mean running for *Mayor* against *me?*

LIBBY. That's what I was trying to tell you.

MR. NOBLE. Will you kindly . . . (*Then to the Boss*) But he can't do that . . . with the election only two days off.

THE BOSS. He can . . . he has.

MRS. NOBLE. You'll have a chance to use *all* your oratory, dear.

MR. NOBLE (*to his wife*). Will you . . . (*Then to the Boss with desk slaps*) He most certainly cannot . . . That's entirely illegal . . . Why if, if, if such was the case, I mean to say, why any Tom, Dick or Harry, any loose character whatsoever . . . fresh from the penitentiary could come along . . .

LIBBY (*forcefully*). A loose character, Mr. Noble . . . Woodrow doesn't happen to be a loose character . . . and he's fresh from a battlefield, not from a penitentiary.

MR. NOBLE. That was a figure of speech.

LIBBY. Well, I don't care for it.

FORREST. Father didn't mean it the way it sounded.

MR. NOBLE. Well, maybe father did. . . . Which side are you *on,* anyway?

MRS. NOBLE. The romantic side, of course, dear.

MR. NOBLE. Because I don't want any spies around *my* office.

FORREST. Father, please.

MRS. NOBLE. Everett, for heaven's sake . . . He doesn't mean that, Libby.

MR. NOBLE. Oh, yes, I do!

LIBBY. Well, if you don't want me around your office, you certainly don't have to have me.

MRS. NOBLE (*shaking her husband*). This is your daughter, you old idiot, this is your son's fiancée.

MR. NOBLE. Well, she isn't my fiancée . . . when I lose confidence in people . . .

MRS. NOBLE. She's going to live in your house with you.

MR. NOBLE. She isn't going to live in *my* house with *me* . . . I'll move into the dog house first.

LIBBY. Then goodbye, Mr. Noble.

MR. NOBLE. Goodbye, Miss . . . whatever your name is . . .

FORREST (*following Libby out*). Libby, for heaven's sake.

MR. NOBLE. That's right . . . abandon the shinking sip, sinking ship, whatever the . . .

MRS. NOBLE. Aren't you ashamed of yourself, Evvy? You're not sunk yet . . . You're very popular . . . in some quarters.

MR. NOBLE. Anyway the whole thing is entirely illegal . . . (*Then getting a thought*) Why his *name* isn't even on the ballot.

THE BOSS. It don't have to be. He's a write-in candidate . . . That's what that blank space is for down at the bottom.

MR. NOBLE. Well, that most certainly is *not* what it's for. It's to, to count them wi . . . it's to put the date on. You call my lawyer.

THE BOSS. I already called him, Evvy. You could take my word for it . . . This is a free country . . . They can vote for anybody they like.

MR. NOBLE. But that's disgraceful.

THE BOSS. I know, but that's how it is, and the way it looks it don't look so *good.*

MR. NOBLE. You mean he actually has a chance?

THE BOSS. A chance! Did you ever see a snowslide?

As Mr. Noble recoils and clutches his collar, as if to protect himself from the cold, the scene dissolves to a view of LIBBY and FORREST walking along.

FORREST (*catching up with Libby*). I'm terribly sorry, Libby. Father is naturally a little upset . . . I guess we *all* are a little bit.

LIBBY (*seething with indignation*). Talking that way about a boy who risked his life so the Noble Chair Company can make its twelve percent.... Business as Usual!

FORREST. The Noble Chair Company makes twenty-four percent, just enough to cover its taxes, but he doesn't mean it, Libby . . . Politicians always talk that way about each other . . . Woodrow is probably calling Father an old . . . windbag, right this minute.

LIBBY. Well, if he is, he's right.

FORREST *(frigidly)*. Thank you.

LIBBY. I'm sorry . . . we *all are* a little upset, I guess.

FORREST. You weren't going to stay on as Father's secretary anyway . . . after our marriage. So what does it matter?

LIBBY. What was I going to do, stay home and weave?

FORREST. You *might* stay home and take care of your children . . . with the servant problem as it is.

LIBBY. Thank you for warning me.

FORREST. Do you mean that?

LIBBY. Of course I don't mean it, I don't mean anything . . . but that ass of a father of yours . . . going around talking about people he doesn't know anything about.

FORREST *(mildly)*. You're still talking about your children's grandfather.

LIBBY. What are you trying to do, depress me? If I thought they'd look anything like him . . .

FORREST. Well, *I* don't look anything like him.

LIBBY. I've noticed that . . . I pin my hopes on it.

FORREST. We're getting a little disagreeable again, aren't we?

LIBBY. We seem to be.

FORREST. Maybe now that the "hero" is home, you feel a little differently about me.

LIBBY. No, I don't. I feel just exactly the same about you as I've always felt . . . that you're upright . . . and honorable, and tall, and handsome, and, and wealthy and exactly what any girl in her right mind would hope for.

FORREST *(gravely)*. Thank you.

LIBBY. I just wish Woodrow hadn't come home exactly when he did; that's all.

FORREST. Well, what's he got to do with us?

LIBBY. It just spoils things a little, that's all.

FORREST. Why should it? . . . Or do you think I ought to offer you to him like the keys to the city, on a silver platter?

LIBBY. Don't talk like an idiot.

FORREST *(wound up)*. And say: Here, oh, noble hero, it happens to be my fiancée, but I'm only a civilian after all, so if you'd rather have her just help yourself . . . Don't bother to stand on ceremony.

LIBBY. In the first place he doesn't want me . . .

FORREST *(quickly)*. Oh, you asked him, did you?

LIBBY. I did not. And in the second place I'm engaged to you and that's all there is to it. I had plenty of time to think it over before I accepted you and that's all there is to it. A girl who kept changing her mind wouldn't be much good, I don't think.

FORREST. She wouldn't be much good to *me*.

LIBBY. She wouldn't be much good to anybody.

FORREST (*taking her arm*). Thank you. (*Suddenly he notices something.*) Where's your ring?

LIBBY. My aunt has it . . . I was afraid of losing it in all that excitement.

FORREST. Oh . . . how did he take the news anyway?

LIBBY (*uneasily*). What news?

FORREST (*surprised*). Of our engagement.

LIBBY (*stalling for time*). Who?

FORREST. Well, how many people did you have to break it to?

LIBBY. Oh, you mean Woodrow.

FORREST. Well, naturally I mean Woodrow.

LIBBY. Well, I didn't *quite* get the chance to tell him yet.

FORREST (*indignantly*). You haven't *told* him yet!

LIBBY. I didn't get the chance.

FORREST. Then what have you been doing all day . . . basking in his glory?

LIBBY. I just didn't get an opening.

FORREST. Well, do you want *me* to tell him? . . . I'll *create* an opening.

LIBBY. No, I don't.

FORREST. Holy mackerel!

They arrive in front of Libby's house.

LIBBY. Don't sound like your father.

FORREST. Well, when *are* you going to tell him?

LIBBY. I'll go over in a little while.

FORREST. Be sure to put on something pretty.

LIBBY. I will.

FORREST. And try not to break his heart.

LIBBY. I won't.

FORREST. Holy mackerel . . . Will I see you any more tonight.

LIBBY. No.

FORREST. Well, then . . . good night.

LIBBY (*holding up her face to be kissed*). Good night, dear.

Forrest kisses her and she turns away. Forrest takes two steps, then looks back.

FORREST. Say . . . you haven't got any *more* boy friends in the Army, the Navy or the Marine Corps, have you?

LIBBY (*quietly*). No, dear . . . he was the only one.

FORREST. I was just wondering . . . Holy Moses.

He strides down the street. Libby looks after him a moment, then sniffs twice, gulps and hurries into the house. Then we see Libby going upstairs in the house.

LIBBY (*at the newel post*). Aunt Martha.

Since there is no answer she continues slowly up the stairs. As she goes into her room, the scene cuts to LIBBY'S BEDROOM. Libby comes in slowly, closes the door behind her and leans against it. We hear the speechmaking in front of Woodrow's house and the band playing. Libby goes to the bureau, looks at a big picture of Forrest, then goes over to her bed. Suddenly she gets up, gets a photo of Woodrow out of a drawer, throws the picture into a corner, then throws herself face down and sobs broken-heartedly.

LIBBY'S AUNT (*entering and seeing Libby, sitting down beside her and patting her shoulder as Libby raises her head*). Well, that's the war for you. It's always hard on women. Either they take your men away and never send them back at all, or they send them back unexpectedly, just to embarrass you. No consideration at all. (*Libby buries her face in her arms and sobs.*)

This dissolves to the CORPORAL addressing the crowd at night. A pitcher of ice water has been placed on the porch.

CORPORAL. And when I say surrounded I mean surrounded, you get me ... they was no hope, we was surrounded. (*He takes a sip of ice water, gargles it, and continues.*) Suddenly a figure comes through the trees, hopping from tree to tree. We can't see who it is, see ... Now there is a little opening, he's gotta cross it ... We hold our breaths ... He makes a dive for it ... Half way across we hear rat, tat, tat, tat, tat, tat, tat, tat, tat. ... He grabs his belly and falls ... He got it, see. We say, So long, Joe. (*He starts to take a sip of ice water. He puts it down suddenly and continues talking.*) But wait a minute! He's on his feet, he's running toward us carrying the machine gun with him. ... He fooled them, see. Their guns begin to chatter, but he's reached the trees. ... We're saved and as he comes staggerin' in to us we see for the first time who it is ... Do I have to tell you who it was?

There is a wild hooray. The Corporal takes a sip of water and pulls Jonesy into view.

CORPORAL. The next speaker will be Texas Jones, who is gonna tell you *his* experience with you know who.

He picks up a drumstick. The crowd hoorays. This cuts to the CHAIRMAN, the PROGRESSIVE BAND LEADER and the SIGN PAINTER, surrounded by people at night. The Chairman is passing out buttons and at the same time supervising the painting of the stanzas of "We Want Woodrow" on the four sides of the box sign. The Progressive Band Leader holds the lyric in his hand.

CHAIRMAN (*passing out buttons*). Be careful, the ink is still a little fresh ... And one for the little boy of course.

PROGRESSIVE BAND LEADER (*to the sign painter*). We Want Woodrow For Our Mayor.

SIGN PAINTER. M-a-r-e?

CHAIRMAN. M-a-y-o-r ... What's the matter with you? What have horses to do with it?

A VOICE IN THE CROWD. Give me a half dozen of them.

CHAIRMAN (*handing them out*). A half dozen by all means ... Be careful, the ink is still a little fresh ... Now don't stick yourself, Lurella ... Why certainly it's all right to wear it on the hat.

PROGRESSIVE BAND LEADER (*shouting up to the sign painter*). Win with Woodrow, Win with Woodrow. Let's give Everett the air.

SIGN PAINTER. I wouldn't want to get in wrong with Mr. Noble.

CHAIRMAN. You paint it the way he tells you or you'll be in wrong with the new administration, I can tell you. (*Then to the crowd*) Win with Woodrow . . . button, button who's got the button? . . . Be careful; the ink is still a little fresh. (*Now he shouts up to somebody.*) Stretch it out, it's all droopy.

We see TWO MEN on two ladders nailing up a sagging banner which reads, "Win With Woodrow." They look around, and the scene cuts to the CHAIRMAN.

CHAIRMAN (*making a lifting movement*). Hoist it up . . . stretch it out flat.

He falls off his box and disappears. This cuts to MR. SCHULTZ.

MR. SCHULTZ (*working the beer barrel*). Step right up . . . A glass of ice cold beer? Free lunch and pickles is to the left. Step right up . . . Not too much foam? We knock it off. Win with Woodrow.

This cuts to the JUDGE and the SHERIFF at the sandwich table.

JUDGE. A Woodrow special? (*Then to the Sheriff*) One Woodrow special . . . That means the best of everything . . . Ice cream? The ice cream is on the lawn . . . No, no, no; everything is free, everything.

This cuts to WOODROW'S MOTHER and LIBBY'S AUNT.

WOODROW'S MOTHER. Ice cream for the children?

LIBBY'S AUNT. It's a good thing that food came in when it did.

WOODROW'S MOTHER. It's a good thing Woodrow came in when he did. . . . Oh, I'm so happy.

This cuts to JONESY at the rail.

JONESY. He said, "Don't give up, kid . . . it may be hard, but we'll git back" . . . I said, "How?" He said, "We'll swim back" . . . and I said, "Look, Woody, there's only one trouble: I don't know how to swim," and he said, "Just hang onto me, partner" . . . and that's how we come back.

During the hooraying that follows this, the scene dissolves to a view of WOODROW'S HANDS, holding a glass and a bottle of cooking wine. This is in the kitchen. The hands clench and unclench nervously, then slap the table with futility. Now, shaking, they pour the wine into the glass, the neck of the bottle rattling against the glass. Then we see BUGSY standing in the kitchen doorway: He is looking out toward the front of the house, listening to the speechmaking with a happy smile. He looks back toward Woodrow and the smile vanishes. He crosses to the kitchen table which brings Woodrow into the shot.

BUGSY (*severely*). Your ma said not to drink any more of that stuff.

He takes the wine away from Woodrow and starts pouring it back into the bottle.

WOODROW (*indignantly*). Say, am I four years old or something . . . You gimme that.

BUGSY. You behave yourself and do like your ma tells you. You made her enough trouble.

WOODROW. I made *her* trouble!

BUGSY (*severely*). That's right.

WOODROW. You made *me* trouble . . . you and your mother complex!

BUGSY (*roughly*). Listen, knucklehead, you take one more crack at your mother and I'll . . .

WOODROW (*belligerently*). Who's taking cracks at my mother? All I said was . . .

BUGSY. Well, don't say it.

WOODROW. Are you nuts or something?

BUGSY. Maybe.

As the two men stand and look at each other, Woodrow's mother hurries into the kitchen.

WOODROW'S MOTHER. Isn't it wonderful, darling? I'm so proud of you. (*She hugs him and kisses him in passing.*) We're running out of ice cream plates, there's so many people out there.

She scoops up a stack of saucers and starts out, kissing him again on the way.

BUGSY. You see that look in her eyes?

WOODROW. Yes, I saw it.

BUGSY. That's what we're working for, see?

WOODROW (*desperately*). Can't you get it through your thick skull that . . .

SERGEANT (*hurrying in*). All right, you're on next. (*He grabs Bugsy's arm.*) Just shoot 'em some bull about how you was in a hot spot with your foot caught in a gizmo and the ringtails is comin' from all sides and just when you ain't got a chancet who should come along but . . . (*He jerks his finger toward Woodrow.*)

WOODROW (*grabbing him, desperately*). Will you quit telling lies and getting me in deeper and deeper so there'll never be a way out?

SERGEANT. They're eatin' it up . . . let 'em enjoy it.

BUGSY (*turning to go*). Can I tell 'em about me and Smitty at Tulagi?

SERGEANT. Maskee, only you gotta be Smitty and he's gotta be you and you both gotta come out *alive*.

BUGSY (*disappearing*). Ding how.

SERGEANT (*reassuringly*). Everything's going great . . . You're gonna win in a walk and once you're in . . . you're *in*.

WOODROW (*holding onto the Sergeant*). Don't you understand an election based on fraud. . . .

SERGEANT (*interrupting him*). Where's the fraud? *You* was in the Marines! Look: I didn't expect this any more than you did . . . but now that it's happened . . . let it happen . . . They want heroes? We got six of 'em . . . All right we throw in a seventh for good luck . . . Who's counting? We're doin' it for your ma, kid . . . They say opportunity's only got one hair on its head and you gotta grab it while it's goin' by and dog it down or you mightn't get another chancet.

WOODROW (*desperately*). I don't *want* the chance . . . I don't want anything to do with it.

SERGEANT. Well, you got it whether you want it or not.

WOODROW. Don't you understand this is all based on lies?

SERGEANT (*indignantly*). What lies? You put on the wrong blouse when

Woodrow: All I ever thought about was being a marine.

Woodrow: You want me to run for m-m-mayor?

The Boss: We got a fight on our hands.

Woodrow: Until a still bigger phony came along . . . then you naturally wanted him.

the train come into the station. That could happen to anybody . . .

WOODROW (*pointing*). The lies they're telling out front!

SERGEANT (*virtuously*). Who's telling lies out front? Every one of those boys is telling the truth . . . except they change the names a little so's not to give out military information. Lies! (*He turns and starts out of the room; now he pauses in the doorway.*) Anyway those ain't lies . . . Those is campaign promises . . . They expect those!

He hurries out, passing Libby, who is just coming in. She wears a very pretty summer dress.

LIBBY. Hello, Woodrow.

This cuts to WOODROW at the kitchen table.

WOODROW (*dejectedly*). Hello, Libby.

He sinks into his chair and starts pouring himself a glass of cooking wine. Then we see LIBBY moving from the doorway to Woodrow. She puts her hand on his shoulder.

LIBBY (*gently*). You shouldn't drink too much of that stuff, dear . . . no matter how much you feel like celebrating.

WOODROW (*looking up at her balefully*). Are you going to start now?

LIBBY (*stepping back, hurt*). Why Woodrow . . . I'm only thinking of your own good.

WOODROW (*violently*). Yes, well there are too many people doing it . . . They're thinking about my own good so much they're going to land me in the calaboose . . . if they haven't already.

LIBBY (*pointing to the bottle*). Woodrow, you've been nipping.

WOODROW (*getting to his feet*). I have not been nipping and I'll tell you something else . . .

LIBBY. I have something to tell *you*, Woodrow.

WOODROW. All right. But the less you hang around *here* and are seen with *me*, the better it's going to be, you understand . . . I'm telling you that for *your* good.

LIBBY (*indignantly*). Oh, you needn't think I want to cash in on your glory! All I came here to tell you . . .

WOODROW. Who said anything about that? (*Outside we hear the crowd starting to sing "We Want Woodrow."*)

LIBBY. All I came to tell you is that I'm going to marry Forrest Noble next Sunday morning at ten o'clock and the only reason I didn't tell you all day . . .

WOODROW (*taking her arms*). But that's marvelous!

LIBBY. . . . was because I didn't want to spoil your homecom . . .

WOODROW. But that's marvelous! That's the first good news I've had all day.

LIBBY (*frigidly*). I'm glad you feel that way about it . . .

WOODROW. At least I don't have to worry about you!

LIBBY. . . . because I think it's marvelous too and, and, and . . . (*She starts to blubber.*) I hope I never see you again as long as I live . . . Here's your frat pin.

She presses it in his hand and turns and runs out the back door.

WOODROW. Will you wait a minute?

He starts after her but is stopped by the sudden entrance of Judge Dennis followed by Mr. Schultz and the Sergeant.

JUDGE DENNIS (*grabbing Woodrow*). Woodrow, you've just *got* to come out and address the crowd again.

MR. SCHULTZ. They will no longer accept substitutes any longer.

WOODROW. Well, I'm not going to address the crowd again. I've already told them how I feel and . . .

JUDGE DENNIS. But that's no way to run for Mayor.

MR. SCHULTZ. Or is it?

WOODROW. How many times do I have to tell you I'm not running for . . .

MR. SCHULTZ. But you *are* running for Mayor.

SERGEANT. Whether you like it or not.

JUDGE DENNIS. You have been drafted.

WOODROW (*to the Sergeant*). Can they do that?

SERGEANT. They done it.

MR. SCHULTZ (*pointing outside*). Listen to them.

He, the Sergeant and Judge Dennis move forward a little.

WOODROW. You listen to them.

He turns and looks in the direction taken by Libby, and the scene cuts to JUDGE DENNIS, MR. SCHULTZ, and the SERGEANT.

MR. SCHULTZ (*beating time to the song*). Beautiful.

And next we see the CHAIRMAN leading the song, behind him the Progressive Party Band, around him the people. He holds aloft the four-sided box, now completed, on each side of which is printed a verse of the song.

FIRST SIDE.
We want Woodrow
We want Woodrow
We want Woodrow for our Mayor

SECOND SIDE.
Win with Woodrow
Win with Woodrow
Let's give Everett the air

THIRD SIDE.
Up with Woodrow
Down with Noble
Let's kick Evvy off the chair.

FOURTH SIDE.
Up our hero goes and down this zero goes
'cause we want Woodrow for our Mayor.

This cuts to the JUDGE, MR. SCHULTZ, and the SERGEANT in the kitchen. The song is now approximately in its third verse.

JUDGE DENNIS. It's like Lincoln said: "You can fool all of the people part of the time and part of the people . . ." Where did he go?

MR. SCHULTZ (*as he and the Sergeant turn*). What happened to him?

They walk back into the deserted kitchen. The Sergeant sticks his head out of the window.

SERGEANT (*pulling his head back in*). We'll find him . . . he won't get far.

This dissolves to a BACK ALLEY: In the distance we hear the crowd singing

HAIL THE CONQUERING HERO

"We Want Woodrow." Libby comes forward. As she gets closer we hear her sobbing. Woodrow appears way in the background. He calls, "hey." She pauses, and he catches up to her.

LIBBY. What do you want?

WOODROW. Look: I'm in enough trouble without *you* turning against me.

LIBBY. When did I turn against you? I've been loyal to you all my life . . . I, I, you know how I felt about you . . . You broke off with *me* . . . I would have waited for always . . . Even so I asked my . . . my fiancé's permission to—to welcome you the way I thought you'd like to be welcomed . . . although I may have been wrong . . . I defended you all afternoon and got fired for it by Mr. Noble and nearly broke off my engagement with Forrest . . . and now you say I'm t-t-turning against you.

WOODROW. I'm sorry.

LIBBY (*starting away*). Well, you can go to . . .

WOODROW (*interrupting her*). Will you quit that.

He catches up with her and they move along together.

LIBBY. No, I won't . . . You made me enough trouble with everybody saying I threw you over while you were fighting overseas to marry F-f-f-forrest . . . as if I'd do such a thing . . . but I couldn't go around wearing your letter in my hat telling me you'd f-f-fallen in love with somebody else . . . which is your perfect right . . . and I'm *deeply* in love with Forrest . . . and then you have to come back a he-he-he . . .

WOODROW (*finishing it for her*). A heel.

LIBBY (*reproachfully*). A hero! So now they can say— "You see? It served her right! She got just what she deser-deser-deserved."

WOODROW (*as she weeps copiously*). Cut it out, will ya? I've got enough troubles.

LIBBY (*indignantly*). You *have* troubles . . .

WOODROW. And *how* I have.

LIBBY. I should say so . . . You can have any girl in town you want and then you get a mom-mo-monument and they b-b-burned your mother's mom-mo-mortgage and you're going to be m-m-m-mayor and I'm going to m-m-m-marry F-f-f-orrest.

WOODROW. But you said you loved him deeply.

LIBBY. Well, of course I do, but what's that got to do w-w-with it?

WOODROW. Libby.

LIBBY. What?

WOODROW. You don't know how well off you are.

LIBBY. Don't talk that way . . . you're going to make me feel worse.

WOODROW. If you knew what a heel *I* was you'd be very happy.

LIBBY. I *am* very happy and I know exactly how much of a heel you are.

WOODROW. You do?

LIBBY. Anybody who could write a letter like you wrote six weeks after we parted, like we parted . . . you wouldn't have to tell me any more about.

WOODROW. Oh . . . then you don't know anything.

LIBBY. I don't *want* to know anything about her . . . whether she's tall or short or thin or fat or blond or . . . I just hope she's awful . . . No I don't, I hope she's beautiful and that you have ten children by her. (*As Woodrow doesn't answer*) Is she?

WOODROW. If you only knew.

LIBBY (*crossly*). Well, I don't want to know. (*They reach her garden gate.*) Do you want to come in a minute? I suppose you shouldn't . . . but we'll have to start being grown-up sometime and it might as well be now.

She opens the gate and he follows her in. They walk to the old apple tree, around the trunk of which there is, as if on purpose, a bench. They sit down, and the scene cuts to a close view of LIBBY and WOODROW.

LIBBY (*archly, after a moment*). It's a beautiful night, isn't it?

WOODROW. Great.

LIBBY. Are you worried about something?

WOODROW (*also archly*). Who? Me? How could I be? . . . ha, ha.

LIBBY. Don't you want to be mayor?

WOODROW. Naturally I want to be mayor . . . I'd like to have a million dollars, too.

LIBBY. Well, then . . . of course I don't know what it's like to be famous . . . I suppose it even has its drawbacks but I should think you'd be so proud, Woodrow . . . so satisfied . . . I know I certainly *am* for you . . . no matter how I talked out there.

WOODROW. I'm going to be famous all right.

LIBBY. I was so proud even sitting beside you this afternoon . . . (*She makes a helpless gesture.*) Do you remember when we used to come and sit here . . . in the cool of the evenings?

WOODROW. Naturally I do.

LIBBY. I thought maybe you'd forgotten . . . so much can happen in a year.

WOODROW. So much can happen in a *day.*

LIBBY. I suppose so . . . Were you surprised when they nominated you for mayor?

WOODROW. Surprised isn't the word for it.

Libby pats his hand then snatches her hand back in her lap.

LIBBY. Excuse me.

WOODROW. That's all right.

LIBBY. Did you ever think of me in Guadalcanal?

WOODROW (*dully*). No.

LIBBY (*slightly hurt*). Oh, I guess that was a pretty busy place.

WOODROW. I guess so. I thought of you in other places though.

LIBBY. Where?

WOODROW. Just other places.

LIBBY. I'm so glad . . . even though it can only be a memory now . . . Do you remember when you cut our initials in the tree?

WOODROW. Naturally.

LIBBY (*pointing to them*). There they are . . . they'll be there always.

WOODROW. Unless something happens to the tree.

LIBBY. I would never allow that.

WOODROW. You'd be better off to chop the tree down and forget me for good . . . That's why I'm so glad you're going to marry Forrest . . . why it's such a load off my mind. There's no hope for Mom . . . she'll just have to leave town, but at least you can say you suspected it all along and that's why you broke off with me and married Forrest, who's all right if you like people like that, and then you won't be hurt, see? . . . Because outside of Mom you're the only thing in the world I care for, the only thing that matters. And now that it's over, I can tell you that letter I wrote you was the hardest thing I ever did in my life . . . and I've thought about you every night . . . and every morning . . . and every afternoon . . . and every girl I saw reminded me of you . . . and every flower, I wanted to send you . . . That's why I'm so happy, see? Because you had such a narrow escape.

LIBBY. I think you're a little bit feverish, dear.

WOODROW. Who? Me? I'm a little bit phony, that's all . . . a little!

LIBBY (*tenderly*). You—a phony!

WOODROW. That's right . . . You don't have to tell anybody; they'll find out soon enough . . . but I'm never going to be mayor or anything else, you understand? And I was never in Guadalcanal or any place else and I never got any medals and I wasn't even in the Marines . . . You understand?

LIBBY (*gently*). You've had a very hard day, dear. (*She looks around as if for help.*)

WOODROW (*prophetically*). Yes, but wait till tomorrow comes.

LIBBY. I don't think you're feeling very well.

WOODROW. Me? I never felt better in my life except I never felt worse.

LIBBY. You'll be all right, dear.

WOODROW. I suppose you despise me now?

LIBBY. Despise you! How can you despise anybody you love . . . even if you are engaged to . . . another man. I'll love you as long as I live, Woodrow, and I might as well tell you so now while we still have a few moments . . . a last few moments . . . together.

WOODROW. I don't think you understand what I said: I'm a phony, I'm a faker, I'm a . . .

LIBBY (*weeping*). I know . . . you're just saying that to make me feel better, but I'm never going to feel any better . . . I'm just brokenhearted, Woodrow, I, I, I, . . .

WOODROW. Now wait a minute . . . (*He takes her in his arms and starts patting her on the back.*) Now wait a minute, will you? (*He looks around to see if anybody is listening and gives a double-take to the gate.*)

This cuts to the Sergeant standing at the GATE.

SERGEANT (*after a soft whistle*). Here he is.

Now he comes through the gate followed presently by the other Marines.

SERGEANT. I almost thought you took it on the lam for a minute . . . Oh, excuse me.

This cuts to WOODROW and LIBBY.

WOODROW. Come here.

Then as the Sergeant comes into view:

WOODROW. Will you tell Libby I've never been in Guadalcanal or any place else—that I'm just a phony?

Libby looks up at the Sergeant tearfully.

SERGEANT. Sure, he's never been in Guadalcal. He's never been no place . . . None of us have . . . We're all phonies, see, 'specially after a hard day; only sometimes we're more phony than others. You get me?

LIBBY. I understand.

SERGEANT. He ain't runnin' for mayor or nothing, you understand . . . he just needs a good night's sleep.

WOODROW (*indignantly*). What are you trying to . . .

SERGEANT (*clamping a heavy arm around his shoulders*). A good night's rest.

WOODROW. Will you take your arm . . .

CORPORAL (*putting his arm around Woodrow*). You oughtta see me in a thunderstorm.

LIBBY. Good night, Woodrow.

She kisses him quickly and runs into the house.

SERGEANT. What are you tryin' to do, make a sucker out of the Marine Corps?

WOODROW (*violently*). Let go of me.

To cover this struggle the Sergeant starts to sing.

SERGEANT (*with a look to the others*). "We Want Woodrow."

The others pick it up as Woodrow is turned around and marched out of the gate. This cuts to LIBBY looking after them; this is from the back door of her house. She looks very miserable. Then the scene dissolves to the BAND and the CROWD going down a street at night, just outside the Noble Chair Company. They sing and play "We Want Woodrow." They are carrying torches. Then we see MR. NOBLE'S OFFICE in the NOBLE CHAIR COMPANY: Present are Mr. Noble, the Boss, and four or five of his minions. The Boss is talking to these aides, but we do not hear what is said because of the deafening noise of the parade. Possibly we see some of the flickering of passing torches and possibly it would not show in the lighted office. Mr. Noble's untouched dinner sits on a tray on the desk. Mr. Noble himself is tossing a Bromo-Seltzer from glass to glass. Now he tosses it down his gullet and nearly strangles. The Boss pounds him on the back, then sends his minions away.

THE BOSS. Feel better?

MR. NOBLE. Thank you . . . brrwulp . . . of all the cheezy songs I ever heard . . . that one certainly takes the crackers . . . brrrwulp.

THE BOSS. Why don't you eat your dinner?

MR. NOBLE. How can you think of food at a moment like this?

THE BOSS (*picking up a piece of cheese*). You gotta live.

MR. NOBLE. It would turn to Russian dressing in my stomach. (*He shakes his head at the thought, then jerks a thumb toward the departed minions.*) What did they say?

THE BOSS. They said it looks very good . . .

MR. NOBLE (*quickly*). They did?

THE BOSS. . . . for Woodrow.

MR. NOBLE. Oh. (*He gives the Boss a dirty look, then paces up and down.*) Don't eat with your mouth open . . . Do you mind? . . . I'm just a little bit irritable.

THE BOSS. I don't blame you. (*He picks up a wedge of pie and contemplates it.*)

MR. NOBLE (*after staring, hypnotized*). Well, are you going to eat it or aren't you?

The Boss bites the end off the pie. Mr. Noble walks down to the end of the room and back.

MR. NOBLE. I mean to say, why did he have to come back at a moment like this? I mean to say, if he *had* to come back why couldn't he have come back *after* the election . . . I mean to say, I don't want to sound unpatriotic or anything, but I mean to say a man like that belongs in . . . Guadaloupe.

THE BOSS. Guadalcanal.

MR. NOBLE. Guadalcanal . . . I mean to say in a war like this— (*Mr. Noble is slapping the desk at the proper places.*) Every man must do what he does best and what *he* does best he does in . . . Guadal . . . canal.

THE BOSS (*with his mouth full*). Shave your voish, Evvy.

MR. NOBLE. What?

The Boss makes a gesture that it doesn't matter anyway.

MR. NOBLE. I mean to say a boy like that needs exercise and violent physical conflict to keep him fit . . . He'll be lost in a town like this . . . The quiet will kill him.

THE BOSS (*swallowing it*). Save your throat, Evvy, you don't have to persuade me.

MR. NOBLE. What I'm trying to say is . . .

THE BOSS. I know what you're trying to say. I've been listening to you long enough.

He picks up a chop and contemplates it.

MR. NOBLE. Do you always eat backwards?

THE BOSS (*biting into the chop*). Hunh?

MR. NOBLE. I mean to say I don't even think he *wants* to be Mayor!

The Boss, having a full mouth, waves this down.

MR. NOBLE (*mimicking his waving*). What does that mean?

THE BOSS (*after swallowing with difficulty*). Everybody wants to be Mayor . . . That's human nature.

MR. NOBLE (*slapping the desk*). Everybody but me! With me it's just civic pride . . . Why don't you look what you're doing? (*He picks up a napkin and stuffs it in the Boss's vest.*)

THE BOSS (*looking down at his vest*). Thanks.

MR. NOBLE (*walking up and down*). I mean to say, soldiers coming back at moments like this can upset a political balance that has taken *years* to adjust.

THE BOSS. You're telling me.

He does something with the food.

MR. NOBLE. I mean to say they take on an importance that, that, that I mean to say, that completely overshadows the, the, the . . . I mean to say if you took all the seats I'm building for the Army and the Navy and the Marine Corps and sat them side by side they'd probably stretch from here to the, the, the . . . Halls of Montezuma . . . but I can't wear one around my neck or pinned on my bosom with a purple ribbon . . . You notice they don't bring MacArthur back on the eve of a National election.

THE BOSS (*putting salt and pepper on the second chop*). I wonder if he really *is* a hero.

MR. NOBLE (*hopefully*). Who, MacArthur? (*Down again*) Why, certainly he's a hero. They're all heroes; and if I didn't happen to have got stuck in the Quartermaster Corps during the last war I'd probably have more stuff on me than you could hang on a Christmas tree.

THE BOSS. How do you know he's a hero?

MR. NOBLE (*tapping his chest*). Because I saw the, the . . . the stuff.

THE BOSS. That don't make it official.

MR. NOBLE. What are you talking about! Don't go chasing moonbeams . . . There're some things you have to accept on faith . . . value . . . face value and one of them is a hero . . . You can't ask him for his . . . union card.

THE BOSS. Then why do you suppose he took off his uniform? That ain't natural.

MR. NOBLE. Because he's home . . . because he's been . . . dismissed . . . or whatever you call it.

THE BOSS. What for?

MR. NOBLE (*angrily*). How do I know what for? . . . Maybe he has corns or, or pyorrhea . . . How do I know?

THE BOSS (*taking the phone off the hook*). It ain't natural to take off a uniform in war time . . . it's just the other way around.

MR. NOBLE (*pointing to the phone*). What are you doing there anyway?

THE BOSS. Get me Western Union . . . I'm just gonna wire the Marine Base in San Diego and check up on our local hero.

MR. NOBLE (*upset*). What's the matter with you? Are you trying to kill me politically *forever*?

THE BOSS. Save your throat, Evvy

MR. NOBLE. You leave me out of this. You understand? . . . I don't want to be mixed up with this in any shape, form, connection or even by innuendo.

THE BOSS. I'm waiting for Western Union.

MR. NOBLE. If you send this it is entirely at your own risk and peril. I challenge his fitness as mayor but the one thing that I do *not* challenge, question or doubt is the fact that he is a hero. I want that definitely. . . .

THE BOSS. Shut up, will ya. Hello, Western Union, I want to send a night letter.

This dissolves to WOODROW in his BEDROOM: He is sleeping fitfully in just enough moonlight to register on the film.

WOODROW (*thickly at first*). Here they come boys, here they come! . . . They're sneaking through the palm trees, they're coming through the palm trees. Here they come, boys, there's thousands of them ... Man the guns ... *Let 'em have it! ... Charge!*

As he makes a wild movement and falls out of bed on the floor, the scene cuts to the DOORWAY of WOODROW'S ROOM.

BUGSY (*coming in*). What's the matter?

WOODROW (*being helped back into bed*). I must have had a nightmare, I guess.

BUGSY. You're lucky.

WOODROW. Hunh?

BUGSY. You're lucky you don't have them all the time ... like some guys.

He laughs, goes out and closes the door. Now Woodrow swings his feet out of bed, turns on the light, and starts to dress with great determination. After pulling on his pants he tiptoes to the door and peeks out.

This cuts to the UPPER HALL as Woodrow suddenly sees Bugsy arranged on two chairs, a magazine in his lap.

BUGSY. You want some more hot milk or somethin'?

WOODROW. I'm all right. You gonna stay *there* all night?

BUGSY. I don't care much about sleeping at night.

Woodrow goes back into his room, and we see him there, closing the door, looking sourly at it, then crossing to the window and looking down.

This cuts to JONESY standing guard below.

JONESY. Was you looking for somethin'?

WOODROW pulls his head back into the room, goes slowly to his bed and sits down on it. Suddenly he scowls at something on the wall, and the scene cuts to the beautifully embroidered "SEMPER FIDELIS," and to WOODROW on the bed as he starts taking off his pants, and the scene fades out.

PART FIVE

The STATUE of GENERAL ZABRISKI fades in at sunrise. Around it and on it the birds are chirping merrily.

This dissolves to WOODROW pacing up and down in his room at sunrise. The tails of his nightshirt flop against his legs. Now he sits dejectedly on the bed. Slowly a ray of sun comes down on his head as it did on the head of General Zabriski.

WOODROW (*suddenly*). I've got it! Oh, boy!

He does a little dance around the room, then opens the door and sticks his head out.

This cuts to the UPPER HALL of WOODROW'S HOUSE: Juke is dozing in the chair formerly occupied by Bugsy.

WOODROW (*ecstatically, as he sticks his head out*). I've got it ... everything is all right.

JUKE. Hunh?

WOODROW. It came to me with the sunrise.

Juke scratches his head and looks after him as Woodrow disappears. Then we again see WOODROW in his room.

WOODROW (*happily*). Oh, boy!

He hops into his bed, pulls the covers up and with a sigh of relief prepares for sleep.

WOODROW (*drowsily*). Oh, boy!

[Then we see a SMALL STEAM ROLLER in full sunlight. It is actually the type run by gasoline, although, I think, still called a steam roller. It is parked in front of the local painter, paperhanger and interior decorator's store. Against the store the painter and his assistants are preparing banners. The steam roller is receiving the personal attention of the Chairman and Mr. Schultz. The banner across it reads: "Help Us Flatten Noble." The big wheel has been filled with a disk sign which reads: "Up With Woodrow." When it turns upside down: "Down With Noble." The Leader of the Progressive Band stands waiting to talk to the Chairman, who, with the assistance of Mr. Schultz, is tying bunting to all the protuberances of the steam roller.

PROGRESSIVE BAND LEADER. Now we start with "Win With Woodrow" . . .

CHAIRMAN. That's right.

PROGRESSIVE BAND LEADER. Then we modulate into "The Halls of Montezuma."

CHAIRMAN. That's right.

PROGRESSIVE BAND LEADER. Then we modulate into . . .

MR. SCHULTZ. Why do you always have to modulate into everything? If you want to go into "The Halls of Montezuma" why don't you just walk in?

PROGRESSIVE BAND LEADER. Why don't you mind your own business? You handle the meat, I'll handle the music.

MR. SCHULTZ. Look, you floor flusher, if I couldn't play a better E flat cornet as you . . .

CHAIRMAN. Gentlemen, gentlemen, please . . . no dissension within the party lines.

PROGRESSIVE BAND LEADER. Then I modulate into "There'll Be a Hot Time in the Old Town Tonight."

MR. SCHULTZ. Then you modulate out of it.

CHAIRMAN. That's absolutely correct, Ed. Now Ewald . . .

PROGRESSIVE BAND LEADER (*leaving*). The name is *Ned*, if it's all the same to you.

MR. SCHULTZ. It could be Shpitzenvogel and it would be all the same to us.

CHAIRMAN. Please, Ewald . . . don't tie your end so tight . . . make the bows lighter . . . airier . . . with more zoom.

MR. SCHULTZ (*crossly*). Look, when you've tied up as many veal roasts as I have . . .

CHAIRMAN. That's just it, Ewald, it's bad enough that it still looks like a steam roller without its looking like a veal roast . . . or even a pork roast . . .

MR. SCHULTZ. You handle the breast, I'll handle the rump.

CHAIRMAN. By the way, you don't happen to *have* a pork roast, do you? I'm drooling for one.

MR. SCHULTZ. With fried apples, smashed potatoes and brown gravy? . . .

CHAIRMAN (*drooling*). That's right.

MR. SCHULTZ. No.

CHAIRMAN (*crestfallen*). Oh.

MR. SCHULTZ. But if Woodrow wins . . . maybe.

CHAIRMAN. Then I practically have my teeth in it.

The Judge and Doc Bissell drive into sight.

JUDGE. Everything ready?

DOC BISSELL. Zero hour is at ten.

CHAIRMAN. Everything is ding how.

DOC BISSELL. What?

CHAIRMAN. That's leatherneck for okay.

JUDGE DENNIS. Oh. Then: Up High Street, down Main. Then we go around into Oak Street . . .

MR. SCHULTZ. We modulate into Oak Street.

JUDGE DENNIS. What?

DOC BISSELL. Is that some more leatherneck?

CHAIRMAN. Pay no attention . . . We go around into Oak Street . . .

JUDGE DENNIS. And pick him up.

CHAIRMAN. Right.

DOC BISSELL. Right.

JUDGE DENNIS. Right.

MR. SCHULTZ. Left.

JUDGE DENNIS. What?

CHAIRMAN (*laughing*). He's just contrary this morning.

JUDGE DENNIS. Oh . . . well come on. (*He drags Doc Bissell away.*)]

We see some FLAP-JACKS sizzling on a griddle and Woodrow's mother's hand adds them to a pile on a plate and as she walks to the table with them we discover ourselves in her kitchen. The Marines are eating hungrily. Only one is missing: Juke.

CORPORAL. Oh, boy!

And now WOODROW is coming down the stairs: He looks spick and span and very happy. He is whistling, "We Want Woodrow." Now he sings the third line.

WOODROW. "We want Woodrow for our mayor."

As he adjusts his cravat, he moves into the kitchen.

WOODROW (*happily*). Good morning, all . . . good morning, Mama. (*He kisses her, then looks around.*) I hope you all had a good night . . . How about a stack of your famous flannel cakes, Mama? Light as a feather and put together by fairy hands . . . taste their crunchy, brunchy munchiness . . . ask your grocer!

The scene cuts to the SERGEANT—next to an empty seat at the table. He watches Woodrow very suspiciously, as the latter comes into the scene and slaps him on the back before sitting down.

WOODROW (*happily*). *Good* morning, Sergeant Heffelfinger . . . Is everybody happy? . . . I trust your conscience didn't keep you awake during the night . . . You know there's nothing like a housebroken conscience . . . Now you take the conscience in its wild or native form . . . when first trapped let us say . . . (*As the Sergeant leans over and smells his breath.*) What's the matter, am I unpleasant? Ah! Is the reason for my unpopularity at last revealed as in a vision?

SERGEANT. I was wondering if you'd been guzzling some more of that cooking wine.

WOODROW (*shocked*). Guzzling! At this hour of the morning, Sergeant . . . You offend me.

SERGEANT. What happened, did somebody leave you some dough or something?

WOODROW. You mean because I'm happy? Wouldn't you be happy if you were about to become mayor of this fair city? Not large, mind you, but fascinating . . . Lives there a man with soul so dead who never to himself hath said . . . Good morning, Libby, won't you join us in a stack of collision mats as we say in the good old Marine Corps . . . and a cup of Jamoke?

This cuts to LIBBY appearing in the doorway.

LIBBY. Good morning, good morning, Woodrow . . . I'm glad you're feeling better. (*She comes into the room.*)

WOODROW (*helping her to a chair*). Just call me Mr. Mayor . . . I never felt better in my life.

Libby catches the Sergeant's eye as he looks back at her very dubiously, then shrugs his shoulders.

LIBBY. You got over all that nonsense then?

WOODROW. What nonsense was that?

LIBBY (*making sure his mother isn't listening*). I mean about . . . never having been in . . . you know . . . Guadalcanal? . . . and all that stuff.

WOODROW (*astounded*). *I* said such a thing?

LIBBY. Well, I certainly understood you to . . .

WOODROW (*interrupting*). But how could I? (*He looks from one Marine to another.*) I'm a great hero . . . People *run* when they see me coming . . . . I kill Nips with a wave of the hand . . . I *blow* them down . . . (*He blows through his lips.*) I shoot them from all angles, backwards, forwards, while looking in mirrors . . . I swim into the water and drown them like rats . . . I pick up machine guns . . .

SERGEANT. I got it.

WOODROW (*severely*). You got what?

SERGEANT. He's gonna play Screwloose from Toulouse.

WOODROW (*waving no, no, no*). Oh, no I'm not . . . I invite an investigation . . . I'm as sane as a Dane . . . and I'm going to be the mayor.

LIBBY. Are you sure you feel all right, Woodrow?

WOODROW'S MOTHER (*coming into view with a stack of wheat cakes for Libby*). What are you talking about, dear?

WOODROW. Well, I'll tell you one thing . . . I certainly feel a lot better than I did yesterday . . . (*As the phone rings*) Ah. (*He looks at the Sergeant with amusement.*)

WOODROW'S MOTHER. I'll get it, dear. (*She hurries out.*)

SERGEANT. What are you trying to pull?

WOODROW (*amiably*). You'll find out.

This cuts to the TELEPHONE in the hall as Woodrow's Mother comes into view and picks up the receiver. Judge Dennis and Doc Bissell come into the house and stand near her.

> WOODROW'S MOTHER. Yes . . . yes, he's here . . . The what? . . . Oh, yes. (*She turns and looks into the kitchen.*) Woodrow, the Marine Base in San Diego wants to talk to you.

We see WOODROW with the MARINES and LIBBY.

> WOODROW (*very innocently*). To *me!* Why, whatever could the Marine Base in San Diego want to talk to *me* about?

He looks brightly from the Sergeant to Libby. The Sergeant looks very worried indeed as he exchanges a look with the Corporal.

> WOODROW. I'd better find out . . . Good morning, Judge, good morning, Doc Bissell . . . I'll be with you in a moment. (*He crosses to the telephone and speaks into it.*) Hello . . . yes, this is Corporal Truesmith . . . Who is it? . . . Yes, sir, Colonel . . .

This cuts to the SERGEANT and the OTHERS.

> SERGEANT. Know about what?

This cuts to WOODROW at the telephone as Judge Dennis and Doc Bissell come forward, a little worried.

> WOODROW. They've taken me back in the Marine Corps for limited service. I'll have to leave for San Diego at once.

The band outside the house starts playing "We Want Woodrow." Doc Bissell checks the time on his wrist watch.

> JUDGE DENNIS. But the parade! The rally! The mayoralty! Aren't you going to be our mayor?

> WOODROW. I'm sorry, Judge, the United States comes first.

This cuts to a TELEPHONE BOOTH in the local DRUGSTORE. The door opens, Juke sticks his head out, looks around like a conspirator to see if he is observed and leaps away from the phone booth, relaxes and walks out of the drugstore whistling "We Want Woodrow."— Then we see WOODROW and the OTHERS in the kitchen: Everybody looks greatly depressed except Woodrow, who is bearing the news with great fortitude.

> WOODROW'S MOTHER (*with her arm around her son*). They won't be sending you anywhere dangerous any more?

> LIBBY (*indignantly*). Well, I should hope not, after what he's been through.

> WOODROW (*to his Mother*). You don't have a thing to worry about, Mama. It'll probably just be, you know, like clerical work or maybe some kind of work in a shipyard or maybe an airplane factory . . . you know, guarding things.

> JUDGE DENNIS (*indignantly*). Then why don't they leave you here . . . where we need you?

> DOC BISSELL. That is one of the weaknesses of the military viewpoint . . . It does not always recognize the importance of civilians in war time.

> JUDGE DENNIS (*almost tearfully*). He could do *so* much more good here.

> DOC BISSELL. I suppose it's natural in a world surrendered to the sword.

> WOODROW. I hope you win, Doc.

> DOC BISSELL. I'm afraid my chances are very slender . . . but thank you.

JUDGE DENNIS. You were our only hope, Woodrow.

WOODROW. I'm terribly sorry, Judge, but when duty calls . . . (*He pauses to look at the Sergeant, who is then seen looking at Woodrow sourly.*) . . . duty calls.

He looks at BUGSY, who is then seen looking at Woodrow with a very cold expression indeed.

WOODROW'S MOTHER. Do you have to leave *today,* dear?

WOODROW. I'm afraid so.

LIBBY. You won't even be here for my . . . wedding?

WOODROW. Well, to tell you the truth that's one thing I don't mind missing . . . although I certainly *wish* you all the happiness in the world.

LIBBY. I know you do.

JUDGE DENNIS. Woodrow.

WOODROW. Yes, sir.

JUDGE DENNIS. You'll ride in the parade anyway, won't you . . . now that it's all dolled up and everything?

WOODROW (*not too anxiously*). Well . . . sure if you want me to, but what good will it do? . . . When you gotta go—you gotta go.

JUDGE DENNIS. It might do some good . . . We won't tell them anything about your bad news . . . until you get to the town hall. Then you can tell them you have to leave suddenly and maybe swing some of your . . . enormous popularity to the Doc here.

DOC BISSELL. Not that I want it for myself *personally,* you understand . . . but I think it would be good for the town.

WOODROW. I know it would.

JUDGE DENNIS. Just your *endorsement* would mean a great deal.

WOODROW. I certainly can't refuse that.

JUDGE DENNIS (*starting out*). Then I'll see if everything's ready.

DOC BISSELL. It's going to be more like a funeral march. (*He goes out also.*)

LIBBY. Can I ride in the parade with you, Woodrow . . . just this last time?

WOODROW. Well, sure . . . if you think it's all right.

LIBBY. Of course it's all right . . . I have the right to say goodbye to you.

WOODROW (*as Woodrow's Mother turns away and her shoulders start to shake*). I'm sorry, Mama . . . I can't do anything about it, I . . .

WOODROW'S MOTHER. It will be so lonely without you.

Woodrow makes a helpless gesture, then catches Bugsy's eye: We see BUGSY, the Sergeant standing behind him. Bugsy makes a slight move as if to come forward. The Sergeant drops a hand on his shoulder to restrain him and gives a double-take at the new arrival in the doorway.

SERGEANT. Where have you been?

We see JUKE in the doorway.

JUKE (*with exaggerated innocence*). Who? me? . . . Oh, I was just taking a little walk.

This cuts to the SERGEANT and BUGSY.

SERGEANT. Since when do you forget to have breakfast?

We again see JUKE in the doorway.

JUKE. Well, I . . . just a . . .

The view moves from Juke onto the wall phone, then cuts to the SERGEANT and BUGSY.

SERGEANT. Oh . . . you were just making a little phone call . . . to that dame in San Diego . . . I got you, Colonel.

Juke smiles a kind of a sickly smile.

JUKE. Well . . . you know.

Bugsy comes from behind the Sergeant like a bat out of hell.

SERGEANT (*making a dive after him*). Hey.

Now the Corporal and the others jump to their feet and also rush forward. Woodrow, his mother and Libby try to get out in the hall also.

BILL. We're very sorry . . . It's nothing . . . There's just a little ill feeling there . . .

He holds his arms out to keep them out of the trouble. Quickly Woodrow forces his way through.

We see the struggling MARINES at the foot of the stairs and hear panting and dull thuds.

SERGEANT (*quietly*). Lay off, will ya? . . . You can settle it later.

With the assistance of the big Corporal he pulls Bugsy off Juke. Juke, slightly dazed, sits on the stairs. His left eye is closed and his mouth is bleeding.

JUKE. What's the big idea?

Bugsy struggles to get at him again. Now Woodrow forces his way into the group. He looks at Juke, then confronts Bugsy. During the following scene the men keep their voices very low, in order not to be heard by the women. Outside the band modulates into "Hail, The Conquering Hero Comes."

WOODROW (*through clenched teeth*). You meant that for me, didn't you?

BUGSY. What about it?

WOODROW. You think I'm afraid, hunh?

BUGSY (*sneeringly*). Well, I'm glad I wasn't never in a foxhole with you. (*He laughs bitterly.*)

WOODROW. Let him go.

BUGSY. You yellow-bellied . . .

WOODROW (*nearly crying with rage*). Let him go, I tell you!

Bugsy laughs in his face and Woodrow hits him a terrible punch in the mouth. The Corporal and the Sergeant exchange a glance, then drop Bugsy's arms. Bugsy looks at Woodrow for a moment, spits some blood out of his mouth, then speaks:

BUGSY. Go find a woman to fight with . . . that's all you know how to hurt. (*He leans over and helps Juke to his feet.*) Come on, kid.

As the two Marines start up the stairs, the scene cuts to WOODROW: He is massaging the knuckles of his right hand. His lips tremble and a couple of tears run down his cheek. The Hero music outside gets louder.

This dissolves to a view of the PARADE in full swing, in the morning. A double banner is carried in front of it. It reads: "Follow Us To The Big Rally, Everybody Welcome." Behind this comes the steam roller with the Chairman running it, assisted by Mr. Schultz' advice. They are having a terrible time. Now comes a sign which reads: "Free Seats, Free Speech, Free Food." Behind this a much larger sign which says: "Free Drinks." After this: "Win With Woodrow." Then: "Honor The Hero—Make

Him 'His Honor.' " Then: "Honor And Courage." Then: "Come and Meet The Mayor." Now the Progressive Party Band followed by the car containing Woodrow, his mother and Libby in the back seat and Judge Dennis and Doc Bissell in the front seat. The five Marines walk alongside as a guard of honor. Behind the car there appears a banner which reads: "A Warrior for War Time." Behind this another car containing the Sheriff, the Rev. Doctor Upperman and the town painter and the other members of the Bissell delegation.

We get a close view of WOODROW, his MOTHER and LIBBY: All three look quite depressed, though they try to smile in answer to the hoorays. Now Woodrow scowls as he sees someone and the view cuts to a view of the CROWD walking down the SIDEWALK as it follows the parade: Bugsy is leaning against a lamp post which parts the crowd. He is chewing gum. Apart from this his face has neither movement nor expression. Then we again see WOODROW, his MOTHER and LIBBY, and Woodrow looks very sore. The view turns around as Woodrow's car goes by and we see the parade, with the church in the background, turning the corner.

This dissolves to the exterior of the NOBLE CHAIR COMPANY. Mr. Noble's followers increase in number on the sidewalk, as the music of the parade approaches. Now Mrs. Noble comes out and looks down the street delightedly.

MRS. NOBLE (*clapping her hands*). Oh, isn't it exciting? I *love* a parade.

This cuts to MR. NOBLE, the BOSS and FORREST in the PRIVATE OFFICE as the music of the parade drifts in faintly.

MR. NOBLE. Parades . . . statues . . . burning mortgages . . .

THE BOSS. I subscribed to *that*.

MR. NOBLE. So did I for that matter, but I mean to say . . .

THE BOSS. Save your voice, Evvy.

MR. NOBLE. For what? I mean to say I have nothing against the boy personally. A hero is a fine thing . . . *in its place*.

FORREST. You mean in a park.

MR. NOBLE. I don't mean that at all . . . I don't wish this young man anything but, ahem, success *in what he can do best. But what can he do best?*

FORREST. Well . . .

MR. NOBLE (*cutting him off instantly*). That is our problem. I speak, not as your candidate for mayor but as the most humble voter. (*He turns to his son.*) Get me a glass of water, will you?

THE BOSS. Why don't you save . . .

MR. NOBLE. Why don't you shut up? (*He puts a cough drop in his mouth.*) I mean to say this problem is not local . . . it is national. . . . In a few years, if this war goes on, heaven forbid, you won't be able to swing a cat without knocking down a couple of heroes . . . And are we to be governed by young men, *very* young men, however well meaning and patriotic they may be, whose principal talent consists in hopping in and out of wolf holes, or . . .

THE BOSS. Foxholes.

MR. NOBLE. What?

THE BOSS. They're called foxholes.

MR. NOBLE (*running all the words together*). Oh . . .'sprincipaltalentconsistsofhoppinginandoutof . . . foxholes, and killing *hundreds* of enemies with one swoop of the sword, or are we going to be governed by respectable civic leaders of mature age who do not seek the appointment but to accept it as a civic duty? I refer to men like . . . well . . . myself. I did not . . . Wait a minute! Did they take out a permit to hold this parade?

FORREST (*appearing with a glass of water*). What does it matter?

MR. NOBLE (*after taking a sip of water*). What does it matter, what does it matter? . . . That's the trouble with the American viewpoint . . . It matters very much indeed. (*He starts out of the office and the others follow him.*) This country is run by permits, that is to say laws, and just because it's war time these soldiers think they can, they can . . .

This cuts to the exterior of the NOBLE CHAIR COMPANY as Mr. Noble comes out followed by the Boss and Forrest.

MR. NOBLE. They'll find out whether it matters or not . . .

MRS. NOBLE. Isn't it exciting, Everett? . . . They make a handsome couple, don't they? . . . Oh, I'm sorry, Forrest.

THE BOSS (*as Mrs. Noble starts forward*). Hold your horses.

MRS. NOBLE. What's the matter now?

We see the little old Western Union man coming through the crowd.

THE WESTERN UNION BOY (*approaching Mr. Noble*). Howdy, Mr. Mayor . . . I got a telegram for ya if I can just remember where I put it.

MR. NOBLE. What kind of a telegram?

THE BOSS. Can you remember where it came from?

THE WESTERN UNION BOY. Now let me see . . . (*He takes off his cap to scratch his head.*) San Diego, I think.

At this the telegram falls to the sidewalk. Mr. Noble and the Boss make a dive for it, bump their heads, pick up the telegram at the same time and tear it in two as they straighten up.

MR. NOBLE (*severely*). You're a big help.

And now they read the two halves of the telegram, which reads:
"Marine Headquarters, San Diego, California
Private Woodrow L. P. Truesmith medically discharged one year ago. Reason: Chronic hay fever.
    A. B. Hilton, Major U.S.M.C.
    Adj. to C.O."

This dissolves slowly to MR. NOBLE, the BOSS, FORREST and MRS. NOBLE.

MR. NOBLE (*deeply puzzled*). But then how could he have been in a . . . Guadal . . . canal?

THE BOSS (*amused*). That's just it . . . he wasn't.

MR. NOBLE (*indignantly*). But then he's a fraud, a faker, a, a, a,—why he ought to be tarred and feathered. (*Now he beams.*) Oh, boy!

FORREST. Oh!

MRS. NOBLE. Who's a fraud and a faker?

MR. NOBLE (*pointing*). Right there. Look at him.

We see the PARADE as Woodrow is just going by; then MR. NOBLE, the BOSS, FORREST and MRS. NOBLE.

MRS. NOBLE. I don't believe it.

MR. NOBLE. You don't believe it. Well, he laughs last who laughs, laughs. Hah!

He puts the halves of the telegram in the hands of his son, who is glaring at something else.

MR. NOBLE. Here . . . glue this together for me and hurry up about it. (*As Forrest does not answer, Mr. Noble follows his gaze.*)

MRS. NOBLE. I'm sure you're mistaken, Everett. Remember, your impulses are *always* wrong, dear.

This cuts to LIBBY in the OFFICIAL CAR as she smiles sweetly to Noble, then to MR. NOBLE, FORREST, the BOSS and MRS. NOBLE.

MR. NOBLE (*taking back the telegram*). Never mind . . . we'll wipe *that* smile off her face, too . . . Personally I wouldn't marry her for that.

MRS. NOBLE. Please, Evvy, you talk such nonsense.

MR. NOBLE (*as he starts after the parade*). Come on.

THE BOSS (*holding him back*). Where are you going?

MR. NOBLE. It says, "Everybody Welcome," doesn't it?

THE BOSS. Be careful, you're fooling with dynamite.

MR. NOBLE. You watch my smoke.

MRS. NOBLE. Evvy, all my intuitions tell me. . . .

He hurries out of sight followed by Mrs. Noble and the Boss. Forrest follows slowly. Now Bugsy walks into sight, and the view moves after him onto the statue of General Zabriski, the town hall, the halted parade and the crowd.

This dissolves to a view of the STEPS of the Town Hall. Halfway up the steps Libby sees Forrest and Woodrow sees Bugsy. As Woodrow, his mother and Libby go up, Mr. and Mrs. Noble and the Boss come to the door.

MR. NOBLE (*happily*). After *you*.

THE BOSS. No, no, after you.

MRS. NOBLE (*pushing Noble through*). Age before beauty.

They go in, following which Forrest comes up, and after him comes Bugsy. Then the scene cuts to the interior of the TOWN HALL while the band is playing its usual tunes. Mr. Noble and the Boss and Mrs. Noble appear and move around to the back seats. This brings them face to face with the the FREE LUNCH table.

MR. NOBLE. Ah. (*He exchanges a look with the Boss.*) I wonder if this would be rubbing it in?

THE BOSS (*pointing to the sign*). It says: "Help Yourself."

MR. NOBLE. Well . . . there's plenty of time.

MRS. NOBLE. Everett, I just have a feeling you're going to make an ass of yourself . . . I'm just going to pretend I don't know you.

She goes on. He makes himself a little sandwich; the Boss takes a sour pickle and they move down to some empty seats just in front of Mrs. Noble. The town hall is decorated with bunting, flags, "We Want Woodrow" signs and other banners.—Then we see FORREST coming in and sitting down in the last row. Now Bugsy comes in, walks down front and takes a seat in the second row.

The PLATFORM is next seen from approximately BUGSY's POSITION. There is a speaker's table with ice water in front and behind this a row of chairs for notables. On these sit the elders of the Bissell delegation, the Sheriff, Reverend Doctor Upperman, the Town Painter, Mr. Schultz, Judge Dennis, Doc Bissell, Woodrow, his mother, Libby and the five Marines. The Chairman is leading the band on one side of the platform. Now Judge Dennis gets up and comes forward to the speaker's table. The Chairman brings the band to a stop and goes over and sits down.

JUDGE DENNIS. Yesterday morning seven Marines got off the Northbound. (*There is a hooray from the crowd.*) Six of them were strangers to us . . . one a local boy who had made good.

There is a wild hooray from the crowd interspersed with "We Want Woodrow."

This cuts to a close view of WOODROW. He smiles wanly at the audience, waves his hand a little, then scowls at Bugsy. We see BUGSY looking at Woodrow, then JUDGE DENNIS and the OTHERS.

JUDGE DENNIS. Yesterday afternoon we asked this local boy to cast his lot with ours—you might call us the "unvested" or shirtsleeve interests of the town—and lead us to victory.

There is a wild hooray from the crowd and the band starts to play "We Want Woodrow."

This cuts to MR. NOBLE and the BOSS: Mr. Noble is busy eating his sandwich. He pantomimes to the Boss that it is very tasty. Mrs. Noble shushes him. Then we again see the JUDGE and the OTHERS.

JUDGE DENNIS (*motioning for silence*). I'm going to ask Woodrow himself to tell you the rest of the story.

The crowd goes wild and the band plays "We Want Woodrow" again, as Woodrow gets to his feet and comes forward. We see WOODROW'S MOTHER and LIBBY: Woodrow's mother cries a little. Libby watches Woodrow proudly. This cuts to FORREST, who watches all of this with some displeasure; to WOODROW looking at BUGSY; to the SERGEANT looking at BUGSY; to WOODROW and behind him the Judge waving for silence; to MR. NOBLE and the BOSS.

MR. NOBLE (*fingering the telegram*). Shall we do it now or let him linger?

THE BOSS. Let him have his moment.

Mrs. Noble behind them shushes them again and Mr. Noble turns and gives her a dirty look. Then we get a close view of WOODROW.

WOODROW. I came here this morning to say good-bye to you.

This cuts to the CROWD as the people look at each other and murmur their displeasure; then to MR. NOBLE and the BOSS as Mr. Noble turns to the Boss in astonishment, then looks back at Woodrow.

MRS. NOBLE. You see?

We see BUGSY taking a toothpick out of his pocket and starting to chew on it. Then we again see WOODROW.

WOODROW. I came here to tell you that I had been called back into the Marine Corps for limited service and that for that reason I would not be able to run for mayor.

There is a murmur of distress again.

WOODROW. Well . . . *I'm not going to do it.* (*He looks straight at Bugsy as he says this.*)

There is a wild hooray from the crowd. This cuts to BUGSY, who looks puzzled; then to MR. NOBLE and the BOSS as Mr. Noble looks utterly bewildered. He starts to pull the telegram out of his pocket, but the Boss motions him to put it back in.

MRS. NOBLE. You see what I told you?

This cuts to the SERGEANT, who looks perplexedly at the Judge; to the JUDGE, who looks hopefully at Woodrow's mother and Libby; to WOODROW's MOTHER, LIBBY and DOC BISSELL as Libby looks hopefully at Doc Bissell, who does not understand at all; then to WOODROW, who is motioning for silence.

WOODROW. You'd better save your hoorays for somebody else . . . for somebody who deserves them . . . like Doc Bissell here . . . who has tried for so long to serve you . . . only you didn't know a good man when you saw one . . . so you always elected a phony instead. (*He nods toward Mr. Noble.*)

This cuts to MR. NOBLE and the BOSS as the crowd laughs.

MR. NOBLE (*getting to his feet*). Oh, I am, am I? . . . Well, let me tell you something, young man. (*He starts to reach for the telegram.*)

There are yells of "Quiet!" and "Sit down!" The Boss, helped by Mrs. Noble, pulls Mr. Noble down. Mr. Noble sits down muttering, "You'll find out."

MRS. NOBLE. Everett, you're making a spectacle of yourself.

This cuts back to WOODROW.

WOODROW. Until a still bigger phony came along . . . then you naturally wanted him.

The Sergeant gets up in the background, walks up to Woodrow and taps him on the shoulder.

WOODROW (*quietly*). Sit down, Sergeant.

SERGEANT. Now wait a minute . . .

There are calls of "Sit down!" and "Quiet!" from the audience.

WOODROW. This should have been the happiest day of my life . . . it could have been . . . instead it is the bitterest. . . . It says in the Bible "my cup runneth over" . . . Well, my cup runneth over . . . with gall. This is the last act . . . the farce is over, the lying is finished . . . and the coward is at last cured of his fear.

SERGEANT (*hurrying up*). Ladies and gentlemen, I think this whole thing had better be called off. He don't feel very good in the head sometimes.

There are yells of "Quiet!" and "Sit down!" as the scene cuts to LIBBY, who is looking at Woodrow anxiously as the Sergeant sits down beside her.

LIBBY. It's the same thing that happened to him last night.

SERGEANT. Yeh, only a lot worse.

WOODROW looks back from the Sergeant.

WOODROW. I was born in this town . . . My father was born here. Most of the town is on my grandfather's homestead . . . His well was just about where I'm standing and it leaks into the cellar sometimes . . . They've had quite a lot of trouble with it . . . (*There is a nervous laugh which Woodrow ignores.*) My grandfather was an honorable man. So was my father . . . I've sold papers on the street to most of you who are here this morning . . . I've known you all my life. Your affection means a great deal to me and now that I've lost the chance forever I want you to know how much it would have

HAIL THE CONQUERING HERO

meant to me to be the mayor . . . or the city clerk, or the assistant city clerk . . . or the dog catcher . . . of this town which was my grandfather's farm . . . By the same token I would gladly have given my life to have earned just one of the many ribbons you see on these brave men's chests . . . If I could have reached as high as my father's shoestrings, my whole life would be justified and I would stand here proudly before you . . . instead of as the thief and coward that I am. (*There is a hubbub of voices and for the first time Woodrow speaks with authority.*) Quiet . . . A coward because I postponed until now what I should have told you a year ago when I was discharged from the Marine Corps for medical unfitness . . . a coward because I didn't want my mother to know . . . Well, it wasn't to save *her*, it was to save *me*.

This cuts to WOODROW'S MOTHER and LIBBY as Woodrow's mother lowers her head, while Libby looks rigidly at Woodrow . . . a look of compassion on her face; to the SERGEANT as he looks around nervously, and fixes his gaze to something at one side of the stage; to the EXIT sign over the back door of the town hall; then to WOODROW again.

WOODROW. . . . A thief because I stole your admiration, I stole the ribbons I wore, I stole this nomination.

We see BUGSY: During the preceding speech he has gotten up from his seat, walked around onto the platform, and taken his place beside the other Marines.

WOODROW (*seen again*). I have never been in Guadalcanal or any place else . . . I've been working in a shipyard for the last year. I've never received a medal of any description . . . naturally, since I've never fought. Two days ago I decided to come home. Since I'd written to my Mother I was overseas I had to come home as a soldier . . . I had to have some ribbons, so I bought them in a hock shop. When I was all dressed up I met some real Marines . . . I brought them home with me to make things look better . . . I fooled them as much as I did the rest of you, not that I really wanted to fool any of you . . . I just wanted to come home.

SERGEANT (*getting to his feet*). That's as dirty a lie as . . . (*But he is greeted with yells of "Quiet!" and "Sit down!"*)

WOODROW. I've told you all this because too many men have bled and died for you . . . and for me . . . to live this lie any longer . . . I *guess* that's why I told you . . . I certainly didn't mean to when I came in . . . I'm gonna pack my things now so this will probably be my last chance to say good-bye to you. I know my mother will give you back the mortgage . . . and I hope you won't hold it against her that her son didn't . . . quite come through . . . There's no use telling you I'm sorry because I wish I was dead. I—that's all.

He turns and looks toward his mother, then walks toward the back door with squeaking shoes.

This cuts to MR. NOBLE and the BOSS.

MR. NOBLE (*confidentially*). I need some air.

He pinches his nose. They rise and start out. After a moment Mrs. Noble goes out, wiping away a tear.

WOODROW'S MOTHER and LIBBY get up and start out. At the gesture from the

Sergeant, the five Marines surround them and escort them toward the door.

> JUDGE DENNIS. If everybody will please keep their seats.

Now the Sergeant turns and comes up to the table beside Judge Dennis.

> SERGEANT. I just wanta tell you one thing, see . . . I seen a lot of brave men in my life . . . that's my business . . . but what that kid just done . . . took *real* courage . . . and now that he's shot his mouth off you might as well hear the rest of it . . . in fact you'd *better* hear it . . . There's six of us, see, and we got fifteen cents between us . . . and we're from Guadalcanal *and no foolin'*, what I mean . . .

The scene dissolves, then we see WOODROW moving along. At first he walks with his hands in his pockets and his head down. Presently he holds his head high. After a while he takes his hands out of his pockets and holds his head still higher. We leave him striding along quite manfully. Way in the background we see Woodrow's mother, Libby and the five Marines.

We get a close view of WOODROW'S MOTHER, LIBBY and the MARINES.

> LIBBY (*taking her departure*). I'll be over in a few minutes.
>
> WOODROW'S MOTHER. You'd better not, dear . . . you've got yourself in enough trouble.
>
> LIBBY. I'll be over in a few minutes.

They move toward the Noble Chair Company, and Libby goes in.—This cuts to MR. NOBLE'S PRIVATE OFFICE, where we find Mr. Noble, the Boss and Forrest.

> MR. NOBLE. Pitiful, pitiful . . . There you see one of the fallacies—I wouldn't want this to go any further, you understand—of the democratic principle: They can vote for anybody they like. *I* was never deceived for an instant, but the poor misguided voters, without a brain to bless themselves with, without a cerebellum to the carload. Make a note of that one, Forrest, I'll use it . . .
>
> THE BOSS. I wouldn't.
>
> MR. NOBLE. . . . open wide their arms to . . . Oh, there you are.

LIBBY appears in the doorway.

> LIBBY (*quite placidly*). Hello.

She comes forward into the group, and Mrs. Noble hurries in after her.

> MRS. NOBLE. I'm so sorry, dear. My heart bled for you.
>
> MR. NOBLE. You have the effrontery to return?
>
> LIBBY. What?
>
> MRS. NOBLE. Oh, shut up, Evvy. Don't pay any attention to him, Libby.
>
> MR. NOBLE. What do you think of your hero now?
>
> FORREST. Don't rub it in, Father. She probably feels badly enough.
>
> MR. NOBLE (*crossly*). Well, she *should* feel badly and if you ask my advice . . .
>
> FORREST. Which I don't.
>
> MRS. NOBLE. You heard him.
>
> MR. NOBLE. You're a sucker if you even consider going through with . . .
>
> THE BOSS (*taking "a quick powder"*). I want to see somebody outside.
>
> MRS. NOBLE. I don't blame you. (*The Boss goes out.*)

LIBBY. But I don't feel badly at all.

MR. NOBLE. You don't?

MRS. NOBLE. Good for you.

FORREST. Father, I wish you'd keep your nose out of my affairs . . . This is a matter entirely between Libby and myself.

LIBBY. . . . and Woodrow.

FORREST. And Woodrow!

MRS. NOBLE. Naturally.

MR. NOBLE. What do you mean "naturally"?

FORREST. You don't mean to tell me that after that disgraceful exhibition you still have any . . . interest . . . in the "hero"?

LIBBY. I guess women feel a little differently than men do about these things, Forrest . . . so if you'll please forgive me and . . . not think too harshly of me . . . (*She starts to take the engagement ring off her finger.*)

MRS. NOBLE. You see what I told you? You walked right into it.

This dissolves to the FIVE MARINES on the porch of Woodrow's house: Nobody seems to have much to say. One is rolling a cigarette, another is whittling.

BILL. What time is the train?

JONESY. Who's got the dough?

CORPORAL. If I could just find a good crap game.

As Bugsy spits over the rail the scene dissolves to WOODROW and his MOTHER in his room. She is sitting on the edge of the bed. He is packing the suitcase on top of his dresser.

WOODROW'S MOTHER. Why couldn't you stay here? Now that you've told everything, nothing much more could happen.

WOODROW. Who's gonna give me a job?

WOODROW'S MOTHER. Well . . .

WOODROW. I'll tell you what I'll do. Mama. If I can find a nice place, I'll send for you and . . .

WOODROW'S MOTHER (*coming behind him and kissing him*). I know you meant it for the best, dear. I know you meant it for me no matter what anyone else might think.

Her lips tremble as she turns and leaves the room. As she does so Libby appears in the background. She comes into the room.

WOODROW. Hello.

LIBBY. Can I help you?

WOODROW. I'll manage all right.

We get a close view of LIBBY and WOODROW.

LIBBY (*after kissing him*). Of course I'm going with you. I've never loved anybody but you and you've never loved anybody but me and . . . (*She starts to weep a little.*) . . . You can't say it's because you're a hero I'm running after you, can you? Oh, Woodrow, when I think I almost lost you, stupid, stupid, stupid . . . (*She kisses him.*)

WOODROW (*interrupting the kiss*). You're crazy, honey.

LIBBY. Then I'm crazy. (*She kisses him again.*)

This dissolves to a view of the hands of the STATION MASTER as the hands are stamping tickets to the music of

"Mademoiselle from Armentières." Then we see WOODROW's MOTHER and BUGSY near the ticket window. He pats her on the shoulder, then looks away. The view moves across the other Marines onto Libby and Woodrow as the latter turns from the ticket window. Libby has an overcoat over her arm. Woodrow's suitcases are at his feet. He starts to pick them up, but the Marines do it for him.

WOODROW (*to the station master*). Is she on time, Mr. Kennedy?

STATION MASTER (*a little hard of hearing*). How was that?

WOODROW. Is the Southbound on time?

STATION MASTER. Be here in four and a quarter minutes. Where you goin'? . . . I thought you was runnin' for Mayor?

WOODROW. I changed my mind.

STATION MASTER. Oh . . . that's very unusual.

WOODROW. Well, this was an unusual case.

STATION MASTER. I said it's very unusual.

WOODROW. You said it.

CORPORAL. How about the Sarge?

WOODROW (*looking at his watch*). Well . . .

JUKE. I told him where you were.

CORPORAL. Go look for him. (*As Juke starts out*) He'll be here . . . He don't never miss nothin'.

This cuts down to a view of the Sergeant, followed apparently by the entire town, coming down the main street. The music is very grim, resolute. A close view then shows the Sergeant and the elders of the town walking along. We also spot the political boss. This cuts to JUKE looking out the door of the station, and he reacts to the oncoming mob and hurries away. We again see the MOB coming forward, then WOODROW, LIBBY, WOODROW's MOTHER, BUGSY, the CORPORAL, BILL and JONESY on the station platform as Juke hurries toward them.

JUKE (*excitedly*). Cheese it, the whole town is coming.

WOODROW. What is it. . . . A lynching?

CORPORAL (*very hard*). With us here. (*He makes a gesture to the other Marines.*) We'll just kind of surround you, see?

WOODROW. Yeah, you were gonna do that before.

His mother and Libby step close to him.

We again see the approaching MOB as seen from the front of the station, then we pick up the Sergeant and the leaders of the mob. They come into position opposite Woodrow and the Marines. The platform is filling up.

SERGEANT. Leave a little room there . . . quiet!

As quiet is established we hear the distant whistle of the Southbound. The Sergeant moves to his place with the other Marines.

JUDGE DENNIS. We had quite a talk after you left, Woodrow. The Sergeant told us a few things.

MR. SCHULTZ. *Quite* a few things.

CHAIRMAN (*severely*). That *you* had forgotten to mention.

JUDGE DENNIS. Naturally the nomination went back to Doc Bissell, but he got up and said . . .

MR. SCHULTZ. "Ladies and Gents . . ."

DOC BISSELL. Don't misquote me.

JUDGE DENNIS. What?

DOC BISSELL. I said, "Ladies and Gentlemen."

CHAIRMAN. Of course you did.

DOC BISSELL. I said, "Ladies and Gentlemen, in all the years that I have been unsuccessfully mixed into politics this is the first and only time that I have seen a candidate for office given an opportunity to prove publicly, permanently and beyond peradventure of a doubt that he was honest, courageous and veracious."

JUDGE DENNIS. That means truthful . . . He likes those big words.

DOC BISSELL. And I said further, that if to act out a little lie to save one's mother humiliation was a fault . . . in other words, if tenderness toward and consideration of one's mother was a fault, it was a fault any man might be proud of.

DOC UPPERMAN. Hear, hear.

A VOICE AMONG THE SPECTATORS. Hooray.

DOC BISSELL. Thank you. I made a very good speech on your behalf . . . better than I have ever made for myself.

JUDGE DENNIS. It was a wonderful speech, Woodrow.

SERGEANT. The guy had us all blubbering.

DOC BISSELL. I meant every word of it straight from the heart, Woodrow. I concluded by pointing out that if this town really wanted an honest, courageous and veracious mayor . . .

JUDGE DENNIS. That means truthful.

DOC BISSELL. They had better catch you before you caught the Southbound and got away.

JUDGE DENNIS. So we come right over. . . . That's why we're here.

The scene cuts to WOODROW, his MOTHER, LIBBY and the SERGEANT.

WOODROW. I'm a little dizzy. I guess I don't quite understand what you meant.

LIBBY. I think they mean they want you as mayor, Woodrow.

WOODROW. They want me as mayor?

SERGEANT. That's right.

WOODROW'S MOTHER. They want you as mayor?

WOODROW. No, no.

This cuts to the JUDGE and the others.

JUDGE DENNIS. We're *all* a little dizzy, Woodrow, but that's what we mean . . . we want you for mayor.

We hear the train pulling into the station and see its shadow. Then we see WOODROW and the OTHERS.

WOODROW. You mean you *still* want me?

This cuts to the JUDGE and the others.

JUDGE DENNIS. We still want you . . . very much.

MR. SCHULTZ. What do we want a soldier for, anyway?

DOC BISSELL. Politics is a very peculiar thing, Woodrow . . . If they want you, they want you . . . They don't need reasons any more . . . They find their own reasons . . . just like when a girl wants a man . . .

LIBBY. That's right . . . You don't need reasons, although they're probably there.

This cuts to the CONDUCTOR of the train as he approaches the group.

CONDUCTOR (*sarcastically*). Pardon me for intruding, but is anybody here interested in getting on this train . . . or is this the Democratic National Convention?

WOODROW (*still thunderstruck*). Oh . . . well . . .

LIBBY. Of course you re not going.

WOODROW'S MOTHER. Of course you're not.

JUDGE DENNIS (*to the Conductor*). We won't detain you any longer . . . Nobody's leaving . . . Thank you very much.

CONDUCTOR. O.K. All aboard!

SERGEANT. Just a minute, Mac. (*Then to Woodrow*) Gimme six of them tickets, will ya? . . . We still got a little work to do . . . in our own line. . . . So long, kid, see youse in church.

WOODROW. Will ya come back?

SERGEANT. Well, we always come back before . . . So long, everybody . . . Come on there, rookies.

As they move toward the train, the scene cuts to the BOSS coming into Mr. Noble's office.

THE BOSS (*coming in*). Save your voice, Evvy, they've just renominated Woodrow.

MRS. NOBLE (*hurrying in*). Oh, isn't it exciting, Evvy. . . . Now the battle is on again.

MR. NOBLE (*horrified*). Shut up! What on?

THE BOSS. I don't know . . . but I think it's a vindication campaign.

Mr. Noble rolls his eyes up and falls flat out of sight.

FORREST. Look out.

As he hurries to pick up his father, the scene dissolves to a view of WOODROW and the gang of MARINES.

WOODROW. So long, gang.

CONDUCTOR'S VOICE. All aboard!

WOODROW (*gratefully, moved*). I don't know how to . . .

This cuts to the MARINES standing on the observation car.

SERGEANT. Don't say it . . . it was a pleasure . . . anything for the son of an old friend.

We hear the bumping of the couplers up ahead as the train starts to move.

WOODROW. I knew the Marines could do almost anything, but I never knew they could do anything like this.

This cuts to the OBSERVATION PLATFORM as it is pulling away.

BUGSY. You got no idea.

He laughs a little and raises his hand in farewell. The other Marines do likewise. The band starts to play "From the Halls of Montezuma to the Shores of Tripoli." WOODROW, seen close, speaks barely audibly:

WOODROW. "Semper Fidelis."

The MARINES, being carried out of sight by the moving train, raise their arms high in salute. The music gets faster and faster and the United States Marine emblem dissolves in.

CASABLANCA

(A Warner Brothers Production)

Screenplay by JULIUS J. & PHILIP G. EPSTEIN
and HOWARD KOCH

From a Play by MURRAY BURNETT and JOAN ALISON

Produced by HAL B. WALLIS

Directed by MICHAEL CURTIZ

The Cast

RICK	Humphrey Bogart
ILSA LUND	Ingrid Bergman
VICTOR LASZLO	Paul Henreid
CAPTAIN LOUIS RENAULT	Claude Rains
MAJOR STRASSER	Conrad Veidt
SENOR FERRARI	Sydney Greenstreet
UGARTE	Peter Lorre
CARL, A WAITER	S. Z. Sakall
YVONNE	Madeleine LeBeau
SAM	Dooley Wilson
ANNINA BRANDEL	Joy Page
BERGER	John Qualen
SASCHA, A BARTENDER	Leonid Kinskey
JAN	Helmut Dantine

and others

Film Editor—OWEN MARKS

Dialogue Director—HUGH MACMULLAN

CASABLANCA. Copyright 1943 by Warner Brothers Pictures, Inc. Screenplay of the Warner Brothers photoplay "Casablanca," copyright 1943 by Warner Brothers Pictures, Inc. By permission of Warner Brothers Pictures, Inc.

CASABLANCA

PART ONE

A long view of a REVOLVING GLOBE fades in, and as it revolves it becomes animated. Long lines of people (in miniature) stream from all sections of Europe to converge upon one point on the tip of Africa. Over this animated scene comes the voice of a Narrator.

NARRATOR. With the coming of the Second World War, many eyes in imprisoned Europe turned hopefully or desperately toward the freedom of the Americas. Lisbon became the great embarkation point. But not everybody could get to Lisbon directly; so a tortuous, roundabout refugee trail sprang up.

This dissolves to the ANIMATED MAP illustrating the trail as the Narrator mentions the points.

NARRATOR (*continuing*). Paris to Marseilles. Across the Mediterranean to Oran. Then by train—or auto—or foot—across the rim of Africa to Casablanca in French Morocco.

This dissolves to a RELIEF MAP of CASABLANCA showing the ocean on one side and the desert on the other. The voice of the Narrator comes over.

NARRATOR. Here the fortunate ones—through money or influence or luck—obtain exit visas and scurry to Lisbon, and from Lisbon to the Americas. But the others wait in Casablanca—and wait and wait.

As the Narrator's voice fades away—the view moves rapidly to: a close view of the RELIEF MAP showing a street, which dissolves to a long view of the OLD MOORISH SECTION of the CITY in daylight. At first only the turrets and rooftops are visible against a torrid sky, in the distance a haze-enveloped sky. The view then moves down the façades of the Moorish buildings to a narrow, twisting street crowded with the polyglot life of a native quarter. The intense desert sun holds the scene in a torpid tranquillity. Activity is unhurried and sounds are muted. . . . Suddenly the screech of a siren shatters the calm, and veiled women run screaming for shelter, while street vendors, beggars and urchins melt into doorways. A police car speeds into view and pulls up before an old-fashioned Moorish hotel—flop-house would be a better word for it.

This cuts to a CORRIDOR of this decrepit hotel. Native French police officers run up the steps, crash into the doors of the various rooms, and come out dragging frightened refugees. This cuts to a DOOR as one police officer flings it open. The shadow of a man hanging by a rope from a chandelier is seen on the wall. The officer slams the door shut.

Next we see a STREET CORNER where two other policemen have stopped a white civilian and are talking to him.

FIRST POLICEMAN. May we see your papers, please?

CIVILIAN (*nervously*). I—I don't think I have them—on me.

Copyright 1943, by *Warner Brothers Pictures, Inc.*

632

FIRST POLICEMAN. In that case, we'll have to ask you to come along.

CIVILIAN (*patting his pockets*). It's just possible that I— Yes, here they are.

He brings out his papers. The second policeman examines them.

SECOND POLICEMAN. These papers expired three weeks ago. You'll have to—

Suddenly the civilian breaks away and starts to run wildly down the street, the scene moving with him. We hear the policeman shout "Halt!" But the civilian keeps going. A shot rings out, and the man falls.

The scene then moves to a close view of JAN and ANNINA BRANDEL huddled in a doorway, the dazed and frightened spectators to this casual tragedy. They are an Austrian couple, very young and attractive, thrust by circumstances from a simple country life into an unfamiliar hectic world. Annina's hand clutches her husband's arm as their eyes follow the police who are examining the victim.—This cuts to JAN and ANNINA as the police car sweeps past them on its way back, and Jan takes his wife by the hand. They both speak with a Central European accent.

JAN. The Prefecture must be this way.

They start off in the direction taken by the police car.

Next we see an INSCRIPTION, reading: "Liberté, Égalité, Fraternité" carved in a marble block along the roofline of a building. The view then moves down the façade, French in architecture, to the high-vaulted entrance over which is inscribed *"Palais de Justice,"* and continues to move down to the entrance. A queue of people of all ages and nationalities overflows from inside the building and down the steps. The view moves over the line of waiting people extending into the square, and we pick up a babel of languages with only a few recognizable words such as, "visa," "Monsieur le Prefect," "Portugal," "a hundred francs." Suddenly the attention of the people is attracted toward the street . . .

We then see the SQUARE (as viewed from the angle of the waiting line), typically French in its landscaping and architecture. This is the center of the modern city of Casablanca. The police car is just pulling up to the curb in front of the Prefecture. A policeman opens the grated door at the back of the car and a nondescript assortment of refugees begins to pour out.

A SIDEWALK CAFÉ on one side of the square: A middle-aged English couple are standing in front of their table for a better view of the commotion in front of the Prefecture. A dark-visaged European smoking a cigarette leans against a lamppost a short distance away. He is watching the English couple more closely than the scene on the street.

ENGLISHWOMAN. What on earth's going on there?

DARK EUROPEAN (*walking over to the couple*). Pardon, Madame . . . have you not heard?

ENGLISHWOMAN. We hear very little —and we understand even less.

DARK EUROPEAN. Two German couriers were found murdered in the desert. (*With an ironic smile*) The . . . unoccupied desert.

IN FRONT of the PALAIS DE JUSTICE (as viewed from the angle of the café) we see the refugees being unloaded from the police car as his voice continues . . .

DARK EUROPEAN'S VOICE. This is the customary roundup of refugees, liberals and . . . (*As a young blonde girl—the last to leave the car—is herded with the others in front of the Prefecture*) Of course, a beautiful young girl for M'sieur Renault, the Prefect of Police.

We again see the SIDEWALK CAFÉ with the speakers.

ENGLISHWOMAN (*puzzled*). I don't understand.

DARK EUROPEAN. As usual, the refugees and the liberals will be released in a few hours. (*Smiling slightly*) The girl will be released in the morning.

ENGLISHWOMAN (*horse-faced and past middle age*). Why, a woman isn't safe in this wretched place!

DARK EUROPEAN (*shrugging*). To get out of Casablanca they say one needs two dollars for an exit visa and two hundred for the Prefect. Unless, of course, one is a beautiful young girl. The rich and the beautiful sail to Lisbon. The poor are always with us.

ENGLISHWOMAN. Dreadful. . . .

DARK EUROPEAN. Unfortunately, along with these unhappy refugees the scum of Europe has gravitated to Casablanca. Some of them have been waiting years for a visa. (*Putting his arms compassionately around the Englishman*) M'sieur, I beg of you, watch yourself. Take care. Be on guard. . . . This place is full of vultures—vultures! Everywhere! Everywhere!

ENGLISHMAN (*rather taken aback by this sudden display of concern*). Er —er—thank you. Thank you very much.

DARK EUROPEAN. Not at all. (*He raises his hat politely.*) Bon jour, Madame. Bon jour, M'sieur.

He walks out of sight, and the Englishman, still a trifle disconcerted by the European's action, looks after him, mopping his brow with his pocket handkerchief.

ENGLISHMAN (*restoring his pocket handkerchief*). Friendly chap, wasn't he?

As he pats his breast pocket, he finds that something is lacking. He opens his coat, and feels inside.

ENGLISHMAN. Silly of me . . .

ENGLISHWOMAN. What, dear?

ENGLISHMAN. Leaving my wallet in the hotel room . . .

He closes his coat, then suddenly he looks off in the direction of the departing dark European, the clouds of suspicion gathering. But now, overhead, the drone of a low-flying airplane is heard. Heads look up; and next we see an AIRPLANE flying overhead, its motor cut for a landing, and a closer view shows that it has a *swastika* on its tail.

A moving view along the waiting line of REFUGEES shows their upturned gazes following the flight of the plane. In their faces is revealed one hope they all have in common—and the plane is the symbol of that hope. The moving scene stops at the last of the line far out on the street, just as Jan and Annina appear and take their places at the very end. Their eyes also follow the droning plane.

ANNINA. Perhaps tomorrow we shall be on the plane. (*Wistfully*) Jan, is it true that in America you can travel a thousand miles without a visa?

JAN (*smiling at his wife with superior knowledge*). Annina, you and your fairy tales . . .

At this the scene dissolves to the AIRPORT as the PLANE is swooping down—past a neon sign on a building on the edge of the airport. The sign reads: "RICK'S." Then we see a GROUP of OFFICERS: CAPTAIN LOUIS RENAULT, a French officer appointed by Vichy as Prefect of Police in Casablanca, stands chatting with the others. He is a handsome, middle-aged Frenchman, debonair and gay, but withal a shrewd and alert official. Around him are clustered the German Consul, HERR HEINZE, a young Italian officer, CAPTAIN TONELLI, and Renault's aide, LIEUTENANT CASSELLE. Behind them is a detail of French native soldiers. The officers watch the approaching plane as it taxies toward them. The German and Italian detach themselves from the group and walk toward the place where the plane will stop. The German walks briskly a step ahead of the Italian, who appears to be making an effort to catch up.

We see the PLANE, with the swastika over the door, and when the door is open, the first passenger to step out is a large German wearing heavy horn-rimmed spectacles. He is bland-faced, with a perpetual smile that seems more the result of a frozen face muscle than a cheerful disposition. On any occasion when MAJOR STRASSER is crossed, the smile melts and the expression hardens into iron. Herr Heinze steps up to him with upraised arm.

HEINZE. Heil Hitler.

STRASSER (*with a more relaxed gesture*). Heil Hitler. (*They shake hands.*)

HEINZE (*in German*). It is good to see you again, Major Strasser.

STRASSER (*in German*). Thank you, thank you.

The Italian steps up with elaborate good will.

TONELLI. Captain Tonelli, at your service, sir.

STRASSER. That is kind of you.

TONELLI. Our staff is anxious to co-operate—

But he gets no further than that. Strasser turns away to greet Renault and Casselle, who have come over. Herr Heinze makes the introduction.

HEINZE (*in English*). May I present Captain Renault, Police Prefect of Casablanca. . . . Major Strasser.

The two shake hands.

RENAULT (*courteously—but with just a suggestion of mockery underneath his words*). Unoccupied France welcomes you to Casablanca.

STRASSER (*in perfect English—beaming on the Frenchman*). Thank you, Captain. It is very good to be here.

RENAULT. Major, may I present my aide, Lieutenant Casselle?

Casselle does not offer to shake hands. They merely salute and bow. Renault leads Strasser toward the edge of the airfield, where their cars await them. Heinze and Casselle follow, with the Italian captain left to bring up the rear. —The view then follows RENAULT and STRASSER walking toward the cars.

RENAULT (*again the suggestion of a double-edged inference*). You may find the climate of Casablanca a trifle warm, Major.

STRASSER. Oh, we Germans must get used to all climates—from Russia to the Sahara. (*Suddenly the smile fades and the eyes harden.*) But perhaps you were not referring to the weather.

RENAULT (*sidestepping the implication with a smile*). What else, my dear Major?

STRASSER (*casual again*). By the way, the murder of the couriers—what has been done?

RENAULT. Realizing the importance of the case, my men are rounding up twice the usual number of suspects. (*At this Strasser again looks at him sharply.*)

HEINZE. Captain Renault means that the round-up is a blind. We already know who the murderer is.

STRASSER. Good. Is he in custody?

RENAULT. There is no hurry. Tonight he will come to Rick's. (*Indicating the café at the airport's edge*) Everybody comes to Rick's. (*Heinze shrugs to indicate that he can do nothing with Renault.*)

STRASSER. I have already heard about this café—and also about M'sieur Rick himself.

As they arrive at the car, the scene dissolves to a view of RENAULT'S CAR as it proceeds through the narrow, crooked streets of the Medina (the old city of Casablanca).

RENAULT. . . . But naturally, so important a man as Major Strasser did not come all the way to Casablanca merely because two couriers are murdered.

STRASSER (*smiling benignly*). I suspect, Captain, you are a very clever man. Perhaps you are even clever enough to tell me the real reason for my coming?

RENAULT. I might offer a guess. It has perhaps something to do with Victor Laszlo?

STRASSER. Very clever indeed. . . . Has Laszlo arrived?

RENAULT. This morning, from Oran. With a beautiful woman. Otherwise he traveled light.

STRASSER (*all business now*). Captain Renault, it is of the utmost importance to the German government that M'sieur Laszlo travels no further than Casablanca.

RENAULT. Naturally.

STRASSER (*casually, but watching the Frenchman closely*). It is well known that M'sieur Laszlo is prepared to offer a fabulous bribe for an exit visa.

RENAULT (*briefly*). And I am prepared to refuse it.

STRASSER (*smiling*). Then we understand each other. We shall perhaps have a little talk with M'sieur Laszlo. Where do you suggest?

RENAULT. Everybody goes to Rick's, Major—or did I mention that before?

The scene dissolves to an ELECTRIC SIGN reading "RICK'S"; then the view moves down to reveal a COUPLE entering RICK's through the revolving door as the sound of music and laughter comes from the café. And this cuts to the interior of RICK'S, an expensive and chic night club which definitely possesses an air of sophistication and intrigue. The view moves around the room, soaking in the atmosphere: A woman, just past the first blush of youth, is singing to the accompaniment of a four-piece orchestra. The piano is a small, salmon-

Rick: You're right, Ugarte. I am a little more impressed with you.

Rick: Hello, Ilsa.

Sam: Don't just sit and look a hole in that drink, Boss.

Rick: Nobody is going to be arrested, Louis. Not for a while yet.

colored instrument on wheels. There is a Negro on the stool, SAM. He is dressed in bright blue slacks and sport shirt. He is playing and singing "It had to be you, it had to be you, etc. Wonderful you! Had to be you!" and " 'Cause my teeth are pearly, etc." About him there is a hum of voices, chatter and laughter. The occupants of the room are varied. There are Europeans in their dinner jackets, their women beautifully begowned and bejeweled. There are Moroccans in silk robes, Turks wearing fezzes, Levantines, Naval officers, members of the Foreign Legion, distinguished by their kepis. Across the room, stretching the entire length of the wall, is a tremendous, resplendent bar.

The view moves from the piano to the bar, and as it passes the various tables we hear a babel of foreign tongues. Here and there we catch a scattered phrase or sentence in English—"I have an idea for a little business in Brazil—" A very beautiful young woman at another table is being nostalgic. She is saying to an elderly male admirer: "It used to take a Villa at Cannes, or the very least, a string of pearls—Now all I ask is an exit visa."

As the moving view nears the bar we see a man staring hopelessly into space. His companion is trying to cheer him up, but the man says tonelessly, "I'll never get out of here—I'll die in Casablanca." From the table next to the bar there is a burst of feminine laughter.— And now we are at the bar.

We see the RUSSIAN BARTENDER, a young, foreign-looking man, wearing a silk smock. He hands a drink to a customer, with the Russian equivalent of "Bottoms Up." Then he calls out to a passing waiter.

RUSSIAN BARTENDER. Carl—

The waiter stops, turns, and walks to the bar. He is a small, mild-mannered man with spectacles.

CARL. Yes, Sascha—

SASCHA (*with a heavy Russian accent*). Carl, my frien'— (*He hands him a huge sheaf of bar checks.*) You will make the computations, plees? I am so busy—

Carl just glances quickly through the checks, then hands them back to Sascha.

CARL (*with a German accent*). Two hundred and seventy-eight francs. You undercharged on the last check.

SASCHA (*gratefully, as Carl walks away*). Thank you, my frien', thank you— (*To the customer; with great admiration for Carl*) All in his head, like an adding machine—Three books he wrote on mathematics—astronomy—the greatest professor in the whole University of Leipzig.

CUSTOMER (*turning to look at Carl in the distance*). Really? Is that so?

SASCHA (*nodding vehemently*). And the mos' vonderful t'ing of all—he's not a bad waiter!

CUSTOMER. And what did you do before you came here?

SASCHA (*sadly*). I was the Czar's favorite sword swallower. Whenever he felt depressed— (*Leaning closer to the customer*) Tell me, my frien', do you think there's a future in America for a sword swallower?

We see CARL, tray in hand, walking up to a private door, over which a burly man stands guard.

CARL (*to the burly man*). Open up, Abdul.

ABDUL (*respectfully, as he opens the door*). Herr Professor.

Carl goes in and the scene cuts to a long view of the GAMBLING ROOM, full of activity at the various tables, as Carl comes in; following which the scene cuts to the BACCARAT TABLE where a woman hands a check to the dealer. He, in turn, turns around and hands it on to a tuxedoed Overseer who looks at the check, then at the woman.

OVERSEER (*to the woman*). Just one minute, please.

And as he walks toward a table, the scene cuts to a close view of a MAN's HAND holding a drink. The Overseer's body comes into the scene, and his hand places a check on the table. The other man's hand picks up the check.— Obviously, the man is studying it. Then his hand comes into the scene and on the back of the check, in pencil, it writes:
"Okay—Rick"
The Overseer's hand takes the check as the view draws back to RICK, an American of indeterminate age, sitting at the table alone. He just sits staring at the drink, with no expression in his eyes.

A TABLE, at which TWO WOMEN and A MAN are seated, comes into view. The women are glancing off scene at Rick's table, fascinated. Carl is in the scene, preparing Turkish coffee.

WOMAN (*to Carl*). Will you ask Rick if he'll have a drink with us?

CARL. Madame, he never drinks with customers unless he invites them to his table.

SECOND WOMAN (*disappointedly; glancing toward Rick*). What makes saloon-keepers so snobbish?

MAN (*to Carl; holding out a bill*). Perhaps if you told him I ran the second largest banking house in Amsterdam . . . ?

CARL (*shaking his head*). That wouldn't impress Rick. The leading banker in Amsterdam is now the pastry chef in our kitchen.

He takes the bill from the man's hand and walks away. The view then moves with him, disclosing RICK glancing toward the open door and indicating that the person seeking admittance is not to be let in. But at this point there is a commotion at the door, and a voice with a German accent is heard shouting.

GERMAN VOICE. Of all the nerve! Who do you think—

Thereupon, Rick gets up, and with no change of expression, walks across the floor to the door, the view moving with him, following which we see a RED-FACED GERMAN outside the door. He is protesting to Abdul.

GERMAN. I know there's gambling in there! I . . . (*At this the door opens, and Rick comes out.*)

RICK (*coldly*). Yes?

The scene cuts to the ENTRANCE TO RICK'S as UGARTE comes in. He is a small, thin man with a nervous air. If he were an American he would look like a tout. As he looks interestedly in the direction of Rick and the German, the scene cuts to a closer view of the two.

GERMAN (*waving his card*). I've been in every gambling room between Honolulu and Berlin and if you think I'm going to be kept out of a saloon like this, you're very much mistaken.

Rick just looks at him calmly, and takes the newspaperman's card out of the German's hand.

RICK (*tearing up the card*). Your cash is good at the bar.

Carl, tray in hand, comes out of the gambling room, and walks right between the German and Rick.

CARL. S'cuse me.

GERMAN (*to Rick*). Why—what—Do you know who I am??

RICK (*coldly*). I do. You're lucky the bar's open to you.

GERMAN. This is outrageous! I shall report it to the *Angriff*.

Rick turns away from the sputtering German, and catches the Negro's eye at the piano. The Negro, who while still playing, has been watching the byplay, winks at Rick, and Rick acknowledges the wink with some friendly gesture. It isn't quite a smile, but it is probably the closest thing to a smile that Rick can manage. Anyway, it establishes the fact that as far as Rick is concerned the Negro is a privileged person.

And now, as Rick goes back into the bar, the view cuts to a TABLE in the GAMBLING ROOM with Rick approaching it. A moment later, Ugarte appears, following him.

UGARTE (*with the manner of a man who curries favor*). M'sieur Rick.

RICK (*barely looking at him*). Hello, Ugarte.

Rick sits on a stool at the end of the bar, and again Ugarte follows him. There is nobody near them.

UGARTE (*fawning*). Watching you just now with the Deutsches Bank, one would think you had been doing this all your life.

RICK (*stiffening*). Well, what makes you think I haven't?

UGARTE (*vaguely*). Oh, nothing. When you first came to Casablanca, I thought—

RICK (*coldly*). Yes?

UGARTE (*fearing to offend Rick, laughing*). What right have I to think? (*Hastily changing the subject*) Too bad about those German couriers, wasn't it?

RICK (*indifferently*). They got a break. Yesterday they were just two German clerks; today they're the Honored Dead.

UGARTE (*shaking his head*). You are a very cynical person, Rick, if you'll forgive me for saying so.

RICK (*shortly*). I forgive you.

We see the BARTENDER coming into the scene with two drinks, which he sets before the men.

UGARTE (*his eyes lighting up*). Oh, Rick—you are going to drink with me?

RICK. No.

UGARTE (*sadly*). You despise me, don't you?

RICK (*indifferently*). If I gave you any thought, I probably would.

UGARTE. You object to the work I do. But think of the poor refugees who must rot in this place if I did not help them. Is it so bad that through ways of my own I provide them with exit visas?

RICK (*staring at his drink*). For a price, Ugarte, for a price.

UGARTE. Yes—but those poor devils who cannot meet Renault's price, I get it for them for half. Is that so parasitic?

RICK (*turning to look at Ugarte*). I don't mind a parasite. I object to a *cut-rate* one.

UGARTE. Well, after tonight I'll be through with the whole business. Rick, I am leaving Casablanca.

RICK. Who did you bribe for your visa? Renault or yourself?

UGARTE (*ironically*). Myself. I found myself much more reasonable. (*He takes an envelope from his pocket, and taps it on his hand.*) Do you know what these are? Something that not even you have ever seen— (*Lowering his voice*) Letters of Transit signed by Marshal Weygand. They cannot be rescinded or questioned.

Rick looks at him, then holds out his hand for the envelope.

UGARTE. In a moment. Tonight I will sell these for more money than even I ever dreamed of. Then—farewell to Casablanca. You know, Rick, I have many friends in Casablanca, but somehow just because you despise me you're the only one I trust. Will you keep these Letters for me?

RICK. For how long?

UGARTE. Oh, perhaps an hour, perhaps a little longer.

RICK (*taking them*). I don't want them here overnight.

UGARTE. Oh, don't be afraid of that. Waiter—

We see the WAITER coming into the scene.

UGARTE (*to the waiter*). Any messages for me?

WAITER. No, M'sieur.

UGARTE. I'll be expecting some people. If, er, anyone asks for me, I'll be right here. (*The waiter nods, and leaves, and Ugarte turns once more to Rick.*) Rick, I hope you are more impressed with me. Excuse me, I go to share my good luck with your roulette wheel. (*And he starts across the floor.*)

RICK. Wait a minute—

As Ugarte stops and Rick comes up to him, the scene cuts to a close view of RICK and UGARTE, and Rick's voice is barely audible.

RICK. I heard a rumor that those German couriers were carrying Letters of Transit.

UGARTE (*hesitating for a moment*). Yes—I heard that rumor, too. Poor devils.

RICK (*looking at Ugarte steadily, then slowly*). You're right, Ugarte. I am a little more impressed with you.

At this, Ugarte smiles and almost swaggers toward the gambling table. And as Rick starts for the door, the scene cuts to the area AT THE PIANO where a very fat man in a tropical dinner coat stands beside Sam, the Negro, who is improvising on the piano "Say, who's got trouble?" with the musicians singing in reply, "We got trouble, etc." The fat man is SENOR FERRARI, boss of the Black Market. His voice is high-pitched and he seems to be perpetually out of breath.

SENOR FERRARI. Sam, how would you like to work for me at the Blue Parrot?

SAM. Ah likes it fine with Mister Rick.

SENOR FERRARI. I'll double whatever Rick pays you.

SAM. But ah ain't got time to spend what ah makes here.

RICK'S VOICE (*heard at this point*). My competition getting a little stiff for you, Senor Ferrari?

Sam gives a worried glance over his shoulder, but continues to play the piano. Senor Ferrari turns around very deliberately—not the least flustered by being discovered trying to lure Sam away. Then the scene includes Rick, who is smiling now, but not a pleasant smile.

FERRARI. Hello, Rick.

RICK. Hello, Ferrari. How's business at the Blue Parrot?

FERRARI. Fine, but I'd like to buy your café.

RICK. It's not for sale.

SENOR FERRARI. You're doing very well, here, Rick. But then, I always like to see a man doing well.

RICK. So out of your good will, you try to rob me of my piano player?

SENOR FERRARI. "Rob" is a strong word.

RICK. Is it?

SENOR FERRARI (*thinking it over*). Well, perhaps it isn't . . . but what I can't steal, I'm willing to pay for. What do you want for Sam?

RICK. I don't buy or sell human beings.

SENOR FERRARI. Too bad. That's Casablanca's leading commodity. In refugees alone we could make a fortune if you would work with me through the Black Market.

RICK. Suppose you let me run my business, and you run yours.

Senor Ferrari walks toward the door of the gambling room, shakes his head, and sighs.

SENOR FERRARI. My dear Rick, when will you realize that in the world today, isolationism is no longer a practical policy? (*And he goes out into the next room.*)

Rick walks over to the piano, lifts the lid casually, and drops in the envelope Ugarte has given him. Sam looks up, and smiles.

SAM. I didn't see nothin', Boss.

Rick nods in reply, and walks toward the bar, following which a woman customer comes into view, leans over, and whispers to Sam.

SAM. All right.

Sam gives a signal, the wall lights dim, and the spotlight focusses on him as he begins to play.

AT THE LONG BAR in the café proper, we see a young woman, YVONNE, sitting on a stool, drinking brandy. Sascha, who is looking at her with lovesick eyes, is filling her tumbler.

SASCHA. The boss' private stock. Because—Yvonne—I loff you.

YVONNE (*morosely*). Oh, shut up.

SASCHA (*fondly*). For you, Yvonne, I shot opp.

Rick saunters into the scene, and leans against the bar next to Yvonne. But he pays no attention to her. She looks at him bitterly, without saying a word.—The scene cuts to a view of SAM playing —he is in the midst of a number— then back to RICK and YVONNE, with Sam alone spotlighted at the piano, while Rick and Yvonne stand in the gloom. Yvonne, who has never taken her eyes off Rick, finally blurts out.

YVONNE. Where were you last night?

RICK. That's so long ago. I don't remember.

YVONNE (*after a pause*). Will I see you tonight?

RICK (*calmly*). I never make plans that far ahead.

Yvonne turns, looks at Sascha, and extends her glass to him, saying "Give me another." As Sascha is about to fill the glass Rick turns, and stops him with a gesture.

RICK. Sascha, she's had enough.

YVONNE. Don't listen to him, Sascha. Fill it up.

SASCHA (*hesitating, looking at Rick, then putting the bottle down*). Yvonne, I loff you, Yvonne, but he pays me.

YVONNE (*wheeling on Rick with drunken fury*). Rick, I'm sick and tired of having you—

RICK. Sascha, call a cab.

SASCHA (*accepting the order fatalistically*). Yes, Boss. (*And he walks toward the café entrance.*)

RICK (*taking Yvonne by the arm*). Come on, we're going to get your coat. You're going home.

YVONNE. Take your hands off me—

As he pulls her along toward the hall door, the scene cuts to the STREET in front of RICK'S. SASCHA stands at the curb signalling a cab, and finally one pulls up. Then Rick and Yvonne are seen coming out of the café entrance. He is putting a coat over her shoulders. She is objecting violently.

YVONNE. Who do you think you are, pushing me around? I'm a lady. I sang in America. I've been married twice. What a fool I was to fall in love with a man like you.

RICK (*to Sascha—as he and Yvonne approach the waiting cab*). You'd better go with her, Sascha, and be sure she gets home.

SASCHA (*delighted at the opportunity*). Yes, Boss.

One on each arm, they help Yvonne into the cab. Sascha follows her in.

RICK. And, Sascha. . . . (*As Sascha looks out through the window*) Come right back.

SASCHA (*his face falling*). Yes, Boss.

The cab starts off, following which we see RICK walking back toward the café entrance. At this we hear Renault—

RENAULT'S VOICE. How extravagant you are—throwing away women like that. Some day they may be rationed.

And as Rick turns toward the voice, we see a TABLE on the CAFÉ TERRACE where Renault is sipping some brandy, his eyes expressing amusement. Rick walks into view.

RICK. Hello, Louis.

RENAULT. I think now I shall pay a call on Yvonne—maybe get her on the rebound, eh?

RICK (*as he takes a seat at the table*). Well, when it comes to women, you're a true democrat.

Renault laughs at this and pours Rick a drink. There is the sound of a plane warming up on the adjacent airfield, and Rick looks in the direction of the sound, Renault following his gaze.— We see a TRANSPORT PLANE in the full glare of the floodlights, standing poised on the runway, its motors racing, ready for the take-off. Then we see RICK and RENAULT again as Rick is still looking steadfastly at the plane.

RENAULT. The plane to Lisbon— (*Looking at Rick shrewdly*) You would like to be on it?

RICK (*curtly*). Why? What's in Lisbon?

RENAULT. The Clipper to America.

Rick doesn't answer; he looks at the plane warming up, but his look isn't a happy one.

RENAULT. I have often speculated on why you do not return to America. Did you abscond with the church funds? Did you run off with the President's wife? I should like to think you killed a man. It is the romantic in me.

RICK (*still looking at the plane—sardonically*). It was a combination of all three.

RENAULT. And what in Heaven's name brought you to Casablanca? (*The plane's motors grow louder.*)

RICK. My health. I came to Casablanca for the waters.

RENAULT. The waters? What waters? We are in the desert.

RICK. I was misinformed.

Renault shakes his head but can say nothing, for the plane is speeding down the runway, its lights shining on the faces of Rick and Renault. Rick cannot take his eyes from the plane. Now it leaves the ground and passes almost directly over them. He watches the plane until its lights disappear into the distance.

A CROUPIER, so identified by the green visor over his eyes, comes into view.

CROUPIER. Excuse me, M'sieur Rick, but a gentleman inside has won ten thousand francs. The cashier would like some money.

RICK (*not at all perturbed*). I'll get it from the safe.

CROUPIER. I am so upset, M'sieur Rick. I do not understand how—

RICK (*consoling him*). It's all right, Emil. Mistakes like that happen all the time.

Rick and Renault both rise. As they start toward the door, a French and an Italian officer come out, arguing violently on some political subject. As they meet Renault they both come to attention and salute; then move on, still arguing. Rick and Renault start in.

RENAULT. Rick, there is going to be some excitement here tonight. We are going to make an arrest in your café.

RICK (*not at all excited*). What, again?

This cuts to the interior of the CAFÉ as Rick and Renault come in.

RENAULT. Oh, this is no ordinary arrest. A murderer, no less.

A close view of RICK shows his eyes reacting to the news. Involuntarily they glance toward the gambling room.— Then RICK and RENAULT are seen starting for the steps alongside the bar.

RENAULT (*who has caught the look*). If you are thinking of warning him —don't put yourself out. He can't possibly escape.

RICK (*starting up the steps*). I stick my neck out for nobody.

RENAULT. A wise foreign policy—

There is a drink at the end of the bar waiting to be picked up by a waiter. Renault takes the drink as he starts upstairs after Rick. The waiter turns around—to find no drink.

RENAULT (*up the steps—drink in hand*). We could have made this arrest earlier in the evening at the Blue Parrot—

Rick enters a room on the landing, then the scene cuts to RICK'S OFFICE as he comes in, followed by Renault.

RENAULT. —But out of my high regard for you we are staging it here. It will amuse your customers.

RICK (*opening a door*). Our entertainment is enough.

We see a small, dark room off the office, where the safe is kept. Rick goes in, and starts to open the safe, while Renault leans against the door jamb.

RENAULT. Rick, we are to have an important guest tonight—Major Strasser of the Third Reich—no less. We want him to be here when we make the arrest. A little demonstration of the efficiency of my administration.

RICK. I see. And what's Strasser doing here? He hasn't come all the way to Casablanca to witness a demonstration of your efficiency.

RENAULT. Perhaps not.

RICK. Louis, you have something on your mind. Why don't you spill it?

RENAULT (*admiringly*). You are very observant. As a matter of fact, I wanted to give you a word of advice.

RICK. Yes?

RENAULT. There are many exit visas sold in this café, but we know that you have never sold them. That is the reason we permit you to remain open.

RICK (*amiably*). I thought it was because we let you win at roulette.

RENAULT. Yes, that is another reason. . . . My dear Rick, there is a man who has arrived in Casablanca on his way to America. He will offer a fortune to anyone who will furnish him with an exit visa.

RICK. Yes? What's his name?

RENAULT. Victor Laszlo.

RICK. Laszlo here in Casablanca!

RENAULT (*watching Rick's reaction*). Rick, this is the first time I have ever seen you so impressed.

RICK (*casual again*). Well (*laughing*), he's succeeded in impressing half the world.

RENAULT. It's my duty to see that he does not impress the other half. (*Now intensely serious*) Rick, Laszlo must never reach America. He stays in Casablanca.

RICK. It'll be interesting to see how he manages.

RENAULT. Manages what?

RICK. His escape.

RENAULT. But I just told you—

RICK. Stop it, Louis. He escaped from a concentration camp, didn't he? The Nazis have been chasing him all over Europe.

RENAULT (*grimly*). This is the end of the chase.

RICK. Ten thousand francs says it isn't.

RENAULT. Is that a serious **wager**?

RICK. I just paid out twenty. I'd like to get it back.

RENAULT. Make it ten. I am only a poor corrupt official. (*As Rick nods*) Done. No matter how clever he is, he still needs an exit visa—or I *should* say, two.

They start out of the room and down the steps, the scene moving with them.

RICK. Why two?

RENAULT. He is traveling with a lady.

RICK. Well, he'll take one.

RENAULT. I think not. I have seen the lady. And if he did not leave her in Marseilles, nor in Oran, he will not leave her in Casablanca.

RICK. Well, maybe he's not as romantic as you.

RENAULT. It does not matter—one or two—romanticist or not—there is no exit visa for him.

RICK. Louis, where did you get the idea I might be interested in helping Laszlo?

RENAULT. Because, my dear Rick, I suspect under that cynical shell, you are at heart a sentimentalist. (*As Rick breaks into a laugh*) Laugh if you will, but I happen to be familiar with your record. Let me point out just two items. In 1935, you ran guns to Ethiopia; in 1936, you fought in Spain on the Loyalist side.

RICK (*trying to make light of this*). And got well paid for it on both occasions.

RENAULT (*pointedly*). The winning side would have paid you much better.

RICK (*casually*). Maybe. (*Anxious for a change of subject*) Well, it seems that you are determined to keep Laszlo here.

RENAULT. I have my orders.

RICK. I see. Gestapo spank.

There is a closer view of RENAULT: They are down now. As he speaks he faces the huge mirror over the bar.

RENAULT. You overestimate the influence of the Gestapo, Rick. We do not interfere with them and they do not interfere with us. In Casablanca I am master of my fate. I am captain of my—

He stops short as in the mirror he sees the reflection of Major Strasser who is coming into the café. Then we see both RICK and RENAULT.

RENAULT (*hurriedly*). Excuse me, Rick—

He hurries toward Strasser. Rick looks in the mirror, sees whom Renault is hurrying toward, and smiles cynically. The Croupier, who has been waiting, comes into the scene.

RICK (*handing the money to the Croupier*). There you are.

CROUPIER (*with grim determination*). It shall not happen again, M'sieur!

He hurries away. Rick picks up a drink from the bar.

In the CAFÉ, Renault is now walking with Carl.

RENAULT. Carl, see that Herr Strasser gets a good table—close to the ladies.

CARL. I have already given him the best, M'sieur! (*Sadly*) . . . Knowing he is German and would take it anyway.

Renault beckons to a NATIVE OFFICER who is apparently waiting for the word. The latter approaches and salutes.

RENAULT (*in a low voice*). Take him quietly. Two guards at every door.

NATIVE OFFICER. Yes, sir.

He salutes and starts toward the door of the gambing room. The scene travels with Renault, who walks to a table on one side of the café where Strasser and Heinze are seated. At the adjoining table are some German officers. Strasser beams as Renault approaches the table.

RENAULT. Good evening, gentlemen.

STRASSER. Good evening, Captain.

HEINZE. Won't you join us?

RENAULT (*sitting down*). Thank you. It is a pleasure to have you here, Major.

STRASSER. A very interesting club.

RENAULT. Especially so this evening. (*In a low voice*) In just a minute you will see the arrest of the man who murdered your couriers.

STRASSER. I expected no less, Captain.

A close view shows UGARTE at the roulette table in the gambling room. Piled in front of him is a huge stack of chips. He is having a run of luck and his eyes are feverish as they follow the marble that is bouncing on the wheel. The marble stops on number 13. Exultantly Ugarte reaches for the chips which the Croupier shoves on the table. But just then another hand closes onto Ugarte's arm, and a look of terror crosses his face as the Native Officer is heard.

NATIVE OFFICER'S VOICE. You will come with me, Monsieur Ugarte.

UGARTE (*in a low voice*). Allow me to cash my chips.

The Native Officer nods assent, and follows Ugarte to the Cashier, following which we see the CASHIER'S BOOTH where the Cashier pays Ugarte the amount of his chips. Ugarte thrusts the money in his inside coat pocket, but as his hand comes out of the pocket, it grips a small revolver, pointed at the Native Officer. The Officer makes a jump for Ugarte, and the gun goes off. The Officer clasps his shoulder. A woman screams. People at the gambling tables duck for cover. Ugarte runs toward the hallway.

QUICK FLASHES show Rick crossing the floor of the café, and turning abruptly toward the door to the gambling room; a woman in a booth jumping to her feet, looking in the direction of the sound; a man at the bar lifting his glass to drink, and abruptly putting the glass down; the music stopping as Sam's hands hold on the piano keys; Carl, behind the bar, flashing an expectant look toward Strasser's booth; and Renault, Strasser and Heinze all jumping to their feet.

We then see the HALLWAY BETWEEN THE ROOMS as Ugarte rushes into the hallway. Rick appears from the opposite direction.

UGARTE. Rick, help me!

RICK (*in a low voice*). Don't be a fool. You can't get away.

UGARTE. Hide me. Do something. You must help me, Rick! Do something.

RICK (*indistinctly*). Shut up!

Before he can finish, Renault, Strasser, Heinze and others rush in from behind Rick. Other police officers appear from the gambling room and grab Ugarte.

Without a word, Rick pushes his way through the group to the café.

MAN (*half kiddingly, half in earnest*). When they come to get me, Rick, I hope you'll be of more help.

RICK. I stick my neck out for nobody.

We see the CAFÉ again as Rick comes out on the floor. An air of tense expectancy pervades the room, and a few customers are on the point of leaving. Rick speaks in a very calm voice.

RICK. I'm sorry there was a disturbance, but it's all over. Everything's all right. (*He glances toward his piano player.*) All right, Sam . . .

AT THE PIANO, SAM nods, and begins to play.

SAM. Ol' Noah, what'd he do? (*He shouts at the audience.*) C'mon, folks— (*He starts again.*) Ol' Noah, what'd he do?

He waits and plays the next phrase. There is a full view of the café, taking in several tables as there is a half-hearted response from the people.

THE PEOPLE. Ol' Noah, what'd he do?

SAM (*grinning, playing louder and faster*). Dat's right. He built a floatin' zoo.

The people at the TABLES, under Sam's spell again, join in and sing. The gloom is somewhat lifted. The view roves over various tables, picking up all types of people during the course of the song.— Then we see STRASSER'S TABLE as the song is finished and the excitement has quieted down. Renault, Strasser and Heinze are now back at their table. The headwaiter is taking their order.

STRASSER. . . . Champagne and a tin of caviar—very cold.

RENAULT. Let me recommend Veuve Cliquot twenty-six, Major.

WAITER (*leaving*). Very well, sir.

RENAULT (*calling to Rick, who is not yet seen*). Oh, Rick . . . (*At this Rick appears.*)

RENAULT. Rick, this is Major Heinrich Strasser of the Third Reich.

STRASSER. How do you do.

RENAULT. And you already know Herr Heinze.

STRASSER (*as Rick nods to Strasser and Heinze*). Please join us, Herr Rick.

Rick sits down beside Heinze, facing Renault and Strasser.

RENAULT (*changing the subject*). Rick, we are very honored tonight. Major Strasser is one of the reasons why the Third Reich enjoys the reputation it has today (*Rick nods.*)

STRASSER (*smiling*). You repeat "Third Reich" as though you expected there to be others.

RENAULT. Well, personally, Major, I will take what comes.

The waiter appears with drinks, and begins to open the bottles and pour during the ensuing conversation.

STRASSER. Do you mind if I ask you a few questions? Unofficially, of course.

RICK (*shrugging*). Make it official, if you like.

STRASSER. What is your nationality?

RICK (*looking at him a moment before replying, then with a poker face*). I'm a drunkard. (*Strasser looks closely at him.*)

RENAULT. And that makes Rick a citizen of the World.

There is a closer view of RICK, RENAULT and STRASSER.

RICK. I was born in New York City, if that'll clear things up any.

STRASSER (*to Rick—very amiably*). I understand you came here from Paris at the time of the Occupation.

RICK. Well, there seems to be no secret about that.

STRASSER. Are you one of those people who cannot *imagine* the Germans in their beloved Paris?

RICK. It's not particularly *my* beloved Paris.

HEINZE (*with a slight laugh*). Can you imagine us in London?

RICK. When you get there, ask me.

RENAULT (*laughing*). Oh! Diplomatist!

STRASSER (*digging into the caviar*). How about New York?

RICK. There are certain sections of that city I would not advise you to try to invade.

STRASSER. Um-huh. . . . Who do you think will win the war?

RICK. I haven't the slightest idea.

RENAULT. Rick is completely neutral about everything. And that takes in the field of women, too.

Strasser takes a little black book from his pocket, and riffles through the pages.

STRASSER (*to Rick*). You weren't always so carefully neutral. We have a complete dossier on you. (*He reads.*) "Richard Blaine, American. Age thirty-seven. Cannot return to his country."— (*Looking up from the book*) The reason is a little vague. We also know what you did in Paris— (*Renault, very curious, tries to look over Strasser's shoulder.*) Also, Herr Blaine, we know why you left Paris.

At this Rick reaches over, and takes the book from Strasser's hand.

STRASSER. Don't worry. We are not going to broadcast it.

RICK (*looking in the book*). Are my eyes really brown?

STRASSER. You will forgive my curiosity, Herr Blaine. The point is, an enemy of the Reich has come to Casablanca and we are checking up on anyone who can possibly be of help to us.

RICK. Well, my interest in Victor Laszlo's staying or going—(*with a glance toward Renault*)—is purely a sporting one.

STRASSER. In this case, you have no sympathy for the fox, huh?

RICK. Not particularly. I understand the point of view of the hound, too.

STRASSER. Victor Laszlo published the foulest lies in Prague newspapers until the very day we marched in, and even after that he continued to print scandal sheets in a cellar.

RENAULT. Of course, one must admit he has great courage.

STRASSER. I admit he is very clever. Three times he slipped through our fingers. In Paris he continued his activities. We intend not to let it happen again.

RICK (*rising with a slight smile*). Er, you'll excuse me, gentlemen? Your business is politics. Mine is running a saloon.

STRASSER. Good evening, Herr Blaine. (*Rick walks out of the scene, toward the gambling room.*)

RENAULT. You see, Major, you have nothing to worry about Rick.

STRASSER (*his eyes following the direction Rick has gone*). Perhaps . . .

The scene cuts to ANOTHER TABLE where the dark-appearing foreigner we had seen in the opening sequence is busily engaged with a middle-aged prosperous-looking man.

DARK FOREIGNER (*his arms thrown solicitously around the other man*). I beseech you, my friend—be on guard. Take care. Use every precaution.

SAM is again seen AT THE PIANO as he is idling away at something sentimental. The people at the tables have resumed their chatter. As he plays Sam glances casually around. Suddenly, as his eyes look toward the entrance, his playing falters, then stops altogether.

We see what Sam is staring at toward the ENTRANCE: A couple has just come in: Victor Laszlo and a beautiful companion. She wears a simple white gown. Her beauty is such that people turn to stare. The headwaiter comes up to them.

HEADWAITER. Yes, M'sieur.

LASZLO (*in quiet, even tones*). I reserved a table. Victor Laszlo.

A closeup shows a small blond man looking intently at Laszlo, and this is followed by a close view of the WOMAN —who has been looking around casually. When she sees Sam, her face registers a startled surprise for just an instant while we hear the headwaiter.

HEADWAITER'S VOICE. Yes, M'sieur Laszlo. Right this way.

A close view of SAM, as he sees her looking at him, shows him turning his gaze away, and resuming his piano playing; following which there is a moving view of the GROUP as the headwaiter takes them to a table. Although they pass right by the piano and the woman (who is later to be identified as ILSA LUND) looks directly at Sam, the latter with a conscious effort keeps his eyes on the keyboard. Ilsa smiles slightly. After she has gone out of sight, Sam steals a look in her direction.

AT LASZLO'S TABLE: The headwaiter seats Ilsa and leaves. Laszlo takes the chair opposite. He surveys the room with a sweeping glance.

LASZLO. I saw no one of Ugarte's description.

ILSA. Victor, are you sure we should have come here—so in public? I, I feel, somehow, we shouldn't stay here.

LASZLO. If we should walk out so soon it would only call attention to us. Perhaps Ugarte's in some other part of the café.

MAN'S VOICE. Excuse me, but you look like a couple who are on their way to America.

The small blond man, later identified as BERGER, walks into the scene.

LASZLO. Well?

The man reaches into his vest pocket, and brings out a ring with a large aquamarine stone.

BERGER. You will find a market there for this ring. I am forced to sell it at a great sacrifice.

LASZLO. Thank you, but I hardly think—

BERGER. Then perhaps for the lady. The ring is quite unique.

He holds it down to their view, and begins to twist the stone, which is apparently screwed into the setting.

We then see the RING *in* BERGER'S HAND *as the stone comes loose in his fingers. In the setting underneath, on a gold plate, is a faint impression of the Lorraine Cross of General De Gaulle.*

LASZLO'S VOICE. Oh, yes, I am *very* interested.

BERGER. Good.

LASZLO (*in a lower voice*). What is your name?

BERGER. Berger . . . Norwegian . . . I'm at your service, sir.

ILSA (*looking off, then giving Laszlo a signal*). Victor!

LASZLO (*to Berger, in a low voice as he comprehends the signal*). I'll meet you in a few minutes at the bar. (*In a louder voice, obviously intended for the benefit of someone out of sight*) No, I do not think we want to buy the ring. But thank you for showing it to us.

BERGER (*taking the cue, sighing, and putting the ring away*). Such a bargain. But if that is your decision—

He bows and turns away, the scene moving with him. As he walks away, he brushes by Captain Renault and Major Strasser, who are approaching the table. They glance sharply at Berger as he passes.—Then Renault beams as the scene moves back with him to the table.

RENAULT. Monsieur Laszlo, is it not?

LASZLO (*sharply*). Yes.

RENAULT. I am Captain Renault, Prefect of Police.

LASZLO. Yes. What is it you want?

RENAULT. Merely to welcome you to Casablanca and to wish you a pleasant stay. It isn't often we have so distinguished a visitor. (*As Strasser appears*) May I present Major Heinrich Strasser . . . Mademoiselle Ilsa Lund—and M'sieur Victor Laszlo.

The German bows, but there is not the slightest recognition from either Ilsa or Laszlo. Renault and Strasser wait to be asked to seat themselves. But Laszlo is plainly blocking their approach to the table.

LASZLO. I am sure you will excuse me if I am not gracious . . . but you see, Major Strasser . . . I am a Czechoslovakian.

STRASSER. You *were* a Czechoslovakian—now you are a subject of the German Reich.

LASZLO. I am on French soil. What is it you want of me?

STRASSER. Merely to discuss some matters arising from your presence on . . . French soil.

LASZLO. This is hardly the time or the place . . .

STRASSER (*hardening*). Then we shall state another time and another place. Tomorrow at ten, in the Prefect's office. With Mademoiselle.

LASZLO (*turning to the Prefect*). Captain Renault, I am under your authority. Is it *your* order that we come to your office?

RENAULT (*amiably*). Let us say it is my request. That is a much more pleasant word.

LASZLO. Very well.

He bows and turns back to the table, where he sits next to Ilsa, and Renault and Strasser leave them. At this moment the wall lights are going down, as the floor show is about to begin.

We see the DANCE FLOOR, where a Master of Ceremonies stands in the spotlight.

MASTER OF CEREMONIES. And now, ladies and gentlemen, we continue the evening's entertainment with that sensational South American chanteuse, Senorita Andreya.

The girl appears in the spotlight, a guitar strapped over her shoulders. As she acknowledges the introduction, there is a smattering of applause from the audience.

LASZLO and ILSA are again seen at their table.

LASZLO. Strasser. . . . This time they *really* mean to stop me.

ILSA. Victor, I am afraid for you.

LASZLO. We have been in difficult places before.

He puts a hand over hers, and Ilsa smiles back at him, but her eyes are still troubled.

LASZLO (*after the scene has cut to a view of the café crowd and the Senorita singing in Spanish "Alla donde las rosas crecen"—"There where the roses grow"*). I must find out what Berger knows. If you see anyone watching me, remember his face. We must learn who are our enemies and who are our friends.

Ilsa nods, saying anxiously, "Be careful." Laszlo rises, and starts toward the end of the bar, which is on the far corner of the café.—Laszlo moves across the room in the comparative darkness. Though most people watch the singer, some heads turn.—ILSA, from the table, watches him anxiously.

AT THE BAR, BERGER is sipping a drink while we hear the Spanish entertainer. Laszlo walks into the scene, and casually takes a place at the bar next to Berger.

LASZLO (*to Sascha*). Champagne cocktail, please.

SASCHA. Yes, M'sieur.

As Sascha moves down the bar to make the cocktail, Laszlo takes out a cigarette, and Berger leans over to give him a light.

BERGER (*in a low voice*). . . . I recognize you from news photographs, M'sieur Laszlo.

LASZLO. In a concentration camp, one is apt to lose a little weight.

BERGER. We read five times that you were killed in five different places.

LASZLO (*smiling wryly*). As you see, it was true every time. . . . Thank the good Lord you found me, Berger. I am looking for a man by the name of Ugarte. He is to help me.

BERGER (*shaking his head silently*). M'sieur Laszlo, Ugarte cannot even help himself. He is under arrest for murder. He was arrested here tonight.

LASZLO (*absorbing the shock quietly*). I see.

BERGER (*with intense devotion*). But we who are still free will do all we can. We are organized, M'sieur—underground like everywhere else. Tomorrow night there is a meeting. If you would come— (*He stops as he sees a gendarme approaching in the background.*)

AT ILSA'S TABLE: Renault moves up behind her, unnoticed until he speaks.

RENAULT. Mademoiselle . . . (*Ilsa is startled, but she covers up with a smile.*)

ILSA. Captain Renault. . . .

RENAULT. Does the cold blanket of inhospitality also cover me? (*He gestures toward the chair by her side, plainly indicating that he would like to sit down with her.*)

ILSA. Since we are in Casablanca under your protection, Captain. . . . (*She nods toward the chair. Her manner is friendly, but reserved.*)

RENAULT. Thank you. (*As he sits down, he gestures to a hovering waiter, and addresses him.*) Your best champagne, and put it on my bill.

ILSA. No . . . please. . . .

RENAULT (*shooing the waiter away*). It is a little game we play. They put it on my bill, I tear the bill up. It is most convenient.

The song finishes and there is some applause. The lights come up.—As seen from their perspective, the songstress acknowledges the applause and leaves, and Sam wheels out his piano. Then we see ILSA, at the TABLE with RENAULT, looking off at Sam.

RENAULT. Mademoiselle, I was informed you were the most beautiful woman ever to visit Casablanca. That is a gross understatement.

ILSA. You are very kind. What a lovely uniform, Captain.

RENAULT (*pleased*). I have a uniform for every occasion— (*Significantly; on the make, definitely*) Every occasion. (*He indicates his medals,* which *cover his entire breast in a row.*) What do you think of my medals?

ILSA. One of them is out of line.

RENAULT. That is the one I really earned. It should be a little conspicuous.

As Ilsa laughs, she hears Sam's piano, and she looks off again in his direction. —We see SAM at the piano again—and as he plays, he steals a nervous glance in Ilsa's direction, and looks away again, following which we return to ILSA'S TABLE. Ilsa looks back to Renault.

ILSA. Captain, the boy who is playing the piano . . . somewhere I have seen him.

RENAULT. Sam? He came here from Paris with Rick.

ILSA. Rick? Who is he?

RENAULT (*smiling*). Mademoiselle, you are in Rick's. Well, Rick is. . . .

ILSA (*with an air of being casual, but pursuing her own line of inquiry*). Is what?

RENAULT. He is the kind of man that. . . . Well, if I were a woman and *I* . . . (*tapping his chest*) were not around, I would be in love with Rick. But what a fool I am! Talking to a beautiful woman about another man! . . .

The gendarme (who appeared in the background of the scene at the bar between Laszlo and Berger) enters the scene during the above beside Renault and waits to catch his attention. Renault looks up, annoyed.

GENDARME. Mon Capitaine. . . .

RENAULT (*annoyed*). What is it?

GENDARME (*to Ilsa*). Excusez-moi. . . . (*He stoops and whispers something in Renault's ear.*)

RENAULT (*annoyed—in a low voice*). Not now, fool.

GENDARME. But, mon Capitaine. . . . (*To Ilsa*) Excusez-moi. . . . (*And he whispers again.*)

RENAULT (*giving up, and rising with a sigh*). Will you excuse me? I'll only be a moment.

ILSA (*with a little smile*). I shall try to live until you return.

Renault doesn't quite know how to take this, but decides to take it as a compliment. He bows and leaves, the gendarme following. As soon as they have gone, Ilsa looks off and calls. . . .

ILSA. Sam. . . .

Sam looks up, startled. Ilsa motions him to come over. Sam hesitates—then starts to wheel the piano over, following which there is a close view at Ilsa's table. On Sam's face, as he wheels in the piano, is that curious fear. And to tell the truth, Ilsa herself is not as self-possessed as she tries to appear. There is something behind this, some mysterious, deep-flowing feeling.

ILSA. Hello, Sam.

SAM. Hello, Miss Ilsa. Ah never expected to see you again.

ILSA. It's been a long time. A lot of the Seine has flowed under the Pont-Neuf since then.

SAM. Yes, Miss Ilsa. A lot of water under the bridge. (*He sits down and is ready to play.*)

ILSA. Some of the old songs, Sam.

Sam begins to play a number. He is nervous, waiting for anything. But even so, when it comes he gives a little start. . . .

ILSA. Where's Rick?

SAM (*evading*). I don't know. Ain't seen him all night.

Ilsa gives him a tolerant smile. Sam looks very uncomfortabe.

ILSA. When will he be back?

SAM. Not tonight no more. He ain't coming. Er, he went home.

ILSA. Does he always leave so early?

SAM. He never—I mean— (*Desperately*) Well, he's got a girl up at the—Blue Parrot— He goes there all the time . . .

ILSA. You used to be a much better liar, Sam.

SAM. Leave him alone, Miss Ilsa. You're bad luck to him.

ILSA (*softly*). Sam, play it once for old time's sake.

SAM. Ah don't know what you mean, Miss Ilsa.

ILSA. Play it, Sam. Play "As Time Goes By."

SAM. I can't remember it, Miss Ilsa! (*Of course he can. He doesn't want to play it. He seems even more scared.*)

ILSA. I'll hum it for you. (*And she starts to hum.*)

SAM. I can't seem to get it!

ILSA. Somehow I didn't think you would. I'll play it for you.

SAM. No, Miss Ilsa. I think I've got it now. (*And he begins to play it very softly.*)

ILSA. Sing it, Sam.

SAM. I don't know the words!

ILSA (*softly*). I'll give them to you. (*She feeds him the first line, speaking it.*) "You must remember this. . . ."

—and Sam picks it up, singing.

"You must remember this,
A kiss is still a kiss,
A sigh is just a sigh . . ."

THE ENTRANCE TO THE GAMBLING ROOM: RICK comes swinging out. He has heard the music and he is livid.

RICK. What the—! Sam, I thought I told you never to play it.

He stops abruptly, stops speaking, and stops moving. SAM and ILSA are seen from his perspective—at the piano.— A closer view of SAM and ILSA follows as Sam looks over his shoulder at Rick and stops playing. Ilsa knows why even before she turns and looks. She knows whom she'll see when she turns. She turns slowly. She isn't breathing much.

A closeup of RICK shows that he isn't breathing at all. It's a "wallop," a shock. For a long moment he just looks at her and you can tell what he is thinking. He starts moving forward, his eyes riveted on her. He moves in a closeup across the café. Ilsa is looking directly at Rick, too. Sam is plainly terrified. He puts his stool on top of the piano and with a plaintively accusing . . .

SAM. Now you've done it!

—he wheels the piano quickly away. Ilsa doesn't notice. She still looks at Rick. At the same time, Renault and Laszlo are seen approaching from the bar.

Then we see the GROUP of three (Ilsa, Renault, Laszlo) at the TABLE as Renault approaches with Laszlo, arm in arm.

RENAULT (*to Ilsa*). See what I have found for you—a wandering escort.

She doesn't seem to have heard, and Renault looks off in the direction she is looking.

RENAULT. Well, you were asking about Rick and here he is.

Now Rick moves into the scene.

RENAULT. Ricky, my dear friend, here are some nice people. I have the honor of introducing—

RICK. Hello, Ilsa.

ILSA (*under her breath*). Hello, Rick. (*She offers her hand and he takes it.*)

RENAULT. Oh, you've already met Rick, Mademoiselle? (*Receiving no answer from either*) Well, then, perhaps you also know—

ILSA. This is Mr. Laszlo.

She says this in a funny way—as if she's frightened to say it and yet would rather say it herself than have someone else do it. Rick measures Laszlo with a look, then looks at Ilsa and smiles. You would say there is some mockery in the way he smiles.

LASZLO. How do you do?

RICK. How do you do?

LASZLO. One hears a great deal about Rick in Casablanca.

RICK (*looking back at him*). And about Victor Laszlo everywhere.

LASZLO. Won't you join us for a drink?

RICK. I'll join you. I never drink unless I'm alone.

LASZLO (*with a laugh as they sit*). Well, that is a new turn on the old phrase—"Drink alone and like it."

(*He is making conversation.*) This is a most interesting café—I congratulate you.

RICK. And I congratulate you.

LASZLO. What for?

RICK. Oh—your work. (*Why does he look at Ilsa?*)

LASZLO. Thank *you*. I try.

RICK. We all try. You succeed.

RENAULT. I can't get over—you two. She was asking about you earlier, Rick, in a way that made me extremely jealous.

ILSA (*to Rick*). I wasn't sure you were the same. Let's see, the last time we met . . .

RICK. Was it "La Belle Aurore"?

ILSA. How nice. You remembered! But of course—that was the day the Germans marched into Paris.

RICK. Not an easy day to forget, was it?

ILSA. No.

RICK. I remember every detail—the Germans wore gray, you wore blue.

ILSA. Yes. I put that dress away. When the Germans march out I'll wear it again.

RENAULT. Ricky, you're becoming quite human. I suppose we have to thank you for that, Mademoiselle.

LASZLO. Ilsa, I don't wish to be the one to say it—but it's late.

RENAULT (*glancing at his wristwatch*). So it is. And we have a curfew here in Casablanca. It would never do for the Chief of Police to be caught drinking after hours and have to fine himself.

LASZLO (*signalling the waiter*). I'm afraid we're almost the last ones left. I hope we haven't overstayed our welcome.

RICK. Not at all. (*He takes the check from the waiter.*)

LASZLO. Oh, please. I'd rather. . . .

RICK. Oh, it's my party.

RENAULT. Another precedent broken. This has been a most interesting evening. (*They all rise.*)

LASZLO (*to Rick as he helps Ilsa on with her wrap*). I'd like to come back.

RICK. Any time.

ILSA (*extending her hand to Rick*). Will you say good night to Sam for me?

RICK. I will.

ILSA. There's still nobody in the world who can play "As Time Goes By" like Sam.

RICK. He hasn't played it for a long time.

ILSA (*after a pause, smiling*). Good night.

Rick and Laszlo nod good night to each other. Laszlo and Ilsa start to the door, Renault with them.

We get a close view of RICK as he watches them go. Renault can be heard speaking.

RENAULT'S VOICE. I'd better get you a cab—this time of night—gasoline rationing—

The revolving door is heard turning.

We see the exterior of the CAFÉ as the three come out. Renault walks to the curb and is heard to blow his whistle.

Laszlo lights a cigarette, and speaks very casually . . .

> LASZLO. A very puzzling fellow, this Rick. Just what sort is he?

Ilsa doesn't look at him. With an effort she keeps her voice steady.

> ILSA. I really can't say. I met him in Paris. We were acquaintances . . .

A cab is heard drawing up. Ilsa moves forward; Laszlo follows her. And at this the view moves up to the sign "Rick's."

This dissolves to THE SIGN—now dark—illuminated only as the revolving beacon from the airport strikes it. Then we see the interior of RICK's: The customers have all gone. Sam switches off the last of the house lights. The revolving beacon from the airfield sends its beam through the window. As it slowly circles the room, the finger of light reveals Rick still sitting at the same table. There is a jigger glass of Bourbon on the table directly in front of him—and another glass empty on the table before an empty chair. Near at hand is a bottle from which this one drink, exactly, has been poured. Rick just sits, staring at the drink. His face is entirely expressionless.

During the following scene the beacon continues its gyration, picking up first one speaker and then the other in its sweep around the room. (The effect should be to create a mood of unreality that will make the flashback a plausible device.)

> SAM. Boss. (*Receiving no answer*) Boss, ain't you going to bed? (*Receiving no answer*) Don't just sit and look a hole in that drink, Boss. (*Receiving no answer*) Pour it back and come to bed!
>
> RICK. Not tonight, Sam. Tonight I've got a date with the heeby-jeebies.

> SAM (*scared*). Boss, no. Listen to me, Boss. (*He comes quickly to him.*) I've been with you a long time now. She's bad luck. You was doing fine until she come. Boss, let's get out of here!
>
> RICK. I've got a date with the little green men—and pink elephants, dancing in the moonlight in the Place Concorde— And a ferris wheel at Montmartre, and the lights of La Belle Aurore, and the rotten smell of the flowers in the Bois.
>
> SAM (*pleading*). Boss, we'll take a car and drive all night. We'll get drunk. We'll go fishin' and stay away until she's gone.
>
> RICK. Shut up and go home, will yuh?
>
> SAM. No, suh. Ah'm stayin' right here.
>
> RICK (*strangely*). They grab Ugarte, then she walks in. That's the way it goes. One in and one out—Sam.
>
> SAM. Yes, Boss . . .
>
> RICK. If it's December 1941 in Casablanca, what time is it in New York?
>
> SAM (*puzzled; muttering*). What? My watch stopped.
>
> RICK. I bet they're asleep in New York. I bet they're asleep all over America . . . (*Returning to his thought*) Of all the gin joints in all the towns in all the world, she walks into mine (*As Sam begins to play softly*) What's that you're playin'?
>
> SAM. Oh, just a little somethin' of my own.
>
> RICK. Well, stop it. You know what I want to hear—
>
> SAM (*hesitating*). No, I don't.

RICK. You played it for her. You can play it for me.

SAM. Well, I don't think I can remember it—

RICK. If she can stand it (*with bitter resolve*) I can!— Play it!

SAM (*sadly*). Yes, Boss . . .

Softly Sam begins to play "As Time Goes By," and the view moves up to Rick, who is staring into the past, then concentrates on the drink on the table before him. We get the effect of the glass slowly turning into an hour-glass —the liquid flowing instead of sand.

And this dissolves into FLASHBACKS: A quick view of PARIS, dissolving to the CHAMPS-ÉLYSÉES on a spring day—Rick is driving a small, open car slowly along the boulevard, and close beside him, with her arm linked in his, sits Ilsa. This dissolves to an EXCURSION BOAT on the Seine at night, an orchestra playing French music. By themselves, at the rail of the boat, stand Rick and Ilsa; they are transported by the night, by the music, by each other.—This dissolves to RICK'S PARIS APARTMENT, Ilsa at the window fixing flowers, Rick opening champagne and Ilsa joining him.

RICK. Who are you really? What were you before? What did you do? What did you think?

ILSA. We said "no questions."

RICK. Here's looking at you, kid. (*They drink.*)

We then see a swank PARIS CAFÉ, where Rick and Ilsa are dancing; then ILSA'S PARIS APARTMENT, with Rick and Ilsa.

ILSA. A franc for your thoughts.

RICK. In America they'd only bring a penny . . . it'd be about all they're worth, I guess.

ILSA. I'm willing to be overcharged— come on—tell me.

RICK. Well, I was wondering.

ILSA. Yes?

RICK. Why I was so lucky—why I should find you waiting for me to come along.

ILSA. Why there is no other man in my life? (*As Rick nods*) Well, that's easy. There was. And he's dead.

RICK. I'm sorry. I forgot we said "no questions." I'll never ask another.

ILSA (*kissing him*). This should be answer enough.

A STREET in Paris appears as people are staring down from their windows. We see a loudspeaker wagon, around which is clustered a group of frightened French people. A harsh German voice is barking out the tragic news of the Nazi push toward Paris. Parisians are being told how to act when the conquerors march in.—Then RICK and ILSA are seen together.

RICK. Nothing will stop them now. Wednesday—Thursday at the latest —they'll be in Paris.

ILSA (*frightened*). Richard, they'll find out your record. It won't be safe for you here.

RICK (*smiling*). I'm on their blacklist already—their roll of honor.

This dissolves to a SMALL CAFÉ in the Montmartre, a sign over the café reading "LA BELLE AURORE,' and this in turn dissolves to a view of SAM playing at the piano, "As Time Goes By," blending in with the background music.

He looks happily over his shoulder.—And now Ilsa is leaning on the piano, listening. Nobody else is in the room—everyone being in the street, listening to the loudspeaker. Ilsa's attitude, as she listens, is very distraught. There is evidently something on her mind—and it isn't all concerned with the war.

ILSA (*trying to shake off her mood*). Sam—all the—how do you call them?—"hot" piano players say they never took a lesson in their lives. Of course, you never did, did you, Sam?

SAM (*gravely*). Studied twelve years. Juilliard Foundation, New York.

ILSA (*wryly*). Well—all the best theories are going under these days.

Rick, bearing a champagne bottle and glasses, comes into the scene. His manner is wry, but not the bitter wryness we have seen in Casablanca.

RICK. Henri wants us to finish this bottle and then three more. (*Pouring*) He says he'll water his garden with champagne before he lets the Germans drink any of it. (*He hands the glasses to Ilsa and Sam.*)

SAM (*looking at his glass*). This sorta takes the sting outa bein' Occupied, doesn't it, Mister Rick?

But now a shout is heard from the people in the street, and Rick and Ilsa look at each other, then hurry to the window.—Thereupon the scene cuts to an OPEN WINDOW as Rick and Ilsa approach it. The loudspeaker is blaring in German.

RICK. My German's a little rusty . . .

ILSA (*sadly*). It's the Gestapo. They say they expect to be in Paris tomorrow. They are telling us how to act when they come marching in.

They are silent, depressed.

ILSA (*smiling faintly*). With the whole world crumbling we pick this time to fall in love.

RICK (*with an abrupt laugh*). Yeah. It's pretty bad timing. (*He looks at her.*) Where were you ten years ago?

ILSA (*trying to cheer him up*). Ten years ago? Let's see . . . (*She laughs.*) Oh, yes. I was having a brace put on my teeth. Where were you?

RICK. I was looking for a job.

ILSA (*after a pause, looking at him tenderly*). Rick—Hitler or no Hitler, kiss me.

Rick takes her in his arms, and kisses her hungrily. But while they are locked in an embrace the dull boom of cannon is heard, and Rick and Ilsa separate.

ILSA (*frightened, but trying not to show it*). Was that cannon fire—or was it my heart pounding?

RICK (*grimly*). That was the new seventy-seven. And, judging by the sound, only about thirty-five miles away— (*Another booming is heard—Rick smiles grimly.*) And getting closer every minute.—Drink up. We'll never finish the other three.

In the MONTMARTRE STREET as viewed by Ilsa and Rick through the window, a crowd has collected around the loudspeaker.—Then we see SAM appearing at the window beside Ilsa and Rick.

SAM. The Germans'll be here pretty soon now and they'll come lookin' fer you. . . . And don't forget there's a price on your head. (*Ilsa reacts to this with anxiety.*)

RICK (*drily*). I left a note in my apartment. They'll know where to find me.

Sam shrugs helplessly, and leaves. Ilsa looks carefully at Rick.

ILSA. Oh, it's strange, Rick—I really know so very little about you.

RICK. I know very little about you—just the fact that you had your teeth straightened.

ILSA. Don't joke, Rick. You are in danger. You must leave Paris.

RICK. No, no, no. *We* must leave.

ILSA (*without looking at him*). Yes, of course—we . . .

RICK. Well, the train for Marseilles leaves at five. I'll pick you up at the hotel at four-thirty.

ILSA (*quickly*). No, not at the hotel. I—I have things to do in the city before I leave. I'll meet you at the station.

RICK. All right. The Gare de Leon at a quarter to five. (*A thought strikes him.*) Say—why don't we get married in Marseilles?

ILSA (*evasively*). That's too far ahead to plan . . .

RICK (*happy, excited at the thought of leaving with Ilsa*). Yes, that is too far ahead. I wonder if the engineer on the train could marry us?

ILSA (*laughing nervously*). Oh, Rick . . .

RICK. Why not? The Captain on a ship can. It doesn't seem fair . . . (*But suddenly Ilsa starts to cry softly.*)

RICK. Ilsa—what's the matter?

ILSA (*controlling herself*). Nothing, darling. It's just that I—I love you so much and I hate the Germans so much. It sort of . . . (*She stops and looks at Rick.*) Oh, Rick—it's a crazy world—anything can happen— If you shouldn't get away— If—if something should keep us apart. Wherever they put you—Wherever I'll be—I want you to know— (*She can't go on—she lifts her face to his.*) Rick— (*He kisses her gently.*) No. Kiss me as though—as though it were the last time.

He looks into her eyes, then kisses her—as though it *were* the last time. Sam is again heard playing "As Time Goes By."

This dissolves to the CLOCK OVER THE GARE DE LEON. The hands stand at three minutes to five. A teeming rain spatters against the roof of the building. The view then moves along the station platform, where a crowd of bedraggled refugees stand shivering in the cold rain. There is a hectic, fevered excitement evident in the faces we pass. This is the last train out of Paris! The moving view stops at Rick, who is glancing at his watch, then up at the clock. It is two minutes before train time. Rain is pouring over his head and shoulders, but he seems not to notice. Suddenly Sam appears with an envelope clasped in his hand.

RICK. Where is she? Have you seen her?

SAM. No, Mr. Richard. I can't find her. She checked out of the hotel. But this note came just after you left.

Rick grabs the letter. He fumbles as he tries unsuccessfully to open it, but at this moment the train pulls into the station, and there is a hubbub among the crowd. Finally Rick gets the envelope open, and stares down at the letter.—We see the LETTER, which reads:

"Richard:
I cannot go with you or ever see you again. You must not ask why. Just believe that I love you. Go, my darling, and God bless you.
Ilsa."

SAM'S VOICE (*frantically*). That's the last call, Mr. Richard. Do you hear me? Come on, Mr. Richard. Come on!

The raindrops pour down on the letter, smudging the writing. We hear the Train Announcer calling *En voiture* (*All aboard!*) The train gives a long, mournful whistle.

The scene dissolving, we watch the hour-glass changing into the drink. The view draws back from the glass, then moves to a closeup of Rick. He still stares at the drink. There is no sound of music now, only utter silence. Sam has gone home. The circle of light passes over Rick's face and sweeps out, and only by a flicker on his face do we follow the light around the room.

The next time it passes, Rick's eyes are caught by the light and his head turns, following it. The circle reaches the door, and we see Ilsa standing in the doorway. The circle passes on, and in the darkness it is hard to tell that she is still there.

RICK is then seen staring at the doorway. It is probable that at first he thinks it is imagination that is playing a trick on him. The light sweeps over him again. His expression hardens.

ILSA is now seen at the doorway in the darkness.

ILSA (*calling out*). Rick.

As she starts forward, the light passes over her. Her face is eager and pleading.

At the TABLE Rick gets half to his feet as she enters the scene. The light sweeps by.

RICK. We closed up at one o'clock.

ILSA. I came back. I have to talk to you.

Her manner is a little uncertain, a little tentative—but with a quiet determination beneath it.

RICK. I saved my first drink to have with you. (*He reaches for the bottle.*)

ILSA. No. No, Rick, not tonight.

She sits down in the chair before the empty glass. Her eyes are searching his face, but there is no expression on it except a cold and impassive one. He sits down, too, and reaches for his glass and half-gestures with it toward her.

RICK. Mind if I . . . ?

ILSA. No. . . .

RICK. *Especially* tonight.

He drains his glass and, reaching for the bottle, pours himself another drink. She watches this with a look which says that she wishes he wouldn't drink tonight.

RICK. Why did you have to come to Casablanca? There are other places.

ILSA. I wouldn't have come if I had known that you were here. Believe me, Rick, that's the truth, I didn't know.

RICK. Funny about your voice. How it hasn't changed. I can still hear it— "Rick dear, I'll go with you anyplace. We'll get on a train together and we'll never stop. All my life, forevermore–"

ILSA. Please don't. (*As she watches him taking another drink*) I can understand how you feel.

RICK. And funny about your looks. *They've* changed a little. At least from that first day. And the other days.— How long was it we had, honey?

ILSA. I didn't count the days.

RICK. All hail the happy days! (*He takes another drink.*) When there were no questions asked, and faith was something all in one piece—

ILSA. Do you remember, Rick? I can remember. The day at the circus— the excursion boat—

RICK. Mostly I remember the wow finish. A guy standing on a platform, and the last train about to pull out, and Sam pushing him to get on—and the guy just standing there with a comical look on his face, because his insides had been kicked out by a pair of French heels.

ILSA (*after a pause*). Can I tell you a story, Rick?

RICK. Has it got a wow finish, honey, has it got a twist?

ILSA. I don't know the finish yet.

RICK. Well, go on, tell it. Maybe one will come to you as you go along.

ILSA. It's about a girl who was very young. She had just come to Paris from her home in Oslo. At the house of some friends she met a man—a very great and good man. They became friends—he became her teacher. She had been brought up very provincially, and he opened up for her a whole beautiful world of knowledge and thoughts and ideals. Everything she ever knew or ever became was because of his goodness. And she looked up at him and worshipped him with a feeling she supposed was love—

RICK (*definitely interrupting*). Yes, that's very pretty. I heard a story once. In fact, I've heard a lot of stories in my time. They went along with the sound of a tinny piano in the parlor downstairs. "Mister, I met a man when I was only a kid," they'd always begin.

ILSA (*shuddering as she gets up*). I'll go now.

RICK (*as she walks away*). Well, I guess neither one of our stories was very funny. (*Then in a moment he adds.*) But you might tell me just who it was you left me for. Was it Laszlo—or were there others in between—or aren't you the kind that tells?

ILSA is too proud to answer him. She goes to the doorway and walks out.— Rick's head slumps over the table. Gradually his body sags over the table. The glass tips over, spilling its contents over the cloth, as the scene fades out.

PART TWO

RENAULT'S OFFICE fades in. It is day. Strasser is with Renault.

STRASSER. I strongly suspect that Senor Ugarte left the Letters of Transit with Herr Blaine. I would suggest you search the Café immediately and thoroughly.

RENAULT. If Rick has the Letters, he is much too smart to let us find them there.

STRASSER. You give him credit for too much cleverness. My impression was that he's just another blundering American.

RENAULT. Quite so. But we mustn't underestimate American blundering. (*Innocently*) I was with them when they "blundered" into Berlin in 1918.

As Strasser looks at him, the scene cuts to the DOOR which opens, and a native policeman enters.

NATIVE POLICEMAN (*saluting*). Captain Renault—

RENAULT (*to Strasser and the others*). You will excuse me for one moment—

As he walks toward the door, the scene cuts to another view of the DOOR, which the native policeman has left slightly ajar. Through the opening two beautiful women can be seen standing down the hall. When Renault comes into the scene the native policeman whispers to him. Renault looks through the opening at the two women.

RENAULT (*thoughtfully*). Which one? (*He sighs.*) Ten years ago there would have been no problem— Oh, well, tell the dark one to wait in my private office and we'll go into the visa matter thoroughly.

NATIVE POLICEMAN (*starting away*). Yes, Captain.

RENAULT (*taking another quick look down the hall*). And it wouldn't hurt to have the other one leave her address and phone number.

This cuts to STRASSER as Renault comes up to him.

RENAULT. Now—where were we?

STRASSER (*annoyed*). Don't you think, Captain Renault, that with so much important work to be done you could devote a little less time to personal matters?

RENAULT (*shrugging*). Well—you enjoy war; I enjoy women. We are both very good at our jobs.

STRASSER. I think the German viewpoint is a much healthier one.

RENAULT. You are probably right, Major Strasser. At least your work keeps you outdoors.

Strasser shakes his head. It is hopeless to argue with Renault.

STRASSER. As to Herr Laszlo, we want him watched twenty-four hours a day.

RENAULT (*reassuringly*). It may interest you to know that at this very moment M'sieur Laszlo is on his way here.

This cuts to the exterior of the PREFECTURE OF POLICE. People are packed around the entrance as Laszlo and Ilsa make their way through the jam.

This scene dissolving, we see the door being opened by the Native Officer, who ushers in Laszlo and Ilsa. Both Renault and Strasser, in the foreground, rise, facing the couple as they walk toward them. Renault moves forward to offer Ilsa his hand.

RENAULT. I am delighted to see you both. Did you have a good night's rest?

LASZLO (*calmly*). I slept very well.

RENAULT (*laughing*). That's strange. No one is supposed to sleep well in Casablanca.

LASZLO (*briefly*). May we proceed with the business?

RENAULT. With pleasure. Won't you sit down?

LASZLO. Thank you.

STRASSER (*now as cold as Laszlo*). Very well, Herr Laszlo, we will not mince words. You are an escaped prisoner of the Reich. So far you have been fortunate in eluding us. You have reached Casablanca—it is my duty to see that you stay in Casablanca.

LASZLO. Whether or not you succeed in fulfilling your duty is, of course, problematical.

STRASSER. Not at all. Captain Renault's signature is necessary on every exit visa.

LASZLO. I am perfectly aware of the Captain's official duties.

STRASSER (*turning to Renault*). Captain, would you think it is possible that M'sieur Laszlo will receive a visa?

RENAULT. I am afraid not. I regret, M'sieur.

LASZLO (*casually*). Well, perhaps I shall like it in Casablanca.

STRASSER. And Mademoiselle?

ILSA. You need not be concerned about me.

LASZLO (*preparing to rise*). Is that all you wish to tell us?

STRASSER (*smiling*). Do not be in such a hurry, M'sieur Laszlo. You have all the time in the world. You may be in Casablanca indefinitely. ... (*He suddenly leans forward and speaks intently.*) Or you may leave for Lisbon tomorrow. On one condition.

LASZLO. And that is?

STRASSER (*leaning forward, speaking intently*). You know the leaders of the Underground Movement in Prague, in Paris, in Amsterdam, in Brussels, in Oslo, in Belgrade, in Athens ...

LASZLO. Yes—even in Berlin.

STRASSER. Even in Berlin. If you will furnish me with their names and their exact whereabouts—you will have your exit visa in the morning ...

RENAULT (*tongue in cheek again*). And the honor of having served the Third Reich!

LASZLO. Before France fell I was in a German concentration camp for a year. That is honor enough for a lifetime.

STRASSER. You will give us the names?

LASZLO. If I didn't give them to you in the concentration camp where you had more "persuasive methods" at your disposal, I certainly won't give them to you now. (*The passionate conviction in his voice now revealing the crusader*) And what if you track down these men and kill them? What if you murdered all of us? From every corner of Europe hundreds of men—thousands—would rise up to take our places. Even Nazis cannot kill that fast. ...

STRASSER. Herr Laszlo, you have a reputation for eloquence which I can now understand. But in one respect you are mistaken. You said the enemies of the Reich could all be replaced. But there is one exception—*no one could take your place* in the event anything ... er ... unfortunate should occur to you while you were trying to escape.

LASZLO. You will not dare to interfere with me here. This is still Unoccupied France. Any violation of neutrality will reflect on Captain Renault.

RENAULT. M'sieur, in so far as it is in my power. . . .

LASZLO. Thank you.

RENAULT. By the way, last night you evinced an interest in Senor Ugarte.

LASZLO (*warily*). Yes.

RENAULT. I believe you have a message for him.

LASZLO (*pretending ignorance*). Nothing important, but may I speak to him now?

STRASSER (*wryly*). You would find the conversation a trifle one-sided. (*After a pause*) Senor Ugarte is dead.

ILSA (*as Laszlo and Ilsa look at each other*). Oh.

RENAULT (*picking up the papers on his desk*). I am making out the report now— (*Coming around the desk*) We haven't quite decided yet whether he committed suicide or died trying to escape.

LASZLO (*after a pause*). You are quite finished with us?

STRASSER (*bowing*). For the time being.

LASZLO. Good day.

As Ilsa and Laszlo leave, the young officer comes in. When the door has closed on Ilsa and Laszlo, Renault addresses him.

RENAULT (*to the young officer*). Undoubtedly their next step will be to the Black Market. (*Significantly*) You will—

YOUNG OFFICER. Yes, Captain. By the way—another visa problem has come up.

RENAULT (*happily, as he looks at himself in the mirror*). Show her in.

This scene dissolves to the exterior of the BLUE PARROT CAFÉ in the native section of the city. It is flanked on all sides by bazaars, shops and stalls, selling all kinds of merchandise.—We then see the BAZAAR which obviously sells linens, tablecloths, laces, etc. Two young American men come up to the bazaar.

FIRST AMERICAN (*to the vendor*). Has the bus from Tangiers arrived yet?

VENDOR. In a few minutes, M'sieur. (*At this point a Frenchman comes into the scene.*)

FRENCHMAN (*to the vendor*). The bus from Tangiers—?

VENDOR. Very soon now.

The Frenchman nods, leans up against the wall and waits. A well-to-do Arab approaches and converses with the vendor.

SECOND AMERICAN (*to the first American*). Did he ask after the bus from Tangiers?

FIRST AMERICAN. Obviously.

SECOND AMERICAN. What's it made of —gold?

FIRST AMERICAN (*laughing*). The bus driver is the attraction. (*He looks at his watch.*) In a little while he'll pull up and come out carrying cases of sugar, American cigarettes, English tobacco, strips of leather—everything that is rationed or illegal to sell in Casablanca. This spot is the center of the Black Market in Casablanca. I wouldn't mind having a piece of it—

The scene cuts to the ENTRANCE TO THE BLUE PARROT. SENOR FERRARI comes out, and looks impatiently up and down the street, whereupon the view cuts to the TWO AMERICANS.

FIRST AMERICAN. That's Senor Ferrari. He's pretty near got a monopoly on the Black Market here.

SENOR FERRARI is about to go back into the café when Annina and Jan walk up to him.

JAN. Excuse me—you are Senor Ferrari, are you not?

FERRARI. Yes?

JAN. We were told that you might be able to help us. (*At this Ferrari looks at them a moment before answering.*)

FERRARI. Come in.

As he leads the way into the Blue Parrot, the scene dissolves to SENOR FERRARI'S OFFICE. He is seated behind his desk talking to Jan and Annina.

FERRARI. Exit visas?— Well, now—that's Captain Renault's province. Have you tried him?

JAN (*nodding*). His price is 2,000 francs.

ANNINA. We haven't got that much.

FERRARI. Of course, I'm not saying I can get you exit visas—or not—but, incidentally, how much money have you got?

JAN. We have 300 francs left, Senor.

At this Ferrari leans back in his chair and laughs until his whole huge frame shakes.

FERRARI (*wiping the tears from his eyes*). 300 francs! What innocents! In the Black Market in Casablanca 300 francs will get you a lump of sugar—nothing more.

Jan and Annina look at each other in consternation. Ferrari, still laughing, opens his desk drawer, takes out a cigarette case, and opens it, revealing several lumps of sugar in it, instead of cigarettes.

FERRARI (*handing Annina a lump*). Here—with my compliments. But exit visas—that's another matter. (*And he gets up from behind the desk.*)

We see the interior of the BLUE PARROT CAFÉ, much less pretentious than RICK'S. The bar is well populated, but there are only a few people at the tables. Rick comes into the scene, and walks toward Ferrari. He is wearing his usual dead pan.—This cuts to the OUTSIDE DOOR TO THE OFFICE. As Rick comes into the scene the door opens and Ferrari comes out, ushering out Jan and Annina, who look very downhearted.

FERRARI (*patting Annina's shoulder*). There—don't be too downhearted. Perhaps you can come to terms with Captain Renault.

JAN. Thank you very much, Senor.

He leads Annina away. Rick watches the couple as they move toward the door. Then he walks in the direction of Ferrari.

RICK. Hello, Ferrari. (*At this Senor Ferrari turns around, pleased to see Rick.*)

FERRARI. Good morning, Rick.

RICK. I see the bus is in. I'll take my shipment with me.

FERRARI. No hurry. I shall have it sent over. Have a drink with me.

RICK. I never drink in the morning. And every time you send my shipment over, it's a little short.

FERRARI (*chuckling*). Carrying charges, my friend, carrying charges . . . (*Pulling out a chair*) Here—sit down. There's something I want to talk over with you, anyhow. (*Rick sits down—Ferrari hails a waiter.*) The Bourbon . . . (*To Rick—sighing deeply*) The news about Ugarte upset me very much.

RICK. You're a fat hypocrite. You don't feel any sorrier for Ugarte than I do.

FERRARI (*eying Rick closely*). Of course not. What upsets me is the fact that Ugarte is dead and no one knows where those Letters of Transit are.

RICK (*dead pan*). Practically no one.

FERRARI. If I could lay my hands on those Letters, I could make a fortune.

RICK. So could I. And I'm a poor businessman.

FERRARI. I have a proposition for whoever has those Letters. I will handle the entire transaction, get rid of the Letters, take all the risk—for a small percentage.

RICK. And the carrying charges.

FERRARI (*smiling*). Naturally there will be a few incidental expenses—(*Looking at Rick squarely*) That is the proposition I have for whoever has those Letters.

RICK (*drily*). I'll tell him when he comes in.

FERRARI. Rick—I'll put my cards on the table. I think you know where those Letters are.

RICK (*shrugging*). Well, you're in good company. Renault and Strasser probably think so too. I came here to give them a chance to ransack my place.

FERRARI. Rick—don't be a fool. Take me into your confidence. You need a partner—

But Rick isn't listening to him. He is looking through the open door in the direction of the linen bazaar.

We see the LINEN BAZAAR in front of which ILSA and LASZLO have paused. Laszlo leaves Ilsa and starts walking toward the BLUE PARROT CAFÉ. Thereupon the scene cuts to RICK and SENOR FERRARI.

RICK (*interrupting Ferrari, as he gets up*). Excuse me. I'll be getting back.

Ferrari nods, and takes a long drink. The scene moves with Rick as he walks toward the door, where he meets Laszlo coming in. Laszlo stops, and addresses him politely.

LASZLO. Good morning . . .

RICK (*with a jerk of his head, not pausing*). Senor Ferrari is the fat gent at the table.

He continues out, leaving Laszlo looking after him with a puzzled expression.

We see a LINEN STALL where Ilsa is examining a napkin set which an Arab vendor is endeavoring to sell. There is a sign on the counter by the display which reads: "700 francs." From Ilsa's manner it is apparent that she is aware of Rick's approach and is pretending to be absorbed in the article to escape his notice.

ARAB. . . . You will not find a treasure like this in all Morocco, Mademoiselle. Only seven hundred francs.

RICK (*appearing*). You're being cheated.

Ilsa takes a split second to compose herself. When she turns to Rick, her manner is politely formal.

ILSA. It doesn't matter, thank you.

ARAB. Ah—the lady is a friend of Rick's? For friends of Rick's we have a small discount. Seven hundred francs, did I say? You can have it for two hundred.

Reaching under the counter, he takes out a sign reading "200 francs" and replaces the other sign with it.

RICK. If my fuzzy memory can be relied on, I wasn't very cordial to you when you called on me last night.

You can't tell just how he means it—whether he is sorry or not. Rick isn't giving anything away.

ILSA. That doesn't matter, either.

ARAB (*beaming*). For *special* friends of Rick's we have a *special* discount. One hundred francs. Shall I wrap it up? (*Business of replacing sign with one reading "100 francs."*)

RICK. Your exit line was a humdinger —but it left me a little confused. Or maybe it was the Bourbon. If you care to clear it up a little more . . .

ARAB. Wait. I have some lace tablecloths— Will you excuse me—?

ILSA. I'm really not interested.

ARAB (*already on his way to the rear*). Please, one moment. . . . Please.

The Arab is now out of sight. There is a short silence between Ilsa and Rick. Ilsa pretends to be interested in the goods on the counter. Rick is just looking at her. We can guess now that he really would like to know—that beneath his enigmatic and rather hard exterior, his feelings are at work, but his hurt pride doesn't let them show.

RICK. Why did you come back? To tell me why you ran out on me at the railway station?

ILSA. Yes.

RICK. Well, you can tell me now. (*Wryly*) I'm reasonably sober.

ILSA (*softly*). I don't think I will, Rick.

RICK. Why not? After all, I got stuck with a railroad ticket. I think I am entitled to know.

ILSA. Last night I saw what has happened to you. The Rick I knew in Paris, I could tell him. He'd understand. But the one who looked at me with such hatred— I'll be leaving Casablanca soon and we'll never see each other again. We knew very little about each other when we were in love in Paris. If we leave it that way maybe we'll remember those days, not Casablanca, not last night.

RICK. Did you run out on me because you couldn't take it? Because you knew what it would be like, hiding from the police, running away all the time?

ILSA (*proudly*). You can believe that, if you want to.

RICK. Well, I'm not running away any more. I'm settled now; above a saloon, it's true. But (*ironically*) . . . walk up a flight. I'll be expecting you.

We again see the Moroccan crowd as Rick and Ilsa continue.

RICK. Well, all the same you'll come to me. Some day you'll lie to Laszlo. You'll be there.

Ilsa smiles at him, and shakes her head.

RICK (*bitterly*). How is it—what you wouldn't do for me, you're doing for Laszlo? All along the refugee trail— you've done plenty of running away.

Don't tell me you're in love with him!

ILSA (*after a pause*). Victor Laszlo is a great and important man.

RICK (*sarcastically*). I know. That's what attracted you to him. But enough to make you leave all the comforts of Paris?

ILSA (*steadily*). It also happens that Victor Laszlo is my husband and has been for some time. (*After a pause*) Even when I knew you in Paris.

The Arab returns with some lace.

ILSA. Please don't bother. Some other time perhaps.

She turns away, and walks in the direction of the BLUE PARROT. Rick stares after her.

ARAB (*to Rick*). M'sieur Rick, would you be interested in some lace tablecloths? A special price for any friend of Madame's. . . .

As Rick turns to go, the plainclothesman we saw shadowing Ilsa and Laszlo on the street saunters into the scene, and leans up against the bazaar.

The scene cuts to the BLUE PARROT CAFÉ with LASZLO, SENOR FERRARI and ILSA. Ferrari is helping Ilsa into a chair.

FERRARI. I was just telling M'sieur Laszlo that, unfortunately, I am not able to help him.

ILSA (*troubled*). Oh.

LASZLO (*to Ilsa*). You see, my dear, the word has gone around. I am a marked man.

FERRARI (*to Ilsa*). As leader of all illegal activities in Casablanca, I am an influential and respected man, but it would be worth my life to do anything for M'sieur Laszlo. You, however, are a different matter.

LASZLO. Senor Ferrari thinks it might just be possible to obtain an exit visa for you.

ILSA. You mean—for me to go on alone?

FERRARI. And *only* alone.

LASZLO. I will stay here, Ilsa, and keep on trying. Perhaps in a little while . . .

FERRARI. We might as well be frank, M'sieur. It will take a miracle to get you out of Casablanca. And the Germans have outlawed miracles.

ILSA (*to Ferrari*). We are only interested in two visas, Senor.

LASZLO. Please, Ilsa. We mustn't be hasty.

ILSA (*firmly*). No, Victor. No.

FERRARI (*getting to his feet*). Excuse me. I will be at the bar. (*He bows and goes.*)

LASZLO. Ilsa, I won't let you stay here. You must get to America. And believe me—somehow—I'll get out— I'll join you . . .

ILSA (*slowly*). Do you really want me to go on alone, Victor? Do you really want to stay here—without me?

LASZLO (*after a pause—honestly*). No.

ILSA. Very well then, the subject is closed. We'll have a drink and go back to the hotel.

LASZLO. No, Ilsa, you must listen to me . . .

ILSA (*interrupting*). Victor—if the situation were different—if I had to stay and there were only a visa for you—would you take it?

LASZLO (*after some hesitation—not very convincingly*). Ye-es, I would.

Ilsa smiles faintly.

ILSA. I see. When I had trouble getting out of Lilles, why didn't you leave me there? And when I was sick in Marseilles and held you up for two weeks and you were in danger every minute of the time—why didn't you leave me then?

LASZLO (*with a wry smile*). I meant to, but something serious always held me up. My—my laundry was late coming back—or there was a cinema I wanted to see . . .

ILSA (*smiling at him fondly*). We'll just forget about the drink. A pack of American cigarettes—and we'll go home.

LASZLO (*reaching over, putting his hand over hers*). I love you very much, Ilsa.

ILSA (*affectionately*). That makes me feel very good.

LASZLO. I also need you very much.

ILSA. And that makes me feel very important.

LASZLO (*smiling faintly*). Don't tell anyone. Leaders of the Underground are not supposed to be in love.

ILSA (*smiling*). Your secret is safe with me. (*As she gets up*) Ferrari is waiting for our answer.

We see FERRARI at the bar talking to the bartender.

BARTENDER (*shaking his head*). Three of our silver shakers were stolen last night.

FERRARI (*not disturbed*). Hassid El Bey, most likely. Go over there later and buy them back. Not more than fifty francs though.

Ilsa and Laszlo come into the scene.

LASZLO. We've come to a decision. For the present we'll go on looking for two visas. Thank you very much.

FERRARI (*his manner indicating it is hopeless*). Well—good luck. But be careful— (*With a flick of his eyes in the direction of the bazaar*) You know you're being shadowed?

LASZLO (*not turning*). Of course. It becomes an instinct.

FERRARI (*shrewdly—looking at Ilsa*). I observe that you in one respect are a very fortunate man . . . M'sieur, I am moved to make one more suggestion— Why, I do not know. Because it cannot possibly profit me, but . . . have you heard about Senor Ugarte and the Letters of Transit?

LASZLO. Yes. Something.

FERRARI. Those Letters were not found on Ugarte when they arrested him.

LASZLO (*after a moment's pause*). Do you know where they are?

FERRARI. Not for sure, M'sieur. But I will venture a guess—that Ugarte left those Letters with M'sieur Rick.

Ilsa's face darkens. Laszlo quietly observes her.

LASZLO. Rick?

FERRARI. He is a difficult customer, that Rick. One never knows what he will do, or why. But it is worth a chance.

LASZLO (*starting to rise*). Thank you very much.

ILSA. And for your coffee, Senor— (*Bravely*) I shall miss that when we leave Casablanca.

FERRARI (*bowing*). You were gracious to share it with me. Good day, Mademoiselle . . . M'sieur.

LASZLO. Good day.

Ferrari walks toward the entrance of his café, and the scene moves with Ilsa and Laszlo as they start down the marketplace.

LASZLO. Always Rick.

He watches Ilsa out of the corner of his eye as they go along, and the scene fades out.

The ENTRANCE TO RICK's in the late afternoon: An attendant is sweeping out some broken glass. Rick appears and walks to the entrance. He just pauses a moment and notes the broken glass, kicks some of it with his foot, exchanges a look with the attendant, and goes in. —Then we see the interior of the CAFÉ. The place has been ransacked thoroughly—some things broken, but mostly things scattered around. The waiters and bartenders are trying to put things back together again. Rick notes it all as he walks through. In the foreground Sam is disconsolately trying to fit together his broken piano bench. He looks up as Rick comes to him.

RICK. Renault's boys gave us a nice massage.

SAM. They went through everything.

RICK. Everything?

He opens the piano and looks in. He reaches in and brings out the envelope and puts it in the breast pocket of his coat. He winks at Sam. Sam's eyes are popping.

RICK. Not quite everything. (*And he starts away.*)

The scene fades out.

The exterior of RICK's fades in, at night. The DARK EUROPEAN is entering the café, his arm around a prosperous male tourist.

DARK EUROPEAN (*solicitously*). Put yourself in my hands. There are vultures in there—vultures— Be on guard—

This cuts to the BAR where SASCHA is gazing intently at a slip of paper. He has many bottles lined up in front of him—and as he looks at the slip of paper he mixes ingredients. Carl comes into the scene.

CARL. Two brandies for the Leuchtags, please.

SASCHA (*not even looking at him*). Bottle's down de bar. Halp yourself. I'm too busy.

CARL. Too busy?

SASCHA (*nodding*). A Yankee gave me dis recipe for American drink. In two or t'ree years I will be in America, please Heaven—so I'm prectisink.

CARL (*reaching for the brandy bottle*). What is the name of the drink?

SASCHA (*peering very closely at the slip of paper*). It sounds vunderful— (*Reading with difficulty*) Meecky— Feen—Dere are coint'nly some strange things in it.

CARL. Sounds good. When you perfect it—try it out on me. (*And he walks away.*)

The scene cuts to the LEUCHTAGS, a middle-aged couple, at a TABLE as Carl appears with the brandy.

MR. LEUCHTAG. Carl, have a brandy with us.

MRS. LEUCHTAG (*beaming with happiness*). To celebrate our leaving for America tomorrow.

CARL (*pouring*). Thank you very much. I thought you would ask me, so I brought the good brandy.

MR. LEUCHTAG. Frau Leuchtag and I are speaking nothing but English now.

MRS. LEUCHTAG. So we should feel at home ven ve get to America.

CARL (*handing them the drinks*). A very wise idea.

MR. LEUCHTAG (*raising his glass*). To America.

Mrs. Leuchtag and Carl repeat "To America." They clink glasses and drink.

MR. LEUCHTAG (*proudly, to display his good English, addressing his wife*). Liebchen—what watch?

MRS. LEUCHTAG (*glancing at her wrist watch*). Ten watch.

MR. LEUCHTAG (*surprised*). Such much?

CARL (*reassuringly*). You will get along beautifully in America.

This cuts to the BAR where we see RICK and RENAULT: Rick is drinking steadily.

CARL (*handing him a drink*). Monsieur Rick, you are getting to be your best customer.

RENAULT (*genially*). Well, Ricky, I'm very pleased with you. Now you're beginning to live like a Frenchman.

RICK. That was some going-over your men gave my place this afternoon. We just got it cleaned up in time to open.

RENAULT. Well, I told Strasser he would not find the Letters here. But I told my men to be especially destructive. You know how that impresses Germans. (*He pours himself a drink.*) Rick, have you got those Letters of Transit? (*At this Rick looks at him a moment.*)

RICK (*steadily*). Louis—are you Pro-Vichy or Free French?

RENAULT (*promptly*). Serves me right for asking a direct question. The subject is closed.

This cuts to RICK and RENAULT as Rick is gazing at Yvonne and a German officer approaching the bar.

RICK. I see Yvonne has gone over to the enemy.

RENAULT. Who knows? In her own way she may constitute an entire second front— (*Out of the corner of his eye he sees Annina approaching—he gets up.*) I think it is time for me to flatter Major Strasser a little. See you later, Rick. (*He strolls away.*)

Next, at the BAR we see YVONNE and the OFFICER.

GERMAN OFFICER (*arrogantly—to Carl*). French seventy-fives.

YVONNE (*somewhat tight already*). Put up a whole row of 'em, Sascha— (*indicating on the bar with her hand*)—starting here and ending there.

GERMAN OFFICER. We will begin with two.

One of the French officers, standing near her, turns to her: "*Dites—donc, vous n'êtes pas Française vous, d'aller avec les boches comme ça.*" ("Say, you, you are not French to go with the Germans like this.") She replies angrily

"De quoi vous melez-vous." ("What are you butting in for?") At this the German officer turns to the French officer.

GERMAN OFFICER (*clipping his words*). What did you say? Would you kindly repeat it? (*At this, the French officer steps out from the group.*)

FRENCH OFFICER (*drunk enough to be reckless*). What I said is none of your business.

GERMAN OFFICER. I will make it my business—

The German officer raises his fist and the French officer prepares to defend himself. There are exclamations from the people nearby, and Yvonne cries out *"Arretez, je vous en prie."* ("Stop. I beg of you.") Thereupon Rick walks between the two men, and addresses the German.

RICK. I don't like disturbances in my place. Either lay off politics or get out.

The French officer retires, muttering, *"Sale boche, un jour vous aurons notre revanche!"* ("Dirty boche, some day we'll have our revenge!") Then the scene cuts to STRASSER'S TABLE where Renault, Strasser and the other German officers have settled back in their chairs.

STRASSER. ... You see, Captain, the situation is not as much under control as you believe.

RENAULT. My dear Major, we are trying to cooperate with your government. But we cannot regulate the feelings of our people.

STRASSER (*eying him closely*). Captain Renault, are you entirely certain which side you're on?

RENAULT. Frankly, I have no conviction, if that is what you mean. I blow with the wind, and the prevailing wind is blowing from Vichy.

STRASSER. And if it should change?

RENAULT (*smiling*). Oh, surely the Reich does not admit that possibility?

STRASSER. We are concerned about more than Casablanca. We know that every French province in Africa is honeycombed with traitors just waiting their chance—waiting, perhaps, for a leader.

RENAULT (*casually, as he lights a cigarette*). A leader like. ... Laszlo?

STRASSER (*nodding*). I have been thinking. It is too dangerous if we let him go. It may be too dangerous if we let him stay.

RENAULT (*thoughtfully*). I see what you mean. ...

At this point, the scene cuts to the CASHIER'S BOOTH in the GAMBLING ROOM, where Annina is emptying her bag of bills, which she lays on the counter.

ANNINA. Two hundred francs' worth, please.

The Cashier hands out the chips, and takes in the bills. The scene moves with Annina as she crosses to the roulette table, where Jan is bending over the spinning wheel. Annina watches breathlessly over his shoulder. The wheel stops. The Croupier takes in the chips. Jan wipes his forehead.

JAN. Black again ...

ANNINA (*handing him the chips*). This is all we have, Jan. Do you think we should?

JAN (*bitterly*). We might as well have nothing as two hundred francs.

He begins to scatter the chips recklessly over the board. Annina looks at him for a moment, comes to a silent resolve, and walks toward the hallway.— This cuts to ANNINA as she stops, looks in Rick's direction, and steels herself to approach him. Then, her mind made up, she makes her way to his table.

ANNINA. M'sieur Rick . . .

RICK. Yes?

ANNINA. Could I speak to you—just for a moment?

RICK (*looking at her*). How did you get in here? You're under age.

ANNINA. I came with Captain Renault.

RICK (*cynically*). I should have known.

ANNINA. My husband is with me, too.

RICK. He is? (*Looking over to where Renault is seated*) Captain Renault is branching out. (*To Annina*) Sit down.

ANNINA. Thank you.

RICK. Drink? Ah, of course not—Mind if I . . . ?

ANNINA. Oh, no— (*Nervously, as Rick pours himself a drink*) M'sieur Rick—what sort of man is Captain Renault?

RICK (*shrugging*). Like any other man . . . (*After a pause*) Only more so.

ANNINA. I mean—is he trustworthy?—Is his word . . . ?

RICK. Just a minute. Who told you to ask me that?

ANNINA. He did. Captain Renault did.

RICK. I thought so. (*After a pause*) Where's your husband?

ANNINA (*wryly*). At the roulette table—trying to win enough for our exit visas. Of course he is losing.

RICK (*looking at her closely*). How long are you married?

ANNINA (*simply*). Six weeks. (*Rick nods.*) We come from Bulgaria. Things are very bad there, M'sieur. A devil has the people by the throat. So Jan and I, we . . . we did not want our children to grow up in such a country.

RICK (*wearily*). So you decided to go to America.

ANNINA. Yes. But we do not have much money, and travel is so difficult and expensive, M'sieur. It took much more than we thought to get here. Then Captain Renault sees us and he is so kind. He wants to help.

RICK. I'll bet.

ANNINA. He tells me that he can get an exit visa for us. But . . . (*Again she hesitates.*) But we have no money.

RICK. Does Renault know?

ANNINA. Oh, yes.

RICK. And he is *still* willing to give you an exit visa?

ANNINA. Yes, M'sieur. (*At this Rick looks down at his drink for a moment.*)

RICK. And you want to know . . . ?

ANNINA. Will he keep his word, M'sieur?

RICK (*still looking at his drink*). He always has.

There is a silence, and then we see RICK and ANNINA together more closely. Annina is very disturbed.

ANNINA. M'sieur, you are a man. If someone loved you . . . very much, so that your happiness was the only thing in the world that she wanted and . . . she did a bad thing to make certain of it, could you forgive her?

RICK. No one has ever loved me that much.

ANNINA. But, M'sieur, if he never knew . . . if the girl kept this bad thing locked in her heart . . . that would be all right, wouldn't it?

RICK (*harshly*). You want my advice?

ANNINA. Oh, yes, M'sieur, please.

RICK. Go back to Bulgaria.

ANNINA. Oh, b-but if you knew what it means to us to be able to leave Europe—to get to America . . . (*After a pause, sighing*) But if Jan should find out— He is such a boy. In many ways I am so much—so much older than he is.

RICK (*getting up—noncommittally*). Yes. Well—everyone in Casablanca has a problem. Yours may work out. Excuse me.

We get a close view of ANNINA as she looks down at the tablecloth. Her lips are trembling.

ANNINA (*tonelessly*). Thank you— M'sieur.

She gets up, and goes out.—Then we see RICK, dead-pan, as usual, walking among the tables. But he stops short as he sees someone entering. And this cuts to ILSA and LASZLO appearing through the REVOLVING DOOR. Rick comes up to them.

RICK. Good evening.

LASZLO. Good evening. You see, we are here again.

RICK. I take that as a great compliment to Sam. (*To Ilsa*). I suppose to you Sam means Paris of—well—happier days.

ILSA (*quietly*). He does. Could we have a table very close to Sam?

LASZLO (*who has been looking around*). And as far from Major Strasser as possible.

RICK. Well, the geography might be a little difficult to arrange— (*He snaps his fingers for the headwaiter.*)

We get a close view of ILSA as Rick confers with the headwaiter. She is looking at Rick intently. Then we see RICK, ILSA, LASZLO and the HEADWAITER.

HEADWAITER (*to Ilsa and Laszlo*). Right this way, if you please—

LASZLO (*to Rick*). Thank you very much.

RICK (*to Ilsa*). I'll have Sam play "As Time Goes By." I think that's your favorite number?

ILSA (*smiling*). It is. Thank you.

She follows Laszlo to their table. Rick walks to Sam, bends over and whispers something to him. Thereupon Sam shakes his head, but starts to play "As Time Goes By."—Rick looks in Ilsa's direction, but she seems to be paying no particular attention, and Rick saunters toward the gambling room.

The scene cuts to the GAMBLING ROOM as Rick comes in. He looks toward the roulette wheel. Jan and Annina are there. Two players walk away from the table. Jan and Annina are alone then.—We then see the group at the ROULETTE TABLE. Jan's eyes are tragic. As Rick comes into the scene, the croupier is speaking to Jan:

CROUPIER. Do you wish to place another bet, M'sieur?

JAN. No, no, thank you— (*He juggles the two remaining chips in his hands wryly.*) We can't leave without tipping, can we, Annina? (*She just looks at him, dumb with misery.*)

RICK (*to the croupier*). I'll take over the wheel. (*To Jan; dead-pan*) Have you tried twenty-four tonight?

Jan looks at Rick, then at the two chips in his hand. He pauses. He puts the two chips on twenty-four.—Rick spins the wheel.—This cuts to a close view of JAN looking straight ahead; then to a close view of the CROUPIER looking at Rick; then to a close view of CARL in the background, looking at the wheel, fascinated; then to the group at the WHEEL, as it stops spinning.

RICK (*calling out*). Twenty-four.

The croupier pushes a pile of chips onto the number. Jan reaches for it.

RICK (*not even looking at Jan*). Leave it there.

Jan hesitates. Annina looks at Rick.

ANNINA (*to Jan*). Leave it there.

Jan withdraws his hands. In the background, Carl draws a little closer. Rick spins the wheel. Nobody speaks while it spins. When it stops Rick calls out.

RICK. Number twenty-four.

In the background Carl gasps. The croupier shoves a pile of chips towards Jan.

RICK (*to Jan*). Now, take it—and don't ever come back.

In the background the last two customers are seen walking out. One of them is complaining to Carl.

CUSTOMER. Had terrible luck tonight. You sure this place is honest?

CARL (*fervently*). As honest as the day is long!

ANNINA (*to Rick; all choked up*). M'sieur Rick, I—

She kisses him and goes toward Jan —at the cashier's desk. Then we get a close view of JAN and ANNINA together there.

ANNINA. He is an American, Jan. You see, America *must* be a wonderful place.

As Annina and Jan hurry from the room, the scene cuts to a close view of RICK and the CROUPIER.

RICK (*to the croupier*). How were the receipts tonight?

CROUPIER (*drily*). Well—a couple of thousand less than I thought they would be. (*At this, Rick smiles slightly and goes toward the bar.*)

We see the HALLWAY leading to the bar as Rick enters from the gambling room. Carl comes up to Rick as they walk toward the bar.

CARL (*solicitously*). May I get you a cup of coffee, M'sieur Rick?

RICK. No, thanks.

CARL. I wish to tell you that it is a privilege to work for you. I will tell Sascha. Nothing exciting ever happens at the bar.

And now we see RENAULT, ANNINA and JAN in a corner near the bar. Jan is pressing the bills upon him.

RENAULT. No, no, not here. Come to my office in the morning. We'll do everything business-like.

JAN. We'll be there at six.

RENAULT. I'll be there at ten. (*Smiling broadly, but insincerely*) How happy I am for both of you. Still—it's very strange that you should have won—

As he looks off, the scene cuts to a view of RICK at the bar, then back to RENAULT, ANNINA and JAN.

RENAULT (*seeing Rick*). Well, perhaps not so strange after all— Run along, now. I'll see you in the morning.

ANNINA. Thank you so much, Captain Renault.

She and Jan, beaming with happiness, go off. Renault looks after her, regretfully. Then he walks toward Rick.

We see RICK, who, pretending not to do so, is glancing in Ilsa's direction. Renault comes up to him.

RENAULT. As I suspected, you're a rank sentimentalist.

RICK. Why?

RENAULT (*chidingly*). Why do you interfere with my little romances? When it comes to women you have charm, I have only visas.

RICK. I don't know what you're talking about.

RENAULT (*goodnaturedly*). I forgive you this time. However, I will be in tomorrow night with a breath-taking brunette. It will make me very happy if she loses. (*He smiles, and walks into the gambling room.*)

This cuts to SASCHA and CARL whispering together. Sascha looks toward Rick with great admiration. Then, with giant strides he moves toward Rick, the scene moving with him. He reaches Rick.

SASCHA (*grandly*). You haf done a beyootiful t'ing!

And he takes Rick's face between his two hands and plants a resounding kiss on Rick's forehead. Then, before the astonished Rick can recover, he walks back to the bar with huge strides.

RICK (*recovering*). Go away, you crazy Russian—! (*He swears under his breath.*)

This cuts to LASZLO approaching Rick.

LASZLO. M'sieur Blaine, I wonder if I could talk to you.

RICK. Go ahead.

LASZLO. Well, isn't there some other place? This is rather confidential what I have to say.

RICK (*nodding toward it*). To my office.

As they start up, the scene quickly dissolves to RICK'S OFFICE, where RICK is at his desk with LASZLO.

LASZLO. You must know that it's very important I get out of Casablanca.

RICK. Why you more than any of the other thousands who are stuck here?

LASZLO (*simply*). Whether Victor Laszlo, the man, gets out is not important at all. But it's my privilege to be one of the leaders of a great movement. You know what I have been doing. You know what it means to the work—to the lives—of thousands and thousands of little people that I be free to reach America and continue my work.

RICK. I'm not interested in politics. The problems of the world are not in my department. I'm a saloon-keeper.

LASZLO (*looking at him closely*). That wasn't always your attitude.

RICK (*lighting a cigarette*). Wasn't it?

LASZLO. My friends here in the Underground tell me that you have quite a record. You ran guns to Ethiopia. You fought against the Fascists in Spain.

RICK. What of it?

LASZLO. Isn't it strange that you always happened to be on the side of the underdog?

RICK (*thinking a moment*). Yes. I found that a very expensive hobby, too. But then I never was much of a businessman.

LASZLO. Are you enough of a businessman to appreciate an offer of a hundred thousand francs?

RICK. I appreciate it—but I don't accept it.

LASZLO. I'll raise it to two hundred thousand francs.

RICK. My friend, if you offered me a million francs—or three francs—my answer would be still the same.

LASZLO. I see. You intend using the Letters yourself some day?

RICK. Not at all. (*Bitterly*) I'm much too comfortable here to travel.

LASZLO. Then you are saving them for someone else?

RICK. No. I may even put a match to them some day.

LASZLO. Then I don't understand. There must be some reason why you won't let me have them.

From the café we hear the sound of male voices raised in song. Rick gets up.

RICK. There is. I suggest that you ask your wife.

LASZLO (*looking at him, puzzled*). I beg your pardon?

RICK. I said—ask your wife.

LASZLO. My wife! (*The sound of the male singing grows louder.*)

RICK. Yes. (*As he hears the singing*) Who's singing that? (*And he goes out, leaving Laszlo to stare after him.*)

The scene cuts to the CAFÉ as TWO GERMAN OFFICERS, beer mugs in hand, are standing by the piano, singing the "Wacht am Rhine." Sam, looking very uncomfortable, is accompanying them. Everybody in the room is looking at them. Suddenly Sam stops playing.

SAM (*to the officers*). Dat's all I know of dat song.

An officer swears at Sam in German, grabs Sam and lifts him off the stool. A German officer sits at the piano. The officers resume their singing. This cuts to the BAR as a FRENCH OFFICER starts forward. Sascha leans forward quietly and lays a restraining hand on his arm.

RICK appears on the STEPS. He listens to the officers sing—his expression deadpan. Laszlo has come out of the room. His lips are very tight as he listens to the song.—The view then takes in the entire ROOM, which grows deadly quiet. Strasser is on his feet, singing too. As the moving view passes the Dark European we see that he is singing the "Wacht am Rhine" too. But nobody else in the room is. Renault has come in from the gambling room, and stands by the door. We can't tell from his expression what he is thinking

This cuts to LASZLO crossing the floor to the orchestra, reaching the orchestra, and turning to Sam.

LASZLO (*looking at her closely*). We'll discuss it later. Come— (*Noting the secret agent watching for them outside*) Our faithful friend is still there.

We see the BAR as people are hastily downing their drinks, and leaving. One of the German officers addresses Sascha.

GERMAN OFFICER. Think I'll have a quick one before I go. What's that you're mixing?

SASCHA (*looking at the slip of paper*). Some new drink—

GERMAN OFFICER. I'll have it.

He reaches over, takes it and drinks it. Then he throws some change on the bar and starts out, the scene moving with him. After a few steps a glazed expression comes into his eyes. He clutches convulsively at his stomach. He is running hell-bent for the door as the scene fades out.

PART THREE

The scene dissolves to a dark HOTEL ROOM: A door is heard to open and then the light is switched on, revealing Ilsa and Laszlo as they enter the room. Ilsa takes off her wrap while her husband walks over to the window and starts to draw the shades. There are no words spoken—and we sense a tension between the two. Ilsa's eyes follow him, but Laszlo apparently takes no notice. He looks out of the window.—We see a MAN across the STREET standing in the doorway of a house. Then we again see the HOTEL ROOM as Ilsa moves to Laszlo at the window, and stands close beside him.

LASZLO (*as he draws the shade*). Our faithful friend is still there.

ILSA. Victor, please don't go to the Underground meeting tonight.

LASZLO (*soberly*). I must. (*With a smile*) And besides, it isn't often that a man has the chance to display heroics before his wife.

ILSA. Don't joke. After Strasser's horrible threats tonight—Victor, I'm frightened!

LASZLO (*with another quiet smile*). To tell you the truth, my dear, I am frightened, too. So shall I remain hiding here in a hotel room in that unpraiseworthy condition—or shall I carry on the best I can?

ILSA. Whatever I would say, you'd carry on.

LASZLO. Since our friend Rick has refused us there is little alternative, as I see it.

Ilsa turns away to conceal her emotion. She sits on the edge of the bed. Laszlo follows her with his eyes. He is looking at her steadily and thoughtfully— but in no way antagonistically.

LASZLO. One would think that if sentiment wouldn't persuade him, the money would.

ILSA (*ill at ease, trying to keep her voice steady*). Did he—did he give any reason?

LASZLO. He suggested that I ask you.

ILSA. Ask *me*?

LASZLO (*walking across to her and looking down at her*). He said, "Ask your wife." I don't know why he said that.

Ilsa finds it impossible to look at him. She looks away. Laszlo turns off the light switch, making the room dark except for the dim light that comes from the shaded windows.

LASZLO. Our friend outside will think we have retired now. That is what I want him to think. I will go in a few minutes.

He sits down on the bed beside her. A silence falls between them. It grows strained. Finally—

LASZLO (*quietly*). Ilsa—?

ILSA. Yes?

LASZLO (*after a pause*). Ilsa, when I was in the concentration camp—were you lonely in Paris?

Their faces are now barely visible in the darkness.

ILSA. Yes, Victor. I was.

LASZLO (*sympathetically*). I know how it is to be lonely— (*Very quietly*) Is there anything you want to tell me?

We get a close view of ILSA in the darkness: Her lips tremble as she controls herself.

ILSA (*very low*). No, Victor, there isn't. (*This is followed by a moment of silence; then we hear Victor.*)

VICTOR'S VOICE. I love you very much, my dear.

ILSA (*barely able to speak*). Yes. Yes, I know. Victor— Whatever I do, will you believe that—that—

LASZLO. You do not even have to say it. I will believe.

We see the TWO together: After a moment he gets up.

LASZLO (*quite cheerfully*). Well, our friend must be convinced I'm sound asleep. (*He bends down and kisses her cheek.*) Good night, dear.

ILSA. Good night, dear.

He walks out of sight. She watches him, then calls after him.

ILSA. Victor!—

She gets up and goes after him, following which the scene cuts to a view of the TWO at the door: He is just opening it. Ilsa comes over to him. In the slit of light from the partially opened door, we can see her face, which is strained and worried.

LASZLO. Yes, dear?

ILSA (*after a moment of hesitation, in a tone which suggests this is not what she has been tempted to say*) Please be careful.

LASZLO. Of course.

He kisses her on the forehead and goes out the door. She stands there for a few seconds, then goes to look out of the same window as before. Thereupon we observe that the figure in the doorway outside has gone.

ILSA in the HOTEL ROOM watches for a moment longer. This cuts to a WALL, back of the hotel, and Laszlo's figure is visible against the wall, going down the narrow street. Then we again see ILSA in the HOTEL ROOM: She leaves the window and crosses the room to the place she dropped her wrap. She puts it on. Then, after a second's pause, she walks to the door and goes out. This dissolves to RICK'S OFFICE where RICK and CARL are bent over ledgers. Carl is very busy figuring.

CARL (*looking up*). Well, you are in pretty good shape, Herr Rick.

RICK. How long can I afford to stay closed?

CARL. Two weeks—maybe three.

RICK (*getting up*). Maybe we won't have to. A bribe has worked before. In the meantime, everyone stays on salary. (*He walks to the door.*)

CARL. Oh, thank you, Herr Rick. Sascha will be very happy to hear it. I owe him money.

RICK (*at the door*). You lock up, Carl.

CARL. I will. Then I am going to the meeting of the—

RICK (*interrupting*). Don't tell me where you're going.

CARL (*with a smile*). I won't. Good night, Herr Rick.

RICK. Good night, Carl.

He goes out, and the scene cuts to the BALCONY outside the office as RICK walks toward his apartment, then to RICK'S APARTMENT, which is dark. The door is opened by Rick, letting in some light from the hall. A figure is revealed in the room. Rick lights a small lamp. There is Ilsa facing him, her face white but determined. Rick pauses for a moment in astonishment.

RICK. How did you get in?

ILSA. The stairs from the street.

RICK. I told you this morning you'd come around—but this is a little ahead of schedule. (*With mock politeness*) Won't you sit down?

ILSA (*as she takes the chair*). Richard, I had to see you.

RICK. So I'm Richard again? We're back in Paris. I've recovered my lost identity.

ILSA. Please . . .

RICK (*lighting a cigarette*). Your unexpected visit isn't connected by any chance with the Letters of Transit? (*Ilsa remains silent.*) It seems while I have those Letters, I'll never be lonely.

ILSA (*looking at him steadily*). Richard, you can ask any price you choose. You can impose any condition you want. But you must give me those Letters.

RICK. I went all through that with your husband. It's no deal.

ILSA. I know how you feel about me, and I don't blame you. But I'm asking you to put your feelings aside for something more important.

RICK. Do I have to hear again what a great man your husband is? And what an important Cause he's fighting for?

ILSA. It was your Cause, too. In your own way, you were fighting for the same thing.

RICK. Well, I'm not fighting for anything any more—except myself. I'm the only Cause I'm interested in now.

A pause, then Ilsa deliberately takes a new approach.

ILSA. Richard, we loved each other once. If those days meant anything at all to you—

RICK (*harshly*). I wouldn't bring up Paris if I were you. It's poor salesmanship.

ILSA. Please listen to me. If you knew what really happened. If you knew the truth—

RICK (*cutting in*). I wouldn't believe you, no matter what you told me

You'll say anything now, to get what you want.

ILSA (*her temper flaring—scornfully*). You *want* to feel sorry for yourself, don't you? With so much at stake, all you can think of is your own feeling. One woman has hurt you, and you take your revenge on the rest of the world. You're a coward, and— (*Breaking*) Oh, Richard, I'm sorry. But *you're* our last hope. If you don't help us, Victor Laszlo will die in Casablanca.

RICK. What of it? I'm going to die in Casablanca. It's just the spot for it. Now, if you— (*He stops short as he looks closely at Ilsa.*)

A close view shows ILSA holding a small revolver in her hand.

ILSA. All right. I tried to reason with you. I tried everything. Now I want those Letters.

A close view discloses RICK as, for a moment, a look of admiration comes into his eyes. Then we see ILSA and RICK together.

ILSA. Get them for me.

RICK. I don't have to. (*Reaching into his inner pocket*) They're right here. (*He has the Letters in his hand.*)

ILSA. Put them on the table.

RICK (*shaking his head*). No.

ILSA. For the last time, put them on the table.

RICK. You'll have to kill me to get them. If Laszlo—if the Cause means so much, you won't stop at anything. . . . Well, go ahead, shoot. You'll be doing me a favor.

ILSA, seen close, rises, still pointing the gun at Rick. Her finger rests on the trigger. It seems as if she is summoning nerve to press it. Then, suddenly, her hand trembles and the pistol falls to the table. She breaks up, covering her face with her hands. Rick walks into the scene and stands close to her. Suddenly, she flings herself into his arms.

ILSA (*almost hysterical*). Richard, I tried to stay away. I thought I would never see you again . . . that you were out of my life. The day you left Paris, if you knew what I went through! How much I loved you . . . how much I still love you—

Her words are smothered as he presses her tight to him, kisses her passionately. She is lost in his embrace as the scene fades out.

PART FOUR

RICK'S APARTMENT fades in. Then, a little while later there is a close view of a TABLE BEFORE A COUCH. There is a bottle of champagne on the table and there are two half-filled glasses. We hear Ilsa talking as the scene moves to her and Rick. She is gazing into space as she talks. Rick is listening intently, but not looking at her.

ILSA. . . . We were married three weeks when Victor got word they needed him in Prague. Just a two-line item in the paper, "Victor Laszlo apprehended. Sent to concentration camp." The months went by. Then came a rumor that he was dead. (*She pauses for a moment.*) I was lonely before, but now I had nothing left—not even hope. (*She puts her hand on his.*) Until I met you.

RICK. But why didn't you tell me all this?

ILSA. Victor made me promise to keep our marriage a secret. I knew his plans and his friends. If the Gestapo found out I was his wife, Victor felt it would be dangerous for me and for those working with us . . . I kept my promise.

RICK. Then you got word he escaped?

ILSA. You remember there was a telephone call? (*Rick nods.*) A friend of Victor's. They were hiding him in a freight car on the outskirts of Paris. He was sick and he needed me. I didn't tell you because you wouldn't have left Paris—and they would have caught you. So . . . well, you know the rest.

RICK. It's still a story without an ending. (*He looks at her directly.*) What about now?

ILSA (*simply*). I'll never have the strength to go away from you again.

RICK. And Laszlo?

ILSA. Richard, you'll help him now, won't you? You'll see he gets out? (*Rick nods.*) Then he'll have his work—all the things he's been living for.

There is a pause.

RICK. All except one. He wouldn't have you.

ILSA. I can't fight it any more. I ran away from you once. Some morning I may wake up to find that you've gone, and if it lasts fifty years or ten days I know there'll be more heartache in it than happiness. I don't know what's right any longer. You'll have to think for both of us, Richard—for all of us.

RICK (*taking her in his arms*). I've already made up our minds.

ILSA (*in a whisper*). I wish I didn't love you so much. (*She draws his face down to hers.*)

We see an ALLEY as LASZLO and CARL appear, making their way through the darkness toward Rick's. The headlights of a speeding car sweep toward them and they flatten themselves against a wall to avoid detection. The lights move past them and they continue down the alley. Then the scene quickly dissolves to the interior of RICK'S as LASZLO and CARL enter and go toward the bar, out of breath from their exertion.

CARL. I think we lost them, Herr Laszlo.

LASZLO. I'm afraid they caught some of the others.

This cuts to RICK'S APARTMENT as RICK and ILSA hear voices below and Rick goes to the door. Then we see RICK at the door upstairs, with ILSA standing just in back of him. Her expression shows her anxiety for Laszlo. She makes a move as if to come out on the balcony but Rick's arm bars her way.

RICK (*in a low tone*). He's all right. Keep out of sight and leave it to me.

She withdraws behind the door as Rick walks out to the balcony railing. This cuts to a full view of the CAFÉ.

RICK. What's happened? (*At this both Carl and Laszlo look up.*)

CARL (*excitedly*). Herr Rick, the police break up our meeting! We get away so close a shave like this. (*He indicates with his fingers the tiniest margin.*)

RICK. Come up here, Carl.

Carl, who is just about to pour a drink, looks up wonderingly, then puts the bottle down and starts toward the stairway.

CARL. Yes, I come.

RICK (*to Carl, as he comes up the stairs*). I want you to put out the light at the rear entrance. It might attract the police.

CARL. But Sascha always puts out that light before . . .

RICK (*cutting in*). Tonight he forgot.

We see the BALCONY where Rick stands, as Carl climbs into view.

RICK (*in a low voice—jerking his head toward the door*). Miss Lund. I want you to take her home. (*At this, Carl's eyes grow enormous but he asks no questions.*)

CARL. Yes, Herr Rick.

As Carl goes to the door, Rick starts downstairs, and the scene cuts to LASZLO in front of the BAR. He is wrapping one of the small bar towels around a cut in his wrist. Rick comes into sight, and looks questioningly at the injured hand.

LASZLO. It's nothing. Just a little cut. We had to get through a window.

He buttons his cuff down over the towel to hold it in place as Rick walks in back of the bar, picks up a bottle of whiskey and pours a drink.

RICK. This might come in handy.

He shoves the glass across the bar to Laszlo.

LASZLO. Thank you.

Laszlo takes it in a swallow. Rick is now pouring one for himself.

RICK. Had a close one, eh?

LASZLO. Yes, rather.

RICK. Huh. Don't you ever wonder if it's worth all this? (*Laszlo looks at him, puzzled.*) I mean what you're fighting for?

LASZLO. We might as well question why we breathe. If we stop breathing, we die. If we stop fighting our enemies, the world will die.

RICK. What of it? Then it'll be out of its misery.

LASZLO. Do you know how you sound, M'sieur Rick? Like a man trying to convince himself of something that in his heart he doesn't believe. Each of us has a destiny. For good or for evil. It is our . . . Letter of Transit, M'sieur Rick, from birth to death. Neither we nor the world will be *allowed* to die until we have reached our destination.

RICK (*drily*). Yes, I get the point.

With the bottle in his hand, Rick starts around toward the front of the bar, Laszlo's body turning as he presses Rick closely.

LASZLO. I wonder if you do. I wonder if you know that you're trying to escape from yourself and that you'll never succeed. What you're meant to do will follow you wherever you go. That is what I mean by your destiny.

Rick looks at Laszlo for a moment, then sits down at a table and begins to pour himself another drink.

RICK (*ironically*). You seem to know all about my "destiny."

LASZLO. You see, M'sieur Rick, I know a good deal more about you than you suspect. I know, for instance, that you are in love with a woman.

Rick has lifted his glass to drink. He puts it down and stares at Laszlo, who stands facing him from the bar.

LASZLO (*smiling just a little*). It is perhaps a strange circumstance that we should be in love with the same woman.

Rick straightens up in his chair and watches Laszlo closely. Laszlo walks over to the table.

LASZLO. The first evening I came here to this café I knew there was something between you and Ilsa. Since no one is to blame, I demand no explanation. I ask only one thing.

He sits down. Their eyes hold across the table.

LASZLO. You won't give me the Letters of Transit. All right! But I want my wife to be safe . . . M'sieur Rick, I ask you as a favor to use the Letters to take her away from Casablanca.

Rick looks at Laszlo incredulously.

RICK. You love her that much?

LASZLO. Apparently you think of me only as the leader of a Cause. Well, I am also a human being and . . . (*Looking away for a moment, then quietly*) Yes, I love her that much.

At this moment there is a sharp knock on the front door of the café, followed by the entrance of several gendarmes. Rick and Laszlo rise as a French Officer walks into the lighted area and addresses Laszlo.

FRENCH OFFICER. M'sieur Laszlo, you will come with us. We have a warrant for your arrest.

LASZLO. On what charge?

FRENCH OFFICER. Captain Renault will discuss that with you later.

Laszlo looks at Rick, who smiles ironically.

RICK. It seems "destiny" has taken a hand.

In dignified silence Laszlo crosses to the Police Officer. Together they walk toward the door. Rick's eyes follow them, but his expression reveals nothing of his feelings.

The scene dissolves to RENAULT'S OFFICE with RICK and RENAULT.

RENAULT. . . . If we can prove at the trial that he was at the meeting, we will have grounds to hold him.

RICK. You haven't any actual proof, and you know it. (*Renault shrugs.*) You might just as well let him go now.

RENAULT. Ricky, I would advise you not to interest yourself too much in what happens to Laszlo. If by any chance you were to help him escape—

RICK (*cutting in*). What makes you think I'd stick my neck out for Laszlo?

RENAULT. Because one: You have bet ten thousand francs that he'd escape. Two: You've got the Letters of Transit. . . . Now don't bother to deny it. . . . And, well, you might do it simply because you don't like Strasser's looks. As a matter of fact, I don't like him either.

RICK (*grinning*). Well, they're all excellent reasons . . .

RENAULT. Don't count on my friendship, Ricky. In this matter I am powerless. Besides, I might lose the ten thousand francs.

RICK (*thinking quickly*). You're not very subtle, but you are effective. I get the point. Yes, I have the Letters, Louis. But I intend using them myself. I'm selling out my place and leaving Casablanca on tonight's plane . . . the last plane.

RENAULT. What!

RICK. And I'm taking a friend with me. (*He smiles.*) One you'll appreciate.

RENAULT. What friend?

RICK. Ilsa Lund. (*An amazed incredulity is written on Renault's face.*) That ought to put your mind to rest about my helping Laszlo escape. He's the last man I want to see in America.

RENAULT (*shrewdly*). You didn't come here to tell me this. You have the Letters of Transit. You can fill in your name and hers and leave any time you please. Why are you still interested in what happens to Laszlo?

RICK. I'm not. But I *am* interested in what happens to Ilsa and me. We have a legal right to go, that's true. But people have been held in Casablanca in spite of their legal rights.

RENAULT. What makes you think we want to hold you?

RICK. Ilsa is Laszlo's wife. She probably knows a good deal that Strasser would like to know . . .

RENAULT. I see.

RICK. Louis, I'll make a deal with you. Instead of this petty charge you have against him you can get something really big, something that would chuck him in a concentration camp for years. Be quite a feather in your cap, wouldn't it?

RENAULT. It most certainly would. Germany . . . er (*correcting himself*), Vichy, would be very grateful.

RICK. Then release him. You be at my place a half hour before the plane leaves. I'll arrange for Laszlo to come there to pick up the Letters of Transit, and that will give you the criminal grounds on which to make the arrest. You get him, and we get away. In catching the whale, two small fish will slip through your fingers. To the Germans that last will be just a minor irritation.

RENAULT (*puzzled*). There's still something I don't quite understand about this business. Miss Lund—she's very beautiful, yes . . . but you were never interested in any women.

RICK. Well, she isn't just any woman.

RENAULT. I see. How do I know you will keep your end of the bargain?

RICK. I'll make the arrangements with Laszlo right now in the visitors' pen.

RENAULT. Ricky, I will miss you. Apparently you're the only one in Casablanca that has even less scruples than I.

RICK (*drily*). Oh, thanks . . . (*He rises.*) And, by the way, call off your watchdogs after you let him go. I don't want them around this afternoon. I'm taking no chances, Louis—not even with you.

The scene thereupon dissolves quickly to the VISITORS' PEN: There is the wire netting that separates the visitors from the prisoners. Rick is seated on his side. There is nobody else in the room. Then a door opens and a guard leads Laszlo into the room. As Laszlo, looking coldly at Rick, seats himself, the guard leaves the room . . .

This cuts to a closer view of RICK and LASZLO facing each other across the netting.

RICK (*sotto voce*). I haven't much time. I've bribed a release for you.

LASZLO (*looking at him closely*). Thank you—

RICK. I've decided to let you have the Letters of Transit—(*as Laszlo stares at him*)—for a hundred thousand francs.

LASZLO. Very well.

RICK. Better get down to my café a few minutes before the Lisbon plane leaves.

LASZLO. They'll shadow me.

RICK. I've taken care of that.

We see RENAULT in his OFFICE listening over a sort of a dictaphone.

LASZLO'S VOICE (*coming through in Renault's office*). And Ilsa?

There is a pause. Renault strains his ears.

RICK'S VOICE. Bring her with you all ready to leave.

As Renault in his office smiles broadly, the scene cuts to another view of RICK and LASZLO facing each other.

LASZLO (*gratefully*). M'sieur Rick—

RICK (*curtly*). Skip it. This is strictly a matter of business. (*He gets up and walks out.*)

The scene then dissolves to FERRARI'S OFFICE, with RICK and FERRARI at the table.

FERRARI. Shall we draw up papers, or is our handshake good enough?

RICK (*getting up*). It's certainly not good enough. But being I'm in a hurry, it'll have to do.

FERRARI (*shaking hands, sighing enviously*). Oh—to get out of Casablanca—to go to America. . . . You are a lucky man.

RICK. Oh, by the way—my agreement with Sam's always been he gets twenty-five per cent of the profits. That still goes.

FERRARI. I happen to know he gets ten per cent. But he's worth twenty-five.

RICK. And Abdul and Carl and Sascha—they stay with the place, or I don't sell.

FERRARI. Of course they stay. Rick's wouldn't be Rick's without them.

RICK. So long. (*He walks to the door, stops and turns.*) Don't forget, you owe Rick's a hundred cartons of American cigarettes.

FERRARI (*smiling*). I shall remember to pay it to myself.

As Rick walks off, the scene dissolves to a PLANE at the AIRPORT at night. A crew of workmen are giving it the last-minute inspection. Fuel is being pumped into its tanks. On the fuselage is painted: "LISBON—CASABLANCA." As the view moves across the field, this dissolves to the exterior of RICK's: On the door a huge placard is pasted. It reads:

CLOSED
By Order of The Prefect of Police

And this dissolves to a close view of a SPINNING ROULETTE WHEEL as three pairs of hands are shoving huge stacks of chips on the numbers. Then the view draws back to disclose CARL, SASCHA and ABDUL gathered round the wheel. They all look bored. The wheel stops.

ABDUL. Number twenty-nine.

CARL (*very bored*). Ve all lose seven million francs.

SASCHA. To who?

CARL. To each udder.

SASCHA. Now let's play de dice table de same way. It's more exercise.

Next we see the CAFÉ as SAM is playing the piano for his own enjoyment. Rick comes down the steps from his office. He looks at his watch.

RICK (*indicating the gambling room*). Sam—do you mind taking the piano inside? I'm expecting some people.

SAM (*getting up*). Not at all, Boss.

He starts pushing the piano. Rick follows him to the door, locks it behind him, then crosses to the bar, where he pours himself a stiff drink. There is a knock on the front door. Rick takes the drink in one swallow, and starts across.

At the FRONT DOOR—Rick comes to it and opens it to admit Renault.

RICK. You're late.

RENAULT. I was informed when Laszlo was about to leave the hotel, so I knew I would be on time.

RICK. I thought I asked you to tie up your watchdogs.

RENAULT. Laszlo will not be followed here. (*He looks around the empty café, and sighs.*) This place won't be the same without you, Ricky.

RICK. It'll be all right, Louis. I've arranged with Ferrari. You'll still win at roulette.

RENAULT (*who merely smiles in acknowledgment*). Is everything ready?

RICK (*tapping his breast pocket*). I have the Letters right here.

RENAULT. Tell me, Rick—when we searched the place, where were they?

RICK. In Sam's piano.

RENAULT. Serves me right for not being musical!

The sound of a car pulling up is heard.

RICK. Oh, here they are. You'd better wait in my office.

As Renault walks toward the office, the scene cuts to the exterior of the CAFÉ as LASZLO is paying the cab driver. Ilsa is walking toward the entrance. Then in the CAFÉ we see RICK opening the door to admit Ilsa. She goes into his arms, and a close view of ILSA and RICK follows. Her intensity reveals the strain she is under.

ILSA. Victor thinks I'm leaving with him. Haven't you told him?

RICK (*looking at her for a moment, then answering, with a quiet emphasis*). No, not yet.

ILSA (*anxiously*). But it's all right, isn't it? You were able to arrange everything?

RICK (*quietly*). Everything is quite all right.

ILSA. Oh, Rick—

RICK. We'll tell him at the airport. The less time to think the easier for all of us. Please trust me.

ILSA. Yes, I will.

We get a full view of the CAFÉ as Laszlo comes in.

LASZLO. M'sieur Blaine, I don't know how to thank you.

RICK (*cutting him short*). Oh, save it. We've still got lots of things to do.

LASZLO. I brought the money, M'sieur Blaine. (*He is about to give it to him.*)

RICK (*gruffly*). Keep it. You'll need it in America.

LASZLO (*protesting*). But we made a deal.

RICK. Oh, never mind that. You won't have any trouble in Lisbon, will you?

LASZLO. No. That is all arranged.

RICK. Good. (*He takes out the Letters.*) Here are the Letters. They're all made out in blank. You'll just have to fill in the signatures.

He hands them to Laszlo, who takes them gratefully.

LASZLO. M'sieur Blaine, I—

RENAULT'S VOICE (*suddenly heard*). Victor Laszlo!

At this they wheel toward the office door, and we next see RENAULT coming down the steps.

RENAULT. Victor Laszlo, you are under arrest . . .

A fairly close view of ILSA and LASZLO shows that they are both caught completely off guard, and are speechless. They turn toward Rick. Horror is in Ilsa's eyes.

RENAULT'S VOICE. . . . on a charge of accessory to the murder of the couriers from whom those Letters were stolen.

He walks into the scene and notices their bewildered expressions.

RENAULT. Oh, you are surprised about my friend Rick? The explanation is quite simple. Love, it seems, has triumphed over virtue.

Obviously, the situation delights Renault. He is laughing as he turns toward Rick, but suddenly the laughter dies in his throat. In Rick's hand is a gun, which he is levelling at Renault.

RICK. Nobody is going to be arrested, Louis. Not for a while yet.

RENAULT (*staring open-mouthed for a moment*). Have you lost your mind, Rick?

RICK. Yes. Sit down over there.

As Renault hesitates, the scene cuts to a close view of ILSA showing that her belief in Rick comes back. Then we see the entire group, the view favoring RICK and RENAULT.

RENAULT (*walking toward Rick*). Put that gun down.

RICK (*not retreating a step*). Louis, I wouldn't like to shoot you. But I will if you take one more step.

Renault halts for a moment and studies Rick. Then he shrugs.

RENAULT. Under the circumstances, I will sit down.

He walks to a table, sits down, and reaches into his pocket.

RICK (*sharply*). You will keep your hands on the table . . . away from your pistol pocket.

RENAULT (*taking out a cigarette case*). I suppose you know what you are doing, but I wonder if you realize what this means?

RICK. Perfectly. But we'll have plenty of time to discuss that later.

LASZLO. There won't be any trouble at the airport, will there?

RENAULT (*sighing*). I'm afraid not. (*Reproachfully, to Rick*) Call off your watchdogs, you said!

Rick takes a phone on a long cord, and slides it across the table to Renault.

RICK. Just the same, call the airport and let me hear you tell them. And remember—I've got this gun pointed right at your heart.

RENAULT (*as he dials*). That is my least vulnerable spot. (*Into the phone*) Hello, airport?—Captain Renault calling from Rick's Café. There'll be two Letters of Transit for the Lisbon plane. There's to be no trouble about them.— Good.

We see STRASSER on the phone in the German Consulate.

STRASSER (*jiggling the receiver violently*). Hello, hello. . . . What was that? (*He hangs up, reaches for his hat, and calls out to an officer*) My car quickly! (*Telephoning*) This is Major Strasser. Have a squad of police meet me at the airport at once. At once! Do you hear?

We again see RICK, ILSA, LASZLO and RENAULT while an orderly announces the departure of the Lisbon plane in ten minutes over a loudspeaker system.

RICK. Louis, have your man go with Mr. Laszlo, and take care of his baggage.

RENAULT (*smiling*). Certainly, Rick. Anything you say. (*To the Orderly*) Find Mr. Laszlo's luggage and put it on the plane.

ORDERLY (*to Laszlo*). Yes, sir. This way, please.

Laszlo and the Orderly go out and the scene cuts to a closer view of Rick, Renault and Ilsa, who is tense with expectation. She has no inkling of Rick's real intentions any more than has Renault.

RICK (*to Renault*). If you don't mind, you fill in the names. That'll make it official.

RENAULT (*with an ironical smile*). You think of everything, don't you?

RICK (*without expression*). And the names are Mr. and Mrs. Victor Laszlo. (*This astounds Renault.*)

ILSA (*dazed; startled*). I don't understand. What about you?

RICK. I'm staying here to keep Captain Renault company until the plane gets safely away.

ILSA (*as Rick's intention fully dawns on her*). No, Richard, no. What's happened to you? Last night we said—

RICK. You said I was to do the thinking for both of us. Well, I've done a lot of it since then and it all adds up to one thing. You're getting on that plane with Victor where you belong.

ILSA. But Richard, no, I—I—

RICK. Now you've got to listen to me. Do you have any idea what you'd have to look forward to if you stayed on here? Nine chances out of ten we'd both wind up in a concentration camp.—Isn't that true, Louis?

RENAULT (*who has been watching him ironically*). I'm afraid Major Strasser would insist.

ILSA (*dully*). You're saying this only to make me go.

RICK. I'm saying it because it's true. Inside of us we both know you belong with Victor. You're part of his work. The thing that keeps him going. If that plane leaves the ground and you're not with him, you'll regret it.

ILSA (*crying out, in torment*). No.

RICK. Maybe not today, maybe not tomorrow, but soon, and for the rest of your life.

ILSA. What about us?

RICK (*tenderly*). We'll always have Paris. We didn't have. We'd—we'd lost it until you came to Casablanca. (*Softly*) We got it back last night.

ILSA. And I said I would never leave you!

RICK. And you never will.—But I've got a job to do, too. Where I'm going you can't follow. What I've got to do, you can't be any part of.

The scene cuts to a close view of ILSA listening to him, moved.

RICK'S VOICE. Ilsa, I'm no good at being noble. But it doesn't take much to see that the problems of three little people don't amount to a hill o' beans in this crazy world. Some day you'll understand that. (*As she is crying*) Now, now . . .

We see the room again, with the three of them, as Rick pours a drink.

RICK. Here's looking at you, kid!

And now LASZLO returns.

LASZLO. Everything is in order.

RICK (*his eyes on her*). All except one thing. There's something you should know before you leave.

LASZLO. Monsieur Blaine, I don't ask you to explain anything.

RICK. I'm going to anyway, because it may make a difference to you later on. You said you knew about Ilsa and me.

LASZLO. Yes.

RICK. But you didn't know she came to my place last night. She came, there for the Letters of Transit.—Isn't that true, Ilsa?

ILSA. Yes.

RICK (*his voice more harsh, almost brutal*). She tried everything to get them and nothing worked. She did her best to convince me she was still in love with me. But that was long ago. For your sake, she pretended it wasn't—and I let her pretend.

LASZLO. I understand.

We get a close view of ILSA as she looks at Rick for the last time. Then we see the GROUP: Laszlo looks at Rick. Sam is heard playing in the other room.

LASZLO (*quietly*). Thanks. I appreciate it. Welcome back to the fight. This time I know our side will win. (*To Ilsa, who has been standing there silently*). Are you ready, Ilsa?

ILSA (*going over to Rick; deeply moved*). Yes, I am ready. (*To Rick*) Good-bye, Rick. God bless you.

RICK (*covering his emotion*). You'd better hurry or you'll miss that plane.

Ilsa and Laszlo go out, and we get a close view of Renault and Rick.

RENAULT (*looking at Rick triumphantly*). Well, I was right. You *are* a sentimentalist. (*He tries to rise.*)

RICK (*sharply*). Stay where you are! (*As Renault subsides*) I don't know what you are talking about!

RENAULT. What you just did for Laszlo. And that fairy tale you invented to send Ilsa away with him. I know a little about women, my friend. She went, but she knew you were lying.

RICK. Anyway, thanks for helping me out.

Rick's face reveals nothing. With his free hand, he takes out a cigarette and lights it.

RENAULT. Do you have to keep me here any longer?

RICK. Yes. There's still the telephone.

RENAULT. I suppose you know this is not going to be pleasant for either of us—and especially for you. I'll have to arrest you, of course.

RICK. As soon as the plane leaves, Louis.

Renault shrugs and listens. Rick looks inscrutably out of the window toward the airport, from where we still hear the plane engine warming up. Suddenly from the street, the shriek of automobile tires coming to a sudden stop is heard; then the sound of an automobile door slamming, followed by the sound of running footsteps. Renault half rises from his chair.

RICK. Stay where you are, Louis.

Strasser comes bursting in. Rick has his gun ready, but concealed from Strasser.

STRASSER (*to Renault*). What was the meaning of that phone call?

RENAULT. Victor Laszlo is on the plane for Lisbon.

STRASSER. What! (*For a moment, dazed; then recovering*) Well, why do you sit there? Why don't you stop them?

RENAULT. Ask M'sieur Rick—

STRASSER (*as he spies the telephone and starts toward it*). I will call them to stop the plane.

RICK (*pointing the revolver at Strasser*). Stay away from that phone!

Strasser stops in his tracks, looks at Rick, and sees that he means business.

STRASSER (*steelly*). I would advise you not to interfere with an official of the Third Reich.

RICK (*wryly*). I am a true neutral. I was willing to shoot Captain Renault and I am willing to shoot you.

We get a quick glimpse of the AIR FIELD: The plane is now taxiing to the edge of the runway. Then we again see RICK, STRASSER and RENAULT in the CAFÉ. Rick still has the gun pointed at Strasser. The sound of the plane taxiing is heard. Suddenly Strasser, in desperation, throws a lamp at Rick, then leaps at him. The gun goes off harmlessly. The men struggle. Sam, Carl, Sascha and Abdul are seen pounding at the closed door in the GAMBLING ROOM, trying to get in. They start to shout.

RICK and STRASSER are still struggling. Finally Strasser, with a tremendous effort, throws Rick across the room— then leaps for the phone.

STRASSER (*desperately—into the phone*). Operator—! Get me the Radio Tower.

This is as far as he gets, for a shot rings out. Strasser crumples slowly to the floor. Renault stares at him, fascinated. At this moment the door to the gambling room is broken down. Carl, Sam, Sascha and Abdul burst in.

SAM. Boss—!

But they all stop in their tracks and stare at the sight of Strasser on the floor. Through the front door two gendarmes come bursting in. They look at Strasser—then at Renault.—RENAULT is looking at Rick.—RICK returns Renault's gaze. His eyes are expressionless.—Then we see the CAFÉ filled with the men who have burst in.

RENAULT (*to the gendarme*). Major Strasser has been shot. (*After a pause—as he looks at Rick, then at the gendarmes*) Round up the usual suspects.

Suddenly the beacon light from the airport sweeps into the room and the roar of an ascending airplane is heard. And at this Rick walks slowly toward the terrace.

THE TERRACE as Rick comes out and looks up: In the background the plane —the beam light on it—is seen rising into the air. Rick's eyes are glued on it. Renault comes into the scene and stands beside Rick. Suddenly they look up. The plane soars right above their heads. Renault looks at Rick, his face expressing sympathy.

RENAULT. Well, Rick, you're not only a sentimentalist, but you've become a patriot.

RICK. Maybe, it seemed like a good time to start.

RENAULT. I think perhaps you're right. It might be a good idea for you to disappear from Casablanca for a while. There's a Free French garrison over at Brazzaville. I could be induced to arrange your passage.

RICK (*his eyes still glued on the fast-disappearing plane*). My letter of transit? I could use a trip, but it doesn't make a bit of difference about our bet. You still owe me ten thousand francs.

RENAULT (*smiling*). And that ten thousand should pay our expenses.

RICK. *Our* expenses?

RENAULT. Uh-huh?

RICK (*seeing him in a new light; pleased*). Louis, I think this is the beginning of a beautiful friendship.

The lights of the plane disappear, and the scene fades out.

OHIO UNIVERSITY LIBRARY

Please return this book as soon as you have finished with it. In order to avoid a fine it must be returned by the latest date stamped below.

SEP 2 0 1996
0 4 1996
2004
2004